HISTORY OF UTAH
1540–1886

Indexers, copyists and a team of writers are busy on the fifth floor in Bancroft's History Company, in the 19th century.

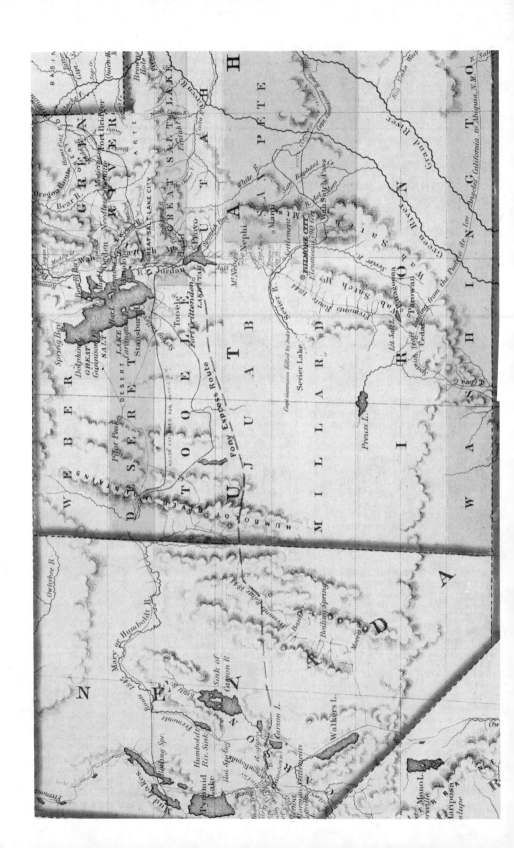

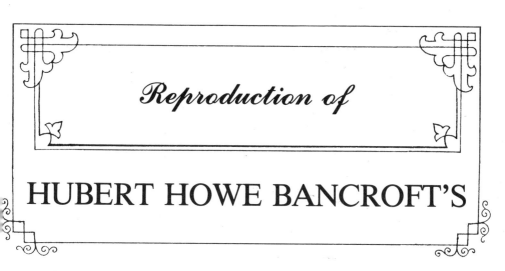

Reproduction of

HUBERT HOWE BANCROFT'S

HISTORY OF UTAH
1540–1886

With Illustrations provided by
The Bancroft Library
Berkeley, California

Nevada Publications
Box 15444
Las Vegas, Nevada 89114
1982

*Hubert Howe Bancroft
in middle age.*

PREFACE.

In the history of Utah we come upon a new series of social phenomena, whose multiformity and unconventionality awaken the liveliest interest. We find ourselves at once outside the beaten track of conquest for gold and glory; of wholesale robberies and human slaughters for the love of Christ; of encomiendas, repartimientos, serfdoms, or other species of civilized imposition; of missionary invasion resulting in certain death to the aborigines, but in broad acres and well filled storehouses for the men of practical piety; of emigration for rich and cheap lands, or for colonization and empire alone; nor have we here a hurried scramble for wealth, or a corporation for the management of a game preserve. There is the charm of novelty about the present subject, if no other; for in our analyses of human progress we never tire of watching the behavior of various elements under various conditions.

There is only one example in the annals of America of the organization of a commonwealth upon principles of pure theocracy. There is here one example only where the founding of a state grew out of the founding of a new religion. Other instances there have been of the occupation of wild tracts on this continent by people flying before persecution, or desirous of greater religious liberty; there were the quakers, the huguenots, and the pilgrim fathers, though their spiritual interests were so soon subordinated to political necessities; religion has often played a conspicuous part in the settlement of the New World, and there has at times been present in some degree the theocratic, if not indeed the hierarchal, idea; but it has been long since the world, the old continent or the new, has witnessed anything like a new religion successfully established and set in prosperous running order upon the fullest and combined principles of theocracy, hierarchy, and patriarchy.

With this new series of phenomena, a new series of difficulties arises in attempting their elucidation: not alone the perplexities always attending unexplored fields, but formidable embarrassments which render the task at once delicate and dangerous.

If the writer is fortunate enough to escape the many pitfalls of fallacy and illusion which beset his way; if he is wise and successful enough to find and follow the exact line of equity which should be drawn between the hotly contending factions; in a word, if he is honest and capable, and speaks honestly and openly in the treatment of such a subject, he is pretty sure to offend, and bring upon himself condemnation from all parties. But where there are palpable faults on both sides of a case, the judge who unites equity with due discrimination may be sure he is not in the main far from right if he succeeds in offending both sides. Therefore, amidst the multiformity of conflicting ideas and evidence, having abandoned all hope of satisfying others, I fall back upon the next most reasonable proposition left—that of satisfying myself.

In regard to the quality of evidence I here encounter, I will say that never before has it been my lot to meet with such a mass of mendacity. The attempts of almost all who have written upon the subject seem to have been to make out a case rather than to state the facts. Of course, by any religious sect dealing largely in the supernatural, fancying itself under the direct guidance of God, its daily doings a standing miracle, commingling in all the ordinary affairs of life prophecies, special interpositions, and revelations with agriculture, commerce, and manufactures, we must expect to find much written which none but that sect can accept as true.

And in relation to opposing evidence, almost every book that has been put forth respecting the people of Utah by one not a Mormon is full of calumny, each author apparently endeavoring to surpass his predecessor in the libertinism of abuse. Most of these are written in a sensational style, and for the purpose of deriving profit by pandering to a vitiated public taste, and are wholly unreliable as to facts. Some few, more especially among those first appearing, whose data were gathered by men upon the spot, and for the purpose of destroying what they regarded as a sacrilegious and pernicious fanaticism, though as vehement in their opposition as any, make some pretensions to honesty and sincerity, and are more worthy of credit. There is much in government reports, and in the writings of the later residents in Utah, dictated by honest patriotism, and to which the historian should give careful attention. In using my authorities, I distinguish between these classes, as it is not profitable either to pass by anything illustrating principles or affecting progress, or to print pages of pure invention, palpable lies, even for the purpose of proving them such. Every work upon the subject, however, receives proper bibliographical notice.

The materials for Mormon church history are exceptionally full. Early in his career the first president appointed a historiographer, whose office has been continuous ever since. To his people he himself gave their early history, both the inner and intangible and the outer and material portions of it. Then missionaries to different posts were instructed to make a record of all pertinent doings, and lodge the same in the church archives. A sacred obligation seems to have been implied in this respect from the beginning, the *Book of Mormon* itself being largely descriptive of such migrations and actions as usually constitute the history of a people. And save in the matters of spiritual manifestations, which the merely secular historian cannot follow, and in speaking of their enemies, whose treatment we must admit in too many instances has been severe, the church records are truthful and reliable. In addition to this, concerning the settlement of the country, I have here, as in other sections of my historical field, visited the people in person, and gathered from them no inconsiderable stores of original and interesting information.

Upon due consideration, and with the problem fairly before me, three methods of treatment presented themselves from which to choose: first, to follow the beaten track of calumny and vituperation, heaping upon the Mormons every species of abuse, from the lofty sarcasm employed by some to the vulgar scurrility applied by others; second, to espouse

the cause of the Mormons as the weaker party, and
defend them from the seeming injustice to which from
the first they have been subjected; third, in a spirit of
equity to present both sides, leaving the reader to
draw his own conclusions. The first course, however
popular, would be beyond my power to follow; the
second method, likewise, is not to be considered; I
therefore adopt the third course, and while giving
the new sect a full and respectful hearing, withhold
nothing that their most violent opposers have to say
against them.

Anything written at the present day which may
properly be called a history of Utah must be largely
a history of the Mormons, these being the first white
people to settle in the country, and at present largely
occupying it. As others with opposing interests and
influences appear, they and the great principles thereby
brought to an issue receive the most careful consideration. And I have deemed it but fair, in presenting the
early history of the church, to give respectful consideration to and a sober recital of Mormon faith and
experiences, common and miraculous. The story of
Mormonism, therefore, beginning with chapter iii., as
told in the text, is from the Mormon standpoint, and
based entirely on Mormon authorities; while in the
notes, and running side by side with the subject-
matter in the text, I give in full all anti-Mormon
arguments and counter-statements, thus enabling the
reader to carry along both sides at once, instead of
having to consider first all that is to be said on one
side, and then all that is to be said on the other.

In following this plan, I only apply to the history
of Utah the same principles employed in all my historical efforts, namely, to give all the facts on every

side pertinent to the subject. In giving the history of the invasion and occupation of the several sections of the Pacific States from Panamá to Alaska, I have been obliged to treat of the idiosyncrasies, motives, and actions of Roman catholics, methodists, presbyterians, episcopalians, and members of the Greek church: not of the nature or validity of their respective creeds, but of their doings, praising or blaming as praise or blame were due, judged purely from a standpoint of morals and humanity according to the highest standards of the foremost civilization of the world. It was not necessary—it was wholly outside the province of the historian, and contrary to my method as practised elsewhere—to discuss the truth or falsity of their convictions, any' more than when writing the history of Mexico, California, or Oregon to advance my opinions regarding the inspiration of the scriptures, the divinity of Christ, prophecies, miracles, or the immaculate conception. On all these questions, as on the doctrines of the Mormons and of other sects, I have of course my opinions, which it were not only out of place but odious to be constantly thrusting upon the attention of the reader, who is seeking for facts only.

In one respect only I deem it necessary to go a little further here: inasmuch as doctrines and beliefs enter more influentially than elsewhere into the origin and evolution of this society, I give the history of the rise and progress of those doctrines. Theirs was not an old faith, the tenets of which have been fought for and discussed for centuries, but professedly a new revelation, whose principles are for the most part unknown to the outside world, where their purity is severely questioned. The settlement of this section sprung primarily from the evolution of a new religion, with all its attendant trials and persecutions. To give their actions without their motives would leave the work obviously imperfect; to give their motives without the origin and nature of their belief would be impossible.

In conclusion, I will say that those who desire a knowledge of people and events impartially viewed, a statement of facts fairly and dispassionately presented, I am confident will find them here as elsewhere in my writings.

The dedication of the present Bancroft Library building was made May 1973. The library was moved from San Francisco to Berkeley in 1906 just after the great fire.

H. H. Bancroft's firm, the History Company, was housed in this newly constructed building in 1886 until it was destroyed by the great fire of 1906.

CONTENTS OF THIS VOLUME.

CHAPTER IV.

THE STORY OF MORMONISM.

1830–1835.

CHAPTER V.

THE STORY OF MORMONISM.

1835–1840.

CHAPTER VI.

THE STORY OF MORMONISM.

1840–1844.

CHAPTER XXVI.

SETTLEMENT, SOCIETY, AND EDUCATION.

1862–1886.

CHAPTER XXVII.

AGRICULTURE, STOCK-RAISING, MANUFACTURES, AND MINING.

1852–1886.

CHAPTER XXVIII.

COMMERCE AND COMMUNICATION.

1852–1885.

AUTHORITIES CONSULTED

IN THE

HISTORY OF UTAH.

Adams (G. J.), A Few Plain Facts, etc. Bedford (Eng.), 1841; Letter to
    President John Tyler. New York, 1844.
Address by a Minister of the Church of Jesus Christ of Latter-day Saints to
    the People of the United States. Printed while the Mormons were at
    Nauvoo. Philadelphia, n.d.
A Friendly Warning to the Latter-day Saints. London, 1860.
Albany (Or.), Journal.
Aldrich (Hazen), The Olive Branch, monthly. Kirtland (O.), 1851-2.
Alegre, Hist. Comp. Jesus, i. 233-8.
Alexander (W. C.), Princ. Mag., xxiv. 687.
Alta (Utah), Times.
Amberley, in Fortnightly Rev., xii. 511.
American Almanac. Boston and New York, 1830 et seq.
American Geog. and Statis. Soc. Mag. New York, 1850 et seq.
American Quarterly Register and Magazine. Philadelphia, 1848 et seq.
American Whig Review. New York, 1845-51. 13 vols.
Among the Mormons, in All the Year Round. x. 1863.
Among the Mormons, in Gent. Mag., new ser., vii.
Ampére (J. J.), Promenade en Amérique, etc. Paris, 1855. 2 vols. Paris,
    1860. 2 vols.
Ancient American Records. n.d.
Ancient and Modern Michilimackinac. (History of James J. Strang's Move-
    ment.) n.d.
Anderson (R. R.), Salt Lake City Street-Railroad. MS.
Andouard, Far West.
Andree (Karl), Die Mormonen und ihr Land. Dresden, 1859.
An Exposure of Mormonism. Dunstable (Eng.), n.d.
Anti-Mormon Almanac. New York, 1842.
Antioch (Cal.), Ledger.
A Plan to Solve the Utah Problem. Salt Lake City, 1880.
Apples of Sodom. Cleveland (O.), 1883.
Appleton (D. & Co.), Amer. Cycloped., N. Y., 1873, 1875; Journal, N. Y.
Appleton's Illustrated Hand-book of Amer. Travel. New York, 1856 et seq.
Arch. Cal., Prov. Rec. MS., i. 47-8, vi. 59.
Archives du Christianisme (1852-3).
Ashland (Or.), Tidings.
Astoria (Or.), Astorian.
Athrawiaeth a Chyfammodau (Wales). n.d.
Atlantic Monthly. Boston, 1858 et seq.

Austin (Nev.), Reese River Reveille.
Authentic History of Remarkable Persons, etc. New York, 1849.
A Visit to the Mormons, in Westm. Rev., lxxvi. 1861.
A Voice from the Mountains. Salt Lake City, 1881.

Balch (W. R.), Mines of the U. S. Philadelphia, 1882.
Ballantyne (Richard), Proclamation of the Gospel. Madras (Hind.), 1853;
    Only Way to be Saved. Madras (Hind.), 1853; Replies to Rev. J. Rich-
    ards. Madras (Hind.), 1853; Millennial Star. Madras (Hind.), 1854.
Bancroft (H. H.), History of California; History of Nevada; History of
    New Mex.; History of North Mex. States; History of Northwest Coast;
    Native Races, etc.
Barber (F. C.), in De Bow, Comml. Rev., xvi. 368.
Barber (J. W.), History of the Western States, etc. Cincinnati, 1867.
Barclay (Jas W.), Mormonism Exposed. London, 1884.
Barfoot (J. L.), Brief History of the Deseret Museum. MS.; Hand-book
    Guide to the Salt Lake Museum. Salt Lake City, 1880.
Barneby (W. H.), Life and Labor in the Far, Far West. London, Paris, and
    New York, 1884.
Barnes (D.), From the Atlantic to the Pacific, Overland. New York, 1866.
Barr, Treatise on the Atonement, etc.
Bates (Geo. C.), Argument on Jurisdiction of Probate Courts, etc. Salt Lake
    City, n.d.
Battle of Bear River, 1863.
Bays (Joseph), The Blood of Christ. Chatteris (Eng.), 1849.
Beadle (J. H.), Bill Hickman, Brigham's Destroying Angel. New York,
    1872; Life in Utah. Philadelphia, 1870; Undevel. West. Philadelphia,
    1873; Western Wilds. Cincinnati, 1879; in Harper's Mag., liii. 641; Pop.
    Sci. Monthly, ix. 479; Scribner's Monthly, xiv. 397.
Beatie (A. S.), The First in Nevada. MS.
Beaumont, Hist. Mich. MS., 407-22, etc.
Beaver City (Utah) Chronicle; Enterprise.
Beckwith (E. G.), Report on Route, etc. Washington, 1855; Washington,
    1856.
Belden (J.), Statement. MS.
Bell (J. F.), Reply to John Theobald. Liverpool, n.d.
Belmont (Nev.), Courier.
Bennett (J. C.), History of the Saints, or Mormonism Exposed. Boston, 1842.
Benton (Thos H.), Speech in U. S. Senate, 1861.
Benzoni, Hist. Mundo Nuevo, 107.
Bernal Diaz, Hist. Verdad., 235.
Bertrand (L. A.), Autorité Divine, ou Réponse, etc. Paris, 1853; Mémoires
    d'un Mormon. Paris, 1862.
Bidwell, Cal., 184-8. MS.
Bigamy and Polygamy, Review of the Opinion of the Supreme Court of the
    U. S., Oct. 1878.
Bigler (Henry W.), Diary of a Mormon. MS., passim.
Bill to Establish a Territorial Government for Utah. Liverpool, 1852.
Bingham (Utah), Pioneer.
Bird (Isabella L.), Lady's Life in the Rocky Mountains. New York, 1881.
Bishop (Gladden), Address to the Sons and Daughters of Zion, etc. Kirtland,
    (O.), 1851.
Black (Judge), Argument on Federal Jurisdiction in the Territories. Salt
    Lake City, 1883.
Bliss (C. H.), Is Baptism Essential? Baptism for the Remission of Sins. Salt
    Lake City, n.d.
Blodget (L.), Meteorological Report. Washington, 1855.
Boadicea, The Mormon Wife. New York, etc., 1855.
Boisé (Idaho), News; Statesman.
Boller (H. A.), Among the Indians. Philadelphia, 1868.

Bonanza City (Idaho), Yankee Fork Herald.
Bonner (T. D.), Life and Advent. of James P. Beckwourth, 71–3.
Bonwick (J.), The Mormons and the Silver Mines. London, 1872.
Book of Commandments. Independence, Missouri, 1833.
Book of Mormon. Kirtland, 1837; Liverpool, 1841, 1852, 1854, 1883; New
    York, n.d. Salt Lake City (First Utah ed.), 1871; Salt Lake City,
    1879, and many others.
Book of Mormon Examined, etc. (Anon.) n.d.
Book of Mormon; Littell's Museum of For. Lit., xlii.
Boston Christ. Exam., 5th ser. ii., 1858.
Boston Journal.
Bowes (John), in Christian Magazine, nos. 13–18; Mormonism. London, Man-
    chester, Glasgow, and Edinburgh, 1848; Mormonism Exposed, 1851.
Bowles (S.), Across the Continent. Springfield (Mass.), 1866; Our New
    West. Hartford, 1869.
Bowne, Jr. (A. G.), in Atlantic Monthly, iii., 361, 474, 570.
Boyer (Lanson), From Orient to Occident. New York, 1878.
Brackett (A. G.), History of the U. S. Cavalry. New York, 1865.
Bradford (W. J. A.), Origin and Fate of Mormonism, in Christ. Exam., liii.
    201.
Brewster (James C.), Address to the Church of Latter-day Saints. Spring-
    field (Ill.), 1848; Very Important to the Mormon Money-diggers.
    Springfield (Ill.), 1843.
Briggs (E. C.), and Attwood (R. M.), Address to the Saints in Utah and Cali-
    fornia. Plano (Ill.), 1869.
Brigham (C. H.), in No. Amer. Rev., xcv. 189; Old and New, i. 628, ii. 320.
Brigham (Wm J.), The Church of Latter-day Saints, in Old and New. Sept.
    and Oct. 1870.
Brigham Young Academy—Circulars.
Brigham Young and his Women, in Galaxy, Dec. 1866.
Brigham Young's Will.
Brighamism; Its Promises and Failure. Plano (Ill.)
British and American Commercial Joint-stock Company, Deed of Settlement.
    Liverpool, 1846.
Brit. Quat. Rev., xxxv. 175.
Bromfield (Edward T.), Picturesque Journeys, etc. New York, 1883.
Brother Bertrand's Conversion, in All the Year Round, ix. 68.
Brotherton (Edward), Mormonism, etc. Manchester (Eng.), n.d.
Brown (Albert G.), The Utah Expedition, in Atlantic Monthly, March, April,
    and May, 1859.
Brown (Benjamin), Testimonies for the Truth, etc. Liverpool, 1853.
Brown (Joseph E.), Speech in U. S. Senate. Washington, 1884.
Brown (Mrs M.), Letter. MS.
Brown's Statement. MS.
Brown (Thos D.), Utah! Its Silver Mines, etc.
Browne (Charles F.), Artemus Ward's Lecture. London, 1882.
Browne (J. R.), Report upon the Mineral Resources of the States and Terri-
    tories west of the Rocky Mountains. Washington, 1867, 1868. San
    Francisco, 1868; Resources of the Pacific Slope. San Francisco, 1869.
Budge (Wm), Views of the Latter-day Saints on Marriage. Liverpool, 1879;
    The Gospel Message. Liverpool, 1879; The Only True Gospel. Liver-
    pool, 1878.
Bulfinch (S. G.), The Mormons, in Christ. Exam., lxiv. 421.
Burchard (H. C.), Director, Report upon the Statistics of the Production
    of the Precious Metals in the U. S. Washington, 1881.
Burgess (J. M.), The Book of Mormon. Liverpool, 1850.
Burnett (Peter H.), Recollections, etc., of an Old Pioneer. New York, 1880.
Burton (R. F.), The City of the Saints. London, 1861. New York, 1862.
Burton's City of the Saints, Review of, Edinb. Rev., cxv. 185; Littell's Liv.
    Age, lxxi. 630.

Busch (M.), Die Mormonen. Leipzig, 1855; Geschichte der Mormonen. Liepzig, 1870.
Bush (C. S.), Plain Facts. Macclesfield (Eng.), 1840.
Byers (W. N.), The Mormons at the Missouri. MS.

California: Its Past History, etc. London, 1850.
California Journals of Assembly and Senate, 1850–1881.
Californian. San Francisco, 1880 et seq.
Call (Anson), and Others, Fragments of Experience. Salt Lake City.
Call to the Unconverted, etc. Liverpool; n.d.
Camp (D. W.), The American Year-Book, 1869 et seq. Hartford.
Campbell (A.), Analysis of the Book of Mormon. Boston, 1832; Mormonism Weighed in the Balances. London, Edinburgh, and Nottingham, n.d. The Millennial Harbinger. Bethany, Va.
Campbell (A.), and Hines (J. V.), Delusions, and Mormon Monstrosities. Boston, 1842.
Campbell (J. H.), My Circular Notes. London, 1876.
Campbell (J. L.), Idaho; Six Months in the New Gold-diggings. Chicago, 1864.
Campbell (Robt), in Pac. R. Rept, xi. 35.
Cannon (Geo. Q.), Speeches in the U. S. House of Rep. for his admission to a seat. Salt Lake City, 1882; The Western Standard. San Francisco, Cal., 1856 et seq; Sunday Schools in Utah. MS.; Juvenile Instructor, Ills. Salt Lake City, 1866 et seq.; Review of Decision of U. S. Supreme Court in the case of Geo. Reynolds. Salt Lake City, 1879; Speech in U. S. House of Rep. Washington, 1882; Utah and its People in No. Amer. Rev., cxxxii. 451; George Q. Pukuniahi He Olelo Hoolaha, etc. San Francisco, 1855; My First Mission. Salt Lake City, 1879; The Life of Nephi. Salt Lake City, 1883; Writings from the Western Standard. Liverpool, 1864.
Carson (Nev.), Appeal; State Register.
Carvalho (S. N.), Incidents of Travel and Adventure in the Far West. New York, 1858.
Carver (J.), Travels through the interior parts of North America. London, 1778.
Caswall (Henry), The City of the Mormons, etc. London, 1843; The Prophet of the 19th Century, etc. London, 1843; Joseph Smith and the Mormons, etc. London, 1851; Mormonism and its Author, etc. London, 1852.
Catechism Cards. Salt Lake City.
Cavo, Tres Siglos, i. 127–9.
Chalmers, Jr (E. B.), Mormonism a Delusion. London, 1852.
Chambers, History of the Mormons. Edinburgh and London, n.d.; History and Ideas of the Mormons, in Westm. Rev., Jan. 1853; Religious Impostors. Edinburgh, n.d.
Champagnac (J. B. L.), Le Jeune Voyageur en Californie. Paris, n.d.
Chandless (W.), A Visit to Salt Lake. London, 1857.
Cherry Creek (Nev.), White Pine News.
Chicago (Ill.), Inter-Ocean; Journal.
Christ or Barabbas? Weston—super mare. London and Bristol, n.d.
Cincinnati (O.), Commercial Advertiser; Gazette; Inquirer.
Circular of the First Presidency. Salt Lake City, July 11, 1877.
Circular from the Twelve Apostles. Salt Lake City, 1880.
Clagett (Wm H.), Speech in House of Rep., Jan. 28, 29, 1873. Washington, 1873.
Clark (John A.), Gleanings by the Way. New York and Philadelphia, 1842.
Clarke (F. W.), The Mormon Widow's Lament, in Galaxy, May 1871.
Clarke (Mrs H. T.), The Emigrant Trail. MS.
Clarke, The Mormons in a Fix. London, n.d.
Clarke (R.), Mormonism Unmasked. n.d.

Clavigero, Storia Cal., 153.
Clay (Edmund), Tracts on Mormonism. London, Leamington, and Liverpool, 1851, 1852.
Clayton (W.), Journal. MS.
Clemens (S. L.), (Mark Twain), Roughing It. Hartford, etc., 1874.
Coast Review. San Francisco, 1871–80. 15 vols.
Cobb (J. J.), The Mormon Problem. MS.
Codman (J.), in Intern. Rev., xi. 1881; The Round Trip. New York, 1879; Through Utah, in The Galaxy, xx. 1875, in Intl. Rev., ii. 227; The Mormon Country. New York, 1874.
Coffin (C. C.), Our New Way round the World. Boston, 1869.
Colburn's United Service Mag., etc. London, 1829 et seq.
Cole (Wm L.), California, etc. New York, 1871.
Colfax (Schuyler), Speech at Salt Lake City, Oct. 5, 1869; Letter in New York Independent, Dec. 2, 1869.
Col. Doc., xiv. 321–3.
Comettant (O.), Les Civilisations Inconnues. Paris, 1863.
Como (Nev.), Lyon County Sentinel.
Concordance and Reference Guide to the Book of Doctrine and Covenants. Plano (Ill.), 1870.
Congressional Globe. Washington, 1836 et seq.
Constitution of State of Deseret, and Memorial to Congress. S. L City, 1872.
Constitution of the State of Utah. Salt Lake City, 1882.
Contested Election. Maxwell vs Cannon. Argument. n.d.
Contributor. Salt Lake City, 1879 et seq.
Conybeare (J. W.), Mormonism. London, 1854.
Conyer (Josiah B.), The Leading Causes of the Hancock Mob, etc. Quincy (Ill.), 1846.
Cook (Joseph), Speeches, etc. n.d.
Cooke (Mrs S. A.), Theatrical and Social Affairs in Utah. MS.
Cooper (A. R.), Polygamy and Prostitution. MS.
Copenhagen Skandinavisk Stjerne. Ungdommens Raadgiver. n.d.
Copperopolis (Cal.), Courier.
Corinne (Utah), Enterprise; Reporter.
Cornaby (H.), Autobiography and Poems. Salt Lake City, 1881.
Correspondence between Joseph Smith and Col John Wentworth, Gen. Jas A. Bennett, and Hon. John C. Calhoun. New York, 1844.
Correspondence, Orders, etc., in Relation to the Disturbances with the Mormons. Fayette (Mo.), 1841.
Corrill (John), Brief History of the Church, etc. St. Louis, 1839.
Cortez (J.), Report on Indian Tribes. Washington, 1856.
Country Clergyman's Warning to his Parishioners. London, n.d.
Coyner (J. M.), Letters to Bost. Educ. Jour. Salt Lake City, 1878–9; Handbook of Mormonism. Salt Lake City, 1882.
Cradlebaugh (John), Mormonism. S. L. City, 1877; Nevada Biography. MS.; Speech in House of Rep., Feb. 7, 1863. Washington, 1863.
Cragin (Aaron H.), Speech in U. S. Senate, May 18, 1870, on Execution of Laws in Utah. Washington, 1870.
Cram (Capt. T. J.), Topog. Memoir on the Department of the Pacific. Washington, 1859; 35th cong. 2d sess., H. Ex. Doc. 114.
Crawford (P. W.), Narrative. MS.; Overland to Oregon. 2 vols. MS.
Crimes of Latter-day Saints. San Francisco, 1884.
Crocheron (A. J.), Representative Women of Deseret. Salt Lake City, 1884; Wild Flowers of Deseret. Salt Lake City, 1881.
Crofutt (G. A.), New Overland Tourist. Chicago, 1879.
Crouise (T. F.), Nat. Wealth of Cal. San Francisco, 1868.
Culmer (H. L. A.), Tourists' Guide-book to Salt Lake City. Salt Lake City, 1879; Utah Directory and Gazetteer. Salt Lake City, 1879.
Curtis (W. E.), in Amer. Christ. Rev., viii. 367.

Dall (Caroline H.), My First Holiday. Boston, 1881.
Dallas (Tex.), Herald.
Dalles (Or.), Mountaineer.
Dalton (Mrs L. L.), Autobiography. MS.
Damon (S. C.), The Friend. Honolulu, 1843–7.
Dana (C. W.), The Great West. Boston, 1861.
Daniels (Wm N.), A Correct Account of the Murder of Generals Joseph and Hyrum Smith. Nauvoo, 1844.
Das Buch Mormon. n.d.
Davies (John), Yr hyn sydd o ran, etc.; Epistol Cyffredinol Cyntaf; Traethawd ar Wyrthiau; Etto Adolygiad, etc.; Chwech Rhifyn; Pregethu i'r Ysbrydion yn Ngharchar, etc.; Ewch a Dysgwch; Darlithiau ar Ffydd; Y Doniau Ysbrydol yn Mrawdlys y Gelyn; Traethawd ar Fedydd; Corff Crist; neu yr Eglwys; Ffordd y Bywyd Tragywyddol; Yr Achos Mawr Cyntaf, gan O. Pratt; Profivch Bob Peth, etc.; Athraniaeth Iachus; Ymddyddanion yn Gymraeg a Saesonaeg; Llythyron Capt. Jones o Ddyffryn y li. H. Mawr, yn desgrifio arderchawgrwydd Seion: no dates (pub. in Wales).
Davis (E. J.), Manufacture and Sale of Intoxicating Liquors. MS.
Davis (Geo. T. M.), Massacre of Joseph Smith, etc. St Louis, 1844.
Davis (John E.), Mormonism Unveiled. Bristol (Eng.), 1856, second edition.
Dawson's Hist. Mag., new series, vi. 1869.
Dayton (Nev.), Lyon County Sentinel.
De Bow (J. D. B.), De Bow's Review and Industrial Resources. New Orleans, etc., 1854–7. 7 vols.
Declarations of Principles of Utah Territorial Convention, People's Party. Salt Lake City, 1882.
Deek (J. G.), The Mormons, etc. Bombay, 1853.
Deer Lodge (Mont.), New Northwest.
Defence of the Constitutional and Religious Rights of the People of Utah, 1882.
De Groot (Henry), Report on Mineral Deposits, etc. San Francisco, 1871; Sketches of Washoe Silver Mines. San Francisco, 1860.
Delano (A.), Life on the Plains. New York, 1861.
Democrat, Bear River, 1880 et seq.
Democratic Review.
Demoralizing Doctrines and Disloyal Teachings of the Mormon Hierarchy. New York, 1866.
Denver (Col.), News.
Derby (E. H.), The Overland Route to the Pacific. Boston, 1869.
Der Mormonismus. Bern (Switz.), 1872.
De Rupert (A. E. D.), Californians and Mormons. New York, 1881.
Description of Huntsville, Weber Co., Utah. MS.
Deseret Agric. and Manufac. Soc. Reports. Salt Lake City, 1867 et seq.; List of Premiums. Salt Lake City, 1878.
Deseret Alphabet: The following works printed in—Deseret First Book, by the Regents of the Deseret University, 1868; Book of Mormon, part i. New York, 1869; Book of Mormon. New York, 1869.
Deseret and Nauvoo, Natl. Mag., iv. 481, v. 343.
Deseret Home, A Monthly Journal. Salt Lake City, Jan. 1882 et seq.
Deseret News. Salt Lake City, 1850 et seq.; Extra, Sept. 14, 1852.
Deseret Sunday-school: Catechism, no. i., Joseph the Prophet. Salt Lake City, 1882; Reader, First and Second Books. Salt Lake City, 1880, 1881, and 1883; Union Music Book. Salt Lake City, 1884.
Deseret Telegraph Company. Memoranda. MS.
De Smet (P. J.), Western Missions and Missionaries. New York, 1868.
D'Haussonville, One Day in Utah. Salt Lake City, 1883.
Dialogues: Between Joseph Smith and the Devil. Salt Lake City and New York, 1844; between Tradition, Reason, and Scriptus. n.d. (Liverpool).

Diamond (Utah), Rocky Mountain Husbandman.
Diario, in Doc. Hist. Mex., ser. ii. tom. i. 378, 392.
Dickeson (M. W.), The American Numismatic Manual. Philadelphia, 1860.
Dickinson (E. E.), in Scribner's Monthly, xx. 613.
Diehl (C.), History of the Masonic Fraternity in Utah. MS.
Dilke (C. W.), Greater Britain. Philadelphia, 1869. 2 vols.
Directories: Utah, Pacific Coast, San Francisco, Nevada.
Discourses delivered by Joseph Smith (30th June, 1843) and Brigham Young
    (18th February, 1855) on the Relation of the Mormons to the Govern-
    ment of the U. S. Salt Lake City.
Dixon, in All the Year Round. No. 17,252.
Dixon (W. H.), New America. London and New York, 1867; White Con-
    quest. London, 1876. 2 vols.
Doctrine and Covenants, etc. Nauvoo, 1846; Liverpool, 1854; Liverpool, n.d.;
    Liverpool, 1882; Salt Lake City, 1876.
Doctrines of Mormonism. London, n.d.
Documentos Historicos Mexicanos, three ser. Mexico, 1853, 1854, 1856.
Documentos Historicos Mexicanos. MS.
Domenech (Abbé Em.), Seven Years' Residence in the Great Deserts of North
    America. London, 1860.
Dooly (J. E.), History of the Express and Banking Business in Utah. MS.
D'Orbigny (A.), Voyage dans les deux Amèriques. Paris, 1859.
Douglas' Private Papers. MS. 2d ser., i.
Drummond (P.), Mormonism an Imposture. n.d.; The Mormons' Only Way
    to be Saved not the Way to be Saved. Stirling (Scot.), 1854.
Duffus-Hardy (Lady), Through Cities and Prairie Lands. London, 1881.
Dunbar (E. E.), The Romance of the Age. New York, 1867.
Dunn (B. S.), How to Solve the Mormon Problem. New York, 1877.
Dutton (J. R.), in Gent. Mag., new ser., vii. 675.

Early Scenes in Church History. Salt Lake City, 1882.
East Portland (Or.), Democratic Era.
Eaton (Mrs), Origin of Mormonism.
Ebey's Journal. MS.
Eckman (E.), Medicinal Herbs and their Use. MS.
Edinburgh Review. Edinburgh, 1850 et seq.
Eine Gottliche Offenbarung; und Belehrung uber den Chestand. n.d.
Elder's Journal, Kirtland, Ohio, and Far West, Missouri, 1838-9.
Elko (Nev.) Independent.
Engelmann (H.), Geolog. Survey of Utah. Washington, 1860.
Enoch's Advocate, 1874.
Epistle of the Twelve Apostles, etc. Salt Lake City, 1877.
Epitome of the Faith and Doctrines of the Reorganized Church of Jesus
    Christ of Latter-day Saints. Plano (Ill.)
Epitre du President de la Mission Française à l'Eglise des Saints des Der-
    niers-jours en France et dans les Iles de la Manche. n.d.
Erb (G. S.), Recollections. MS.
Escalante, Carta de 28 Oct., 1775. MS.
Etourneau (M.), Les Mormons. Paris, 1856.
Eureka (Nev.), Leader; Sentinel.
Eustis (W. T.), Rev. of Ferris, Utah, etc., in New Englander, xii. 553.
Evidence Taken on the Trial of Mr Smith, before the Municipal Court of
    Nauvoo, on Saturday, July 1, 1843. Nauvoo.
Exposures of a Rotten Priesthood. Salt Lake City, 1878.
Eyring (Henry), Ein Wort der Vertherdigung, etc. Bern (Switz.), 1875.

F. (W. B.), The Mormons, the Dream and the Reality, etc. London, 1857.
Fabian (B.), Statistics concerning Utah. Salt Lake City, 1874.
Farmer (E. J.), The Resources of the Rocky Mountains.
Farnham (A.), The Zion's Watchman. Sidney (N. S. W.), Aug. 1853 et seq.

Farnham (T. J.), Travels in the Great Western Prairies. Poughkeepsie, 1841; New York, 1843.
Far West (Mo.), Elder's Journal.
Faulconer (M. A.), Fulness of the Atonement. Plano (Ill.); Questions for the Use of Scholars in the Latter-day Saints Sunday-schools. Plano (Ill.), 1869.
Favez, Fragments sur J. Smith et les Mormons. n.d.
Female Life among the Mormons. New York, 1855.
Ferris (B. G.), Utah and the Mormons. New York, 1854, 1856.
Ferris (Mrs G. B.), The Mormons at Home. New York, 1856.
Fiftieth Annual Conference of the Church of Jesus Christ of Latter-day Saints. Salt Lake City, 1880.
Findlay (Hugh), The Mormons, or Latter-day Saints. Bombay (India), 1853.
Fire Department, Report of Chief Engineer. Salt Lake City, 1880.
Fisher (L. P.), Advertiser's Guide. San Francisco, 1870.
Fisher (R. S.) and Colby (C.), American Statistical Annual. N. Y., 1854.
Fitch (Mrs Thos), in Overland Monthly, vii. 235.
Fitch (Thos), Speeches in House of Rep., Feb. 23, 1870, and April 29, 1870. Washington, 1870; Speech in Utah Constitutional Convention, Feb. 20, 1872. Salt Lake City, 1872; Argument before House Judiciary Committee, Feb. 10, 1873. Washington, 1873.
Flanigan (J. H.), Reply to Palmer's Internal Evidence against the Book of Mormon. Liverpool, 1849.
Font's Journal. MS.
Forbes' Hist. Cal., 157–62.
Ford (Thomas), Message, Dec. 23, 1844, to Illinois Senate, etc. Springfield, 1844; History of Illinois. Chicago, 1854.
Fort Jones (Utah), Scott Valley News.
Foster (J. E.), Prehistoric Races of U. S. of America. Chicago, 1873.
Fraser's Magazine. London, 1830 et seq.
Fremont (J. C.), Narrative of Exploring Expedition. New York, 1849; Report of Exploring Expedition. Washington, 1845.
Friendly Warnings on the Subject of Mormonism. London, 1850.
Frignet, La Californie, 58–60.
Frisco (Utah), Times.
Froiseth (Jennie Anderson), Women of Mormonism. Detroit (Mich.), 1882.
Frost (W.), Dialogue between a Latter-day Saint and a Methodist. Aylsham (Eng.), 1849.
Fry (F.), Traveler's Guide, etc. Cincinnati, 1865.
Fuller (Metta Victoria), (M. F. Victor), Lives of Female Mormons. Philadelphia, 1860; Mormon Wives, etc. New York, 1856.
Fullmer (John S.), Assassination of Joseph and Hyrum Smith, etc. Liverpool, 1855; Expulsion from Nauvoo. Liverpool, n.d.

Garcés, Diario, 246–348.
Garden of the World. Boston, 1856.
Gardener (A.), Mormonism Unmasked. Rochdale (Eng.), 1841.
Gardner (J. G.), Iron Ore and Iron Manufacture. MS.
Geese of Ganderica. Salt Lake City, 1883.
Geikie (A.), in Nature, xxii. 324.
Gems for the Young Folks. Salt Lake City, 1881.
General Epistle from the Council of the Twelve Apostles, etc., dated at Winter Quarters, Omaha Nation (now Florence, Neb.), Dec. 23, 1847.
Geneva, (Switzerland), Le Reflecteur.
Genoa (Carson Valley), Territorial Enterprise, 1858 et seq.
Gerstäcker (Freidrich), Adventures d'une Colonie d'émigrants en Amèrique, Paris, 1855; Travels, London, 1854; Western Lands and Western Waters. London, 1864.
Gibbon (J. G.), in Phila. Cath. Quart. Rev., iv. 664.

Gibson (Wm), Three Nights' Public Discussion, etc. Liverpool, 1851.
Glad Tidings of Great Joy. Salt Lake City.
Goddard (F. B.), Where to Emigrate, and Why. New York, 1869.
Gold Hill (Nev.), News.
Gomara, Hist. Ind., 272–4.
Gooch (Daniel W.), Speech in the U. S. House of Rep. April 4, 1860, on
    Polygamy in Utah. Washington.
Goodrich (E. S.), Mormonism Unveiled; The Other Side. Salt Lake City,
    1884.
Goodrich (L. D.), Rocky Mountain Rovings. MS.
Good Tidings, etc. Liverpool, n.d.
Goodwin (C. C.), in Harper's Mag., lxiii. 756; No. Amer. Rev., cxxxii. 276.
Gordon (J. B.), Historical and Geographical Memoir of the N. A. Continent.
    Dublin, 1820.
Gospel, The [broadsheet]. Plano (Ill.)
Gospel Witness (Anon.) Liverpool, 1848.
Graham (J. C.), Utah Directory. Salt Lake City, 1883–4.
Grant (J. M.), A Collection of Facts Relative to the Course of Sidney Rigdon.
    Philadelphia, 1844, 1884; Three Letters to the "N. Y. Herald," etc.,
    1852; Letter to the President (of the U. S.), May 1, 1852.
Grass Valley (Cal.), Republican.
Gray (J. H.), Principles and Practices of the Mormons. Douglas (Isle of
    Man), 1853.
Gray (W. H.), History of Oregon. Portland, S. F., and N. Y., 1870.
Great Contrast, etc. Liverpool, n.d.
Great Proclamation, etc. Liverpool, n.d.
Greeley (H.), Overland Journey. New York, 1860.
Green (N. W.), Fifteen Years among the Mormons. New York, 1858; Mor-
    monism, etc. Hartford, 1870; Narrative of Mrs Mary Ettie V. Smith.
    New York, 1860.
Greene (John P.), Facts Relative to the Expulsion of the Mormons from
    Missouri. Cincinnati, 1839.
Greenhow (R.), History of Oregon and California. Boston and London, 1844;
    New York, 1845; Boston, 1845; Boston, 1847.
Greenlagh (James), Narrative, To Nauvoo and Back. Liverpool, 1842.
Greenwood (Grace), New Life in New Lands. New York, 1873.
Guers, L'Irvingisme et le Mormonisme jugés par la parole de Dieu. n.d.
Gunnison (J. W.), The Mormons, or Latter-day Saints. Philadelphia, 1852,
    1857, 1860.
Gurley (Z. H.), The Polygamic Revelation. Lamoni (Iowa), 1882.
Gurley (Z. H.) and Kelley (E. L.), The Utah Problem and the Solution.
    Washington, 1882.
Gwin (W. M.), Memoirs on History. MS.

Haefeli (L.), One Day in Utah. Ogden, 1883.
Haefeli (L.) and Cannon (F. J.), Directory of Ogden City and Weber County.
    Ogden City, 1883.
Haefer, Biographie Générale. 1858.
Haining (Samuel), Mormonism Weighed, etc. Douglas (Isle of Man), 1840.
Hakluyt's Voy., iii. 373–9.
Hall (E. H.), Guide to the Great West. New York, 1865; New York, 1866.
Hall (William), Abominations of Mormonism. Cincinnati, 1852.
Hand-book Guide to Salt Lake Museum. Salt Lake City, 1881.
Hand-book on Mormonism. Salt Lake City, Chicago, and Cincinnati, 1882.
Hand-book of Reference. Salt Lake City, 1884.
Hardy (J. D.), in Gent. Mag., xxv. 233.
Harper (C.), Agricultural Products of Utah. MS.
Harper's New Month. Mag. New York, 1856 et seq.
Harris (W.), Mormonism Portrayed, etc. Warsaw (Ill.), 1841.
Hartley (R.) and Rich (B. E.), Public Discussion. Salt Lake City, 1884.

Hassard (J. R. G.), in Cath. World, xxvi. 227.
Hastings (L. W.), Emigrants' Guide to Oregon and California. Cin. 1845.
Have You Read the Book of Mormon ? n.d.
Havilah (Cal.), Courier.
Hawthornwaite, Adventures among the Mormons. Manchester (Eng.), 1857.
Hay (John), The Mormon Prophet's Tragedy, in Atlantic Monthly, xxiv. 669.
Hayden (F. V.), Survey. Meteor. Obsver., by Gannett. Washington, 1872;
    Report. Washington, 1872.
Hayden (——), Early History of the Disciples in the Western Reserve.
Hayes (Benjamin), Diary of a Journey Overland, 1849–50. MS.; Emigrant
    Notes. MS., and Scraps; California Politics (Scraps); Utah (Scraps).
Haynes (John), The Book of Mormon Examined. Brighton and London,
    1853; Refutation of the Mormon Doctrines. Brighton and London, 1853.
Hays (Rev.), Addresses on Mormonism. Douglas (Isle of Man), 1839.
Head (F. H.), in Overland Monthly, v. 270; Chamb. Jour., xxxvii. 29.
Healdsburg (Cal.) Enterprise; Russian River Flag.
Heap (G. H.), Central Route to the Pacific. Philadelphia, 1854.
Helena (Mont.), Independent.
Hepburn (A. B.), Mormonism Exposed. London and Swansea, 1855.
Herrera, dec. vi. lib. ix. cap. xi.-xii.
Hewitt (W.), Exposure of the Errors and Fallacies of the Self-named Latter-
    day Saints. Staffordshire, n.d.
Hewlett (Alfred), One Wife, or Many Wives. Manchester and London, n.d.
Hickman (Edward B.), Mormonism Sifted. London, Norwich, and Brandon,
    1850.
Higbie (Rev. A.), Polygamy vs Christianity. San Francisco, 1857.
Hill (H. A.), in Penn. Monthly, ii. 129.
Hill (H. C.), Remarks on Mines and Mining in Utah. MS.
Hines (G.), Voyage round the World. Buffalo, 1850.
Hist. Nevada. Oakland (Cal.), 1881.
Historical Magazine, and Notes and Queries. Boston, etc., 1857–69. 15 vols.
Hittell (John S.), Comm. and Indus. of the Pac. Coast. San Francisco, 1882.
    Scraps.
Hollister (O. J.), Resources and Attractions of Utah. Salt Lake City, 1882.
Holman (J.), The Peoria Party. MS.
'Homespun,' Lydia Knight's History. Salt Lake City, 1883.
Honolulu Friend. Polynesian, 1845 et seq.
Hooper (W. H.), Speeches in House of Rep., Feb. 25, 1869, March 23, 1870;
    and 28th and 29th Jan., 1873. Washington, 1870, 1873.
Hopper, Narrative. MS.
Horn (H. B.), The Overland Guide. New York, 1852.
Horne (Mrs J.), Migration and Settlement of the Latter-day Saints. MS.
Hours at Home. New York, 1865 et seq.
Howe (E. D.), Mormonism Unvailed. Painesville (O.), 1834, 1841.
Howe (Mrs J.), Migration and Settlement of the Latter-day Saints. MS.
Howitt (Mary), History of the U. S. New York, 1860.
Hoyt (J. P.), Arizona Events. MS.
Hübner (Le Baron de), A Ramble round the World. New York, 1874.
Huffaker's Early Cattle Trade. MS.
Hughes (Elizabeth), Voice from the West to the Scattered People of the
    Twelve, and all the Seed of Abraham. San Francisco, 1879.
Hunt (J. H.), Mormonism: Origin, Rise, and Progress. St Louis, 1844.
Hunt's Merchants' Magazine. New York, 1839 et seq.
Huntington (D. B.), Vocabulary of the Utah and Shoshone Dialects. Salt
    Salt Lake City, 1872.
Hurlburt, Mormonism Unveiled. n.d.
Hutchings' Illus. Cal. Mag. San Francisco, 1857–61.
Hyde, Jr (John), Mormonism: Its Leaders and Designs. York, 1857
Hyde (Mrs M. A. P.), Autobiograhpy. MS.

Hyde (Orson), Address to the Hebrews. Rotterdam (Holland), 1841; Cry out of the Wilderness, 1842 (first published in Germany and in German); News from the Old World; Sketch of Travels and Ministry. Salt Lake City, 1869; Speech on Sidney Rigdon. Nauvoo, 1844.
Hyde (Mrs Orson), Workings of Mormonism. MS.
Hygiene of U. S. Army, etc. Washington, 1875.
Hymns, A Collection of Sacred. Voree (Wis.), 1850, second edition; New York, 1838; The Saints' Harp, etc. Plano (Ill.), 1870; Of Latter-day Saints. Liverpool, 1841, 1881; London, 1851; Salt Lake City, 1st Utah ed. (14th ed.), 1871.

Idaho City, Idaho World.
Idolatry. Plano (Ill.)
L'Illustration. Journal Universel, 1858 et seq.
Important Documents Bearing on Political Questions in Utah. Logan, 1882.
Independence (Mo.), Elder's Journal; Evening and Morning Star, 1832 et seq.; Upper Missouri Advertiser, 1832.
Indian Hostilities: Letter Sec. of War. 41st cong. 2d sess., H. Ex. Doc. 44; Memorial Leg. Assemb. Utah. 41st cong. 1st sess., H. Misc. Doc. 19. 1869.
Indictment for the Murder of James Monroe, etc. Liverpool, 1851.
Insane Ayslum of Utah, Report of Board of Directors. Salt Lake City, 1884.
Intemperance. Salt Lake City, 1881.
Internat. Rev. New York, 1870 et seq.
Interview between Pres. John Taylor and U. S. Int. Rev. Col. O. J. Hollister. Salt Lake City, Jan. 13, 1879.
Investigation into the Murder of Dr J. K. Robinson. Salt Lake City, 1866.
Irving (Edward), and the Catholic and Apostolic Church. London and Liverpool, 1856.
Irving (Wash.), Bonneville's Adven., 186.
Is Mormonism True or Not? (Religious Tract Society.) London, n.d.
Items of Church History. Salt Lake City, 1884.

J. (H. S.), The Latter-day Saints, and their Spiritual Views. n.d.
Jackson (D. J.), Early Overland Emigration. MS.
Jackson (Helen H.), (H. H.), Bits of Travel at Home. Boston, 1878.
Jacksonville (Or.), Dem. Times.
Jacob (May), Peace-maker. Nauvoo (Ill.), 1842.
Jacob (U. H.), Extract from a Manuscript Entitled The Peace-maker. Nauvoo, n.d.
Jaques (John), Der Katechismus für Kinder. Bern (Switz.), 1872; Catechism for Children. Salt Lake City, 1870, 1877; Exclusive Salvation; Salvation: A Dialogue in Two Parts. n.d.; The Church of Jesus Christ of Latter-day Saints, etc. Salt Lake City, 1882.
Jenkins (H. D.), The Mormon Hymn-book, in Our Monthly, Dec. 1870.
Jennings (Wm), Carson Valley. MS. Material Progress of Utah. MS.
Jepson (Ring), Among the Mormons. San Francisco, 1879.
Johnson (Benjamin F.), Why the Latter-day Saints Marry a Plurality of Wives, etc. San Francisco, 1854.
Johnson (J. H.), Voice from the Mountains. Salt Lake City, 1881.
Johnston (James F. W.), Joe Smith and the Mormons, in Harper's Mag., June 1851.
Jones (Dan.), Yr Eurgrawn Ysgrythyrol; Pwy yw Duw y Saint; Yr Hen Grefydd Newydd; Annerchiad i'r Peirch, etc.; Gwrthbrofion i'r Spaulding Story am Lyfr Mormon; Anmhoblogrwydd Mormoniaeth; Arweinydd i Seion; Pa beth yw Mormoniaeth? Pa beth yw gras Cadwedigol? Dadl ar Mormoniaeth? Anffyddiaeth Sectyddiaeth; Amddiffyniad rhag Camgyhuddiadau; Y Lleidr ar y Groes; "Peidiwch a'u Gwrando;" Egwyddorion Cyntaf a Gwahoddiadau; Ai duw a Ddanfonodd Joseph Smith; Llofruddiad Joseph a Hyrum Smith; Tarddiad Llfyr Mormon; Dammeg y Pren Ffrwythtawn; Darlun o'r Byd Crefyddol. n.d. (Pub. in Wales.)

Jones (Nathaniel V.), Reply to 'Mormonism Unveiled.' Calcutta, 1853.
Jones (Wm A.), Reconnoissance of Northwestern Wyoming. 1873. Washington, 1875.
Jonveaux L'Amérique Actuelle. Paris, 1869.

Kane (Thos L.), The Mormons: Discourse before Hist. Soc. of Penn., March 26, 1850. Philadelphia.
Kanesville (Iowa), Frontier Guardian.
Kelley (E. L.) and Braden (C.), Public Discussion. St Louis, 1884.
Kelly (Wm.), An Excursion to Cal. London, 1851. 2 vols.; The Pretensions of Mormonism. Guernsey (Chan. Isles), 1848.
Kelson (J. H.), Seth's Work is Done. Salt Lake City, 1883.
Kendall (H.), A Week in Great Salt Lake City, in Hours at Home, i. 63.
Kidder (Dan'l P.), Mormonism and the Mormons. New York, 1842.
Kimball (David C.), Fireside Visitor. Liverpool, n.d.
Kimball (H. C.), Journal. Salt Lake City, 1882; Journal. MS.
Kimball (H. C.) and Woodruff (W.), The Word of our Lord to the Citizens of London. 1839.
King (Hannah Tapfield), An Epic Poem. Salt Lake City, 1884; Brief Memoir of Early Mormon Life of. MS.; Songs of the Heart. Salt Lake City, 1876; Women of the Scriptures. Salt Lake City, 1874.
Kinney (John F.), Speech in House of Rep., Jan. 27, 1864, on Loyalty of Utah to U. S.; Speech on March 17, 1864, on Territories and Settlement of Utah. Washington, 1864.
Kirchhoff (Theodor), Reisebilder und skissen aus Amerika. New York, 1875–6. 2 vols.
Kirtland (Ohio), Latter-day Saints Messenger and Advocate; Northern Times.
Kneeland (S.), The Wonders of Yosemite. Boston, 1871.

Labors in the Vineyard. Salt Lake City, 1884.
Lapham (F.), in Dawson's Hist. Mag., 2d ser., vii. 1870.
Latter-day Saints. Cape Town (Africa).
Latter-day Saints in Utah. Opinion of Judge Snow, etc. n.d.
Lausanne (Switzerland) Reflecteur.
Lawrence (C. W.), A Few Words from a Pastor. n.d.
Laws concerning Naturalization, etc., quoted from statutes, etc.
Lee (John D.), Trial. Salt Lake City, 1875.
Leslie (Mrs Frank), California: A Pleasure Trip from Gotham to the Golden Gate. New York, 1877.
L'Étoile du Déseret. Paris, 1851–2.
Lewis (M. G.), Coöperation in Theory and Practice. MS.
Liberty (Mo.), Missouri Enquirer.
Libro de Mormon, Trozos Selectos. Salt Lake City, 1875.
Libro di Mormon. n.d.
Lieber (F.), in Putnam's Monthly, v. 225.
Life among the Mormons, in Putnam's Monthly, Aug. to Dec. 1855.
Life among the Mormons. By an Officer of the U. S. A. New York, 1868.
Life of Bill Hickman, Brigham Young's Destroying Angel. New York, 1872.
Linforth (James), Reply to "Few Words from a Pastor," etc. Liverpool, n.d.; Route from Liverpool to Great Salt Lake Valley. Liverpool, 1855.
Lippincott's Magazine, etc. Philadelphia, 1868 et seq.
Littell's Living Age. Boston, 1844 et seq.
Little (F.), Mail Service across the Plains. MS.
Little (J. A.), Jacob Hamlin. Salt Lake City, 1881.
Littlefield (L. O.), Narrative of the Massacre of Joseph and Hyrum Smith. Nauvoo, 1844; The Martyrs. Salt Lake City, 1882.
Liverpool Mormon.
Livesey (Richard), An Exposure of Mormonism. Preston (Eng.), 1838.
Livre de Mormon. n.d.
Llyfr Hymnau (Wales). n.d.
Llyfr Mormon (Wales). n.d.

Logan (Utah), Journal; Leader.
London Monthly Rev., new. ser., iii. 1842, vi. 1852.
Lorenzana, in Cortés, Hist. Mex., 325.
Los Angeles Herald; News; Star.
Lossing (B. J.), The Mormons, in Harper's Mag., vi. 605.
Louisville Courier-Journal.
Lovejoy (A. L.), Founding of Portland. MS.
Lowe (J. B.), Mormonism Exposed. Liverpool, 1852.
Ludlow (F. H.), Among the Mormons, in Atlantic Monthly, xiii. 479; The Heart of the Continent. New York, 1870.
Lynn (Catherine Lewis), Narrative of Some of the Proceedings of the Mor-mons, etc. 1848.
Lyon (J.), The Harp of Zion. London and Liverpool, 1853.

Mac (R. W.), Mormonism in Illinois, in Amer. Whig Review, April, June, and Dec. 1852.
Mackay (Chas), The Mormons, or Latter-day Saints. London, 1851; London, 1852; Auburn, N. Y., 1853; London, 1854. London. 2 vols. n. impr.
Madan (M.), Thelyphthora; or, A Treatise on Federal Ruin. London, 1781.
Magasin Pittoresque. Paris, 1859 et seq.
Marcy (Col R. B.), Thirty Years of Army Life on the Border. N. Y., 1866.
Mariposa (Cal.), Gazette.
Marsh (R. K.), Cotton Growing and Manufacture. MS.
Marshall (C.), Characteristics of Mormonism, in Transatlantic Mag., Aug. 1871; Id., in Frazer's Mag., no. 83, 692; no. 84, 97.
Marshall (W. G.), Through America. London, 1881.
Martin (Moses), A Treatise on the Fulness of the Everlasting Gospel. New York, 1842.
Martin (T. S.), Narrative of Fremont's Expedition. 1845-7. MS.
Marurier (X.), Les Voyageurs Nouveaux. Paris, 1860.
Marysville (Cal.), Appeal.
Mather (F. G.), Early Days of Mormonism, in Lippincott's Mag. August, 1880.
Mayer (B.), Mexico, Aztec, Spanish, and Republican. Hartford, 1852.
Mayhew (H.), The Mormons. London, 1851, 1852.
McBride (J. R.), The Route by Which the Mormons Entered Salt Lake Val-ley in 1847. MS.; Utah and Mormonism, in Internat. Rev. New York, February, 1882.
McCabe, Jr (J. D.), A Comprehensive View of our Country and its Re-sources. Philadelphia, 1876.
McCarthy (Justin), Brigham Young, in Galaxy, Feb. 1870.
McCauley (I. H.), History of Franklin County, Pennsylvania.
McChesney (James), An Antidote to Mormonism. New York, 1838.
McClellan (R. G.), The Golden State. San Francisco, 1872.
McClure (A. K.), Three Thousand Miles through the Rocky Mountains. Philadelphia, 1869.
McGlashan (C. F.), History of the Donner Party. Truckee, 1879; San Francisco, 1880.
McGrorty vs Hooper; 40th cong. 2d sess., H. Com. Rept, 79.
McKinley (Henry J.), Brigham Young, etc. San Francisco, 1870.
McLaughlin (A. C.), Mormonism Measured by the Gospel Rule. Covington (Ky.), 1842.
McNierce (R. G.), in Presb. Rev., ii. 331.
Memoir of the Mormons. South. Lit. Messenger, Nov. 1848.
Memorial of Citizens of Salt Lake City, March 31, 1870, against "Cullom" Bill. Washington, 1870.
Memorial of Legislative Assembly of Utah. Salt Lake City, 1882; Washing-ton (D. C.), 1884.
Memorial to Congress. Plano (Ill.), 1870.

Mendocino (Cal.), Democrat.
Merewether (H. A.), By Sea and by Land. London, 1874.
Merrish (W. J.), The Latter-day Saints, etc. Ledbury, n.d.
Meteor. Observations. Washington, 1826.
Meteor. Register. Washington, 1851.
Mexico, Anales del Ministerio de Fomento. Mex. 1854, vol. 1, 1855, vol. 2.
Miles (J.) vs The U. S.
Millennial Star. Manchester, 1841; Liverpool, 1842–54; Liverpool and Lon-
    don, 1855 et seq.
Miller (Joaquin), Danites in the Sierras. Chicago, 1881; First Families of the
    Sierras. Chicago, 1876.
Miller (N. K.), Federal Affairs in Utah. MS.
Miller (Reuben), James J. Strang Weighed in the Balances, etc. Burlington
    (Iowa), 1846.
Mines of Utah, List of. Salt Lake City, 1882.
Missions, Reports of the Scandinavian, Italian, and Prussian. Liverpool,
    1853.
Mokelumne Hill (Cal.), Calaveras Chronicle.
Möllhausen (B.), Tagebauch einer Reise vom Mississippi, etc. Liepzig, 1858;
    Der Halbindianes. Leipzig, 1861; Das Mormonmädchen. Jena and
    Leipzig, 1864.
Monogamy and Polygamy. Boston, 1882.
Montonus (A.), De Nieuwe Weereld. Amsterdam, 1671.
Moore (Aug.), Pioneer Experience. MS.
Morgan (J.), Doctrines of the Church; Plan of Salvation. Salt Lake City, n.d.
Morgan (Martha M.), A Trip across the Plains. San Francisco, 1864.
Morgan (Wm B.), Mormonism and the Bible. London and Bristol, n.d.
Mormon Battalion, Report of the First General Festival of the Renowned.
    Salt Lake City, n.d.
Mormon Doctrine. Salt Lake City.
Mormon Hymn-book. Liverpool and London, 1851.
Mormonism: Additional Articles on in the following magazines: All the Year
    Round, x. 247; Amer. Bib. Repos., 2d ser., ix.; Amer. Ch. Rev., viii.;
    Amer. Natur., ix.; Bentley, Miscel., xxxviii. 61; Brit. Quart. Rev.,
    xxiii. 62, xxxv., cxxii. 450; Chamb. Jour., xxxvii., liii. 193; Christ.
    Exam., liii.; Christ. Obser., lxii. 183; Christ. Rememb., iv. 278, xxxiii.
    257, xlv. 185; Colburn Monthly, cxiv. 239, cxxi. 253, cxxxvi. 369; Cong.
    Mag., xxvii. 641; De Bow, Com. Rev., xvi.; Dem. Rev., xl. 184, xliii.
    294; Dub. Rev. xxxiii. 77; Dub. Univ. Mag., xxi. 288, lviii.; Eclec.
    Mag., xxi. 400, xcvii. 773; Eclec. Rev., xcvi. 669, xcviii. 479; Edinb.
    Rev., xcix.; Evan. Rev., x.; Every Sat. xi. 291, 541; Fraser Mag., lxxxiii.,
    lxxxiv.; Galaxy, ii., iv., xiv. 677, 822; Gent. Mag., new ser., vii. xxv.;
    Hogg, Instruc., viii. 107, 321; Hours at Home, i.; Lakeside Monthly, i.;
    Lippincott, Mag., vi. 41; Littell, Liv. Age, xxx. 429, xlii. 99, 147, xlix.
    602, l. 429, lvi. 494, lxxviii. 124, 2d ser., xx.; Id., Mus. For. Lit., xlii.,
    xlv.; Lond. Quart. Rev., ii. 95, xviii. 351; Meth. Quart., iii.; Monthly
    Rev., clix. 190; Museum For. Lit., xlii. 370; Natl. Mag., iv., v.; Natl.
    Quart. Rev., xxxix.; New Englander, xii.; New Quart. Rev., iv.; No.
    Brit. Rev., xxxix. 207, 485; Penn. Monthly, ii.; Potter, Amer. Monthly,
    xvii. 298; Presbt. Rev., ii.; Princeton Rev., xxiv.; Putnam Mag., v. 641,
    vi. 144, 602; Sharpe, London Mag., xx. 55, l. 29; South. Lit. Messen.,
    x. 526, xiv. 641, xvii. 170; South. Rev., new ser., xx. 438; Tait, Edinb.
    Mag., xxiv. 763; Temp. Bar, iv. 181; U. S. Cath. Mag., iv. 354; U. S.
    Westm. lxxxvii. 401; Westminst. Rev., lix., lxxvi. 360, lxxxvii.
Mormonism. Cuttack (Ind.), 1855.
Mormonism Examined, etc. Birmingham, 1855.
Mormonism, Its Character, Origin, and Tendency. n.d.
Mormonism. London, n.d.
Mormonism or the Bible, etc. Cambridge and London, 1852.
Mormonism, Past and Present. Nor. Brit. Review, Aug. 1863.

Mormonism Self-refuted (by D. K.) London, n.d.
Mormonism Unveiled. Calcutta, 1852.
Mormonism Unveiled, etc. London, 1855.
Mormonism Unveiled, Life and Confessions of John D. Lee. St Louis, 1877.
Mormonismen och Swedenborgianismen. Upsala, 1854.
Mormon Pamphlets. A collection of thirteen brochures referred to by titles.
Mormon Politics and Policy in San Bernardino Co., Cal. Los Angeles, 1856.
Mormons Bog. n.d.
Mormons (The), History of their Leading Men, in Phren. Jour., Nov. 1866.
Mormons (The), in Utah. Bentley's Miscel., Jan. 1855.
Mormons (The). London, 1851, 1852.
Mormons: their Politics and Policy. Los Angeles, 1856.
Mormon's Wife (The), in Putnam's Monthly, June 1855.
Mormon Women in Mass Meeting. Salt Lake City, Nov. 16, 1878.
Morris (Annie), A Week among the Mormons. Lipp. Mag., July 1870.
Morrish (W. J.), Latter-day Saints and Book of Mormon. Ledbury (Eng.), 1840.
Morse, Washington Territory. MS.
Mota-Padilla, Conq. N. Gal., iii. 14, 158–69.
Mountain Meadows Massacre. Trial of John D. Lee. Salt Lake City, 1875.
Mountain of the Lord's House. Plano (Ill.)
Muhlenpfordt (E.), Versuch einer getreuen Schilder. Repub. Mex. Hanover, 1844. 3 vols.
Mulholland (James), An Address to Americans. Nauvoo, 1841.
Murdock (John), Persecutions of the Latter-day Saints, etc.; Sydney (Australia), 1852; Zion's Watchman. Sydney, 1852.
Murphy (J. R.), Mineral Resour. of Utah. San Francisco, 1872.
Murray (Eli H.), Message to the Legislative Assembly, 1884; Remarks on the Way out of the Difficulty. MS.
Musser (A. M.), Defence of our People. Philadelphia, 1877; Fruits of Mormonism. Salt Lake City, 1878.

Napa County Reporter.
Narrative of Some of the Proceedings of the Mormons. n.d.
Narrative of the Massacre of Joseph and Hyrum Smith. (Anon.) n.d.
Natl. Almanac. Phila., San Francisco, London, and Paris, 1863 et seq.
Natl. Democ. Quart. Rev. Washington, 1859 et seq.
Nauvoo (Ill.), Ensign and Zarahemla Standard; L'Étoile du Deseret; Expositor; Neighbor; Patriot; Wasp.
Nebeker (John), Early Justice. MS.
Neill (E. D.), in Hist. Mag., xvi. 68.
Nelson's Picture Guide Books. New York, n.d.
Nevada (Cal.), Journal.
Nevada, Journals of Assembly and Senate, 1864 et seq
Nevers, Nevada Pioneers. MS.
New Amer., in All the Year Round, xvii. 1867.
New Amer. Religions, in Lond. Quart. Rev., cxxii. 1867.
Newman (J. P.), A Sermon with an Answer by O. Pratt. Salt Lake City, 1870.
New Orleans Picayune.
Newspapers of Utah and other territories of the Pacific U. S., etc. The most important are cited under the name of the town where published, and many of them named in this list.
New York Courier and Enquirer; Herald; Mail; Mormon Intelligence; Observer; Prophet; Sun; Times; Wall St Journal.
Nicholay (C. G.), Oregon Territory. London, 1846.
Nicholson (John), Comprehensive Salvation. Liverpool, 1880; The Latter-day Prophet. Salt Lake City, n.d.; The Means of Escape. Liverpool, 1878; The Modern Prophet; The Preceptor. Salt Lake City, 1883.
Nickerson (Freeman), Death of the Prophet. Boston, 1844.

Nidever, Life and Adv. MS.
Niles' Register, Baltimore, etc., 1847 et seq.
Nineteenth Century. London, 1884.
Nordoff (Chas), California for Health, Pleasure, etc. New York, 1873.
North American Review. Boston, 1850 et seq.
Noticias, in Doc. Hist. Mex., 671–2.
Nouvelles Annales des Voyages. Paris, 1847 et seq.

Oakland Monthly Review; Tribune.
O'Bit O Tauk between Two Berry Chaps obeawt th' Latter-day Saints, etc.
    Bury (Eng.), 1848.
Observations in Utah. MS.
Ogden (Utah), Freeman; Herald; Junction; Times.
Olive Branch. Kirtland (O.), and Springfield (Ill.), 1848–50.
Olshausen (Theodor), Geschichte der Mormonen, etc. Göttingen, 1856.
Olympia (Wash.), Pioneer and Democrat; Puget Sound Courier; Puget Sound
    Herald; Washington Standard.
Omaha (Neb.), New West, Republican.
Onderdonk (J. L.), in Nat. Quart. Rev., xxxix. 80.
Ontario Mining Company, Report, 1881–3.
Origin and History of the Mormonites, in Eclectic Mag., Nov. 1850.
Origin of the Morm. Imposture, in Littell's Liv. Age, xxx. 1851.
Orr (Adrian), Mormonism Dissected. Bethania (Pa.), 1841.
Overland Monthly. San Francisco, 1868 et seq.
Oviedo, iv. 19.
Oxford, Idaho Enterprise.

Pacific Railroad Reports. Washington, 1855–60. 13 vols.
Paddock (Cornelia), Fate of Madame La Tour. New York, 1881; In the
    Toils, etc. Chicago, 1879.
Page (John E.), The Spaulding Story, etc., Exposed. Plano (Ill.), 1866.
Palmer (Joel), Journal of Travels over the Rocky Mountains, 1845–6. Cin-
    cinnati, 1852.
Palmer (W.), Mormonism Briefly Examined. London, n.d.
Palou, Not., ii. 281–2.
Panama, Star and Herald.
Park (J. R.), Educational Affairs in Utah. MS.
Parker (Samuel), Journey beyond the Rocky Mountains. Ithaca (N. Y.),
    etc., 1840, 1842, 1846.
Parry (C. C.), in Amer. Natural., ix. 14–346.
Parry (J. H.), The Mormon Metropolis. Salt Lake City, 1883.
Parsons (T.), Mormon Fanaticism Exposed. Boston, 1841.
Patterson (R.), History of Washington County, Pa. Philadelphia, 1882.
Patterson (Robt), Who Wrote the Book of Mormon? Philadelphia, 1882.
Pearl of Great Price. Salt Lake City, 1878.
Peck (G.), in Meth. Quart., iii. 111.
Penrose (C. W.), Mormon Doctrine. Salt Lake City, 1882.
Perpetual Emigrating Fund. MS.
Petaluma (Cal.), Argus; Crescent; Journal and Argus.
Peters (De W. C.), Life and Adventures of Kit Carson. New York, 1859.
Phelps (W. W.), Deseret Almanac, 1851 et seq.
Philadelphia (Pa), Gospel Reflector.
Philip Harry, in Simpson's Explor., 490.
Pierrepont (Edward), Fifth Avenue to Alaska. N. Y. and Lond. 1884.
Pioche (Nev.), Record.
Pittsburg (Pa), Baptist Witness; Latter-day Saints Messenger and Advocate.
Placer (Cal.), Herald; Times.
Placerville (Cal.), Tri-weekly Register, June 24, 1858.
Plain Questions for Mormonites. By One Who Knows They are not Saints.
    London, 1852.

Plano (Ill.), True Latter-day Saints' Herald; Saints' Advocate.
Player-Frowd (J. G.), Six Months in California. London, 1872.
Political Pamphlets. A collection of twenty brochures referred to by title
    and number. Salt Lake City, 1879.
Polygamy and Monogamy Compared. The History and Philosophy of Mar-
    riage. Boston, 1875.
Popular Science Monthly. New York, 1872 et seq.
Portland (Or.), Bee; Deutsch Zeitung; Herald; Lantern; Oregonian; Stand-
    ard.
Port Townsend (Wash.), Democratic Press.
Powell (J. W.), Explor. of the Colorado River of the West. Washington,
    1875; Geol. of East. Uinta Mountains. Wash., 1876; Geol. Surv. of
    Rocky Mountains. Wash., 1877; Rept on Lands of Arid Region. Wash.,
    1879.
Pratt (Belinda Marden), Defence of Polygamy by a Lady of Utah. Salt Lake
    City, 1854. Republished in Millennial Star of July 29, 1854.
Pratt (Orson), Remarkable Visions. Edinburgh, 1840; Liverpool, 1848; Ac-
    count of Several Remarkable Visions. New York, 1841, 1842; Was
    Joseph Smith Sent of God ? Liverpool, 1848; Kingdom of God, in 4 parts.
    Liverpool, 1848–9; New Jerusalem, etc. Liverpool, 1849; Divine Authen-
    ticity of the Book of Mormon. 6 nos. Liverpool, 1850–1; Reply to '' Re-
    marks on Mormonism,'' etc. Liverpool, 1849; Reply to T. W. P. Taylder.
    Liverpool, 1849; Great First Cause, etc. Liverpool, 1851; Twenty-four
    Miracles. Liverpool, 1857; Spiritual Gifts. Liverpool and London, 1857;
    Universal Apostacy, etc. Liverpool, 1857; The Seer, vol. i. 12 numbers,
    ii. 8 numbers. Washington, 1853 et seq.; A Series of Pamphlets on Faith,
    Repentance, Baptism, Holy Spirit, Spiritual Gifts, etc. Liverpool, 1851,
    1857; Reply to Newman's Sermon. Salt Lake City, 1870; Bible and
    Polygamy. Salt Lake City, 1877; Cubic and Biquadratic Equations.
    London and Liverpool, 1866; Key to the Universe. London and Liver-
    pool, (——); Salt Lake City, 1879; Works, A Series of Pamphlets on the
    Doctrines of the Gospel. Salt Lake City, 1884.
Pratt (Orson) and Newman (J. P.), Discussion on Polygamy. Salt Lake
    City, Aug. 12–14, 1870.
Pratt (Orson), Smith (G. A.), and Cannon (G. Q.), Discourses on Celestial
    Marriage. Salt Lake City, Oct. 7, 1869.
Pratt (Parley P.), Journal of the Elders and their Missions. Liverpool,
    1837–8; The Millennium and Other Poems, etc. New York, 1840; Late
    Persecution. New York, 1840; Appeal to the Inhabitants of New York
    State. Nauvoo (Ill.), 1841; Letter to Queen Victoria. Manchester,
    1841; Heaven on Earth. Liverpool, 1841; Voice of Warning and In-
    struction. New York, 1837; Liverpool (——); London, 1854; Salt Lake
    City, 1874; Mormon Herald. San Francisco (Cal.), 1855 et seq.; Voix
    d'Avertissement. n.d.; Fountain of Knowledge. n.d.; Intelligence and
    Affection. n.d.; Immortality of the Body. n.d.; Priodas a Moesau yn
    Utah (Wales). n.d.; Key to the Science of Theology. Liverpool and
    London, 1855; Salt Lake City, 1874; Marriage and Morals in Utah.
    Liverpool, 1856; Autobiography. New York, 1874; An Address to the
    People of England, etc. Manchester, 1840; Mormonism Unveiled, etc
    New York, 1838; Proclamation, etc. Sydney (N. S. W.), 1852; Repent,
    Ye People of California. San Francisco, 1854; Scriptural Evidences in
    Favor of Polygamy. San Francisco, 1856; The Angel of the Prairies.
    Salt Lake City, 1880; Treatise on the Regeneration and Eternal Duration
    of Matter. New York, 1840.
Prescott (Ariz.), Miner.
Price (R. L.), The Two Americas. Philadelphia, 1877.
Prichard (Jas C.), Researches into the Physical History of Mankind. Lon-
    don, 1836; London, 1847. 5 vols.
Prieto (G.), Viaje à los Estados Unidos. Mexico, 1877–9. 3 vols.
Prime (E. D. G.), Around the World. New York, 1872.

Proclamation of the Twelve Apostles, etc.   N. Y. and Liverpool, 1845.
Prophwyd y Jubili.   Merthyr Tydvil, South Wales.
Provo (Utah), Enquirer; Times.
Putnam's Magazine.   New York, 1863 et seq.

Quigley (Hugh), The Irish Race in California, etc.   San Francisco, 1878.

Rae (W. F.), Westward by Rail.   London, 1870.
Raffensperger (Mrs), in Scribner's Monthly, iii. 672.
Ramusio, Viaggi, iii. 359–63.
Randolph's Oration, 313–14.
Raymond (Rossiter W.), Mining Industry of the States and Territories of
    the Rocky Mountains.   New York, 1874; Silver and Gold.   New York,
    1873; Statistics of Mines and Mining.   Washington, 1873.
Reasons Why I cannot Become a Mormonite.   London, n.d.
Red Bluff (Cal.), Independent; Sentinel.
Reese (J.), Mormon Station.   MS.
Reid (Mayne), The Mormon Monsters, in Onward, Nov. 1869.
Rejection of the Church.   Plano (Ill.)
Relacion de Castañeda.   Ternaux-Compans, serie i. tom. ix. 61–5.
Religious Pamphlets.   A collection of 25 pamphlets.   S. L. City, 1879.
Remarks on Mormonism.   Glasgow (Scot.), n.d.
Remé, Orientale et Americane.   n.d.
Remonstrance and Resolutions adopted by a mass meeting of the citizens of
    Utah against the Cullom Bill.   Salt Lake City, 1870.
Remy (Jules), Voyage au pays des Mormons.   Paris, 1860.   2 vols.
Remy (Jules) and Julius Brenchley, A Journey to Great Salt Lake City.
    London, 1861.   2 vols.
Reno (Nev.), Gazette; State Journal.
Reorganization of the Legislative Power of Utah Territory.   Minority Report
    of Committee on Territories.   Washington, 1884.
Report of the First General Festival of the Renowned Mormon Battalion.
    Salt Lake City, 1855.
Report of the Grand Jury, 1878.
Report of Three Nights' Public Discussion in Bolton (Eng.), etc.   Liverpool,
    1851.
Report of Utah Commission.   Washington, 1884.
Report on Governor's Message.   Salt Lake City, 1882.
Review of the Opinion of the U. S. Supreme Court in Reynolds vs U. S.
    Salt Lake City, 1878.
Revised Laws of the Nauvoo Legion.   Nauvoo, 1844.
Revised Ordinances of Provo City.   Salt Lake City, 1877.
Révoil, Les Harems du Nouveau Monde.   Paris, 1856.
Revue des Deux Mondes.   Paris, 1839 et seq.
Revue Orientale et Americaine.   Paris, 1859 et seq.
Reynolds (George), Are We of Israel?   Salt Lake City, 1883; Myth of the
    Manuscript Found.   Salt Lake City, 1883; The Book of Abraham.   Salt
    Lake City, 1879; Plaintiff in Error vs U. S.   n.d.
Rhinehart Memoranda.   MS.
Ribas, Hist. Triumphos, 26–7.
Richards (Franklin D.), Bibliography of Utah.   MS.; European Emigra-
    tion to Utah.   MS.; Compendium of the Faith and Doctrines of the
    Church, etc.   Liverpool, 1857.   Narrative.   MS.; Private Journal.   MS.;
    The Book of Mormon.   MS.; The Pearl of Great Price.   Liverpool, 1851;
    Revised.   Salt Lake City, 1878; Tracts.
Richards (F. D.) and Little (James A.), Compendium of the Doctrines of the
    Gospel.   Salt Lake City, 1882, 1884.
Richards (Franklin S.), Bennett, Harkness, and Kirkpatrick, Argument on
    the Elections in Utah.   Salt Lake City, 1884.
Richards (J.), What is Mormonism?   Madras (Hind.), 1853.

Richards (Mrs F. D.), Reminiscences. MS.; The Inner Facts of Social Life in Utah. MS.
Richards (Willard), Address to Chancellor and Regents of Deseret University. Great Salt Lake City, April 17, 1850.
Richardson (A. D.), Beyond the Mississippi. Hartford, 1867.
Richardson (D.), Preëxistence of Man, etc. n.d.; Faith of the Latter-day Saints.
Richardson (David M.), Address to Congress. Detroit (Mich.), 1882.
Rise and Progress of the Mormon Faith and People, in South. Lit. Messenger, Sept. 1844.
Roberts (C. M.), Politics and Religion: MS.
Robinson (Phil.), Sinners and Saints. Boston, 1883.
Rockwell (O. P.), The Destroying Angels, etc. San Francisco, 1878.
Rockwood (A. P.), Report on Zion Coöp. Fish Association. S. L. City, 1878.
Rodenbough (Theo. F.), From Everglade to Cañon with the Second Dragoons. New York, 1875.
Rollo (J. B.), Mormonism Exposed. Edinburgh, 1841.
Ross (James) and George Gary, From Wisconsin to Cal. and Return. Madison, 1869.
Ruby City (Idaho), Avalanche.
Ruby Hill (Nev.), Mining News.
Ruffner (E. H.), Report of Reconnais. in the Ute Country. Wash., 1876.
Rules and Practice of the District Court, etc. Salt Lake City, 1868.
Rusling (Jas F.), Across America. New York, 1874.
Ruxton (Geo. F.), Life in the Far West. New York, 1855.

Sacramento (Cal.), Bee; Record-Union; Union.
Safford (A. K. P.), Narrative. MS.
Saint Abe and his Seven Wives. A Tale of Salt Lake City. (Poem.) London, 1872.
Sala (George A.), America Revisited. London, 1882. 2 vols.
Salem (Or.), Oregon Argus; Oregon Statesman.
Salmeron, in Doc. Hist. Mex., 3d ser., pt iv. 7-9.
Salt Lake City (Utah), Newspapers: Anti-Polygamy Standard; Birkuben (Scandinavian); Christian Advocate; City Review; College Lantern; Contributor; Deseret News; Educational Journal; Footlights; Grocer; Herald; Independent; Journal; Juvenile Instructor; Leader; Mail; Miner; Monthly Record; Mormon Expositor; Mormon Tribune; Mountaineer; New Endowment; News; Peep o' Day; Press; Real Estate Circular; Rocky Mountain Christian Advocate; Skandinav; Telegraph; Tribune; Union Vidette; Utah Commercial; Utah Magazine; Utah Mining Gazette; Utah Mining Journal; Utah Musical Times; Utah Posten (Danish); Utah Reporter; Utah Review; Valley Tan; Western Magazine (Utah ed.); Woman's Exponent.
Salt Lake Fruit. Boston, 1884.
Samson (G. W.), in Scribner's Monthly, iii. 1872.
San Bernadino Guardian.
San Buenaventura Ventura Free Press.
San Diego News; Union.
San Francisco (Cal.), Newspapers: Abend Post; Alta California; Cal. Christian Advocate; Cal. Courier; Cal. Farmer; Cal. Mercantile Journal; Cal. Star; Cal. Teacher; Call; Chronicle; Commercial Herald and Market Review; Despatch and Vanguard; Echo du Pacifique; Evening Bulletin; Examiner; Golden Era; Herald; Mercantile Gazette; Mercantile Journal; Mining Review, etc.; Mining and Scientific Press; Monitor; News Letter; Occident; Pacific Baptist; Pacific Churchman; Pacific News; Pacific Observer; Pacific Rural Press; Picayune; Pioneer; Post; Scientific Press; Stock Exchange; Stock Report; Times; Town Talk; Visitor; Western Standard, 1856-8; Wide West.
San José (Cal.), Argus; Mercury; Pioneer; Times.

San Luis Obispo Tribune.

Santa Barbara Index.

Santa Cruz Sentinel.

Santa Rosa Times.

Sargent (A. A.), Speech in House of Rep., Feb. 23, 1870. Washington, 1870.

Saxon (Isabella), Five Years within the Golden State. Philadelphia, 1868.

Scenes in the Rocky Mountains. Philadelphia, 1846.

Schiel (Doct. J.), Reise durch die Felsengebirge Schaffhausen. 1859.

Schott (Chas A.), Tables of Temperature, etc. Washington, 1876; Tables of Rain and Snow, etc. Washington, 1872.

Scribner's Monthly Magazine (later the Century). New York, 1871 et seq.

Seattle (Wash.), Intelligencer; Pacific Tribune; Puget Sound Despatch.

Second General Epistle of the Presidency of the Church of Jesus Christ of Latter-day Saints. Salt Lake City, 1849; Third ditto. Salt Lake City, 1850.

Seeley (R. H.), The Mormons and their Religion, in Scribner's Monthly, iii. 396.

Seer (The). Washington and Liverpool.

Serra, Memorial, March 1873. MS.

Sexton (Geo.), A Portraiture of Mormonism. London, 1849.

Shearer (Joel), Mysteries Revealed. Council Bluffs (Iowa), 1854.

Shearer (Joel) and Swett (Wm), Comments on the Kingdom of God. Council Bluffs (Iowa), 1854.

Shearer, Journal of a Trip to California. 1849. MS.

Sheen (Isaac), The Narrow Way. Plano (Ill.); The Plan of Salvation. Plano (Ill.)

Shepherd (M. L.), Colonizing of San Bernardino. MS.

Shuck (O. T.), Cal. Scrap-book. San Francisco, 1869; Rep. Men. San Francisco, 1870, 1875.

Silliman (Benjamin), Amer. Jour. of Science and Art. New Haven, 1846 et seq.

Silver City (Idaho), Avalanche.

Silver Reef (Utah), Echo; Miner.

Simonin (L.), Le Grand-Ouest des Etats-Unis. Paris, 1869; Les Mines d'Or et d'Argent aux Etats-Unis, in Reveue des Deux Mondes. Nov. 1875.

Simons (John), A Few More Facts, etc. Dymock (Eng.), 1840.

Simpson (J. H.), On the Change of Route West from Omaha, proposed by the U. P. Railroad. Washington, 1865; Rept. on U. P. Railroad and Branches. Washington, 1865; Shortest Route to Cal. Philadelphia, 1869; Report of Explorations across the Great Basin, etc. Washington, 1876.

Simpson (S.), Mormonism: Its History, Doctrine, etc. London, n.d.

Siskiyou Couuty Affairs. MS.

Skelton (Robt) and Meik (J. P.), Defence of Mormonism. Calcutta, 1855.

Sketches of Mormonism, as Drawn by Brigham Young and the Elders, in Western Lit. Messenger, July 1856.

Slater (N.), Fruits of Mormonism. Coloma (Cal.), 1851.

Sloan (E. L.), Gazetteer of Utah. Salt Lake City, 1874.

Sloan (R. W.), Utah Gazetteer. Salt Lake City, 1884.

Sloan (Robt W.), and Others, Utah, Her Attractions and Resources. S. L. City, 1881.

Smith (Alexander H.), Polygamy, etc. Plano (Ill.)

Smith (Charles H.), The Mormonites. Bristol (Eng.), 1849.

Smith (Clark), Mystery and Crime in the Land of the Ute. Cornelius (Or.), 1878.

Smith (David H.), The Bible versus Polygamy. Plano (Ill.)

Smith (Emma), Selection of Hymns. Independence (Mo.), 1832.

Smith (Geo. A.), Plea on Trial of Howard Egan. Liverpool, 1852; Rise, Progress, etc., of Latter-day Saints. Salt Lake City, 1869, 1872; Liverpool and London, 1873; Discourse on Celestial Marriage. Oct. 8, 1869.

Smith (J.), Items of Church History, etc. Salt Lake City, 1884.
Smith (J. L.), Einige Worte on die Heiligen der Lezten Tage. Zurich (Switz.), 1861.
Smith (Joseph), Reply to Orson Pratt. Plano (Ill.); "Who then can be Saved?" Plano (Ill.)
Smith, Jr (Joseph), Book of Mormon. Palmyra (N. Y.), 1830; Completely Revised by the Translator. Nauvoo (Ill.), 1840; Liverpool, 1852; New York, (——); Salt Lake City, 1871, 1879; The Holy Scriptures Translated and Corrected by the Spirit of Revelation. Plano (Ill.), 1867; Book of Doctrine and Covenants, etc. Nauvoo, 1846; Liverpool, 1854; Liverpool, n.d.; Liverpool, 1882; Salt Lake City, 1876; Views of the Powers and Policy of the Government of the United States. Nauvoo, 1844.
Smith, Jr (Joseph), Correspondence between, and John Wentworth, James A. Bennett, and John C. Calhoun. New York, 1844; and Young (Brigham), Discourses on the Relation of the Mormons to the Government. Salt Lake City, 1855.
Smith (Lucy), Biog. Sketches of Joseph Smith, etc. Liverpool, 1853.
Smith (Mary Ettie V.), Fifteen Years among the Mormons. N. Y., 1858.
Smith, Narrative of the Assassination of Joseph and Hyrum. By an Eyewitness.
Smith (The Prophet Joseph), Questions and Answers. Salt Lake City, 1882.
Smith (T. W.), Spiritualism Viewed from a Scriptural Standpoint. Plano (Ill.); The "One Baptism," etc. Plano (Ill.) The "One Body." Plano (Ill.)
Smith (Wm), Revelation Given to. Philadelphia, 1848; Slanders Refuted, etc., n.d.
Smithsonian Institution, Annual Reports. Washington, 1853 et seq.
Smoot (Margaret S.), Experience of a Mormon Wife. MS.
Smucker (Sam'l H.), The Religious, Social, and Political History of the Mormons. N. Y., 1856, 1860.
Smyth (John H.), Homestead Law, etc.
Snow (Eliza R.), Hymns and Songs. Salt Lake City, 1880; Poems, Religious, Historical, and Political. Liverpool and London, 1856. vol. i.; Salt Lake City, 1877. vol. ii.; Women's Organizations in Utah. MS.; Bible Questions and Answers. Salt Lake City, 1881 and 1884; Brief Sketch. MS.; Biography of Lorenzo Snow. Salt Lake City, 1884; Children's Primary Hymn Book. Salt Lake City, 1880 and 1882; Correspondence of Palestine Tourists. Salt Lake City, 1875; Recitations for the Primary Associations, Books nos. 1 and 2. Salt Lake City, 1882; Sketch of my Life. MS.; Time Book. Salt Lake City, 1880.
Snow (Erastus), En röst från landet Zion. Copenhagen (Den.), 1852; One Year in Scandinavia, etc. n.d.; Skandinabieus Stierne. Copenhagen, 1851.
Snow (E.) and Winchester (B.), Address to the Citizens of Salem (Mass.), 1841.
Snow (Lorenzo), Voice of Joseph, etc. Liverpool and Lond. 1852; Only Way to be Saved. London, 1851; Madras, 1853; Italian Mission. n.d.; La Voix de Joseph, etc. Turin (Italy), 1851; Exposition des Premier Principes de la Doctrine de l'Eglise de Jesus Christ, etc. Turin (Italy), 1851.
Snow (Z.) (Atty-Genl.), Communications to Utah Legislature. Salt Lake City, 1872; Salt Lake City, 1874; Correspondence with Wm Clayton (Auditor, etc.) Salt Lake City, 1872; Opinion on Brigham Young. Liverpool, 1852.
Sonoma (Cal.), Democrat.
Southern Quarterly Review. New Orleans, etc., 1842 et seq.
Spaulding (Samuel J.), Spaulding Memorial; A Genealogical History, etc. Boston, 1872.
Spence (Thos), Settlers' Guide. New York, 1862.
Spencer (Orson), Letters Exhibiting the Most Prominent Doctrines of the Church, etc. Liverpool, 1848; London, 1852; Patriarchal Order, or Plurality of Wives, etc. Liverpool, 1853; Report to President Young on the Prussian Mission. Liverpool and London, 1853; Most Prominent Doctrines of the Latter-day Saints. Salt Lake City, 1874.

Spiritual Courtship and Marriage of the Mormons. London, n.d.
Spiritual-Wife Doctrine of the Mormons. Report of the Judges of Utah
    Territory. Cheltenham (Eng.), 1852.
Spring Lake Villa (Utah), Farmer's Oracle.
Stanford (Jos), Sketch of Weber County. MS.; Ogden City. MS.
Stansbury (Howard), Die Mormonen, etc. Stuttgart, 1854; Exped. to Valley
    of Great Salt Lake. Philadelphia, 1855. 2 vols.
Staples (Dav. J.), Incidents and Information. MS.
Statistical Report of Stakes of Zion. MS.
Stayner (Arthur), Report on the Manufacture of Sugar. Salt Lake City,
    1884.
Stayner (C. W.), Farmers' and Miners' Manual. Salt Lake City, 1883.
St Clair (D. L.), To the Followers of the Latter-day Saints. Cheltenham
    (Eng.), 1840.
Stenhouse (T. B. H.), Exposé of Polygamy. New York, 1872; Les Mormons,
    etc. Lausanne, 1854; The Rocky Mountain Saints. New York, 1873.
Stenhouse (Mrs T. B. H.), Tell it All, etc. Hartford, 1879; An Englishwoman
    in Utah. London, 1880; A Lady's Life among the Mormons. New
    York, 1872.
Stevenson (H.), Lecture on Mormonism. Newcastle (Eng.), 1839.
St George (Utah), Pomologist and Gardener.
Stillman (Jas W.), Speech on the Mormon Question. Boston, 1884.
St Louis Democrat; Luminary.
Stockton (Cal.), Herald; Independent.
Stone (W. F.), The Mormon Problem. MS.; The Saints at Pueblo. MS.
Sturtevant (J. M.), Review of Mormonism in All Ages, in Amer. Bib. Repos.,
    2d ser., ix. 109.
Successor in the Prophet's Office, etc. Plano (Ill.)
Suisun (Cal.), Republican.
Sunday-school Dialogues and Recitations, Book no. 1. Salt Lake City, 1884.
Sunderland (L.), Mormonism Exposed, 1841; New York, 1842.
Sutter Co. Hist. 17.
Sweet (J. B.), The Book of Mormon and the Latter-day Saints. London,
    1857.

Talmage (De Witt), Speeches, etc.
Tanner (Mary J.), Fugitive Poems. Salt Lake City, 1880.
Taylder (T. W. P.), Mormon's Own Book, etc. London, 1845, 1857; Material-
    ism of the Mormons, etc. Woolwich (Eng.), 1849.
Taylor (B. F.), Summer Savory, etc. Chicago, 1879.
Taylor (John), Three Nights' Public Discussion, at Boulogne-sur-mer.
    Liverpool, 1850; Aux Amis de la Vérité Religieuse. n.d.; De la Né-
    cessité de Nouvelles Révélations prouvée par la Bible. n.d.; Traité sur
    le Baptême. n.d; Buch der Mormonen. Hamburg, 1851; Zion's Panier.
    Hamburg, 1851; Government of God. Liverpool and London, 1852; Re-
    plies to Vice-President Colfax. Salt Lake City, 1870; On the decision of
    the Supreme Court of the U. S. in the case of Geo. Reynolds. Jan. 13,
    1879, Salt Lake City; Discourse at the General Conference. Salt Lake
    City, April 9, 1882; Early Recollections. MS.; Epistle to the Presidents
    of Stakes, etc. Salt Lake City, 1882; Items on Priesthood. Salt Lake
    City, 1881, 1882; On Marriage and Succession in the Priesthood. Salt
    Lake City, 1882; Reminiscences of the First Year's Journey across the
    Plains. MS.; The Mediation and Atonement of Our Lord and Savior
    Jesus Christ. Salt Lake City, 1882; Truth Defended, etc. Liverpool,
    1840.
Taylor (John) and Others, Epistle of the Twelve Apostles, etc. S. L. City,
    1877; Circular from the Twelve Apostles. S. L. City, April 16, 1880;
    A String of Pearls. Salt Lake City, 1882.
T. C. R., What I Saw in Utah. MS.
Testimony of the Great Prophet, etc. Liverpool, n. impt.

The Book of Mormon a Forgery. London and Leamington, 1850.
The Book of Mormon, History and Contents. London and Leamington, 1850.
The Church of Latter-day Saints, in Old and New, ii. 1870.
The City of the Saints, in Littell's Liv. Age, lxxi. 1861.
The Delegate from Utah (Geo. Q. Cannon). n.d.
The Diamond. Voree (Wis.), 1848.
The Doctrine of the Latter-day Saints. London, n.d.
The Doctrines of Mormonism. London, n.d.
The Emigrant Caravan, in Chambers's Jour., liii. 1876.
The External Evidences of the Book of Mormon Examined. London, n.d.
The Fowlers' Snare. London, 1 360.
The Galaxy. New York, 1866 et seq.
The Gates of the Mormon Hell Opened. London, n.d.
The Hand-book of Reference to History, etc., of Latter day Saints. Salt
      Lake City, 1884.
The Latter-day Saints, in Fortnightly Rev., xii. 1869.
The Life and Character of Joseph Smith. London and Leamington, 1850.
The Mining Industry. Denver (Col.), 1881.
The Mormon Doctrine of Polygamy. London, 1853.
The Mormon Imposture, etc. London, 1851.
The Mormon Metropolis. Salt Lake City, 1883.
The Mormon Problem, in Old and New, i. 1870.
The Mormonites, in Lond. Month. Rev., new ser., iii. 1842.
The Mormons in Utah, in Littell's Liv. Age, xlvi. 1855.
The Mormons or Latter-day Saints, with Memoirs of the Life of Joseph
      Smith, the American Mahomet. London (——).
The Mormons, or Life in Utah. Birmingham, n.d.
The Mysteries of Mormonism. New York, 1882.
The Restorer (in English and Welsh), Monthly; Merthyr Tydfil. Wales,
      1864.
The Spiritual-Wife Doctrine of the Mormons. Manchester (Eng.), n.d.
The Two Prophets of Mormonism, in Cath. World, xxvi. 1878.
The Utah Magazine, 1868–69.
The Voice of Truth, etc. Nauvoo, 1844.
The Yankee Mahomet, in Am. Whig Rev., new ser., vii. 1851.
Theobald (J.), Mormonism Dissected.
Thomas (E. A.), in No. Amer. Rev.; 1884. Fortnightly Rev., xxxvi. 414;
      Potter's Amer. Monthly, xvii. 298.
Thomas (John), Rise, Progress, and Dispersion of the Mormons. London,
      Edinburgh, and Nottingham.
Thompson (Charles), Evidences in Proof of the Book of Mormon; Batavia
      (N. Y.) and New York, 1841; Proclamation and Warning to the Inhab-
      itants of America.
Thornton (J. Q.), Oregon and California in 1848. N. Y., 1849. 2 vols.
Three Nights' Public Discourse at Boulogne-sur-mer, etc. Liverpool, 1850.
Tice (J. H.), Over the Plains, etc. St Louis, 1872.
Times and Seasons. Commerce (Ill.), 1830; Nauvoo (Ill.), 1840–46. 6 vols.
      in 2.
Tithing. Plano (Ill.)
Todd (John), The Sunset Land. Boston, 1870.
Torquemada, i. 609–10.
Townsend (G. A.), The Mormon Trials at Salt Lake City. New York, 1871.
Townsend (J. K.), Narrative of a Journey, etc. Philadelphia, 1839.
Townsend, Mormon Trials. n.d.
Townshend (F. T.), Ten Thousand Miles of Travel, etc. London, 1869.
Tracy (Mrs N. N.), Narrative. MS.
Trial of Jos Smith, Jr, and Others, for High Treason and Other Crimes
      against the State of Missouri. 26th cong. 2d sess., Sen. Doc. 189, Feb.
      15, 1841.
Trial of the Witnesses to the Resurrection of Jesus. Plano (Ill.), 1870.

Tribune Almanac. N. Y., 1838 et seq.
Triplett (Frank), Conquering the Wilderness. New York and St Louis, 1883.
True Latter-day Saints' Herald. Cincinnati (O.) and Plano (Ill.), 1860–72.
Truth by Three Witnesses: A Warning Voice. Plano (Ill.)
Truth made Manifest: A Dialogue. Plano (Ill.)
Tucker (Pomeroy), Origin, Rise, etc., of Mormonism. New York, 1867.
Tullidge (Edward W.), Life of Brigham Young. N. Y., 1876; Life of Jo-
    seph the Prophet. Salt Lake City, 1878; Women of Mormondom. N. Y.,
    1877; Quarterly Magazine. S. L. City, 1880 et seq.; Morm. Common-
    wealth, in Galaxy, ii. 356. Morm. Theoc., in Id., ii. 209, iv. 541; Refor-
    mation, etc., Harper's Mag., xliii. 602; Autobiograhpy. MS.; Brigham
    Young and Mormonism, in Galaxy, Sept. 1867; Views of Mormorism, in
    Id., Oct. 1, 1866; Leaders in the Mormon Reform Movement, in Phren.
    Jour., July 1871; The Mormons, etc., in Id., Jan. 1870; The Utah Gen-
    tiles, etc., in Id., May 1871; Wm H. Hooper, of Utah, in Id., Nov. 1870;
    History of Salt Lake City.
Tullidge's Quarterly Magazine. Salt Lake City, 1880 et seq.
Turnbull (W.), A Call to the Unconverted. Liverpool, n.d.
Turner (J. B.), Mormonism in All Ages. New York, 1842.
Turner (O.), Origin of the Mormon Imposture, in Littell's Liv. Age, Aug. 30,
    1851.
Tuscarora (Nev.), Times; Review.
Tuthill, Colorado.
Tuthill, Hist. Cal. San Francisco, 1866.
Tyler (Daniel), History of the Mormon Battalion. Salt Lake City, 1881.
Tyson (Thomas), Joseph Smith, the Great American Impostor. London,
    1852.

Udgorn Seion. Wales.
Unionville (Nev.), Silver State.
United States Geolog. Explor. of 40th Parallel, by Clarence King. Wash-
    ington, 1870.
United States Geolog. Surv. West of 100th Merid. (Geo. W. Wheeler);
    Bulletins; Reports and Various Publications. Washington, 1874 et seq.
    4to. Atlas sheets. Maps.
United States Government Documents: Accounts; Agriculture; Army Reg-
    ulations; Army Meteorological Register; Banks; Bureau of Statistics;
    Census; Commerce, Foreign and Domestic; Commerce and Navigation;
    Commercial Relations; Congressional Directory; Education; Engineers;
    Finance; Indian Affairs; Interior; Land Office; Meteorological Reports;
    Mint; Ordnance; Pacific Railroad; Patent Office; Postmaster-General;
    Post-offices; Quartermaster-general; Revenue; U. S. Official Register—
    cited by their dates.
United States Government Documents: House Exec. Doc.; House Journal;
    House Miscel. Doc.; House Com. Reports; Message and Documents;
    Senate Exec. Doc.; Journal; Miscel. Doc.; Com. Repts—cited by con-
    gress and session. Many of these documents have, however, separate
    titles, for which see author or topic.
University of Deseret. Annual Catalogues, 1868 et seq.; Circulars; Bien-
    nial Reports.
Upper Missouri Advertiser. 1838.
U. P. R. R., Report of Saml B. Reed.
U. S. Charters and Constitutions. Washington, 1877. 2 vols.
Utah: A Bill to Establish a Territorial Government. Washington. 1850.
Utah Almanac.
Utah and its People. New York, 1882.
Utah and the Mormons, in The New Englander, vi. 1854.
Utah Board of Trade, Resources and Attractions, etc. Salt Lake City, 1879.
Utah Central R. R. Company, Grants, Rights and Privileges, etc. Salt Lake
    City, 1871.
Utah Commission, Special Report. Washington, 1884.

Utah Commission, the Edmunds Act, Reports of the Commissioners, Rules, Regulations, etc. Salt Lake City, 1884.
Utah, Constitution of the State of. Salt Lake City, 1882.
Utah, County Sketches by various authors. MS.
Utah, Election Laws. Salt Lake City. n.d.
Utah, in Beadle's Monthly, July 1866.
Utah: Its Silver Mines and Other Resources. n.d.
Utah Journals of Council and House, 1851 et seq., together with the other Public Documents printed by the territory, which are cited in my notes by their titles and dates, the title consisting of 'Utah,' followed by one of the following headings: Act; Adjutant General's Report; Agricultural; Chancellor of University Reports; Corporations; Council and House Bills, County Financial Reports, Deseret Agric. and Manufac. Society; Stat. Reports; Domestic Relations; Elections, Fisheries; Inaugural Addresses of Governors, Messages and Documents; Joint Resolutions; Land Acts; Laws; Memorials; Militia; Mines and Mining; Political Code; Revenue Laws; School Law; Secretary of Territory Reports; Superintendent of District Schools Reports; Territorial Auditor Reports; Territorial Librarian Reports; Transportation; Warden of Penitentiary Reports.
Utah Miscellany. MS.
Utah Notes. MS.
Utah Pamphlets, Political, containing the following: Argument before Commr of Intl Revenue, etc.; Bates (George C.), Argument in Baker habeas corpus case; Cannon (Geo. Q.), Review of decision of U. S. Supreme Court; Clagett (Wm H.), Speech against admission of Utah as a state; Constitution of State of Deseret and Memorial; Cragin (A. H.), Speech on execution of laws in Utah; Fitch (Thos), Speech on Utah Bill; Speech on Land Grants and Indian Policy; Speech on the Utah Problem; Reply to Memorial of Salt Lake Bar; Hooper (W. H.), Speech against the "Cullom Bill;" Reply to Clagett; Kinney (Jno. F.), Reply to Fernando Wood; Laws concerning Naturalization, etc.; Memorial of Citizens of Salt Lake City; Musser (A. M.), Fruits of Mormonism; Paine (H. E.), Argument in Contested Election, etc.; Review of Opinion of U. S. Supreme Court by an old Lawyer; Reynolds (Geo.), vs U. S.; Snow (Z.), (Terrtl Atty.-Genl.), Communication to Legislative Assembly; Communication to Terr. House of Rep.; Taylor (John), Interview with O. J. Hollister, etc.
Utah Pamphlets, Religious, containing the following: Minutes of Special Conference of August 28, 1852, at Salt Lake City; Extract from a MS. entitled The Peace-maker; Skelton (Robt) and Meik (J. P.), A Defence of Mormonism; Pratt (O.), Smith (Geo. A.), and Cannon (Geo. Q.), Discourses on Celestial Marriage; Hyde (O.), Sketch of Travels and Ministry; Colfax (S.), The Mormon Question; Taylor (John), Reply to Colfax; Newman (Rev. Dr.), A Sermon on Plural Marriage; Pratt (O.), Reply to Newman; Zion's Cöoperative Mercantile Institution, Constitution and By-laws; Utah Central R. R. Grants, Rights and Privileges; Smith (Geo. A.), Rise, Progress, and Travels of the Church, etc.; Young (B.), The Resurrection; Circular of the First Presidency; Death and Funeral of Brigham Young; Young, Sen. (Joseph), History of the Organization of the Seventies; Gibbs (G. F.), Report of Convention of Mormon Women, etc.; The Great Proclamation, etc.; Good Tidings, etc.; The Testimony of the Great Prophet; The Great Contrast; Death of the Prophets Joseph and Hyrum Smith; Smith (Jos), Pearl of Great Price; Reynolds (Geo.), Book of Abraham.
Utah. Perpetual Emigration Fund. MS.
Utah Pioneers, Anniversary Meetings; Proceedings 33d Anniversary. Salt Lake City, 1880.
Utah, Speeches on the Edmunds Bill.
Utah Tracts, A collection of eleven pamphlets cited by titles and dates. Salt Lake City, 1879.

Vancouver (Wash.), Register.
Van Deusen (Increase and Maria), Hidden Orgies of Mormonism. Notting-
ham (Eng.), n.d.; Spiritual Delusions. New York, 1855; Startling
Disclosures of the Great Mormon Conspiracy. New York, 1849; Sub-
lime and Ridiculous Blended. New York, 1848.
Van Dyke (Walter), Recollections of Utah. MS.
Van Sickles (H.), Utah Desperadoes.
Van Tramp (John C.), Prairies and Rocky Mountains. St Louis, 1860.
Venegas, Not. Cal., i. 167-9.
Vest, Morgan, Call, Brown, Pendleton, and Lamar, in U. S. Senate. Salt
Lake City, 1882.
Vetromile (Eugene), Tour in Both Hemispheres. New York, etc., 1880.
Victor (Frances F.), All Over Oregon and Washington. San Francisco, 1872;
River of the West. Hartford, 1870.
"Vidette" (The Union). Camp Douglas and Salt Lake City, 1864 to 1867.
Villagrä, Hist. N. Mex., 19 et seq.
Virginia (Mont.), Madisonian.
Virginia and Helena (Mont.), Post.
Virginia City (Nev.), Chronicle; Territorial Enterprise.
Visit of the Wyoming Legislature to Utah. Salt Lake City, 1884.
Visit to the Crazy Swede. MS.
Visit to the Mormons, in Westmin. Rev., Oct. 1861.
Voice from the West, etc.; History of the Morrisites. San Francisco, 1879.
Voice of the Good Shepard. Plano (Ill.)

Wadsworth (W.), National Wagon-road Guide. San Francisco, 1858.
Waite (C. B.), The Western Monthly. Salt Lake City, 1869 et seq.; in
Lakeside, i. 290.
Waite (Mrs C. V.), Adventures in the Far West, etc. Chicago, 1882; The
Mormon Prophet and his Harem. Chicago, 1857; Cambridge, 1866.
Walker (W.), Industrial Progress and Prospects of Utah. MS.
Walla Walla (Wash.), Statesman.
Wandell (C. W.), History of the Persecutions Endured by the Church, etc.
Sidney (N. S. W.), 1852; Reply to "Shall we Believe in Mormon?"
Sidney (N. S. W.), 1852.
Ward (Austin N.), Husband in Utah. New York, 1857; Male Life among
the Mormons. Philadelphia, 1863.
Ward (J. H.), Gospel Philosophy. Salt Lake City, 1884; The Hand of Provi-
dence. Salt Lake City, 1883.
Ward (Maria), Female Life among the Mormons. New York, 1855; The
Mormon Wife, etc. Hartford, 1873.
Warner, Rem. MS., 21-9.
Warren (G. K.), Preliminary Report, etc. Washington, 1875.
Warsaw (Ill.), Signal.
Washington (D. C.), Natl Intelligencer; Seer; Star.
Waters (——), Life among the Mormons. New York, 1868.
Watsonville (Cal.), Pajaronian; Pajaro Times.
Way to End the Mormon War, in Littell's Liv. Age, 2d ser., xx. 1858.
Webster (Thomas), Extracts from the Doctrine and Covenants. Preston
(Eng.), n.d.
Wedderburn (D.), Mormonism from a Mormon Point of View, in Fortnightly
Rev., 1876; Pop. Scien. Monthly, x. 156.
Weightman (Hugh), Mormonism Exposed; The Other Side. Salt Lake City,
1884.
Weiser (R.), in Evang. Rev., x. 80.
Wells (D. H.), Journal. MS.
Wells (E. B.) and Williams (Z. Y.), Memorial to U. S. Congress. Washing-
ton, 1879.
Wells (J. F.), The Contributor, A Monthly Magazine. Salt Lake City, Oct.
1879 et seq.

Wells (Samuel R.), The Mormon Question, in Phren. Jour., Dec. 1871; Our Visit to Salt Lake City, in Id., Dec. 1870.
Wentworth, Great West.
West (P. R.), The Brewing Business. MS.
Westbrook (G. W.), Appendix to Hunt's Mormonism. St Louis, 1844; The Mormons in Illinois. St Louis, 1844.
West Coast Reporter, iv. 415.
Westmins. Rev., lix. 196.
Whatcom (Wash.), Bellingham Bay Mail.
White (F. P.), Cattle Raising and Grazing. MS.
Whitney (H.), Journal. MS.
Whitney (H. M.), Plural Marriage. Salt Lake City, 1882.
Whittier (J. G.), in Howitt, Journal, ii. 157; Littell's Liv. Age, xv. 461.
Why We Practise Plural Marriage. Salt Lake City, 1884.
Wight (Lyman), Abridged Account of my Life. n.d.
Willard (Emma), Last Leaves of American History. New York, 1853.
Willes (W.), What is Mormonism? Calcutta, n.d.; The Mountain Warbler. Salt Lake City. 1872.
Williams (H. T.), Pacific Tourist. New York, 1876.
Williams (S.), Mormonism Exposed. 1842.
Willmore (Benj.), Mormonism Unmasked. West Bromwich (Eng.), 1855.
Winchester (Benj.), A History of the Priesthood. Philadelphia, 1843; Origin of the Spaulding Story. Philadelphia, 1840; Synopsis of the Holy Scriptures, etc. Philadelphia, 1842.
Winnemucca (Nev.), Silver State.
With the False Prophet, in Scrib. Monthly, iii. 1872.
Wolfe (J. M.), Gazetteer. Omaha, 1878.
Woodruf (W.) and Richards (F. D.), Historial Events of Mormonism. MS.
Woodruff (Phebe W.), Autobiog. Sketch. MS.
Woodruff (W.), Leaves from my Journal. Salt Lake City, 1881, 1882; Overland to Utah. MS.; Private Journal. MS.
Woods (C. L.), Recollections. MS.
Worthington (C. J.), The Woman in Battle, etc. Hartford, 1876.
Wray (G. W.), Mormonism Exhibited in its Own Minor. Middlesbrough (Eng.), 1854.

Yankee Mahomet (The), in Amer. Whig Rev., June 1851.
Year of Jubilee, etc. Salt Lake City, 1880.
Young (Ann Eliza), Wife No. 19, etc. Hartford, 1876.
Young (Brigham), Resurrection: A Discourse. Salt Lake City, 1875; Death of, etc. Salt Lake City, 1877; History and Private Journal. MS.
Young (Brigham) and Others, Circular of the First Presidency, etc. Salt Lake City, July 11, 1877; Journal of Discourses. Liverpool and London, 1854 et seq.
Young (L.), Early Experiences. MS.
Young (Mrs C. D.), A Woman's Experiences with the Pioneer Band. MS.
Young, Sen. (Jos), Organization of the Seventies, etc. Salt Lake City, 1878.
Y Perl o Fawr Bris. n.d. (Wales).
Yr Curgrawn Ysgrythyrol. Merthyr Tydvil, South Wales.
Yuma (Arizona), Sentinel.

Zabriskie (Jas C.), Public Land Laws of the U. S. San Francisco, 1870.
Zion's Coöperative Mercantile Institution; Constitution, By-Laws, and Articles óf Incorporation. S. L. City, 1870. MS.; Argument before U. S. Commissioner of Internal Revenue. S. L. City, 1878; Mercantile and Manufacturing Establishments. S. L. City, 1884; Semi-annual Statement. S. L. City, 1880; Wholesale Price List. S. L. City, 1880.
Zion's Watchman (Australia and New Zealand).

HISTORY OF UTAH.

CHAPTER I.

DISCOVERIES OF THE SPANIARDS.

1540-1777.

FRANCISCO VAZQUEZ DE CORONADO AT CÍBOLA—EXPEDITION OF PEDRO DE
TOBAR AND FATHER JUAN DE PADILLA—THEY HEAR OF A LARGE
RIVER—GARCÍA LOPEZ DE CÁRDENAS SENT IN SEARCH OF IT—THE FIRST
EUROPEANS TO APPROACH UTAH—ROUTE OF CÁRDENAS—MYTHICAL
MAPS—PART OF THE NORTHERN MYSTERY—JOURNEY OF DOMINGUEZ
AND ESCALANTE—THE COURSE THEY FOLLOWED—THE RIVERS THEY
CROSSED—THE COMANCHES—REGION OF THE GREAT LAKES—RIVERS
TIMPANOGOS, SAN BUENAVENTURA, AND OTHERS—THE COUNTRY OF
THE YUTAS—ROUTE FROM SANTA FÉ TO MONTEREY—THE FRIARS TALK
OF THE LAKE COUNTRY—RETURN OF THE SPANIARDS TO ZUÑI AND
MARCH TO SANTA FÉ.

As Francisco Vazquez de Coronado was journeying
from Culiacan to the north and east in 1540, he rested
at Cíbola, that is to say Zuñi, and while waiting for
the main army to come forward, expeditions were sent
out in various directions. One of these, consisting
of twenty men under Pedro de Tobar, and attended
by Father Juan de Padilla, proceeded north-westward,
and after five days reached Tusayan, or the Moqui
villages, which were quickly captured. Among other
matters of interest, information was here given of a
large river yet farther north, the people who lived
upon its banks being likewise very large.

Returning to Cíbola, Tobar reported what had been
said concerning this river; whereupon Captain García
Lopez de Cárdenas was sent with twelve men to
explore it, Pedro de Sotomayor accompanying to

(1)

chronicle the expedition. Obtaining at Tusayan, where
he was well received, guides and carriers, with an
ample supply of provisions, Cárdenas marched for
twenty days, probably in a north-westerly direction,[1]

[1] I say probably, though in my own mind there is little doubt. The Spaniards were exploring northward. They had lately traversed the region to
their south-west, and instead of wishing to retrace their steps they would be
likely to keep up well away from their former track. It is true that one narrative gives the direction as west; but then the same writer places Tusan, or
Tusayan, west of Cíbola, which if the latter be Zuñi, and the former Moqui,
is incorrect. Then, if their direction from the Moqui towns was the same
as this writer declares it to have been in travelling to that place, the
Spaniards at this time certainly struck the Colorado within the limits of the
present Utah. Escalante, *Carta de 28 Oct. 1775*, MS., placed Moqui west
of Zuñi, but a little north of west, with the Yutas their neighbor on the
north. It is sufficiently plain that Cíbola was Zuñi, and Tusayan Moqui,
and as a matter of fact the latter is in a north-westerly direction from the
former. That they went due west and crossed the Little Colorado without
any mention of that stream is not likely; because, first, it is not twenty days
distant from the Moquis, and the stream when reached does not answer to
their description. It was the great river they wished to find, and a north-
west course would be the most direct. Further than this, it is stated plainly
that the point at which they discovered the river was much nearer its source
than where the Spaniards had previously seen it. Upon the direction then
taken hangs the question as to the first Europeans to enter Utah. I deem the
matter of sufficient importance to give both the originals and the translations
of two of the most complete and reliable narratives of the expedition. The
first and fullest we find in the *Relation de Castañeda* of Coronado's expedition, *Ternaux-Compans*, série i. tom. ix. 61–5, which reads as follows:
  'Comme don Pédro de Tobar avait rempli sa mission, il revint sur ses pas
et rendit compte au général de ce qu'il avait vu. Celui-ci fit partir sur-le-
champ don Garci-Lopez de Cardenas et douze autres personnes pour aller
visiter cette rivière; cet officier fut très-bien reçu et parfaitement traité par
les indiens de Tusayan, qui lui donnèrent des guides pour continuer sa route.
Nos soldats partirent chargés de vivres, les indiens les ayant avertis qu'il
fallait traverser un désert de vingt journées de long avant d'entrer dans un
pays habité. Après ces vingt journées de marche ils arrivèrent en effet à
cette rivière, dont les bords sont tellement élevés qu'ils croyaient être à trois
ou quatre lieues en l'air. Le pays est couvert de pins bas et rabougris; il est
exposé au nord, et le froid y est si violent, que, quoique l'on fût en été, ou
pouvait à peine le supporter. Les Espagnols marchèrent pendant trois jours
le long de ces montagnes, espérant toujours trouver une descente pour arriver
à la rivière qui, d'en haut, ne paraissait pas avoir plus d'une brasse de large,
et qui, selon les Indiens, avait plus d'une demi-lieue; mais il fut impossible
de s'y rendre. Étant parvenus deux ou trois jours après dans un endroit où
la descente leur parut plus facile, le capitaine Melgosa, Juan Galeras et un
soldat qui étaient les plus légers de la bande, résolurent de faire une tenta-
tive. Ils descendirent jusqu'à ce que ceux qui étaient restés en haut les
eussent perdus de ven. Ils revinrent vers les quatre heures du soir, disant
qu'ils avaient trouvé tant de difficultés, qu'ils n'avaient pu arriver jusqu'en
bas; car ce qui d'en haut semblait facile, ne l'était pas du tout quand on
approchait. Ils ajoutèrent qu'ils étaient parvenus à environ un tiers de la
descente, et que de là, la rivière paraissait déjà très grande, ce qui confirmait
ce que les indiens avaient dit. Ils assurèrent que quelques rochers que l'on
voyait d'en haut, et qui paraissait à peine de la hauteur d'un homme étaient
plus hauts que la tour de la cathédrale de Séville. Les Espagnols cessèrent

through a desert country until he discovered the river, but from such high banks that he could not reach it. It was the river called the Tizon, and it flowed from the north-east toward the south-west. It seemed to the Spaniards when they first descried it that they were on mountains through which the river had cut

de suivre les rochers qui bordent la rivière, parce qu'on y manquait d'eau. Jusque-là ils avaient été obligés chaque soir de s'avancer une lieue ou deux dans l'intérieur pour en trouver. Quand ils eurent marché pendant trois ou quatre jours, les guides leur déclarèrent qu'il était impossible d'aller plus loin, qu'on ne trouverait pas d'eau de quatre jours; que quand les Indiens passaient cette route, ils emmenaient avec eux des femmes chargées de calebasses remplies d'eau, et qu'ils en enterraient une partie pour les retrouver au retour; que d'ailleurs ils parcouraient en un jour autant de chemin que les Espagnols en deux. Cette rivière était celle del Tizon. On arriva beaucoup plus près de sa source que de l'endroit où Melchior Diaz et ses gens l'avaient traversée, et l'on sut plus tard que les Indiens dont on avait parlé étaient de la même nation que ceux que Diaz avait vus. Les Espagnols revinrent donc sur leurs pas, et cette expédition n'eut pas d'autre résultat. Pendant la marche, ils arrivèrent à une cascade qui tombait d'un rocher. Les guides dirent que les cristaux blancs qui pendaient à l'entour étaient du sel. On en recueillit une quantité que l'on emporta, et qu'on distribua à Cibola, où l'on rendit compte par écrit au général de tout ce que l'on avait vu. Garci-Lopez avait emmené avec lui un certain Pédro de Sotomayor, qui était chroniqueur de l'expédition. Tous les villages de cette province sont restés nos alliés, mais on ne les a pas visités depuis, et l'on n'a tenté aucune découverte de ce côté.'

As soon as Don Pédro de Tobar had fulfilled his mission, he returned and gave the general an account of what he had seen. The latter immediately ordered Don Garci-Lopez de Cárdenas, and 12 other persons, to go and visit that river; this officer was well received and politely treated by the Indians of Tusayan, who furnished him with guides to continue his journey. Our soldiers departed loaded with provisions, the Indians having notified them that it was necessary to travel 20 days through a desert before entering any inhabited country. After this 20 days' march, they arrived at that river whose banks are of such a height that it seemed to them that they were three or four leagues up in the air. The country is covered with low and stunted pines, exposed to the north, and the cold is so violent that, although it was summer, one could hardly endure it. The Spaniards during three days skirted those mountains, always in the hope of finding a descent to reach the river, which from above appeared to be no more than a fathom in width, and which, according to the Indians, was more than half a league wide; but all their efforts were vain. Two or three days later, they arrived at a place where the descent seemed easier; Captain Melgosa Juan Galeras and a soldier who were the lightest men of the band, resolved to make an attempt. They descended until those who had remained on the top had lost sight of them. They returned at about four o'clock in the afternoon, saying they had found so many difficulties that they could not reach the bottom; for, what seemed easy from above was not at all so when approaching the water. They added that they came down about one third of the descent, and that even from there the river seemed very large. This statement confirmed what the Indians had said. The three men affirmed that some rocks seen from above and which appeared to be of the height of a man, were higher than the tower of the cathedral of Seville. The Spaniards stopped following the rocks that bordered the river on account of the lack of water. Until then, they had been obliged to advance one or two leagues in the interior to find a chasm only a few feet wide, but which if they might believe the natives was half a league across. In vain for several days, with their faces toward the south and west, they sought to escape from the mountains that environed them, and descend to the river, for they were suffering from thirst. At length

some. When they had marched during three or four days, the guides declared to them that it was impossible to go further, that water would not be found before four days; that when the Indians travelled on this road, they took with them women who carried calabashes filled with water, and they buried a certain part, so that they might find it when returning; and besides they made in one day as many miles as the Spaniards would in two. This was the river del Tizon. They arrived much nearer to its source than the place where Melchor Diaz and his people had crossed, and it was known later that the Indians spoken of belonged to the same nation as those seen by Diaz. The Spaniards therefore came back, and the expedition had no other result. While marching, they arrived at a cascade falling from a rock. The guides affirmed that the white crystals hanging around were salt. A quantity of it was gathered, carried away, and distributed at Cíbola, where a written account of all that had been seen was sent to the general. Garci-Lopez had taken with him a certain Pedro de Sotomayor, who was the chronicler of the expedition. All the villages of this province have remained our allies, but they have not been visited since, and no attempt at discovery has been made in that direction.

The other is from a relation by an unknown author, found in the archives of the Indies, and printed in *Pacheco* and *Cárdenas, Col. Doc.*, xiv. 321–3, under title of *Relacion del suceso de la Jornada que Francisco Vazquez hizo en el descubrimiento de Cíbola*, and from which I give the extract covering the same incident:

'Vuelto D. Pedro de Tobar, é dada relacion de aquellos pueblos, luego despachó á D. García Lopez de Cárdenas, maestre de campo, por el mesmo camino que habia venido D. Pedro, é que pasase de aquella provincia de Tuzan, al Poniente, é para ida é vuelta de la jornada é descobrimiento, le señaló ochenta dias de término de ida é vuelta, el qual fué echado adelante de Tuzan con guias de los naturales que decian que habia adelante, poblado, aunque lejos, andadas cincuenta leguas de Tuzan al Poniente, é ochenta de Cíbola, halló una barranca de un rio que fué imposible por una parte ni otra hallarle baxada para caballo, ni aun para pié, sino por una parte muy traba-xosa, por donde tenia casi dos leguas de baxada. Estaba la barranca tan acantillada de peñas, que apenas podian ver el rio, el cual, aunque es segun dicen, tanto ó mucho mayor que el de Sevilla, de arriba aparescia un arroyo; por manera que aunque con harta diligencia se buscó pasada, é por muchas partes no se halla, en la cual estuvieron artos dias con mucha necesidad de agua, que no la hallaban, é la del rio no se podian aprovechar della aunque la vian; é á esta causa le fué forzado á don García Lopez volverse á donde hallaron; este rio venia del Nordeste é volvia al Sur Sudueste, por manera que sin falta ninguna es aquel donde llegó Melchor Diaz.'

Don Pedro de Tobar having returned, and having made a report concerning those towns, D. García Lopez de Cárdenas, maestre de campo, was ordered to take the same route by which Don Pedro had come, and to go on from the province of Tuzan to the westward. He was given 80 days in which to make the journey, from his departure until his return. He went on beyond Tuzan, accompanied by Indian guides, who told him that farther on there was a settlement. Having gone 50 leagues to the westward of Tuzan, and 80 from Cíbola, he came to the cañon of a river adown the side of which there was no descent practicable for horse, nor even for those on foot, except

one morning three of the lightest and most active of the party crept over the brink and descended until they were out of sight. They did not return till toward evening, when they reported their failure to reach the bottom, saying that the river, and distances and objects, were all much larger than they seemed to the beholder above, rocks apparently no higher than a man being in fact larger than the cathedral at

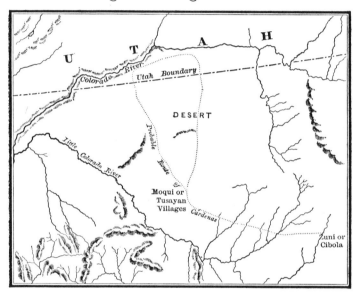

PROBABLE ROUTE OF CÁRDENAS.

Seville. Compelled by thirst they retired from the inhospitable stream, and finally returned to Tusayan and Cíbola.

by a way full of difficulties, and nearly two leagues in length. The side of the cañon was of rock so steep that the river was barely discernible, although, according to report, it is as great as the river of Seville, or greater; and from above appeared a brook. During many days, and in many places, a way by which to pass the river was sought in vain. During this time there was much suffering from a lack of water, for although that of the river was in view, it was unattainable. For this reason Don Garcia Lopez was forced to return. This river comes from the north-east, and makes a bend to the south-south-eastward; hence, beyond a doubt, it must be that reached by Melchor Diaz.

Thus the reader will be able to determine the matter for himself as clearly as may be. For details on Coronado's expedition see the following author-

It was not necessary in those days that a country
should be discovered in order to be mapped; even
now we dogmatize most about what we know least.
It is a lonely sea indeed that cannot sport mermaids
and monsters; it were a pity to have so broad an extent of land without a good wide sheet of water in it;
so the *Conibas Regio cum Vicinis Gentibvs* shows a
large lake, called Conibas, connecting by a very wide

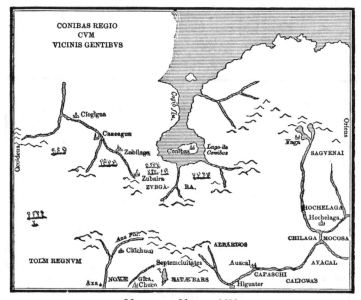

MAP FROM MAGIN, 1611.

river apparently with a northern sea. I give herewith
another map showing a lake large enough to swallow

ities, though comparatively few of them make mention of the adventures
of Captain Cárdenas on the Colorado: *Ramusio, Viaggi*, iii. 359-63; *Hakluyt's Voy.*, iii. 373-9; *Mota-Padilla, Conq. N. Gal.*, iii. 14, 158-69; *Torquemada*, i. 609-10; *Herrera*, dec. vi. lib. ix. cap. xi.-xii.; *Beaumont, Hist.
Mich.*, MS., 407-22, 482-546, 624-5; *Oviedo*, iv. 19; *Villagrá, Hist. N.
Mex.*, 19 et seq.; *Gomara, Hist. Ind.*, 272-4; *Bernal Diaz, Hist. Verdad.*,
235; *Benzoni, Hist. Mundo Nuovo*, 107; *Ribas, Hist. Triumphos*, 26-7; *Venegas, Not. Cal.*, i. 167-9; *Clavigero, Storia Cal.*, 153; *Alegre, Hist. Comp.
Jesus*, i. 233-8; Salmeron, in *Doc. Hist. Mex.*, 3d ser. pt. iv. 7-9; *Noticias*, in
Id., 671-2; *Cavo, Tres Siglos*, i. 127-9; Lorenzana, in *Cortés, Hist. Mex.*,
325. These might be followed by a long list of modern writers, for which I
will refer the reader to *Hist. North Mexican States*, this series.

Utah and Idaho combined, and discharging its waters by two great rivers into the Pacific. This species of geography was doubtless entirely satisfactory to the wise men of this world until they came to know better about it. If the reader will look over the chapters on the Northern Mystery in my *History of the*

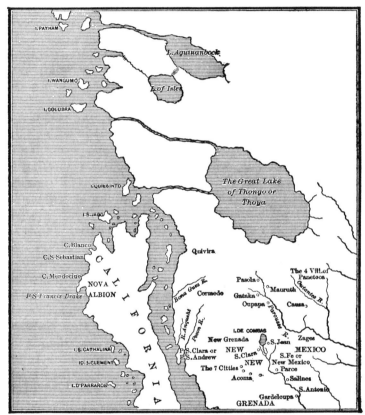

MAP BY JOHN HARRIS, 1705.

Northwest Coast he may learn further of absurdities in map-making.

A more extended and pronounced exploration was that of two Franciscan friars, one the *visitador comi-*

sario of New Mexico, Francisco Atanasio Dominguez,
and the other *ministro doctrinero* of Zuñi, Silvestre
Velez de Escalante, who set out from Santa Fé July
29, 1776, for the purpose of discovering a direct route
to Monterey, on the seaboard of Alta California.
New Mexico had now been known nearly two and a
half centuries; the city of Santa Fé had been founded
over a century and a half, Monterey had been occupied since 1770, and yet there had been opened no
direct route westward with the sea, communication
between Mexico and Santa Fé being by land, the
road following the Rio Grande.   In his memorial of
March 1773, while in Mexico, Father Junípero Serra
had urged that two expeditions be made, one from
Sonora to California, which was carried out the following year by Captain Anza, and one from New
Mexico to the sea, which Dominguez and Escalante
now proposed to undertake.   Again in 1775 Anza
made a similar journey, this time leaving at the junction of the Colorado and Gila Father Garcés who
ascended the former stream to the Mojave country,
whence crossing to Mission San Gabriel he proceeded
to the Tulare Valley.   There he heard from the natives of a great river coming in from the east or north-
east.[2]   Indeed it was long the prevailing opinion that
there existed such a stream in that vicinity.   From
the Tulare country Garcés returned to San Gabriel
and Mojave, and thence proceeded to the villages of
the Moquis.   From this place he probably wrote to
Santa Fé concerning the rumor of this river; for all
through the journey of Dominguez and Escalante
they were in search of it.[3]

[2] On Father Font's map, 1777, are laid down two rivers entering the region
of the Tulare lakes from the north-east, one the *Rio de San Phelipe*, and the
other called the *Rio de que se Viene Noticia por el P. Garces.*   See *Font's
Journal*, MS.; *Serra, Memorial*, March 1773, MS.; *Garcés, Diario*, 246–348;
Forbes' Hist. Cal., 157–62; *Arch. Cal., Prov. Rec.*, MS., i. 47–8, vi. 59;
Palou, Not., ii. 281–2; *Hist. Cal.; Hist. New Mex.; Hist. North Mex. States*,
this series.
[3] Probably it was the San Joaquin, or the Sacramento, of which they
heard.   Concerning a route from New Mexico to California Humboldt says:
' En considérant les voyages hardis des premiers conquerans espagnols au

The party consisted in all of nine persons. Besides the two priests there were Juan Pedro Cisneros, *alcalde mayor* of Zuñi, Bernardo Miera y Pacheco, *capitan miliciano* of Santa Fé, and five soldiers.[4] Having implored divine protection, on the day before named they took the road to Abiquiú, passed on to the Rio Chama, and on the 5th of August reached a point called Nieves, on the San Juan River, three leagues below the junction of the Navajo. Thence they passed down the north bank of the San Juan, crossing the several branches, until on the 10th they found themselves on a branch of the Mancos, some distance from the San Juan, and beyond the line of the present state of Colorado.[5] The 12th they camped on the north bank of the Rio Dolores, in latitude 38° 13',[6] and were there joined by two natives from Abiquiú, who had deserted their homes to follow the expedition.[7]

They now followed the general course of the Dolores[8] until the 23d, when they left the San Pedro, which flows into the Dolores near La Sal, and crossed

Mexique, au Pérou, et sur la rivière des Amazones, on est étonné de voir que depuis deux siècles cette même nation n'a pas su trouver un chemin de terre dans la Nouvelle-Espagne, depuis Taos au port de Monterey.' *Essai Pol.*, i. 317.

[4] 'Don Joaquin Lain, vecino de la misma villa, Lorenzo Olivares de la villa del Paso, Lucrecio Muñiz, Andrés Muñiz, Juan de Aguilar y Simon Lucero.' *Diario*, in *Doc. Hist. Mex.*, ser. ii. p. 378.

[5] At the beginning of the journey their route was identical with what was later known as the old Spanish trail from Santa Fé to Los Angeles. Their course was at first north-west, but shortly after passing Abiquiú it pointed due north into Colorado, then west, and again north-west into Utah, being about the same as was later called the old Spanish trail from Santa Fé to Great Salt Lake. Captain J. N. Macomb of the topographical engineers has surveyed and mapped essentially the same trail.

[6] Probably not so far north by some 40'.

[7] 'Esta tarde nos alcanzaron un coyote y un genízaro de Abiquiú, nombrados el primero Felipe y el segundo Juan Domingo; por vagar entre los gentiles, se huyeron sin permiso de sus superiores del dicho pueblo, pretestando querer acompañarnos. No necesitábamos de ellos; mas por evitar las culpas, que ó por su ignorancia ó por su malicia podian cometer andando mas tiempo solos entre los yutas, si intentábamos que regresasen, los admitimos por compañeros.' *Diario, Doc. Hist. Mex.*, ser. ii. tom. i. 392.

[8] These streams are doubtless those emptying into the Colorado not far from its junction with the Bunkara. Latitude 39° 13' is here given, but that must be too high. Philip Harry, in *Simpson's Explor.*, 490, says that up to the point first touched on the Dolores the priests' path and Macomb's survey are identical, but that they here diverge.

over north-east to Rio San Francisco,[9] and again to
the Rio San Javier[10] on the 28th, their course being
for some distance east of north.

Not far from their path was a ranchería of Yutas,
which the Spaniards visited, endeavoring to obtain
guides to the land of the Timpanogos, Timpangotzis,
or Lagunas, where they had been told to look for

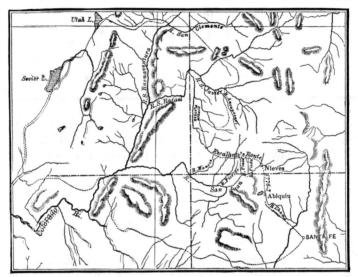

ESCALANTE'S ROUTE FROM SANTA FÉ TO UTAH LAKE.

Pueblo towns.   A Laguna guide was there, but the
Yutas did all in their power to dissuade the explorers

---

[9] An affluent of the San Javier, or Grand River.

[10] Called by the Yutas *T'omiche;* to-day Grand River. It may here be
observed that the route toward this region had been visited by Spaniards
before, notably by Juan María de Ribera in 1761, and Spanish names had
been given to places, though the present Utah was probably not entered by
him.   Escalante states that the San Javier is formed by four small streams
coming in above the point at which he crossed, and these, says Harry, *Simpson's Explor.,* 490, correspond 'remarkably with the Uncompagre River,
Grand River, Smith's Fork, and another large fork...It seems evident that
after crossing the San Xavier he follows up stream a different fork from what
we call Grand River, but which fork he calls the main river, or San Xavier.'
Gunnison maps his explorations, showing the mouth of this last named
stream.   In *Simpson's Explor.,* 489, is given a map of the present expedition,
but it does not conform in every particular to Escalante's text.

from proceeding, pretending ignorance of the country
and danger from the Comanches. But the 3d of September saw them again on their way. Pursuing a
north-west course, the second day they crossed and
camped on the north bank of the Rio San Rafael, or
Colorado,[11] in latitude 41° 4'. Their course thence
was north-westerly, and on the 9th they crossed a
river called San Clemente,[12] flowing west. Signs of
buffaloes were abundant, and on the 11th they killed
one. Two days afterward they crossed the Rio de
San Buenaventura,[13] the boundary between the Yutas
and the Comanches, in latitude 41° 19', at a place
which the priests call Santa Cruz. Here were six large
black poplars, on one of which they left an inscription.
After resting two days they took the course of the
San Buenaventura south-west ten leagues, and from
a hill saw the junction of the San Clemente. Descending a little farther they found a river flowing in from
the west, following which they reached a branch the
17th, naming it the San Cosme.[14]

From this point they proceeded westward, following up the Uintah, across the Duchesne, and over the
mountains, with no small difficulty, to a river which
they called Purísima,[15] and which they followed till
on the 23d they came in sight of the lake which the
natives called Timpanogos, but which is known now
as Utah Lake.

Several reasons combined to bring the Spaniards
so far to the north of what would be a direct road

[11] Grand River; but the latitude given was about 1° 30' too high.
[12] White River, the point of crossing being near the Utah line.
[13] Green River. The latitude given is at least 50' too high. The crossing
was above the junctions of White River and the Uintah with Green River.
See Rep. Fr. Alonso de Posada, custodio de N. Mex., in *Doc. Hist. Mex.*, i.
439.
[14] This is the north branch of the Uintah. Indeed the narrative of the
explorers makes their route in this vicinity unmistakable.
[15] Now the Timpanogos. 'Proseguimos al noroeste media legua, pasamos á
la otra banda del rio, subimos una corta cuesta y divisamos la laguna y dila-
tado valle de Nuestra Señora de la Merced de los Timpanogotzis—así lo nom-
bramos desde aquí.' *Diario, Doc. Hist. Mex.*, série ii. tom. i. 454.

from Santa Fé to Monterey. First, Escalante entertained a theory that a better route to the Pacific
could be found northward than toward the south.
Then there was always a fascination attending this
region, with its great and perpetual Northern Mystery; perhaps the Arctic Ocean came down hereabout,
or at least an arm of the Anian Strait might be
found; nor were forgotten the rivers spoken of by
different persons on different occasions as flowing
hence into the Pacific. And last of all it may be
that the rumor of Pueblo villages in this quarter carried the explorers further north than otherwise they
would have gone.

However this may have been, they were now of
opinion that they had penetrated far enough in a
northerly direction, and from this point must take a
southerly course. There were here no town-builders
like the Moquis and Zuñis, as the priests had been
led to suppose, but there were wild Indians, and the
first they had seen in this vicinity. At first these
savages manifested fear, but when assured that the
strangers had not come to harm them, and were in no
way leagued with the dreaded Comanches, they welcomed them kindly and gave them food. They were
simple-minded and inoffensive, these native Yutas,
very ready to guide the travellers whithersoever they
would go; but they begged them to return and establish a mission in their midst; in token of which, and
of their desire to adopt the Christian faith, they gave
the priests a kind of hieroglyphic painting on deer-
skin.[16]

[16] The Spaniards asked from them some token to show that they wished
them to return, and the day after they brought them one; 'pero al traer la
seña vió un compañero, que no sabia el órden dado, á las figuras de ella, y
mostrándole la cruz del rosario, les dió á entender, que la pintasen sobre una
de las figuras, y entonces la volvieron á llevar, y sobre cada una pintaron
una cruz pequeña; lo demas quedó como antes y nos la dieron diciendo que
la figura que por uno y otro lado tenia mas almagre, ó como ellos decian,
sangre, representaba al capitan mayor, porque en las batallas con los cumanches habia recibido mas heridas: las otras dos que no estaban tan ensangren-
tadas, á los otros dos capitanes inferiores al primero, y la que no tenia sangre
ninguna, á uno que no era capitan de guerra, pero era de autoridad entre

Then the Spaniards talk of the country, and of the people about them. They are in the valley and by the lake of Nuestra Señora de la Merced de los Tim-

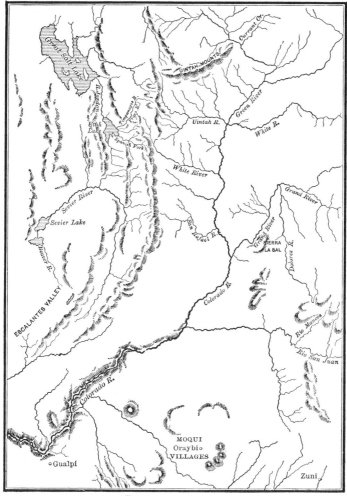

TIMPANOGOS VALLEY.

ellos. Estas cuatro figuras de hombres estaban rudamente pintadas con tierra y almagre en un corto pedazo de gamuza.' *Diario, Doc. Hist. Mex.*, série ii. tom. i. 462-3.

panogos,[17] and north of the river San Buenaventura are
the mountains which they have just crossed, extending north-east and south-west some seventy leagues,
and having a width of forty leagues. From the surrounding heights flow four rivers of medium size,
discharging their waters into the lake, where thrive
fish and wild fowl. The valley which surrounds this
lake extends from south-east to north-west sixteen
Spanish leagues; it is quite level, and has a width of
ten or twelve leagues. Except the marshes on the
lake borders the land is good for agriculture. Of the
four rivers which water the valley the southernmost,
which they call Aguas Calientes, passes through rich
meadows capable of supporting two large towns.
The second, three leagues from the first, flowing
northerly, and which they call the San Nicolás, fer-
tilizes enough good land to support one large town
or two smaller ones. Before reaching the lake it
divides into two branches, on the banks of which
grow tall poplars and alders. The third river, which
is three and a half leagues to the north-east, and which
they call the San Antonio de Padua, carries more
water than the others, and from its rich banks, which
would easily support three large towns, spring groves
of larger trees. Santa Ana, they call the fourth
river, which is north-west of the San Antonio, and
not inferior to the others [18]—so they are told, for they
do not visit it. Besides these rivers, there are good
springs of water both on plain and mountain-side;
pasture lands are abundant, and in parts the fertile
soil yields such quantities of flax and hemp that it
seems they must have been planted there by man.
On the San Buenaventura the Spaniards had been

[17] Or, as it was also called, Timpagtzis, Timpanoautzis, ó Come Pescado.
Doc. Hist. Mex., série ii. tom. i. 464.
[18] There is no difficulty in recognizing these land-marks, the Uintah
Mountains, the San Buenaventura, or Green River; and in the four streams
of the valley, their Aguas Calientes is Currant Creek; the second, their San
Nicolás, though more than three leagues from the first, and not correspond-
ing in every other particular, is the Spanish River; the San Antonio is the
Provo; and the Santa Ana, the River Jordan.

troubied by the cold; but here the climate is so delightful, the air so balmy, that it is a pleasure to breathe it, by day and by night. In the vicinity are other valleys equally delightful. Besides the products of the lake the Yutas hunt hares, and gather seeds from which they make *atole*. They might capture some buffaloes in the north-north-west but for the troublesome Comanches.[19] They dwell in huts of osier, of which, likewise, many of their utensils are made; some of them wear clothes, the best of which are of the skins of rabbits and antelopes. There are in this region many people, of whom he who would know more may consult the *Native Races*.

The Spaniards are further told by the Yutas of a large and wonderful body of water toward the northwest, and this is what Father Escalante reports of it. "The other lake, with which this communicates," he says, "occupies, as they told us, many leagues, and its waters are injurious and extremely salt; because the Timpanois[20] assure us that he who wets any part of his body with this water, immediately feels an itching in the wet part. We were told that in the circuit of this lake there live a numerous and quiet nation, called Puaguampe, which means in our language Sorcerers; they speak the Comanche language, feed on herbs, and drink from various fountains or springs of good water which are about the lake; and they have their little houses of grass and earth, which latter forms the roof. They are not, so they intimated, enemies of those living on this lake, but since a certain time when the people there approached and killed a man, they do not consider them as neutral as before.

[19] This is directly opposite the direction in which we would expect to find the Comanches of to-day; but the Utes applied the term *comanche* to all hostile Indians. Buffaloes were common in aboriginal times in Cache and Powder River valleys as well as in eastern Oregon and Boisé valley.

[20] Yet another form for the name Timpanogos, as indeed before the end of the following page we have 'Timpanosis,' 'Timpanogotzis,' and 'Timpanogo.' See note 17 this chapter. On Froisett's map, published at Salt Lake City in 1875, is the 'Provo, or Timponayas' river.

On this occasion they entered by the last pass of the
Sierra Blanca de los Timpanogos, which is the same in
which they are, by a route north one fourth north-west,
and by that same way they say the Comanches make
their raids, which do not seem to be very frequent."[21]
Continuing their journey the 26th of September
with two guides, the Spaniards bend their course
south-westwardly in the direction of Monterey, through
the Sevier lake and river region, which stream they
call Santa Isabel. The 8th of October they are in
latitude 38° 3' with Beaver River behind them.
Passing on into what is now Escalante Valley they
question the natives regarding a route to the sea, and
as to their knowledge of Spaniards in that direction.
The savages know nothing of either. Meanwhile
winter is approaching, provisions are becoming low, the
way to the sea must be long and difficult; therefore
the friars resolve to abandon the attempt; they will
continue south, turning perhaps to the east until they
come to the Colorado, when they will return to Santa
Fé by way of the Moqui and Zuñi villages.

Some of the party object to this abandonment of

[21] As this is the first account we have of the Great Salt Lake and its people
I will give the original entire: 'La otra laguna con quien esta se comunica,
ocupa, segun nos informaron, muchas leguas y sus aguas son nocivas ó estre-
madamente saladas; porque nos aseguran los timpanois que el que se mojaba
alguna parte del cuerpo con ellas, al punto sentia mucha comenzon en la parte
mojada. En su circuito nos dijeron habita una nacion numerosa y quieta,
que se nombra Puaguampe, que en nuestro vulgar dice hechiceros; la cual
usa el idioma cumanche; se alimenta de las yervas, bebe de varias fuentes ú
ojos de buena agua, que están en el circuito de la laguna, y tienen sus casitas
de zacate y tierra, que era el techo de ellas. No son enemigos de los lagunas,
segun insinuaron, pero desde cierta ocasion que se acercaron y les mataron un
hombre, no los tienen por tan neutrales como antes. En esta ocasion entraron
por la puerta final de la Sierra Blanca de los Timpanosis, que es la misma en
que están, por el norte cuarta al noroeste, y por aquí mismo dicen hacer sus
entradas los cumanches, las que no parecieron ser muy frecuentes.' Diario,
Doc. Hist. Mex., série ii. tom. i. 468.

Mr Harry is evidently not very thoroughly versed in the Spanish language, or his manuscript copy of Escalante's journey is defective. For example he translates echizeros—which being old Spanish he could not find in his
modern dictionary—'throwers or slingers' when the word 'witches,' or rather
'sorcerers,' is clearly implied. Again he queries sacate, not knowing its
meaning—a common enough Mexican word, formerly written zacate, and signifying hay or grass. For further inaccuracies see his summary in Simpson's
Explor., 494. Warren, Pacific Railroad Report, xi. 35, examined the same
copy of Escalante's narrative, then in the Peter Force library, which was
used by Harry.

purpose. They have come far; they can surely find a way: why turn back? To determine the matter prayers are made and lots cast, the decision being against Monterey. As they turn eastward, the 11th, in latitude 36° 52′, they are obliged to make bread of seeds purchased from the natives, for their supplies are wholly exhausted. Reaching the Colorado the 26th, twelve days are passed in searching for a ford, which they find at last in latitude 37°, the line dividing Utah from Arizona. Their course is now south-east, and the 16th of November they reach Oraybi, as they call the residence of the Moquis. There they are kindly received; but when for food and shelter they offer presents and religious instruction the natives refuse. Next day the Spaniards visit Xongopabi, and the day after Gualpi, at which latter place they call a meeting and propose to the natives temporal and spiritual submission. The Moquis will be friendly they say, but the further proposals they promptly decline. Thereupon the friars continue their way, reaching Zuñi November 24th and Santa Fé the 2d of January 1777.[22]

[22] The journey into Utah of Dominguez and Escalante, as given in *Doc. Hist. Mex.*, série ii. tom. i. 375–558, under title of *Diario y derrotero de los R. R. PP. Fr. Francisco Atanasio Dominguez y Fr. Silvestre Velez de Escalante, para descubrir el camino desde el Presidio de Santa Fé del Nuevo Mexico, al de Monterey, en la California Septentrional*, is full and clear as to route and information regarding the country and its inhabitants. As must be expected in all such narratives it is full of trivial detail which is tiresome, but which we can readily excuse for the worth of the remainder. The priests were close and intelligent observers, and have much to say regarding configuration, soil, climate, plants, minerals, animals, and people. A summary is given in *Simpson's Explor.*, app. R by Philip Harry, from a manuscript copy of the original in the archives in the city of Mexico which answers the purpose therein required, but is not sufficiently reliable or exact for historical purposes. The map accompanying the summary is better, being for the most part correct. Of the two padres and what they saw Humboldt says, *Essai Pol.*: 'Ce terrain est la continuation de la Cordillère des Grues, qui se prolonge vers la Sierra Verde et vers le lac de Timpanogos, célèbre dans l'histoire mexicaine. Le Rio S. Rafaël et le Rio S. Xavier sont les sources principales du fleuve Zaguananas, qui, avec le Rio de Nabajoa, forme le Rio Colorado: ce dernir a son embouchure dans le golfe de Californie. Ces régions abondantes en sel gemme out été examinees, en 1777, par deux voyageurs remplis de zéle et d'intrépidité, moines de l'order de S. Francois, le père Escalante et le pere Antonio Velez.' From the last clause it is clear that Humboldt was confused as to names, Velez and Escalante belonging to the same person. Simpson, *Explor.*, 13, enters upon a long dissertation over a simple and very transparent mistake. See also *Hist. North Mex. States; Hist. New Mex.;* and *Hist. Cal.*, this series.

HIST. UTAH. 2

CHAPTER II.

ADVENT OF TRAPPERS AND TRAVELLERS.

1778–1846.

INVASION BY FUR HUNTERS—BARON LA HONTAN AND HIS FABLES—THE POP-
ULAR GEOGRAPHIC IDEA—DISCOVERY OF THE GREAT SALT LAKE—JAMES
BRIDGER DECIDING A BET—HE DETERMINES THE COURSE OF BEAR RIVER
AND COMES UPON THE GREAT LAKE—HENRY, ASHLEY, GREEN, AND
BECKWOURTH ON THE GROUND—FORT BUILT AT UTAH LAKE—PETER
SKEEN OGDEN—JOURNEY OF JEDEDIAH S. SMITH—A STRANGE COUN-
TRY—PEGLEG SMITH—WOLFSKILL, YOUNT, AND BURTON TRAVERSE THE
COUNTRY—WALKER'S VISIT TO CALIFORNIA—SOME OLD MAPS—THE
BARTLESON COMPANY—STATEMENTS OF BIDWELL AND BELDEN COM-
PARED—WHITMAN AND LOVEJOY—FRÉMONT—PACIFIC COAST IMMIGRA-
TIONS OF 1845 AND 1846—ORIGIN OF THE NAME UTAH.

HALF a century passes, and we find United States
fur hunters standing on the border of the Great Salt
Lake, tasting its brackish waters, and wondering if
it is an arm of the sea.[1]

[1] There are those who soberly refer to the Baron la Hontan and his prodi-
gious falsehoods of 1689 for the first information of Great Salt Lake. Because
among the many fabulous wonders reported he somewhere on the western
side of the continent placed a body of bad-tasting water, Stansbury, *Exped.*,
151, does not hesitate to affirm 'that the existence of a large lake of salt water
somewhere amid the wilds west of the Rocky Mountains seems to have been
known vaguely as long as 150 years since.' Perhaps it was salt, and not silver
that the Winnebagoes reported to Carver, *Travels*, 33–6, as coming down in
caravans from 'the mountains lying near the heads of the Colorado River.'
Warren, in *Pacific Railroad Report*, xi. 34, repeats and refutes the La Hontan myth. He says, 'the story of La Hontan excited much speculation, and
received various additions in his day; and the lake finally became represented
on the published English maps.' Long before this date, however, reliable information had been received by the Spaniards, and the same may have come
to English trappers; so that by 1826 reports of the existence of such a sheet
may have reached civilization. It is needless to say that neither La Hontan
nor Carver ever received information from the natives, or elsewhere, sufficient
to justify map-makers in placing a large lake in that vicinity. In Gordon's
Historical and Geographical Memoir of the North American Continent, published in Dublin in 1820, it is written: 'Concerning the lakes and rivers of
this as yet imperfectly explored region we have little to say. Of the former

First among these, confining ourselves to authentic records, was James Bridger, to whom belongs the honor of discovery. It happened in this wise. During the winter of 1824–5 a party of trappers, who had ascended the Missouri with Henry and Ashley, found

we have no certain account. Two have been noticed in the western parts, a salt lake about the thirty-ninth degree of latitude, the western limits of which are unknown, and the lake of Timpanogos, about the forty-first degree, of great but unascertained extent.'

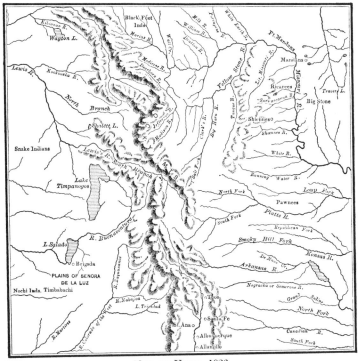

MAP OF UTAH, 1826.

In a report submitted to congress May 15, 1826, by Mr Baylies it is stated that 'many geographies have placed the Lake Timpanogos in latitude 40, but they have obviously confounded it with the Lake Theguayo, which extends from 39° 40' to 41°, and from which it appears separated by a neck or peninsula; the two lakes approaching in one direction as near as 20 miles.' *19th Cong., 1st Sess., House Rept. No. 213.* Such statements as this amount to nothing—the honorable gentleman, with all due respect, not knowing what he was writing about—except as going to show the vague and imperfect impression of the popular mind concerning this region at that time.

I will give for what it is worth a claim, set up in this same congres-

themselves on Bear River, in Cache, or Willow Valley. A discussion arose as to the probable course of Bear River, which flowed on both sides of them. A wager was made, and Bridger sent to ascertain the truth. Following the river through the mountains the first view of the great lake fell upon him, and when he went to the margin and tasted the water he found that it was salt. Then he returned and reported to his companions. All were interested to know if there emptied into this sheet other streams on which they might find beavers, and if there was an outlet; hence in the spring of 1826 four men explored the lake in skin boats.[2]

During this memorable year of 1825, when Peter

sional report, by one Samuel Adams Ruddock, that in the year 1821 he journeyed from Council Bluff to Santa Fé, and thence with a trading party proceeded by way of Great Salt Lake to Oregon. The report says: 'On the 9th of June this party crossed the Rio del Norte, and pursuing a north-west direction on the north bank of the river Chamas, and over the mountains, reached Lake Trinidad; and then pursuing the same direction across the upper branches of the Rio Colorado of California, reached Lake Timpanagos, which is intersected by the 42d parallel of latitude, the boundary between the United States of America and the United States of Mexico. This lake is the principal source of the river Timpanagos, and the Multnomah of Lewis and Clarke. They then followed the course of this river to its junction with the Columbia, and reached the mouth of the Columbia on the first day of August, completing the journey from the Council Bluffs in seventy-nine days.'

    [2] This, upon the testimony of Robert Campbell, *Pac. R. Rept.*, xi. 35, who was there at the time 'and found the party just returned from the exploration of the lake, and recollect their report that it was without any outlet.' Bridger's story of his discovery was corroborated by Samuel Tullock in Campbell's counting-room in St Louis at a later date. Campbell pronounces them both 'men of the strictest integrity and truthfulness.' Likewise Ogden's trappers met Bridger's party in the summer of 1825 and were told of the discovery. See *Hist. Nevada*, this series. Irving, *Bonneville's Adv.*, 186, says it was probably Sublette who sent out the four men in the skin canoe in 1826. Bonneville professes to doubt this exploration because the men reported that they suffered severely from thirst, when in fact several fine streams flow into the lake; but Bonneville desired to attach to his name the honor of an early survey, and detract from those entitled to it. The trappers in their canoes did not pretend to make a thorough survey, and as for scarcity of fresh water in places Stansbury says, *Exped.*, 103, that during his explorations he frequently was obliged to send fifty miles for water. Other claimants appear prior to Bridger's discovery. W. M. Anderson writing to the *National Intelligencer* under date of Feb. 26, 1860, says that Provost trapped in this vicinity in 1820, and that Ashley was there before Bridger. Then it was said by Seth Grant that his partner, Vazquez, discovered the great inland sea, calling it an arm of the ocean because the water was salt. That no white man ever saw the Great Salt Lake before Bridger cannot be proven; but his being the only well authenticated account, history must rest there until it finds a better one.

Skeen Ogden with his party of Hudson's Bay Company trappers was on Humboldt River, and James P. Beckwourth was pursuing his daring adventures, and the region round the great lakes of Utah first became familiar to American trappers, William H. Ashley, of the Rocky Mountain Fur Company, at the head of one hundred and twenty men and a train of well packed horses, came out from St Louis, through the South Pass and down by Great Salt Lake to Lake Utah. There he built a fort, and two years later brought from St Louis a six-pounder which thereafter graced its court. Ashley was a brave man, shrewd and honest; he was prosperous and commanded the respect of his men. Nor may we impute to him lack of intelligence, or of common geographical knowledge, when we find him seriously considering the project of descending the Colorado in boats, by means of which he would eventually reach St Louis. Mr Green, who gave his name to Green River, had been with Ashley the previous year; and now for three years after the establishing of Fort Ashley at Utah Lake, Green with his trappers occupied the country to the west and north.[3]

[3] See *Hist. Northwest Coast*, ii. 447-8, this series. T. D. Bonner in his *Life and Adventures of James P. Beckwourth*, 71-3, gives what purports to be an account of Ashley's descent of Green River to Great Salt Lake on a certain occasion in Ashley's own language. There may be some truth in it all, though Beckwourth is far astray in his dates, as he places the occurrence in 1822. Beckwourth goes on to say that one day in June a beautiful Indian girl offered him a pair of moccasins if he would shoot for her an antelope and bring her the brains, that with them she might dress a deer-skin. Beckwourth started out, but failing to secure an antelope, and seeing as he supposed an Indian coming, he thought he would shoot the Indian and take his brains to the girl, who would not know the difference. Just as he was about to fire he discovered the supposed Indian to be Ashley, who thereupon told him of his adventures down Green River and through the cañon to Great Salt Lake. I have no doubt it is three fourths fiction, and what there is of fact must be placed forward four years. 'We had a very dangerous passage down the river,' said Ashley to Beckwourth, 'and suffered more than I ever wish to see men suffer again. You are aware that we took but little provision with us, not expecting that the cañon extended so far. In passing over the rapids, where we lost two boats and three guns, we made use of ropes in letting down our boats over the most dangerous places. Our provisions soon gave out. We found plenty of beaver in the cañon for some miles, and, expecting to find them in as great plenty all the way, we saved none of their carcasses, which constituted our food. As we proceeded, however, they became more and more scarce, until there were none to be seen, and we were entirely out of provisions. To trace the river was impossible, and to ascend the perpendicu-

From Great Salt Lake in August, 1826, Jedediah
S. Smith sets out on a trapping and exploring tour
with fifteen men. Proceeding southward he trav-
erses Utah Lake, called for a time Ashley Lake,[4] and
after ascending Ashley River, which, as he remarks,
flows into the lake through the country of the Sam-
patches, he bends his course to the west of south, passes
over some mountains running south-east and north-
west, and crosses a river which he calls Adams,[5] in

lar cliffs, which hemmed us in on either side, was equally impossible. Our
only alternative was to go ahead. After passing six days without food, the
men were weak and disheartened. I listened to all their murmurings and
heart-rending complaints. They often spoke of home and friends, declaring
they would never see them more. Some spoke of wives and children whom
they dearly loved, and who must shortly become widows and orphans. They
had toiled, they said, through every difficulty; had risked their lives among
wild beasts and hostile Indians in the wilderness, all of which they were willing to undergo; but who could bear up against actual starvation? I encouraged them all in my power, telling them that I bore an equal part in their
sufferings; that I too was toiling for those I loved, and whom I yet hoped to
see again; that we should all endeavor to keep up our courage, and not add
to our misfortunes by giving way to despondency. Another night was passed
amid the barren rocks. The next morning the fearful proposition was made
by some of the party for the company to cast lots, to see which should be
sacrificed to afford food for the others, without which they must inevitably
perish. My feelings at such a proposition cannot be described. I begged
of them to wait one day more, and make all the way they could meanwhile.
By doing so, I said, we must come to a break in the cañon, where we could
escape. They consented, and moving down the river as fast as the current
would carry us, to our inexpressible joy we found a break, and a camp of
trappers therein. All now rejoiced that they had not carried their fearful
proposition into effect. We had fallen into good hands, and slowly recruited
ourselves with the party, which was under the charge of one Provo, a man
with whom I was well acquainted. By his advice we left the river and proceeded in a north-westerly direction. Provo was well provided with provisions and horses, and he supplied us with both. We remained with his
party until we arrived at the Great Salt Lake. Here I fell in with a large
company of trappers, composed of Canadians and Iroquois Indians, under the
command of Peter Ogden, in the service of the Northwest Fur Company.
With this party I made a very good bargain, as you will see when they arrive
at our camp, having purchased all their peltry on very reasonable terms.'

   [4] Jedediah Smith in 1826 calls the lake Utah, and the stream flowing into
it from the south Ashley River. 'Je traversai le petit lac Utâ, et je remon-
tai le cours de l'Ashley qu'il recoit.' Extrait d'une lettre, in Nouvelles An. des
Voy., xxxvii. 208. For an account of this journey see Hist. Cal., this series,
where are fully discussed the several conflicting authorities. Warner's Rem.,
MS., 21–9, dates the journey 1824, and carries the company from Green
River, south of Salt Lake, and over the mountains near Walker Pass.
Accounts in Cronise's Nat. Wealth Cal.; Hutchings' Mag., v. 351–2; S. F.
Times, June 14, 1867; Randolph's Oration, 313–14; Tuthill's Hist. Cal., 124–5;
Frignet, La Californie, 58–60; Douglas' Private Papers, MS., 2d ser. i.;
Victor's River of the West, 34; Hines' Voy., 110, are mentioned.

   [5] The Sevier; or possibly he crossed from the Sevier to the Vírgen and
supposed them to be one stream.

honor of the president. After ten days' march, still in a south-westerly direction, through the country of the Pah Utes, he recrosses the same stream, and after two days comes to the junction of the Adams with what he calls the Seedskeeder, or Siskadee, river,[6] a stream full of shallows and rapids and flowing through a sterile country. Then he reaches a fertile wooded valley which belongs to the Amajabes, or Mojaves, where the party rests fifteen days, meeting with the kindest treatment from the natives, who provide food and horses. Thence they are guided by two neophytes westward through a desert country, and reach the mission of San Gabriel in December, their appearance causing no small commotion in California. After many strange adventures, fully narrated in my *History of California*, Smith works his way northward up the San Joaquin Valley, and in May 1827 crosses the Sierra Nevada and returns eastward to Great Salt Lake. With Jedediah Smith, during some part of his stay in Utah, was Thomas L. Smith, whom we must immortalize in history as Pegleg Smith. He did not possess a very estimable character, as, I am sorry to say, few of his class did in those days. The leaders of American fur companies, however, were exceptions, and in points of intelligence, integrity, and daring were in no wise behind their British brethren.[7]

From south-east to north-west a portion of Utah was traversed in the autumn of 1830 by a trapping party under William Wolfskill. The company was fitted out in New Mexico, and the great valley of California was their objective point. Wolfskill had been a partner of Ewing Young, who was then in California. Leaving Taos in September they struck

[6] The Adams now is clearly the Rio Virgen, and the Seedskeeder, or Siskadee, the Colorado. See *Hist. Northwest Coast*, ii. 583, this series.
[7] P. W. Crawford, *Nar.*, MS., 27, says he saw Pegleg Smith in 1847 on Ham Fork, in a beautiful valley of the Bear River Mountains, where he then lived with his native wife and a few savage retainers.

north-westerly, crossing the Colorado, Grande, Green, and Sevier rivers, and then turned south to the Rio Vírgen, all the time trapping on the way. Then passing down by the Mojaves they reached Los Angeles in February 1831. George C. Yount and Louis Burton were of the party.[8]

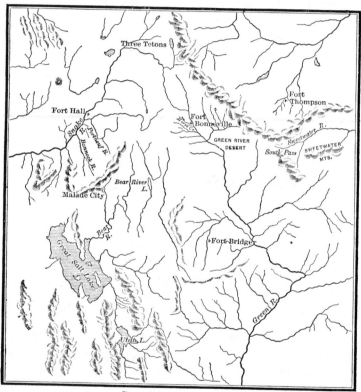

GREEN RIVER COUNTRY.

During the winter of 1832–3 B. L. E. Bonneville made his camp on Salmon River, and in July following was at the Green River rendezvous.[9] Among the several trapping parties sent by him in various direc-

[8] There was little of importance to Utah history in this expedition, for full particulars of which see *Hist. Cal.*, this series.

[9] For an account of Bonneville and his several excursions see *Hist. Northwest Coast*, ii. chap. xxv.; *Hist. Cal.*, and *Hist. Nevada*, this series.

tions was one under Joseph Walker, who with some thirty-six men, among them Joe Meek, went to trap on the streams falling into the Great Salt Lake.

Bonneville affirms that Walker's intention was to pass round the Great Salt Lake and explore its borders; but George Nidever who was of Walker's company, and at the rendezvous while preparations were made, says nothing of such purpose, and it was probably not thought of by Bonneville until afterward. Nidever had suffered severely from the cold during the previous winter, and had come to the Green River rendezvous that season for the express purpose of joining some party for California or of forming such a party himself, having been informed that the climate there was milder than in the mountains where he had been.[10]

If the intention was, as Bonneville asserts, that this party should pass round the great lake, in their endeavor they presently found themselves in the midst of desolation, between wide sandy wastes and broad brackish waters; and to quench their thirst they hastened westward where bright snowy mountains promised cooling streams. The Ogden River[11] region being to them so new, and the thought of California so fascinating, they permitted themselves to stray from original intentions, and cross the Sierra Nevada to Monterey. All that is known of their doings before reaching the Snowy Range is given in my *History of Nevada,* and their exploits after reaching California are fully narrated in that part of this series devoted to the history of the latter country.[12]

---

[10] Such being the case he would hardly have joined Walker's expedition had it been understood that the exploration of Salt Lake was intended. See *Nidever's Life and Adv.,* MS., 58.

[11] Previously called the Mary River, and now the Humboldt. See *Hist. Nevada; Hist. Northwest Coast;* and *Hist. Cal.,* this series.

[12] See *Nidever's Life and Adv.,* MS.; *Warner's Mem.,* in *Pac. R. Report,* xi. pt. i. 31–4. In giving his dictation to Irving, Bonneville professed great interest in the exploration of Great Salt Lake though he had done nothing to speak of in that direction. Irving, however, humored the captain, whose vanity prompted him to give his own name to the lake, although he had not a shadow of title to that distinction.

In Winterbotham's history published in New York
in 1795 is given a map of North America showing an
enormous nameless inland sea above latitude 42° with
small streams running into it, and south of said parallel and east of the meridian of the inland sea is a
smaller body of water with quite a large stream flowing in from the west, besides three smaller ones from
the south and north. As both of these bodies of

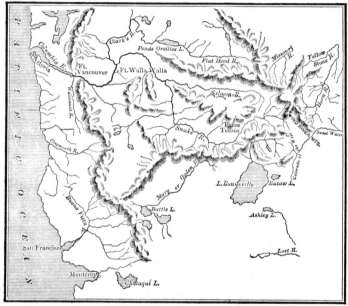

BONNEVILLE'S MAP, 1837.

water were laid down from the imaginations of white
men, or from vague and traditionary reports of the
natives, it may be that only the one Great Salt Lake
was originally referred to, or it may be that the original description was applied to two lakes or inland seas.
The native village on one of the southern tributaries,
Taguayo, refers to the habitations of the Timpanogos,
and may have been derived from the Spaniards; but
more probably the information was obtained through

natives who themselves had received it from other
natives.

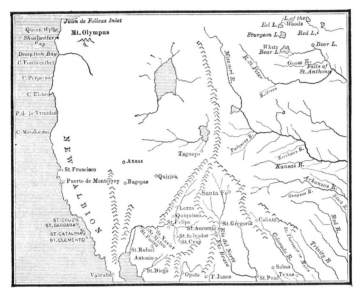

UTAH AND NEVADA, 1795.

In the map of William Rector, a surveyor in the
service of the general government, Utah has open
and easy communication with the sea by way of the

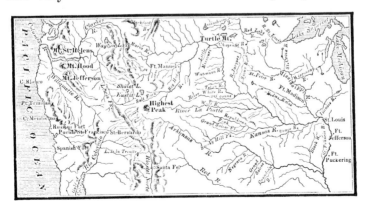

RECTOR'S MAP, 1818.

valley of the Willamette River, whose tributaries
drain the whole of Nevada and Utah.

Mr Finley in his map of North America claimed
to have included all the late geographical discoveries,
which claim we may readily allow, and also accredit
him with much not yet and never to be discovered.
The mountains are artistically placed, the streams
made to run with remarkable regularity and direct-
ness, and they are placed in positions affording the best

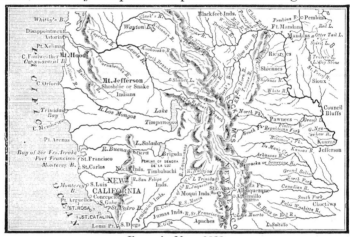

FINLEY'S MAP, 1826.

facilities for commerce. The lakes and rivers Timpanogos, Salado, and Buenaventura, by their position,
not to say existence, show the hopeless confusion of
the author's mind.

A brief glance at the later visits of white men to
Utah is all that is necessary in this place. The early
emigrants to Oregon did not touch this territory, and
those to California *via* Fort Bridger for the most part
merely passed through leaving no mark. The emigrants to Oregon and California in 1841 came together
by the usual route up the Platte, along the Sweetwater, and through the South Pass to Bear River
Valley. When near Soda Springs those for Oregon

went north to Fort Hall, while those for California followed Bear River southward until within ten miles of Great Salt Lake, when they turned westward to find Ogden River. Of the latter party were J. Bartleson, C. M. Weber, Talbot H. Green, John Bidwell, Josiah Belden, and twenty-seven others. Their adventures while in Utah were not startling. Little was known of the Salt Lake region,[13] particularly of the country to the west of it.

Mr Belden in his *Historical Statement*, which I number among my most valuable manuscripts, says: " We struck Bear River some distance below where the town of Evanston now is, where the coal mines are, and the railroad passes, and followed the river down. It makes a long bend to the north there, and comes down to Salt Lake. We arrived at Soda Springs, on Bear River, and there we separated from the company of missionaries, who were going off towards Snake River or Columbia. There we lost the services of the guide Fitzpatrick. Several of our party who had started to go with us to California also left us there, having decided to go with the missionaries. Fitzpatrick advised us to give up our expedition and go with them to Fort Hall, one of the Hudson's Bay stations, as there was no road for us to follow, nothing was known of the country, and we had nothing to guide us, and so he advised us to give up the California project. He thought it was doubtful if we ever got there, we might get caught in the snow of the mountains and perish there, and he considered it very hazardous to attempt it. Some four or five of our party withdrew and went with the mis-

---

[13] 'Previous to setting out,' says Bidwell, *California, 1841-8*, MS., 24-5, 'I consulted maps so as to learn as much as possible about the country...As for Salt Lake, there was a large lake marked in that region, but it was several hundred miles long from north to south, with two large rivers running from either end, diverging as they ran west, and entering the Pacific Ocean.' It was Finley's map of North America, 1826, herein reproduced, which he alludes to. 'My friends in Missouri advised me to bring tools, and in case we could not get through with our wagons to build canoes and go down one of these rivers.' The region to the west of Salt Lake was indeed a *terra incognita* to these explorers.

sionaries. About thirty-one of us adhered to our original intention and declined to give up our expedition."

While the party were slowly descending Bear River four of them rode over to Fort Hall to obtain if possible a "pilot to conduct us to the gap in the California Mountains, or at least to the head of Mary's River," and to make inquiries of Mr Grant, then in charge. No guide could be found, and Grant was not able greatly to enlighten them. The fur-trader could have told them much concerning the route to Oregon, but this way to California as an emigrant road had hardly yet been thought of.

"As we approached Salt Lake," writes Bidwell,[14] "we were misled quite often by the mirage. The country too was obscured by smoke. The water in Bear River became too salt for use. The sage brush on the small hillocks of the almost level plain became so magnified as to look like trees. Hoping to find water, and supposing these imaginary trees to be growing on some stream, and knowing nothing about the distance to Salt Lake, we kept pushing ahead mile after mile. Our animals almost perished for want of water while we were travelling over this salt plain, which grew softer and softer till our wagons cut into the ground five or six inches, and it became impossible to haul them. We still thought we saw timber but a short distance ahead, when the fact really was there was no timber, and we were driving straight for the Great Salt Lake."

The truth is they had wandered from their course; they had passed Cache Valley where they intended to rest and hunt; they were frequently obliged to leave

---

[14] *California, 1841–8*, MS., 33–4. The author, then little more than boy, being but 21, has a long story to tell about straying from camp one day in company with a comrade, James John, bent on a visit to the adjacent heights for a handful of snow; and how they slept in the mountains in a bear's nest, and reached next day their company, some of whom had spent the night in search. They had been given up as slain by the Blackfeet; and there were those so ungracious as to say that it would have served them right had it been so.

the river, turned aside by the hills. It was past mid-summer, and the sun's rays beat heavily on the white salted plain. The signal fires of the Shoshones illuminated the hills at night. "In our desperation we turned north of east a little and struck Bear River again a few miles from its mouth. The water here was too salt to quench thirst; our animals would scarcely taste it, yet we had no other." The green fresh-looking grass was stiffened with salt. Mr Belden says: "After separating from the missionaries we followed Bear River down nearly to where it enters Salt Lake, about where Corinne is now. We had some knowledge of the lake from some of the trappers who had been there. We turned off more to the west and went round the northerly end of Salt Lake. There we found a great difficulty in getting water for several days, all the water near the lake being very brackish. We had to make it into strong coffee to drink it."

On the 20th of August the company rested while two of their number went out to explore. They found themselves encamped ten miles from the mouth of the river. Thence next day, Sunday, they took a north-west course, crossing their track of the Thursday previous; on the 23d they were in full view of Salt Lake. Men and animals were almost dying of thirst, and "in our trouble," says Bidwell, "we turned directly north toward some high mountains, and in the afternoon of the next day found springs of good water and plenty of grass." This was the 27th, and here the company remained while two of their number again advanced and discovered a route to Ogden River. What befell them further on their way across to the mountains the reader will find in my *History of Nevada*.[15]

[15] The expedition entire is given in *Hist. Cal.*, this series. See also *Belden's Hist. Statement*, MS.; *Hopper's Narrative*, MS.; *Taylor's Dis. and Founders*, i. No. 7; *Sutter Co. Hist.*, 17; *S. F. Bulletin*, July 27, 1868; *S F. Alta*, Aug. 5, 1856, and Sept. 1868; *Santa Cruz Sentinel*, Aug. 29, 1868; *Los Angeles News*, Sept. 1, 1868; *San Diego Union*, Jan. 16, 1869; *San José Pioneer*,

In 1842 Marcus Whitman and A. L. Lovejoy, on their way from Oregon to the United States, passed through Utah from Fort Hall, by way of Uintah, Taos, and Santa Fé. For further information concerning them, and the object of their journey, I would refer the reader to my *History of Oregon.*

In 1843 John C. Frémont followed the emigrant trail through the south pass, and on the 6th of September stood upon an elevated peninsula on the east side of Great Salt Lake, a little north of Weber River, beside which stream his party had encamped the previous night. Frémont likens himself to Balboa discovering the Pacific; but no one else would think of doing so. He was in no sense a discoverer; and though he says he was the first to embark on that inland sea, he is again in error, trappers in skin boats having performed that feat while the pathfinder was still studying his arithmetic, as I have before mentioned. It is certainly a pleasing sight to any one, coming upon it from either side, from the cover of rolling mountains or the sands of desert plains, and under almost any circumstance the heart of the beholder is stirred within him. A number of large islands raised their rocky front out of dense sullen waters whose limit the eye could not reach, while myriads of wild fowl beat the air, making a noise " like distant thunder."

Black clouds gathered in the west, and soon were pouring their floods upon the explorers. Camping some distance above the mouth on Weber River, they made a corral for the animals, and threw up a small fort for their own protection. Provisions being scarce, seven of the party under François Lajeunesse were sent to Fort Hall, which place they reached with

Feb. 1877; *Shuck's Scrap Book*, 182–4; *Petaluma Crescent*, Sept. 10, 1872; *Santa Clara News*, Feb. 6, 1869; *Hayes' Scrap Books, Cal. Notes*, iii. 171; *Napa Reporter*, March 23, Sept. 21, 1872; *S. F. Bulletin*, July 19, 1860; *Shuck's Rep. Men*, 920–1.

difficulty, after separation from each other and several days' wanderings.

Leaving three men in camp, with four others, including Kit Carson who was present, Frémont on the 8th embarked in a rubber boat and dropped down to the mouth of the stream, which the party found shallow and unnavigable. Next morning they were out on the lake, fearful every moment lest their air-blown boat should collapse and let them into the saline but beautiful transparent liquid. At noon they reached one of the low near islands and landed. They found there, washed up by the waves, a dark brown bank, ten or twenty feet in breadth, composed of the skins of worms, about the size of oats, while the rocky cliffs were whitened by incrustations of salt. Ascending to the highest point attainable they took a surrounding view, and called the place Disappointment Island,[16] because they had failed to find the fertile lands and game hoped for. Then they descended to the edge of the water, constructed lodges of drift-wood, built fires, and spent the night there, returning next day in a rough sea to their mainland camp. Thence they proceeded north to Bear River, and Fort Hall, and on to Oregon.[17] On his return by way of Klamath and Pyramid lakes, Frémont crossed the Sierra to Sutter Fort, proceeded up the San Joaquin into Southern California, and taking the old Spanish trail to the Rio Vírgen followed the Wahsatch Mountains to Utah Lake.

There was a party under Frémont in Utah also in 1845. Leaving Bent Fort in August they ascended the Arkansas, passed on to Green River, followed its left bank to the Duchesne branch, and thence crossed to the head-waters of the Timpanogos, down which stream they went to Utah Lake. Thence

---

[16] Now Castle Island, or as some call it Frémont Island.

[17] For an account of Frémont's Oregon adventures see *Hist. Oregon;* and for his doings in California see *Hist. Cal.*, this series. We also meet with him again in our *History of Nevada*.

they passed on to Great Salt Lake, made camp near where Great Salt Lake City is situated, crossed to Antelope Island, and examined the southern portion of the lake. After this they passed by way of Pilot Peak into Nevada.[18]

Of the six companies comprising the California immigration of 1845, numbering in all about one hundred and fifty, five touched either Utah or Nevada, the other being from Oregon. But even these it is not necessary to follow in this connection, Utah along the emigrant road being by this time well known to travellers and others. With some it was a question while on the way whether they should go to Oregon or California. Tustin, who came from Illinois in 1845, with his wife and child and an ox team, says in his manuscript *Recollections:* "My intention all the way across the plains was to go on to Oregon; but when I reached the summit of the Rocky Mountains where the trail divides, I threw my lash across the near ox and struck off on the road to California."

For the Oregon and California emigrations of 1846, except when they exercised some influence on Utah, or Utah affairs, I would refer the reader to the volumes of this series treating on those states. An account of the exploration for a route from southern Oregon, over the Cascade Mountains, and by way of Klamath and Goose lakes to the Humboldt River, and thence on to the region of the Great Salt Lake by Scott and the Applegates in 1846, is given in both the *History of Oregon,* and the *History of Nevada,* to which volumes of this series the reader is referred.[19]

[18] *Frémont's Expl. Ex.,* 151–60. *Warner* in *Pac. R. Rep.,* xi. 49–50.
[19] The word Utah originated with the people inhabiting that region. Early in the 17th century, when New Mexico was first much talked of by the Spaniards, the principal nations of frequent mention as inhabiting the several sides of the locality about that time occupied were the Navajos, the Yutas, the Apaches, and the Comanches. Of the Utah nation, which belongs to the Shoshone family, there were many tribes. See *Native Races,* i. 422, 463–8,

this series. There were the Pah Utes, or Pyutes, the Pi Edes, the Gosh ˙Utes, or Goshutes, the Uinta Utes, the Yam Pah Utes, and many others. *Pah* signifies water; *pah guampe*, salt water, or salt lake; *Pah Utes*, Indians that live about the water. The early orthography of the word Utah is varied. Escalante, prior to his journey to Utah Lake, *Carta de 28 Oct. 1775*, MS., finds the 'Yutas' inhabiting the region north of the Moquis. This was a common spelling by the early Spaniards, and might be called the proper one. Later we have 'Youta,' 'Eutaw,' 'Utaw,' and 'Utah.'

CHAPTER III.

A GLANCE EASTWARD—THE MIDDLE STATES SIXTY YEARS AGO—BIRTH AND
PARENTAGE OF JOSEPH SMITH—SPIRITUAL MANIFESTATIONS—JOSEPH
TELLS HIS VISION—AND IS REVILED—MORONI APPEARS—PERSECUTIONS
—COPYING THE PLATES—MARTIN HARRIS—OLIVER COWDERY—TRANSLA-
TION—THE BOOK OF MORMON—AARONIC PRIESTHOOD CONFERRED—CON-
VERSIONS — THE WHITMER FAMILY — THE WITNESSES — SPAULDING
THEORY—PRINTING OF THE BOOK—MELCHISEDEC PRIESTHOOD CON-
FERRED—DUTIES OF ELDERS AND OTHERS—CHURCH OF LATTER-DAY
SAINTS ORGANIZED—FIRST MIRACLE—FIRST CONFERENCE—OLIVER COW-
DERY ORDERED TO THE WEST.

LET us turn now to the east, where have been evolv-
ing these several years a new phase of society and a
new religion, destined presently to enter in and take
possession of this far-away primeval wilderness. For
it is not alone by the power of things material that
the land of the Yutas is to be subdued; that mysterious agency, working under pressure of high enthusiasm in the souls of men, defying exposure, cold, and
hunger, defying ignominy, death, and the destruction
of all corporeal things in the hope of heaven's favors
and a happy immortality, a puissance whose very
breath of life is persecution, and whose highest glory
is martyrdom—it is through this subtile and incom-
prehensible spiritual instrumentality, rather than from
a desire for riches or any tangible advantage that the
new Israel is to arise, the new exodus to be conducted,
the new Canaan to be attained.

Sixty years ago western New York was essentially
a new country, Ohio and Illinois were for the most

part a wilderness, and Missouri was the United States limit, the lands beyond being held by the aborigines. There were some settlements between Lake Erie and the Mississippi River, but they were recent and rude, and the region was less civilized than savage. The people, though practically shrewd and of bright intellect, were ignorant; though having within them the elements of wealth, they were poor. There was among them much true religion, whatever that may be, yet they were all superstitious—baptists, methodists, and presbyterians; there was little to choose between them. Each sect was an abomination to the others; the others were of the devil, doomed to eternal torments, and deservedly so. The bible was accepted literally by all, every word of it, prophecies, miracles, and revelations; the same God and the same Christ satisfied all; an infidel was a thing woful and unclean. All the people reasoned. How they racked their brains in secret, and poured forth loud logic in public, not over problems involving intellectual liberty, human rights and reason, and other like insignificant matters appertaining to this world, but concerning the world to come, and more particularly such momentous questions as election, justification, baptism, and infant damnation. Then of signs and seasons, God's ways and Satan's ways; likewise concerning promises and prayer, and all the rest, there was a credulity most refreshing. In the old time there were prophets and apostles, there were visions and miracles; why should it not be so during these latter days? It was time for Christ to come again, time for the millennial season, and should the power of the almighty be limited? There was the arch-fanatic Miller, and his followers, predicting the end and planning accordingly. "The idea that revelation from God was unattainable in this age, or that the ancient gifts of the gospel had ceased forever, never entered my head," writes a young quaker; and a methodist of that epoch says: "We believed in the gathering of Israel, and in the restoration

of the ten tribes; we believed that Jesus would come
to reign personally on the earth; we believed that
there ought to be apostles, prophets, evangelists, pastors, and teachers, as in former days, and that the
gifts of healing and the power of God ought to be associated with the church." These ideas, of course,
were not held by all; in many respects the strictly
orthodox evangelical churches taught the contrary;
but there was enough of this literal interpretation and
license of thought among the people to enable them
to accept in all honesty and sincerity any doctrine in
harmony with these views.

Such were the people and the place, such the atmosphere and conditions under which was to spring up
the germ of a new theocracy, destined in its development to accomplish the first settlement of Utah—a
people and an atmosphere already sufficiently charged,
one would think, with doctrines and dogmas, with vulgar folly and stupid fanaticism, with unchristian hate
and disputation over the commands of God and the
charity of Christ. All this must be taken into account in estimating character, and in passing judgment on credulity; men of one time and place cannot
with justice be measured by the standard of other
times and places.

Before entering upon the history of Mormonism, I
would here remark, as I have before said in the preface to this volume, that it is my purpose to treat the
subject historically, not as a social, political, or religious partisan, but historically to deal with the sect
organized under the name of the Church of Jesus
Christ of Latter-day Saints as I would deal with
any other body of people, thus carrying over Utah
the same quality of work which I have applied to my
entire field, whether in Alaska, California, or Central
America. Whatever they may be, howsoever righteous or wicked, they are entitled at the hand of those
desirous of knowing the truth to a dispassionate and

respectful hearing, which they have never had. As a matter of course, where there is such warmth of feeling, such bitterness and animosity as is here displayed on both sides, we must expect to encounter in our evidence much exaggeration, and many untruthful statements. Most that has been written on either side is partisan—bitterly so; many of the books that have been published are full of vile and licentious abuse—disgustingly so. Some of the more palpable lies, some of the grosser scurrility and more blasphemous vulgarity, I shall omit altogether.

Again, the history of the Mormons, which is the early history of Utah, is entitled in its treatment to this consideration, as differing from that of other sections of my work, and to this only—that whereas in speaking of other and older sects, as of the catholics in Mexico and California, and of the methodists and presbyterians in Oregon, whose tenets having long been established, are well known, and have no immediate bearing aside from the general influence of religion upon the subjugation of the country, any analysis of doctrines would be out of place, such analysis in the present instance is of primary importance. Ordinarily, I say, as I have said before, that with the religious beliefs of the settlers on new lands, or of the builders of empire in any of its several phases, social and political, the historian has nothing to do, except in so far as belief influences actions and events. As to attempting to determine the truth or falsity of any creed, it is wholly outside of his province.

Since the settlement of Utah grew immediately out of the persecution of the Mormons, and since their persecutions grew out of the doctrines which they promulgated, it seems to me essential that the origin and nature of their religion should be given. And as they are supposed to know better than others what they believe and how they came so to believe, I shall let them tell their own story of the rise and progress of their religion, carrying along with it the commentaries of their opponents; that is, giving in the text the narrative proper, and in the notes further information, elucidation, and counter-statements, according to my custom. All this by no means implies, here or elsewhere in my work, that when a Mormon elder, a catholic priest, or a baptist preacher says he had a vision, felt within him some supernatural influence, or said a prayer which produced a certain result, it is proper or relevant for me to stop and dispute with him whether he really did see, feel, or experience as alleged.

As to the material facts connected with the story of Mormonism, there is but little difference between the Mormons and their opposers; but in the reception and interpretation of acts and incidents, particularly in the acceptation of miraculous assertions and spiritual manifestations, they are as widely apart as the two poles, as my text and notes clearly demonstrate. And finally, I would have it clearly understood that it is my purpose, here as elsewhere in all my historical efforts, to impart information rather than attempt to solve problems.

In Sharon, Windsor county, Vermont, on the 23d of December, 1805, was born Joseph Smith junior, presently to be called translator, revelator, seer, prophet, and founder of a latter-day dispensation. When the boy was ten years old, his father, who was a farmer, moved with his family to Palmyra, Wayne county, New York, and four years afterward took up his abode some six miles south, at Manchester, Ontario county. Six sons and three daughters comprised the family of Joseph and Lucy Smith, namely, Alvin, Hyrum, Joseph junior, Samuel Harrison, William, Don Carlos, Sophronia, Catharine, and Lucy.[1]

---

[1] Much has been said by the enemies of Mormonism against the Smith family. 'All who became intimate with them during this period [1820 to 1830] unite in representing the general character of old Joseph and wife, the parents of the pretended prophet, as lazy, indolent, ignorant, and super-

There was much excitement over the subject of religion in this section at the time, with no small discussion of doctrines, methodist, baptist, and the rest; and about a year later, the mother and four of the children joined the presbyterians.

But young Joseph was not satisfied with any of the current theologies, and he was greatly troubled what to do. Reading his bible one day, he came upon the passage, "If any of you lack wisdom, let him ask of God." He retired to the woods and threw himself upon his knees. It was his first attempt at prayer.

While thus engaged a vision fell upon him. Suddenly he was seized by some supernatural power of evil import, which bound him body and soul. He could not think; he could not speak; thick darkness gathered round. Presently there appeared above his head a pillar of light, which slowly descended and enveloped him. Immediately he was delivered from the enemy; and in the sky he saw two bright personages, one of whom said, pointing to the other, " This is my beloved son; hear him." Then he asked what he should do; to which sect he should unite himself.

stitious, having a firm belief in ghosts and witches; the telling of fortunes; pretending to believe that the earth was filled with hidden treasures, buried there by Kid or the Spaniards. Being miserably poor, and not much disposed to obtain an honest livelihood by labor, the energies of their minds seemed to be mostly directed toward finding where these treasures were concealed, and the best mode of acquiring their possession.' *Howe's Mormonism Unveiled*, 11. In the towns of Palmyra and Manchester, in 1833, documents defamatory to the family were circulated for signature, one receiving 11 and another 51 names. Given with signatures in *Howe's Mormonism Unveiled*, 261–2, and in *Kidder's Mormonism*, 20–1. See also *Olshausen, Gesch. d. Morm.*, 9–14, 103–10, 200–1; *Gazette of Utah, 1874*, 17; *Tucker's Origin and Prog. Mor.*, 11–20. In one of these documents, signed and sworn to by Peter Ingersoll, he said that the Smith family employed most of their time in gold-digging. At one time Joseph Smith senior told Ingersoll to hold a mineral rod in his hand, a piece of witch-hazel, and selected a place to stand where he was to whisper directions to the rod; Smith stood apart, throwing himself into various shapes, but was unable to produce the desired effect. Again he took a stone that Ingersoll had picked up and exclaimed that it was invaluable; looking at it earnestly, he said it revealed to him chests of gold and silver at the back of his house; and putting it into his hat, threw himself into various attitudes, and soon appeared exhausted; then in a faint voice, said, 'If you only knew what I had seen you would believe.' Some time before Joseph's discovery of the gold plates, the elder Smith told Ingersoll that a book had been found in Canada in a hollow tree which treated of the discovery of this continent.

And he was told to join none of them, that all were corrupt, all were abomination in the eyes of the Lord. When he came to himself he was still gazing earnestly up into heaven. This was in the spring of 1820, and Joseph was yet scarcely fifteen.

When the young prophet began to proclaim his vision, the wise men and preachers of the several sects laughed at him; called him a silly boy, and told him that if his mind had really been disturbed, it was the devil's doing. "Signs and revelations," said they, "are of by-gone times; it ill befits one so young to lie before God and in the presence of his people." "Nevertheless," replied Joseph, "I have had a vision." Then they reviled him, and the boy became disheartened and was entangled again in the vanities of the world, under the heavy hand of their oppression.

But the spirit of the Lord could not thus be quenched. The young man repented, and sought and found forgiveness. Retiring to his bed, midst prayer and supplication, on the night of September 21, 1823, presently the room grew light, and a figure robed in exceeding whiteness stood by the bedside, the feet not touching the floor. And a voice was heard, saying, "I am Moroni, and am come to you, Joseph, as a messenger from God." Then the angel told the youth that the Lord had for him a great work to do, that his name should be known to all people, and of him should be spoken both good and evil. He told him of a book written on plates of gold, and containing an account of the early inhabitants of this continent, and the gospel as delivered to them by Christ. He said that deposited with those plates were two stones in silver bows, which, fastened to a breastplate, constituted the Urim and Thummim; and that now as in ancient times the possession and use of the stones constituted a seer, and that through them the book might be translated. After offering many scriptural quotations from both the old and the new testament, and charging the young man that when the book and the breastplate were delivered to him he should show them to no one, under pain of death and destruction—the place where the plates were deposited meanwhile being clearly revealed to his mental vision—the light in the room grew dim, as Moroni ascended along a pathway of glory into heaven, and finally darkness was there as before. The visit was made three times, the last ending with the dawn, when Joseph arose greatly exhausted and went into the field to work.

His father, observing his condition, sent him home; but on the way Joseph fell in a state of unconsciousness to the ground. Soon, however, the voice of Moroni was heard, commanding him to return to his father, and tell him all that he had seen and heard. The young man obeyed. The father answered that it was of God; the son should do as the messenger had said. Then Joseph, knowing from the vision where the plates were hidden, went to the west side of a hill, called the hill Cumorah, near the town of Manchester, and beneath a large stone, part of whose top appeared above the ground, in a stone box,[2] he found the plates,[3] the urim and thum-

[2] Oliver Cowdery stated that he visited the spot, and that 'at the bottom of this [hole] lay a stone of suitable size, the upper surface being smooth. At each edge was placed a large quantity of cement, and into this cement at the four edges of this stone were placed erect four others, their lower edges resting in the cement at the outer edges of the first stone. The four last named when placed erect formed a box, the corners, or where the edges of the four came in contact, were also cemented so firmly that the moisture from without was prevented from entering. It is to be observed also that the inner surfaces of the four erect or side stones were smooth. The box was sufficiently large to admit a breastplate. From the bottom of the box or from the breastplate arose three small pillars, composed of the same description of cement as that used on the edges; and upon these three pillars were placed the records. The box containing the records was covered with another stone, the lower surface being flat and the upper crowning.' *Mackay's The Mormons*, 20.

[3] Orson Pratt thus describes the plates, *Visions*, 14: 'These records were engraved on plates, which had the appearance of gold. Each plate was not far from seven by eight inches in width and length, being not quite as thick as common tin. They were filled on both sides with engravings in Egyptian characters, and bound together in a volume, as the leaves of a book, and fastened at one edge with three rings running through the whole. This volume was about six inches in thickness, and a part of it was sealed. The characters or letters upon the unsealed part were small and beautifully engraved. The whole book exhibited many marks of antiquity in its construction, as well

mim,[4] and the breastplate.[5] But when he was about to take them out Moroni stood beside him and said, "Not yet; meet me here at this time each year for four years, and I will tell you what to do." Joseph obeyed.

The elder Smith was poor, and the boys were sometimes obliged to hire themselves out as laborers. It was on the 22d of September, 1823, that the plates were found. The following year Alvin died, and in October 1825 Joseph went to work for Josiah Stoal, in Chenango county. This man had what he supposed to be a silver mine at Harmony, Pennsylvania, said to have been once worked by Spaniards. Thither Joseph went with the other men to dig for silver,[6]

as much skill in the art of engraving.' In the introduction to the *Book of Mormon* (New York ed.), viii., is given essentially the same description. See also *Bouwick's Mormons and Silver Mines*, 61; *Bertrand, Mem. d'un Mor.*, 25; *Olshausen, Gesch. d. Morm.*, 12–29; *Stenhouse, Les Mormons*, i.–vii.; *Ferris' Utah and The Mormons*, 58; *Mackay's The Mormons*, 15–22; *Smucker's Hist. Mormons*, 18–28. For fac-simile of writing on golden plates, see *Beadle's Life in Utah*, 25. For illustrations of the hill, finding the plates, etc., see *Mackay's The Mormons*, 15; *Smucker's Hist. Mormons*, 24; *Tucker's Origin and Prog. Mor.*, frontispiece. When sceptics ask, Why are not the plates forthcoming? believers ask in turn, Why are not forthcoming the stone tables of Moses? And yet the ten commandments are to-day accepted.

[4] 'With the book were found the urim and thummim, two transparent crystals set in the rims of a bow. These pebbles were the seer's instrument whereby the mystery of hidden things was to be revealed!' Introduction to *Book of Mormon* (New York ed.), viii. 'The best attainable definition of the ancient urim and thummim is quite vague and indistinct. An accepted biblical lexicographer gives the meaning as "light and perfection," or the "shining and the perfect." The following is quoted from *Butterworth's Concordance:* "There are various conjectures about the urim and thummim, whether they were the stones in the high-priest's breastplate, or something distinct from them; which it is not worth our while to inquire into, since God has left it a secret. It is evident that the urim and thummim were appointed to inquire of God by, on momentous occasions, and continued in use, as some think, only till the building of Solomon's temple, and all conclude that this was never restored after its destruction."' *Tucker's Origin and Prog. Mor.*, 32.

[5] 'A breastplate such as was used by the ancients to defend the chest from the arrows and weapons of their enemy.' *Mackay's The Mormons*, 20.

[6] 'Hence arose the very prevalent story of my having been a money digger.' *Hist. Joseph Smith*, in *Times and Seasons*, May 2, 1842. It seems from this, or some other cause, that the followers of Smith have never regarded mining with favor, although some of them at times have engaged in that occupation. Upon the discovery of gold in California, the Mormons were among the first in the field, at Coloma, at Mormon Bar, and elsewhere. Left there a little longer, they would soon have gathered barrels of the precious dust; but promptly upon the call they dropped their tools, abandoned their brilliant prospects, and crossing the Sierra, began to build homes among their people in the untenanted desert.

boarding at the house of Isaac Hale. After a month's fruitless effort Stoal was induced by Joseph to abandon the undertaking; but meanwhile the youth had fallen in love with Hale's pretty daughter, Emma, and wished to marry her. Hale objected, owing to his continued assertions that he had seen visions, and the resulting persecutions; so Joseph took Emma to the house of Squire Tarbill, at South Bainbridge, where they were married the 18th of January, 1827, and thence returned to his father's farm, where he worked during the following season.[7]

Every year went Joseph to the hill Cumorah to hold communion with the heavenly messenger, and on the 22d of September, 1827, Moroni delivered to him the plates,[8] and the urim and thummim with which to translate them, charging him on pain of dire dis-

[7] Among the many charges of wrong-doing ascribed to Smith from first to last, was that of having stolen Hale's daughter. In answer it is said that the young woman was of age, and had the right to marry whom and as she chose.

[8] 'When the appointed hour came, the prophet, assuming his practised air of mystery, took in hand his money-digging spade and a large napkin, and went off in silence and alone in the solitude of the forest, and after an absence of some three hours, returned, apparently with his sacred charge concealed within the folds of the napkin. Reminding the (Smith) family of the original "command" as revealed to him, strict injunction of non-intervention and non-inspection was given to them, under the same terrible penalty as before denounced for its violation. Conflicting stories were afterwards told in regard to the manner of keeping the book in concealment and safety, which are not worth repeating, further than to mention that the first place of secretion was said to be under a heavy hearthstone in the Smith family mansion. Smith told a frightful story of the display of celestial pyrotechnics on the exposure to his view of the sacred book—the angel who had led him to the discovery again appearing as his guide and protector, and confronting ten thousand devils gathered there, with their menacing sulphurous flame and smoke, to deter him from his purpose! This story was repeated and magnified by the believers, and no doubt aided the experiment upon superstitious minds which eventuated so successfully.' *Tucker's Orig. and Prog. Mor.*, 30–31. 'A great variety of contradictory stories were related by the Smith family before they had any fixed plan of operation, respecting the finding of the plates from which their book was translated. One is, that after the plates were taken from their hiding-place by Jo, he again laid them down, looked into the hole, where he saw a toad, which immediately transformed itself into a spirit and gave him a tremendous blow. Another is, that after he had got the plates, a spirit assaulted him with the intention of getting them from his possession, and actually jerked them out of his hands. Jo, nothing daunted, seized them again, and started to run, when his Satanic majesty, or the spirit, applied his foot to the prophet's seat of honor which raised three or four feet from the ground.' *Howe's Mormonism Unveiled*, 275–6. The excavation was at the time said to be 100 feet in extent, though that is probably an ex-

aster to guard them well until he should call for
them. Persecutions increased when it was known
that Joseph had in his possession the plates of gold,
and every art that Satan could devise or put in force
through the agency of wicked men was employed to

aggeration. It had a substantial door of two-inch plank, and a secure lock.
Lapse of time and other causes have almost effaced its existence. *Tucker's
Origin and Prog. Mor.*, 48. 'In 1843, near Kinderhook, Illinois, in excavating a large mound, six brass plates were discovered of a bell-shape four
inches in length and covered with ancient characters. They were fastened
together with two iron wires almost entirely corroded, and were found
along with charcoal, ashes, and human bones, more than twelve feet below
the surface of a mound of the sugar-loaf form, common in the Mississippi
Valley. Large trees growing upon these artificial mounds attest their great
antiquity...No key has yet been discovered for the interpretation of the
engravings upon these brass plates, or of the strange gylphs upon the
ruins of Otolum in Mexico.' Daniel Wedderburn, in *Popular Science Monthly,*
Dec. 1876; see also *Times and Seasons,* iv. 186-7, and engraved cuts in *Taylor's Discussions,* and in *Mackay's The Mormons,* 26-7. On the authority of
Kidder, *Mormonism,* 23-6, Willard Chase, a carpenter, said: 'In the fore
part of September (I believe) 1827, the prophet requested me to make him a
chest, informing me that he designed to move back to Pennsylvania, and expecting soon to get his gold book, he wanted a chest to lock it up, giving me
to understand, at the same time, that if I would make the chest he would
give me a share in the book. I told him my business was such that I could
not make it; but if he would bring the book to me, I would lock it up for
him. He said that would not do, as he was commanded to keep it two years
without letting it come to the eye of any one but himself. This commandment, however, he did not keep, for in less than two years twelve men said
they had seen it. I told him to get it and convince me of its existence, and
I would make him a chest; but he said that would not do; as he must have a
chest to lock the book in as soon as he took it out of the ground. I saw him
a fews days after, when he told me I must make the chest. I told him plainly
that I could not, upon which he told me that I could have no share in the book.
A few weeks after this conversation he came to my house and related the
following story: That on the 22d of September he arose early in the morning
and took a one-horse wagon of some one that had stayed over night at their
house, without leave or license; and, together with his wife, repaired to the
hill which contained the book. He left his wife in the wagon, by the road,
and went alone to the hill, a distance of thirty or forty rods from the road;
he said he then took the book out of the ground and hid it in a tree-top and
returned home. He then went to the town of Macedon to work. After
about ten days, it having been suggested that some one had got his book, his
wife went after him; he hired a horse, and went home in the afternoon, stayed
long enough to drink one cup of tea, and then went for his book, found it
safe, took off his frock, wrapt it round it, put it under his arm, and ran all
the way home, a distance of about two miles. He said he should think it
would weigh sixty pounds, and was sure it would weigh forty. On his return
home he said he was attacked by two men in the woods, and knocked them
both down and made his escape, arrived safe, and secured his treasure. He
then observed that if it had not been for that stone (which he acknowledged
belonged to me) he would not have obtained the book. A few days afterward he told one of my neighbors that he had not got any such book, and
never had; but that he told the story to deceive the damned fool (meaning
me), to get him to make a chest.' Others give other accounts, but it seems
to me not worth while to follow them further.

wrest them from him. But almighty power and wisdom prevailed, and the sacred relics were safely kept till the day the messenger called for them, when they were delivered into his hands, Joseph meanwhile having accomplished by them all that was required of him. And now so fierce becomes the fiery malevolence of the enemy that Joseph is obliged to fly.[9] He is very poor, having absolutely nothing, until a farmer named Martin Harris has pity on him and gives him fifty dollars,[10] with which he is enabled to go with his wife to her old home in Pennsylvania.[11] Immediately after his arrival there in December, he begins copying the

[9] 'Soon the news of his discoveries spread abroad throughout all those parts...The house was frequently beset by mobs and evil-designing persons. Several times he was shot at, and very narrowly escaped. Every device was used to get the plates away from him. And being continually in danger of his life from a gang of abandoned wretches, he at length concluded to leave the place, and go to Pennsylvania; and accordingly packed up his goods, putting the plates into a barrel of beans, and proceeded upon his journey. He had not gone far before he was overtaken by an officer with a search-warrant, who flattered himself with the idea that he should surely obtain the plates; after searching very diligently, he was sadly disappointed at not finding them. Mr Smith then drove on, but before he got to his journey's end he was again overtaken by an officer on the same business, and after ransacking the wagon very carefully, he went his way as much chagrined as the first at not being able to discover the object of his research. Without any further molestation, he pursued his journey until he came to the northern part of Pennsylvania, near the Susquehanna River, in which part his father-in-law resided.' *Pratt's Visions*, 15.

[10] ' In the neighborhood (of Smith's old home) there lived a farmer possessed of some money and more credulity. Every wind of doctrine affected him. He had been in turn a quaker, a Wesleyan, a baptist, a presbyterian. His heterogeneous and unsettled views admirably qualified him for discipleship where novelty was paramount, and concrete things were invested with the enchantment of mystery. He was enraptured with the young prophet, and offered him fifty dollars to aid in the publication of his new bible.' *Taylder's Mormons*, xxviii.-ix.

[11] 'Soon after Smith's arrival at Harmony, Isaac Hale (Smith's father-in-law) heard he had brought a wonderful box of plates with him. Hale "was shown a box in which it is said they were contained, which had to all appearances been used as a glass box of the common window-glass. I was allowed to feel the weight of the box, and they gave me to understand that the book of plates was then in the box—into which, however, I was not allowed to look. I inquired of Joseph Smith, Jr., who was to be the first who would be allowed to see the book of plates. He said it was a young child. After this I became dissatisfied, and informed him that if there was anything in my house of that description, which I could not be allowed to see, he must take it away; if he did not, I was determined to see it. After that the plates were said to be hid in the woods."' *Howe's Mormonism Unveiled*, 264.

characters on the plates, Martin Harris coming to his
assistance, and by means of the urim and thummim
manages to translate some of them, which work is
continued till February 1828. Harris' wife is exceedingly curious about the matter, and finally obtains
possession through her husband of a portion of the
manuscript.[12] About this time Harris takes a copy

[12] Martin Harris 'says he wrote a considerable part of the book as Smith
dictated; and at one time the presence of the Lord was so great that a screen
was hung up between him and the prophet; at other times the prophet would
sit in a different room, or up stairs, while the Lord was communicating to him
the contents of the plates. He does not pretend that he ever saw the wonderful plates but once, although he and Smith were engaged for months in
deciphering their contents.' *Mormonism Unveiled*, 14. 'Harris rendered
Smith valuable assistance by transcribing for him, since he could not write
himself. Poor Martin was unfortunately gifted with a troublesome wife. Her
inquisitive and domineering nature made him dread unpleasant results from
his present engagement. His manuscript had reached 116 pages, and he
therefore begged permission to read it to her "with the hope that it might
have a salutary effect upon her feelings." His request was at length granted;
but through carelessness or perfidy, while in his house, the precious document was irrecoverably lost. Joseph suffered greatly in consequence of this
hinderance, but more from the anger of heaven which was manifested against
him. As soon as possible, he resumed his task, having secured the services
of another scribe, Oliver Cowdery, a school-master in the neighborhood.
Martin Harris, earnest as he was, had never yet been favored with a sight of
the golden plates. He had not attained to sufficient purity of mind; but a
copy of a small portion of their contents was placed in his hands, and this he
was told he might show to any scholar in the world, if he wished to be satisfied. Accordingly he started for New York, sought Professor Anthon
(Charles Anthon, LL.D., then adjunct professor of ancient languages in Columbia College), and requested his opinion.' *Taylder's Mormons*, xxxviii.-ix.
'She (Harris's wife) contrived in her husband's sleep to steal from him the
particular source of her disturbance, and burned the manuscript to ashes.
For years she kept this incendiarism a profound secret to herself, even until
after the book was published. Smith and Harris held her accountable for the
theft, but supposed she had handed the manuscript to some "evil-designing
persons," to be used somehow in injuring their cause. A feud was thus produced between husband and wife which was never reconciled. Great con-
sternation now pervaded the Mormon circles. The reappearance of the mysterious stranger (who had before visited the Smiths) was again the subject of
inquiry and conjecture by observers, from whom was withheld all explanation
of his identity or purpose. It was not at first an easy task to convince the
prophet of the entire innocency of his trusted friend Harris in the matter of
this calamitous event, though mutual confidence and friendship were ultimately
restored.' *Tucker's Orig. and Prog. Mor.*, 46. Of this lost manuscript Smith
afterward wrote: 'Some time after Mr Harris had begun to write for me he
began to tease me to give him liberty to carry the writings home and show
them, and desired of me that I would inquire of the Lord through the urim
and thummim if he might not do so.' To two inquiries the reply was no, but
a third application resulted in permission being granted under certain restrictions, which were, that Harris might show the papers to his brother,
his wife, her sister, his father and mother, and to no one else. Accordingly
Smith required Harris to bind himself in a covenant to him in the most
solemn manner that he would not do otherwise than had been directed. 'He

of some of the characters to New York city, where
he submits them to the examination of Professor
Anthon and Dr Mitchell, who pronounce them to
be Egyptian, Syriac, Chaldaic, and Arabic.[13]   Then

did so,' says Smith. 'He bound himself as I required of him, took the
writings, and went his way. Notwithstanding... he did show them to others,
and by stratagem they got them away from him.' *Smith*, in *Times and Seasons*, iii. 785–6.
[13] In a letter to E. D. Howe, printed in his book, and in the introduction
to the New York edition of the *Book of Mormon*, Prof. Anthon, among other
statements, denies that he ever gave a certificate.   The letter reads as follows:
                                        'NEW YORK, February 17, 1834.
'DEAR SIR: I received your letter of the 9th, and lose no time in making
a reply.   The whole story about my pronouncing the Mormon inscription to
be reformed Egyptian hierogylphics is perfectly false.   Some years ago, a
plain, apparently simple-hearted farmer called on me with a note from Dr
Mitchell, of our city, now dead, requesting me to decipher, if possible, the
paper which the farmer would hand me.   Upon examining the paper in question, I soon came to the conclusion that it was all a trick—perhaps a hoax.
When I asked the person who brought it how he obtained the writing, he gave
me the following account: A gold book consisting of a number of plates, fastened together by wires of the same material, had been dug up in the northern
part of the state of New York, and along with it an enormous pair of spectacles.   These spectacles were so large that if any person attempted to look
through them, his two eyes would look through one glass only, the spectacles
in question being altogether too large for the human face.   "Whoever," he
said, "examined the plates through the glasses was enabled not only to read
them, but fully to understand their meaning."   All this knowledge, however,
was confined to a young man, who had the trunk containing the book and spectacles in his sole possession.   This young man was placed behind a curtain in a
garret in a farm-house, and being thus concealed from view, he put on the
spectacles occasionally, or rather looked through one of the glasses, deciphered
the characters in the book, and having committed some of them to paper,
handed copies from behind the curtain to those who stood outside.   Not a
word was said about their being deciphered by the gift of God.   Everything
in this way was effected by the large pair of spectacles.   The farmer added
that he had been requested to contribute a sum of money toward the publication of the golden book, the contents of which would, as he was told, produce
an entire change in the world, and save it from ruin.   So urgent had been
these solicitations, that he intended selling his farm and giving the amount to
those who wished to publish the plates.   As a last precautionary step, he had
resolved to come to New York, and obtain the opinion of the learned about
the meaning of the paper which he brought with him, and which had been
given him as part of the contents of the book, although no translation had at
that time been made by the young man with spectacles.   On hearing this odd
story, I changed my opinion about the paper, and instead of viewing it any
longer as a hoax, I began to regard it as part of a scheme to cheat the farmer
of his money, and I communicated my suspicions to him, warning him to beware of rogues.   He requested an opinion from me in writing, which, of
course, I declined to give, and he then took his leave, taking his paper with
him.   This paper in question was, in fact, a singular scroll.   It consisted of
all kinds of singular characters disposed in columns, and had evidently been
prepared by some person who had before him at the time a book containing
various alphabets, Greek and Hebrew letters, crosses and flourishes; Roman
letters inverted or placed sideways were arranged and placed in perpendicular
columns, and the whole ended in a rude delineation of a circle, divided into
HIST. UTAH. 4

Joseph buys of his wife's father a small farm and goes to work on it. In February 1829 he receives a visit from his own father, at which time a revelation comes to Joseph Smith senior, through the son, calling him to faith and good works. The month following Martin Harris asks for and receives a revelation, by the mouth of the latter, regarding the plates, wherein the said Harris is told that Joseph has in his possession the plates which he claims to have, that they were delivered to him by the Lord God, who likewise gave him power to translate them, and that he, Harris, should bear witness of the same. Three months later, Harris having meanwhile acted as his scribe, Joseph is commanded to rest for a season in his work of translating until directed to take it up again.

various compartments, arched with various strange marks, and evidently copied after the Mexican calendar given by Humboldt, but copied in such a way as not to betray the source whence it was derived. I am thus particular as to the contents of the paper, inasmuch as I have frequently conversed with friends on the subject since the Mormon excitement began, and well remember that the paper contained anything else but Egyptian hieroglyphics. Some time after, the farmer paid me a second visit. He brought with him the gold book in print, and offered it to me for sale. I declined purchasing. He then asked permission to leave the book with me for examination. I declined receiving it, although his manner was strangely urgent. I adverted once more to the roguery which, in my opinion, had been practised upon him, and asked him what had become of the gold plates. He informed me they were in a trunk with the spectacles. I advised him to go to a magistrate and have the trunk examined. He said the curse of God would come upon him if he did. On my pressing him, however, to go to a magistrate, he told me he would open the trunk if I would take the curse of God upon myself. I replied I would do so with the greatest willingness, and would incur every risk of that nature, provided I could only extricate him from the grasp of the rogues. He then left me. I have given you a full statement of all that I know respecting the origin of Mormonism, and must beg of you, as a personal favor, to publish this letter immediately, should you find my name mentioned again by these wretched fanatics. Yours respectfully, 'CHARLES ANTHON.'

It is but fair to state that Smith never claimed that the characters were the ordinary Greek or Hebrew, but were what he called Reformed Egyptian. Harris says: 'He gave me a certificate which I took and put into my pocket, and was just leaving the house when Mr Anthon called me back, and asked me how the young man found out that there were gold plates in the place where he found them. I answered that an angel of God had revealed it unto him. He then said unto me, Let me see that certificate. I accordingly took it out of my pocket and gave it to him, when he took it and tore it to pieces, saying that there was no such thing now as ministering of angels, and that if I would bring the plates to him he would translate them. I informed him that part of the plates were sealed, and that I was forbidden to bring them; he replied, "I cannot read a sealed book." I left him and went to Dr Mitchell, who sanctioned what Professor Anthon had said respecting both the characters and the translation.' *Pearl of Great Price*, xiii. 54.

The tenor of the book of Mormon [14] is in this wise:
Following the confusion of tongues at the tower of
Babel, the peoples of the earth were scattered abroad,
one colony being led by the Lord across the ocean to
America. Fifteen hundred years after, or six hundred
years before Christ, they were destroyed for their
wickedness. Of the original number was Jared,
among whose descendants was the prophet Ether,
who was their historian. Ether lived to witness the
extinction of his nation, and under divine direction he
deposited his history in a locality where it was found
by a second colony, Israelites of the tribe of Joseph,
who came from Jerusalem about the time of the destruction of the first colony, namely, six hundred
years before Christ. Thus was America repeopled;
the second colony occupied the site of the first, multiplied and became rich, and in time divided into two
nations, the Nephites and the Lamanites, so called
from their respective founders, Nephi and Laman.
The former advanced in civilization, but the Lamanites lapsed into barbarism, and were the immediate
progenitors of the American aboriginals.

The Nephites were the beloved of the Lord. To
them were given visions and angels' visits; to them
the Christ appeared with gifts of gospel and prophecy.
It was, indeed, the golden age of a favored people;
but in a time of temptation, some three or four centuries after Christ, they fell, and were destroyed by

---

[14] 'The word "Mormon," the name given to his book, is the English termination of the Greek word *mormoo*, which we find defined in an old, obsolete
dictionary to mean bugbear, hobgoblin, raw head, and bloody bones.' *Howe's
Mormonism Unveiled*, 21. 'The word "Mormon" is neither Greek nor derived from the Greek, but from the "reformed Egyptian."' *Bell's Reply to
Theobald*, 2. In *Times and Seasons*, Mr Smith writes as follows with regard
to the meaning of the word 'Mormon:' 'We say from the Saxon, *good;* the
Dane, *god;* the Goth, *goda;* the German, *gut;* the Dutch, *goed;* the Latin,
bonus; the Greek, *kalos;* the Hebrew, *tob;* and the Egyptian, *mon.* Hence,
with the addition of *more*, or the contraction *mor*, we have the word "Mormon," which means, literally *more good.*' 'Joseph Smith, annoyed at the
profane wit which could derive the word "Mormon" from the Greek *mormo*, a
bugbear, wrote an epistle on the subject, concluding with an elaborate display
of his philological talent, such as he was accustomed to make on every possible occasion.' *Taylder's Mormon's Own Book*, xxxiv., xxxv.

the wicked Lamanites. The greatest prophet of the Nephites, in the period of their declension, was Mormon, their historian, who after having completed his abridgment of the records of his nation, committed it to his son Moroni, and he, that they might not fall into the hands of the Lamanites, deposited them in the hill of Cumorah, where they were found by Joseph Smith.

On the 5th of April, 1829, there comes to Joseph Smith a school-teacher, Oliver Cowdery by name, to whom the Lord had revealed himself at the house of the elder Smith, where the teacher had been boarding. Inquiring of the Lord, Joseph is told that to Oliver shall be given the same power to translate the book of Mormon,[15] by which term the writing on

[15] *The Book of Mormon; an account written by The Hand of Mormon, upon plates taken from the plates of Nephi. Wherefore it is an abridgment of the record of the people of Nephi, and also of the Lamanites, who are a remnant of the house of Israel; and also to Jew and Gentile; written by way of commandment, and also by the spirit of prophecy and of revelation. Written and sealed up, and hid up unto the Lord, that they might not be destroyed; to come forth by the gift and power of God unto the interpretation thereof; sealed by the hand of Moroni, and hid up unto the Lord, to come forth in due time by the way of Gentile; the interpretation thereof by the gift of God. An abridgment taken from the Book of Ether also; which is a record of the people of Jared; who were scattered at the time the Lord confounded the language of the people when they were building a tower to get to heaven; which is to shew unto the remnant of the House of Israel what great things the Lord hath done for their fathers; and that they may know the covenants of the Lord, that they are not cast off forever; and also to the convincing of the Jew and Gentile that Jesus is the Christ, the Eternal God, manifesting himself unto all nations. And now if there are faults, they are the mistakes of men; wherefore condemn not the things of God, that ye may be found spotless at the judgment-seat of Christ. By Joseph Smith, Jun., Author and Proprietor.* (Printed by E. B. Grandin, for the author, Palmyra, New York, 1830.) Several editions followed. This first edition has 588 pages, and is prefaced among other things by an account of 117 pages, which Mrs Harris burned. This preface is omitted in subsequent editions. The testimony of three witnesses, and also of eight witnesses which in subsequent editions is placed at the beginning, is here at the end. The testimony of witnesses affirms that the signers saw the plates and the engravings thereon, having been shown them by an angel from heaven; they knew of the translation, that it had been done by the gift and power of God, and was therefore true. The book was reprinted at Nauvoo, at New York, at Salt Lake City, and in Europe. An edition printed by Jas O. Wright & Co., evidently by way of speculation, contains eight pages of introduction, and an advertisement asserting that it is a reprint from the third American edition, and that the work was originally published at Nauvoo, which latter statement is incorrect. The publishers further claim that at the time of this printing, 1848, the book was out of print, notwithstanding the several pre-

ceding editions. The edition at present in common use was printed at Salt
Lake City, at the *Deseret News* office, and entered according to act of congress in 1879, by Joseph F. Smith. It is divided into chapters and verses,
with references by Orson Pratt, senior. The arrangement is as follows:

The first book of Nephi, his reign and ministry, 22 chapters; the second
book of Nephi, 33 chapters; the book of Jacob, the brother of Nephi, 7 chapters; the book of Enos, 1 chapter; the book of Jarom, 1 chapter; the book
of Omni, 1 chapter; the words of Mormon, 1 chapter; the book of Mosiah,
29 chapters; the book of Alma, the son of Alma, 63 chapters; the book of
Helaman, 16 chapters; the book of Nephi, the son of Nephi, who was the
son of Helaman, 30 chapters; the book of Nephi, who is the son of Nephi,
one of the disciples of Jesus Christ, 1 chapter; book of Mormon, 9 chapters;
book of Ether, 15 chapters; the book of Moroni, 10 chapters. In all 239
chapters.

I give herewith the contents of the several books. The style, like that of
the revelations, is biblical.

'First Book of Nephi. Language of the record; Nephi's abridgment;
Lehi's dream; Lehi departs into the wilderness; Nephi slayeth Laban; Sariah
complains of Lehi's vision; contents of the brass plates; Ishmael goes with
Nephi; Nephi's brethren rebel, and bind him; Lehi's dream of the tree, rod,
etc.; Messiah and John prophesied of; olive branches broken off; Nephi's
vision of Mary; of the crucifixion of Christ; of darkness and earthquake;
great abominable church; discovery of the promised land; bible spoken of;
book of Mormon and holy ghost promised; other books come forth; bible and
book of Mormon one; promises to the gentiles; two churches; the work of
the Father to commence; a man in white robes (John); Nephites come to
knowledge; rod of iron; the sons of Lehi take wives; director found (ball);
Nephi breaks his bow; directors work by faith; Ishmael died; Lehi and Nephi
threatened; Nephi commanded to build a ship; Nephi about to be worshipped
by his brethren; ship finished and entered; dancing in the ship; Nephi bound;
ship driven back; arrived on the promised land; plates of ore made; Zenos,
Neum, and Zenock; Isaiah's writing; holy one of Israel.

'Second Book of Nephi. Lehi to his sons; opposition in all things; Adam
fell that man might be; Joseph saw our day; a choice seer; writings grow together; prophet promised to the Lamanites; Joseph's prophecy on brass
plates; Lehi buried; Nephi's life sought; Nephi separated from Laman; temple built; skin of blackness; priests, etc., consecrated; make other plates;
Isaiah's words by Jacob; angels to a devil; spirits and bodies reunited; baptism; no kings upon this land; Isaiah prophesieth; rod of the stem of Jesse;
seed of Joseph perisheth not; law of Moses kept; Christ shall shew himself;
signs of Christ, birth and death; whisper from the dust; book sealed up;
priestcraft forbidden; sealed book to be brought forth; three witnesses behold
the book; the words (read this, I pray thee); seal up the book again; their
priests shall contend; teach with their learning, and deny the holy ghost; rob
the poor; a bible, a bible; men judged of the books; white and a delightsome
people; work commences among all people; lamb of God baptized; baptism by
water and holy ghost.

'Book of Jacob. Nephi anointeth a king; Nephi dies; Nephites and
Lamanites; a righteous branch from Joseph; Lamanites shall scourge you;
more than one wife forbidden; trees, waves, and mountains obey us; Jews
look beyond the mark; tame olive tree; nethermost part of the vineyard;
fruit laid up against the season; another branch; wild fruit had overcome;
lord of the vineyard weeps; branches overcome the roots; wild branches
plucked off; Sherem, the anti-Christ; a sign, Sherem smitten; Enos takes the
plates from his father.

'The Book of Enos. Enos, thy sins are forgiven; records threatened by
Lamanites; Lamanites eat raw meat.

'The Book of Jarom. Nephites wax strong; Lamanites drink blood;
fortify cities; plates delivered to Omni.

'The Book of Omni. Plates given to Amaron; plates given to Chemish;

Mosiah warned to flee; Zarahemla discovered; engravings on a stone; Coriantumr discovered; his parents come from the tower; plates delivered to King Benjamin.
'The words of Mormon. False Christs and prophets.
'Book of Mosiah. Mosiah made king; the plates of brass, sword, and director; King Benjamin teacheth the people; their tent doors toward the temple; coming of Christ foretold; beggars not denied; sons and daughters; Mosiah began to reign; Ammon, etc., bound and imprisoned; Limhi's proclamation; twenty-four plates of gold; seer and translator.
'Record of Zeniff. A battle fought; King Laman died; Noah made king; Abinadi the prophet; resurrection; Alma believed Abinadi; Abinadi cast into prison and scourged with fagots; waters of Mormon; the daughters of the Lamanites stolen by King Noah's priests; records on plates of ore; last tribute of wine; Lamanites' deep sleep; King Limhi baptized; priests and teachers labor; Alma saw an angel; Alma fell (dumb); King Mosiah's sons preach to the Lamanites; translation of records; plates delivered by Limhi; translated by two stones; people back to the Tower; records given to Alma; judges appointed; King Mosiah died; Alma died; Kings of Nephi ended.
'The Book of Alma. Nehor slew Gideon; Amlici made king; Amlici slain in battle; Amlicites painted red; Alma baptized in Sidon; Alma's preaching; Alma ordained elders; commanded to meet often; Alma saw an angel; Amulek saw an angel; lawyers questioning Amulek; coins named; Zeesrom the lawyer; Zeesrom trembles; election spoken of; Melchizedek priesthood; Zeesrom stoned; records burned; prison rent; Zeesrom healed and baptized; Nehor's desolation; Lamanites converted; flocks scattered at Sebus; Ammon smote off arms; Ammon and King Lamoni; King Lamoni fell; Ammon and the queen; king and queen prostrate; Aaron, etc., delivered; Jerusalem built; preaching in Jerusalem; Lamoni's father converted; land desolation and bountiful; anti-Nephi-Lehies; general council; swords buried; 1,005 massacred; Lamanites perish by fire; slavery forbidden; anti-Nephi-Lehies removed to Jershon, called Ammonites; tremendous battle; anti-Christ, Korihor; Korihor struck dumb; the devil in the form of an angel; Korihor trodden down; Alma's mission to Zoramites; Rameumptom (holy stand); Alma on hill Onidah; Alma on faith; prophecy of Zenos; prophecy of Zenock; Amulek's knowledge of Christ; charity recommended; same spirit possess your body; believers cast out; Alma to Helaman; plates given to Helaman; twenty-four plates; Gazelem, a stone (secret); Liahona, or compass; Alma to Shiblon; Alma to Corianton; unpardonable sin; resurrection; restoration; justice in punishment; if, Adam, took, tree, life; mercy rob justice; Moroni's stratagem; slaughter of Lamanites; Moroni's speech to Zerahemnah; prophecy of a soldier; Lamanites' covenant of peace; Alma's prophecy 400 years after Christ; dwindle in unbelief; Alma's strange departure; Amalickiah leadeth away the people, destroyeth the church; standard of Moroni; Joseph's coat rent; Jacob's prophecy of Joseph's seed; fevers in the land, plants and roots for diseases; Amalickiah's plot; the king stabbed; Amalickiah marries the queen, and is acknowledged king; fortifications by Moroni; ditches filled with dead bodies; Amalickiah's oath; Pahoran appointed judge; army against king-men; Amalickiah slain; Ammoron made king; Bountiful fortified; dissensions; 2,000 young men; Moroni's epistle to Ammoron; Ammoron's answer; Lamanites made drunk; Moroni's stratagem; Helaman's epistle to Moroni; Helaman's stratagem; mothers taught faith; Lamanites surrendered; city of Antiparah taken; city of Cumeni taken; 200 of the 2,000 fainted; prisoners rebel, slain; Manti taken by stratagem; Moroni to the governor; governor's answer; King Pachus slain; cords and ladders prepared; Nephihah taken; Teancum's stratagem, slain; peace established; Moronihah made commander; Helaman died; sacred things, Shiblon; Moroni died; 5,400 emigrated north; ships built by Hagoth; sacred things committed to Helaman; Shiblon died.
'The Book of Helaman. Pahoran died; Pahoran appointed judge; Kishkumen slays Pahoran; Pacumeni appointed judge; Zarahamia taken; Pacu-

meni killed; Coriantumr slain; Lamanites surrendered; Helaman appointed judge; secret signs discovered and Kishkumen stabbed; Gadianton fled; emigration northward; cement houses; many books and records; Helaman died; Nephi made judge; Nephites become wicked; Nephi gave the judgment-seat to Cezoram; Nephi and Lehi preached to the Lamanites; 8,000 baptized; Alma and Nephi surrounded with fire; angels administer; Cezoram and son murdered; Gadianton robbers; Gadianton robbers destroyed; Nephi's prophecy; Gadianton robbers are judges; chief judge slain; Seantum detected; keys of the kingdom; Nephi taken away by the spirit; famine in the land; Gladianton band destroyed; famine removed; Samuel's prophecy; tools lost; two days and a night, light; sign of the crucifixion; Samuel stoned, etc.; angels appeared.

'Third Book of Nephi. Lachoneus chief judge; Nephi receives the records; Nephi's strange departure; no darkness at night; Lamanites become white; Giddianhi to Lachoneus; Gidgiddoni chief judge; Giddianhi slain; Zemnarihah hanged; robbers surrendered; Mormon abridges the records; church begins to be broken up; government of the land destroyed; chief judge murdered; divided into tribes; Nephi raises the dead; sign of the crucifixion; cities destroyed, earthquakes, darkness, etc.; law of Moses fulfilled; Christ appears to Nephites; print of the nails; Nephi and others called; baptism commanded; doctrine of Christ; Christ the end of the law; other sheep spoken of; blessed are the Gentiles; Gentile wickedness on the land of Joseph; Isaiah's words fulfilled; Jesus heals the sick; Christ blesses children; little ones encircled with fire; Christ administers the sacrament; Christ teaches his disciples; names of the twelve; the twelve teach the multitude; baptism, holy ghost, and fire; disciples made white; faith great; Christ breaks bread again; miracle, bread and wine; Gentiles destroyed (Isaiah); Zion established; from Gentiles, to your seed; sign, Father's work commenced; he shall be marred; Gentiles destroyed (Isaiah); New Jerusalem built; work commence among all the tribes; Isaiah's words; saints did arise; Malachi's prophecy; faith tried by the book of Mormon; children's tongues loosed; the dead raised; baptism and holy ghost; all things common; Christ appears again; Moses, church; three Nephites tarry; the twelve caught up; change upon their bodies.

'Book of Nephi, son of Nephi. Disciples raise the dead; Zarahemia rebuilt; other disciples are ordained in their stead; Nephi dies; Amos keeps the records in his stead; Amos dies, and his son Amos keeps the records; prisons rent by the three; secret combinations; Ammaron hides the records.

'Book of Mormon. Three disciples taken away; Mormon forbidden to preach; Mormon appointed leader; Samuel's prophecy fulfilled; Mormon makes a record; lands divided; the twelve shall judge; desolation taken; women and children sacrificed; Mormon takes the records hidden in Shim; Mormon repents of his oath and takes command; coming forth of records; records hid in Cumorah; 230,000 Nephites slain; shall not get gain by the plates; these things shall come forth out of the earth; the state of the world; miracles cease, unbelief; disciples go into all the world and preach; language of the book.

'Book of Ether. Twenty-four plates found; Jared cries unto the Lord; Jared goes down to the valley of Nimrod; Deseret, honey-bee; barges built; decree of God, choice land; free from bondage; four years in tents at Moriancumer; Lord talks three hours; barges like a dish; eight vessels, sixteen stones; Lord touches the stones; finger of the Lord seen; Jared's brother sees the Lord; two stones given; stones sealed up; goes aboard of vessels; furious wind blows; 344 days' passage; Orihah anointed king; King Shule taken captive; Shule's sons slay Noah; Jared carries his father away captive; the daughters of Jared dance; Jared anointed king by the hand of wickedness; Jared murdered and Akish reigns in his stead; names of animals; poisonous serpents; Riplakish's cruel reign; Morianton anointed king; poisonous serpents destroyed; many wicked kings; Moroni on faith; miracles by faith; Moroni sees Jesus; New Jerusalen spoken of; Ether cast out; records finished in the cavity of a rock; secret combinations; war in all the land; King Gilead murdered by his high priest; the high priest murdered by Lib; Lib slain by Coriantumr; dead bodies cover the land and none to bury them; 2,000,000 men slain; hill Ramah; cries rend the air; sleep on their swords; Coriantumr slays Shiz; Shiz falls to the earth; records hidden by Ether.

'Book of Moroni. Christ's words to the twelve; manner of ordination; order of sacrament; order of baptism; faith, hope and charity; baptism of little children; women fed on their husbands' flesh; daughters murdered and eaten; sufferings of women and children; cannot recommend them to God; Moroni to the Lamanites; 420 years since the sign; records sealed up (Moroni); gifts of the spirits; God's word shall hiss forth.'

From a manuscript furnished at my request by Franklin D. Richards, entitled *The Book of Mormon*, I epitomize as follows: Several families retaining similar forms of speech were directed by God to America, where they became numerous and prosperous. They lived righteously at first, but afterward became sinful, and about 600 B. C. broke up as a nation, leaving records by their most eminent historian Ether. During the reign of Zedekiah, king of Judah, two men, Lehi and Mulek, were warned of God of the approaching destruction of Jerusalem, and were directed how they and their families could make their escape, and were led to this land where they found the records of the former people. Lehi landed at Chili. His people spread to North America, became numerous and wealthy, lived under the law of Moses which they had brought with them, and had their judges, kings, prophets, and temples. Looking confidently for the coming of Christ in the flesh, in due time he came, and after his crucifixion organized the church in America as he had done in Judea, an account of which, together with their general history, was preserved on metallic plates in the language of the times. An abridgment was made on gold plates about A. D. 400 by a prophet named Mormon, from all the historical plates that had come down to him. Thus were given not only the histories of the Nephites and Lamanites—his own people—but of the Jaredites, who had occupied the land before them, and his book was called the Book of Mormon. Destruction coming upon the people, Mormon's son, Moroni, was directed of God where to deposit the plates, the urim and thummim being deposited with them so that the finder might be able to read them. And as Moroni had left them so were they found by Joseph Smith. The *Book of Mormon* was translated in 1851 into Italian, under the auspices of Lorenzo Snow, and into Danish under the direction of Erastus Snow; in 1852 John Taylor directed its translation into French and German, and Franklin D. Richards into Welsh. In 1855 George Q. Cannon brought out an edition in the Hawaiian language at San Francisco; in 1878 N. C. Flygare supervised its publication in the Swedish, and Moses Thatcher in 1884 in the Spanish language.

In December 1874, Orson Pratt, at that time church historian, prepared an article for insertion in the *Universal Cyclopedia*, a portion of which is as follows: 'The first edition of this wonderful book was published early in 1830. It has since been translated and published in the Welsh, Danish, German, French, and Italian languages of the east, and in the language of the Sandwich Islands of the west. It is a volume about one third as large as the bible, consisting of sixteen sacred books...One of the founders of the Jaredite nation, a great prophet, saw in vision all things from the foundation of the world to the end thereof, which were written, a copy of which was engraved by Moroni on the plates of Mormon, and then sealed up. It was this portion which the prophet, Joseph Smith, was forbidden to translate or to unloose the seal. In due time this also will be revealed, together with all the sacred records kept by the ancient nations of this continent, preparatory to the time when the knowledge of God shall cover the earth as the waters cover the great deep.' *Deseret News*, Sept. 27, 1876. Orson Pratt afterward stated that the book of Mormon had been translated into ten different languages. *Deseret News*, Oct. 9, 1878. See also *Taylder's Mormons*, 10. For further criticisms on the book of Mormon, see *Millennial Star*, xix., index v.;

the golden plates is hereafter known, and that he also shall bear witness to the truth.

Two days after the arrival of Oliver,[16] Joseph and he begin the work systematically, the former translating while the latter writes ;[17] for Oliver has a vision, mean-

Times and Seasons, ii. 305–6; *Pratt's Pamphlets*, i. to vi. 1–96; *Hyde's Mormonism*, 210–83; *Olshausen Gesch. der Mormen*, 15–29; *Howe's Mormonism Unveiled*, 17–123; *Salt Lake City Tribune*, Apr. 11, June 5 and 6, and Nov. 5, 1879; *Juvenile Instructor*, xiv. 2–3; *Reynolds' Myth of the Manuscript Found*, passim; *Lee's Mormonism*, 119–26; *Clements' Roughing It*, 127–35; *Pop. Science Monthly*, lvi. 165–73; *Bennett's Mormonism Exposed*, 103–40. See letter from Thurlow Weed, also statement by Mrs Matilda Spaulding McKinstry in *Scribner's Mag.*, Aug. 1880, 613–16.

[16] Oliver Cowdery ' is a blacksmith by trade, and sustained a fair reputation until his intimacy commenced with the money digger. He was one of the many in the world who always find time to study out ways and means to live without work. He accordingly quit the blacksmithing business, and is now the editor of a small monthly publication issued under the directions of the prophet, and principally filled with accounts of the spread of Mormonism, their persecutions, and the fabled visions and commands of Smith.' He was ' chief scribe to the prophet, while transcribing, after Martin had lost 116 pages of the precious document by interference of the devil. An angel also has shown him the plates from which the book of Mormon proceeded, as he says.' *Howe's Mormonism Unveiled*, 15, 265; see also *Pearl of Great Price*, xiii. 54; *Smucker's Hist. Mor.*, 28; *Taylder's Mormons*, xxxii.

[17] 'Instead of looking at the characters inscribed upon the plates, the prophet was obliged to resort to the old peep-stone which he formerly used in money digging. This he placed in a hat, or box, into which he also thrust his face. . . Another account they give of the transaction is, that it was performed with the big spectacles,' which enabled 'Smith to translate the plates without looking at them.' *Howe's Mormonism Unveiled*, 17–18. ' These were days never to be forgotten,' Oliver remarks, 'to sit under the sound of a voice dictated by the inspiration of heaven, awakened the utmost gratitude of this bosom! Day after day I continued, uninterrupted, to write from his mouth, as he translated with the urim and thummim, or, as the Nephites would have said, "interpreters," the history or record called the "Book of Mormon,"' *Pearl of Great Price*, 55. See also *Mackay's The Mormons*, 30–31; *Millennial Star*, iii. 148; *Smucker's Hist. Mormons*, 35; *Pratt's Pamphlets*, iv. 58–9; *Ferris' Utah and the Mormons*, 61–2. In relation to the peep-stone alluded to, Williard Chase says in his sworn testimony that he discovered a singular stone while digging a well in the year 1822. Joseph Smith was assisting him, and borrowed the stone from him, alleging that he could see into it. After he obtained the stone Smith published abroad the wonders that he could see in the stone, and made much disturbance among the credulous members of the community. See *Howe's Mormonism Unveiled*, 241. ' This stone attracted particular notice on account of its peculiar shape, resembling that of a child's foot. It was of a whitish, glassy appearance, though opaque, resembling quartz. . . He (Joseph Jr) manifested a special fancy for this geological curiosity; and he carried it home with him, though this act of plunder was against the strenuous protestations of Mr Chase's children, who claimed to be its rightful owners. Joseph kept this stone, and ever afterward refused its restoration to the claimants. Very soon the pretension transpired that he could see wonderful things by its aid. The idea was rapidly enlarged upon from day to day, and in a short time his spiritual endowment was so developed that he asserted the gift and power (with the stone at his eyes) of revealing both things existing and things to come.' *Tucker's Mormonism*, 19–20.

while, telling him not to exercise his gift of translating
at present, but simply to write at Joseph's dictation.
Continuing thus, on the 15th of May the two men go
into the woods to ask God concerning baptism, found
mentioned in the plates. Presently a messenger descends from heaven in a cloud of light. It is John the
Baptist. And he ordains them, saying, "Upon you,
my fellow-servants, in the name of messiah, I confer
the priesthood of Aaron." Baptism by immersion is
directed; the power of laying-on of hands for the gift
of the holy ghost is promised, but not now bestowed;
then they are commanded to be baptized, each one
baptizing the other, which is done, each in turn laying his hands upon the head of the other, and ordaining him to the Aaronic priesthood. As they come
up out of the water the holy ghost falls upon them,
and they prophesy.

Persecutions continue; brethren of Christ threaten
to mob them, but Joseph's wife's father promises
protection. Samuel Smith comes, and is converted,
receiving baptism and obtaining revelations; and later
Joseph's father and mother, Martin Harris, and
others. Food is several times charitably brought to
the translators by Joseph Knight, senior, of Colesville, New York, concerning whom is given a revelation. In June comes David Whitmer with a request
from his father, Peter Whitmer, of Fayette, New
York, that the translators should occupy his house
thenceforth until the completion of their work, and
brings with him a two-horse wagon to carry them
and their effects. Not only is their board to be free,
but one of the brothers Whitmer, of whom there are
David, John, and Peter junior, will assist in the writing. Thither they go, and find all as promised; David
and Peter Whitmer and Hyrum Smith are baptized,
and receive revelations through Joseph, who inquires
of the Lord for them by means of the urim and thummim. The people thereabout being friendly, meetings
are held, and the new revelation taught, many believ-

ing, certain priests and others disputing. Three special witnesses are provided by Christ, namely, Oliver Cowdery, David Whitmer, and Martin Harris,[18] to whom the plates are shown by an angel after much prayer and meditation in the woods. These are the three witnesses. And there are further eight witnesses, namely, Christian Whitmer, Jacob Whitmer, Peter Whitmer junior, John Whitmer, Hiram Page, Joseph Smith senior, Hyrum Smith, and Samuel H. Smith, who testify that the plates were shown to them by Joseph Smith junior, that they handled them with their hands, and saw the characters engraven thereon.[19]

[18] The objections raised against this testimony are, first, there is no date nor place; second, there are not three separate affidavits, but one testimony signed by three men; third, compare with Smith's revelation *Doctrine and Covenants*, p. 173, and it appears that this testimony is drawn up by Smith himself. But who are these witnesses? Sidney Rigdon, at Independence, Missouri, in 1838, charged Cowdery and Whitmer with 'being connected with a gang of counterfeiters, thieves, liars, blacklegs of the deepest dye, to deceive and defraud the saints.' Joseph Smith (*Times and Seasons*, vol. i. pp. 81, 83-4) charges Cowdery and Whitmer with being busy in stirring up strife and turmoil among the brethren in 1838 in Missouri; and he demands, 'Are they not murderers then at the heart? Are not their consciences seared as with a hot iron?' These men were consequently cut off from the church. In 1837 Smith prints this language about his coadjutor and witness: 'There are negroes who have white skins as well as black ones—Granny Parish and others, who acted as lackeys, such as Martin Harris! But they are so far beneath my contempt that to notice any of them would be too great a sacrifice for a gentleman to make.' *Hyde's Mormonism*, 252-5. Of David Whitmer, Mr Howe says: 'He is one of five of the same name and family who have been used as witnesses to establish the imposition, and who are now head men and leaders in the Mormonite camp. They were noted in their neighborhood for credulity and a general belief in witches, and perhaps were fit subjects for the juggling arts of Smith. David relates that he was led by Smith into an open field, on his father's farm, where they found the book of plates lying upon the ground. Smith took it up and requested him to examine it, which he did for the space of half an hour or more, when he returned it to Smith, who placed it in its former position, alleging that it was in the custody of an angel. He describes the plates as being about eight inches square, the leaves being metal of a whitish yellow color, and of the thickness of tin plates.' *Mormonism Unveiled*, 16. See also *Kidder's Mormons*, 49-51; *Tucker's Origin and Prog. Mor.*, 69-71; *Smucker's Hist. Mor.*, 29-30; *Bertrand's Mémoires d'un Mormon*, 29-31.

[19] 'It will be seen that the witnesses of this truth were principally of the two families of Whitmer and Smith. The Smiths were the father and brothers of Joseph. Who the Whitmers were is not clear, and all clew to their character and proceedings since this date, though probably known to the Mormons themselves, is undiscoverable by the profane vulgar.' *Mackay's The Mormons*, 23.

The theory commonly accepted at present by those not of the Mormon faith, in regard to the origin of the book of Mormon, is thus given in the introduction to the New York edition of the *Book of Mormon*, essentially the same as that advanced previously by E. D. Howe, and subsequently elaborated by others: 'About the year 1809, the Rev. Solomon Spaulding, a clergyman who had graduated from Dartmouth college, and settled in the town of Cherry Valley, in the State of New York, removed from that place to New Salem (Conneaut), Ashtabula county, Ohio. Mr Spaulding was an enthusiastic archæologist. The region to which he removed was rich in American antiquities. The mounds and fortifications which have puzzled the brains of many patient explorers attracted his attention, and he accepted the theory that the American continent was peopled by a colony of the ancient Israelites. The ample material by which he was surrounded, full of mythical interest and legendary suggestiveness, led him to the conception of a curious literary project. He set himself the task of writing a fictitious history of the race which had built the mounds. The work was commenced and progressed slowly for some time. Portions of it were read by Mr Spaulding's friends, as its different sections were completed, and after three years' labor, the volume was sent to the press, bearing the title of *The Manuscript Found*. Mr Spaulding had removed to Pittsburgh, Pa., before his book received the final revision, and it was in the hands of a printer named Patterson, in that city, that the manuscript was placed with a view to publication. This was in the year 1812. The printing, however, was delayed in consequence of a difficulty about the contract, until Mr Spaulding left Pittsburgh, and went to Amity, Washington county, New York, where in 1816 he died. The manuscript seems to have lain unused during this interval. But in the employ of the printer Patterson was a versatile genius, one Sidney Rigdon, to whom no trade came amiss, and who happened at the time to be a journeyman at work with Patterson. Disputations on questions of theology were the peculiar delight of Rigdon, and the probable solution of the mystery of the book of Mormon is found in the fact that, by this man's agency, information of the existence of the fictitious record was first communicated to Joseph Smith. Smith's family settled in Palmyra, New York, about the year 1815, and removed subsequently to Ontario county, where Joseph became noted for supreme cunning and general shiftlessness. Chance threw him in the company of Rigdon soon after Spaulding's manuscript fell under the eye of the erratic journeyman, and it is probable that the plan of founding a new system of religious imposture was concocted by these two shrewd and unscrupulous parties. The fact that the style of the book of Mormon so closely imitates that of the received version of the bible—a point which seems to have been constantly kept in view by Mr Spaulding, probably in order to invest the fiction with a stronger character of reality—answered admirably for the purposes of Rigdon and Smith.' Mr Howe testifies that 'an opinion has prevailed to a considerable extent that Rigdon has been the Iago, the prime mover of the whole conspiracy. Of this, however, we have no positive proof.' *Mormonism Unveiled*, 100.

To prove the foregoing, witnesses are brought forward. John Spaulding, brother of Solomon, testifies: 'He then told me that he had been writing a book, which he intended to have printed, the avails of which he thought would enable him to pay all his debts. The book was entitled *The Manuscript Found*, of which he read to me many passages. It was an historical romance of the first settlers of America,' etc. He goes on to speak of Nephi and Lehi as names familiar, as does also Martha Spaulding, John's wife. Henry Lake, formerly Solomon's partner, testifies to the same effect; also John N. Miller, who worked for Lake and Spaulding in building their forge; also Aaron Wright, Oliver Smith, and Nahum Howard, neighbors; also Artemas Cunningham, to whom Spaulding owed money. To these men Solomon Spaulding used to talk about and read from his *Manuscript Found*, which was an account of the ten lost tribes in America, which he wanted to publish and with the profits pay his debts. After the book of Mormon was printed, and they saw it, or heard it read, they were sure it was the same as Spaulding's *Manuscript Found*. *Id.*, 278-87.

Who Wrote the Book of Mormon? is the title of a 4to pamphlet of 16 pages by Robert Patterson of Pittsburgh. Reprinted from the illustrated history of Washington county, Philadelphia, 1882. This Patterson is the son of printer Patterson, to whose office the Spaulding MS. is said to have been sent. Little new information is brought out by this inquisition. First he extracts passages from Howe's *Mormonism Unveiled*, quoting at second-hand from Kidder's *Mormonism and the Mormons*, in the absence of the original, stating erroneously that Howe's book was first printed in 1835. I give elsewhere an epitome of the contents of Howe's work. Ballantyne in his *Reply to a Tract*, by T. Richards, *What is Mormonism?* wherein is advanced the Spaulding theory, asserts in answer that Spaulding's manuscript was not known to Smith or Rigdon until after the publication of the *Book of Mormon*, and that the two were not the same, the latter being about three times larger than the former. 'Dr Hurlburt,' he says, 'and certain other noted enemies of this cause, having heard that such a manuscript existed, determined to publish it to the world in order to destroy the book of Mormon, but after examining it, found that it did not read as they expected, consequently declined its publication.' The Spaulding theory is advanced and supported by the following, in addition to the eight witnesses whose testimony was given by Howe in his *Mormonism Unveiled.* Mrs Matilda Spaulding Davidson, once wife of Solomon Spaulding, said to Rev. D. R. Austin, who had the statement printed in the *Boston Recorder*, May 1839, that Spaulding was in the habit of reading portions of his romance to his friends and neighbors. When John Spaulding heard read for the first time passages from the book of Mormon he 'recognized perfectly the work of his brother. He was amazed and afflicted that it should have been perverted to so wicked a purpose. His grief found vent in a flood of tears, and he arose on the spot and expressed to the meeting his sorrow and regret that the writings of his deceased brother should be used for a purpose so vile and shocking.' Statements to the same effect are given as coming from Mrs McKinstry, daughter of Spaulding, printed in *Scribner's Monthly*, August 1880; W. H. Sabine, brother of Mrs Spaulding; Joseph Miller, whose statements were printed in the *Pittsburgh Telegraph*, Feb. 6, 1879; Redick McKee in the *Washington Reporter*, April 21, 1869; Rev. Abner Jackson in a communication to the Washington County Historical Society, printed in the *Washington Reporter*, Jan. 7, 1881, and others. See also *Kidder's Mormonism*, 37–49; *California—Its Past History*, 198–9; *Ferris' Utah and Mormons*, 50–1; *Gunnison's Mormons*, 93–7; *Bertrand's Mémoires d'un Mormon*, 33–44; *Hist. of Mormons*, 41–50; *Bennett's Mormonism*, 115–24; *Howe's Mormonism*, 289–90.

Robert Patterson, in his pamphlet entitled *Who Wrote the Book of Mormon?* thus discusses the case of Sidney Rigdon: 'It was satisfactorily proven that Spaulding was the author of the book of Mormon; but how did Joseph Smith obtain a copy of it? The theory hitherto most widely published,' says Patterson, 'and perhaps generally accepted, has been that Rigdon was a printer in Patterson's printing-office when the Spaulding manuscript was brought there in 1812–14, and that he either copied or purloined it. Having it thus in his possession, the use made of it was an after thought suggested by circumstances many years later. More recently another theory has been advanced, that Rigdon obtained possession of the Spaulding manuscript during his pastorate of the first baptist church or soon thereafter, 1822-4, without any necessary impropriety on his part, but rather through the courtesy of some friend, in whose possession it remained unclaimed, and who regarded it as a literary curiosity. The friends of Rigdon, in response to the first charge, deny that he ever resided in Pittsburgh previous to 1822, or that he ever was a printer, and in general answer to both charges affirm that he never at any time had access to Spaulding's manuscript.' Rigdon denies emphatically that he ever worked in Patterson's printing-office or knew of such an establishment; and the testimony, produced by Patterson, of Carvil Rigdon, Sidney's brother, Peter Boyer, his brother-in-law, Isaac King, Samuel Cooper, Robert Dubois, and Mrs Lambdin points in the same direction. On the other hand, Mrs Davidson, Joseph Miller, Redick McKee, Rev. Cephas Dodd, and Mrs Eichbaum are quite positive that either Rigdon worked in the printing-office, or had access to the manuscript. 'These witnesses,' continues Patterson, 'are all whom we can find, after inquiries extending through some three years, who can testify at all to Rigdon's residence in Pittsburgh before 1816, and to his possible employment in Patterson's printing-office or bindery. Of this employment none of them speak from personal knowledge. In making inquiries among two or three score of the oldest residents of Pittsburgh and vicinity, those who had any opinion on the subject invariably, so far as now remembered, repeated the story of Rigdon's employment in Patterson's office as if it were a well known and admitted fact; they could tell all about it, but when pressed as to their personal knowledge of it or their authority for the conviction, they had none.' Nevertheless he concludes, 'after an impartial consideration of the preceding testimony, that Rigdon as early as 1823 certainly had possession of Spaulding's manuscript; how he obtained it is unimportant for the present purpose; that during his career as a minister of the Disciples church in Ohio, he carefully preserved under lock and key this document, and devoted an absorbed attention to it; that he was aware of the forthcoming book of Mormon and of its contents long before its appearance; that the said contents were largely Spaulding's romance, and partly such modifications as Rigdon had introduced; and that, during the preparation of the book of Mormon, Rigdon had repeated and long interviews with Smith, thus easily supplying him with fresh instalments of the pretended revelation.' In a letter to the editors of the *Boston Journal*, dated May 27, 1839, Rigdon says: 'There was no man by the name of Patterson during my residence at Pittsburgh who had a printing-office; what might have been before I lived there I know not. Mr Robert Patterson, I was told, had owned a printing-office before I lived in that city, but had been unfortunate in business, and failed before my residence there. This Mr Patterson, who was a presbyterian preacher, I had a very slight acquaintance with during my residence in Pittsburgh. He was then acting under an agency in the book and stationery business, and was the owner of no property of any kind, printing-office or anything else, during the time I resided in the city.' *Smucker's Mormons*, 45–8.

In Philadelphia, in 1840, was published *The Origin of the Spaulding Story, concerning the Manuscript Found; with a short biography of Dr P. Hulbert, the originator of the same; and some testimony adduced, showing it to be a sheer fabrication so far as its connection with the Book of Mormon is concerned. By B. Winchester, minister of the Gospel*. The author goes on to say that Hulbert, a methodist preacher at Jamestown, N. Y., joined the Mormons in 1833, and was expelled for immoral conduct, whereupon he swore vengeance and concocted the Spaulding story. Hearing of a work written by Solomon Spaulding entitled *The Manuscript Found*, he sought to prove to those about him that the book of Mormon was derived from it, 'not that any of these persons had the most distant idea that this novel had ever been converted into the book of Mormon, or that there was any connection between them. Indeed, Mr Jackson, who had read both the book of Mormon and Spaulding's manuscript, told Mr H. when he came to get his signature to a writing testifying to the probability that Mr S.'s manuscript had been converted into the book of Mormon, that there was no agreement between them; for, said he, Mr S.'s manuscript was a very small work, in the form of a novel, saying not one word about the children of Israel, but professed to give an account of a race of people who originated from the Romans, which Mr S. said he had translated from a Latin parchment that he had found.' Winchester states further that Hurlburt, or Hulbert, wrote *Mormonism Unveiled* and sold it to Howe for $500.

The Myth of the Manuscript Found; or the absurdities of the Spaulding story; By Elder George Reynolds, was published at Salt Lake City in 1883. It is a 12mo vol. of 104 pages, and gives first the history of the Spaulding manuscript, and names Hurlburt as the originator of the story. Chap. iii. is entitled 'the bogus affidavit,' referring to the alleged sworn statement of Mrs

The translation of the book of Mormon being finished, Smith and Cowdery go to Palmyra, secure the copyright, and agree with Egbert B. Grandin to print five thousand copies for three thousand dollars. Meanwhile, a revelation comes to Martin Harris, at Manchester, in March, commanding him to pay for the printing of the book of Mormon, under penalty of destruction of himself and property.[20] The title-

Davison, the widow of Spaulding, published by Storrs, but denied by Mrs Davison. Rigdon's connection, or rather lack of connection with the manuscript is next discussed. Then is answered an article in *Scribner's Magazine* by Mrs Dickenson, grand niece of Mr Spaulding, and probably the most shallow treatment of the subject yet presented on either side. Further discussions on the book are followed by an analysis of the life of Joseph, and finally internal evidences and prophecies are considered. 'It is evident,' Mr Reynolds concludes, 'that if Mr Spaulding's story was what its friends claim, then it never could have formed the ground-work of the book of Mormon; for the whole historical narrative is different from beginning to end. And further, the story that certain old inhabitants of New Salem, who, it is said, recognized the book of Mormon, either never made such a statement, or they let their imagination run away with their memory into the endorsement of a falsehood and an impossibility.'

[20] Speaking of Martin Harris, E. D. Howe says: 'Before his acquaintance with the Smith family he was considered an honest, industrious citizen by his neighbors. His residence was in the town of Palmyra, where he had accumulated a handsome property. He was naturally of a very visionary turn of mind on the subject of religion, holding one sentiment but a short time.' Mortgaged his farm for $3,000, and printed the *Book of Mormon*, as he said, to make money. The price first was $1.75, then $1.25, afterward whatever they could get. 'Since that time the frequent demands on Martin's purse have reduced it to a very low state. He seems to have been the soul and body of the whole imposition, and now carries the most incontestable proofs of a religious maniac...Martin is an exceedingly fast talker. He frequently gathers a crowd around in bar-rooms and in the streets. Here he appears to be in his element, answering and explaining all manner of dark and abstruse theological questions...He is the source of much trouble and perplexity to the honest portion of his brethren, and would undoubtedly long since have been cast off by Smith were it not for his money, and the fact that he is one of the main pillars of the Mormon fabric.' *Mormonism Unveiled*, 13–15. 'The wife of Martin Harris instituted a lawsuit against him [Joseph Smith, Jr], and stated in her affidavit that she believed the chief object he had in view was to defraud her husband of all his property. The trial took place at New York, and the facts, as related even by the mother of the prophet, are strongly condemnatory of his conduct...Harris denied in solemn terms that Smith had ever, in any manner, attempted to get possession of his money, and ended by assuring the gentlemen of the court that, if they did not believe in the existence of the plates, and continued to resist the truth, it would one day be the means of damning their souls.' *Taylder's Mormons*, xxxi.-ii. 'In the beginning of the printing the Mormons professed to hold their manuscripts as sacred, and insisted upon maintaining constant vigilance for their safety during the progress of the work, each morning carrying to the printing-office the instalment required for the day, and withdrawing the same at evening. No alteration from copy in any manner was to be made. These things were "strictly commanded," as they said. Mr

page is not a modern production, but a literal translation from the last leaf of the plates, on the left-hand
side, and running like all Hebrew writing.

And now in a chamber of Whitmer's house Smith,
Cowdery, and David Whitmer meet, and earnestly ask
God to make good his promise, and confer on them
the Melchisedec priesthood, which authorizes the laying-on of hands for the gift of the holy ghost. Their
prayer is answered; for presently the word of the
Lord comes to them, commanding that Joseph Smith
should ordain Oliver Cowdery to be an elder in the
church of Jesus Christ, and Oliver in like manner
should so ordain Joseph, and the two should ordain
others as from time to time the will of the Lord should
be made known to them.[21]   But this ordination must
not take place until the baptized brethren assemble
and give to this act their sanction, and accept the
ordained as spiritual teachers, and then only after the
blessing and partaking of bread and wine.   It is next
revealed that twelve shall be called to be the disciples
of Christ, the twelve apostles of these last days, who
shall go into all the world preaching and baptizing.

John H. Gilbert, as printer, had the chief operative trust of the type-setting
and press-work of the job.   After the first day's trial he found the manuscripts in so very imperfect a condition, especially in regard to grammar,
that he became unwilling further to obey the "command," and so announced
to Smith and his party; when finally, upon much friendly expostulation, he
was given a limited discretion in correcting, which was exercised in the particulars of syntax, orthography, punctuation, capitalizing, paragraphing, etc.
Many errors under these heads, nevertheless, escaped correction, as appear
in the first edition of the printed book.   Very soon, too—after some ten
days—the constant vigilance by the Mormons over the manuscripts was re-
laxed by reason of the confidence they came to repose in the printers.   Mr
Gilbert has now (1867) in his possession a complete copy of the book in the
original sheets, as laid off by him from the press in working...Meanwhile,
Harris and his wife had separated by mutual arrangement, on account of
her persistent unbelief in Mormonism and refusal to be a party to the mortgage.   The family estate was divided, Harris giving her about eighty acres
of the farm, with a comfortable house and other property, as her share of the
assets; and she occupied this property until the time of her death.' *Tucker's
Origin and Prog. Mor.*, 50-7.

[21] Speaking of the manner in which Smith delivered these revelations,
Howe says: 'In this operation he abandoned his spectacles, or peep-stone, and
merely delivered it with his eyes shut.   In this manner he governs his followers, by asking the Lord, as he says, from day to day.' *Mormonism Unveiled,*
102.

By the spirit of prophecy and revelation it is done. The rise of the church of Jesus Christ in these last days is on the 6th of April, 1830, at which date the church was organized under the provisions of the statutes of the state of New York by Joseph Smith junior, Hyrum Smith, Oliver Cowdery, David Whitmer, Samuel H. Smith, and Peter Whitmer. Joseph Smith, ordained an apostle of Jesus Christ, is made by the commandment of God the first elder of this church, and Oliver Cowdery, likewise an apostle, is made the second elder. Again the first elder falls into worldly entanglements, but upon repentance and self-humbling he is delivered by an angel.

The duties of elders, priests, teachers, deacons, and members are as follow: All who desire it, with honesty and humility, may be baptized into the church; old covenants are at an end, all must be baptized anew. An apostle is an elder; he shall baptize, ordain other elders, priests, teachers, and deacons, administer bread and wine, emblems of the flesh and blood of Christ; he shall confirm, teach, expound, exhort, taking the lead at meetings, and conducting them as he is taught by the holy ghost. The priest's duty is to preach, teach, expound, exhort, baptize, administer the sacrament, and visit and pray with members; he may also ordain other priests, teachers, and deacons, giving a certificate of ordination, and lead in meetings when no elder is present. The teacher's duty is to watch over and strengthen the members, preventing evil speaking and all iniquity, to see that the meetings are regularly held, and to take the lead in them in the absence of elder or priest. The deacon's duty is to assist the teacher; teacher and deacon may warn, expound, exhort, but neither of them shall baptize, administer the sacrament, or lay on hands. The elders are to meet in council for the transaction of church business every three months, or oftener should meetings be called. Subordinate officers will receive from the elders a license defining their authority; elders will

receive their license from other elders by vote of
church or conference. There shall be presidents,
bishops, high counsellors, and high priests; the presiding elder shall be president of the high priesthood,
and he, as well as bishops, high counsellors, and high
priests, will be ordained by high council or general
conference. The duty of members is to walk in holiness before the Lord according to the scriptures, to
bring their children to the elders, who will lay their
hands on them and bless them in the name of Jesus
Christ. The bible, that is to say, the scriptures of
the old and new testaments, is accepted wholly, save
such corruptions as have crept in through the great
and abominable church; the book of Mormon is a
later revelation, supplementary thereto. Thus is organized the Church of Jesus Christ of Latter-Day
Saints,[22] in accordance with special revelations and
commandments, and after the manner set forth in the
new testament.

The first public discourse, following the meetings
held in Whitmer's house, was preached on Sunday,
the 11th of April, 1830, by Oliver Cowdery, who the

[22] The church was not at that time so called, nor indeed until after the
4th of May, 1834. See chap. iv., note 50; also *Millennial Star*, iv. 115; *Burton's City of the Saints*, 671-2. Kidder, *Mormonism*, 68, affirms that this
name was not adopted till some years later. Mather is only a year and a day
astray when he says, 'The conference of elders on May 3, 1833, repudiated
the name of "Mormons" and adopted that of "Latter-Day Saints."' *Lippincott's Mag.*, Aug. 1880. The term 'Mormons,' as first applied by their enemies
to members of the church of Latter-Day Saints, was quite offensive to them,
though later they became somewhat more reconciled to it. As at present popularly employed, it is by no means a term of reproach, though among themselves
they still adhere to the appellation 'Saints,' just as quakers speak of themselves as the 'Society of Friends.' The term 'Mormon' seems to me quite fitting for general use, fully as much so as presbyterian, reformed Dutch, uni-
versalist, and others, few of which were of their own choosing. 'Mormon was
the name of a certain man, and also of a particular locality upon the American continent; but was never intended to signify a body of people. The name
by which we desire to be known and to walk worthy of is "Saints."' *Bell's
Reply to Theobald*, 2. At the time of the riots in Missouri, in addressing communications to the governor, and in many other instances, they designate
themselves as 'members of the church of Christ, vulgarly called Mormons.'
See also *De Smet's Western Missions*, 393; *Mackay's The Mormons*, 41-2.
The term 'gentile' was generally applied to unbelievers of the white race.
The Indians, originally, were denominated 'of the house of Israel,' 'of the
house of Joseph,' or 'of the house of Jacob,' also the Lamanites.

same day baptized in Seneca Lake several persons, among whom were Hyrum and Katherine Page, some of the Whitmers, and the Jolly family. The first miracle likewise occurred during the same month, Joseph Smith casting out a devil from Newel Knight, son of Joseph Knight, who with his family had been universalists. Newel had been a constant attendant at the meetings, and was much interested; but when he attempted to pray the devil prevented him, writhing his limbs into divers distortions, and hurling him about the room. "I know that you can deliver me from this evil spirit," cried Newel. Whereupon Joseph rebuked the devil in the name of Jesus Christ, and the evil spirit departed from the young man. Seeing this, others came forward and expressed their belief in the new faith, and a church was established at Colesville.

On the 1st of June the first conference as an organized church was held, there being thirty members. The meeting was opened by singing and prayer, after which they partook of the sacrament, which was followed by confirmations and further ordinations to the several offices of the priesthood. The exercises were attended by the outpouring of the holy ghost, and many prophesied, to the infinite joy and gratification of the elders. Some time after, on a Saturday previous to an appointed sabbath on which baptism was to be performed, the brethren constructed, across a stream of water, a dam, which was torn away by a mob during the night. The meeting was held, however, though amid the sneers and insults of the rabble, Oliver preaching. Present among others was Emily Coburn, Newel Knight's wife's sister, formerly a presbyterian. Her pastor, the Rev. Mr Shearer, arrived, and tried to persuade her to return to her father. Failing in this, he obtained from her father a power of attorney, and bore her off by force; but Emily returned. The dam was repaired, and baptism administered to some thirteen persons the following morning; whereupon fifty men surrounded Mr Knight's house, threatening violence. The same night Joseph was arrested by a constable on a charge of disorderly conduct, and for preaching the book of Mormon. It was the purpose of the populace to capture Joseph from the constable and use him roughly, but by hard driving he escaped. At the trial which followed, an attempt was made to prove certain charges, namely, that he obtained a horse from Josiah Stoal, and a yoke of oxen from Jonathan Thompson, by saying that in a revelation he was told that he was to have them; also as touching his conduct toward two daughters of Mr Stoal; but all testified in his favor, and he was acquitted. As he was leaving the court-room, he was again arrested on a warrant from Broome county, and taken midst insults and buffetings to Colesville for trial. The old charges were renewed, and new ones preferred. Newel Knight was made to testify regarding the miracle wrought in his behalf, and a story that the prisoner had been a money digger was advanced by the prosecution. Again he was acquitted, and again escaped from the crowd outside the court-house, whose purpose it was to tar and feather him, and ride him on a rail. These persecutions were instigated, it was said, chiefly by presbyterians.

While Joseph rested at his home at Harmony further stories were circulated, damaging to his character, this time by the methodists. One went to his father-in-law with falsehoods, and so turned him and his family against Joseph and his friends that he would no longer afford them protection or receive their doctrine. This was a heavy blow; but proceeding in August to Colesville, Joseph and Hyrum Smith and John and David Whitmer continued the work of prayer and confirmation. Fearing their old enemies, who lay in wait to attack them on their way back, they prayed that their eyes might be blinded; and so it came to pass. Then they held service and returned safely, although five dollars reward had been offered

for notification of their arrival. Removing his family
to Fayette, Joseph encountered further persecutions,
to which was added a fresh grief. Hiram Page was
going astray over a stone which he had found, and by
means of which he had obtained revelations at variance with Joseph's revelations and the rules of the
new testament. It was thought best not to agitate
the subject unnecessarily, before the meeting of the
conference to be held on the 1st of September; but
the Whitmer family and Oliver Cowdery seeming
to be too greatly impressed over the things set forth
by the rival stone, it was resolved to inquire of the
Lord concerning the matter; whereupon a revelation
came to Oliver Cowdery, forbidding such practice;
and he was to say privately to Hiram Page that
Satan had deceived him, and that the things which
he had written from the stone were not of God.
Oliver was further commanded to go and preach the
gospel to the Lamanites,[23] the remnants of the house
of Joseph living in the west,[24] where he was to estab-

[23] 'The Lamanites originally were a remnant of Joseph, and in the first
year of the reign of Zedekiah, King of Judah, were led in a miraculous manner from Jerusalem to the eastern borders of the Red Sea, thence for some
time along its borders in a nearly south-east direction, after which they altered
their course nearly eastward, until they came to the great waters, where by
the command of God they built a vessel in which they were safely brought
across the great Pacific Ocean, and landed upon the western coast of South
America. The original party included also the Nephites, their leader being
a prophet called Nephi; but soon after landing they separated, because the
Lamanites, whose leader was a wicked man called Laman, persecuted the
others. After the partition the Nephites, who had brought with them the
old testament down to the time of Jeremiah, engraved on plates of brass, in
the Egyptain language, prospered and built large cities. But the bold, bad
Lamanites, originally white, became dark and dirty, though still retaining a
national existence. They became wild, savage, and ferocious, seeking by
every means the destruction of the prosperous Nephites, against whom they
many times arrayed their hosts in battle; but were repulsed and driven back
to their own territories, generally with great loss to both sides. The slain,
frequently amounting to tens of thousands, were piled together in great heaps
and overspread with a thin covering of earth, which will satisfactorily account
for those ancient mounds filled with human bones, so numerous at the present day, both in North and South America.' *Pratt (Orson), Series of Pamphlets*, vi. 7–8; *Pratt (P. P.), Voice of Warning*, 81–117.
[24] 'The attention of the little band was directed, from the very commencement of their organization, to the policy and expediency of fixing their headquarters in the far west, in the thinly settled and but partially explored
territories belonging to the United States, where they might squat upon or
purchase good lands at a cheap rate, and clear the primeval wilderness.

lish a church and build a city,[25] at a point to be designated later.

"Behold, I say unto thee, Oliver, that it shall be given unto thee that thou shalt be heard by the church in all things whatsoever thou shalt teach them by the comforter concerning the revelations and commandments which I have given. But behold, verily, verily, I say unto thee, no one shall be appointed to receive commandments and revelations in this church, excepting my servant Joseph Smith, Jr, for he receiveth them even as Moses; and thou shalt be obedient unto the things which I shall give unto him, even as Aaron, to declare faithfully the commandments and the revelations with power and authority unto the church. And if thou art led at any time by the comforter to speak or teach, or at all times by the way of commandment unto the church, thou mayest do it. But thou shalt not write by way of commandment, but by wisdom; and thou shalt not command him who is at thy head and at the head of the church; for I have given him the keys of the mysteries and the revelations which are sealed, until I shall appoint unto them another in his stead."

They required elbow-room, and rightly judged that a rural population would be more favorable than an urban one to the reception of their doctrine.' *Mackay's The Mor.*, 63.

[25] The most ancient prophecy which the saints are now in possession of relating to the New Jerusalem was one delivered by Enoch, the seventh from Adam. This was revealed anew to Joseph Smith in December 1830. In it the Lord is represented as purposing 'to gather out mine own elect from the four quarters of the earth unto a place which I shall prepare...But this revelation does not tell in what part of the earth the New Jerusalem should be located. The book of Mormon, which the Lord has brought out of the earth, informs us that this holy city is to be built upon the continent of America, but it does not inform us upon what part of that vast country it should be built.' *Pratt's Series of Pamphlets*, vii. 4; *Pratt's Interesting Account*, 16–25; *First Book of Nephi* in *Book of Mormon.*

CHAPTER IV.

THE STORY OF MORMONISM.

1830–1835.

Parley Pratt's Conversion—Mission to the Lamanites—The Mission-
aries at Kirtland—Conversion of Sidney Rigdon—Mormon Suc-
cess at Kirtland—The Missionaries in Missouri—Rigdon Visits
Smith—Edward Partridge—The Melchisedec Priesthood Given—
Smith and Rigdon Journey to Missouri—Bible Translation—
Smith's Second Visit to Missouri—Unexampled Prosperity—Causes
of Persecutions—Mobocracy—The Saints are Driven from Jackson
County—Treachery of Boggs—Military Organization at Kirtland
—The Name Latter-day Saints—March to Missouri.

One evening as Hyrum Smith was driving cows
along the road toward his father's house, he was
overtaken by a stranger, who inquired for Joseph
Smith, translator of the book of Mormon. "He is
now residing in Pennsylvania, a hundred miles away,"
was the reply.

"And the father of Joseph?"

"He also is absent on a journey. That is his house
yonder, and I am his son."

The stranger then said that he was a preacher of
the word; that he had just seen for the first time a
copy of the wonderful book; that once it was in his
hands he could not lay it down until he had devoured
it, for the spirit of the Lord was upon him as he read,
and he knew that it was true; the spirit of the Lord
had directed him thither, and his heart was full of joy.

Hyrum gazed at him in amazement; for converts
of this quality, and after this fashion, were not common in those days of poverty and sore trial. He
was little more than a boy, being but twenty-three,

and of that fresh, fair innocence which sits only on a youthful face beaming with high enthusiasm. But it was more than a boy's soul that was seen through those eyes of deep and solemn earnestness; it was more than a boy's strength of endurance that was indicated by the broad chest and comely, compact limbs; and more than a boy's intelligence and powers of reasoning that the massive brow betokened.

Hyrum took the stranger to the house, and they passed the night in discourse, sleeping little. The convert's name was Parley P. Pratt. He was a native of Burlington, New York, and born April 12, 1807. His father was a farmer of limited means and education, and though not a member of any religious society, had a respect for all. The boy had a passion for books; the bible especially he read over and over again with deep interest and enthusiasm. He early manifested strong religious feeling; mind and soul seemed all on fire as he read of the patriarchs and kings of the old testament, and of Christ and his apostles of the new. In winter at school, and in summer at work, his life passed until he was sixteen, when he went west with his father William, some two hundred miles on foot, to Oswego, two miles from which town they bargained for a thickly wooded tract of seventy acres, at four dollars an acre, paying some seventy dollars in cash. After a summer's work for wages back near the old home, and a winter's work clearing the forest farm, the place was lost through failure to meet the remaining payments. Another attempt to make a forest home, this time in Ohio, thirty miles west of Cleveland, was more successful; and after much toil and many hardships, he found himself, in 1827, comfortably established there, with Thankful Halsey as his wife.

Meanwhile religion ran riot through his brain. His mind, however, was of a reasoning, logical caste. "Why this difference," he argued, "between the ancient and modern Christians, their doctrines and their practice? Had I lived and believed in the days of the apostles, and had so desired, they would have said, 'Repent, be baptized, and receive the holy ghost.' The scriptures are the same now as then; why should not results be the same?" In the absence of anything better, he joined the baptists, and was immersed; but he was not satisfied. In 1829 Sidney Rigdon, of whom more hereafter, preached in his neighborhood; he heard him and was refreshed. It was the ancient gospel revived—repentance, baptism, the gift of the holy ghost. And yet there was something lacking— the authority to minister; the power which should accompany the form of apostleship. At length he and others, who had heard Rigdon, organized a society on the basis of his teachings, and Parley began to preach. The spirit working in him finally compelled him to abandon his farm and go forth to meet his destiny, he knew not whither. In this frame of mind he wandered eastward, and while his family were visiting friends, he came upon the book of Mormon and Hyrum Smith. Now did his soul find rest. Here was inspiration and revelation as of old; here was a new dispensation with attendant signs and miracles.

As he left Smith's house the following morning, having an appointment to preach some thirty miles distant, Hyrum gave him a copy of the sacred book. Travelling on foot, and stopping now and then to rest, he read at intervals, and found to his great joy that soon after his ascension Christ had appeared in his glorified body to the remnant of the tribe of Joseph in America, that he had administered in person to the ten lost tribes, that the gospel had been revealed and written among nations unknown to the apostles, and that thus preserved it had escaped the corruptions of the great and abominable church.

Returning to Smith's house, Parley demanded of Hyrum baptism. They went to Whitmer's, where they were warmly welcomed by a little branch of the church there assembled. The new convert was bap-

tized by Cowdery, and was ordained an elder. He
continued to preach in those parts with great power.
Congregations were moved to tears, and many heads
of families came forward and accepted the faith.
Then he went to his old home. His father, mother,
and some of the neighbors believed only in part; but
his brother Orson, nineteen years of age, embraced
with eagerness the new religion, and preached it from
that time forth. Returning to Manchester, Parley
for the first time met Joseph Smith, who received him
warmly, and asked him to preach on Sunday, which
he did, Joseph following with a discourse.

Revelations continued, now in the way of command,
and now in the spirit of prophecy. In Harmony, to
the first elder it was spoken: "Magnify thine office;
and after thou hast sowed thy fields and secured them,
go speedily unto the churches which are in Colesville,
Fayette, and Manchester, and they shall support
thee; and I will bless them, both spiritually and
temporally; but if they receive thee not, I will send
on them a cursing instead of a blessing, and thou
shalt shake the dust off thy feet against them as a
testimony, and wipe thy feet by the wayside." And
to Cowdery, thus: "Oliver shall continue in bearing
my name before the world, and also to the church;
and he shall take neither purse nor scrip, neither
staves nor even two coats." To Emma, wife of Joseph: "Thy sins are forgiven thee, and thou art an
elect lady, whom I have called; and thou shalt comfort thy husband, my servant Joseph, and shalt go
with him, and be unto him as a scribe in the absence
of my servant Oliver, and he shall support thee."
Emma was also further directed to make a selection of
hymns to be used in church.[1]

[1] The hymn-book of Emma Smith does not appear to have been published,
but a little book containing hymns selected by Brigham Young passed through
eight editions up to 1849, the eighth being published in Liverpool in that year.
Smucker's Hist. of Mor., 57–61; *Millennial Star*, iv. 150–1. The preface to
the first edition was signed by Brigham Young, Parley P. Pratt, and John

In the presence of six elders, at Fayette, in September 1830, came the voice of Jesus Christ, promising them every blessing, while the wicked should be destroyed. The millennium should come; but first dire destruction should fall upon the earth, and the great and abominable church should be cast down. Hiram Page renounced his stone. David Whitmer was ordered to his father's house, there to await further instructions. Peter Whitmer junior, Parley P. Pratt, and Ziba Peterson were directed to go with Oliver and assist him in preaching the gospel to the Lamanites, that is to say, to the Indians in the west, the remnant of the tribe of Joseph. Thomas B. Marsh was promised that he should begin to preach. Miracles were limited to casting out devils and healing the sick. Wine for sacramental purposes must not be bought, but made at home.[2]

Taking with them a copy of the revelation assigning to them this work, these first appointed missionaries set out, and continued their journey, preaching in the villages through which they passed, and stopping at Buffalo to instruct the Indians as to their ancestry, until they came to Kirtland, Ohio. There they remained some time, as many came forward and embraced their faith, among others Sidney Rigdon, a preaching elder in the reformed baptist church, who presided over a congregation there, a large portion of whom likewise became interested in the latter-day church.[3]

Taylor. The preface to the ninth edition, published at Liverpool and London in 1851, is by Franklin D. Richards, who states that 54,000 copies of the several editions have been sold in the European missions alone within eleven years. Several editions have since been published in Europe and America.

[2] Smith says: 'In order to prepare for this (confirmation) I set out to go to procure some wine for the occasion, but had gone only a short distance when I was met by a heavenly messenger, and received the revelation.' *Millennial Star*, iv. 151; *Times and Seasons*, iv. 117–18.

[3] At the town of Kirtland, two miles from Rigdon's residence, was a number of the members of his church who lived together, and had all things in common, from which circumstance, Smith says, the idea arose that this was the case with the Mormon believers. To these people the missionaries repaired and preached with some success, gathering in seventeen on the first occasion. Rigdon after spending some time in the study of the book of Mor-

Rigdon was a native of Pennsylvania, and was now thirty-seven years of age. He worked on his father's farm until he was twenty-six, when he went to live with the Rev. Andrew Clark, and the same year, 1819, was licensed to preach. Thence he went to Warren, Ohio, and married; and after preaching for a time he was called to take charge of a church at Pittsburgh, where he met with success, and soon became very popular. But his mind was perplexed over the doctrines he was required to promulgate, and in 1824 he retired from his ministry. There were two friends who had likewise withdrawn from their respective churches, and with whom he conferred freely, Alexander Campbell, of his own congregation, and one Walter Scott, of the Scandinavian church of that city. Campbell had formerly lived at Bethany, Virginia, where was issued under his auspices a monthly journal called the *Christian Baptist*. Out of this friendship and association arose a new church, called the Campbellites, its doctrines having been published by Campbell in his paper. During the next two years Rigdon was obliged to work in a tannery to support his family; then he removed to Bainbridge, Ohio, where he again began to preach, confining himself to no creed, but leaning toward that of the Campbellites. Crowds flocked to hear him, and a church was established in a neighboring town through his instrumentality. After a year of this work he accepted a call to Mentor, thirty miles distant. Slanderous reports followed him, and a storm of persecution set in against him; but by his surpassing eloquence and deep reasoning it was not only soon allayed, but greater multitudes than ever waited on his ministrations.

mon concluded to accept its doctrines, and together with his wife was baptized into the church, which now numbered about twenty in this section. *Millennial Star*, iv. 181–4; v. 4–7, 17; *Times and Seasons*, iv. 177, 193–4. Rigdon had for nearly three years already taught the literal interpretation of scripture prophecies, the gathering of the Israelites to receive the second coming, the literal reign of the saints on earth, and the use of miraculous gifts in the church. *Gunnison's Mormons*, 101.

Rigdon was a cogent speaker of imposing mien and impassioned address. As a man, however, his character seems to have had a tinge of insincerity. He was fickle, now and then petulant, irascible, and sometimes domineering. Later, Joseph Smith took occasion more than once to rebuke him sharply, fearing that he might assume the supremacy.

Upon hearing the arguments of Pratt and Cowdery, and investigating the book of Mormon, Rigdon was convinced that he had not been legally ordained, and that his present ministry was without the divine authority. In regard to the revival of the old dispensation, he argued thus: "If we have not familiarity enough with our creator to ask of him a sign, we are no Christians; if God will not give his creatures one, he is no better than Juggernaut." The result was, that he and others accepted the book and its teachings,[4] received baptism and the gift of the holy ghost, and were ordained to preach.

On one occasion Cowdery preached, followed by Rigdon. After service they went to the Chagrin River to baptize. Rigdon stood in the stream and poured forth his exhortations with eloquent fervor. One after another stepped forward until thirty had been baptized. Present upon the bank was a hardheaded lawyer, Varnem J. Card, who as he listened grew pale with emotion. Suddenly he seized the arm of a friend and whispered, "Quick, take me away, or in a moment more I shall be in that water!" One hundred and twenty-seven converts at once, the num-

---

[4] Howe intimates that Rigdon knew more of the book and the people than he pretended. Of the proselytes made in his church he says: 'Near the residence of Rigdon, in Kirtland, there had been for some time previous a few families belonging to his congregation, who had formed themselves into a common stock society, and had become considerably fanatical, and were daily looking for some wonderful event to take place in the world. Their minds had become fully prepared to embrace Mormonism, or any other mysterious ism that should first present itself. Seventeen in number of these persons readily believed the whole story of Cowdery about the finding of the golden plates and the spectacles. They were all reimmersed in one night by Cowdery.' *Mormonism Unveiled*, 103.

ber afterward increasing to a thousand, were here gathered into the fold.[5]

After adding to their number one Frederic G. Williams, the missionaries continued on their way, arriving first at Sandusky, where they gave instructions to the Indians in regard to their forefathers, as they had done at Buffalo, and thence proceeded to Cincinnati and St Louis. In passing by his old forest home, Pratt was arrested on some trivial charge, but made his escape. The winter was very severe, and it was some time before they could continue their journey. At length they set out again, wading in snow knee-deep, carrying their few effects on their backs, and having to eat corn bread and frozen raw pork; and after travelling in all fifteen hundred miles, most of the way on foot, preaching to tens of thousands by the way, and organizing hundreds into churches, they reached Independence, Missouri, in the early part of 1831. There Whitmer and Peterson went to work as tailors, while Pratt and Cowdery passed over the

---

[5] Speaking of the doings at Kirtland after the departure of the Lamanite mission, Mr Howe says: 'Scenes of the most wild, frantic, and horrible fanaticism ensued. They pretended that the power of miracles was about to be given to all those who embraced the new faith, and commenced communicating the holy spirit by laying their hands upon the heads of the converts, which operation at first produced an instantaneous prostration of body and mind. Many would fall upon the floor, where they would lie for a long time apparently lifeless. They thus continued these enthusiastic exhibitions for several weeks. The fits usually came on during or after their prayer meetings, which were held nearly every evening. The young men and women were more particularly subject to this delirium. They would exhibit all the apish actions imaginable, making the most ridiculous grimaces, creeping upon their hands and feet, rolling upon the frozen ground, go through with all the Indian modes of warfare, such as knocking down, scalping, ripping open and tearing out the bowels. At other times they would run through the fields, get upon stumps, preach to imaginary congregations, enter the water and perform all the ceremony of baptizing, etc. Many would have fits of speaking all the different Indian dialects, which ..one could understand. Again, at the dead hour of night the young men might be seen running over the fields and hills in pursuit, as they said, of the balls of fire, light, etc., which they saw moving through the atmosphere...On the arrival of Smith in Kirtland he appeared astonished at the wild enthusiasm and scalping performances of his proselytes there. He told them that he had inquired of the Lord concerning the matter, and had been informed that it was all the work of the devil, as heretofore related. The disturbance therefore ceased.' *Mormonism Unveiled*, 104, 116.

border, crossed the Kansas River, and began their work among the Lamanites, or Indians, thereabout. The chief of the Delawares was sachem of ten tribes. He received the missionaries with courtesy, and set food before them. When they asked him to call a council before which they might expound their doctrines, he at first declined, then assented; whereupon Cowdery gave them an account of their ancestors, as contained in the wonderful book, a copy of which he left with the chief on taking his departure, which soon occurred; for when it was known upon the border settlements what the missionaries were doing, they were ordered out of the Indian country as disturbers of the peace.[6] After preaching a short time in Missouri, the five brethren thought it best that one of their number should return east and report. The choice fell on Pratt. Starting out on foot, he reached St Louis, three hundred miles distant, in nine days. Thence he proceeded by steamer to Cincinnati, and from that point journeyed on foot to Strongville, forty miles from Kirtland. Overcome by fatigue and illness, he was forced to remain at this place some ten days, when he continued his journey on horseback. He was welcomed at Kirtland by hundreds of the saints, Joseph Smith himself being present.

In December 1830 comes Sidney Rigdon to Joseph Smith at Manchester, and with him Edward Partridge, to inquire of the Lord; and they are told what they shall do; they shall preach thereabout, and also on the Ohio.[7]

[6] 'One of their leading articles of faith is, that the Indians of North America, in a very few years, will be converted to Mormonism, and through rivers of blood will again take possession of their ancient inheritance.' *Howe's Mormonism Unveiled*, 145.

[7] 'We before had Moses and Aaron in the persons of Smith and Cowdery, and we now have John the Baptist, in the person of Sidney Rigdon. Their plans of deception appear to have been more fully matured and developed after the meeting of Smith and Rigdon. The latter being found very intimate with the scriptures, a close reasoner, and as fully competent to make

The year 1831 opens with flattering prospects.
On the 2d of January a conference is held at Fayette,
attended by revelations and prophecy. James Col-
ville, a baptist minister, accepts the faith, but shortly
recants, being tempted of Satan, and in fear of persecution.[8] Smith and his wife go with Rigdon and

white appear black and black white as any other man; and at all times prepared to establish, to the satisfaction of great numbers of people, the negative
or affirmative of any and every question from scripture, he was forthwith
appointed to promulgate all the absurdities and ridiculous pretensions of
Mormonism, and call on the holy prophets to prove all the words of Smith.
But the miraculous powers conferred upon him we do not learn have yet been
put in requisition. It seems that the spirit had not, before the arrival of
Rigdon, told Smith anything about the promised land, or his removal to Ohio.
It is therefore very questionable what manner of spirit it was which dictated most of the after movements of the prophet. The spirit of Rigdon, it
must be presumed, however, generally held sway; for a revelation was soon
had that Kirtland, the residence of Rigdon and his brethren, was to be the
eastern border of the promised land, and from thence to the Pacific Ocean.
On this land the New Jerusalem, the city of refuge, was to be built. Upon
it all true Mormons were to assemble, to escape the destruction of the
world which was so soon to take place.' *Howe's Mormonism Unveiled*, 109-10.
Tucker, *Origin and Prog. Mor.*, 76-8, thus speaks of the first appearance of
this first regular Mormon preacher before a Palmyra congregation: 'Rigdon
introduced himself as the messenger of God, declaring that he was commanded
from above to proclaim the Mormon revelation. After going through with a
ceremonious form of prayer, in which he expressed his grateful sense of the
blessings of the glorious gospel dispensation now opening to the world, and
the miraculous light from heaven to be displayed through the instrumentality
of the chosen revelator, Joseph Smith Jr,...he announced his text as follows: First book of Nephi, chapter iv.—"And the angel spake unto me, saying, These last records which thou hast seen among the gentiles shall establish the truth of the first, which is of the twelve apostles of the lamb, and
shall make known the plain and precious things which have been taken away
from them; and shall make known to all kindreds, tongues, and people that
the lamb of God is the son of the eternal father and saviour of the world; and
that all men must come unto him or they cannot be saved." The preacher
assumed to establish the theory that the book of Mormon and the old bible
were one in inspiration and importance, and that the precious things now revealed had for wise purposes been withheld from the book first promulgated
to the world, and were necessary to establish its truth. In the course of his
argument he applied various quotations from the two books to prove his position. Holding the book of Mormon in his right hand, and the bible in his
left hand, he brought them together in a manner corresponding to the emphatic declaration made by him, that they were both equally the word of God;
that neither was perfect without the other; and that they were inseparably
necessary to complete the everlasting gospel of the saviour Jesus Christ.' It
is said that Rigdon, after his return to Kirtland from his visit to Smith, in
one of his eloquent discourses on the new faith, 'gave a challenge to the
world to disprove the new bible, and the pretensions of its authors.' Rigdon's
old friend, Thomas Campbell, hearing of it, wrote him from Mentor accepting, at the same time enclosing an outline of what his line of argument would
be. There the matter dropped.
    [8] See *Millennial Star*, v. 33-5; *Times and Seasons*, iv. 352-4. Mather, in
Lippincott's Mag., Aug. 1880, states that to escape persecution sixty believ-

Partridge to Kirtland, arriving there early in February, and taking up their residence with N. K. Whitney, who shows them great kindness. Among the hundred believers there at the time, certain false doctrines have crept in; these are quickly overcome, and a plan for community of goods which the family of saints had adopted is abolished. Commandment comes by revelation that a house shall be built for Joseph; that Sidney shall live as seems to him good, for his heart is pure; that Edward Partridge shall be ordained a bishop;[9] that all but Joseph and Sidney shall go forth, two by two, into the regions westward and preach the gospel.[10]

"And now, behold, I speak unto the church: thou shalt not kill; thou shalt not steal; thou shalt not lie; thou shalt love thy wife, cleaving unto her and to none else; thou shalt not commit adultery; thou shalt not speak evil of thy neighbor, nor do him any harm. Thou knowest my laws, given in my scriptures; he that sinneth and repenteth not shall be cast out. And behold, thou wilt remember the poor, and consecrate of thy properties for their support, laying the same before the bishop of my church, the residue not to be taken back, but to be used by the church in buying lands and building houses of worship, for I will consecrate of the riches of those who embrace my gospel among the gentiles unto the poor of my people who are of the house of Israel. Let him that goeth to

ers abandoned their homes in the Susquehanna valley and moved westward. 'Some of the followers,' he says, 'were moved by a spirit of adventure, while others placed their property in the common lot and determined to accompany the prophet to his earthly as well as to his heavenly kingdom. Smith Baker was one of the teamsters, and reports that the train consisted of three baggage and eleven passenger wagons. The exodus was along the old state road, north of Binghamton, to Ithaca, and thence across Cayuga Lake to Palmyra.'

[9] 'Smith had appointed as his bishop one Edward Partridge, a very honest and industrious hatter of Painesville, Ohio, who had withal a comfortable stock of the good things of the world. He was stationed at Independence, and had the sole control of all the temporal and spiritual affairs of the colony, always obedient, however, to the revelations promulgated by Smith.'

[10] 'Some of the members pretended to receive parchment commissions miraculously, which vanished from their sight as soon as they had been copied.' For a copy of one of these, with seal attached, see *Howe's Mormonism Unveiled*, 107; *Kidder's Mormonism*, 73.

the east tell them that shall be converted to flee to
the west. And again, thou shalt not be proud; let
thy garments be plain, the work of thine own hand,
and cleanly. Thou shalt not be idle. And whosoever
among you is sick, and has faith, shall be healed;
and if he has not faith to be healed, but believe, he
shall be nourished with all tenderness. If thou wilt
ask, thou shalt receive revelation and knowledge.
Whosoever hath faith sufficient shall never taste death.
Ye shall live together in love; that whether ye live
ye may live in me, or if ye die ye may die in me. So
saith the Lord."

Edward Partridge was born at Pittsfield, Massachusetts, August 27, 1793. At the age of sixteen he
was apprenticed to a hatter. His was an earnest,
thoughtful nature, and his mind much troubled about
religion. In 1828 he entered Sidney Rigdon's Campbellite church, and in that faith remained until met
by the missionaries Pratt, Cowdery, and the others,
when he accepted the new revelation, and was subsequently baptized by Joseph in the Seneca River. He
had a profitable business at the time; but when it was
revealed that he should leave his merchandise and de-
vote his whole time to the church, he obeyed without
a murmur.

Joseph and Sidney were much together now in their
revelations and rulings. A woman attempted prophesying and was rebuked. Sarcasm was employed, and
scurrilous stories were printed in the newspapers; an account of a great Asiatic earthquake was headed "Mormonism in China." Revelations during March were
frequent. In one of them John Whitmer was appointed church historian; and it was revealed that he
should keep the church records, write and keep a regular history, and act as secretary to Joseph, as had
Oliver Cowdery formerly.[11] Lands might be bought

[11] 'Since the organization of the church on the sixth day of April, 1830,
there has been a record kept in our church of its general transactions, of its

for immediate necessity; but remember the city to be presently built, and be prudent.[12] And now from the shaking quakers came one Lemon Copley and accepted the gospel, though not in its fullness, as he retained

persecutions and general history. The one in charge of this duty is called by us "the historian and general church recorder." The first who occupied this position was John Whitmer, until 1838, when he was excommunicated from the church for transgression, and took portions of the church records with him.' *Richards' Bibliography of Utah*, MS., 2. 'The earliest clerk service rendered the prophet Joseph, of which there is any account, was by Martin Harris; Joseph's wife, Emma, then Oliver Cowdery, who, as is claimed, wrote the greater portion of the original manuscript of the *Book of Mormon*, as he translated it from the gold plates by the urim and thummim which he obtained with the plates. In March 1831 John Whitmer was appointed to keep the church record and history continually, Oliver having been appointed to other labors. Whitmer was assisted, temporarily, on occasions of absence or illness by Warren Parrish. At a meeting of high council at Kirtland, Sept. 14, 1835, it was decided that "Oliver Cowdery be appointed, and that he act hereafter as recorder for the church," Whitmer having just been called to be editor of the *Messenger and Advocate*. At a general conference held in Far West April 6, 1838, John Corrill and Elias Higbee were appointed historians, and George W. Robinson "general church recorder and clerk for the first presidency." On the death of Elder Robert B. Thompson, which occurred at Nauvoo on the twenty-seventh of August, 1841, in his obituary it is stated: "Nearly two years past he had officiated as scribe to President Joseph Smith and clerk for the church, which important stations he filled with that dignity and honor befitting a man of God." During the expulsion from Missouri, and the early settlement of Nauvoo, James Mulholland, William Clayton, and perhaps others rendered temporary service in this line until the 13th of December, 1841, when Willard Richards was appointed recorder, general clerk, and private secretary to the prophet, which offices he occupied until his death, in March 1854, when he was succeeded by George A. Smith, who held it until his death on the first of September, 1875, with Wilford Woodruff as his assistant. Soon after, Orson Pratt succeeded to the office, retaining Woodruff as his assistant, until his demise on the third of October, 1881. Directly after President Woodruff was appointed to the office, and in January 1884, Apostle Franklin D. Richards was appointed his assistant.' See *Times and Seasons*, v. 401; *Millennial Star*, v. 82; *Richards' Narrative*, MS., 94–8.

[12] Of the future of this city there were many revelations and many conjectures. 'It was said that it would in a few years exceed in splendor everything known in ancient times. Its streets were to be paved with gold; all that escaped the general destruction which was soon to take place would there assemble with all their wealth; the ten lost tribes of Israel had been discovered in their retreat, in the vicinity of the north pole, where they had for ages been secluded by immense barriers of ice, and became vastly rich; the ice in a few years was to be melted away, when those tribes, with St John and some of the Nephites, which the book of Mormon had immortalized, would be seen making their appearance in the new city, loaded with immense quantities of gold and silver. Whether the prophet himself ever declared that these things had been revealed to him, or that he had seen them through his magic stone or silver spectacles, we will not say; but that such stories and hundreds of others equally absurd were told by those who were in daily intercourse with him, as being events which would probably take place, are susceptible of proof.' *Howe's Mormonism Unveiled*, 127–8. 'Kirtland was never intended to be the metropolis of Mormonism; it was selected as a temporary abiding place, to make money in reference to a removal farther west.' *Ferris' Utah and the Mormons*, 72.

somewhat of his former faith; whereupon a revelation ordered him to go with Parley P. Pratt and preach to the shakers, not according to his old ideas, but as Parley should direct.

"And again, I say unto you that whoso forbiddeth to marry is not ordained of God, for marriage is ordained of God unto man; wherefore it is lawful that he should have one wife, and they twain shall be one flesh. Beware of false spirits. Given May 1831."

The saints from New York began to come in numbers, and Bishop Partridge was ordered to look after them and attend to their requirements. It was ordered that if any had more than they required, let them give to the church; if any had less, let the church relieve their necessities. The 6th of June a conference of elders was held at Kirtland, and several received the authority of the Melchisedec priesthood. The next conference should be held in Missouri, whither Joseph and Sidney should proceed at once, and there it would be told them what to do. And to the same place others should go, two by two, each couple taking different routes and preaching by the way. Among those who went forth were Lyman Wight and John Corrill, John Murdock and Hyrum Smith by the way of Detroit, Thomas B. Marsh and Selah J. Griffin, Isaac Morley and Ezra Booth, David Whitmer and Harvey Whitlock, Parley P. Pratt and Orson Pratt, Solomon Hancock and Simeon Carter, Edson Fuller and Jacob Scott, Levi Hancock and Zebedee Coltrin, Reynolds Cahoon and Samuel H. Smith, Wheeler Baldwin and William Carter, Joseph Wakefield and Solomon Humphrey. With Joseph and Sidney were to go Martin Harris and Edward Partridge, taking with them a letter of recommendation from the church.[13] "And thus, even as I have

---

[13] 'From this point in the history of this delusion,' says Howe, 'it began to spread with considerable rapidity. Nearly all of their male converts, however ignorant and worthless, were forthwith transformed into elders, and sent forth to proclaim, with all their wild enthusiasm, the wonders and mys teries of Mormonism. All those having a taste for the marvellous and de-

said, if ye are faithful, ye shall assemble yourselves together to rejoice upon the land of Missouri, which is the land of your inheritance, which is now the land of your enemies. Behold, I the Lord will hasten the city in its time, and will crown the faithful with joy and with rejoicing. Behold I am Jesus Christ the son of God, and I will lift them up at the last day. Amen."

While preparing for the journey to Missouri, a letter was received from Oliver Cowdery, reporting on his missionary work, and speaking of another tribe of Lamanites, living three hundred miles west of Santa Fé, called the Navarhoes (Navajoes), who had large flocks of sheep and cattle, and who made blankets. W. W. Phelps,[14] with his family joining the society, was commissioned to assist Oliver Cowdery in selecting, writing, and printing books for schools. Thus the move from Ohio to Missouri was begun, Joseph and his party starting from Kirtland the 19th of June, going by wagon, canal-boat, and stage to Cincinnati, by steamer to St Louis, and thence on foot to Independence, arriving about the middle of July.

lighting in novelties flocked to hear them. Many travelled fifty and a hundred miles to the throne of the prophet in Kirtland, to hear from his own mouth the certainty of his excavating a bible and spectacles. Many, even in the New England states, after hearing the frantic story of some of these elders, would forthwith place their all into a wagon, and wend their way to the promised land, in order, as they supposed, to escape the judgments of heaven, which were soon to be poured out upon the land. The state of New York, they were privately told, would most probably be sunk, unless the people thereof believed in the pretensions of Smith.' *Mormonism Unveiled,* 115–16.

[14] Howe writes thus of Phelps: 'Before the rise of Mormonism he was an avowed infidel; having a remarkable propensity for fame and eminence, he was supercilious, haughty, and egotistical. His great ambition was to embark in some speculation where he could shine preëminent. He took an active part for several years in the political contests of New York, and made no little display as an editor of a partisan newspaper, and after being foiled in his desires to become a candidate for lieutenant-governor of that state, his attention was suddenly diverted by the prospects which were held out to him in the gold-bible speculation. In this he was sure of becoming a great man, and made the dupes believe he was master of fourteen different languages, of which they frequently boasted. But he soon found that the prophet would suffer no growing rivalships, whose sagacity he had not well calculated, until he was met by a revelation which informed him that he could rise no higher than a printer.' *Mormonism Unveiled,* 274.

" Harken, O ye elders of my church, saith the Lord
your God, who have assembled yourselves together,
according to my commandments, in this land, which
is the land of Missouri, which is the land which I
have appointed and consecrated for the gathering of
the saints; wherefore this is the land of promise, and
the place for the city of Zion. And thus saith the
Lord your God, if you will receive wisdom here is
wisdom. Behold the place which is now called Independence is the centre place, and the spot for the
temple is lying westward upon a lot which is not far
from the court-house: wherefore it is wisdom that
the land should be purchased by the saints; and also
every tract lying westward, even unto the line running directly between jew and gentile; and also every
tract bordering by the prairies, inasmuch as my disciples are enabled to buy lands."

Further, Sidney Gilbert was made church agent, to
receive money and buy lands; he was also directed to
establish a store. Partridge was to partition the
lands purchased among the people; Phelps was
made church printer. But the last two becoming a
little headstrong on entering upon their new duties,
Joseph found it necessary to reprimand and warn
them. Harris was held up as an example to emulate,
for he had given much to the church. It was ordered that an agent be appointed to raise money in
Ohio to buy lands in Missouri, and Rigdon was commissioned to write a description of the new land of
Zion for the same purpose. Ziba Peterson was dis-
possessed of his lands, and made to work for others,
in punishment for his misdemeanors.

Thus the latter-day saints had come to the border
line of civilization, and looking over it into the west
they thought here to establish themselves forever.
Here was to be the temple of God; here the city of
refuge; here the second advent of the savior. Meanwhile their headquarters were to be at the town of
Independence.

In Kaw township, twelve miles west of Independence, the Colesville branch of the church built a log house; the visible head of the church, on the 2d of August, laying the first log, brought thither by twelve men, in honor of the twelve tribes of Israel. Next day the ground for the temple, situated a little west of Independence,[15] was dedicated, and the day following was held the first conference in the land of Zion.[16] It was now commanded that Smith, Rigdon, Cowdery, and others should return east, and make more proselytes, money for the purpose to be furnished them out of the general fund.[17] Accordingly on the

[15] Of Independence one of them says: 'It is a new town, containing a courthouse built of brick, two or three merchants' stores, and 15 or 20 dwellinghouses built mostly of logs hewed on both sides; and is situated on a handsome rise of ground about three miles south of Missouri River, and about 12 miles east of the dividing line between the United States and the Indian reserve, and is the county seat of Jackson county.' Booth's letter in *Howe's Mormonism Unveiled*, 196. On the south side of the Missouri, Parley Pratt says, *Autobiography*, 78, 'some families were entirely dressed in skins, without any other clothing, including ladies young and old. Buildings were generally without glass windows, and the door open in winter for a light.'

[16] Booth, in *Howe's Mormonism Unveiled*, 196–9, says: 'The designation of the site where the city of Zion was to begin was attended with considerable parade and an ostentatious display of talents, both by Rigdon and Cowdery. And the next day the ground for the temple was consecrated, Smith claiming the honor of laying the corner-stone himself. The location of the stone was marked by a sapling from which the bark was removed on the north and east sides: on the south side a letter T was cut, which stood for temple, and on the east side Zom., for Zomas; which Smith said is the original word for Zion. This stone was placed near the foot of the sapling and covered with bushes cut for the purpose; the spot being on an elevation half a mile from Independence.' 'The Colesville branch was among the first organized by Joseph Smith, and constituted the first settlers of the members of the church in Missouri. They had arrived late in the summer and cut some hay for their cattle, sowed a little grain, prepared some ground for cultivation, and were engaged during the fall and winter in building log cabins, etc. The winter was cold, and for some time about 10 families lived in one cabin, which was open and unfinished, while the frozen ground served for a floor. Our food consisted of beef, and a little bread made of corn which had been grated into coarse meal by rubbing the ears on a tin grater.' *Pratt's Autobiography*, 76. See also *Millennial Star*, v. 131. It was revealed through Joseph the seer that the property of the Colesville branch should be held in common, and that Partridge (its bishop) have charge and distribute from the community storehouse according to the needs of each. *Smith's Doctrine and Covenants* (1876), 187–8. Smith in the beginning of the church attempted to establish communism, each giving their all to the bishop, and only drawing out of the office sufficient to live upon. This was found to be impracticable, and it was silently permitted to glide into the payment of tithing. *Hyde's Mormonism*, 37.

[17] 'This year, 1831, passed off with a gradual increase, and considerable wealth was drawn in, so that they began to boast of a capital stock of ten or

9th Joseph and ten elders started down the river in sixteen canoes, the leaders arriving at Kirtland the 27th,[18] after having suffered hardship and mortification through disaffection among the elders. Titus Billings, who had charge of the church property there, was ordered to dispose of the lands, and prepare to remove to Missouri in the following spring, together with part of the people, and such money as could be raised. It was provided that those wishing to buy land in Zion could do so by forwarding the purchase-money. The account of the new country written by Sidney Rigdon did not please Joseph, and he was ordered to write another; if that should not prove satisfactory, he was to be deprived of office.[19]

On the 12th of September Joseph removed to the town of Hiram, thirty miles away, and prepared to begin again the translation of the bible, with Rigdon as scribe. The farm of Isaac Morley was ordered sold, while Frederic G. Williams should retain his, for it was desirable to keep a footing at Kirtland yet for

fifteen thousand dollars. Their common-stock principles appear to be somewhat similar to those of the shakers.' *Howe's Mormonism Unveiled*, 128–9.

[18] Booth intimates that Smith and Rigdon preferred living in Ohio to enduring the hardships of Missouri. 'Before they went to Missouri their language was, "We shall winter in Ohio but one winter more;" and when in Missouri, "It will be many years before we come here, for the lord has a great work for us to do in Ohio." And the great work is to make a thorough alteration of the bible, and invent new revelations, and these are to be sent to Missouri in order to be printed.' Letter in *Howe's Mormonism Unveiled*, 199.

[19] 'Some dispute, of which the nature is not clearly known, appears to have arisen between Joseph and his friend Sidney Rigdon before their return. It is probable, from the course of subsequent events, that Sidney, even at this time, aspired to greater power in the church than suited the prophet, . . . who saw fit to rebuke him by a revelation accusing him of "being exalted in his heart, and despising the counsel of the lord." They afterward became reconciled."' *Smucker's Mormons*, 75–6, confirmed by *Millennial Star*, v. 149; *Times and Seasons*, v. 467. From this time till January 1832, Joseph continued preaching in various parts of the United States, making converts with great rapidity. He found it necessary, however, further to check the presumption of some new and indiscreet converts who also had revelations from the Lord, which they endeavored to palm off upon the public. Among others, one W. E. McLellan was rebuked for endeavoring to 'write a commandment like unto one of the least of the Lord's.' *Mackay's Mormons*, 67–8. See anecdote of 'The Swamp Angel;' also account of raising the dead by Smith, about this time. *Ward's Mormon Wife*, 10–11, 15–24. For text of rebuke, where the name of the offender is given William E. M'Lellin, see *Millennial Star*, v. 185–6; *Times and Seasons*, v. 496.

five years. The store kept by Newel K. Whitney and Sidney Gilbert should likewise be continued. A system of tithes should be established. Ezra Booth apostatized, and wrote letters against the church.[20] Orson Hyde, clerk in Gilbert and Whitney's store, was baptized, and later make an elder. Phelps was told to buy at Cincinnati a printing-press and type, and start a monthly paper at Independence, to be called the *Evening and Morning Star*, which was done. Oliver Cowdery was instructed in November to return to Missouri, and with him John Whitmer, the latter to visit the several stations, and gather further materials for church history. Newel K. Whitney

[20] Booth's letters were first printed at Ravenna, in the *Ohio Star*, and afterward by E. D. Howe in his book, *Mormonism Unveiled*, 175–221. They are nine in number, and are full of general denunciation and sorrow over his past blindness, and an account of the hardships and disappointments attending his journey to and from Missouri. I quote the more pertinent points. 'When I embraced Mormonism I conscientiously believed it to be of God.' 'The relation in which Smith stands to the church is that of a prophet, seer, revealer, and translator; and when he speaks by the spirit, or says he knows a thing by the communication of the spirit, it is received as coming directly from the mouth of the Lord.' 'This system, to some, carries the force of plausibility, and appears under an imposing form. It claims the bible for its patron, and proffers the restoration of the apostolic church, with all the gifts and graces with which the primitive saints were endowed.' 'Many of them have been ordained to the high priesthood, or the order of Melchisedec, and profess to be endowed with the same power as the ancient apostles were. But they have been hitherto unsuccessful in finding the lame, the halt, and the blind who had the faith sufficient to become the subjects of their miracles, and it is now concluded that this work must be postponed until they get to Missouri; for the Lord will not show those signs to this wicked and adulterous generation. In the commandment given to the churches in the state of New York to remove to the state of Ohio, they were assured that these miracles should be wrought in the state of Ohio; but now they must be deferred until they are settled in Missouri.' 'Everything in the church is done by commandment; and yet it is said to be done by the voice of the church. For instance, Smith gets a commandment that he shall be the head of the church, or that he shall rule the conference, or that the church shall build him an elegant house and give him 1,000 dollars. For this the members of the church must vote, or they will be cast off for rebelling against the commandments of the Lord.' 'Smith describes an angel as having the appearance of a tall, slim, well built, handsome man, with a bright pillar upon his head.' The bishop's 'business is to superintend the secular concerns of the church. He holds a deed of the lands; and the members receive a writing from him signifying that they are to possess the land as their own so long as they are obedient to Smith's commandments.' 'The Lord's storehouse is to be furnished with goods suited to the Indian trade, and persons are to obtain license from the government to dispose of them to the Indians in their own territory; at the same time they are to disseminate the principles of Mormonism among them.'

was appointed bishop, to receive and account for church funds collected by the various elders. Many of the elders who went to Missouri were by this time at work in different parts of the east and the west.[21]

On the 16th of February, 1832, while Smith and Rigdon were translating the gospel of St John, they were favored by a glorious vision from the Lord,[22] which gave them great comfort and encouragement. The revelations about this time were frequent and lengthy, their purport being in great part to direct the movements of missionaries. Simonds Rider and Eli, Edward, and John Johnson now apostatized.

On the night of the 25th of March, Smith and Rigdon were seized by a mob, composed partly of the Campbellites, methodists, and baptists of Hiram, twelve or fifteen being apostate Mormons. The captives were roughly treated, and expected to be killed; but after they had been stripped, beaten, and well covered with tar and feathers, they were released. Smith preached and baptized as usual the next day, Sunday, but Rigdon was delirious for some time afterward.[23] This broke up for the present the translation

[21] 'Thirty or forty elders were sent off in various directions in pursuit of proselytes, and the year passed off with a gradual increase.' *Howe's Mormonism Unveiled*, 128-9. The men, after baptism, are elders, and are empowered to perform the ceremony upon others. *Carvalho's Incidents of Travel*, 148. For names of apostates at this time, see *Smucker's Hist. Mor.*, 77. For instances of young women induced to unite with the sect about this time, see *Ward's Mormon Wife*, 42-81. Mackay erroneously states that the number of saints in Kirtland at this time, including women and children, was but 150. *The Mormons*, 71-2.

[22] In January it was revealed that the work of translating should be proceeded with by Smith and Rigdon until finished; and that several of the elders, among whom was Orson Hyde, a recent convert, should go forth in various directions in pairs as before, and preach. Smith and some of the elders attended a conference at Amherst, Loraine Co., after returning from which both himself and Rigdon were shown the devil in a vision, and had the revelation of St John explained to them. In March it was revealed that steps should be taken to regulate and establish storehouses for the benefit of the poor, both at Kirtland and at Zion. More missionaries were sent out, and word was received that the emigrants had safely reached Missouri. *Times and Seasons*, v. 576-7, 592-6, 608-9.

[23] *Times and Seasons*, v. 611-12. Mackay, *Mormons*, 68-71, erroneously dates the outrage Jan. 25th. One account says aqua-fortis was poured into Smith's mouth. *Deseret News*, Aug. 6, 1862. Smith says 'they tried to force a vial into my mouth, and broke it in my teeth.' One reason assigned for this treatment was that they were attempting to establish communism and

of the bible; Rigdon went to Kirtland, and on the 2d of April, in obedience to a revelation, Smith started for Missouri, having for his companions Whitney, Peter Whitmer, and Gause. The spirit of mobocracy was aroused throughout the entire country. Joseph even feared to go to K:rtland, and escaped by way of Warren, where he was joined by Rigdon, whence the two proceeded to Cincinnati and St Louis by way of Wheeling, Virginia, a mob following them a good part of the way. The brethren at Independence and vicinity welcomed their leaders warmly, but the unbelievers there as elsewhere hourly threatened violence.[24] In May the first edition of the *Book of Commandments*[25] was ordered printed; the following month, pub-

dishonorable dealing, forgery, and swindling. *Burton's City of the Saints*, 672. Smith merely says that Rigdon was mad; but his mother asserts that he counterfeited the madness in order to mislead the saints into the belief that the keys of the kingdom had been taken from the church, and would not be restored, as he said, until they had built him a new house. This, she says, gave rise to great scandal, which Joseph however succeeded in silencing. Rigdon repented and was forgiven. He stated that as a punishment for his fault, the devil had three times thrown him out of his bed in one night. *Remy's Journey to Great Salt Lake*, i. 283 (note).

[24] The 26th of April Smith called a general council, which acknowledged him as president of the high priesthood, to which he had been ordained at the Amherst conference in January, and Bishop Partridge and Rigdon, who had quarrelled, were reconciled, probably by Smith, as Rigdon was supposed to be at Kirtland at the time. This greatly rejoiced Smith; and he immediately received a revelation, in which it was announced that the stakes must be strengthened, and all property was to be held in common. *Times and Seasons*, v. 624–5; *Mackay's The Mormons*, 71.

[25] The first edition of *Doctrine and Covenants* presents the following title page: *A Book of Commandments for the Government of the Church of Christ organized according to law on the 6th of April, 1830. Zion: Published by W. W. Phelps & Co., 1833*. This edition contains the revelations given up to September, 1831. There were 3,000 copies printed of this edition. Then there was *The Book of Doctrine and Covenants of the Church of Jesus Christ of Latter-Day Saints; Selected from the Revelations of God. By Joseph Smith, President. First European Edition, Liverpool*, no date. The preface, however, by Thomas Ward, is dated Liverpool, June 14, 1845. There are two principal divisions and an appendix. The first consists of seven lectures on faith, delivered by Sidney Rigdon before a class of elders at Kirtland; the second is called Covenants and Commandments, and consists chiefly of revelations given 1830–42, to Joseph Smith, the same for the most part that are also printed in *Times and Seasons*, under title of History of Joseph Smith. There are also rules, minutes of council, visions, and expositions. The appendix contains rules on marriage, a dissertation on government and laws, and a brief account of Joseph and Hyrum Smith. 'The book of Mormon, although most known, is not the chief book of the sect. The *Book of Teachings and Covenants*, containing some of the revelations which Smith pretended to have received from heaven, is regarded by his disciples as a book of the law which God

lished in connection with the *Upper Missouri Advertiser*, appeared the first number of the *Evening and
Morning Star*, under the auspices of W. W. Phelps,
whose printing-press was the only one within a hundred and twenty miles of Independence. On the 6th
of May Smith, Rigdon, and Whitney again set out
on their return to Kirtland.[26] On the way Whitney
broke his leg. Smith was poisoned, and that so badly
that he dislocated his jaw in vomiting, and the hair
upon his head became loosened; Whitney, however,
laid his hands on him, and administered in the name
of the Lord, and he was healed in an instant.[27]

Some three or four hundred saints being now gathered in Missouri, most of them settled on their own
inheritances in this land of Zion, besides many others
scattered abroad throughout the land, who were yet to
come hither, it was deemed best to give the matter of
schools some attention. Parley P. Pratt was laboring in Illinois. Newel K. Whitney was directed in
September to leave his business in other hands, visit

has given this generation. Smith also published other revelations, which are
contained in a little book called *The Pearl of Great Price.' De Smet's Western
Missions*, 393. 'This book abounds in grammatical inaccuracies, even to a
greater extent than the book of Mormon.' *Mackay's The Mormons*, 43. A
bungling statement is made by Mather, *Lippincott's Mag.*, Aug. 1880, to the
effect that in 1835 'Rigdon's *Book of Doctrine and Covenants* and his *Lectures
on Faith* were adopted.'

[26] Arrangements were early made for the establishment of a store. *Ferris'
Utah and Mormons*, 75. When the printing press was bought—see *Deseret
News*, June 30, 1869—a supply of goods was purchased; and arrangements
were made at the May council to keep up the supply, which, with few exceptions, were considered satisfactory. On April 27th considerable business was
transacted 'for the salvation of the saints who were settling among a ferocious set of mobbers, like lambs among wolves.' On the 28th and 29th Smith
visited the settlement above Big Blue River in Kaw township, 12 miles west
of Independence, including the Colesville branch, and returned on the 30th,
when it was revealed that all minors should be supported by their parents,
but after becoming of age 'they had claims upon the church, or in other
words, the Lord's storehouse,' as was also the case with widows left destitute.
Times and Seasons, v. 625–6.

[27] On May 6th, leaving affairs as he supposed in a flourishing condition,
Smith started for Kirtland to look after the mill, store, and farm in that
neighborhood, but owing to an accident which resulted in the breaking of
Whitney's leg, Smith was delayed 4 weeks en route. Rigdon, who was also of
the party, proceeded through without stopping, and the other two arrived
some time in June. The season was passed by Smith in his work of translating the scriptures, and in attending to business affairs. *Times and Seasons*,
v. 626.

the churches, collect money, and administer to the wants of the poor. The new translation of the bible was again taken up and continued through the winter, the new testament being completed and sealed up, not to be opened till it reached Zion.[28]

On January 23, 1833, the ceremony of washing feet is instituted after John's gospel. Each elder washes his own feet first, after which Joseph girds himself with a towel and washes the feet of them all. "Behold, verily, thus saith the Lord unto you, in consequence of evils and designs, which do and will exist in the hearts of conspiring men in the last days, I have warned you, and forewarned you, by giving unto you this word of wisdom by revelation, that inasmuch as any man drinketh wine or strong drink among you, behold it is not good, nor meet in the sight of your father. And again, tobacco is not for the body, neither for the belly, and it is not good for man. And again, hot drinks are not for the body or belly."

[28] Hardly had President Smith turned his back upon Zion, when dissensions broke out among the saints there. He corresponded regularly with the *Star*, giving advice and warning, but matters apparently grew worse, for in January 1833 a conference of twelve high priests was held at Kirtland, or Kirtland Mills, as they now called their settlement, at which Orson Hyde and Hyrum Smith were appointed to write an epistle to the brotherhood of Zion. The document was dated Jan. 14th, and began: 'From a conference of 12 high priests to the bishop, his council, and the inhabitants of Zion.' After premising that Smith and certain others had written on this all-important subject, and that the replies received had not given satisfactory assurances of confession and repentance, charges were made that old grievances, supposed to be settled, had been again brought up in a censorious spirit, and that they had accused Brother Smith of seeking after monarchical power and authority. This complaint was made by Carroll in a letter dated June 2d. Again, Brother Gilbert, on Dec. 10th, wrote a letter which contained 'low, dark, and blind insinuations, which they declined to entertain, though the writer's claims and pretensions to holiness were great.' Brother Phelps, Dec. 15th, wrote a letter betraying 'a lightness of spirit that ill becomes a man placed in the important and responsible station that he is placed in.' To a request that Smith should come to Zion, made by Phelps in a previous letter, it was answered that 'Brother Smith will not settle in Zion until she repent and purify herself...and remember the commandments that have been given her to do them as well as say them.' Finally, it was threatened that unless these disturbances should cease, they should all be cut off, and the Lord would seek another place. Brother Ziba Peterson was delivered 'over to the buffetings of Satan, in the name of the Lord, that he may learn not to transgress the commandments of God.' *Times and Seasons*, v. 801.

The first presidency is organized on the 8th of March, Sidney Rigdon and Frederick G. Williams being Smith's councillors. Money flows in, and a council of high priests, March 23d, orders the purchasing for $11,100 of three farms at Kirtland, upon which the saints may build a stake, or support, in Zion,[29] and the foundations of the temple are laid, for here they will remain for five years and make money until the western Zion shall be made ready and a temple built there also. On the land is a valuable quarry of stone, and good clay for bricks; they also buy a tannery. In April the school of the prophets closes, to reopen in the autumn. Shederlaomach is made by revelation a member of the united firm. It is not the will of the Lord to print any of the new translation in the *Star*; but when it is published, it will all go to the world together, in a volume by itself, and the new testament and the book of Mormon will be printed together. Those preparing to go to Zion should organize.

Commandment comes to lay at Kirtland the foundation of the city of the stake in Zion, with a house of the Lord, a school-house for the instruction of elders, a house for the presidency, a house of worship and for the school of the prophets, an endowment house with a room for the school of apostles, and a house in which to print the translation of the scriptures. A church is established in Medina county,

[29] 'The church that was to be established in Jackson county was called Zion, the centre of gathering, and those established by revelation in other places were called stakes of Zion, or stakes; hence the stake at Kirtland, the stake at Far West, etc. Each stake was to have a presidency, consisting of three high priests, chosen and set apart for that purpose, whose jurisdiction was confined to the limits of the stake over which they took the watch care.' *Kidder's Mormonism*, 121–2. A stake of Zion is an organization comprising a presidency, high priests, and its council of 12 high priests. The latter is a tribunal for the trial of brethren. It is a court of appeal from the bishops, and has also jurisdiction in spiritual matters. *Richards' Narrative*, MS., 55. For origin of name, see *Doctrine and Convenants* (1876), 263. 'The next year, 1833, commenced with something like a change of operations. Instead of selling their possessions in Ohio, they again began to buy up improved land, mills, and water privileges. It would seem that the Missouri country began to look rather dreary to the prophet and his head men, supposing that they could not enjoy their power there as well as in Ohio.' *Howe's Mormonism Unveiled*, 130.

Ohio, by Sidney Rigdon, who sometimes proves himself unruly. Dr Hurlbut is tried before the bishop's council of high priests on a charge of unchristianlike conduct with the female sex, and condemned, but on confession is pardoned.[30] Temples are ordered built in the city of Zion, in Missouri, as follow: a house of the Lord for the presidency of the high and most holy priesthood after the order of Melchisedec; the sacred apostolic repository,

[30] Four years after the first printing of the *Book of Mormon*, at Palmyra, New York, was issued in Ohio the following work: *Mormonism Unveiled: or, A faithful account of that singular Imposition and Delusion, from its rise to the present time. With sketches of the characters of its Propagators, and a full detail of the manner in which the famous Golden Bible was brought before the World. To which are added inquiries into the probability that the historical part of the said bible was written by one Solomon Spaulding, more than twenty years ago, and by him intended to have been published as a romance. By E. D. Howe. Painesville, Printed and Published by the Author, 1834.* 12mo, 290 pages. Painesville is situated but a short distance from Kirtland, then the headquarters of Mormonism, where about that time was ordained the first quorum of the twelve apostles, and Sidney Rigdon was delivering Joseph Smith's famous lectures on faith, subsequently printed in *Doctrine and Covenants*, already noticed. Here also, shortly afterward, the first Mormon temple was dedicated. Great excitement prevailed throughout that section regarding religion, and the book was widely circulated. It was a powerful weapon, and promptly and skillfully handled; yet it seems to have been no serious barrier to the dissemination of the new doctrines. The work is well written; and while not vehement in its denunciations, it brings forward a large mass of evidence to prove, as he says, 'the depths of folly, degradation, and superstition to which human nature can be carried.' He observes that 'the difficulty of procuring, or arriving at the whole truth, in relation to a religious imposition which has from its birth been so studiously veiled in secrecy, and generally under a belief that the judgments of God would follow any disclosures of what its votaries had seen or heard, will be readily discovered.' The author begins with some account of the Smith family. Their thoughts turned greatly toward gaining possession of hidden treasures. Young Joseph 'had become very expert in the arts of necromancy, juggling, the use of the divining rod, and looking into what they termed a peep-stone, by which means he soon collected about him a gang of idle, credulous young men, to perform the labor of digging into the hills and mountains, and other lonely places in that vicinity in search of gold.' After comments on Cowdery, Harris, and Whitmer, Mr Howe gives a commentary on the golden bible. Some 63 pages are devoted to this, and to observations on the credibility of the three and the eight witnesses. Sarcasm is the weapon employed, and generally with effect; the exposition in regard to contradictions and historical inaccuries might apply with equal force to the bible, the koran, or any other sacred book. Mention is next made of Pratt's conversion, which, he intimates, was not accidental, followed by an account of the expedition to the Lamanites. Thus the line of events is followed by Mr Howe to the time of the publication of his book, at the end of which are given letters and testimonials to disprove the statements and doctrines of the Mormons, and also to prove that the book of Mormon was the work of Spaulding. On the whole, besides being the first book published in opposition to the Mormons, it is also one of the most ably written, the most original, and the most respectable.

for the use of the bishop; the holy evangelical house, for the high priesthood of the holy order of God; house of the Lord for the elders of Zion; house of the Lord for the presidency of the high priesthood; house of the Lord for the high priesthood after the order of Aaron; house of the Lord for the teachers in Zion; house of the Lord for the deacons in Zion; and others. There are also to be farms, barns, and dwellings. The ground secured for the purpose is a mile square, and will accommodate fifteen or twenty thousand people.[31]

Affairs in Missouri were very prosperous. "Immigration had poured into the county of Jackson in great numbers," says Parley P. Pratt, "and the church

[31] A plan and specifications for the new city of Zion were sent out from Kirtland. The plot was one mile square, drawn to a scale of 660 feet to one inch. Each square was to contain ten acres, or 660 feet fronts. Lots were to be laid out alternately in the squares; in one, fronting north or south; in the next east or west; each lot extending to the centre line of its square, with a frontage of 66 feet and a depth of 330 feet, or half an acre. By this arrangement in one square the houses would stand on one street, and in the square opposite on another street. Through the middle of the plot ran a range of blocks 660 feet by 990 feet set apart for the public buildings, and in these the lots were all laid off north and south, the greatest length of the blocks being from east to west: thus making all the lots equal in size. The whole plot was supposed to be sufficient for the accommodation of from 15,000 to 20,000 people. All stables, barns, etc., were to be built north or south of the plot, none being permitted in the city among the houses. Sufficient adjoining ground on all sides was to be reserved for supplying the city with vegetables, etc. All streets were to be 132 feet (8 perches) wide, and a like width was to be laid off between the temple and its surrounding streets. But one house was to be built on a lot, and that must front on a line 25 feet from the street, the space in front to be set out with trees, shrubs, etc., according to the builder's taste. All houses to be of either brick or stone. The house of the Lord for the presidency was to be 61 feet by 87 feet, 10 feet of the length for a stairway. The interior was so arranged as to permit its division into 4 parts by curtains. At the east and west ends were to be pulpits arranged for the several grades of president and council, bishop and council, high priests and elders, at the west; and the lesser priesthood, comprising presidency, priests, teachers, and deacons, at the east. Provision was also made to seat visiting officers according to their grades. The pews were fitted with sliding seats, so that the audience could face either pulpit as required. There was to be no gallery, but the house was to be divided into 2 stories of 14 feet each. A bell of very large size was also ordered. Finally, on each public building must be written, Holiness to the Lord. When this plot was settled, another was to be laid out, and so on. *Times and Seasons*, vi. 785–7, 800. Zion City —its prototype in Enoch's City. *Young's History of the Seventies*, 9–15, no. 10, in *Mormon Pamphlets*. It was revealed to Smith that the waters of the gulf of Mexico covered the site of a prehistoric city, built by and named for Enoch; and that it was translated because its inhabitants had become so far advanced that further earthly residence was unnecessary. Zion, Smith's ideal city, was finally to reach a like state of perfection.

in that county now numbered upward of one thousand souls. These had all purchased lands and paid for them, and most of them were improving in buildings and in cultivation. Peace and plenty had crowned their labors, and the wilderness became a fruitful field, and the solitary place began to bud and blossom as the rose. They lived in peace and quiet, no lawsuits with each other or with the world; few or no debts were contracted, few promises broken; there were no thieves, robbers, or murderers; few or no idlers; all seemed to worship God with a ready heart. On Sundays the people assembled to preach, pray, sing, and receive the ordinances of God. Other days all seemed busy in the various pursuits of industry. In short, there has seldom, if ever, been a happier people upon the earth than the church of the saints now were." They were for the most part small farmers, tradesmen, and mechanics, and were not without shrewdness in the management of their secular affairs.

But all this must now be changed. The saints ot God must be tried as by fire. Persecutions such as never before were witnessed in these latter days, and the coming of which were foretold by Joseph, are upon them; they shall be buffeted for five years, and the end is not yet. "Political demagogues were afraid we should rule the country," says Parley, "and religious priests and bigots felt that we were powerful rivals."[32] Moreover, there is no doubt that they were indiscreet; they were blinded by their prosperity; already the kingdom of God and the kingdom of this world had come unto them; now let the gentiles tremble![33]

---

[32] *Autobiography*, 103.

[33] 'Their prophet had declared that Zion should be established, and should put down her enemies under her feet. Why, then, should they hesitate to proclaim their anticipations? They boasted openly that they should soon possess the whole country, and that the unbelievers should be rooted out from the land.' *Edinburgh Review*, April 1854. 'We have been credibly informed that Rigdon has given it as his opinion that the Mormons will be able to elect a member of congress in five years, and that in three years they would take the offices in the town of Kirtland. They say that when they get the

And the gentiles did tremble, as they saw so rapidly increasing their unwelcome neighbors, whose compact organization gave them a strength disproportionate to their numbers. Since there was no law to stop their coming, they determined to face the issue without law.[34]

In April the people held consultations as to the best way of disposing of the Mormons; and again about the middle of July three hundred persons met at Independence to form a plan for driving them out. A declaration, in substance as follows, was drawn up and signed by nearly all present. The citizens of Jackson county fear the effect upon society of a pretended religious sect, fanatics or knaves, settling among them, and mean to get rid of them at any hazard, and for the following reasons: They blasphemously pretend to personal intercourse with the deity, to revelations, miracles, healing the sick, casting out devils, and other delusions; they are the dregs of society, held together by the acts of designing leaders, and are idle and vicious. They are poor. They tamper with the slaves and free negroes. They declare the Indian region to be theirs by heavenly inheritance.

In answer, Parley P. Pratt asks if their supernatural pretensions are more extravagant than those of the old and new testament; if it is anywhere written that there shall be no more spiritual manifestations as of old; does the word of God or the law of man make poverty a crime? and have they not paid for all the land they occupy? They are no more dregs than their neighbors, and the charge of fraternizing with the blacks is not true; neither is that of vice or crime, as

secular power into their hands, everything will be performed by immediate revelations from God. We shall then have Pope Joseph the First and his hierarchy.' *Howe's Mormonism Unveiled,* 145.

[34] 'So early as April 1832, the saints were made to feel themselves unwelcome sojourners in Jackson co. Stones and brickbats were thrown through the windows of their houses, and they were otherwise annoyed and insulted. Meetings were held during that year and the early part of 1833, at which resolutions were sometimes passed, and sometimes the assembly indulged in a fight among its members; but nothing more serious resulted. Stoning houses, however, was resumed in the early summer of the last-mentioned year.' *Times and Seasons,* i. 17; vi. 851.

the county records will show. In regard to the lands of the Indians, no violence or injustice is contemplated; and if it were, what record of robbery, murder, and treacherous betrayal could excel that already made by the people of Missouri and others in the United States for our example?[35] On the 20th the people again met according to appointment. The old charges were reiterated, and the old resolutions renewed, with some additions.[36] To put them into action the men of Jackson county

[35] *Persecution of the Saints*, 21–8. Mackay, *The Mormons*, 72–4, says 'the manner in which the Mormons behaved in their Zion was not calculated to make friends. The superiority they assumed gave offense, and the rumors that were spread by some false friends, who had been turned out of the church for misconduct, excited against them an intense feeling of alarm and hatred. They were accused of communism, and not simply a community of goods and chattels, but of wives...Joined to the odium unjustly cast upon them for these reasons, they talked so imprudently of their determination to possess the whole state of Missouri, and to suffer no one to live in it who would not conform to their faith, that a party was secretly formed against them, of which the object was nothing less than their total and immediate expulsion from their promised Zion...The anti-Mormon press contained at the same time an article entitled "Beware of false prophets," written by a person whom Joseph called a black rod in the hand of Satan. This article was distributed from house to house in Independence and its neighborhood, and contained many false charges against Smith and his associates, reiterating the calumny about the community of goods and wives.' Smith calls this man 'one Pixley,' and says he was sent by the missionary society, to civilize and christianize the heathen of the west, and that he was not only a black rod, but 'a poisoned shaft in the power of our foes, to spread lies and falsehoods'...It is also probable that the more indolent Missourians gazed with jealous eyes as the new-comers exhibited that agricultural thrift which has always characterized them as a people; for we find the twelve high priests, through Hyde and Hyrum Smith, reprimanding Brother Phelps as follows: "If you have fat beef and potatoes, eat them in singleness of heart, and boast not yourselves in these things."' *Times and Seasons*, v. 721; vi. 816. 'It was conjectured by the inhabitants of Jackson county that the Mormonites as a body are wealthy, and many of them entertain fears that next December, when the list of land is exposed for sale, they will outbid others, and establish themselves as the most powerful body in the county.' Booth, in *Howe's Mormonism Unveiled*, 195.

[36] It was further declared: ' 1st, That no Mormon shall in future move and settle in this county. 2d, That those now here, who shall give a definite pledge of their intention, within a reasonable time, to remove out of the county, shall be allowed to remain unmolested until they shall have sufficient time to sell their property and close their business without any sacrifice. 3d, That the editor of the *Star* be required forthwith to close his office, and discontinue the business of printing in this county; and as to all other stores and shops belonging to the sect, their owners must in every case comply with the terms strictly, agreeably to the 2d article of this declaration; and upon failure, prompt and efficient measures will be taken to close the same. 4th, That the Mormon leaders here are required to use their influence in preventing any further emigration of their distant brethren to this county, and

sallied forth for the office of the *Star*,[37] and demanded that the publication be discontinued. Compliance being refused, Phelps' house, containing the printing-office, was torn down, materials and paper destroyed,[38] and Bishop Partridge and Elder Allen were tarred and feathered.[39]   Meanwhile, clergymen of other denominations, and officers of the state and county, looked on, saying, "Mormons are the common enemies of mankind, and ought to be destroyed," and "You now know what our Jackson boys can do, and you must leave the country."[40]

Again the mob appeared on the morning of the 23d, bearing a red flag, and demanding the departure of the Mormons. Seeing no way of escape, the elders entered into treaty with the assailants, and promised to leave the county within a certain time.[41]   Cowdery

counsel and advise their brethren to comply with the above requisitions. 5th, That those who fail to comply with the above requisitions be referred to those of their brethren who have the gift of tongues, to inform them of the lot that awaits them.' *Howe's Mormonism Unveiled*, 141.

[37] 'Six of the principal elders met the mob's committee. The latter demanded that the printing-office, the shops, and the store, be closed forthwith, and that the society leave the county immediately. The elders asked for three months' delay, which was refused; then for ten days, which was also refused; the latter refusal being accompanied with a notification that fifteen minutes was the longest time that could be granted. Each elder having declined to accede to the terms, one of the mob remarked on leaving that he was sorry, for, said he, "the work of destruction will commence immediately."' *Times and Seasons*, i. 18.   Phelps, the editor, Partridge, the bishop, and Gilbert, the store-keeper, are mentioned. *Smucker's Hist. Mor.*, 89.

[38] 'In a short time time hundreds of the mob gathered around the printing-office (a two-story brick building), which they soon threw down. The press was thrown from the upper story, and all the books, stock, and material scattered through the streets.   After destroying the printing house, they proceeded to Gilbert and Whitney's store for the same purpose, but Gilbert agreeing to shut it, and box the goods soon, they concluded to let it alone.' *Times and Seasons*, i. 18; *Pratt's Persecution of the Saints*, 29.

[39] 'A number more were taken, but succeeded in escaping through the over-anxiety of their keepers, who crowded forward to enjoy the sport.' *Times and Seasons*, i. 18.   Phelps the editor was one. *Smucker's Hist. Mor.*, 89.   Partridge says the mob was led by George Simpson. *Times and Seasons*, vi. 819.

[40] Spoken by Lilburn W. Boggs, lieutenant-governor, a man who thenceforward appears to have persecuted the Mormons with unrelenting hostility. He 'was in the immediate neighborhood of the riot, but declined to take any part in preserving the peace.' *Smucker's Hist. Mor.*, 89–90; *Times and Seasons*, vi. 819.

[41] Six persons signed the agreement that one half of the Mormons should leave in January and one half in April 1834, the publication of the paper to be discontinued. *Mackay's The Mormons*, 76; *Pratt's Persecution*, 30.

was despatched to Kirtland to consult as to what was best to be done. Meanwhile, incendiary articles appeared in the *Western Monitor*, printed at Fayette, Missouri. "Two years ago," said that journal, "some two or three of this people made their appearance on the upper Missouri, and they now number some twelve hundred souls in this county." They look at the land as theirs to inherit, by either fair means or foul; and when the officers of law and government shall be Mormon, we must go. "One of the means resorted to by them, in order to drive us to emigrate, is an indirect invitation to the free brethren of color in Illinois to come up like the rest to the land of Zion." True, they deny this, but that is only subterfuge. So it is resolved that no more Mormons shall be permitted to come; that those here must go within a reasonable time; and that the *Star* printing-office shall be declared confiscated.

An appeal was made to the governor, Daniel Dunklin, for redress, and while awaiting the answer matters were continued much in the usual way. The brethren were instructed by their elders not to retaliate, but to bear all with meekness and patience. At length a letter came from the governor, assuring them of his protection, and advising them to resort to the courts for damages. The church leaders ordered that none should leave Independence except those who had signed an agreement to that effect. Four lawyers were engaged for one thousand dollars to carry the matter into the courts. No sooner was this known than the whole country rose in arms and made war upon the Mormons. On the nights of October 30th, 31st, and November 1st, armed men attacked branches of the church west of Big Blue, and at the prairie unroofed the houses and beat the men. Almost simultaneously attacks were made at other points. Stones flew freely in Independence, and houses were destroyed and the inmates wounded. Gilbert's store was broken open, and the goods scat-

tered in the streets.   On November 2d thirty saints
retired with their families and effects to a point half a
mile from town.   Next day four of the brethren went to
Lexington for a peace warrant, but the circuit judge
refused to issue one through fear of the mob.   "You
had better fight it out and kill the outlaws if they
come upon you," said the judge.[42]   The saints then
armed, and on the 4th there was a fight, in which two
gentiles and one Mormon were killed, and several on
both sides wounded.   One of the store-breakers was
brought before the court, and during the trial the
populace became so furious that Gilbert, Morley, and
Corrill were thrust into jail for protection.   The morning of the 5th broke with signs of yet more bloody
determination on both sides.   The militia were called
out to preserve the peace, but this only made matters
worse.   The lieutenant-governor, Boggs, pretending
friendship, got possession of the Mormons' arms, and
seized a number to be tried for murder.[43]   Further
and yet more violent attacks were made; hope was
abandoned; the now defenceless saints were forced to
fly in every direction, some out into the open prairie,
some up and some down the river.   "The struggle
was over," writes Pratt, "our liberties were gone!"
On the 7th both banks were lined with men, women,
and children, with wagons, provisions, and personal
effects.   Cold weather came on with wind and rain,
to which most of the fugitives were exposed, few of
them having tents.   Some took refuge in Clay county,
some in Lafayette county, and elsewhere.[44]

   Throughout all these trying scenes, Governor

[42] *Pratt's Autobiography*, 105; *Mackay's The Mormons*, 77–8; *Pratt's
Persecution*, 31–6.
   [43] In a memorial to the legislature of Missouri, dated Far West, Dec. 10,
1838, and signed by nine prominent Mormons, is this statement: 'A battle
took place in which some two or three of the mob and one of our people were
killed.   This raised, as it were, the whole county in arms, and nothing could
satisfy them but an immediate surrender of the arms of our people, and they
forthwith had to leave the county.   Fifty-one guns were given up, which
have never been returned or paid for to this day.'
   [44] 'About 1,500 people were expelled from Jackson co. in Nov. 1833, and
about 300 of their houses burned.' Geo. A. Smith, in *Deseret News*, June 30,

Dunklin endeavored to uphold the law, but Boggs, lieutenant-governor, was with the assailants. Wells, attorney-general, wrote to the council for the church, the 21st, saying that if they wished to replace their houses in Jackson county the governor would send them an adequate force, and if they would organize themselves into companies, he would supply them with arms. Application was made accordingly. "It is a disgrace to the state," writes Judge Ryland, "for such acts to happen within its limits, and the disgrace will attach to our official characters if we neglect to take proper means to insure the punishment due such offenders." In view of this advice from the state authorities, the saints resolved to return to their homes as soon as protection should be afforded them, and it was ordered by revelation that they should do so, but with circumspection and not in haste.[45]

All this time President Joseph Smith was at Kirtland, harassed with anxiety over affairs in Missouri, still pursuing the usual tenor of his way, and not knowing what moment like evils might befall him and his fold there.[46] It was resolved by the first presidency that the *Star* should be published at Kirtland

1869, 247. 'Several women thus driven from their homes gave birth to children in the woods and on the prairies.' *Greene's Facts*, 18. Pratt says 203 houses were burned, according to the estimate of the enemy.

[45] On Dec. 15th, Phelps writes to Smith from Clay co.: 'The situation of the saints, as scattered, is dubious, and affords a gloomy prospect...We are in Clay, Ray, Lafayette, Jackson, Van Buren, etc. [counties], and cannot hear from each other oftener than we do from you...The governor is willing to restore us, but as the constitution gives him no power to guard us when back, we are not willing to go. The mob swear if we come we shall die! Our people fare very well, and when they are discreet, little or no persecution is felt. The militia in the upper counties is in readiness at a moment's warning, having been ordered out by the governor, to guard a court-martial and court of inquiry, etc., but we cannot attend a court of inquiry on account of the expense, until we are restored and protected.' *Times and Seasons*, vi. 944.

[46] Smith wrote to the saints about this time that he had heard they had surrendered their arms and fled across the river. If this report was true, he advised them not to recommence hostilities; but if they were still in possession, they should 'maintain the ground as long as there is a man left.' They were also advised to prosecute to the extent of the law; but must not look for pecuniary assistance from Kirtland, for matters there were by no means in a flourishing condition. It was recommended that a tract of land be purchased in Clay co. for present necessaries. *Times and Seasons*, vi. 914–15.

until it could be reinstated in Missouri; another journal, the *Latter-day Saints' Messenger and Advocate,*
was also established at Kirtland, and a mission organized for Canada.[47]

The work of proselyting continued east and west
without abatement through the year 1834. Two by
two and singly the elders went forth: Lyman Johnson and Milton Holmes to Canada, also Zebedee Coltrin and Henry Harriman; John S. Carter and Jesse
Smith should go eastward together, also James Durfee and Edward Marvin. Elders Oliver Granger,
Martin Harris, and Brigham Young preferred to
travel alone. To redeem the farm on which stood
the house of the Lord, elders Orson Hyde and Orson
Pratt were sent east to solicit funds. The movements
of many others of the brethren are given. Parley
Pratt and Lyman Wight were instructed not to return
to Missouri until men were organized into companies of

---

[47] 'Concerning our means of diffusing the principles we profess, we have
used the art of printing almost from the beginning of our work. At Independence, Missouri, in 1832-3-4, two volumes of the *Evening and Morning
Star* were issued by William W. Phelps and Oliver Cowdery. This was a
monthly octavo of 16 pages, devoted to the faith and doctrines of the church,
and was continued from Independence from June 1832 until July 1833, when
its publication was transferred to Kirtland, Ohio, from whence it was continued until September 1834, when it gave place to the *Latter-day Saints' Messenger and Advocate,* which continued to cheer the persecuted saints until
August 1837, when there appeared in its columns a prospectus for a new
paper to be published at Kirtland, called the *Elders' Journal of the Church
of Latter-day Saints,* also a monthly, the first number of which bore date
October 1837. The gathering of the people from Kirtland to Far West in
Missouri transferred the publication of the journal also to that place, from
whence it issued until stopped by the persecution and extermination of the
saints in the fall and winter of 1838 from the state of Missouri. The first
number of the *Millennial Star* was issued at Liverpool in May 1840, at first a
monthly, then fortnightly, and for many years a weekly, with at one time a
circulation of 22,000 copies, edited and published variously by elders appointed
and sent to edit the paper, manage the emigration, and preside over the
work generally in the European countries. This work is still issued weekly,
and greatly aids the cause in Europe. The *Skandinaviens' Stjerne* has been
published in Copenhagen nearly thirty years in the Danish language, edited
by those who have from time to time presided over the Scandinavian missions.
The first number was issued in 1851, and is well supported, being a great aid
in the missionary service in northern Europe. For several years a periodical
entitled the *Udgorn Seion* was published at Merthyr Tydfil, and was continued until the number of saints in the Welsh mission was so reduced by emigration as to render its further publication impracticable.' *Richards' Bibliography of Utah,* MS., 7-9.

ten, twenty, fifty, or one hundred. Thereupon these and others went out in various directions to raise men and means for a religio-military expedition to Missouri. There were churches now in every direction, and the brethren were scattered over a broad area.

Several appeals for redress were made by the saints at Independence to the governor of Missouri, and to the president of the United States. The president said it was a matter for the governor to regulate, and the governor did not see what could be done except through the courts. A court of inquiry was instituted, which decided, but to little purpose, that there was no insurrection on the 5th of November, 1833, and therefore the arms taken by the militia from the Mormons on that occasion must be restored to them.[48] "And now a commandment I give unto you concerning Zion, that you shall no longer be bound as an united order to your brethren of Zion, only in this wise; after you are organized you shall be called the united order of this stake of Zion, the city of Shinehah,[49] and your brethren, after they are organized, shall be called the united order of the city of Zion."

On the 7th of May, 1834, a military company was organized at Kirtland under the name of Zion's camp, consisting of one hundred and fifty brethren, mostly young men, elders, priests, teachers, and deacons, with

---

[48] 'About this time a court of inquiry held at Liberty for the purpose of investigating the action of Col Pitcher, in connection with the expulsion of the saints from Jackson co., found sufficient evidence against that officer to result in his being placed in arrest for trial by court-martial. The plant of the printing-office was given by the citizens to Davis & Kelly, who removed it to Liberty, where they commenced the publication of a weekly paper called the *Missouri Enquirer*.' 'The citizens also paid $300 on the $1,000 note given by the elders to their lawyers, thus acknowledging their action had been wrong.' *Times and Seasons*, vi. 961. 'The governor also ordered them to restore our arms which they had taken from us, but they never were restored.' *Pratt's Persecution*, 52. See also *Tayl er's Mormons*, xliii.–xlvi.; *Deseret News*, Dec. 27, 1851, and June 30, 1869; *Utah Tracts*, no. 4, 56–64; *Millennial Star*, xxv. 535–6, 550–2; *Gunnison's Mormons*, 104–14; *Ferris' Utah and Mormons*, 87–8.

[49] They 'called their Kirtland colony Shinahar.' *Gunnison's Mormons*, 167.

F. G. Williams paymaster and Zerubbabel Snow commissary general. They had twenty wagons loaded
with arms and effects, and next day set out for Missouri, President Smith joining them, leaving Rigdon
and Cowdery to look after matters in Ohio. They
passed through Ohio, Indiana, and Illinois, reaching
Missouri[50] in June, Pratt and others still continuing

[50] 'They were trying times, requiring the combined wisdom of the prophet
and his head men...But the prophet more readily discovered the new advantages that would ultimately accrue to his cause by a little perseverance. He
well knew that the laws could not continue to be violated in our country for
any length of time, and that he and his followers would, in the end, be the
greatest gainers by the cry of persecution which they could raise...A revelation was printed in the form of a handbill. It was taken up by all their
priests and carried to all their congregations, some of which were actually sold
for one dollar per copy. Preparations immediately began to be made for a
crusade to their holy land to drive out the infidels...Old muskets, rifles, pistols, rusty swords, and butcher knives were soon put in a state of repair and
scoured up. Some were borrowed and some were bought, on a credit if possible, and others were manufactured by their own mechanics...About the first
of May the grand army of fanatics commenced its march in small detachments
from the different places of concentration. On the 3d the prophet, with a life
guard of about 80 men, the elite of his army, left his quarters in Kirtland
with a few baggage wagons, containing their arms, ammunition, stores, etc.
...On arriving at Salt Creek, Illinois, they were joined by Lyman Wight
and Hyrum Smith, brother of the prophet, with a reënforcement of twenty
men, which they had picked up on the way. Here the grand army, which
being fully completed, encamped for the space of three days. The whole
number was now estimated at 220, rank and file. During their stay here the
troops were kept under a constant drill of manual exercise with guns and
swords, and their arms put in a state of repair; the prophet became very expert with a sword, and felt himself equal to his prototype Coriantumr. He
had the best sword in the army; probably a true model of Laban's, if not the
identical one itself, an elegant brace of pistols, which were purchased on a
credit of six months, a rifle, and four horses. Wight was appointed second
in command, or fighting general, who, together with the prophet, had an armor-bearer appointed, selected from among the most expert tacticians, whose
duty it was to be in constant attendance upon their masters with their arms.'
Howe's Mormonism Unveiled, 147–59. 'Cholera broke out in his camp on
the 24th of June, and Joseph attempted to cure it by laying on of hands and
prayer...Joseph lost thirteen of his band by the ravages of the disease...
He arrived in Clay co. on the 2d, and started back for Kirtland on the 9th...
Short as was the time he stayed, he did not depart without organizing and
encouraging the main body...and establishing the community in Clay co. on
a better footing than when he arrived.' *Mackay's The Mormons*, 85. Churches
were visited in New York, Pennsylvania, and the New England States, about
100 recruits obtained, and 50 more in the vicinity of Kirtland. The first detachment, about 100 strong, left Kirtland May 5th, and by the next Sunday
about 60 more had joined, part from Ohio and part from the east. The body
was organized in companies of tens, each being furnished with camp equipage.
Messes for cooking purposes were formed, and guards mounted at night.
Deseret News, Oct. 19, 1869. These men were well armed. A detachment of
twenty men had preceded them as an advanced guard. *Remy's Journey*, i.
297. They were divided into companies of 12, consisting of 2 cooks, 2 fire-
men, 2 tent-makers, 2 watermen, one runner or scout, one commissary, and 2

their efforts en route as recruiting officers. It was an army of the Lord; they would not be known as Mormons, which was a name they hated; moreover, they would be incognito; and the better to accomplish all these purposes, three days before they started, Sidney Rigdon proposed in conference that the name by which hereafter they would call themselves should be The Church of Jesus Christ of Latter-day Saints, which proposal was adopted.[51] On the way the breth-

wagoners. 20 wagons accompanied them, and they had fire-arms and all sorts of munitions of war of the most portable kind for self-defence. *Smucker's Hist. Mor.*, 95; *Times and Seasons*, vi. 1074. On June 3d, when in camp on the Illinois River, Smith had a mound opened and took out a skeleton, between whose ribs an arrow was sticking. A revelation followed, in which the prophet was informed that the bones were those of a white Lamanite, a warrior named Zelph, who served under the great prophet Omandagus. *Times and Seasons*, vi. 1076; *Smucker's Hist. Mor.*, 95–6; *Remy's Journey*, i. 297; *Ferris' Utah and the Mormons*, 83–4. June 4th to 6th was occupied in crossing the Mississippi, there being but one boat. The company now consisted of 205 men and 25 wagons, with 2 or 3 horses each. The company camped on Rush Creek, Clay co., on June 23d, and on the night of the 24th the cholera broke out among them, causing several deaths. On the 25th Smith broke up his command, and the men were scattered among their neighbors. *Times and Seasons*, vi. 1076, 1088, 1105–6; *Deseret News*, Oct. 19, 1864. Up to June 22d, Smith had travelled incognito, apparently fearing assassination. *Times and Seasons*, vi. 1104. A list of the members of Zion's camp will be found in *Deseret News*, Oct. 19, 1864, and those living in 1876 in *Id.*, Apr. 26, 1876. Smith disbanded his forces in obedience to a revelation. *Doctrine and Covenants*, 345–9. As the prophet approached Missouri he selected a body-guard of 20 men, appointing his brother Hyrum as their captain, and another brother, George, his armor-bearer. He also appointed a general, who daily inspected the army and drilled them. *Smucker's Hist. Mor.*, 99. On April 10, 1834, the president was again petitioned from Liberty, Mo. (a petition had been sent on in October 1833); the persecutions were recounted, it was related that an unavailing appeal had been made to the state executive, and it was asked that they be restored to the lands in Jackson co. they had purchased from the U. S. For text of correspondence, etc., see *Times and Seasons*, vi. 1041–2, 1056–9, 1071–8, 1088–92, 1103, 1107–9, 1120–4. On the march Pratt still acted as recruiting officer, and visited the churches in Ohio, Indiana, Illinois, and Missouri, obtaining men and money which he forwarded to the main body from time to time. *Pratt's Autobiog.*, 122–3. The band finally numbered 205 in all. *Utah Pioneers, 33d Anniversary*, 17. The march to Clay co., Mo., occupied 46 days, 9 of which were spent in camp. During the existence of the body 2 deserted because they could not fight the mob, and one left without a discharge; the rest remained faithful. *Deseret News*, Oct. 19, 1864. Further details of the march will be found in *Mackay's Mormons*, 80–5; *Kidder's Mormonism*, 111–16; *Howe's Mormonism Unveiled*, 156–63. Campbell and others who threatened to attack Smith were drowned by the upsetting of a boat whilst attempting to cross the Missouri. Campbell's vow, and what became of it. *Smucker's Hist. Mor.*, 100. When the prophet returned to Kirtland, in August, the council met and proceeded to investigate charges against Smith and others on this march. *Deseret News*, Nov. 15 and 29, 1851.

[51] The society never styled themselves Mormons; it is a name popularly attached to them. The true name is Latter-day Saints. *Pratt's Persecution*, 21.

ren learned of the outrages which had again occurred in Jackson county.

Just before his arrival in Clay county, Missouri, a committee of citizens waited on President Smith and proposed the purchase of the lands in Jackson county from which the Mormons had been driven. The offer was declined, the president and council making the following proposal in return: Let each side choose six men, and let the twelve determine the amount of damages due to the Mormons, and also the value of the possessions of all those who do not wish to live near them in peace, and the money shall be paid within a year. The offer was not accepted.[52]

On the 3d of July a high council of twelve was organized by the head of the church, with David Whitmer as president and W. W. Phelps and John Whitmer as assistant presidents. The twelve were: Simeon Carter, Parley P. Pratt, Wm E. McLellan, Calvin Beebe, Levi Jackman, Solomon Hancock, Christian Whitmer, Newel Knight, Orson Pratt, Lyman Wight, Thomas B. Marsh, and John Murdock. Later Phelps became president of the church in Missouri. In company with his brother Hyrum, F. G. Williams, and W. E. McLellan, President Joseph returned to Kirtland, arriving about the 1st of August.

"Now, that the world may know that our faith in the work and word of the Lord is firm and unshaken, and to shew all nations, kindreds, tongues, and peoples that our object is good, for the good of all, we come before the great family of mankind for peace, and ask their hospitality and assurance for our comfort, and the pres-

Hyde, *Mormonism*, 202, states that the sect was first called The Church of Jesus Christ of Latter-day Saints by Sidney Rigdon at a convention at Kirtland May 4, 1834. See chap. iii., note 22.

[52] When the camp arrived near Salt River, Orson Hyde and Parley P. Pratt were despatched to Jefferson City to request military aid from Gov. Dunklin, in repossessing the saints of their lands in Jackson co., which aid was refused. *Pratt's Autobiog.*, 123–4. Upon the approach of Smith and his party the people of Jackson co. held a meeting and sent a committee to Smith with proposals to buy all the Mormon property in the county. The offer was declined, and the Mormons in turn offered to buy out the Missourians. See correspondence in *Howe's Mormonism*, 164–76.

ervation of our persons and property, and solicit their charity for the great cause of God. We are well aware that many slanderous reports and ridiculous stories are in circulation against our religion and society; but as wise men will hear both sides and then judge, we sincerely hope and trust that the still small voice of truth will be heard, and our great revelations read and candidly compared with the prophecies of the bible, that the great cause of our redeemer may be supported by a liberal share of public opinion, as well as the unseen power of God. The faith and religion of the latter-day saints are founded upon the old scriptures, the book of Mormon, and direct revelation from God." Thus far have I given the History of Joseph Smith, in substance as written by himself in his journal,[53] and

[53] The most complete history of the early Mormon church is the *Journal of Joseph Smith*, extracts from which were made by himself, so as to form a consecutive narrative, under title of *History of Joseph Smith*, and published in *Times and Seasons*, beginning with vol. iii. no. 10, March 15, 1842, and ending Feb. 15, 1846, after the prophet's death. The narrative would fill a good-sized 12mo volume. It is composed largely of revelations, which, save in the one point of commandment which it was the purpose specially to give, are all quite similar. Publication of the *Times and Seasons* was begun at Commerce, afterward called Nauvoo, Illinois, Nov. 1839, and issued monthly. The number for May 1840 was dated Nauvoo. Later it was published semi-monthly, and was so continued till Feb. 1846. It is filled with church proceedings, movements of officers, correspondence of missionaries, history, and general information, with some poetry. To write a complete history of the Mormons down to 1846 without these volumes would not be possible. The names of E. Robinson and D. C. Smith first appear as publishers, then Robinson alone, then D. C. Smith, then E. Robinson and G. Hills, next Joseph Smith, and finally John Taylor. The organ of that branch of the church which remained in Iowa was the *Frontier Guardian*, published by Orson Hyde at Potawatamie, or Kanesville, 1849–52, and of the church in Utah the *Deseret News*, which was first issued at Salt Lake City in June 1850.

'At the organization of this church, the Lord commanded Joseph the prophet to keep a record of his doings in the great and important work that he was commencing to perform. It thus became a duty imperative. After John Whitmer and others had purloined the records in 1838, the persecution and expulsion from Missouri soon followed. When again located, now in Nauvoo, Illinois, and steamboat loads of emigrants were arriving from England via New Orleans, the sound thereof awakened an interest in the country that led Hon. John Wentworth, of Chicago, to write to the prophet, Joseph Smith, making inquiries about the rise, progress, persecution, and faith of the Latter-day Saints, the origin of this work, the *Book of Mormon*, the plates from which the record was translated, etc.; and it is the answer to this letter contained in *Times and Seasons*, March 1, 1842, that precedes or prefaces the present history of Joseph Smith, which is the history of the Church of Jesus Christ of Latter-day Saints. This request of Mr Wentworth's seemed to forcibly remind the prophet of the importance of having the history of his wonderful work restored to such a condition that correct

printed in the *Times and Seasons,* which ends here.
It is taken up in the *Millennial Star,* in diary form,
beginning with volume xv. and continuing to the day
of his death.

information could be given to editors, authors, publishers, and any or all
classes of inquirers that might apply, and he undertook with his clerks, recorder, and all available aid from private journals, correspondence, and his
own indelible memory, and made it a labor to get his own history, which was
indeed that of the church in all the stages of its growth, while he remained
with his people, compiled and written up to date, which with his own current journal enabled the historian to complete the history to the time of his
assassination, with the utmost fidelity to facts as they occurred.   Our method
of verification, after compilation and rough draft, was to read the same before a session of the council, composed of the First Presidency and Twelve
Apostles, and there scan everything under consideration.' *Richards' Bibliography of Utah,* MS., 2-6.

CHAPTER V.

THE STORY OF MORMONISM.

1835–1840.

PRESIDENT SMITH AT KIRTLAND—FIRST QUORUM OF TWELVE APOSTLES—THE
KIRTLAND TEMPLE COMPLETED—KIRTLAND SAFETY SOCIETY BANK—IN
ZION AGAIN—THE SAINTS IN MISSOURI—APOSTASY—ZEAL AND INDIS-
CRETION—MILITARY ORGANIZATION—THE WAR OPENS—DEPREDATIONS
ON BOTH SIDES—MOVEMENTS OF ATCHISON, PARKS, AND DONIPHAN—
ATTITUDE OF BOGGS—WIGHT AND GILLIAM—DEATH OF PATTEN—DANITE
ORGANIZATION—ORDER LODGE—HAUN MILL TRAGEDY—MOBS AND
MILITIA—THE TABLES TURNED—BOGGS' EXTERMINATING ORDER—LUCAS
AND CLARK AT FAR WEST—SURRENDER OF THE MORMONS—PRISONERS—
PETITIONS AND MEMORIALS—EXPULSION—GATHERING AT QUINCY—
OPINIONS.

MEANWHILE, although the frontier of Zion was receiving such large accessions, the main body of the
church was still at Kirtland, where President Smith
remained for some time.

On the 14th of February, 1835, twelve apostles
were chosen at Kirtland, Brigham Young, Orson
Hyde, and Heber C. Kimball being of the number;
likewise a little later Parley P. Pratt. Thence, the
following summer, they took their departure for the
east, holding conferences and ordaining and instructing elders in the churches throughout New York and
New England, and the organization of the first quorum
of seventies was begun. Classes for instruction, and
a school of prophets were commenced, and Sidney
Rigdon delivered six lectures on faith, of which Joseph
Smith was author.[1] Preaching on the steps of a

---

[1] They were printed and bound in *Doctrine and Covenants*. See *Hyde's
Mormonism*, 202; *Remy's Journey*, 504; *Pratt's Autobiography*, 139. Mather,
in *Lippincott's Mag.*, Aug. 1880, states that the twelve apostles started in
May.

Campbellite church at Mentor, Parley P. Pratt was mobbed midst music and rotten eggs.

The temple at Kirtland being finished, was dedicated on the 27th of March, 1836, and on the 3d of April Joseph and Oliver had interviews with the messiah, Moses, Elias, and Elijah, and received from them the several keys of priesthood, which insured to their possessors power unlimited in things temporal and spiritual for the accomplishment of the labors assigned by them for him to perform.[2] The building of this structure by a few hundred persons, who, during the period between 1832 and 1836, contributed voluntarily of their money, material, or labor, the women knitting and spinning and making garments for the men who worked on the temple, was regarded with wonder throughout all northern Ohio. It was 60 by 80 feet, occupied a commanding position, and cost $40,000.

During its erection the saints incurred heavy debts for material and labor. They bought farms at high prices, making part payments, and afterward forfeiting them. They engaged in mercantile pursuits,

[2] 'A square mile was laid out in half-acre lots, and a number of farms were bought, the church farm being half a mile down one of the most beautiful valleys which it is possible to conceive in a range of country so uniformly level.' Mather, in *Lippincott's Mag.*, Aug. 1880. In May 1833 it was revealed that building should begin. Two houses 55 by 65 feet each were ordered, one for the presidency, the other for printing. Hyrum Smith and two others were presented with lots, and directions were sent to the faithful to subscribe money to aid in building a temple at Kirtland. *Times and Seasons*, vi. 769-70. Before its completion, private assemblies were held at the houses of the faithful, frequently at Smith's. When partly finished, schools were opened in several of the apartments. It was begun in June 1833, and dedicated March 27, 1836. A brief description of the building, arrangement of interior, etc., and a full account of the dedication and ordinary services are given in *Tullidge's Women,* 76, 80-95, 99-101. Daniel Tyler, in *Juvenile Instructor*, xiv. 283; *Busch, Gesch. der Morm.*, 74; *Kidder's Mormonism*, 124-6. Probably but little work was done on it in 1833, for about the front entrances the gilded inscription,' Built by the church of Jesus Christ, 1834,' still shines bright as ever. *Salt Lake Herald*, June 6, 1877. See also Smith's account in *Times and Seasons*, vi. 708-11, 723-6, and *Remy's Journey*, i. 302-4. For cuts of building, see *Young's Hist. of the Seventies*, 8; *Juvenile Instructor*, xiv. 283; *Pratt's Autobiog.*, 140. When nearly finished there was a debt on the building of from $15,000 to $20,000. *Kidder's Mormonism*, 124-6. Most of the workmen were dependent upon their labor for their daily food, which often consisted of corn meal alone, and that had been donated. *Juvenile Instructor*, 283. Writing in 1880, Mather says: 'The residences of Smith and Rigdon are almost under the eaves of the temple, and the theological seminary is now occupied by the methodists for a church.' *Lippincott's Mag.*, Aug. 1880.

buying merchandise in New York and elsewhere in excess of their ability to pay. They built a steam-mill, which proved a source of loss, and started a bank, but were unable to obtain a charter; they is-sued bills without a charter, however, in consequence of which they could not collect the money loaned, and after a brief struggle, and during a period of great apostasy, the bank failed. It was called the Kirtland Safety Society Bank, of which Rigdon was president and Smith cashier. All this time, writes Corrill, "they suffered pride to arise in their hearts, and became desirous of fine houses and fine clothes, and indulged too much in these things, supposing for a few months that they were very rich." Upon the failure of the bank in 1838, Smith and Rigdon went to Missouri, leaving the business in the hands of others to wind up.[3]

[3] 'They also suffered jealousies to arise among them, and several persons dissented from the church, and accused the leaders of the church with bad management, selfishness, etc....On the other hand, the leaders of the church accused the dissenters with dishonesty, want of faith and righteousness,... and this strife or opposition arose to a great height,...until Smith and Rig-don were obliged to leave Kirtland.' Corrill, in *Kidder's Mormonism*, 126–7. 'Subsequently they had a revelation,' another says, 'commanding them to establish a bank, which should swallow up all other banks. This was soon got into operation on a pretended capital of four millions of dollars, made up of real estate round about the temple.' John Hyde, *Mormonism*, 201, says that the bank, a store, and mill were started in Aug. 1831. Before me is one of their bills, dated Jan. 17, 1837, payable to C. Scott, or bearer. Mather says, *Lippincott's Mag.*, Aug. 1880: 'Richard Hilliard, a leading merchant of Cleveland, received their bills for a few days, and then took possession of all their available assets. They were also in debt for their farms, and for goods bought in New York. The bubble burst, and many in the vicinity of Kirtland were among the sufferers. Smith and Rigdon fled to Far West, after having been tarred and feathered for their peculiar the-ories of finance.' 'Chauncey G. Webb (father of Ann Eliza Young) assisted in founding this bank, giving Smith all he possessed outside of his house and shop toward completing the amount necessary for a capital on which to start the new enterprise. With the failure of the bank Webb lost everything.' *Young's Wife No. 19*, 33, 40–41; see account of formation of bank in *Ben-nett's Mormonism*, 135–6. 'Smith had a sort of bank issue on what was then called the wild-cat principle. His circulating medium had no redeeming basis, and was worthless in the hands of the people.' *Tucker's Mormonism*, 154–5. 'Smith had a revelation from the Lord, to the effect that his bank would be a pattern of all the banks in the United States, that it would speedily break, and that all the rest would follow the example. The bank was closed the same day.' *Hall's Mormonism*, 19. The bank failed in Nov. 1837. *Remy's Journey*, i. 504; *Busch, Gesch. der Morm.*, 84. 'By means of great activity and an actual capital of about $5,000, they succeeded in set-ting afloat from $50,000 to $100,000. The concern was closed up after

An endowment meeting, or solemn assembly, held in 1836 in the temple at Kirtland, is thus described by William Harris: "It was given out that those who were in attendance at that meeting should receive an endowment, or blessing, similar to that experienced by the disciples of Christ on the day of pentecost.

flourishing 3 or 4 weeks.' *Kidder's Mormonism*, 128. The building is now occupied by a private family. *Salt Lake S. W. Herald*, June 6, 1877. 'In order to pay the debt on the temple, they concluded to try mercantile business, and ran in debt in New York and elsewhere some $30,000 for goods, and shortly after, $50,000 or $60,000 more. In consequence of their ignorance of business and extravagance, the scheme proved a failure.' *Kidder's Mormonism*, 126, 128; *Smucker's Hist. Mor.*, 76. 'Gilbert and Whitney's store is still used for original purposes.' *Salt Lake Herald*, June 6, 1877. 'A poorly furnished country store, where commerce looks starvation in the face.' *Id.*, Nov. 17, 1877. 'Smith's store was seized and goods sold in Nov. 1839.' *Hyde's Mormonism*, 203; *Bennett's Mormonism*, 135. They also spent some thousands of dollars in building a steam-mill, which never profited them anything. *Kidder's Mormonism*, 126. 'The skeleton of a superannuated engine and its contrivances half buried in a heap of ashes—the shed that covered it having recently burned to the ground—marks the spot where stood the ashery and its successor, the Mormon saw-mill, at the foot of Temple hill.' *Salt Lake Herald*, Nov. 17, 1877. Heber C. Kimball, who went to Nauvoo in 1839, built a pottery at Kirtland, the ruins of which were to be seen in 1877. *Ibid.* 'After the temple was dedicated, the Kirtland high school was taught in the attic story by H. M. Hawes, prof. of Greek and Latin. There were from 130 to 140 students, divided into three departments—the classic, where only languages were taught; the English, where mathematics, common arithmetic, geography, English grammar, and reading and writing were taught; and the juvenile department. The last two departments were under assistant instructors. The school was begun in Nov. 1836.' *Tullidge's Women*, 99. 'On the 3d floor are a succession of small rooms containing crippled benches, blackboards, ruined walls, and other paraphernalia, which indicated that at some period of the temple's history this part had been used as a primary school.' *Salt Lake S. W. Herald*, June 6, 1877. A Hebrew professorship is also mentioned. *Remy's Journey*, i. 504. 'Immediately after the closing of the bank, and before the news of its failure had time to spread, Smith with some 4 or 5 terriers (understrappers in the priesthood) went to Toronto, Canada, where he preached, whilst his followers circulated the worthless notes of the defunct bank. Brigham Young also succeeded in spreading about $10,000 of the paper through several states.' *Hall's Mormonism*, 19-20. 'In January 1838 Smith and Rigdon, being at Kirtland together, were both arrested on charges of swindling in connection with their worthless paper bank,' etc. 'The prisoners, however, escaped from the sheriff in the night and made their way on horseback to Missouri.' *Tucker's Mormonism*, 155-6. Smith and Rigdon ran away on the night of Jan. 12, 1838. *Hyde's Mormonism*, 203. 'A new year dawned upon the church at Kirtland,' writes Smith, 'in all the bitterness of the spirit of apostate mobocracy, which continued to rage and grow hotter and hotter, until Elder Rigdon and myself were obliged to flee from its deadly influence, as did the apostles and prophets of old, and as Jesus said, "When they persecute you in one city, flee ye to another;" and on the evening of the 12th of January, about ten o'clock, we left Kirtland on horseback to escape mob violence, which was about to burst upon us, under the color of legal process to cover their hellish designs and save themselves from the just judgment of the law.'

When the day arrived great numbers convened from the different churches in the country. They spent the day in fasting and prayer, and in washing and perfuming their bodies; they also washed their feet, and anointed their heads with what they called holy oil, and pronounced blessings. In the evening they met for the endowment. The fast was then broken."

Midsummer of 1837 saw Parley P. Pratt in New York city, where he printed the first edition of his *Voice of Warning*,[4] and where he labored with great earnestness, at first under many discouragements, later with signal success. After that he went once more to Missouri. Others were going in the same direction from Kirtland and elsewhere during the entire period between 1831 and 1838. The *Messenger and Advocate* having been discontinued, the *Elder's Journal* was started by Joseph Smith in Kirtland in October 1837.

After the émeutes which occurred in Jackson county in the autumn of 1833, as before related, the saints escaped as best they were able to Clay county, where they were kindly received. Some took up their abode in Lafayette and Van Buren counties, and a few in Ray and Clinton counties.[5] For their lands, stock, furniture, buildings, and other property destroyed in Jackson county, they received little or no compensation; on the contrary, some who went back for their effects were caught and beaten.[6] Nevertheless, there

---

[4] It consisted of 4,000 copies. The author states that 'it has since been published and republished in America and Europe, till some 40,000 or 50,000 copies have not been sufficient to supply the demand.' *Pratt's Autobiography,* 184.

[5] Most of these fled into Clay co., where they were received with some degree of kindness, and encamped on the banks of the Missouri. Those who went into Van Buren and Lafayette counties were soon expelled, and had to move. *Pratt's Persecution,* 51; *Mackay's Mormons,* 78; *Times and Seasons,* vi. 913. The Missouri River bends to the east as it enters the state, and runs in a generally east direction through the western counties. Jackson co. is immediately south of Clay—the river being the dividing line—and Van Buren lies next south of Jackson. All west of the state line was Indian territory, as I have said. See map, p. 121 this vol.

[6] The Jackson co. exiles being in a destitute condition, a conference was

were three years of comparative rest for the people of
God, the effect of which soon appeared in Zion's
wilderness.

The men of Missouri were quite proud of what they
had done; they were satisfied on the whole with the
results, and though their influence was still felt, no
further violence was offered till the summer of 1836.
Then the spirit of mobocracy again appeared. The
Jackson-county boys had served themselves well;
why should they not help their neighbors? So they
crossed the river, in small squads at first, and began
to stir up enmity, often insulting and plundering their
victims, until the people of Clay county, fearing
actions yet worse, held a meeting, and advised the
saints to seek another home.[7]

For their unrelenting hostility toward the latter-
day saints, for the services rendered to their country
in defying its laws and encouraging the outrages upon
citizens at Independence and elsewhere during the
first Mormon troubles in Missouri, Boggs was made
governor of that state, Lucas major-general, and
Wilson brigadier-general.[8] After his election, as before, Boggs did not hesitate to let it be known that

held at P. P. Pratt's house in Clay co. (some time during the winter of 1833–
4—date not given), at which it was resolved to appeal to Smith, at Kirtland,
for aid and counsel; and P. P. Pratt and Lyman Wight, having volunteered
their services, were despatched with the message. Starting from Liberty on
Feb. 1, 1834, on horseback, but penniless, on a journey of from 1,000 to 1,500
miles, through a country but partially settled, they arrived at their destination early in the spring with plenty of money received from friends along their
route. *Pratt's Autobiog.*, 114–16; *Utah Pioneers, 33d Aniversary*, 17; *Horne's
Migrations*, MS., 3; *Young's Woman's Experiences*, MS., 2.

[7] 'From threats, public meetings were called, resolutions were passed, vengeance and destruction were threatened, and affairs again assumed a fearful
attitude.' *Cor. Joseph Smith, etc.*, 5. See also *Greene's Facts*, 12. 'A meeting of the citizens was held at Liberty on the 29th of June, 1836, in which
these matters were taken into consideration. The Mormons were reminded
of the circumstances under which they were received, and requested to leave,
time being given them to harvest their crops and dispose of their property.
Fortunately for all concerned, the saints...agreed to leave on the terms proposed, denying strenuously that they had ever tampered with the slaves, or
had any idea of exciting an Indian war.' *Ferris' Utah and the Mormons*, 82–3.

[8] These officers 'all very readily received their commissions from their accomplice, Gov. Boggs; and thus corruption, rebellion, and conspiracy had
spread on every side, being fostered and encouraged by a large majority of
the state; and thus treason became general.' *Pratt's Persecution*, 55–6.

any reports of misconduct, however exaggerated, would, if possible, be accepted as reliable. Such reports were accordingly circulated, and without much regard to truth. Right or wrong, law or no law, and whether in accord with the letter or spirit of the constitution or government of the United States or not, the people of Missouri had determined that they would go any length before they would allow the saints to obtain political ascendency in that quarter. It was well understood that war on the Mormons, war on their civil, political, and religious rights, nay, on their presence as members of the commonwealth, or if need be on their lives, was part of the policy of the administration.

Thereupon the Mormons petitioned the legislature to assign them a place of residence, and the thinly populated region afterward known as Caldwell county was designated. Moving there, they bought the claims of most of the inhabitants, and entered several sections of government lands. Almost every member of the society thus became a landholder, some having eighty acres, and some forty. A town was laid out, called Far West, which was made the county seat; they were allowed to organize the government of the county, and to appoint from among their own people the officers.[9] Again they found peace for a season, during which their numbers increased, while settlements were made in Daviess county and elsewhere.[10] Those in Daviess county were on terms of amity with their gentile neighbors. Wight was there, and when Smith and Rigdon arrived from the east they laid out a town named Diahman,[11] which soon rivalled Gallatin, and gradually the

[9] John Hyde, *Mormonism*, 203, says that on their arrival in Missouri, Smith and Rigdon began 'to scatter the saints in order to obtain political ascendency in other counties.'

[10] Of the officers then appointed, two of the judges, thirteen magistrates, all the military officers, and the county clerk were Mormons. 'These steps were taken, be it carefully observed, by the advice of the state legislature, and the officers were appointed in the manner directed by law.' *Greene's Facts*, 18. The gentiles murmur because of their being under Mormon rule. *Hyde's Mormonism*, 203.

[11] 'Smith gave it the name of Adamondiamon, which he said was formerly

people of Daviess, like the rest, began to war upon the Mormons.[12]

To add to the ever-thickening troubles of the prophet, a schism broke out in the church about this time, and there were apostates and deserters, some because of disappointed ambition, and some from shame of what they now regarded as a delusion, but all carrying away with them vindictive feelings toward their former associates, whom they did not hesitate to denounce as liars, thieves, counterfeiters, and everything that is vile. Among these were Joseph's old friends Martin Harris, Oliver Cowdery, and David Whitmer, the three witnesses to the book of Mormon; Orson Hyde, Thomas B. Marsh, and W. W. Phelps also seceding.[13]

given to a certain valley where Adam, previous to his death, called his children together and blessed them.' *Corrill's Brief History*, in *Kidder's Mormonism*, 131. 'The earth was divided,' says Mr Richards, 'all the land being together and all the water. Adam dwelt there with his people for some time previous to his death. Adam constructed an altar there, and it was there that he bestowed his final blessings upon his descendants.' The place was also called Adam-On-Diahman, Adam-on-di-ahman, and again Diahman. The second of these names appears to have been the one in use among the saints. After the foundations of the temple at Far West were relaid, between midnight of the 25th and dawn of the 26th of April, 1839, the quorum sang the song which they called Adam-on-di-ahman. *Tullidge's Life of Brigham Young*.

[12] They were afraid the Mormons would 'rule the county, and they did not like to live under the laws and administration of Jo Smith.' *Ibid.*

[13] The first three were themselves accused of counterfeiting coin, and defaming Smith's character; and others charged Smith with 'being accessory to several murders and many thefts, and of designing to rule that part of the state of Missouri, and eventually the whole republic.' *Hyde's Mormonism*, 204; *Mackay's The Mormons*, 86. 'At Independence, Rigdon publicly charged Oliver Cowdery and David Whitmer with being connected with a gang of counterfeiters, etc. Cowdery was afterward arraigned before the church, and found guilty of "disgracing the church by being connected with the bogus business, as common report says."' *Tucker's Origin and Prog. Mor.*, 158–9. 'Brother Turley could not be surpassed at "*bogus*." A press was prepared, and the money, composed of zinc, glass, etc., coated with silver, was executed in the best style. Imitations both of gold and silver were in general circulation and very difficult to detect. In fact, for a time, scarcely any other circulating medium was to be found among them.' When leaving Illinois for Council Bluffs, Hall carried in his wagon for some distance on the way a bogus press, which was afterwards sold on credit in Missouri, but the seller never got his money, being afraid to go for it. *Hall's Mor.*, 20–1. Hall, who was a Mormon from 1840 to 1847, mentions this counterfeiting in connection with the Kirtland bank swindle, but does not state when the work was begun. It may have originated in Kirtland, but probably was not carried on to any great extent before the migration to Illinois. These rambling and general charges should be received with every allowance. 'From some

At Far West on the 4th of July, 1838, assemble from the surrounding districts thousands of the saints, to lay the corner-stone of a temple of God, and to declare their rights as citizens of the commonwealth to safety and protection, as promised by the constitution. They are hated and despised, though they break not the laws of God; they are hunted down and killed, though they break not the laws of the land. To others their faith is odious, their words are odious, their persons and their actions are altogether detestable. They are not idlers, or drunkards, or thieves, or murderers; they are diligent in business as well as fervent in spirit, yet they are devils; they worship what they choose and in their own way, like the dissenters in Germany, the quakers in Pennsylvania, and the pilgrims from England, yet their spiritual father is Satan. And now, though thus marked for painful oppression by their fellow-citizens, they come together on the birthday of the nation to raise the banner of the nation, and under it to declare their solemn prerogative to the enjoyment of life, liberty, and the pursuit of happiness, to the maintainance of which they stand ready to pledge their lives, their fortunes, and their sacred honor. This they do. They raise the pole of liberty; they unfold the banner of liberty; they register their vows. Is it all in irony? Is it all a mockery? Or is it the displeasure of omnipotence, which is now displayed because of the rank injustice wrought by the sons of belial under this sacred emblem? God knoweth. We know only that out of heaven comes fire, blasting the offering of the saints![14]

distant bank,' continued Hall, 'they would buy quantities of its unsigned bank notes, which they took home, and after having them signed by competent artists, placed in circulation. In procuring these bills, no persons met. The package would be left by a window of the bank, with a pane out, and the package taken and its price left by the purchaser.'

[14] 'In a day or two after these transactions, the thunder rolled in awful majesty over the city of Far West, and the arrows of lightning fell from the clouds, and shivered the liberty pole from top to bottom; thus manifesting to many that there was an end to liberty and law in that state, and that our little city strove in vain to maintain the liberties of a country which was ruled by wickedness and rebellion.' *Pratt's Persecution*, 57.

Sidney Rigdon delivered the oration on this occasion; and being an American citizen, and one of the founders of an American religion, it was perhaps natural for him to indulge in a little Fourth-of-July oratory; it was natural, but under the circumstances it was exceedingly impolitic. "We take God to witness," cries Sidney, "and the holy angels to witness this day, that we warn all men, in the name of Jesus Christ, to come on us no more forever. The man or the set of men who attempt it, do it at the expense of their lives; and that mob that comes on us to disturb us, there shall be between us and them a war of extermination, for we will follow them till the last drop of their blood is spilled, or else they will have to exterminate us; for we will carry the war to their own houses, and their own families, and one party or the other shall be utterly destroyed."

On the 8th of July there was a revelation on tithing. Early in August a conference was held at Diahman, and a military company, called the Host of Israel, was organized after the manner of the priesthood, including all males of eighteen years and over. There were captains of ten, of fifty, and of a hundred; the organization included the entire military force of the church, as had the Kirtland army previously a part of it.[15]

At length the storm burst. The state election of 1838 was held in Daviess county at the town of Gallatin on the 6th of August. Soon after the polls were opened, William Peniston, candidate for the legislature, mounted a barrel and began to speak, attacking the Mormons with degrading epithets, calling them horse-thieves and robbers, and swearing they should not vote in that county. Samuel Brown, a Mormon, who stood by, pronounced the charges untrue, and said that for one he should vote. Immediately Brown was struck by one Weldin, whose arm, in attempting to repeat the blow, was caught by

[15] 'Every man obeyed the call.' *Lee's Mormonism*, 57.

another Mormon, named Durfee. Thereupon eight
or ten men, with clubs and stones, fell upon Durfee,
whose friends rallied to his assistance, and the fight
became general, but with indecisive results. The
Mormons voted, however, and the rest of the day
passed quietly.

THE WAR IN MISSOURI.

On the next day two or three of Peniston's party,
in order it was said to stir up the saints to violence,
rode over to Far West, one after another, and re-

ported a battle as having been fought at Gallatin, in which several of the fraternity were killed. Considerable excitement followed the announcement, and several parties went to Diahman to learn the truth of the matter. Ascertaining the facts, and being desirous of preventing further trouble, one of the brethren went to the magistrate, Adam Black, and proposed bonds on both sides to keep the peace. The proposition was accepted, Joseph Smith and Lyman Wight signing for the Mormons, and Black for the gentiles. The Mormons then returned to Far West; but the people of Daviess county, not approving the action of the magistrate, disputed Black's right to bind them; whereupon, to appease them, Black went to the circuit judge and obtained a writ for the arrest of Smith and Wight on a charge of having forced him, by threats of violence, to sign the agreement. Brought before Judge King at Gallatin, Smith and Wight were released on their own recognizances.

Nevertheless the excitement increased. In Daviess and adjacent counties, three hundred gentiles met and armed. The Mormons say that the gentiles made prisoners, and shot and stole cattle, and the gentiles say that the Mormons did the same.[16] Finally affairs became so alarming that Major-General Atchison concluded to call out the militia of Ray and Clay counties, under command of generals Doniphan and Parks, the latter being stationed in Daviess county.[17] Their purposes in that quarter being thus defeated, the men of Missouri threw themselves on a small settlement of saints at Dewitt, where they were joined by a party with a six-pounder from Jackson county. Setting fire

[16] In Daviess county the saints killed between 100 and 200 hogs and a number of cattle, took at least forty or fifty stands of honey, and at the same time destroyed several fields of corn. The word was out that the Lord had consecrated through the bishop the spoils unto his host. *Harris' Mormonism Portrayed*, 30–1.

[17] 'One thousand men were then ordered into service under the command of Major-General Atchison and brigadier-generals Parks and Doniphan. These marched to Daviess co., and remained in service thirty days. But judging from the result, they had no intention of coming in contact with the mob, but only to make a show of defending one neighborhood while the mob was allowed to attack another.' *Pratt's Autobiography*, 191.

to the houses, they drove off the inmates and destroyed their property. General Parks then moved his troops to Dewitt, but found the mob too many for him. They openly defied him, would make no compromise, and swore "they would drive the Mormons from Daviess to Caldwell, and from Caldwell to hell." General Atchison then went to Dewitt and told the Mormons that his men were so disaffected[18] that they had better apply for protection to Governor Boggs. This official returned answer that, as they had brought the war upon themselves, they must fight their own battles, and not look to him for help. Thereupon they abandoned the place, and fled to Far West.

In order to intercept the mob General Doniphan entered Daviess county with two hundred men, and thence proceeded to Far West, where he camped for the night. In consultation with the civil and military officers of the place, who, though Mormons, were nevertheless commissioned by the state, Doniphan advised them to arm and march to Daviess county and defend their brethren there. Acting on this advice, all armed, some going to Daviess county and some remaining at Far West.[19] The former were met by Parks, who inquired of them all particulars. Shortly afterward some families came in from beyond Grand River, who stated that they had been driven away and their houses burned by a party under C. Gilliam.[20] Parks then ordered Colonel Wight, who held a commission under him as commander of the

[18] 'At length the general (Atchison) informed the citizens that his forces were so small, and many of them so much in favor of the insurrectionists, that it was useless to look any longer to them for protection...After the evacuation of Dewitt, when our citizens were officially notified that they must protect themselves,...they assembled in Far West to the number of one thousand men, or thereabout, and resolved to defend their rights to the last.' *Pratt's Autobiography*, 192–3.

[19] 'The Mormons in Caldwell were the regular state militia for that county, and were at the time acting under the legal authorities of the county.' *Greene's Facts*, 20.

[20] 'A noted company of banditti, under the command of Cornelius Gilliam, who had long infested our borders and been notorious for their murders and daring robberies, and who painted themselves as Indian warriors, came pouring in from the west to strengthen the camp of the enemy.' *Pratt's Autobiography*, 202.

Mormon militia, to disperse the party, which was done, and the cannon in their possession seized, without firing a shot. Spreading into other counties, Gilliam's men raised everywhere the cry that the Mormons were killing people and burning property.

Soon afterward the Mormon militia returned from Daviess county to Far West, where they learned that a large force under Samuel Bogart, a methodist clergyman, was plundering and burning houses south of that point, in Ray county, and had taken three men prisoners, one only of whom was a Mormon. Elias Higbee, county judge, ordered the Mormon militia under Captain Patten[21] to retake the prisoners. In passing through a wood Patten came without knowing it upon the encampment of Bogart, whose guard fired without warning, killing one of Patten's men. Patten then attacked, routing Bogart's force, but not preventing the shooting of the Mormon prisoner, though he afterward recovered. In the charge one man was killed, and Patten and one other were mortally wounded. The company captured forty wagons.[22]

About this time arose the mysterious and much dreaded band that finally took the name of Danites, or sons of Dan, concerning which so much has been said while so little is known, some of the Mormons even denying its existence. But of this there is no question. Says Burton: "The Danite band, a name of fear in the Mississippi Valley, is said by anti-Mormons to consist of men between the ages of seventeen and forty-nine. They were originally termed Daughters of Gideon, Destroying Angels—the gentiles say devils—and, finally, Sons of Dan, or Danites, from one of whom was prophesied he should be a serpent in the path. They were organized about 1837 under D.

[21] Pratt, *Persecution*, 68, says that the detachment was under the command of Captain Durphey, aided by Patten.

[22] 'The enemy had left their horses, saddles, camp, and baggage in the confusion of their flight, which fell into our hands.' *Pratt's Persecution*, 72. 'We delivered the horses and spoils of the enemy to Col. Hinckle, the commanding officer of the regiment.' *Id.*, 74.

W. Patten, popularly called Captain Fearnot, for the purpose of dealing as avengers of blood with gentiles; in fact, they formed a kind of death society, desperadoes, thugs, hashshashiyun—in plain English, assassins in the name of the Lord. The Mormons declare categorically the whole and every particular to be the calumnious invention of the impostor and arch apostate, Mr John C. Bennett."[23]

John Hyde, a seceder, states that the Danite band, or the United Brothers of Gideon, was organized on the 4th of July, 1838, and was placed under the command of the apostle David Patten, who for the purpose assumed the name of Captain Fearnot.[24]

[23] John Corrill says that some time in June a secret society was formed of a few individuals who should be agreed in all things, and stand by each other, right or wrong, under all circumstances. Next to God was the first presidency; and they bound themselves by the most solemn covenants before the almighty that the presidency should be obeyed. 'Who started this society I know not,' writes Corrill; 'but Doctor Samson Avard was the most prominent leader and instructor, and was assisted by others. The first presidency did not seem to have much to do with it,...but I thought they stood as wireworkers behind the curtain.' 'Avard was very forward and indefatigable in accomplishing their purposes, for he devoted his whole talents to it, and spared no pains; and, I thought, was as grand a villain as his wit and ability would admit of...They ran into awful extremes,' seeming to think that they were called upon to execute the judgments of God on all their enemies. 'Dr Avard received orders from Smith, Rigdon, and company to destroy the paper containing the constitution of the Danite society, as, if it should be discovered, it would be considered treasonable. He did not, however, obey the orders, but after he was made prisoner he handed it to General Clark.' Kidder's Mormonism, 143. The constitution is published in Bennett's Mormonism Exposed, 265. 'The oath by which the Danites were bound in Missouri was altered in a secret council of the inquisition at Nauvoo so as to read: "In the name of Jesus Christ, the Son of God, I do solemnly obligate myself ever to regard the prophet and first presidency of the church of Jesus Christ of Latter-Day Saints, as the supreme head of the church on earth, and to obey them in all things the same as the supreme God; that I will stand by my brethren in danger or difficulty, and will uphold the presidency, right or wrong; and that I will ever conceal, and never reveal, the secret purposes of this society, called the Daughter of Zion. Should I ever do the same, I hold my life as the forfeiture, in a caldron of boiling oil."' Id., 267. The origin of the name Daughter of Zion may be found in Micah iv. 13.

[24] Hyde's Mormonism, 104. In Id., 104–5, Hyde writes as follows: 'When the citizens of Carroll and Daviess counties, Mo., began to threaten the Mormons with expulsion in 1838, a death society was organized under the direction of Sidney Rigdon, and with the sanction of Smith. Its first captain was Captain Fearnot, alias David Patten, an apostle. Its object was the punishment of the obnoxious. Some time elapsed before finding a suitable name. They desired one that should seem to combine spiritual authority with a suitable sound. Micah iv. 13, furnished the first name. "Arise and thresh, O daughter of Zion! for I will make thy horn iron, and thy hoofs brass; and thou shalt beat in pieces many people; and I will consecrate their gain unto the Lord, and their substance unto the Lord of the whole earth." This furnished them with

It is the opinion of some that the Danite band, or Destroying Angels as again they are called, was organized at the recommendation of the governor of Missouri as a means of self-defence against persecutions in that state.[25] Thomas B. Marsh, late president of the twelve apostles, and president of the church at Far West, but now a dissenter, having "abandoned the faith of the Mormons from a conviction of their immorality and impiety," testifies that in October, 1838, they "had a meeting at Far West, at which they appointed a company of twelve, by the name of the Destruction Company, for the purpose of burning and destroying."[26]

The apostate Bennett gives a number of names by which the same society, or divisions of it, were known, such as Daughter of Zion, Big Fan,[27] "inasmuch as it fanned out the chaff from the wheat," Brother of Gideon, Destructive, Flying Angel. The explanation of Joseph, the prophet, was that one Doctor Sampson Arvard, who after being a short time in the church, in order to add to his importance and influence secretly initiated the order of Danites, and held meet-

a pretext; it accurately described their intentions, and they called themselves the Daughters of Zion. Some ridicule was made at these bearded and bloody daughters, and the name did not sit easily. Destroying Angels came next; the Big Fan of the thresher that should thoroughly purge the floor was tried and dropped. Genesis, xlix. 17, furnished the name that they finally assumed. The verse is quite significant: "Dan shall be a serpent by the way, an adder in the path, that biteth the horse's heels, so that his rider shall fall backward." The sons of Dan was the style they adopted; and many have been the times that they have been adders in the path, and many a man has fallen backward, and has been seen no more.'

[25] See *Smucker's Hist. Mor.*, 108.

[26] 'The members of this order were placed under the most sacred obligations that language could invent...to stand by each other unto death,...to sustain, protect, defend, and obey the leaders of the church under any and all circumstances unto death.' To divulge a Danite secret was death. There were signs and tokens, the refusal to respect which was death. 'This sign or token of distress is made by placing the right hand on the right side of the face, with the points of the fingers upwards, shoving the hand upwards until the ear is snug up between the thumb and forefinger.' *Lee's Mormonism*, 57–8.

[27] 'The society was instituted for the purpose of driving out from the holy land, their earthly paradise, in Missouri, all apostates or dissenters... They make no scruple whatever to commit perjury, when deemed requisite for the welfare of their church...The number of Danites is now, 1842, about 2,000 or 2,500. From the élite of the Danites, or Daughters of Zion, twelve men are selected, who are called Destructives, or Destroying Angels, or Flying Angels.' *Mormonism Exposed*, 265–9.

ings organizing his men into companies of tens and
fifties, with captains. Then he called the officers
together and told them that they were to go forth
and spoil the gentiles; but they rejected the proposal,
and Arvard was cut off from the church. All the
present leaders of the Mormon church deny emphatically the existence of any such band or society as a
part of or having anything to do with their organization.[28]

[28] 'It was intended to enable him,' Smith, 'more effectually to execute
his clandestine purposes.' '"Milking the gentiles" is a kind of vernacular
term of the Mormons, and signifies the obtaining of money or property from
those who are not members of the Mormon church.' *Id.*, 272-8. 'In an examination before Judge King, Samuel (Samson?) Arvard testified that the
first object of the Danite band was to drive from the county of Caldwell all
those who dissented from the Mormon church, in which they succeeded admirably... The prophet Joseph Smith, Jr, together with his two counsellors Hyrum
Smith and Sidney Rigdon, were considered the supreme head of the church,
and the Danite band felt themselves as much bound to obey them as to obey
the supreme God.' John Corrill swore: 'I think the original object of the
Danite band was to operate on the dissenters; but afterwards it grew into a
system to carry out the designs of the presidency, and if it was necessary, to use physical force to uphold the kingdom of God.' John Cleminson
said: 'Whoever opposed the presidency in what they said or desired done
should be expelled the county or have their lives taken.' Wm W. Phelps,
for a season an apostate, testified: 'If any person spoke against the presidency they would hand him over to the hands of the Brothers of Gideon.'
'The object of the meeting seemed to be to make persons confess and repent
of their sins to God and the presidency.' 'Wight asked Smith, Jr, twice if
it had come to the point now to resist the laws. Smith replied the time had
come when he should resist all law.' *Ferris' Utah and the Mormons*, 92-3.
Arvard 'swore false concerning a constitution, as he said, that was introduced
among the Danites, and made many other lying statements in connection
therewith.' *Mem. to Leg.*, in *Greene's Facts*, 32-3. Says John Corrill in his
Brief History, 'A company, called the Fur Company, was raised for the purpose of procuring provisions, for pressing teams, and even men sometimes,
into the army in Caldwell.' Reed Peck testified that small companies were
sent out on various plundering expeditions; that he 'saw one of these companies on its return. It was called a fur company. Some had one thing,
some another; one had a feather-bed; another some spun yarn, etc. This fur
they were to take to the bishop's store, where it was to be deposited, and if
they failed to do this it would be considered stealing.' *Kidder's Mormonism*,
147-8. Affidavit of the city council, Nauvoo: 'We do further testify that
there is no such thing as a Danite society in this city, nor any combination
other than the Masonic of which we have any knowledge.' Signed by Wilson Law, John Taylor, Wilford Woodruff, and 10 others. *Millennial Star*, xix.
614. References to authorities speaking of the Danites: *Mackay's The Mormons*, 89-90, 116; *Lee's Mormonism*, 57-8, 156-60; *Olshausen, Gesch. d. Morm.*,
48; *Ferris' Utah and the Mormons*, 89; *Beadle's Life in Utah*, 389-90; *Burton's
City of the Saints*, 359; *Smucker's Hist. Mor.*, 108-9; *Young's Wife No 19*,
47-8, 268; *Busch, Gesch. der Morm.*, 87; *Marshall's Through Am.*, 215-16;
Hyde's Mormonism, 104-5; *Bennett's Mormonism Exposed*, 263-72; *Miller's
First Families*, 64-5; *Hickman's Brigham's Destroying Angel; Hall's Mormonism*, 94-5; *E. M. Webb*, in *Utah County Sketches*, MS., 49-50, the last named
referring to the rules and principles of the order of Enoch.

Meanwhile was being matured the bloody tragedy which occurred on the 30th of October near Haun's[29] mill, on Shoal creek, about twenty miles below Far West. Besides the Mormons living there, were a number of emigrants awaiting the cessation of hostilities before proceeding on their journey. It had been agreed between the Mormons and Missourians of that locality that they would not molest each other, but live together in peace. But the men of Caldwell and Daviess counties would not have it so. Suddenly and without warning, on the day above mentioned, mounted and to the number of two hundred and forty, they fell upon the fated settlement. While the men were at their work out of doors, the women in the house, and the children playing about the yards, the crack of a hundred rifles was heard, and before the firing ceased, eighteen of these unoffending people were stretched dead upon the ground, while many more were wounded. I will not enter upon the sickening details, which are copious and fully proven; suffice it to say, that never in savage or other warfare was there perpetrated an act more dastardly and brutal.[30] Indeed, it was openly avowed by the men of Missouri that it was no worse to shoot a Mormon than to shoot an Indian, and killing Indians was no worse than killing wild beasts.

A somewhat singular turn affairs take at this juncture. It appears that Boggs, governor, and sworn enemy of the saints, does not like the way the war is going on. Here are his own soldiers fighting his own voters, the state forces killing the men who have put

---

[29] Spelled also Hahn, Hohn, Hawn.

[30] 'Immediately after this, there came into the city a messenger from Haun's mill, bringing the intelligence of an awful massacre of the people who were residing in that place, and that a force of two or three hundred, detached from the main body of the army, under the superior command of Col. Ashley, but under the immediate command of Capt. Nehemiah Compstock, who, the day previous, had promised them peace and protection, but on receiving a copy of the governor's order to exterminate or to expel, from the hands of Col. Ashley, he returned upon them the following day, and surprised and massacred the whole population, and then came on to the town of Far West, and entered into conjunction with the main body of the army.' *Mackay's The Mormons*, 88-9.

him in office! This will not do. There is bad blundering somewhere. It is the Mormons only that are to be killed and driven off, and not the free and loyal American Boggs voters. Ho, there! Let the state arms be turned against these damned saints! On what pretext? Any. Say that they are robbing, and burning, and killing right and left, and that they swear they will never stop until they have the country. Easy enough. No doubt they do kill and burn; the men of Missouri are killing them and burning; why should they not retaliate? No doubt there are thieves and bad men among them, who take advantage of the time to practise their vile calling. No doubt there are violent men among them, who swear roundly at those who are hunting them to death, who swear that they will drive them off their lands and kill them if they can. But this does not make insurrectionists and traitors of the whole society. No matter; down with the Mormons! And so Boggs, the governor, seats himself and coolly writes off to his generals to drive out or exterminate the vermin.[31]

[31] Several of them write to Boggs: 'There is no crime, from treason down to petit larceny, but these people, or a majority of them, have been guilty of; all, too, under the counsel of Joseph Smith, Jr, the prophet. They have committed treason, murder, arson, burglary, robbery, larceny, and perjury. They have societies formed under the most binding covenants in form, and the most horrid oaths, to circumvent the laws and put them at defiance; and to plunder and burn and murder, and divide the spoils for the use of the church.' Tucker's Mormonism, 164.

And thus Boggs makes answer, Oct. 27th: 'Since the order of the morning to you directing you to cause four hundred mounted men to be raised within your division, I have received by Amos Rees, Esq., and Wiley E. Williams, Esq., one of my aids, information of the most appalling character, which changes entirely the face of things, and places the Mormons in the attitude of an open and avowed defiance of the laws, and of having made open war upon the people of this state. Your orders are therefore to hasten your operations, and endeavor to reach Richmond in Ray county, with all possible speed. The Mormons must be treated as enemies, and must be exterminated or driven from the state if necessary, for the public good. Their outrages are beyond all description. If you can increase your force, you are authorized to do so to any extent you may think necessary. I have just issued orders to Maj.-Gen. Wollock of Marion county to raise 500 men, and to march them to the northern part of Daviess, and there unite with Gen. Doniphan of Clay, who has been ordered with 500 men to proceed to the same point for the purpose of intercepting the retreat of the Mormons to the north. They have been directed to communicate with you by express. You can also communicate with them if you find it necessary. Instead, therefore, of proceeding as at first directed, to reinstate the citizens of Daviess in their homes, you will pro-

HIST. UTAH. 9

Thus it appears that the Missouri state militia, called out in the first instance to assist the Mormon state militia in quelling a Missouri mob, finally joins the mob against the Mormon militia. In none of their acts had the saints placed themselves in an attitude of unlawful opposition to the state authorities; on the other hand, they were doing all in their power to defend themselves and support law and order, save in the matter of retaliation.

The first the saints of Caldwell county know of the new tactics is the appearance, within half a mile of Far West,[32] of three thousand armed men, under General Lucas, generals Wilson and Doniphan being present, and General Clark with another army being a few days' march distant. General Lucas states that the main business there is to obtain possession of three individuals, whom he names, two of them not Mormons; and for the rest he has only to inform the saints that it is his painful duty either wholly to drive them from the state or to exterminate them.[33] Gilliam and his comrades, who as disguised Indians and white men had been fighting the Mormons, now that the state espouses their cause, join Lucas.[34] General Atchison was at Richmond, in Ray county, when the governor's exterminating order was issued. "I will have nothing to do with so infamous a proceeding," he said, and immediately resigned.

ceed immediately to Richmond and there operate against the Mormons. Brig.-Gen. Parks of Ray has been ordered to have 400 men of his brigade in readiness to join you at Richmond. The whole force will be placed under your command.'

[32] 'The governor's orders and these military movements were kept an entire secret from the citizens of Caldwell and Daviess...even the mail was withheld from Far West.' *Pratt's Autobiography*, 200.

[33] 'This letter of the governor's was extremely unguarded, and seems to have been too literally construed...Making all due allowance for the exasperated state of the public mind, these threats of extermination sound a little too savage in Anglo-Saxon ears...But they were impolitic, because they gave plausibility to the idea that the saints were the victims of a cruel and unrelenting religious persecution, and furnished them with one of the surest means of future success.' *Ferris' Utah and the Mormons*, 90-1.

[34] 'About the time that Lucas came out to Far West, Smith assembled the Mormon troops, and said that for every one they lacked in number of those who came out among them, the Lord would send angels, who would fight for them, and they should be victorious.' *Kidder's Mormonism*, 143.

The day following his arrival General Lucas orders
George M. Hinckle, colonel commanding the Mormon
militia, to bring before him Joseph Smith, junior,
Hyrum Smith, Lyman Wight, Sidney Rigdon, Parley
P. Pratt, Caleb Baldwin, and Alexander McRae,
which is done, though not without charge of fraud and
treachery on the part of Hinckle. A court-martial
is immediately held; the prisoners are all condemned,
and sentenced to be shot next morning at eight o'clock.
"In the name of humanity I protest against any
such cold-blooded murder," says General Doniphan
who further threatens to withdraw his men if such
a course is persisted in; whereupon the sentence is
not executed. All the Mormon troops in Far West,
however, are required to give up their arms and consider themselves prisoners of war.[35]   They are further
required to execute a deed of trust pledging all
Mormon property to the payment of the entire cost
of the war, and to give a promise to leave the state
before the coming spring.

Thus in the name of law and justice the Mormon
soldiery, whose chief crime it would seem was that, in
common with the rest of the militia, they had assisted

[35] They were 'confined to the limits of the town for about a week.' During
this time much property was destroyed, and women abused.   The number of
arms taken was 630, besides swords and pistols, worth between $12,000 and
$15,000. *Mem. to Leg.*, in *Greene's Facts*, 15.   'General Lucas demanded the
Caldwell militia to give up their arms, which was done to the number of upward of 500, the rest of the troops having fled during the night.   After the
troops had surrendered, the city of Far West was surrounded by the robbers,
and all the men detained as prisoners, none being permitted to pass out of
the city, although their families were starving for want of sustenance.'
Pratt's Persecution, 84.   'We determined not to resist anything in the shape
of authority, however tyrannical or unconstitutional might be the proceedings against us.   With this request (to surrender ourselves as prisoners), we
readily complied as soon as we were assured by the pledge of the honor of
the principal officers that our lives should be safe...We were marched into
camp, surrounded by thousands of savage-looking beings, many of whom
were painted like Indian warriors.   These all set up a constant yell, like so
many blood-hounds let loose on their prey...A hint was given us that the
general officers held a secret council...in which we were all sentenced to be
shot.' *Pratt's Persecution*, 80–2.   'If the vision of the infernal regions could
suddenly open to the mind, with thousands of malicious fiends, all clamoring,
exulting, deriding, blaspheming, mocking, railing, raging, and foaming like
a troubled sea, then could some idea be formed of the hell which we had entered.' *Pratt's Autobiography*, 204.   See *Young's Woman's Experience*, MS.;
Horne's Migrations, MS.

the state in putting down a mob, were forced at the point of the bayonet to sign an obligation, binding not only themselves but the civilians within their settlements to defray the entire expense of the war. This proceeding was sufficiently peculiar; but, as a climax to their conduct, some of the officers and men laid hands on the Mormons' property wherever they could find it, taking no thought of payment.

General Clark [36] now comes forward, and entering the town of Far West, collects the saints in the public square, reads them a lecture,[37] and selecting fifty of their number, thrusts them into prison. Next day forty-six of the fifty are taken to Richmond,[38] and after a fortnight's confinement half are liberated,[39]

[36] Pratt says that Clark has been commended by some writers for his heroic, merciful, and prudent conduct toward the Mormons, but that the truth is that he openly avowed his approval of all the proceedings of Gen. Lucas, and said that he should not alter his decrees. *Autobiography*, 227-8.

[37] It runs as follows: 'Gentlemen, You whose names are not attached to this list of names will now have the privilege of going to your fields to obtain corn for your families, wood, etc. Those that are now taken will go from thence to prison, to be tried, and receive the due demerit of their crimes, but you are now at liberty, all but such as charges may be hereafter preferred against. It now devolves upon you to fulfil the treaty that you have entered into, the leading items of which I now lay before you. The first of these you have already complied with, which is, that you deliver up your leading men to be tried according to law. Second, that you deliver up your arms; this has been attended to. The third is, that you sign over your property to defray the expenses of the war; this you have also done. Another thing yet remains for you to comply with, that is, that you leave this state forthwith, and whatever your feelings concerning this affair, whatever your innocence, it is nothing to me. Gen. Lucas, who is equal in authority with me, has made this treaty with you. I am determined to see it executed. The orders of the governor to me were, that you should be exterminated, and not allowed to continue in the state, and had your leaders not been given up and the treaty complied with before this, you and your families would have been destroyed, and your houses in ashes.'

[38] Pratt says in his *Autobiography*, p. 210, that a revelation to Joseph Smith buoyed up their spirits continually during their captivity. 'As we arose and commenced our march on the morning of the 3d of November, Joseph Smith spoke to me and the other prisoners in a low but cheerful and confidential tone; said he, "Be of good cheer, brethren; the word of the Lord came to me last night that our lives should be given us, and that whatever we may suffer during this captivity, not one of our lives should be taken."' 'When we arrived in Richmond as prisoners there were some fifty others, mostly heads of families, who had been marched from Caldwell on foot, distance thirty miles, and were now penned up in a cold, open, unfinished court-house, in which situation they remained for some weeks, while their families were suffering severe privations.' *Id.*, 227.

[39] A court of inquiry was instituted at Richmond before Judge Austin A. King, lasting from the 11th to 28th of November. Pratt says: 'The judge could not be prevailed on to examine the conduct of the murderers and rob-

most of the remainder being set free a week later on giving bail. Lucas [40] then retires with his troops, leaving the country to be ravaged by armed squads that burn houses, insult women, and drive off stock *ad libitum*.[41] The faint pretext of justice on the part of the state, attending forced sales and forced settlements, might as well have been dispensed with, as it was but a cloak to cover official iniquity.[42]

bers who had desolated our society, nor would he receive testimony except against us...The judge in open court, while addressing a witness, proclaimed that if the members of the church remained on their lands to put in another crop they should be destroyed indiscriminately, and their bones be left to bleach on the plains without a burial...Mr Doniphan, attorney for the defence, and since famed as a general in the Mexican war, finally advised the prisoners to offer no defence; "for," said he, "though a legion of angels from the opening heavens should declare your innocence, the court and populace have decreed your destruction."...Joseph and Hyrum Smith, Sidney Rigdon, Lyman Wight, Caleb Baldwin, and Alexander McRay were committed to the jail of Clay co. on charge of treason; and Morris Phelps, Lyman Gibbs, Darwin Chase, Norman Shearer, and myself were committed to the jail of Richmond, Ray co., for the alleged crime of murder, said to be committed in the act of dispersing the bandit Bogart and his gang.' *Id.*, 230–3.

[40] Ingloriously conspicuous in the Missouri persecutions were generals Clark, Wilson, and Lucas, Colonel Price, Captain Bogart, and Cornelius Gilliam, 'whose zeal in the cause of oppression and injustice, ' says Smith, 'was unequalled, and whose delight has been to rob, murder, and spread devastation among the saints...All the threats, murders, and robberies which these officers have been guilty of are entirely ignored by the executive of the state, who to hide his own iniquity must of course shield and protect those whom he employed to carry into effect his murderous purposes.' *Times and Seasons*, i. 7.

[41] Pages of evidence, both Mormon and anti-Mormon, might be given, and can indeed at any time be produced, to prove the commission of innumerable wrongs and revolting atrocities on the part of the people of Missouri, while abetted therein by state forces, commanded by state officers, and all under guidance of the state governor.

[42] There is abundance of testimony from disinterested sources, even from the opposers of Mormonism themselves, to prove the persecution on the part of the people of Missouri unjust and outrageous. I will quote only three from many similar comments that have been made on this subject, and all, be it remembered, emanating from the open and avowed enemies of this religion.

Says Prof. Turner of Illinois college: 'Who began the quarrel? Was it the Mormons? Is it not notorious, on the contrary, that they were hunted like wild beasts, from county to county, before they made any desperate resistance? Did they ever, as a body, refuse obedience to the laws, when called upon to do so, until driven to desperation by repeated threats and assaults from the mob? Did the state ever make one decent effort to defend them as fellow-citizens in their rights, or to redress their wrongs? Let the conduct of its governors, attorneys, and the fate of their final petitions answer. Have any who plundered and openly massacred the Mormons ever been brought to the punishment due to their crimes? Let the boasting murderers of begging and helpless infancy answer. Has the state ever remunerated even those known to be innocent, for the loss of either their property or their arms? Did either the pulpit or the press through the state raise a note of remonstrance or alarm? Let the clergymen who abetted and the editors

It did not seem possible to a community convicted of no crime, and living in the nineteenth century, under the flag of the world's foremost republic, that such flagrant wrongs as the Boggs exterminating order, and the enforced treaty under which they were deprived of their property, could be carried into effect. They appealed, therefore, to the legislature,[43] demanding justice. But that body was too much with the people and with Boggs to think of justice. To make a show of decency, a committee was appointed and sent to Caldwell and Daviess counties, to look into the matter, but of course did nothing. Another was appointed with like result. Debates continued with more or less show of interest through the month of December. In January, 1839, the Mormons were plainly told that they need expect no redress at the hand of the legislature or other body of Missouri.

who encouraged the mob answer.' *Correspondence Joseph Smith*, 2. On the 16th of March, 1839, the editor of the *Quincy Argus* wrote as follows: 'We have no language sufficiently strong for the expression of our indignation and shame at the recent transaction in a sister state, and that state Missouri, a stc'e of which we had long been proud, alike for her men and history, but r .v so fallen that we could wish her star stricken out from the bright constellation of the Union. We say we know of no language sufficiently strong for the expression of our shame and abhorrence of her recent conduct. She has written her own character in letters of blood, and stained it by acts of merciless cruelty and brutality that the waters of ages cannot efface. It will be observed that an organized mob, aided by many of the civil and military officers of Missouri, with Gov. Boggs at their head, have been the prominent actors in this business, incited, too, it appears, against the Mormons by political hatred, and by the additional motives of plunder and revenge. They have but too well put in execution their threats of extermination and expulsion, and fully wreaked their vengeance on a body of industrious and enterprising men who had never wronged nor wished to wrong them, but on the contrary had ever comported themselves as good and honest citizens, living under the same laws, and having the same right with themselves to the sacred immunities of life, liberty, and property.' 'By enlightened people the Mormons were regarded as the victims of misguided vengeance in Missouri. The ruffianly violence they encountered at the hands of lawless mobs, in several instances eventuating in deliberate murder, finds no extenuation in any alleged provocation. The due process of law might have afforded adequate redress for the criminalities of which they should be found guilty on legal trial. Such was the view of the subject rightly taken by the people of Illinois and of the world, though it may have been wrongfully applied in favor of the cause of the persecuted.' *Tucker's Mormonism*, 166.

[43] A memorial was sent to the legislature of Missouri, dated Far West, Dec. 10, 1838, setting forth these facts, and praying that the governor's novel, unlawful, tyrannical, and oppressive order be rescinded. It was signed by Edward Partridge, Heber C. Kimball, John Taylor, Theodore Turley, Brigham Young, Isaac Morley, George W. Harris, John Murdock, John M. Burk.

There was no help for them; they must leave the state or be killed; of this they were assured on all sides, publicly and privately.

And now begins another painful march—painful in the thought of it, painful in the telling of it. It is midwinter; whither can they go, and how? They have homes, but they may not enjoy them; land which they have bought, houses which they have built, and barns and cattle and food, but hereabout they are hunted to death. Is it Russia or Tartary or Hindostan, that people are thus forced to fly for opinion's sake? True, the people of the United States do not like such opinions; they do not like a religious sect that votes solid, or a class of men whom they look upon as fools and fanatics talking about taking the country, claimed as theirs by divine right; but in any event this was no way to settle the difficulty. Here are men who have been stripped in a moment of the results of years of toil—all that they have in the world gone; here are women weighed down with work and care, some whose husbands are in prison, and who are thus left to bear the heavy burden of this infliction alone; here are little children, some comfortably clad, others obliged to encounter the wind and frozen ground with bare heads and bleeding feet.

Whither can they go? There is a small following of the prophet at Quincy, Illinois; some propose to go there, some start for other places. But what if they are not welcome at Quincy, and what can they do with such a multitude? There is no help for it, however, no other spot where the outcasts can hope for refuge at the moment. Some have horses and cattle and wagons; some have none. Some have tents and bedding; some have none. But the start is made, and the march is slowly to the eastward. In the months of February and March[44]

[44] 'On the 20th of April, 1839, the last of the society departed from Far West. Thus had a whole people, variously estimated at from ten to fifteen

over one hundred and thirty families are on the west bank of the Mississippi unable to cross the river, which is full of floating ice. There they wait and suffer; they scour the country for food and clothing for the destitute; many sicken and die.

Finally they reach Quincy, and are kindly received. Not only the saints but others are there who have human hearts and human sympathies. Indeed, upon the expulsion of the Mormons from Missouri the

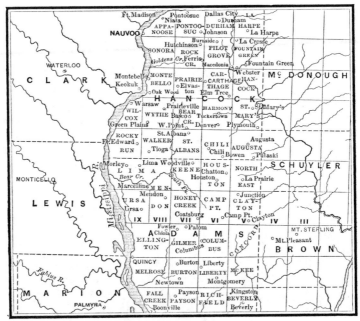

SETTLEMENTS IN ILLINOIS.

people of Illinois took a stand in their favor. The citizens of Quincy, in particular, offered their warmest sympathy and aid, on the ground of humanity. A select committee, appointed to ascertain the facts in the case, reported, on the 27th of February, 1839, "that the

thousand souls, been driven from houses and lands and reduced to poverty, and had removed to another state, during one short winter and part of a spring. The sacrifice of property was immense.' *Pratt's Autobiography*, 245.

strangers recently arrived here from the state of Missouri, known by the name of latter-day saints, are entitled to our sympathy and kindest regard." The working-men of the town should be informed "that these people have no design to lower the wages of the laboring class, but to procure something to save them from starving." Finally it was resolved: "That we recommend to all the citizens of Quincy, in all their intercourse with the strangers, that they use and observe a becoming decorum and delicacy, and be particularly careful not to indulge in any conversation or expressions calculated to wound their feelings, or in any way to reflect upon those who, by every law of humanity, are entitled to our sympathy and commiseration."[45]

How in regard to neighboring states? In case the people of Illinois soon tire of them, what will they then do? From Commerce, Isaac Galland writes to Robert Lucas, governor of Iowa, asking about it. The answer is such as one would expect from the average American citizen—neither better nor worse. It is such, however, as to condemn throughout all time the conduct of the people of Missouri.[46]

---

[45] *Pratt's Persecution of the Saints*, 185.

[46] 'On my return to this city,' writes Lucas from the executive office at Burlington, Iowa, 'after a few weeks' absence in the interior of the territory, I received your letter of the 25th ult. [Feb. 1839], in which you give a short account of the sufferings of the people called Mormons, and ask whether they could be permitted to purchase lands and settle upon them in the territory of Iowa, and there worship Almighty God according to the dictates of their own consciences, secure from oppression, etc. In answer to your inquiry, I would say that I know of no authority that can constitutionally deprive them of this right. They are citizens of the United States, and are all entitled to all the rights and privileges of other citizens. The 2d section of the 4th article of the constitution of the United States (which all are solemnly bound to support) declares that "the citizens of each state shall be entitled to all the privileges and immunities of citizens in the several states;" this privilege extends in full force to the territories of the United States. The first amendment to the constitution of the United States declares that "congress shall make no law respecting an establishment of religion or prohibiting the free exercise thereof." The ordinances of congress of the 13th July, 1787, for the government of the territory north-west of the river Ohio, secures to the citizens of said territory and the citizens of the states thereafter to be formed therein, certain privileges which were by the late act of congress organizing the territory of Iowa extended to the citizens of this territory. The first fundamental article in that ordinance, which is

During these trying times the prophet was moving about among his people, doing everything in his power to protect and encourage them. Late in September he was in the southern part of Caldwell county, whence in October he passed into Carroll county, where he soon found himself hemmed in by an enraged populace. He appealed to the people, he applied to the governor, but all to no purpose. Afterward he went to Daviess county, and then back to Far West, where he was arrested and incarcerated with the others. Shortly afterward the prisoners, now

declared to be forever unalterable except by common consent, reads as follows, to wit: No person demeaning himself in a peaceable and orderly manner shall ever be molested on account of his mode of worship or religious sentiments in said territory. These principles I trust will ever be adhered to in the territory of Iowa. They make no distinction between religious sects. They extend equal privileges and protection to all; each must rest upon its own merits and will prosper in proportion to the purity of its principles, and the fruit of holiness and piety produced thereby. With regard to the peculiar people mentioned in your letter, I know but little. They had a community in the northern part of Ohio for several years, and I have no recollection of ever having heard in that state of any complaint against them of violating the laws of the country. Their religious opinions I conceive have nothing to do with our political transactions. They are citizens of the United States, and are entitled to the same political rights and legal protection that other citizens are entitled to. The foregoing are briefly my views on the subject of your inquiries.'

In a memorial sent to Washington in the autumn of 1839, it was claimed by the Mormons that their property destroyed in Jackson co. was worth $120,000; that 12,000 souls were banished; that they purchased and improved lands in Clay co., and in three years were obliged to leave there with heavy loss; that they then purchased and improved lands in Daviess and Carroll counties; that for the most part these counties were wild and uncultivated; that they had converted them into large and well improved farms, well stocked, which were rapidly advancing in cultivation and wealth; and that they were finally compelled to fly from these counties. In a petition presented by Sidney Rigdon to the state of Pennsylvania, it is stated that 'Lilburn Boggs, governor of the state, used his executive influence to have us all massacred or driven into exile; and all this because we were not lawless and disobedient. For if the laws had given them a sufficient guaranty against the evils complained of...then would they have had recourse to the laws. If we had been transgressors of laws, our houses would not have been rifled, our women ravished, our farms desolated, and our goods and chattels destroyed, our men killed, our wives and children driven into the prairies, and made to suffer all the indignities that the most brutal barbarity could inflict; but would only have had to suffer that which the laws would inflict, which were founded in justice, framed in righteousness, and administered in humanity... Why, then, all this cruelty? Answer: because the people had violated no law; and they could not be restrained by law, nor prevented from exercising the rights according to the laws, enjoyed, and had a right to be protected in, in any state of the Union.' Mr Corrill remarks: 'My opinion is, that if the Mormons had been let alone by the citizens, they would have divided and subdivided, so as to have completely destroyed themselves and their power as a people in a short time.'

consisting of the prophet Joseph Smith, with Sidney Rigdon, Hyrum Smith, Parley P. Pratt, Lyman Wight, Amasa Lyman, and George W. Robinson, were removed to Independence; why they did not know, but because it was the hot-bed of mobocracy, they said, and peradventure they might luckily be shot or hanged. A few days later they were taken to Richmond and put in irons, and later to Liberty jail in Clay county, where they were kept confined for four months. Habeas corpus was tried, and many petitions were forwarded to the authorities on their behalf, but all to no purpose. At length they obtained a hearing in the courts, with a change of venue to Boone county where they were still to be incarcerated. Rigdon had been previously released on habeas corpus, and one night, when the guard was asleep, Smith and the others escaped and made their way to Quincy.

"I was in their hands as a prisoner," says Smith, "about six months; but notwithstanding their determination to destroy me, with the rest of my brethren who were with me, and although at three different times we were sentenced to be shot without the least shadow of law, and had the time and place appointed for that purpose, yet through the mercy of God, in answer to the prayers of the saints, I have been preserved, and delivered out of their hands."[47]

[47] In 1839 Carlin was governor of Illinois, and on him the governor of Missouri made a formal demand for the surrender to the authorities of Smith and Rigdon, but little attention was paid to it. One of the most complete documents extant covering this period is, *Facts Relative to the Expulsion of the Mormons, or Latter-day Saints, from the State of Missouri under the Exterminating Order. By John P. Greene*, an *authorized representative of the Mormons* (Cincinnati, 1839). The work consists of 43 8vo pages, and was written for the purpose of showing to what wrongs the Mormons had been subjected at the hands of the people and politicians of Missouri, and also to obtain contributions for the destitute. The contents are largely documentary, and if we allow for some intensity of feeling, bear the impress of truth. Pointing in the same direction but less pretentious and less important is *Correspondence between Joseph Smith, the prophet, and Col. John Wentworth, editor of the 'Chicago Democrat,' and member of congress from Illinois; General James Arlington Bennett, of Arlington House, Long Island; and the Honorable John C. Calhoun, Senator from South Carolina, in which is given a sketch of t.. life of Joseph Smith, Rise and Progress of the Church of Latter-day , and their persecution by the state of Missouri; with the peculiar views .eph Smith in relation to Political and Religious matters generally; to .h is added a concise account of the present state and prospects of the city of*

Notwithstanding their enormous losses, and the extreme indigence of many, the saints were not all as
destitute of credit as they were of ready means, if
we may judge by their business transacted during
the year 1839. Bishop Knight bought for the church
part of the town of Keokuk, Iowa, situated on the
west bank of the Mississippi, forty miles above Quincy,
Illinois. He also purchased the whole of another
town-site called Nashville, six miles above Keokuk.
Four miles above Nashville was a settlement called
Montrose, part of which Knight bought, together
with thirty thousand acres of land.[48]
Opposite Montrose, on the east bank of the Mississippi where was a good landing, stood a village

Nauvoo. (New York, 1844). With a title-page from which so much information is to be derived, we must not expect too much from the book itself.
A portion of this correspondence was published in the *Times and Seasons*.
  *Late Persecution of the Church of Jesus Christ of Latter-day Saints. Ten
thousand American citizens robbed, plundered, and banished; others imprisoned, and others martyred for their Religion. With a sketch of their Rise, Progress, and Doctrine. By P. P. Pratt, Minister of the Gospel. Written in prison*
(New York, 1840). This is a 16mo vol. of 215 pages, most of which is devoted
to the Missouri persecutions, with but little other history, except what is thrown
in incidentally. An appendix of 37 pages is made up mostly from *Greene's
Facts*. Pratt gives a graphic account of his life in prison, and of the means
whereby, with the coöperation of his wife, he rescued from jail the manuscript
of this book, which was written there. After mentioning them, he says:
'Thus, kind reader, was this little book providentially, and I may say miraculously, preserved, and by this means you have it to read.' The first edition
was published at Detroit, Michigan, the book consisting then of 84 pages.
  Full reference for the persecutions of the Mormons in Missouri, 1831-39.
Memorial to Legislature Mass. in 1844, against such conduct, in *Times and
Seasons*, i. 17-20, 33-6, 49-56, 65-6, 81-6, 94, 97-104, 113-16, 128-34, 145-50,
161-7, 177; v. 514-19; *Pratt's Persecution of the Saints*, 21-215; *Utah Tracts*,
no. 4, 56-64; *Pratt's Autobiography*, 190-237, 311-22, 336-40; *Smucker's Hist.
Mor.*, 86; *Deseret News*, Dec. 27, 1851, Nov. 29 and Dec. 27, 1851, June
30, 1869; *Mackay's The Mormons*, 106-14; *Tucker's Origin and Prog. Mor.*,
160-6; *Howe's Mormonism Unveiled*, 138-76; *Ferris' Utah and the Mormons*,
87-8, 90; *White's Ten Years in Or.*, 144; *Taylder's Mormon's Own Book*, xliii.-
xlvi.; *Gunnison's Mormons*, 104-14; *Millennial Star*, xxv., 535-6, 550-2, 599-
600, 614-16, 631; *Burnett's Rec.*, 56; *Beadle's Life in Utah*, 60; *Lee's Mormonism*, 55-96; *Tullidge's Women*, 116-74; *Richards' Narrative*, MS., 6-9;
Young's Wife No. 19, 43-53; *Atlantic Monthly*, Dec. 1869; *Stenhouse, Les
Mormons*, 154-71; *Liberty Tribune; Margaret Smoot's Experiences of a Mormon Wife*, MS., 2-3; *Farnham's Travels Rocky Mts.*, 6; *Bertrand's Mem.
Mor.*, 51; *Busch, Gesch. der Mor.*, 85-7, 90-7; *Juvenile Instructor*, xv. 78;
Kidder's Mormonism, 133-5; *Iowa Frontier Guardian*, March 21, 1849; *Rabbi-
son's Growth of Towns*, MS., 2-5.
  [48] 'Since their expulsion from Missouri a portion of them, about one hundred families, have settled in Lee county, Iowa Territory, and are generally
considered industrious, inoffensive, and worthy citizens.' *Letter from Robert
Lucas, governor of Iowa, to A. Ripley*, dated Jan. 4, 1840.

called Commerce, where were some twenty houses. This was purchased by the saints, with the lands surrounding, and a town laid out which was named Nauvoo, "from the Hebrew, which signifies fair, very beautiful, and it actually fills the definition of the word; for nature has not formed a parallel on the banks of the Mississippi from New Orleans to Galena." The post-office there was first called Commerce, after the Mormons had purchased the village, but the name was changed to that of Nauvoo in May, 1840.[49] The place was started by a company from New York, but it was so sickly that when the agent for the Mormons came they were glad to sell. The Mormons drained it and made the place comparatively healthy.

On his escape from prison, Smith visited Commerce among other places, and seeing at once the advantages of its site, determined to establish there the headquarters of the church. For so great had his power now become, so extensive his following, that he might choose any spot whereon to call into existence a city, had but to point his finger and say the word to transform a wilderness into a garden. During the winter of 1840 the church leaders applied to the legislature of Illinois for several charters, one for the city of Nauvoo, one for agricultural and manufacturing purposes, one for a university, and one for a military body called the Nauvoo Legion. The privileges asked were very extensive, but were readily granted; for the two great political parties were pretty equal in numbers in Illinois at this time, and the leaders of the party in office, perceiving what a political power these people were, determined to secure them.

[49] 'Nauvoo was one of the names of one of the numerous petty chiefs in British India.' *Ferris' The Mor.*, 97. 'Nauvoo is a Hebrew word, and signifies a beautiful habitation for man, carrying with it the idea of rest; it is not, however, considered by the Mormons their final home, but a resting place only; for they only intend to remain there until they have gathered force sufficient to enable them to conquer Independence in Jackson co., Missouri, which is one of the most fertile, pleasant, and desirable countries on the face of the earth, possessing a soil unsurpassed in any region. Independence they consider their Zion, and there they intend to rear their great temple, the corner-stone of which is already laid. There is to be the great gath-

There were now saints everywhere, all over the United States, particularly throughout the western portion; there were isolated believers, and small clusters, and small and great congregations. There were also many travelling preachers, men full of the holy ghost, or believing themselves so, who travelled without purse or scrip, whom no buffetings, insults, hunger, or blows could daunt, who feared nothing that man could do, heaven's door being always open to them. See now the effects of these persecutions in Missouri. Twelve thousand were driven from their homes and set moving by Boggs and his generals; three fourths of them found new homes at Quincy, Nauvoo, and elsewhere; but three thousand, who, but for the persecutions, would have remained at home and tilled their lands, were preaching and proselyting, making new converts and establishing new churches wherever they went. One of their number, William Smith, was a member of the Illinois legislature. In the very midst of the war they were preaching in Jackson county, among their old enemies and spoilers, striving with all their souls to win back their Zion, their New Jerusalem. From New York, February 19, 1840, Brigham Young, H. C. Kimball, Orson Pratt, and Parley P. Pratt indited a letter to the saints at Commerce, speaking of the wonderful progress of the faith, and of their own intended departure for England.[50]

Thus, despite persecution, the saints increased in number year by year. Before the end of 1840 there were fifteen thousand souls at Nauvoo, men, women, and children, not all of them exiles from Missouri, but from every quarter, old believers and new converts from different parts of the United States, from Canada, and from Europe; hither came they to the city of their God, to the mountain of his holiness.

ering place for all the saints, and in that delightful country they expect to find their Eden, and build the New Jerusalem.' Bennett's *Mormonism Exp.*, 192–3.

[50] See J. D. Hunter's letter of Dec. 26, 1839, from Jackson county, Ill., in *Times and Seasons*, i. 59.

CHAPTER VI.

THE STORY OF MORMONISM.

1840-1844.

THE CITY OF NAUVOO—ITS TEMPLE AND UNIVERSITY—THE NAUVOO LE-
GION—THE MORMONS IN ILLINOIS—EVIL REPORTS—REVELATION ON
POLYGAMY—ITS RECEPTION AND PRACTICE—THE PROPHET A CANDI-
DATE FOR THE PRESIDENCY—THE 'NAUVOO EXPOSITOR'—JOSEPH AR-
RESTED—GOVERNOR FORD AND HIS MEASURES—JOSEPH AND HYRUM
PROCEED TO CARTHAGE—THEIR IMPRISONMENT—THE GOVERNOR'S
PLEDGE—ASSASSINATION OF THE PROPHET AND HIS BROTHER—CHAR-
ACTER OF JOSEPH SMITH—A PANIC AT CARTHAGE—ADDRESSES OF RICH-
ARDS AND TAYLOR—PEACEFUL ATTITUDE OF THE MORMONS.

To the saints it is indeed a place of refuge, the
city of Nauvoo, the Holy City, the City of Joseph.[1]
It stands on rolling land, covering a bed of limestone
yielding excellent building material, and bordered on
three sides by the river which here makes a majestic
curve, and is nearly two miles in width. The aborigines were not indifferent to the advantages of the
spot, as the presence of their mounds testifies. In
area it is three miles by four. The city is regularly
laid out in streets at right angles, of convenient width,
along which are scattered neat, whitewashed log cabins,
also frame, brick, and stone houses, with grounds and
gardens. It is incorporated by charter,[2] and contains
the best institutions of the latest civilization; in the

[1] 'Among the more zealous Mormons, it became the fashion at this time
(1845) to disuse the word Nauvoo, and to call the place the holy city, or the
city of Joseph.' *Mackay's The Mormons*, 191.
[2] The charter granted by the legislature was signed by Gov. Carlin Sept.
16, 1840, to take effect Feb. 1, 1841. 'So artfully framed that it was found
that the state government was practically superseded within the Mormon corporation. Under the judicial clause its courts were supreme.' McBride in
International Review, Feb. 1882. Charters were also granted to the university
and the Nauvoo legion. *Times and Seasons*, ii. 281.

(143)

country are hundreds of tributary farms and planta-
tions. The population is from seven to fifteen thousand, varying with the ebb and flow of new converts
and new colonizations.[3]

Conspicuous among the buildings, and chief archi-
tectural feature of the holy city, is the temple, glistening in white limestone upon the hill-top, a shrine in
the western wilderness whereat all the nations of the
earth may worship, whereat all the people may inquire of God and receive his holy oracles.[4] Next in

---

[3] The blocks contain 'four lots of eleven by twelve rods each, making all
corner lots...For three or four miles upon the river, and about the same distance back in the country, Nauvoo presents a city of gardens, ornamented
with the dwellings of those who have made a covenant by sacrifice...It will
be no more than probably correct, if we allow the city to contain between
700 and 800 houses, with a population of 14,000 or 15,000.' *Times and Seasons*, iii. 936. A correspondent of the *New York Herald* is a little wild when
he writes about this time: 'The Mormons number in Europe and America
about 150,000, and are constantly pouring into Nauvoo and the neighboring
country. There are probably in and about this city and adjacent territories
not far from 30,000.' Fifteen thousand in 1840 is the number given in
Mackay's The Mormons, 115, as I mentioned in the last chapter. A correspondent's estimate in the *Times and Seasons*, in 1842, was for the city 7,000,
and for the immediate surroundings 3,000. Phelps, in *The Prophet*, estimates
the population during the height of the city's prosperity in 1844 at 14,000, of
whom nine tenths were Mormons. Some 2000 houses were built the first year.
Joseph Smith in *Times and Seasons*, March 1842, says: 'We number from six
to eight thousand here, besides vast numbers in the county around, and in
almost every county in the state.'

[4] The structure was 83 by 128 feet, and 60 feet high. The stone was quarried within city limits. There was an upper story and basement; and in the
latter a baptismal font wrought after the manner of King Solomon's brazen
sea. A huge tank, upon whose panels were painted various scenes, and ascent
to which was made by stairs, was upborne by twelve oxen, beautifully carved,
and overlaid with gold. 'The two great stories,' says a Mormon eye-
witness, 'each have two pulpits, one at each end, to accommodate the Melchizedek and Aaronic priesthoods, graded into four rising seats, the first
for the president of the elders and his two counsellors, the second for the
president of the high priesthood and his two counsellors, and the third for
the Melchizedek president and his two counsellors, and the fourth for the president of the whole church and his two counsellors. There are thirty hewn
stone pilasters which cost about $3,000 apiece. The base is a crescent new
moon; the capitals, near 50 feet high; the sun, with a human face in bold relief, about two and a half feet broad, ornamented with rays of light and
waves, surmounted by two hands holding two trumpets.' All was crowned
by a high steeple surmounted with angel and trumpet. The cost was nearly
$1,000,000, and was met by tithes contributed by some in money or produce,
and by others in labor. The four corner-stones of the temple were laid with
much ceremony on the 6th of April, 1841, on the celebration of the anniversary of the church. Sidney Rigdon delivered the address, and upon the
placing of the first stone, said: 'May the persons employed in the erection of
this house be preserved from all harm while engaged in its construction, till the
whole is completed—in the name of the father, and of the son, and of the holy

the City of Joseph in prominence and importance is
the house of Joseph, hotel and residence, called the
Nauvoo House,[5] which is to the material man as the

ghost; even so, amen.' *Times and Seasons*, ii. 376. A revelation was published
in Jan. 1841. 'Let all my saints come from afar, and send ye swift messengers, yea, chosen messengers, and say unto them: "Come ye with all your gold
and your silver and your precious stones, and with all your antiquities, and with
all who have knowledge of antiquities, that will come, may come; and bring
the box-tree and the fir-tree and the pine-tree, together with all the precious
trees of the earth, and with iron and with copper and with brass and with
zinc and with all your precious things of the earth, and build a house to my
name for the most high to dwell therein."' *Smucker's Hist. Mor.*, 132. For
reference notes on temple: minutes of conference, relating to building a
church, etc., see *Times and Seasons*, i. 185-7. Laying the foundation stone, *Id.*,
ii. 375-7, 380-2; *Mackay's The Mormons*, 118-20; *Smucker's Hist. Mor.*, 133.
Laying of the capstone, *Times and Seasons*, vi. 926. Progress of its building,
Id., iii. 775-6; iv. 10-11; *The Prophet*, in *Mackay's The Mormons*, 189-91.
Description of the temple with cut, *Smucker's Mormons*, 129; *Ferris' The Mormons*, 137-9; *Pratt's Autobiography*, 378; without cut, *Smucker's Mormons*,
202-4; *Bertrand Mem. Morm.*, 61; *Cincinnati Times; Deseret News*, March
22, 1876; church claims, *Times and Seasons*, iii. 735-8; 767-9; v. 618-20; *Kimball*, in *Times and Seasons*, vi. 972-3; misappropriation of funds, *Hall's Mormonism Exposed*, 7-8. 'One of the most powerful levers which he had invented for moving his disciples in temple building was the doctrine of baptism
for the dead...which baptism must be performed in the temple; no other
place would give it the requisite efficacy.' *Ferris' The Mormons*, 97-8. 'Another mode of making the dimes was that of giving the blessing, as it was said,
from heaven. This was the sole province of the patriarch, which office, till
his death, was exercised by Hiram Smith. No blessing could be obtained for
less than one dollar; but he frequently received for this service twenty,
thirty, and even forty dollars.' *Hall's Mormonism*, 22.

[5] It was ordered by revelation given to Joseph Smith, Jan. 19, 1841, that
a hotel should be built and called the Nauvoo House; that it should be
erected under the supervision of George Miller, Lyman Wight, John Snider,
and Peter Haws, one of whom should be president of a joint-stock company
to be formed for the purpose, and that stock subscriptions should be for not
less than fifty dollars nor more than fifteen thousand dollars by any one
man, and that only by a believer in the book of Mormon. Vinson Knight,
Hyrum Smith, Isaac Galland, William Marks, Henry G. Sherwood, and William Law were directed by name to take stock. 'And now I say unto you,
as pertaining to my boarding-house, which I have commanded you to build
for the boarding of strangers, let it be built unto my name, and let my name
be named upon it, and let my servant Joseph and his house have place therein
from generation to generation.' The Nauvoo House Associaton was incorporated Feb. 23, 1841, by George Miller, Lyman Wight, John Snider, and
Peter Haws, and associates. Copy of act in *Bennett's Hist. Saints*, 204-5.
Plan of city, with cuts of temple, baptismal font, and Nauvoo Legion,
with description, in *Bennett's Hist. Saints*, 188-91, which is quite erroneous,
the building being then not completed. I have taken this account chiefly
from Phelps' description in *The Prophet*. The Nauvoo House, says Bennett,
'though intended chiefly for the reception and entertainment of strangers
and travellers, contains, or rather when completed is to contain, a splendid
suite of apartments for the special accommodation of the prophet Joe Smith,
and heirs and descendants forever.' Cut of temple, and best description of
Nauvoo institutions, in *Mackay's The Mormons*, 115, 190-1. The Nauvoo
House, in form of an L, had a frontage on two streets of 120 feet each,
by a depth of 40 feet; the estimated cost was $100,000. *Times and Seasons*,
ii. 369. Another building opened in Nov. 1843 was the Nauvoo mansion.

temple to the spiritual man. Unfortunately both the
one and the other are destined to an occupancy and
enjoyment all too brief in view of the vast labor bestowed upon them. Besides these buildings are the
Hall of Seventies, in which is a library, the Masonic
Hall, and Concert Hall; also there a university and
other institutions are established, though having as
yet no separate edifices.

The president of the university and professor of
mathematics and English literature is James Kelly,
a graduate of Trinity College, Dublin, and a ripe
scholar; Orson Pratt, a man of pure mind and high order of ability, who without early education and amidst
great difficulties had to achieve learning as best he
could, and in truth has achieved it; professor of languages, Orson Spencer, graduate of Union College
and the Baptist Theological Seminary, New York;
professor of church history, Sidney Rigdon, versed
in history, belles-lettres, and oratory. In the board
of regents we find the leading men of the church;[6]
connected with the university were four common-
school wards, with three wardens to each.

In 1840 all the male members of the church between the ages of sixteen and fifty were enrolled in
a military organization known as the Nauvoo Legion,
which eventually numbered some four thousand men,
and constituted part of the state militia. It was divided into two cohorts, and then into regiments, battalions, and companies, Lieutenant-general Joseph
Smith being commander-in-chief.[7] The organization

[6] Chancellor, John C. Bennett; registrar, William Law; regents, Joseph
Smith, Sidney Rigdon, Hyrum Smith, William Marks, Samuel H. Smith,
Daniel H. Wells, N. K. Whitney, Charles C. Rich, John T. Barnett, Wilson
Law, John P. Greene, Vinson Knight, Isaac Galland, Elias Higbee, Robert
D. Foster, James Adams, Samuel Bennett, Ebenezer Robinson, John Snider,
George Miller, Lenos M. Knight, John Taylor, Heber C. Kimball. The
tuition fees were five dollars per quarter, payable twice each quarter in ad-
vance.

[7] Among his generals were Robert D. Foster, George W. Robinson, Charles
C. Rich, W. P. Lyon, Davison Hibbard, Hirum Kimball, A. P. Rockwood;
majors, Willard Richards, Hosea Stout; colonels, John F. Weld, Orson Pratt,
Francis M. Higbee, Carlos Gove, C. L. Higbee, James Sloan, George Schindle,
Amasa Lyman, D. B. Smith, George Coulson, Alexander McRea, J. R. Back-

was modelled after the Roman legion. The men were well disciplined, brave, and efficient. These troops carried their name to Utah, where they were reörganized in May 1857.

Though all are soldiers, there are no dandy warriors in their midst. Each one returns after drill to his occupation—to his farm, factory, or merchandise. Among other workshops are a porcelain factory established by a Staffordshire company, two steam sawmills, a steam flouring-mill, a foundry, and a tool-factory. A joint-stock company is organized under the style of the Nauvoo Agricultural and Manufacturing Association. Just outside the city is a community farm, worked by the poor for their own benefit; to each family in the city is allotted one acre of ground; the system of community of property does not obtain.

Most of the people in and about Nauvoo are Mormons, but not all. The population is made up chiefly from the farming districts of the United States and the manufacturing districts of England; though uneducated, unpolished, and superstitious, they are for the most part intelligent, industrious, competent, honest, and sincere.[8] With a shrewd head to direct,

enstos, L. Woodworth; captains, D. B. Huntington, Samuel Hicks, Amos Davis, Marcellus Bates, Charles Allen, L. N. Scovil, W. M. Allred, Justus Morse, John F. Olney, Darwin Chase, C. M. Kreymyer, and others. 'Col. A. P. Rockwood was drill-master. Rockwood was then a captain, but was afterward promoted to colonel of the militia, or host of Israel. I was then fourth corporal of a company. The people were regularly drilled and taught military tactics, so that they would be ready to act when the time came for returning to Jackson county, the promised land of our inheritance.' *Lee's Mormonism*, 112. 'Reviews were held from time to time, and flags presented, and Joseph appeared on all those occasions with a splendid staff, in all the pomp and circumstance of a full-blown military commander.' *Ferris' Utah and the Mormons*, 100-1. 'At the last dress parade of the legion, he was accompanied in the field by a display of ten of his spiritual wives or concubines, dressed in a fine uniform, and mounted on elegant white horses.' *Tucker's Mormonism*, 170. After the force reached Utah it was 'regularly drilled by competent officers, many of whom served in Mexico with the Mormon battalion under Gen. W. Scott. They are well armed, and perfectly fearless.' *Hyde's Mormonism*, 183. See further *Times and Seasons*, ii. 321-2, 417-18, 435, 517; iii. 654, 700-1, 718, 733-4, 921; *Stenhouse's Tell It All*, 306; *Deseret News*, April 15 and July 1, 1857, July 6, 1859; *Gunnison's Mormons*, 133; *Smucker's Hist. Mor.*, 149; *Kidder's Mormonism*, 182-9.

[8] Says the *St Louis Atlas* of September 1841: The people of Nauvoo 'have

like that of the prophet, a wisdom like his to concentrate, a power like his to say to ten thousand men, do this, and it is done, with plenty of cheap, virgin land, with a collective knowledge of all arts, and with habits of economy and industry, it were a wonder if they did not rapidly accumulate property, and some of them acquire wealth. This they do, though tithed by the church, and detested by the gentiles, and they prosper in a remarkable degree. Of course, in political, as in spiritual and pecuniary affairs, the prophet's word is law.

"Nauvoo is the best place in the world!" exclaims an enthusiastic saint. Nauvoo, the beautiful indeed! And "as to the facilities, tranquillities, and virtues of the city, they are not equalled on the globe." Here the saints find rest. "No vice is meant to be tolerated; no grog-shops allowed; nor would we have any trouble, if it were not for our lenity in suffering the world,[9] as I shall call them, to come in and trade, and

been grossly misunderstood and shamefully libelled...The present population is between eight and nine thousand, and of course it is the largest town in Illinois. The people are very enterprising, industrious, and thrifty. They are at least quite as honest as the rest of us in this part of the world, and probably in any other. Some peculiarities they have, no doubt. Their religion is a peculiar one; that is, neither Buddhism, nor Mahometanism, nor Judaism, nor Christianity, but it is a faith which they say encourages no vice nor immorality, nor departure from established laws and usages; neither polygamy, nor promiscuous intercourse, nor community of property...Ardent spirits as a drink are not in use among them...Tobacco, also, is a weed which they seem almost universally to despise. We don't know but that the Mormons ought to be expatriated for refusing to drink whiskey and chew tobacco; but we hope the question will not be decided hastily, nor until their judges have slept off the fumes of their own liquor and cigars.' 'They have enclosed large farms on the prairie ground, on which they have raised corn, wheat, hemp, etc., and all this they have accomplished within the short space of four years. I do not believe there is another people in existence who could have made such improvements in the same length of time under the same circumstances. And here allow me to remark, that there are some here who have lately emigrated to this place, who have built themselves large and convenient homes in the town; others on their farms on the prairie, who, if they had remained at home, might have continued to live in rented houses all their days, and never once have entertained the idea of building one for themselves at their own expense.' *Smucker's Mormonism*, 159.

[9] Gentiles were not excluded from the holy city. In *Bennett's Hist. Saints*, 158, is given an ordinance, dated March 1, 1841, running as follows: 'Be it ordained by the city council of the city of Nauvoo, that the catholics, presbyterians, methodists, baptists, latter-day saints, quakers, episcopalians, universalists, unitarians, mohammedans, and all other religious sects and denominations whatever, shall have toleration and equal privileges in this city;

enjoy our society, as they say." "They are a wonderfully enterprising people," writes a gentile. "Peace and harmony reign in the city. The drunkard is scarcely ever seen, as in other cities, neither does the awful imprecation or profane oath strike upon your ear; but while all is storm and tempest and confusion abroad respecting the Mormons, all is peace and harmony at home."[10]

About this time there comes to Joseph Smith a somewhat singular individual making somewhat singular advances. He is a yankee huckster of the first class, only for his merchandise, instead of patent clocks and wooden nutmegs, he offers for sale theology, medicine, and a general assortment of political and military wares. The thing is a fraud, and before long he openly announces himself as such. As his manhood is far inferior to his duplicity, so his name—the Reverend General John C. Bennett, M. D., U. S. A., president, chancellor, and master in chancery—as we may observe, is subordinate to his titles. He has ability, he has brains and fingers; but

and should any person be guilty of ridiculing, abusing, or otherwise depreciating another in consequence of his religion, etc., he shall be fined and imprisoned.' On the 17th of March, 1842, the Female Relief Society of Nauvoo was organized.

[10] In the *Salem Advertiser* was published an account of the visit to Nauvoo in 1843 of one Newhall, a lecturer, who says: 'I sought in vain for anything that bore the marks of immorality, but was both astonished and highly pleased at my ill success. I could see no loungers about the streets nor any drunkards about the taverns. I did not meet with those distorted features of ruffians, or with the ill-bred and impudent. I heard not an oath in the place, I saw not a gloomy countenance; all were cheerful, polite, and industrious.' *Smucker's Mormons*, 154-5. 'The mayor of Nauvoo deserves praise for the stand he has taken in favor of temperance. The retailing of ardent spirits is not permitted within the bounds of the corporation.' *Kidder's Mormons*, 189. For city ordinance prohibiting the sale of intoxicating liquors in less quantity than a quart except as a physician's prescription, see *Bennett's Hist. Saints*, 27. On the 12th of Nov. 1841, B. Winchester writes from Nauvoo: 'You would be astonished, if you were here, at the vast improvement made in so short a space of time...You will see nothing like idleness, but will hear the hum of industry, nay, may I not say more, the voice of merriment...Now as to the morality of the people here:...you know if you should throw cold water into melted iron the scene would be terrific, because the contrast would be so great; so it is with the saints: if a small portion of wickedness happens among them, the contrast between the spirit of Christ and that of darkness is so great that it makes a great upstir and tremendous excitement; this is the case here; but in other communities the same amount of crime would hardly be noticed.'

he has no soul. He comes to Joseph and says,
"Hail, master!" and worships him. He professes all
that the Mormons profess, and more; he does all
that the Mormons do, and more. So the prophet
makes him general of his legion, mayor of the city,
chancellor of the university, not to mention his functions as attorney, doctor, and privy counsellor. All
this is done with quick despatch; and the result
is that the great man soon tires of his greatness,
or thinks to become yet greater by turning renegade, and writing a book against his late friends and
associates.[11]

[11] Representative of a class of anti-Mormon literature, not altogether
creditable to either its authors or supporters, are the following:
  *The History of the Saints; or, An Exposé of Joe Smith and Mormonism.
By John C. Bennett.* (Boston, 1842.)
  *The Abominations of Mormonism Exposed; containing many Facts and
Doctrines concerning that singular people during seven years' membership with
them, from 1840 to 1847. By William Hall.* (Cincinnati, 1852.)
  *Mormonism: Its Leaders and Designs. By John Hyde, Jun., formerly a
Mormon elder and resident of Salt Lake City.* (New York, 1857.)
  *Mormonism Unveiled; or, The Life and Confessions of the late Mormon
bishop, John D. Lee; Written by Himself; Embracing a history of Mormonism
from its inception down to the present time, with an exposition of the secret history, signs, symbols, and crimes of the Mormon Church; also the true history
of the horrible butchery known as the Mountain Meadow Massacre.* (St Louis,
1877.)
  The role of traitor is not one which in any wise brings credit to the
performer, either from one side or the other. However great the service he
may render us, we cannot but feel that he is false-hearted and vile. Many
of the apostates, though they may not have written books, declare that they
joined the sect only to learn their secrets and then expose them. These are
the most contemptible of all. There may be cases where a young or inex-
perienced person, through ignorance or susceptibility, has been carried away
for a time contrary to the dictates of cooler judgment; but the statements of
such persons are justly regarded with more or less suspicion. Far better is
it, far more honest and praiseworthy, for him who, having unwittingly made
a mistake, seeks to rectify it, to go his way and say nothing about it; for if
he talks of writing a book for the good of others, as a warning, and that
they may avoid his errors, few will believe him. 'If he has proved traitor
once,' they say, 'he will deceive again; and if he is sincere, we cannot more
than half believe him, for such an individual is never sure of himself.' John
C. Bennett, general, doctor, methodist preacher, and quack, is from his own
showing a bad man. He devotes some fifty pages to the vindication of his
character, which would not be necessary were he honest; other fifty are
given to defaming his late worshipful patron Joseph Smith, which would
never have been written were he true. When a man thrusts in your face
three-score certificates of his good character, each signed by from one to a
dozen persons, you may know that he is a very great rascal. Nor are we
disappointed here. This author is a charlatan, pure and simple; such was
he when he joined the Mormons, and before and after. We may credit him
fully when he says, 'I never believed in them or their doctrines;' although
in a letter to Dr Dyer, dated Nauvoo, Jan. 20, 1842, he declares: 'My heart is

There is another individual of similar name, and yet more similar character, James Arlington Ben-

filled with indignation, and my blood boils within me, when I contemplate the vast injustice and cruelty which Missouri has meted out to the great philanthropist and devout Christian, General Joseph Smith, and his honest and faithful adherents.' When, however, he affects patriotism and lofty devotion to the welfare of his fellow-men, pretending to have joined the society in order to frustrate 'a daring and colossal scheme of rebellion and usurpation throughout the north-western states, ... a despotic military and religious empire, the head of which, as emperor and pope, was to be Joseph Smith,' we know that the writer is well aware that it is all nonsense. Nor do we believe that he was induced to print his book 'by a desire to expose the enormous iniquities which have been perpetrated by one of the grossest and most infamous impostors that ever appeared upon the face of the earth.' We have heard and are still hearing so much of that kind of talk from some of the worst men in the community that it is becoming somewhat stale, and if the general really does not know better than this why he wrote his book, perhaps he will excuse me for telling him that it was, first, for notoriety; second, for money; and third, in order to make people think him a better and greater man than he is. When a man's ambition is pitched so low, it is a pity that he should not have the gratification of success. Bravely, then, the general proceeded to offer himself on the altar of his country, 'to overthrow the impostor and expose his iniquity' by 'professing himself a convert to his doctrines;' for 'the fruition of his hopeful project would, of course, have been preceded by plunder, devastation, and bloodshed, and by all the countless horrors which invariably accompany civil war.' We are still more impressed when we read: 'I was quite aware of the danger I ran'—that of being kicked out of some back door—'but none of these things deterred me.' Without wasting more time and space upon the man, we are well enough prepared to place a proper estimate upon his statements, particularly when we take into account that, in May of the very year in which his book was published, he went before Alderman Wells and made affidavit that Joseph Smith was an honest, virtuous, sincere, high-minded, and patriotic man. He says himself that he solemnly swore to be true to the Mormons and not reveal their secrets, and now in breaking that oath he has the audacity to ask us to regard him as an honest and truthful man! In some measure, at least, the statements of such men as this, taken up by the press and people, and reiterated throughout the land, have given the latter-day saints a worse name than they deserve. Some of his charges are too coarse and filthy for repetition. I will cite a few specimens, however, to show how far mendacity is sometimes carried in this direction.

Joseph Smith is a 'monster who is using the power he possesses to gratify a brutal lust;' 'a Giovanni or some dozens of mistresses;' 'must be branded as a consummate knave;' one 'of the most heaven-daring liars the world ever saw;' 'notoriously profane;' 'gets most gloriously drunk,' etc. In the most vulgar and licentious language, he goes on to describe what he calls the 'Mormon seraglio,' 'the female inquisition,' 'Joe's cloistered, chambered, and cyprian maids.' He revels in all the wickedness of this kind during past ages which he can make up, rolling it as a sweet morsel under his tongue, finally affirming that 'the holy Joe outdoes them all!' He says that any woman belonging to the society who lapses from virtue is condemned to a life of secret prostitution, the most trustworthy members of the church having knowledge of it; another class indulge in illicit intercourse by special permission of the prophet; another class are the spiritual wives. All this is said, be it remembered, within two or three months of the time he made oath that Smith was one of the best and purest of men. Next comes an exposé of several secret societies, the Danites, Destroying Angel, etc., and finally a list of murders and robberies perpetrated in that section during a certain time, all of

nett, also called general, whom Mackay, Smucker,
a reviewer in the *Edinburgh,* and others have mis-

which are charged to these agencies. Sidney Rigdon is praised by Bennett;
so much the worse for Sidney.   Doubtless this book played its part in bringing about the assassination of Joseph Smith. Says John Taylor of John C.
Bennett: 'At one time he was a good man, but fell into adultery, and was
cut off from the church for his iniquity;...he was also expelled from the municipal court, of which he was a member.' *Public Discussion,* 5-6.
    William Hall was an old gentleman of simple mind and manners when he
wrote his book; he appears to be earnest and truthful.   As he says of the
saints, so I should say of him: he meant well, but he should beware of bad
leaders.   Hall was not a great man in the church, like Bennett; nevertheless,
like Bennett he wrote a book, but unlike Bennett's, his book reads like that
of an honest man, although it is full of bitter accusations against the Mormons.   All such works should be taken with some degrees of allowance; for
when a person begins to rail against any people or individual, he is apt to be
carried away and misrepresent, intentionally or unintentionally. The period
that Hall's experiences cover is quite an important one, including as it does the
Illinois expulsion and the exodus to Great Salt Lake.
    Quite different from any of his brother apostates is John Hyde, Jr, who
cannot by right be placed in the category of vulgar ranter or hypocritical reformer.   I regard him as an able and honest man, sober and sincere.   He
does not denounce the sect as hypocrites.   'I know your sincerity; I know
also your delusion,' he writes. He does not even denounce all the leaders;
even to Brigham Young, whom he mercilessly scourges, he gives credit for
ability and sincerity.   'That you are sincere in your confidence in Joseph
Smith, and in your own pretensions,' he writes to him, 'I believe and acknowledge; but at the same time, that you are leading confiding thousands
to misery and ruin is evident...I admire your genius, but I deplore its exercise.
...I admire the industry of your people, their notable labors, and their general
sincerity; but I deplore their delusion, and I denounce their deceivers.' His
book is dedicated 'To the honest believers in Mormonism,' and he says to
them: 'In writing the following work I was not actuated by the base design
of helping to malign an unpopular people, nor by the unworthy one of administering to a mere idle curiosity.' John Hyde was born in England, in
1833, and joined the Mormons there when fifteen years of age. He was almost immediately ordained a priest and began to preach.   In 1851 he was
ordained one of the seventies, an office of equal power but inferior jurisdiction to that ot one of the twelve, and joined John Taylor in France.   With
about 400 Mormon converts he sailed from Liverpool in Feb. 1853, visited Nauvoo, and thence crossed the plains in company with 2,500 brethren to Salt Lake
City, where he married and began teaching school.   In Feb. 1854 he was 'initiated into the mysteries of the Mormon endowment,' became shaken in the
faith, and the following year, having accepted a mission to the Hawaiian Islands, he threw off Mormonism and preached and wrote against it instead of
for it.   In his book he gives a description of Salt Lake City in 1853-4, a chapter entitled 'Practical Polygamy,' and others on Mormon Mysteries, Education, Brigham Young, Book of Mormon, Theoretical Polygamy, and Suppression of Mormonism. Hyde's book would be quite useful were he not so
loose about his dates; it would appear from the way he throws statements
together that in the absence of a date he guessed at it.
    Still another style of book is that of John D. Lee, purporting to have
been written by him, but as a matter of fact written for the most part by
W. W. Bishop while Lee was in prison condemned to death.   The work, therefore, though the story of a Mormon, and of one who under the circumstances
could not be expected to be very friendly, is not by a Mormon. The book
is not essentially different from the matter published in the newspapers about
the time of Lee's execution, under the title of 'Confessions.' Lee gives the

taken for the original. The quality of impudence appears as fully in the second Bennett as in the first.[12]

As I have before observed, the misfortunes of the saints by no means dampened their ardor, or impoverished them as a society. Some lost their all; in that case the others helped them. Old scores were

story of his life, simply and honestly enough; to this is added an account of the Mountain Meadow massacre, and of the arrest, trial, and execution of Lee. He was a native of Illinois, born in 1812, worked hard and with success while a young man, became an enthusiastic Mormon in 1837, and went to Missouri. With everything there he was highly delighted; he attended devoutly all the services of the church, and was duly promoted. He was with his people at Nauvoo, migrated with them to Utah, and was adopted by Brigham Young. In 1877 he was executed for participation in the Mountain Meadow massacre, excusing himself while cursing others.

Mormonism and the Mormons; A Historical View of the rise and progress of the sect self-styled Latter-day Saints; by Daniel P. Kidder, is the title of a 16mo vol. of 342 pages, published in New York, and bearing no date, though entered for copyright in the year 1842. Mr Kidder certainly wrote a book on short acquaintance with the subject; as he says up to Nov. 1840, he knew little about it. On the 13th of that month he found himself on board a Mormon steamboat called the *Fulton City*, on the Mississippi River, bound for Nauvoo. Nearly all the passengers and crew were Mormons. Desirous of knowing more of them, and holding to the maxim that by teaching most is to be learned, he procured copies of the *Book of Mormon, Doctrine and Covenants, Howe's Mormonism Unveiled*, and *Corrill's Brief History*, and seating himself before them made his book, which consists chiefly of extracts from the above sources tied together with occasional remarks neither startling nor original. In Nauvoo, without date, but probably about 1841, were published two chapters of nonsense about women and their relations and duties to men, entitled, *An Extract from a Manuscript entitled The Peace-maker, or the Doctrines of the Millennium, being a Treatise on Religion and Jurisprudence, or a New System of Religion and Politics. For God, my Country, and my Rights. By Adney Hay Jacob, an Israelite, and a Shepherd of Israel. Nauvoo, Ill. J. Smith, Printer*. In a preface the reader is told: 'The author of this work is not a Mormon, although it is printed by their press.'

[12] In a letter to the prophet dated October 24, 1843, which has become quite famous, James A. Bennett pretends to have been baptized by Brigham Young, a ceremony that he alludes to as 'a glorious frolic in the clear blue ocean' with 'your most excellent and worthy friend, President B. Young.' 'Nothing of this kind,' he goes on to say, 'would in the least attach me to your person or cause. I am capable of being a most undeviating friend, without being governed by the smallest religious influence...I say, therefore, go ahead, you have my good wishes. You know Mahomet had his right-hand man,' etc. Smith replied at length in a religio-philosophic strain. More has been made of this correspondence than it deserves. It was printed in *Times and Seasons*, iv. 371-3, in *Cor. between Joseph Smith... Wentworth...and ...Calhoun*, as well as in *Mackay's The Mormons*, and *Smucker's Hist. Mor*. See also *Edinburgh Review*, April 1854, 334. Mackay observes: 'Joseph's reply to this singular and too candid epistle was quite as singular and infinitely more amusing. Joseph was too cunning a man to accept, in plain terms, the rude but serviceable offer; and he rebaked the vanity and presumption of Mr Bennett, while dexterously retaining him for future use.' All this would have some significance if Smith had been in the least deceived, or had the writer of this letter and the original rascal been one.

cancelled, old debts forgiven.[13]   There were no great
riches among them; yet he who had nothing could
not be called poor amid such surroundings.   Head
over all, temporal and spiritual, was Joseph Smith,
not only prophet and president, but general and
mayor.[14]   He had now approached the summit of his
career, and for a brief space was permitted to enjoy
his fame, wealth, and power in some degree of quiet.

They were salutary lessons that the prophet and
his people had received in Missouri, and for a time
their speech and manner were less arrogant than of
old.   But soon prosperity was far greater here than
ever before, and as with Israel of old the chastise-
ments of the Lord were soon forgotten.   From the
moment they crossed the river from Missouri into
Illinois their position as men and members of the
commonwealth was changed.   In the one state they
were regarded as fanatics, dangerous to the government and to the people, having associated assassins to
do their bidding, and holding to a doctrine of divine
inheritance with regard to all that country; in the

---

[13] 'At the conference in April 1840, the prophet delivered a lengthy address upon the history and condition of the saints. He reminded the brethren that all had suffered alike for the sake of the gospel. The rich and the
poor had been brought to a common level by persecution; that many of the
brethren were owing debts that they had been forced to contract in order to
get out of Missouri alive. He considered it was unchristian-like for the
brethren to demand the payment of such debts; that he did not wish to
screen any one from the just payment of his debts, but he did think that it
would be for the glory of the kingdom if the people would, of their own will,
freely forgive each other for all their existing indebtedness, one to the other,
then renew their covenants with almighty God and with each other; refrain
from evil, and live their religion; by this means, God's holy spirit would support and bless the people. The people were then asked if they were in favor
of thus bringing about the year of jubilee. All that felt so inclined were
asked to make it known by raising their hands; every hand in the audience
was raised.' The prophet then declared all debts of the saints, to and from
each other, forgiven and cancelled. He then gave the following words of
advice to the people: 'I wish you all to know that because you were justified
in taking property from your enemies while engaged in war in Missouri,
which was needed to support you, there is now a different condition of things
existing. We are no longer at war, and you must stop stealing. When the
right time comes we will go in force and take the whole state of Missouri. It
belongs to us as an inheritance; but I want no more petty stealing.' *Lee's
Mormonism*, 110–11.

[14] Smith was first mayor. Feb. 1, 1841, Bennett was elected mayor and
so continued till May 19, 1842, when Smith again assumed the office.

other they were esteemed as hard-working and thrifty American citizens, whose votes, to the party in power, were worth as much as those of the baptist or the methodist.

Such was their past and present status in the community. They were now treated, politically and socially, with conside[,] ation, especially by politicians. Thomas Carlin, governor of Illinois, was their friend, and granted them all the privileges they asked; Robert Lucas, governor of Iowa, was their friend, and promised them the protection due to every citizen of the United States, of whatsoever religion, creed, superstition, fanaticism, craze, or whatever people might choose to call it.

But soon there came a governor, named Thomas Ford, who knew not Joseph. He was a well meaning man enough, not blood-thirsty like Boggs, nor strong and cool-headed like Carlin, nor yet a man of positive action and opinion like Lucas; still, Ford was not a bad man, and if the saints had conducted themselves according to the wisdom of the world, they might in time, perhaps, have overcome the prejudices of the people. But prosperity seemed as fatal to them as adversity was profitable. All the best of heaven and earth was now theirs, and again Jeshurun waxed fat and kicked, revelations becoming less frequent as the cares of this world, the lusts of the flesh, and the pride of life crept in among the people.

The city charter of Nauvoo [15] allowed the enactment of any laws not in conflict with those of the state or of the United States, and particularly that a writ of *habeas corpus* might be issued in all cases arising under city ordinance. In the interpretation of this

[15] Describing Nauvoo at this period, Linforth remarks: 'Before the close of 1842 a vast improvement had taken place. The city, which then extended 3 or 4 miles on the river, and about the same distance back, had been regularly laid off into blocks, containing 4 lots of 11 by 12 rods each, between 700 and 800 houses had been erected, and the population numbered about 15,000. Two steam-mills and 2 printing-presses existed, and buildings for various manufactures were rapidly going up. In the mean time the temple and Nauvoo House were progressing.' *Route from Liverpool to G. S. L. Valley*, 62.

provision the saints allowed themselves rather a wide latitude, even assuming authority opposed to superior powers, and sometimes questioning the validity of state documents not countersigned by the mayor of Nauvoo. The counties surrounding Hancock, in which was Nauvoo, were fearful of the prosperity of the saints, and of their political influence; there were angry words and bickerings between the opposing societies, and then blows. The old Missouri feud was kept alive by suits instituted against Smith and others.[16] An attempt made to assassinate Governor Boggs was, of course, charged to the Mormons, and probably with truth. In fact, if we may believe their enemies, they did not deny it. Boggs had unlawfully ordered all the Mormons in Missouri killed if they did not leave the state: why had not they the same right, they argued, to break the law and kill him?[17]

Among the reports circulated, besides those of assassination and attempted assassination, the following will serve as specimens: That the plan of Smith

[16] When on his return from Quincy, to which place he had accompanied Hyrum Smith and William Law, who were on a mission to the east, Joseph was arrested the 5th of June, 1841, on a warrant from Gov. Carlin to deliver him to the Missouri state authorities. In return, Joseph Smith brought suit against J. H. Reynolds and H. G. Wilson for false imprisonment. This as well as other affairs of the kind kept up a bitter excitement.

[17] On the 6th of May, 1842, Gov. Boggs was fired at through a window, and narrowly escaped being killed. The crime was charged to O. P. Rockwell, 'with the connivance and under the instructions of Joseph Smith.' *Hyde's Mormonism*, 105, 206. Boggs swore he believed Smith a party to the attempted assassination, and instituted legal proceedings. *Mackay's The Mormons*, 139. Bennett, *Hist. Saints*, 281-2, labors hard to prove that Smith wanted Boggs killed, and said as much, which it seems to me few would deny. Bennett states that in 1841 Smith prophesied that Boggs would die by violent hands within a year. 'In the spring of the year 1842 Smith offered a reward of $500 to any man who would secretly assassinate Gov. Boggs.' Joseph O. Boggs, brother of the governor, writes Bennett, Sept. 12, 1842, 'We have now no doubt of the guilt of Smith and Rockwell.' *Id.*, 286. Rockwell was arrested, discharged, and went to Utah. 'Brigham has had him into the pulpit,' says Hyde, 'to address the meetings.' We read: 'Orin Porter Rockwell, the Mormon confined in our county jail some time since for the attempted assassination of ex-governor Boggs, was indicted by our last grand jury for escaping from the county jail some weeks since, and sent to Clay county for trial. Owing, however, to some informality in the proceedings, he was remanded to this county again for trial. There was not sufficient proof adduced against him to justify an indictment for shooting at ex-governor Boggs; and the grand jury, therefore, did not indict him for that offence.' *Independent Expositor; Niles' Register*, Sept. 30, 1843.

was to take the county, then the state, after that the
United States, and finally the whole world; that any
section making a move against the saints should be
destroyed by the Danites; that Smith declared his
prophecies superior to law, and threatened that if not
let alone he would prove a second Mahomet, and send
streams of blood from the Rocky Mountains to the
sea.

In an address to the saints at Nauvoo, September
1, 1842, Joseph stated that on account of the enemies
in pursuit of him, both in Missouri and in Illinois, he
deemed it best to retire for a time, and seek safety.[16]
He ordered his debts paid as they fell due, his property to be sold if necessary to meet requirements,
and exhorted all officers to be faithful to their trust.
"When the storm is past I will return," he said; "and
as for perils, they seem small things to me, for the
envy and wrath of man have been my common lot all
the days of my life." And again: "Verily thus saith
the Lord, let the work of my temple, and all the works
which I have appointed unto you, be continued and
not cease. Let all the records be had in order, that
they may be put in the archives of my holy temple.
I will write the word of the Lord from time to time
and send it to you by mail. I now close my letter for
the present, for the want of more time, for the enemy
is on the alert; and as the savior said, the prince of
this world cometh, but he hath nothing in me."

Five days later the prophet sent an address to the
saints, mainly touching the baptism for the dead, of
which more hereafter. "Now what do we hear in the
gospel which we have received? A voice of gladness!
A voice of mercy from heaven; and a voice of truth
out of the earth, glad tidings for the dead; a voice
of gladness for the living and dead; glad tidings of
great joy. And again what do we hear? Glad tidings
from Cumorah! Moroni, an angel from heaven, declaring the fulfilment of the prophets—the book to
be revealed. A voice of the Lord in the wilderness

of Fayette, Seneca county, declaring the three witnesses to bear record of the book. The voice of Michael on the banks of the Susquehanna, detecting the devil when he appeared as an angel of light. The voice of Peter, James, and John in the wilderness between Harmony, Susquehanna county, and Colesville, Boone county, on the Susquehanna River, declaring themselves as possessing the keys of the kingdom, and of the dispensation of the fulness of times. And again, the voice of God in the chamber of old Father Whitmer, in Fayette, Seneca county, and at sundry times and in divers places, through all the travels and tribulations of this church of Jesus Christ of Latter-day Saints."

We come now to a most momentous epoch in the history of the church, to the most important act of the prophet during the entire course of his wonderful life, to the act of all others pregnant with mighty results, if we except the primary proceedings relative to the sacred book and its translation.

Twenty years had passed since the plates of Mormon had been revealed to Joseph, during which time he had suffered divers and continued persecution. He and his followers had been reviled and spit upon from the beginning; some of them had been robbed, and beaten, hunted down, imprisoned, and slain. Yet they had prospered; the church had rapidly increased, and its members were blessed with plenty. Their neighbors spoke much evil of them and committed many violent acts. The saints were exceedingly annoying; they voted solid and claimed the whole world as theirs, including Jackson county, Missouri; they were wild in their thoughts, extravagant in their pretensions, and by no means temperate in the use of their tongues; they were not always prudent; they were not always without reproach.

Just how far certain members or leaders erred, bringing evil on all, it is impossible at this day to determine. The evidence comes to us in the form of rumors, general assertions, and bold statements from the mouths of men filled with deadly hate, and cannot be altogether trusted. Some of these have said that the leaders of the church, finding their power over the minds and bodies of their female associates so greatly increased, so rapidly becoming absolute, could not resist temptation, but fell into grievous sins like Jeroboam and David, and were thereby obliged to adopt some plan either to cover or make right their conduct.

It was easy for the gentiles to make such a charge appear plausible, in view of the fact that about this time the doctrine of plurality of wives as practised and promulgated in the scriptures attracted much attention. Most of the other acts, customs, and ordinances of the old and new testaments had been adopted in common with those contained in the book of Mormon by the latter-day church; why should not this? Wives and concubines without restriction had been permitted to the worthy men of old; the holy scriptures had nowhere condemned the custom; God had at no time ordered otherwise. On the contrary, it seemed in the line of example and duty; it seemed necessary to make the holy fabric symmetrical and complete. True, it was not now in vogue with either Jews or Christians; but neither were miracles nor special revelations. Surely, if God disapproved, he would have so declared; his commands he makes clear; particularly acts heinous in his sight he denounces loudly and with many repetitions.

Thus argued the elders. They did not consider, nor indeed care for, the fact that, viewed from the standpoint of intellectual progress, the revival of polygamy, or concubinage, in common with other practices of the half-savage Hebrews, was a retrogression, a turning back toward savagism. They found it sanctioned in the holy book in use by the most civilized nations of the earth, and they felt themselves able to make

it appear plausible.   If any had the right to adopt part
of the bible as their rule of conduct, accepting it all as
true, they claimed the right to adopt the whole of it
for their rule of conduct if they chose.   It was civilization, and not the holy scriptures, that forbade
polygamy, and they cared very little comparatively
for civilization.

Finally, on the 12th of July, 1843, while the chief
men of the church were thinking the matter over,
though saying little even among themselves, it is
stated that there came to Joseph a revelation, the last
of the prophet's revelations of which there is any
record.

"Verily, thus saith the Lord unto you, my servant
Joseph, that inasmuch as you have inquired of my
hand to know and understand wherein I, the Lord,
justified my servants Abraham, Isaac, and Jacob; as
also Moses, David, and Solomon, my servants, as touching the principles and doctrine of their having many
wives and concubines: Behold! and lo, I am the Lord
thy God, and will answer thee, as touching this matter.

"Abraham received concubines, and they bare him
children, and it was accounted unto him for righteousness, because they were given unto him, and he abode
in my law; as Isaac also, and Jacob, did none other
things than that which they were commanded.
David also received many wives and concubines, as
also Solomon, and Moses, my servant, as also many
others of my servants, from the beginning of creation
until this time, and in nothing did they sin, save in
those things which they received not of me.

"David's wives and concubines were given unto him
of me by the hand of Nathan, my servant, and others
of the prophets who had the keys of this power; and
in none of these things did he sin against me, save in
the case of Uriah and his wife: and, therefore, he hath
fallen from his exaltation, and received his portion;
and he shall not inherit them out of the world, for I
gave them unto another, saith the Lord.

"Verily, I say unto you, a commandment I give unto mine handmaid, Emma Smith, your wife, whom I have given unto you, that she stay herself, and partake not of that which I commanded you to offer unto her; for I did it, saith the Lord, to prove you all, as I did Abraham, and that I might require an offering at your hand by convenant and sacrifice; and let mine handmaid, Emma Smith, receive all those that have been given unto my servant Joseph, and who are virtuous and pure before me.

"And I command mine handmaid, Emma Smith, to abide and cleave unto my servant Joseph, and to none else. And again, verily, I say, let mine handmaid forgive my servant Joseph his trespasses, and then shall she be forgiven her trespasses, wherein she hath trespassed against me; and I, the Lord thy God, will bless her and multiply her, and make her heart to rejoice.

"And again, as pertaining to the law of the priesthood: if any man espouse a virgin, and desire to espouse another, and the first give her consent; and if he espouse the second, and they are virgins, and have vowed to no other man, then he is justified; he cannot commit adultery, for they are given unto him; for he cannot commit adultery with that belonging unto him, and to none else; and if he have ten virgins given unto him by this law he cannot commit adultery, for they belong to him, and they are given unto him; therefore he is justified."

It is said that as early as 1831 the will of the Lord in this respect had been revealed to Joseph. In translating the bible he had come upon the passages relating to plural wives and concubines, and had inquired of the Lord what he should do. He was told to wait, and not make the matter public then, the people not yet having faith to receive it. It was one of the severest trials the church had yet been called upon to undergo, and the wisest circumspection was necessary lest Joseph should be repudiated by his followers as a false prophet.   So he approached persons singly, first the man of the family and then the woman.   In 1841 Joseph began to take to himself plural wives, and his example was followed by some of the others. Finally, in order that all might know that he was not acting on his own responsibility alone, the revelation came, sanctioning and enforcing the system.   This, as I have given it, is the orthodox and authorized explanation of the matter.

Thus came to the saints the doctrine of polygamy, first to the leaders and for a time kept secret, and finally to the whole church, as one of its most prominent tenets.[18]   For years it was known only to a few, and it was not formally promulgated until after the great exodus, when the church had become well established in the valleys of the Yutas.[19]

There were several reasons for adopting this course. First, the hate and obloquy which would be engendered by its publication, and the wide-spread and bitter opposition it would meet.   The work of missionaries in the field would greatly suffer.   Many in the church would oppose it; women would rebel, while their sisters throughout christendom would hold them in derision. It was all so new and strange.   Even in theory it was startling enough; but put it in practice, and who could foretell the result?   The very foundations of

[18] John Hyde mentions a previous revelation. He says that about the year 1838 'Smith pretended to obtain a revelation from God authorizing him to practise polygamy, and began to practise it accordingly.' *Mormonism*, 203. See also *Slater's Mormonism*, 84, and *Deseret News*, Oct. 22, 1879.   There is no truth whatever in this assertion.   And yet John Hyde is regarded as pretty good authority; but in this loose way thousands of false statements have been made regarding the secrets of the saints.

[19] This revelation was first published in the *Deseret News* in 1852, and next in the *Millennial Star* at Liverpool, England, in 1853.   It is given entire elsewhere in this volume.   The *Edinburgh Review* of April 1854, 335, says, 'Not many months have yet passed since the Mormon leaders have decided on a bolder policy and have publicly avowed this portion of the system,' which shows that the fact of publication was not generally known to the gentile European world until two years after the official notice in Salt Lake City appeared. Copies of it will also be found in *Doc. and Cov.*, 423–32; *Young's Wife No. 19*, 77–86; *Ferris' Utah and the Mormons*, app.; *Burton's City of the Saints*, 451–7; *Tucker's Mormonism*, 172–82; *Smith's Rise, Prog. and Travels*, 42–8; *Pearl of Great Price*, 64–70; *Stenhouse's Tell It All*, 135–8; and *Stenhouse's Exposé of Polygamy*, 207–15.

the church might thereby be broken up.   If it must needs be, then let discretion be used.   Let the matter be broken to the church as it is able to receive it; let the system be introduced gradually, and practised secretly; by the chief men at first, and later by all.[20]

It was indeed a heavy load that the saints thus took upon themselves, willingly or unwillingly, in the service of God or in the service of Satan.   Up to this

[20] It is denied by some that polygamy was practised by the Mormons at this date.   In the *Deseret News* of Oct. 22, 1879, are several statements under oath to the effect that between 1840 and 1843 Joseph taught the doctrine of celestial or plural marriage, that several women were sealed to him according to this doctrine, and this with the consent of Joseph's wife, Emma Smith. On the other hand, it is stated in the *Salt Lake City Tribune*, Oct. 3, 1879, that Emma denied that her husband was ever married to another, or that, so far as she knew, he ever had improper relations with any woman.   Elder Pratt reported at Plano, Ill., in the summer of 1878, several instances of Joseph's having had wives sealed to him, one at least as early as April 5, 1841.   'Smith introduced (at Nauvoo) the system of spiritual wifeism, and had largely increased his household by celestial ensealment.   This was the preliminary step of polygamy, or its practical adoption, though it had not yet been revealed as a tenet in the Mormon creed.' *Tucker's Mormonism*, 170.   The revelation was written after he had taken other wives. *Stenhouse's Exposé of Polygamy*, 70.   Jos. Smith adopts it and is sealed to Eliza Snow. *Tullidge's Life of Young*, Suppl. 22.   In a letter to the *Deseret News*, Oct. 22, 1879, Eliza R. Snow signs her name as 'a wife of Joseph Smith the prophet.' 'Brigham Young delivered over to Jo Smith all his wives except one, and soon after Smith had a revelation that Young should be his successor as head of the church.' *Slater's Mormonism*, 84.   John D. Lee says: 'I understood that Brig. Young's wife was sealed to Joseph.   After his death Brig. Young told me that Joseph's time on earth was short, and that the Lord allowed him privileges that we could not have.' *Mormonism*, 147.   Jos. Smith had taken some more wives, but the revelation required that he should do it without publicity (for fear of the mob). *Richards' Reminiscences*, MS., 18.   'Joseph Smith lost his life entirely through attempting to persuade a Mrs Dr Foster, at Nauvoo, that it was the will of God she should become his spiritual wife; not to the exclusion of her husband, Dr Foster, but only to become his in time for eternity.   This nefarious offer she confessed to her husband.   Some others of a similar nature were discovered, and Dr Foster, William Law, and others began to expose Smith.   Their paper was burned, type and press demolished, for which Smith was arrested, and afterward shot by Missourians, at Carthage, Ill.' *Hyde's Mormonism*, 85.

'Smith and Noble repaired by night to the banks of the Mississippi, where Noble's sister was sealed to Smith by Noble, and the latter to another woman by Smith.   These were the first plural marriages, and a son born to Noble the first child born in polygamy.' *Young's Wife No. 19*, 72–3.   'That polygamy existed at Nauvoo, and is now a matter scarcely attempted to be concealed among the Mormons, is certain.' *Gunnison's Mormons*, 120.   On the other side, in *Times and Seasons*, iv. 143 (March 15, 1843), we read, 'The charge of advocating a plurality of wives is as false as the many other ridiculous charges brought against us.' In *Id.*, v. 474 (March 15, 1844), Hyrum Smith declares that no such doctrine is taught or practised; and on p. 715 it is declared that 'the law of the land and the rules of the church do not allow one man to have more than one wife alive at once.' For additional denials by Parley Pratt, John Taylor, and others, see *S. L. Tribune*, Nov. 11, 1879.

time, though citizens of the commonwealth, they had
not been in sympathy with other citizens; though
religionists, they were in deadly opposition to all other
religions; as a fraternity, bound by friendly compact,
not alone spiritually but in temporal matters, in buying
and selling, in town-building, farming, and stock-raising, in all trades and manufactures, they stood on vant-
age-ground. They were stronger than their immediate
neighbors—stronger socially, politically, and industrially; and the people about them felt this, and while
hating, feared them.

It is true, that on their first arrival in Zion they
were not wealthy; neither were their neighbors. They
were not highly educated or refined or cultured;
neither were their neighbors. They were sometimes
loud and vulgar of speech; so were their neighbors.
Immorality cropped out in certain quarters; so it did
among the ancient Corinthians and the men of modern Missouri; there was some thieving among them;
but they were no more immoral or dishonest than
their persecutors who made war on them, and as
they thought without a shadow of right.

There is no doubt that among the Mormons as
among the gentiles, perhaps among the Mormon
leaders as among the gentile leaders, fornication and
adultery were practised. It has been so in other ages
and nations, in every age and nation; it is so now,
and is likely to be so till the end of the world. But
when the testimony on both sides is carefully weighed,
it must be admitted that the Mormons in Missouri
and Illinois were, as a class, a more moral, honest,
temperate, hard-working, self-denying, and thrifty
people than the gentiles by whom they were surrounded. Says John D. Lee on entering the Missouri fraternity and, at the time of this remarking, by
no means friendly to the saints, "The motives of the
people who composed my neighborhood were pure;
they were all sincere in their devotions, and tried to
square their actions through life by the golden rule. . .

The word of a Mormon was then good for all it was pledged to or for. I was proud to be an associate with such honorable people." And thus Colonel Kane, a disinterested observer, and not a Mormon: As compared with the other "border inhabitants of Missouri, the vile scum which our society, like the great ocean, washes upon its frontier shores," the saints were "persons of refined and cleanly habits and decent language."

Nevertheless the sins of the entire section must be visited on them. Were there any robberies for miles around, they were charged by their enemies upon the Mormons; were there any house-burnings or assassinations anywhere among the gentiles, it was the Danites who did it. Of all that has been laid at their door I find little proved against them. The charges are general, and preferred for the most part by irresponsible men; in answer to them they refer us to the records. On the other hand, the outrages of their enemies are easily followed; for they are not denied, but are rather gloried in by the perpetrators. To shoot a Mormon was indeed a distinction coveted by the average gentile citizen of Illinois and Missouri, and was no more regarded as a crime than the shooting of a Blackfoot or Pawnee. Of course the Mormons retaliated.

Polygamy was a heavy load in one sense; in another sense it was a bond of strength. While in the eyes of the world its open avowal placed the saints outside the pale of respectability, and made them amenable to the law, among themselves as law-breakers, openly defying the law, and placing themselves and their religion above all law, the very fact of being thus legal offenders, subject to the penalties and punishments of the law, brought the members of the society so acting into closer relationship, cementing them as a sect, and making them more dependent on each other and on their leaders. It is plain that while thus bringing upon themselves ignominy and reproach,

while laying themselves open to the charge of being
law-breakers, and assuming an attitude of defiance
toward the laws and institutions of the country in
which they lived, this bond of sympathy, of crim-
inality if you will, particularly when made a matter of conscience, when recognized as a mandate from
the almighty, higher than any human law, and in
whose obedience God himself was best pleased, and
would surely afford protection, could but prove in the
end a bond of strength, particularly if permitted to
attain age and respectability among themselves, and
assume the form of a concrete principle and of sacred
obligation.

If instead of falling back upon the teachings of the
old testament, and adopting the questionable practices
of the half-civilized Jews; if instead of taking for their
models Abraham, David, and Solomon, the saints at
Nauvoo had followed the advice of Paul to the saints
at Ephesus, putting away fornication and all uncleanness, and walking worthy of their vocation, in all
lowliness and meekness, as children of light, they would
probably have remained in their beautiful city, and
come into the inheritance of their Missouri Zion as
had been prophesied. Had they consulted more
closely the signs of the times, had they been less
orthodox in their creed, less patriarchal in their practices, less biblical in their tenets, less devoted in their
doctrines—in a word, had they followed more closely
the path of worldly wisdom, and, like opposing christian sects, tempered religion with civilization, giving
up the worst parts of religion for the better parts of
civilization, I should not now be writing their history,
as one with the history of Utah.

But now was brought upon them this overwhelming
issue, which howsoever it accorded with ancient scripture teachings, and as they thought with the rights
of man, was opposed to public sentiment, and to the
conscience of all civilized nations. Forever after they
must have this mighty obstacle to contend with; for-

ever after they must live under the ban of the christian world; though, with unshaken faith in their
prophet and his doctrine of spiritual wedlock, they
might scorn the world's opinion, and in all sincerity
and singleness of heart thank God that they were
accounted worthy to have all manner of evil spoken
of them falsely.

During this period of probation the church deemed
it advisable to deny the charge, notably by Elder
Pratt in a public sermon, and also by Joseph Smith.
"Inasmuch as this Church of Christ has been re-
proached with the crime of fornication and polygamy,
we declare that we believe that one man should have
one wife, and one woman but one husband, except in
case of death, when either is at liberty to marry
again."[21] In the *Times and Seasons* of February 1,
1844, we have a notice signed by Joseph and Hyrum
Smith: "As we have lately been credibly informed
that an elder of the Church of Jesus Christ of Latter-
day Saints, by the name of Hiram Brown, has been
preaching polygamy and other false and corrupt doctrines in the county of Lapeer, state of Michigan, this
is to notify him and the church in general that he
has been cut of from the church for his iniquity."

Notwithstanding these solemn denials and denunciations in high places, the revelation and the practices which it sanctioned were not easily concealed.[22]
As yet, however, the calumny of the gentiles and
the bickering of the saints vexed not the soul of Joseph. He was now in the zenith of his fame and
power; his followers in Europe and America numbered

[21] *Doctrine and Covenants*, app. 331.
[22] 'It is believed,' writes Governor Ford not long afterward to the Illinois
legislature, 'that Joseph Smith had announced a revelation from heaven
sanctioning polygamy, by some kind of spiritual-wife system, which I never
could well understand; but at any rate, whereby a man was allowed one
wife in pursuance of the laws of the country, and an indefinite number of
others, to be enjoyed in some mystical and spiritual mode; and that he himself, and many of his followers, had practised upon the precepts of this
revelation, by seducing a large number of women.' *Message to Ill. Sen.*, 14th
Ass. 1st Sess., 6. A copy of Ford's message will be found in *Utah Tracts*,
no. 11.

more than a hundred thousand; his fortune was estimated at a million dollars; he was commander-in-chief of the Nauvoo Legion, a body of troops "which," remarks an artillery officer, from his own observation, "would do honor to any body of armed militia in any of the states, and approximates very closely to our regular forces;" he was mayor of the city; and now, as the crowning point of his earthly glory, he was announced in February 1844 as a candidate for the presidency of the United States, while Sidney Rigdon was named for vice-president. Whether this was done for effect or in earnest is somewhat doubtful, for it appears that the prophet's head was a little turned about this time; but it is certain that the people of Illinois and Missouri believed him to be in earnest. Addressing letters to Clay and Calhoun, near the close of 1843, he asked each of them what would be his rule of action toward the Mormons as a people should he be elected to the presidency. The reply in both cases was non-committal and unsatisfactory;[23] whereupon Joseph issues an address setting forth his views on the government and policy of the United States, and foreshadows his own policy, in which we find many excellent features and many absurdities. "No honest man can doubt for a moment," he says, "but the glory of American liberty is on the wane; and that calamity and confusion will sooner or later destroy the peace of the people. Speculators will urge a national bank as a savior of credit and comfort. A hireling pseudo-priesthood will plausibly push abolition doctrines and doings and 'human rights' into congress, and into every other place where conquest smells of fame or opposition swells to popularity."[24]

[23] Copies of the correspondence may be found in *Times and Seasons*, v. 393–6, 544–8; *Mackay's The Mormons*, 151–62; *Olshausen, Geschichte der Mormonen*, 202–19.

[24] 'Now, oh people!' he continues, 'turn unto the Lord and live; and reform this nation. Frustrate the designs of wicked men. Reduce congress at least one half. Two senators from a state and two members to a million of population will do more business than the army that now occupy the halls

The aspirations of the prophet, pretended or otherwise, to the highest office in the republic, together with renewed, and at this juncture exceedingly dangerous, claims, pointing toward almost universal empire,[25] brought upon him afresh the rage of the surrounding gentile populace, and resulted in an awful tragedy, the circumstances of which I am now about to relate. "The great cause of popular fury," writes Governor Ford shortly after the occurrence, " was that the Mormons at several preceding elections had cast their vote as a unit; thereby making the fact apparent that no one could aspire to the honors or offices of the country, within the sphere of their influence, without their approbation and votes."

Indeed, a myriad of evils about this time befell the church, all portending bloody destruction. There were

of the national legislature. Pay them two dollars and their board per diem, except Sundays; that is more than the farmer gets, and he lives honestly. Curtail the offices of government in pay, number, and power, for the philistine lords have shorn our nation of its goodly locks in the lap of Delilah. Petition your state legislature to pardon every convict in their several penitentiaries, blessing them as they go, and saying to them in the name of the Lord, Go thy way and sin no more...Petition also, ye goodly inhabitants of the slave states, your legislators to abolish slavery by the year 1850, or now, and save the abolitionist from reproach and ruin, infamy and shame. Pray congress to pay every man a reasonable price for his slaves out of the surplus revenue arising from the sale of public lands, and from the deduction of pay from the members of congress...Give every man his constitional freedom, and the president full power to send an army to suppress mobs; and the states authority to repeal and impugn that relic of folly which makes it necessary for the governor of a state to make the demand of the president for troops in cases of invasion or rebellion. The governor himself may be a mobber, and instead of being punished as he should be for murder and treason, he may destroy the very lives, rights, and property he should protect. Like the good Samaritan, send every lawyer as soon as he repents and obeys the ordinances of heaven, to preach the gospel to the destitute, without purse or scrip, pouring in the oil and the wine...Were I the president of the United States, by the voice of a virtuous people, I would honor the old paths of the venerated fathers of freedom; I would walk in the tracks of the illustrious patriots, who carried the ark of the government upon their shoulders with an eye single to the glory of the people... When a neighboring realm petitioned to join the union of the sons of liberty, my voice would be, Come; yea, come Texas; come Mexico; come Canada; and come all the world—let us be brethren; let us be one great family; and let there be universal peace.' A full copy of the address is given in *Times and Seasons*, v. 528–533; *Mackay's The Mormons*, 141–51; *Remy's Jour. to G. S. L. City*, 353–71.

[25] Two months after announcing himself a candidate for the presidency, Joseph again publicly declared that all America, from north to south, constituted the Zion of the saints, theirs by right of heavenly inheritance.

suits and counter-suits at law; arrests and rearrests;
schisms, apostasies, and expulsions; charges one against
another of vice and immorality, Joseph himself being
implicated. Here was one elder unlawfully trying
his hand at revelations, and another preaching polygamy. Many there were whom it was necessary not
only to cut off from the church, but to eradicate with
their evil influences from society. Among the prophet's most inveterate enemies were William Law, who
sought to betray Smith into the hands of the Missourians, and almost succeeded—Doctor Foster and
Francis M. Higbee, who dealt in scandal, charging
Joseph, Hyrum, Sidney, and others with seducing
women, and having more wives than one. Suits of
this kind brought by the brethren against each other,
but more particularly by the leaders against high
officials, were pending in the Nauvoo municipal court
for over two years.

Early in June 1844 was issued the first number of
the *Nauvoo Expositor*, the publishers being apostate
Mormons and gentiles.[26] The primary object of the
publication was to stir up strife in the church, and
aid its enemies in their work of attempted extermination. Its columns were at once filled with foul abuse
of the prophet and certain elders of the church,
assailing their character by means of affidavits, and
charging them with all manner of public and private
crimes, and abusing and misrepresenting the people.
The city council met, and pronouncing the journal
a nuisance, ordered its abatement. Joseph Smith
being mayor, it devolved on him to see the order
executed, and he issued instruction to the city marshal and the policemen accordingly. The officers
of the law forthwith entered the premises, and de-

[26] In *Remy's Jour. to G. S. Lake City*, i. 388, it is stated that, among others,
a renegade catholic priest, J. H. Jackson by name, 'conceived the idea of
starting at Nauvoo a newspaper called the *Expositor*, with the avowed object
of opposing the Mormons.' I find no confirmation of this statement. The
first number of the *Nauvoo Neighbor* had been issued May 3, 1843, in place
of the *Wasp*, suspended.

stroyed the establishment, tearing down the presses and throwing the type into the street.[27] For this act the proprietors obtained from the authorities of the town of Carthage, some twenty miles distant, a warrant for the arrest of Joseph Smith, which was placed in the hands of the Carthage constable to be served.

It was a proceeding not at all to the taste of the Mormons that their mayor should be summoned for misdemeanor before the magistrate of another town, and Smith refused to go. He was willing to be tried before a state tribunal. Meanwhile the offenders were brought before the municipal court of Nauvoo, on a writ of habeas corpus, and after examination were discharged. The cry was then raised throughout the country that Joseph Smith and associates, public offenders, ensconced among their troops in the stronghold of Nauvoo, defied the law, refusing to respond to the call of justice; whereupon the men of Illinois, to the number of two or three thousand, some coming even from Missouri, rallied to the support of the Carthage constable, and stood ready, as they said, not only to arrest Joe Smith, but to burn his town and kill every man, woman, and child in it.

As the forces of the enemy enlarged and grew yet more and more demonstrative in their wrath, the town prepared for defence, the Nauvoo Legion being called out and placed under arms, by instructions from Governor Ford to Joseph Smith, as general in command. This gave rise to a report that they were about to make a raid on the neighboring gentile settlements.[28]

[27] Letter of John S. Fullmer to the *New York Herald*, dated Nauvoo, Oct. 30, 1844 (but not publshed until several years later). A copy of it will be found in *Utah Tracts*, ix. p. 7. Smith had been elected mayor on the resignation of John C. Bennett April 19, 1842. Mackay, *The Mormons*, 168, says: 'A body of the prophet's adherents, to the number of two hundred and upward, sallied forth in obedience to this order, and proceeding to the office of the *Expositor*, speedily razed it to the ground.' Remy states that 'an order to destroy the journal signed by Joseph was immediately put into execution by a police officer, who proceeded the same day to break up the presses.' *Journey*, i. 389. Ford declares that the marshal aided by a portion of the legion executed his warrant by destroying the press and scattering the type and other materials of the office. Message to *Ill. Sen.*, 14th Ass. 1st Sess., 4.

[28] 'At a meeting of the citizens of Hancock co. held at Carthage, on the

In consequence of these rumors and counter-rumors the governor went to Carthage. Previous to this, frequent communications were sent to him at Springfield by Joseph Smith, informing him of the position of affairs in and around Nauvoo. The governor in his *History of Illinois,* referring to these times, writes: "These also were the active men in blowing up the fury of the people, in hopes that a popular movement might be set on foot, which would result in the expulsion or extermination of the Mormon voters. For this purpose public meetings had been called, inflammatory speeches had been made, exaggerated reports had been extensively circulated, committees had been appointed, who rode night and day to spread the reports and solicit the aid of neighboring counties, and at a public meeting at Warsaw resolutions were passed to expel or exterminate the Mormon population. This was not, however, a movement which was unanimously concurred in. The county contained a goodly number of inhabitants in favor of peace, or who at least desired to be neutral in such a contest. These were stigmatized by the name of Jack Mormons, and there were not a few of the more furious exciters of the people who openly expressed their intention to involve them in the common expulsion or extermination."

Thomas Ford, governor of Illinois, was as a man rather above the average politician usually chosen among these American states to fill that position. Not specially clear-headed, and having no brain power to spare, he was quite respectable and had some conscience, as is frequently the case with mediocre men. He had a good heart, too, was in no wise vindictive, and though he was in no sense a strong man, his sense of right and equity could be quite stubborn upon oc-

6th inst, it was resolved to call in the people of the surrounding counties and states, to assist them in delivering up Joe Smith, if the governor of Illinois refused to comply with the requisition of the governor of Missouri. The meeting determined to avenge with blood any assaults made upon citizens by the Mormons. It was also resolved to refuse to obey officers elected by the Mormons, who have complete control of the country, being a numerical majority.' *Missouri Reporter,* in *Niles Register,* lxv. 70, Sept. 30, 1843.

casion. Small in body, he was likewise small in mind;
indeed, there was a song current at the time that
there was no room in his diminutive organism for such
a thing as a soul. Nevertheless, though bitterly censured by some of the Mormons, I do not think Ford
intended to do them wrong. That he did not believe
all the rumors to their discredit is clearly shown in
his statement of what was told him during the days
he was at Carthage. He says: "A system of excitement and agitation was artfully planned and executed
with tact. It consisted in speading reports and rumors
of the most fearful character. As examples: On
the morning before my arrival at Carthage, I was
awakened at an early hour by the frightful report,
which was asserted with confidence and apparent con-
sternation, that the Mormons had already commenced
the work of burning, destruction, and murder, and that
every man capable of bearing arms was instantly
wanted at Carthage for the protection of the county.
We lost no time in starting; but when we arrived at
Carthage we could hear no more concerning this
story. Again, during the few days that the militia
were encamped at Carthage, frequent applications
were made to me to send a force here, and a force
there, and a force all about the country, to prevent
murders, robberies, and larcenies which, it was said,
were threatened by the Mormons. No such forces
were sent, nor were any such offences committed at
that time, except the stealing of some provisions, and
there was never the least proof that this was done
by a Mormon."

On the morning to which he refers, the report was
brought to him with the usual alarming accompaniments of fears being expressed of frightful carnage,
and the like. Hastily dressing, he assured the crowd
collected outside of the house in which he had lodged
that they need have no uneasiness respecting the matter, for he was very sure he could settle the difficulty
peaceably. The Mormon prophet knew him well,

and would trust him. What he purposed doing was to demand the surrender of Joseph Smith and others. He wished them to promise him that they would lend their assistance to protect the prisoners from violence, which they agreed to do.

After his arrival at Carthage the governor sent two men to Nauvoo as a committee to wait on Joseph Smith, informing him of his arrival, with a request that Smith would inform him in relation to the difficulties that then existed in the county. Dr J. M. Bernhisel and Elder John Taylor were appointed as a committee by Smith, and furnished with affidavits and documents in relation both to the proceedings of the Mormons and those of the mob; in addition to the general history of the transaction they took with them a duplicate of those documents which had previously been forwarded by Bishop Hunter, Elder James, and others. This committee waited on the governor, who expressed an opinion that Joseph Smith and all parties concerned in passing or executing the city law in relation to the press had better come to Carthage; however repugnant it might be to their feelings, he thought it would have a tendency to allay public excitement, and prove to the people what they professed, that they wished to be governed by law. The next day the constable and a force of ten men were despatched to Nauvoo to make the arrests. The accused were told that if they surrendered they would be protected; otherwise the whole force of the state would be called out, if necessary, to take them.

Upon the arrival of the constable and his posse, the mayor and the members of the city council declared that they were willing to surrender. Eight o'clock was the hour appointed, but the accused failed to make their appearance; whereupon the constable returned, and reported that they had fled. The governor was of opinion that the constable's action was part of a plot to get the troops into Nauvoo and exterminate the Mormons. He called a council of officers and proposed to march on the town with the small force under his command, but was dissuaded. He hesitated to make a further call on the militia, as the harvest was nigh and the men were needed to gather it. Meanwhile, ascertaining that the Mormons had three pieces of cannon and two hundred and fifty stand of arms belonging to the state, the possession of which gave offence to the gentiles, he demanded a surrender of the state arms, again promising protection.

On the 24th of June[29] Joseph and Hyrum Smith, the members of the council, and all others demanded, proceeded to Carthage, gave themselves up, and were charged with riot. All entered into recognizances before the justice of the peace to appear for trial, and were released from custody. Joseph and Hyrum, however, were rearrested, and, says Ford, were charged with overt treason, having ordered out the legion to resist the posse comitatus, though, as he states, the degree of their crime would depend on circumstances. The governor's views on this matter are worthy of note. "The overt act of treason charged against them," he remarks, "consisted in the alleged levying of war against the state by declaring martial law in Nauvoo, and in ordering out the legion to resist the posse comitatus. Their actual guiltiness of the charge would depend upon circumstances. If their opponents had been seeking to put the law in force in good faith, and nothing more, then an array of a military force in open resistance to the posse comitatus and the militia of the state most probably would have amounted to treason. But if those opponents merely intended to use the process of the law, the militia of the state, and the posse comitatus as cat's-paws to compass the possession of their persons for the purpose of murdering them afterward, as the

---

[29] Report, ut supra, 10–11. In *Times and Seasons*, v. 560, it is stated that 'on Monday, June 24th, after Ford had sent word that eighteen persons demanded on a warrant, among whom were Joseph Smith and Hyrum Smith, should be protected by the militia of the state, they in company with ten or twelve others start for Carthage.'

sequel demonstrated the fact to be, it might well be doubted whether they were guilty of treason."

With the Nauvoo Legion at their back, the two brothers voluntarily placed themselves in the power of the governor who, demanding and accepting their surrender, though doubting their guilt, nevertheless declared that they were not his prisoners, but the prisoners of the constable and jailer. Leaving two companies to guard the jail, he disbanded the main body of his troops, and proceeding to Nauvoo, addressed the people, beseeching them to abide by the law. "They claimed," he says, "to be a law-abiding people; and insisted that as they looked to the law alone for their protection, so were they careful themselves to observe its provisions. Upon the conclusion of my address, I proposed to take a vote on the question, whether they would strictly observe the laws, even in opposition to their prophet and leaders. The vote was unanimous in favor of this proposition." The governor then set forth for Carthage, and such in substance is his report when viewed in the most favorable light.[30]

It is related that as Joseph set forth to deliver himself up to the authorities he exclaimed: "I am going like a lamb to the slaughter; but I am calm as a summer's morning; I have a conscience void of offence toward God and toward all men. I shall die innocent, and it shall yet be said of me, He was murdered in cold blood."[31] Nevertheless, for a moment he hesitated. Should he offer himself a willing sacrifice, or should he endeavor to escape out of their hands? Thus meditating, he crossed the river thinking

[30] *Message*, ut supra. The above appear to be the facts of the case, so far as they can be sifted from a lengthy report, which consists mainly of apology or explanation of what the governor did or left undone.

[31] *Smith's Doc. and Cov.*, app. 335. The same morning he read in the fifth chapter of Ether, 'And it came to pass that I prayed unto the Lord that he would give unto the gentiles grace, that they might have charity. And it came to pass that the Lord said unto me, If they have not charity it mattereth not unto you, thou hast been faithful; wherefore thy garments are clean. And because thou hast seen thy weakness, thou shalt be made strong, even unto the sitting down in the place which I have prepared in the mansions of my father.'

to depart. On reaching the opposite bank he turned and gazed upon the beautiful city, the holy city, his own hallowed creation, the city of Joseph, with its shining temple, its busy hum of industry, and its thousand happy homes. And they were his people who were there, his very own, given to him of God; and he loved them! Were he to leave them now, to abandon them in this time of danger, they would be indeed as sheep without a shepherd, stricken, and scattered, and robbed, and butchered by the destroyer. No, he could not do it. Better die than to abandon them thus! So he recrossed the river, saying to his brother Hyrum, "Come, let us go together, and let God determine what we shall do or suffer."

Bidding their families and friends adieu, the two brothers set out for Carthage. Their hearts were very heavy. There was dire evil abroad; the air was oppressive, and the sun shot forth malignant rays. Once more they returned to their people; once more they embraced their wives and kissed their children, as if they knew, alas! that they should never see them again.

The party reached Carthage about midnight, and on the following day the troops were formed in line, and Joseph and Hyrum passed up and down in company with the governor, who showed them every respect—either as guests or victims—introducing them as military officers under the title of general. Present were the Carthage Greys, who showed signs of mutiny, hooting at and insulting the prisoners—for such in fact they were, being committed to jail the same afternoon until discharged by due course of law.

A few hours later Joseph asked to see the governor, and next morning Ford went to the prison. "All this is illegal," said the former. "It is a purely civil matter, not a question to be settled by force of arms." "I know it," said the governor, "but it is better so; I did not call out this force, but found it assembled; I pledge you my honor, however, and the faith and honor of the state, that no harm shall come to you while undergoing this imprisonment." The governor took his departure on the morning of the 27th of June. Scarcely was he well out of the way when measures were taken for the consummation of a most damning deed. The prison was guarded by eight men detailed from the Carthage Greys, their company being in camp on the public square a quarter of a mile distant, while another company under Williams, also the sworn enemies of the Mormons, was encamped eight miles away, there awaiting the development of events.

It was a little after five o'clock in the evening. Joseph and Hyrum Smith were confined in an upper room. With the prisoners were John Taylor and Willard Richards, other friends having withdrawn a few moments before. At this juncture a band of a hundred and fifty armed men with painted faces appeared before the jail, and presently surrounded it. The guard shouted vociferously and fired their guns over the heads of the assailants, who paid not the slightest attention to them.[32] I give what followed from *Burton's City of the Saints*, being the statement of President John Taylor, who was present and wounded on the occasion.

"I was sitting at one of the front windows of the jail, when I saw a number of men, with painted faces, coming around the corner of the jail, and aiming toward the stairs. The other brethren had seen the same, for, as I went to the door, I found Brother Hyrum Smith and Dr Richards already leaning against it. They both pressed against the door with their shoulders to prevent its being opened, as the lock and latch were comparatively useless. While in this position, the mob, who had come up stairs, and tried to open the door, probably thought it was

[32] Littlefield says the Carthage Greys were marched in a body, 'within about eight rods of the jail, where they halted, in plain view of the whole transaction, until the deed was executed.' *Narrative*, 9.

locked, and fired a ball through the keyhole; at this Dr Richards and Brother Hyrum leaped back from the door, with their faces toward it; almost instantly another ball passed through the panel of the door, and struck Brother Hyrum on the left side of the nose, entering his face and head. At the same instant, another ball from the outside entered his back, passing through his body and striking his watch. The ball came from the back, through the jail window, opposite the door, and must, from its range, have been fired from the Carthage Greys, who were placed there ostensibly for our protection, as the balls from the fire-arms, shot close by the jail, would have entered the ceiling, we being in the second story, and there never was a time after that when Hyrum could have received the latter wound. Immediately, when the balls struck him, he fell flat on his back, crying as he fell, 'I am a dead man!' He never moved afterward.

"I shall never forget the deep feeling of sympathy and regard manifested in the countenance of Brother Joseph as he drew nigh to Hyrum, and, leaning over him, exclaimed, 'Oh! my poor, dear brother Hyrum!' He, however, instantly arose, and with a firm, quick step, and a determined expression of countenance, approached the door, and pulling the six-shooter left by Brother Wheelock from his pocket, opened the door slightly, and snapped the pistol six successive times; only three of the barrels, however, were discharged. I afterward understood that two or three were wounded by these discharges, two of whom, I am informed, died.[33] I had in my hands a large, strong hickory stick, brought there by Brother Markham, and left by him, which I had seized as soon as I saw the mob approach; and while Brother Joseph was firing the pistol, I stood close behind him. As soon

[33] 'He wounded three of them, two mortally, one of whom, as he rushed down out of the door, was asked if he was badly hurt. He replied, "Yes; my arm is shot all to pieces by old Joe; but I don't care, I've got revenge; I shot Hyrum!"' *Id.*, 11.

as he had discharged it he stepped back, and I immediately took his place next to the door, while he occupied the one I had done while he was shooting. Brother Richards, at this time, had a knotty walking-stick in his hands belonging to me, and stood next to Brother Joseph, a little farther from the door, in an oblique direction, apparently to avoid the rake of the fire from the door. The firing of Brother Joseph made our assailants pause for a moment; very soon after, however, they pushed the door some distance open, and protruded and discharged their guns into the room, when I parried them off with my stick, giving another direction to the balls.

"It certainly was a terrible scene: streams of fire as thick as my arm passed by me as these men fired, and, unarmed as we were, it looked like certain death. I remember feeling as though my time had come, but I do not know when, in any critical position, I was more calm, unruffled, energetic, and acted with more promptness and decision. It certainly was far from pleasant to be so near the muzzles of those fire-arms as they belched forth their liquid flames and deadly balls. While I was engaged in parrying the guns, Brother Joseph said, 'That's right, Brother Taylor, parry them off as well as you can.' These were the last words I ever heard him speak on earth.

"Every moment the crowd at the door became more dense, as they were unquestionably pressed on by those in the rear ascending the stairs, until the whole entrance at the door was literally crowded with muskets and rifles, which, with the swearing, shouting, and demoniacal expressions of those outside the door and on the stairs, and the firing of the guns, mingled with their horrid oaths and execrations, made it look like pandemonium let loose, and was, indeed, a fit representation of the horrid deed in which they were engaged.

"After parrying the guns for some time, which now protruded thicker and farther into the room, and

seeing no hope of escape or protection there, as we
were now unarmed, it occurred to me that we might
have some friends outside, and that there might be
some chance to escape in that direction, but here
there seemed to be none. As I expected them every
moment to rush into the room—nothing but extreme
cowardice having thus far kept them out—as the
tumult and pressure increased, without any other
hope, I made a spring for the window which was
right in front of the jail door, where the mob was
standing, and also exposed to the fire of the Carthage
Greys, who were stationed some ten or twelve rods
off. The weather was hot, we had our coats off, and
the window was raised to admit air. As I reached
the window, and was on the point of leaping out, I
was struck by a ball from the door about midway of
my thigh, which struck the bone and flattened out
almost to the size of a quarter of a dollar, and then
passed on through the fleshy part to within about
half an inch of the outside. I think some prominent
nerve must have been severed or injured, for, as soon
as the ball struck me, I fell like a bird when shot, or
an ox when struck by a butcher, and lost entirely and
instantaneously all power of action or locomotion. I
fell upon the window-sill, and cried out, 'I am shot!'
Not possessing any power to move, I felt myself falling outside of the window, but immediately I fell
inside, from some, at that time, unknown cause.
When I struck the floor my animation seemed restored, as I have seen it sometimes in squirrels and
birds after being shot. As soon as I felt the power
of motion I crawled under the bed, which was in a
corner of the room, not far from the window where I
received my wound. While on my way and under
the bed I was wounded in three other places; one ball
entered a little below the left knee, and never was
extracted; another entered the forepart of my left
arm, a little above the wrist, and passing down by the
joint, lodged in the fleshy part of my hand, about

midway, a little above the upper joint of my little finger; another struck me on the fleshy part of my left hip, and tore away the flesh as large as my hand, dashing the mangled fragments of flesh and blood against the wall.

"It would seem that immediately after my attempt to leap out of the window, Joseph also did the same thing, of which circumstance I have no knowledge only from information. The first thing that I noticed was a cry that he had leaped out of the window. A cessation of firing followed, the mob rushed down stairs, and Dr. Richards went to the window. Immediately afterward I saw the doctor going toward the jail door, and as there was an iron door at the head of the stairs adjoining our door which led into the cells for criminals, it struck me that the doctor was going in there, and I said to him, 'Stop, doctor, and take me along.' He proceeded to the door and opened it, and then returned and dragged me along to a small cell prepared for criminals.

"Brother Richards was very much troubled, and exclaimed, 'Oh! Brother Taylor, is it possible that they have killed both Brothers Hyrum and Joseph? it cannot surely be, and yet I saw them shoot them;' and, elevating his hands two or three times, he exclaimed, 'Oh Lord, my God, spare thy servants!' He then said, 'Brother Taylor, this is a terrible event;' and he dragged me farther into the cell, saying, 'I am sorry I can not do better for you;' and, taking an old filthy mattress, he covered me with it, and said, 'That may hide you, and you may yet live to tell the tale, but I expect they will kill me in a few moments.' While lying in this position I suffered the most excruciating pain. Soon afterward Dr. Richards came to me, informed me that the mob had precipitately fled, and at the same time confirmed my worst fears that Joseph was assuredly dead." It appears that Joseph, thus murderously beset and in dire extremity, rushed to the window and threw himself out, receiving in the act several shots, and with the cry, "O Lord, my God!" fell dead to the ground.[34] The fiends were not yet satiated; but setting up the lifeless body of the slain prophet against the well-curb, riddled it with bullets.[35]

Where now is the God of Joseph and of Hyrum, that he should permit this most iniquitous butchery? Where are Moroni and Ether and Christ? What mean these latter-day manifestations, their truth and efficacy, if the great high priest and patriarch of the new dispensation can thus be cruelly cut off by wicked men? Practical piety is the doctrine! Prayer

[34] Joseph dropped his pistol, and sprang into the window; but just as he was preparing to descend, he saw such an array of bayonets below, that he caught by the window casing, where he hung by his hands and feet, with his head to the north, feet to the south, and his body swinging downward. He hung in that position three or four minutes, during which time he exclaimed two or three times, 'O Lord, my God!' and fell to the ground. While he was hanging in that situation, Col. Williams halloed, 'Shoot him! God damn him! shoot the damned rascal!' However, none fired at him. He seemed to fall easy. He struck partly on his right shoulder and back, his neck and head reaching the ground a little before his feet. He rolled instantly on his face. From this position he was taken by a young man who sprung to him from the other side of the fence, who held a pewter fife in his hand, was barefooted and bareheaded, having on no coat, with his pants rolled above his knees, and shirt-sleeves above his elbows. He set President Smith against the south side of the well-curb that was situated a few feet from the jail. While doing this the savage muttered aloud, 'This is old Jo; I know him. I know you, old Jo. Damn you; you are the man that had my daddy shot' —intimating that he was a son of Boggs, and that it was the Missourians who were doing this murder. *Littlefield's Narrative*, 13.

[35] After President Taylor's account in *Burton's City of the Saints*, the best authorities on this catastrophe are: *Assassination of Joseph and Hyrum Smith, the Prophet and the Patriarch of the Church of Jesus Christ of Latter-day Saints; also a Condensed History of the Expulsion of the Saints from Nauvoo, by Elder John S. Fullmer (of Utah, U. S. A.)*, Pastor of the Manchester, Liverpool, and Preston Conferences. Liverpool and London, 1855; *Message of the Governor of the State of Illinois, in relation to the disturbances in Hancock County, December 23, 1844.* Springfield, 1844; *Awful assassination of Joseph and Hyrum Smith; the pledged faith of the State of Illinois stained with innocent blood by a mob*, in *Times and Seasons*, v. 560–75; *A Narrative of the Massacre of Joseph and Hyrum Smith by an Outsider and an Eye-witness*, in *Utah Tracts*, i.; and *The Martyrdom of Joseph Smith, by Apostle John Taylor*, a copy of which is contained in *Burton's City of the Saints*, 625–67. Brief accounts will be found in *Utah Pamphlets*, 23; *Lee's Mormonism*, 152–5; *Remy's Jour. to G. S. L. City*, 388–96; *Hall's Mormonism Exposed*, 15–16; *Green's Mormonism*, 36–7; *Tullidge's Women*, 297–300; *Olshausen, Gesch. der Mor.*, 100–3; *Tucker's Mormonism*, 189–92; *Mackay's The Mormons*, 169–72; *Smucker's Hist. Mor.*, 177–9; *Ferris' Utah and Mormons*, 120–5, and in other works on Mormonism. In the *Atlantic Monthly* for Dec. 1869 is an article entitled 'The Mormon Prophet's Tragedy,' which, however justly it may lay claim to Boston 'smart' writing, so far as the facts are concerned is simply a tissue of falsehoods.

and faith must cease not though prayer be unan-
swered; and they ask where was the father when the
son called in Gethsemane? It was foreordained that
Joseph and Hyrum should die for the people; and the
more of murder and extermination on the part of their
enemies, the more praying and believing on the part
of saints, and the more praise and exultation in the
heavenly inheritance.

The further the credulity of a credulous people is
taxed the stronger will be their faith. Many of the
saints believed in Joseph; with their whole mind
and soul they worshipped him. He was to them as
God; he was their deity present upon earth, their
savior from evil, and their guide to heaven. Whatever he did, that to his people was right; he could
do no wrong, no more than king or pope, no more
than Christ or Mahomet. Accordingly they obeyed
him without question; and it was this belief and
obedience that caused the gentiles to fear and hate.
There are still open in the world easier fields than this
for new religions, which might recommend themselves
as a career to young men laboring under a fancied in-
exorable necessity.

Whatever else may be said of Joseph Smith, it
must be admitted that he was a remarkable man.
His course in life was by no means along a flowery
path; his death was like that which too often comes
to the founder of a religion. What a commentary on
the human mind and the human heart, the deeds of
those who live for the love of God and man, who die
for the love of God and man, who severally and col-
lectively profess the highest holiness, the highest
charity, justice, and humanity, higher far than any
held by other sect or nation, now or since the world
began—how lovely to behold, to write and meditate
upon their disputings and disruptions, their cruelties
and injustice, their persecutions for opinion's sake,
their ravenous hate and bloody butcheries!

The founder of Mormonism displayed a singular genius for the work he gave himself to do. He made thousands believe in him and in his doctrines, howsoever good or evil his life, howsoever true or false his teachings. The less that can be proved the more may be asserted. Any one possessing the proper abilities may found a religion and make proselytes. His success will depend not on the truth or falsity of his statements, nor on their gross absurdity or philosophic refinement, but on the power and skill with which his propositions are promulgated. If he has not the natural and inherited genius for this work, though his be otherwise the greatest mind that ever existed, he is sure to fail. If he has the mental and physical adaptation for the work, he will succeed, whatever may be his abilities in other directions.

There was more in this instance than any consideration short of careful study makes appear: things spiritual and things temporal; the outside world and the inside workings. The prophet's days were full of trouble. His people were often petulant, his elders quarrelsome, his most able followers cautious and captious. While the world scoffed and the neighbors used violence, his high priests were continually asking him for prophecies, and if they were not fulfilled at once and to the letter, they stood ready to apostatize. Many did apostatize; many behaved disgracefully, and brought reproach and enmity upon the cause. Moreover, Joseph was constantly in fear for his life, and though by no means desirous of death, in moments of excitement he often faced danger with apparent indifference as to the results. But without occupying further space with my own remarks, I will give the views of others, who loved or hated him and knew him personally and well.

Of his physique and character, Parley P. Pratt remarks: "President Joseph Smith was in person tall and well built, strong and active; of a light complexion, light hair, blue eyes, very little beard, and of an

expression peculiar to himself, on which the eye naturally rested with interest, and was never weary of be-
holding.   His countenance was ever mild, affable,
and beaming with intelligence and benevolence, mingled with a look of interest and an unconscious smile
of cheerfulness, and entirely free from all restraint, or
affectation of gravity; and there was something connected with the serene and steady, penetrating glance
of his eye, as if he would penetrate the deepest abyss
of the human heart, gaze into eternity, penetrate the
heavens, and comprehend all worlds.   He possessed
a noble boldness and independence of character; his
manner was easy and familiar, his rebuke terrible as
the lion, his benevolence unbounded as the ocean,
his intelligence universal, and his language abounding
in original eloquence peculiar to himself."

And thus a female convert who arrived at Nauvoo
a year or two before the prophet's death: "The first
time I ever saw Joseph Smith I recognized him from a
vision that once appeared to me in a dream.   His countenance was like that of an angel, and such as I had
never beheld before.   He was then thirty-seven years
of age, of ordinary appearance in dress and manner,
but with a child-like innocence of expression.   His hair
was of a light brown, his eyes blue, and his complexion light.   His natural demeanor was quiet; his character and disposition were formed by his life-work; he
was kind and considerate, taking a personal interest in
all his people, and considering every one his equal."[36]

On the other hand, the author of *Mormonism Unveiled* says: "The extreme ignorance and apparent
stupidity of this modern prophet were by his early
followers looked upon as his greatest merit, and as
furnishing the most incontestable proof of his divine
mission...His followers have told us that he could
not at the time he was chosen of the Lord even write
his own name.   But it is obvious that all these defi-

---

[36] Another account says that at 36 he weighed 212 lbs, stood 6 feet in his
pumps, was robust, corpulent, and jovial, but when roused to anger his ex
pression was very severe.

ciencies are fully supplied by a natural genius, strong inventive powers of mind, a deep study, and an unusually correct estimate of the human passions and feelings. In short, he is now endowed with all the requisite traits of character to pursue most successfully the humbug which he has introduced. His address is easy, rather fascinating and winning, of a mild and sober deportment when not irritated. But he frequently becomes boisterous by the impertinence or curiosity of the skeptical, and assumes the bravado, instead of adhering to the meekness which he professes. His followers, of course, can discover in his very countenance all the certain indications of a divine mission."

One more quotation will serve to show the impression that Joseph Smith's doctrines and discourse made not only on his own followers but on the gentiles, and even on gentile divines. In 1843 a methodist minister, named Prior, visited Nauvoo and was present during a sermon preached by the prophet in the temple. "I took my seat," he remarks, "in a conspicuous place in the congregation, who were waiting in breathless silence for his appearance. While he tarried, I had plenty of time to revolve in my mind the character and common report of that truly singular personage. I fancied that I should behold a countenance sad and sorrowful, yet containing the fiery marks of rage and exasperation. I supposed that I should be enabled to discover in him some of those thoughtful and reserved features, those mystic and sarcastic glances, which I had fancied the ancient sages to possess. I expected to see that fearful faltering look of conscious shame which from what I had heard of him he might be expected to evince. He appeared at last; but how was I disappointed when, instead of the head and horns of the beast and false prophet, I beheld only the appearance of a common man, of tolerably large proportions.

"I was sadly disappointed, and thought that, although his appearance could not be wrested to indicate anything against him, yet he would manifest all I had heard of him when he began to preach. I sat uneasily and watched him closely. He commenced preaching, not from the book of Mormon, however, but from the bible; the first chapter of the first of Peter was his text. He commenced calmly, and continued dispassionately to pursue his subject, while I sat in breathless silence, waiting to hear that foul aspersion of the other sects, that diabolical disposition of revenge, and to hear that rancorous denunciation of every individual but a Mormon. I waited in vain; I listened with surprise; I sat uneasy in my seat, and could hardly persuade myself but that he had been apprised of my presence, and so ordered his discourse on my account, that I might not be able to find fault with it; for instead of a jumbled jargon of half-connected sentences, and a volley of imprecations, and diabolical and malignant denunciations heaped upon the heads of all who differed from him, and the dreadful twisting and wresting of the scriptures to suit his own peculiar views, and attempt to weave a web of dark and mystic sophistry around the gospel truths, which I had anticipated, he glided along through a very interesting and elaborate discourse, with all the care and happy facility of one who was well aware of his important station and his duty to God and man." [37]

No event, probably, that had occurred thus far in the history of the saints gave to the cause of Mormonism so much of stability as the assassination of Joseph Smith. Not all the militia mobs in Illinois, in Missouri, or in the United States could destroy this cause, any more than could the roundheads in the

---

[37] *Mackay's The Mormons*, 131-3. Of course views as to Joseph Smith's character are expressed in nearly all the works published on Mormonism. With the exception, perhaps, of Mahomet, no one has been so much bespattered with praise by his followers and with abuse by his adversaries as the founder of this faith.

seventeenth century destroy the cause of monarchy. The deed but reacted on those who committed it.

When two miles on his way from Nauvoo, the governor was met by messengers who informed him of the assassination, and, as he relates, he was "struck with a kind of dumbness." At daybreak the next morning all the bells in Carthage were ringing. It was noised abroad throughout Hancock county, he says, that the Mormons had attempted the rescue of Joseph and Hyrum; that they had been killed in order to prevent their escape, and that the governor was closely besieged at Nauvoo by the Nauvoo Legion, and could hold out only for two days. Ford was convinced that "those whoever they were who assassinated the Smiths meditated in turn his assassination by the Mormons," thinking that they would thus rid themselves of the Smiths and the governor, and that the result would be the expulsion of the saints, for Ford had shown a determination to defend Nauvoo, so far as lay in his power, from the threatened violence. Arriving at Carthage at ten o'clock at night, he found the citizens in flight with their families and effects, one of his companies broken up, and the Carthage Greys also disbanding, the citizens that remained being in instant fear of attack. At length he met with John Taylor and Willard Richards, who, notwithstanding the ill-usage they had received, came to the relief of the panic-stricken magistrate, and addressed a letter to their brethren at Nauvoo, exhorting them to preserve the peace, the latter stating that he had pledged his word that no violence would be used.

The letter of Richards and Taylor, signed also by Samuel H. Smith, a brother of the deceased, who a few weeks afterward died, as the Mormons relate, of a broken heart, prevented a threatened uprising of the saints.[38] On the 29th of June, the day after the news was received, the legion was called out, the letter read,

[38] To the letter was appended a postscript from the governor, bidding the Mormons defend themselves until protection could be furnished, and one from

and the fury of the citizens allayed by addresses from
Judge Phelps, Colonel Buckmaster, the governor's
aid, and others. In the afternoon the bodies of
Joseph and Hyrum arrived in wagons guarded by
three men. They were met by the city council, the
prophet's staff, the officers of the legion, and a vast
procession of citizens, crying out "amid the most
solemn lamentations and wailings that ever ascended
into the ears of the Lord of hosts to be avenged of
their enemies." Arriving at the Nauvoo House, the
assemblage, numbering ten thousand persons, was
again addressed, and "with one united voice resolved
to trust to the law for a remedy of such a high-handed
assassination, and when that failed, to call upon God
to avenge them of their wrongs. Oh! widows and
orphans! Oh Americans! weep, for the glory of freedom has departed!"

Meanwhile the governor, fearing that the Mormons
would rise in a body to execute vengeance, issued an
address to the people of Illinois, in which he attempted
to explain his conduct,[39] and again called out the
militia. Two officers were despatched to Nauvoo,
with orders to ascertain the disposition of the citizens,
and to proceed thence to Warsaw, where were the
headquarters of the anti-Mormon militia, and forbid
violent measures in the name of the state. On arriving at the former place they laid their instructions
before the members of the municipality. A meeting
of the council was summoned, and it was resolved that
the saints rigidly sustain the laws and the governor,
so long as they are themselves sustained in their
constitutional rights; that they discountenance vengeance on the assassins of Joseph and Hyrum Smith;
that instead of an appeal to arms, they appeal to the
majesty of the law, and, should the law fail, they

General Deming, telling them to remain quiet, that the assassination would
be condemned by three fourths of the people of Illinois, but that they were
in danger of attack from Missouri, and 'prudence might obviate material
destruction.' *Times and Seasons*, v. 561.

[39] Copies of it will be found in *Id.*, v. 564-5; *Mackay's The Mormons*, 178-
9; and *Smucker's Hist. Mor.*, 186-7.

leave the matter with God; that the council pledges itself that no aggressions shall be made by the citizens of Nauvoo, approves the course taken by the governor, and will uphold him by all honorable means. A meeting of citizens was then held in the public square; the people were addressed, the resolutions read, and all responded with a hearty amen.

The two officers then returned to Carthage and reported to the governor, who was so greatly pleased with the forbearance of the saints that he officially declared them "human beings and citizens of the state." He caused writs to be issued for the arrest of three of the murderers—after they had taken refuge in Missouri.[40] The assassins escaped punishment, however; and now that order was restored, the chief magistrate disbanded the militia, after what he termed "a campaign of about thirteen days."

On the afternoon of July 1st a letter was addressed by Richards, Taylor, and Phelps to the citizens of Nauvoo, and a fortnight later, an epistle signed by the same persons and also by Parley P. Pratt was despatched to all the saints throughout the world. "Be peaceable, quiet citizens, doing the works of righteousness; and as soon as the twelve and other authorities can assemble, or a majority of them, the onward course to the great gathering of Israel, and the final consummation of the dispensation of the fulness of times, will be pointed out, so that the murder of Abel, the assassination of hundreds, the righteous blood of all the holy prophets, from Abel to Joseph, sprinkled with the best blood of the son of God, as the crimson sign of remission, only carries conviction to the business and bosoms of all flesh, that the cause is just and will continue; and blessed are they that hold out faithful to the end, while apostates, consenting to the shedding of innocent blood, have no forgiveness in this world nor in the world to come...Let no vain

[40] In *Message to Ill. Legis.*, 20, it is stated that some of the murderers afterward surrendered on the understanding that they should be admitted to bail. There was not sufficient proof to convict them.

and foolish plans or imaginations scatter us abroad and divide us asunder as a people, to seek to save our lives at the expense of truth and principle, but rather let us live or die together and in the enjoyment of society and union."[41]

At this time the saints needed such words of advice and consolation. Some were already making preparations to return to the gentiles; some feared that their organization as a sect would soon come to an end. To reassure them, one more address was issued on August 15th, in the name of the twelve apostles,[42] and signed by Brigham Young, the president of the apostles. The saints were told that though they were now without a prophet present in the flesh, the twelve would administer and regulate the affairs of the church; and that even if they should be taken away, there were still others who would insure the triumph of their cause throughout the world.

In 1830, as will be remembered, the church of Jesus Christ of Latter-day Saints was organized in a chamber by a few humble men; in 1844 the prophet's followers mustered scores of thousands. Speedy dissolution was now predicted by some, while others argued that as all his faults would lie buried in the tomb, while on his virtues martyrdom would shed its lustre, the progress of the sect would be yet more remarkable. The latter prediction was verified, and after the Mormons had suffered another period of persecution, Joseph Smith the martyr became a greater power in the land than Joseph Smith the prophet.

[41] The full text of both letters is given in *Times and Seasons*, v. 568, 586–7; *Mackay's The Mormons*, 180–2; *Smucker's Hist. Mormons*, 189–92.

[42] Who are thus described in a letter addressed by Phelps to the editor of the *New York Prophet*, a small journal established to promulgate the views of the sect: 'Brigham Young, the lion of the Lord; Heber C. Kimball, the herald of grace; Parley P. Pratt, the archer of paradise; Orson Hyde, the olive branch of Israel; Willard Richards, the keeper of the rolls; John Taylor, the champion of right; William Smith, the patriarchal staff of Jacob; Wilford Woodruff, the banner of the gospel; George A. Smith, the entablature of truth; Orson Pratt, the gauge of philosophy; John E. Page, the sun-dial; and Lyman Wight, the wild ram of the mountains. They are good men; the best the Lord can find.' See *Mackay's The Mormons*, 186.

CHAPTER VII.

BRIGHAM YOUNG SUCCEEDS JOSEPH.

1844–1845.

UPON the death of Joseph Smith, one of the questions claiming immediate attention was, Who shall be his successor? It was the first time the question had arisen in a manner to demand immediate solution, and the matter of succession was not so well determined then as now, it being at present well established that upon the death of the president of the church the apostle eldest in ordination and service takes his place.

Personal qualifications would have much to do with it; rules could be established later. The first consideration now was to keep the church from falling in pieces. None realized the situation better than Brigham Young, who soon made up his mind that he himself was the man for the emergency. Then to make it appear plain to the brethren that God would have him take Joseph's place, his mind thus works: "The first thing that I thought of," he says, "was whether Joseph had taken the keys of the kingdom with him from the earth. Brother Orson Pratt sat on my left; we were both leaning back on our chairs. Bringing my hand down on my knee, I said, 'The keys of the kingdom are right here with the church.'" But who held the keys of the kingdom? This was the all-absorbing question that was being discussed at Nauvoo when Brigham and the other members of the quorum arrived at that city on the 6th of August, 1844.

Brigham Young was born at Whitingham, Windham county, Vermont, on the 1st of June, 1801. His father, John, a Massachusetts farmer, served as a private soldier in the revolutionary war, and his grandfather as surgeon in the French and Indian war.[1] In 1804 his family, which included nine children,[2] of whom he was then the youngest, removed to Sherburn, Chenango county, New York, where for a time hardship and poverty were their lot. Concerning Brigham's youth there is little worthy of record. Lack of means compelled him, almost without education, to earn his own livelihood, as did his brothers, finding employment as best they could. Thus, at the age of twenty-three, when he married he had learned how to work as farmer, carpenter, joiner, painter, and glazier, in the last of which occupations he was an expert craftsman.

In 1829 he removed to Mendon, Monroe county, where his father then resided; and here, for the first time, he saw the book of Mormon at the house of his brother Phineas, who had been a pastor in the reformed methodist church, but was now a convert to Mormonism.[3]

[1] *Waite's The Mormon Prophet and his Harem.* Linforth, *Route from Liverpool*, 112, note, states that his grandfather was an officer in the revolutionary war; this is not confirmed by Mrs Waite, who quotes from Brigham's autobiography. Again, Nabby Howe was the maiden name of Brigham's mother, as given in his autobiography; while Linforth reads Nancy Howe; and Remy, *Jour. to G. S. L. City*, i. 413, Naleby Howe.

[2] Born as follow: Nancy, Aug. 6, 1786, Fanny, Nov. 8, 1787, Rhoda, Sept. 10, 1789, John, May 22, 1791, Nabby, Apr. 23, 1793, Susannah, June 7, 1795, Joseph, Apr. 7, 1797, Phineas, Feb. 16, 1799, and Brigham, June 1, 1801. Two others were born later: Louisa, Sept. 25, 1804, and Lorenzo Dow, Oct. 19, 1807.

[3] In *Ibid.*, it is mentioned that before the organization of the latter-day

About two years later he himself was converted[4] by the preaching of Elder Samuel H. Smith, brother of the prophet; on the 14th of April, 1832, he was baptized, and on the same night ordained an elder, his father[5] and all his brothers afterward becoming proselytes. During the same month he set forth to meet the prophet at Kirtland, where he found him and several of his brethren chopping wood. "Here," says Brigham, "my joy was full at the privilege of shaking the hand of the prophet of God...He was happy to see us and bid us welcome. In the evening a few of the brethren came in, and we conversed together upon the things of the kingdom. He called upon me to pray. In my prayer I spoke in tongues. As soon as we rose from our knees, the brethren flocked around him, and asked his opinion...He told them it was the pure Adamic language;...it is of God, and the time will come when Brother Brigham Young will preside over this church." In 1835 he was chosen, as will be remembered, one of the quorum of the twelve, and the following spring set forth on a missionary tour to the eastern states. Returning early in the winter, he saved the life of the prophet, and otherwise rendered good service during the great apostasy of 1836, when the church passed through its darkest hour.[6]

Brigham was ever a devoted follower of the prophet, and at the risk of his own life, shielded him against the persecutions of apostates. At the close of 1837 he was driven by their machinations from Kirtland,[7]

church, Phineas had wrought a miracle, 'whereby a young girl on the point of death had been restored to life.' Remy does not give his authority.

[4] At a branch of the church at Columbia, Penn. *Tullidge's Life of Young*, 78.

[5] John Young was made first patriarch of the church. He died at Quincy, Ill., Oct. 12, 1839. *Waite's The Mormon Prophet*, 2.

[6] *Tullidge's Life of Brigham Young*, 83. In a speech delivered after he became president, Brigham says: 'Ascertaining that a plot was laid to waylay Joseph for the purpose of taking his life, on his return from Monroe, Michigan, to Kirtland, I procured a horse and buggy, and took brother William Smith along to meet Joseph, whom we met returning in the stage-coach. Joseph requested William to take his seat in the stage, and he rode with me in the buggy We arrived at Kirtland in safety.'

[7] 'On the morning of Dec. 22d I left Kirtland in consequence of the fury

and took refuge at Dublin, Indiana, where he was soon
afterward joined by Joseph Smith and Sidney Rigdon.
Thence, in company with the former, he went to Missouri, arriving at Far West a short time before the
massacre at Haun's Mill. Once more Brigham was
compelled to flee for his life, and now betook himself
to Quincy, where he raised means to aid the destitute
brethren in leaving Missouri,[8] and directed the first
settlement of the saints in Illinois, the prophet Joseph,
Parley P. Pratt, and others being then in prison.

By revelation of July 8, 1838,[9] it was ordered that
eleven of the quorum should "depart to go over the
great waters, and there promulgate my gospel, the
fulness thereof, and bear record of my name. Let
them take leave of my saints in the city Far West, on
the 26th day of April next; on the building spot of my
house, saith the Lord." As the twelve had been banished from Missouri and could not return with safety,
many of the church dignitaries urged that the latter
part of this revelation should not be fulfilled. "But,"
says Brigham, "I felt differently, and so did those of
the quorum who were with me." The affairs of the
church were now in the hands of the twelve, and their
president was not the man to shrink from danger.
"The Lord had spoken, and it was their duty to obey."

The quorum started forth, and reaching Far West
toward the end of April, hid themselves in a grove.
Between midnight of the 25th and dawn of the 26th

of the mob, and the spirit that prevailed in the apostates, who threatened to
destroy me because I would proclaim publicly and privately that I knew, by
the power of the holy ghost, that Joseph Smith was a prophet of the most
high God, and had not transgressed and fallen, as apostates declared.' *Id.*, 84.

[8] 'I held a meeting with the brethren of the twelve and the members of
the church in Quincy, on the 17th of March, when a letter was read to the
people from the committee, on behalf of the saints at Far West, who were
left destitute of the means to move. Though the brethren were poor and
stripped of almost everything, yet they manifested a spirit of willingness to
do their utmost, offering to sell their hats, coats, and shoes to accomplish the
object. At the close of the meeting $50 was collected in money and several
teams were subscribed to go and bring the brethren.' *Id.*, 89–90.

[9] This is the date given in *Doctrine and Covenants*, 381 (ed. S. L. City,
1876). See also *Linforth's Route from Liverpool*, 112, note. Tullidge gives
July 8, 1836. *Life of Brigham Young*, 90.

they held a conference, relaid the foundation of the house of the Lord,[10] and ordained Wilford Woodruff and George A. Smith as apostles in place of those who had fallen from grace. "Thus," says Brigham, "was this revelation fulfilled, concerning which our enemies said, if all the other revelations of Joseph Smith came to pass, that one should not be fulfilled."

Upon the excommunication of Thomas B. Marsh, in 1839, the office of president of the twelve devolved by right on Brigham by reason of his seniority of membership. On the 14th of April, 1840, he was publicly accepted by the council as their head, and at the reorganization of the church councils at Nauvoo he was appointed by revelation on the 19th of January, 1843, president of the twelve travelling council.

After the founding of Nauvoo, the president, together with three others of the quorum,[11] sailed for Liverpool, where they arrived on the 6th of April, 1840, the tenth anniversary of the organization of the church. Here he was engaged for about a year in missionary work, of which more hereafter. Taking ship for New York on the 20th of April, 1841, he reached Nauvoo on the 1st of July, and was warmly welcomed by the prophet, who a few days afterward[12] received the following revelation: "Dear and well-beloved brother Brigham Young, verily thus saith the Lord unto you, my servant Brigham, it is no more required at your hand to leave your family as in times past, for your offering is acceptable to me; I have seen your labor and toil in journeyings for my name. I therefore command you to send my word abroad, and take special care of your family from this time henceforth and forever. Amen."

Already the mantle of the prophet was falling upon the president of the twelve; already the former had

<hr />

[10] 'Elder Cutler, the master workman of the house, recommenced laying the foundation by rolling up a large stone near the south-east corner.' *Id.*, 92.

[11] Heber C. Kimball, George A. Smith, and Parley P. Pratt. Reuben Hedlock also accompanied them.

[12] On July 9th. *Doctrine and Covenants*, 409.

foretold his own death; but notwithstanding the revelation, Brigham was sent as a missionary to the eastern states, and at Peterborough, New Hampshire, received news of the tragedy at Carthage jail.

When Governor Ford and his militia were preparing to march on Nauvoo for the purpose of forestalling civil war, the only course open to the prophet and his followers was a removal from Illinois. In 1842 an expedition had been planned to explore the country toward or beyond the Rocky Mountains; but when Joseph Smith put himself forward as a candidate for the presidency of the United States, all other matters were for the time forgotten. Brigham claimed that had he been. present the assassination would never have occurred; he would not have permitted the prophet's departure for Carthage: rather would he have sent him to the mountains under a guard of elders. But Brigham had no reason to complain of the dispensation of providence which was now to bring his clear, strong judgment and resolute will to the front.

Prominent among the aspirants for the presidency of the church was Sidney Rigdon, one of the first and ablest to espouse the cause, and not altogether without grounds for his pretensions. He had performed much labor, had encountered many trials, and had received scanty honors, being at present nothing more than preacher, and professor of history, belles-lettres, and oratory. By revelation of January 19, 1841, he had been offered the position of counsellor to the prophet,[13]

---

[13] *Doctrine and Covenants*, 406. In this same revelation the officers of the priesthood were likewise named: Hyrum Smith, patriarch; Joseph Smith, presiding elder over the whole church, also translator, revelator, seer, and prophet, with Sidney Rigdon and William Law as councillors, the three to constitute a quorum and first presidency. Brigham Young, president over the twelve travelling council, who were Heber C. Kimball, Parley P. Pratt, Orson Pratt, Orson Hyde, William Smith, John Taylor, John E. Page, Wilford Woodruff, Willard Richards, George A. Smith, and some one to be appointed in place of David Patten; a high council, Samuel Bent, H. G. Sherwood, George W. Harris, Charles C. Rich, Thomas Grover, Newel Knight, David Dort, Dunbar Wilson, Aaron Johnson, David Fulmer, Alpheus Cutler, Will

if he would consent to humble himself. But Sidney would not humble himself. Soon after Joseph's death, at which he was not present, he had a revelation of his own, bidding him conduct the saints to Pittsburgh.[14] Visiting that city, he found the time not yet ripe for this measure; and meanwhile returning to Nauvoo, the 3d of August, he offered himself on the following day as a candidate for the presidency, aided by Elder Marks.

Sidney now put forth all his strength to gain influence and secure retainers. He must have Joseph's mantle; he must have the succession, or henceforth he would be nothing. It was a momentous question, not to be disposed of in a day. To substantiate his claim, Sidney could now have visions with the best of them; on various occasions he told how the Lord had through him counselled the people to appoint him as their guardian. He requested that a meeting should be held on the following sabbath, the 8th of August, for the further consideration of the matter. But prior to this meeting Parley Pratt and two others of the twelve bade the candidate go with them to the house of John Taylor, who yet lay prostrate with his wounds. Taylor expostulated with him, but to no purpose. Sidney continued to press his claims, even assuming the sacred office, prophesying and ordaining. On the sabbath named, according to appointment, Sidney and his supporters met in the grove near the temple; but were confronted by the apostles, with Brigham at their head. Standing before them, Sidney addressed the

iam Huntington; president over a quorum of high priests, Don Carlos Smith, with Amasa Lyman and Noah Packard for counsellors; a priesthood to preside over the quorum of elders, John A. Hicks, Samuel Williams, and Jesse Baker; to preside over the quorum of seventies, Joseph Young, Josiah Butterfield, Daniel Miles, Henry Herriman, Zera Pulsipher, Levi Hancock, James Foster—this for elders constantly travelling, while the quorum of elders was to preside over the churches from time to time; to preside over the bishopric, Vinson Knight, Samuel H. Smith, and Shadrach Roundy, and others.

[14] See his memorial to the Pennsylvania legislature, in *Times and Seasons*, v. 418–23. Remy says that he was also instructed to pay a visit to Queen Victoria, and overthrow her if she refused to accept the gospel. *Jour. to G. S. L. City*, i. 411; a statement for which I find no authority.

brethren for nearly two hours. Yet he seemed to
make no impression. "The Lord has not chosen
him," said one to another. The assembly then adjourned to two o'clock, when the saints in and about
Nauvoo gathered in great numbers. After singing
and prayer, through the vast assemblage was heard a
voice, strikingly clear, distinct, and penetrating.[15] It
was the voice of Brigham, who said: "Attention, all!
For the first time in my life I am called to act as chief
of the twelve; for the first time in your lives you are
called to walk by faith, your prophet being no longer
present in the flesh. I desire that every one present
shall exercise the fullest liberty. I now ask you, and
each of you, if you want to choose a guardian, a prophet,
evangelist, or something else as your head to lead you.
All who wish to draw away from the church, let them
do it, but they will not prosper. If any want Sidney
Rigdon to lead them, let them have him; but I say unto
you that the keys of the kingdom are with the twelve."[16]

It was then put to vote, Brigham meanwhile saying, "All those who are for Joseph and Hyrum, the
book of Mormon, book of Doctrine and Covenants, the
temple, and Joseph's measures, they being one party,
will be called upon to manifest their principles boldly,
the opposite party to enjoy the same liberty."[17] The
result was ten votes for Sidney, the quorum with
Brigham at their head getting all the rest. Elder
Philips then motioned that all "who have voted for
Sidney Rigdon be suspended until they can have a
trial before the high council."[18]

The truth is, Sidney was no match for Brigham.
It was a battle of the lion and the lamb; only Brig-

---

[15] 'He [Brigham] said, as he stood on the stand, he would rather sit in sack-
cloth and ashes for a month than appear before the people, but he pitied their
loneliness, and was constrained to step forward, and we knew he was, because
he had the voice and manner of Joseph, as hundreds can testify.' *Reminiscences
of Mrs F. D. Richards*, MS., p. 14.

[16] *Woodruff's Journal*, MS., Aug. 8, 1844.

[17] *Hist. Brigham Young*, 1844, MS., 25.

[18] Wilford Woodruff states that Rigdon did not receive a single vote.
Reminiscences, MS., 2.

ham did not know before that he was a lion, while Sidney received the truth with reluctance that he was indeed a lamb. Something more than oratory was necessary to win in this instance; and of that something, with great joy in his heart, Brigham found himself in possession. It was the combination of qualities which we find present primarily in all great men, in all leaders of men—intellectual force, mental superiority, united with personal magnetism, and physique enough to give weight to will and opinion; for Brigham Young was assuredly a great man, if by greatness we mean one who is superior to others in strength and skill, moral, intellectual, or physical. The secret of this man's power—a power that within a few years made itself felt throughout the world—was this: he was a sincere man, or if an impostor, he was one who first imposed upon himself. He was not a hypocrite; knave, in the ordinary sense of the term, he was not; though he has been a thousand times called both. If he was a bad man, he was still a great man, and the evil that he did was done with honest purpose. He possessed great administrative ability; he was far-seeing, with a keen insight into human nature, and a thorough knowledge of the good and evil qualities of men, of their virtues and frailties. His superiority was native to him, and he was daily and hourly growing more powerful, developing a strength which surprised himself, and gaining constantly more and more confidence in himself, gaining constantly more and more the respect, fear, and obedience of those about him, until he was able to consign Sidney to the buffetings of Satan for a thousand years, while Brigham remained president and supreme ruler of the church.[19]

[19] Sidney had a trial, and was convicted and condemned. Sidney Rigdon was a native of Saint Clair, Penn., where he was born in 1793. Until his 26th year he worked on his father's farm, but in 1819 received a license to preach, from the society known as the regular baptists, being appointed in 1822 to the charge of the first baptist church in Pittsburgh, where he became very popular. In 1824 he resigned his position, from conscientious motives, and joined the Campbellites, supporting himself by working as a journeyman tanner. Two years later he accepted a call as a Campbellite preacher at Bainbridge, O.,

Thus Brigham Young succeeded Joseph Smith. The work of the latter was done. It was a singular work, to which he was singularly adapted; the work yet to be done is no less remarkable, and a no less remarkable agent is raised up at the right moment. Matters assume now a more material turn, and a more material nature is required to master them—if coarser-grained, more practical, rougher, more dogmatical, dealing less in revelations from heaven and more in self-protection and self-advancement here on earth, so much the better for the saints. "Strike, but hear me!" Joseph with Themistocles used to cry; "I will strike, and you shall hear me," Brigham would say.

No wonder the American Israel received Brigham as the gift of God, the Lion of the Lord,[20] though the explanation of the new ruler himself would have been nearer that of the modern evolutionist, who would account for Brigham's success as the survival of the fittest. It was fortunate for the saints at this juncture that their leader should be less prophet than priest and king, less idealist than business manager, political economist, and philosopher. Brigham holds communion with spiritual powers but distantly, perhaps distrustfully; at all events, he commands the spirits rather than let them command him; and the older he grows the less he has to do with them; and the less he has to do with heavenly affairs, the more his mind dwells on earthly matters. His prophecies are eminently practical; his people must have piety that will pay. And later, and all through his life, his position is a strange one. If the people about Nauvoo are troublesome, God orders him west; and then he tells

and afterward built up churches at Mantua and Mentor in that state. In 1830 he joined the Mormon church, being converted by the preaching of Parley. Further particulars will be found in *Times and Seasons,* iv. 177–8, 193–4, 209–10; *Cobb's Mormon Problem,* MS., 12; *Tucker's Mormonism,* 123–7; *Pittsburgh Gaz.,* in *S. F. Bulletin,* Aug. 4, 1876. Returning to Pittsburgh after his excommunication, Sidney led a life of utter obscurity, and finally died at Friendship, Alleghany County, N. Y., July 14, 1876. *Lippincott's Mag.,* Aug. 1880.

[20] See note 41, p. 192, this vol.

him if roads are opened and canals constructed it will please him. From these practical visions come actions, and on a Sunday the great high-priest rises in the tabernacle and says: "God has spoken. He has said unto his prophet, 'Get thee up, Brigham, and build me a city in the fertile valley to the south, where there is water, where there are fish, where the sun is strong enough to ripen the cotton plants, and give raiment as well as food to my saints on earth. Brethren willing to aid God's work should come to me before the bishop's meeting.'" "As the prophet takes his seat again," says an eye-witness, "and puts on his broad-brimmed hat, a hum of applause runs around the bowery, and teams and barrows are freely promised."

To whatsoever Brigham applied himself he directed his whole strength, provided his whole strength was necessary to the accomplishment of his purpose. There were others in the field against him, aspirants for the late prophet's place, besides Sidney; but directing his efforts only against the most powerful of them, the president of the twelve summoned the quorum and the people, as we have seen, crushed Rigdon and his adherents by one of the master-strokes which he was now learning, declared the revelations of Rigdon to be of the devil, cut him off, cursed him, and was himself elected almost without a dissenting voice, giving all ostensibly the fullest liberty to act, yet permitting none of them to do so, and even causing ten to be tried for dissenting. Henceforth none dared to gainsay his authority; he became not only the leader of the Mormons, but their dictator; holding authority for a time as president of the twelve apostles, and finally in the capacity of the first presidency, being made president of the whole church in December 1847.

Brigham Young was now in his forty-third year, in the prime of a hale and vigorous manhood, with exuberant vitality, with marvelous energy, and with unswerving faith in his cause and in himself. In stat-

ure he was a little above medium height; in frame
well-knit and compact, though in later years rotund
and portly; in carriage somewhat stately; presence
imposing, even at that time, and later much more so;
face clean shaven now, but afterward lengthened by
full beard except about the mouth; features all good,
regular, well formed, sharp, and smiling, and wearing
an expression of self-sufficiency, bordering on the supercilious, which later in life changed to a look of subdued sagacity which he could not conceal; deep-set,
gray eyes, cold, stern, and of uncertain expression,
lips thin and compressed, and a forehead broad and
massive—his appearance was that of a self-reliant and
strong-willed man, of one born to be master of himself and many others.   In manner and address he was
easy and void of affectation, deliberate in speech, conveying his original and suggestive ideas in apt though
homely phrase.[21]   When in council he was cool and
imperturbable, slow to decide, and in no haste to act;
but when the time for action came he worked with an
energy that was satisfied only with success.

Like his predecessor, he was under all circumstances
naturally a brave man, possessing great physical
strength, and with nerves unshaken by much excess
or sickness.   That he was given to strong drink has
often been asserted by his enemies, but never by his
friends, and rarely by impartial observers.   He was
always in full possession of himself, being far too
wise a man to destroy himself through any indiscre-
tion.

He was undoubtedly the man for the occasion,
however, for no other could, at this juncture, save
the Mormons from dissolution as a sect and as a
people.   If the saints had selected as their leader a
man less resolute, less confident, less devoted to his
cause and to his people, a man like Sidney Rigdon,

<hr>

[21] Bowles, *Across the Continent*, 86, says that even at 64 he spoke ungram-
matically.   This criticism is a fair commentary on the difference between a
Bowles and a Brigham.

for example, Mormonism would have split into half a dozen petty factions, the strongest of which would hardly be worthy of notice.

Discussing the great Mormon leaders, Hyde, who though an apostate was one of the most impartial of writers, says: "Brigham Young is far superior to Smith in everything that constitutes a great leader. Smith was not a man of genius; his forte was tact. He only embraced opportunities that presented themselves. He used circumstances, but did not create them. The compiling genius of Mormonism was Sidney Rigdon. Smith had boisterous impetuosity, but no foresight. Polygamy was not the result of his policy, but of his passions. Sidney gave point, direction, and apparent consistency to the Mormon system of theology. He invented its forms and many of its arguments. He and Parley Pratt were its leading orators and polemics. Had it not been for the accession of these two men, Smith would have been lost, and his schemes frustrated and abandoned. That Brigham was superior not only to Smith but also to Rigdon is evident."

Burton says: "His manner is at once affable and impressive, simple and courteous,...shows no sign of dogmatism,...impresses a stranger with a certain sense of power; his followers are, of course, wholly fascinated by his superior strength of brain." Temper even and placid, manner cold, but he is neither morose nor methodistic. Often reproves in violent language; powers of observation acute; has an excellent memory, and is a keen judge of character. "If he dislikes a stranger at the first interview, he never sees him again. Of his temperance and sobriety there is but one opinion. His life is ascetic; his favorite food is baked potatoes with a little buttermilk, and his drink water."[22]

---

[22] *City of the Saints*, 292–3; *Mormonism*, 170. Hyde is by no means one of Brigham's flatterers, but appears to speak from conviction. On the same page he remarks: 'Brigham may be a great man, greatly deceived, but he

Further: though he made his people obey him, he shared their privations. Soon we shall find him rousing his followers from the lethargy of despair, when their very hearts had died within them, and when all cheeks blanched but his; speaking words of cheer to the men, and with his own sick child in his arms, sharing his scant rations with women and children who held out their hands for bread.

For a brief space after the election of Brigham the saints had rest. The city of Nauvoo continued to thrive;[23] a portion of the temple was finished and dedicated,[24] the building of the Nauvoo house and council-house was progressing rapidly.

Their buildings were erected with great sacrifice of time, and amidst difficulties and discouragement in consequence of poverty. Money was exceedingly scarce.[25] The revelation requiring tithing, made in 1838, was first practically applied in Nauvoo; the tenth day was regularly given to work on the temple; the penny subscriptions of the sisters are mentioned, which was a weekly contribution, and was intended for the purchase of glass and nails. Every effort was made to encourage manufacture, and to utilize their water-power. At a meeting of the trades delegates

is not a hypocrite;' and on the next page: 'Brigham, however deceived, is still a bad man, and a dangerous man; and as much more dangerous, being sincere in thinking he is doing God's work, as a madman is than an impostor.' In *Id.*, 136-40, we have a short and succinct narrative of Brigham's career up to the assassination of Joseph Smith, probably the best that has yet been written in such brief space.

[23] 'Almost every stranger that enters our city is excited with astonishment that so much has been done in so short a time.' Likewise there was always work enough for them among the gentiles, who 'did not know how to make a short johnny-cake until our girls taught them.' Speech of Elder Kimball, April 8, 1845, in *Id.*, vi. 973. Says John Taylor: 'When we first settled in Nauvoo,...farming lands out of the city were worth from $1.25 to $5 per acre; when we left they were worth from $5 to $50 per acre. We turned the desert into a city, and the wilderness into a fruitful field or fields and gardens.' *Millennial Star*, viii. 115. Bennett mentions a community farm near Nauvoo, which was cultivated in common by the poorer classes. *History of the Saints*, 191.

[24] It was dedicated May 1, 1846, by Wilford Woodruff and Orson Hyde. Two days later they held their last meeting there. *Woodruff's Rem.*, MS., 3.

[25] 'When corn was brought to my door at ten cents a bushel, and sadly needed, the money could not be raised.' *Utah Notes*, MS., p. 6.

there was intelligent discussion as to the place becoming a great manufacturing centre.[26]

In January 1845 it was proposed that a building for the high-priests should be erected, to cost $15,000, and the work was cheerfully undertaken. There were frequent entertainments given in the way of dances and public dinners in the Nauvoo mansion and in the bowery six miles out of the city.[27] At their conference in April, thousands gathered. The temple was pushed forward, as the people were counselled to receive their endowments there as early as possible. On the 24th of May the walls were finished, and the event was duly celebrated.[28] On the 5th of October their first meeting in the temple was held.[29] From mites and tithings it was estimated that a million dollars had been raised. Brigham, Parley, and others of the quorum administered in the temples to hundreds of people, the services often continuing all day and night.[30] At the end of December one thousand of the people had received the ordinances. And all this was done midst renewed persecutions, and while the people were making preparations to evacuate the city.

The masons withdrew the dispensation previously granted to Nauvoo, and to this day they refuse to admit Mormons into their order.

[26] There was $500 or $600 already collected from the penny subscriptions, which was drawn by order of Brigham to meet a debt on land which must be immediately paid. *Hist. B. Young*, MS., Dec. 5, 1844. John Taylor says it was intended to establish manufactures at Nauvoo on a large scale, for which the services of English emigrants were to be secured. At the head of the rapids, near Nauvoo, stood an island, to which it was proposed to build a dam, leaving spaces for water-wheels, and thus securing power for mills. *Rem.*, MS., 19–20.

[27] In *Hist. B. Young*, MS., July 9, 1845, is a description of a public dinner for the benefit of the church, where Young, Kimball, Taylor, and others officiated at the table.

[28] At six o'clock in the morning the people assembled. The 'Cap-stone March,' composed for the occasion, was played by Pitt's band; Brigham laid on the last stone, and pronounced the benediction, and the whole congregation shouted, 'Hosanna! hosanna to God and the lamb! amen, amen, and amen!' *Hist. B. Young*, MS., 83.

[29] The first stone was laid April 6, 1841.

[30] 'I commenced administering the ordinances of endowment at five o'clock and continued until half-past three in the morning.' *Id.*, MS., Dec. 10, 1845.

Fresh disaster now approached Nauvoo. The whigs and the democrats of Illinois had both sought to secure the Mormon vote, until finally they began to declare that Mormonism signified a government not in accord with that of the United States. The city charter had been repealed in January 1845, and Daniel Spencer, who had been elected to fill the remainder of the term of the murdered mayor, was deposed, as were all the other city officers; a new charter was before the legislature, but never granted. These and like measures, followed as they were by the discharge of Joseph Smith's assassins, imparted to the gentiles renewed courage. The crimes of the whole country were laid at the door of the saints. Nauvoo was denounced as a den of counterfeiters, cattle-thieves, and assassins,[31] the leaders of the gang being men who in the name of religion outraged all sense of decency. The saints retaliated in kind; and shortly it came about that in sections settled by Mormons gentiles feared to travel, and in sections settled by gentiles Mormons feared to travel. In view of this state of affairs, which was more like old-time feudalism than latter-day republicanism, Governor Ford made an inspection of the city, and declared that fewer thefts were committed in Nauvoo in proportion to population than in any other town in the state. The cause of this, however, may have lain in the fact that the population of Nauvoo was chiefly Mormon, and whatever might be their depredations upon the gentiles, the saints were not accustomed to steal from each other.

At a place called the Morley settlement, in Hancock county, in September 1845, the people held a meeting to devise means for the prevention of thievery. Though few definite charges were advanced, there was much said derogatory to Mormon honesty. Presently the discharge of a gun was heard, once or twice, perhaps more. It was said the shots were fired

[31] For specimens of the accusations brought against them, see *Hall's Mormonism Exposed*, 24–34.

by Mormons, and that they took aim at the house in which the meeting was held. Soon the cry went abroad that the Mormons were in arms, and there were quickly volunteers at hand to help the men of Morley. A meeting was held, and it was resolved to expel the saints. At the time appointed, armed bands appeared and burned some twenty Mormon dwellings, driving the inmates into the bushes.[32] The people of Illinois were evidently now determined to adopt the previous policy of the men of Missouri. This was not all. Word had come that forces from Nauvoo were moving to the aid of the Mormons at Morley, whereupon the gentiles throughout all that region banded, threatening to burn and drive out the saints until not one should remain. As a beginning, Buel's flouring mill and carding machine, near Lima, the property of a Mormon, was reduced to ashes.[33]

And now the men of Quincy, their old friends and benefactors, turned against them; and though not manifesting the deadly hate displayed in some quarters, were nevertheless resolved that the Mormons should depart from the state. On the 22d the citizens met and agreed that further efforts to live in peace with the Mormons were useless.[34]

Indeed, the saints themselves had reached the

[32] Says the *Quincy Whig*: 'If the Mormons have been guilty of crime, why, punish them; but do not visit their sins on defenceless women and children. This is as bad as the savages.' Sheriff Backenstos thus testifies: 'It is proper to state that the Mormon community have acted with more than ordinary forbearance, remaining perfectly quiet, and offering no resistance when their dwellings, other buildings, stacks of grain, etc., were set on fire in their presence, and they have forborne until forbearance is no longer a virtue.' *Fullmer's Expulsion*, 19.

[33] 'Mobs commenced driving out the Mormons in the lower part of Hancock co., and burning their houses and property...The burning was continued from settlement to settlement for ten or eleven days without any resistance whatever. The people at Nauvoo sent out wagons and teams to bring those people in whom the mob had driven out of their homes.' *Wells' Narrative*, MS., 35-6. 'The mob said they would drive all into Nauvoo, and all Nauvoo into the Mississippi.' *Richards, Rem.*, MS., 16.

[34] 'It is a settled thing that the public sentiment of the state is against the Mormons, and it will be in vain for them to contend against it; and to prevent bloodshed and the sacrifice of so many lives on both sides it is their duty to obey the public will, and leave the state as speedily as possible. That they will do this, we have a confident hope, and that, too, before the last extreme is resorted to, that of force.' *Fullmer's Expulsion*, 20.

HIST. UTAH. 14

same conclusion. It was no new idea to them, seeking a home elsewhere. It was a rough element, that by which they were surrounded, an element which brought upon them more of evil than of good. Comparatively few additions were made to their number from the bold border men of Missouri and Illinois, most of their proselytes coming from other parts of the United States and from Europe. The whole great west was open to them; even during the days of Joseph there had been talk of some happy Arcadian retreat far away from every adverse influence;[35] and in the fertile brain of Brigham the idea assumed proportions yet broader and of more intensified form, significant of western empire and isolation somewhere in California or the Pacific isles, with himself as leader, and followers drawn from every quarter of the globe.

A general council was held on the 9th of September, at which it was resolved that a company of fifteen hundred men be selected to go to Salt Lake Valley, and a committee of five was appointed to gather information relative to the subject.[36] There were frequent meetings of the authorities and consultations in regard to emigrating to California.[37]

The saints would go, they said, but they must have a reasonable time in which to dispose of their prop-

[35] On the 20th of Feb., 1844, according to the *Millennial Star*, xxii. 819, Joseph counselled the twelve to send out a delegation and 'investigate the locations of California and Oregon, and hunt out a good location where we can remove to after the temple is completed, where we can build a city in a day and have a government of our own.' In Taylor's *Reminiscences*, MS., 19, is the following: 'A favorite song in Nauvoo, and of my own composition, was entitled "The Upper California, O that's the land for me!" what is now Utah being known by that name. Joseph Smith was the first who talked of the latter-day saints coming to this region. As early as August 1842 he prophesied that the saints would be driven to the Rocky Mountains, and there become a mighty people.'

[36] See *Hist. B. Young*, 1845, MS., 19.

[37] F. D. Richards read *Fremont's Journal* to the twelve, and later Hastings' account of California was read. *Hist. B. Young*, MS., 308–16. A letter was also read to the authorities from Brother Sam Brannan, stating that the secretary of war and others of the cabinet were planning to prevent their moving west—alleging that it was against the law for an armed body to go from the U. S. to any other government; that it would not do to let them go to California or Oregon, but that they must be obliterated. *Hist. B. Young*, MS., 305.

erty and leave the country.[38] The meeting at Quincy, notice of which with a copy of the resolutions was sent to Nauvoo, named six months as the time within which the Mormons must depart. In answer, the council of the church replied, on the 24th of September, that they could not set forth so early in the spring, when there would be neither food for man or beast, nor even running water, but that it was their full intention to depart as soon as possible, and that they would go far enough, God helping them, forever thereafter to be free from their enemies. Meanwhile all they asked was that they should not be further molested by armed bands or suits at law, but rather assisted in selling their property and collecting their effects.[39]

To this the men of Quincy gave assent; at the same time pledging themselves to prompt action in case of failure on the part of the saints to keep their promise, and taking measures to secure a military organization of the people of Adams county.[40]

It was not to be expected that Carthage would remain idle while other towns were acting. A convention of delegates from nine surrounding counties was held there about the end of September, and four commissioners, among whom were Hardin, commander of the state militia, and Douglas, senator,[41] were sent to Nauvoo to demand the departure of the Mormons. The deputation was met by the council of the twelve with the president at their head, and answer was promptly made that the removal would

[38] One thousand families, including 5,000 or 6,000 souls, would remove in the spring. *Hist. B. Young*, MS., 1845, 134. Hundreds of farms and some 2,000 houses were offered for sale in Nauvoo city and county. 'There was grain enough growing within 10 miles of Nauvoo, raised by the Mormons, to feed the whole population for two years, if they were to do nothing but gather it in and feast upon it.' *Id.*, MS., 35.

[39] A lengthy communication to this effect was drawn up and signed by Brigham Young, president, and Willard Richards, clerk. Printed in full in *Fullmer's Expulsion*, 20–1.

[40] Answer in full in *Id.*, 22.

[41] The other two were W. B. Warren and J. A. McDougal. *Tullidge's Life of Young*, 8.

take place as speedily as possible. "What guarantee will you give us?" asked Hardin. "You have our all as guarantee," answered Brigham. "Young is right," said Douglas. But this reply would not satisfy all the commissioners, and the twelve were requested to submit their intentions in writing, in order that they might be laid before the governor and people of the state. This was done.[42]

The commissioners then returned home; but not even yet were the men of Carthage content. To the resolutions passed at Quincy were added others of similar nature, and the whole adopted. A plan of organization was agreed upon, and arrangements were made for calling meetings and securing volunteers, who were to select their own officers and report to the Quincy military committee. The judge of Hancock county was requested by this convention not to hold

[42] In answer to the letter of the commissioners, the saints on the same day said, after referring to their communication of the 24th to the Quincy committee: ' In addition to this, we would say that we had commenced making arrangements to remove from the country previous to the recent disturbances; that we have four companies of 100 families each, and six more companies now organizing, of the same number each, preparatory to a removal. That 1,000 families, including the twelve, the high council, the trustees, and general authorities of the church, are fully determined to remove in the spring, independent of the contingencies of selling our property; and this company will comprise from 5,000 to 6,000 souls. That the church, as a body, desire to remove with us, and will if sales can be effected so as to raise the necessary means. That the organization of the church we represent is such that there never can exist but one head or presidency at any one time. And all good members wish to be with the organization; and all are determined to remove to some distant point, where we shall neither infringe nor be infringed upon, so soon as time and means will permit. That we have some hundreds of farms and some 2,000 houses for sale in this city and county, and we request all good citizens to assist in the disposal of our property. That we do not expect to find purchasers for our temple and other public buildings; but we are willing to rent them to a respectable community who may inhabit the city. That we wish it distinctly understood that although we may not find purchasers for our property, we will not sacrifice it, nor give it away, or suffer it illegally to be wrested from us. That we do not intend to sow any wheat this fall, and should we all sell, we shall not put in any more crops of any description. That as soon as practicable we will appoint committees from the city, La Harpe, Macedonia, Bear Creek, and all necessary places in the country, to give information to purchasers. That if these testimonies are not sufficient to satisfy any people that we are in earnest, we will soon give them a sign that cannot be mistaken—we will leave them.' In *Hist. B. Young*, MS., Nov. 1845, it is stated that there were families organized 3,285; wagons on hand 1,508; wagons commenced 1,892.

court during that autumn, for fear of collision between
saints and gentiles, and the governor was recommended
to station in that vicinity a small military force to
keep peace during the winter.

During the height of the troubles at Nauvoo, Orson
Pratt was in New York, where on the 8th of November, 1845, he addressed a farewell message to the
brethren in the east, calling upon such of them as
had means to sell their property, buy teams, and join
the overland emigration, and those who had none to
take passage in the ship *Brooklyn*, chartered for the
purpose by Elder Samuel Brannan, and which was to
sail round Cape Horn, via the Hawaiian Islands, for
California. Shortly after, the *Brooklyn* sailed with
238 emigrants, the price of passage being $50 for
adults, with $25 additional for subsistence. The de-
tails of this expedition, with names of the emigrants,
their doings in California, and the departure for the
Great Salt Lake of a large portion of them, is given
in volume V. chapter XX. of my *History of California*.
Upon his return to Nauvoo, Pratt brought $400 worth
of Allen's six-shooting pistols.

CHAPTER VIII.

EXPULSION FROM NAUVOO.

1845–1846.

A Busy City—Meeting in the Temple—Sacrifice of Property—Detachments Move Forward—A Singular Exodus—The First Encampment —Cool Proposal from Brother Brannan—The Journey—Courage and Good Cheer—Swelling of their Numbers—The Remnant of the Saints in Nauvoo—Attitude of the Gentiles—The Mormons Attacked—Continued Hostilities—The Final Departures—The Poor Camp—A Deserted City.

THE holy city now presented an exciting scene. Men were making ready their merchandise, and families preparing to vacate their homes. Hundreds were making tents and wagon covers out of cloth bought with anything they happened to have; companies were organized and numbered, each of which had its own wagon-shop, wheelwrights, carpenters, and cabinet-makers, who were all busily employed.[1] Green timber was prepared for spokes and felloes, some kiln-dried, and some boiled in salt and water. At the Nauvoo house shops were established as well as at the mason's hall and arsenal. Iron was brought from different parts of the country, and blacksmiths were at work night and day.[2] Some three years previous, the prophet Joseph had ordered that there should not be another general con-

[1] Parley Pratt's calculation for an outfit of every family of 5 persons was 1 good wagon, 3 yoke cattle, 2 cows, 2 beef cattle, 3 sheep, 1,000 lbs flour, 20 lbs sugar, 1 rifle and ammunition, a tent and tent-poles, from 10 to 20 lbs seed to a family, from 25 to 100 lbs tools for farming, and a few other items, the cost being about $250, provided they had nothing else but bedding and cooking utensils. *Hist. B. Young*, MS., 125.

[2] In December the drying-house of emigrating company no. 18 was burned to the ground, consuming $300 worth of wagon timber. *Id.*, MS., Dec. 1845.

ference until it could be held in the temple. And now, on the 5th of October, 1845, five thousand persons assembled, and on the following day began the great conference, which lasted three days. The saints, however, were permitted but short enjoyment of their beautiful structure, a meagre reward for all the toil and money expended. Holiness to the Lord was the motto of it; and there was little else they could now carry hence; the hewn stone, the wood-work, and the brass they must leave behind. This building was to them as a temple "where the children of the last kingdom could come together to praise the Lord." As they cast one last gaze on their homes and the monuments reared to their faith, they asked, "Who is the God of the gentiles? Can he be our God?"[3]

In the same number of the *Times and Seasons* in which appeared a notice of this meeting was published a circular signed by Brigham Young, and addressed to the brethren scattered abroad throughout America, informing them of the impending change. "The exodus of the nations of the only true Israel from these United States to a far distant region of the west, where bigotry, intolerance, and insatiable oppression will have lost its power over them, forms a new epoch, not only in the history of the church, but of this nation."[4]

[3] Kane, with the carelessness usual in his statements, says that the temple was completed and consecrated in May, and that the day after its consecration its ornaments were carried away. 'For that one day the temple shone resplendent in all its typical glories of sun, moon, and stars, and other abounding figured and lettered signs, hieroglyphs, and symbols; but that day only. The sacred rites of consecration ended, the work of removing the sacrasancta proceeded with the rapidity of magic. It went on through the night; and when the morning of the next day dawned, all the ornaments and furniture, everything that could provoke a sneer, had been carried off; and except some fixtures that would not bear removal, the building was dismantled to the bare walls. It was this day saw the departure of the last elders, and the largest band that moved in one company together. The people of Iowa have told me that from morning to night they passed westward like an endless procession. They did not seem greatly out of heart, they said; but at the top of every hill, before they disappeared, were to be seen looking back, like banished Moors, on their abandoned homes and the far-seen temple and its glittering spire.' *The Mormons*, 21.

[4] *Times and Seasons*, vi. 1018. In this number is a notice, signed by Willard Richards, cutting off William Smith, the prophet's brother, for apostasy.

The arbitrary acts of the people of Illinois in forcing the departure of the saints lays them open to the grave charge, among others, of a desire to possess their property for less than its value. Houses and lots, farms and merchandise, could not be turned into money, or even into wagons and live-stock, in a moment, except at a ruinous sacrifice. Granted that the hierarchy was opposed to American institutions, that the Mormons wished to gain possession of the United States and rule the world: no one feared the immediate consummation of their pretentious hopes. Granted that among them were adulterers, thieves, and murderers: the gentiles were the stronger, and had laws by which to punish the guilty. It was not a noble sentiment which had actuated the people of Missouri; it was not a noble sentiment which now actuated the people of Illinois, thus to continue their persecutions during the preparations for departure, and drive a whole cityful from their homes out upon the bleak prairie in the dead of winter.

In January 1846 the council ordered that a detachment should set forth at once, and that the remainder of the saints should follow as soon as possible. "Beloved brethren," said their leader, "it now remains to be proven whether those of our family and friends who are necessarily left behind for a season, to obtain an outfit through the sale of property, shall be mobbed, burned, and driven away by force. Does any American want the honor of doing it? or will any Americans suffer such acts to be done, and the disgrace of them to remain on their character, under existing circumstances. If they will, let the world know it."

The world was soon to know it. Driven almost at the point of the sword, a large number of the saints, soon afterward followed by the president, the twelve, the high council, and other companies, gathered on the eastern bank of the Mississippi early in February. There was but little money in circulation through-

out the west at this time. Over vast wild sections
skins were the only currency, and at the settlements
traffic for the most part assumed the form of barter
or exchange of labor. It was, therefore, exceedingly
difficult, as I have said, for the saints to get their
property into portable form, even after selling their
lands at half or quarter their value. The gentiles,
of course, could pay what they pleased, being the only
buyers, and the saints being forced to sell. Moreover, there was more property thrown upon the
market than could be taken at once, and the departure of so large and thrifty a portion of the population was of itself sufficient to depreciate property.
The best they could do was to exchange their lands
for wagons and horses and cattle, and this they did
to as large an extent as possible, scouring the country for a hundred miles around in search of live-stock.[5]

And now, putting upon their animals and vehicles
such of their household effects as they could carry, in
small detachments the migratory saints began to leave
Nauvoo.[6] Before them was the ice-bound river, and
beyond that the wilderness.

There is no parallel in the world's history to this
migration from Nauvoo. The exodus from Egypt
was from a heathen land, a land of idolaters, to a fertile region designated by the Lord for his chosen people, the land of Canaan. The pilgrim fathers in flying
to America came from a bigoted and despotic people—

[5] 'The Mormons went up and down with their furniture, etc., and traded
for anything that could travel, such as an animal or a wagon...Another
company went out in May, but they did not sell their property, leaving it
in the hands of trustees to sell.' *Wells' Narrative*, MS., 37. Their two-
story brick house, which they had occupied but three months, and which
they had denied themselves in every way to build, Mrs Richards says was
sold for 'two yoke of half-broken cattle and an old wagon.' *Reminiscences*,
MS., 20.

[6] 'When we were to leave Mo., the saints entered into a covenant not to
cease their exertions until every saint who wished to go was removed, which
was done...We are better off now than we were then;...he [B. Y.] wants
to see this influence extend from the west to the east sea.' Brigham moved:
'That we take all the saints with us, to the extent of our ability, that is, our
influence and property; seconded by Elder Kimball, and carried unanimously.'
This covenant was entered into Oct. 6, 1845. *Times and Seasons*, vi. 1011.

a people making few pretensions to civil or religious liberty. It was from these same people who had fled from old-world persecutions that they might enjoy liberty of conscience in the wilds of America, from their descendants and associates, that other of their descendants, who claimed the right to differ from them in opinion and practice, were now fleeing. True, the Mormons in various ways had rendered themselves abominable to their neighbors: so had the puritan fathers to their neighbors. Before this the Mormons had been driven to the outskirts of civilization, where they had built themselves a city; this they must now abandon, and throw themselves upon the mercy of savages.

The first teams crossed about the 10th, in flat boats, which were rowed over, and which plied forth and back from early dawn until late into the night, skiffs and other river craft being also used for passengers and baggage. The cold increased. On the 16th snow fell heavily; and the river was frozen over, so that the remainder of the emigration crossed on the ice. Their first camp, the camp of the congregation, was on Sugar Creek, a few miles from Nauvoo and almost within sight of the city.[7] All their movements were directed by Brigham, who with his family and a quorum of the twelve, John Taylor, George A. Smith, Heber C. Kimball, Willard Richards, Orson Hyde, Orson Pratt, Parley P. Pratt, and Amasa Lyman, joined the brethren on Sugar Creek on the 15th. Wilford Woodruff, who had been sent to preside over the mission to England, joined the emigration later at Mount Pisgah.

On the morning of the 17th, all the saints in camp being assembled near the bridge to receive their leader's instructions, the president stood upright in his wagon, and cried with a loud voice, "Attention! the

---

[7] 'We encamped at Sugar Creek, in the snow, while two of my children were very ill. We slept in our wagons, which were placed close to our tents.' *Horne's Migrations*, MS., 16.

whole camp of Israel."[8] He then went on to say that as the Lord had been with them in times past, howsoever singular had been his method of proving his presence, so would he be with them in the future. His empire, the empire of his people, was established, and the powers of hell should not prevail against it.[9]

After this, with comparatively light hearts, they broke camp, and slowly wending their way westward, disappeared at length beyond the horizon, in pursuit once more of the ever-mocking phantom of home. Whither they journeyed they were as yet uncertain. They knew only that they were to search out, probably beyond the Rocky Mountains, if not indeed among them, some isolated spot, where, far away from the land of boasted freedom, the soil, the skies, and mind and manners were free. If they were offensive to the laws, if the laws of the land were offensive to them, they would go where they might have land and laws of their own.

Considering their situation, and what they had been lately called to undergo—ignominy, insult, the loss of property, the abandonment of home—there was little complaint. It was among their opponents, and in the midst of a general recital of their wrongs, that the saints were accustomed to put on a long face and strike into a doleful strain. Among themselves there were

---

[8] The camp of Israel was wherever the president and apostles were.

[9] It has been stated that after dismissing his congregation on the 17th the president led several of the twelve aside to a valley east of the camp, and held a council. A letter was then read from Samuel Brannan, a Mormon elder then in New York, together with a copy of an agreement between him and one A. G. Benson. Brannan was at that time in charge of a company of saints bound for the Pacific coast by way of Cape Horn, and the agreement which he forwarded for Brigham's signature required the pioneers to transfer to A. G. Benson and company the odd numbers of all the town lots that they might acquire in the country where they settled. 'I shall select,' writes Brannan, 'the most suitable spot on the bay of San Francisco for the location of a commercial city.' The council refused to take any action in the matter. In case they refused to sign the agreement, Tullidge soberly relates, *Life of Brigham Young*, 19–23, the president, it was said, would issue a proclamation, setting forth that it was the intention of the Mormons to take sides with either Mexico or Great Britain against the United States, and order them to be disarmed or dispersed! Further mention of this matter is made in *History of California*, vol. v. cap. xx., this series.

few people more free from care, or more light-hearted
and happy.

In the present instance, though all were poor and
some destitute, and though man and beast were exposed to driving rain and hail, and the chill blasts of a
western winter often sweeping down upon them un-
checked from the limitless prairie, they made the best
of it, and instead of wasting time in useless repining,
set themselves at work to make the most of their
joys and the least of their sorrows. On the night of
March 1st, when the first camp was pitched beyond
Sugar Creek, after prayer they held a dance, and
as the men of Iowa looked on they wondered how
these homeless outcasts from Christian civilization
could thus praise and make merry in view of their
near abandoning of themselves to the mercies of savages and wild beasts.[10] Food and raiment were provided for all; for shelter they had their tents and
wagons, and after the weather had spent somewhat of
its ruggedness, no extreme hardships were suffered.
Without attempting long distances in a single day,
they made camp rather early, and after the usual
manner of emigrants, the wagons in a circle or semicircle round the camp-fire, placed so as best to shield
them from the wind and wild beasts and Indians,
with the animals at a convenient distance, some staked,
and some running loose, but all carefully guarded.
The country through which they passed was much of
it well wooded; the land was fertile and afforded abundant pastures, the grass in summer being from one to
ten feet high. Provisions were cheap: corn twelve
cents and wheat twenty-five to thirty cents a bushel,

---

[10] ' In the latter part of March we started for Council Bluffs, 400 miles distant, and were three months on the way. Crossing a long prairie in a fearful
storm, the mud became so soft that we could not travel, and we were obliged
to encamp; the water was several inches deep all over our camping-ground;
we had no wood for a fire, and no means of drying our soaked clothing. In
the morning everything was frozen fast; and a squirrel was found frozen....
Frequently boughs were laid on the ground before the teams could pass...
We had to camp in mud until the roads were dry enough to travel.' *Horne's
Migrations*, MS., 18-19.

beef two cents a pound, and all payable in labor at what was then considered good wages, say forty or fifty cents a day.

Into the wilderness they went, journeying day after day on toward the setting sun, their hearts buoyant, their sinews strengthened by a power not of this world. Forever fades the real before the imaginary. There is nothing tougher than fanaticism. What cared they for wind and rain, for comfortless couches or aching limbs?—the kingdom of the Lord was with them. What cared they for insults and injustice when the worst this world could do was to hasten heaven to them? So on toward the west their long train of wagons rolled, leaving each day farther and farther behind the old, cold, fanatical east, with its hard, senseless dogmas, and its merciless civilization, without murmurings, without discord, the man above any other on earth they most loved and feared riding at their head, or standing with uplifted and extended hands as his people passed by, blessing and comforting them. "We were happy and contented," says John Taylor, "and the songs of Zion resounded from wagon to wagon, reverberating through the woods, while the echo was returned from the distant hills."[11]

There were brass or stringed instruments in every company, and night and morning all were called to prayers[12] at the sound of the bugle. Camp-fires drew around them the saints when their day's work was finished, and singing, dancing, and story-telling enlivened the hour.

As they went on their way their ranks were swelled by fresh bands, until there were brought together 3,000 wagons, 30,000 head of cattle, a great number of mules and horses, and immense flocks of sheep.

[11] 'It is true,' he writes, 'that in our sojourning we do not possess all the luxuries and delicacies of old-established countries and cities, but we have abundance of the staple commodities, such as flour, meal, beef, mutton, pork, milk, butter, and in some instances cheese, sugar, coffee, tea, etc.' Letter in *Millennial Star*, viii. 114.

[12] Each family had prayers separately. *Taylor's Rem.*, MS., 9.

Richardson Point[13] they made their second stationary
camp, the third at Chariton River, the fourth at
Locust Creek, where a considerable time was spent.
Then there were—so named by the saints—Garden
Grove,[14] a large timbered tract which had been burned
over, Mount Pisgah,[15] and finally Winter Quarters, in
Nebraska, on the west side of the Missouri, a little above
the modern Omaha, on the site of the present town
of Florence.[16]   At Garden Grove and Mount Pisgah
were established farming settlements for the benefit
of those who were to follow.   In July the main body
reached the Missouri at the spot now known as Council
Bluffs, and soon afterward many crossed the river in a
ferry-boat of their own construction, and pitched their
tents at Winter Quarters.   Other large encampments

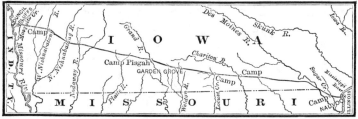

BETWEEN THE MISSISSIPPI AND MISSOURI.

[13] In Lee County, Iowa, three weeks from their starting-point.

[14] About 150 miles from Nauvoo, on the east fork of the Grand River.
'Many located there, ploughing and sowing, and preparing homes for their
poor brethren for a longer period.' *Horne's Migrations*, MS., 19. 'On the
morning of the 27th of April the bugle sounded at Garden Grove, and all
the men assembled to organize for labor.   Immediately hundreds of men
were at work, cutting trees, splitting rails, making fences, cutting logs for
houses, building bridges, making ploughs, and herding cattle.   Quite a number were sent into the Missouri settlements to exchange horses for oxen, valuable feather-beds and the like for provisions and articles most needed in the
camp, and the remainder engaged in ploughing and planting.   Messengers
were also despatched to call in the bands of pioneers scattered over the country seeking work, with instructions to hasten them up to help form the new
settlements before the season had passed; so that, in a scarcely conceivable
space of time, at Garden Grove and Mount Pisgah, industrious settlements
sprung up almost as if by magic.' *Tullidge's Life of Brigham Young*, 41.

[15] This site was discovered by Parley, who was sent forward to reconnoitre
by Brigham.   It was situated on a branch of Grand River, and for years was
the resting-place for the saints on their way to Utah. *Autobiog. P. Pratt*, 381.

[16] Here 700 log cabins and 150 dugouts (cabins half under ground) were
built.   A large quantity of hay was cut, and a flouring mill erected. *Id.*, 383.

were formed on both banks of the river, or at points near by, where grass was plentiful. In early autumn about 12,000 Mormons were assembled in this neighborhood, or were on their way across the plains.

Leaving here the advance portion of the emigration, let us return to Nauvoo and see how it fared with those who were still engaged in preparations for their pilgrimage. It had been stipulated, the reader will remember, that the Mormons should remove from the state in the spring, or as soon afterward as they could sell their property, and that meanwhile they should not be molested. Long before spring, thousands had crossed the Mississippi, among whom were all the more obnoxious members of the sect. Meanwhile, how had the gentiles kept their faith?

But passing the cause, what a picture was now presented by the deserted city and its exiled inhabitants!—the former, as Colonel Kane viewed it—but which view must be regarded as ideal rather than strictly historical—with "its bright new dwellings set in cool green gardens, ranging up around a stately dome-shaped hill, which was crowned by a noble marble edifice, whose high tapering spire was radiant with white and gold. The city appeared to cover several miles; and beyond it, in the background, there rolled off a fair country, checkered by the careful lines of fruitful husbandry."

To the *Nauvoo Eagle* Major Warren sent notice from Carthage, on the 16th of April, that he had been directed by the governor to disband on the 1st of May the force which had been kept there ostensibly for the protection of the saints, as the time appointed for their departure would expire on that day.[17] The day arrived, and there were yet many Mormons remaining, many who had found it impossible to remove on ac-

[17] 'The removal of the entire population,' the major adds, 'has been locked forward to as an event that could alone restore peace and quiet to this portion of our state.' *Fullmer's Expulsion*, 24.

count of sickness, failure to dispose of their property, or other adverse fortune; whereat the men of Illinois began to bluster and threaten annihilation. Warren, who had disbanded his troops on the 1st, received an order from the governor on the following day to muster them into service again. This he did; for he would, if possible, see the treaty between the Mormons and the governor faithfully carried out, and while urging the saints to haste, he endeavored to stand between them and the mob which now threatened their lives and the destruction of their property.[18]

Major Warren appears to have performed his duty firmly and well, and to have done all that lay in his power to protect the Mormons. In a letter to the *Quincy Whig*, dated May 20th, he writes: "The Mormons are leaving the city with all possible despatch. During the week four hundred teams have crossed at three points, or about 1,350 souls. The demonstrations made by the Mormon people are unequivocal. They are leaving the state, and preparing to leave, with every means God and nature have placed in their hands." It was but the lower class of people that clamored for the immediate expulsion of the remnant of the saints—the ignorant, the bigoted, the brutal, the vicious, the lawless, and profligate, those who hated their religion and coveted their lands.

---

[18] 'Thus while with one hand he pushed the saints from their possessions across the river to save their lives, with the other he kept at bay the savage fiends who thirsted for blood, and who would fain have washed their hands in the blood of innocence, and feasted their eyes on the smoking ruins of their martyred victims.' *Id.*, 24–5. From Nauvoo, May 11, 1846, Warren writes: 'To the Mormons I would say, Go on with your preparations, and leave as fast as you can. Leave the fighting to be done by my detachment. If we are overpowered, then recross the river and defend yourselves and property. The neighboring counties, under the circumstances, cannot and will not lend their aid to an unprovoked and unnecessary attack upon the Mormons at this time; and without such aid the few desperadoes in the county can do but little mischief, and can be made amenable to the law for that little. The force under my command is numerically small; but backed as I am by the moral force of the law, and possessing as I do the confidence of nine tenths of the respectable portion of the old citizens, my force is able to meet successfully any mob which can be assembled in the county, and if any such force does assemble, they or I will leave the field in double-quick time.'

On the 6th of June the people of Hancock county met at Carthage to arrange for celebrating the 4th of July. One of the citizens rose and said that since the Mormons were not all removed they could not rejoice as freemen. Mormon affairs then took precedence, and another meeting was appointed for the 12th, an invitation being sent to the gentiles at Nauvoo who had occupied the deserted dwellings of the saints. It happened that this was the day appointed for the assembling of the militia, with a view to raise volunteers for the Mexican war; and now, it was thought, was a good opportunity to show the Mormons the military strength of the county. The officers conferred, and without authority from the governor, marched their troops, some three or four hundred in number, to a place called Golden Point, five miles from Nauvoo, where they encamped, and opened communication with the city. It happened, however, at this juncture, that Colonel Markham and others had returned with teams from Council Bluffs for some of the church property, and arming a force of six or eight hundred, prepared to sally forth; the name of Colonel Markham was a terror to evil-doers, and the militia fled, no one pursuing them.

There were yet remaining, as late as August, certain sturdy saints who, having committed no crime, would not consent to be driven from their homes or barred from their occupations. Among these was a party engaged in harvesting wheat at a settlement eight miles from Nauvoo, in company with one or two of the gentiles, although it was forbidden by the men of Illinois that any Mormon should show himself outside the city, except en route for the west. The harvesters were seized and beaten with clubs, whereupon the people of Nauvoo, both Mormons and gentiles, took up the matter. Some arrests were made, and the culprits taken to Nauvoo, but by writ of habeas corpus were removed to Quincy, where they met with little trouble. While in Nauvoo, a gun in the hands of a militia officer was recognized by William Pickett as belonging to one of the harvesters. Pickett took possession of the weapon, and a warrant was issued against him for theft; when an officer came to arrest him, he refused to surrender. As the Mormons stood by him in illegal attitude, the affair caused considerable excitement.

In short, from the 1st of May until the final evacuation of the city, the men of Illinois never ceased from strife and outrage. Of the latter I will mention only two instances: "A man of near sixty years of age," writes Major Warren in the letter just referred to, "living about seven miles from this place, was taken from his house a few nights since, stripped of his clothing, and his back cut to pieces with a whip, for no other reason than because he was a Mormon, and too old to make a successful resistance. Conduct of this kind would disgrace a horde of savages." In August a party consisting of Phineas H. Young, his son Brigham, and three others who were found outside the city, were kidnapped by a mob, hurried into the thickets, passed from one gang to another—men from Nauvoo being in hot pursuit—and for a fortnight were kept almost without food or rest, and under constant threat of death.

Fears are now entertained that, by reason of the popular feeling throughout the country, Nauvoo city will be again attacked; the gentile citizens therefore ask Governor Ford for protection, whereupon Major Parker is sent to their relief.[19] All through August

---

[19] 'Sir—I have received information that another effort is to be made on Monday next to drive out the inhabitants of Nauvoo, new as well as old, and destroy the city. I am informed that it is believed in the surrounding counties that the new citizens in Nauvoo are all Mormons, and that the remnant of the old Mormon population are determined to remain there, although I am assured that the contrary in both particulars is the truth. You are therefore hereby authorized and empowered to repair to Nauvoo, and there remain until you are relieved. You will immediately inquire how many of the inhabitants are new citizens, and how many of them are Mormons; how many of the old Mormon population remain, and what the prospect is of their removal in a reasonable time; and in case an attack on the city should be attempted or threatened, you are hereby authorized to take command of such

troubles continue, the anti-Mormons almost coming to blows among themselves. Before the end of the month about six hundred men are assembled at Carthage, by order of Thomas Carlin, a special constable, ostensibly to enforce the arrest of Pickett, but in reality to enforce the expulsion of the Mormons. Major Parker orders the constable's posse to disperse, otherwise he threatens to treat them as a mob. The constable replies that if the major should attempt to molest them in discharge of their duty he will regard him and his command as a mob and so treat them. "Now, fellow-citizens," declares a committee selected from four counties,[20] in a proclamation issued at Carthage, "an issue is fairly raised. On the one hand, a large body of men have assembled at Carthage, under the command of a legal officer, to assist him in performing legal duties. They are not excited—they are cool, but determined at all hazards to execute the law in Nauvoo, which has always heretofore defied it. They are resolved to go to work systematically and with ample precaution, but under a full knowledge that on their good and orderly behavior their character is staked. On the other hand, in Nauvoo is a blustering Mormon mob, who have defied the law, and who are now organized for the purpose of arresting the arm of civil power. Judge ye which is in the right."

Intending, as it seems, to keep his word, Carlin places his men under command of Colonel Singleton, who at once throws off the mask, and on the 7th of September announces to Major Parker that the Mormons must go. On the same day a stipulation is made, granting to the saints sixty days' extension of time, and signed by representatives on both sides.[21]

volunteers as may offer themselves, free of cost to the state, to repel it and defend the city.' *Fullmer's Expulsion*, 29–30.

[20] Among the members was the Rev. Thomas S. Brockman, who afterward took command of the posse.

[21] Hostilities to cease; the city to be evacuated in 60 days, 25 men remaining to see the stipulation carried out. *Id.*, 34–5.

But to the terms of this stipulation the men of Illinois would not consent. They were sore disgusted, and rebelled against their leaders, causing Singleton, Parker, and others to abandon their commands, the posse being left in charge of Constable Carlin, who summoned to his aid one Thomas Brockman, a clergyman of Brown county, and for the occasion dubbed general. On the 10th of September the posse, now more than a thousand strong, with wagons, equipments, and every preparation for a campaign, approached Nauvoo and encamped at Hunter's farm.

At this time there were in the city not more than a hundred and fifty Mormons, and about the same number of gentiles, or, as they were termed, 'new citizens,' capable of bearing arms, the remainder of the population consisting of destitute women and children and of the sick. Many of the gentiles had departed, fearing a general massacre, and those who remained could not be relied upon as combatants, for they were of course unwilling to risk their lives in a conflict which, if successful, would bring them no credit. Nothing daunted, the little band, under command of colonels Daniel H. Wells[22] and William Cutler, took up its position on the edge of a wood in the suburbs of Nauvoo, and less than a mile from the enemy's camp.[23]

Before hostilities commenced, a deputation from Quincy[24] visited the camp of the assailants, and in vain attempted to dissuade them from their purpose. No sooner had they departed than fire was opened on the Mormons from a battery of six-pounders, but without effect. Here for the day matters rested. At sunrise the posse changed their position, intending to take the city by storm, but were held in check by

[22] Who afterward became lieut.-gen. of the Nauvoo legion in Utah.
[23] There were about 300 Mormons and new citizens who could then bear arms against the mob, but on the day of the fight no more than 100 could be found to go, as the Mormons were continually leaving.' Wells' Narrative, MS., 39.
[24] John Wood, the mayor, Major Flood, Dr Conyers, and Joel Rice. See Wells' Narrative, MS., passim.

Captain Anderson[25] at the head of thirty-five men, termed by the saints the Spartan band. The enemy now fired some rounds of grape-shot, forcing the besieged to retire out of range; and after some further cannonading, darkness put an end to the skirmish, the Mormons throwing up breastworks during the night.[26]

On the morning of the 12th the demand of unconditional surrender was promptly rejected; whereupon, at a given signal, several hundred men who had been stationed in ambush, on the west bank of the river, to cut off the retreat of the Mormons, appeared with red flags in their hands, thus portending massacre. The assailants now opened fire from all their batteries, and soon afterward advanced to the assault, slowly, and with the measured tramp of veterans, at their head being Constable Carlin and the Reverend Brockman, and unfurled above them—the stars and stripes. When within rifle-range of the breastworks the posse wheeled toward the south, attempting to outflank the saints and gain possession of the temple square. But this movement had been anticipated, and posted in the woods to the north of the Mormon position lay the Spartan band. Leading on his men at double-quick, Anderson suddenly confronted the enemy and opened a brisk fire from revolving rifles.[27] The posse advanced no farther, but for an hour and a half held their ground bravely against the Spartan band, the expense of ammunition in proportion to casualties being greater than has yet been recorded in modern warfare. Then they retreated in excellent order to the camp. The losses of the Mormons were three killed and a few slightly wounded; the losses of the gentiles are variously

[25] He was more than brave, he was presumptuous. Wells, in *Utah Notes*, MS., p. 7.

[26] 'Many of our log houses were torn down by the mob, which numbered 1,000 men; we made barricades of corn-stalks stacked up.' Wells, in *Utah Notes*, MS., 7.

[27] Elder John S. Fullmer, then a colonel in the Nauvoo legion, claims that he directed this movement. *Expulsion*, 38.

stated.[28] Among those who fell were Captain Anderson and his son, a youth of sixteen, the former dying, as he had vowed that he would die, in defence of the holy sanctuary.

The following day was the sabbath, and hostilities were not renewed; but on that morning a train of wagons, despatched by the posse for ammunition and supplies, entered the town of Quincy. It was now evident that, whether the men of Illinois intended massacre or forcible expulsion, it would cost them many lives to effect either purpose. With a view, therefore, to prevent further bloodshed, a committee of one hundred proceeded to Nauvoo and attempted mediation. At the same time the Reverend Brockman sent in his ultimatum, the terms being that the Mormons surrender their arms, and immediately cross the river or disperse, and that all should be protected from violence.[29] There was no alternative. The armed mob in their front was daily swelling in number, while beyond the river still appeared the red flag; their own ranks, meanwhile, were being rapidly thinned by defection among the new citizens.[30]

[28] 'But three in all were killed...Meetings were held to stop the effusion of blood,...but there was no necessity for such action, when no blood was shed.' Wells, in *Utah Notes*, 7.

[29] ' 1st. The city of Nauvoo will surrender. The force of Reverend Brockman to enter and take possession of the city to-morrow, the 17th of September, at three o'clock P. M. 2d. The arms to be delivered to the Quincy committee, to be returned on crossing the river. 3d. The Quincy committee pledge themselves to use their influence for the protection of persons and property, and the officers of the camp and the men likewise pledge themselves. 4th. The sick and helpless to be protected and treated with humanity. 5th. The Mormon population of the city to leave the state or disperse as soon as they can cross the river. 6th. Five men, including the trustees of the church, and five clerks with their families (William Pickett not one of the number), to be permitted to remain in the city for the disposition of property, free from all molestation and personal violence. 7th. Hostilities to cease immediately, and ten men of the Quincy committee to enter the city in the execution of their duty as soon as they think proper.' It will be observed that nothing is said about the surrender of Pickett. He was not even arrested.

[30] 'The mob entered the temple, instituted an inquisition, and regardless of the Mormons or new citizens, went from house to house plundering cowyards, pig-pens, hen-roosts, and bee-stands indiscriminately; thus turning some of their best friends into enemies, bursting open trunks and chests, searching for arms, keys, etc.' p. 343. 'In the temple ringing the bells, shouting, and

On the 17th of September the remnant of the
Mormons crossed the Mississippi, and on the same
day the gentiles took possession of Nauvoo.[31]

It was indeed a singular spectacle, as I have said,
this upon the western border of the world's great
republic in the autumn of 1846. A whole cityful,
with other settlements, and thousands of thrifty agri-

hallooing; they took several to the river and baptized them, swearing, throwing them backward, then on to their faces, saying: "The commandments must
be fulfilled, and God damn you." *Hist. B. Young*, MS., 345.

[31] The best narrative, and indeed the only one that enters circumstantially
into all the details of the expulsion from Nauvoo, is contained in the *Assassination of Joseph and Hyrum Smith, the Prophet and the Patriarch of the Church
of Latter-day Saints. Also a Condensed History of the Expulsion of the Saints
from Nauvoo by Elder John S. Fullmer (of Utah, U. S. A.), Pastor of the Manchester, Liverpool, and Preston Conferences.* Liverpool and London, 1855. The
work is written from a Mormon standpoint, but including as it does copies of
the despatches of Illinois officers and officials, of the stipulations between the
belligerents, and of some comments made by the *Quincy Whig*, appears in
the main reliable. The author's comments on the gentiles are sufficiently
bitter, and his description of the fight at Nauvoo and the valor of the saints
militant must of course be taken with due allowance. For instance: 'Seeing
our men take possession of some vacant buildings on the line of their approach, they took a position on an elevated spot of ground, and opened a
heavy cannonade at a distance of something less than half a mile. This was
returned with great spirit on our part from guns made of steam shafts that
carried six-pound balls. Many were the balls that we picked up as they
came rolling and bounding among us, and we sent them back with as much
spirit and precision as they were first sent.' p. 37. Col Kane says: 'A vindictive war was waged upon them, from which the weakest fled in scattered
parties, leaving the rest to make a reluctant and almost ludicrously unavailing defence.' *The Mormons*, 54. In the General Epistle of the Twelve,
Dec. 23, 1847, in *Snow's Voice of Joseph*, 14–15, we read: ' In September
1846 an infuriated mob, clad in all the horrors of war, fell on the saints who
had still remained in Nauvoo for want of means to remove, murdered some,
and drove the remainder across the Mississippi into Iowa, where, destitute of
houses, tents, food, clothing, or money, they received temporary assistance
from some benevolent souls in Quincy, St Louis, and other places, whose
names will ever be remembered with gratitude. Their property in Hancock
co., Illinois, was little or no better than confiscated; many of their houses
were burned by the mob, and they were obliged to leave most of those that
remained without sale; and those who bargained sold almost for a song; for
the influence of their enemies was to cause such a diminution in the value of
property that for a handsome estate was seldom realized enough to remove
the family comfortably away; and thousands have since been wandering to
and fro, destitute, afflicted, and distressed for the common necessaries of life,
or unable to endure, have sickened and died by hundreds; while the temple
of the Lord is left solitary in the midst of our enemies, an enduring monu-
ment of the diligence and integrity of the saints.' Mention of the expulsion
from Nauvoo is of course made in most of the books published on Mormonism, but in none of them, except perhaps in one or two of the most rabid
anti-Mormon works, which I have not thought it worth while to notice, is
the conduct of the Illinois mob defended.

culturists in the regions about, citizens of the United
States, driven beyond the border by other citizens: not
by reason of their religion alone, though this was made
a pretence; not for breaking the laws, though this was
made a pretence; not on account of their immorality,
for the people of Illinois and Missouri were not immaculate in this respect; nor was it altogether on
account of their solid voting and growing political
power, accompanied ever by the claim of general inheritance and universal dominion, though this last
had more to do with it probably than all the rest
combined, notwithstanding that the spirit of liberty
and the laws of the republic permitted such massing
of social and political influence, and notwithstanding
the obvious certainty that any of the gentile political
parties now playing the role of persecutors would
gladly and unscrupulously have availed themselves of
such means for the accomplishment of their ends.   It
was all these combined, and so combined as to engender deadly hate.   It gave the Mormons a power in
proportion to their numbers not possessed by other
sects or societies, which could not and would not endure
it; a power regarded by the others as unfairly acquired,
and by a way and through means not in accord with
the American idea of individual equality, of equal
rights and equal citizenship.   In regard to all other
sects within the republic, under guard of the constitution, religion was subordinated to politics and government; in regard to the Mormons, in spite of the
constitution, politics and government were subordinated to religion.

And in regard to the late occupants of the place,
the last of the Mormon host that now lay huddled to
the number of 640 on the western bank of the river
in sight of the city:[32] if the first departures from Nauvoo
escaped extreme hardships, not so these.   It was the

[32] A few months before, Nauvoo with the neighboring Mormon settlements
had contained some 20,000 saints, of whom in July about 15,000 were encamped
on the Missouri River, or were scattered through the western states in search
of employment.

latter part of September, and nearly all were pros-
trated with chills and fevers;[33] there at the river bank,
among the dock and rushes, poorly protected, without
the shelter of a roof or anything to keep off the force
of wind or rain, little ones came into life and were left
motherless at birth.[34] They had not food enough to
satisfy the cravings of the sick, nor clothing fit to
wear. For months thereafter there were periods
when all the flour they used was of the coarsest, the
wheat being ground in coffee and hand mills, which
only cut the grain; others used a pestle; the finer meal
was used for bread, the coarser made into hominy.
Boiled wheat was now the chief diet for sick and well.
For ten days they subsisted on parched corn. Some
mixed their remnant of grain with the pounded bark
of the slippery elm which they stripped from the
trees along their route.

This encampment was about two miles above
Montrose on the Mississippi, and was called the
Poor Camp. Aid was solicited, and within three
weeks a little over one hundred dollars was collected,
mostly in Quincy, with provisions and clothing,
though the prejudice against them was deep and
strong.[35] Some of the people were crowded into
tents, made frequently of quilts and blankets; others
in bowers made of brush; others had only wagons for
shelter. They suffered from heavy thunder-storms,
when the rain was bailed out with basins from their
beds. Mothers huddled their children in the one
dress which often was all they possessed, and shaking
with ague or burning with fever, took refuge from
the pitiless storms under wagons and bushes.[36]

[33] While at Montrose, Heber C. Kimball writes thus in his journal of the
condition of his family, his wife having a babe a few days old, and he himself
ill with ague. 'I went to the bed; my wife, who was shaking with the ague,
having two children lying sick by her side;...the only child well was little
Heber Parley, and it was with difficulty he could carry a two-quart pail full
of water from a spring at the bottom of the hill.'

[34] 'Such deaths occurred from exposure and fright in Nauvoo. The camp
journalist recorded: Effect of persecution by the Illinois mob.'

[35] The trustees from Nauvoo also distributed clothing, and molasses, salt,
and salt pork. *Hist. B. Young*, MS., 1846, 383.

[36] *Mrs Clara Young's Experience*, MS., 3.

" While the people for the most part were ill with chills and fever," says Wells, "quail fell into camp and were picked up with ease.[37] This supply was looked upon as miraculous by the half-famished people. So long had they been lashed by the fierce winds of misfortune, that now they accepted with gratitude this indication of providential care.

Wagons were sent from Winter Quarters for the removal of the people from Poor Camp; and gradually all reached the various stations in which the Mormons had gathered.[38]

Of their long journey many painful incidents are recorded. Weakened by fever or crippled with rheumatism, and with sluggish circulation, many were severely frost-bitten. Women were compelled to drive the nearly worn-out teams, while tending on their knees, perhaps, their sick children. The strength of the beasts was failing, as there were intervals when they could be kept from starving only by the browse or tender buds and branches of the cotton-wood, felled for the purpose.[39]

At one time no less than two thousand wagons could be counted, it was said, along the three hundred miles of road that separated Nauvoo from the Mormon encampments. Many families possessed no wag-

[37] ' On the 9th of October, while our teams were waiting on the banks of the Miss. for the poor saints...left without any of the necessaries of life,...and nothing to start their journey with, the Lord sent flocks of quail, which lit upon their wagons and on their empty tables, and upon the ground within their reach, which the saints, and even the sick, caught with their hands until they were satisfied.' Hist. B. Young, MS., 1847, 9. This phenomenon extended some 30 or 40 miles along the river, and was generally observed. The quail in immense quantities had attempted to cross the river, but it being beyond their strength, had dropped into the river boats or on the bank.' Wells, in Utah Notes, MS., 7.

[38] See The Mormons: A Discourse delivered before the Historical Society of Pennsylvania, March 26, 1850, by Thomas L. Kane. Philadelphia, 1850. A copy of it will be found at the end of Orson Pratt's Works, and in Mackay's The Mormons, 200–45. The story of the Mormon exodus, as handed down to us by a man of Colonel Kane's powers of observation, would have been a valuable record were it not plainly apparent that truth is too often sacrificed to diction. Among Mormon writers we find no detailed narrative of this exodus, and among others little that is not borrowed from the colonel's discourse.

[39] Snow's Biography, 89.

ons, and in the long procession might be seen vehicles of all descriptions, from the lumbering cart, under whose awning lay stretched its fever-stricken driver, to the veriest makeshifts of poverty, the wheelbarrow or the two-wheeled trundle, in which was dragged along a bundle of clothing and a sack of meal—all of this world's goods that the owner possessed.

On arriving at the banks of the Missouri, the wagons were drawn up in double lines and in the form of squares. Between the lines, tents were pitched at intervals, space being left between each row for a passage-way, which was shaded with awnings or a lattice-work of branches, and served as a promenade for convalescents and a playground for children.

And what became of Nauvoo? The temple was destroyed by fire and tempest,[40] and all the wood-work consumed, while the rock was utilized for miles around as foundations of houses, for door-steps, and other purposes. A French company coming in later bought the stone from those in possession, and built wine-vaults. Foundations of buildings were broken up, and houses once surrounded by carefully tended flower-gardens, pillaged of all that was valuable, were now abandoned by their ruthless destroyers.[41] "At present," writes Linforth, "the Icarians form the most important part of the population of Nauvoo...They live in a long ugly row of buildings, the architect of which and of the school-house was a cobbler." In the house built for the prophet and his family dwelt in 1854 the prophet's widow, his mother, and his family.[42]

[40] The temple was half destroyed by fire on Nov. 19, 1848. *Nauvoo Patriot*, in *Millennial Star*, xi. p. 46; and on May 27, 1850, further damaged by a tornado. *Hancock Patriot*, in *Mackay's The Mormons*, 210. For cut of remnants, see *Linforth's Route from Liverpool to G. S. L. Valley*, 62, and *Hyde's Mormonism*, 140. See also George Q. Cannon, in *Juvenile Instructor*, vol. ix. no. 5, and *Wells' Narrative*, MS., 41; *Deseret News*, Aug. 24, 1850; *Frontier Guardian*, July 24, 1850.

[41] As James Linforth describes in writing of Nauvoo in 1858.

[42] *Route from Liverpool to G. S. L. Valley*, 63.

CHAPTER IX.

AT THE MISSOURI.

1846-1847.

NATIVE RACES OF THE MISSOURI—THE POTTAWATTAMIES AND THE OMAHAS—
THE MORMONS WELCOMED AS BRETHREN—WAR WITH MEXICO—CALIFOR-
NIA TERRITORY—MEXICAN BOUNDARIES—APPLICATION TO THE UNITED
STATES GOVERNMENT FOR AID—AN OFFER TO SERVE AS SOLDIERS AC-
CEPTED—ORGANIZATION OF THE MORMON BATTALION—DEPARTURE OF
THE BATTALION—BOUNTY MONEY—MARCH ACROSS THE CONTINENT—
THE BATTALION IN CALIFORNIA—MATTERS ON THE MISSOURI.

AMONG the savages on either side of the Missouri,
the Pottawattamies on the east side and the Omahas
on the west side, the outcasts from Nauvoo were
warmly welcomed. "My Mormon brethren," said
the chief Pied Riche,[1] "the Pottawattamie came sad
and tired into this unhealthy Missouri bottom, not
many years back, when he was taken from his beautiful country beyond the Mississippi, which had abundant game and timber and clear water everywhere.
Now you are driven away in the same manner from
your lodges and lands there, and the graves of your
people. So we have both suffered. We must help
one another, and the great spirit will help us both."
Extreme care was taken not to infringe in any way
upon the rights of the Indians or the government.
Brigham counselled the brethren to regard as sacred
the burial customs of the natives; frequently their
dead were deposited in the branches of trees, wrapped
in buffalo robes and blankets, with pipes and trinkets

---

[1] Surnamed Le Clerc, on account of his scholarship.

beside them. At Cutler Park there were friendly negotiations made with Big Elk, chief of the Omahas, who said: "I am willing you should stop in my country, but I am afraid of my great father at Washington."[2]

As the United States pretended to hold the title to the land, it was thought that the Pottawattamies had no right to convey their timber to others; so Brigham enjoined that there should be no waste of timber within these limits, but that as much as was necessary might be used. A permit for passing through their territory, and for remaining while

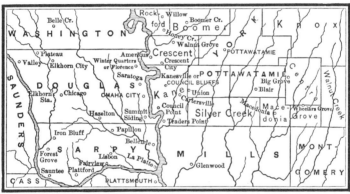

ABOUT THE MISSOURI.

necessary, was obtained from Colonel Allen, who was acting for the United States.[3]

Although it was late in the season when the first bands of emigrants crossed the Missouri, some of them still moved westward as far as the Pawnee villages on Grand Island, intending to select a new home before winter. But the evil tidings from Nauvoo, and the destitute condition in which other parties of the

[2] 'The Omahas caused them some trouble, as they would steal with one hand while we fed them with the other.' *Hist. B. Young*, MS., 46, Oct. 18th.

[3] *Hist. B. Young*, MS., 1846, 98-9. Maj. Harvey brought the Mormons at Winter Quarters letters from Washington, expecting them to leave the Pottawattamie lands in the spring. See cor., *Hist. B. Young*, MS., 441-52.

saints reached the Mormon encampments, forbade further progress, and all prepared to spend the winter on the prairie. To the Mormon encampment on the site of the present town of Council Bluffs was afterward given the name of Kanesville.[4]

While the saints were undergoing their infelicities at Nauvoo, war had broken out between the United States and Mexico. At that time New Mexico and California were a part of Mexico, and Utah and Nevada were a part of California.[5] Journeying west from Nauvoo, California or Oregon would be reached. The latter territory was already secured to the United States; people were there from the United States, composing religious sects and political parties as jealous of their holdings as any in Missouri or Illinois. Vancouver Island[6] was practically unoccupied, but the Hudson's Bay Company would scarcely regard with favor its occupation by a large body of American citizens whose government was at that moment crowding them out of the Oregon territory and across the Columbia River.

But had the Mormons known their destination, had they known what point among the mountains or

---

[4] So called after Thomas L. Kane. Here was first issued on Feb. 7, 1849, the *Frontier Guardian*, and its publication was continued till March 22, 1852. *Richards' Narr.*, MS., 65; *Richards' Bibliog. of Utah*, MS., 13. The paper was edited by Orson Hyde, and makes a very creditable appearance. The subscription was $2 per year. In the second number we read: 'Flour nicely put up in sacks of from 50 to 100 lbs each will be received in exchange for the *Guardian* at the rate of $2 per hundred pounds, if good.' The last number of the *Times and Seasons* bears date Feb. 15, 1846.

[5] I frequently find California and Utah confounded by writers of this early period. The limits of California on the east were not then defined, and it was not uncommon, nor indeed incorrect, to apply that term to territory east of the sierra. I find this written in *Snow's Voice of the Prophet*, 15: 'The pioneers discovered a beautiful valley beyond the pass of the great Rocky Mts, being a portion of the great basin of Upper California.' As we shall see later, the Mormons knew even less about Utah than they did about California.

[6] Brigham Young at first suggested Vancouver Island. 'There are said to be many good locations for settlements on the Pacific, especially at Vancouver Island.' Circular to the brethren, in *Times and Seasons*, vi. 1019. In 1845 the report was current that the Mormons of Illinois had chosen V. I. as their future home, the metropolis to be situated at Nootka. *Niles' Register*, lxix. 134. The *Quincy Whig* thinks the Mormons intend to settle at Nootka Sound. *Polynesian*, ii. 1846.

beside the sea was to be their final resting-place, they would not have told it. When they turned their back on Nauvoo, the whole western coast was before them, with its multitudinous mountains and valleys, its rivers and lakes, and long line of seaboard. Of the several parts of this immense territory, ownership and right of occupation were not in every instance determined. The question of the boundary line between England's possessions and those of the United States had stirred up no small discussion and feeling, and out of the present war with Mexico would doubtless arise some changes.[7] It was a foregone conclusion in the minds of many, before ever the migratory saints had reached the Missouri River, that when the present troubles with Mexico were ended the United States would have California. But however this might be, the saints had a firm reliance on an overruling providence, and once adrift upon the vast untenanted west, their God and their sagacity would point out to them their future home. Thus it was that while the Mormons in the western states took the route overland, another portion living at the east took passage round Cape Horn, the intention being that the two bodies of brethren should come together somewhere upon the Pacific slope, which indeed they did.[8]

The national title to what is now the Pacific United States being at this time thus unsettled, and the Mormons having been driven from what was then

[7] In a letter to Pres. Polk, dated near Council Bluffs, Aug. 9, 1846, the determination was expressed, 'that as soon as we are settled in the great basin, we design to petition the U. S. for a territorial govt, bounded on the north by the British and south by the Mexican dominions, east and west by the summits of the Rocky and Cascade Mts.' And again elsewhere: 'We told Col Kane we intended settling in the great basin on Bear River Valley; that those who went round by water would settle in S. F. That was in council with the twelve and Col Kane.' *Hist. B. Young*, MS., 133, 140.

[8] In his address to the saints in Great Britain, dated Liverpool, 1849, Elder John Taylor says: 'When we arrive in California, according to the provisions of the Mexican government, each family will be entitled to a large tract of land, amounting to several hundred acres; but as the Mexican and American nations are now at war, should Cal. fall into the hands of the American nation, there has been a bill before congress in relation to Or., which will undoubtedly pass, appropriating 640 acres of land to every male settler.' *Millennial Star*, viii. 115.

the United States, it was considered but natural, as
indeed it seemed to be a necessity, that they would
take possession of such unoccupied lands in the region
toward the Pacific as best suited them.   But it was
not necessary that they should hold possession of such
lands in opposition to the government of the United
States, as they have been charged with doing.

They now applied to the government at Washington for work, offering to open roads, transport military stores, or perform any other service which the
government might require in this farthest west, even
to assist in fighting its battles.   Such occupation
would be of the greatest advantage to them in this
new country, where land was fertile and plenty and
free, and possessing as they did large herds of cattle
and horses and sheep, with no market and but little
money.   And on the other hand, being on the ground,
accustomed to work, and having every facility at
hand without long and expensive transportation, they
could give more and better work for the pay than
the government could obtain by any other means.

They even asked for aid direct about the time the
exodus began, being represented at Washington by
Elder Jesse C. Little,[9] who, aided by Colonel Kane,
Amos Kendall, and others, brought the matter before
President Polk.   While negotiations were yet in
progress, news arrived that General Taylor had already won two victories over the Mexicans; whereupon the elder addressed a petition to the president,
stating that from twelve to fifteen thousand Mormons
had set forth from Nauvoo for California, while some
had departed by sea, and in Great Britain alone were
forty thousand converts, all resolved to join the saints
in their promised land.   Many of them were without
means; they were compelled to go; they wanted as-

---

[9] In the letter appointing and giving instructions to Elder Little is the
following: 'If our government should offer facilities for emigrating to the
western coast, embrace those facilities if possible.   As a wise and faithful
man, take every advantage of the times you can.' *Tullidge's Life of Brigham
Young*, 48.

sistance either in the way of work or otherwise. The Mormons were true-hearted Americans, the memorial went on to say, and if the government would assist them in their present emergency, the petitioner stood ready to pledge himself as their representative to answer any call the government might make upon them for service on the field of battle.

Elder Little was taken at his word. At a cabinet meeting, held a day or two after his petition was presented, the president advised that the elder be sent at once to the Mormon camps, and there raise a thousand men to take possession of California in the name of the United States, while a thousand more be sent by way of Cape Horn for the same purpose, on board a United States transport. It was finally arranged that the elder, in company with Kane, should proceed westward, the latter bearing despatches to Kearny, then at Fort Leavenworth, with a view to raising a corps of about five hundred men.

On the 19th of June, Kearny issued an order to Captain James Allen of the 1st dragoons to proceed to the Mormon camp, and there raise four or five companies of volunteers, to be mustered into the service of the United States and receive the pay and rations of other infantry volunteers. They were then to be marched to Fort Leavenworth, where they would be armed; after which they would proceed to California by way of Santa Fé. They were to enlist for twelve months, after which time they were to be discharged, retaining as their own property the arms furnished them.

In pursuance of his orders, Captain Allen proceeded to Mount Pisgah, where on the 26th he made known his mission. After a conference with the church council at that point, Allen went to Council Bluffs, where on the 1st of July it was determined by President Young that the battalion should be raised. In two weeks the corps was enrolled, and mustered in on the 16th of July, the president of the church

promising to look after the wants of the families of
those enlisting.

Though in reality a great benefit to the brethren,
there were some hardships connected with the measure.[10]   As Brigham and others were on their way from
Council Bluffs to Pisgah to aid in obtaining these
recruits, they passed 800 west-bound wagons.   At
their encampments on each side the river there was
much serious illness, and as many of the teamsters
had been withdrawn for this campaign, much heavy
work fell upon the women and children, and the aged
and infirm.[11]

After a ball on the afternoon of the 19th, the volunteers next day bade farewell to their families and
friends, and accompanied by eighty women and children,[12] set forth on their march,[13] on the 1st of August
arriving at Fort Leavenworth.   Here the men re-

[10] So ingrafted in their minds was the idea of persecution, and so accustomed were they now to complaining, that when the government acceded to
their request, there were many who believed, and so expressed themselves,
that this was but an act of tyranny on the part of the United States, whose
people, after driving them from their borders, had now come upon them to
make a draft on their healthiest and hardiest men, forcing them to separate
from their wives and children now in the time of their extremest need, under
penalty of extermination in case of refusal.   And this idea, which was wholly
at variance with the facts, is present in the minds of some even to this day.
In order to facilitate enlisting, or for some other cause best known to himself,
Brigham deemed it best to preserve this idea rather than wholly disabuse
their minds of it; for in his address to the brethren on the 15th of July he
said: ' If we want the privilege of going where we can worship God according to the dictates of our consciences, we must raise the battalion.'   In his
address at the gathering of the pioneers on the 24th of July, 1880, Wilford
Woodruff said: ' Our government called upon us to raise a battalion of 500
men to go to Mexico to fight the battles of our country.   This draft was ten
times greater, according to the population of the Mormon camp, than was
made upon any other portion of our nation...Whether our government expected we would comply with the request or not, is not for me to say.   But
I think I am safe in saying that plan was laid by certain parties for our destruction if we did not comply.' Utah Pioneers, 33d Ann., 20.

[11] ' Most of our people were sick; in fact, the call for 500 able-bodied men
from Council Bluffs for Mexico, by the government, deprived us of about all
our strength.' Richards' Rem., MS., 25.

[12] Compare official report in U. S. House Ex. Doc., no. 24, 31st Cong.,
1st Sess., and Tyler's Hist. Mormon Battalion, and note discrepancies in regard
to numbers enlisted and discharged.   The names of those who reached California will be found in my pioneer register, Hist. Cal., this series.

[13] 'The members started upon their pilgrimage cheerfully,' says Woodruff,
' understanding that they occupied the place of a ram caught in a thicket, and
were making a sacrifice for the salvation of Israel.' Utah Pioneers, 20.

ceived their arms and accoutrements, and to each was given a bounty of forty dollars, most of the money being sent back to the brethren by the hands of elders Hyde, Taylor, and others, who accompanied the battalion to that point, and there bade them God speed.[14]

About the middle of August the corps resumed its march toward Santa Fé, a distance of seven hundred miles, arriving at that place in two parties on the 9th and 12th of October. There eighty-eight men were invalided and sent back to Pueblo for the winter, and later a second detachment of fifty-five, being found unfit for service, was also ordered to Pueblo.[15] Many of them found their way during the following year to the valley of Great Salt Lake.

From Santa Fé the remainder of the troops set forth for San Diego, a journey of more than eleven hundred miles, the entire distance between that town and the Mormon camps on the Missouri exceeding two thousand miles. Much of the route lay through a pathless desert; at few points could food be obtained in sufficient quantity for man or beast, and sometimes even water failed. Wells were sunk in the wilderness; but on one occasion, at least, the men travelled for a hundred miles without water.[16] Before leaving Santa

[14] 'Here they received 100 tents, one for every 6 privates.' 'The paymaster remarked that every one of the Mormon battalion could write his own name, but only about one third of the volunteers he had previously paid could do so.' *Hist. B. Young*, MS., 1846, 18. 'Five thousand eight hundred and sixty dollars was brought in by Parley Pratt from Ft Leavenworth, being a portion of the allowance for clothing paid the battalion. It was counselled that this money be expended in St Louis for the families; three prices have to be paid here;...we wish they should all act voluntarily, so that they may have no reflections to cast upon themselves or counsellors.' *Id.*, MS., 1846, 150. 'When the goods were bought, prices had advanced and ferriage was very high, all of which brought the goods higher than was anticipated, and produced some grumbling in camp.' *Id.*, MS., 1847, 12.

[15] Families accompanying the battalion were ordered to Pueblo for winter quarters. *Hist. B. Young*, MS., 1846, 260. A detachment was sent to Pueblo consisting of 89 men and 18 laundresses. Later in this vol., I refer to affairs at Pueblo as furnished me in a very valuable manuscript by Judge Stone of Colorado.

[16] In a general order issued at San Diego on Jan. 30, 1847, by command of Lieut-col St George Cooke, then in charge of the battalion, vice Col Allen, deceased, the men are thus complimented on their safe arrival at the shores of the Pacific: 'History may be searched in vain for an equal march of infantry; nine tenths of it through a wilderness, where nothing but savages and

Fé rations were reduced,[17] and soon afterward further reduced to one half and finally to one quarter allowance, the meat issued to the troops being the flesh of such animals as were unable to proceed further, though their hides and entrails were eagerly devoured, being gulped down with draughts of water, when water could be had.[18] While suffering these hardships the men were compelled to carry their own knapsacks, muskets, and extra ammunition, and sometimes to push the wagons through heavy sand, or help to drag them over mountain ranges.

Passing through a New Mexican pueblo on the 24th of October, some of the men were almost as naked as on the day of their birth, except for a breech-clout, or as their colonel termed it, a 'centre-clothing,' tied around the loins. In this plight, near the middle of December, the battalion reached the San Pedro River, some three hundred and forty strong, and here occurred the only battle which the saints militant fought during their campaign—an encounter with a

wild beasts are found; or deserts where, for the want of water, there is no living creature. There, with almost hopeless labor, we have dug deep wells, which the future traveller will enjoy. Without a guide who had traversed them, we have ventured into trackless prairies, where water was not found for several marches. With crowbar and pickaxe in hand, we have worked our way over mountains which seemed to defy aught save the wild goat, and hewed a passage through a chasm of living rock, more narrow than our wagons.' *Smith's Rise, Progress, and Travels*, 10.

[17] 'Until further orders, three fourths pound of flour, also three fourths rations sugar and coffee will be issued. Beef, one and a half pounds will be issued for a day's ration.' *Order No. 11, Headquarters Mormon Battalion*, Santa Fé. A copy of it will be found in *Tyler's Hist. Mor. Battalion*, 175–6.

[18] During the march from Santa Fé to San Diego a song was composed by Levi W. Hancock, a musician belonging to company E. It was entitled the 'Desert Route,' and commences:

> While here beneath a sultry sky,
> Our famished mules and cattle die;
> Scarce aught but skin and bones remain,
> To feed poor soldiers on the plain.
>
> *Chorus:* How hard to starve and wear us out
> Upon this sandy desert route.
>
> We sometimes now for lack of bread,
> Are less than quarter rations fed,
> And soon expect, for all of meat,
> Naught else than broke-down mules to eat.
>
> Now half-starved oxen, over-drilled,
> Too weak to draw, for beef are killed;
> And gnawing hunger prompting men,
> To eat small entrails and the skin.

Id., 181–2.

herd of wild bulls. Thence, without further adventure worthy of note, they continued their march, and reaching the Pacific coast on the 29th of January, 1847, found the stars and stripes floating peacefully over the town of San Diego.[19]

A more detailed account of the career of the Mormon battalion will be found in my *History of California*. It remains only to add here that about one hundred of the men reached Salt Lake City in the winter of 1847, while some remained on the Pacific coast.[20]

The alacrity displayed by the Mormon president in raising this battalion has been ascribed to various causes; to the fear of further persecution should the levy be refused, and to a desire of showing that, notwithstanding their maltreatment, the saints were still

[19] In *A Concise History of the Mormon Battalion in the Mexican War, 1846 -1847*, by *Sergeant Daniel Tlyer*, (Salt Lake City,) 1881, 8vo, 376 pp., we have a most valuable book, and one that forms the leading authority on this subject. Though written, of course, from a Mormon standpoint, and marked by the credulity of his sect, the execution of the work is all that its title-page promises. In the introduction, occupying 109 pages, we have President John Taylor's account of the martyrdom of Joseph Smith, Colonel Kane's discourse on the Mormons, and a poem by Eliza R. Snow, entitled *The Mormon Battalion, and First Wagon Load over the Great American Desert*. The remainder of the volume consists of original matter. Tyler was a member of company C in the battalion, and no doubt speaks the truth when he says in his preface that 'neither labor, pains, nor expense has been spared in the effort to make this a just and authentic history.' Among other authorities may be mentioned *Horne's Migr. and Settlem't, L. D. Saints*, MS., 32–3; *Nebeker's Early Justice*, MS., 3; *Woodruff's Rem.*, MS., 76; *Henry W. Bigler's Diary of a Mormon in California*, MS., in which last we have a faithful and interesting record of the Mormon battalion and Mr Bigler's account of the discovery of gold in California. *The Conquest of New Mexico and California: an Historical and Personal Narrative, by P. St. George Cooke, Brigadier and Brevet Major-general U. S. A.*, N. Y., 1878, 12mo, gives some additional matter, as do the journal and report of that officer in *U. S. Sen. Doc. No. 2*, 30th Cong., Special Sess., and in *House Ex. Doc.*, 30th Cong., 1st Sess., no. 41, pp. £49–63. Cooke, it will be remembered, was in command of the battalion. Items have also been gathered from *U. S. House Ex. Doc.*, 31st Cong., 1st Sess., no. 24, p. 22; Apostle Wilford Woodruff's Speech, in *Utah Pioneers*, 33d ann., 19–22; *Smith's Rise, Progress, and Travels*, 8–11; *Tullidge's Life of Brigham Young*, 41–76; *Olshausen, Gesch. de Mor.*, 142–4; and *Kane's The Mormons*, 27–9. Biographical notices of some of the members, and the names of the women who accompanied the battalion, are given in *Tullidge's Women*, 427, 432, 443–4.

[20] In the *Frontier Guardian*, March 7, 1849, is a notice copied from the *St Joseph Gazette*, stating that the members of the battalion can at once receive their extra pay at Fort Leavenworth. The notice is signed by Paymaster Thos S. Bryant.

unswerving in their loyalty to the United States. While all this carried weight, the bounty of twenty thousand dollars was no insignificant consideration, nor the hope that this battalion might serve as vanguard to Brigham's host, provided he carried out his partially formed purpose to settle in California.

At the close of 1846, about twelve thousand souls had assembled in the Mormon camps, a portion of them being yet stationed as far eastward as Garden Grove. Of the rest a few had made their way to some Atlantic port and taken ship for California; many had dispersed throughout the country, some of whom were now gathering at the rendezvous. Though the first bands that crossed the Mississippi encountered no very severe hardships, as I have said, the sufferings of those who set forth later have few parallels, even among the pioneers, who, a year or two afterward, followed their track westward in search of gold.[21]

Mount Pisgah, the next encampment west of Garden Grove, was on the middle fork of Grand River. Through this winter of 1846-7, which was one of severest struggle, there was great lack of food and clothing. They could not go on because they had no teams, most of them being employed in bringing forward the emigration from the Mississippi. Many

[21] Instance the experiences of Mrs Richards, *Reminiscences*, MS., passim. While on their journey toward the Missouri, having parted from her husband who was about starting on a mission to England, her little daughter was taken dangerously ill, and the mother was prematurely confined in a wagon with a son, who died soon after. 'Our situation was pitiable; I had no suitable food for myself or my child; the severe rain prevented our having any fire; on the third day we resumed our journey. In ten days we reached Mt Pisgah; my little girl was very ill, and I was also. We continued our journey till we reached my mother at Cutler Park, and here, after weeks of almost incredible suffering, my little daughter died. A few days previously she had asked for some potato soup, the first thing she had shown any desire for for weeks, and as we were then travelling, we came in sight of a potato-field. One of the sisters eagerly asked for a single potato. A rough woman impatiently heard her story throug, and putting her hands on her shoulders, marched her out of the house, say ig, "I won't give or sell a thing to one of you damned Mormons." I turned on my bed and wept, as I heard them trying to comfort my little one in her disappointment. When she was taken from me I only lived because I could not die.'

families were entirely out of provisions, and their destitute neighbors were sorely taxed.[22] A fatal sickness swept through the camp, and soon there were not sufficient persons to nurse the sick; frequently burials were hastened with little ceremony. In the spring of 1847, Lorenzo Snow was made president of the camp. The men were put to work wherever they could get it. Seed was planted, and the result was enough not only for themselves, but they were enabled to send supplies to the camp at Council Bluffs.[23] Snow instituted religious ceremonies and amusements to brighten and encourage them. He describes a dance in his log cabin, where clean straw was spread over the ground floor, and the walls draped with sheets. Turnips were scooped out and in them were placed lighted candles, which, suspended from the ceiling of earth and cane, or fastened on the walls, imparted a picturesque effect. Dancing, speeches, songs, and recitations varied the exercises, which opened and closed with prayer.

On each side of the hills where now stands Council Bluffs could be seen the white canvas tents of a Mormon encampment, from which arose at sunrise the smoke of hundreds of fires. After the morning meal, the men employed themselves in tending herds, in planting grain and vegetables, or in building houses for winter. Many of them were excellent craftsmen, and could fell a tree, and split its trunk into boards, scantling, rails, posts, or whatever were needed, as

---

[22] It cannot be said that any considerable number died of starvation. 'Only those died of it outright,' says Kane in *The Mormons*, 'who fell in out-of-the-way places that the hand of brotherhood could not reach...If but part of a group were supplied with provisions, the whole went on half or quarter ration.' 'Articles of diet, such as tea, coffee, sugar, with every species of clothing, were eagerly stored up, as possibly the last we should ever see.' *Brown's Testimonies*, MS., 24. ' When starting from Nauvoo, a gentile neighbor gave me a pound of tea, which through sickness and great suffering was about all the sustenance I had for some time.' *Mrs Richards' Rem.*, MS., 20.

[23] 'Parties were sent to the gentile settlements to look for work, food, and clothing, and elders Dana and Campbell collected about $600 from the rich gentiles in Ohio and elsewhere.' *Snow's Biography*, 91.

readily as the most expert backwoodsmen of their day.[24]

During the summer and autumn months of 1846, the Papillon camp, near the Little Butterfly River, in common with the others, was stricken with fever, and with a scorbutic disease which the Mormons termed the black canker. In the autumn drought, the streams that discharge into the Missouri at this point are often little better than open sewers, pestilential as open cesspools, and the river, having lost more than half its volume, flows sluggishly through its channel of slime and sedge. Of the baked mud on either bank is formed the rich soil on which lay the encampments, the site being called, in their own phrase, Misery Bottom. In the year previous the Indians in this neighborhood had lost one ninth of their number; and now that the earth was for the first time upturned by the plough, the exhalations from this rank and steaming soil were redolent of disease and death.

In the camp nearest to Papillon more than one third of the company lay sick at the beginning of August; elsewhere matters were even worse; and as the season advanced there were in some of the encampments not one who escaped the fever, the few who were able to stagger from tent to tent carrying food and water to their comrades. For several weeks it was impossible to dig graves quickly enough for the burial of the dead,[25] and one might see in the open tents the wasted forms of women brushing away the flies from the putrefying corpses of their children.

Through all these months building was continually going on at Winter Quarters.[26] The axe and saw were

[24] 'There were among them many skilled mechanics, who could work at forge, loom, or turning-lathe. A Mormon gunsmith is the inventor of the excellent repeating rifle that loads by slides instead of cylinders; and one of the neatest finished fire-arms I have ever seen was of this kind, wrought from scraps of old iron, and inlaid with the silver of a couple of half-dollars.' *Kane's The Mormons*, 36.

[25] At the camp situated on the site of the town of Florence, there were over 600 burials. *Kane's The Mormons*, 51.

[26] 'Here we suffered terribly from scurvy, for want of vegetables. I was a victim, and even my little children as young as three years of age. The

incessantly at work night and day. It was a city of
mud and logs; the houses had puncheon floors and
roofs of straw and dirt, or of turf and willows; they
were warm and not unwholesome, but would not endure the thaw, rain, and sunshine.[27]

There was a camp at Cutler Park which was moved
to Winter Quarters. Great difficulty was experienced in getting flour and meal; a little grain was
ground at the government mill, and the rest was obtained in Missouri, a hundred and fifty miles distant.[28]
Brigham kept everybody busy, and everything was
well organized and systematically executed.[29] Schools
were soon established, officers of the church appointed,
and men sent on missions. The whole machinery was
apparently in as active operation as it had been at
Nauvoo. The gathering continued through the sum-

first relief experienced was when a bag of potatoes was brought in from
Missouri...It was observed that those who had milk escaped the trouble.'
Horne's Migrations, MS., 20.

[27] 'The buildings were generally of logs from 12 to 18 feet long, a few
were split, and made from lynn and cotton-wood timber; many roofs were
made by splitting oak timber into boards, called shakes, about 3 ft long and
6 in. wide, and kept in place by weights and poles; others were made of
willows, straw, and earth, about a foot thick; some of puncheon. Many
cabins had no floors; there were a few dugouts on the sidehills—the fire-
place was cut out at the upper end. The ridge-pole roof was supported by
two uprights in the centre and roofed with straw and earth, with chimneys
of prairie sod. The doors were made of shakes, with wooden hinges and
string latch; the inside of the log houses was daubed with clay; a few had
stoves.' *Hist. B. Young*, MS., 1846, 534. 'The roofs were made of logs laid
across with flags spread over them, and earth spread over these. This was
partial protection from the rain, but when once it was soaked through in a
heavy storm, we were at the mercy of the rain.' *Richards' Rem.*, MS., 27. In
Dec. 1846, at Winter Quarters there were '538 log houses and 83 sod houses,
inhabited by 3,483 souls, of whom 334 were sick.' *Church Chronology*, 65.

[28] '$8,000 was sent by Whitney to St Louis to purchase stones and machin-
ery for flouring mills; and through A. H. Perkins a carding machine was
ordered from Savannah.' *Hist. B. Young*, MS., Aug. 30, 1846. 'Sugar and
coffee were 16⅔ cts per lb.; domestics and calicoes from 18 to 25 cts; $3 a cwt.
for flour,' etc.; all of which could be purchased in St Louis for a third of these
rates. These prices seemed exorbitant to the Mormons, though in reality
they were not unreasonable. In transporting the goods from St Louis later,
ferriage became so high and prices were so advanced that the brethren burst
forth: 'Woe unto you, Missourians! but we are independent of them and
can live without them, for we have thousands of cattle left.'

[29] 'At a meeting of the council July 14th, it was voted that colonies be
established on the east side of the river to put in buckwheat, and winter;
that a fort be built on Grand Island and a settlement made there; and that
Bishop Miller and a company go over the mountains.' *Hist. B. Young*, MS.,
1846, 50.

mer, but it was deemed inexpedient to move forward
that year.   Some twelve hundred cattle were herded
on the rush bottoms, about a hundred miles up the
river.

The building of a water flouring mill was in process
of construction, and Brigham superintended the work.
As the camp journalist writes: "He sleeps with one
eye open and one foot out of bed, and when anything
is wanted he is on hand."   The tithing collected was
distributed among the destitute at Mount Pisgah.
To the gentiles who visited their camps such hospitality
was extended as their means permitted, which though
often scant was never stinted.

Within the camp the women attended not only to
their ordinary household duties, but were busily occupied spinning, knitting, making leggings from deer and
elk skins, and in weaving willow baskets for market.[30]
With cheerfulness and courage they adapted themselves to their many vicissitudes, their faith in their
religion never swerving, and supported by it to a patient endurance beyond human strength.   Most of
them had exchanged their household treasures and
personal effects, even to their table and bed furniture,
for stores of maize or flour, which with milk were
their only articles of diet.   As evening approached,
the tinkling of cattle bells announced the return of the
men, when the women went forth to meet them, and
welcome them back to their log hut and frugal meal.
Then a little later all sounds were hushed, save that on
the still night arose the strains of the evening hymn
and the murmur of the evening prayer, the day
closing, as it had commenced, with a supplication for
the blessing of the Almighty, and with heartfelt
thanksgiving that he had been pleased to deliver his
people from the hands of their persecutors.

During the latter part of the winter and toward
the early spring matters assumed a brighter look.

[30] Several loads of willow baskets were manufactured. *Hist. B. Young*,
MS., 534.

New-year's day was ushered in at Winter Quarters by the firing of cannon.[31] There were frequent assemblies for dancing, and in February several picnics were held. In inaugurating these festivities, Brigham told the people he would show them how to go forth in the dance in an acceptable manner before the Lord,[32] and to the sound of music led the dance. A picnic lasting for three days was also given, at which three hundred of the poor were feasted.[33]

[31] The thermometer was during that week from 2° to 8° below zero, later falling several degrees lower.

[32] 'I then knelt down and prayed to God in behalf of the meeting,...and dedicated the meeting and house to the Lord,...and led forth in the dance.' *Hist. B. Young*, MS., 1847, 27. In an address Brigham said: 'For some weeks past I could not wake up at any time of the night but I heard the axe at work,...and now my feelings are, dance all night if you desire to do so.' p. 48. 'The "Silver Greys" and spectacled dames,...some nearly a hundred years old,...dancing like ancient Israel.' p. 49.

[33] 'There were 117 poor adults,...divided into three wards...Shortly after noon I met with 66 of my family, including my adopted children.' *Id.*, p. 53.

CHAPTER X.

MIGRATION TO UTAH.

1847.

IN the spring of 1847 we find the saints still in camp in the vicinity of the Missouri. Considering what they had been called upon to undergo, they were in good health and spirits. There is nothing like the spiritual in man to stimulate and sustain the physical; and this result is equally accomplished by the most exalted piety of the true believer, or by the most stupid fanaticism or barbaric ignorance; for all of us are true believers, in our own eyes. There is nothing like religion to sustain, bear up, and carry men along under trying circumstances. They make of it a fight; and they are determined that the world, the flesh, and the devil shall not conquer.

In the present instance it was of course a miracle in their eyes that so many of their number were preserved; it was to this belief, and to the superhuman skill and wisdom of their leader, and partly to their own concert of action, that their preservation was due.

Frequent meetings had been held by the council to consider plans for further explorations by a pioneer band.[1] A call was made for volunteers of young and able-bodied men, and in April a company was organized, with Brigham Young as lieutenant-general, Stephan Markham colonel, John Pack major, and fourteen captains. The company consisted of 143 persons, including three women, wives of Brigham Young, Lorenzo Young, and Heber C. Kimball. They had 73 wagons drawn by horses and mules, and loaded chiefly with grain and farming implements,[2] and with provisions which were expected to last them for the return journey.

Early in April a detachment moved out of Winter Quarters for the rendezvous on the Elkhorn, and on the 14th the pioneer band, accompanied by eight members of the council,[3] began the long journey westward in search of a site for their new Zion. If none were found, they were to plant crops and establish a settlement at some suitable spot which might serve as a base for future explorations.[4]

The route was along the north branch of the Platte, and for more than 500 miles the country was bare of

[1] The octagon house of Dr Richards in which the council met is described as a queer-looking thing, much resembling a New England potato-heap in time of frost. 'Council voted a load of wood for each day they met in his house.' *Hist. B. Young*, MS., 1847, 2.

[2] *Woodruff's Journal*, MS., Apr. 17, 1847.

[3] John Taylor, Parley Pratt, and Orson Hyde were engaged in missionary work abroad. *Pratt's Autobiog.*, 383.

[4] The impression was that they would reach as soon as possible 'the foot of the mountains somewhere in the region of the Yellowstone River, perhaps at the fork of Tongue River, say 2 days' ride north of the Oregon road, and a week's travel west of Ft Laramie...I informed Bishop Miller that when we moved hence it would be to the great basin.' *Hist. B. Young*, MS., 79. No one knew whither they were going, not even the leaders. 'We have learned by letter to Elder G. D. Watt that a company left Council Bluffs for the mountains on the 12th of April to seek a location for a stake in Zion.' *Millennial Star*, ix. 235. 'The pioneers started for the mountains to seek out a resting-place for the saints.' *Brown's Testimonies for the Truth*, 26. In *Niles' Register*, lxxii. 206 (May 29, 1847), we read: 'Their intention is to proceed as far as possible up to the period of necessary planting-time, when they will stop and commence a crop. The leaders will make but a short delay at this point, and will proceed over into California and communicate with or join the disbanded forces of the Mormon battalion, whose period of service will expire about the 1st of July next.' 'When President Young was questioned by any of the pioneers as to the definite point of our destination, all he could say to them was, that he would know it when he should see it.' Erastus Snow, in *Utah Pioneers, 33d ann.*, 44.

vegetation.   Roused by the call of the bugle at five
o'clock in the morning, they assembled for prayers;
then they breakfasted, and upon a second call of the
bugle at seven o'clock they started, and travelled
about twenty miles for the day.   At night the note
of the bugle sent each to his own wagon to prayers
and at nine o'clock to bed.   They rested on Sunday,
giving up the day to fasting and prayer.   They were
careful in marching to preserve order, with loaded guns
and powder-horn ready.   And the better to present a
compact front, the wagons were kept well together,
usually two abreast where the ground would permit,
and the men were required to walk by the wagons.

   They felled cotton-wood trees for their horses and

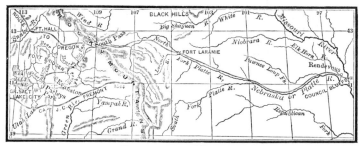

ROUTE OF THE MORMONS.

cattle to browse upon, and at last were obliged to feed
them from the grain, flour, and biscuit they carried,
subsisting meanwhile themselves on game and fish.
In the valley of the Platte roamed such vast herds of
buffaloes that it was often necessary to send parties in
advance and clear the road before the teams could
pass.   At night the wagons would be drawn up in a
semicircle on the bank, the river forming a defence
upon one side.   The tongues of the wagons were on
the outside, and a fore wheel of each was placed
against the hind wheel of the wagon before it; all the
horses and cattle were brought inside of the enclosure.   The corral thus formed was oblong, with an

opening at either end, where was stationed a guard. The tents were pitched outside of the corral.[5]

In crossing the Loup River on the 24th, they used a leathern boat made for this expedition, and called *The Revenue Cutter.* On the 4th of May letters were sent back to Winter Quarters by a trader named Charles Beaumont. On the 22d they encamped at Ancient Bluff Ruins. Here the spirits of the people reached such high hilarity that their commanding

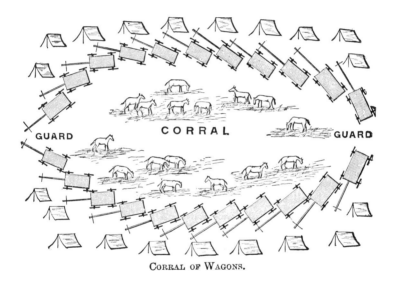

GUARD   **C O R R A L**   GUARD

CORRAL OF WAGONS.

officer was obliged to rebuke them, whereupon all covenanted to humble themselves.[6]

Early in June they reached the Black Hills by way of Fort Laramie.[7] Here they rested for two or three

[5] *Woodruff's Journal,* MS., April 19, 1847. On May 4th they 'established a post-office and guide system for the benefit of the next camp following. Every ten miles...we put up a guide-board.'

[6] 'I have told the few who did not belong to the church that they were not at liberty to introduce cards, dancing, or iniquity of any description.' *Hist. B. Young,* MS., 1847, 90.

[7] Fort John, or Laramie, was occupied by 'James Bordeaux and about eighteen French half-breeds and a few Sioux...There had been no rain for the last two years...Two or three of us visited Mr Bordeaux at the fort.

weeks to build ferry-boats and recruit their animals. Grass was now plentiful; most of the brethren depended upon their rifles for food, and after having prepared sufficient dried meat for the rest of the journey, they continued on their way.

No sooner had they crossed the river than a horseman, who had followed their trail from Laramie, rode up and begged them to halt, as near by was a large company bound for Oregon, for which he asked conveyance over the stream. The pioneers consented, stipulating that they should receive payment in provisions. Other parties following, the larder of the saints was replenished.[8]

Travelling rapidly, and a little to the south of what was known as the Oregon track,[9] the Mormons arrived at South Pass in the latter part of June, about the time when the tide of emigration usually passed the Missouri. Thence skirting the Colorado desert and reaching the Green River country, the monotony was broken. Here the brethren were met by Elder Brannan, who had sailed from New York for California in the ship *Brooklyn*, the previous February, with 238 saints, as before mentioned. He reported that they were all busy making farms and raising grain on the San Joaquin River.[10] As several of the present

We paid him $15 for the use of his ferry-boat. Mr Bordeaux said that this was the most civil and best-behaved company that had ever passed the fort.' *Id.*, MS., 1847, 91.

[8] Snow, in *Utah Pioneers*, 44. ' Capt. Grover and eight others of the pioneers were left at North Platte ferry and ford to ferry the companies that should arrive, and especially to ferry the emigration from Winter Quarters.' *Hist. B. Young*, MS., 1847.

[9] 'Making a new road for a majority of more than one thousand miles westward, they arrived at the great basin in the latter part of July.' *General Epistle of the Twelve*, in *Millennial Star*, x. 82. 'He [Brigham] and the company arrived on the 24th of July, having sought out and made a new road 650 miles, and followed a trapper's trail nearly 400 miles. *Smith's Rise, Progress, and Travels*, 16; see also *Tullidge's Life of Young*, 161. Remy says that an odometer was attached to a wheel of one of the wagons, and careful notes taken of the distances. *Jour. to G. S. L. City*, i. 433–4. 'As I remember, there was no trail after leaving Laramie, going over the Black Hills, except very rarely. For a short distance before reaching the Sweetwater, we saw a wagon track; it was a great surprise and a great curiosity.' *Hist. B. Young*, MS., 1848, 7.

[10] *Hist. B. Young*, MS., 1847, 95; *Tullidge's Life of Young*, 166.

company were ill with mountain fever, they encamped for a few days. Thirteen battalion brethren who were out searching for stolen cattle now surprised them, and Brigham led in three hearty cheers.[11] Again en route, passing through the Green River country, they reached Fort Bridger. Soon after leaving this point the real difficulties of the journey commenced. Led, as the saints relate, only by the inspiration of the Almighty,[12] Brigham and his band crossed the rugged spurs of the Uintah range, now following the rocky bed of a mountain torrent, and now cleaving their way through dense and gnarled timber until they arrived at Echo Cañon, near the eastern slope of the Wasatch Mountains, where for a brief space the main body rested, the president and many others being attacked with mountain fever.[13]

Impatient of the delay, Brigham, after a formal

[11] 'I exclaimed, "Hosanna! hosanna! give glory to God and the lamb, amen!" in which they all joined.' *Hist. B. Young*, MS., 1847, 96. 'Left Phineas Young and four others, who had volunteered to return to guide the immigrants.'

[12] *Smith's Rise, Progress, and Travels*, 16. ' For,' says the author, 'no one knew anything of the country.' Snow, in *Utah Pioneers, 33d ann.*, 44, remarks: ' The president said we were to travel "the way the spirit of the Lord should direct us."' Snow states that James Bridger, who had a trading post which still bears the name of Fort Bridger, when he met the president on the Big Sandy River about the last of June, and learned that his destination was the valley of Great Salt Lake, offered $1,000 for the first ear of corn raised there. 'Wait a little,' said the president, 'and we will show you.' Again, on p. 45 he says that, being encamped on what is now known as Tar Springs, the pioneers were met by a mountaineer named Goodyear, who had wintered on the site of the present city of Ogden, after planting grain and vegetables in the valley, but with meagre results. The mountaineer's report was very discouraging, but to him also Brigham replied, 'Give us time and we will show you.' There is no evidence that as yet the president knew anything about the Salt Lake Valley except what he heard from Bridger and Goodyear, or had gleaned from the reports of Frémont's expedition. 'On the 15th of June met James H. Grieve, Wm Tucker, James Woodrie, James Bouvoir, and six other French-men, from whom we learned that Mr Bridger was located about 300 miles west, that the mountaineers could ride to Salt Lake from Fort Bridger in two days, and that the Utah country was beautiful.' *Hist. B. Young*, MS., 1847, 92. 'Half-mile west of Fort Bridger some traded for buckskins, their cloth-ing being worn out.' *Id.*, 97. Note also the following: 'Met Capt. Bridger, who said he was ashamed of Frémont's map of this country. Bridger con-sidered it imprudent to bring a large population into the great basin until it was ascertained that grain could be raised.'

[13] 'We had to stop at Yellow Creek and again at the head of Echo Cañon, stopping and travelling as the sick were able to endure the journey, until we reached the Weber at the mouth of Echo Cañon, and struck our camp a few miles below the present railroad station.' *Utah Pioneers, 33d ann.*, 45.

HIST. UTAH. 17

meeting, directed Orson Pratt[14] to take the strongest of their number and cut through the mountains
into the valley, making roads and bridges as they
went. After crossing what were designated as Big
and Little mountains, the party, consisting of some
forty-two men having twenty-three wagons, encamped
in Emigration Cañon.[15]

Thus the saints are reaching their resting-place.
Their new Zion is near at hand; how near, they are
as yet all unaware. But their prophet has spoken;
their way is plain; and the spot for them prepared
from the foundation of the earth will presently be
pointed out to them. The great continental chain is
penetrated. In the heart of America they are now
upon the border of a new holy land, with its Desert

[14] 'Voted, that Orson Pratt take charge of an expedition to go on and make
a road down the Weber River.' *Hist. B. Young*, MS., 1847, 97. O. Pratt was
appointed to take 23 wagons and 42 men, and precede the main company.
Church Chron., 65.   Erastus Snow says, in a discourse on the Utah pioneers,
delivered in the tabernacle July 25, 1880: 'I well remember, as we called at
the wagon to bid the president good-by, Brother Willard Richards...asking
if he had any counsel to give to guide our movements...Resting his elbow
on the pillow with his head in his hand, he spoke feebly,...'' My impressions
are," said he, " that when you emerge from the mountains into the open
country you bear to the northward, and stop at the first convenient place for
putting in your seed." '

[15] 'The emigration route previous to 1847 was via Laramie through South
Pass to Big Sandy River.   Then to avoid a desert stretch, down the Big
Sandy to its junction with Green River, and across, then up Black's Fork to
junction with Ham's Fork, and thence up Black's Fork to Fort Bridger.   The
Mormons here took the road made by Hastings and the Donner company in
1846, bearing almost due west, crossing Bear River, down Echo Cañon to
junction with the Weber.   The Mormons here chose the Donner trail, which
passed up the Weber southerly from Echo about twelve miles, then westerly
into Parley's Park, then across the hills northerly to the head of Emigration
Cañon, then into the valley.   As the Donner company had passed over this
route more recently than any other, it seems to have been followed as
probably the best, and was usually travelled for many years.   In 1847, when
the Mormons entered the valley, there were three wagon routes into it.   The
first, down Bear River from Soda Springs, through Cache Valley—Capt. Bart-
lett's route in 1841, followed by Frémont in 1843; the second, Hastings'
California emigration through Echo and Weber cañons in 1846; and the third,
the Donner route of 1846, described.   The Mormons found a plain road into
a fertile, unoccupied country;...its isolation alone was the cause of its non-
occupation.' *McBride's Route of the Mormons*, MS.   This manuscript, to
which among other favors I am indebted to Judge McBride, throws fresh
light on the question of passes and routes in early times.   The author, one of
the first to enter Utah, was second to none in ability and position at a later
period.

and Dead Sea, its River Jordan, Mount of Olives, and Gallilee Lake, and a hundred other features of its prototype of Asia.

Through the western base of the mountains extends the cañon, the two sides of which are serrated by a narrow stream, which along the last five miles flings itself from one side to the other a score or two of times, in places tumbling over bowlders, again quietly threading its way over a pebbly bottom, but everywhere cutting up the narrow and rugged gorge so as to make it most difficult and dangerous of passage.

The primeval silence is now broken; the primeval songs are now disturbed by sounds strange to the surrounding hills, accustomed only to the music of running water and the notes of birds and wild beasts. There is the rumbling of the caravan as it comes slowly picking its way down the dark ravine, the tramping of the horses upon the hard ground, and the grinding of the wheels among the rocks as they plunge down one bank and climb another, or thread their way along the narrow ledge overhanging an abyss, the songs of Israel meanwhile being heard, and midst the cracking of whips the shouts now and then breaking forth of a leader in Israel awe-struck by the grandeur of the scene, "Hosanna to the Lord! hosanna to the creator of all! hallelujah! hallelujah!"

Emerging from the ravine upon a bench or terrace, they behold the lighted valley, the land of promise, the place of long seeking which shall prove a place of rest, a spot whereon to plant the new Jerusalem, a spot of rare and sacred beauty. Behind them and on either hand majestic mountains rear their proud fronts heavenward, while far before them the vista opens. Over the broad plain, through the clear thin air, bathed in purple sunlight, are seen the bright waters of the lake, dotted with islands and bordered by glistening sands, the winding river, and along the creek the broad patches of green cane which look like waving corn. Raising their hats in reverence from their heads, again hosannas burst from their lips, while praise to the most high ascends from grateful hearts.

It was near this terrace, being in fact a mile and a half up the cañon, that Orson Pratt and Erastus Snow, with their detachment of pioneers, encamped on the 20th of July, 1847. Next day, the ever-memorable 21st, to reach this bench, whence was viewed with such marvellous effect the warm, pulsating panorama before them, Pratt and Snow crept on their hands and knees, warned by the occasional rattle of a snake, through the thick underbrush which lined the south side of the mountain and filled the cañon's mouth, leaving their companions on the other side of the brush. After drinking in the scene to the satisfaction of their souls, they descended to the open plain, Snow on horseback, with his coat thrown loosely upon his saddle, ard Pratt on foot. They journeyed westward three miles, when Snow missing his coat turned back, and Pratt continued alone. After traversing the site of the present city, and standing where later was temple block, he rejoined his comrade at the mouth of the cañon. Together they then returned to camp late in the evening and told of their discoveries.

The following morning the advance company, composed of Orson Pratt, George A. Smith,[16] and seven others, entered the valley and encamped on the bank of Cañon Creek. They explored the valley toward the lake, and about three miles from the camp found two fine streams with stony bottoms, whose banks promised sufficient pasturage. Proceeding northward, they found hot springs at the base of the mountain spur. Upon their return they were greeted by the working camp five miles from the mouth of the cañon, at what was subsequently known as Parley Cañon

[16] Geo. A. Smith says in his autobiography that on this journey he walked 1,700 miles and rode some 800 miles on horseback. He had 25 lbs of flour, which he used by the cupful for those who were ill; for six weeks he was without bread, and like the rest of the company, lived on buffalo meat and other game.

creek.[17] On the 23d the camp moved some two or
three miles northward, the site chosen being near the
two or three dwarf cotton-woods,[18] which were the only
trees within sight, and on the bank of a stream of pure
water now termed City Creek, overgrown with high
grass and willows. Pratt called the men together,
dedicated the land to the Lord, and prayed for his
blessing on the seeds about to be planted and on the
labors of the saints. Before noon a committee returned a report that they had staked off land suitable
for crops; that the soil was friable, and composed
of loam and gravel. The first furrow was thereupon
turned by William Carter, and through the afternoon
three ploughs and one harrow were at work. A dam
was commenced and trenches cut to convey water to
the fields. Toward evening their energetic labors
were interrupted by a thunder-storm.[19] The ground
was so dry that they found it necessary to irrigate it
before ploughing, some ploughs having been broken;
and it was not until after the arrival of Brigham that
planting was begun.

The coming of the leader had been impatiently
awaited, although in their ambition to have as much
as possible accomplished, the time quickly passed.
Brigham was slowly following with the remainder of
the company, and was still so weak as to be obliged
to be carried on a bed in Wilford Wordruff's carriage.
As they reached a point on Big Mountain where the
view was unbroken, the carriage was turned into
proper position, and Brigham arose from his bed and
surveyed the country. He says: "The spirit of light
rested upon me and hovered over the valley, and I
felt that there the saints would find protection and

---

[17] Parley was always quite popular among the brethren, though his judgment was not always the best.

[18] 'My poor mother was heart-broken because there were no trees to be seen;
I don't remember a tree that could be called a tree.' *Clara Young's Experiences*, MS., 5.

[19] 'July 23d, 96° Fah. A company commenced mowing the grass and preparing a turnip-patch.' *Hist. B. Young*, MS., 1847, 99.

safety."[20]   Woodruff in describing the scene says of
Brigham: "He was enwrapped in vision for several
minutes.   He had seen the valley before in vision,
and upon this occasion he saw the future glory of
Zion...planted in the valley."[21]   Then Brigham said:
"It is enough.   This is the right place.   Drive on."
Toward noon on the 24th they reached the encampment.   Potatoes were planted in a five-acre patch of
ploughed ground, and a little early corn.[22]

Their first impressions of the valley, Lorenzo Young
says, were most disheartening.[23]   But for the two or
three cotton-wood trees, not a green thing was in sight.
And yet Brigham speaks almost pathetically of the
destruction of the willows and wild roses growing
thickly on the two branches of City Creek, destroyed
because the channels must be changed, and leaving
nothing to vary the scenery but rugged mountains,
the sage bush, and the sunflower.   The ground was
covered with millions of black crickets which the
Indians were harvesting for their winter food.[24]   An
unusual number of natives had assembled for this purpose, and after dinner gathered about the new-comers,
evincing great curiosity as to their plans.

Lumber was made in the cañons, or from logs drawn
thence, with whip-saws, through the entire winter;

[20] *Hist. B. Young*, MS., 1847, 99.
[21] Woodruff, in *Utah Pioneers*, 1880, 23.   See also *Woodruff's Journal*, MS.;
Clara Young's Experiences, MS.; *Utah Early Record*, MS.; *Pioneer Women*,
MS.; *Taylor's Rem.*, MS.
[22] 'I had brought a bushel of potatoes with me, and I resolved that I would
neither eat nor drink until I had planted them.' Woodruff, in *Utah Pioneers*,
1880, 23.   'I planted the first potato...in Salt Lake Valley,' says Geo. A.
Smith in his autobiography.
[23] Mrs Clara Decker Young speaks of the distress she suffered at leaving
Winter Quarters, where there were so many people and life so social; but that
when she finally reached her destination she was satisfied.   'It didn't look
so dreary to me as to the other two ladies.   They were terribly disappointed
because there were no trees, and to them there was such a sense of desolation
and loneliness.' *Experience of a Pioneer Woman*, MS., 5.
[24] 'The Indians made a corral twelve or fifteen feet square, fenced about
with sage brush and grease-wood, and with branches of the same drove them
into the enclosure.   Then they set fire to the brush fence, and going amongst
them, drove them into the fire.   Afterward they took them up by the thousand, rubbed off their wings and legs, and after two or three days separated
the meat, which was, I should think, an ounce or half an ounce of fat to each
cricket.' *Early Experiences of Lorenzo Young*, MS., 4.

afterward, on account of alarm at the apparent scarcity of timber, restrictions were put upon the manner of cutting and quantity used. Certain fines were imposed as a penalty for disobedience; for fuel only dead timber was allowed, and while there was sufficient, the restraint excited some opposition.[25]

The next day was the sabbath; and as had been the custom at Nauvoo, two services were held, George A. Smith, followed by Heber C. Kimball and Ezra T. Benson, preaching the first sermon, and in the afternoon the meeting was addressed by Wilford Woodruff, Orson Pratt, and Willard Richards. One cause for thankfulness was that not a man or an animal had died on the journey. The sacrament was administered, and before dismissing the saints, the president bade them refrain from labor, hunting, or fishing. "You must keep the commandments of God," he said," or not dwell with us; and no man shall buy or sell land, but all shall have what they can cultivate free, and no man shall possess that which is not his own."

On the 27th,[26] the president, the apostles, and six others crossed a river which was afterward found to be the outlet of Utah Lake, and thence walked dryshod over ground subsequently covered by ten feet of water to Black Rock, where all bathed in the lake, Brigham being the first to enter it.[27] The party returned to camp on the following day, when a council was held, after which the members walked to a spot midway between the north and south forks of a neighboring creek, where Brigham stopped, and striking the ground with his cane, exclaimed, " Here will

[25] ' Taylor and Pratt took the lead; through them this understanding about the timber occurred.' *Nebeker's Early Justice*, MS., 4.

[26] On Monday, the 26th, the president and his apostles ascended Ensign Peak, so called on account of a remark made by Brigham: ' Here is a proper place to raise an ensign to the nations.' *Ibid.* See also *Utah Early Records*, MS., 4; *Woodruff's Journal*, MS.; *Nebeker's Early Justice*, MS. Woodruff was the first who stood on the top of the peak.

[27] On this day was commenced the first blacksmith's shop, the property of Burr Frost.

be the temple of our God."[28]   This was about five
o'clock in the afternoon.   An hour later it was agreed
that a site should be laid out for a city in blocks or
squares of ten acres, and in lots of an acre and a
quarter, the streets to be eight rods wide, with sidewalks of twenty feet.

At eight o'clock on the same evening a meeting was
held on the temple square, and it was decided by vote
that on that spot the temple should be built,[29] and from
that spot the city laid out.

On the 29th of July a detachment of the battalion, which had wintered at Pueblo,[30] to the number of
150, under Captain James Brown, arrived in the valley; they were accompanied by fifty of the brethren
who had started the year previous from the Mississippi.   On the following evening a praise service for
their safe arrival was held in the brush bowery,[31] has-

[28] 'This was about the centre of the site of the Temple we are now building.' *Utah Pioneers, 33d ann.*, 23.

[29] 'Some wished for forty acres to be set apart for temple purposes, but it
was finally decided to have ten acres;...the base line was on the south-east
corner, and government officials afterward adopted it as the base meridian
line.' *Taylor's Reminiscences*, MS., 21.   When the elders arrived from England
they brought with them to Winter Quarters, just before the starting of the
pioneers, 'two sextants, two barometers, two artificial horizons, one circular
reflector, several thermometers, and a telescope.' *Hist. B. Young*, MS., 1847,
82.   Thus Orson Pratt was enabled to take scientific observations.   He reported
the latitude of the north line of temple square, which was ten acres in size, to
be 40° 45' 44" N., and its longitude 111° 26' 34" W.   From George W. Dean's
observations in 1869, taken at the temple block, the results were lat. 40° 46'
2", long. 111° 53' 30". *Rept Coast Survey*, 1869-70.   In taking lunar distances for longitude, it is usual to have four observers, but Orson Pratt had no
assistant; hence probably the discrepancy.   On August 16th it was determined that the streets around the temple block should be called respectively
North, South, East, and West Temple streets, the others to be named, as required, First North street, Second North street, First South street, Second
South street, etc.

[30] Says Mrs Clara Young: 'Before reaching Laramie three of the pioneers
were sent to Pueblo to tell the families there to strike their trail and follow
them to their settlement.' *Ex. of a Pioneer Woman*, MS., 7.   'The men of
this detachment were on their way to San Francisco, but their wagons breaking down and their cattle being in very poor condition, they were compelled
to turn aside and await further orders.' *Utah Early Records*, MS., 8.

[31] For many years these boweries of trees and brush had been constructed
when any large number of the people needed a temporary place of shelter.
This one was 40 x 28 feet.   Col Markham reported at this meeting 'that 13
ploughs and 3 harrows had been stocked during the past week, 3 lots of ground
broken up, one lot of 35 acres planted in corn, oats, buckwheat, potatoes,
beans, and garden seed.' *Hist. B. Young*, MS., 1847, 103-4.   'On the 20th
H. G. Sherwood, in returning from an excursion to Cache Valley, brought an

tily constructed for the purpose by the battalion brethren.

During the next three weeks all were busily at work, tilling the soil, cutting and hauling timber, making adobes, and building, ambitious to accomplish as much as possible before the main body of the pioneer band should start on its return journey to report to the brethren and to promote further emigration. The battalion brethren moved their wagons and formed a corral between the forks of City Creek. Brigham exhorted the brethren to be rebaptized, himself setting the example, and reconfirming the elders. On the 8th of August three hundred were immersed, the services commencing at six o'clock in the morning. During the month twenty-nine log houses had been built, either with roofs or ready for the usual substitute, a covering of poles and dirt. These huts were so arranged as to carry out their plan of forming a rectangular stockade,[32] the president and Heber C. Kimball being the first to take possession of their dwellings.

On the 17th of August twenty-four pioneers and forty-six of the battalion set out on their return to Winter Quarters.[33]

On the afternoon of the 22d a conference was held, at which it was resolved that the place should be called the City of the Great Salt Lake. The term 'Great' was retained for several years, until changed by legislative enactment. It was so named in contradistinction to Little Salt Lake, a term applied

Englishman with him, named Wells, who had been living in New Mexico for some years.' *Hist. B. Young*, MS., 1847, 109. On the 21st A. Carrington, J. Brown, W. W. Rust, G. Wilson, and A. Calkins made the ascent of the Twin Peaks, 15 miles south-east of the stockade, and the highest mountain in the Wasatch Range, its elevation being, as they reported, 11,219 feet. These were probably the first white men who ascended this mountain.

[32] They were 8 or 9 feet high, and 16 or 17 feet long, by 14 wide. *Hist. B. Young*, MS., 1847, 110. 'We were the first to move into the fort; our house had a door and a wooden window, which through the day was taken out for light, and nailed in at night...There was also a port-hole at the east end of the fort, which could be opened and closed at pleasure...We had adobe chimneys and a fire-place in the corner, with a clay hearth.' *Young's Pioneer Women*, MS., 6.

[33] 'With 34 wagons, 92 yoke of oxen, 18 horses, and 14 mules, in charge of Shadrach Roundy and Tunis Rappelye. Lt Wesley Willis was in charge of the battalion men.' *Richards' Narr.*, MS., 13–14.

to a body of water some two hundred miles to
the south, situated in what was later known as Iron
county, near Parowan, and.which has since almost
disappeared. The stream connecting the two great
lakes was named the Western Jordan, now called the
Jordan, and the whole region whose waters flow into
the lake was distinguished as the great basin.[34] On
the 26th a second company, consisting of 107 persons,[35] started for Winter Quarters. Brigham Young
and Heber C. Kimball set forth on horseback a little
in advance of the others, but turning back, they waved
their hats with a cheery "Good-by to all who tarry,"
and then rode on.

"We have accomplished more this year," writes
Wilford Woodruff, " than can be found on record concerning an equal number of men in the same time
since the days of Adam. We have travelled with
heavily laden wagons more than a thousand miles,
over rough roads, mountains, and cañons, searching
out a land, a resting-place for the saints. We have
laid out a city two miles square, and built a fort of
hewn timber drawn seven miles from the mountains,
and of sun-dried bricks or adobes, surrounding ten
acres of ground, forty rods of which were covered
with block-houses, besides planting about ten acres of
corn and vegetables. All this we have done in a
single month."[36]

At Winter Quarters active preparations had been
making for following the pioneers at the earliest opportunity. Throughout the spring all was activity.
Every one who had teams and provisions to last a
year and a half was preparing to move, and assisting those who were to remain to plough and sow.
Parley P. Pratt, having returned[37] from England short-

[34] 'It was also called The Great North American Desert.' *Taylor's Rem.*,
MS., 22.
[35] With 36 wagons, 71 horses, and 49 mules.
[36] *Woodruff's Journal*, MS., 78.
[37] 'I found my family all alive and dwelling in a log cabin; they had, however, suffered much from cold, hunger, and sickness...The winter had been

ly before Brigham's departure, was left in charge of
the first companies ordered westward. On the 4th of
July, 1847, they set forth for the Rocky Mountains,
numbering in all 1,553 persons.[38]

A complete organization of the people was effected,
according to a revelation of the Lord made through
Brigham on the 14th of January, 1847.[39] They
were divided into companies, each with one hundred
wagons, and these into companies of fifty wagons,
and ten wagons, every company under a captain or
commander. Two fifties travelled in double columns
if practicable. When a halt was called the wagons
were arranged as in the march of the pioneers, forming a temporary fort, with its back opening upon the
corral formed by the two semicircles. The cattle
were then driven into the corral under charge of the
herdsmen. When ready to march, the captain of
each ten attended to his company, under the supervision of the captain of fifty. Advance parties each
day selected the next camping-ground. In the absence of wood, fires were made from buffalo chips and
sage brush. The wagons had projections extending
over the sides, making the interior six feet wide.
Hen-coops were carried at the end of each wagon,
and a few young pigs were brought for use in the
valley. Great care was used to prevent a stampede
of the animals, as they appeared to recognize the
peculiarities and dangers of the new country and

very severe, the snow deep, and consequently horses and cattle had been lost.
...My wagons were overhauled and put in order, tires reset, chains repaired,
yokes and bows arranged in order, wagon bows made and mended.' *Pratt's
Autobiog.*, 397-8. 'The companies were organized by Elder P. P. Pratt and
myself, as near as we could in accordance with instructions left by Pres.
Young.' *Taylor's Rem.*, MS., 7.

[38] This company is distinguished as the first immigration. It was supplied
with 580 wagons, 2,213 oxen, 124 horses, 887 cows, 358 sheep, 716 chickens, and
35 hogs. *Utah Early Records*, MS., 17. Smith says about 700 wagons. *Rise,
Progress, and Travels*, 16. Kearny's and Frémont's parties met Pratt's companies at Loup River; and according to *Martin's Narr.*, '42 *in Cal.*, MS.,
122, John Young was appointed president and John Van Cott marshal.

[39] This was called 'the word and will of the Lord concerning the camp
of Israel.' Like all revelations, it was in scriptural phraseology, and very
explicit in its directions. It was also read by Brigham to his people in Salt
Lake City on the 1st of August.

were easily alarmed.   The organization and order in
the camp was so perfect that not unfrequently half
an hour after a halt the people sat down to a comfortable meal of fresh bread and broiled meat.[40]

At the beginning of their journey, jealousy, bickering, and insubordination arose among them, and a halt
was called for the purpose of holding a council and
adjusting matters.   For several hundred miles they
followed the trail of the pioneers, and now were approaching the president and his men, who, encamped
between Green River and the Sweetwater, had sent
forward two messengers[41] to ascertain the progress
and condition of the company.   Upon hearing of the
difficulties that had arisen, Brigham sent for Pratt
and censured him severely for defects in the management of the party at the start, and for misunderstand-
ings on the road.   Pratt humbly acknowledged his
faults and was forgiven.   While the president and
council were at prayer, the Sioux improved the occasion by stealing a number of horses, which proved a
serious loss.

Pratt now returned to his command, and without
special incident reached the Salt Lake settlement on
the 19th of September; the companies arriving in detachments at intervals of several weeks.

Brigham's band was scantily provisioned for the
journey to Winter Quarters.[42]   The number that had
already gathered at Salt Lake had drawn heavily on
the pioneers' resources, and they set out depending for
subsistence on game and fish.   They travelled more
rapidly in returning,[43] although most of them were
compelled to walk.   A few days after the Indian dep-

---

[40] From account of their journeyings furnished me in *Taylor's Rem.*, 7–12.

[41] O. P. Rockwell and E. T. Benson.

[42] Among them was a party of battalion men who were entirely destitute except for a very small quantity of beef, which was soon exhausted.   General Epistle of the Twelve, in *Millennial Star*, x. 83.

[43] 'Camped on the south side of the Platte.   We were 42 days in going to the valley from this point, and only 23 days in returning.' *Hist. B. Young*, MS., 1847, 115.

redation mentioned during the council, the Mormons were attacked by a large war party of Sioux, who again carried off many horses. The meeting of the battalion and pioneer brethren with Parley Pratt's company was an occasion of rejoicing to all.[44] On the 7th of September the former arrived at the Sweetwater. Here, with the assembled companies, a jubilee was held and a feast of good things prepared. While the men cut down brush and constructed a bowery, the women, with great trouble, unpacked their dishes and table furniture, delighted at the opportunity of assisting at such an event. A fat heifer was killed, and whatever luxuries were in camp were now produced. A slight snow fell, but in no degree marred their merriment; the feast was followed by music and dancing, and by accounts of the pioneers' experiences in entering upon and settling their new Zion; after prayer the company dispersed.[45] The remnants of the banquet were left with the eastern-bound train, and as they separated each bade the other God speed. A fortnight before reaching Winter Quarters a small delegation met Brigham's company with most welcome supplies. On the 31st of October, when within one mile of the settlement, Brigham called his men together, praised them for their good conduct, blessed and dismissed them. They drove into town in order an hour before sunset. The streets were crowded, and friends pressed forward, shaking hands as they passed through the lines.[46]

During this season an abundant harvest had been gathered by the brethren at their encampments near

[44] 'Met Spencer's advance company Sept. 3d, with 76 wagons; we had a joyful meeting; on the 4th met encampment of 75 wagons; on the 5th 162; and on the 8th met the last company of saints.' *Hist. B. Young*, MS., 1847.

[45] 'All felt greatly encouraged. We now knew for the first time our destination; we had talked of California, and knew not until now where we should settle.' *Horne's Migrations*, MS., 22.

[46] 'We were truly rejoiced once more to behold our wives, children, and old friends, after an absence of six months, having travelled over 2,000 miles... and accomplished the most important mission in this last dispensation.' *Hist. B. Young*, MS., 1847, 122.

the Missouri, though sickness was an ever-present
guest; and many of their number who could least be
spared were scattered throughout the world as missionaries in Europe, and as far westward as the Sandwich Islands, as soldiers in California, or as laborers
wherever they could find a livelihood in the western
states. The winter was passed quietly and in content,
most of the saints preparing for their migration in the
spring. Meanwhile, on the 23d of December, 1847,
a general epistle of the twelve was issued to the
brethren and to the gentiles. In this it was stated
that they were at peace with all the world, that their
mission was to extend salvation to the ends of the
earth, and an invitation was extended to "all presidents, and emperors, and kings, and princes, and no-
bles, and governors, and rulers, and judges, and all
nations, kindreds, tongues, and people under the whole
heaven, to come and help us to build a house to the
name of the God of Jacob, a place of peace, a city of
rest, a habitation for the oppressed of every clime."
Then followed an exhortation for the saints to gather
unto Zion, promising that their reward should be a
hundred-fold and their rest glorious. They must
bring "their gold, their silver, their copper, their
zinc, their tin, and brass, and iron, and choice steel,
and ivory, and precious stones; their curiosities of
science,...or anything that ever was, or is, or is to
be for the exaltation, glory, honor, and salvation of
the living and the dead, for time and for all eternity."[47]

Such a gathering of saints and gentiles would of
itself have constituted an earthly Zion, especially for
the president and the twelve, who held virtual control
over their brethren's property. Among the gentiles
one would think that such rhodomontade could not
fail to bring discredit on the Mormon faith and the
Mormon cause, but no such result followed. As will
be mentioned later, their missions were never more
prosperous than during the years when at their new

[47] The full text of this epistle is given in the *Millennial Star*, x. 81-8.

stake of Zion the saints were employed, not in adorning their temple with gold, silver, and precious stones, but in building rough shanties, hewing timber, hoeing corn, and planting potatoes.

The trite maxim commencing *Æquam memento* was one which the saints had taken well to heart, and on few was the *mens æqua in arduis* more firmly stamped than on the brow of him who, on christmas eve, the day after his invitation to the princes and potentates of all the earth, was appointed president of the church of Jesus Christ of latter-day saints. And while in adversity there were none more steadfast, it must be admitted there were few in whom success developed so little of pride and of vainglory. From this time forth Brigham Young was to the saints as a prophet —yea, and more than a prophet: one on whom the mantle had fallen not unworthily. By his foresight he had saved his people from dispersion, and perchance his faith from annihilation. Hounded by a mob, he had led his followers with consummate tact throughout their pilgrimage, and in a wilderness as yet almost untrodden by man had at length established for them an abiding-place.

After the departure of Brigham from Salt Lake, John Smith, the prophet's uncle, was nominally president of the camp;[48] but upon the arrival of John Taylor and Parley P. Pratt their precedence was acknowledged and they were placed in charge.[49] There were no laws until the latter part of this year, though certain penalties were assigned for certain crimes and executed by the people. As there was no jail, the whipping-post was substituted, but used only two or three times. In such cases the high council tried the

---

[48] Affairs were controlled by the high council, consisting of twelve high-priests. Salt Lake City was a stake of Zion, with president and other officers. 'At the conference on Oct. 3d Father John Smith was elected president of the stake of Zion and patriarch of the church. Brigham Young was sustained as president of the whole church.' *Hist. B. Young,* MS., 117.

[49] *Nebeker's Early Justice,* MS., 4.

prisoner, and sentenced him. "President Young was decidedly opposed to whipping,"[50] says George Q. Cannon, "but matters arose that we considered required punishment at the time."[51]

During this period men and women voted by ballot in matters relating to government. Women had already voted in religious meetings by the uplifted hand, but this is probably the first instance in the United States where woman suffrage was permitted. Utah at that time, however, was not a part of the United States, and before its admission as a territory the privilege was withdrawn.[52]

[50] 'I had to chastise one in that way for stealing.' *Id.*, MS., 4.

[51] 'For instance, one of our best men now, who was then young, was accused of riding on horseback with a girl in front of him. This was looked upon as indecorous. He and others guilty of the same thing were severely reprimanded.' G. Q. Cannon, in *Taylor's Rem.*, MS., 12–13.

[52] *Taylor's Rem.*, MS., 14. Herewith I give a list of the Utah pioneers of 1847: Adams, Barnabas L.; Angel, Truman O.; Allen, Rufus; Attwood, Millen; Badger, Rodney; Barney, Lewis; Barnham, Charles D.; Benson, Ezra T.; Billings, Geo. P.; Boggs, Francis; Brown, Geo.; Brown, John; Brown, Nathaniel Thomas; Bullock, Thos; Burke, Charles; Burnham, Jacob D.; Byard, Robert; Carrington, Albert; Carter, William; Case, James; Chamberlin, Solomon; Chessley, Alexander P.; Clayton, William; Cloward, Thos P.; Coltrin, Zebedee; Craig, James; Crosby, Oscar; Curtis, Lyman; Cushing, Hosea; Davenport, James; Dewey, Benjamin F.; Dixon, John; Driggs, Starling; Dykes, William; Earl, Sylvester H.; Eastman, Ozro; Egan, Howard; Egbert, Joseph; Eldredge, John S.; Ellsworth, Edmund; Empey, William A.; Ensign, Datus; Everett, Addison; Fairbanks, Nathaniel; Farr, Aaron; Fitzgerald, Perry; Flake, Green (colored); Fowler, John S.; Fox, Samuel; Freeman, John M.; Frink, Horace M.; Frost, Burr; Gibbons, Andrew S.; Gleason, John S.; Glines, Eric; Goddard, Stephen H.; Grant, David; Grant, Geo. R.; Greene, John Y.; Grover, Thomas; Hancock, Joseph; Hanks, Sidney A.; Hanson, Hans C.; Harmon, Appleton M.; Harper, Charles A.; Henrie, William; Hewd, Simeon; Higbee, John S.; Holman, John G.; Ivory, Matthew; Jackman, Levi; Jacobs, Norton; Johnson, Artemas; Johnson, Luke; Johnson Philo; Kelsey, Stephen; Kendall, Levi N.; Kimball, Ellen S. (wife of H. C. K.); Kimball, Heber C.; King, William A.; Klineman, Conrad; Lark, Hark (colored); Lewis, Tarlton; Little, Jessie C.; Losee, John G.; Loveland, Chancey; Lyman, Amasa; Marble, Samuel H.; Markham, Stephen; Matthews, Joseph; Mills, George; Murray, Carlos; Newman, Elijah; Norton, John W.; Owen, Seely; Pack, John; Pierce, Eli H.; Pomeroy, Francis M.; Powell, David; Pratt, Orson; Reddin, Jackson; Rappelye, Tunis; Richards, Willard; Rockwell, Orrin P.; Rockwood, Albert P.; Rolfe, Benjamin W.; Rooker, Joseph; Roundy, Shadrach; Schofield, Joseph S.; Scholes, George; Sherwood, Henry G.; Shumway, Andrew P.; Shumway, Charles; Smith, George A.; Smoot, Wm C. A.; Snow, Erastus; Stevens, Roswell; Stewart, Benjamin F.; Stewart, James W.; Stringham, Briant; Summe, Gilburd; Taft, Seth; Tanner, Thomas; Taylor, Norman; Thomas, Robert T.; Thornton, Horace M.; Thorpe, Marcus B.; Tippitts, John H.; Vance, William P.; Walker, Henson; Wardel, George; Weiler, Jacob; Wheeler, John; Whipple, Edson; Whitney, Horace K.; Whitney, Orson K.; Williams, Almon L.; Woodard, George; Woodruff, Wilford; Woolsey, Thomas; Words-

On the 16th of November, O. P. Rockwell, E. K. Fuller, A. A. Lathrop, and fifteen others set forth for California to buy cows, mules, mares, wheat, and seeds. They bought two hundred head of cows at six dollars each, with which they started from California, but lost forty head on the Mojave; being ninety days on the return trip. During the autumn, several parties of the battalion men arrived from California, bringing a quantity of wheat. Captain Grant came to Salt Lake City from Fort Hall in December to arrange for opening trade between the two points. After due discussion, the matter was referred to the headquarters of the Hudson's Bay Company.

In regard to affairs at Pueblo and on the Missouri, I am indebted for further and later information to my esteemed friends Wilbur F. Stone and William N. Byers of Colorado. A detachment of the Mormons that wintered at Pueblo underwent many hardships, and there have been found relics in that vicinity, in the shape of furnace and cinders, significant of their industrial occupation at the time.

On the Missouri, the Indians, who at first had so heartily welcomed the saints during the year 1847, complained to the government that they were intruding on their domain. The government therefore ordered away the Mormons, but gave them permission to occupy lands on the east bank of the river for five years. There they built a town, named Kanesville, opposite Omaha, and occupied the best part of the country up and down the left bank of the river for a distance of twenty miles in each direction. Many of them lived in dugouts, that is, artificial caves made by digging out a space for occupancy in the bank of the river or on the side of a bluff. Most

worth, William; Young, Brigham; Clarissa D. (wife of B. Y.); Young, Harriet P. (wife of Lorenzo D.); Young, Isaac P. D.; Young, Lorenzo D.; Young, Lorenzo Z.; Young, Phineas H.

of them were farmers, and they had three or four grist-mills and two or three saw-mills.

The first emigrants did not stop on the east side of the river, but passed over at once on arrival, making their first settlement, as before mentioned, at Winter Quarters, situated six miles from the present city of Omaha, at the north end of the plateau, nearly all of which they ploughed up in the spring of 1847, and planted seed corn brought by those who the previous winter had returned to the Mississippi to work for wages. Hereabout they built many log houses, Brigham having a little cluster of them for his wives in a cosey nook apart from the others.

On their final departure for the west, the Mormons left a few of their number under A. J. Mitchell, who was assisted by A. J. Smith. They lived on the east side of the Missouri at first, and had a ferry across the river as early as 1851, with other ferries west, one at Loup Fork, and one on the Elkhorn. A large emigration up the river from New Orleans set in about this time. In the spring of 1852 the steamboat *Saluda*, having six hundred souls on board, was blown up at the mouth of the Platte.

In 1854 the lands of the Omahas, on the west side of the river, came into market, through a treaty made during the summer of that year with the natives, who ceded that section to the United States. Mitchell and Smith then moved to the western side, and changed the name of Winter Quarters to that of Florence, at the same time selling their interests on the eastern side to the gentiles, who changed the name of Kanesville to that of Council Bluffs.

CHAPTER XI.

IN THE VALLEY OF THE GREAT SALT LAKE.

1848.

FOOD AND RAIMENT—HOUSES—HOME MANUFACTURES—THE FORT—WILD
BEASTS—CANNON FROM SUTTER'S FORT—INDIAN CHILDREN FOR SALE—
MEASLES—POPULATION—MILLS AND FARMING MACHINERY—THE PLAGUE
OF CRICKETS—THEY ARE DESTROYED BY GULLS—SCARCITY OF PROVISIONS
—THE HARVEST FEAST—IMMIGRATION—FIVE THOUSAND SAINTS GATH-
ERED IN THE VALLEY—FENCING AND FARMING—DISTRIBUTION OF LOTS—
ORGANIZATION OF COUNTY GOVERNMENT—ASSOCIATION FOR THE EXTER-
MINATION OF WILD BEASTS.

AT the opening of January 1848, the saints were
housed, clad, and fed in moderate comfort, and general
content prevailed.[1]   The season was exceptionally
mild; there were occasional light falls of snow, but
not enough to interfere with ploughing and sowing,[2]
and a large tract of land was partially enclosed and
planted with wheat and vegetables.

So many people were now in the valley that notwithstanding the abundant crops food at length became scarce.   Families weighed out their flour and
allowed themselves so much a day.   The wheat was
ground at a mill on City Creek, but as there was no
bolting-cloth, the shorts and bran could not be separated.   The beef was very poor,[3] as most of the cattle

[1] Parley P. Pratt says: 'Here life was as sweet as the holidays, as merry
as in the Christian palaces and mansions of those who had driven us to the
mountains.'

[2] 'It was a strange sight to see sometimes furrows on one side and snow
on the other.   In Feb. men worked out of doors in their shirt sleeves.' *Horne's
Migrations*, MS., 24.

[3] 'It was so tough that Brother Taylor suggested we must grease the saw
to make it work.' *Horne's Migrations*, MS., 26.

had been worked hard while driven to the valley and
after their arrival, while those turned out to range did
not fatten quickly.   Butter and tallow were needed.
One wild steer, well fattened, was brought in from
Goodyear's rancho.   A herd of deer crossing from one
range of mountains to another was startled by the
unexpected obstruction of the fort, and one sprang
into the enclosure and was killed.   Wild sago and
parsnip roots constituted the vegetable food of the
settlers.   A few deaths occurred from poisonous
roots.   The bracing air and hard work stimulated
appetite as stores decreased.   For coffee parched barley and wheat were used, and as their sugar gave out,
they substituted some of home manufacture.[4]   In the
spring thistle tops were eaten, and became an important article of diet.[5]

Anxiety began to be felt about clothing, and the
hand-looms were now busily at work, although wool
was scarce.[6]   As shoes wore out, moccasins were substituted, and goat, deer, and elk skins were manufactured into clothing for men and women, though
most unsuitable for use in rain and snow.

At the time of Parley P. Pratt's arrival, the city
of Great Salt Lake consisted of a fort enclosing a
block of ten acres, the walls of part of the buildings
being of adobes and logs.   There were also some
tents.[7]   As additional companies came in, they ex-

[4] 'We manufactured our own sugar and molasses from beets, corn-stalks,
and watermelons, and made preserves for winter, which were excellent, by
boiling the rinds of the melons in this molasses.' *Horne's Migrations*, MS.,
30.   'I attempted to make sugar out of corn.   A rude apparatus was made
to squeeze the corn stalks, but the manufacture was not altogether a success.
After this, beet molasses followed.   The boiler I used this time I made out
of some stove piping and lumber.   Brother Cannon and I assisted to saw our
lumber.' *Taylor's Reminiscences*, MS., 16.
[5] Geo. Q. Cannon, in *Juv. Inst.*, xix. no. 5, 68.
[6] 'They collected the hair of the buffalo from the sage brush as they
travelled, and used also the hair of cows.' *Horne's Migrations*, MS., 35.
From this blankets were woven and used in exchange with the Indians.   Mrs
Horne remarks that 'in Nauvoo there was a man dressed throughout in a suit
made from the curly hair of his dog, which was sheared annually.'
[7] It stood on what was later known as the 6th Ward Square.

tended the south divisions, which were connected with
the old fort by gates. Wagon-boxes were also brought
into line, and served for habitations until better accom-
modations were provided. The houses were built of
logs, and were placed close together, the roofs slanting
inward, and all the doors and windows being on the
inside, with a loop-hole to each room on the outside.
As everything indicated a dry climate, the roofs were
made rather flat, and great inconvenience resulted.
In March the rains were very heavy, and umbrellas
were used to protect women and children while cooking, and even in bed. The clay found in the bottoms
near the fort made excellent plaster, but would not
stand exposure to rain, and quickly melted. All breadstuffs were carefully gathered into the centre of the
rooms, and protected with buffalo skins obtained from
the Indians. The rooms in the outer lines all ad-
joined, and many of the families had several rooms.
On the interior cross-lines rooms were built on both
sides, the streets being eight rods wide.

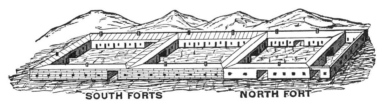

FORT, GREAT SALT LAKE CITY, 1848.

There were serious depredations committed by
wolves, foxes, and catamounts, and great annoyance
occasioned by the howling of some of these animals.[8]
Further discomfort was caused by innumerable swarms
of mice. Digging cavities and running about under
the earthen floor, they caused the ground to tremble,
and when the rain loosened the stones of the roofs,

[8] 'One night soon after our arrival I spread some strychnine about, and in
the morning found fourteen white wolves dead.' *Lorenzo Young's Ex.*, MS., 8.

scampered off in hordes. Frequently fifty or sixty had to be caught and killed before the family could sleep.[9]

The furniture was home-made, and very little of it at that. The table was a chest, and the bedstead was built into the corner of the house, which formed two of its sides, rails or poles forming the opposite sides; pegs were driven into the walls and rails, and the bed-cord tightly wound around them.[10] The chimneys were of adobe, and sometimes there was a fireplace in the corner with a clay hearth.

In the early part of the year two brass cannon were purchased at Sutter's Fort for the church, by the battalion brethren.[11]

During the winter of 1847–8, some Indian children were brought to the fort to be sold. At first two were offered, but the settlers peremptorily refused to buy them. The Indian in charge said that the children were captured in war, and would be killed at sunset if the white men did not buy them. Thereupon they purchased one of them, and the one not sold was shot. Later, several Indians came in with two more children, using the same threat; they were bought and brought up at the expense of the settlers.[12]

Measles now appeared for the first time among the natives, who did not know where the disease came from or what to do. They assembled in large numbers at the warm springs, bathed in the waters, and died.[13]

[9] 'One contrivance for catching them was a bucketful of water with a board sloping at each end, greased and balanced on the edge. The first cat and her progeny were invaluable. The green timber from the mountains was full of bed-bugs, another serious trouble.' *Horne's Migrations*, MS., 31.

[10] This describes the furniture of the first house occupied in the fort by Brigham Young's family. *Mrs Clara Young's Pioneer Ex.*, MS., 8.

[11] Forty-five of the battalion brethren contributing $512 for the purpose. *Hist. B. Young*, MS., 1848, 35.

[12] 'Charles Decker bought one of the prisoners, a girl, who was afterward brought up in President Young's family. She married an Indian chief named Kanosh.' *Wells' Narr.*, MS., 48.

[13] 'Some they buried, but not all. We buried thirty-six in one grave. They killed their dogs when their masters died.' *Nebeker's Early Justice*, MS., 2.

Public meetings were generally held near the liberty-pole in the centre of the fort; religious and secular meetings were also held in private houses. In March 1848 the population of the city was reported at 1,671, and the number of houses 423.[14] Bridges were built over Mill Creek and Jordan River. Daniel Spencer was appointed road-master, and authorized to call on men to assist in making roads. In order that the burden might fall equally on all, a poll and property tax were instituted.

There were several mills soon in working order. A small grist-mill on City Creek was built by Charles Crismon near the pioneer garden; then there were Chase's saw-mill and Archibald and Robert Gardiner's on Mill Creek, and Nebeker, Riter, and Wallace's in a cañon ten miles north of the city. A carding machine was erected near Gardiner's saw-mill by Amasa Russell, and a flouring mill during the summer by John Neff. Leffingwell constructed a threshing machine and fanning mill on City Creek, with a capacity of two hundred bushels per day. Mill-stones cut out of the basalt in the valley were of very good quality. Mill-irons, mill-stones, printing-presses, type, paper, and the carding machine were brought by the first bands of emigrants in 1848.[15]

The spring saw everybody busy, and soon there were many flourishing gardens, containing a good variety of vegetables. In the early part of March ploughing commenced. The spring was mild and rain plentiful, and all expected an abundant harvest. But in the latter part of May, when the fields had put on their brightest green, there appeared a visitation in the form of vast swarms of crickets, black and baleful as the locust of the Dead Sea.[16] In their track

[14] *Juv. Inst.*, ix. no. 1, 9.
[15] *Hist. B. Young*, MS.; *Horne's Migrations*, MS.; Geo. Q. Cannon, in *Juv. Inst.; Taylor's Reminiscences*, MS.; *Woodruff's Journal*, MS.; *Young's Ex.*, MS.; *Wells' Narr.*, MS.; *Richards' Narr.*, MS.; *Nebeker's Early Justice*, MS.; *Jenning's Material Progress*, MS., passim.
[16] *Utah Early Records*, MS., 29–30.

they left behind them not a blade or leaf, the appearance of the country which they traversed in countless and desolating myriads being that of a land scorched by fire.[17] They came in a solid phalanx, from the direction of Arsenal Hill, darkening the earth in their passage. Men, women, and children turned out en masse to combat this pest, driving them into ditches or on to piles of reeds, which they would set on fire, striving in every way, until strength was exhausted, to beat back the devouring host. But in vain they toiled, in vain they prayed; the work of destruction ceased not, and the havoc threatened to be as complete as was that which overtook the land of Egypt in the last days of Israel's bondage. "Think of their condition," says Mr Cannon—"the food they brought with them almost exhausted, their grain and other seeds all planted, they themselves 1,200 miles from a settlement or place where they could get food on the east, and 800 miles from California, and the crickets eating up every green thing, and every day destroying their sole means of subsistence for the months and winter ahead."[18]

I said in vain they prayed. Not so. For when everything was most disheartening and all effort spent, behold, from over the lake appeared myriads of snow-white gulls, their origin and their purpose alike unknown to the new-comers! Was this another scourge God was sending them for their sins? Wait and see. Settling upon all the fields and every part of them, they pounced upon the crickets, seizing and swallowing them. They gorged themselves. Even after their stomachs were filled they still devoured them. On Sunday the people, full of thankfulness, left the fields to the birds, and on the morrow found on the edges of the ditches great piles of dead crickets that had been swallowed and thrown up by the

---

[17] *Autobiog. P. P. Pratt,* 405; *Smith's Rise, Progress, and Travels,* 17.
[18] *Juv. Inst.,* ix. no. 2, 22.

greedy gulls. Verily, the Lord had not forgotten to be gracious!

To escape the birds, the crickets would rush into the lake or river, and thus millions were destroyed. Toward evening the gulls took flight and disappeared beyond the lake, but each day returned at sunrise, until the scourge was past.[19] Later grasshoppers seem to have taken the place of crickets. They were of a kind popularly called iron-clad, and did much mischief.[20]

Though the crops of this year of 1848 were thus saved from total destruction, fears were entertained that there would not be food enough for those already in the valley, and the expected arrival of large additional numbers was looked upon as a calamity.[21] The stock of provisions was therefore husbanded with care, many living principally on roots and

[19] Kane says that the gulls soon grew to be as tame as poultry, and that the children called them their pigeons. They had clear, dark eyes, small feet, and large wings that arched in flight. *The Mormons*, 67. 'No one is allowed to kill a gull in Utah, and they are consequently very tame.' *Jenning's Material Progress*, MS., 7. 'I am sure that the wheat was in head, and that it averaged two or three crickets on every head, bending them down. One couldn't step without crushing under foot as many as the foot could cover.' *Mrs Clara Young's Experiences of a Pioneer*, MS., 9. 'Channels were dug and filled with water to prevent their travel, but they would throw themselves across; it was impossible to fight them back.' *Nebeker's Early Justice*, MS., 2. 'In the spring, when thousands of young trees had been started and were several inches in height, came the crickets. The wheat, too, was well in head.' *Horne's Migrations*, MS., p. 28.

[20] Says Mr Jennings: 'They would devastate hundreds of acres, and as they would rise and fly high in the air, the air would be darkened with them. They seemed to be massed together, and to take but one direction, flying eight or ten miles perhaps, then settling upon another field...The only exterminator seems to be the sea-gulls. They gorge themselves on this rich diet; they suddenly appear in the wake of the grasshoppers, and will swallow them, throw them up, and swallow them again...Sometimes the grasshoppers come like a cloud, and apparently alighting not knowing where; on one occasion a quarter of their number perhaps dropped into the lake, and were blown on shore by the wind, in rows of sometimes two feet deep for a distance of two miles.' *Material Progress*, MS., 6–7.

[21] 'Word was sent back that probably no crops could be raised that year, and advising that no further emigrations should come in that season.' *Mrs Clara Young's Experiences of a Pioneer*, MS., 9. John Young wished to send an express to his brother, the president, advising him not to bring any more people to the valley, as there was danger of starvation. *Utah Early Records*, MS., 30–2. Parley P. Pratt writes: 'I had a good harvest of wheat and rye without irrigation, but those who irrigated had double the quantity. Wheat harvest commenced early in July...Oats do extremely well, yielding sixty bushels for one.' *Hist. B. Young*, MS., 1848, 54.

thistles, to which fare was sometimes added a little flour or milk. The wheat crop, however, turned out better than was expected, and pumpkins, melons, and corn yielded good returns.[22]

On the 10th of August, however, the harvest being then gathered, a feast was held in the bowery, at which the tables were loaded with a variety of viands, vegetables, beef, and bread, butter and cheese, with cakes and pastry. Sheaves of wheat and other grain were hoisted on harvest poles; "and," says Parley, "there was prayer and thanksgiving, congratulations, songs, speeches, music, dancing, smiling faces, and merry hearts."

The rendezvous for westward-bound brethren in the spring of 1848 was the Elkhorn River, and thither at the end of May came the president, who organized the people and gave them instructions to be observed on the way. Good order was to be preserved in camp; there must be no shouting; prayers were to be attended to, and lights put out at 9 o'clock. Drivers of teams must walk beside their oxen, and not leave them without permission. Brigham was general superintendent of the emigrating companies, with Daniel H. Wells as aide-de-camp, H. S. Eldredge marshal, and Hosea Stout captain of the night-guard. Moving west early in June, on the 14th the emigrants were fired on by Indians, two being wounded. At this time also there was sickness in the camp. To secure grass and water, the emigration was separated into divisions, of which there were two principal

---

[22] 'Wheat harvest good. Corn crop good. The worms ate some in the ear. Price of wheat, $2 a bushel. Population, 1,800; main fence, 12 miles long. Had a surplus of bread-stuff this year.' *Hist. B. Young*, MS., Aug. 1, 1848, 52. Parley states that he and his family, in common with many others, suffered much for want of food. He had ploughed and planted, in grain and vegetables, nearly 40 acres, nearly every women and child in his family toiling in the field so far as their age and strength would permit. *Autobiog.*, 405. 'One family had nothing but milk to live upon;...they would let a portion thicken, and then mix it with new milk and eat it for bread. They lived upon it for six weeks, and thrived.' Eliza Snow, in *Utah Notes*, MS., 6.

ones, under Brigham Young and H. C. Kimball, with several subdivisions.[23]

The first letters received at Great Salt Lake City from Brigham came twelve months after his departure from the valley, and were sent on in advance from the encampments. The excitement was great as Taylor and Green rode into the city and distributed the letters, without envelopes, tied round and round with buckskin thongs, and bearing the cheering news that a large body of brethren was on the way, and bringing plenty of food.[24]

In June and July two small parties left the city to meet the immigration, and another in August. In September Brigham and the first companies arrived; and under the organization of the president and his two counsellors, Willard Richards and Heber C. Kimball, during the autumn months most of the brethren from Winter Quarters and other camps reached the valley.[25]

Before the expiration of the year, there were nearly

[23] The first division consisted of 1,229 persons, with 397 wagons, 74 horses, 91 mules, 1,275 oxen, 699 cows, 184 loose cattle, 411 sheep, 141 pigs, 605 chickens, 37 cats, 82 dogs, 3 goats, 10 geese, 2 hives of bees, 8 doves, and 1 crow; the second of 662 persons, with 226 wagons, 57 horses, 25 mules, 737 oxen, 284 cows, 150 loose cattle, 243 sheep, 96 pigs, 299 chickens, 17 cats, 52 dogs, 3 hives of bees, 3 doves, 5 ducks, and 1 squirrel.

[24] As recorded in Mrs Clara Decker Young's very valuable manuscript. She shows now the first letter received, still tied with buckskin thongs.

[25] The first companies under Brigham arrived on Sept. 20th; Kimball's party reached the valley a few days later. At the beginning of August Lorenzo Snow, A. O. Smoot, and others, with 47 wagons and 124 yoke of oxen, were sent from Salt Lake City to assist the emigrants. On the 28th of the same month a party well supplied with wagons and cattle was sent back to Winter Quarters from the camp of the president, then on the Sweetwater. *Utah Early Records*, MS., 33. The companies under Richards reached their destination toward the end of October. *Richards' Narr.*, MS., 38. In relating the incidents of his journey, Richards states that his was the last party to leave Winter Quarters during that summer. His men were ill supplied with provisions; feed was scarce, and many of the cattle died from drinking alkali water, so that he was compelled to yoke to the wagons even his yearlings and his milch-cows. Many families, including the children, were compelled to walk the entire distance; yet not a single death occurred. *Id.*, 34–5. 'The companies behind were kept well informed of the progress of those in advance...Sometimes a copy of the camp journal was written and placed in a notch in a tree,...sometimes in a post stuck in the ground; but whenever a large buffalo skull or other suitable bone was found,...some particulars were written on them.' Cannon, in *Juv. Inst.*, xix. no. 3, 36.

three thousand,[26] and including the pioneers, the battalion men, and the companies that arrived under Parley, at least five thousand of the saints assembled in the valley.

Thus about one fourth of the exiles from Nauvoo were for the present beyond reach of molestation. That five thousand persons, including a very large proportion of women and children, almost without money, almost without provisions, excepting the milk of their kine and the grain which they had raised near their own camps, should, almost without the loss of a life, have accomplished this journey of more than twelve hundred miles, crossing range after range of mountains, bridging rivers, and traversing deserts, while liable at any moment to be attacked by roaming bands of savages, is one of the marvels that this century has witnessed. To those who met them on the route, the strict order of their march, their coolness and rapidity in closing ranks to repel assault, their method in posting sentries around camp and corral, suggested rather the movements of a well-organized army than the migration of a people; and in truth, few armies have been better organized or more ably led than was this army of the Lord.[27] To the skill of their leaders, and their own concert of purpose and action, was due their preservation. And now, at length, they had made good their escape from the land of their bondage to the promised land of their freedom, in which, though a wilderness, they rejoiced to dwell.

In a private letter written in September 1848, Parley writes: "How quiet, how still, how free from excitement we live! The legislation of our high council, the decision of some judge or court of

---

[26] White persons 2,393, and 24 negroes, with 792 wagons, 2,527 oxen, about 1,700 cows, 181 horses, 1,023 sheep, and other live-stock. *Utah Early Records*, MS., 41.

[27] 'So well recognized were the results of this organization, that bands of hostile Indians have passed by comparatively small parties of Mormons to attack much larger but less compact bodies of other emigrants.' *Kane's The Mormons*, 34.

the church, a meeting, a dance, a visit, an exploring tour, the arrival of a party of trappers and traders, a Mexican caravan, a party arrived from the Pacific,[28] from the States, from Fort Bridger, a visit of Indians, or perhaps a mail from the distant world once or twice a year, is all that breaks the monotony of our busy and peaceful life... Here, too, we all are rich—there is no real poverty; all men have access to the soil, the pasture, the timber, the water power, and all the elements of wealth, without money or price."[29]

On his arrival in the autumn, Brigham stirred up the people to the greatest activity. Fencing material being scarce, and the city lands all appropriated, it was proposed that a large field for farming purposes adjoining the city should be selected and fenced in common. By October there were 863 applications for lots, amounting to 11,005 acres.

A united effort was made to fence the city, which was done by enclosing each ward in one field, and requiring the owner of every lot to build his proportion of the fence.[30] No lots were allowed to be held for speculation, the intention, originally, being to assign them only to those who would occupy and improve them. The farming land nearest the city was surveyed in five-acre lots to accommodate the mechanics and artisans; next beyond were ten-acre lots, followed by forty and eighty acres, where farmers could build and reside. All these farms were enclosed in one common fence, constituting what was called the 'big field,' before mentioned.[31]

[28] 'In July 1848, William and Nathan Hawks, Sanford Jacobs, and Richard Slater came from California with copies of Brannan's *Star* of April 1st, and tidings that the brethren at San Francisco were doing well, and that those who had settled on the San Joaquin River had vacated in favor of the mosquitoes.' *Hist. B. Young*, MS., 1848, 46.

[29] The letter was afterward published in part in *Snow's Voice of Joseph*, 16, and portions copied into *Utah Early Pioneers*, MS., 34–5.

[30] 'Every man is to help build a pole, ditch, or a stone fence... in proportion to the land he draws, also a canal on each side for the purpose of irrigation.' *Hist. B. Young*, MS., 1849, 55.

[31] 'The fence will be 17 miles and 53 rods long, and 8 ft high.' *Hist. B. Young*, MS., 1848, 68–9; *Juv. Inst.*, ix. no. 3, 34. It had been decided by the high council in Jan. that fencing be commenced, and that the farm lands be

The streets were kept open, but were barely wide enough for travel, as the owners cultivated the space in front of their houses. At a meeting on the 24th of September, permission was granted to build on the lots immediately, all buildings to be at least twenty feet from the sidewalk; and a few days later it was voted " that a land record should be kept, and that $1.50 be paid for each lot; one dollar to the surveyor and fifty cents to the clerk for recording." A council-house was ordered to be built by tithing labor; and it was suggested that water from the Big Cottonwood be brought into the city; the toll for grinding grain was to be increased,[32] and a resolution was passed against the sale or use of ardent spirits. That all might be satisfied, the lots were to be distributed "by ballot, or casting lots, as Israel did in days of old."[33]

On the 1st of October Brigham called the battalion brethren together, blessed them, and thanked them for the service they had rendered. "The plan of raising a battalion to march to California," he said, "by a call from the war department, was devised with a view to the total overthrow of this kingdom, and the destruction of every man, woman, and child."[34]

Winter was now at hand, and there was sore need that the saints should bestir themselves. The presi-

located as near together as possible, and immediately south of the city. The line of the fence began at a steep point in the bluffs just south of the warm springs, thence straight to the north-west corner of the fort, then from the south-east corner of the fort, east of south, to some distance south of Mill Creek, thence east to the bluffs again, its entire length, including two sides of the fort, being 3,638 rods. *Utah Early Records*, MS., 20-1. The entire tract was 5,153 acres, of which 872 acres were sown with winter-wheat, the remainder being intended for spring and summer crops.

[32] 'Chas Crismon petitions that it be increased from 1-16 to 1-10; granted.' *Hist. B. Young*, MS., 1848, 64.

[33] 'The city plat is already allotted, and many families are at present without lots; therefore we have deemed it expedient to run off an addition to the city, commencing at the eastern line of the city and running east as far as the nature of the land will allow for building purposes. Not only is this addition necessary, but we are going to lay off a site for a city about ten miles north, and another site about ten miles to the south of our city.' *Hist. B. Young*, MS., 1848, 69.

[34] *Hist. B. Young*, MS., 1848, 65. This was not the case. See *Hist. Cal.*, vol. v. chap. xviii., this series.

dent and others of the church dignitaries worked in-
defatigably with their people, carrying mortar and
making adobes, hauling timber and sawing it.   There
were but 450 log cabins within the stockade, and
one thousand more well-filled wagons had arrived this
season.

A county government was organized, and John D.
Barker elected sheriff, Isaac Clark judge of probate,
and Evan M. Green recorder and treasurer.[35]   Two
hunting companies in December were formed, under
the leadership of John D. Lee and John Pack, for
the extermination of wild beasts.   There were eighty-
four men in all, and their efforts were successful.[36]
From the 1st of December until the end of February
there were heavy snow-storms.   On the coldest day
the mercury fell below zero,[37] and on the warmest
marked 21° of Fahrenheit.   On account of the snow
in the cañons it was difficult to bring in the necessary
fuel.   As the previous winter had been warm, the
settlers were unprepared for such cold weather, and
there was much suffering.[38]

[35] 'George Coulson, Andrew H. Perkins, and David D. Yearsley, county
commissioners; James Sloan, district clerk; Jacob G. Bigler, William Snow,
Levi Bracken, and Jonathan C. Wright, magistrates.' *Hist. B. Young*, MS., 77.

[36] 'The two hunting companies organized last Dec. report that they have
killed 2 bears, 2 wolverenes, 2 wild-cats, 783 wolves, 409 foxes, 31 minks,
9 eagles, 530 magpies, hawks, and owls, and 1,026 ravens.' *Hist. B. Young*,
MS., March 1849.

[37] 'To 33° below freezing-point on Feb. 5th.' General Epistle of the Twelve,
in *Frontier Guardian*, May 30, 1849.

[38] 'At Fort Bridger the winter had been unusually severe, and the traders,
it was reported, had suffered almost starvation.' It was resolved that no
corn should be made into whiskey, and that if any man was preparing to distil
corn into whiskey or alcohol, the corn should be taken and given to the poor.
Hist. B. Young, MS., 1849, 4.

CHAPTER XII.

IN THE VALLEY OF THE GREAT SALT LAKE.

1849.

FOOD SUPPLY AND SHELTER—BUILDING LOTS—CURRENCY ISSUE—BANK
NOTES AND COINAGE—PRIVATE AND PUBLIC BUILDINGS—WIDE AREA OF
THE CITY—SECOND ANNIVERSARY OF THE PIONEERS—FESTIVALS AND
AMUSEMENTS—LABOR A DUTY AMONG THE SAINTS—EFFECT OF THE CALI-
FORNIA GOLD DISCOVERY—IMMIGRATION—CARRYING COMPANY—CALI-
FORNIA-BOUND EMIGRANTS—THEIR TRAFFIC WITH THE MORMONS—PROD-
UCTS AND PRICES—GOLD-HUNTING FROWNED UPON BY THE CHURCH.

THROUGHOUT the winter of 1848–9 food was scarce
among the settlers. Many still subsisted mainly on
roots, thistles, and even on rawhides.[1] Milk, flesh,
and the small quantity of breadstuffs that remained
were, however, distributed among the poor in such
quantities as to prevent actual starvation. On April
1, 1849, each household was required to state the
smallest allowance of breadstuffs that would suffice
until the forth-coming harvest. Some received half
a pound a day, and others four ounces.[2]

[1] 'Many were necessitated to eat rawhides, and to dig sago and thistle
roots for mouths to subsist upon.' *Hist. B. Young*, MS., 1849, 95.

[2] The committee on breadstuffs reported on the 8th of Feb. that there
was $\frac{78}{100}$ lb. per capita for the next five months. *Utah Early Records*, MS., 45.
'In the former part of Feb. the bishops took an inventory of the breadstuff
in the valley, when was reported a little more than $\frac{3}{4}$ lb. per day for each
soul, until the 9th of July; and considerable was known to exist which was
not reported. Hence while some were nearly destitute others had abundance.
The price of corn since harvest has been $2; some has sold for $3; at present
there is none in the market at any price. Wheat has ranged from $4 to $5,
and potatoes from $6 to $20, a bushel; and though not to be bought at present, it is expected that there will be a good supply for seed by another
year.' General Epistle of the Twelve, in *Frontier Guardian*, May 30, 1849.
'Those persons who had imparted measurably to those who had not, so that
all extremity of suffering from hunger was avoided.' *Hist. B. Young*, MS.,
1849, 95.

Until the first fruits were reaped the famine continued, but the harvest of 1849 was a bountiful one,[3] and for six years thereafter none wanted for bread in the city of Salt Lake.[4]

During part of this season many women and children were without shelter or fuel. To each family as it arrived was given a city lot, until the site was exhausted, as we have seen; but for most a wagon served for dwelling during the coldest months, and later an adobe hut, roofed with unseasoned lumber, and thatched with hay or frozen mud.[5] Before summer all were housed in log or adobe dwellings,[6] the fort

---

[3] It was not injured by crickets. *Kane's The Mormons*, 67. 'Our prophet predicted that if we would exercise patience under our difficulties during the immediate future, our necessities would be supplied as cheaply as they could be in the city of St Louis; and this proved to be true, for in 1849 we raised fair crops.' *Smoot's Mormon Wife*, MS., 5–6.

[4] The peculiar chemical formations in earth and water proved of great practical value when once understood. 'For two years all the saleratus used was obtained from Saleratus Lake, near Independence Rock; the salt from the lake became an article of value in local use and among their exports. The alkali swept down from the mountains, and composed of a great variety of ingredients, such as magnesia, soda, salt, etc., when once subdued, makes the most durable of soils, which needs no enriching.' Richards, in *Utah Notes*, MS., 8.

[5] 'Now as regards my beginning at Salt Lake. Soon after my arrival a city lot was assigned to me for a home and residence, on which I placed my wagon box or wagon bed, which contained our provisions, bedding, and all our earthly goods, placed them upon the ground, turned away our stock upon the winter range, and looked about us. I soon disposed of some of my clothing for some adobes, and put the walls up of a small room, which we covered with a tent-cloth, that answered us during the winter, until lumber could be procured next spring.' *Richards' Narr.*, MS., 38; *Early Records*, MS., 36–8.

[6] On Feb. 18th the people began to move out of the fort to their city lots. *Id.*, 47. A number of temporary farm buildings had been completed before this date. *Pratt's Autobiography*, 406; *Millennial Star*, x. 370. A correspondent of the *New York Tribune*, writing from Salt Lake City, July 8, 1849, gives an exaggerated account of the place, which has been copied by several writers on Mormonism. 'There were no hotels, because there was no travel; no barbers' shops, because every one chose to shave his neighbor; no stores, because they had no goods to sell nor time to traffic; no centre of business, because all were too busy to make a centre. There was abundance of mechanics' shops, of dressmakers, milliners, and tailors, etc.; but they needed no sign, nor had they time to paint or erect one, for they were crowded with business. I this day attended worship with them in the open air. Some thousands of well-dressed, intelligent-looking people assembled, some on foot, some in carriages, and on horseback. Many were neatly and even fashionably clad. The beauty and neatness of the ladies reminded me of some of our congregations in New York.' The letter is in *Mackay's The Mormons*, 282. It is unnecessary to expose the absurdity of this description, as the reader is well aware that hundreds of California-bound emigrants passed through the valley this year. Harvesting began July 9th, and until that date the Mormons were

being rapidly broken up by the removal of the houses on to the city lots. The city was divided into nineteen bishops' wards;[7] the ten-acre blocks were divided into allotments of an acre and a quarter, the five-acre lots in similar proportion, each building facing the garden of the one adjoining, the space of twenty feet left between the houses and the surrounding fence being afterward planted with trees and shrubbery.[8]

The need of a circulating medium had been felt ever since the valley had been settled.[9] Their currency was blankets, grain, and seeds; and even after gold-dust was brought in by the miners great inconvenience was experienced in its use, and many refused to take it, as there was a waste in weighing it. To meet this emergency, bank bills for one dollar

often without their daily bread, as we have seen. The following is probably much nearer the truth: 'The houses are small, principally of brick (adobe), built up only as temporary abodes, until the more urgent and important matters of enclosure and cultivation are attended to; but I never saw anything to surpass the ingenuity of arrangement with which they are fitted up, and the scrupulous cleanliness with which they are kept. There were tradesmen and artisans of all descriptions, but no regular stores or workshops, except forges. Still, from the shoeing of a horse to the mending of a watch there was no difficulty in getting it done, as cheap and as well put out of hand as in any other city in America.' *Kelly's Excursion to California*, 226.

[7] The bishops were David Fairbanks, John Lowry, Christopher Williams, William Hickenlooper, William J. Perkins, Addison Everett, Seth Taft, David Pettigrew, Benjamin Covey, Edward Hunter, John Murdock, Abraham O. Smoot, Isaac Higbee, Joseph L. Heywood, James Hendrix, Benjamin Brown, Orville S. Cox, and Joel H. Johnson. *Utah Early Records*, MS., 47-8, 69. The valley is settled for 20 miles south and 40 miles north, and divided into 19 wards. *Hist. B. Young*, MS., 1849, 57.

[8] At a council held Feb. 17, 1849, the committee on fencing reported that the enclosure termed the big field would include 291 ten-acre lots, 460 five-acre lots, the church farm of 800 acres, and 17 acres of fractional lots, the whole requiring 5,240 rods of fencing, of which it was recommended that 3,216 should be of adobes, 663 of adobes or stone, and 1,361 of ditch, posts, and rails. 'When the Mormons first arrived they did not quarrel for best lands, but cultivated a whole district in common, dividing the harvest according to work done, seed supplied, and need of family. On dividing the town into lots, each received his plat, and so with fields, for south of the town lay a field of 6 square miles, cultivated in common; this was divided into 5-acre square lots and given to heads of families, by lot or distribution, in tracts of one to eight lots each. After the distribution some began to speculate with their lots, but to this the church objected, saying that none should sell his land for more than first cost and improvements, for it belonged to God, and was merely held in use by the holder. Still, secret speculations occurred.' *Olshausen's Mormonen*, 166-7.

[9] 'Owing to the absence of small change, the tax collector was instructed to give due-bills for sums less than a dollar, and redeem them when presented in sufficient amount.' *Hist. B. Young*, MS., 1849, 23.

were issued on the 1st of January, 1849, signed by Brigham Young, Heber C. Kimball, and Thomas Bullock, clerk. In September, Brigham had brought eighty-four dollars in small change into the valley, which had been distributed, but was no longer in circulation. On the 6th of January, resolutions were passed by the council to the effect that "the Kirtland bank bills be put into circulation for the accommodation of the people, thus fulfilling the prophecy of Joseph, that the Kirtland notes would one day be as good as gold." The first printing was in connection with the manufacture of paper money.[10]

Previous to the issue of this currency an attempt was made by John Kay to coin gold-dust, but the crucibles broke in the attempt. All the dies and everything connected with the coining were made in Salt Lake City.[11] Subsequent attempts were more successful. The coin was made of pure gold, without alloy, which made it deficient in weight; it was therefore sold as bullion. Brigham then proposed the issue of paper currency until gold could be coined.[12] There was also a paper currency issued some years later by a company in Salt Lake City known as the Deseret Currency Association, its capital being in cattle, but this was merely a temporary convenience.[13] Cur-

[10] Fifty-cent and one-dollar paper currency was issued. *Hist. B. Young,* MS., 1849, 3. On the 22d, type was set for 50-cent bills—the first type-setting in the city. *Id.,* 42–3; *S. L. C. Contributor,* ii. 209.

[11] 'Robert Campbell engraved the stamps for the coin.' *Wells' Narr.,* MS., 42. Brigham says, 'I offered the gold-dust back to the people, but they did not want it.' *Hist. B. Young,* MS., 1849, 1. 'Thos L. Smith, a mountaineer, wrote me from Bear River Valley, offering to sell me $200 or $300 in small coin...and take our currency for the same, and he would trade his skins, furs, robes, etc., with us.' *Id.,* 79.

[12] 'John Kay coined $2.50, $5, and $20 pieces.' *Nebeker's Early Justice,* MS., 3. A description is given in *Juv. Inst.* of coins with beehive and spread eagle on one side, with inscription 'Deseret Assay Office, Pure Gold,' and at the base '5 D.' On the reverse is a lion, surrounded by 'Holiness to the Lord,' in characters known as the Deseret alphabet. Vol. ix. no. 4, p. 39. In 1849 and 1850, coins of the value of $20, $10, $5, and $2.50 were struck off. Their fineness was 899-1000, and no alloy was used except a little silver. *S. L. C. Contributor,* ii. 209. 'The gold-dust was sufficient in quantity for all ordinary purposes...In the exchange the brethren deposited the gold-dust with the presidency, who issued bills or a paper currency; and the Kirtland safety fund re-signed it on a par with gold.' *Id.,* 56.

[13] See *Taylor's Reminiscences,* MS., 23.

rency, in either gold or paper, was afterward designated as valley tan, a name synonymous with home-made or of Utah manufacture, the origin of which will be explained later.[14]

Of the houses built early in 1849, few had more than two rooms, many had only board windows, and some were without doors. Several of the adobe houses in the fort had fallen down from the effects of the thaw. When at last they had learned how to make adobes, they were of the best kind. Alkali at first was mixed with the clay, which, when exposed to rain, would expand and burst the bricks. After this year more commodious structures were erected for public and private use, the means being supplied in part by traffic with emigrants for California. Conspicuous among them was the council-house on East Temple street, a two-story stone edifice, forty-five feet square,[15] used originally for church purposes, and afterward occupied by the state and territorial legislatures. In front of the council-house was temple block, on the south-west corner of which stood the tabernacle, built in 1851-2, on the ground now occupied by the assembly hall, with accommodation for 2,500 persons,[16] and consecrated on April 6th of the latter year.[17] Dur-

[14] See chap. xix., note 44, this vol.

[15] 'I was appointed superintendent of public works in the fall of 1848. The first house that was built was a little adobe place that was used for the church office...The little office that was the first place built was one story, about 18 by 12 feet, slanting roof covered with boards and dirt. This remained the church office for about two years...The foundation of the council-house was laid in the spring of 1849, and then the first story put up.' *Wells' Narr.*, MS., 41-2. Built by tithing. *Hist. B. Young*, MS., 1849, 55. At a meeting held Oct. 1, 1848, it was resolved to build a council-house, and on the 7th of November masons commenced laying the foundation. *Utah Early Records*, MS., 36, 38.

[16] Linforth gives its dimensions at 126 ft by 64, and states that the roof was arched, without being supported by pillars. *Route from Liverpool*, 109. In *Utah Early Records*, MS., 125, 127, it is stated that the dimensions were 120 by 60 ft, and that work was begun May 21st. See also *Deseret News*, May 17, 1851; *The Mormons at Home*, 112-13, 147-9; *Burton's City of the Saints*, 270.

[17] At a general conference, the proceedings of which are related in the *Contributor*, ii. 333. The conference lasted several days, and at its conclusion a collection was made to provide funds for a sacramental service, $149 being given in coin, together with several pounds' weight of silver watch-cases, spoons, rings, and ornaments. From the silver, cups were made, which are still in use at the tabernacle.

ing its construction, the saints in every part of the world were urged to self-denial, and it was voted to dispense with the use of tea, coffee, snuff, and tobacco, the sums thus saved to be also used for the building of the temple, which was to stand on the same block. The latter was to be built of stone quarried in the mountains, and a railroad from temple block to the quarry was chartered for the conveyance of building material.

Adjoining the tabernacle was the bowery, 100 by 60 feet, made of posts and boarding, completed three or four years later, and large enough to contain 8,000 people, a temporary structure having been erected in 1848. Among other buildings may be mentioned the tithing office, the social hall, and the seventies' hall of science. Several bridges were also built, which were paid for by the one per centum property tax.[18]

Thus at the western base of the Wasatch Mountains was laid out the city of Great Salt Lake, its buildings being distributed over a greater area than that on which stood, in 1850, the commercial metropolis of the United States.[19] Its site was on a slope, barely perceptible except toward the north, where it was enclosed by the Wasatch Range and a spur trending to the westward. Resting on the eastern bank of the Jordan, it was watered by several creeks; a canal, twelve miles long, crossing three streams, being proposed to convey the waters of the Big Cottonwood to the farm-lands south of the city; and through each street flowed a rivulet of pure water, which was thence diverted into the garden plats.

On the 24th of July, 1849, was held the second anniversary of the arrival of the pioneers.[20] At day-

[18] Resolved that a tax of one per ct per annum be assessed on property to repair public highways. *Hist. B. Young*, MS., 1849, 5.

[19] *Kane's The Mormons*, 74; *New York Tribune*, Oct. 7, 1849.

[20] The 4th and 24th of July were at first celebrated together, but on the latter date because bread and vegetables were more plentiful at the end of this month than at the beginning. *Utah Early Records*, MS., 91.

break cannon were fired and bands of music passed through the city, arousing the citizens for the great events of the day. A flag brought from Nauvoo was prominently displayed, and a larger flag was hoisted from the liberty-pole. A procession was formed of young men and maidens, who in appropriate costumes, bearing banners and singing, escorted Brigham to the bowery. They were received with shouts of "Hosanna to God and the Lamb!" While the governor and the church dignitaries were passing down the aisle cheers and shouts of "Hail to the governor of Deseret!" greeted them on every side. The declaration of independence and the constitution were then read, followed by patriotic addresses. The procession was then re-formed and marched to the feast served on tables fourteen hundred feet in length. "The tables were heavily loaded," says Brigham, "with all the luxuries of field and garden, and with nearly all the vegetables of the world; the seats were filled and refilled by a people who had been deprived of those luxuries for years, and they welcomed to their table every stranger within their border."[21] A greater variety was provided, as the saints had exchanged for many luxuries their flour, butter, potatoes, and other produce, with passing emigrants.

Not only on the pioneer anniversary but on the 4th of July,[22] at christmas week, and on other occa-

---

[21] 'The hospitalities of the occasion were not confined to the saints alone, but included several hundreds of California emigrants who had stopped to recruit, as well as threescore Indians,' says Eliza Snow. See *Snow's Biography*, 95–107, for description of the celebration; also *Kane's The Mormons*, 80–1; *Hist. B. Young*, MS., 108–116, 143; *Mrs Horne's Migrations*, MS., 30; *Frontier Guardian*, Sept. 19, 1849. After dinner four and twenty toasts were drunk, followed by volunteer toasts. President Young declared that he never saw such a dinner in his life. One of the elders remarked that 'it was almost a marvellous thing that everybody was satisfied, and...not an oath was uttered, not a man intoxicated, not a jar or disturbance occurred to mar the union, peace, and harmony of the day.' *Frontier Guardian*, Sept. 19, 1849. Among the guests was the Indian chief Walker, who, accompanied by Soweite, chief of the Utahs, and several hundred Indians, men, women, and children, had visited the city in Sept. 1848. *Utah Early Records*, MS., 33.

[22] For a description of 4th of July festivities, see *Frontier Guardian*, July 10, 1850, Oct. 3, 1851; *Deseret News*, July 12, 1851, July 10, 1852; *S. L. C. Contributor*, ii. 271.

sions festivities were held.[23]   Sometimes the guests
contributed toward the expense of the entertainment,
the amount that each one was expected to pay being
stated on the card of invitation.[24]

In winter, theatrical performances were given by
the Deseret Dramatic Association at the social hall,
and in summer at the bowery, the parts being well
sustained and the orchestra and decorations well appointed.[25]   At the former, private parties were given
when the gathering was too large for the residence of
the host; in the basement were appliances for cooking,
and adjoining was a dining-room with seats and tables
sufficient for three hundred persons.   All entertainments were opened with prayer; then came dancing,
songs, and music, followed by supper, the guests being
dismissed with a benediction at an early hour.

The public festivities of the Mormons were always
conducted under the auspices of the church, and none
were allowed to join in them who were not in good
standing.   To sing, dance, and rejoice before the
Lord was regarded almost as a religious duty, but
only those must rejoice whose hearts were pure and
whose hands were clean.   Thus, toward christmas of
this year, 1849, regulations were issued by the high
council for the observance of the approaching holidays.   They were to commence on the 20th of December and last until the council should declare them
at an end, officers being appointed to preside over the
dances.   No person who had been disfellowshipped

[23] The-christmas festival of 1851 is described in the *Deseret News*, Jan.
24, 1852.   ' On the 24th,' writes Brigham in regard to another occasion, ' I invited the wives of the twelve apostlcs, and other elders who were on missions,
with a number of my relatives, to dine at my house.   Seventy ladies sat down
at the first table.   I employed five sleighs to collect the company; the day
was stormy; near my house the snow drifted three feet deep.' *Hist. B. Young*,
MS., 1850, 2.

[24] Contributions were often made in the shape of eatables, and an in-door
picnic extemporized. *Ferris' Utah and the Mormons*, 306.

[25] In May 1851, the second act of ' Robert Macaire' was performed at the
bowery, the performance concluding with the farce of ' The Dead Shot.' *Contributor*, ii. 271.

or excommunicated was allowed to go forth to the dance.   Those who had sold liquor for gain, thereby corrupting the morals of society, were also disqualified.   All friends and well-wishers to society, all who remembered the poor and needy,[26] were invited to participate, though not members of the church.   But declares the council: "Woe unto them that dance with guile and malice in their hearts toward their neighbor!   Woe unto them that have secretly injured their neighbor or his or her property!   Woe unto them that are ministers of disorder and of evil!   If these shall go forth in the dance without confessing and forsaking their guilt, the faith of the council is that they seal their doom by it."

After their festivities the people returned, each to his calling, with renewed zest.   It was an article of faith among them that labor was honorable, and all who were not missionaries were expected to do their part.   By revelation, Joseph Smith was released from this obligation, but Brigham Young worked as a carpenter in his own mills.   Labor was regarded as a duty no less than prayer or temple service, each one working with his hands at whatsoever he found to do, and cheerfully contributing his tithes toward the church revenues, which were expended for public improvements, for the support of missions, and the relief of the sick and destitute.[27]

[26] ' Bring all your tithes and offerings to the proper place for the poor, that there be none hungry among us, and let the poor rejoice; and then you may rejoice in the dance to your heart's content.' Regulations of the High Council, in *Frontier Guardian*, Nov. 28, 1849.   Brigham, in an address at the state-house in 1852, at a party given to the legislature, said: 'I want it distinctly understood that fiddling and dancing are no part of our worship. My mind labors like a man logging.   This is the reason why I am fond of these pastimes; they give me a privilege to throw everything off and shake myself, that my body may exercise and my mind rest.'   And again: 'This company is controlled like the ship by the rudder in a gentle breeze, that can be turned hither and thither at the will and pleasure of him who commands.' *Hist. B. Young*, MS., 1852, 22.

[27] *Olshausen's Mormonen*, 164–5.   On July 28, 1850, the president writes to Orson Hyde, then at Kanesville.   'Our celebration was well attended.   It is a general time of health with the saints, and peace and plenty of hard work, as every one has been so busy that they can hardly get time to eat or sleep. You speak about hurry and bustle at Kanesville; but if you were here, to see, feel, and realize the burdens, labors, and responsibilities, which are daily,

Among the causes that led to the prosperity of the people of Utah at this period was the migration of gold-seekers to California. Hundreds of emigrants, turning aside to Salt Lake City, wearied and dispirited, their cattle worn out and their wagons broken, were glad to exchange them, together with their tools, household furniture, and spare clothing, for provisions and pack animals at very low rates.[28] Many were glad to remain during winter, and work for their livelihood. Though reports were freely circulated to the contrary, there is sufficient evidence that as a rule they were kindly treated, and not a few abandoned their search for gold to cast in their lot with the saints.[29]

The arrival in November of the first pack-mule train from California, laden with many luxuries and necessities, was an important event. The people formed in line, waiting hours for their turn to buy the limited amount allowed.[30] When a sack of potatoes was

hourly, momentarily, rolling, piling, tumbling, and thundering upon us, you would at least conclude that there was no danger of our getting the gout from idleness or too much jollity.' *Frontier Guardian*, Sept. 18, 1850. Mention of cholera on the Mississippi and Missouri rivers in the spring of 1849 is made by Brigham. 'Many Mormon brethren and sisters emigrating on those rivers died; 60 died going from St Louis to Kanesville, mostly from England and Wales, under Capt. Dan. Jones.' *Hist. B. Young*, MS., 1849, 85.

[28] Horses, harnesses, carriages, wagons, etc., were bought of eager emigrants at one fifth of their cost in the states. *Utah Early Records*, MS., 113.

[29] In the autumn of 1849 many emigrants, while resting in Salt Lake City, wrote letters to their friends, in which they acknowledged the kindness and hospitality shown them by the saints. Extracts from these letters were published in newspapers throughout the states. Gunnison, *The Mormons*, 65, says: 'Their many deeds of charity to the sick and broken-down gold-seekers all speak loudly in their favor, and must eventually redound to their praise.' See also *Kane's The Mormons*, 76-7; Stansbury's *Expedition to G. S. Lake*, i. 134. In March 1851, numbers of emigrants were baptized, and most of them remained in Utah. *Id.*, 123. D. J. Staples, who remained at S. L. City for two or three weeks with a Boston party bound for California in 1849, says: 'The Mormons showed their kindness in every possible way, supplying all wants and taking care of the sick.' *Incidents and Inform.*, in *Cal.*, MS., D. 1-3. See also *Van Dyke's Statement*, in *Id.*, 1. Among later instances may be mentioned that of John C. Frémont, who with nine white men and twelve Indians arrived at Parowan Jan. 7, 1854, in a starving condition. He was supplied with provisions and fresh animals, setting forth eastward on the 20th.

[30] Brown sugar was $1 a lb.; and everything else in proportion. No one was allowed more than one pound of anything. *Mrs Horne's Migrations*, MS., 30.

brought into the valley in the spring, they were eagerly bought at any price. From four small ones, costing fifty cents, was obtained a bushel of good-sized potatoes which were saved for seed.

The immigration during the season numbered some 1,400 souls, who were added to the settlers in the valley,[31] and who, with the number remaining of those originally bound for California, made a large population to clothe, feed, and shelter.

A carrying company was also established[32] in December for the purpose of conveying passengers and goods from the Missouri River to the gold regions of California. In their prospectus, the proprietors set forth that, residing as they did in the valley, and being acquainted with the route, they could provide fresh animals as they were needed and save the loss of hundreds and thousands of dollars that had been incurred by former parties through inexperience. For passengers to Sutter's Fort, the rate was $300, of which $200 must be paid in advance, and the remainder on reaching Salt Lake City. For freight, the terms were $250 per ton, of which two thirds must also be paid in advance.

A small company under Captain Lamoreaux left the valley for Green River, and there established a ferry and trading post; among them were wagon-makers and blacksmiths, whose services would be invaluable.

When the immigrants of this year arrived in the valley of the Great Salt Lake, many of them were

[31] 'Our cattle stampeded, and at the south pass of the Platte we were overtaken by a heavy storm, in which 70 animals were frozen. We made our journey to Salt Lake City, 1,034 miles, in 145 days, arriving Oct. 27th.' *Geo. A. Smith's Autobiog.*, in *Tullidge's Mag.*, July 1884. The cattle of the California Enterprise Company, under Judge Thos K. Owen of Ill., stampeded near the forks of the Platte and ran back 130 miles in about 26 hours; they were brought along by Capt. Allen Taylor's company, which received from their owners a series of resolutions expressive of their gratitude. *Hist. B. Young*, MS., 1849, 157–8.

[32] Termed the Great Salt Lake Valley Carrying Company. The proprietors were Shadrach Roundy, Jedediah M. Grant, John S. Fullmer, George D. Grant, and Russell Homer. *Utah Early Records*, MS., 101; *Hist. B. Young*, MS., 1849, 168.

almost destitute of clothing,[33] bedding, and household furniture, such articles as they possessed having been exchanged for food during their journey. In 1848 it had been prophesied by Heber C. Kimball that the commodities, known among the brethren as 'states goods,' would be as cheap in Salt Lake City as in New York; while Brigham Young, soon after setting forth from Nauvoo, had made a similar prediction, declaring that within five years his people would be more prosperous than they had ever been. Both prophecies were fulfilled,[34] when, during the first years of the gold fever, company after company came pouring into Utah, which might now be termed the half-way house of the nation. Several hundred California-bound emigrants arrived in the valley in 1849, too late to continue their journey on the northern route, and proposed to spend the winter in the valley. There was scarcely provision enough for those already there, and as Jefferson Hunt of the battalion offered to pilot the company over the southern route, they decided to undertake the trip, and started on the 8th of October, arriving in California on the 22d of December.[35] On the 1st of December nineteen men came into the city on foot, nearly famished, having been two days making their way over Big Mountain. Their wagons had been left on Echo Creek, and their animals at Willow Springs, where the snow, they said, was six feet deep on a level. Though many of these adventurers were poor, some of the trains were loaded with valuable merchandise, for which their owners

[33] Parley relates that during 1848 he and his family were compelled to go barefooted for several months, reserving their Indian moccasins for extra occasions. *Autobiog.*, 405.

[34] In the summer of 1849, almost every article except tea and coffee sold at 50 per cent below the prices ruling in eastern cities. *Frontier Guardian*, Sept. 5, 1849.

[35] 'The company became dissatisfied at the continued southern direction. At Beaver Creek, one Capt. Smith came up with a company of packers, saying that he had maps and charts of a new route, called Walker's cut-off. All the packers and most of Capt. Hunter's co. joined Smith. After wandering about the mountains for a time many turned back and took the southern route, while Capt. Smith and a few others struggled through and arrived in California on foot.' *Hist. B. Young*, MS., 1849, 167.

expected to find a ready market on reaching their destination. But while sojourning in the valley, news arrived that vessels laden with similar merchandise had arrived in San Francisco, or were far on their way, and that already the market was greatly over-stocked.[36] The emigrants were therefore glad to exchange their costly outfits and their trading goods for whatever they could get in exchange, a single horse or a mule, with a small stock of provisions, be-ing sometimes accepted as an equivalent for property that had cost the owner thousands of dollars. The cattle thus obtained by the settlers, in barter, after being fattened on the nutritious grasses of the valley, were driven to California, where a sure and profitable market was found.

As a result of the California-bound migration, there followed an enormous advance in the price of provi-sions, flour selling before the harvest of 1850 at one dol-lar per pound, and after harvest at twenty-five dollars per cental.[37] Throughout the autumn of this year the grist-mills were run to their utmost capacity, grinding wheat for the passing emigrants, who at any cost must procure sufficient to carry them to the gold mines. Some other articles of food were for a time equally scarce, sugar selling at the rate of three pounds for two dollars;[38] though beef was plentiful, and could be had for ten cents per pound.[39] It is probable,

[36] 'Thousands of emigrants...have passed through Salt Lake City this sea-son, exchanging domestic clothing, wagons, etc., for horses and mules.' *Hist. B. Young*, MS., 1849, 143.

[37] *Utah Early Records*, MS., 112; *Contributor*, ii. 240. See also *Frontier Guardian*, Sept. 18, 1850, where is a copy of an address delivered by Brigham Young at the bowery, S. L. City. 'I say unto you, farmers, keep your wheat, for I foresee if you are not careful starvation will be on our heels.' It was not intended, however, that food should be withheld from the destitute; in another address from Brigham, published in the same paper, we read: 'I say to you, latter-day saints, let no man go hungry from your doors; divide with them and trust in God for more.' 'Emigrants, don't let your spirits be worn down; and shame be to the door where a man has to go hungry away.'

[38] On Nov. 21, 1849, Mr Vasquez opened a store in Salt Lake City, and met with ready sale for his sugar at this rate. *Utah Early Records*, MS., 100.

[39] Fuel and building material were costly, firewood being worth, in 1850, ten dollars per cord, adobe bricks a dollar a hundred, and lumber five dollars the hundred feet. Two years later, 'states goods' had also become scarce throughout the territory, linen selling for 20 to 30 cents per yard, flannel for

however, that these rates represent the prices charged to passing emigrants, for at this period the wages of laborers did not exceed $2 per day, and of skilled mechanics $3. The saints prided themselves upon their honorable dealings with these strangers, and the moderate prices demanded, though frequently charged with swindling.[40] They could afford to part with their produce, because they had learned to dispense with many articles which among other communities were considered necessaries. For men who had fed during their first winter in the valley on hides and roots, it was no great hardship to dispense for a season with a portion of their provisions, their grain, beef, and butter, their coffee and sugar, in return for which they received such value.

It was not of course to be expected that while thousands of California-bound emigrants were passing each year through the Mormon settlements, the saints should themselves entirely escape the gold fever. In November 1848, several small parties of the battalion found their way to Salt Lake City,[41] some of them bringing considerable quantities of gold-dust, which, as they relate, had come into their possession in this wise.

In September 1847 about forty of the battalion men arrived at Sutter's Fort in search of employment and were hired by Sutter to dig the races for a flour mill about six miles from the fort and for a saw-mill some forty-five miles distant.[42] The latter work being completed in January 1848, and the frame of the

---

30 to 40 cents, prints for 25 to 50 cents, and jeans for 75 cents to $1.25; while a bottle of ink cost $2, and a ream of writing-paper $10 to $12. *Deseret News*, Nov. 6, 1852, where it is stated that on some classes of goods traders realized from 200 to 10,000 per cent profit.

[40] ' I saved straw that spring and braided forty hats...I made one to order and sold to an emigrant at the usual price, $1. He was surprised at its cheapness, but in all our dealings with emigrants we took no advantage of them. I took boarders at five or six dollars a week.' *Mrs Richards' Rem.*, MS., 36.

[41] Others had already arrived in June and Sept. of this year. *Utah Early Records*, MS., 30–1.

[42] Their pay was to be 12½ cents per cubic yard, with rations and free pasture for their stock. *Tyler's Hist. Mormon Battalion*, 332.

building erected, water was turned into the flume
on the 24th, and the fall being considerable, washed
out a hole near the base of the mill on reaching the
tail-race, whereupon Marshall, Sutter's partner, and
superintendent of the party, examined the spot, fearing that the water would undermine the foundations.
While thus engaged, he observed there pieces of yellow glistening metal, and picking up a handful put
them in his pocket, not knowing what they were, and
supposing probably that he had found nothing more
valuable than iron pyrites.

They were no iron pyrites, however, that Marshall
had found, but, as it proved, nuggets of gold, the
largest of them being worth about five dollars.   The
discovery was revealed in confidence to three of the
saints, who unearthed a few more specimens, and soon
afterward removed to a sand-bar in the Sacramento
river, since known as Mormon Island.   Here was gold
in paying quantities, the average earnings of each
man being twenty to thirty dollars per day.   But
though dust and nuggets were freely shown to the
brethren, there were few who would believe their
senses, and for weeks the matter caused no excitement.
At length, however, the secret was disclosed, which
soon transformed the peaceful valleys of California into
busy mining camps, changing as if by magic the entire
face of the country.   How throughout the settlements
on seaboard and on river the merchant abandoned his
wares, the lawyer his clients, the parson his flock, the
doctor his patients, the farmer his standing grain—all
making one mad rush for the gold-fields, some on
horseback, some with pack-mules, some with wheelbarrows, some with costly outfits, and some with no
outfit save the clothes on their backs—is fully set forth
in my *History of California*.

When the disbanded soldiers arrived in the valley
of the Great Salt Lake and displayed their treasures,
a cry was raised among the saints, "To California; to
the land of Ophir that our brethren have discovered!"

But from the twelve came a stern rebuke. "The true use of gold is for paving streets, covering houses, and making culinary dishes; and when the saints shall have preached the gospel, raised grain, and built up cities enough, the Lord will open the way for a supply of gold to the perfect satisfaction of his people. Until then, let them not be over-anxious, for the treasures of the earth are in the Lord's storehouse, and he will open the doors thereof when and where he pleases."[43]

President John Smith wrote to the saints in California in March 1848, urging them to gather at the Great Salt Lake, "that they might share in the blessings to be conferred on the faithful; and warned them against settling down at ease in California with an eye and a half upon this world and its goods, and half an eye dimly set towards Zion on account of the high mountains and the privations to be endured by the saints."

"If we were to go to San Francisco and dig up chunks of gold," said Brigham to the returned battalion on the 1st of October, 1848, "or find it in the valley, it would ruin us." In an address on the sabbath he said: "I hope the gold mines will be no nearer than eight hundred miles...There is more delusion and the people are more perfectly crazy on this continent than ever before...If you elders of Israel want to go to the gold mines, go and be damned. If you go, I would not give a picayune to keep you from damnation."[44] "I advise the corrupt, and all who want, to go to California and not come back, for I will not fellowship them...Prosperity and riches blunt the feelings of man. If the people were united, I would send men to get the gold who would care no more about it than the dust under their feet, and then we would gather millions into the church...

[43] Second General Epistle of the Twelve, dated Salt Lake City, Oct. 12, 1849, in *Frontier Guardian*, Dec. 26, 1849.
[44] *Hist. B. Young*, MS., 1849, 100-2, 123.

Some men don't want to go after gold, but they are the very men to go."[45]

Thus the threatened migration was stayed; a few companies departed,[46] and were asked in all kindness never to return. "If they have a golden god in their hearts," said Brigham, "they had better stay were they are." But the majority of the settlers were well content to abide in the valley, building up towns, planting farms, and tending stock in their land of promise.

[45] On the 7th of December, 1848, Brigham writes in his journal: 'Some few have caught the gold fever; I counselled such, and all the saints, to remain in the valleys of the mountains, make improvements, build comfortable houses, and raise grain against the days of famine and pestilence with which the earth would be visited.'

[46] The gold fever first broke out in June 1848, news of the discovery being brought by a party of battalion men that arrived from California in that month. In March 1849, about a dozen families departed or were preparing to depart for the mines. In March 1851, about 520 of the saints were gathered at Payson, Utah county, most of them for the purpose of moving to California. *Utah Early Records*, MS., 31, 69, 122.

CHAPTER XIII.

SETTLEMENT AND OCCUPATION OF THE COUNTRY.

1847–1852.

FOUNDING OF CENTREVILLE—BOUNTIFUL—OGDEN—LYNNE—EASTON—MAR-
RIOTSVILLE—SAN PETE—PROVO—INDIAN WAR—WALLED CITIES—EV-
ANSVILLE—LEHI—BATTLE CREEK—PLEASANT GROVE—AMERICAN FORK
—PAYSON—NEPHI—MANTI—CHIEF WALKER—FILLMORE—SITE CHOSEN
FOR THE CAPITAL—TOOELE—GRANTSVILLE—KAYSVILLE—LITTLE SALT
LAKE—PAROWAN—CEDAR CITY—PARAGOONAH—FORTS WALKER AND
HARMONY—BOX ELDER CREEK—BRIGHAM CITY—WILLARD CITY—
SAN BERNARDINO IN CALIFORNIA.

IN the autumn of 1847 one Thomas Grover arrived
with his family on the bank of a stream twelve miles
north of Salt Lake City, and now called Centreville
Creek. His intention was to pasture stock for the
winter; and for this purpose a spot was chosen where
the stream spreading over the surface forms plats of
meadow-land, the soil being a black, gravelly loam.
Here Grover, joined by others in the spring, resolved
to remain, though in the neighborhood were encamped
several bands of Indians, and this notwithstanding
that as yet there was no white settlement north of
Salt Lake City. Land was ploughed and sown in
wheat and vegetables, the crops being more promising
than those to the south. But in May of the following year the settlers were startled, not by the war-
whoop of the Utahs, but by hordes of black monster
crickets, swarming down from the bench-lands, as at
Salt Lake City, and bringing destruction on field and
garden. They turned out to do battle with the foe;
ditches were dug around the grain-fields, and the

HIST. UTAH. 20

water of the stream diverted into them, while men,
women, and children, armed with clubs, checked the
advance of the devouring host.   Enough of the crop
was saved to supply the wants of the settlers, and
their energy, on this occasion, coupled with a supposed

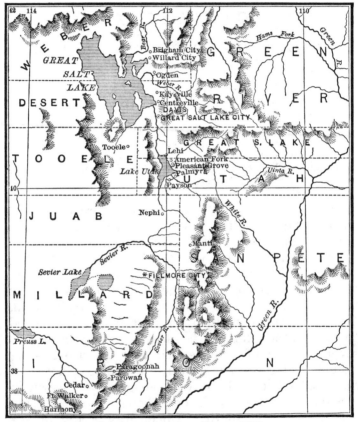

SETTLEMENTS AT THE END OF 1852.

miraculous visitation of gulls, probably saved a fore-
taste of the disaster of 1848.[1]   A site for a town was

[1] After this incident the water in the creek began to fail, thus for a time
preventing the growth of the settlement. In 1880 there was a good flow of
water, sufficient for the wants of forty families, with their orchards, gardens,
and farm lands. N. T. Porter, in *Utah Sketches*, MS., 177.

surveyed in the autumn of 1849, and the place was named Centreville.

Near Centreville, in what was afterward Davis county, a settlement was begun in the spring of 1848 by Peregrine Sessions, the place being called Bountiful.[2]

As early as 1841 the country round where the city of Ogden was laid out was held as a Spanish grant by Miles M. Goodyear, who built a fort, consisting of a stockade and a few log houses, near the confluence of the Weber and Ogden rivers.[3] On the 6th of June, 1848, James Brown, of the battalion, coming from California with $5,000, mostly in gold-dust, purchased the tract from Goodyear.[4] As it was one of the most fertile spots in all that region, grain and vegetables being raised in abundance, not only numbers of the brethren from Salt Lake City, but after a while gentiles from the western states, settled there. In August 1850 Brigham Young, Heber C. Kimball, Orson Hyde, and others laid out the city of Ogden, so called from the name of the river.[5] The

[2] A little to the south of Centreville was a small settlement which at first went by the name of Call's settlement, afterward taking the name Bountiful. *Utah Early Records*, MS., 132. In *Sloan's Utah Gazetteer*, 130-1, it is stated that there were three settlements of this name—East, West, and South Bountiful—West Bountiful being settled in 1848 by James Fackrell and his family, South Bountiful by George Meeyers and Edwin Page. All are now on the line of the Utah Central railroad. In January of this year Sessions also founded a settlement which bore his name, about 15 miles north of S. L. City. *Harrison's Crit. Notes on Utah*, MS., 45.

[3] The tract is described as commencing at the mouth of Weber Cañon, following the base of the mountains north to the hot springs, thence westward to the Great Salt Lake, along the southern shore of the lake to a point opposite Weber Cañon, and thence to the point of beginning. *Stanford's Ogden City*, MS., 1; *Richards' Narr.*, MS., passim.

[4] Some say for $1,950; others place the amount at $3,000. See *Richards' Narr.*, MS.; *Stanford's Ogden City*, MS.

[5] *Utah Early Records*, MS., 112. See also *S. L. C. Contributor*, ii. 240; and *Deseret News*, Sept. 7, 1850. *Stanford's Ogden City*, MS., 1-2. The site was selected as early as Sept. 1849, on the south side of the Ogden River, at the point of bench-land between the forks of the Ogden and Weber rivers, so that water from both streams might be used for irrigation. *Utah Early Records*, MS., 94. North Ogden, formerly called Ogden Hole, once the resort of a noted desperado, was laid out in 1851. Amos Maycock, in *Utah Sketches*, MS., 114. 'Heber C. Kimball, Willard Richards, J. M. Grant, Brigham Young, and several others ascended a sand hill, Sept. 3d, to discover the best location for a town, which we finally decided should be on the south side of

president urged the people to move at once to their city lots, and to build for themselves substantial dwellings, a meeting-house, and a school-house, to fence their gardens and plant fruit-trees, so that the place might become a permanent settlement, and the headquarters of the northern portion of the territory. Before the end of the year a log structure was finished, which served for school and meeting house, and soon afterward the settlers commenced to build a wall for protection against the Indians, completing it about three years later at a cost of some $40,000.[6] So rapid was the growth of the town, that in 1851 it was made a stake of Zion,[7] divided into wards, and incorporated by act of legislature.[8]

In 1848 Isaac Morley and two hundred others settled in the southern part of the valley of the San Pete[9]—particulars to be mentioned hereafter.

In the spring of 1849 a stockade was built and log houses erected by the pioneer settlers of Utah county, numbering about thirty families,[10] near the Timpanogos or Provo River, and below the point where a small creek issuing from it discharges into Lake Utah. To

Ogden...A dance was instituted in the evening.' *Hist. B. Young*, MS., 1849, 124.

[6] Raised by taxation. *Stanford's Ogden City*, MS., 4.

[7] Of which Lorin Farr was appointed president, and R. Dana and David B. Dillie councillors. *Id.*, 3.

[8] The first municipal election was held on Oct. 23d, Farr being chosen mayor, Gilbert Belnap marshal, David Moore recorder, and William Critchellow justice of the peace. Four aldermen and twelve councillors were also elected. *Id.*, 4. According to the statement of John Brown, a resident of Ogden in 1884, there were 100 families in Ogden in 1852. Brown, a native of Yorkshire, England, came to Winter Quarters in 1849, remained in the church for 21 years, and was then cut off at his own request. In 1883 he was the proprietor of the hotel which bears his name. Two miles north of Ogden a settlement named Lynne was formed in 1849. *Stanford's Weber Co.*, MS., 1. Near Lynne a few families formed a settlement named Slaterville in 1852-3, but on account of troubles with Indians, moved into Lynne in 1854. *Id.*, 3. Eight miles south-east of Ogden, at the mouth of Weber Cañon, on the line of the railway, a small settlement named Easton was formed in 1852, a branch of the church organized, and A. Wadsworth appointed bishop. Three miles northwest of Ogden a settlement named Marriotsville was formed in 1850 by three families. The neighborhood was infested with wolves and bears, and near by were the lodges of 200 Indian warriors. *Id.*, 10.

[9] So called from the name of an Indian chief. *Richards' Narr.*, MS., 66.

[10] Under the leadership of John and Isaac Higbee and Jefferson Hunt of the battalion. Albert Jones, in *Utah Sketches*, MS., 54.

this settlement was given the name of Fort Utah. Within the space enclosed by the stockade was a mound, the top of which was levelled, and on a platform built thereon were mounted several twelve-pounders for the purpose of intimidating the Indians. But the Indians were not to be thus intimidated. In the autumn they began to steal the grain and cattle of the white men, and one of their number being killed while in the act of pilfering, hostilities broke out and the fort was soon in a state of siege.

Indeed, ill feeling on the part of the Indians had begun to show itself the previous year. Vasquez and Bridger wrote to Brigham on the 17th of April, 1849, that the Utes were badly disposed toward Americans, and that chiefs Elk and Walker were urging the Utes to attack the settlements in Utah Valley. The brethren were advised to protect themselves, but if the Indians were friendly, to teach them to raise grain, and "order them to quit stealing." Brigham was persuaded that Bridger was his enemy, and expressed the conviction that he and the other mountaineers were responsible for all the Indian trouble, and that he was watching every movement of the Mormons and reporting to Thomas H. Benton at Washington.[11] Alexander Williams and D. B. Huntington were empowered by the council to trade exclusively with the Indians on behalf of the community.

On the 31st of January, 1850, Isaac Higbee, of Fort Utah, reported at Salt Lake that the Indians of Utah Valley had stolen fifty or sixty head of cattle or horses, threatening further depredations, and asked permission to chastise them, which was granted. General Daniel H. Wells then called for volunteers from the militia, and on the 4th of February Captain George D. Grant started with a company for Utah Fort, followed soon after by Major Andrew Lytle.

[11] 'I believe that old Bridger is death on us, and if he knew that 400,000 Indians were coming against us, and any man were to let us know, he would cut his throat...His letter is all bubble and froth...Vasquez is a different sort of man.' *Hist. B. Young*, MS., 1849, 77.

The Indians were attacked on the 8th, and took refuge in a log house, whence they were dislodged next day, and driven into the thicket along the Provo River. In this encounter Joseph Higbee was killed, and Alexander Williams, Samuel Kearns, Albert Miles, Jabez Nowland, and two men named Orr and Stevens were wounded.

On the 11th the Indians fled from the thicket to Rock Cañon, whither the volunteers pursued them; but failing to find them, the white men proceeded to the west and south sides of Utah Lake, and shot all they could find there.

During the expedition twenty-seven warriors were killed. The women and children threw themselves upon the settlers for protection and support, and were fed and cared for in Salt Lake City until spring. Thus Utah Valley was entirely rid of hostile Indians. Until 1852 there was no further trouble with them of a serious nature;[12] and thus ended the first Indian war of Utah, which like all the others was rather a tame affair. It was the mission of the Mormons to convert the Indians, who were their brethren, and not to kill them.

Later in the year was founded the city of Provo,[13] somewhat to the eastward of Fort Utah, near the western base of the Wasatch Mountains, on a site where timber and pasture were abundant,[14] and where the gradual fall of the Timpanogos affords excellent water-power. In March 1851 it was organized as a stake of Zion. The settlement was pushed forward with the energy characteristic of the settlers. Before the close of 1850 more than twenty dwellings

[12] 'I was ordered not to leave that valley until every Indian was out of it.' *Wells' Narr.*, MS., 45-6.

[13] At a general conference of the church, held in October 1849, it was ordered that a city be laid out in the Utah Valley, and called Provo. *Utah Early Records*, MS., 97.

[14] A heavy growth of cotton-wood and box-elder covered the river bottom, with a large belt of cedar extending some four miles north from the river and about half a mile in width. Bunch-grass was very plentiful. Albert Jones, in *Utah Sketches*, MS., 55.

had been completed;[15] and before the end of 1851 the place began to wear the appearance of a town, among the buildings in course of erection being a flouring-mill and two hotels; manufactures were started; all were busy the livelong day at farm or workshop, and in the evening, writes Elder Isaac Higbee, in February 1852, "We have on Monday singing-school, on Tuesday lyceum, on Wednesday seventies' meeting, on Thursday prayer-meeting, on Friday spelling-school, and on Saturday the meeting of the lesser priesthood."[16]

On Dry Creek, near the head of Lake Utah and about sixteen miles northwest of Provo, a settlement was formed in 1851, named Evansville.[17] The neighboring lands were surveyed in lots of forty acres, and to each new settler as he arrived was given a plat of this size until the tract was exhausted. The soil was rich; but here, as elsewhere in the northern part of Utah county, water was scarce. A supply was obtained by diverting a portion of the waters of American Fork creek,[18] and thereafter the affairs of the settlement prospered so rapidly that, in February 1852, the place was incorporated under the name of Lehi, or as it is sometimes written, Lehigh.

South-east of Lehi, on a plain about three miles east of Lake Utah, was founded, in 1850, a settle-

[15] *Deseret News*, Jan. 24, 1852. Ross R. Rogers l·uilt the first adobe house in 1851. Albert Jones, in *Utah Sketches*, MS., 53. A large building was erected in 1852 for George A. Smith, the prophet's cousin, then president of Utah co. stake. It was afterward used as a school-house and known as the seminary. In 1851 an adobe wall was commenced, 14 feet in height and four feet at the base. Three sides of it, with bastions, port-holes, and gates, were completed in 1855, the finished length being then two and a half miles. A portion of this wall remained in 1880. *Id.*, 57. These walls were built about several of the settlements. 'It was usual for our people to protect themselves by building what we call a fort—a place the people could get into in the event of a raid. Our wall was a kind of concrete. In Mount Pleasant their walls were built of cobble rock, parts of which are now standing. At that place they put a grist-mill inside, so the Indians couldn't cut them off. At Nephi the Indians did cut them off from their grist-mill.' *Wells' Narr.*, MS., 60.

[16] Letter in *Deseret News*, Feb. 21, 1852.

[17] A few houses were built on an adjacent site by David Savage and others in 1850. David Evans, in *Utah Sketches*, MS., 37.

[18] By a ditch seven miles in length.

ment first known as Battle Creek, and afterward called
Pleasant Grove. It was here that the first engagement with the natives occurred. Captain Scott with
a band of thirty or forty men started south in pursuit
of Indians who had stolen fourteen horses from Orr's
herd, on Wilson Creek, in Utah Valley, and several
cattle from Tooele Valley. The band was found encamped on a creek in the midst of willows and dense
brushwood in a deep ravine. After a desultory fight
of three or four hours, four Indians were killed, but
none of the settlers. As was their custom, the women
and children of the slain followed the victorious party
to their camp.[19]

In the neighborhood of Pleasant Grove were good
farming land, good range for stock, and water-power,
inducements which quickly attracted emigrants, and
caused the place to thrive rapidly. In 1853 the present site was laid out,[20] and to this spot were transferred,
on July 24th of that year, the effects of the community, then numbering seventy-five families.

Between Lehi and Pleasant Grove the village of
American Fork was founded in 1850, on a site where
were farming and grazing land of fair quality, a little
timber, springs of fresh water, and a stream that could
be easily diverted for purposes of irrigation.[21]

About twenty miles south of Provo the settlement
of Payson was laid out on the banks of the Peteetneet
Creek;[22] a few miles to the north-east of Payson was
founded a village named Palmyra, containing, at the
close of 1852, fifty families; and in 1851, on Salt Creek,

[19] Hist. B. Young, MS., 1849, 24–5; John Brown, in Utah Sketches, MS.,
30. The first Indian trouble was a little skirmish between some sheep-herders
and Indians. Wells' Narr., MS., 43.

[20] By George A. Smith and Ezra T. Benson.

[21] The site was laid out by George A. Smith, assisted by L. E. Harrington,
Arza Adams, Stephen Chipman, William Greenwood, and Stephen Mott. A.
J. Stewart was the surveyor. The first house was built by Adams and Chip-
man in 1850; the first grist-mill by Adams in 1851; and the first store was
opened by Thomas McKenzie in the same year. L. E. Harrington, in Utah
Sketches, MS., 121.

[22] The first settlers were James Pace, Andrew Jackson Stewart, and John
C. Searle. Joseph S. Tanner, in Utah Sketches, MS., 3.

twenty-five miles to the south, the site of Nephi, in
Juab county, was first occupied by Joseph L. Heywood. Nephi was surveyed in the autumn of 1852,
the spot being selected on account of its beauty and convenience. A fort was afterward built, surrounded by
a wall twelve feet in height and six feet at the base.[23]
Through this town passed the old California or southern road made by the pioneers in 1849; and here, in
cabins built of mud and willows, lived, at the close of
1852, more than forty families.[24]

I have mentioned that Isaac Morley with two
hundred settlers went into the San Pete country in
1848. On the 14th of June, 1849, a council was held
at Salt Lake City, at which were present a Ute chief
named Walker,[25] and twelve of his tribe. After the
pipe of peace had been passed around, Walker declared
himself a friend of the settlers, and asked their sachem
to send a party southward to the valley of San Pete,
where they might teach his people how to build and
farm. "Within six moons," answered Brigham, "I
will send you a company." In the spring of this
year the party sent to explore this valley had already
selected the site of the present town of Manti, on a
branch of the San Pete Creek, though there was little
in the neighborhood to invite the settler, sage brush
and rabbit brush, the red man and the coyote, being

[23] Its length was 420 rods, and its cost $8,400. Portions of it remained in
1880. Geo. Teasdale, in *Id.*, 111.

[24] The first settler was Timothy B. Foote, who, with his wife and six children, took up his abode in this neighborhood in the autumn of 1851. Before
the end of the year he was joined by seven other families. *Id.*, 107; and before the end of 1852, 35 additional families settled at Nephi. *Deseret News*,
Dec. 11, 1852.

[25] 'Walker was the chief of the Ute Indians...Uinta was the great chief
of this region, and Ora was the head chief of the Ute nation...Walker's headquarters were the Sevier, generally; he would pay a visit to San Pete once a
year.' *Wells' Narr.*, MS., 48, 56. 'Walker used to go into California to steal
horses; had a place of concealment among the mountains. At one time, while
there, people were so incensed that they turned out to capture him and his
band. In the dead of night he quietly took possession of their horses and
trappings and came into Utah triumphant. He would boast of his proceedings some time later. He never brought stolen goods into the settlements,
but secreted them among his people.' *Utah Notes*, MS., 8.

the principal features. In November the town was laid out.[26] The name of Manti was suggested by Brigham, who declared that on this spot should be raised one of the cities spoken of in the book of Mormon, and here he built with his own hands an adobe house, which in 1883 was still pointed out to visitors as one of the curiosities of the place.[27]

On Chalk Creek, in Pahvan Valley, south-west of Manti and about a hundred and fifty miles from Salt Lake City, a site was chosen by Brigham, in October 1851, for the capital of the territory, and named Fillmore, in honor of the president.[28] During 1852 the foundations of the state-house were laid, and many private buildings erected, the settlement numbering about seventy families at the close of the year.

In the autumn of 1849, John Rowberry, Cyrus Tolman, and others set forth from Salt Lake City to explore the country west of the Jordan Valley, in search of grazing lands whereon to pasture their stock. Crossing the mountain range which forms the western boundary of Cedar and Jordan valleys,[29] they discovered a spot where grass, timber, and water were abundant, and encamped for the winter on the banks of a stream now called Emigrant Cañon creek. Returning in the spring, they made their report to Brigham, who recommended them to form a settlement in that neighborhood. To this the men consented. "By what name will you call it?" asked the

[26] Including 110 blocks, each 26 rods square, with eight lots to each block. *Utah Early Records*, MS., 111. The site was surveyed by Jesse W. Fox, under Brigham's direction. J. B. Maiben, in *Utah Sketches*, MS., 172.

[27] In June 1852 a fort was completed, the walls being eight feet high and two feet thick. *Deseret News*, July 10, 1852.

[28] In the *Deseret News* of Jan. 24, 1852, is a letter to Brigham from Anson Call, one of the first settlers, dated Nov. 24, 1851. 'We have had an addition of three to our camp since you left; have built a corral according to your instructions, including about two and a half acres of ground. We found, upon trial, that the ground was so dry and hard, being also rocky, that it was next to an impossibility to stockade or picket in our houses with the tools we have to work with; so we have built our houses in close order, having our doors or windows on the outside.'

[29] Now called the Oquirrh Mountains, Oquirrh being probably an Indian word.

president. Tolman suggested Cedar Valley, a large belt of cedar having been found there; but Brigham recommended Tule, as reeds were plentiful in that neighborhood. And so it was ordered; and this word, spelled Tooele by Thomas Bullock, the president's private secretary, is still applied to the town, the site of which was di.covered by Rowberry and his comrades.[30]

In the winter of 1849–50, Edward Phillips and John H. Green proceeded northward from Salt Lake City, intending to settle in the neighborhood of Ogden. When within twelve miles of that place, the snow-drifts prevented further progress, and turning aside to Sandy Creek, or as it was later termed, Kay Creek, where the land was covered with bunch-grass, they resolved to take up their abode in that neighborhood. After passing the winter in Salt Lake City, the two men set forth in the spring of 1850, accompanied by William Kay and others, and founded the settlement of Kaysville.[31] In September it was organized as a ward, Kay being appointed bishop, with Green and Phillips as councillors.[32]

In the winter of 1849–50, it was ordered by the first presidency that Parley P. Pratt, with a company of fifty men, should explore the southern part of the territory in the neighborhood of Little Salt Lake. They found the brethren at Manti well pleased with their location, there being a good stone quarry and an abun-

[30] The site was surveyed by Jesse W. Fox, under Rowberry's direction. The first house was built by Tolman, who in partnership with Rowberry erected a saw-mill nine miles north of the settlement. The first grist-mill was built by Ezaias Edwards, and the first store opened by Isaac Lee. John Rowberry and F. M. Lyman, in *Utah Sketches*, MS., 150. A meeting-house 24 feet square had been finished in March 1852. *Deseret News*, April 17, 1852. Twelve miles to the west of Tooele was a small settlement named Grantsville.

[31] From 5 bushels of club-wheat, planted during this year, 250 bushels were raised. Edward Phillips, in *Utah Sketches*, 81–2.

[32] A mile and a half south of Sandy Creek was a herd-house, the property of S. O. Holmes. Near this spot a fort was built, surrounded with a mud wall.

dance of cedar at hand.   At the Sevier River they met
Charles Shumway, James Allred, and Elijah Ward;
also Walker, the Utah war chief, and his people, many
of whom were sick with the measles.   They proceeded
to explore the country for some distance round.   On
the 1st of January, 1850, they were on Virgen River,
whence they passed up the Santa Clara, and came to
"the valley subsequently named Mountain Meadows."
One division of the party explored Little Salt Lake.
Beaver Creek was pronounced an excellent place for
a settlement.   In a half-frozen condition they reached
Provo the 30th, and next day some of them were in
Salt Lake.

The report of Parley being favorable, a party of
about one hundred and seventy persons, well supplied with wagons, implements, live-stock, seeds, and
provisions,[33] set forth, in charge of George A. Smith,
on the 7th of December, 1850, toward the south;
and on Centre Creek, in a valley of the Wasatch
Range, about two hundred and fifty miles from Salt
Lake City, built a fort near the site of the present town of Parowan.[34]   Pasture and timber were
plentiful, the soil was of good quality, and in the season of 1851 a bountiful harvest was gathered from
about one thousand acres of land.[35]   The main attraction, however, was the immense deposits of magnetic
iron ore found in the neighboring mountains.   In
May, Brigham and others visited Parowan and addressed the people in the fort.   The Indian name
Parowan was then recommended and adopted.   Brig-

[33] John Urie, in *Utah Sketches*, MS., 88, says that there were 119 men
and 48 women and children, with 101 wagons, 368 oxen, 146 cows, and about
22 tons of seed; that they were well supplied with implements, and had 300
lbs of flour *per capita*. Richards, in *Utah Early Records*, MS., 117, mentions 163 souls, of whom 30 were women.

[34] James G. Bleak, in *Utah Sketches*, MS., 67–8.   On the south-east corner
of the fort a meeting-house in the shape of a St Andrew's cross was built of
hewn logs. *Utah Early Records*, MS., 163.   The name was first spelt Paroan.
Frontier Guardian, Aug. 8, 1851.   A view of the fort, with Little Salt Lake
in the distance, painted by W. Majors, was presented by Brigham Young to
the Deseret University in 1870. *Contributor*, ii. 270.

[35] In the *Deseret News* of March 6, 1852, is an account of the pioneer anniversary celebrated at Parowan on July 24, 1851.

ham urged the people to buy up the Lamanite children as rapidly as possible, and educate them in the gospel, for though they would fade away, yet a remnant of the seed of Joseph would be saved.[36]

At Cedar City—or, as it was then called, Cedar Fort—seventeen miles to the south-west of Parowan, a furnace was built in 1852, but at the close of the year stood idle for lack of hands.[37] Here, in May 1851, coal had been discovered near what was then known as the Little Muddy, now Coal Creek. In November of that year the site was occupied[38] by a company from Parowan. The winter was passed amid some privation, mainly from lack of warm clothing; but on the 30th of January a dry-goods pedler making his appearance—probably the first who had ventured so far south into the land of the Utahs—the settlers were soon clad in comfort.[39] In October it was re-solved to move the settlement to a point farther to the west and south, and before the end of the year a number of iron-workers and farmers arrived from Salt Lake City.[40]

In 1851 a party under Simeon A. Carter, sent to explore the country north of Ogden, founded a small settlement at Box Elder Creek.[41] The soil was of the

[36] *Hist. B. Young*, MS., 1851, 46. On the same page is mentioned the first use in the country of the stone-coal at Parowan, used in blacksmith work.

[37] George A. Smith, in *Frontier Guardian*, Aug. 8, 1851, and in *Deseret News*, Dec. 11, 1852.

[38] This valley had been explored as early as 1847. In December of that year, a party of the pioneers passed through it, as already mentioned, on their way to California to purchase live-stock and provisions.

[39] Building progressed rapidly, and during the following summer one Burr Frost, a blacksmith from Parowan, started the manufacture of iron, making nails enough to shoe a horse. *Deseret News*, Nov. 27, 1852.

[40] John Urie, in *Utah Sketches*, MS., 93–4. See also *Deseret News*, July 24, 1852. The scarcity of nails hindered building. Workmen were brought from England to manufacture them from native ore, but the experiment failed; as the work could not be done on a sufficiently large scale to make it profit-able, and it was abandoned. Years later, when the soldiers were ordered away from Camp Floyd, the settlers bought old iron cheap, and nails were manu-factured to advantage. The price in market then was 30 or 40 cts a lb.; afterward the railroad brought them in and they were sold at 3 to 5 cents a pound.

[41] About 60 miles north of Salt Lake City. A. Christensen, in *Utah Sketches*, MS., 102.

poorest, but near by were a few spots of meadow and farm land, on which, with irrigation, a fair crop could be raised.   A number of emigrants, principally Welsh and Scandinavian, joined the party, and two years later a new site was surveyed[42] under the direction of Lorenzo Snow.   To the town then laid out was afterward given the name of Brigham City.

A few weeks later a small settlement was formed about five miles south of this point, and in 1853 was removed to the present site of Willard City.[43]

On Red Creek, about twenty miles north of Cedar City, a small settlement was formed in the autumn of 1852, named Paragoonah, the Pi-Ede name for Little Salt Lake.[44] Six miles south of Cedar City, Fort Walker was built, containing at the close of 1851 only nine men capable of bearing arms; and on Ash Creek, nineteen miles farther south, was Fort Harmony, the southernmost point in the valley occupied by white men,[45] and where John D. Lee located a rancho in 1852.

[42] In blocks of six acres, each lot being half an acre.

[43] The first settlers on the old site were Jonathan S. Wells, who built the first house, and was the first to commence farming, Elisha Mallory, who with his brother Lemuel built the first grist-mill, M. McCreary, Alfred Walton, and Lyman B. Wells. George W. Ward, in *Utah Sketches*, MS., 44–5.   The city was named after Willard Richards. *Richards' Narr.*, MS., 67.

[44] In December, 15 or 20 families had settled there. *Deseret News*, Dec. 11, 1852.   On June 12, 1851, a company with a few wagons started for this point from Salt Lake City. *Utah Early Records*, MS., 128.

[45] This settlement was 20 miles north of the Rio Virgen.   It was thought that the route to California might be shortened by way of the fort about 35 miles. *Deseret News*, Dec. 11, 1852.   In addition to those mentioned in the text, a number of small settlements had been made in various parts of the territory.   Farmington, now the county seat of Davis co., and on the line of the Utah Central railroad, was first settled in 1848 by D. A. Miller and four others.   In 1849 it was organized as a ward.   Mill Creek, in S. Lake co., was settled in 1848–9 by John Neff and nine others; Alpine City and Springville, in Utah co., in 1850, the former by Isaac Houston with ten others, the latter by A. Johnson and three comrades.   Santaquin, in the same county, was settled in 1852; abandoned in 1853 on account of Indian raids, and reoccupied in 1856 by B. F. Johnson and 23 associates.   The site of Harrisville, a few miles north of Ogden, was occupied in the spring of 1850 by Ivin Stewart, abandoned the same autumn on account of an Indian outbreak, and resettled in 1851 by P. G. Taylor and others.   In 1883 Taylor was bishop of this ward.   Slaterville, in Weber county, was first settled in the fall of 1850 by Alex. Kelley, who was soon afterward joined by several families; in 1853—the year of the Walker war—it was abandoned, the inhabitants taking refuge in Bingham Fort, but was again occupied in 1854.   South Weber, in the same county,

Thus we see that within less than two years after the founding of Salt Lake City, the population there had become larger than could be supported in comfort on the city lots and the lands in their vicinity, and it had been found necessary to form new settlements toward the north and south, the latter part of the territory being preferred, as water, pasture, and land fit for tillage were more abundant. Instead of merely adding suburb to suburb, all clustering around the parent centre, as might have been done by other communities, the church dignitaries, while yet Salt Lake City was but a village, ordered parties of the brethren, some of them still barely rested from their toilsome journey across the plains, to start afresh for remote and unprotected portions of a then unknown country. As new locations were needed, exploring parties were sent forth, and when a site was selected, a small company, usually of volunteers, was placed in charge of an elder and ordered to make ready the proposed settlement. Care was taken that the various crafts should be represented in due proportion, and that the expedition should be well supplied with provisions, implements, and live-stock.

When, for instance, at the close of 1850, it had been resolved to form a settlement in the neighborhood of Little Salt Lake, a notice appeared in the *Deseret News* of November 16th, giving the names of those who had joined the party, and calling for a hundred additional volunteers. They must take with them 30,000 pounds of breadstuffs, 500 bushels of seed wheat, 34 ploughs, 50 horses, 50 beef-cattle, 50 cows, and 25 pairs of holster pistols; each man must be supplied with an axe, spade, shovel, and hoe,[46] a gun and 200 rounds

was located in 1851 by Robt Watts and nine others. Uintah, at the mouth of Weber Cañon, was settled in 1850 by Dan. Smith and a few others. It was first called East Weber, and received its present name on the 4th of March, 1867, at which date the Union Pacific railroad was finished to this point. *Sloan's Utah Gazetteer*, 1884, passim. Of the above settlements, those which became prominent will be mentioned later.

[46] The party must also have 17 sets of drag teeth, and of grain and grass scythes, sickles, and pitchforks, 50 each.

of ammunition. Among them there should be five carpenters and joiners, a millwright, a surveyor, and two blacksmiths, shoemakers, and masons. Thus equipped and selected, the settlers, with their marvellous energy and thrift, made more progress and suffered less privation in reclaiming the waste lands of their wilderness than did the Spaniards in the garden spots of Mexico and Central America, or the English in the most favored regions near the Atlantic seaboard.

A company was organized in March 1851, at the suggestion of Brigham, to go to California and form the nucleus of a settlement in the Cajon Pass, where they should cultivate the olive, grape, sugar-cane, and cotton, gather around them the saints, and select locations on the line of a proposed mail route.[47] The original intention was to have twenty in this company, with Amasa M. Lyman and C. C. Rich in charge. The number, however, reached over five hundred, and Brigham's heart failed him as he met them at starting. "I was sick at the sight of so many of the saints running to California, chiefly after the god of this world, and was unable to address them."[48]

[47] In *Hist. B. Young*, MS., 1851, 85, it is stated that, at the next session of congress, it was expected that a mail route would be established to San Diego by way of Parowan. At this date there was, as we shall see later, a monthly mail between S. L. City and Independence, Mo. There was also a mail to Sacramento, leaving that and S. L. City on the 1st of each month, a bi-monthly mail to The Dalles, Or., a weekly mail to the San Pete valley, and a semi-weekly mail to Brownsville.

[48] *Hist. B. Young*, MS., 1851, 14. The object of the establishment of this colony was that the people gathering to Utah from the Islands, and even Europe, might have an outfitting post. In 1853, Keokuk, Iowa, on the Mississippi River, was selected by the western-bound emigrants as a rendezvous and place of outfitting.

CHAPTER XIV.

EDUCATION, MANUFACTURES, COMMERCE, AGRICULTURE, SOCIETY.

1850-1852.

IN the year 1850 Utah, bounded on the south and east by New Mexico, Kansas, and Nebraska, on the west by California, on the north by Oregon, which then included Idaho, was one of the largest territories in the United States. Its length from east to west was 650 miles, its breadth 350 miles, and its area 145,-000,000 acres. The portion known as the great basin, beyond which were no settlements in 1852, has an elevation of 4,000 to 5,000 feet, and is surrounded and intersected by mountain ranges, the highest peaks of the Humboldt Range near its centre being more than 5,000 feet, and of the Wasatch on the east about 7,000 feet, above the level of the basin.

For 300 miles along the western base of the Wasatch Range is a narrow strip of alluvial land.[1] Elsewhere in the valley the soil is not for the most part fertile until water is conducted to it, and some of the alkali washed out. Rain seldom falls in spring

---

[1] *Gunnison's The Mormons*, 15.

or summer, and during winter the snow-fall is not
enough to furnish irrigating streams in sufficient number and volume. Throughout the valley, vegetation
is scant except in favored spots. With the exception
of the Santa Clara River in the south-west, the Green
River in the east, the Grand and other branches of
the Colorado in the south and east, the streams all
discharge into lakes or are lost in the alkali soil of
the bottom-lands. On the hillsides bunch-grass is
plentiful the year round, and in winter there is pasture in the cañons. Around Salt Lake the soil is poor;
in the north and east are narrow tracts of fertile land;
toward the valleys of the Jordan and Tooele, separated by the Oquirrh Range, and on the banks of the
Timpanogos and San Pete, is soil of good quality,
that yielded in places from sixty to a hundred bushels
of grain to the acre.

The Jordan and Timpanogos furnished good water-
power, and on the banks of the latter stream was
built a woollen-mill that ranked as the largest factory of the kind west of the Missouri River. In
the Green River basin, immense deposits of coal
were known to exist, and the Iron Mountains near
Little Salt Lake were so called from the abundance of ore found in their midst. Other valuable
minerals were afterward discovered, among them being
gold, silver, copper, zinc, lead, sulphur, alum, and borax;
the waters of Great Salt Lake were so densely impregnated that one measure of salt was obtained from five
of brine.[2]

In the streams were fish of several varieties;[3] in

---

[2] An analysis of the mineral matter forty years ago showed 97.8 per cent
of chloride of sodium, 1.12 of sulphate of lime, .24 of magnesium, and .23
of sulphate of soda. *Linforth's Route from Liverpool*, 101. The specific gravity of the water is given by L. D. Gale, in *Stansbury's Expedition to G. S. Lake*,
at 1.117. Out of 22.422 parts of solid matter Gale found 20.196 of common
salt, 1.834 of soda, .252 of magnesium, and of chloride of calcium a trace.
See also *Sloan's Utah Gazetteer*, 1884, 177–8; *Hist. Nev.*, 11, this series. In
chap. i. of that vol. is a further description of the great basin, its topography,
climate, soil, springs and rivers, fauna and flora.

[3] 'The angler can choose his fish either in the swift torrents of the cañons,
where the trout delights to live, or in the calmer currents on the plains,

the mountains roamed the deer, elk, antelope, and bear, and on the marshy flats amid the plains were smaller game.[4] Timber was scarce and of poor quality, except in places difficult of access;[5] but with this exception there was no great lack of resources in the territory which the saints had made their abode.

During the first years that followed their migration, while yet engaged in building houses, fencing lands, planting crops, and tending herds, the Mormons provided liberally for the cause of education. In the third general epistle of the twelve, dated the 12th of April, 1850, it is stated that an appropriation of $5,000 per annum, for a period of twenty years, had been made for a state university[6] in Salt Lake City, branches to be established elsewhere throughout the territory as they were needed. In the curriculum the Keltic and Teutonic languages were to rank side by side with the Romanic, and all living languages spoken by men were to be included. Astronomy, geology, chemistry, agriculture, engineering, and other branches of science were to be studied; for having sought first the kingdom of heaven, the saints were now assured that knowledge and all other things should be added unto them.[7] The world of science was to be revolu-

where he will find abundance of the pike, the perch, the bass, and the chub. *Gunnison's The Mormons*, 20.

[4] Wild ducks and geese were abundant in 1852. *Ibid.* There were also quail and herons. In summer, boys filled their baskets with eggs found among the reeds on the banks of streams or on the islands in the Great Salt Lake.

[5] 'Hidden away in the profound chasms and along the streams, whose beds are deeply worn in the mountain-sides, are the cedar, pine, dwarf-maple, and occasionally oak, where the inhabitants of the vale seek their fuel and building timber, making journeys to obtain these necessaries twenty to forty miles from their abodes.' *Id.*, 21.

[6] Under the supervision and control of a chancellor, twelve regents, a secretary, and a treasurer. *Frontier Guardian*, June 12, 1850.

[7] 'But what,' says Phelps in an oration delivered July 24, 1851, 'will all the precious things of time, the inventions of men, the records, from Japheth in the ark to Jonathan in congress, embracing the wit and the gist, the fashions and the folly, which so methodically, grammatically, and transcendentally grace the libraries of the élite of nations, really be worth to a saint, when our father sends down his regents, the angels, from the grand library of Zion above, with a copy of the history of eternal lives, the records of worlds, the genealogy of the gods, the philosophy of truth, the names of our spirits from

tionized; the theories of gravitation, repulsion, and attraction overthrown, the motion of atoms, whether single or in mass, being ascribed to the all-pervading presence of the holy spirit. The planetary systems were to be rearranged, their number and relations modified, for in the book of Abraham it was revealed that in the centre of the universe was the great orb Kolob, the greatest of all the stars seen by that patriarch, revolving on its axis once in a thousand years, and around which all other suns and planets revolved in endless cycles.[8]

At first, however, education among the settlers was mainly of an elementary nature. There were many, even among the adults, who could not write or spell, and not a few who could not read. A parents' school was therefore established at Salt Lake City, for the heads of families and for the training of teachers, among the pupils being Brigham Young.[9] Primary and other schools were opened in all the principal settlements,[10] and for those who were sufficiently advanced, classes were organized as early as the winter of 1848–9, for the study of ancient and modern languages.[11]

the Lamb's book of life, and the songs of the sanctified?' *Deseret News*, July 26, 1851.

[8] 'I saw the stars that they were very great, and that one of them was nearest unto the throne of God; and there were many great ones that were near it; and the Lord said unto me, These are the governing ones: and the name of the great one is Kolob, because it is near unto me, for I am the Lord thy God; I have set this one to govern all those which belong to the same order of that upon which thou standest. And the Lord said unto me, By the urim and thummim, that Kolob was after the manner of the Lord, according to its times and seasons in the revolution thereof, that one revolution was a day unto the Lord, after his manner of reckoning, it being one thousand years according to the time appointed unto that whereon thou standest.' *Reynolds' Book of Abraham*, 29. See also Orson Pratt's lecture on astronomy in *Deseret News*, Dec. 27, 1851.

[9] The parent school is in successful operation in the council-house, and schools have been built in most of the wards. *Hist. B. Young*, MS., 1851, 32; *Gunnison's The Mormons*, 80; *Utah Early Records*, MS., 115. Lyons Collins was appointed teacher by the chancellor and board of regents.

[10] Jesse W. Fox taught the first school at Manti in 1850. *Utah Sketches*, MS., 172. The first school at Nephi was opened in 1851. *Id.*, 111. The best school-house in Utah county was at Palmyra; at Provo, Evan M. Greene opened a select school in the second ward. *Deseret News*, Dec. 11, 1852.

[11] 'There have been a large number of schools the past winter, in which the Hebrew, Greek, Latin, French, German, Tahitian, and English languages

In 1850, by vote of congress, twenty thousand dollars were appropriated for the building of a state-house, and the sum of five thousand dollars was appropriated for the foundation of a library in Salt Lake City. The delegate from Utah was authorized to make a selection of books, and several thousand volumes were forwarded from the east during this and the following year.[12] Rooms were prepared in the council-house for their reception, and many periodicals, both Mormon and gentile, were added to the stock of reading matter. Among the former was the *Millennial Star*, already mentioned, and the *Frontier Guardian*, published bi-monthly at Kanesville, Iowa, between February 1849 and March 1852, and afterward as a weekly paper under the style of the *Frontier Guardian and Iowa Sentinel*.[13]

have been taught successfully. First General Epistle of the Twelve, in *Utah Early Records*, MS., 74, and *Frontier Guardian*, May 30, 1849. 'German books were bought in order that the elders might learn that language.' *Hist. B. Young*, MS., 1849, 3.

[12] Dr Bernhisel was appointed by the president of the U. S. as special agent to expend the U. S. appropriation of $5,000. *Hist. B. Young*, MS., 80. Many valuable donations of maps, papers, etc., were received. *Contributor*, 270; *Gunnison's The Mormons*, 83; *Utah Early Records*, MS., 130; *Millennial Star*, xii. 330-1. William C. Staines was appointed librarian. *Deseret News*, Feb. 21, 1852.

[13] Of the *Frontier Guardian*, brief mention has already been made. The first number, published Feb. 7, 1849, with Orson Hyde as editor and proprietor, will bear comparison with many of the leading newspapers in eastern or European cities. In the prospectus Mr Hyde states that 'it will be devoted to the news of the day, to the signs of the times, to religion and prophecy, both ancient and modern; to literature and poetry; to the arts and sciences, together with all and singular whatever the spirit of the times may dictate.' Published, as was the *Guardian*, on the extreme frontier of the states, Mr Hyde was enabled to furnish the latest news from Salt Lake City, and many valuable items have been gleaned from its pages. Glancing at them for the first time, one asks, How did he contrive to bring out his newspaper in such creditable shape, at a place which one year before was only an encampment of emigrants en route for the valley? During this year, however, Kanesville—later Florence—had made very rapid progress, due, in part, to the migration to California. Glancing over the first numbers of the *Guardian*, we find advertised for sale dry goods, groceries, provisions, hardware, clothing, and most of the commodities needed by emigrants. There was a hotel, a fashionable tailor, a lawyer, a doctor, and of course a tabernacle, which served for social parties and religious worship. Provisions rose to very high rates, thr gh not to the prices demanded in Salt Lake City. On Feb. 7, 1849, flour, beef, and pork were selling at Kanesville for about $2 per 100 lbs. On May 1, 1850, flour was worth $6 to $6.50, beef $3.50 to $4.50, and pork $5 to $6. Potatoes had risen meanwhile from 25 cents to $1, corn from 20 cents to $2.25, and wheat from 50 cents to $1.75, per bushel. On March 4, 1852, appeared the first num-

On the 15th of June, 1850, was published at Salt
Lake City, under the editorship of Willard Richards,
the first number of the *Deseret News*, a weekly paper,
and the church organ of the saints.[14] In this number, a copy of which I have before me, is a report of
the conflagration which occurred in San Francisco on
christmas eve of 1849, and of Zachary Taylor's message to the house of representatives relating to the
admission of California as a state.

ber of the *Frontier Guardian and Iowa Sentinel*, the paper having then passed
into the hands of Jacob Dawson & Co.

[14] Until Aug. 19, 1851, it was issued as an eight-page quarto, the pages
being about 8½ by 6½ in., and without column rules. After that date it was
suspended for want of paper until Nov. 19th. 'We got short of type, and
I happened to have some stereotyped plates,...which we melted down and
used for type.   We were short, too, of paper, and all went to work to make it.
We collected all the rags we could and made the pulp, sifted it through a sieve,
and pressed it as well as we could.' *Taylor's Rem.*, MS., 17.   The terms were
$5 per year, payable half-yearly in advance, single copies being sold for fifteen
cents.   There seems to have been some difficulty in collecting subscriptions,
for in the issue of November 15, 1851, the editor states that payment will be
due at the office on receipt of the first number, 'and no one need expect the
second number until these terms are complied with, as credit will not create
the paper, ink, press, or hands to labor.' In his prospectus, Richards said
that the *Deseret News* is designed ' to record the passing events of our state,
and in connection refer to the arts and sciences, embracing general education,
medicine, law, divinity, domestic and political economy, and everything that
may fall under our observation which may tend to promote the best interest,
welfare, pleasure, and amusement of our fellow-citizens...We shall ever take
pleasure in communicating foreign news as we have opportunity; in receiving
communications from our friends at home and abroad; and solicit ornaments
for the *News* from our poets and poetesses.' In the first issue is the following,
perhaps by Beta, who afterward wrote a number of papers styled the *Chron-
icles of Utah* in the *Salt Lake City Contributor:*

To my Friends in the Valley.
Let all who would have a good paper,
   Their talents and time ne'er abuse;
Since 'tis said by the wise and the humored,
   That the best in the world is the *News.*

Then ye who so long have been thinking
   What paper this year you will choose,
Come trip gayly up to the office
   And subscribe for the *Deseret News.*

And now, dearest friends, I will leave you;
   This counsel, I pray you, don't lose;
The best of advice I can give you
   Is, pay in advance for the *News.*

Fortunately for the prospects and reputation of the paper, such effusions were
rare even in its early pages. The *Deseret News* was at first less ably edited,
and inferior, as to type and paper, to the *Frontier Guardian*. It appears,
indeed, to have lacked support, for in the first number are only two adver-
tisements, one from a blacksmith and the other from a surgeon-dentist, who
also professes to cure the scurvy. In Nov. 1851 it appeared in folio and in
greatly improved form; for years it was the only paper, and is still the leading Mormon journal, in the territory.

At Salt Lake City and elsewhere throughout the country manufactures began to thrive. Isolated, poor, having brought little or nothing with them, these settlers were peculiarly dependent for necessaries and comforts upon themselves, and what they could do with their hands. And it would be difficult to find anywhere in the history of colonization settlers who could do more. Among them were many of the best of Europe's artisans, workers in wood, iron, wool, and cotton, besides farmers, miners, and all kinds of laborers.

At Tooele and several other settlements grist-mills and saw-mills were established before the close of 1852.[15] Near Salt Lake City, a small woollen-mill was in operation.[16] At Parowan and Cedar City, iron-works were in course of construction; at Paragoonah, a tannery had been built; and at Salt Lake City, in addition to other branches of manufacture, flannels, linseys, jeans, pottery, and cutlery were produced,[17] and sold at lower prices than were asked for eastern goods of inferior quality. "Produce what you consume," writes Governor Brigham Young in his message of January 5, 1852; "draw from the native elements the necessaries of life; permit no vitiated taste to lead you into indulgence of expensive luxuries which can only be obtained by involving yourselves in debt; let home industry produce every article of home consumption."[18] This excellent advice

[15] The first grist-mill built at Tooele was erected by Ezaias Edwards; in 1849 a saw-mill was built at Provo by James Porter and Alex. Williams, and in 1850 a grist-mill, by James A. Smith and Isaac Higbee. At American Fork Azra Adams built a grist-mill in 1851; at Manti a grist-mill was built by Brigham Young and Isaac Morley, and a saw-mill by Charles Shumway; in 1848 Samuel Parish built a grist-mill at Centreville. *Utah Sketches*, MS., passim. In Salt Lake county there were, in the autumn of 1851, four grist-mills and five saw-mills. *Utah Early Records*, MS., 158. Near Ogden, Lorin Farr built a grist-mill and saw-mill in 1850. *Stanford's Ogden City*, MS., 3.

[16] In March 1851 the general assembly appropriated $2,000 for this purpose. *Utah Early Records*, MS., 123.

[17] 'Our pottery is nearly completed;...cutlery establishments are completed.' *Hist. B. Young*, MS., 1851, 26.

[18] In *Id.*, Nov. 6, 1852, similar advice is given to the saints: 'Buy no article from the stores that you can possibly do without. Stretch our means, skill, and wisdom to the utmost to manufacture what we need, beginning with

was not unheeded; but the supply of home-manufactured goods did not, of course, keep pace with the demand. Such commodities as were not the products of home industry were, for the most part, obtained by barter with passing emigrants, or were brought in wagon trains by way of Kanesville;[19] though already traffic had been opened with regions far to the westward on either side of the Sierra Nevada.[20]

According to the United States census returns for the year 1850, the population of the valley of Great Salt Lake mustered 11,354 persons, of whom about 53 per cent were males, and 6,000 residents of Salt Lake City.[21] There were 16,333 acres under cultivation, on which were raised 128,711 bushels of grain. The value of live-stock was estimated at $546,698, and of farming implements at $84,288. At the close of 1852, the total population was variously estimated at from 25,000 to 30,000,[22] of whom perhaps 10,000 resided in the metropolis. The assessed value of

a shoestring (if we cannot begin higher).' 'When we have manufactured an article, sell it for cash or its equivalent, as low, or lower, than it can be bought for at the stores.' In the fifth general epistle is the following: 'Beach and Blair have opened a general manufacturing establishment;...are now making molasses and vinegar. Several grain and lumber mills have been erected in the various settlements,...chairs and various articles of furniture are multiplying,...two or three threshing-machines have been in successful operation.' *Hist. B. Young*, MS., 1851, 24. 'We are going in extensively for home manufactures. My own family alone have this season manufactured over 500 yds of cloth, and the home-made frequently makes its appearance in our streets'—a great blessing, 'if it will prove an inducement to the people to depend and rely upon their own resources for their own supplies.' *Id.*, 1852, 16.

[19] On May 1, 1851, the first train of merchandise for the season arrived in the city, laden partly with sugar, coffee, and calicoes. *Utah Early Records*, MS., 127.

[20] On Nov. 19, 1848, Capt. Grant of the Hudson's Bay Company arrived from Fort Hall with pack-horses laden with skins, groceries, and other goods. On April 17, 1851, a small party arrived from Fort Hall in search of provisions and Indian trading goods. On the 10th of the same month, Col Reese sent ten or twelve wagon-loads of flour to Carson Valley for trading purposes. *Id.*, 39, 125, 127.

[21] The returns were made under the direction of Brigham Young, who was appointed census agent. *Utah Early Records*, MS., 112; *Deseret News*, Oct. 5, 1850.

[22] Early in 1853 the *Deseret Almanac* places the number at 30,000, while in Orson Pratt's *Seer* it is given at 30,000 to 35,000. *Olshausen's Mormonen*, 192. At this date it was estimated at 25,000 by the gentiles. *Burton's City of the Saints*, 357. Probably the Mormons exaggerated, as they desired to

taxable property at the latter date was $1,160,883.80, or an average of more than $400 per capita. The entire revenue amounted to $26,690.58,[23] of which sum $9,725.87 was expended for public improvements, the encouragement of industries, or educational purposes.

Little more than five years had elapsed since the pioneer band entered the valley of Great Salt Lake, and now the settlers found themselves amidst plenty and comfort in the land of promise, where until their arrival scarce a human being was to be seen, save the Indians whose clothing was the skins of rabbits and whose food was roasted crickets.[24] There was no destitution in their midst;[25] there was little sickness.[26] In these and some other respects, the wildest misstatements have been made by certain gentile writers, among them Mr Ferris, who, as we shall see, was appointed secretary for Utah.[27] In this pure show as soon as possible a population of 100,000, which would entitle them to claim admission as a state.

[23] Not more than one tenth was collected in cash, payment being usually made in grain. *Contributor*, 332. 'Securing a territorial revenue of $23,000, including merchants' licenses and tax on liquors.' *Hist. B. Young*, MS., 1852, 2.

[24] The most exposed parts of the country are annually run over by the fires set by the Indians to kill and roast the crickets, which they gather in summer for winter food.' *Gunnison's The Mormons*, 21.

[25] The country was canvassed to ascertain how many inmates there would be for a poor-house, then projected. Only two were found, and the Mormons concluded that it was not yet time for such an institution. *Id.*, 34.

[26] The number of deaths in the territory during the year ending June 1, 1850, was 239. *U. S. Census, 1850*, 997; and in Salt Lake county, which virtually meant Salt Lake City, 121; in both, the mortality was therefore less than 20 per thousand, or about the average death-rate in San Francisco during recent years. Moreover, the population of Utah included a very large proportion of infants. Of 64 deaths reported in the *Deseret News* of March 8, 1851, 34 occurred between the ages of one and ten.

[27] *Utah and the Mormons: the History, Government, Doctrines, Customs, and Prospects of the Latter-day Saints; from personal observation during a six months' residence at Great Salt Lake City. By Benjamin G. Ferris, late secretary of Utah Territory, New York, 1854.* Mr Ferris is not the first one whom in his own opinion a six months' residence in the west justifies in writing a book. It was the winter of 1852–3 which he spent there, and while professing that he writes wholly from an anti-Mormon standpoint, as a rule he is comparatively moderate in his expressions. The illustrations in this volume are many of them the same which are found in several other works. Beginning with the physical features of Utah, he goes through the whole range of Mormon history, and concludes with chapters on government, doctrines, polygamy, book of Mormon proselytizing, and society. While sometimes interesting, there is little original information; and aside from what the author saw during his residence in Utah, the book has no special value.

mountain air, with its invigorating embrace, the aged and infirm regained the elasticity of a second youth. Here was no rank vegetation, here were no stagnant pools to generate miasma, no vapors redolent of death, like those amid which the saints encamped on the banks of the Missouri. In the valley were mineral springs, the temperature of which ranged from 36° to 150° of Fahrenheit, some of them being prized for their medicinal properties. From the warm spring[28] in the vicinity of Salt Lake City, waters which varied between 98° in summer and 104° in winter[29] were conducted by pipes to a large bath-house in the northern part of the city.[30]

[28] The water was analyzed in 1851 by L. D. Gale. Its specific gravity was found to be 1.0112; it was strongly impregnated with sulphur, and 100 parts of water yielded 1.082 of solid matter. The specific gravity of the hot spring in the same neighborhood was 1.013, and 100 parts yielded 1.1454 of solid matter. Detailed analyses are given in *Stansbury's Expedition to G. S. Lake*, i. 419-20. An analysis of the warm spring given by Joseph T. Kingsbury in *Contributor*, iv. 59-60, differs somewhat from that of Gale. Further information on these and other springs and mineral waters will be found in *Id.*, iv. 86-9; *Hist. Nev.*, 17, this series; *Salt Lake Weekly Herald*, July 29, 1880; *S. L. C. Tribune*, Jan. 5, 1878; *Wheeler's Surveys*, iii. 105-17; *Hollister's Resources of Utah*, 83-5; *Hardy's Through Cities and Prairie*, 121; *Burton's City of the Saints*, 222; *Sac. Union*, Aug. 7, 1860.

[29] *Contributor*, iv. 59. One of the brethren, writing to Orson Hyde from Salt Lake City, Sept. 10, 1850, says that the temperature stands, winter and summer, at about 92°. *Frontier Guardian*, Jan. 8, 1851.

[30] On Nov. 27, 1850, the warm-spring bath-house was dedicated and opened with prayer, festival, and dance. *Utah Early Records*, MS., 116.

The material for the preceding chapters has been gathered mainly from a number of manuscripts furnished at intervals between 1880 and 1885. As I have already stated, to F. D. Richards I am especially indebted for his unremitting effort in supplying data for this volume. The period between Feb. 1846 and the close of 1851—say between the commencement of the exodus from Nauvoo and the opening of the legislature of Utah territory—is one of which there are few authentic printed records. From *Kane's The Mormons*, from *Fullmer's Expulsion*, and other sources, I have gleaned a little; but as far as I am aware, no work has yet been published that gives, or pretends to give, in circumstantial detail the full story of this epoch in the annals of Mormonism. In the *Utah Early Records*, MS., I have been supplied with a brief but full statement of all the noteworthy incidents from the entrance of Orson Pratt and Erastus Snow into the valley of the Great Salt Lake to the close of the year 1851. In the *Narrative of Franklin D. Richards*, MS.; the *Reminiscences of Mrs F. D. Richards*, MS.; *Inner Facts of Social Life in Utah*, MS., by the same writer; *History of Brigham Young*, MS., which is indeed a continuation of the *History of Joseph Smith*, or the history of the church; *Martin's Narrative*, MS.—I have been kindly furnished with many details that it would have been impossible to obtain elsewhere. Some of them I have already noticed, and others I shall mention in their place.

In *Reminiscences of President John Taylor*, MS., we have an account of the migration from Nauvoo to Winter Quarters, the organization of the various companies, and much information of a miscellaneous nature, relating to house-building in Salt Lake City, the first manufactures, the location of the temple, and other matters. The manuscript also makes mention of his visit to England as a missionary in 1846, in company with Parley P. Pratt and Orson Hyde. The *Narrative of General Daniel H. Wells*, MS., gives an account of the disturbances in Hancock county, the troubles at Nauvoo before the exodus, the journey to Winter Quarters, the organization of the Nauvoo legion, and of the state of Deseret; but perhaps the most valuable portion is a condensed narrative of all the Indian outbreaks between 1849 and 1864, a task for which General Wells, who during this period had charge of the Nauvoo legion and aided in suppressing some of the disturbances, is specially qualified.

Wilford Woodruff's Journal, MS., commencing with the claims of Sidney Rigdon to the guardianship of the church, in 1846, and closing with a summary of the operations of the pioneers in the following year. Mr Woodruff gives some valuable details concerning this most interesting period in the annals of Mormonism. Being himself a pioneer, he furnishes minute particulars as to their journey and their early labors in the valley.

In *A Woman's Experiences with the Pioneer Band, by Mrs Clara Decker Young*, MS., we have also some information as to the work accomplished during the single month that the pioneers remained in the valley, among other matters being the building of the old fort. Items of interest are also given concerning those who were left alone in the valley after the pioneers' departure, until the arrival of Parley Pratt's companies. Clara Decker Young, a native of Freedom, N. Y., moved with her parents to Daviess co., Mo., in 1837, the family being driven, during the persecutions of that year, to Far West, whence they removed to Quincy, and later to Nauvoo. When 16 years of age she became the fifth wife of Brigham Young.

From the *Material Progress of Utah, by William Jennings*, MS., I have gathered many details as to the industrial condition of the Mormons from the earliest settlement of S. L. City up to a recent date, among them being items relating to manufactures, agriculture, stock-raising, the grasshopper plague, and the influence of the railroad on the population of Utah.

Early Justice, by John Nebeker, MS., besides describing the punishment of offenders in the days of 1847, when, as I have already stated, the whipping-post was substituted for imprisonment, furnishes other material of value relating to early times. In his capacity of public complainer, Mr Nebeker prosecuted one culprit before the high council for stealing, and himself administered the flogging. Mr Nebeker, a native of Delaware, came to Nauvoo in the winter of 1846; crossed the plains with the first companies, and left Winter Quarters with Parley Pratt's detachment.

In *The Migration and Settlements of the Latter-day Saints, by Mrs Joseph H. Horne*, MS., is an account of her conversion, her experiences at Far West, Quincy, and Nauvoo, and the hardships suffered during the migration. Then follows a description of the first years in S. L. City, the food, dress, and dwellings of the saints, their make-shifts and privations, with some mention of the Mormon battalion, and the ill feeling caused by the withdrawal of 500 able-bodied men at this crisis in their affairs. Mrs Horne, a native of Rainham, England, moved with her parents to New York (now Toronto, Canada) when ten years of age. In 1836, the year of her marriage, she was converted by the preaching of Parley and Orson Pratt, her house being afterward open to the elders, who frequently held meetings there.

From the *Utah Sketches*, MS., I have gathered much information as to the founding of various settlements and their progress up to the year 1880, of which mention will be made later. Most of them were written by persons who were themselves among the earliest settlers, and of whom some are still prominent members of the several communities among which their lot was cast. In this connection may be mentioned the *Brief Historical Sketch of the Settlements in Weber County, by Joseph Stanford*, MS., and the *Historical Sketch of Ogden City*, by the same author.

In addition to the manuscripts and journals constituting the vast original sources upon which I have drawn, I would mention also the following printed and secondary authorities: *Millen. Star*, iv. 187–90, v. 174–7, vi. 41–2, vii. 71–2, 87–9, 103–4, 149–53, viii. 68–71, 97–8, 102–3, 113–21, 149–58, ix. 11–22, xi. 46–7; *Times and Seasons*, i. 30–1, 44, 185–7, 517, ii. 273–4, 281–6, 309, 319, 321–2, 336, 355–6, 370–1, 375–7, 380–2, 417–18, 435, 517, 567–70, iii. 630–1, 666, 638, 654, 683–6, 700, 718, 733–4, 743, 767–9, 775–6, 806–7, 831–2, 902–3, 919–21, 936–7, iv. 10–11, 33–6, 65–71, 154–7, 198–9, 241–78, v. 392–6, 418– 23, 455, 471–2, 536–48, 560–75, 584–99, 618–22, vi. 762, 773–80, 926, 972–3; *Beadle, Life in Utah*, 58–9, 63–121, 125–54, 161–2, 280; *Bennett, Morm. Exposed*, 5–10, 140–62, 188–214, 278–302, 307–40; *Bertrand, Mem. Morm.*, 61, 65–70; *Bonwick, Morm. and Silv. Mines*, 3; *Burton, City of Saints*, 183–4, 433, 625–67; *Busch, Gesch. Morm.*, 43–5, 97–113, 125–30, 205–17, 254–98; *Death of the Prophets, with Offic. Doc.*, no. 23, in *Utah Pamph. Relig.; Deseret News*, 1851, Apr. 8, Nov. 29, Dec. 13, 27; 1867, July 24; 1868, July 1, Dec. 16, 30; 1869, Apr. 7, Sept. 1; 1876, Mar. 22; 1877, Nov. 14; *Hall, Morm. Exposed*, 7– 8, 15–16, 24–7, 28–34, 55–70, 91–9, 106–7; *Tucker, Morm.*, 37, 167–207; *Tullidge, Life of Young*, 6–191, 204; *Women of Morm.*, 297–300, 425–32, 443–4, 488–95; *Edinburg Rev.*, Apr. 1854, 319–83; *Ford (Thos, Gov. Ill.)*, in *Utah Tracts*, no. 11; *Ferris, Utah and Morm.*, 51, 92–107, 114–15, 137–46, 151–4. 120–30; *Gunnison, Morm.*, 133, 115–39; *Stansbury, Exped.*, 135–7; *Green, Morm.*, 28–9, 36–7, 54–64; *Hickman, Destroying Angel*, 41–5; *Hyde, Morm.*, 140, 144–6, 152–3, 155–7, 172–5, 183–5, 189–92; *Kidder, Morm.*, 157–9, 182– 92; *Kanesville (Ia), Front. Guard.*, 1849, Feb. 7, 21, Mar. 7, June 27, Aug. 8, Nov. 14; *Id.*, 1850, May 1, 29, Oct. 2, 30; *Id.*, 1852, Mar. 18, 25; *Linforth, Route from Liverpool*, 61–9, 72–5; *Lee, Morm.*, 109–12, 144–8, 152–5, 167–8, 173–4, 179–80; *Mackay, The Morm.*, 115–206; *Niles' Reg.*, lxix. 70, 134, lxx. 208, 211, 327, lxxii. 206, 370, lxxiii. 6; *Olshausen, Gesch.*, 59–65, 88–90, 100–3, 144–51, 202–34; *Hon. Polynesian*, ii. 1846, 91; *Pratt (P.), Autobiog.*, 378, 398–401, 405–6; *Remy, Journey to G. S. L. City*, i. 336–406, 434–8, ii. 258–63; *Smucker, Hist. Morm.*, 119–34, 148–276, passim; *Snow (Eliza)*, in *Utah Pioneers, 33d Ann.*, 41–50, in *Times and Seasons*, iv. 287; *Snow (Lorenzo)*, with *Taylor, Govt of God*, no. 12, 9–11; *Stenhouse, Tell It All*, 306; *Crimes of L. D. Saints*, 11–15; *Dunbar, Romance of Age*, 45; *Ebberts, Trapper's Life*, MS., 18; *Fullmer*, in *Utah Tracts*, no. 9, 1–40; *Mather*, in *Lippincott's Mag.*, Aug. 1880; *McGlashen, Hist. Donner Party*, 34–56; *Spence, Settler's Guide*, 268–9; *Sala, Amer. Revisited*, ii. 289; *Salt Lake City, Contributor*, ii. 86, 134–7, 195–8, 239, 301, 354–6, 366, iii. passim, iv. 370–6; *Salt Lake City, Deseret News*, 1850, July 27; 1851, July 26, Aug. 19; 1852, Feb. 7, Aug. 7, 21; 1854, July 27, Aug. 3; 1855, Sept. 26; 1857, July 29, Aug. 5; 1858, June 30; *Salt Lake City, Herald*, 1880, July 3, 29; *Salt Lake City, Telegraph*, 1868, May 30, Oct. 10, 12–14; *Smith, Rise, Progress*, etc., 6–18, 314–22, 334–6; *Smoot (Margaret S.), Experience*, etc., MS., 4–5; *Cal., Its Past Hist.*, 219; *Tracy (Mrs N. N.), Narr.*, MS., 10–19; *Thornton, Or. and Cal.*, i. 158–9; *Utah Pioneer, 33d Ann.*, 50–2; *Narrative of the Murders of the Smiths*, in *Utah Tracts*, no. 1, passim; *The Murder of Jos Smith*, in *Utah Tracts*, no. 1, 54–5; *Tyler, Hist. Morm. Battalion*, passim; *U. S. Ex. Doc.*, 24, 31 Cong. 1st Sess.; *Van Tramp, Adventures*, 313–38; *Woodruff (W.)*, in *Utah Pion., 33d Ann.*, 19–24; *Ward, Mormon Wife*, 81–4, 109–40, 165; *White (Mrs C. V.), The Mormon Prophet*, etc., 4–8; *Young (Ann Eliza), Wife No. 19*, 54–7; *Marshall, Through Amer.*, 184; *Murphy, Mineral Resour.*, 84–5; *Miller (J.), First Families*, etc., 65–73; *Martin (Thos S.), Narrative*, etc., MS., 42; *San Francisco, Alta Cal.*, 1851, Aug. 8; *Id., Cal. Star*, 1848, Feb. 26; *Id., Call*, 1869, Sept. 5, 1877, Aug. 31; *Id., Chronicle*, 1881, Jan. 9; *Id., Herald*, 1851, Oct. 12, 1859, Nov. 15; *Sacramento, Placer Times*, 1849, May 26; *Id., Union*, 1855, Sept. 10, 27, 1859, Aug. 24; *Portland (Or.), Telegram*, 1879, Mar. 15; *Salem (Or.), Argus*, 1858, Feb. 13, Aug. 28; *Id., Statesman*, 1851, Dec. 23; *Or. City (Or.), Spectator*, 1846, July 4; *Ogden (Utah), Freeman*, 1879, May 2; *Gold Hill (Nev.), News*, 1872, May 1, Oct. 24; *Eureka (Nev.), Leader*, 1880, July 24; *Carson (Nev.), State Register*, 1872, Nov. 24; *Rae, Westward by Rail*, 125–7.

CHAPTER XV.

MORMONISM AND POLYGAMY.

WHAT IS MORMONISM?—TENETS OF THE CHURCH—SACRED BOOKS AND PERSON-
AGES—ORGANIZATION — PRIESTHOOD—FIRST PRESIDENCY — THE TWELVE
APOSTLES—PATRIARCHS—ELDERS, BISHOPS, PRIESTS, TEACHERS, AND
DEACONS—THE SEVENTIES—STAKES AND WARDS—MARRIAGE—TEMPLE
BUILDING—TABERNACLE—POLITICAL ASPECT—POLYGAMY AS A CHURCH
TENET—CELESTIAL MARRIAGE—ATTITUDE AND ARGUMENTS OF CIVILI-
ZATION—POLYGAMY'S REPLY—ETHICS AND LAW—THE CHARGE OF DIS-
LOYALTY—PROPOSED REMEDIES.

WE are now prepared to ask the question with some
degree of intelligence, What is Mormonism? In for-
mulating an answer, we must consider as well the
political as the religious idea. I will examine the
latter first.

Mormonism in its religious aspect is simply the acceptation of the bible, the whole of it, literally, and
following it to its logical conclusions.

As the Christian world has advanced in civilization
and intelligence these two thousand years or so, it has
gradually left behind a little and a little more of its
religion, first of the tenets of the Hebraic record, and
then somewhat even of those of the later dispensation.
Long before religionists began to question as myths
the stories of Moses, and Jonah, and Job, they had
thrown aside as unseemly blood-sacrifice and burnt-
offerings, sins of uncleanness, the stoning of sabbath-
breakers, the killing in war of women, children, and
prisoners, the condemnation of whole nations to perpetual bondage, and many other revolting customs of
the half-savage Israelites sanctioned by holy writ.

This they did of their own accord, not because they were so commanded, but in spite of commandments, and by reason of a higher and more refined culture—a culture which had outgrown the cruder dogmas of the early ages. Then came the putting away of slavery and polygamy, the former but recently permitted in these American states, and the latter being here even now. Among the discarded customs taught and encouraged by the new testament are, speaking in tongues, going forth to preach without purse or scrip, laying on of hands for the healing of the sick, raising the dead, casting out devils, and all other miracles; and there will be further repudiations as time passes, further ignoring of portions of the scriptures by orthodox sects, a further weeding out of the unnatural and irrational from things spiritual and worshipful.

The tenets of the Mormon church are these:

The bible is the inspired record of God's dealings with men in the eastern hemisphere; the book of Mormon is the inspired record of God's dealings with the ancient inhabitants of this continent; the book of Doctrine and Covenants of the Church of Jesus Christ of Latter-day Saints consists of revelations from God concerning the present dispensation to Joseph Smith, who was inspired to translate the book of Mormon and organize the church of Christ anew. Joseph Smith to the present dispensation is as Moses was to Israel; there is no conflict, either in personages or books. The statements, assertions, promises, and prophecies of the books, and the precepts and practices of the personages, are accepted, all of them, and held to be the revealed will to man of one and the same God, whose will it is the duty and endeavor of his people to carry out in every particular to the best of their ability.

There are more gods than one. There are spiritual gifts. Not only must there be faith in Christ, but faith in the holy priesthood, and faith in continual revelation.[1] Man is a free agent. The laying on of hands for ordination, and for the healing of the sick, descends from the early to the later apostles.[2] There will be a resurrection of the body and a second coming of Christ. Israel is a chosen people; there has been a scattering of Israel, and there will be a gathering. Joseph Smith was the fulfiller not only of bible prophecies, but of the book of Mormon prophecies, and of his own prophecies. Foreordination, election, and dispensation of the fulness of times are held. There was an apostasy of the primitive church, and now there is a return. There was the Jerusalem of the eastern hemisphere; on the continent of North America is planted the new Jerusalem. Miracles obtain; also visions and dreams, signs and tokens, and angels of light and darkness. There are free spirits and spirits imprisoned; the wicked will be destroyed, and there will be a millennial reign. The saints are largely of the house of Israel, and heirs to the promises made to Abraham, Isaac, and Jacob. The aboriginal inhabitants of America and the Pacific isles were the

[1] In 1853, Benjamin Brown, high-priest, and pastor of the London, Reading, Kent, and Essex conferences, published at Liverpool a tract entitled, *Testimonies for the Truth; a Record of Manifestations of the Power of God, Miraculous and Providential*, witnessed by him in his travels and experiences. The author was a native of New York, and born in 1794. He was a firm believer in latter-day revelations from God, and that the ancient gifts of the gospel still remained, long before he joined the Mormons. He labored long and in various places. He held property in Nauvoo when the saints were driven out, and was obliged to take $250 for what was worth $3,000. Afterward he underwent all the sufferings and vicissitudes of the overland journey to Salt Lake. Mr Brown was an earnest and honest man; his book is the record of his life, and is simple and attractive in style and substance.

[2] Healing the sick. Joseph early laid it down as a rule that all diseases and sickness among them were to be cured by the elders, and by the use of herbs alone. Physicians of the world were denounced as enemies to mankind, and the use of their medicines was prohibited. Afterw 'd, anointing with oil, prayer, and laying on hands were resorted to in add. 'on to the first mentioned. Says Mrs Richards, 'In all sicknesses we use. no medicines, with the exception of herb teas that we ourselves prepared, trusting exclusively to the efficacy of the anointing with oil and prayer.' *Reminiscences*, MS., 34. Joseph said, 'All wholesome herbs God hath ordained for the constitution, nature, and use of man. Every herb in the season thereof, and every fruit in the season thereof.' The use of flesh was not forbidden, but rather restricted to seasons of cold and famine. All grain was pronounced good for man, but wheat was particularly recommended, with corn for the ox, oats for the horse, rye for fowls and swine, and barley for all useful animals, and for mild drinks; as also other grain. *Times and Seasons*, v. 736.

seed of Joseph, divided into numerous nations and
tribes.   The Lamanites were of the house of Ma-
nasseh.

We believe, say their articles of faith, in God the
father, in Jesus Christ the son, and in the holy ghost.
For their own sins, and not for any transgression of
Adam, men will be punished; but all may be saved,
through the atonement, by obedience to the ordinances of the gospel, which are: faith in Christ, repentance, baptism by immersion,[3] and laying on of

[3] Baptism, a prerequisite to church membership, as well as to final salvation, to be of avail, must be by immersion, and performed by one of the sect.
The person who is called of God, and has authority from Jesus Christ to baptize, shall go down into the water with the person to be baptized, and shall say,
calling him or her by name: ' Having been commissioned of Jesus Christ, I
baptize you in the name of the father, and of the son, and of the holy ghost.
Amen.' *Doctrine and Covenants*, 115, 118.   Baptisms are entered in the general church records, giving the name, place, and date of birth, quorum, date
of baptism, first time or re-baptism, by whom baptized, when and by whom
confirmed. *Deseret News*, Feb. 22, 1851.   In 1844, complaints were made that
members of the church, dismissed by the council, had been re-baptized by
elders who were themselves excluded, and declaring such baptisms invalid.
Times and Seasons, v. 458-9.

In 1836, Joseph introduced the ceremony of anointing with consecrated oil.
He first anointed his father, who, having been blessed by the first presidency,
anointed them in turn, beginning with the eldest.   The bishops of Kirtland
and Zion, together with their counsellors, were next anointed, and afterward the presiding officers of each quorum performed the ceremony on their
subordinates, assisted in some instances by the Smith brothers.   Joseph describes the ceremony of consecrating the oil, as follows: ' I took the oil in my
left hand, Father Smith being seated before me, and the remainder of the
presidency encircled him round about.   We then stretched our right hands
towards heaven, and blessed the oil, and consecrated it in the name of Jesus
Christ.' *Mil. Star*, xv. 620.   Olive-oil is commonly used. *Mrs Richards,
Reminiscences*, MS., 34.   Many remarkable cures are mentioned.   A sea-
man, belonging to H. B. M. ship *Terror*, was rendered deaf and dumb by
a stroke of lightning, at Bermuda.   Several years after, he was baptized
by elders in a canal in England, and instantly recovered both speech and
hearing. *Frontier Guardian*, Jan. 23, 1850.   In 1840, a young woman then
living at Batavia, N. Y., who had been deaf and dumb for four and one
half years, was first restored to her hearing by the laying on of the
hands of the elders of the church, and a second ministration, some time
afterward, enabled her to speak. *Times and Seasons*, ii. 516-17.   During
the building of Nauv̄   , nearly every one was attacked with malarial fever,
caused by breaking ..p the new land, and even the prophet himself succumbed for a time.   But hearing the voice of the Lord calling on him,
he arose and went through the camp healing all to whom he drew near.
Woodruff (Mrs), Autobiog., 2-3.   Brigham declares he was among the number healed at this time. *Mil. Star*, xxv. 646.   While Joseph was in the midst
of his sick, an unbeliever, living a few miles distant, came to him, beseeching
him to come and heal his twin children, who were near death's door.   The
prophet was unable to go himself, but sent Wilford Woodruff in his place.
Says the latter, ' He [Joseph] took a red silk handkerchief out of his pocket
and gave it to me, and told me to wipe their faces with the handkerchief

hands for the gift of the holy ghost. We believe in
the same organization and powers that existed in

when I administered to them, and they should be healed.' He also said unto
me: "As long as you will keep that handkerchief, it shall remain a league
between you and me." I went with the man, and did as the prophet commanded me, and the children were healed. I have possession of the handkerchief unto this day [1881].' *Leaves from my Journal*, 65.   F. D. Richards,
who had been sick for several months, was baptized, anointed, and confirmed;
immediately after which he was restored to health.   Some time afterward,
being then an elder, he cured a severe toothache by touching the tooth with
his finger. *Narrative*, MS., 15–16.   Mrs Richards' brother, afterward Elder
Snyder, was raised from a sick-bed after having been baptized and administered to by Elder John E. Page.   Mrs Richards was taken by her brother
from a sick-bed to a lake from the surface of which ice more than a foot thick
had been removed, and there baptized, whereupon she immediately recovered.
Similar cases might be given by the score.
   Baptism for the dead is first alluded to by the prophet, who, in a revelation dated Jan. 19, 1841, declares, 'A baptismal font there is not upon the
earth, that they, my saints, may be baptized for those who are dead.' It is
intimated that a reasonable time will be allowed in which to build a temple
and a permanent font, and that during this time a temporary substitute
for the font may be employed; but after the completion of the temple, no
baptisms for the dead will be of avail unless conducted within the building. See *Doctrine and Covenants*, 392, 395.   Brigham says he first heard of
the new doctrine when he was in Europe (1840), and that he believed in it
before anything was said or done about it in the church. *Times and Seasons*,
vi. 954.   Daniel Tyler says the doctrine was first taught in Nauvoo, although
Joseph told some of the elders in Kirtland that it was part of the gospel, and
would yet be practised as such. *Juvenile Instructor*, xv. 56.   He also says
that before other provision was made, many were baptized in the Mississippi
River.   The first baptismal font, a temporary structure, intended for use only
until the completion of the temple, was erected in the basement of that building, and dedicated on Nov. 8, 1841, Joseph being present and Brigham delivering the address.   Joseph thus describes the font: It is constructed of pine
staves, tongued and grooved, and is oval-shaped, 'sixteen feet long east and
west, and twelve feet wide, seven feet high from the foundation, the basin
four feet deep; the mouldings of the cap and base are formed of beautiful
carved work in antique style.   The sides are finished with panel-work.   A
flight of stairs in the north and south sides lead up and down into the
basin, guarded by a side railing.   The font stands upon twelve oxen, four on
each side and two at each end, their heads, shoulders, and fore legs project-
ing out from under the font; they are carved out of oak plank, glued together,
and copied after the most beautiful five-year-old steer that could be found in
the country, and they are an excellent striking likeness of the original; the
horns were geometrically formed after the most perfect horn that could be
procured.   The oxen and the mouldings were carved by Elder Elijah Fordham, from the city of New York, the work occupying eight months.   The
whole was enclosed in a temporary frame building.' *Mil. Star*, xviii. 744.   On
Sept. 6, 1842, Joseph writes to the church that all baptisms must be recorded by a person appointed for the purpose, and whose duty it will be to
note every detail of the ceremony in each case.   One of the officials is to
be appointed in each ward, and his returns properly certified to are to be
forwarded to the general recorder, who will enter them on the church records,
together with the names of all witnesses, etc., and finally add his own certificate as to the genuineness of the signature of the ward recorder.   This detail
is necessary for the proper identification hereafter of those baptized, for the
authority for which the prophet quotes *Revelations*, xx. 12.   'And I saw the

the primitive church, namely, apostles, prophets, pastors, teachers, evangelists; in the gift of tongues,[4]

dead, small and great, stand before God; and the books were opened,' etc. He also states that it was revealed to him on Sept. 1, 1842, that a general recorder must be appointed. *Mil. Star*, xx. 5-6; *Doctrine and Covenants*, 409-13. For the ceremony itself, he finds warrant in *1st Cor.*, xv. 29. 'Else what shall they do who are baptized for the dead? If the dead rise not at all, why are they then baptized for the dead?'

Confirmation follows baptism, with frequently an interval of a few days. Baptism may take place on any day in the week, and the confirmation be deferred until the church assembles on the following, or even a later, Sunday. Two or more elders commonly attend, all taking part in the ceremony. Mrs Stenhouse thus describes her own confirmation: 'Four elders placed their hands solemnly upon my head, and one of them said: "Fanny, by virtue of the authority vested in me, I confirm you a member of the church of Jesus Christ of latter-day saints; and inasmuch as you have been obedient to the command of God, through his servants, and have been baptized for the remission of your sins, I say unto you that those sins are remitted. And in the name of God I bless you, and say unto you, that inasmuch as you are faithful and obedient to the teachings of the priesthood, and seek the advancement of the kingdom, there is no good thing that your heart can desire that the Lord will not give unto you. You shall have visions and dreams, and angels shall visit you by day and by night. You shall stand in the temple in Zion, and administer to the saints of the most high God. You shall speak in tongues and prophecy; and the Lord shall bless you abundantly, both temporally and spiritually. These blessings I seal upon your head, inasmuch as you shall be faithful; and I pray heaven to bless you; and say unto you, be thou blessed, in the name of the father, and of the son, and of the holy ghost. Amen."' *Englishwoman in Utah*, 19–20.

[4] The gift of tongues is the power to speak in a strange language, but not to translate. It first appeared about 1830, when it was pronounced of the devil. Howe says it was revived in the early part of 1833, and that at one meeting Joseph passed around the room laying his hand upon each one, and speaking as follows: 'Ak man, oh son, oh man, ah ne commene en holle goste en haben en glai hosanne en holle goste en esac milkea jeremiah, ezekiel, Nephi, Lehi, St John,' etc. *Mormonism Unveiled*, 132–6. In this year, it was suggested that 'no prophecy spoken in tongues should be made public, for this reason: many who pretend to have the gift of interpretation are liable to be mistaken, and do not give the true interpretation of what is spoken; ... but if any speak in tongues a word of exhortation or doctrine, or the principles of the gospel, etc., let it be interpreted for the edification of the church.' *Times and Seasons*, vi. 865. The gift was not confined to men; many women were noted for eloquence when thus inspired. Says Mrs Stenhouse of a Sister Ellis: 'Her hands were clenched, and her eyes had that wild and supernatural glare which is never seen save in cases of lunacy or intense feverish excitement. Every one waited breathlessly, listening to catch what she might say; you might have heard a pin drop. They [her utterances] seemed to be chiefly the repetition of the same syllables, something like a child repeating la, la, la, le, lo; ma, ma, ma, mi, ma; dele, dele, dele, hela; followed, perhaps, by a number of sounds strung together, which could not be rendered in any shape by the pen.' *Englishwoman in Utah*, 27–8. Says Orson Hyde: 'We believe in the gift of the holy ghost being enjoyed now as much as it was in the apostles' days, and that it is imparted by the laying on of hands of those in authority; and that the gift of tongues, and also the gift of prophecy, are gifts of the spirit, and are obtained through that medium.' *Frontier Guardian*, Dec. 12, 1849. Mrs Stenhouse remarks that 'in later days, the exercise of this gift has been discouraged by the elders, and especially by Brigham.' Going to the Lion House one day, she was blessed by one of Brigham's wives,

prophecy, revelation, and visions. In the scriptures is found the law of tithing, which law is now revived, and the keeping of it made one of the first duties of the saints. The ten commandments, and all other commandments, ordinances, promulgations, and possibilities, are in force now as at the time they were given. Marriage is a sacred and an eternal covenant. Plural marriage, sanctioned under the old dispensation and revived under the new, is open to all, and is, in some instances, commanded, when it becomes a sacred obligation.

Seldom does a good Mormon appear in a court of law arrayed against a brother Mormon. And this is why, as the saints allege, the twenty-five or fifty lawyers in Utah who are compelled to derive their living almost entirely from the gentiles, are so bitter against the saints. When two Mormons disagree, they present themselves before the president of the stake, who with twelve councillors, six facing six, their selection having been agreed to by the litigants, is ready to try the case without delay. Plaintiff and defendant, each with his witnesses, take their places before the president, and between the rows of councillors. Prayer is then offered, almighty aid being asked in bringing the affair to a righteous and amicable conclusion. The litigants state the case, each from his own standpoint; the witnesses are heard; the councillors decide. Prayer is again offered. The adversaries shake hands; there is nothing to pay. Until the gentiles came, there were in Utah no police or police courts; no houses of drinking, or of gambling, or of prostitution. Of the administration of justice among the saints I shall speak more at length in a later chapter.

and the blessing interpreted by another wife; the latter, however, cautioned her not to repeat what had occurred, for 'Brother Brigham does not like to hear of these things.' *Englishwoman in Utah*, 29. Tullidge mentions the names of many women who were distinguished as possessing this gift, and relates an instance of a party whose wagon was surrounded by Indians, escaping with their lives and property; the captors being induced to abandon their prize by Jane Grover, a girl of seventeen, who addressed them in their own language. *Women of Mormondom*, 474–8.

The doctrine of blood atonement was early inculcated
by the church, as a sacrifice necessary for salvation, and
not, as many have asserted, in order to legalize murder.
There were the altars and the offerings of the old
testament, and the great god-man sacrifice of the
new.   Christ made the atonement for the sins of the
world by the shedding of his blood.   By the laws of
the land, he who commits murder must atone for it
by his own death.[5]   There are sins of various de-

---

[5] The theory of blood atonement is that for certain sins the blood of the
transgressor must be shed to save his soul.   Among these sins are apostasy,
the shedding of innocent blood, and unfaithfulness to marriage obligations
on the part of the wife.   Says Brigham, in a discourse delivered in Salt Lake
City: 'There are sins which men commit for which they cannot receive forgiveness in this world, or in that which is to come, and if they had their
eyes open to their true condition, they would be perfectly willing to have
their blood spilled upon the ground, that the smoke thereof might ascend to
heaven as an offering for their sins; and the smoking incense would atone for
their sins; whereas, if such is not the case, they will stick to them and remain upon them in the spirit world.   I know, when you hear my brethren
telling about cutting people off from the earth, that you consider it is strong
doctrine; but it is to save them, not to destroy them...I do know that there
are sins committed, of such a nature that if the people did understand the
doctrine of salvation they would tremble because of their situation.   And
furthermore, I know that there are transgressors who, if they knew themselves and the only condition upon which they can obtain forgiveness, would
beg of their brethren to shed their blood, that the smoke thereof might ascend to God as an offering to appease the wrath that is kindled against them,
and that the law might have its course.   I will say further: I have had men
come to me and offer their lives to atone for their sins...There are sins that
can be atoned for by an offering upon an altar, as in ancient days; and there
are sins that the blood of a lamb, of a calf, or of turtle-doves cannot remit,
but they must be atoned for by the blood of the man.'   And at another
time: 'All mankind love themselves, and let these principles be known by
an individual, and he would be glad to have his blood shed.   That would be
loving themselves, even unto an eternal exaltation.   Will you love your
brothers or sisters likewise when they have committed a sin that cannot be atoned for without the shedding of their blood?   Will you love
that man or woman well enough to shed their blood?   That is what Jesus
Christ meant...I could refer you to plenty of instances where men have
been righteously slain in order to atone for their sins.   I have seen scores
and hundreds of people for whom there would have been a chance in the
last resurrection if their lives had been taken and their blood spilled on the
ground as a smoking incense to the almighty...I have known a great many
men who have left this church for whom there is no chance whatever for
exaltation; but if their blood had been spilled it would have been better for
them.   This is loving our neighbor as ourselves; if he needs help, help him;
and if he wants salvation, and it is necessary to spill his blood on the earth
in order that he may be saved, spill it.' *Deseret News*, Oct. 1, 1856, Feb.
18, 1857.   Following Brigham's lead, Heber C. Kimball and Jedediah M.
Grant taught the same doctrine during the religious revival, or so-called
reformation, in Utah, in 1856-7, of which more later, Grant being the most
vehement of the three.   The reader will find these discourses reported at
length in the *Deseret News*.   The doctrine is very clearly explained in *Pen-*

grees of heinousness; some requiring only public confession and promised reformation by way of atonement, whilst others are characterized by an enormity so vast that pardon on earth is impossible. Of the first class are all minor offences against church discipline, breach of which has been publicly acknowledged by nearly every leader, from Joseph himself down to the humblest official.

For the proper carrying out of the instructions revealed in the sacred books, an organization has been effected in these latter days, based upon books and on former organizations. There are two principal priesthoods, the Melchisedek and the Aaronic, the latter including the Levitical. The Melchisedek is the higher, comprising apostles, patriarchs, high-priests, seventies, and elders. It holds the right of presidency, with authority to administer in all the offices, ordinances, and affairs of the church. It holds the keys of all spiritual blessings, receives the mysteries of the kingdom of heaven, whose doors are ever open, and holds communion with God the father, Jesus Christ the mediator, Joseph Smith the prophet, and all departed saints.[6]

The Aaronic is a subordinate priesthood, being an appendage to the Melchisedek, and acting under its

rose's *Blood Atonement*, passim. See also *Lee's Morm.*, 282–3; *Morm. Proph.*, 157–60; *Young's Wife No. 19*, 182–99; *Paddock's La Tour*, 305–8; *Bertrand's Mem. Morm.*, 139–72, 250–8, 296–316.

[6] In regard to the two priesthoods, the Melchisedek and the Aaronic, or Levitical, all authority in the church is subordinate to the first, which holds the right of presidency and has power over all the offices in the church. The presidency of the high-priesthood of this order has the right to officiate in all the offices of the church. High-priests are authorized to officiate in any lower positions in the church, as well as in their own office. Elders are of this priesthood, and are authorized to officiate instead of high-priests, in the absence of the latter. The twelve apostles are charged with the duty of ordaining all the subordinate officers of the church, and also with its missionary work. Together they form a quorum whose authority equals that of the first presidency, but action by either body must be unanimous. A majority may form a quorum when circumstances render it impossible to assemble the whole body. They also constitute a travelling, presiding high-council, under the direction of the presidency of the church, and it is their duty to ordain ministers in all large branches. The seventies are also missionaries—assistants to the twelve, and united they are equal in authority with the twelve.

supervision. It comprises bishops, priests, teachers, and deacons, who hold the keys of the ministering angels, having power to administer in certain ordinances and in the temporal affairs of the church, baptizing and sitting as judges in Israel. The bishopric is the presidency of the Aaronic priesthood. The office of a bishop is to administer in temporal matters. First-born sons, lineal descendants of Aaron, and no others, have a legal right to the bishopric. But a high-priest of the order of Melchisedek may officiate in all lesser offices, including that of bishop, when no lineal descendant of Aaron can be found, and after he has been ordained to this power by the first presidency. There is also the patriarchal priesthood,[7]

[7] About 1834, Joseph Smith had a revelation to the effect that it was the will of the Lord that every father should bless his own children, and that patriarchs should be set apart to bless those without a father in the church. This revelation was due to an expressed desire on the part of Brigham Young's father to bless his own children before dying, after the manner of the patriarchs of old. *Young's Wife No. 19*, 581. Several years before this, it had been directed that every member of the church having children should bring them to the elders before the church, who were to lay their hands upon them in the name of Jesus Christ, and bless them. *Doctrine and Covenants*, 72. During the life of the first patriarch—Jos. Smith, sen.—these blessings were nominally free to the recipients. A high-council held at Kirtland in Sept. 1835 decided that when the patriarch was occupied in blessing the church, he should be paid at the rate of ten dollars a week, and his expenses; also that Frederick G. Williams be appointed to attend blessing meetings, and record the proceedings, for which services he should receive the same compensation. The payment of twelve dollars for a book in which to record the blessings caused discussion in this council, and brother Henry Green, who had intimated that a suitable book could be procured for less money, was excluded from the church for his presumption. *Mil. Star*, xv. 308–9. In Jan. 1836, Smith, sen., was anointed with oil by the prophet, blessed by each of the presidency in turn, and was thenceforth known as Father Smith. *Id.*, 620. In 1837, the pay of the patriarch was fixed at a dollar and fifty cents a day, and that of the recorder at ten cents for each 100 words. *Mil. Star*, xvi. 109. When Hyrum became patriarch, says the author of *Young's Wife No. 19*, 581, the demand for blessings had so increased that one dollar each was charged for them; and in 1875 the price had advanced to two dollars. Upon the death of his father in 1840, Hyrum Smith succeeded to the office of patriarch, pursuant to a revelation entailing it on the eldest son. The revelation is dated in Jan. 1841. *Doctrine and Covenants*, 305–6; *Mil. Star*, xviii. 363. The following notice appears in *Times and Seasons*, Nov. 1, 1841: 'The brethren are hereby notified that our well-beloved brother, Hyrum Smith, patriarch of the church, has erected a comfortable office opposite his dwelling-house [in Nauvoo], where himself, together with his scribe and recorder, James Sloan, will attend regularly every Monday, Wednesday, and Friday, during the entire day, or upon any other day if urgent circumstances require it, to perform the duties of his high and holy calling. A copy of the blessings can be received immediately after being pronounced, so that the brethren who live

the patriarch to be the oldest man of the blood of Joseph or of the seed of Abraham. Likewise there are mothers in Israel.[8]

Head over all is the First Presidency of the Church, known also as the First Presidency of the High-Priesthood, and consisting of a president and two councillors.[9] The first presidency presides over and governs

at a distance can have it to take with them.' Hyrum's successor was his brother William, who was disfellowshipped in 1845, John Smith, brother to the prophet, being ordained patriarch over the church, and holding that office until his death in 1854. In the following year Hyrum's son John was ordained patriarch, and since that date has been sustained in his office at each successive conference. A child is first blessed when eight days old, and again so soon as the mother is able to present her child on a regular fast-day. The first Thursday in each month is set apart for fasting. *Mrs Richards' Reminiscences*, MS., 34–5. The second ceremony is usually attended by both parents, and in addition to a blessing, the child receives its name. Each birthday it is customary for the parents to hold a family gathering, when the child is again blessed, and prayers offered for its welfare. When eight years old, the child is baptized. See *Horne's Migrations*, MS., 37. The blessings are not only pronounced, but also written out. *Id.*, 34. 'These blessings are rather wonderful affairs; they promise all sorts of things, in a vague, indefinite way, if only the recipient proves faithful. Some are assured they shall never taste death, but live until Christ comes, and be caught up to meet him in the air; others are assured that they are to have the privilege of redeeming their dead so far back that there shall not be a broken link in the chain. Absurd as this all seems, there are hundred of saints who believe that every word shall be fulfilled.' *Young's Wife No. 19*, 581.

[8] Hall says there is a class of women, mothers in Israel, whose business it is to instruct females as to their duty in matters not suitable to be taught from the stand. *Mormonism Exposed*, 39–44.

[9] Early in 1833 the first presidency was established, with Joseph Smith at the head, his associates in the management of affairs being Sidney Rigdon and Frederick G. Williams. The revelation creating this triumvirate is dated March 8th, and in it Joseph's coadjutors are instructed first to finish the translation of the prophets, and afterward preside over the affairs of the church and the school. *Times and Seasons*, v. 736–7. William Hall, who was a member of the church for seven years, erroneously states that the presidency at first consisted of Smith, Rigdon, and William Law. *Abominations*, 8. At a conference held in Sept. 1837, Joseph appealed to the church to ascertain if he was still regarded as its head, when the vote was unanimous. He then introduced Rigdon and Williams as his councillors. According to the minutes of the conference, Williams was not accepted at first, but this action appears to have been rescinded afterward. *Mil. Star*, xvi. 56. Oliver Cowdery, Jos. Smith, sen., Hyrum Smith, and John Smith were accepted as assistant councillors, and these seven were henceforth to be regarded the heads of the church. At a general conference of the branch of the church at Far West in Nov. 1837, the action of the Kirtland conference was sustained so far as Smith and Rigdon were concerned, but Williams was rejected. Hyrum Smith was unanimously chosen in Williams' place. *Mil. Star*, xvi. 106–7. At a conference held at Far West in April 1838, the first presidency was appointed to sign the licenses of the official members of the church. In Jan. 1841, Joseph had a revelation to the effect that he was presiding elder over all the church, translator, revelator, a seer, and prophet; and that his councillors were Sidney Rigdon and William Law. These three were to consti-

all the affairs of the church, temporal and spiritual;
the first president is the prophet of God, seer, revelator, and translator.

Next in authority are twelve apostles, who are a
travelling presiding high-council, and with whom, on
the death of the president of the church, the supreme
rulership rests until another first presidency is in-
stalled.[10] The president of the twelve, chosen in the

tute a quorum and first presidency, to receive the oracles for the whole
church. Law's selection was to fill the vacancy caused by the appointment
of Hyrum Smith to be patriarch. *Mil. Star*, xviii. 363. In this same month
Joseph notified the recorder of Hancock county that he (Joseph) had been
elected sole trustee of the church of Jesus Christ of latter-day saints by the
church at Nauvoo, to hold office during life. *Id.*, 373. Smith, Rigdon, and
Law were continued in office by the annual conference, convened in April 1843.
After the murder of the Smiths in 1844, the first presidency lapsed, and for
more than three years the church was governed by the quorum of the twelve
apostles, of which Brigham was president. At a meeting of the twelve apostles, high-council, and high-priests at Nauvoo, in August 1844, Sidney Rigdon
offered himself as guardian to the church, claiming that his action was in
obedience to revelation. Young opposed Rigdon's claims, and the assembly
decided that the twelve should govern the church, with Young at their head.
Mil. Star, xxv. 215-17, 263-4. In Dec. 1847 Brigham Young, Heber C. Kimball, and Willard Richards were chosen to constitute the first presidency.
Juv. Inst., xiv. 128. Young died in 1877, and the presidency remained vacant
until October 1880, when John Taylor was chosen, with George Q. Cannon and Joseph F. Smith as councillors. *Marshall, Through America*, 161.
This conference lasted five days. *S. L. Tribune*, Oct. 11, 1880. On the death
of the president the quorum is dissolved, and its members, as a presidency,
have no status. *Richards' Narr.*, MS., 51.

[10] On Feb. 14, 1835, the church at Kirtland met for the purpose of choosing and ordaining the twelve apostles. The business occupied several days.
Briefly, the ceremonies were as follows: The assemblage consented to accept
the names presented by the three witnesses who had been appointed to make
the selection. P. P. Pratt says, in his *Autobiog.*, 127-28, the ceremonies were
performed by Smith, Whitmer, and Cowdery, and that they acted in accordance with the revelation of June 1829; but in the history of Jos. Smith, *Mil.
Star*, Mar. and Apr. 1853, the three witnesses only are mentioned. Martin
Harris' name does not appear in the revelation referred to. See *Doctrine
and Covenants*, 190-2. In an article by 'R. A.' in the *Juv. Inst.*, xiv. 128,
the selection is accredited to the three witnesses, who are mentioned by
name. As Pratt was one of the ordained, it would seem that his account
should be reliable. Each candidate came forward as summoned, and in return received a blessing, and a charge from one of the three. The order of
ordination was as follows: On Feb. 14th, Lyman E. Johnson, Brigham
Young, and Heber C. Kimball. On the next day, Orson Hyde, David W.
Patten, Luke Johnson, Wm E. McLellin, John F. Boynton, and William
Smith. On Feb. 21st, Parley P. Pratt, Orson Pratt, and Thos B. Marsh, who
were absent on a mission, were ordained upon their return to Kirtland, which
occurred later. *Mil. Star*, xv. 206-12. Shortly after, the names were arranged
according to seniority, when they stood, Marsh, Patten, Young, Kimball,
Hyde, McLellin, P. P. Pratt, Luke Johnson, Smith, O. Pratt, Boynton, and
L. E. Johnson. Four of the above apostatized in 1838, viz.: McLellin, the
Johnsons, and Boynton; John Taylor, John E. Page, Wilford Woodruff, and
Willard Richards were appointed instead. Shortly after this, Marsh, the

first instance by reason of seniority or ordination, usually becomes president of the church. The office of the twelve is to preach and teach throughout the world, regulating the affairs of the church everywhere under the direction of the first presidency, calling to their aid therein the seventies.

An apostle may administer in the several offices of the church, particularly in spiritual matters.[11] The office of a patriarch is to give patriarchal blessings; the office of a member of a seventy is to travel and preach the gospel; but a patriarch, a high-priest, a

president of the twelve, apostatized, and in 1838 Patten was killed, which left Young at the head of the list, and he became president of the twelve. Geo. A. Smith was ordained in 1839, and Lyman Wight not long after. In 1844, according to Elder Phelps, the following names were on the roll: Young, Kimball, Parley P. Pratt, Hyde, Richards, Taylor, William Smith, Woodruff, George A. Smith, Orson Pratt, Page, and Wight. During this year Wm Smith and Page apostatized, and were replaced by Amasa M. Lyman and Ezra T. Benson. Early in 1845, Young, Kimball, and Richards were chosen to the first presidency, and Wight was disfellowshipped for apostasy; the vacancies thus caused were filled by appointing Chas C. Rich, Lorenzo and Erastus Snow, and Franklin D. Richards. In 1857, Geo. Q. Cannon was appointed, vice P. P. Pratt, deceased. In 1867, Lyman was dropped and Jos. F. Smith appointed. In 1868, Geo. A. Smith became one of the first presidency, and Brigham Young, jun., succeeded him. Albert Carrington was appointed in 1869 in place of Benson, deceased, and Moses Thatcher in 1879, vice Hyde, deceased in 1878; which left the twelve in the following order: John Taylor, Wilford Woodruff, Orson Pratt, Chas C. Rich, Lorenzo Snow, Erastus Snow, Franklin D. Richards, George Q. Cannon, Brigham Young, Joseph F. Smith, Albert Carrington, Moses Thatcher, Pratt being the only remaining member of the original twelve. *Juv. Inst.*, xiv. 128–9. The vacancies caused by the elevation of John Taylor to the presidency in 1880, with George Q. Cannon and Joseph F. Smith as councillors, were partially filled by the appointment of Francis M. Lyman and John H. Smith. *S. L. Tribune*, Oct. 11, 1880. Orson Pratt died Oct. 1881, and a year later Geo. Teasdale and Heber J. Grant were elected. *Hand-book of Ref.*, 89–90. Up to 1877, the twelve received no pay for their services; but the conference of Oct. voted $1,500 a year to each apostle. 'This is the first sum that has ever been publicly appropriated to any council of the church for the performance of their duties to the people. When I went to Europe in 1866, I borrowed the means and gave my note; on my return I had to pay back my indebtedness.' *Richards' Narr.*, MS., 59–60.

[11] In 1845 was issued at New York and Liverpool, *Proclamation of the Twelve Apostles of the Church of Jesus Christ of Latter-day Saints; to all the Kings of the World; to the President of the United States of America; to the Governors of the several states, and to the rulers and people of all nations*, Greeting, 'Know ye that the kingdom of God has come,' etc. The tract goes on to say that 'Jehovah has been pleased once more to speak from the heavens,' by which means the apostleship of Christ has been restored, in preparation for his coming, which is now near at hand. Then are recited the leading points of faith, with allusions to the history of the church, and calls to repentance.

member of a seventy, and an elder may, in common
with an apostle, administer in other spiritual offices.

All superior officers are frequently called elders.
Thus an apostle is an elder; and he may baptize, and
ordain other elders, priests, teachers, and deacons.
It is his calling to administer bread and wine, or bread
and water, emblems of the flesh and blood of Christ;
to confirm the baptized by the laying on of hands for
the baptism of fire and the holy ghost; to teach, expound, exhort, and to lead in meetings as he is led by
the holy ghost.

A bishop who is a first-born and a lineal descendant of Aaron may sit as a common judge in the church
without councillors, except in the trial of a president
of the high-priesthood. But a bishop from the high-
priesthood may not sit as a judge without his two
councillors. Over all the bishops in the church there
is a presiding bishop.

The duties of a priest are to preach, baptize, administer the sacrament, and visit families and pray
with them. The duties of a teacher are to watch over
and strengthen the church, and see that no iniquity
creeps into it, and that every member performs his
obligations and conducts himself without guile. The
duties of the deacon are to assist the teacher and the
bishop, attending to the temporal affairs of the church,
looking after the houses of worship and the necessities
of the poor. Teachers and deacons may instruct and
exhort, but they are not authorized to baptize, lay on
hands, or administer the sacrament. No one can hold
office except by authoritative call and ordination, or
by special appointment of God.

The seventies are organized into various councils of
seventy, commonly called quorums. Each council of
seventy has seven presidents, chosen out of the seventy, one of the seven presiding over the others and over
the whole seventy. The seven presidents of the first
council of seventies also preside over all the councils

of seventies.[12] According to Elder John Jaques, to whose little book on the priesthood I am indebted for this information, there were in 1882 seventy-six councils of seventies, with seventy members in each council when complete. Elders are organized in councils of ninety-six, each council having a president and two councillors. Priests are organized in councils of forty-eight, each with a president—who must be a bishop—and two councillors. Teachers are organized in councils of twenty-four, and deacons in councils of twelve, each with a president and two councillors.[13]

In the society of saints, there are territorial divisions into what are called Stakes of Zion. In Utah, these divisions correspond usually, but not necessarily, with the counties, each county being a stake.

[12] In February 1835, Joseph Smith, with the aid of the recently appointed apostles, proceeded to organize two quorums of the seventies, whose duties were to assist in the missionary work of the church. Each quorum had seven presidents, and these constituted the councils of the two organizations. Joseph Youngsen, who gives an account of the seventies, gives the names of the presidents of the first quorum only, as follows: Hazen Aldrich, Joseph Young, Levi W. Hancock, Leonard Rich, Zebedee Coltrin, Lyman Sherman, and Sylvester Smith. After noting the changes in the interval, he states that in 1878 the presidents were Young, sen., Hancock, Henry Herriman, Albert P. Rockwood, Horace S. Eldredge, Jacob Gates, and John Van Cott. *Hist. of Organ. of Seventies*, 1–8. In an account of the dedication of their hall at Nauvoo, in 1844, it is stated there were fifteen quorums—one thousand and fifty in all, if each quorum was full. *Times and Seasons*, vi. 794.

[13] For act of incorporation of Mormon church, 1851, see *Utah, Acts Legisl.* (ed. 1866), 108; *S. L. C. Contributor*, ii. 270; number and wealth of churches, *Seventh Census Rept*, 1851-2, 45; prayer in the family, *Robinson's Sinners and Saints*, 243–4; church property, and law regulating it, *Richards' Narr.*, MS., 83; church government, *Ward's Husband in Utah*, 16–17; *Mil. Star*, iii. 67; positions of church officials, *Id.*, xv. 709. As showing the relative standing of the church dignitaries, the order of voting, as prescribed at the conference which elected Taylor to the presidency in 1880, is given. The twelve apostles and their councillors; the patriarchs; presidents of stakes and their councillors, and the high-councils; the high-priests; the seventies; the elders; the bishops and their councillors; the lesser priesthood—priests, teachers, and deacons. The members of each order voted standing and with the right hand uplifted, and finally the congregation voted in the same manner. *S. L. City Tribune*, Oct. 11, 1880. On faith and doctrine, see *Jaques' Church of Jesus Christ*, passim; *Hand-book of Reference*, passim; *Jaques' Catechism*, passim; *Book of Doctrine and Covenants*, passim; *Richards' and Little's Compendium*, passim; *Articles of Our Faith*, passim; *Pearl of Great Price*, passim; *Times and Seasons*, passim; *Millennial Star*, passim; *Deseret News*, passim; *Moffat's Catechism*, passim; *Pratt's Persecutions*, passim; *Pratt's Voice of Warning*, passim; *Reynolds' Book of Abraham*, passim; and many other books, pamphlets, and periodicals by various members and dignitaries of the church.

Every stake has a president, with his two councillors, and a high-council, consisting of twelve high-priests.[14] The high-priests assemble in council, having its president and two councillors, at stated times, usually once a month, for conference and instruction. The president of a stake, with his two councillors, presides over the high-council of that stake, which has original and appellate jurisdiction, and whose decisions are usually, but not invariably, final. Appeals are had to a general assembly of the several councils of the priesthood, but such appeals are seldom taken. The jurisdiction of the several councils is ecclesiastical, affecting fellowship and standing only, the extreme penalty being excommunication.

Each stake is divided into wards, the number being according to territory and population; over each ward presides a bishop, with his two councillors. Each stake and each ward, as a rule, has its own meeting-house. There are about twenty-five stakes, divided into some three hundred wards. Salt Lake City is divided into twenty-one wards, each containing for the most part nine ten-acre blocks, though in the outskirts they are larger. Each stake holds a quarterly conference; and the church holds a general conference every April and October.

It will be observed that the orders of priesthood and organization of the church are copied essentially from the bible. As before remarked, the Mormons believe and practise what their sacred books teach, and all that they teach, without intended misinter-

---

[14] The standing high-council at the stakes of Zion forms a quorum equal in authority in the affairs of the church, in all its decisions, to the quorum of the presidency, or to the travelling high-council. Each order is governed as follows: the seventy, by seven presidents, one of whom presides over the other six; and as many additional seventies may be organized as the increase of the church shall demand. The president of the high-priests is to preside over the whole church; the president of the elders presides over ninety-six elders; the president of the Aaronic priesthood over forty-eight priests; the president of the teachers over twenty-four teachers, and the president of the deacons over twelve deacons. Should the president of the church transgress, he is to be tried before the common council of the church.

pretation, elimination, or repudiation. And as the book of Mormon is held to be a continuation of the historical portion of the bible, and equally with it the word of God; and as the ideas and instructions contained in the book of Doctrine and Covenants have been derived, for the most part, from a study and literal interpretation of the bible—though with something added—it is safe to say that in the main the Mormons believe what the bible teaches, and that Mormonism is the acceptation of the bible, the whole of it, literally, and following it to its logical conclusions.

Tithing, though enjoined by divine command, is a free-will offering.[15] The law of tithing in its

[15] Upon the matter of tithing, Joseph Smith in 1831 had three several revelations, each containing a clause requiring money and other property to be set apart for general use in the church. The first was received in Feb., the second in May, and the last in Aug. See *Times and Seasons*, iv. 369; v. 416, 466. But it was not until several years later that an organized system was established, by revelation dated Far West, July 8, 1838. See *Doctrine and Covenants*, 382–3. During the progress of settlements at Far West, the question of taxation was brought up and referred to the prophet, who inquired of the Lord, and received answer that all surplus property must be turned over to the bishop as the first step, after which one tenth of each annual interest was also to be paid. These payments were to be devoted to the building of a place of worship, and for the debts of the presidency. In the *Millennial Star*, xxv. 474, it is denied that the priesthood receive any support from the tithing fund, and asserted that it is expended for general purposes solely, such as public buildings, roads, assisting immigration. The twelve apostles, in an epistle dated Nauvoo, Dec. 13, 1841, declare that the tithing required is 'one tenth of all any one possessed at the commencement of the building of the temple, and one tenth part of all his increase from that time till the completion of the same, whether it be money, or whatever he be blessed with. Many in this place are laboring every tenth day for the house, and this is the tithing of their income, for they have nothing else.' *Times and Seasons*, iii. 626. Says William Hall: 'When I came to Illinois, I gave, as was required, one tenth of the amount of my whole estate to be appropriated to the building of the temple. After this, annually, I gave one tenth of the products of my farm; even the chickens, cabbages, and other vegetables in kind were turned over, with a like share of the grain.' *Mormonism Exposed*, 6. Mrs Stenhouse, during her first winter in Salt Lake City, made bonnets for Brigham Young's wives, for which a bill of $250 was presented to Young, when the latter gave orders that the amount should be credited to the Stenhouses for tithing. *Englishwoman in Utah*, 187–8. There are two colonies of Mormons in Arizona that are free from territorial and county taxes. They are so isolated that the cost of collecting amounts to more than the taxes. They do not escape tithes, however. *Elko (Nev.) Daily Independent*, Jan. 28, 1882. During the construction of the railroad through Utah, Mormon agents collected tithings from the railroad laborers. *Salt Lake Reporter*, Feb. 9, 1869, in *S. F. Times*, Feb. 19, 1869. Should a laborer be idle thirty days, the tithing office claims three

fulness requires the tenth of the surplus property of
members coming to Zion to be paid into the church as
a consecration, and after that one tenth of increase or
earnings annually.   This is to be used for the poor, for

days from him, on the grounds that he may do as he pleases with twenty-seven
days, but he has no right to idle away three days belonging to the Lord.
Vedette, in *San José Mercury*, Mar. 14, 1867.   Says Richards: 'If they do not
pay their tithes, nothing is done to compel them to do it; they are only reminded of the case, as with neglect to attend meeting, or of any other duty.'
Narr., MS., 60-1.   At the conference held at Salt Lake City on April
6, 1880, it was reported that the total tithing receipts for the year ending
Dec. 31, 1879, were $458,333; which amount it had cost $18,956.75—paid
the bishops—to collect.   *S. L. C. Tribune*, April 7, 1880.   This report includes
only the branches of the church in Utah.   Coyner, in a letter to the *Boston
Educational Journal*, dated S. L. City, Nov. 20, 1878, states that the church
has an income of about $1,000,000 from tithing.   Numerous complaints are
made from the church's pulpits against delinquents who have failed to pay.
In a book of travels, entitled *My First Holiday*, Boston, 1881, Caroline H.
Dall wrongly asserts that the Scandinavian Mormons refuse to pay tithes.   In
almost any number of the *Deseret News* the reader may find a notice calling
upon delinquents to pay their tithing.   In the issue of May 14, 1853, the
bishop within whose jurisdiction a saw-mill is in operation is reminded that
lumber is wanted at the public yard; and in the number of July 20, 1854, the
first presidency calls on every bishop throughout the territory to furnish at
once lists showing who have paid and who still owe.   In a speech by Brigham,
April 7, 1873, he said: 'When I reached here I could not pay one tenth, I
could not pay my surplus, I could not give my all, for I had nothing.'   *Deseret
News*, April 23, 1873.   Finally, at the jubilee conference, held in celebration
of the semi-centennial of the church's organization, one half of the delinquent
tithes throughout the whole church, the amount being about $75,900, was re-
mitted.   The deserving poor of the church were further assisted on this occasion by the gift of 6,000 head of milch-cows and sheep, and a loan of about
34,000 bushels of wheat until after harvest, without interest.   *Circulars from
the Twelve Apostles*, S. L. City, Apr. 16, 1880.
   If tithing dues are satisfied by manual labor, the workman is paid from
the public stores at rates which, though fixed from time to time, are probably never so low as those paid in ready money elsewhere.   Captain Burton
copies a price-current list for 1860, too long for me to repeat here, but
which will be referred to again elsewhere, and remarks that wheat is quoted
at $1.50 per bushel, more than double its current value at the time in the
valley of the Mississippi.   *City of the Saints*, 389.   Mrs Waite states that
when the poor clamored, in 1862-3, because the tithing-office price of flour
was $6 per hundred, they were assured that though flour would undoubtedly
still advance in price, the cost to them would be no greater.   But the following winter, when, owing to the demand from the mining regions of Idaho
and elsewhere, flour rose rapidly in price, the tithing-office charged $12 per
hundred.   This caused so great an excitement that Brigham deemed it necessary to interfere, and the price was reduced to $6 again.   It is complained
in the *Deseret News* of Jan. 10, 1852, that merchants are paying 33 per cent
more for butter than tithing-house rates, and that this action had drawn the
saints away from the tithing-house, and thus forced the laborers on the temple to eat their bread without butter.   This was in the midst of winter, when
such action might not be altogether unexpected; but we find six months
later another complaint, reporting that from March 29th to July 11th there
had only been received 5,115¾ pounds of butter, 2,534½ of cheese, and 1,182½
dozens of eggs, and inquiring how fast the work would proceed at this rate of
supply.   *Id.*, July 24, 1852.   The revelation establishing tithing was followed

building or other church purposes, and for the support
of those engaged in church business. There are no
salaried preachers. Tithing is paid in kind to the
bishop, who renders a strict account, the whole finan-

ten days later by another, in which it was declared that the church fund
should be disposed of by a council composed of the first presidency, the
bishop and his council, and the high-council. This revelation, which is not
given in the earliest editions of *Doctrine and Covenants*, will be found, however, on p. 383 of the edition of 1876, and also in the *Mil. Star*, xvi. 183. The
twelve, in an epistle dated Nauvoo, Dec. 13, 1841, direct that all money and
other property designed for tithings be paid to President Joseph Smith,
trustee in trust. *Times and Seasons*, iii. 627. Smith had been chosen to this
office some time before by a general conference, at Quincy, Ill. *Id.*, ii. 579.
After Smith, each president has held the position in turn. W. Richards,
editor of the *Deseret News*, describes the system of accounts in use at the
general tithing-office, in his number of Nov. 29, 1851. A debtor and credit
account was kept on a ledger, with all persons who paid tithing. When an
account was settled in full, the name was transferred to the general tithing
record, or the book of 'The Law of the Lord,' and a certificate of non-in-
debtedness given to the person paying, which was evidence in case of a
demand from the bishop of his ward. Four kinds of certificates were issued at this time: one for property tithing due previous to Sept. 10, 1851;
one for property tithing due in accordance with the vote of a conference of the date mentioned; and one each for labor and produce tithing.
These were all for the year 1851, after which only the labor and produce
tithes would be required until a future conference should authorize a new levy.
The business of appraising property belongs of right to the presiding bishop,
but he may send one of his clerks to attend to the matter. It has been
charged against Joseph Smith that his entire wealth was acquired by the
diversion of tithes. The prophet, at his own estimate, had property worth
one million dollars about the time of his death. He was then at the head of
affairs in planning and laying out the city of Nauvoo. His estimates, based
upon his faith in the prosperity of the city, may have been not unreasonable;
but with the crash of the falling walls of his temple came ruin to his estate.
As the general conduct of the church under Brigham was peaceful, and
therefore progressive compared with the disastrous rule of his predecessor,
so opportunities increased, not only for augmenting private fortunes, but
for the circulation of scandal. A writer in the *Salt Lake Tribune* of June
25, 1879, asserts that during Brigham's term of office he received about
$13,000.000 in tithes, of which 'about $9,000,000 was squandered on his
family,' and dying, left the remainder to be quarrelled over by his heirs and
assigns, including the church. In July 1859 Horace Greeley visited Brigham, who said: 'I am the only person in the church who has not a regular
calling apart from the church's service, and I never received one farthing
from her treasury. If I obtain anything from the tithing-house, I am charged
with and pay for it, just as any one else would...I am called rich, and consider myself worth $250,000; but no dollar of it was ever paid me by the
church, nor for any service as a minister of the everlasting gospel. I lost
nearly all I had when we were broken up in Missouri and driven from that
state. I was nearly stripped again when Joseph Smith was murdered, and
we were driven from Illinois; but nothing was ever made up to me by the
church, nor by any one. I believe I know how to acquire property, and how
to take care of it.' *Overland Journey to California*, 213–14. The governor, in
his message to the legislature in 1882, stated that tithing should be prohibited. The message was referred to a committee, which reported that the question being one of a purely religious character did not call for legislative
action. 'The payment of tithing, like contributions for missionary, charita-

cial system being in the hands of the bishopric, but supervised by the trustee in trust through the aid of an auditing committee. The names of those who do not keep the law of tithing shall not be enrolled with the people of God; neither shall their genealogy be kept.

The doctrine of divine revelation is continued. God's ways are immutable; past and present to him are as one; what he has done, that he continues to do; what was right five thousand years ago is right now. If God spoke to Abraham and Solomon, and gave them more wives than one, even giving to David his neighbor's wives, there is no reason why he should not do the same with Joseph and Brigham. There is nothing which God has ever done and sanctioned that he may not do and sanction now; otherwise he is not an omniscient, omnipotent, unchangeable, all-wise, and perfect being. Every member of the church may hold communion with God relative to his own affairs; revelations for the church are only given through its head.

As through Christ alone man may be saved, in order that the souls of many millions who never heard of him may not be all of them lost, baptism for the dead, and thereby salvation, was revealed, as was also celestial marriage.

Nature is dual. An unmarried man or woman is and forever must be an imperfect creature. There are marriages for time and marriages for eternity. A celestial marriage is a marriage of God, and those thus

ble, and other church purposes, by the members of other religious bodies, is clearly an ecclesiastical matter, with which, as law-makers, we have nothing whatever to do, so long as the free exercise thereof does not interfere with the rights and liberties of others. Tithing is not, as we understand it, a new doctrine, for, as a religious privilege and duty, Abraham paid tithes to Melchisedek about four thousand years ago. We are not aware, however, that exactions of tithings are made in this territory, even by ecclesiastical authority; but supposing they were, there is no law by which payment can be enforced, nor is it likely there ever will be, for it is a matter not within the constitutional province of legislative enactment. If any citizen in the territory feels aggrieved by reason of the payment of tithes or other church donations, he holds the remedy in his own hands by simply renouncing connection with any religious body requiring such donations.'

joined can never be divorced, except by the power of God. If a man's wife dies and he marries another, and she dies and he marries a third, believing in resurrection and a life of purity beyond the grave but repudiating polygamy, how will he manage with his plural wives in heaven? She who dies unmarried cannot enter into the full enjoyment of God; but as a man may be baptized for the dead and so save their souls, so he may be sealed to a husbandless woman in heaven. There is a difference between marriage and sealing; the former is secular, and the latter both secular and celestial, as it may be either for time or for eternity, in person or by proxy, and with the living or with the dead. A woman may be sealed to one man for time and to another for eternity, the former being still living.[16]

[16] Gentile marriage and divorce are not recognized as valid in the Mormon church. In its early days, the church had no marriage ordinances of its own, and the requirements, conditions, and ceremonies incident to the rite were similar to those of the various protestant sects. Nor had it officials legally qualified to marry, other, perhaps, than a few such men as Sidney Rigdon, who, having been duly appointed to preside over churches of other denominations, were still competent to join in legal marriage. In 1836, when the church was three years old and the Kirtland temple about to be dedicated, we find Joseph petitioning the court of Medina county, Ohio, for licenses permitting his elders to perform marriage ceremonies, which authority had been refused them by the Geauga county court. *Mil. Star,* xv. 708.

Later, when the church had gained power, the result of more complete organization, Joseph announced, as its belief respecting marriage, that it 'should be solemnized in a public meeting, or feast, prepared for that purpose,' and that the celebrant should be 'a presiding high-priest, bishop, elder, or priest.' But no prohibition was issued against marriage by any other authority. Neither were church-members forbidden to marry out of the church, though any so doing would be considered weak in the faith. In the edition of *Doctrine and Covenants,* published at S. L. City in 1876, a revelation of the prophet's purporting to explain 1st Cor., vii. 14, is construed as forbidding marriages between believers and unbelievers. Ann Eliza Webb, who was twice married according to Mormon practice, once by Brigham, and afterward to him, thus describes the ceremonies: After registration, which includes name, age, place of birth, with county, state, or country, 'we went before Brigham Young, who was waiting for us,' and who asked, 'Do you, Brother James Dee, take Sister Ann Eliza Webb by the right hand, to receive her unto yourself, to be your lawful and wedded wife, and you to be her lawful and wedded husband, for time and eternity, with a covenant and promise on your part that you will fulfil all the laws, rights, and ordinances pertaining to this holy matrimony, in the new and everlasting covenant, doing this in the presence of God, angels, and these witnesses, of your own free will and accord?' 'Yes.' 'Do you, Sister Ann Eliza Webb, take Brother James Dee by the right hand, and give yourself to him, to be his lawful and wedded wife, for time and for all eternity, with a covenant and promise on your part that you will fulfil all the laws, rights, and ordinances pertaining to this holy matrimony, in the new and everlasting covenant, doing this in

A sacred duty is the constant effort to convert all
men throughout the world to a belief in the divinity

the presence of God, angels, and these witnesses, of your own free will and
accord?' 'Yes.' 'In the name of the Lord Jesus Christ, and by the authority of the holy priesthood, I pronounce you legally and lawfully husband and
wife, for time and for all eternity. And I seal upon you the blessings of the
holy resurrection, with power to come forth in the morning of the first resurrection, clothed with glory, immortality, and everlasting lives; and I seal
upon you the blessings of thrones, and dominions, and principalities, and
powers, and exaltations, together with the blessings of Abraham, Isaac, and
Jacob. And I say unto you, Be fruitful, and multiply and replenish the
earth, that you may have joy and rejoicing in your prosperity in the day of
the Lord Jesus. All these blessings, together with all other blessings pertaining to the new and everlasting covenant, I seal upon your heads, through
your faithfulness unto the end, by the authority of the holy priesthood, in
the name of the father, and of the son, and of the holy ghost. Amen.' 'The
scribe then entered the date of the marriage, together with the names of my
mother and the one or two friends who accompanied us.' When the marriage
is a polygamous one, the wife stands on the left of her husband, and the bride
at her left hand. The president then puts this question to the wife: 'Are
you willing to give this woman to your husband, to be his lawful and wedded
wife for time and for all eternity? If you are, you will manifest it by placing her right hand within the right hand of your husband.' The right hands
of the husband and bride being thus joined, the wife takes her husband by
the left arm, as in walking, and the ceremony then proceeds as in the manner
quoted above. *Young's Wife No. 19*, 388. Mrs Stenhouse, who gave a polygamous wife to her husband, states that in her case the ceremony was performed at the altar, her husband kneeling on one side, and the two women
opposite him; the wife being required to join the hands of the contracting
parties as in the other case; but it does not appear that she afterward took
her husband's arm. Indeed, the position of the three would render this impracticable. See *Tell It All*, 453–4. Of course, as these ceremonies took place
in the endowment house, the temple robes were worn.

But apart from ordinary marriage as known among gentiles, remarriage of
converts and polygamous unions, the church in its beneficence, by an additional marriage rite, secures to her children eternal salvation accompanied
with permanent positions of rank. This is effected by the ceremony known
as spiritual marriage, based upon the following tenets: No unmarried man or
woman can be eternally saved. One woman can save one man only; but a
man can be instrumental in the salvation of an indefinite number of women.
Sealing may be either for the dead, or for those yet alive. Persons sealed on
earth need not necessarily live together. Brigham, in a discourse delivered
in Nauvoo, Apr. 6, 1845, announces the doctrine in the following language:
'And I would say, as no man can be perfect without the woman, so no woman can be perfect without a man to lead her. I tell you the truth as it is
in the bosom of eternity; and I say so to every man upon the face of the earth:
if he wishes to be saved, he cannot be saved without a woman by his side.
This is spiritual wifeism, that is, the doctrine of spiritual wives.' *Times and
Seasons*, vi. 955. ' No woman can be sealed to two husbands; she must choose
which it shall be whom she will marry for eternity. The man can be sealed
to as many wives as he pleases. If the husband will be baptized for a former
husband who perhaps died out of the church, then it leaves the wife at liberty to make that choice. If she feels that her second husband is her pref-
erence, she can be baptized for some dead female, and have her sealed to her
dead husband, so as to secure his conjugal happiness forever.' *Mrs Richards'
Inner Facts*, MS., 5. ' If a husband has lost his wife by death, before he had
the opportunity of attending to this holy ordinance, and securing her as his
lawful wife for eternity, then it is the duty of the second wife, first, to be

of Joseph Smith's mission.   To this end are sent forth proselyting ministers, elders of the church, selected by

sealed or married to the husband, for and in the name of the deceased wife, for all eternity; and, secondly, to be married for time and eternity herself, to the same man.   Thus, by this holy ordinance, both the dead and the living wife will be his in the eternal worlds.   But if, previous to marriage for eternity, a woman lose her husband by death, and marry a second, and if her first husband was a good man, then it is the duty of the second husband to be married to her for eternity, not for herself, but in the name of her deceased husband, while he himself can only be married to her for time; and he is obliged to enter into a covenant to deliver her up, and all her children, to her deceased husband, in the morning of the first resurrection.' *Waite's Mormon Prophet*, 173.   'A man can either have a woman sealed to him as his consort for this world only, or he can have her sealed to him both for this world as well as for the world to come—she is A.'s wife while she is on earth, but she becomes B.'s as soon as she has reached heaven.   Or again, a woman—a spinster, for instance—who has taken a particular fancy to any deceased saint, and who wishes to become his consort in the world to come, can be sealed to him by proxy by becoming the wife of some living saint.   She has first to be sealed on earth before she can obtain the necessary introduction into heaven.   When a woman is said to be sealed to a man, it does not necessarily imply that she is married to him.   It may mean marriage, or it may simply amount to an arrangement to marry, to be consummated in the next world, made either directly between the two parties, or by proxy by another party in place of one of the two interested parties who is dead, ... even if she prefers being the consort of Abraham, Isaac, Moses, Job, etc., for the Mormon spiritual-wife doctrine even ventures to go the length of this!' *Marshall, Through America*, 186.   Mrs Stenhouse says President Heber C. Kimball upon one occasion introduced her to five of his wives in succession, and upon being asked, 'Are these all you have got?' replied, 'O dear! no.   I have a few more at home, and about fifty more scattered over the earth somewhere.   I have never seen them since they were sealed to me in Nauvoo, and I hope I never shall again.' *Exposé of Polygamy in Utah*, 91–2.   See also, in this connection, *Green's Mormonism*, 180–92; *Lee's Mormonism Unveiled*, 165–72.

Brigham, as head of the church, claimed authority not only to marry, but also to divorce at will.   No law's delay, no filing of bills, summoning witnesses, or learned decision granting absolute or partial severance, accompanied by partial or impartial award of property and the custody of infants, was required.   Given the approbation of the chief, and the rest followed as speedily as a clerk could write the certificate and receive the fee.   In a district removed from the capital, only the consent of the bishop is necessary, and the bill of divorcement is a very simple writing.   'March 18, 1871.   To whomsoever it may concern.   This is to certify, in the beginning of 1869 when I gave a bill of divorce to Sarah Ann Lowry I gave to her for the good of her four children the following property, viz.: a parcel of land of about nine acres enclosed all around, with a house of two rooms and one cow and heifer.   William C. Ritter.'   The customary fee is ten dollars, and Mrs Waite relates an instance in which a woman who had been granted a divorce was told by Brigham that the act was null until the money was paid. *The Mormon Prophet*, 239.   The following is copied from note G, app. to *Paddock's Madame La Tour:* 'An Englishwoman who abandoned her husband and children for the purpose of gathering with the saints to Zion has been divorced and remarried five times since she came to Utah.   The present writer has lived within half a block of a woman who, after being divorced from five husbands, is now living in polygamy with the sixth; and one of our district judges reports the case of an elderly saintess, living near the place in which he holds court, who has been divorced fourteen times.'

the authorities and called by the saints assembled at
the general semiannual conferences held in Salt Lake
City.   Neither age nor pecuniary condition governs
the selection.   They may be men or boys, rich or
poor; but they must have faith and integrity, and go
forth without purse or scrip, relying alone upon the
hand of God to feed them.   An elder is likewise
selected by the church authorities to preside over
each mission.   Thus has been visited almost every
quarter of the globe, the book of Mormon being meanwhile translated into many languages.   And a Perpetual Emigration Fund Company has been established, which has advanced the funds to bring out
thousands to Zion, the money being paid back by the
immigrant after his arrival, as he has been able to
earn it.

Temple building is a characteristic work, and is
prompted by the belief that Jesus Christ will some
day come suddenly to his temple.   Hence the devotion
and self-sacrifice practised by Christ's people in order
to prepare for him a fitting place of reception.   Wonders in this direction have been accomplished by a
poor and wandering people, at Kirtland, at Nauvoo,
at Salt Lake City, St George, Manti, and Logan.

In the north-west corner of Temple block, Salt
Lake City, in which is the tabernacle, the smaller
church building, and the new temple, stands a plain
two-story adobe structure known as the Endowment
House.   Here are conducted the most secret and
solemn mysteries of the church, which may be termed
religio-masonic ceremonies, illustrative of the origin
and destiny of man.   Here also are performed the
rites of baptism for the dead, anointing with oil, marriage, and other ceremonies, by which the convert is
endowed with the special grace of God, receives his
inheritance as a child of God, and is made a partaker
of the fulness of all the blessings of religion.   All
these rites should properly be performed in the temple,
which on its completion will supersede the endowment

house, and in which special apartments are being constructed for these purposes.[17]

[17] The ceremony of Endowment, or as it is termed, going through the endowment house, occupies usually about eight hours. It has been described at length by several persons who have experienced it, and I give herewith a condensation of the most reliable accounts. Minor changes have been introduced since the days of Joseph Smith, but, in the main, the rites are as they were in the beginning. Certain days in each week, throughout the year, are set apart, upon which candidates present themselves at the endowment house, as early as seven o'clock A. M. Each is required to bring a bottle of the best olive-oil, and supposed to bring his robes also, although it is common to borrow the latter from friends, for the first appearance, after which every good Mormon possesses his own. These garments are described as follows: The temple robe, alike for both sexes, is a long, loose, flowing garment, made of white linen or bleached muslin, and reaching to the ankle. It is gathered to a band sufficiently long to pass around the body from the right shoulder underneath the left arm, thus leaving the latter free. A linen belt holds it in place. The women wear a head covering made of a large square of Swiss muslin, gathered in one corner so as to form a sort of cap to fit the head, the remainder falling down as a veil. For the men, a round piece of linen, drawn up with a string and a bow in front, something after the fashion of a Scotch cap, is used. The under garment, which is also alike for both sexes, is a sort of jacket and trousers together, something like the night-dresses made for children; and is worn night and day. When changed, only an arm or a leg must be removed at once, the fresh garment being thus put on as the other is taken off. This garment protects from disease, and even death, for the bullet of an enemy will not penetrate it. The prophet Joseph carelessly left off this garment on the day of his death, and had he not done so, he would have escaped unharmed. Over the inner garment the men wear an ordinary shirt, and the women a white skirt. White stockings and a pair of white linen slippers complete the costume. Entering the building, the candidate's own name and age are registered, and also the names of the parents. The candidates hand in their oil, remove their shoes, and pass with their bundles of clothing into a bath-room divided down the middle by a heavy curtain which separates the sexes. Here the ceremony of purification is performed, the women being washed by women, and the men by men. The person washed is informed that he or she is now cleansed from the blood of this generation, and if faithful, shall never be subject to the plagues and miseries which are about to come upon the earth. Next follows the anointing. The oil is poured from a large horn into the hand of the person officiating, and applied to the crown of the head, eyes, ears, mouth, and feet of the candidate. The eyes are touched, that they may be quick to see; the ears, that the hearing may be sharp; the mouth, to bestow wisdom upon speech; and the feet, that they be swift to run in the ways of the Lord. Then a new name, which is rarely to be mentioned, is whispered into the ear, and all are marched into room No. 2, where they are seated, the sexes on opposite sides of the room, and facing each other. Here they are told by a priest that any person not strong enough to proceed may retire; but if any portion of the ceremony is disclosed, the throat of the person so offending will be cut from ear to ear. Those faltering, if any, having retired, the remainder are taken into room No. 3, where a representation of the creation, the temptation, and fall is given. Each candidate then puts on over his robe an apron of white linen, upon which are sewn pieces of green silk representing fig-leaves, and also the cap or veil. All good Mormons are buried in their endowment robes, and the veil worn by the women covers their faces when they are consigned to the grave. In the morning of the resurrection, this veil is to be lifted by the husband; otherwise no woman can see the face of the almighty in the next world. This ends the first degree; and the initiated are now driven out of Eden into room No.

The order of exercises in the tabernacle, which
seats seven thousand persons, is much the same as
in orthodox evangelical churches, beginning and ending with prayer and singing, and sometimes singing
and administering the sacrament in the middle of a
discourse. The speaker seldom knows that he is to
speak until called upon by the moderator, who regu-
lates the services, and makes the selection under inspiration, announcing the name of the person sometimes
without knowing whether he is in the house, or even
in the city. The singing is very fine, the organ, constructed wholly by Mormon artisans, being the largest

4, which represents the world, where they encounter many temptations, the
chief of which is the false gospel preached by methodists, baptists, etc. Finally
St James and St John appear and proclaim the true gospel of Mormonism, which
all gladly embrace. After this they receive certain grips and pass-words, and
all are arranged in a circle, kneel, and the women lower their veils. Then,
with the right hand uplifted, an oath is taken to avenge the death of Joseph
Smith, jun., upon the gentiles who had caused his murder, to teach the children
of the church to do likewise, to obey implicitly and without murmur or question
all commands of the priesthood, to refrain from adultery, and finally, eternal
secrecy concerning all that transpired in the endowment house is promised.
Then comes an address, after which another room is entered, leading from
which is a door with a hole in it, covered with a piece of muslin. The men
approach this door in turn and ask to enter. Then a person behind the door
reaches through the opening, and with knife in hand cuts a certain mark on
the left breast of the shirt, another over the abdomen, and one over the right
knee, which marks are faithfully copied by the women in their own garments
after returning to their homes. The man then mentions his new name, gives
the grip of the third degree, and is permitted to pass in. This is called going behind the veil. When the men are all in, each woman is passed through
by her husband, or having none, by one of the brethren. This concludes the
ceremony, with the exception of marriage, which will be noticed elsewhere.
Of these ceremonies Mrs Stenhouse, from whose account the foregoing is partly
taken, says: 'About what was done in Nauvoo, I can only speak by hearsay, but have been told many strange and revolting stories about the ceremonies which were there performed. Of the endowments in Utah, everything
was beautifully neat and clean, and I wish to say most distinctly that, although the initiation appears now to my mind as a piece of the most ridiculous
absurdity, there was, nevertheless, nothing in it indecent or immoral. *Englishwoman in Utah*, 190-2. For more on endowment ceremonies, see *Morm.
at Home*, 209; *Stenhouse's Englishwoman*, 155-201; *Tell It All*, 253-6, 514-15;
Beadle's Life in Utah, 486-502; *Hyde's Morm.*, 89-101, 108-9; *Worthington's
Woman in Battle*, 591-2; *Burton's City of Saints*, 271-2; *Young's Wife No.
19*, 356-72; *S. L. Herald*, Mar. 31, 1881; *Tribune*, Nov. 16, 1878; Sept. 28,
1879; *Utah Rev.*, Dec. 12, 1871; *S. F. Bulletin*, 1878, Nov. 16; 1879, May 5,
Oct. 25; *Herald*, July 27, 1852; *Red Bluff Sentinel*, Nov. 30, 1878; *Sac.
Union*, Sept. 25, 1858; *Rec.-Union*, Oct. 1, 1879; *San José Argus*, Sept. 15,
22, 1877; *Sta Cruz Cour.*, May 10, 1878; *Stockton Indep.*, May 6, 1879; *Te-
hama Tocsin*, Nov. 1, 1879; *Yreka Union*, Nov. 22, 1879; *Salem (Or.)
Statesman*, Nov. 7, 1879; *Carson City (Nev.) Tribune*, Oct. 6, 1879; *Elko
Indep.*, Dec. 12, 1878; *Gold Hill News*, 1878, Oct. 29-31.

and finest in America at the time it was built. The acoustic properties of the oval-shaped room and ceiling are wonderful; stationed at one point, a pin may be heard drop at the opposite end. The singers, thirty or forty in number, are stationed on the main stage, facing the audience in front of the organ. In front of them are the church officials, seated on a series of platforms according to their respective grades, the first presidency highest, next the twelve apostles, and finally the teachers, priests, and bishops, who have charge of administering the sacrament of the Lord's supper, which is done regularly every Sunday. In the first organization of the church, bread and wine were specified as the proper elements to be used, but it was soon after revealed that it makes no difference what the emblems are, and now bread and water are used. Tabernacle services are held Sunday afternoons; there are Sunday-schools at the ward meeting-houses Sunday mornings, and preaching at the same places in the evening by subordinate officials, who often repeat the main points of the morning tabernacle discourse. In the tabernacle, several rows of the best seats are reserved for gentile strangers, and are filled for the most part by travellers and tourists, American and European, who take no pains to hide their contempt for all about them, and return the courtesy extended by smiles and sneers, which, to say the least, is in bad taste for people pretending to a superior culture.[18]

[18] One or two other matters of belief I may mention here. There was early established the order of Enoch. The prophet Joseph not only indorsed the biblical account of the translation of Enoch, but added to it. There was not only one Enoch, but a whole city full. This city of Enoch was located where are now the waters of the gulf of Mexico, and its inhabitants were absolutely perfect. Many sought to reach this place, for its fame had become noised abroad; but none were successful, owing to wanderings and bickerings by the way. Within its gates all things were held in common, and unalloyed happiness reigned. And inasmuch as the people of Enoch were unfitted by their moral excellence to mingle with other earthly inhabitants, they were removed to celestial realms. Joseph's idea at this time seems to have been to induce his followers to surrender all rights, including that of property, into the hands of the church. In May 1831 it was revealed, 'And again, let the bishop appoint a storehouse unto this church, and let all

After all that can be said about Mormonism and
polygamy in their social or moral relations, it is only
when we come to consider them in their political aspect, in their relations to government and governing,

things, both in money and in meat, which is more than is needful for the wants
of this people, be kept in the hands of the bishop.' *Times and Seasons,* v.
416. This revelation was for the information and guidance of the first bishop,
Partridge, who is authorized therein to take what he wants for himself and
family. The prophet's revelation concerning the order of Enoch is without
date, and is entitled ' Revelation given to Enoch concerning the order of the
church for the benefit of the poor.' In it is prescribed that there shall be
two treasuries: from the first, to be called ' the sacred treasury of the Lord,'
nothing can be taken but by the voice of the order, or by commandment;
into the second treasury are to be cast all moneys except those reserved for
sacred purposes. It is also provided that general consent is necessary for the
withdrawal of funds from this, as in the case of the first repository, but
common consent in this case is construed to be, if any man shall say to the
treasurer, ' I have need of a certain sum,' he shall receive it, provided the asker
shall be in full fellowship. The revelation in full will be found in *Doctrine
and Covenants,* 283–9. One of the grounds of complaint brought against the
saints in Caldwell county, by the Missourians, was that the former were communists, as has been narrated already. Says the *Salt Lake Tribune* of May
9, 1874: ' The Mormons paid the United States authorities $318,000 for public
lands in Missouri, but were not allowed to enjoy one acre of their purchase.'
See also *Deseret News,* May 13, 1874. At Nauvoo, Joseph had himself
appointed trustee in trust of the whole church, and thereafter we hear no
more of the order of Enoch until some years subsequent to the establishment
of the Deseret colonies. Soon after Joseph's death we find Brigham sole
trustee of affairs. During the scenes following the murder of the Smiths,
the expulsion from Illinois, and up to the settlement of the migratory saints
in Utah, there was little property to care for; but after that, attention was
again turned to the matter. Robinson, in his *Sinners and Saints,* gives a
copy of a deed: ' Be it known by these presents, that I, Jessie W. Fox, of
Great Salt Lake City, in the county of Great Salt Lake, and territory of
Utah, for and in consideration of the sum of one hundred ($100) dollars and
the good-will which I have to the church of Jesus Christ of latter-day
saints, give and convey unto Brigham Young, trustee in trust for the said
church, his successor in office and assigns, all my claims to and ownership of
the following-described property, to wit: One house and lot, $1,000; one city
lot, $100; east half of lot 1, block 12, $50; lot 1, block 14, $75; two cows,
$50; two calves, $15; one mare, $100; one colt, $50; one watch, $20; one
clock, $12; clothing, $300; beds and bedding, $125; one stove, $20; household
furniture, $210; total, $2,127; together with all the rights, privileges, and
appurtenances thereunto belonging or appertaining. I also covenant and
agree that I am the lawful claimant and owner of said property, and will
warrant and forever defend the same unto the said trustee in trust, his successor in office and assigns, against the claims of my heirs, assigns, or any
person whomsoever.' Then follows the attestation of the witness, and the
formal certificate of the judge of the probate court that the signer of the
above transfer personally appeared before him on April 2, 1857, and made
the customary acknowledgment. Robinson also gives a list of rules, which
I have not room for in detail, but which the reader may find in pp. 223–5, in
the work already quoted. William Hall, who was a member of the church
from 1840 until 1847, says that at the time of the exodus from Nauvoo a
mercantile firm was appointed to act as trustees, not only for the church
property, but also for individuals. These trustees were to sell the property

that we touch the core of the matter. Those who wax the hottest against the latter-day saints and their polygamous practices are not as a rule among the purest of our people. They care no more, indeed,

left behind, and account to the proper owners. *Mormonism Exposed*, 66–70. Says Ex-elder John Hyde, jun.: 'In 1854 Brigham Young commanded the people to consecrate by legal transfer all right and title to all personal property. Quitclaim deeds were drawn up, and from their land to their wearing apparel the majority transferred everything to Brigham or his successor as trustee in trust for the latter-day saints; and some, in the exuberance of enthusiasm, threw in their wives and families.' *Mormonism*, 37–9. The legislature, by act approved Jan. 18, 1855, legalized these transfers, and provided a form in blank therefor. See *Utah Laws* (ed. 1855), 268–9; (ed. 1866), 92–3. At the semiannual conference held in Oct. 1873, the subject of reviving the order was again agitated. Elder David McKenzie touched upon the ultimate establishment of the order of Enoch in a very emphatic manner. *Deseret News*, Oct. 15, 1873. The *Salt Lake Tribune* of March 21, 1874, quotes the elder as follows: ' We should give thanks and praise to almighty God that there is a chance, a door opened, by which we may take a step towards establishing the order of Enoch.' Mrs Stenhouse says efforts were made to revive the order before the completion of the railways, which were not finished until 1869. *Englishwoman in Utah*, 371–2. Rev. Clark Smith, author of a 12mo pamphlet entitled *Mystery and Crime in the Land of the Ute*, states that the plan for reviving the order was matured during the winter of 1873–4 at St George, where Brigham and a few of his leaders were at that time. During the early part of 1874, scarcely a sermon was delivered without a reference to the order and an assurance that all joining would be benefited both spiritually and temporally. On May 9th an election of officers was held. Brigham was was chosen president; Geo. Smith, Danl H. Wells, and the twelve apostles, vice-presidents; David McKenzie, George Goddard, D. O. Calder, P. A. Schettler, John T. Caine, and James Jack, secretaries; Thos W. Ellerbeck, general book-keeper; Edward Hunter, treasurer; and Horace J. Eldridge, John Sharp, Ferezmore Little, James Van Cott, Moses Thatcher, Thos Dinwiddie, and Elijah Sheets, directors. *S. L. C. Tribune*, May 16, 1874.

The dogma of adoption for eternity originated after Joseph's time. Hall says he first heard of it about the date of the expulsion from Nauvoo. *Mormonism Exposed*, 70. It was ascertained that many of the saints had intermarried with gentile stock, and were thus debarred from a full enjoyment of the rights and privileges of the house and lineage of Abraham. But these lost blessings could be restored by ingraftment upon the stock of one of the twelve tribes of Israel, represented by the twelve apostles, each of whom was deemed as in lineal descent from Abraham, tracing his consanguinity to Isaac and Jacob, and thence to himself as a chief of one of the tribes. Romans, xi. 16, is quoted as authorizing the doctrine, which requires every member of the church, except the twelve, to choose a father from one of the latter. The father may be either younger or older than the son, but in any case assumes the character of guardian, with full control of the labor and estate of the adopted son. Many young men give themselves over to the leaders as ' eternal sons,' in the hope of sharing the honor of their adopted parents. W. C. Staines was Brigham's adopted son, and D. Candland, Heber C. Kimball's. *Hyde, Mormonism*, 110. Wilbert Earls is also mentioned as Kimball's son. *Hall, Mormonism Exposed*, 70.

About 1840, in obedience to a special revelation, Joseph Smith established a secret society known as the Order Lodge. None save persons of high standing in the church could gain admission, the avowed object of the organization being induction into the higher mysteries of the priesthood. J. C. Bennett writes as follows of this order: ' The lodge-room is carefully prepared and

about the half-dozen wives of the Mormon than about
the half-dozen mistresses of the congressman. As
Judge Roseborough, in a very able dictation to my
stenographer, remarks: "When I came here I was a

consecrated; and from 12 to 24 sprigs of cassia, olive branches, cedar boughs,
or other evergreens, are tastefully arranged about it. These are intended to
represent the eternal life and unmingled bliss, which, in the celestial kingdom,
will be enjoyed by all who continue in full fellowship.'...The candidate is
stripped naked, blindfolded, and in this condition marched around the lodge-
room, the most excellent Grand Master repeating: 'I will bring the blind by
a way they know not; I will lead them in paths that they have not known;
I will make darkness light before them, and crooked things straight. These
things will I do unto them, and not forsake them.' The candidate having
knelt before the altar, the following oath is administered: 'In the name of
Jesus Christ, the son of God, I now promise and swear, truly, faithfully, and
without reserve, that I will serve the Lord with a perfect heart and a willing
mind, dedicating myself, wholly and unreservedly, in my person and effects,
to the upbuilding of his kingdom on earth, according to his revealed will. I
furthermore promise and swear that I will regard the first president of the
church of Jesus Christ of latter-day saints as the supreme head of the church
on earth, and obey him the same as the supreme God, in all written revelations, given under the solemnities of a "thus saith the Lord," and that I will
always uphold the presidency, right or wrong. I furthermore promise and
swear that I will never touch a daughter of Adam unless she is given me of
the Lord. I furthermore promise and swear that no gentile shall ever be
admitted to the secrets of this holy institution, or participate in its blessings.
I furthermore promise and swear that I will assist the Daughter of Zion
in the utter destruction of apostates, and that I will assist in setting up the
Kingdom of Daniel in these last days, by the power of the highest and the
sword of his might. I furthermore promise and swear that I will never communicate the secrets of this degree to any person in the known world, except
it be to a true and lawful brother, binding myself under no less a penalty
than that of having melted lead poured into my ear. So help me God and
keep me faithful.' *Hist. of the Saints*, 275–6.

I have thousands of references to articles written and sermons preached on
the doctrines of the church. The tabernacle and bowery sermons have been
reported and published in the *Deseret News*, from its first publication up to
1860. Besides President Young, the prominent speakers were Parley P.
Pratt, Orson Hyde, Orson Pratt, Lorenzo Snow, Heber C. Kimball, George
A. Smith, John Taylor, Franklin D. Richards, David Fullmer, J. W. Cummings, John Young, Wilford Woodruff, Joseph Young, John D. McAllister, Joseph Young,
Daniel H. Wells, Cyrus H. Wheelock, Robert T. Burton, Jacob Gates, Charles
H. Bassett, and many others. For duties of bishops, see *Deseret News*, 1850,
Aug. 10; patriarchal notice, Sept. 21; revelation, Dec. 28; 1851, for religious
questions and answers, Jan. 11; minutes special conference of seventies, Jan.
25; appel. presidency and apostolate, Mar. 8; min. gen. con., 19; Patriarch
Smith's letter to the saints throughout the world, and letter from P. P.
Pratt to Brigham Young, Nov. 29; letter from Thos Bullock, president
of seventies, Dec. 27; 1852, letter from O. Jones to Pres. Young, Jan.
10; offices in church, authority explained, Jan. 24; signs of the times, and
advice to the saints, Feb. 7; disc. by Brigham, Feb. 9; letter, Patriarch
Smith, Feb. 20; opinions about Mormonism (from *Harper's Mag.*), Feb.
21; min. con. new tabernacle, Apr. 17; Mormon question (*N. Y. Tribune* and *Herald*), May 1; letter of defence (in *N. Y. Herald*), May 15;
reflections, O. Pratt, June 26; disc. by Kimball, Aug. 15; gen. funeral sermon by O. Pratt, Aug. 21; Brigham on apostles, *News* extra, p. 25; remarks
by Taylor and Kimball, Sept. 4; speech by Kimball, Sept. 14; special con.,

democrat. They pretended to be democrats, but I found them such democrats as hell is full of. They are neither democrats nor republicans. I did not care about matters of belief, if they were American citizens.

Sept. 18; disc. by Brigham, Oct. 2; min. gen. con., Oct. 16 and Nov. 6; epistle by Young, Oct. 16; the Mormons the Mahometans of 19th cent. (*N. Y. Herald*), Nov. 2; remarks, Young, Aug. 26, Nov. 6; 1853, sermon by P. P. Pratt, Jan. 19; address by Taylor, Jan. 19; disc. by Benson, Feb. 1; sermon, Pratt, Mar. 2; Brigham and Pratt, address, Apr. 2; Brigham, disc., Apr. 13; min. gen. con., Apr. 16, 30; epistle pres., rept quorum seventies, Apr. 16; ad., Hyde, May 14; ad., Brigham, May 14; disc., Brigham, July 6 and 20; speech, Hyde, July 30; disc., Brigham, Aug. 24, 31, and Oct. 1; min. gen. con., Oct. 15 and 29; ep. pres., Oct. 15; disc., Brigham, Sept. 7; ad., H. Kimball, Nov. 12; ad., tabernacle, Nov. 24; Mormon vs gentile, Nov. 24; ad., Brigham, Dec. 8; Mormonism, Dec. 8; sermon, Taylor, Dec. 22; 1854, disc., H. Kimball, Jan. 4; Smith, Jan. 18; reg. dialogue, and art. on restitution, Jan. 12; bible and Mormonism, Jan. 19; repts of quorums of seventies, Mar. 2, Apr. 13, Apr. 27; gen. epis., Apr. 13; gen. confer., Apr. 13; address, Hyde, Apr. 27; disc., Pratt, Apr. 27; address, Kimball, Apr. 27; disc., Taylor, May 11; Brigham, May 11; Smith, May 11; Grant, June 8; Brigham, July 27; Grant, July 27; Brigham, Aug. 3; Kimball, Aug. 17; epis. pres., Sept. 14; disc., Kimball, Sept. 14; a Mormon leader (from *Sem. Wy. Jour.*, Tex.), Sept. 21; disc., Grant, Sept. 21; epis. against litigation, Sept. 21; remarks, Grant, Sept. 28; disc., Kimball, Sept. 28; Hyde, Oct. 5, Oct. 19; Kimball, Oct. 19; Benson, Oct. 19; Smith, Oct. 26; Pratt, Oct. 26; Brigham, Oct. 26; Hyde, Nov. 9; Grant, Nov. 23; Kimball, Nov. 23; Pratt, Nov. 30; Grant, Dec. 7; Kimball, Dec. 14; Pratt, Dec. 21; local recog. of Morm. (from *Democracy*), Dec. 21; disc., Pratt, Dec. 28; 1855, Grant, Jan. 25; testimony, Kimball, Jan. 25; disc., Brigham, Feb. 8; rept of 27 quor., Jan. 11; disc. on prophecies, Pratt, Feb. 22; Morm. worldliness, etc., Harrison; address, Brigham, Mar. 1; belief in superiority, Hyde, Mar. 14; sermon, Woodruff, Mar. 21; Hyde, Mar. 28; Smith, Apr. 4; testimony, faith, and confidence; gen. confer., Apr. 11; sermon, Grant, Apr. 11; gen. epist., Apr. 25; disc., Brigham, Apr. 25, May 9; remarks, Pratt, May 2; elders' corresp., May 16; disc., Pratt, May 16; on inspection, Brigham, May 23; elders' corresp., May 23, May 30; remarks, Brigham, June 6; disc., Brigham, June 20; the word of wisdom (in *Doctrines and Covenants*), June 27; sermon, Smith, July 11; Morm., July 18; disc., Brigham, July 18; lecture, Grant, July 25; disc., Brigham, Aug. 1; Smith, Aug. 22; Benson, Aug. 22; Smith, Aug. 29; comments (*N. Y. Papers*), Sept. 12; remarks, Benson, Sept. 12; disc., Pratt, Sept. 12; remarks, Pratt, Sept. 19; disc., Brigham, Sept. 26; Smith, Oct. 10; gen. confer., Oct. 10; disc., Oct. 10; bowery meeting, Oct. 17; confer., Oct. 17, 24; tabernacle meeting, Oct. 24, 31; gen. epis., Oct. 31; sermon, Brigham, Oct. 31; to the truth-loving, Nov. 7; disc., Nov. 7; remarks, Grant, Nov. 7; tabernacle meeting, Nov. 7; remarks, Kimball, Nov. 7; sermon, Brigham, Nov. 28; disc., Kimball, Dec. 4; Pratt, Dec. 12, 19; Lyman, Dec. 19, 26; 1856, disc., Lyman, Jan. 2; Pratt, Jan. 30; Kimball, Feb. 6; Brigham, Feb. 6; Grant, Feb. 6; Lyman, Feb. 20; Brigham, Feb. 27; remarks, Kimball, Mar. 5; Brigham, Mar. 5, 12; epis. to high priest's quorum, Mar. 12; disc., Kimball, Mar. 12; remarks, Grant, Mar. 12; fair weather disc., Mar. 12; disc., Wells, Mar. 19; Kimball, Mar. 19; Brigham, Mar. 26; Vernon, Mar. 26; remarks, Brigham, Mar. 26; disc., Grant, Apr. 2; Brigham, Apr. 2; Kimball, Apr. 2; gen. confer., Apr. 9; disc., Kimball, Apr. 9; sacrifice, Apr. 9; disc., Smith, Apr. 16; obedience, Apr. 23; disc., Pratt, Apr. 23; Brigham, Apr. 30; Pratt, May 14; the world and the saints, May 28; remarks, Brigham, June 18; disc., Brigham, June 25; counsel, July 9; obedience, July 16; disc., Pratt, July 16; Kimball, Aug. 20; sermon, Brigham, Aug. 27; confer. at Kayville, Sept. 24; disc., Pratt, Sept. 24; sermon, Brigham, Sept. 27; disc., Grant, Sept. 27; disc.,

They might worship the devil if they were citizens and discharged their duties as citizens. But I found that in a military way, in a political way, and in a judicial way they controlled matters; and nearly all of them

Brigham, Oct. 1; meetings, Oct. 1; disc., Kimball, Oct. 1; Brigham, Oct. 1; remarks, Grant, Oct. 1; confer., Oct. 8; remarks, Kimball, Oct. 8; Brigham, Oct. 8, 15; disc., Richards, Oct. 15; confer., Oct. 15; remarks, Spencer, Oct. 15; condition of saints, Oct. 22; remarks, Kimball, Nov. 5; disc., Grant, Nov. 5; special confer., Nov. 5; quart. confer., Nov. 12; remarks, Nov. 12; disc., Brigham, Nov. 12; Grant, Nov. 12; appointments, Nov. 12; disc., Grant. Nov. 19; Kimball, Nov. 19; remarks, Brigham, Nov. 19; Young (Jos. A.), Nov. 19; Woodruff, Nov. 26; Brigham, Nov. 26; Kimball, Nov. 26; address, Pratt, Dec. 1; remarks, Brigham, Dec. 10; gen. epist., Dec. 10; disc., Pratt. Dec. 24; high priest's meeting, Dec. 31; sermon, Kimball, Dec. 31; remarks, Woodruff, Dec. 31; 1857, disc., Kimball, Jan. 7: remarks, Grant, Jan. 7; disc., Snow, Jan. 14; Richards, Jan. 21; Kimball, Jan. 21; Snow, Jan. 28; remarks, Woodruff, Feb. 4; toleration, Feb. 4; remarks, Grant, Feb. 4; morals, Feb. 11; disc., Brigham, Feb. 11; Kimball, Feb. 11; Cummings, Feb. 18; Brigham, Feb. 18; remarks, Kimball, Feb. 25; Hyde, Mar. 4; disc., Richards, Mar. 4; Woodruff, Mar. 4; remarks, Wells, Mar. 4; disc., Brigham, Mar. 11; Kimball, Mar. 11; Snow, Mar. 11; remarks, Wells, Mar. 11; disc., Brigham, Mar. 18; Young (Jos.), Mar. 18; Brigham, Mar. 25; Kimball, Mar. 25; Grant. Mar. 25; remarks, McAllister, Mar. 25; Kimball, Apr. 1; Richards, Apr. 1; disc. Woodruff, Apr. 1; sermon, Brigham, Apr. 8; remarks, Burton, Apr. 8; gen. confer., Apr. 15; remarks, Wells, Apr. 15; Stout, Apr. 15; Wells, Apr. 15; disc., Kimball, Apr. 22; Brigham, Apr. 22, 29; remarks, Herriman, Apr. 29; Wheelock, Apr. 29; remarks, Snow, May 6; Brigham, May 6; Woodruff, May 13; disc., Brigham, May 13; disc., May 20; the bible, May 20; remarks, Brigham, May 20; Ferguson, May 20; Fullmer, May 20; Davis, May 20; McKnight, May 20; Bassett, May, 27; disc., Gates, May 27; remarks, Woodruff, May 27; disc., Woolley, June 3; Mills, June 3; remarks, Brigham, June 10; Smith, June 10; Kimball, June 10; disc., Kimball, June 17; remarks, Brigham, June 17, 24; Rich, June 24; Brigham, June 24; Hyde, June 24; Lyman, June 24; disc., Kimball, June 24; Chislett, July 8; remarks, Brigham, July 8; Cummings, July 8; Brigham, July 15; Kimball, July 15; Carn, July 15; Lyman, July 22; Ellsworth, July 22; Brigham, July 22; disc., Lyman, July 29; pol. move. against Utah, July 29; remarks, Brigham, Aug. 5; Smoot, Aug. 5; Smith, Aug. 5; disc., Hyde, Aug. 5; Smith, Aug. 12; Kimball, Aug. 12; Smith (E.), Aug. 12; remarks, Brigham, Aug. 12; Kimball, Aug. 12; Taylor, Aug. 19; Brigham, Aug. 19; Kimball, Aug. 26; Brigham, Aug. 26; disc., Hyde, Aug. 26; Taylor, Sept. 2; remarks, Brigham, Sept. 9; Stewart, Sept. 9; disc., Kimball, Sept. 9, 16; Taylor, Sept. 16, 23; remarks, Smith, Sept. 23; Brigham, Sept. 23; Kimball, Sept. 30; Brigham, Sept. 30; disc., Taylor, Sept. 30; remarks, Woodruff, Oct. 7; disc., Kimball, Oct. 7; sem. ann. confer., Oct. 14; remarks, Brigham, Oct. 14; Spencer, Oct. 14; Snow, Oct. 14; disc., Hyde, Oct. 14; Kimball, Oct. 14; Snow, Oct. 21; sermon, Lyman, Oct. 21; remarks, Spencer, Oct. 21; remarks, Brigham, Oct. 21; Rich, Oct. 21; Young, Oct. 21; Snow, Oct. 21; Brigham, Oct. 28; by bishops and elders, Oct. 28; Brigham, Nov. 11, 25, Dec. 2, 9, 30; 1858, confer., Apr. 14; 1859, Mar. 9, Apr. 13, Oct. 12, Dec. 28; disc., 1858, Jan. 27, Feb. 17, Apr. 14, July 14, 28; 1859, May 25, June 1, 8, 15, July 6, Aug. 10, 17, Nov. 16, 23, 30; 1860, remarks, Brigham, Mar. 14, Apr. 4, 25, May 2, 16, 30, June 6, 27, July 18, 25, Aug. 1, 8, 15, 22, 29, Sept. 5; 1864, June 15; 1865, Jan. 4; 1866, Mar. 15; 1867, Feb. 3; 1868, Jan. 15; 1869, Jan. 20, Feb. 2, Dec. 10; 1870, Mar. 30; 1871, Apr. 19; 1879, Feb. 12; confer., 1860, Feb. 8, Apr. 11, Oct. 10; 1861, Apr. 10, Oct. 23; 1862, Apr. 9, 16, 29, Oct. 15; 1863, Apr. 15, 22; 1864, Apr. 13, May 25, Oct. 12, Dec. 14; 1865, Apr. 12, Oct. 12; 1866, Mar. 8, Apr. 12, Oct. 10; 1867, Apr. 10, Oct. 9; 1868, Apr. 8, 15, Oct.

are aliens. I found that I had got out of the United States and come to Utah. I have never got over that feeling yet, and I think I will get out of Utah and back into the United States again."

14; 1869, Apr. 14, July 7, Oct. 13; 1870, Apr. 13, May 11, Oct. 12, Nov. 2; 1871, Apr. 12, May 24, Oct. 11; 1872, Apr. 10, 17, 24, May 1, Aug. 28, Oct. 9, 16; 1873, Apr. 9, 16, May 7, Aug. 13, Oct. 8; 1874, Apr. 8, May 13, Oct. 14; 1875, Mar. 3, Apr. 14, 21, Oct. 13; 1876, Apr. 12, Oct. 11; 1877, May 16, June 6, 13, Oct. 10; 1878, Mar. 9, Apr. 10, Oct. 9, 16; 1879, Apr. 9, 16; Oct. 15; 1884. Apr. 7; high council, 1877, Oct. 24; meetings of priesthood, 1877, Oct. 10, Dec. 5; 1878, Feb. 6; 1879, Mar. 12; epist., 1879, Apr. 2; elders' disc., 1872, Jan. 24; 1873, Jan. 22, Apr. 16; 1874, Jan. 21, Apr. 22, May 6, 27; 1876, May 3, Oct. 11; 1877, May 16, 23; 1878, Feb. 13; hist. of Morm. (from *St Louis Weekly Union*), Dec. 27, 1851; miscel. (from *St Louis Republican*), *S. F. Herald*, Sept. 25, 1851.

For sermons and discourses, see also *Millennial Star*, passim; address, Kimball, *Young's Journal of Discourses*, ii. 354–7; sermons, *Ferris, Utah and the Mormons*, 217–32, 302–3; sermon, Brigham, *Salem (Or.) Statesman*, Feb. 5, 1856; repts of confer., among others, *Frontier Guardian*, 1851, June 13, Oct. 31, Nov. 28; gen. epist., in *Id.*, Nov. 14; various sermons, *Young's Jour. of Disc.*, ii. passim; disc., Pratt, *Ward's Husband in Utah*, 79–103; sermons, Brigham, *Sac. Union*, 1855, Oct. 25, Dec. 13; 1857, June 16; sermons by Brigham and Kimball, *et al.*, *S. F. Alta*, 1854, May 16; 1855, Apr. 6, May 1; 1857, Jan. 12, June 4, Oct. 14; *S. F. Bulletin*, 1857, May 2; 1866, Apr. 18; lecture, Hyde, *S. F. Herald*, 1857, Apr. 14; rites and ceremonies, *Ferris, Utah and the Mormons*, 311–17; *Gunnison's Mormons*, 37–8; *Remy's Journey to G. S. L. City*, ii. 4–82; *Derby, Overland Route*, 30–2; *Rae's Westward by Rail*, 123–4; *Beadle's Life in Utah*, 255–9; *Rusling's Across America*, 166–9; *Life among the Mormons*, 173–9; *Boller's Among the Indians*, 401–3; *Bowles' Our New West*, 242–7; *Stenhouse, Tell It All*, 251, 387–9; *Ward's Husband in Utah*, 204–8; *Schiel, Reise durch Felsengeb*, 103–24; *Smith's Rise, Progress, and Travels*, 64–5; *Utah Scraps*, 5, 16; *Burton's City of Saints*, 365–75. On faith and doctrines, see *Smith, Doc. and Cov.*, passim; *S. F. Gol. Era*, Dec. 1, 1867; *Des. News*, Sept. 14, 1864; *Mackay's The Morm.*, 51–4; *Ferris, Utah and Morm.*, 201–16; *Gunnison's Morm.*, 39–63; *Frontier Guardian*, Feb. 20, 1850; *Busch, Morm.*, 72–105; *De Rupert's Cal. and Morm.*, 138–46; *Times and Seasons*, vi. 971; *Tucker's Morm.*, 174–9; *S. L. C. Contributor*, ii. 192–324; church gov., *Tullidge, Hist. S. L. City*, 57–8; *Todd's Sunset Land*, 185–93; *S. L. Direc.*, 1869, 58; *Head*, in *Overland Monthly*, v. 275–7; *Utah Scraps*, 8–9; *Mackay's Morm.*, 298–305; *Ferris, Utah and Morm.*, 171–7; *Stansbury's Expor. Exp.*, 135–9; *Richards' Narr.*, MS., 42; *Smith's Rise, Prog.*, etc., 17–18, 27–8; *Green's Morm.*, 150–66, 308–19; *Hyde's Morm.*, 18, 25, 101–2, 188–9; *The Morm. Proph.*, 120–1, 114–19; *Beadle's Life in Utah*, 381–9; *Remy's Journey to G. S. L. City*, ii. 229–34; *Young's Wife No. 19*, 577; *Gunnison's Morm.*, 23–5, 57–61, 78–9; *Sac. Union*, June 26, 1857; theory of creation, *Stenhouse's R. M. Saints*, 485–94; order of Enoch, *Id.*, 495–503; law of adoption, *Id.*, 503–6; book of Abraham, *Id.*, 507–20; res. of infants, 483–4; Washington bap. by prox., *Id.*, 475–82; Hyde expelled, *Id.*, 640; negro Mormons, *S. F. Bulletin*, Nov. 14, 1884; pub. discuss., *Pratt, Ser. of Pamph.*, no. 10, 1–46, no. 11, 1–46; *Taylor's Govt of God*, passim; Morm. pro and con, *Chandless' Visit to S. Lake*, 156; *Ward's Husband in Utah*, 140–283; *Gunnison's Morm.*, 35, 164; *Salem (Or.) Statesman*, Dec. 5, 1854; *S. F. Herald*, 1854, Jan. 26, Aug. 23, Sept. 27; *Alta*, 1851, July 24, Aug. 6, 7; 1852, Dec. 21; 1853, Nov. 26; 1854, June 25, 26; 1856, May 10, 15, June 13, Sept. 15, Dec. 17; 1858, Jan. 22; *Cal. Chris. Advoc.*, Apr. 6, 1865; *Bulletin*, 1856, Aug. 21; 1877, Sept. 8; *Sac. Union*, 1855, Mar. 16, July 17, Dec. 13; 1856, June 14; *Morm. at Home*, 65, 122–3, 142–5, 220–1; *N. Y. Jour. of Com.*, in *Pan. Star and Her.*,

Thus, notwithstanding the iniquities of the saints, together with their impudence and arrogance, as charged
upon them by their enemies, the impossibility of others
living with them as members of one community, of

Feb. 18, 1869; *Smucker's Hist. Morm.*, 323–99; *Young's Wife No. 19*, 333–40;
Olshausen, Morm., 170–5; *Jonveaux, L'Amerique*, 235–6, 244–8; *Mackay's
The Mcrm.*, 271–326; *Ferris, Utah and Morm.*, 171–7; *Young's Resurrection*,
11; *Smet's Western Missions*, 390–7; *32 Cong. 1st Sess.*, H. Ex. Doc., 19–20;
Frontier Guardian, 1850, Feb. 6, 20, Mar. 6, 20, June 12, July 10, Sept. 4,
Oct. 30, Dec. 25; 1851, Jan. 8, Mar. 21, Apr. 18, May 16, 30, June 13, 27,
July 25, Aug. 8, Sept. 5, Oct. 31, Dec. 12, 26; 1852, Jan. 9, 23, Feb. 6, 20;
Ward's Husband in Utah, 283–9; *Hyde's Morm.*, 50, 179–81, 306–30; *Burton's City of Saints*, 437–97; *Hickman's Dest. Angel*, 10–15.
    In addition to these authorities, it is safe to assert that every gentile paper
of importance in the U. S. has at some time extracted from the Salt Lake
papers, and commented freely thereon.   During the existence of the *Kanesville (Iowa) Frontier Guardian*, 1849–52, nearly every issue contained articles explanatory of the dogmas of the church, a few of which I have referred
to.   The *Millennial Star*, although devoted more especially to missionary
effort abroad, has always copied freely from home publications.   I append a
few additional authorities, as follows: On religion, *S. F. Alta*, Jan. 19, 1860;
Bulletin, June 19, 1871; *S. L. Rev.*, Sept. 22, 1871; *Gaz. Utah*, 1874; *S. L.
Trib.*, Jan. 29, 1876, May 19, 1877; *Juv. Inst.*, xv.; doc., *Pratt, Key to Scien.
Theol.*, passim; *Bonwick, Morm. and Silv. Mines*, 34–61; *S. L. Trib.*, Jan. 25,
1872, Mar. 28, 1874; *S. L. C. Contributor*, ii. 39, 70, 135; bible and book of
Morm., *S. L. Trib.*, May 16, 1874; rev., *Eureka Sent.*, Apr. 16, 1875; *Silv.
City Avalan.*, Mar. 31, 1876; *S. L. Trib.*, June 2, Oct. 20, 1877; Sept. 24, Oct.
26, 1879; *Silv. Reef Miner*, June 11, 1879; *Stenhouse, Englishwoman in Utah*, 34,
74; *S. F. Stock Rept*, Jan. 1, 1880; church, *Sac. Union*, Feb. 4, Sept. 1, 1860;
S. F. Bulletin, Dec. 22, 1868, Oct. 10, 1870; *Chronicle*, Oct. 7, 1883; priesthood, *Sac. Union*, Oct. 20, 1860; *S. L. Trib.*, in *Unionville Silv. State*, Mar.
23, 1872; *Eureka Sent.*, Apr. 15, 1873; *S. F. Alta*, Apr. 14, 1873; *S. L. Trib.*,
July 4, 1874, July 10, 1875; *Gold Hill News*, Dec. 14, 1875; *Smith's Mystery
and Crime*, 16–23, 27–30; *Circulars of First Presid.*, 1877; Pratt's prophecy,
Austin, Reese Riv. Rev., Apr. 23, 1880; worship and preachers, *Burton, City
of Saints*, 316; sermons, *Young*, 1860; *Burton, City of Saints*, 320; *Sac. Union*,
May 30, Oct. 9; *Morm. Expos.*, i. no. 1; *S. F. Call*, May 11, 1865; *Bulletin*,
Oct. 17, 1867; *Alta*, July 19, 1869; *S. L. Rev.*, Dec. 7, 1871; *Hubner's Round
the World*, 109; *The Resurr.*, S. L. City, 1875; *Prescott Miner*, Aug. 17, 1877;
by elders, *S. L. Tel.*, June 15, 1869; *Corinne Reptr*, in *Elko Indpt*, Aug. 21,
1869; *Greenwood's New Life*, 144–7; *Taylor's Summer Savory*, 21–5; *S. L.
Herald*, 1878, Sept. 2, 17, 24, Oct. 1, 22, 29, Nov. 5, 12, 19; *Marshall's
Through Amer.*, 198–205; *Silver Reef Min.*, June 18, 1879; character of, *Sala's
Amer. Revis.*, 296; *Richardson's Beyond Miss.*, 356–7; *Sac. Union*, Feb. 28,
1861; relig. freedom, *Cannon, Rev. of Decis. of Supm. Ct*; confer., *S. F. Alta*,
1869, Oct. 9; 1872, Apr. 29; *Bulletin*, 1870, Apr. 12; 1871, Oct. 6, 7; 1872,
Apr. 9, 29; 1873, Apr. 7, 9; 1874, Oct. 7; 1876, Nov. 3; 1877, Apr. 11, Oct. 8;
1879, Apr. 9; 1883, Oct. 6, 15; *Call*, 1864, Apr. 7; 1871, Apr. 11; 1872, Apr.
9; 1873, Apr. 7; *Chronicle*, 1883, Oct. 6; *Post*, 1875, Apr. 12; 1877, Apr. 6;
Times, 1868, Apr. 21; *Sac. Union*, 1860, Oct. 20; *Carson Union*, Apr. 12, 1873;
Jackson (Amador) Ledger, Dec. 29, 1877; *S. L. Herald*, 1878, Oct. 8; 1879,
Apr. 9, 12, 22, May 20, June 10, 24, Oct. 7; 1880, Jan. 6; *Telegraph*, 1869,
Apr. 6, 7, 8, 9; 1870, May 7, 8, 9; *Tribune*, 1873, May 10; 1874, Apr. 4; 1875,
Apr. 17, Aug. 6, Oct. 9, 10, 12; 1876, Apr. 8–15, Oct. 7; 1877, May 19, 26,
Oct. 13; 1878, Apr. 13, July 13, Oct. 12; 1879, Apr. 5, 8, Oct. 7; 1880, Apr.
10, Sept. 23; *Townsend's Morm. Trials*, 44; *Beadle's Life in Utah*, 278–89;
Robinson's Sinners and Saints; bishops, *Des. News*, Nov. 29, 1851; book of

one commonwealth, is the real difficulty—not their religion, their so-called blasphemies, their pretended revelations and miracles, their opposition bible, their latter-day dispensations, and the rest; nor yet their crimes and misdemeanors, their robberies and murders; nor even yet their secret ceremonies, their endowments, Danite bands, blood atonement, and the rest. The copy or counterpart of very many of these, in greater or smaller degree, is, or has been, practised by the gentiles; or if not, few care enough for any of them to go to war on their account. The trouble is this, and this will continue to be the trouble, in Utah or elsewhere in the United States, and that whether polygamy stands or falls—the saints are too exclusive, industrially and politically, for their neighbors.

The theory of government of this republic is numerical equality, each man and each hundred men being equal to every other man or every other hundred men as industrial and political factors. In this case, however, it is not so, and it never can be so. Spiritual manifestations and spiritual wives have nothing to do with it. A hundred or a thousand Mormons are a unit, socially, politically, and commercially, in a community organized theoretically upon the basis of only one man to the unit. And until the principles of the United States republic are remodelled, Mormons and gentiles cannot live together in peace and amity. It is folly for gentiles to enter a Mormon

Abraham, *Smith's Pearl of Gt Price*, 25–30; *Mil. Star*, xv. 549–50, passim. For additional sermons on theology, see *Mil. Star*, i. passim, vi. 33–8, 49–56, 65–70, 97–9, viii. 35–8; *Times and Seasons*, ii., iii., iv., and v. passim, vi. 808–9, 823–5, 957–8, 1001–5; anal. of, *Beadle's Life in Utah*, 311–31; *Townsend's Morm. Trials*, 40; on creed and faith, *Times and Seasons*, i. 68–70, iii. 863–5, 931–3; *Spencer's Letters*, etc., 1–252; *Young's Wife No. 19*, 58–60; *Bennett's Hist. of Saints*, 103–32, 302–7, 340–1; *Eden Rev.*, Apr. 1854, 352; *Pratt, Inter. Acct*, 27–36; *Id.*, *Series of Pamph.*, nos 2–6; *Tucker's Morm.*, 139–52; *Vetromile, A Tour*, 70–1; *Ferris' Utah and Morm.*, 211–13, 299–300; *Stenhouse's Tell It All*, 295–300; *Reynolds' Bk of Abraham*, 15; *Grass Valley, Foothill Tidings*, July 5, 1879; *Pratt, in Des. News*, Aug. 21, 1852; *Smith, in Times and Seasons*, iii. 709; *Id.*, *Pearl of Gt Price*, 63; *Smucker's Morm.*, 61–6; *Pratt's Persecutions*, iii.–v.; *Id.*, *Voice of Warn.*, passim; *Dixon, White Conquest*, 182–8, 193–7, 223–8; preachers and preaching, *Greeley's Overland Jour.*, 218–22; *Seventies, Mil. Star*, xxxvi. 369–72; church charter, *S. F. Bulletin*, Nov. 26, 1858; sincerity of Morm., *S. F. Alta*, Mar. 30, 1858.

community and think to rule, or to have any part in the government as at present existing, and following the line of law and order. This is why the people of Missouri and Illinois drove them out—not because of their religion or immorality, for their religion was nothing to the gentiles, and their morals were as good or better than those of their neighbors. It may as well be understood and agreed upon that, in the United States or out of the United States, the Mormons are, and ever will be, a people self-contained and apart.

Thus the matter continues to be discussed by the world at large, as a question of theology or morality, and not of active political and judicial control, or of the domination of a politico-religious organization, with aspirations and purposes diverse from those of the American people generally.

The theory and assumption of the Mormon church as a politico-religious organization is that the church is a government of God, and not responsible to any other government on earth conflicting with it, if not indeed bound from necessity to overturn and supplant all civil governments. This assumption lies at the very foundation of the Mormon creed; and from this point, in practical operation as well as in theory, there is a divergence between that organization and the United States government. Grant that any man believes what the Mormons believe, say their enemies, and where will his allegiance rest—with the government of the United States, or with this politico-religious organization which ought to and will, as they imagine, supplant all other governments? Many of them are alien born, and, from the treatment they receive on their arrival, learn to distrust the government of the United States, and to cling all the closer to the institutions of their sect.

" It is not consistent that the people of God," says Orson Pratt, " should organize or be subject to man-made governments. If it were so, they could never be perfected. There can be but one perfect government—that organized by God, a government by apostles, prophets, priests, teachers, and evangelists; the order of the original church of all churches acknowledged by God."

Early in this narrative we saw plainly, and remarked upon it as we proceeded, that it has been chiefly the political character and aspirations of the church that have brought it into all its difficulties everywhere—in Ohio, in Missouri, in Illinois. And its thirty years of isolation and independence in Utah, during which time it came in contact with the American people or with the government only in a limited degree, intensified its desire for control. The only way the Mormons can live in peace with gentile neighbors is for them to follow the example of their brethren, the Josephites—leave politics and government out of their ethics, and not combine for the purpose of controlling counties, states, or territories. But this strikes at the very root of their religion, which has already given them for an inheritance all counties and countries and peoples throughout the world, as they modestly claim.

There is here much more than the religious unity of ancient Israel. As a coöperative association, Mormonism has not its equal in the history of the world. In every conceivable relation, position, interest, and idea; in every sentiment of hope and fear, of joy and sorrow—there is mutual assistance and sympathy. It enters into all affairs, whether for time or eternity; there is an absolute unity in religion, government, and society, and to the fullest extent short of communism, mutual assistance in agriculture, commerce, and manufactures. If a foreign convert wishes to come to America, he is helped hither; if he wants land, farming implements, seed, stock, he is helped to them; trade and manufactures are largely coöperative. And this bond of strength, whether it be called the holiness of saints or

the bigotry of fanatics, causes them to be feared and
hated by their neighbors.

Polygamy, as a tenet of the Mormon church, is
based upon scripture example, and if this is unlawful, it says, all is unlawful.   Marriage is ordained of
God, and essential to salvation.   Christian sects
hold up the patriarchs as examples in their sacred
instruction, and yet condemn in these personages a
practice which Christ nowhere condemns.   While
in polygamy, God blessed them and their polygamous seed, saying never a word about their plural
wives.   Polygamy was common in Asia at the time
of the apostles; yet none of them preached against
it, nor does John the revelator mention it, writing
to the seven churches.   In the days of Justin Martyr,
the Jews practised polygamy.   It is true that the
emperor Theodosius, about A. D. 393, promulgated a
law against polygamy, but it was repealed sixty years
after by Valentinian.   Nevertheless, as the civilized
world, particularly Christian sects, regarded the practice with abhorrence, the prophet Joseph inquired of
the Lord as to what he should do.   And the Lord
answered, commanding him to restore all things, the
practice of polygamy among the rest.   The revelation
on this subject is given entire in note 19 of this chapter.   The inferior order of wifehood, known in the
sacred scriptures as concubinage, is not recognized in
the Mormon church.   By the marriage covenant, all
are made wives, and all children are legitimate.

Celestial marriage and the plural-wife system, as
incorporated parts of the Mormon religion, are essential to the fulness of exaltation in the eternal world.
The space around us, it declares, is inhabited by spirits,
thousands of years old, awaiting tabernacles in the
flesh, which can be legitimately furnished them only
by marriage and procreation; and bodies cannot be
obtained for these spirits fast enough unless men have
more wives than one.   It is the will and glory of God

that these spirits have bodies as speedily as possible, that they become saints on earth and in his kingdom, those who keep this commandment thus to multiply being as gods; otherwise these spirits will take refuge in the bodies of unbelievers, and so sink to perdition.

But civilization has pronounced polygamy a curse and a crime, a retrogression, an offence against society and against morality, a beastly abomination, immoral, incestuous, degrading, a relic of barbarism, a sin, a shame, a vice, and as such has discarded it and passed laws against it. And the issue between polygamy and monogamy is one purely for civilization to determine; christianity has not a foot of ground to stand upon in the matter.

Culture cares nothing for religion; it is what a man does, not what he believes, that affects progress. It will not do to break the law in the name of religion. Suppose a man's religion authorizes him to commit murder: does that make it right? Civilization seeks the highest morality; and the highest morality, it says, is not that of the bible, of the book of Mormon, or of any other so-called holy book. The highest morality is based on nature, and by a study of nature's laws men may find it. Long before Christ, civilization awoke to the evils of this custom, which is not in accord with its morality. The religious reformer, Buddha, who died 470 years before Christ was born, and whose followers now number about one third of the whole human race, preached against polygamy. When Greece and Rome were the foremost nations of the world, they did not practise polygamy, nor has ever the highest civilization entertained it. Polygamy is to monogamy as Greece to China, or as England to India.

All very religious people, as well as science fanatics, are partially insane. This insanity may be passive and harmless, or aggressive and hurtful. We have innumerable instances of both kinds in the history of the Christian church. But as the world progresses, religion becomes less dogmatic, and the insanity assumes more and more the milder form. Thus it is with the Mormons as with others; they would not feel justified in doing now some things which were done by their predecessors, any more than gentile Christians would wish to burn heretics, or slaughter millions in the name of the redeemer; or any more than they would accept Joseph Smith as a prophet from God, or believe in his metal book of Mormon, or his pretended revelations.

But admitting man's obligation to follow the precepts and example of the bible, which, if done literally, would lead him into all manner of contrarieties and absurdities, even as it does the Mormons to-day, the scriptural argument in support of polygamy does not go for much. Among the half-savage Israelites the custom obtained, but as they grew more civilized, it died out. The first apostles had none of them two wives, and St Paul maintained that it was best not to have any; the spirit of the new testament is all against plurality of wives, and, though it nowhere in so many words condemns the system, the books of Mormon and doctrine and covenants do.

Thus we see that holy books are contradictory and unreliable, not being consistent in themselves, or producing consistent followers. Codes of morality depending on the divine will are without foundation: are, indeed, not codes of morality, which to be genuine must be based on nature as the law-giver and punisher; for otherwise all men to whom the will of God has not been revealed, or who do not believe in any god or revelation, would be without any knowledge of right and wrong, or any standard of morality.

Innate perceptions, supernatural intuitions, or a conscience divinely given, instead of one evolved from the ever-increasing accumulation of human experiences, are not safe guides to right conduct, as the doctrines and doings of the Mormons clearly show. By the result of an act, not by supernatural revelation, we know whether it is good or bad; and here, the result being bad, the act is wrong, immoral.

The result is bad because by reason of the act civilization takes a step backward, woman is degraded, and the progress of the race hampered. The monogamic is the highest type of family, and the highest type of society, yet evolved. Polygamy is better than promiscuity or polyandry, but it is not equal to monogamy. Polygamy springs from the desire to extend the sexual gratification at the expense of the better sense of the better part of the world's inhabitants. It is but a few removes from the old way among savages, where women were property, and bought by husbands to be used as slaves. To monogamy is due the fullest development of the emotions, of the higher sentiments, motherly tenderness, fatherly care, and the dutiful respect and obedience on the part of children. It is here that the passion of love assumes its most refined form; it is here that we find in family, social, and political relations, the greatest good to the greatest number.

For if we degrade woman, we degrade her children, her husband, and the whole community. Throughout all ages the position of woman has fixed the advancement of the nation in the scale of refinement and intelligence. Polygamy makes of woman, not the equal and companion of man, but his subordinate, if not indeed his serf or slave. The charm of her influence is gone; the family circle becomes incongruous and less cohesive; and there is an absence of those firm relations, filial and paternal, which, continued through successive generations, engender the highest type of society yet known. Make of American women Circassian slaves, and you will make of American men Turks.

The nations having the highest and best literature, laws, commerce, and religion, the nations that are enlightening the world with their books, telegraphs, steamboats, and railroads, are monogamic. Polygamy encourages, if it does not necessitate, a domestic despotism, which, united with a religious and political despotism, constitutes one of the worst possible of social evils. It adds to the Mormons numbers and strength, banding them in a peculiar brotherhood, politically and socially.

The system is not an equitable one. There are born a tolerably even number of males and females, so that under this arrangement, where one man had a dozen wives, a dozen or so men would have none. Then, as to the relationships of the individual members, injustice is wrought, some of them being but little better than those existing among animals. There is an instinct in every woman which tells her that to be second or third is to be no wife at all. Neglect must exist. One man cannot properly care for so many women and children. Even if he is wealthy, he has not the time. Differences of origin and interests breed jealousies, foster selfishness, and are injurious to character. Then, when the reproductive age has passed, there is nothing left for the wife but a lonely and miserable old age.

Further than this, if reproduction be the chief incentive to the plural-wife system among the Mormons, and if it be true, as is often asserted, that as a rule the sexes are born numerically equal, then the system will in the end defeat its own object, for more children will be born and cared for where there is one man for every woman than where some women have to go without a husband, or with a fraction of one. It might pertinently be asked, in this connection, what is the benefit in multiplying the population? Are there not enough people already in the world? and is it not better to improve the stock than unduly to multiply it? This prevention is practised often for improper motives and by injurious methods; but millions do it because they think they cannot afford to raise children, and have no right to bring them into existence.

True, the evils of the practice are not so great under a theocratic and patriarchal system like that of the Mormons, as it would be if allowed to run riot round the world, giving libertines the widest opportunity to deceive and then desert women; in which case there would be no need of prostitution to satisfy men's passions, as the great barriers between the virtuous and the lewd would be for the most part broken down. Among the Mormons, this is prevented by strong religious feeling, and by the patriarchal influence of the leaders. But the majority of mankind in the great outside world are not controlled by religion or reason —they simply drift.

Whether for this reason or some other reason, Mormons are not loyal to the government, and the issue is between polygamic theocracy and American republicanism. Nor are the fears of the friends of the latter wholly groundless; for, as one writer said of it, "the Mormon church is one of the best organized systems in the world. The cunning of the devil and the sophistry of error are so mingled with truth as to make it one of the most powerful agencies to delude the ignorant." The truth is, the theocratic organization has already become absolute. Opposition stimulates propagandism, and persecution brings only defiance of federal authority and the moral sense of the nation. Legislation is defeated at every turn. The history of Utah is the history of the Mormon priesthood in its attempt to subordinate the state to the church, and make the authority of the priesthood superior to that of the United States government.

So says civilization.

In answer, polygamy reiterates scriptural example and divine command, and repudiates civilization wherever it interferes with religion. Culture and progress, which set at defiance God's law, are of the devil. There is no retrogression in keeping the commands of the most high. God blessed Abraham, and

David, and Solomon; polygamy is no curse. And that cannot be a sin which God commands; that cannot be a vice which has for its accomplishment only the highest and holiest purposes of the almighty; that cannot be against morality which is practised only by the righteous, and for the pure and eternal welfare of the human race.[19]

[19] For a time, in so far as possible, the practice of polygamy in Illinois and Utah was kept secret by the missionaries in England and in Europe. Says Parley P. Pratt in Manchester, and in the *Millennial Star* of 1846, 'Such a doctrine is not held, known, or practised as a principle of the latter-day saints;' and John Taylor at the Boulogne discussion, in France, in July 1850, says, 'We are accused here of polygamy and actions the most indelicate, obscene, and disgusting, such as none but a corrupt heart could have conceived. These things are too outrageous to be believed.'

On the morning of Aug. 29, 1852, before a special conference in session at S. L. City, Orson Pratt preached on the subject of marriage, in which discourse he stated, 'It is well known, however, to the congregation before me, that the latter-day saints have embraced the doctrine of a plurality of wives as part of their religious faith.' In the evening, whilst the sacrament was being passed, Brigham addressed the audience, saying in the course of his remarks, 'Though that doctrine [polygamy] has not been preached by the elders, this people have believed in it for many years.' At the close of Brigham's address, the revelation of July 12, 1843, was read by Elder Thomas Bullock. The proceedings of this conference were published in full in an 8vo pamphlet of 48 pages, issued as an extra by the *Deseret News*, on Sept. 14, 1852, when the revelation first saw the light. It next appeared in the *Millennial Star*, and may now be found in the book of *Doctrine and Covenants*. Herewith I give the revelation entire.

Revelation given to Joseph Smith, at Nauvoo, July 12, 1843: 'Verily, thus saith the Lord unto you, my servant Joseph, that inasmuch as you have inquired of my hand to know and understand wherein I, the Lord, justified my servants Abraham, Isaac, and Jacob, as also Moses, David, and Solomon, my servants, as touching the principle and doctrine of their having many wives and concubines: behold, and lo! I am the Lord thy God, and will answer thee as touching this matter; therefore, prepare thy heart to receive and obey the instructions which I am about to give unto you; for all those who have this law revealed unto them must obey the same; for behold! I reveal unto you a new and an everlasting covenant, and if ye abide not that covenant, then are ye damned; for no one can reject this covenant and be permitted to enter into my glory; for all who will have a blessing at my hands shall abide the law which was appointed for that blessing, and the conditions thereof, as were instituted from before the foundations of the world; and as pertaining to the new and everlasting covenant, it was instituted for the fulness of my glory; and he that receiveth a fulness thereof must and shall abide the law, or he shall be damned, saith the Lord God. And verily I say unto you, that the conditions of this law are these: All covenants, contracts, bonds, obligations, oaths, vows, performances, connections, associations, or expectations that are not made and entered into and sealed by the holy spirit of promise, of him who is anointed, both as well for time and for all eternity, and that, too, most holy, by revelation and commandment, through the medium of mine anointed, whom I have appointed on the earth to hold this power (and I have appointed unto my servant Joseph to hold this power in the last days, and there is never but one on the earth at a time on whom this power and the keys of this priesthood are conferred), are of no efficacy, virtue, or force in and after the resurrection from the dead; for all contracts

Whatever may be the blessings attending civilization, they are insignificant as compared with the blessings of religion, a life of faith and holiness, and the pure worship of God.   Civilization with its one-wife or no-wife system breeds licentiousness, fosters pros-

that are not made unto this end have an end when men are dead.   Behold mine house is a house of order, saith the Lord God, and not a house of confusion.   Will I accept an offering, saith the Lord, that is not made in my name ? Or will I receive at your hands that which I have not appointed ?   And will I appoint unto you, saith the Lord, except it be by law, even as I and my father ordained unto you, before the world was ?   I am the Lord thy God, and I give unto you this commandment that no man shall come unto the father but by me, or by my word, which is my law, saith the Lord; and everything that is in the world, whether it be ordained of men, by thrones, or principalities, or powers, or things of name, whatsoever they may be that are not by me, or by my word, saith the Lord, shall be thrown down, and shall not remain after men are dead, neither in nor after the resurrection, saith the Lord your God; for whatsoever things remain are by me, and whatsoever things are not by me shall be shaken and destroyed.   Therefore, if a man marry him a wife in the world, and he marry her not by me, nor by my word, and he covenant with her so long as he is in the world, and she with him, their covenant and marriage are not of force when they are dead, and when they are out of the world; therefore, they are not bound by any law when they are out of the world; therefore, when they are out of the world, they neither marry nor are given in marriage, but are appointed angels in heaven, which angels are ministering servants, to minister for those who are worthy of a far more and an exceeding and an eternal weight of glory; for these angels did not abide my law, therefore they cannot be enlarged, but remain separately and singly, without exaltation, in their saved condition to all eternity, and from henceforth are not gods, but are angels of God forever and ever.   And again, verily I say unto you, if a man marry a wife, and make a covenant with her for time and for all eternity, if that covenant is not by me or by my word, which is my law, and is not sealed by the holy spirit of promise, through him whom I have anointed and appointed unto this power, then it is not valid, neither of force when they are out of the world, because they are not joined by me, saith the Lord, neither by my word; when they are out of the world, it can not be received there because the angels and the gods are appointed there, by whom they cannot pass; they cannot, therefore, inherit my glory, for my house is a house of order, saith the Lord God.   And again, verily I say unto you, if a man marry a wife by my word, which is my law, and by the new and everlasting covenant, and it is sealed unto them by the holy spirit of promise, by him who is anointed, unto whom I have appointed this power and the keys of this priesthood, and it shall be said unto them, Ye shall come forth in the first resurrection; and if it be after the first resurrection, in the next resurrection; and shall inherit thrones, kingdoms, principalities, and powers, dominions, all heights and depths; then shall it be written in the Lamb's book of life, that he shall commit no murder whereby to shed innocent blood, and if he abide in my covenant, and commit no murder whereby to shed innocent blood, it shall be done unto them in all things whatsoever my servant hath put upon them, in time and through all eternity; and shall be of full force when they are out of the world, and they shall pass by the angels and the gods which are set there, to their exaltation and glory in all things, as hath been sealed upon their heads, which glory shall be a fulness and a continuation of the seeds forever and ever.   Then shall they be gods, because they have no end; therefore shall they be from everlasting to everlasting because they continue; then shall they be above all, because all things

titution, and brings much misery on the human race
in this world, not to mention the world to come.
The laws of God we know; civilization's laws we
know not.   Civilization has little to boast of in the

are subject unto them.   Then shall they be gods, because they have all power,
and the angels are subject unto them.

'Verily, verily, I say unto you, except ye abide my law ye cannot attain
to this glory; for straight is the gate and narrow the way that leadeth unto the
exaltation and continuation of the lives, and few there be that find it, because
ye receive me not in the world, neither do ye know me.   But if ye receive me
in the world, then shall ye know me, and shall receive your exaltation, that
where I am ye shall be also.   This is eternal lives, to know the only wise and
true God, and Jesus Christ whom he hath sent.   I am he.   Receive ye,
therefore, my law.   Broad is the gate and wide the way that leadeth to the
deaths, and many there are that go in thereat, because they receive me not,
neither do they abide in my law.   Verily, verily, I say unto you, if a man
marry a wife according to my word, and they are sealed by the holy spirit of
promise, according to mine appointment, and he or she shall commit any sin
or transgression of the new and everlasting covenant whatever, and all manner of blasphemies, and if they commit no murder wherein they shed innocent
blood, yet they shall come forth in the first resurrection and enter into their
exaltation; but they shall be destroyed in the flesh, and shall be delivered
unto the buffetings of Satan, unto the day of redemption, saith the Lord God.
The blasphemy against the holy ghost, which shall not be forgiven in the
world nor out of the world, is in that ye commit murder wherein ye shed innocent blood, and assent unto my death, after ye have received my new and
everlasting covenant, saith the Lord God; and he that abideth not this law
can in no wise enter into my glory, but shall be damned, saith the Lord.   I
am the Lord thy God, and will give unto thee the law of my holy priesthood
as was ordained by me and my Father before the world was.   Abraham received all things whatsoever he received by revelation and commandment by
my word, saith the Lord, and hath entered into his exaltation and sitteth
upon his throne.   Abraham received promises concerning his seed and of the
fruit of his loins—from whose loins ye are, viz., my servant Joseph—which
were to continue so long as they were in the world; and as touching Abraham
and his seed out of the world, they should continue; both in the world and
out of the world should they continue as innumerable as the stars, or if ye
were to count the sand upon the seashore, ye could not number them.   This
promise is yours also, because ye are of Abraham, and the promise was made
unto Abraham, and by this law are the continuation of the works of my
father, wherein he glorifieth himself.   Go ye, therefore, and do the works of
Abraham; enter ye into my law, and ye shall be saved.   But if ye enter not
into my law, ye cannot receive the promise of my Father which he made
unto Abraham.   God commanded Abraham, and Sarah gave Hagar to Abraham to wife.   And why did she do it?   Because this was the law, and from
Hagar sprang many people.   This, therefore, was fulfilling, among other
things, the promises.   Was Abraham, therefore, under condemnation?   Verily I say unto you, nay; for I, the Lord, commanded it.   Abraham was commanded to offer his son Isaac; nevertheless it was written thou shalt not
kill.   Abraham, however, did not refuse, and it was accounted unto him for
righteousness.

'Abraham received concubines, and they bare him children, and it was
accounted unto him for righteousness, because they were given unto him and
he abode in my law; as Isaac also, and Jacob, did none other things than
that which they were commanded; and because they did none other things
than that which they were commanded, they have entered into their exaltation, according to the promises, and sit upon thrones, and are not angels, but

line of its moralities. It is true that monogamy was early enforced in Greece; but outside of marriage limits, there was gross indulgence in every form, which was as freely permitted and practised as among

are gods. David also received many wives and concubines, as also Solomon and Moses, my servants, as also many others of my servants, from the beginning of creation until this tim , and in nothing did they sin, save in those things which they received not of me. David's wives and concubines were given unto him of me by the hand of Nathan, my servant, and others of the prophets who had the keys of this power; and in none of these things did he sin against me, save in the case of Uriah and his wife; and therefore he hath fallen from his exaltation and received his portion; and he shall not inherit them out of the world, for I gave them unto another, saith the Lord. I am the Lord thy God, and I gave unto thee, my servant Joseph, an appointment, and restore all things; ask what ye will, and it shall be given unto you, according to my word; and as ye have asked concerning adultery, verily, verily, I say unto you, if a man receiveth a wife in the new and everlasting covenant, and if she be with another man, and I have not appointed unto her by the holy anointing, she hath committed adultery, and shall be destroyed. If she be not in the new and everlasting covenant, and she be with another man, she has committed adultery; and if her husband be with another woman, and he was under a vow, he hath broken his vow and hath committed adultery; and if she hath not committed adultery, but is innocent, and hath not broken her vow, and she knoweth it, and I reveal it unto you, my servant Joseph, then shall you have power, by the power of my holy priesthood, to take her and give her unto him that hath not committed adultery, but hath been faithful, for he shall be made ruler over many; for I have conferred upon you the keys and power of the priesthood, wherein I restore all things and make known unto you all things in due time. And verily, verily, I say unto you, that whatsoever you seal on earth shall be sealed in heaven, and whatsoever you bind on earth, in my name and by my word, saith the Lord, it shall be eternally bound in the heavens; and whosoever sins you remit on earth shall be remitted eternally in the heavens, and whosoever sins you retain on earth shall be retained in heaven. And again, verily I say, whomsoever you bless, I will bless; and whomsoever you curse, I will curse, saith the Lord; for I the Lord am thy God. And again, verily I say unto you, my servant Joseph, that whatsoever you give on earth, and to whomsoever you give any one on earth, by my word and according to my law, it shall be visited with blessings, and not cursings, and with my power, saith the Lord, and shall be without condemnation on earth and in heaven; for I am the Lord thy God, and will be with thee even unto the end of the world, and through all eternity; for verily I seal upon you your exaltation and prepare a throne for you in the kingdom of my father, with Abraham, your father. Behold! I have seen your sacrifices, and will forgive all your sins; I have seen your sacrifices, in obedience to that which I have told you; go, therefore, and I make a way for your escape, as I accepted the offering of Abraham, of his son Isaac.

'Verily I say unto you, a commandment I give unto mine handmaid, Emma Smith, your wife, whom I have given unto you, that she stay herself and partake not of that which I commanded you to offer unto her; for I did it, saith the Lord, to prove you all, as I did Abraham, and that I might require an offering at your hand by covenant and sacrifice; and let my handmaid Emma Smith receive all those that have been given unto my servant Joseph, and who are virtuous and pure before me; and those who are not pure, and have said they were pure, shall be destroyed, saith the Lord God; for I am the Lord thy God, and ye shall obey my voice; and I give unto my servant Joseph that he shall be made ruler over many things, for he hath been faithful over a few things, and from henceforth I will strengthen him. And I command mine handmaid Emma

the foremost nations of to-day. Plato even advocated plurality of wives, chiefly on patriotic grounds. In Rome, the one-wife system was more firmly established, though in the absence of marriage, chastity was little regarded. Marcus Aurelius, indeed, was eulogized by his biographer for bringing into his

Smith to abide and cleave unto my servant Joseph and to none else. But if she will not abide this commandment, she shall be destroyed, saith the Lord, for I am the Lord thy God, and will destroy her if she abide not in my law; but if she will not abide this commandment, then shall my servant Joseph do all things for her even as he hath said, and I will bless him and multiply him, and give unto him a hundred-fold in this world, of fathers and mothers, brothers and sisters, houses and lands, wives and children, and crowns of eternal lives in the eternal worlds. And again, verily I say, let mine handmaid forgive my servant Joseph his trespasses, and then shall she be forgiven her trespasses, wherein she has trespassed against me, and I, the Lord thy God, will bless her and multiply her, and make her heart rejoice. And again, I say, let not my servant Joseph put his property out of his hands, lest an enemy come and destroy him—for Satan seeketh to destroy—for I am the Lord thy God, and he is my servant; and behold! and lo I am with him, as I am with Abraham, thy father, even unto his exaltation and glory. Now as touching the law of the priesthood, there are many things pertaining thereunto. Verily, if a man be called of my Father, as was Aaron, by mine own voice, and by the voice of him that sent me, and I have endowed him with the keys of the power of this priesthood, if he do anything in my name, and according to my law, and by my word, he will not commit sin, and I will justify him. Let no one, therefore, set on my servant Joseph, for I will justify him; for he shall do the sacrifice which I require at his hands, for his transgressions, saith the Lord your God. And again, as pertaining to the law of the priesthood; if any man espouse a virgin, and desire to espouse another, and the first give her consent, if and he espouse the second, and they are virgins, and have vowed to on other man, then is he justified; he cannot commit adultery, for they are given unto him; for he cannot commit adultery with that that belonged unto him, and to none else; and if he have ten virgins given unto him by this law, he cannot commit adultery, for they belong to him and they are given unto him; therefore is he justified. But if one or either of the ten virgins after she is espoused shall be with another man, she has committed adultery and shall be destroyed; for they are given unto him to multiply and replenish the earth, according to my commandment, and to fulfil the promise which was given by my father before the foundation of the world, and for their exaltation in the eternal worlds, that they may bear the souls of men; for herein is the work of my father continued, that he may be glorified. And again, verily, verily, I say unto you, if any man have a wife who holds the keys of this power, and he teaches unto her the law of my priesthood as pertaining to these things, then shall she believe and administer unto him, or she shall be destroyed, saith the Lord your God; for I will destroy her; for I will magnify my name upon all those who receive and abide in my law. Therefore it shall be lawful in me, if she receive not this law, for him to receive all things whatsoever I, the Lord his God, will give unto him, because she did not administer unto him according to my word; and she then becomes the transgressor, and he is exempt from the law of Sarah, who administered unto Abraham according to the law, when I commanded Abraham to take Hagar to wife. And now, as pertaining to this law, verily, verily, I say unto you, I will reveal more unto you hereafter; therefore let this suffice for the present. Behold I am Alpha and Omega. Amen.'

house a concubine, upon the death of his wife, instead of inflicting upon his children a step-mother.

If monogamy is the only natural form of sexual relationship, how happens it that, throughout the lifetime of the race, there have been and still are so many other forms of relationship? From time immemorial polygamy has existed, and has been sanctioned by all religions. Bramin, Parsee, and Rajpoot all indulged in it. Though nothing is said of it in the new testament, we learn from the Talmud that it was lawful among the Jews about the time of Christ's coming. Among the early converts to christianity in Syria and Egypt were many polygamists who remained uncensured. The rabbies of the west prohibited it eight or nine centuries ago, but those of the east, where it is practised by nearly all nations, permit it even now. It is common to-day throughout a large part of the world. Take all the peoples of the earth, of all times and cultures, and those among whom plural wives obtained are far in excess of the others.

Pre-nuptial unchastity was scarcely censured either in Greece or Rome. "If there be any one," said Cicero, "who thinks that young men should be altogether restrained from the love of courtesans, he is indeed very severe." Even that most austere of Stoics, Epictetus, makes a wide distinction between what he regards as comparatively innocent pre-nuptial indulgences, and those which were regarded as adulterous and unlawful. While the utmost license was allowed the husband, the wife was held under close restrictions. Courtesans were the real companions of men, and the only free women in Athens. Apelles painted them; Pindar and Simonides sang their praises. Aspasia was worshipped before Pericles, and sage philosophers did not hesitate to pay homage at her shrine, and receive words of wisdom from her lips.

In imperial Rome, while the courtesan class never

attained to such distinction as in Greece, divorce was
so easy and frequent as to render the marriage ceremony almost a nullity.   There were periods when the
term 'adultery' had no significance as applied to men;
only women were punished for this crime.   Persons
five, ten, twenty times married and divorced were not
uncommon.   Though monogamy obtained, female life
was lower there than in England under the restoration,
or in France under the regency.   Alexander Seve-
rus, the most persistent of all the Roman emperors,
in vainly legislating against vice, provided his provin-
cial governors, if unmarried, with a concubine as well
as with horses and servants.

The privilege of royalty in having many mistresses,
tolerated until all the people arose and usurped royalty, was but a modified form of polygamy, and is still
secretly practised by individuals.

The question of sensualism has nothing to do with
it.   The polygamist, as a rule, is no more sensual
than the monogamist.   Your true sensualist does not
marry at all.   He holds himself free to taste pleasure
as he can find it.   The trammels of matrimony and
the responsibilities of parentage he alike avoids.   He
is the most selfish of beings; for his own gratification he is willing to sacrifice society, debase manhood,
and doom to perdition the highest inspirations and
holiest affections of the race.

Beastliness is hardly a fit word to apply to the
exercise of an animal impulse, the gratification of
animal appetite.   It too often maligns the brute creation.   Eating and sleeping are in one sense beastly;
while smoking and dram-drinking are worse than
beastly.   Beasts are natural in all things.   In many
respects they are less open to the charge of beastliness, as we commonly employ the term, than men;
they indulge less in excess; they are sometimes glut-
tonish, but they do not intoxicate themselves; if they
do not regulate intercourse by numbers, they do by
seasons.   Their passions are in subordination to the

laws of nature. Man's passions are not. Taking this charge of beastliness as it is meant, the polygamist is less beastly than the monogamist, who in the majority of cases is more beastly in his sexual intercourse than the beast, being less obedient to the laws of nature, less considerate for the health and strength of his one only wife. Millions of gentle, uncomplaining women have been killed by beastly husbands putting upon them more children than they should bear, not to mention innumerable cruelties of other kinds. In so far as any system is not in accordance with the laws of nature, nature will in due time assert her rights and put it down. It is said that the Mormon women are martyrs: so are other women; part of them because they are married, and part because they are not.

The readers must bear in mind that these are the assertions and arguments of polygamy, and must be prepared to take them for what they are worth, and answer them each according to the light of his own reason. I have already presented the current arguments against polygamy; these are the opinions and dogmas of the Mormons themselves, the doctrines they everywhere preach and print, teaching them to their children, inculcating them into the minds of young men and women, until they have fully imbibed them.

And thus they continue. How many husbandless women there are who drag out a miserable existence in the effort to sustain themselves without sin! how many fall into shame under the effort! Society lays no heavier burden on any of its members than on its poverty-stricken single women, reared in luxury, and unable to support themselves by work.

If you are so tender of woman, her position and morals, why not turn your batteries against the ten thousand of your own people of all classes, including preachers and legislators, who tamper with other men's wives, seduce and abandon innocent girls, keep mistresses. and frequent the haunts of prostitution?

That the race deteriorates under the polygamous system is not true, they say. The single wife is very often hurried to a premature grave by an inconsiderate or brutal husband, the offspring which she meanwhile bears being puny and ill-developed. And again, it is only the better class of men, the healthy and wealthy, the strongest intellectually and physically, who as a rule have a plurality of wives; and thus, by their becoming fathers to the largest number of children, the stock is improved.

The charge of immorality, as laid upon the Mormons as a community, is likewise untenable. Morality is the doctrine of right and wrong, the rule of conduct implying honesty and sobriety. In all honesty and sobriety the Mormons live up to their standard of right and wrong, they claim, more completely than any other people. They indulge in fewer vices, such as drunkenness, prostitution, gambling, and likewise fewer crimes. There is nothing necessarily immoral in the practice of polygamy; if it is not immoral for a man to take one wife, it is not for him to take twelve wives.

The Mormons are loyal to their consciences and convictions. They are essentially a moral people, moral in the highest sense of the term, more so, they claim, than the average American or European. They do not drink, cheat, or steal; adultery is scarcely known among them; they are not idle, profligate, or given to lying. They are true to themselves, true to their principles, and true to the world. Of what other society can you fairly say as much? They are honest in all things, and law-abiding when the law does not touch their rights or their religion; when it does, all who are not dastards will fight. Judge them by their fruits; if a sect is to be regarded from the standpoint of its imperfections and inconsistencies rather than from its results, what shall be said of christianity, which has butchered millions for the faith, and has further committed all the wickedness flesh is heir to, or of which Satan could conceive?

It is not right to place the polygamist on a par with the bigamist. The one, without deception, and in conformity with the proclaimed tenets of his faith, takes to wife the second, or third, or twentieth—the more the better for all, it is said—promising to her the same life-long care and protection as to the first; the other breaks his contract with his first wife, and deserts her for another woman. Neither can the polygamist be justly placed on a level with the adulterer. Mormons abhor everything of the kind. The sacred ceremony of marriage signifies far more with them than with those who mark the difference between morality and immorality by a few insignificant rites.

The Mormons lay no small stress on the fact that there is always a large number of women who have no husbands, and can get none, on account of women being always so greatly in the preponderance. They deny that there are more men than women.

Whatever may be true with regard to the numerical equality or inequality of the sexes at birth, it is certain, dating back almost from the beginning, that there have always been more women than men in the world. Particularly in primitive times, owing to war or exposure, the death rate was much greater among the males than among the females. To obviate the evil —for it was early recognized that the sexes should be mated—in some instances the female children were killed, but more frequently the excess of women was divided among the men. Where wars were frequent and continuous, everything else being equal, the monogamous nation could not long stand before a polygamous neighbor.

Coming down to later times, it is safe to say that there are a million more women than men in christendom to-day; there are here five millions of women who would like to marry but cannot, being denied one of the fundamental rights of humanity by statutory law,

A large class of men refuse to take upon themselves the cost and cares of matrimony, preferring more free and cheaper indulgence.   Of very many of these five millions thus left to themselves, unmated, unsupported, forbidden to become plural wives, Christian civilization makes prostitutes or paupers.   And this is the orthodox idea of the elevation of woman!   Make angels of light and happiness of one portion, while dooming the rest, under the hard heel of social despotism, to the depths of misery and despair.   Nay, more: while the men are thus busied working upon the affections of women, taking advantage of their loneliness and poverty, and constantly adding to the numbers of the lost by seducing the pure from the paths of respectability, their sisters, mothers, wives, and daughters are applying the scourge with all their might to these unfortunates, hoping thereby to gain further favor with the men by showing how much better are they than their most foully wronged sisters.

Such are the men, such the society, in which the foulest wrongs to women are so universally and constantly committed—wrongs which would put to blush savages, yea, and all the devils of darkness; such are the men who wage war on the plural-wife system, which would give to this class and all classes of women home and honorable alliance.

Further than all this, polygamy claims that men or governments have no natural or moral right to forbid the practice, pass laws against it, and inflict punishments.   Inherent human rights are above statutory law.   Governments have no right to pass laws against gambling, prostitution, drunkenness, or any act of the individual resulting in injury only to himself.   He who harms another may be punished, not he who harms himself; otherwise, who is to determine what is or what is not harmful?   All men and women are every day doing things harmful to themselves, but which no one thinks of checking by legislation.   By no line of logic can polygamy be rightly placed in the criminal category. In its worst aspect, it can only be called a vice. Drunkenness is not a crime: it is a vice. Statutory law cannot justly make criminal that which by the law of human rights is only a vice. Governments may repress crime, but they never can uproot vice; and the sooner legislators realize and act upon this truth, the fewer failures they will have to record. Public sentiment and moral force are the only agencies which can be brought against this class of evils with any hope of success.

The right and wrong of the matter, as usually discussed, are not the right and wrong of nature and common sense, but of divine and human enactment, variously interpreted and viewed from different standpoints. The bible forbids prostitution, but permits polygamy; the supporters of the bible and its civilization forbid polygamy, but permit prostitution.

The Mormons are held to be a most unphilosophical sect, and yet the sentiment against them is more unphilosophical than their doctrines or practices. The American congress is not a Sunday-school, neither is it within the province of government to establish and enforce a code of ethics. Congress has no more right to legislate, against their consent, for the territories than it has for the states. I do not know that all Mormons hold to this opinion, but many of them do. The idea of political nonage is only an idea; it is not a fact. Murder, theft, breach of contract, malefeasance in office, unjust monopoly, cheating, slave-holding, adulteration, bigamy, etc., are crimes to be punished by law. Drunkenness, gambling, prostitution, and the like, are vices to be uprooted by precept and example. A crime is an injury to one's neighbor; a vice is an injury to one's self. I have no right to injure my neighbor, but I have the right to do as I will with my own and myself, howsoever foolish may be the act. Congress, indeed, would have its hands full were it to undertake to pass laws to keep men from making fools of themselves. If polygamy must be

placed in one category or the other, it must be denominated a vice, and not a crime.   If one man and three
women contract to live in a connubial relationship,
neither God nor nature pronounces it a crime.   In
bigamy the marriage contract is broken; in polygamy
it is kept.   Admit that monogamy is best, that one
man for one woman tends to the highest culture, it
still does not prove that coercion in morals is better
than precept and example.   Is woman less chaste than
in the days of feudalism, now that she is less watched?
If the law has the right to l'mit a man to one wife, it
may if it chooses deny him any wife, as many orders
among the Greeks and Armenians, the heathens and
christians, have declared.   If one man is restricted
by law to one woman, the least the law can do in
common justice is to compel every man to marry one
woman.   Why does not the United States war upon
the catholic priest or the unprincipled debauchee, who
by refusing to take a wife repudiates the laws of
nature, and sets an example which if universally followed would prove the strangulation of the race?
Better punish those who denaturalize themselves
rather than those who are too natural.

This is what Utah polygamy says to civilization.[20]

[20]My references to articles, both printed and in manuscript, relating to
polygamy, are no less voluminous than those touching upon other church
matters.   I note as follows: early polygamists, *Ferris' Utah and Morm.*, 117;
Smucker's Hist. Morm., 161–2; *Young's Wife No. 19*, 150–5; *Stenhouse's Exposé*, 85–93; *Atlantic Monthly*, 1859, 576–7; denial of exist., *Stenhouse's Tell
It All*, 103–4, 499–500; Pratt, in *Millennial Star*, vi. 22; *Lee's Morm.*, 167;
Young's Wife No. 19, 329–31; favored by women, *Des. News*, 1870, Jan. 12,
19; 1871, Nov. 8, Dec. 20; *S. F. Gol. Era*, June 13, 1868; *Woodruff's Auto-
biog.*, MS., 4–6; *The Morm. at Home*, 145–7, 159; *S. L. Herald*, Feb. 1, 1879;
Burton's City of Saints, 525–34; *Ward's Husband in Utah*, 130–4, 216–22;
Tanner's Letter, MS., passim; *Smoot's Experience*, etc., MS., 4, 8–9; *Tracy's
Narr.*, MS., 30–2; *Richards' Remin.*, MS., 18–19, 36–7, 48–9; Pratt (Belinda
M.), in *Utah Pamph. Relig.*, no. 3, 27–33; *Marshall's Through Amer.*, 185–8;
Millennial Star, xvii. 36–7; *Brown's Letter*, MS., passim; arg. in favor of,
Smith's Rise, Progress, etc., 48–56; *Millennial Star*, xix. 636–40, xxxvii. 340–
1; *Beadle's Life in Utah*, 252–4; *Paddock's La Tour*, 324–5; *Ferris' Utah and
Morm.*, 115–17; Johnson, in *Utah Tracts*, no. 10; Richardson, with *Taylor's
Govt of God*, no. 19; Spencer, with *Id.*, no. 18; *Taylor vs Hollister, Sup. Ct
Decis.*, no. 2, in *Morm. Pamph.; Cannon's Rev. of Decis.*, no. 11, in *Id.; Rob-
inson's Sinners and Saints*, 82–109; *Dilke's Greater Brit.*, i. 130; *Stenhouse's
Exposé*, 218–21; *Tell It All*, 256–8; *Richards' Narr.*, MS., 79–81; *Worthing-
ton's Women*, etc., 592–3; *Busch, Gesch. Morm.*, 340–52, 407–44; *Times and

In reply to the charge of disloyalty, of maintaining an anti-American attitude toward the people of America, of endeavoring by any illegal or indirect means to undermine the institutions of the country

Seasons, vi. 798–9; *Tullidge's Women*, etc., 367–78; *Boisé City Statesman*, Sept. 30, 1879; *S. F. Alta*, Nov. 13, 1857; *Chronicle*, 1880, Dec. 12; 1882, Feb. 15, July 29; *Stock Rept*, Jan. 8, 1880; *Des. News*, 1857, May 13, July 16; 1866, Mar. 15; 1867, Apr. 17, 24; 1871, Oct. 11; *S. L. Contrib.*, ii. 213; *Tribune*, 1875, July 17; 1879, Oct. 10, 11; *S. F. Herald*, 1852, Sept. 17; 1853, Mar. 1; 1869, Aug. 28; 1880, Jan. 6, 18; sermons, Young, *Dilke's Greater Brit.*, i. 129; Young, *Jour. of Disc.*, ii. 75–90; *S. F. Bulletin*, 1856, Sept. 16; 1862, Sept. 10; 1866, Oct. 26; 1869, Mar. 3; 1874, Nov. 13; *Call*, 1867, Sept. 11; 1868, Sept. 5; *Occident*, July 10, 1873; *Sac. Union*, Jan. 12, 1856; *Elko Indpt*, Sept. 6, 1873; *Pan. Star and Her.*, Jan. 1867; *Boisé City Statesman*, July 24, 1869; *Salem (Or.) Statesman*, May 5, 1857; *S. L. Herald*, June 6, 1877; *Ward's Husband in Utah*, 104–30, 245–6, 303–7; *Des. News*, May 25, 1870; Pratt, Smith, and Cannon, *Discourses*, passim; disc., Pratt, *Des. News*, Oct. 20, 1869; Hyde, *S. F. Herald*, Nov. 23, 1854; *Des. News*, May 9, 1860; Young (John), *Id.*, Apr. 22, 1857; origin and prog., *S. F. Bulletin*, 1858, July 23; 1859, Apr. 16; 1868, July 18; 1869, Mar. 1; 1870, Nov. 12; 1871, July 6; 1872, Feb. 21, June 25; 1882, Mar. 3; *Call*, 1865, Aug. 2; 1868, Aug. 29; 1869, Feb. 28; 1874, July 15, Oct. 21; *Gol. Era*, July 3, 1869; *Plac. Times*, Feb. 2, 1850; *N. Y. Her.*, in *Watsonville Pajar.*, June 6, 1872; *Cal. Chris. Advoc.*, Oct. 15, 1874; *Cal. Farm.*, June 16, 1870; *Des. News*, 1866, Mar. 22, Apr. 19, May 17; 1879, May 7, 14; *S. L. Contrib.*, iii. 61; *Herald*, May 23, 77; *Review*, 1871, Dec. 11, 19; *Telegraph*, May 26, 1868; *Tribune*, 1874, May 16; 1883, Oct. 20; *Sac. Union*, Nov. 26, Dec. 5, 1856; *S. L. Herald*, in *Helena Gaz.*, Apr. 27, 1872; *Cole, Cal.*, 18; *Beadle's Letter*, Jan. 1, 1869; *Life in Utah*, 346–7; *The Morm. at Home*, 94–5, 102, 111–12; *Young's Wife No. 19*, 124–6, 135–59; *Olshausen, Gesch. Morm.*, 175–84; *Smucker's Hist. Morm.*, 402–24; *Bertrand's Mem. Morm.*, 173–217; *Busch, Gesch. Morm.*, 105–33, 313–17; *Marshall's Through Amer.*, 221; *Stenhouse's Englishwoman in Utah*, 38–9, 76–87, 153–4; *Slater, Morm.*, 85–6; *Burton's City of Saints*, 217, 301–2; *The Morm. Proph.*, 211–14; *Ferris' Utah and Morm.*, 239, 248–64, 309–11; *Mackay's The Morm.*, 287; *Olympia, Pion. and Dem.*, Feb. 6, 1857; women's opposition, *Stenhouse's Exposé*, 34–41, 72–84; *Tell It All*, 393–404, 420–58.

For arguments against polygamy, see *Ward's Husband in Utah*, 180, 303–5; *Beadle's Life in Utah*, 262–4, 354–80; *Nouv. Ann. Voy.*, cxliii. 183–4; *Carvallo's Inc. of Travel*, 151–4, 166–71; *Hall's Morm. Exp.*, 52–5; *Overland Monthly*, vii. 551–8; *De Rupert, Cal. and Morm.*, 153–62; *Todd's Sunset Land*, 161–212; *Dilke's Greater Brit.*, i. 144–52; *Remy's Journey*, etc., ii. 137–72; *Young's Wife No. 19*, 98–109, 591–7; *Pop. Scien. Month.*, lii. 479–90, lvi. 160–5; *Codman's Round Trip*, 173–277; *Froiseth's Women*, etc., passim; *Jonveaux, L'Amer.*, 230–49; *Waite's Morm. Proph.*, 216–60; *Book of Morm.*, 83, 132; *Doc. and Cov.*, 218, 330; *Tucker's Morm.*, 184–6, 267, 283; *Times and Seasons*, iv. 369; *Ferris' Utah and Morm.*, 309–10; *Marshall's Through Amer.*, 178–9; *Harper's Mag.*, liii. 647–51; *Stansbury's Explor. Exp.*, 4–5; *Life Among Morm.*, 123–59; *Utah Scraps*, 15–17; *Townsend's Morm. Trials*, 42–3; *Greenwood's New Life*, 131–71, 161–3; *Hubner's Ramble*, 90, 116; *Olshausen, Morm.*, 175–82; *McClure's Three Thous. Miles*, etc., 158–9; *Nordhoff's Cal.*, 43; *Burton's City of Saints*, 517–25; *Crimes of L. D. Saints*, 30–4; *Hyde's Morm.*, 284–5; *Dixon's White Conq.*, i. 200–14; *Stenhouse's Exposé*, 47–51, 146–53; *Taylder's Morm.*, 148–83; *Barnes' Atlan. to Pac.*, 56–8; *Greeley's Overland Jour.*, 238–41; *Howitt's Hist. Amer.*, ii. 356; *Richardson's Beyond Miss.*, 360–2; *S. F. Advocate*, Aug. 4, 1870; *Alta*, Mar. 26, 1877; Feb. 7, 1882; *Bulletin*, 1856, Aug. 18; 1860, Apr. 28; 1864, Jan. 18; 1865, Aug. 24; 1867, Oct. 25; 1870, Apr. 22, Sept. 2; 1871, Nov. 6; 1872, Sept. 25; 1873, Jan. 17, Dec. 17;

and eventually usurp the government, the Mormons
say that it is not true.   It is not true that Mormons
are not good citizens, law-abiding and patriotic.   Even
when hunted down and robbed and butchered by the

1875, Apr. 9; 1877, June 1, Aug. 3; 1878, Jan. 8, Nov. 1; 1879, Jan. 7, 10, 21;
1881, Aug. 22; *Call,* 1870, Mar. 27; 1871, June 30, Aug. 9, 18; 1872, Feb. 21,
Sept. 6; 1873, Feb. 11; 1874, Jan. 14; 1879, Aug. 11; *Cal. Farm.*, Apr. 17,
1863; *Chronicle,* 1869, June 26, July 28, Aug. 11, 17, 18, 22, Nov. 12, 28,
Dec. 14; 1870, Jan. 28, Feb. 27, May 8, 17; 1871, Sept. 21, Oct. 4, 8, 14, 17,
31, Nov. 5, Dec. 2; 1872, Feb. 3, 10, Apr. 20, Oct. 10; 1873, Apr. 11, 12,
July 17, 27, 31, Aug. 1, 6, 26, Mar. 4; 1880, Oct. 14, 24, Nov. 6, 14, 28; 1881,
Jan. 9; *Gol. Era,* Sept. 26, 1869; *News Letter,* Mar. 16, 1867; *Pacif. Observ.*,
Nov. 10, 1871; *Pioneer,* Sept. 15, 1873; *Post,* 1879, Sept. 11, Dec. 5; *Times,*
1869, Jan. 5, Mar. 25; *Town Talk,* Nov. 26, 1856; *Sac. Union,* May 11, 1859;
San José Herald, Apr. 20, 1877; *Jackson (Am.) Ledger,* Dec. 15, 1877;
Sta Barbara Index, Mar. 8, 1877; *San Rafael Jour.*, Oct. 16, 1879; May 20,
1880; *Red Bluff Sentinel,* Nov. 16, 1878; Jan. 18, 1879; *Ukiah Democ.*, Sept.
6, 1879; *Cres. City Cour.*, Oct. 15, 1879; *Roseburg Plaindealer,* Dec. 20, 1879;
Marin Co. Jour., Oct. 16, 1879; *Monterey Cal.*, Feb. 4, 1879; *Antioch Ledger,*
Nov. 23, 1878; *Healdsburg, Russ. Riv. Flag,* Aug. 22, 1872; *Ogden (Utah)
Freeman,* Mar. 28, 1879; *S. L. Anti-Polyg. Standard,* June 1880; *Contributor,*
iii. passim; *Des. News,* 1854, Aug. 24, Oct. 5; 1858, Aug. 11, 25; 1866, Mar.
29; 1867, July 3; 1869, Aug. 5, Sept. 22; 1870, Feb. 2; 1871, Nov. 1; 1878,
Nov. 20; 1884, Sept. 10; *Utah Rev.,* 1871, Aug. 18, Dec. 5; 1872, Jan. 12, 26;
Tribune, 1872, May 25, June 1; 1874, Mar. 21, Apr. 4, Oct. 24; 1875, Aug. 21;
1876, Jan. 5, Nov. 19; 1877, Apr. 14, Aug. 25; 1878, Oct. 1, Nov. 22, Dec.
21; Apr. 20, May 9, June 25, 29, July 17, Aug. 23, Sept. 24, Oct. 3, 10, 29,
Nov. 16; 1883, June 7; 1884, Sept. 7, 14; *Austin (Nev.) Reese Riv. Reveil.*,
Feb. 15, 1866, Mar. 5, 1872; *Carson State Regis.*, Oct. 24, 1871; *Elko Indep.*,
Aug. 11, 1879; *Eureka Sentinel,* Aug. 28, 1879; *Gold Hill News,* Dec. 6, 1878;
Tuscarora Times-Rev., Nov. 22, 1878; *Virg. City Chron.*, Dec. 12, 1877; *Win-
nemucca, Silv. State,* Apr. 26, 1880; *Prescott (Ariz.) Miner,* Aug. 15, 1879;
Helena (Mont.) Indep., Mar. 12, 1875; *Boisé (Idah.) News,* Aug. 27, 1864; *City
Statesman,* May 24, 1879; *Oxford (Idah.) Enterprise,* Oct. 9, 1879; *Portland
(Or.) Bee,* Oct. 30, 1878; *Oregonian,* July 28, 1865; *Ev. Telegram,* May 1,
1879; *Astoria, Astorian,* Jan. 19, 1878; *Eugene City Guard,* Feb. 1, 1879;
Salem Mercury, Oct. 29, 1870; *Dy Talk,* Nov. 7, 1879; socialism, *Woods (J.
O.),* in *N. Y. Church Union,* Aug. 15, 1884; suggest. for suppress. polyg.,
Colfax, in *Froiseth, Women,* 360–2; *Bliss in Id.*, 367–71; *Ward's Husband in
Utah,* 55–62; *Crimes of L. D. Saints,* i.–iii.; *Russling, Across Amer.*, 191–5;
S. F. Alta, Jan. 8, 1880; *Bulletin,* Feb. 8, 1859; Nov. 29, 1883; *Inyo Indep.*,
July 27, 1872; sermons against, *Smith (T. W.),* in *N. Y. Herald,* Feb. 20,
1882; *Higbee, A Discourse,* etc., passim; *Sac. Union,* May 12, 1855; Nov. 15,
1856; *S. L. Review,* Sept. 15, 1871; *S. F. Call,* Nov. 8, 1878; *Ogden Freeman,*
May 30, 1879; marriage, social and moral effects, *Young's Wife No. 19,* 388–9;
S. F. Alta, Oct. 14, 1857; *Pratt,* in *Des. News,* Jan. 16, 1856; sealing for eter-
nity, *Chandless, Visit to S. L.*, 161–2; *Stenhouse's Exposé,* 69–70; *Rocky Mtn
Saints,* 586–8; *Englishwoman in Utah,* 120–1; *Tell It All,* 405–19, 550, 607; *S.
F. Bulletin,* Jan. 27, 1872; Oct. 29, 1878; *Ferris' Utah and Mormons,* 233–46;
Young's Wife No. 19, 310–18; *Ward's Husband in Utah,* 12–38, 208–12; *Hyde's
Morm.*, 83–9; *Tucker's Morm.*, 270–5; *San Jose Herald-Argus,* Nov. 22, 1878;
Dall, My First Holiday, 91; first monog. marriage, *S. F. Call,* Feb. 8, 1865;
divorce, *Utah Laws,* 1878, 1–2; *Utah Scraps,* 19; *Stenhouse's Tell It All,* 390–1,
554–8; *S. F. Alta,* 1873, July 31, Aug. 9, 23; *Bulletin,* 1877, Sept. 27, Oct. 11;
Cal. Farm., May 12, 1870; *Post,* Feb. 13, 1873; *Stock Exch.*, Feb. 23, 1878; *Sta
Rosa Times,* Nov. 1, 1877; *S. L. Tribune,* 1874, Mar. 28; 1877, June 9, July 14,
Sept. 29; *Virg. City Chron.*, Sept. 27, 1877; dower, *Paddock's La Tour,* 293;

enemies to their faith, they have not retaliated.—On this point they are naturally very sore.—When deprived of those sacred rights given to them in common with all American citizens, when disfranchised, their

Utah, Gov. Mess., 1882, 14; adultery, *Dilke's Greater Brit.*, i. 127; *Kanesville (Iowa) Front. Guard.*, June 13, 1851; *Crimes of L. D. Saints*, 2–6; condition of women, *Duffus-Hardy's Through Cities*, etc., 103–4; *Leslie, California*, etc., 76–102; *Putnam's Mag.*, 144–607, passim; *Utah Scraps*, 18–19; *Young's Wife No. 19*, 224–531, passim; *Cradlebaugh, Speech of*, 4–7; *Bowles' Our New West*, 249–53; *Ward's Husband in Utah*, 23–303, passim; *The Morm. Proph.*, 218–77; *Life Among Morm.*, 183–6; *Prime's Around the World*, 31–2; *Dilke's Greater Brit.*, i. 129; *Hyde's Morm.*, 51–82, 158–67; *Hall's Morm.*, 113; *Tucker's Morm.*, 173–82, 275–6; *Appleton's Jour.*, xi. 547–8; *Morm. at Home*, 116–85; *Clark's Sights*, MS., 7–11; *Mackay's The Morm.*, 298, 303; *Smith's Mys. and Crimes*, 38–43; *Bonwick's Morm. and Silv. Mines*, 110–140; *Jackson's Bits of Trav. at Home*, 22–7; *Greenwood's New Life*, 160–1; *Gunnison's Morm.*, 75, 159–61; *Stenhouse's Englishwoman*, 202–339; *Exposé*, 96–190; *Tell It All*, passim; *S. F. Alta*, July 17, 1873; *Call*, Oct. 8, 1876; *Bulletin*, 1856, Nov. 24; 1858, Nov. 17; 1871, May 4, July 25; 1872, Sept. 30; 1872, Aug. 20; 1877, July 19; *Herald*, Nov. 24, 1856; *Mail*, Jan. 4, 1876; *Pacif. Baptist*, Sept. 17, 1874; *Post*, Nov. 18, 1872; *Eureka Sentinel*, Jan. 22, 1875; *Placer Herald*, Nov. 4, 1871; *Red Bluff Indept*, Apr. 3, 1867; *Sac. Union*, Aug. 25, 1855; Aug. 19, 1857; *Bee*, Nov. 9, 1878; *S. L. Obispo Tribune*, May 5, 1877; *Stockton Indept*, Mar. 8, 1879; *S. L. Des. News*, Oct. 5, 1850; Jan. 15, 1868; Apr. 27, 1870; *Herald*, Nov. 12, 1878; June 25, 1879; *Utah Rev.*, 1871, Aug, 21, Oct. 7, Dec. 7, 19; 1872, Jan. 17, 20, 24; *Tribune*, 1877, Apr. 28, May 19, 26, June 9; *Kanesville (Iowa) Front. Guard.*, June 13, 1849; *Belmont (Nev.) Cour.*, Jan. 12, 1878; *Portland (Or.) Oregonian*, Dec. 24, 1863; *Ev. Telegram*, May 5, 1879; *Young's wives, Stenhouse's Englishwoman*, 168–78; *Exposé*, 154–97; *Tell It All*, 510–14; *Ward's Husband in Utah*, 243–4; *Morm. at Home*, 130–1; *Young's Wife No. 19*, 598–605; *S. L. Tribune*, 1874, Apr. 25, May 23, July 18; *S. F. Call*, 1874, Aug. 27, Oct. 4; 1866, Mar. 29, Aug. 2; 1867, Feb. 1; *Deer Lodge (Mont.) New N. West*, Jan. 31, 1874. For references to polygamy in presidential messages, see *S. F. Times*, June 27, 1869; *U. S. H. Ex. Doc.*, i., 42 Cong., 2d Sess.; *S. F. Bulletin*, Aug. 1, 1872; *Post*, Feb. 15, 1873; *Elko Indept*, Dec. 18, 1875; *S. L. Herald*, Dec. 8, 1881; *N. Y. The Nation*, Dec. 15, 1881.

In his message to the congress of 1883–4, the president favors a repeal of the organic act, and recommends a federal commission as a substitute. In commenting upon this, the *Des. News* declares that the destruction of the local government will fail to destroy polygamy, neither can 'commissions, edicts, or armies, or any other earthly powers,' for the plural marriages of the Mormons are ecclesiastical, perpetual, and eternal. Says W. S. Godbie, a well-known writer on Mormonism, in a letter to the *S. L. Tribune* of Dec. 9, 1883, after first quoting George Q. Cannon as preaching in the tabernacle 'it is not vox populi vox Dei,' but 'vox Dei vox populi,' 'The essence of the whole Utah question lies couched in these telling words of the church organ and the leading apostle.'

For the messages of Utah governors touching polygamy, see *Utah Jour. Legis.*, 1862–3, app. v.–viii.; 1872, 32–4; 1876, 31–3, 34, 240; 1878, 43, 44–5, 47–9; *Utah, Gov. Mess.*, 1882, 11; *S. F. Call*, Jan. 28, 1872; Jan. 17, 1878; *Prescott Miner*, Apr. 30, 1875; *Morm. Prophet*, 79–84; Hazen's report, in *Hayes' Scraps*, R. R. iii. 212; discussions in congress, *S. F. Bulletin*, Mar. 23, 1870; *Call*, 1870, Feb. 19, Mar. 24, Aug. 16; *Chronicle*, Feb. 16, 1882; *Deer Lodge New N. West*, Apr. 29, 1870; *S. L. Dy Telegraph*, Mar. 23, 24, 1870; *Des. News*, May 16, 1860; Apr. 26, 1866; Apr. 3, 1867; Mar. 9, 1870; Apr. 6, 1870; Nov. 29, 1871; Mar. 6, 1872; *Tribune*, May 15, 1875; *Millennial Star*, xxxiv. 257–63, 268–

homes broken up, their families scattered, the husband
and father seized, fined, and imprisoned, they have not
defended themselves by violence, but have left their
cause to God and their country.

71; *Antioch Ledger*, Jan. 17, 1874; *Gooch's Speech*, Apr. 1860; *Green, Morm.*,
457–65; *Beadle's Life in Utah*, 523–6; *Utah Pamph.*, *Polit.*, no. 2; *Id.*, *Relig.*,
no. 7; *Colfax's Morm. Quest.*, passim; *Prescott Miner*, Apr. 30, 1875; also
Cong. Globe, passim; bills introd. in congress, *U. S. H. Jour.*, 34 Cong., 1st-
2d Sess., 1117–18; *U. S. Acts*, 37 Cong., 2d Sess., 208–9; *S. F. Bulletin*, Apr.
1, 1870; *S. L. Dy Telegraph*, Mar. 25, 1870; *Cong. Globe*, 1870–1, 966; *N. Y.
Herald*, Jan. 27, 1872; *Utah, Jour. Legis.*, 1872, 84; 1878, 203–4; *Nat. Quart.
Rev.*, July 1879, 91–2; *U. S. Dist Atty*, in *Froiseth's Women*, etc., 334–5, 346
–51, 355; *S. L. Herald*, Dec. 15, 1881; *Robinson's Sinners and Saints*, 74–81;
S. L. Contributor, iii. 204–13; *S. F. Alta*, 1874, Mar. 1, June 3, Dec. 6; *S. F.
Bulletin*, Dec. 14, 1881; *Call*, Jan. 9, 1879; Feb. 17, 1882; *Chronicle*, 1881, Dec.
13; 1882, Jan. 25, Feb. 17; 1884, June 18; *Post*, Feb. 27, 1873; June 3, 1874;
S. José Mercury, Dec. 1878; *Austin, Reese Riv. Reveil.*, Aug. 12, 1879; *Eureka
Sentinel*, Jan. 28, 1879; *Gold Hill News*, Jan. 3, 1878; *S. L. Tribune*, Feb. 2,
1878; *U. S. Acts and Res.*, passim.

Arthur G. Sedgwick, in the *Century Mag.* for Jan. 1882, under the heading
Leading Aspects of the Mormon Problem, refers to the various bills introduced,
and mentions the most important prosecutions and their results: decis. of U. S.
Supreme Ct, *S. L. Herald*, 1879, Jan. 8, May 23; *Tribune*, Aug. 2, 1879; *S.
F. Bulletin*, 1879, Jan. 7, 8, Feb. 24; *Eureka Sentinel*, Jan. 16, 1879; evasion
of the Edmunds law, *S. F. Bulletin*, 1883, Apr. 30, Sept. 29; grand juries,
charges to, *S. F. Bulletin*, Dec. 9, 1858; *Salem (Oregon) Argus*, Aug. 28, 1858;
Sac. Union, Apr. 20, 22, 1867; *S. F. Call*, Oct. 14, 1875; competency of polygamists as jurors, *S. L. Utah Rev.*, 1871, Sept. 19, 27; report of, *Deseret News*,
Oct. 3, 1877; rept of commission, *Utah, Rept on Gov. Mess.*, 9–13; *S. F. Bulletin*, Dec. 7, 1882; *Chronicle*, Oct. 3, 1882; cause of trouble with U. S., *Richards'
Narr.*, MS., 74; discuss. between Colfax and Morm., *Bowles' Our New West*,
238–41; *Des. News*, Feb. 9, 1870; Chaplain Newman and others, *Pratt and Newman*, etc., 3–67; *Tullidge's Life of Young*, 403–6; *Newman, Sermon*, passim;
Des. News, Aug. 17, 1870; corresp. Newman and Young, *Id.*, 1870, Aug. 10, 17;
mass-meetings, memorials, petitions, and protests, *Tullidge's Life of Young*,
389–413; *Women of Morm.*, 379–402, 528–31; *Coyner's Letters*, etc., vii.; *Stenhouse's Englishwoman*, etc., 373–4; *Tell It All*, 606–7; *U. S. H. Ex. Doc.*, 58, 45
Cong., 3d Sess., 1–6; *Utah Pamph.*, *Relig.*, no. 18; *The Cullom Bill*, in *Morm.
Pamph.*, no. 6; *S. F. Alta*, Apr. 22, 1872; *Bulletin*, Jan. 18, 1870; Nov. 9, 1878;
Jan. 21, 1879; Feb. 17, 23, 1882; *Call*, Nov. 8, 1878; *Chronicle*, Feb. 3, 27, 1882;
Petaluma Argus, Nov. 22, 1878; *Sac. Bee*, Nov. 16, 1878; *Stockton Indept*, Jan.
21, 1878; *Elko Indept*, Nov. 15, 1878; *Eureka Sentinel*, Nov. 17, 1878; *Gold Hill
News*, Nov. 8, 1878; *Reno Gazette*, Nov. 21, 1878; *S. L. Contributor*, iii. 155–6;
Des. News, 1867, Jan. 16; 1870, Apr. 6; 1872, May 22, 29; *Herald*, June 14,
1879; *Telegraph*, Apr. 1, 1870; *Tribune*, 1878, Nov. 16, 23; the Reynolds case,
Froiseth's Women, 401–12; *Utah Pamph.*, *Polit.*, no. 17, 20; *Review of Opin.*,
etc., in *Morm. Pamph.*, no. 1; *S. F. Bulletin*, Aug. 21, 1874; *Call*, Dec. 22,
1875; Dec. 10, 1878; *Elko Indept*, 1878, Oct. 30, Nov. 13; 1879, Jan. 8; *Eureka
Sentinel*, Aug. 6, 1879; *Gold Hill News*, Nov. 15, 1878; *Tuscarora Times-Rev.*,
Nov. 21, 1878; *S. L. Contributor*, ii. 154–7, 188–90; *Des. News*, 1874, Oct. 28;
1875, Apr. 7; 1878, Oct. 9; 1879, Jan. 15, 29, Dec. 3; *Herald*, July 19, 1879;
the Miles case, *S. F. Bulletin*, May 7, 1879; *Call*, Oct. 31, 1878; *Sac. Rec.-
Union*, May 5, 7, 1879; *Elko Indept*, June 5, 1879; *Virg. City Eve. Chron.*,
Oct. 30, 31, Nov. 8, 1878; *S. L. Des. News*, 1878, Nov. 6, 13; 1879, May 7,
14, June 4; *Herald*, 1878, Oct. 27, 29, Nov. 5; 1879, Apr. 29, 30, May 1–4, 6, 7.

On March 10, 1863, the president of the church was arrested, as we shall
see later, the charge being polygamy, and brought under the act of July
1, 1862; the accused was placed under bonds in the sum of $2,000 to appear

Much has been said in terms of reproach against the unity and brotherhood of the Mormons, or as it is more often denominated, their exclusiveness or clannishness, as applied to their social, business, and religious relations. It is said that they hold to one another, band against all societies and interests except their own; that they hold all the agricultural lands, coöperate in commerce and manufactures, vote all one way, and so work into one another's hands in every way; that no other people can stand up in competition with them.

at the next sitting of the U. S. ct for the 3d judic. dist. On Oct. 2, 1871, he was again arrested on an indictment of the grand jury, found under the statutes of Utah; see *Utah Laws*, 58, sec. 32, which prohibits the cohabitation of persons not married to each other. On Jan. 2, 1872, Brigham was for the third time arrested, the accusation on this occasion being complicity in the murder of one Richard Yates in Echo Cañon, in 1857. There being no government jail, and the prisoner old and feeble, he was allowed to remain in his own house under charge of the U. S. marshal. It does not appear that, beyond the annoyance caused by restraint of liberty, Brigham suffered in consequence of either of these charges. For details of the arrests, I refer to *Millennial Star*, xxv. 273-4, xxxiii. 696-700, 708-14, 728, xxxiv. 58-60, 70-1, 120-3, 209-15; *S. F. Alta*, 1871, Oct. 3, 4, 8, 13, 28, 29, Nov. 1, 22, 24, 1872, Apr. 26; *Bulletin*, 1871, Oct. 3, 9, 13, 25, 27, 30, 31, Nov. 21, 28; 1872, Jan. 3, 8, Apr. 26; *Call*, 1870, Jan. 3; 1871, Oct. 3, 5, 11, 17, Nov. 22, 28; 1872, Apr. 26; *Examiner*, 1871, Oct. 6, 9, 13, 17, 19, 25, Nov. 2, 22, 28; 1872, Jan. 3, Feb. 14; *Gol. Era*, Nov. 12, 1871; *Sac. Union*, 1871, Oct. 6, 18; *S. L. Des. News*, 1871, Oct. 11, 18, Nov. 1, 8, 22; 1872, May 1; *Tribune*, 1872, Feb. 1, Apr. 27; *Utah Review*, 1871, Oct. 12, 13, 20, 21, Nov. 25, 27, Dec. 1, 4; 1872, Jan. 16, Feb. 10; *Carson State Regis.*, Oct. 14, 1871; *Elko Indept*, Jan. 6, 1872; *Silver City (Id.) Avalanche*, Oct. 7, 1871; *Portland (Or.) Deutsche Zeit.*, Nov. 4, 1871.

On Oct. 28, 1871, Thomas Hawkins, of Salt Lake City, having been found guilty of adultery with two women, under a territorial statute approved by Gov. Young on Mar. 6, 1852, was sentenced to three years' imprisonment and to pay $500 fine; see *S. F. Alta*, Oct. 4, 1871; *Bulletin*, Nov. 3, 1871; *Sac. Union*, 1871, Oct. 24, 30, Nov. 1. On Mar. 6, 1879, Dan. H. Wells was imprisoned for two days and fined $100 for contempt of court in refusing to testify as to the garments worn during the endowment ceremonies. *Juv. Inst.*, xiv. 114-15; *McClellan, Golden State*, 587-9. In 1873, Ann Eliza Young, known as Wife No. 19, began suit against Brigham for divorce, with alimony. About two years later she was awarded $500 per month, which decision was afterward set aside, but not, Tullidge says, until Brigham had been imprisoned for contempt of court, and had paid two months' alimony and $4,000 counsel fees; see *Young's Wife No. 19*, 553-65; *Tullidge's Life of Young*, 431-3; *Helena (Mont.) Indept*, Nov. 25, 1875; *Virginia Madisonian*, June 9, 1877; *S. F. Bulletin*, 1873, July 29, 31; 1875, Feb. 26, May 11; 1876, Nov. 1, 8; *Call*, July 10, 1875; *Los Angeles Star*, May 5, 1877; *Dayton (Lyon Co.) Times*, May 2, 1877; *Eureka Sentinel*, Jan. 10, 1879; *Gold Hill News*, Apr. 28, 1877; *S. L. Des. News*, Apr. 24, 1872; Sept. 2, 1874; Mar. 3, Nov. 3, 24, 1875; Aug. 2, Nov. 8, 1876; *Tribune*, Nov. 16, 1875; July 22, 1876; Apr. 28, 1877.

Herewith I give a table, brought down to include 1882, compiled from census of 1880, police and penitentiary statistics, and report of commissioners appointed under the Edmunds bill, comparing the distribution of criminals

Grant it, they answer; is it a crime? May not people legally labor hard, practise frugality, worship God after their own fashion, and vote as they choose? Is this contrary to the free enlightenment of American institutions?

Of what are the people of the United States afraid, with their fifty millions of free, intelligent, progressive men and women, that they should deem it their duty to be seized with such a savage hate toward this handful of poor and despised religionists? In the evolution of society as an organism, the fittest is sure to remain. If this principle be true, it is perfectly safe to let the Mormons alone. Their evil practices, as well as those of their enemies, are sure in due time to be dissipated by the ever-increasing enlightenment of

between Mormon and non-Mormon. The table includes the Mormon settlements in Idaho.

	Mormon.	Non-Mormon.
Murder, manslaughter, and all assaults endangering life	41	317
Rape	1	5
Prostitution	..	95
Keeping brothels	..	27
Lewd conduct, insulting women, exposing person, nuisance, obscene and profane language	4	47
Forgery and counterfeiting	..	8
Drunkenness, etc	109	594
Violation of liquor ordinance	..	18
Gambling	..	52
Robbery and burglary	4	62
Disturbing the peace	34	111
Bigamy	..	1
Destroying property	15	26
Arson	..	2
Obtaining property under false pretences	..	25
Opium-smoking, etc	..	16
Stealing railroad rides	..	19
Vagrancy	..	147
Violating prison rules	..	6
	208	1,578

	Mormon.	Non-Mormon.
Confined in Utah penitentiary	6	22
Confined in S. L. co. jail	14	97
Confined in Oneida co. jail	1	30
Confined in Idaho penitentiary	..	6
Confined in Bear Lake co. jail	..	1

The prostitutes enumerated are those in S. L. City only; to these it will be safe to add as many more living in the outside towns and mining camps. In 1880, the population of Utah was 143,963, that of Oneida co., Idaho, was 6,964, and there were 3,235 souls in Bear Lake county. About 7,000 women were in 1885 living in polygamy in Utah. See *Richards' Crime in Utah*, MS., passim.

civilization. The best will remain, while the rest will be destroyed.

As a remedy against the Mormon evil, many plans have been put forth. "Send an army and wipe them out," say the unthinking masses. An army was sent once, but when it came to Utah there was nothing at hand to wipe out. But should an army go and find them there, it would hardly be prepared to enter upon the wholesale slaughter of 140,000 men, women, and children while in pursuit of their daily vocations. Education has been urged. This means is already employed; but while there are gentile schools, the Mormons still teach Mormonism, and the more they educate, the stronger and more widely extended becomes their faith. Senator Hoar suggested seizing the perpetual emigration fund, but this appeared too much like robbery. Make marriage a civil compact, give the wife the right of dower, and so make her less dependent on the husband, some have said. Amend the constitution, prohibiting polygamy, others have urged. But if congressional enactment fails, what can constitutional amendment do? Admit Utah as a state, and let the people split into parties, and so fight out their own issues. But they will not split into parties, is the reply. If they were like other people, this might be the result; but they are not like other people. For the people to differ from their chiefs on matters of government, or on any other matters, would throw them outside the category of Mormons. Such a thing cannot be. Their government, ecclesiastical and civil, is a government of God; their chief is God's prophet and vicegerent, and his will is God's will and cannot be questioned.

By the Edmunds act, approved March 22, 1882, congress made polygamy punishable by disfranchisement, and a fine of not more than five hundred dollars, with imprisonment for not more than three years, the children to be deemed illegitimate. There have been numerous convictions under this law, bringing serious injury upon individuals, and greatly alarming the entire brotherhood.   Many other schemes have been urged.   Cut up the territory and divide it among the adjacent states; permit the wife to testify against her husband; compel marriages to be registered; throw in more gentile population, establishing milliners' shops for the women and whiskey-shops for the men, so that the full force of civilization may be brought to bear upon them.   A proposed remedy is for congress to assume the political powers, and govern the country by a commission of nine or thirteen members appointed for that purpose, and which, the majority being always gentiles, would adopt the necessary laws for the government of the territory, instead of congress or a legislature.   Executive and judicial affairs would go on in the usual way; and as for the municipal, the commission as a legislature could make such regulations as they pleased, providing for the appointment of mayors by the governor if necessary.   In such an event there would not be held any elections of any kind.   A board of five commissioners was appointed under act of congress of March 22, 1882, but nothing extraordinary came of it.

In conclusion, it is scarcely necessary to say that an intelligent and well-balanced mind, free from the bias of religion, and regarding the well-being and refinement of the race as most greatly to be desired, cannot look upon polygamy as conducive to the highest culture.   On the other hand, it may as truthfully be said that coercion is not consistent with the highest type of morality, and that a social despotism, in the name of freedom and pure republicanism, can become the severest of tyrannies.

CHAPTER XVI.

Mormon Missionaries—Parley Pratt and his Colleagues—Missionary Labor in Canada—In Great Britain—Missionaries in Europe—And in Other Parts of the World—The Perpetual Emigration Fund— A General Epistle of the Twelve—From Liverpool to Salt Lake City for Fifty Dollars—Emigrant Ships—Report of a Liverpool Manager—The Passage to New Orleans—Overland Travel— Classes of Emigrants—George A. Smith's Companies at South Pass —The Hand-cart Emigration—Biographical.

Of the twenty-five or thirty thousand latter-day saints gathered in the valley of the Great Salt Lake at the close of the year 1852, less than one third came from Nauvoo; nearly seven thousand proselytes had arrived from various parts of Europe, and the remainder consisted principally of converts made in the United States.[1] As to the number of those who

---

[1] The pioneer band included, as we have seen, 143 members. Parley Pratt's companies, which arrived in Sept. 1847, mustered 1,540. In August 1848 the inhabitants at Salt Lake City were estimated at nearly 1,800, and there were at this date no other settlements with any considerable population. The emigrants from Winter Quarters during the autumn of this year numbered 2,393, and in 1849, 1,400. Smaller bands arrived from time to time, but with the close of the latter year the migration from Nauvoo practically came to an end. The number of Mormons from Nauvoo gathered in the valley at this date may be roughly estimated at not more than 8,000, for there were still large numbers scattered throughout the western states. According to the statistics of emigration from Great Britain and Europe, in *Linforth's Route from Liverpool*, 14–15, 2,877 proselytes left the United Kingdom between 1846 and 1849. This would make a total of 10,877. As the reader will remember, the entire population is stated at 11,380 in the *U. S. Census Rept* of 1850. Add to this number 3,714 emigrants who arrived from Great Britain and Europe between 1850 and 1852, as reported in Linforth's tables, we have a total of 15,094. The remainder were not all converts from the U. S., for there was a considerable number of persons who were not Mormons, probably 500 in all.

had been baptized into the faith in various parts of the world, and were waiting for means or opportunity to emigrate, there are no reliable data; but they probably amounted to not less than 150,000, and possibly to a larger number.

Thus within little more than twenty years the church of Jesus Christ of latter-day saints had increased from a handful to an army. And theirs was a new religion, a new revelation, not an ancient faith; they chose for their proselytizing efforts civilized rather than savage fields. In their missionary adventures no sect was ever more devoted, more self-sacrificing, or more successful. The catholic friars in their new-world excursions were not more indifferent to life, wealth, health, and comfort, not more indifferent to scorn and insult, not more filled with high courage and lofty enthusiasm, than were the Mormon elders in their old-world enterprises. In all their movements they were circumspect, moderate, studying the idiosyncrasies of the several nations in which they labored, and careful about running unnecessarily counter to their prejudices.

On reaching the scene of his labors, the missionary earned his daily bread by some trade or handicraft, not even refusing domestic service, in order to provide for his wants, and meanwhile studying the language of the people among whom he lived. Many were cast into dungeons, where they were forced to live on bread and water; many travelled on foot from district to district, with no other food than the roots which they dug near the wayside; many journeyed under the rays of a tropical sun, the water trickling from the rocks and the berries hanging from the bushes forming at times their only sustenance.[2]

The term of their labors had no certain limit, depending entirely on the will of the first presidency. For the more distant missions it was seldom less than two years or more than six. They must remain at

[2] Remy, *Jour. to G. S. L. City,* ii. 199.

their post until ordered home; and when recalled, they were often forced to earn by their own labor the means of crossing seas and deserts. Restored at length to their families, they were ready to set forth at a day's notice to new fields of labor; and for all this self-denial they sought no earthly reward, esteeming it as their greatest privilege thus to give proof of their unfailing devotion to the church.

One of the first Mormon missions of which we have any record was sent forth in October 1830, in which year, as will be remembered, it was ordered that Pratt, Cowdery, Whitmer, and Peterson should go and preach the gospel to the Lamanites. During their progress they labored for a season among the Wyandots in western Ohio. Thence they journeyed to Cincinnati, but meeting there with little success, proceeded to St Louis, preaching at several points on their way to large congregations. Starting forth westward early in the spring, they travelled for 300 miles through the snow, sometimes knee-deep, their food being corn bread and raw frozen pork. After a journey of 1,500 miles, occupying about four months, they reached Independence, having preached the gospel to thousands of the gentiles, baptizing and confirming many hundreds, and establishing several churches.[3]

[3] *The Autobiography of Parley Parker Pratt, one of the Twelve Apostles of the Church of Jesus Christ of Latter-day Saints, embracing his Life, Ministry, and Travels, with Extracts, in Prose and Verse, from his Miscellaneous Writings, Edited by his son Parley P. Pratt,* New York, 1874, is one of the most valuable works extant on the subject of Mormon missions. The author relates in simple phrase the hardships, persecutions, and adventures which he and other missionaries encountered in various parts of the United States, and though probably he makes the most of them, there can be little doubt that so far his narrative is in the main reliable. Chosen a member of the first quorum in 1835, he was on terms of intimacy with Joseph and Hyrum Smith, Brigham Young, Heber C. Kimball, and others of the church dignitaries, and as the editor remarks, 'his history, therefore, was so interwoven with that of the church, that many of the most interesting sketches of church history will be found therein.' In the autobiography, which covers a period of twenty years, from his early boyhood to his betrayal into the hands of his enemies, of which more hereafter, is an account of his life and travels, his missionary labors, and the labors of those with whom he was associated, together with some of his miscellaneous writings in prose and verse. Other works of this author are: *An Appeal to the Inhabitants of the State of New York,* a pamphlet

For twenty-five years Parley labored at intervals
as a missionary in various parts of the Union,[4] and
in 1845 was appointed president of the churches in
New England and the middle states. During his

of six pages calling for help and deliverance from the persecutions of the people of the United States, particularly from their enemies in Missouri; *Letter to Queen Victoria* is a dissertation on the fundamental principles of the faith, dated Manchester, May 22, 1841. *The Fountain of Knowledge* is a short essay on the scriptures. *Immortality and Eternal Life of the Material Body* is an attempt to prove the proposition as named. *Intelligence and Affection* comprises a few pages on these qualities in man, more particularly in regard to their immortality. The above five pamphlets, besides being published separately, were issued as one pamphlet at Nauvoo. The third son of Jared and Charity Pratt, Parley, was born at Burlington, Otsego co., N. Y., his ancestors being among the earliest settlers at Hartford, Conn., in 1839, and probably among the party that accompanied Thomas Hooker from Newtown, now Cambridge, Mass., in 1836. Of his conversion to Mormonism I have already spoken, and of the leading incidents in his life and the manner of his death mention is made elsewhere. One of those who set forth from Nauvoo in Feb. 1846, he was sent from Winter Quarters, as will be remembered, during the same year, on a mission to England. But for this circumstance his *Autobiography* would probably have included a complete and reliable account of the great Mormon exodus, and one that would have been a most valuable addition to the records of the latter-day saints. Parley was a man of many miracles and visions. In fact, with him all was miraculous; the voice of nature was the voice of God, and in one current ran revelation and human happenings. He was miraculously directed in the first instance to the book of Mormon and Joseph Smith. Myriads of false spirits were rebuked by him and driven back into the darkness. During an illness he had a dream. 'I thought I saw myself dressed in a clean and beautiful linen robe, white as snow,' on which was written the words 'holy prophet' and 'new Jerusalem.' At the elder's conference in Missouri, February 1832, he was obliged to keep his bed, as he had not yet recovered from his illness. At the close of it, he says, 'I requested the elders to lay their hands on me and pray. They did so. I was instantly healed.' Again, when detained by a severe fever, he whispered to Brother Murdock to lay hands on him unobserved while giving him water. 'I drank of it,' he says, 'bounded on my feet, dressed myself, put on my shoes and hat, and told him I was ready to start.' Still travelling with Murdock, he was again taken ill, and again miraculously cured. While engaged in fencing and ploughing six acres for wheat, he heard a voice at night saying, 'Parley, Parley!' I answered, 'Here am I.' Said the voice, 'Cease splitting rails, for the Lord hath prepared you for a greater work.' He dreamed one night, during the troubles in Missouri, of an attack by enemies at a distance, and learned afterward that the vision was true. About to set out from Kirtland on a mission to Canada in April 1836, being in debt and deeply depressed, his wife sick and childless, Heber C. Kimball and other elders, filled with the spirit of prophecy, entered his house late one night and said: 'Brother Parley, thy wife shall be healed from this hour, and shall bear a son, and his name shall be Parley, and he shall be a chosen instrument in the hands of the Lord to inherit the priesthood, and to walk in the steps of his father.' Instances might be multiplied. Scores of sick women and children in obedience to the command, 'In the name of Jesus Christ, be thou made whole,' arose and walked.

[4] In 1831 among the Delawares; in 1832 in the states of Ohio, Indiana, Illinois, and Missouri; in 1833, after the exodus from Independence, in New York; in 1835 in New England, N. Y., and Penn.; in 1837 and 1845 in N. Y. ...y, where in the latter year he commenced the publication of *The Prophet;* and in 1856 in St Louis, Phil., N. Y., and elsewhere. *Autobiog.*, passim.

career he made several thousand proselytes, and wheresoever he set foot, seldom failed of success.

"Of all the places in which the English language is spoken," writes Parley in 1838, "I find the city of New York to be the most difficult as to access to the minds or attention of the people. From July to January we preached, advertised, printed, published,[5] testified, visited, talked, prayed, and wept in vain." Elijah Fordham was with him, and for several weeks only six proselytes were made, of whom two or three sometimes met in a small upper room in an obscure street.

Sorely discouraged, the two elders invited their converts to a last prayer-meeting, intending to set forth for New Orleans. Each prayed in turn, when suddenly the room was filled with the holy spirit, and all began to prophesy and speak in tongues. "They should tarry in the city and go not thence as yet; for the Lord had many people in that city, and he had now come by the power of his holy spirit to gather them into his fold."

Among the converts was a chairmaker, named David Rogers, who now fitted up a large chamber at his own expense and invited the elders to preach. The room was crowded at the first meeting, and soon afterward the elders were ministering at fifteen different places throughout the city, all of which were crowded, sometimes preaching twice a day almost every day in the week, besides visiting from house to house.[6]

Mention has already been made of the labors of Brigham Young and other missionaries in various

[5] ' My first production in that city was a book of upwards of two hundred pages, entitled the *Voice of Warning*. The first edition of this work consisted of four thousand copies; it has since been published and republished in America and Europe till some forty or fifty thousand copies have not been sufficient to supply the demand.' *Id.*, 184.

[6] Branches of the church were formed during 1838 at Sing Sing and in New Jersey, also at Brooklyn and elsewhere on Long Island. *Id.*, 188. In the *S. L. Herald*, June 16, 1877, is a sketch of the Mormon mission in New York at that date.

parts of the United States. To relate them in detail
for each succeeding year would more than occupy
the space alotted to this volume, and for further particulars I refer the reader to the note subjoined.[7]   It

[7] In Jan. 1838, B. Winchester left Ohio on a missionary tour, during which
he preached in Md, Penn., and N. J. At this time Orson Pratt was in New
York city, and L. Barnes and H. Sayers in the states of N. Y. and Penn.
Times and Seasons, i. 9-11. About April 1, 1839, Jno. D. Lee and Levi Stew-
art started on foot from Vandalia, Ill., and, preaching as they went, passed
through several towns in O., returning to their starting-point in October.
During this journey they depended entirely on donations for subsistence. *Lee's
Mormonism*, 97-108. During 1839, Lorenzo Barnes, H. Sayers, E. D. Woolly,
Elisha H. Davis, J. Huston, Henry Dean, Benjamin Winchester, Jas Blaks-
lee, and Saml James preached in O., Va, Del., Penn., N. J., and N. Y.; A.
Petty, G. H. Brandon, J. D. Hunter, Benjamin Clapp, Jeremiah Mackley,
Jno. E. Page, and Daniel and Norman B. Shearer, in Mo., Tenn., and Ill.;
Almon Babbitt, Jacob K. Chapman, and Orson Hyde, in Ind.; Stephen Post,
Julian Moses, and M. Sirrine, in Mich.; Nathan Holmes, in Mass.; and Ly-
sander M. Davis, in S. C. *Times and Seasons*, i. 25-9, 39-40, 59-63, 71-4.
Francis G. Bishop writes, under date Feb. 4, 1840, that since 1832, when he
joined the church, he has preached in fourteen states, spending two years in
Va and N. C. Jos. Smith, jr, made a visit of inspection through the middle
states at this time and presided at several assemblies. Edward M. Webb
and others preached in Ill. and Ia; Duncan McArthur and others, in Me and
N. H.; Orson Hyde, in Philadelphia and N. J.; and Geo. J. Adams, in Philadelphia, New York, and Brooklyn. *Id.*, i. 77-80, 87-9, 108-10, 116-23, ii.
204-5, 220-1; *Millennial Star*, i. 274-6. In 1840-1, Elder Snyder and others
established a church, baptizing about 100, in Laporte, Ind.; *Richards' Rem.*,
MS., 8-9; and in northern Ind., Ohio, Penn., and N. Y. some converts were
made. *Id.*, *Narr.*, MS., 11-12, 16-18, 20-1. At a conference held at Phil.
Oct. 17, 1840, reports were received from various churches in N. Y., N. J.,
and Penn., showing a membership of 896 (details given). In 1840-1, Benj.
C. Elsworth, Chas Thompson, and Isaac C. Haight were preaching in N. Y.;
Erastus Snow, in Penn. and R. I.; Jos. Ball, Phineas Richards, and Saml
Bent, in Mass. and Conn.; Zadock Parker and P. Brown, in Vt; Norwell M.
Head, Danl Tyler, and others, in Tenn. and Miss.; E. Luddington and others,
in N. O.; A. J. Lumereaux, in Ohio; and J. M. Adams, Amasa Lyman, and
W. O. Clark, in Ill. *Times and Seasons*, ii. 215-17, 219-21, 253-4, 339-40,
348-50, 384-6, 399-402, 415-16, 451-2, 468, 515-16. In 1841-3, Erastus
Snow and others were in Mass.; Joshua Grant, in Va and N. C.; Jacob Gates,
in Ind.; Jas Blakeslee, in N. Y.; and A. Young and Saml B. Frost, in Tenn.
Id., iii. 602-6, 620, 696-7, 792-8, 820-1. In 1842-3, A. L. Lamareaux was
preaching in Ind.; E. M. Webb, M. Serrine, and several others, in Mich.;
Edwin D. Woolley and L. A. Shirtliff, in Mass.; Wesley Wandell, in Conn.;
F. M. Edwards, in Tenn.; and R. H. Kinnamon and O. White, in Ky. *Id.*,
iv. 89, 166-7, 194-5, 226-7, 280-1, 300, 302, 354, v. 508. In 1843-4, G. J.
Adams was preaching in Penn.; Benj. Brown and Jesse W. Crosby, in N. Y.;
Alfred Hall and S. Braman, in Ind.; Benj. L. Clapp, W. Huitt, S. Gully,
and H. W. Church, in Miss.; Danl Botsford, Jos. Coon, Levi Stewart, and
W. O. Clark, in Ill.; W. O. Clark, in Iowa; R. H. Kinnamon, in Va and N.
C.; and P. Haws and John Brown, in Alabama. *Id.*, v. 387-8, 444, 460-1,
468-9, 484-5, 507-8, 520-2, 702-3. In the *Frontier Guardian*, July 25 and
Oct. 17, 1851, also in the *Deseret News*, Dec. 13, 1851, are further reports
from missionaries in various parts of the U. S. Between the date of Joseph
Smith's assassination and the settlement of the saints in the valley of the
Great Salt Lake, missionary work was partially suspended. For further
missionary work in New York, see *S. L. Herald*, June 16, 1877; *S. F. Alta*,

remains only to add that, throughout the Union, the Mormons were less successful in making proselytes than in some other parts of the world, especially in Great Britain and northern Europe.

In the year 1833, Orson Pratt was sent as a missionary to southern Canada, and [8] about the same date Joseph Smith and Sidney Rigdon organized a church near Hamilton. In 1836, Parley Pratt, brother to Orson, being then one of the twelve, was sent to Upper Canada[9] to preach and establish a church; and from this ministry it was foretold that the gospel should spread into England. With him went Brother Nickerson, who parted company at Hamilton. Left alone, knowing no one, having no money, what should he do? His destination was Toronto; fare by steamer two dollars; it would be a tedious journey on foot. He entered his closet and prayed to the Lord, then stepped out upon the street and began chatting with the people. Presently he was accosted by a stranger who asked his name, and whither he was going, and if he did not want money. Parley answered, explaining his position, whereupon the stranger gave him ten dollars, and a letter of introduction to John Taylor, a merchant of Toronto, where he arrived the same day. He was kindly received by Mr and Mrs

Nov. 6, 1869; in Boston, *S. F. Bulletin*, Aug. 16, 1870; in Washington, *Deseret News*, Apr. 30, 1853; in Pa, *S. F. Bulletin*, July 22, 1881; in Va, *Juvenile Instructor*, xv. 128-9; in N. C., *Id.*, xv. 21-2; in Georgia, *S. F. Bulletin*, Aug. 12, 1881; in Tex., *Millennial Star*, xxxviii. 588-9; in the southern states generally, *Juvenile Instructor*, xv. 63; in Iowa, *Millennial Star*, xxxviii. 381; *Deseret News*, Aug. 8, 1877; in Ark., *Millennial Star*, xxxviii. 380-1; in Col., *S. F. Bull.*, Nov. 11, 1864; in Ar., *S. F. Bulletin*, Apr. 12, 1873; *S. F. Call*, July 14, 1873; *Prescott Miner*, Aug. 9, 1873; *Millennial Star*, xxxviii. 170-1; in Cal., *S. F. Herald*, June 26, 1854, Feb. 9, June 4, 1855; in Or., *S. F. Alta*, Jan. 21, 1858; *Sac. Union*, Aug. 12, 1857. In 1882 there were about 110 Mormon missionaries in the United States. *Contributor*, iii. 128.

[8] Preaching in Potten, Canada, north of Vermont, the first sermon, so far as is known, that was ever delivered in the British dominions. *Utah Pioneers, 33d Ann.*, 25.

[9] After retiring to rest on a certain evening in April 1835 he was aroused by Heber C. Kimball, who, being filled with the spirit of prophecy, said: 'Thou shalt go to Upper Canada, even to the city of Toronto, the capital, and there thou shalt find a people prepared for the fulness of the gospel, and they shall receive thee.' *Pratt's Autobiog.*, 141-2.

Taylor, but they could give him no direct encouragement; he took tea with them, and then sought lodgings at a public house. In the morning he visited the clergymen of the place, none of whom would open to him their dwellings or places of worship. Then he applied to the sheriff for the use of the court-house, then to the authorities for a public room in the market-place, and with no better result. The prospect was dark, considering the prophecies concerning this mission. Again and again he tried with no better success. His resources were exhausted; he could do nothing more; he must depart.

He retired to a grove just outside the town and prayed. His heart was very heavy. He returned to the house of John Taylor, where he had left his handful of baggage, and bade his friends farewell. Mr Taylor was touched with pity, and held him for a moment in conversation,.during which a Mrs Walton entered and began talking in an adjoining room with Mrs Taylor, who spoke of Parley's failure, saying: "He may be a man of God, and I am sorry to have him' depart." The visitor was at once deeply interested. "Indeed," she said, "I feel that it is so, and that I was directed hither by the spirit of the Lord. I am a widow; but I have a spare room and bed, and food in plenty. My son will come and guide him to my house, which shall be his home; and there are two large rooms to preach in." Parley gladly accepted the offer. His labors were thenceforth attended with success. Mrs Walton soon received baptism; a friend of hers, a poor widow, was miraculously cured of blindness, and many in consequence believed.

There was a Mr Patrick, a wealthy and influential man, whose custom it was every sabbath to hold in his house a meeting, wherein were discussed questions concerning salvation, without regard to doctrine or dogma. Both John Taylor and Mrs Walton were in the habit of attending these meetings, the former frequently taking a part in the discussions. On one occasion Parley attended, and was invited to speak, but declined, preferring to give a special call, which he did. At the appointed hour the rooms were filled; at the close of a powerful discourse another meeting was called for, and then another. Taylor became more and more interested; he once accompanied Parley into the country where he had promised to preach; at length, with Mrs Taylor, he was baptized. Thus was a shining light brought into the church, a branch of which was now established in Toronto, and was the forerunner of the mission work in Great Britain.[10]

During the year 1837, Heber C. Kimball and Orson Hyde, of the quorum of the twelve, accompanied by Willard Richards, were placed at the head of a mission to England, the members of which were drawn from elders of the church in Canada, and several of whom were English, or had friends in England. The elders chosen were Joseph Fielding, Isaac Russell, John Goodson, and John Snider.[11] Taking ship for Liverpool, where they arrived on the 20th of July,[12] apostles Kimball, Hyde, and Willard Richards landed without the means of paying for their first night's lodging; but the remainder of the party furnishing the funds, all secured apartments in the same dwelling, and two days later took coach for Preston. Here at Vauxhall Chapel, then in charge of the Rev. James Fielding, brother to Elder Fielding, the doctrines of Mormonism were first proclaimed in Great Britain, Kimball giving a brief account of the origin of the church, and of the teachings of the book of Mormon.

[10] After ministering at Toronto and its neighborhood for about two months, the apostle announced that he must return to Kirtland, and, as he relates, on the eve of his departure several hundred dollars were placed in his hands, though he had asked no one for money, and none knew that the main reason for returning was to arrange for the payment of his debts. Parley again visited Toronto in April 1836, and labored there until spring of the following year. *Id.*, 166. In 1841, elders Morrison and Bates were preaching near Kingston. *Times and Seasons*, ii. 415. About two years later, Ben. Brown and Jesse W. Crosby preached in Montreal and Quebec. *Id.*, vi. 766-7.

[11] *Utah Pioneers, 33d Ann.*, 26; *Pratt's Autobiog.*, 183; *Times and Seasons*, iii. 879.

[12] On board the *Garrick.*

The work prospered, and within a few months about
1,500 converts were made,[13] not only at Preston, but
also at Manchester, Leeds, Birmingham, and as we
shall see later, in Glasgow and in the south of Wales.
In April 1840, when was held, at Preston, the first
council of the twelve in a foreign land, Brigham
Young, who arrived in England during this year,[14] being elected their president, the church claimed in the
British Islands nearly 2,000 proselytes,[15] in April 1841
more than 6,000,[16] and at the close of 1852 more than
32,000. According to a statistical report of the church
throughout the United Kingdom for the half-year
ending December 31, 1852, there were at that date 742
branches, 17 of the quorum of seventies, 10 high-priests,
1,913 priests, 2,752 elders, 1,446 teachers, and 856

[13] Smith, Rise, Progress, and Travels, 30-1. In Tullidge's Women, 246, it
is stated that 2,000 were baptized within eight months. This is probably exaggerated. The first converts, nine in number, were baptized in the Ribble,
July 30, 1837. Names given in Id., 241.

[14] On board the Patrick Henry, together with Parley and Orson Pratt, Geo.
A. Smith, Heber C. Kimball, and Reuben Hedlock. Brigham left his home
in Montrose on Sept. 14, 1839. Being in feeble health, he was carried to the
house of Heber C. Kimball, where he remained until the 18th, when they set
forth together. Mrs Mary Ann Young was left with an infant only ten days
old, and the youngest child of Mrs Kimball, who was then sick with chills
and fever, was only three weeks old. Heber, who was also suffering from
ague, relates that when he took leave of his family, it seemed as if his very
heart would melt within him. 'This is pretty tough, is it not?' he remarked
to Brigham. 'Let us rise up and give them a cheer.' They arose, and swinging their hats, cried, 'Hurrah, hurrah, hurrah for Israel!' Neither were in
condition to travel, and both were almost penniless. Arriving at Kirtland,
which place they visited on their way, Brigham had one New York shilling
left, and Heber claims that meanwhile the necessary funds had been supplied by some heavenly messenger. The vessel sailed on the 19th of March,
and reached Liverpool on the 6th of April, the tenth anniversary of the organization of the church. Brigham left the ship in company with Heber and
Parley, and when he landed shouted with a loud voice, 'Hosanna!' On the
next day they went to Preston by rail. Hist. B. Young, MS.; Young's Jour., in
Millennial Star, xxv. 711-12; Times and Seasons, ii. 223; Whitney's Woman's
Exper., MS. A parting hymn, composed by Parley a few days before the
vessel sailed, will be found in Pratt's Autobiog., 332, and Times and Seasons,
i. 111. On Dec. 8, 1839, elders Hiram Clark, Alex. Wright, and Sam. Mulliner
had arrived at Preston, and on Jan. 13, 1840, elders Wilford Woodruff, John
Taylor, and Theodore Turley. Id., iii. 884.

[15] In the Millennial Star, i. 20, is a list of most of the towns in which
branches were established, with the number of members in each.

[16] In Id., i. 302, the number is given at 5,814, besides 800 who had emigrated to America during that season. These figures include the Welsh, Irish,
Scotch, and Manx converts.

deacons.[17] It is worthy of note that the number of members at this date was about the same as is stated in the report dated June 1, 1851,[18] no interval of this length having previously occurred during which the number of proselytes was not largely increased. Meanwhile, however, the number of branches had increased by 100, and during the last half of the year 1852 more than 2,000 members had emigrated.

Manchester conference, with its starved factory operatives, heads the list with 3,282 members, and those who have visited any of the great manufacturing towns of Lancashire, where in winter men, women, and children may be seen hastening from their ill-drained hovels through the snow and slush of the dark streets to the cotton-mill, returning exhausted with toil to their supper of bread and tea, will not wonder that these hapless human beings were glad to exchange their hard lot for the plenty of the promised land. In London the number of proselytes was 2,464, in Birmingham 1,883, in Norwich 1,061, and in Liverpool 1,041. In no other town or city does the number amount to one thousand, though most of the shires of England are represented in the list of branches.

At this period the British Islands were justly termed the stronghold of Mormonism; and that Mormon missionaries made in that country a deep and abiding impression is shown by the fact that their 32,000 proselytes, nearly all of them being mechanics, laborers, or factory operatives, expended of their scant earnings nearly one dollar *per capita* a year for the purchase of Mormon books, periodicals, and insignia.[19]

[17] During that term 3,400 persons had been baptized, 85 had emigrated, and 234 had died. *Id.*, xv. 78.

[18] A copy of which will be found in *Id.*, xiii. 207, and in condensed form in *Mackay, The Mormons*, 246–7.

[19] In the *Millennial Star*, xiii. 208, it is stated that, between May 30 and June 16, 1851, £255–8–1 was received, or at the rate of about 80 cents *per capita* for that period. In *Ibid.* we have a list of £1,965–2–1¾ due from the various conferences for books, badges, etc.

The first number of the *Millennial Star* was published in May 1840, some few weeks after the arrival of Brigham Young and his party, Parley P.

In later years a strong reaction set in, the members
of the church at the close of 1878 mustering only
2,904, the number of branches having decreased to

Pratt being the first editor. Issued originally as a monthly, and afterward
as a bi-monthly and then as a weekly periodical, the circulation at one time
reached 22,000 copies. *Richards' Bibliog. of Utah*, MS., 8–9. But for this
publication and the *Frontier Guardian*, it would be impossible to fill the gap
which occurs in the records of the Mormon people between Feb. 15, 1846,
the date of the last issue of the *Times and Seasons*, and June 15, 1850, when
appeared the first number of the *Deseret News*. For conferences at which
reports were received as to the condition of the church branches at Manchester and elsewhere in 1840–1, see *Millennial Star*, i. 67–71, 84–9, 165–8, 301–5;
Times and Seasons, ii. 404, 463; *Pratt's Autobiog.*, 341–2, 344, 348–50; in
1842, *Millennial Star*, iii. 28–32; *Times and Seasons*, iv. 76–80; in 1843,
Millennial Star, iv. 32–6, 81–5; in 1845, *Id.*, v. 166–7; in 1846–7, *Id.*, vii.
passim. For reports of church progress, giving minor details of no particular
value between 1840 and 1846, see *Times and Seasons*, ii. 529, 543, 557; iii.
596–9, 618, 636–7, 682–3, 789–90, 843, 924–5; *Millennial Star*, iv. 129–30,
145–8, 161–2, 174–5, 203–4; v. 25–6, 195; vi. 6–7, 13–14, 23–4, 28–9, 39–40,
73–5. For condensed reports showing progress during latter half of 1840
and spring of 1841, see *Kidder's Mormonism*, 191–200. For missionary work
in different towns in 1840–1, see *Millennial Star*, i. 71–2, 90–3, 184–5, 212–15,
238–40, 255–6, 283–6, 305–9. With the conference of April 6, 1841, the mission of Brigham Young and his associates ended in Eng., and soon afterward
they returned home, first sending an epistle to the church in Great Britain,
and leaving Parley in charge. For text of epistle, see *Millennial Star*, i. 309–
12. Brigham, Heber, O. Pratt, Woodruff, Taylor, Smith, and Richards left
for New York on the ship *Rochester*, on Apr. 20, 1841. Young arrived in
Nauvoo July 1st. *Tullidge's Life of Young*, 99–100. Parley remained at the
head of affairs until Oct. 29, 1842, when he sailed for the U. S. on the
Emerald, arriving in New Orleans early in Jan. 1843, leaving Thomas Ward
to succeed him, with Lorenzo Snow and Hiram Clark as assistants. During
Parley's administration, several parties of emigrants were sent to the U. S.
Pratt's Autobiog., 359, 361. The *Times and Seasons* of Feb. 1, 1843, announces Pratt's arrival at Nauvoo. In June 1843, Elder Reuben Hadlock
was appointed president of the English mission, *Id.*, iv. 232; and again in
1846, *Millennial Star*, vii. 42, where the name is spelled Hedlock. Ward
was associated with Hedlock in the presidency. *Id.*, v. 140, 142. In
1846–7 Orson Hyde was president of the European mission. *Richards' Narr.*,
MS., 27. For 1879, 32 missionaries were appointed for the United States.
A list is given in *Millennial Star*, xli. 692. Further mention of missionary
work in England will be found in the pages of the *Millennial Star*, *Frontier
Guardian*, Apr. 4, July 25, Sept. 19, 1849, July 24, Dec. 11, 1850, July 13,
Aug. 8, 1851; *Lyon's Harp of Zion*, 64–6; *Deseret News*, Nov. 29, Dec. 27,
1851, July 24, 1852, Feb. 5. 1853, Oct. 5, 1854, July 25, 1855, Feb. 26, 1862,
Sept. 9, 1863, March 9, Dec. 7, 1864, March 22, 1865, June 7, 1865, May 8,
Nov. 20, 1867, March 15, 1871, July 15, 1874, June 30, 1875, Sept. 11, 1878;
Utah Scraps, 5; *S. F. Bulletin*, June 11, Nov. 24, 1883; *Sac. Union*, July 2,
1855, May 14, 1869. In the autumn of 1846 John Taylor, Parley Pratt, and
Orson Hyde were ordered to proceed to England, the saints being then encamped at Council Bluffs. Procuring a flat-bottomed boat, they voyaged
down the Missouri River to Fort Leavenworth, where they met with some
of the battalion men, and thence took the steamer for St Louis. From that
city they reached England by way of New York, Parley, however, returning
to Council Bluffs and Winter Quarters with money contributed by the saints in
the eastern states for the assistance of their families and brethren, joining his
comrades later. The missionaries visited the various churches in England,

98, of priests to 182, of elders to 521, of teachers to 105; and of deacons to 128.[20]

In Wales and Scotland the Mormons were at first no less successful, the number of proselytes at the close of 1852 being in the former country nearly 5,000,[21] and in the latter more than 3,000;[22] but in these countries also a reaction occurred, the number of Welsh members at the close of 1878 having fallen to 325 and of Scotch to 351.[23] In Ireland, as in other catholic countries, their missionaries were regarded with little favor, the converts mustering in 1852 only 245, though between 1846 and 1852 Ireland was passing through the years of her sorest tribulation, and those of her people who accepted Mormonism

Scotland, and Wales, and were well received.   Taylor relates that the converts were in the habit of getting up tea-parties, at which he was often requested to sing, one of the songs composed by himself being 'The Upper California, O that's the land for me!' He also states that a marked feeling among the English was the desire to emigrate. *Reminiscences*, MS., 18–19.

[20] *Millennial Star*, xli. 110.

[21] *Millennial Star*, xv. 78. On July 6, 1840, Henry Royle and Frederick Cook were appointed to Flintshire, and on Oct. 30th a church of 32 members was established there.   Jas Burnham reported from Wrexham on Dec. 23, 1840, that there were about 100 saints in that neighborhood.   On Feb. 10, 1841, the 2 churches had an aggregate membership of 150. *Utah Pioneers, 33d Ann.*, 26.   In 1844 Elder Henshaw was in South Wales and meeting with good success. *Millennial Star*, iv. 203.   In 1845, Stratton and Henshaw were in Wales, the latter preaching in the south the language of the country. Capt. Dan. Jones was preaching in Wrexham. *Times and Seasons*, vi. 988–9. Jones writes from Rhyd-y-bont, Feb. 7, 1846, that he has more places to preach in than he can possibly attend to. *Millennial Star*, vii. 63.   For several years a periodical entitled *The Udgorn Seion* was published at Merthyr Tydvil, and continued until emigration greatly reduced the numbers at the Welsh mission. *Richards' Bibliog. of Utah*, MS., 9.

[22] Alexander Wright and Samuel Mulliner were sent to Scotland in Dec. 1839, shortly after their arrival in England.   At the beginning of March, they had baptized a few converts at Paisley. *Times and Seasons*, i. 110; *O. Pratt*, in *Utah Pioneers, 33d Ann.*, 26.   At a general conference on Apr. 17, 1840, it was reported the Scotland branch had 3 elders and 21 members. *Times and Seasons*, i. 120.   Elder H. Clark left Liverpool for Scotland July 27, 1840. *Id.*, ii. 229.   About May 1, 1840, Elder Orson Pratt was sent to Edinburgh. *Id.*, ii. 91.   At a conference at Glasgow April 6, 1841, the membership was 368.   In 1842 Jno. McAuley was stationed there.   In 1843, Elder Jno. Cairns was appointed to Scotland, and at the Glasgow conference of Nov. 5, 1843, the membership had increased to 768. *Id.*, ii. 191, iv. 129–30; *Times and Seasons*, iv. 232.   In 1845 Peter McCue was president of the Glasgow conference and Jno. Banks of the one at Edinburgh. *Millennial Star*, v. 182–3.   In 1846 Franklin D. Richards was appointed to the presidency of the church in Scotland, assisted by his brother Samuel. *Richards' Narr.*, MS., 27.

[23] *Millennial Star*, xli. 110.

had an opportunity, as we shall see later, of improving their condition.[24]

In British India,[25] Ceylon, British Guiana, at the cape of Good Hope, in the West Indies,[26] in Australia, Tasmania, New Zealand,[27] Malta, and Gibraltar, there were also branches of the church, though in none of the British colonies were the missionaries received so cordially as in the mother country.

[24] On July 27, 1840, Apostle John Taylor, Elder McGaffe, and Priest Black sailed from Liverpool for Ireland, staying about a week at Newry and Lisburn. They were followed in Sept. by Elder Theodore Curtis. *Utah Pioneers, 33d Ann.*, 26. On May 29, 1843, Elder Jas Sloan was appointed to Ireland. *Times and Seasons*, iv. 232. Mackay, *The Mormons*, 247, says that Mormonism was not preached in Dublin till 1850, but this statement is doubtful. In Sept. 1840 Taylor visited the Isle of Man, accompanied by Hiram Clark and one or two brethren from Liverpool. *Utah Pioneers, 33d Ann.*, 26. Taylor remained but a short time, being replaced by J. Blakeslee in Nov. A church was organized at Douglas. Clark returned to Liverpool on Jan. 8, 1841, and Blakeslee on Feb. 16th, leaving a membership of 70. *Times and Seasons*, ii. 484; *Millennial Star*, iv. 147.

[25] Wm Donaldson sailed from England for Calcutta early in August 1840. *Times and Seasons*, ii. 229. Wm Willes landed in Calcutta Dec. 25, 1851, and during his sojourn baptized some 300 natives and established a church of about 40 Europeans. *Utah Pioneers, 33d Ann.* 26. Jos. Richards was also in Calcutta in 1851. *Id.*, 28. Elders Nathaniel V. Jones, Robert Skelton, Samuel A. Woolley, Wm Fotheringham, Richard Ballantyne, Truman Leonard, Amos Milton Musser, Robert Owen, and Wm F. Carter arrived in Calcutta and held a conference in April 1853. *Smith's Rise, Progress, and Travels*, 34–5. For further items, see *Deseret News*, May 14, 1853, Jan. 5, Oct. 19, 1854, March 8, 1855; *Sac. Union*, May 17, 1856.

[26] Elders Aaron F. Farr, Darwin Richardson, Jesse Turpin, and A. B. Lambson landed at Jamaica Jan. 10, 1853. They called on the American consul, who told them that the law extended toleration to all religious sects, and soon afterward held a meeting; but a mob gathered round the hall where service was being held and threatened to tear it down, as they had heard that the elders were polygamists. Two of the missionaries were shot at while making their escape from the island. *Smith's Rise, Progress, and Travels*, 36.

[27] Wm Barrett was sent to Australia from Burslem, England, by Geo. A. Smith in July 1840. *Smith's Rise, Progress, and Travels*, 34. In 1845 Andrew Anderson had organized a church of 9 members at Montipeer township. *Times and Seasons*, vi. 989. In March 1852 Jno. Murdock and Chas W. Wandell had organized a church with a membership of 36 at Sydney. Early in 1853 Augustus Farnham, Wm Hyde, Burr Frost, Josiah W. Fleming, and others landed at Sydney, and afterward extended their labors to Van Dieman's Land and New Zealand. *Utah Pioneers, 33d Ann.*, 26. *Smith's Rise, Progress, and Travels*, 34. In August of this year Farnham published the first number of *Zion's Watchman* at Sydney. It was continued until Apr. 1855. *Richards' Bibliog. of Utah*, MS., 13. A brief account of the work in the above countries is given in *Utah Pion.*, 26, and *Smith's Rise, Progress, and Travels*, 34–6. In 1852 the Australian missions were prosperous. *Deseret News*, May 28, 1853. In later years they were less successful. On the 6th of April, 1876, Elder Croxall writes from Sidney that the brethren are working faithfully in Australia, but meet with little encouragement. *Millennial Star*, xxxviii. 381. In this year there were four Mormon missionaries at Christ Church, and one at Wellington, N. Z. There were also two or more at Hobart Town, Tasmania. *Id.*, 379, 509.

In France and Germany few proselytes were made. In the former country there were, in June 1850, branches of the church at Paris, Boulogne, Calais, and Havre; but the total number of members was probably little more than a hundred.[28] In Germany the Mormons were even less successful. In 1853 Elder Carn, who, two years before, had been imprisoned and afterward expelled from the confederation for preaching Mormonism, applied at Berlin for permission to hold meetings. The answer was that he must leave the city immediately under pain of transportation.[29] In Holland,[30] Denmark,[31] Scandinavia,[32]

[28] An elder, name not given, was in France in 1845 and baptized two. *Times and Seasons*, vi. 989. John Pack and Curtis E. Bolton left Salt Lake City in company with Apostle Jno. Taylor, on Oct. 19, 1849, and arrived in Paris in June 1850, having been joined in England by Fred Piercy, Arthur Stayner, and Wm Howell, the last of whom had been in France before. For success, etc., see *Utah Pioneers, 33d Ann.*, 27; *Smith's Rise, Progress, and Travels*, 32. Further information concerning the branches in France will be found in *Frontier Guardian*, Feb. 6, Aug. 21, 1850, June 13, Sept. 19, 1851; *Deseret News*, Jan. 10, Oct. 2, 1852. In 1861 a petition was presented to Napoleon III., asking for the privilege of preaching the gospel. *Millennial Star*, xxiii. 220–1.

[29] For affairs in Germany and Prussia see *Deseret News*, Apr. 17, 1852, May 28, 1853, Aug. 14, 1867, Oct. 11, 1876; Spencer Orson, in *Taylor's Govt of God's Tracts*, no. 20; Bertrand, *Mem. Morm.*, 285–6. At the close of 1878 the German mission claimed 152 members of the church. *Millennial Star*, xli. 111.

[30] After several months' labor, a church was organized at Amsterdam, numbering 14 members. *Utah Pioneers, 33d Ann.*, 19. In 1866 the Dutch mission was fairly prosperous. See letter of Elder Joseph Weiler, in *Deseret News*, Oct. 24, 1866. In 1877 there was 72 members of the church at Amsterdam. *Millennial Star*, xl. 91.

[31] Apostle Erastus Snow and three elders, appointed by Salt Lake conference of Oct. 1849, arrived at Copenhagen June 1, 1850. For results of early Danish mission, see *Utah Pioneers, 33d Ann.*, 27; *Smith's Rise, Progress, and Travels*, 32–3; *Deseret News*, May 1, Dec. 11, 1852; *Frontier Guardian*, Sept. 18, Oct. 16, 1850, March 7, May 16, July 11, 1851, Jan. 10, Nov. 6, 1852. In 1851 the book of Mormon was translated into Danish, and later *The Doctrine and Covenants*. *Richards' Bibliog. of Utah*, MS., 11. There were in 1851, 261 converts in Denmark, of whom 150 were at Copenhagen. *Frontier Guardian*, Aug. 22, 1851. About 600 are claimed in *Utah Pioneers, 33d Ann.*, 27. In July 1877 the first two chapters of *Joseph Smith the Prophet* were published in Danish, bringing his history up to the time of the first publication of the book of Mormon.

[32] By order of Apostle Snow, who had charge of the Scandinavian mission, Elder John Forsgren proceeded to northern Sweden in 1850, where, at Geffle, he baptized 20 persons, but was sent out of the country by the authorities. In 1851 Elder Peterson was ordered to Norway, and organized a branch at Bergen. *Utah Pioneers, 33d Ann.*, 27. In 1879 the work had so greatly increased that 23 missionaries were appointed for Scandinavia. A list of them is given in *Millennial Star*, xli. 692–3. At the close of 1878 there were in this mission 46 branches, 467 elders, and 4,158 members of the church, 1,255 persons having been baptized during the year. *Id.*, 111. For further particulars, see

Iceland,[33] where was published *The Voice of Joseph*,[34] in Italy, Switzerland,[35] in Mexico,[36] in Chili, in China, in Siam,[37] in the Sandwich and Society islands,[33]

Deseret News, July 19, 1865, May 3, 1866; *Juvenile Instructor*, xv. 92–3; *Carson State Register*, June 26, 1872. Several pamphets were published in the Swedish language, and in 1853 the *Scandinavien Stjerne* was established at Copenhagen, which 30 years later was still the organ of the Mormon church and was well supported. *Richards' Bibliog. of Utah*, MS., 9.

[33] *Utah Pioneers, 33d Ann.*, 27; *Deseret News*, July 21, 1875, Sept. 20, 1876.

[34] See letter of Francois Stoudeman, in *Deseret News*, Oct. 16, 1852. Lorenzo Snow, with three elders, arrived at La Tour Sept. 19, 1820. For results, see *Id.*, 27; *Millennial Star*, xii. 370–4; *Smith's Rise, Progress, and Travels*, 32; *Frontier Guardian*, Feb. 21, 1850. Further missionary items will be found in the *Deseret News*, Apr. 2, 1853, March 8, 1855, Aug. 14, 1867. The book of Mormon and other works were translated into Italian in 1852. *The Voice of Joseph: A Brief Account of the Rise, Progress, and Persecutions of the Church of Jesus Christ of Latter-day Saints; with their present position and prospects in Utah Territory, together with American Exiles' Memorial to Congress, by Lorenzo Snow, one of the Twelve Apostles, Liverpool and London, 1852*, abbreviated from the Italian edition, was published for general circulation in various languages, and is a well-written historical sketch, admirably adapted to the purpose. Besides the expulsion from Missouri and Illinois, a general view of their 'location, settlements, and government in Upper California' is well presented. There is also an account of the missionary labors of the elders in the United States, Canada, England, Wales, Scotland, and elsewhere.

[35] Branches of the church were established in Switzerland, under the direction of Lorenzo Snow, about the year 1850. *Utah Pioneers, 33d Ann.*, 28. Soon afterward Elder T. B. H. Stenhouse published at Geneva a volume, entitled *Le Reflecteur*, and organized a branch of the church in the French quarter of that city. *Richards' Bibliog. of Utah*, MS., 11. In 1856–7 Elder Jno. L. Smith published two volumes of a monthly periodical styled *Der Darsteller der heiligen der letzen tage*. Other books and pamphlets innumerable were published in Switzerland and elsewhere in Europe. *Richards' Bibliog. of Utah*, MS., 11. For further mention of the Swiss mission, see *Deseret News*, Sept. 21, 1854, Aug. 14, 1867, Oct. 11, 1867. At the close of 1878 there were in Switzerland 17 branches, 31 elders, and 494 members of the church, 127 baptisms being recorded during that year. *Millennial Star*, xli. 111.

[36] A letter from Elder D. W. Jones, dated Concepcion, Chihuahua, Mex., Apr. 21, 1876, states that he and his fellow-missionaries were hard at work. About this time Jones preached at the theatre in the city of Chihuahua, but was ill received. *Millennial Star*, xxxviii. 381, 509. Portions of the book of Mormon were translated into Spanish for the use of Mexicans, and entitled *Trozos Selectos del Libro de Mormon* (S. L. City, 1875).

[37] *Smith's Rise, Progress, and Travels*, 33, 35. The Chinese mission was a failure. See *Deseret News*, Oct. 29. Dec. 22, 1853.

[38] *Deseret News*, Nov. 29, 1851, May 1, 15, July 24, Nov. 27, 1852. In 1856 the book of Mormon was published in Hawaiian by George Q. Cannon. See *Honolulu Friend*. An account of Cannon's mission to the Sandwich Islands in 1853–4 is given in his work entitled *My First Mission*. For further missionary labors in these islands, see *Deseret News*, Apr. 2, July 30, Oct. 29, Dec. 15, 1853, Aug. 6, 1856, Jan. 21, Dec. 9, 1857, June 1, Aug. 17, Nov. 30, 1864, June 12, 1867, Aug. 19, 1868, July 3, 1874; *Millennial Star*, xxxviii. 380; *Contributor*, v. 240; *Juvenile Instructor*, xv. 21. In 1844 Addison Pratt was stationed on the island of Tooboui, Society group, where he had organized a church with about a dozen members. At the same time, Noah Rogers and Benj. F. Grouard were stationed at Tahiti, but met with little success. In Oct. Rogers went to the island of Huahine. *Millennial Star*, v. 178–9, vi. 5–

and even in Jerusalem, was the Mormon gospel preached.[39]

It may be stated in general terms that the success of Mormon evangelism has been the most pronounced in countries where the climate is harsh, where wages are low, and the conditions of life severe, where there is freedom of conscience, and where there is a large class of illiterate men and women, prone to superstition and fanaticism. Elsewhere no lasting impression has been made. Thus for many years the stronghold of Mormonism was, as we have seen, in England, while in the British colonies, where for the most part food is cheap, labor is in demand at living rates, and the people are somewhat more enlightened than in the mother country, missionaries have met with little encouragement. In Norway, Sweden, and Denmark large numbers of proselytes have also been baptized; but in central and southern Europe, with the exception perhaps of Switzerland, the results have been meagre, and accomplished with great effort. The Scandinavian and British missions, the former including Denmark, claimed, at the close of 1878, nearly 8,000 members of the church;[40] and it is probable that in other parts of Europe there could not be

6, 57–60, vii. 14; *Times and Seasons*, vi. 812–14, 835–8, 882, 1019. These elders started in Oct. 1843, their passage being paid by P. B. Lewis as a donation to the mission. One of their number, K. F. Hanks, died on the voyage and was buried at sea. They baptized over 1,200 natives. Other missionaries at these islands were Jas S. Brown, Alva Hanks, and one Whittaker; but all were expelled by the French in 1851. *Smith's Rise, Progress, and Travels*, 31. See also *Utah Early Records*, MS., 35, 37, 84.

[39] Orson Hyde was appointed by a general conference held at Nauvoo Apr. 6, 1840, to a mission to the Jews in London, Amsterdam, Constantinople, and Jerusalem. He arrived in the last-mentioned city Oct. 24, 1841, and returned to Nauvoo in 1842. *Utah Pioneers, 33d Ann.*, 26. By his own efforts, he raised the money for his passage, often suffering great privation during his labors, his only food at times being snails. Of Jewish descent, he stirred up his unbelieving race in the towns to which he was sent to a livelier faith in the promises of their gathering, and consecrated their land anew to their restoration, when the glory of their latter house should be greater than the glory of their former house. *Richards' Utah Miscell.*, MS., 18. See also *Smith's Rise, Progress, and Travels*, 31; *Millennial Star*, ii. 166–9. For mission to Palestine in 1872, see *Corresp. of Pal. Tourists*, passim.

[40] A statistical report is given in *Millennial Star*, xli. 110–11.

found more than 2,000 or 3,000 additional members. If to these figures be added 15,000 converts distributed throughout the United States, 4,000 in British America, 3,000 in the Sandwich and Society islands, and perhaps 2,000 elsewhere in the world, we have a total of 35,000 latter-day saints scattered among the gentiles; and estimating the population of Utah at 140,000, a total of 175,000 professing the Mormon faith.[41]

Of the present population of Utah, about one third are of foreign birth, and at least another third of foreign parentage, converts having been gathered to Zion as speedily as the means could be furnished, from the earliest days of Mormon evangelism.

Between 1837 and 1851 about 17,000 proselytes set sail from England,[42] among them a considerable percentage belonging to other nationalities. In the latter year, not more than 3,000 persons arrived in the valley of the Great Salt Lake, including converts from the United States; although at this time it was published in American and copied in European papers that proselytes by the hundred thousand were on their way. In 1852 immigration was on a somewhat larger scale.[43] During a single month 352 converts

[41] Remy, *Jour. to G. S. L. City*, ii. 212–13, gives a table of the approximate number of Mormons in each country in 1859. The total is 186,000, of whom 80,000 were in Utah, 40,000 in other states and territories, 32,000 in England and Scotland, 8,000 in British America, 5,000 in Norway, Sweden, and Denmark, and 7,000 in the Sandwich and Society islands. His figures are at least 20 per cent too high. The entire population of Utah, for instance, was not more than 60,000 at this date. A writer in the *Hist. Mag.*, March 1859, p. 85, places the total at 126,000, of whom 38,000 were residents of Utah. Add 20,000 more for Utah, and we have a total of 146,000 which may be accepted approximately as the correct figures. Other estimates differ widely, the Mormons themselves, in an official statement published in the *Deseret News*, in 1856, claiming 480,000 members of the church in all parts of the world. See *American Almanac*, 1858, 338.

[42] Linforth gives the number despatched by the British agency between 1840 and 1852 at 11,296. *Route from Liverpool*, 15. The first vessel sent from England was the *North America*, which sailed June 16, 1840. The ship started on another voyage Sept. 8th of the same year. In *Burton's City of the Saints*, 361–2, is a list of vessels that sailed between 1851 and 1861.

[43] Estimated by Ezra T. Benson at 10,000 souls. It was probably less than half that number. The census of 1850 places the population of the territory at a little over 11,000; the reports of the bishops of wards at the Oct. conference in 1853, as given in *Richards' Hist. Incidents of Utah*, MS., 39, at 18,206.

took ship from Liverpool, of whom 108 were laborers, the remainder being farmers, joiners, shoemakers, rope-makers, watch-makers, engine-makers, weavers, tailors, masons, butchers, bakers, painters, potters, dyers, iron-moulders, glass-cutters, nail-makers, basketmakers, sawyers, gun-makers, saddlers, miners, smiths, and shipwrights.[44] Of the total emigration between 1850 and 1854, it was estimated that 28 per cent were laborers, 14 per cent miners, and about 27 per cent mechanics, among every two hundred being found one domestic servant, a shepherd, and a printer, and among every five hundred a schoolmaster, with here and there a university graduate, usually of no occupation, a dancing-master, a doctor, a dentist, and a retired or cashiered army officer.[45] For each emigrant as he arrived was apportioned an allotment of ground, and thus all became landed proprietors; though few brought with them capital, save the ability to labor, and many had not the means wherewith to pay for their passage.

On October 6, 1849, was organized at Salt Lake City the Perpetual Emigration Fund Company, for the purpose of aiding the poor to remove from Europe and the United States.[46] The company has con-

[44] *Mayhew, The Mormons*, 245; *Edinburgh Review*, Apr. 1854, 351. In *Linforth's Route from Liverpool*, 16-17, is a table showing the occupations of emigrants sent through the British agency between 1849 and 1854.

[45] *Remy's Jour. to S. L. City*, ii. 224-5.

[46] *Utah Perpetual Emigrating Fund*, MS. On Sunday Sept. 9, 1849, it was voted that a perpetual fund be instituted in aid of the poor among the latter-day saints, and that Willard Snow, John D. Lee, Lorenzo Snow, Franklin D. Richards, and John S. Fullmer be appointed a committee. At a general conference of the church, held Oct. 6th and 7th, it was ordered that the committee should raise funds for this purpose, to be placed in charge of Edward Hunter, and that the control of the funds be under the direction of the first presidency. On Sept. 15th Brigham Young was chosen president and Willard Richards was afterward appointed secretary. *Utah Early Records*, MS., 95, 97, 113, 114. The company was incorporated by the provisional government of the state of Deseret, Sept. 14, 1850, and the act of incorporation was made legal Oct. 4, 1851, and amended and confirmed by the same body Jan. 12, 1856. The company began rendering material aid on the 13th of March, 1850. On Sept. 3, 1852, the first company of emigrants assisted by this fund arrived at S. L. City in charge of Abraham O. Smoot. *Richards' Hist. Incidents of Utah*, MS., 18; *Deseret News*, Sept. 18, 1852; *Utah Emi-*

tinued in operation for nearly forty years, and through it fifty thousand persons have been assisted in removing to Utah. "The fund was gotten up," says Woodruff, "on the principle of perpetual succession, to continue increasing on condition of the people acting honestly, and in accordance with their covenants repaying the amounts...which had been advanced.[47] The sum thus loaned was usually refunded as soon as possible, for this obligation was held sacred by most of the saints, some working out their indebtedness at the public ateliers of the tithing office, and receiving meanwhile half the value of their labor, besides being supplied with food. There were many, however, who neglected or were unable to pay the advance, the amount due to the funds increasing gradually, until, in 1880, it had reached, with interest, $1,604,-000. At the jubilee conference, held in April of this year, one half of the debt was remitted in favor of the most worthy and needy of the assisted emigrants.[43]

On the 1st of May, 1852, Samuel W. Richards was placed in charge of the British mission, and on September 30th was appointed agent of the emigration company. During this and the following year emigration parties were organized with better system, and the benefits of the fund extended to larger numbers than during any previous period. On July 17, 1852, was published in the *Millennial Star* the seventh general epistle of the twelve. "Finally, brethren, fear God;

grating Fund, MS. For further particulars concerning the fund, see *Snow's Voice of Joseph*, 16; *Frontier Guardian*, Apr. 3, 1856; *Deseret News*, Sept. 18, 1852, Dec. 1, 1853; *Contributor*, ii. 177; *Ferris' Utah and the Mormons*, 163-4; *Mackay's The Mormons*, 260-2; *Olshausen, Mormonen*, 167; *Bertrand, Mem. d'un Mormon*, 73-4; *Hist. B. Young*, MS.; *Linforth's Route from Liverpool*, 13; *Young's Jour. of Disc.*, ii. 49-74; *Todd's Sunset Land*, 182-4.

[47] *Utah Pioneers*, 1880, p. 47. In a letter to Orson Hyde, Brigham says: 'When the saints thus helped arrive here, they will give their obligations to the church to refund the amount of what they have received as soon as circumstances will admit,...the funds to be appropriated as a loan rather than a gift.' *Hist. B. Young*, MS., 1849, 152-3. Immigrants nearly all came to Salt Lake and were distributed from this point.

[48] *Utah Emigrating Fund*, MS.; *Circular from the Twelve Apostles*, in *Mormon Pamphlets*, no. 3.

work righteousness, and come home speedily. Prepare against another season to come by tens of thousands; and think not that your way is going to be
opened to come in chariots, feasting on the fat of all
lands. We have been willing to live on bread and
water, and many times very little bread too, for years,
that we might search out and plant the saints in a
goodly land. This we have accomplished, through
the blessing of our heavenly father; and we now invite you to a feast of fat things, to a land that will
supply all your wants with reasonable labor; therefore let all who can procure a bit of bread, and one
garment on their back, be assured there is water
plenty and pure by the way, and doubt no longer, but
come next year to the place of gathering, and even in
flocks, as doves fly to their windows before a storm."

These words were repeated by hundreds of elders
throughout the United Kingdom, and no second invitation was needed. Men offered themselves by thousands, begging for passage to the land of the saints,
promising to walk the entire way from St Louis to
Salt Lake City, and to assist in hauling the provisions
and baggage. To meet this demand, it was determined to despatch emigrants for the ensuing season
at the low rate of £10 sterling per capita for the entire journey,[49] including provisions, and nearly one
thousand persons availed themselves of the opportunity. There were now four classes of emigrants:
first, those assisted from the fund by order from Salt
Lake City; second, assisted emigrants selected in
Great Britain; third, the £10 emigrants; fourth, emigrants who paid all their own expenses and sent forward money to procure teams.[50] The entire outlay

[49] *Linforth's Route from Liverpool*, 12. In the *Millennial Star*, xv. 618, is
a notice that the first ship of the season would sail early in Jan. 1853. Each
application must be accompanied by a statement of the name, age, occupation, and nativity of the applicant, and by a deposit of £1. Parties were to
provide their own bedding and cooking utensils. Richards, *Narr.*, MS., 32,
remarks that vessels from New Orleans could be chartered at low rates, as
they could seldom obtain return freight.

[50] At this date the price of a team, including wagon, two yoke of oxen, and
two milch cows, was about £40. *Linforth's Route from Liverpool*, 12.

for the season's emigration was not less than £30,000.
A year or two later it was found necessary to increase
the minimum charge from £10 to £13, on account of
the greater cost of provisions, wagons, and cattle,
caused by the California emigration.

Of emigrant travel by sea and land we have interesting records. Excepting perhaps some parts of
Soudan, there were, at this date, few places in the
world more difficult to reach than the valley of the
Great Salt Lake. After arriving at New Orleans, a
journey of more than three thousand miles awaited
the emigrants by way of St Louis and Council Bluffs,
from which latter point they must proceed in wagons
or on foot across the wilderness, travelling in this
primitive fashion for three weary months before reaching their destination. Of all the thousands who set
forth on this toilsome pilgrimage, few failed to reach
the city of the saints, the loss of life, whether of man
or beast, being very much below that which was suffered by parties bound for the gold-fields of California. While at sea, every provision was made for their
health and comfort, and after reaching Council Bluffs
none were allowed to start until their outfit was complete and their party fully organized.

The Liverpool manager of one of the New Orleans
packet lines speaks in the highest terms of his intercourse with the Mormons during the year 1850. He
states that they were generally intelligent and well
behaved, and many of them highly respectable. After
mentioning the vocations of the emigrants, he declares that the precautions taken for the preservation
of order, decency, and cleanliness on board were ad-
mirable, and well worthy of imitation; and that from
his observation of the slovenly and dirty habits of
other classes of emigrants, it would not only conduce
to their comfort and health, but would absolutely save
the lives of many if similar regulations were introduced.[51]

[51] *Mackay, The Mormons*, 270–3. 'The most scrupulous cleanliness was
thought to be necessary; frequent fumigation and sprinkling with lime; and

The Mormons objected to take passage in ships which carried other emigrants; or, if they embarked in such vessels, it was always arranged that a partition should be built to separate them from the gentiles. The dietary was on a scale[52] that gave to most of them better fare than that to which they had before been accustomed. Many of the vessels chartered for New Orleans were of large tonnage, some of them carrying as many as a thousand passengers. When on board, the brethren were divided into wards, each with its bishop and two councillors, who were implicitly obeyed. The centre of the ship was occupied by married couples, single men being placed in the bow and single women in the stern. Strict discipline was enforced on the voyage.[53] Divine service was held each day, morning and evening, when the weather was favorable, and on Sundays an awning was spread over the main deck, and spare spars so arranged as to furnish seats. Among many of the companies were excellent choirs, which rendered the church music; and during the passage there were frequent entertainments, concerts, and dance-parties, in which the captain and officers of the ship participated.

After landing, the same organization was maintained. Remaining for a few days at New Orleans, the emigrants were conveyed in companies by steamer to St Louis, and thence proceeded to Council Bluffs.[54] Here

on warm days all sick persons, whether willing or not, were brought into the air and sunshine.' *Linforth's Route from Liverpool*, 25. 'For each party were appointed watchmen (or committeemen) to see that no improprieties occurred among the people, or between our people and the sailors.' *Richards' Narr.*, MS., 31. In 1855 the line of route was changed to Philadelphia and New York, and thence to Cincinnati. *Richards' Incidents in Utah Hist.*, MS., 6.

[52] For each adult, weekly, 2½ lbs bread or biscuit, 1 lb. wheat flour, 5 lbs oatmeal, 2 lbs rice, ½ lb. sugar, 2 oz. tea, 2 oz. salt. Three quarts of water were allowed per diem. *Linforth's Route from Liverpool*, 20. Twenty pounds of breadstuffs per capita and an allowance of butter and cheese were provided by the Mormon superintendent. *Mackay, The Mormons*, 270. Meat was often issued in lieu of meal or bread.

[53] All were required to be in their berths at 8 o'clock, and before 7 the beds were made and the decks swept. *Mackay, The Mormons*, 272.

[54] In the *Deseret News*, May 29, June 12, 1852, and the *Juvenile Instructor*, xiv. 143, is an account of a boiler explosion that occurred on board a steamer from St Louis, with a list of those who were killed by the accident.

they rested for a time to recruit themselves and their cattle, and those who were without funds worked for the means wherewith to continue their journey, or waited until supplied with money from the emigration fund.

When the brethren were ready to set forth for Salt Lake City, they were divided into companies of ten, fifty, and a hundred, and the order of march was the same as that adopted in 1848, during the migration from Nauvoo. For every party of ten, a wagon, two oxen, two milch cows, and a tent were provided. Each wagon was examined by one of the bishops, and none were allowed to start that did not contain the requisite quantity of provisions[55] and ammunition. All who were capable of bearing arms were required to carry a rifle or musket. Any surplus means that the members might possess was invested in breadstuffs, groceries, dry goods, clothing, cattle, seeds, or implements.

Of the journey of the emigrant trains from Council Bluffs to the city of the saints, little remains to be said, as mention of this matter has been made in a previous chapter. To each emigrant as he travelled his wagon served for bedroom, parlor, and kitchen, and sometimes even as a boat in which to convey his effects over river or swamp. The average day's journey did not exceed thirteen miles, though the trains were in motion almost from sunrise until even-fall, a halt being made for the mid-day meal, and in order to give the cattle time to graze. Many of the caravans consisted of several hundred wagons, some of them drawn by six or eight oxen, and with every company went large bands of live-stock.[56] The procession, as it moved

[55] For those assisted by the emigration fund in 1853 was supplied for each wagon 1,000 lbs of flour, 50 lbs each of sugar, rice, and bacon, 30 of beans, 20 of dried apples or peaches, 25 of salt, 5 of tea, a gallon of vinegar, and 10 bars of soap. *Linforth's Route from Liverpool*, 19.

[56] Describing one of these trains which he encountered in the valley of the Weber on Sept. 2, 1850, Capt. Stansbury says: 'Ninety-five wagons were met to-day containing the advance of the Mormon emigration to the valley of the Salt Lake. Two large flocks of sheep were driven before the train; and geese

slowly along with its endless train of vehicles and its hundreds of cattle, sheep, horses, and mules, formed a picturesque and motley spectacle.   Among the members of the party were to be found the New England man with his stock of trading goods, the southerner with his colored attendant, the Englishman with his box of mechanic's tools, the Dane, the Swiss, and the Scandinavian with their implements of agriculture. There were few trades and few nationalities not represented, and few professions save that of the lawyer. Among the proselytes were university graduates, physicians, ministers, army and navy officers, school-masters, merchants, storekeepers, and even pawnbrokers. Yet amidst all this heterogeneous gathering, throughout all the hardships and privations of the march, there was little strife or discord; and never did it happen, as was often the case with parties bound for the gold-fields, that a Mormon company broke up into fragments through the dissension of its members.[57]

Those who set forth early in the season—not later than the middle of June—seldom met with any serious disaster; and it was recommended that none should leave Council Bluffs after that time of year, on account of the severe snow-storms that sometimes prevailed in the mountains during autumn.   In October 1849, for instance, while crossing Rocky Ridge, near the summit of South Pass, a party in charge of George A. Smith, the prophet's cousin, encountered a storm, in which more than sixty of their cattle perished.   Toward night on the 2d a strong wind set in from the north-east, accompanied with driving snow. The company encamped on a branch of the Sweet-

and turkeys had been conveyed in coops the whole distance without apparent damage...The appearance of this train was good, most of the wagons having from three to five yoke of cattle, and all in fine condition.   The wagons swarmed with women and children, and I estimated the train at one thousand head of cattle, 100 head of sheep, and 500 human souls.' *Exped. to G. S. Lake,* 223.
[57] For letters and news from emigrants on their way across the plains and matters concerning the organization of emigrant bands, see *Frontier Guardian,* Dec. 16, 1849, June 12, July 10, 24, Sept. 4, Oct. 2, 1850, Jan. 22, March 21, July 11, Aug. 8, 1851.

water, driving their cattle into a willow copse near by, as to build a corral was impossible. The wind freshened into a gale, and then into a hurricane, howling incessantly for thirty-six hours, and drifting the snow in every direction. For two nights women and children lay under their frail covering, exposed to the blast, with no food but a morsel of bread or biscuit. Tents and wagon-tops were blown away, and the wagons buried almost to the tops of their wheels in the snow-drifts. No fires could be lighted; little food could be had; no aid was nigh; and now, in this wintry solitude, though within a few days' march of the valley, the saints expected no other fate than to leave their bodies a prey to the wolves and the vultures.

At length the storm abated, and making their way toward the willow copse, the men found nearly half their cattle lying stiff amid the snow-banks, while others died from the effects of the storm. Not a human life was lost, however, though in this neighborhood many a grave was passed, some of friends near and dear, some of gold-seekers, whose bodies had been disinterred and half devoured by the wolves, and some of their persecutors in Illinois and Missouri, whose bones lay bleaching in the sun, a head-board with name, age, and date of decease being all that remained to mark their resting-place.[58]

Until the year 1856 the poorer classes of emigrants were supplied with ox-teams for the overland portion of the trip, the total cost of the journey from Liverpool, including provisions, never exceeding sixty dollars. There were thousands of converts in Europe, however,

[58] In a letter dated Muddy Fork—930 miles from Winter Quarters—Oct. 18, 1849, and published in the *Frontier Guardian*, Dec. 26th, of that year, George A. Smith writes: 'Among others we noticed at the South Pass of the Rocky Mountains the grave of one E. Dodd, of Gallatin, Mo., died on the 19th of July last of typhus fever. The wolves had completely disinterred him. The clothes in which he had been buried lay strewed around. His under jawbone lay in the grave, with the teeth complete, the only remains discernable of him. It is believed he was the same Dodd that took an active part, and a prominent mobocrat, in the murder of the saints at Haun's Mills, Mo. If so, it is a righteous retribution.'

who were anxious to be gathered unto Zion, but could not command even this sum, and measures were now considered whereby the expense could be reduced. After much discussion, it was decided that parties should cross the plains with hand-carts, in which they were to carry their baggage, wagons being provided only for tents, extra provisions, and those who were unable to walk. Instructions to this effect were issued from Brigham Young, September 30, 1855, and in a general epistle of the twelve, dated October 29th, a circular being published in Liverpool about four months later by the presidency of the British Isles, in which the rate of passage was fixed at £9 sterling per capita.[59] "The Lord, through his prophet, says of the poor, 'Let them come on foot, with hand-carts or wheelbarrows; let them gird up their loins, and walk through, and nothing shall hinder them.'"

Iowa City was selected as the point of outfit, and there the hand-carts were built. They were of somewhat primitive fashion, the shafts being about five feet long and of hickory or oak, with cross-pieces, one of them serving for handle, forming the bed of the cart, under the centre of which was a wooden axle-tree, the wheels being also of wood, with a light iron band, and the entire weight of the vehicle about sixty pounds.[60] Better carts were provided in subsequent years. When the hand-cart emigrants, about thirteen hundred in number, set forth from Liverpool, they were assured that everything would be provided for them on their arrival at Iowa City; but on reaching that point many of them were delayed for weeks until the carts were built. Three companies started early in the season and made the journey without mishap.[61] The next company, under Captain James G. Willie,

---

[59] The letter, epistle, and circular will be found in the *Millennial Star*, xvii. 812–15, xviii. 49–55, 121–3.

[60] *Stenhouse's Rocky Mountain Saints*, 314. The construction of the cart will be seen in a cut facing this page.

[61] The first arrived Sept. 26th, and were met by the first presidency and a large number of the citizens, with an escort of cavalry and the bands of the Nauvoo legion. *Deseret News*, Oct. 6, 1856.

was not in motion until the middle of July, and the last that season, under Captain Edward Martin, not until the end of that month. They were divided, as usual, into hundreds, Willie's company being somewhat below that number; and for each hundred were furnished twenty hand-carts, five tents, three or four milch cows, and a wagon with three yoke of oxen to convey the provisions and tents, the quantity of clothing and bedding being limited to seventeen pounds per capita, and the freight of each cart, including cooking utensils, being about one hundred pounds.

Willie's company reached Winter Quarters, or Florence, as it was now termed, near the middle of August, and here a meeting was held to decide whether they should continue their journey or encamp for the winter. They had yet more than a thousand miles to travel, and with their utmost effort could not expect to arrive in the valley until late in November. The matter was left with the elders, all of whom, except one named Levi Savage, counselled them to go forward and trust in the Lord, who would surely protect his people. Savage declared that they should trust also to such common sense as the Lord had given them. From his certain knowledge, the company, containing as it did so large a number of the aged and infirm, of women and children, could not cross the mountains thus late in the season, without much suffering, sickness, and death. He was overruled and rebuked for want of faith. "Brethren and sisters," he replied, "what I have said I know to be true; but seeing you are to go forward, I will go with you. May God in his mercy preserve us."

The company set forth from Florence on the 18th, and on each hand-cart was now placed a ninety-eight-pound sack of flour, as the wagons could not carry the entire load. At first they travelled about fifteen miles a day, although delays were caused by the breaking of wheels and axles, the heat and aridity of the plains and mountain country speedily making many of the cart-wheels rickety, and unable to sustain their burdens without frequent repairs. Some shod the axles of their carts with old leather, others with tin from the plates and kettles of their mess outfit; and for grease they used their allowance of bacon, and even their soap, of which they had but little. On reaching Wood River, the cattle stampeded,[62] and thirty head were lost, the remainder being only sufficient to allow one yoke to each wagon. The beef cattle, milch cows, and heifers were used as draught animals, but were of little service, and it was found necessary to place another sack of flour on each hand-cart. The issue of beef was then stopped, the cows gave no milk, and the daily ration was reduced to a pound of flour, with a little rice, sugar, coffee, and bacon, an allowance which only furnished breakfast for some of the men, who fasted for the remainder of the day.

While encamped on the north fork of the Platte, the emigrants were overtaken by F. D. Richards, W. H. Kimball, G. D. Grant, and a party of elders, returning from foreign missions, who gave them what encouragement they could. "Though it might storm on their right and on their left, the Lord would keep open their way before them, and they would reach Zion in safety." After camping with them for one night, the elders went on their way, promising to leave provisions for them at Fort Laramie if possible, and to send aid from Salt Lake City. On reaching Laramie no provisions were found, and rations were again reduced, men able to work receiving twelve ounces of flour daily, women and old men nine ounces, and children from four to eight ounces.

As the emigrants travelled along the banks of the Sweetwater, the nights became severe, and their bed-covering was now insufficient. Before them were the mountains, clad almost to the base with snow, where already the storms of winter were gathering. Gradually the old and infirm began to droop, and soon deaths became frequent, the companies seldom leaving

[62] At this point the country was alive with buffaloes.

their camping-ground without burying one or more of
the party. Then able-bodied men began to succumb,
a few of them continuing to pull their carts until the
day before they died, and one or two even on the day of
their death. On the morning when the first snow-
storm occurred, the last ration of flour was issued, and
a march of sixteen miles was before them to the nearest camping-ground on the Sweetwater. The task
seemed hopeless; but at noon a wagon drove up, containing Joseph A. Young and Stephen Taylor, from
Salt Lake City, who told them that a train of supplies
was on the way, and would reach them in a day or
two. Young and Taylor immediately went on to
meet Martin's company, which it was feared was even
in worse plight than that of Captain Willie. Thus
encouraged, the emigrants pushed forward, and by
doubling their teams, while the strongest of the party
helped the weak to drag along their carts, all reached
the camping-ground, though some of the cattle perished, and during the night five persons died of cold
and exhaustion.

In the morning the snow was a foot deep; and now
there remained only two barrels of biscuit, a few pounds
of sugar and dried apples, and a quarter of a sack of
rice. Two of the disabled cattle were killed, their
carcasses issued for beef, and on this and a small dole
of biscuit the emigrants were told that they must
subsist until supplies reached them, the small remnant
of provisions being reserved for the young children
and the sick. It was now decided to remain in camp,
while Captain Willie with one of the elders went in
search of the supply trains. The small allowance of
beef and biscuit was consumed the first day, and on
the second day more cattle were killed and eaten
without biscuit. On the next day there was nothing to
eat, for no more cattle could be spared, and still the supplies came not, being delayed by the same storm which
the emigrants had encountered. During these three

days many died and numbers sickened, some expiring in the arms of those who were themselves almost at the point of death, mothers clasping with their dying clutch the remnants of their tattered clothing around the wan forms of their perishing infants, and, most pitiful sight of all, strong men begging for the morsel of food that had been set apart for the sick and helpless.

It was now the evening of the third day, and the sun was sinking behind the snow-clad ranges, which could be traced far to the west amid the clear, frosty atmosphere of the desert. There were many who, while they gazed on this scene, did not expect to see the light of another day, and there were many who cared no longer for life, having lost all that makes life precious. They retired to their tents, and commending themselves to their maker, lay down to rest, perchance to die. But presently a shout of joy was raised, as from an eminence near the western portion of the camp covered wagons were seen approaching, with Willie at their head. In charge of the train were Kimball and Grant, who distributed to the companies about half of their provisions, together with a quantity of warm clothing, blankets, and buffalo-robes, the remainder being sent forward under charge of Grant for the use of Martin's company, while Kimball now took command of Willie's detachment.

But the troubles of the hand-cart emigrants were not yet at an end. Some were already beyond all human aid; some had lost their reason, and around others the blackness of despair had gathered, all efforts to rouse them from their stupor being unavailing. Each day the weather grew colder, and many were frost-bitten, losing fingers, toes, or ears, one sick man who held on to the wagon-bars, to avoid jolting, having all his fingers frozen. At a camping-ground on Willow Creek, a tributary of the Sweetwater, fifteen corpses were buried, thirteen of them being

frozen to death. Near South Pass another company
of the brethren met them, with supplies from Salt
Lake City, and from the trees near their camp several
quarters of fat beef were suspended—"a picture," says
Chislett, who had charge of one of the companies,
"that far surpassed the paintings of the ancient masters." From this point warmer weather prevailed,
and fresh teams from the valley constantly met them,
distributing provisions sufficient for their needs, and
then travelling eastward to meet Martin's company.

On reaching Salt Lake City on the 9th of November, it was found that sixty-seven out of a total of four
hundred and twenty had died on the journey. Of
the six hundred emigrants included in Martin's detachment, which arrived three weeks later, a small percentage perished, the storm which overtook Willie's
party on the Sweetwater reaching them on the North
Platte. There they encamped, and waited about ten
days for the weather to moderate. Their rations were
reduced to four ounces of flour per head per day, for a
few days, until relief came. On arriving at Salt Lake,
the survivors were received with the utmost kindness,
arrangements being made with the bishops of wards
to provide for those who had no relatives in the territory; and throughout the settlements, wherever it was
known that a family had crossed the plains with the
hand-cart companies, that alone was sufficient to insure
for them substantial aid from the brethren.[63]

[63] My account of the hand-cart emigration is taken principally from Mr
Chislett's narrative in *Stenhouse's Rocky Mountain Saints*, 312–338. The story
as told in *Stenhouse's Tell It All*, 206–36, though it claims to have been written
by one of the women of the party, and perhaps was so written, is merely an
adaptation of the above. Another version will be found in *Young's Wife No.
19*, 206–21. For other mention of the hand-cart emigration, see *Siskiyou Co.
Affairs*, MS., 18; *Paddock's La Tour*, 345; *Deseret News*, Nov. 12, 19, 30,
1856; *S. L. Herald*, Jan. 4, 1879; *S. F. Alta*, Nov. 12, 13, 1856; *S. F. Bulletin*, Jan. 12, 1857. In hundreds of newspapers and magazines appeared
grossly exaggerated descriptions of this disaster, of which the following,
taken from the *Or. Statesman*, June 15, 1857, may serve as a specimen: 'Of
the 2,500 persons who started from the frontier, only about 200 frost-bitten,
starving, and emaciated beings lived to tell the tale of their sufferings. The
remaining 2,300 perished on the way of hunger, cold, and fatigue.' The emi-

There remains yet one more incident in the story of the hand-cart emigration. On arrival at Devil's Gate on the Sweetwater, twenty men, belonging to Martin's company, were left in charge of stock, merchandise, and baggage, with orders to follow in the spring. The snow fell deep, and many of the cattle were devoured by the wolves, while others perished from cold. The rest were slaughtered, and on their frozen carcasses the men subsisted, their small stock of flour and salt being now exhausted. Game was scarce in the neighborhood, and with their utmost care the supply of food could not hold out until spring. Two of the men, with the only horses that remained, were sent to Platte Bridge to obtain supplies; but the animals were lost, and they returned empty-handed. Presently the meat was all consumed; and then their only resource was the hides, which were cut into small pieces and soaked in hot water, after the hair had been removed. When the last hides had been eaten, nothing remained but their boot-tops and the scraps of leather around their wagons, even the neck-piece of a buffalo skin which had served as door-mat being used for food. Thus they kept themselves alive until spring, when they subsisted on thistle roots and wild garlic, until at length relief came from Salt Lake City.

Even the worst enemies of Brigham Young admit that he was in no sense to blame for this disaster, and that he spared no effort to prevent it. When tidings of the emigrants' condition arrived in Salt Lake City, he at once suspended all other business,[64] and declared that nothing more should be done until every available team was sent to their relief. He himself set

grants were happy and content, until winter overtook them in the mountains, singing as they journeyed, one of their songs commencing:

'We're going to Zion with our carts,
And the spirit of God within our hearts;'

the chorus of another, sung to the tune of 'A little more cider:'

'Hurrah for the camp of Israel!
Hurrah for the hand-cart scheme!
Hurrah! Hurrah! 'tis better far
Than wagon and ox-team.'

[64] The October conference was then in session.

the example by sending several of his best teams
laden with provisions and clothing, other large supplies being forwarded by Heber C. Kimball and the
more wealthy of the elders. Each one contributed
according to his means, those who had no teams furnishing apparel, bedding, and food, and this at a time
when, as will presently appear, the territory was
almost in a state of famine, on account of a second
plague of grasshoppers.

The catastrophe was due mainly to the error in
starting so late in the season from Iowa City, and
to the fact that the companies did not contain a
sufficient number of able-bodied men in proportion
to the infirm, the women, and children.[65] Moreover,
the winter was one of the earliest and most severe
that has ever been known in Utah. The hand-cart
scheme was perfectly feasible, if carried out under
proper management, as was proved by the success of
the first companies, and, in the spring of 1857, by a
party of seventy-four missionaries, who accomplished
the trip to the Missouri in forty-eight days, or less
than half the time needed when the journey was
made by wagon.[66]

After the hand-cart disaster, and perhaps partly on
account of the reports sent home by the survivors,
there was a gradual diminution in the rate of emigration, though with many fluctuations. In 1876 only
1,184 proselytes were despatched from Liverpool, this
being one of the smallest movements recorded. In
1877 the number increased to 1,479, and in 1878 to
1,864, but in 1879 fell off to 1,456, about 55 per cent
of the emigrants for the last of these years being of

[65] It was from Iowa City that the late start was made. Stenhouse and
others delight in making out something horrible in the hand-cart business,
and the leaders no better than the vilest criminals. It was an unfortunate
affair, in which the leaders suffered with the rest, but nothing further than
this can be justly charged to any one. *Rocky Mountain Saints*, 341-2. A biographical notice of Spencer and his funeral sermon, delivered by Brigham,
will be found in *S. Lake Tel.*, Dec. 9, 10, 1868.

[66] *Sloan's Utah Gazetteer*, 1884, 26. In the *Deseret News*, Apr. 29, 1857, it
is stated that they hoped to make the trip in 40 days.

British nationality, and 35 per cent Swedish, Norwegian, and Danish.[67] In the church records, the total emigration from foreign countries, between 1840 and 1883, is stated at 78,219 souls, or an average of nearly 2,000 a year, the proselytes taking passage in companies of from 12 to 800 in 243 different vessels, all of which reached their destination in safety.[68] Probably the main cause of the decrease in emigration during later years was the advance in the rate of fare, which in 1878 was fixed at £14-14, a sum for which passage could be secured to almost any portion of the world.

Between 1850 and 1856 the movement appears to have reached its culmination, proselytes being gathered by the thousand to the promised land, and thousands more preparing to follow. The elders were exhorted to "thunder the word of the almighty to the saints to arise and come to Zion."[69] The brethren were commanded to shake from their feet the dust of Babylon and hasten to the holy city. "Every saint who does not come home," says the sixth general epistle of the twelve,[70] "will be afflicted by the devil." "Every particle of our means that we use in Babylon," remarks Elder Erastus Snow,[71] "is a loss to ourselves; and it is so much means expended upon Babylon that shall perish." "O ye poor and oppressed saints!" writes Elder Samuel Richards, "and ye rich ones too, in these lands, do not your bosoms burn with the good spirit of God, which fills his saints always with a desire to congregate together, and become a holy and

---

[67] *Millennial Star*, xli. 680; *Deseret News*, Nov. 19, 1879. There were also 90 Swiss, 34 Germans, and 8 of other nationalities.

[68] Though some were driven back to port, and one was dismasted on the voyage to New Orleans. *Richards' Emigr. to Utah*, MS., 1.

[69] *Millennial Star*, xiv. 201.

[70] Published July 15, 1852, in *Id.*, xiv. 20.

[71] At a special council, held at 23 Ratcliffe Terrace, Islington, London, on the 6th, 7th, 8th, and 9th of April. An account of the proceedings will be found in *Id.*, xiv. 209-12, 225-8, 243-7. At the close of the conferences a memorial was presented to Franklin D. Richards, who was then about to return to Salt Lake City.

peculiar people? Do you not long to gather to your brethren and sisters in the heights of Zion, where sinners cannot dwell? Do you not fondly wish to assemble with the elders of Israel in the sacred resting-places of the excellent of the earth, and there inherit the earth and enjoy the bountiful blessings of a munificent creator?"

Such sayings, freely circulated among the toiling myriads of Europe, where for twelve and fifteen hours a day men worked for a wage barely sufficient to supply their needs, were not without effect. Under such conditions, a new religion, which promised to exchange the penury and drudgery of its converts for plenty and moderate labor, could not fail to receive a hearing. Moreover, the story of the prophet's assassination and of the expulsion from Illinois was yet fresh in the minds of the people. The saints were still looked upon as martyrs, and as martyrs who, having boldly launched forth into an untrodden wilderness, had at length established for themselves an abiding-place, and now stretched forth the hand of christian fellowship to the weary and heavy-laden in all the earth. Never since the founding of the sect was their cause held in more esteem; never had they dwelt together in more perfect harmony, less disturbed by outside influences, or less mindful of the events that were transpiring in the great world beyond. The years that had elapsed since their departure from Nauvoo had witnessed the rise and fall of an empire, the crash of a throne, the great revolutions in the world of science and the world of commerce. But, except so far as they seemed to fulfil the predictions of their seer, all these matters concerned them less than did the building of a saw-mill or a nail-factory in the land of which their prophet had foretold: "And they who are in the north countries shall come in remembrance before the Lord,...and a highway shall be made in the midst of the great deep,...and in the barren deserts there shall come forth pools of living water; and the parched ground shall no longer be a thirsty land."[72]

[72] *Revelation of Joseph Smith*, in *Docrine and Covenants*, 327.

Among the Mormon works largely circulated throughout the British Isles and Europe was one published in 1852, and entitled *The Government of God, by John Taylor, one of the Twelve Apostles of the Church of Jesus Christ of Latter-day Saints.* In a preface by James Linforth, the writer states that it had been the author's intention to superintend the publication of this work, an 8vo volume of 118 pages, in person; but the cares pretaining to his missionary labors and literary work, then more urgently needed, prevented him. He therefore, on his departure for Salt Lake City in the spring of 1852, left with Mr Linforth the manuscript, the printing of which was superintended by him. As a dissertation on a general and abstract subject, it probably has not its equal in point of ability within the whole range of Mormon literature. The style is lofty and clear, and every page betokens the great learning of the author. As a student of ancient and modern history, theologian, and moral philosopher, President Taylor is justly entitled to the front rank; while his proficiency in foreign languages and his knowledge of men and of practical affairs rendered his services no less important as manager abroad than as executive officer at home.

I will here begin the biographical notices of the leading men of Utah, and of some of the pioneers, carrying the same along in the notes to the end of the volume as I have done in other cases in my historical works. The lives of some have already been fully given; and in regard to some of the others who have not yet finished playing their part in the history of the country, their biographies will be given here but partially, and finished as the work proceeds.

First after Joseph Smith and Brigham Young should be mentioned John Taylor, third president of the entire church. A native of Milnthorpe, England, where he was born in November 1808, Taylor emigrated in 1829 to Toronto, Canada, to which city his father had removed two years before. Here, joining a methodist society, he searched the scriptures earnestly, and became convinced that the churches had fallen from grace and were corrupt. With prayer and fasting he besought the Lord that if there were a true church on earth he would send a messenger to him. Shortly afterward he was visited by Parley P. Pratt, to whom he gave but a cool reception, as many evil reports concerning Mormonism were then current. But after close scrutiny, he and several of his friends believed and were baptized. In 1838 it was ordered by revelation that he should be appointed an apostle, and after the schism of that year he filled the vacancy in the quorum caused by the apostasy of John Boynton. In 1840 he arrived in England as a missionary, his labors extending to Ireland and to the Isle of Man, where he was the first to preach the doctrines of Mormonism. While on a visit to Scotland, he corrected the proof-sheets of the book of Mormon, and helped to prepare a hymn-book for the use of converts in the British Islands. He also wrote several pamphlets in reply to charges against the church. Returning to America in 1841, in company with Brigham Young, he proceeded to Nauvoo, where he was selected one of a committee to petition congress for a redress of wrongs, and presented the petition. He also purchased and took charge of the *Times and Seasons*, at the request of the prophet, the last three volumes being published under his direction, and was chosen a member of the city council, a regent of the university, and judge-advocate of the Nauvoo legion. He was firmly attached to the prophet, and at Carthage jail, as we have seen, almost lost his life in attempting to save him. After the expulsion he went, with others of the twelve, to Winter Quarters, where he assisted in organizing the Mormon battalion. At this juncture he was again ordered to England, in company with Parley P. Pratt and Orson Hyde, and returning the following spring, accompanied Pratt's companies to Salt Lake City. In October 1849 he was sent as a missionary to France, where he published a monthly paper, styled *L'*

Etoile du Deseret.   Before leaving Europe he translated the book of Mormon into the French language, and preached the gospel of the saints at Hamburg, where under his direction the same work was translated into German, and where he also published a monthly paper named *Zion's Panier.*   Returning to Salt Lake City in 1852, he was elected, two years afterward, a member of the legislature, but resigning this office, went as a missionary to New York, where he superintended the affairs of the church in the eastern states, and established a journal, the first number of which appeared Feb. 17, 1855, under the title of *The Mormon,* the paper being discontinued in 1857, when Taylor was recalled at the outbreak of the Utah war.   After that date, his labors were mainly confined to the territory, where he was partly engaged in literary work for the church, serving also for a brief term as probate judge of Utah county, and for several terms as a member of the Utah legislature and speaker of the house.   In Oct. 1880 he was appointed, as we shall see later, president of the church of Jesus Christ of latter-day saints.   Further details as to his early career will be found in *Hist. B. Young,* MS.; *Woodruff's Journal,* MS.; *Richards' Narr.,* MS., and many other manuscripts and books.

George Q. Cannon, a native of Liverpool, England, was trained in the Mormon faith, his parents having been converted in 1839, when he was twelve years of age, through the preaching of John Taylor, who some time before had married his father's sister.   A short time before the assassination of Joseph Smith the family arrived at Nauvoo, where George found employment as a printer in the office of the *Times and Seasons* and *Nauvoo Neighbor.*   In 1847 he set out for S. L. City with Parley Pratt's companies, and for two years was engaged in farming, house-building, and other labor incidental to new settlements.   In the autumn of 1849 he went to California in company with Chas C. Rich, and there worked in the gold mines until the summer of 1850, when he was sent on a mission to the Sandwich Islands.   On arriving at Honolulu he began to study the Hawaiian language, which he mastered in six weeks, and then travelled and preached among the natives, organizing several branches of the church.   In 1854 he returned to Salt Lake City, and the following year went as a missionary to California, where he established and edited a newspaper called the *Western Standard.*   When news arrived of the Utah war, he again returned to the valley, and during the exodus of 1858 took charge of the press and printing materials of the *Deseret News,* which were conveyed to Fillmore City.   In October 1859 he was chosen an apostle to fill the vacancy caused by the death of Parley Pratt, and was afterward appointed president of the European mission.   In 1862 he was ordered to Washington to support the claims of Utah to admission as a state, of which more later.   After the adjournment of congress he repaired to England, where he labored until August 1864, 13,000 converts being forwarded to Zion during this period.   Being then summoned home, he was elected a member of the legislative council, and was for three years private secretary to Brigham Young.   In 1867 he became editor and publisher of the *Deseret News,* which was then a semi-weekly paper, and started the *Deseret Evening News,* which was issued daily, his connection with the latter continuing until the autumn of 1872, when he was chosen delegate to congress.   In 1880 Mr Cannon was appointed first councillor to President John Taylor.   For further particulars, see authorities before quoted; also *Sala's America Revisited,* 302; *Reno Daily Gazette,* Jan. 24, 1882.

Joseph F., the son of Hyrum Smith, who with his brother, the prophet, was assassinated at Carthage jail, was born at Far West, Mo., in 1838.   After passing his early youth among the vicissitudes attending the expulsion from Nauvoo and the colonization of Utah, he was ordered, when 16 years of age, to proceed as a missionary to the Sandwich Islands, where he labored earnestly and with marked success.   'By the blessing of the almighty,' he writes, 'I acquired the language of the islanders, and commenced my labors, preaching, baptizing, etc., among the natives, in one hundred days after my arrival at Honolulu.'   At the beginning of the Utah war he returned to S. L. City and served in the militia up to the time when Johnston's army entered the valley. In 1860 he was sent on mission work to England, where he remained till 1863, being again ordered, the following year, to the Sandwich Islands in company with A. L. Smith, L. Snow, E. T. Benson, and W. W. Cluff. Returning in 1865, he was soon after elected an apostle and a member of the legislature, in which latter capacity he served until 1872. In 1874 and 1875 he presided over the British mission, and in 1880 was chosen second councillor to President Taylor. For additional items, see above authorities.

Wilford, the third son of Aphek and Beulah Thompson Woodruff, was born at Farmington (now Avon), Conn., his ancestors for at least three generations being residents of that neighborhood. In 1832 he was converted to Mormonism, together with his brother Azmon, and soon afterward cast in his lot at Kirtland, where, for a time, he was the guest of Joseph Smith. Two years later he started on a missionary tour in company with an elder named Brown, journeying on foot through southern Missouri, northern Arkansas, and western Tennessee. In 1837 he was appointed a member of the first quorum of the seventies, and in April of this year, was married to Phœbe W. Carter at the house of Joseph Smith. In 1839 he was chosen an apostle, and soon afterward was sent on a mission to England, where, in a few months, he and his fellow-missionaries baptized more than 1,800 proselytes, their success being so remarkable as to alarm the orthodox clergy, who brought the matter before the notice of parliament. In 1841 he was shipwrecked at Lake Michigan while on his way to Nauvoo, but escaped with his life and reached that city in October. A few weeks before the assassination of Joseph and Hyrum Smith, he was again ordered to England as a missionary, returning in 1846, when he crossed the plains with the pioneer band. In 1848 we find him once more a missionary, this time in the eastern states, whence he returned to Salt Lake City in 1850, being elected in December of that year a senator for the provisional state of Deseret. After that date he became one of the foremost men in Utah, the church annals being largely compiled from his records. In his public career he is regarded as one of the founders of the territory; his apostolic labors have earned for him among the saints the title of 'Wilford the faithful.' *Woodruff's Leaves from Journal,* 1–96; *Millennial Star,* xxvii. passim; *Times and Seasons,* v. 692; *Deseret News,* July 7, 14, 1858.

Among the pioneers was Willard Richards, born at Hopkinton, Middlesex county, Mass., on the 24th of June, 1804. Under the instruction of his parents, Joseph and Rhoda Richards, he applied himself during his youth to the study of theology, but could not discern in the doctrines of any of the sects around him the fulness of truth. In 1835 he obtained a copy of the book of Mormon, and reading it through twice in ten days, became convinced of its divine authenticity. At this date he was practising medicine at Boston, but at once resolved to remove to Kirtland, where a year later he was baptized and ordained an elder by his cousin, Brigham Young. Proceeding on a mission to England, he labored successfully, and in April 1840 was chosen by revelation one of the twelve. Returning to America, he was appointed historian and general recorder to the church, which offices he held until his decease in March 1854. He was an intimate friend of the prophet's, and, as will be remembered, was present at his assassination in Carthage jail. In 1848, after the return of the pioneer band, he was appointed second councillor to the president. He was also editor of the *Deseret News,* the official organ of the church, and wrote most of the general epistles of the twelve to the brethren throughout the world. After the organization of the state of Deseret he was made secretary of state, and afterward presided over the council of the legislative assembly. The last occasion on which he left his house was for the purpose of addressing the council at the close of its session. 'I will go and perform this duty,' he said, 'if, like John Quincy Adams, I die in the attempt; but no one knows the aggravated extent of my bodily malady. Death stares me in the face, waiting for his prey.' Further particulars will be found in *The Millennial Star,* xxvii. 118–20, 133–6, 150–2, 165–6; *Linforth's Route from*

Liverpool, 75–6; *Deseret News*, March 16, 1854, June 23, 30, 1858, Dec. 9, 1874; *Richards' Narr.*, MS., 107–8.

Franklin Dewey Richards, nephew to Willard, was born at Richmond, Berkshire co., Mass., on April 2, 1821. After receiving a common-school education, he was employed at farm labor, or at his father's trade—that of carpenter. His attention was first called to Mormonism during a visit of Brigham to the house of his grandfather, Joseph Richards. On the 3d of June, 1838, he relates that after being baptized and anointed with oil, he was cured, by the efficacy of prayer, of a severe sickness. In October following, he set forth for Far West, but finding that Gen. Clark had issued an order requiring all Mormons to leave the state, he went to St Louis, where he found employment. In the spring of 1840 he attended a conference at Nauvoo, and was soon afterward sent as a missionary to Indiana, where he established a church. After some further missionary work in the United States, he repaired to Nauvoo where he married, and by great self-denial obtained the means of building a brick house in the eastern part of the city. This he sold before the expulsion for two yoke of oxen and an old wagon. In the spring of 1844 he was ordered with several others to proceed on a mission to England, but after reaching New York he heard of the assassination of the prophet, and returned to Nauvoo. In 1845 he assisted at the completion of the temple, working as a carpenter and painter. When the first bands of the saints crossed the Mississippi in Feb. 1856, Mr Richards accompanied them as far as their camping-ground on Sugar Creek, where he bade adieu to his wife and family, and soon afterward sailed for Liverpool in company with Parley P. Pratt and others. Of further incidents in his life, I shall have occasion to speak elsewhere.

Heber Chase Kimball was a native of Sheldon, Vt, where he was born in 1801. When ten years of age his family removed to West Bloomfield, N. Y., in which town he afterward worked as a blacksmith in his father's shop. In 1820, his father having lost his property, he was compelled to seek his own livelihood, and after suffering much hardship, found employment with his brother, who was a potter by trade, and removed with him to Mendon. He was converted to Mormonism by the preaching of Phineas H. Young, and in 1832 was baptized, and soon afterward ordained an elder. In Sept. of this year he went to Kirtland with Brigham and Joseph Young, and there met the prophet. In 1835 he was chosen a member of the first quorum of the twelve, and from that date until the expulsion from Nauvoo his time was mainly spent in missionary labors in the eastern states and in England. Returning from Salt Lake City to Winter Quarters with the main body of the pioneers, he was appointed first councillor to the president, which office he held until his decease, in June 1868. On the organization of the state of Deseret, he was elected lieutenant-governor and chief justice, and later became president of the council of the legislative assembly. A man of singular generosity, integrity, and purity of heart, there are few whose names are held in more esteem among the latter-day saints than that of President Kimball.

In March 1850 occurred the decease of Oliver Cowdery, at Richmond, Ray co., Mo. His connection with the church from its earliest days, and the part which he took in the translation of the book of Mormon, have already been mentioned. He was cut off, as we have seen, in 1838, but in 1848 was rebaptized. 'His relation of events,' remarks S. W. Richards, 'was of no ordinary character, maintaining unequivocally all those written testimonies he had furnished to the church in earlier days. Moroni, Peter, James, and John, and other heavenly messengers who had ministered to him in connection with the prophet, Joseph Smith, were familiarly but sacredly spoken of.' After his second conversion he devoted the brief remainder of his life entirely to the cause of the church, declaring his willingness to go forth among the nations and bear testimony of that which had been revealed to him—a testimony which none but he could bear. *Contributor*, 1884, p. 446.

In addition to the authorities already quoted on the subject of missions and immigration, I append the following: *Millennial Star*, i. 302, iv. 17–19, 33–6, viii. 142, ix. 244–5, x. and xi. passim, xiv. 618, xxi. 638, xxii. 18. xxiii.

220–1, xxiv. 510, xxv. 640, 744, 760, 807, xxix. 64, xxxvi. 666, xli. 545–680, passim; *Times and Season,* i. passim, ii. 273–7, iii. 593–6, 682–3, 895–6, iv. passim, v. 556, 558–9; *S. L. Deseret News,* 1850, Aug. 10, Oct. 5, Dec. 14; 1851, Mar. 22, June 14, Nov. 15, 29, Dec. 13, 27, 1852, passim; 1853, Feb. 5, 19, Mar. 19, May 14, July 9, Oct. 29, Dec. 1, 8; 1854, Jan. 5, Mar. 2, May 11, June 22, Aug. 10, Sept. 21, Oct. 5; 1855, Jan. 4, Feb. 22, Apr. 4, May 9, July 25, Oct. 17, Dec. 19; 1856, Feb. 27, Apr. 16, May 14, June 4, July 2, Aug. 6, Oct. 8; 1857, Jan. 21, Mar. 18, Apr. 15, May 13, Aug. 26, Dec. 9, 23; 1858, May 19, June 9, July 7, Oct. 27; 1859, Mar. 30, May 11, June 29, Aug. 3, Sept. 21; 1860, May 30, June 13, July 4, Aug. 15, Oct. 24, Nov. 21; 1861, Jan. 2, Mar. 6, Apr. 3, May 15, Sept. 11; 1862, Feb. 26, July 2, Sept. 17; 1863, Mar. 18, May 6, July 15, Sept. 16; 1864, Mar. 9, June 1, Aug. 17, Oct. 19, Nov. 30, Dec. 7; 1865, Mar. 22, June 7, July 12, Oct. 12; 1866, Mar. 8, Apr. 12, May 3, Aug. 30, Oct. 3, 24; 1867, Jan. 23, Feb. 13, May 8, June 12, Aug. 7, Dec. 25; 1868, Feb. 12, July 1, Aug. 19, Dec. 23; 1869, Feb. 10, Apr. 28, June 2, Sept. 29, Oct. 13; 1870, Jan. 26, June 8, Aug. 10; 1871, Mar. 15, June 14; 1872, Jan. 24, Mar. 6, June 12, July 31; 1873, Feb. 12, Aug. 27, Oct. 15, Nov. 19; 1874, Feb. 4, July 3, 15; 1875, Feb. 3, June 30, July 21, Oct. 20; 1876, Feb. 2, July 19, Sept. 20, Oct. 11, Nov. 29; 1877, Feb. 14, Apr. 11, July 4, Aug. 8, Sept. 26; 1868, Mar. 13, Sept. 11, Nov. 13; 1879, Mar. 12, Sept. 10, Nov. 19; *Taylor's Remin.,* MS., 18–19; *Woodruff's Pion. Incid.,* MS., 1; *Utah Early Records,* MS., passim; *Richard's Bibliog. Utah,* MS., 8–14; *Richards' Ear. Emig. to Utah,* MS., 1–2; *Cooke's Theatr. and Soc. Aff. in Utah,* MS., 10–11; *Hyde's Autobiog.,* MS., 2; *Never's Nev. Pion.,* MS., 1–2; *Richards' Incidents in Utah Hist.,* MS., 82; *Kanesville (Iowa) Frontier Guardian,* 1849–51, passim; 1852, Jan. 9; *Linforth's Route from Liverpool,* 1–22, 81–108, 117–20; *Hall's Mormonism Exposed,* 103–5; *Smith's Rise, Progress, and Travels,* etc., 31, 33–7; Pratt (O.), in *Utah Pioneers, 33d Ann.,* 27–8; *Id.,* in *Millennial Star,* x. 244–5; *Id., Series of Pamphlets,* no. 7, 1–16; *Pratt's (P. P.) Autobiog.,* 348–62, 383, 398, 414–26, 428–55, 458–65; *Utah Pamphlets, Religious,* no. 1, 9–14; *Utah, Perpetual Emigrating Fund,* MS., passim; *Honolulu (H. I.) Friend,* iv. 133, 151; *Olshausen's Mormonen,* 165–7, 192; *Busch's Gesch. Mormonen,* 320–36; *Bertrand's Mem. Mormonen,* 73–4, 284–90; *Richards' Narrative,* MS., 30–8; *Richards' (Mrs) Reminiscences,* MS., 34–5; Snow (Lorenzo), in *Millennial Star,* xii. 370–4; *Mackay's The Mormons,* 116, 246–7, 260–75; *Smucker's Hist. of Mormons,* 302–3; *Stenhouse's (Mrs T. B. H.) Exposé of Polygamy,* 19–25, 27–32; *Id., Tell It All,* 91, 101–2, 105–6, 118–19, 171–96, 216–18; *Gunnison, The Mormons,* 64–7, 143–4; *Burton, City of the Saints,* 5–7, 169–70, 275–9, 359–66; *Beadle's Life in Utah,* 159–67, 233–70, 527–32; *Ferris' Utah and the Mormons,* 38–9, 163–4, 178, 318–22; *Waite (Mrs C. V.), The Mormon Prophet,* etc., 144–52; *Kidder's Mormonism,* etc., 200; *Smucker's Hist. of Mormons,* 131, 297–302, 438–9; *Tucker, Mormonism,* 168, 213–21, 277; *Utah Scraps,* 5, 13, 17; *Lyon's Harp of Zion,* 17–19, 41–2, 64–6; *Snow (Eliza), Poems,* i. 219, 260–70; *Rae's Westward by Rail,* 118–43; *S. L. City Contributor,* ii. 59–61, 147–8, 177, iii. 128; *Ferris' (Mrs G. B.) The Mormons at Home,* 69–70, 163, 172–215; *Robinson's Sinners and Saints,* 167, 181, 196–205; Hedlock (R.), in *Millennial Star,* v. 154–5; *Utah Pioneers, 33d Ann.,* passim; *Juvenile Inst.,* xiv. 143, xv. 21–129, passim; *Young (Ann Eliza), Wife No. 19,* 166–80; *Remy and Brenchley, Journey to G. S. L. City,* ii. 194–226, 314–15; *Sac., Placer Times,* Aug. 1, 1849; *Lee (Jno. D.), Morm. Unveiled,* 97–108; *Vetromile, A Tour,* etc., 71–2; *Amer. Almanac,* 1857, 338; 1858, 338; *McClure, Three Thousand Miles,* etc., 184–6; *U. S. Bur. of Statis.,* no. 2, 179–80, 188; *Coyner's Letters,* ii. passim; *Todd's Sunset Land,* 182–4; Spencer (O.), in *Taylor's Govt of God,* passim; *Circular from the Twelve,* etc., 1, 3; *Young's Jour. of Disc.,* ii. 49–74; *A String of Pearls,* passim; *Spencer's Labors in the Vineyard,* 9–61; *Kimball's Gems for Young Folks,* 26–9; *U. S. Comr Ind. Aff. Rept,* 1856, 229–30; 1871, 173, 188, 191–2; *Utah, Jour. Legis.,* 1854–5, 102–3; *Acts,* 1855–6, 38–41; 1866, 111–12; *Marshall's Through Amer.,* 225–7; *Hist. Mag.,* iii. 85; *Hyde's Mormon.,* 191–2; *Stat. Rept Stakes of Zion,* MS., passim; *Nor. Amer. Rev.,* xcv. 191–2; *Dall's First Holiday,* 99–104; *Bowles' Our New West,* 211–12; *Life among the Mormons,* 159–73; *Jon-*

veaux, L'Amerique, 242–3; *Carvalho's Incid. of Travel,* 144–5; *Huber's Round the World,* 100–5; *Comettant's Civ. Inconnues,* 20–5; *Bonwick's Morm. and Silver Mines,* 106; *Codman's Round Trip,* 274; *Paddock's Fate of Mme. La Tour,* 350-2; *Ward's Husband in Utah,* 36, 111–23, 278; *Corres. Palestine Tourists,* passim; *S. L. Herald,* 1877, June 16; 1878, Oct. 31; 1879, Mar. 22, Apr. 2, Aug. 10, Nov. 13; 1880, Feb. 6, June 17; *Telegragh,* 1868, Aug. 5, 17, 18, Sept. 15, 25; *Tribune,* 1876, Apr. 29; 1877, June 2, 6, Aug. 31, Oct. 25, Nov. 2; *S. F. Alta,* 1854, Mar. 10, Apr. 27; 1856, Nov. 17, Dec. 9; 1857, May 15, June 14, Sept. 7, Oct. 13; 1858, Jan. 6, 21, Apr. 13, May 29, June 13, 27, Aug. 3, 10; 1863, July 6; 1867, June 25; 1868, Aug. 4; 1869, May 14, Nov. 6; 1870, Oct. 9; 1873, Sept. 21; 1878, July 1; *Bulletin,* 1856, July 31; 1857, May 15, Oct. 21; 1861, Oct. 3; 1863, June 29, July 9, 11, Aug. 6; 1864, Aug. 22, Nov. 11; 1865, July 29; 1866, May 14; 1867, Sept. 13; 1868, May 25; 1870, Aug. 16; 1872, June 13, Nov. 20; 1873, Apr. 12; 1877, June 15, July 17; 1881, May 4, July 8, 22, Aug. 12, Nov. 3; 1883, June 11, July 2, Sept. 5, Nov. 14, 24; *Call,* 1863, Dec. 1; 1864, July 8, 23; 1865, Feb. 21, June 21, July 13; 1867, Feb. 15, Mar. 31; 1868, July 14, Sept. 5; 1869, Aug. 21; 1870, Oct. 6; 1871, Oct. 6; 1872, May 2; 1873, July 14; 1875; *Chronicle,* 1879, Aug. 6, 20; 1884, June 22; *Examiner,* 1878, July 22; *Gold. Era,* 1865, June 18, July 25; *Herald,* 1850, Aug. 1; 1851, July 25; 1852, June 4; 1853, Feb. 12; 1854, June 26, Aug. 6; 1855, Feb. 9, June 4; *Pac. Churchman,* 1868, Nov. 5; 1870, Nov. 24; *Post,* 1876, June 3; *Times,* 1867, July 16; 1868, Aug. 6, 14, Sept. 2; 1869, Apr. 8, 13, July 3, Sept. 17; *Sac. Union,* 1855, July 2, Sept. 20; 1856, May 17, June 24; 1857, June 26, July 1, 14, 15, Aug. 1, 12, Sept. 21, Oct. 5, Nov. 5; 1858, Mar. 15; 1859, June 21, Nov. 2; 1860, Sept. 24, Oct. 6; 1861, Aug. 22, May 17; 1867, Aug. 5; *S. José Mercury,* Aug. 31, 1871; *Prescott (Ariz.) Miner,* 1873, Aug. 9; 1879, Apr. 4; *Roseburg (Or.) Plaindealer,* Aug. 2, 1879; *Astoria Astorian,* Oct. 12, 1878; *Or. City Argus,* Sept. 1, 1855; *Salem (Or.) Statesman,* 1854, Sept. 26; 1856, Dec. 2; 1857, Sept. 15, 29, Nov. 3; 1858, Jan. 5; *Helena (Mont.) Republican,* Sept. 6, 1866; *Olympia (Wash.) Standard,* Oct. 25, 1862; *Gold Hill (Nev.) News,* 1863, Oct. 28; 1866, Mar. 3; 1878, Oct. 30; 1880, June 15; 1881, July 14; *Austin Reese Riv. Reveil.,* Sept. 8, 1867; *Carson State Regis.,* 1871, Mar. 30; 1872, June 26; *Eureka Sentinel,* 1878, Jan. 13.

CHAPTER XVII.

UTAH AS A TERRITORY.

1849-1853.

UNTIL the year 1849 the Mormons were entirely
under the control of their ecclesiastical leaders, regarding the presidency not only as their spiritual head, but
as the source of law in temporal matters. Disputes
were settled by the bishops, or, as they were also
termed, magistrates of wards, appointed by the presidency. The brotherhood discountenanced litigation,
as before mentioned, but the population did not consist entirely of members of the church. There was
already in their midst a small percentage of gentile
citizens, gathered, as we have seen, from nearly all
the civilized nations of the earth. It was probable
that, as the resources of the territory were developed, this number would increase in greater ratio, and
it was not to be expected that they would always remain content without some form of civil government.
Not infrequently litigation arose among the gentiles,
or between Mormon and gentile; and though strict
justice may have been done by the bishops, it was

difficult for the latter to believe that such was the case. When the loser appealed to the presidency,[1] their judgment always confirmed the decision of the bishops, and hence was further ground for dissatisfaction. The saints regarded their courts as divinely commissioned and inspired tribunals; but not so the gentiles, by whom reports were freely circulated of what they termed the lawless oppression of the Mormons. Thus it became advisable to establish for the benefit of all some judicial authority that could not be questioned by any, whether members of the church or not, and this authority must be one that, being recognized by the government of the United States, would have the support of its laws and the shield of its protection. Further than this, if the Mormons neglected to establish such government, the incoming gentiles would do so erelong.

Early in 1849, therefore, a convention was summoned of "the inhabitants of that portion of Upper California lying east of the Sierra Nevada Mountains," and on the 4th of March assembled at Salt Lake City. A committee[2] was appointed to draught a constitution, under which the people might govern themselves until congress should otherwise provide by law. A few days later the constitution was adopted, and a provisional government organized, under the name of the State of Deseret.[3] An immense tract of country was claimed, extending from latitude 33° to the border of Oregon, and from the Rocky Mountains to the Sierra Nevada, together with a section of the territory now included in southern California, and the strip of

---

[1] The president desired no litigation among his people. 'Most of them,' he said, 'have learned that it is a condescension far beneath them, and that it opens a wide door, when indulged in, for the admission of every unclean spirit.' *Hist. B. Young*, 1852, MS., 15.

[2] Albert Carrington, Joseph L. Heywood, William W. Phelps, David Fullmer, John S. Fullmer, Charles C. Rich, John Taylor, Parley P. Pratt, John M. Bernhisel, and Erastus Snow. *Utah Early Records*, MS., 51.

[3] The word 'Deseret' is taken from the book of Mormon, and means honeybee. As it is written in the book of Ether of the people who came over the great water from the old world to the new: 'And they did also carry with them "deseret," which, by interpretation, is a honey-bee.'

coast lying between Lower California and 118° 30′ of west longitude.[4] The seat of government was to be at Salt Lake City, and its powers were to be divided, as in other states, into three branches, the legislative, executive, and judiciary. The legislative authority was to be vested in a general assembly, consisting of a senate and house of representatives, both to be elected by the people.[5] The executive power was placed in the hands of a governor, elected as elsewhere for four years;[6] a lieutenant-governor, who was chosen for the

[4] After the preamble, in which it is stated that since the treaty with Mexico all civil organization originating with that republic was abrogated, and that congress had failed to provide for the civil government of the territory lying in the great interior basin of Upper California, or any portion of it, the constitution declares: 'We, the people, grateful to the supreme being for the blessings hitherto enjoyed, and feeling our dependence on him for a continuation of those blessings, do ordain and establish a free and independent government by the name of the State of Deseret, including all the territory of the United States within the following boundaries, to wit: commencing at the 33d degree of north latitude, where it crosses the 108th degree of longitude west of Greenwich; thence running south and west to the northern boundary of Mexico; thence west to and down the main channel of the Gila River, on the northern line of Mexico, and on the northern boundary of Lower California to the Pacific Ocean; thence along the coast north-westerly to 118° 30′ of west longitude; thence north to where the said line intersects the dividing ridge of the Sierra Nevada Mountains; thence north along the summit of the Sierra Nevada Mountains to the dividing range of mountains that separates the waters flowing into the Columbia River from the waters running into the great basin; thence easterly along the dividing range of mountains that separates said waters flowing into the Columbia River on the north from the waters flowing into the great basin on the south, to the summit of the Wind River chain of mountains; thence south-east and south by the dividing range of mountains that separates the waters flowing into the gulf of Mexico from the waters flowing into the gulf of California, to the place of beginning, as set forth in a map drawn by Charles Preuss, and published by order of the senate of the United States in 1848.' *Id.*, 52–4; *Hist. B. Young*, MS., passim; *Burton's City of the Saints*, 350–1; *Mackay's The Mormons*, 258–9.

[5] Annual sessions of the general assembly were to be held, the first one to convene on the first Monday in July 1849, and thereafter on the first Monday in December, unless summoned by the governor of the state during the interim. Members of the house of representatives were elected biennially. They must be at least twenty-five years of age, free white male citizens of the United States, residents of the state for one year preceding their election, and of the district or county 30 days preceding. Senators were elected for four years, must be at least 30 years of age, and possess, as to residence and citizenship, the same qualifications as representatives. The number of senators must not be less than one third, nor more than one half that of the representatives. Each house was to choose its own officers, and a majority in each house was to constitute a quorum for the transaction of business. Each member of the assembly must take an oath or affirmation to support the constitution of the United States and of the state of Deseret, the oath to be administered by the members to each other. To the governor was granted the usual power of veto. *Utah Early Records*, MS., 54–6.

[6] The qualifications, powers, and duties of the governor were similar to those of the governors of other states.

same term, and became ex officio president of the senate; a secretary of state; an auditor; and a treasurer.[7] The judiciary was to consist of a supreme court, and such inferior courts as the general assembly might establish. A chief justice and two associate judges were to be elected by a joint vote of the senate and house of representatives.[8]

All free white male residents of the state over the age of twenty-one were allowed a vote at the first election,[9] and all between the ages of eighteen and forty-five, except those exempt by the laws of the United States and of the state of Deseret, were to be armed, equipped, and trained as a state militia, embodied a few weeks later in the Nauvoo legion, which was now reorganized and divided into two cohorts, each cohort containing four regiments, each regiment two battalions, and each battalion five companies, Daniel H. Wells being major-general, and Jedediah M. Grant and Horace S. Eldredge brigadier-generals.[10]

[7] The returns of each election for executive officials were to be sealed up and transmitted to the speaker of the house of representatives, who, during the first week of the session, must open and publish them in the presence of both houses. They were required to take the same oath or affirmation as did the members of the assembly. *Id.*, 60.

[8] The judges were to hold office for four years, or until their successors were elected.

[9] No person in the service of the U. S. government was to be considered a resident on account of his being stationed within the territory, unless otherwise provided by law. Vote was of course by ballot. *Utah, Acts Legisl.* (ed. 1855), 53.

[10] Military districts were organized, one in each county. At the first there were only sufficient men in each district for a company or battalion. As the number increased, a brigade was formed, with a brigadier-general in command, and afterward a division, in charge of a major-general. Each district made returns direct to the adjutant-general's office. *Wells' Narr.*, MS., 10. In May, Charles C. Rich and Daniel H. Wells of the committee on military affairs reported that they had organized the legion. Grant was brigadier-general of the first cohort, John S. Fullmer being colonel of the first regiment, Willard Snow major of the first battalion, and George D. Grant captain of the first company, first battalion. The first regiment consisted entirely of cavalry, and the first company, first battalion—termed life-guards—of selected men, whose duty it was to protect Salt Lake City and its vicinity from Indian depredations. Eldredge was in command of the second cohort, with John Scott as colonel of the first regiment, Andrew Little major of the first battalion, and Jesse P. Harmon captain of the first company, first battalion, called the silver grays, and composed of men over 50 years of age. The second and third companies of this battalion were artillery. The second company, second battalion, of this regiment was termed the juvenile rifle company, and consisted of youths under eighteen. *Hist. B. Young*, MS., 79;

On the 12th of March a general election was held at the bowery in Salt Lake City, this being the first occasion on which the saints had met for such a purpose. For the successful ticket 624 votes were polled, Brigham Young being chosen governor; Willard Richards, secretary; Horace S. Eldredge, marshal; Daniel H. Wells, attorney-general; Albert Carrington, assessor and collector; Newell K. Whitney, treasurer; and Joseph L. Heywood, supervisor of roads. As no session of the assembly had yet been held, the judiciary was also elected by the people, Heber C. Kimball being chosen chief justice, and John Taylor and Newell K. Whitney associate judges.[11]

The general assembly was first convened on the 2d of July, and on the 3d Willard Snow, being appointed speaker of the house of representatives, administered the oath or affirmation to the executive officials.

Thus did the brethren establish, in the valley of the Great Salt Lake, the state of Deseret. It was certainly a novel and somewhat bold experiment on the part of the saints, mustering then little more than one sixth of the number required for admission as a state, thus to constitute themselves a sovereign and independent people, with a vast extent of territory, and calmly await the action of congress in the matter. It will be remembered that they themselves had lent their aid, in howsoever slight degree, in wresting a portion of this territory from Mexico, and they did not claim more than they believed that they could in time subdue and occupy. Already they felt assured that prose-

S. L. City Contributor, ii. 177. In the Deseret News of Oct. 19, 1850, is an account of a three days' muster of the legion. In Id., Sept. 14, 24, 1850, Feb. 22, 1851, July 30, 1853, are copies of general orders issued to the legion during certain Indian troubles, of which more later. Other general orders will be found in Id., Dec. 8, 1853, Jan. 26, 1854, Oct. 3, 1855, July 11, Sept. 10, 1856, Apr. 1, 15, June 17, 1857. For additional items concerning the legion, see Id., Jan. 25, March 21, Apr. 4, 1855; S. F. Herald, Feb. 22, 1854; Sen. Doc., 32d Cong. 2d Sess., no. 33; Fisher's Am. Stat. Ann., 1854, 120; Burton's City of the Saints, 408.

[11] Utah Early Records, MS., 66; Harrison's Crit. Notes on Utah, MS., 5–6; S. L. City Contributor, ii. 177; Smith's Rise, Progress, and Travels, 19. At the same election 25 magistrates or bishops of wards were elected. The number of votes polled was 674. Hist. B. Young, MS., 1849, p. 38.

lytes would gather by myriads under the banner of the prophet. Nor was their assurance unfounded; for, as we have seen, not less than fifteen thousand arrived in the valley before the close of 1852, and were content to remain there, believing that they had found better prospects than were to be had even in the gold-fields of California, which lay but a few weeks' journey beyond.

The Mormons did not, however, hope to remain an independent republic, nor did they probably wish to do so. Well they knew that the tide of westward-bound migration, soon to be increased by the establishing of a stage line and possibly by the building of a railroad, which, as we shall see later, was already projected, would sorely disturb the peace of their mountain home unless their claims were recognized by the United States. On the 30th of April a memorial had already been signed by more than two thousand persons, asking for a "territorial government of the most liberal construction authorized by our excellent federal constitution, with the least possible delay."[12] On the 5th of July Almon W. Babbitt was elected delegate to congress in a joint session of the senate and representatives, and on the 6th a memorial was adopted by the representatives, in which the senate concurred three days later, asking for admission as a state.

The latter memorial is a somewhat remarkable document, and serves to show the slight esteem in which the Mormons held the legislature of the United States, and the unbounded confidence which they placed in themselves. Congress is reminded that it has failed

---

[12] In the preamble we read: 'Whereas we are so far removed from all civilized society and organized government, and also by natural barriers of trackless deserts, everlasting mountains of snow, and savages more bloody than either, so that we can never be united with any other portion of the country, in territorial or state legislature, with advantage to ourselves or others;...and whereas we have done more by our arms and influence than any other equal number of citizens to obtain and secure this country to the government of the United States;...and whereas a large portion of this territory has recently been ceded to the United States'—then follows the body of the petition, which was signed by Brigham on the 30th, 2,270 signatures having been appended at that date. *Utah Early Records,* MS., 75-7.

to provide a civil government for any portion of the territory ceded by the republic of Mexico; that the revolver and bowie-knife have so far been the law of the land; and that, since the gold discovery, many thousands have emigrated to California, all well supplied with the implements and munitions of war. Fears are expressed that, through the failure to provide civil jurisdiction, political aspirants may subject the government to great loss of blood and treasure in extending its authority over this portion of the national domain. The memorial declares that, for their own security, and for the preservation of the rights of the United States, the people of the state of Deseret have organized a provisional government, under which the civil policy of the nation is duly maintained;[13] also that there is now a sufficient number of individuals to support a state government, and that they have erected at their own expense a hall of legislature which will bear comparison with those in the older states. "Your memorialists therefore ask your honorable body to favorably consider their interests; and if consistent with the constitution and usages of the federal government, that the constitution accompanying this memorial be ratified, and that the state of Deseret be admitted into the Union on an equal footing with other states, or to such other form of civil government as your wisdom and magnanimity may award to the people of Deseret; and upon the adoption of any form of government here, that their delegate be received, and their interests properly and faithfully represented in the congress of the United States."[14]

[13] Then follow two clauses in the preamble in which are mentioned the natural barriers between the state of Deseret and other portions of the Union, and the importance of meting out the boundaries of states and territories in such a manner that the heads of departments may be able to communicate with all parts of the U. S. territory with as little delay as possible. Next comes a brief homily on the science of government and its application to the state of Deseret. A copy of the memorial will be found in *Id.*, 87–90.

[14] The assembly at S. L. City resolved that 2,000 copies of the memorial, together with copies of the constitution, and an abstract of all records, jour-

The remarks made in this memorial on the danger of failing to provide a civil government, at a time when California was occupied by thousands of armed and resolute men, seem the more pertinent when it is remembered that, between 1846 and 1849, occurred the great struggle in congress on the question of slavery or no slavery in the ceded territory. When congress adjourned on the 4th of March, 1849, all that had been done toward establishing some form of government for the immense domain acquired by the treaty with Mexico was to extend over it the revenue laws, and to make San Francisco a port of entry. Thus 'Upper California,' as the entire region was still termed, had at this time the same political status as was held by Alaska between 1867 and 1884, at which latter date the national legislature placed that territory within pale of the law.

It is worthy of note, also, that, in September 1849, the people of California, incensed by the dilatory action of congress, followed the example of the Mormons by framing a constitution of their own. On the 6th of that month, by order of President Taylor, General John Wilson, then United States Indian agent, held a consultation with Brigham Young, Heber C. Kimball, Willard Richards, and others, with a view to the temporary amalgamation of the states of California and Deseret, in order to avoid possible difficulties on the slavery question. It was agreed that a memorial should be drawn up, asking for a convention of all the people of Upper California, both east and west of the Sierra Nevada, for the purpose of consolidating the two states in one that should include all the territory acquired from Mexico. At the beginning of 1851 the union was to be dissolved, each state retaining its own constitution, and the people being allowed to determine for themselves to which they would belong. John Wilson and Amasa Lyman were sent as dele-

nals, and other documents pertaining to the organization of the state, be printed and furnished to members of congress. *Id.*, 90-1.

gates to California, and presented the memorial to the legislature; but the governor of that state, reviewing the proposals in his message, one by one, condemned them all. " The two communities were too far apart," he declared, " to be combined even temporarily, and Texas and Maine might as well have been made one state as Deseret and California." Thereupon the legislature refused to entertain the memorial, and nothing was accomplished.[15]

While Babbitt and his colleagues[16] are fulfilling their mission to Washington, let us inquire how justice is administered and the affairs of the people managed in the self-constituted state of Deseret, through which lay the principal routes to the gold-fields of California. Some of the emigrant parties arrived at Salt Lake City with no effects save their jaded cattle, their wagons, and a scant outfit, while others brought with them valuable merchandise, for which they hoped to find a market in the mining camps. When they made a division of their property, as frequently happened on arriving in the valley, difficulties arose among them, and the discontented parties applied for redress to the courts of Deseret. In these instances there is sufficient evidence that impartial justice was rendered,[17] and whatever the decision, appeal to a higher court was useless, for the judgment was invariably confirmed. If the losing party rebelled, or expressed in unseemly language his opinion of Mormon justice, he was severely fined, or sometimes imprisoned for a term long enough to teach him respect for the civil law.

Trespass of emigrants' cattle on the imperfectly

[15] *Cal. Sen. Jour. 1850*, 429–42, 1296; *Frontier Guardian*, May 29, 1850; *Deseret News*, July 6, 1850; *Utah Early Records*, MS., 94–5; *Hist. B. Young*, MS., 1850–1.

[16] R. L. Campbell, Oliver G. Workman, and Edgar Blodgett. *Utah Early Records*, MS., 93.

[17] Lieut Gunnison and Capt. Stansbury, who may be considered impartial observers, both state that this was the case. The former says: ' There was every appearance of impartiality and strict justice done to all parties.' *The Mormons*, 65. The latter remarks: ' Justice was equitably administered alike to saint and gentile.' *Expedition to Valley of G. S. Lake*. 130.

fenced lands of the Mormons was a frequent cause of trouble between saint and gentile. For this a fine was imposed, and the injured party must be fully recompensed. Protests were often made and the case taken before the bishops, but the only result was that the costs were added to the original demand. From the ruling of the bishop, who acted somewhat in the capacity of county court judge, an appeal was sometimes made to the bench of bishops; but seldom to any purpose. A final appeal could be made, however, to Brigham, who administered practical justice in patriarchal fashion, and whose opinion of the bishops was the reverse of flattering. " They are not fit to decide a case between two old women, let alone two men," he remarked on one occasion, while at the same time he threatened to dismiss the entire bench if they did not improve.

The organization of a civil government was intended mainly for the better control of the gentiles,[18] since, to its own members, the authority of the church sufficed. The judicial system of the saints was founded on the doctrines of the book of Mormon rather than on common law, and later, as we shall see, became obnoxious to federal judges and lawyers, none of whom succeeded in making much impression on the pockets of the community. For other reasons the Mormon code was distasteful, especially so far as it related to women. To marry out of the church was an offence. Those who had been sealed were advised not to cast in their lot with the gentiles;[19] any one found guilty of seducing a Mormon's wife must surely be put to death.[20]

[18] Although we read in *Doctrine and Covenants*, 332, ' We believe that all governments necessarily require civil officers and magistrates to enforce the laws of the same.'

[19] Gunnison relates an instance where an emigrant, on his way to California, took in his train, at her own request, a woman who represented that the person to whom she was sealed had not visited or provided for her three years, and that she wished to join a young man in California to whom she had been betrothed. When about 100 miles from Salt Lake City he was overtaken by a party of Mormons and compelled to surrender the woman. *The Mormons*, 72.

[20] At the trial of a man named Egan for killing the seducer of a Mormon

As with the judiciary so with the legislature. The people were instructed by their spiritual law-givers whom to elect as law-makers in matters temporal, and these were always the dignitaries of the church. Vote by ballot obtained, indeed, in name, but there was practically no freedom of election, and there were seldom even opposing candidates, the strife between political parties, as republican and democrat, being something unknown among them. It is this that the gentiles find fault with; though the Mormons boasted, they say, and still boast of this feature in their polity, as showing the harmony which prevails in their midst, it is in fact tyranny, and tyranny of the worst kind—an oligarchy with the form but without any of the spirit of republican institutions. Here we have one of the worst phases of Mormonism. It must be remembered, however, that a great majority of the Mormons were foreigners or of foreign extraction, most of them being men who had never enjoyed political rights, and therefore did not miss them in the land of their adoption.

In the proceedings of the general assembly of the state of Deseret there is little worthy of record, and that little relates mainly to municipal affairs, and the establishment of courts of justice, no expense being incurred for this or other branches of government.[21] During the winter of 1849–50 a portion of the territory was divided into counties, which were named Salt Lake, Weber, Utah, San Pete, Tooele, and Juab.[22] To these were added, in 1850, Iron county; in 1851, Mil-

---

woman, during the husband's absence, the judge declared: 'The principle, the only one that beats and throbs through the heart of the entire inhabitants of this territory, is simply this: The man who seduces his neighbor's wife must die, and her nearest relative must kill him.' *Id.*, 72. See also *Utah Early Records*, MS., 159–60.

[21] *Utah Early Records*, MS., 117.

[22] *Third General Epistle of the Twelve*, in *Frontier Guardian*, June 12, 1850, where the two last are spelled Yoab and Tuille. In *Smith's Rise, Progress, and Travels*, 20, it is stated that Juab county was not organized until 1852. The same statement is made in *Utah Sketches*, 106. Juab is a Ute word, signifying flat or level. San Pete, sometimes called Sanpitch, was the name of an Indian chief. Weber is named after an explorer along the river of that name. *Richards' Utah Miscell.*, MS., 1.

lard and Box Elder counties; and in 1852, Washington county. The limits of Davis county were settled as early as 1848, and the boundaries of several other counties, together with the county seats, were defined in 1850.[23] Acts were passed whereby it was ordered that county courts should be established, and judges, clerks, and sheriffs appointed for each, together with justices and constables for the several precincts. At Salt Lake City, the supreme court was to hold annual sessions, and a system of jurisprudence was instituted, whereby every case, whether civil or criminal, could receive a hearing before the proper officers, and be determined without delay, according to law and equity.

In January 1851 Salt Lake City was incorporated[24] by charter of the general assembly, powers being granted to levy and collect taxes; to establish a system of common schools; to provide a water supply; to open streets, light them, and keep them in repair; to organize a police; and to tax, regulate, restrain, or suppress gambling-houses, houses of ill-fame, and the sale of spirituous and fermented liquors.[25] Acts of incorporation were also passed, between this date and 1865, for Payson, Tooele, Palmyra, Parowan, Nephi, Springville, Lehi, Manti, American Fork, Pleasant Grove, Spanish Fork, Fillmore, Cedar City, Ogden, and Provo,[26] the privileges granted being similar to those conferred on the capital.

[23] *Utah, Compend. Laws*, 113–18. For organization of Millard co., see *Utah, Acts Legisl.* (ed. 1855), 224. It was called after Millard Fillmore; Davis co. after Capt. Davis of the Morm. battalion; Iron co., of course, from the deposits of iron ore found thereabout; and Box Elder from the trees on Box Elder creek. *Richards' Utah Miscell.*, MS., 7.

[24] Jedediah M. Grant was appointed mayor; Nathaniel H. Felt, William Snow, Jesse P. Harmon, and Nathaniel V. Jones, aldermen; Vincent Shirtleff, Benjamin L. Clapp, Zera Pulsipher, William G. Perkins, Lewis Robinson, Harrison Burgess, Jeter Clinton, John L. Dunyon, and Samuel W. Richards, councillors. *Deseret News*, Jan. 11, 1851. See also *Tullidge's Hist. S. L. City*, 77, where the name of Lewis Robinson does not appear in the list of councillors.

[25] *Utah, Acts Legisl.* (ed. 1855), 64–72; *Tullidge's Hist. S. L. City*, 72–7. In 1860 this charter was repealed, and a new act of incorporation passed. In 1864 'an act amending the charter of Great Salt Lake City' passed the legislative assembly, and was approved by the governor. *Utah, Acts Legisl.* (ed. 1866), 113–20.

[26] *Id.* (ed. 1855), 74–102, 321–57; (ed. 1866), 120–72; *Utah, Comp. Laws*, 770, 823–42; *Deseret News*, Feb. 19, 1853.

Perhaps the most remarkable feature in the proceedings of the assembly is the liberality with which valuable timber and pasture lands and water privileges were granted to favored individuals. By act of December 9, 1850, the control of City Creek and cañon was granted to Brigham Young, who was required to pay therefor the sum of five hundred dollars. A month later the right to the timber in the cañons of the mountain range that lay to the west of the Jordan was bestowed on George A. Smith. To Ezra T. Benson was granted the control of the timber in the cañons and mountains at the entrance of Tooele Valley, of the cañons between that point and Salt Lake Valley, and of the waters of Twin and Rock Springs in Tooele Valley. To Heber C. Kimball were given the waters of North Mill Creek cañon—all these grants, with the exception of the first, being made without consideration.[27]

On his arrival at Washington, Babbitt met with a somewhat cool reception. That the Mormons, not deigning to pass through the years of their political minority, should now ask admission as a state, and meanwhile constitute themselves a free and independent community, an imperium in imperio, issuing full-fledged, as did Minerva from the cranium of Jove, into the society of republics, was a proceeding that of course failed to meet with the approval of congress. The memorial, accompanied by the constitution of the state of Deseret, was presented to the senate on the 27th of December, 1849, by Stephen A. Douglas, who moved that it be referred to the committee on territories,[23] and about one month later it was so

[27] *Utah, Acts Legisl.* (ed. 1855), 63–4, 72–3.

[28] On Dec. 31st, Joseph R. Underwood of Kentucky presented a memorial from William Smith and Isaac Sheen—the former a brother of the prophet—representing themselves to be the legitimate presidents of the church of Jesus Christ of latter-day saints, and from twelve members of that church. It is there set forth that, prior to the migration from Nauvoo, 1,500 of the Mormons had taken the following oath: 'You do solemnly swear, in the presence of almighty God, his holy angels, and these witnesses, that you will avenge the blood of Joseph Smith upon this nation, and so teach your children; and that

referred.[29] On the 28th of January, 1850, it was
ordered by the house of representatives that a memorial presented by the delegate praying to be admitted
to a seat in that body be referred to the committee
on elections.[30] The committee unanimously recommended the adoption of the following resolution:
"That it is inexpedient to admit Almon W. Babbitt,
Esq., to a seat in this body, as a delegate to the
alleged state of Deseret." In a committee of the
whole the report of the comm'ttee on elections was
read, and among the reasons alleged against the admission of Babbitt the following is most cogent:
"The memorialist comes as the representative of a
state; but of a state not in the Union, and therefore
not entitled to a representation here; the admission
of Mr Babbitt would be a quasi recognition of the
legal existence of the state of Deseret; and no act
should be done by this house which, even by implica-
tion, may give force and vitality to a political organization extra-constitutional and independent of the
laws of the United States." After considerable debate the report was adopted by a vote of 108 to 77,
and the state of Deseret thus failed to receive recognition from congress.[31]

you will from this day henceforth and forever begin and carry out hostility
against this nation, and keep the same a profound secret now and ever. So
help you God.' The memorial was referred to the committee on territories.
Cong. Globe, 1849–50, xxi. 92. A second memorial from the same parties
was presented to Mr Underwood on March 14, 1850, preferring grievous complaints against the people of Deseret, and stating that the Mormons around
Council Bluffs controlled the post-office in that district and obstructed the
free circulation of newspapers. It was referred to the committee on post-
offices and post-roads. *Id.*, 524.

[29] On Jan. 22d. On the same date a bill introduced by Henry S. Foote of
Mississippi to establish suitable territorial governments for California, Deseret,
and New Mexico, and for other purposes, was referred to the committee on
territories. *Id.*, 212–13.

[30] *House Jour.*, 31st Cong. 1st Sess., 414.

[31] A report of the debates in the senate and house with regard to the
admission of Utah as a state or territory will be found in *Cong. Globe*, 1849–50,
passim. In *Id.*, xxi. 1221, is a copy of a memorial drawn up by James J.
Strang, George J. Adams, and William Marks, and presented to the senate. It
sets forth that ten thousand men, women, and children were illegally expelled
from Missouri, plundered of their effects, exiled from their homes, driven in
destitution, hunger, and want in midwinter to a distant land, passing much
of the way in the midst of foes who not only refused them shelter and food

Some action must be taken in the matter, however, for while yet the struggle on slavery was at its fiercest, the inhabitants of the territory ceded by Mexico had formed themselves into two separate states, each with its own constitution, the people of California having declared against slavery, and the people of Deseret having taken the reins into their own hands. Finally, on the 7th of September, 1850, on which date the celebrated compromise measures became law and were supposed to have settled forever the slavery question, a bill passed the senate for the admission of California as a state, without slavery, while the self-constituted state of Deseret, shorn somewhat of its proportions, was reduced to the condition of New Mexico, under the name of the Territory of Utah, with a proviso that, "when admitted as a state, the said territory, or any portion of the same, shall be received into the Union, with or without slavery, as their constitution may prescribe at the time of their admission." Two days later, both bills passed the house of representatives, and afterward received the president's signature. It is worthy of remark that the final discussion on the bill for the admission of Utah turned entirely on the question of allowing slavery in that territory, for throughout the magnificent domain acquired from Mexico, the only chance now remaining to the south was in the desert portion of the great basin, which, as Senator Seddon of Virginia remarked, "had been abandoned to the Mormons for its worthlessness."

The act to establish a territorial government for

but kept them in continual danger. 'If you tell us, as some of your predecessors told our martyred prophets while they were yet alive, that you have no power to redress our wrongs, then there is presented to the world the melancholy spectacle of the greatest republic on earth, a christian nation, acknowledging itself powerless to judge; unable to protect the right; a nation on whose righteousness half the earth rest the hopes of man, confessing that there is a power above the law.' The memorialists beg that congress pass a law granting the saints the right to settle on and forever occupy the uninhabited lands in the islands of Lake Michigan. Although there probably were no unoccupied lands in these islands in 1850, the petition was referred to the committee on public lands.

Utah[32] placed the southern boundary at the thirty-seventh parallel, the section between that limit and the thirty-third parallel being included in the territory of New Mexico, with the exception of the part transferred to California, by which state Utah was to be bounded on the west. On the north, Oregon was to remain as the boundary, and on the east the Rocky Mountains. The remaining provisions of the organic act differ but little from those framed for other territories, for New Mexico, admitted at the same date as was Utah, or for Nevada, admitted in 1861.

Thus the Mormons were shut in between the mountain walls of the great basin, the strip of coast which was claimed under the constitution of the state of Deseret, and would have included the port of San Diego, being denied to them. It is probable that, if they could have foreseen all the results of the war with Mexico, the treaty of Guadalupe Hidalgo, and the gold discovery, which now threatened to place them almost in the centre of the United States, and not, as they had intended, in a remote and untravelled solitude, they would have selected the site of their new Zion elsewhere than in the valley of the Great Salt Lake.

On the 5th of April, 1851, the general assembly of the state of Deseret was dissolved,[33] though it was

---

[32] Copies of it will be found in *U. S. Public Laws*, 31st Cong. 1st Sess., 453–8; *U. S. Charters and Const.*, ii. 1236–40; *U. S. Acts and Res.*, 31st Cong. 1st Sess., 53–8; *Utah, Acts Legisl.* (ed. 1866), 25–8; (ed. 1855), 111–19; *Deseret News*, Dec. 30, 1850; *Frontier Guardian*, Oct. 16, 1850.

[33] Ten days before, the governor had formally notified the assembly, in a special message, of the passing of the organic act. 'Upon the dissolving of this legislature,' he says, 'permit me to add, the industry and unanimity which have ever characterized your efforts, and contributed so much to the pre-eminent success of this government, will, in all future time, be a source of gratification to all; and whatever may be the career and destiny of this young but growing republic, we can ever carry with us the proud satisfaction of having erected, established, and maintained a peaceful, quiet, yet energetic government, under the benign auspices of which unparalleled prosperity has showered her blessings upon every interest.' *Linforth's Route from Liverpool*, 107–8; *Tullidge's Hist. S. L. City*, 79. On March 28th the legislature, in joint session, passed resolutions cordially accepting the legislation of congress and appropriating the union square for the public buildings. *Id.*, 80.

not until one year later that the state was officially merged into the territory of Utah. The territorial form of government was accepted only as a temporary measure, applications being made to congress for admission as a state, at intervals, as we shall see later, until 1882. Meanwhile, for many years, the shadow of a state government was preserved, the members of the ideal state assembly, after each session, reënacting and sanctioning by vote and in due form the laws which they had previously passed as a territorial legislature.

On the 1st of July a proclamation was issued by the governor, ordering that an election for members of the assembly and for a delegate to congress be held throughout the territory on the first Monday in August. On July 21st three Indian agencies were established,[34] an agent and two sub-agents, of whom the latter had already arrived, and were now assigned to their districts, having been appointed by the government. On the 8th of August three judicial districts were defined. Judges were assigned to each, and the times and places appointed for holding courts in the several counties appointed,[35] these powers being temporarily conferred on the governor by the organic act.

The appointment of governor and superintendent of

[34] The first or Parvan agency included all that lay within the limits of the territory north of the Parvan Valley and west of the Shoshones. The second, or Uintah agency, included the Shoshones, Ewintes or Uintahs, Yampas, 'and all other tribes south within said territory, and east of the eastern rim of the great basin.' The third or Parowan agency included 'all the country lying west of the eastern rim of the great basin, and south of the south line of the Parvan Valley, to the western bounds of the territory.' *Governor Young's Proclamation*, in *Utah, Jour. Legisl.*, 1851–2, 160.

[35] The first judicial district included the city and county of G. S. Lake, Tooele county, and the region east and west to the limits of the territory. Two terms were to be held each year at S. L. City, commencing on the second Tuesday of April and October. The second district included Davis and Weber counties, and the region east, west, and north. Semiannual terms were to be held at Ogden, commencing on the second Tuesday in May and December. Utah, San Pete, and Iron counties, with the country east, west, and south, formed the third district, and sessions were to be held twice a year at Provo, beginning on the second Tuesday of August and February. Each term in the several districts was to continue one week, if necessary, after which the court might adjourn to any other county if business should require it. *Id.*, 160–1.

Indian affairs was given to Brigham,[36] and it is probable that no better selection could have been made. It is at least certain that if any other had been made, the rupture which occurred a few years later between the Mormons and the United States government would have been hastened.   B. D. Harris of Vermont was chosen secretary; Joseph Buffington of Pennsylvania, chief justice; Perry E. Brocchus of Alabama and Zerubbabel Snow of Ohio, associate judges; Seth M. Blair of Deseret, United States attorney; and Joseph L. Heywood of Deseret, United States marshal.   As Buffington declined to serve, Lemuel H. Brandebury was selected to fill his place.[37]   Snow, Heywood, and Blair being Mormons, the government patronage was thus fairly distributed between saints and gentiles.   Although these appointments were made on the 20th of September, 1850, none of the gentile officials arrived in Salt Lake City until the following summer, and all were not assembled until the first week in August.   With them came Almon W. Babbitt, who was intrusted with the sum of $20,000 appropriated by congress toward the building of a state-house.   Harris also brought with him $24,000 for the expenses of the legislature.

The authorities were kindly received by the saints; and had they been men of ability and discretion, content to discharge their duty without interfering with the social and religious peculiarities of the people, all would have been well; but such was not their character or policy.   Judge Brocchus especially was a vain and ambitious man, full of self-importance, fond of intrigue, corrupt, revengeful, hypocritical.   Between

---

[36] Stenhouse, *Rocky Mountain Saints*, 275, says that Brigham owed his appointment to the recommendation of Kane. He took the oath of office Jan. 3, 1851. On the same day a special session of the county court was held, and a grand jury impanelled for the first time. The prisoners, who were emigrants en route for California, were convicted of stealing, and sentenced to hard labor, but were afterward pardoned by the executive, and sent out of the country. *Hist. B. Young*, MS., 1851, 28.

[37] Brandebury was assigned to the first district, Snow to the second, and Brocchus to the third. *Utah, Jour. Legisl.*, 1851-2, 161.

the 7th and 10th of September, a general conference of the church was held, at which the judge obtained permission to address the assembly. During his remarks he drifted into the subject of polygamy, directing this part of his discourse to the women, whom he exhorted to a life of virtue.[38] He also took to task some of the Mormon leaders, who on a previous occasion had spoken disrespectfully of the government, one of them having gone so far as to consign the late President Zachary Taylor to the nether regions.

The Mormons were sorely exasperated, and but that they were held in restraint by Brigham, would have done violence to the judge. "If," said the former, "I had but crooked my little finger, he would have been used up; but I did not bend it. If I had, the sisters alone felt indignant enough to have chopped him in pieces."[39] The governor contented himself with rebuking the judge, who, he declared, must be either profoundly ignorant or perversely wicked. It had become a matter of history throughout the enlightened world, he declared, that the government of the United States regarded the persecution of the saints with indifference, and by their silence gave sanction to such proceedings. Hundreds of women and children had in consequence gone to their graves prematurely, and their blood cried to heaven against those who had caused or consented to their death. Nevertheless, he loved the government and the constitution of the United States; but he did not love corrupt ministers of the governmel... He was indignant that such men as Brocchus should come there to lecture the people on morality and virtue, and should make such insinuations as he had done; and he repeated the statement that Zachary Taylor was then in tophet. At this last remark, Brocchus jumped to his feet and protested angrily, whereupon Heber C. Kim-

[38]*Utah Early Records*, MS., 134–5; *Stenhouse's Rocky Mountain Saints*, 276.
[39]*Journal of Discourses*, ii. 186–7. After this occurrence, Brigham frequently warned the troublesome of the danger they incurred should he but crook his finger. *Stenhouse's Rocky Mountain Saints*, 277.

ball touched him lightly on the shoulder, and told him
that he need have no doubt of it, for he would see him
when he went there.

A few days later Brigham invited the judge to attend a meeting, to be held on the 19th, and explain
or apologize for his conduct. The latter declared that
he had neither apology nor explanation to make; that
he did not intend any insult, especially to the women,
but that his remarks were deliberate and premeditated,
and that his purpose was to vindicate the government.
Then followed a lengthy reply from the governor, in
which Brocchus was severely handled, the judge and
his colleagues being thereafter condemned to social
ostracism.

Soon afterward it was reported to Brigham that
the secretary, together with Brocchus and the chief
justice, intended to return to Washington, whereupon
the governor called on them to ascertain if this was
so. He was assured that such was their purpose, and
that the secretary would also take with him the funds
placed in his hands, and the seal, records, and documents pertaining to his office. The governor considered this course illegal, and immediately issued a
proclamation declaring the result of the election,[40]
and ordering the assembly to convene on the 22d of
September, only four days later.[41] On the 24th a

---

[40] The members of the council were Heber C. Kimball, Willard Richards,
Dan. H. Wells, Jedediah M. Grant, Ezra T. Benson, and Orson Spencer for
Salt Lake co.; John S. Fullmer for Davis co.; Loren Farr and Chas R. Dana
for Weber co.; Alex. Williams and Aaron Johnson for Utah co.; Isaac Morley for San Pete co.; and Geo. A. Smith for Iron co. Representatives: Wilford Woodruff, David Fullmer, Dan. Spencer, Willard Snow, W. W. Phelps,
Albert P. Rockwood, Nathaniel H. Felt, Edwin D. Woolley, Phinehas Richards, Jos. Young, Henry G. Sherwood, Ben. F. Johnson, and Hosea Stout
for Salt Lake co.; Andrew L. Lamoreaux, John Stoker, and Wm Kay for
Davis co.; Jas Brown, David B. Dille, and Jas G. Browning for Weber co.;
John Rowberry for Tooele co.; David Evans, Wm Miller, and Levi W. Hancock for Utah co.; Chas Shumway for San Pete co.; and Elisha H. Groves
for Iron co. *Utah, Jour. Legisl.*, 1851-2, 162. Thus it will be seen there were
13 members of the council and 25 representatives. In the organic act it was
provided that there should be 26 representatives, the number of members for
either house being based on the census of 1850. George Brimhall, the remaining member for Iron co., was elected Nov. 15, 1851.

[41] This proceeding did not conflict with the organic act, which provides
—section iv.—that the first election shall be held and the members elected shall

resolution was passed, enjoining the United States marshal to take into his custody all the government funds and other public property in possession of the secretary.[42] This resolution was presented to Harris, together with an order for $500 to defray the incidental expenses of the assembly. The secretary ignored the resolution and refused to pay the order, under the plea that the members were not legally elected.

Among the grounds on which the secretary declared the election illegal was, that before the votes were cast the governor had failed to take a census of the territory, as provided in the organic act; this the latter attributed to the miscarriage of instructions and blanks, which had not even yet arrived.[43] On the other hand, it was clearly the duty of the secretary, as stated in that act, to remain in the territory during his tenure of office. Moreover, the judges organized and held a session of the supreme court before any time or place was appointed for such session by the executive or legislative authorities, and apparently for the purpose of shielding the secretary. On the 26th Brigham addressed a letter to the court, asking their opinion as to his duty with reference to the organic act, which required that the governor should take care that the laws were faithfully executed, and that the secretary should reside within the territory. No answer was returned; and after the district attorney had been

meet at such places and on such day as the governor shall appoint, but that thereafter the time, place, and manner of conducting elections, and the day for the opening of the regular sessions, shall be prescribed by law.

[42] *Hist. B. Young*, MS., 1851, p. 99.

[43] In a letter to Willard Richards, president of the council, and W. W. Phelps, speaker of the representatives, dated Sept. 25, 1851, Harris declares the election illegal on the grounds—1st. That no census had been taken; 2d. That the governor's proclamation was faulty in form and substance; 3d. That 'aliens voted indiscriminately with American citizens, and those recognized as such by the treaty with Mexico;' 4th. That 'aliens acted as officers at the polls, and were elected to office;' 5th. That 'officers not authorized to be chosen were voted for and elected;' 6th. That legal and timely notice of the election was not given; 7th. That the time and place for the first meeting were not duly appointed. *House Ex. Doc.*, 32d Cong. 1st Sess., no. 25, pp. 25-6. Albert Carrington was chosen clerk of the representatives, and James Cragun sergeant-at-arms; Howard Coray secretary of the council, and Wm H. Kimball sergeant-at-arms. *Utah, Jour. Legisl.*, 1851-2, pp. 5, 46.

ordered to file a petition, in which the request was couched in legal form and phrase, no further action was taken. Finally, on the 28th of September, the secretary, and judges Brandebury and Brocchus, set forth for Washington, taking with them the territorial seal, the records, documents, and funds, which were returned to the proper authorities.[44] On the follow-

TERRITORIAL SEAL.

[44] *Young's Despatch to Fillmore*, in *House Ex. Doc.*, 32d Cong. 1st Sess., v. no. 25, pp. 28–32. See also *Utah Early Records*, MS., 249–51. Stenhouse says that on their return Harris and his colleagues published an account of the matter, remarking 'that polygamy monopolized all the women, which made it very inconvenient for the federal officers to reside there.' This remark disgusted the authorities, and the officials met with a cool reception at Washington. *Rocky Mountain Saints*, 277–8. Their official report will be found in *House Ex. Doc.*, 32d Cong. 1st Sess., v. no. 25, pp. 8–22. The principal charge alleged against the Mormons was that a citizen of Utica, N. Y., named James Munroe, while on his way to S. L. City, was murdered by one of the saints, that his remains were brought into the city and buried without an inquest, and that the murderer was not arrested. There is no proof of this statement. In the *Utah Early Records*, MS., 161–3, we have a synopsis of their report, which was afterward circulated among the people. They alleged that they had been compelled to withdraw in consequence of the lawless acts and seditious tendencies of Brigham Young and the majority of the residents, that the Mormon church overshadowed and controlled the opinions, actions, property, and lives of its members—disposing of the public lands on its own terms, coining and issuing money at will, openly sanctioning polygamy, exacting tithes from members and onerous taxes from non-members, penetrating and supervising social and business circles, and requiring implicit obedience to the council of the church as a duty paramount to all the obligations of morality, society, allegiance, and law. On the other side, we have in *Id.*, 148–158, a copy of the letter addressed by Brigham to the president. After reviewing his proceedings and policy since taking the oath of office, the governor says: 'Mr Harris informed me, in a conversation which I had with him, that he had private instructions designed for no eye but his own, to watch every movement, and not pay out any funds unless the same should be strictly legal, according to his own judgment.' He states that there are none more friendly

ing day the legislative assembly signed a memorial praying that the vacancies be filled as soon as possible from residents of the territory.[45] Meanwhile, to prevent further derangement, and for the safe-keeping of the territorial records, Willard Richards was temporarily appointed secretary.

The successors to the runaway officials were Lazarus H. Reid of New York, who was appointed chief justice; Leonidas Shaver, who succeeded Brocchus; and as secretary, Benjamin G. Ferris. The new officials enjoyed but a brief tenure of office. After remaining in Utah for about a year, Reid returned to New York, where he died in 1855.[46] Shaver retiring to rest one night, soon after his arrival, was found dead in his room next morning, thereby giving rise to an unfounded rumor that he had been poisoned on account of a supposed difficulty with the governor.[47] Secretary Ferris, after a six months' residence, pro-

toward the government than the people of Utah, that they revere the constitution, seek to honor the laws, and complain only of their non-execution, and the abuse of power at the hands of those intrusted with them. He states that Brocchus had never even been in his district, and that, so far as the public interests were concerned, it would have been quite as well if neither the judges nor the secretary had troubled themselves to cross the plains. 'What good and substantial reason can be given that the people of this territory should be deprived, for probably near a year to come, of a supreme court, of the official seal of a secretary of state, of the official publication of the laws, and other matters pertaining to the office of secretary? Is it true that officers coming here by virtue of any appointment by the president have private instructions that so far control their actions as to induce the belief that their main object is not the strict and legal performance of their respective duties, but rather to watch for iniquity, to catch at shadows, and make a man "an offender for a word," to spy out our liberties, and by manifold misrepresentations seek to prejudice the minds of the people against us? If such is the case, better, far better, would it be for us to live under the organization of our provisional government, and entirely depending upon our own resources, as we have hitherto done, until such time as we can be admitted as a state.' A copy of the report will be found in *House Ex. Doc.*, 32d Cong. 1st Sess., v. no. 25, pp. 28–32. It is also mentioned in *Hist. B. Young*, MS., 1851, p. 136.

[45] *Utah, Jour. Legisl.*, 1851–2, p. 53; *Hist. B. Young*, MS., 1851, p. 109.

[46] At his home in Bath, Steuben co., *Waite's The Morm. Prophet*, 25; in his 40th year. *Richards' Incidents in Utah Hist.*, MS., 5.

[47] *Stenhouse's Rocky Mountain Saints*, 279. Brigham said of him: 'One of our judges, Judge Shaver, has been here during the winter, and, as far as he is known, he is a straightforward, judicious, upright man.' The heads of the church took great pains to investigate the matter, and came to the conclusion that 'he had died of some disease of the head.' See *Richards' Incidents in Utah Hist.*, MS., 78. Beadle, *Life in Utah*, 170, says that the Mormons believed him to be an opium-eater, and that he died from being suddenly deprived of that drug.

ceeded to California. The next batch of officials
were, as chief justice, John F. Kinney; associate
judges, George P. Stiles and W. W. Drummond; and
secretary, Almon W. Babbitt, who were appointed
in 1854–5. Of these, Stiles and Babbitt were Mormons, though the former was not in harmony with
the priesthood, and, as we shall see, Kinney and
Drummond play a prominent part in the history of
the saints.

Although there were no funds wherewith to pay
the members, the sessions of the legislature were continued, with occasional adjournments, until February
1852, when a special session was ordered by the governor,[48] and lasted until the 6th of March. The laws
enacted by the assembly of the state of Deseret were
declared to be in force, so far as they did not conflict
with the organic act.[49] Other laws were passed relating to the punishment of crime, the organization of
courts, the administration of estates, the training of the
militia, the incorporation of cities, the distribution of
lands, the construction of roads, bridges, and canals,
and such matters as lay within the range of territorial legislation.[50] It was determined to remove the
site of the capital from Salt Lake City[51] to some
point in the Pahvan Valley, and a committee appointed
for that purpose selected the town of Fillmore.

Memorials to congress were also adopted, one of
which asked that provision be made for the construction of "a national central railroad from some eligible
point on the Mississippi or Missouri River to San
Diego, San Francisco, Sacramento, Astoria, or such

[48] As the 40 days allowed by the organic act were about to expire, and
further time was required for the completion of the necessary business of the
session. For copy of proclamation, see *Utah, Jour. Legisl.*, 1851–2, 166.

[49] By joint resolution, approved Oct. 4, 1851. *Utah, Acts Legisl.* (ed. 1866),
108.

[50] They will be found in *Utah, Acts Legisl.* (ed. 1855), 120–232. 'It is questionable,' says Richards in his *Hist. Incidents of Utah*, MS., 8, 'whether any
of the sister territories had a code of laws framed by its own legislature that
would compare favorably with those enacted during this session.'

[51] The foundation for a state-house was laid in S. L. City Sept. 1, 1851.
Utah Early Records, MS., 133.

other point on or near the Pacific coast as the wisdom
of your honorable body may dictate." The memorialists stated that for want of proper means of transport
about five thousand persons had perished on the different routes within the three preceding years; that
there was no great obstacle to the construction of a
road between Salt Lake City and San Diego; that
at various points on the route iron, coal, and timber
were abundant; that on the completion of the line
the entire trade of China and the East Indies would
pass through the United States; and that the road
would consolidate the relations of the country with
foreign powers in times of peace, and furnish means
of defence in times of war.[52]   In 1854 a second memorial was presented, stating the opinion of the Mormons as to the best route for an overland railroad,
and a demonstration was held in favor of the project,
the inhabitants, male and female, attending en masse.
In the preceding year congress had also been petitioned to provide for the construction of a telegraph
line from some convenient point on the Mississippi or
Missouri to a suitable port on the Pacific.

As early as April 1849 Captain Howard Stansbury,
of the topographical engineers, had been ordered to
Fort Leavenworth, for the purpose of making a survey of the Great Salt Lake and an exploration of its
valley, with a view to the construction of a transcontinental railroad.   Among his party was Lieutenant
J. W. Gunnison, who was placed in charge of the
astronomical department.   Before reaching Salt Lake
City the captain was informed that no survey would
be permitted, and it was even hinted that his life
would be in danger should he attempt it.   Giving no
heed to these warnings, he at once called on Brigham,
aware that if the good-will of the governor were not

[52] A copy of the memorial will be found in *Tullidge's Life of Young*, 213–
14; *Smith's Rise, Progress, and Travels*, 22.   For other memorials passed during the sessions of 1851–2, see *Utah, Acts Legisl.* (ed. 1855), 401–5.

obtained every obstacle, short of open resistance, would be thrown in his way, that neither provisions nor labor would be furnished, and that no information would be afforded. At first Brigham demurred. He was surprised, he said, that the valley should be thus invaded so soon after the Mormons had established their settlements; he had heard of the expedition since its departure from Fort Leavenworth, and the entire community was anxious to know what was the purpose of the government. Moreover, an attaché of General Wilson, the newly appointed Indian agent for California, whose train had passed through the city a few days before, had boasted that the general was authorized to expel the Mormons from the territory. They supposed, therefore, that the arrival of the two parties was a concerted movement, and that Stansbury was sent for the purpose of dividing the land into townships and sections, and of establishing thereto the claims of government. Upon all these subjects Brigham was undeceived, and, the true object of the expedition being explained, he laid the matter before the council. Stansbury was then informed that the authorities were well pleased with the proposed exploration, that they had themselves contemplated such a measure, but could not yet afford the expense, and that they would cheerfully render all the assistance in their power.[53]

After exploring a route to Fort Hall, and making a reconnoissance of Cache Valley and the western shore of the lake, Stansbury and his men returned to Salt Lake City, and there passed the winter of 1849–50. During this winter Lieutenant Gunnison gathered most of the material for his well-known book on the Mormons, one of the most valuable and impartial works yet published by a gentile writer.[54]

[53] *Stansbury's Exped. to Valley of G. S. Lake*, 84–6.
[54] *The Mormons or Latter-day Saints in the Valley of the Great Salt Lake: A History of their Rise and Progress, Peculiar Doctrines, Present Condition, and Prospects, Derived from Personal Observation during a Residence among Them. By Lieut J. W. Gunnison of the Topographical Engineers. Philadelphia,*

Early in the spring the captain and his staff again took the field, and on the 16th of April were engaged in surveying both sides of Bear River Bay, Gunnison with several of the men being out in a storm all

1857. The first six chapters of this work are mainly devoted to a description of the valley of G. S. Lake, the civil and theocratic system of the Mormons, and the tenets of the Mormon church. In chapter vi.–vii., which complete the first part, we have an interesting description of the social condition of the settlers, and of the influence of the priesthood. The second part contains a sketch of the rise and early progress of Mormonism. Unlike most writers on this topic, Mr Gunnison appears to have given the subject some thought. 'This treatise on the faith and condition of the Mormons,' he says, 'results from a careful observation of that strange and interesting people during more than a year's residence among them in an official capacity. The writer has undertaken neither the task of criticism nor controversy. His aim is not "to shoot folly as it flies," but to let folly tire on its own pinions, and reason regain its sway over erratic feeling, when the mists of prejudice on one side and of fanaticism on the other are dispelled by the light of knowledge. For those who desire facts in the history of humanity on which to indulge in reflection, is this offered.' The book is dedicated to Captain Stansbury.

An Expedition to the Valley of the Great Salt Lake of Utah, including a Description of its Geography, Natural History, and Minerals, and an Analysis of its Waters; with an Authentic Account of the Mormon Settlement. Illustrated by numerous beautiful plates from drawings taken on the spot. Also a Reconnoissance of a New Route through the Rocky Mountains, and two large and accurate maps of that region. By Howard Stansbury, Captain Corps Topographical Engineers, U. S. Army. Philadelphia, 1855. The first six chapters of this work contain an account of the captain's journey to the valley of G. S. Lake, and of the explorations mentioned above. Travelling, as he did, during the early days of the gold-fever, his narrative is full of interest. Leaving the valley of Warm Spring Branch near Fort Laramie on July 19, 1849, he writes: 'We passed to-day the nearly consumed fragments of about a dozen wagons that had been broken up and burned by their owners; and near them was piled up in one heap from six to eight hundred weight of bacon, thrown away for want of means to transport it farther. Boxes, bonnets, trunks, wagon-wheels, whole wagon-bodies, cooking utensils, and in fact almost every article of household furniture, were found from place to place along the prairie, abandoned for the same reason.' Two days later he found the road strewn with immense quantities of white beans, which seemed to have been thrown out of the wagons by the sackful, their owners being tired of carrying them farther, or afraid to eat them from danger of cholera. Crossing a spur of the Red Buttes on the 27th, he says: 'To-day we find additional and melancholy evidence of the difficulties encountered by those who are ahead of us. ...Bar iron and steel, large blacksmith's anvils and bellows, crowbars, drills, augers, gold-washers, chisels, axes, lead, trunks, spades, ploughs, large grindstones, baking-ovens, cooking-stoves without number, kegs, barrels, harness, clothing, bacon, and beans were found along the road in pretty much the order in which they have been here enumerated.' In the seventh chapter is a description of the settlements and industrial condition of the Mormons in the winter of 1849–50, together with some excellent remarks on the polity of the state of Deseret. In the remainder of the volume we have an account of various explorations and adventures in the valley and on the return journey. In the appendices are tables of distances, papers on zoölogy, botany, geology, and paleontology, meteorological observations, and chemical analyses of mineral waters. The work is well written, sketchy and entertaining in style, and impartial in its comments on the Mormons. A German edition of it on a smaller scale was published at Stuttgart in 1854, entitled *Die Mor-*

HIST. UTAH. 30

night in the mud-flats on the eastern shore. On the 12th of August Stansbury had completed his survey, which included Great Salt Lake with its islands, Lake Utah, the Jordan, and several of its tributaries, his observations extending over an area of more than five

monen—Ansiedlungen, die Felsengebirge und der grosse Salzsee, nebst einer Beschreibung der Auswanderer—Stratze und der interessanter Abenteuer der Auswanderungen nach jenen Gegenden Geschildert auf einer Untersuchungs Expedition.

Among other works covering about the same period as Lieut Gunnison's book, may be mentioned the following: *The Mormons, or Latter-day Saints; with memoirs of the Life and Death of Joseph Smith, the American Mahomet. Edited by Charles Mackay. Fourth edition, London, 1856.* The first edition of this work was published in 1851. It claims to have been, as indeed it was, the first work upon the subject which could justly be entitled a historical statement of the case. It is a work full of valuable information, much of it of an original character and nowhere else existing. It is written with marked ability, and in a spirit of exceeding fairness, though taking decidedly an anti-Mormon view. Yet the author says: 'It presents the history of Joseph Smith, a great impostor or a great visionary, perhaps both, but in either case one of the most remarkable persons who has appeared on the stage of the world in modern times.' In the fourth edition, 'the whole of the doctrinal chapter, which formed the conclusion of the work in the previous editions, has been excluded in the present instance to make room for matter of a more historical character. Polygamy, which the Mormons attempted to deny, or explain by the euphemism of the spiritual-wife doctrine, has now been unblushingly avowed; and this practice, which has become the most distinctive, as it is the most odious, characteristic of the sect, has received more notice in this edition than was bestowed upon it in the original publication.'

The Religious, Social, and Political History of the Mormons, or Latter-day Saints, from their Origin to the Present Time; containing full statements of their Doctrines, Government, and Condition, and memoirs of their founder, Joseph Smith; edited with important additions, by Samuel M. Smucker. New York, 1860. What it is that Mr Smucker edits, and to what he makes additions, does not appear, but the student with this book and that of Mackay's before him soon discovers that the former is taken almost verbatim from the latter, and without a word of credit. Smucker evidently worked at so much a day for the publishers, who desired something by that name to sell. Considering the circumstances, the work is fairly done; the saints are abused with moderation and decorum, and the publishers probably made money out of it.

Origin, Rise, and Progress of Mormonism. Biography of its Founders and History of its Church. Personal Remembrances and historical collections hitherto unwritten. By Pomeroy Tucker. Palmyra, N. Y., 1867. This author claims a personal acquaintance with Joseph Smith and the Smith family since their arrival at Palmyra, the birthplace of the writer, in 1816. He also knew Martin Harris, Oliver Cowdery, and others of the first converts. He was editorially connected with the *Wayne Sentinel* when the book of Mormon was printed in the office of that journal. His book is published for the purpose of proving Joseph Smith an impostor and the book of Mormon a fraud. The author has ability, and is accustomed to writing; he has done his work well. He employs with no small skill and success that most powerful of weapons in the hand of a ready writer—sarcasm. Much space is devoted to sustaining the Spaulding theory. Historically, the book is of little value after the departure of the Mormons from the vicinity of the writer's home; but up to that point, and not forgetting that it is the plea of an advocate rather than the decision of a judge, it may be called a first-class authority.

thousand square miles.[55]   He then resolved to search
out on his return journey some practicable route to
the southward of South Pass, though a part of it
lay through the territory where Sioux, Blackfoot,
Snake, and Utah were used to meet in conflict.   Disposing of his wagons and spare instruments to the
Mormons, by whom he was furnished with a sufficient
escort, he bade them a kindly farewell, and returned
by way of Bridger's and Cheyenne passes to Fort
Leavenworth.

The route recommended by Stansbury for the portion
of a transcontinental railroad between the Missouri,
near Independence, and Salt Lake City was by way
of the Republican fork and the south fork of the
Platte; thence by way of Lodge Pole Creek, and
skirting the southern extremity of the Black Hills to
the Laramie Plains; thence crossing the north fork of
the Platte to South Pass; thence by way of Bear
River Valley to Fort Bridger; from that point by
way of Black Fork and turning the Uintah Range
to the Kamas prairie, whence the route to the capital
lay through the valley of the Timpanogos.[56]

In 1853 Gunnison, who had now been promoted to
the rank of captain, was ordered to survey a route
farther to the south, by way of the Huerfano River
and the pass of Coochetopa; thence through the valleys of the Grand and Green rivers; thence to the
vegas de Santa Clara and the Nicollet River; thence
northward on a return route to Lake Utah, from
which point he was to explore the most available

[55] Stansbury's field-work is thus summarized: 1. The selection and meas-
urement of a base-line 6 miles in length; 2. The erection of 24 principal
triangulation stations; 3. The survey of G. S. Lake, the shore-line of which
is stated at 291 miles; 4. The survey of the islands, 96 miles; 5. The survey of Lake Utah, 76 miles; 6. The survey of the Jordan and some of its
tributaries, 50 miles, making in all 513 miles; 7. The observations from different triangular stations extending from the northern extremity of G. S. Lake
to the southern boundary of the valley of Lake Utah. *Exped. to Valley of G.
S. Lake*, 216.

[56] *Id.*, 227, 261–3; *Gunnison's The Mormons*, 152.   There is little differ-
ence in the line of route laid down by either.   Stansbury suggests that from
Kamas prairie the road might fork, one branch descending the Wasatch
Range by the Golden Pass, and the other following the Timpanogos Valley.

passes and cañons of the Wasatch Range and South
Pass. The party included Lieutenant E. G. Beckwith, R. H. Kern as topographer and artist, Sheppard
Homans astronomer, Dr James Schiel surgeon and
geologist, F. Creutzfeldt botanist, J. A. Snyder assistant topographer, a number of employés, and an
escort of mounted riflemen in charge of Captain R.
M. Morris. On the 24th of October the party was
encamped on the Sevier River, fifteen or eighteen
miles from the point where it discharges into the lake
of that name, and on the following day Gunnison
started out to explore the lake, accompanied by Kern,
Creutzfeldt, the guide, and a corporal with six men of
the escort, the remainder of the party, under Captain
Morris, proceeding up the river in a north-easterly
direction. The following day several men of Morris'
detachment were sent to ascertain whether a route
were practicable northward from that point to Great
Salt Lake. While the men were yet within a hundred
yards of camp, the corporal came running toward them,
breathless and exhausted, and sinking to the ground,
gasped out a few broken sentences, the purport of
which was that Gunnison and his party had been massacred by Indians, and that, as far as he knew, he was
the only survivor. Morris at once ordered his men
to arm and mount, and within half an hour was on his
way to the scene of the disaster; meanwhile a second
member of Gunnison's escort reached camp on horseback, and two other survivors came in later.

Gunnison had encamped, with no thought of danger, in a sheltered nook under the river bank, where
wood and pasture were abundant. He was aware that
a large band of Pah Utes was in the neighborhood,
and their camp-fires had been seen daily since entering the valley of the Sevier. A recent quarrel with
an emigrant band had resulted in the killing of one of
the natives and the wounding of two others, but they
had made no raids on the Mormon settlements, and
peace had recently been confirmed at a parley held

with some of them by an agent of Brigham. At daybreak all arose and prepared for their day's work, but while seated quietly at breakfast the men were startled by a volley of rifles, a flight of arrows, and the yells of a band of Pah Utes, who had crept, under cover of the bushes, to within twenty-five yards of the spot. The surprise was complete. In vain Gunnison, running forth from his tent, called out to them that he was their friend. He fell, pierced by fifteen arrows, and of the rest only four escaped, after being pursued for several hours by the Indians.[57]

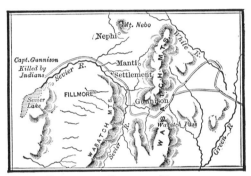

SITE OF THE GUNNISON MASSACRE.

When Captain Morris reached the scene of the massacre no bodies were found. There was hope, therefore, that others were still alive, and a signal-fire was lighted to assure them of safety; but all the night long no response was heard, nor any sound save the howling of wolves. Still the men remained at their post, though not more in number than the party that had been massacred. At daylight the corpses were discovered, and though none were scalped, they were mutilated with all the atrocity common to the most savage tribes. Some of them, among whom was that of Captain Gunnison, had their arms hacked off at the

[57] One of the survivors was thrown from his horse into a bush, where he lay for several hours, the Indians passing him on every side. *Beckwith*, in *Rept. Explor. and Surveys*, ii. 74.

elbow, their entrails cut open and torn by wolves, and were in such condition that they were buried where they lay. It is related that Gunnison's heart was cut out while he was yet alive, and that it was so full of blood that it bounded on the ground.

By many the Gunnison massacre has been and is still ascribed to the agency of the Mormons; and it has even been asserted that Mormons, disguised as Indians, were among those who committed the deed. Here we have a fair specimen of the hundreds of defamatory stories which have been told about the Mormons from the beginning. In this instance not only is there no valid proof against them, but there are many circumstances pointing in the opposite direction,[58] one of them being that among the slain was a Mormon guide. The Gunnison massacre was brought on by gentiles; it was the direct result of the killing of the Pah Ute by California emigrants. As no compensation had been made to his tribe, they avenged themselves, as was their custom, on the first Americans— for thus they termed all white men, other than Mormons—whom they found in their territory.[59] The

[58] A full account of Gunnison's survey, prepared mainly by himself, and of the massacre will be found in *Beckwith's Reports*, in *Id.*, ii. Lieut Beckwith writes: 'The statement which has from time to time appeared or been copied in various newspapers of the country, since the occurrence of these sad events, charging the Mormons or Mormon authorities with instigating the Indians to, if not actually aiding them in, the murder of Captain Gunnison and his associates is, I believe, not only entirely false, but there is no accidental circumstance connected with it affording the slightest foundation for such a charge.' Captain Morris, in his official report to the adjutant-general, says nothing about the Mormons being implicated in the matter. See *House Ex. Doc.*, 33d Cong. 1st Sess., no. 18, pp. 5–6. The names of those who were killed, besides Captain Gunnison, were R. H. Kern, F. Creutzfeldt, William Potter, a Mormon guide, privates Caulfield, Liptoote, and Mehrteens, mounted riflemen, and an employé named John Bellows. *House Ex. Doc.*, 33d Cong. 1st. Sess., no. 18, pp. 6. For other accounts and comments on the Gunnison massacre, see *Möllhausen, Tagelbuch*, 429–30; *Carvalho's Incidents of Travel*, 196–9; *S. F. Alta*, June 25, 1854, Nov. 11, 1857; *S. F. Herald*, May 7, 1855.

[59] On hearing of the massacre, Brigham took measures for the recovery of the property and the disposal of the bodies. Gunnison was somewhat of a favorite among the Mormons. In the *Deseret News* of Nov. 12, 1853, where is a copy of Beckwith's report of the massacre, is the following: 'We feel to commiserate deeply with the friends of those who have been so suddenly and unexpectedly cut off, but more especially with the wife and children of Captain Gunnison, who was endeared to us by a former and fondly cherished acquaintanceship in 1849–50, while he was engaged with Captain Howard Stansbury in the survey of the Great Salt and Utah lakes.' The following is

survey of which Gunnison was placed in charge was completed by Beckwith and the other survivors of the party, who reached Salt Lake City by way of Nephi, Payson, and Provo.

The Mormon maxim with regard to the Indians was that it was cheaper to feed than to fight them. Hence their intercourse with the Utes and Shoshones [60] was generally peaceable. [61] They taught them

a sworn statement from the private journal of Anson Call, a Mormon residing in Fillmore City in 1853, and in 1883 one of the most prominent citizens of East Bountiful, Davis co.: 'From Fillmore to the site of the Gunnison massacre is about 35 miles. The settlements were in a state of alarm on account of the "Walker war," and just before the massacre a party of emigrants from Missouri, on their way to California, came to Fillmore. During their stay they made many threats concerning the Indians, and declared repeatedly that they would kill the first one who came into their camp. I remonstrated with them and cautioned them. After this party had left, I learned that some Indians around had gone into their camp, and that they had killed two of them and wounded three others. This so enraged the Indians that nothing short of blood would appease their wrath. At this time Capt. Gunnison and his exploring party came along. I told him what had happened, and spoke of the exasperation of the Indians. He expressed deep regret, and remarked: "The Indians are sure to take their revenge."' Then follows an account of the massacre, and of the burial of the dead. Call states that Captain Gunnison's remains were interred at Fillmore. At Lieut Beckwith's request he furnished men for an express to Brigham with news of the massacre. *Utah Co. Sketches*, MS., 163–8. Call's statement is confirmed by Wells in his *Narr.*, MS., 15–19. Wells states that Capt. Gunnison's brother at first believed the report that the Mormons were implicated, and met Call by appointment at S. L. City. The latter produced his diary, from which he read extracts, and after a full investigation, declared himself satisfied that the Mormons had nothing to do with the massacre. F. D. Richards says that he and Erastus Snow rescued four of the survivors near Cedar Springs. *Hist. Incidents of Utah*, MS., 42–3.

[60] Although the Indian tribes of Utah were at this period very numerous, the word 'Utahs' was commonly applied to those south of G. S. Lake, and 'Shoshones' or 'Snakes' to those north and west of the lake, especially in the valley of the Humboldt River. The Snakes and Utahs were both Shoshone tribes. See my *Native Races*, i. passim.

[61] *Richards' Narr.*, MS., 47; *Wells' Narr.*, MS., 13; *Young's Early Experiences*, MS., 5–6. In the latter MS. it is related that when the pioneers entered the valley Indians were very numerous, but that the only trouble which occurred in early times was with a lame and vicious savage whom the Mormons named 'the old cripple.' One day this man entered Mrs Young's cabin during her husband's absence, and asked for some biscuits. She gave him all that she could spare, and when he demanded more replied that she had none. The Indian then strung his bow and threatened to shoot her. 'Wait a moment,' said Mrs Young, 'and I will bring more biscuits.' Stepping into an adjoining shed, she let loose at him a huge mastiff, which seized him by the leg, causing him to howl with pain. The savage now gave up his arrows, whereupon his wound was dressed and he was sent about his business. He was never seen again in that neighborhood. This incident is also related in *Tullidge's Women of Morm.*, 442.

Lorenzo Dow Young, brother to Brigham, by whom this MS. was presented to me, arrived in the valley on the 24th of July, 1847, with the pioneer

how to till their lands; they assured them that they
would suffer no wrong; but they also told them that if
they inflicted wrong, punishment would follow. Nevertheless, when the tide of gentile emigration set in for
California, outbreaks among the Indians were of frequent occurrence. The troubles caused to the early
settlers in the Utah Valley in 1849–50 have already
been mentioned. In the autumn of the latter year,
a disturbance occurred in the northern part of the territory, caused by a party of emigrants, who, while encamped on the Malade River, shot two Shoshone
women as they were crossing the stream on horseback,
stole their horses, and then set forth on their journey.
Thereupon the warriors of the tribe began to commit
depredations on the northern settlements, slaying a
Mormon named Campbell, who was engaged in building a saw-mill, near Ogden, and threatening to massacre the inhabitants of that village. General Eldredge
of the Nauvoo legion, being sent with a detachment
to the scene of action, found that the Shoshones had
moved northward, carrying off a number of horses

band, and encamped near the present site of Main Street, S. L. City. During my visit to Utah, in August 1884, he described to me the cabin that he
built soon after his arrival near the spot where the 'Beehive' later stood.
Its roof was of dirt, and its flooring of planks, sawn by his own hands. This
was the first house built in the city, and as it had glass for windows, was
long considered one of the most comfortable. Around this residence locust
trees were planted, but only those were saved which were covered with
buckets. At the time of my visit I found Mr Young living at his country
home, within two or three miles of the capital, in company with the eldest
of his three wives, Harriet Page Wheeler Young, a native of Hillsborough,
N. H., who was baptized into the faith in Feb. 1836, and was married to Lorenzo at Nauvoo in 1844, a few weeks before the assassination of Joseph Smith.
The house was long and narrow, plainly built and furnished, indicating no surplus of this world's goods. Mrs Harriet Young is the heroine of the story related above. In a double brick house near by lived the other wives of Mr
Young. They were honest, good-natured, credulous people, and were thoroughly contented with their lot. Their simple needs were all supplied; their
barn was filled with hay, and the yard well stocked with poultry. All the
wives addressed Lorenzo as 'father,' and the entire party seemed to form one
patriarchal family, living quietly, happily, and in accordance with their faith.
At this date Mr Young was 77 years of age; he was a man of medium height,
ruddy, and cheerful of countenance, with kindly blue eyes, thin, white, curly
locks, and except for a slight deafness, showed little trace of age. He said that
on his 75th birthday he counted 122 living descendants, but had since lost
track of the number of his grandchildren. He expressed a wish that the doctrine of polygamy should be studied in the light of the old testament, and the
facts laid bare by some honest and impartial inquirer.

and cattle. A number of Utahs were on the ground, and a portion of them were made prisoners and retained as hostages, the tribe being advised to move south to their usual place of abode and avoid all further intercourse with the Shoshones. Thus the matter was settled without further bloodshed.[62]

No serious outbreaks occurred among the Indian tribes during 1851–2, though emigrant parties, both Mormon and gentile, were sometimes molested,[63] and in October of the former year, the mail for California was captured within a few days after leaving Salt Lake City.[64]

During 1853 and a portion of the following year occurred what was known as the Walker war, in which the Mormons suffered serious loss of life and property throughout their territory. Walker, a favorite chief of the Utahs, was at this time a man in the prime of life, one versed in all manly exercises, an excellent shot, and a capital judge of horse-flesh. In addition to several of the native dialects, he could converse fluently in Spanish, and make himself understood in English. Long before the advent of the Mormons he made frequent raids into the Mexican states, where he laid the people under contribution, and took captive persons of rank and condition whom he held to ransom. When setting forth on one of these forays he was attired in a suit of the finest broadcloth, cut

[62] *Deseret News*, Sept. 21, 1850; *Smith's Rise, Progress and Travels*, 28. Smith states that on arriving at the spot, the detachment ascertained the cause of the outbreak from some friendly Indians, and restored peace by reimbursing the Shoshones.

[63] When near a branch of the Loupe fork of the Platte, Orson Hyde and his party were robbed by a band of 300 Pawnees, the plunder amounting to about $1,000. *Frontier Guardian*, Aug. 22, 1851. In 1852 there was also some trouble in Tooele co. between the settlers and the Indians, and a company of the legion was sent there, but the Indians got the best of it, carrying away the Mormons' cattle. *Wells' Narr.*, MS., 13.

[64] The party with the mail left S. L. City on Oct. 1st, and reached Goose Creek on the 6th. Here they encamped and lighted a fire for the first time. In the morning, when ready to start, 200 or 300 Indians made their appearance, and pressed so closely on the mail-wagon that the men were forced to abandon it and retreat, some on mules and some on foot, keeping up a fight with the Indians for several miles. At least five of the assailants were killed. *S. F. Alta*, Nov. 2, 1851. In *Id.*, June 2, 5, 1852, are reports of murders committed by Indians.

in the latest fashion, and donned a cambric shirt and a beaver hat. Over this costume he wore his gaudy Indian trappings, and as he rode at the head of his braves, with their gayly accoutred steeds and embroidered saddles glittering with metal ornaments, he might have been taken for a Soldan among the dusky Painims of the west.[65]

At first Walker received the exiled saints with open arms, gave them information as to the nature of the country, advised them where to establish settlements, and guarded them from depredation. But when he saw that they had occupied his choicest lands; when game disappeared from the cañons and mountain sides; and when his people were shot down without provocation, and their cattle stolen by bands of emigrants, his friendship turned to hate, and he longed to rid himself of the white man. On the 17th of July, 1853, hostilities broke out, and continued with little interruption until winter. During this year twelve Mormons were killed and a number wounded; about four hundred cattle and horses were stolen, and the expense incurred in building forts and removing settlements amounted to $200,000.[66] That the loss was not still greater was due to the vigilance of

[65] Richards and others state that even after the gold discovery Walker made raids into California, and that on one occasion, about the year 1849, the people turned out en masse to capture him and his band in their lurking place among the mountains. The chief quietly secured their horses and trappings at dead of night and returned with them to Utah. *Utah Notes*, MS., 8. Wells, *Narr.*, MS., 17, says that Walker did not inherit the chieftainship, but obtained it through the success of his raids into California. When an Indian possessed cattle and horses enough to mount and feed others, he was at once regarded as a big man among the Utahs, and thus Walker obtained his prestige. Ora, now dead, was the head chief of the Ute nation, and Uintah was a great chief among the Utahs.

[66] Governor's message, in *Utah, Jour. Legisl.*, 1853–4, 121–2. On July 17th the Utahs made a raid on Springville, but, the inhabitants being forewarned, no damage was done. On the 18th Alexander Keele, who was on sentry near Payson, was shot dead by Arapeen, Walker's brother. The Indians then moved up Peteetneet Cañon, firing on the settlers as they passed. On the 19th Col Conover started from Provo with 150 men to assist the smaller settlements. On the same day the savages attempted to surprise the settlement at Pleasant Creek, and stole horses and cattle at Manti and Nephi. On the 20th the guard at Nephi was fired upon. On the 24th Clark Roberts and John Berry were wounded at Pleasant Creek, while on their way to Provo, in charge of an express. On the 23d Conover sent forth a scouting party

the governor, for in the spring an émeute had already been threatened, and was only prevented by the prompt measures of Brigham, who visited the Indian camps in person, and for a time averted the outbreak.

Among the causes that led to disturbance with the Utahs was the presence of trading parties from New Mexico, who supplied the Indians with horses, fire-arms, and ammunition, often taking in exchange Indian women and children, who were afterward sold into slavery.[67] To remedy this evil, an act was passed by the Utah legislature in 1852, legalizing the enforced apprenticeship of Indian children, but only for the purpose of inducing the brethren to purchase those who would otherwise have been sold to the Mexicans or abandoned by their parents.[68] So frequent were

which encountered a band of 20 or 30 Indians near Pleasant Creek, and killed six of them. On the night of August 10th a party under Lieut Burns, en-camped on Clover Creek, was attacked, and one of them wounded, several animals being lost. On the 17th four men, who were hauling lumber near Parley Park, were fired on and two of them killed. *Deseret News*, July 30, Aug. 25, 1853; *Wells' Narr.*, MS., 56. Sept. 30th, four men on their way to Manti with ox teams loaded with wheat were killed and mutilated at Uintah Springs. Oct. 2d, eight Indians were killed and others captured in a skirmish at Nephi. Oct. 4th, two Mormons named John E. Warner and William Mills were killed at the grist-mill near Manti. *Id.*, Oct. 15, 1853. Oct. 31st, news of the Gunnison massacre was received at Salt Lake City by letter from Capt. Morris. *Id.*, Nov. 12, 1853. For other accounts of Indian disturbances, see *S. F. Herald*, Sept. 30, Dec. 24, 1853; *S. F. Alta*, Aug. 27, Sept. 30, 1853; *Olshausen's Mormonen*, 186-7.

[67] In the *Deseret News* of Nov. 15, 1851, it is stated that a copy of a license granted to one Pedro Leon, dated Santa Fé, Aug. 14, 1851, and signed by James S. Calhoon, superintendent of Indian affairs, was shown to Willard Richards, who states that on the 3d of that month Leon, with 20 Mexicans, was at Manti, for the purpose of trading horses for Indian children, and that two other companies were about to follow. Wells, *Narr.*, MS., 23, and Richards, *Hist. Incidents of Utah*, MS., 25-6, state that the Utahs were in the habit of stealing children from the Piutes and selling them to Mexican traders. The latter relates that Arapeen had a stolen child who was taken sick, and as the savage could not sell it, he took it by the heels, swung it round his head, and dashed out its brains. The act was witnessed by several Mormons, who were only prevented from shooting him on the spot through fear of provoking a general uprising. By virtue of his authority as governor and superintendent of Indian affairs, Brigham Young forbade all trading of this nature, and told the Mexicans that their license was not valid. *Hist. B. Young*, MS., 1851, 115.

[68] In the preamble it is stated that the purchase of Indian women and chil-dren by Mexican traders has been carried on from time immemorial; that it is a common practice with Indians to gamble away their women and children; that the captives thus obtained, or obtained by war or theft, were often car-ried from place to place, packed on horses or mules, lariated out to subsist on grass or roots, bound with thongs of rawhide, until their feet and hands were

the visits of the slave-traders, that in April 1853 a proclamation was issued by the governor, ordering the arrest of all strolling parties of Mexicans, and forbidding any Mexican to leave the territory until further advised.[69]

Between 1854 and 1856 troubles with the Indians were less frequent,[70] and these were mainly with the

swollen; and when they fell sick, were frequently slain by their masters. It was therefore enacted that whenever any white person within the territory should have in his possession an Indian prisoner, whether by purchase or otherwise, he should immediately take his captive before the probate judge or one of the selectmen, and if in their opinion the applicant was a fit person to retain and educate him, he was to be bound by indenture for a term not exceeding 20 years, during which he must be decently clad at the owner's expense, and attend school for three months in each year. Selectmen were authorized to obtain such prisoners and have them trained to useful vocations. A copy of the act will be found in *Utah, Acts Legisl.* (ed. 1866), 87-8, and *Burton's City of the Saints*, 297-9, note. In a message to the legislature, dated Jan. 6, 1852, Brigham, reviewing at length the internal policy of the territory, said that the system of slavery was obnoxious to humanity, but that the negro should serve the seed of Abraham, and not be a ruler nor vote for men to rule over him. 'My own feelings are, that no property can or should be recognized as existing in slaves, either Indian or African.' *Utah, Jour. Legisl.*, 1851-2, pp. 108-10. Nevertheless, a few years later, there were slaves in Utah. Horace Greeley, during an interview with Brigham, in 1859, asked him, 'What is the position of your church in regard to slavery?' 'We consider it,' he answered, 'of divine institution.' 'Are any slaves now held in this territory?' 'There are.' 'Do your territorial laws uphold slavery?' 'These laws are printed—you can read for yourself. If slaves are brought here by those who owned them in the states, we do not favor their escape from the service of those owners.' *Greeley's Overland Journey*, 211-12. 'The constitution of Deseret is silent upon this; we mean it should be. The seed of Canaan cannot hold any office, civil or ecclesiastical. They have not wisdom to act like white men...The day will come when the seed of Canaan will be redeemed.' *Hist. B. Young*, MS., 1852, p. 2.

[69] A copy of the proclamation will be found in the *Deseret News* of April 30, 1853.

[70] On Jan. 1, 1854, a wagon-train on its way from S. L. City to California for supplies was attacked by Indians, and three Mormons were wounded. When the party arrived at San Bernardino they had only 30 out of nearly 100 head of stock remaining. *S. F. Alta*, Feb. 22, 1854. In Sept. certain Indians were arrested for killing two boys, named William and Warren Weeks. On Sept. 4th Brigham returned from an official visit to the Shoshones. The Indians declared that they desired peace, and had always done so, except when maltreated by passing emigrants. *Deseret News*, in *Id.*, Oct. 19, 1854. During this trip Brigham met the chief Walker at Chicken Creek, made a truce with him, and gave him presents. Walker afterward became very friendly to the Mormons. During the negotiations Walker said, through an interpreter, that Brigham was a great chief, and that he was himself as great —holding up both thumbs to indicate that both were equally great. By the terms of the truce Walker agreed to give up all the stolen horses, or all that could be found. *Wells' Narr.*, MS., 21. On the 17th of August, while a train of Mormon emigrants was passing a Sioux encampment near Fort Laramie, one of their cattle strayed into the Indian camp and was killed. The Mormons complained to the commandant, who ordered Lieut J. L. Grattan to

Utahs. On the 7th of August, 1855, a treaty was negotiated by the Indian agent with the Shoshones, whereby, for a consideration of $3,000, peace and friendship were to be confirmed with the United States, and the passage of United States citizens through their territory without molestation was to be guaranteed.[71] In January of this year the chief Walker died,[72] at peace, as it seems, with the Mor-

proceed to the camp with two howitzers and 29 men of the sixth infantry, and arrest the offender, if it could be done without unnecessary risk. This at the instance of a Sioux chief named The Bear, who stated that the culprit would doubtless be surrendered. Arriving at the outskirts of the camp, Grattan sent for The Bear, who said that his people had determined not to deliver up the accused; whereupon the lieutenant resolved to enter the camp and arrest him at all hazards. Thus far the statements of witnesses agree, but from this point there is a conflict of testimony. It can only be stated with certainty that a fight ensued, in which the lieutenant and his entire command were killed. The whole matter wears the appearance of a well-planned attempt on the part of the Indians to gain possession of Fort Laramie, and of the warehouses of a trading company near by, where the Sioux were awaiting the arrival of the Indian agent to distribute their annuity goods. In the latter attempt they were successful. Various reports of the massacre will be found in *House Ex. Doc.*, 33d Cong. 2d Sess., viii. no. 63. See also *Rept of Sec. of Inter.*, in *Id.*, i. pt i. 224–5. Toward the end of the year a party of Crows captured the mail from S. L. City, destroyed the mail-bags, and secured plunder to the amount of $12,000. *S. F. Alta*, Jan. 1, 1855. In Sept. three Mormons were murdered near the Elk Mountains. For particulars, see *Deseret News*, Oct. 10, 17, 1855; *S. F. Alta*, Nov. 8, 1855; *S. F. Bulletin*, Nov. 9, 1855. In Feb. 1856 there was some trouble with Indians in the Utah and Cedar valleys, during which a Mormon named George Carson was mortally wounded, and two herdsmen killed. *Deseret News*, Feb. 27, March 5, 1856. In May of this year Carlos Murray and his family were massacred in Thousand Spring Valley. *Ind. Aff. Rept*, 1856, 227–30. It is probable that this massacre was caused by the misconduct of California-bound emigrants. In *House Ex. Doc.*, 34th Cong. 1st Sess., i. pt i. 519, Garland Hurt, then Indian agent, in his report to Brigham dated Sept. 30, 1855, says: 'On our return trip we were exceedingly anxious to meet with some Indians whom we had reason to believe were haunting the road between the Humboldt and Bear River. In Thousand Spring Valley we saw but one, and had to chase him on horseback before we came up with him. I asked him why he and his people were so wild when I came so far just to see them and give them presents. He said they were afraid we were Californians and would kill them.'

[71] *Id.*, 267. The treaty was not ratified, and only a copy of it was received at Washington.

[72] At Meadow Creek, near Fillmore. In a letter to Brigham, dated Fillmore City, Jan. 29th, David Lewis says that on the previous day he met Walker, who was so feeble that he had to be supported on his horse. He asked whether Brigham 'talked good.' Lewis replied that he talked very good, and gave him a letter and a number of presents from the governor. The chieftain then went his way, asking Lewis to visit him at Meadow Creek the next morning. Before daybreak a number of Indians came running into the fort (at Fillmore) with news of Walker's death. Walker, in his last words, asked his people not to kill the cattle of the Mormons or steal from them. *Deseret News*, Feb. 8, 1855. For biography and portrait of Walker, see *Linforth's Route from Liverpool*, 104–5; for mention of his death, *Incidents in*

mons, and was succeeded by his brother Arapeen.[73]
Thus the leading spirit of the Utahs was taken from
their midst, and starved though the Indians were,[74]
they ceased for a time from open hostility, contenting
themselves with occasional raids on the Mormons'
cattle and horses, and accepting with thankfulness
such small presents as the Indian agents were pleased
to give them.[75]

It is worthy of note that the United States
should have deemed Utah fit to be organized as a
territory, and should yet have considered the sum of
$3,000 a fair compensation to the Indian tribes for
its occupation. Though no territory was of course
acquired by the informal treaty with the Shoshones,
Utah was then the abode of more than forty thousand

Utah Hist., MS., 63; *Millennial Star*, 269-70; *S. F. Alta*, Apr. 6, 1855; *Sac. Union*, Apr. 9, 1855.

[73] Walker had three brothers, named Arapeen, Sanpitch, and Tabby. Sanpitch succeeded Arapeen, and Tabby was afterward chief of the Utahs. *Wells' Narr.*, MS., 22. In his summary of the Walker war, Richards mentions a brother named Ammon. *Incidents in Hist. Utah*, MS., 30.

[74] In his report to Brigham Young, in *House Ex. Doc.*, i. 34th Cong. 1st Sess., pt i. 518, Garland Hurt states that while in the Humboldt Valley 400 Indians came to his camp within three days, and that many had travelled 100 miles without food. Again, p. 520, he mentions that a party of Utahs were put to work on a farm at Nephi, but they had nothing to eat, and most of them were compelled to betake themselves to the mountains and streams, where there were fish and game.

[75] In 1849 John Wilson was appointed Indian agent at Salt Lake. In *House Ex. Doc.*, 17, 31st Cong. 1st Sess., pp. 182-4, is a copy of his instructions. The total sum allowed him for presents to Indians, rent, fuel, stationery, forage, the purchase of two horses, travelling and incidental expenses, was $1,500. What portion of this amount the Indians were likely to receive in the way of presents the reader will judge for himself. In *Id.*, no. 17, pp. 104-111, is a copy of the agent's report, which contains much that was already known about the geography of the country, but very little about the Indian tribes. Wilson states that to gain anything like a personal knowledge of the actual situation of these tribes would require five years' travel. One would think that he might at least have learned something from the Mormons. In 1851 Jacob H. Holman was appointed Indian agent, and Henry R. Day and Stephen B. Rose sub-agents. *Amer. Almanac*, 1852. Day was removed in 1852. In 1854 Garland Hurt succeeded Holman, and Edward A. Bedell was also appointed agent. In 1855-6 the agents were Garland Hurt and G. W. Armstrong, Brigham being still superintendent of Indian affairs. *Id.*, 1854-7. The reports of the various agents and of the superintendent will be found in *Ind. Aff. Repts*, passim. In his report to the secretary of the interior, dated Nov. 22, 1856, Geo. W. Manypenny, commissioner of Indian affairs, says: 'The Indians in the territory of Utah have, with but few exceptions, continued quiet and peaceable.' Nevertheless, in Feb. of this year there were a few war parties in the field. See Brigham Young's proclamation, in *Deseret News*. Feb. 27, 1856.

citizens, and on the highway of travel between the verges of the continent. Between July 1853 and August 1856 more than $11,000,000 were expended for the occupation or acquisition of Indian territory.[76] Of this total less than the three-hundredth part of one per cent was paid to the Shoshones, and to the Utahs nothing. For the five years ending the 30th of June, 1855, the sum paid to the Mormons for losses incurred through Indian depredations, for the expense of suppressing Indian outbreaks, and of negotiating treaties, amounting probably to not less than $300,-000 was $95,940.65; and, small as it was, when drafts were presented at the treasury, excuses were found for not paying them.[77]

The occupation of territory under such conditions was of course resented by the original owners of the soil, and it is no matter for surprise that the small detachments of United States troops lost more in number between the years 1853 and 1856 than did the Mormons.[78] The saints seldom used their rifles

[76] *Ind. Aff. Repts*, 1856, 264–7.

[77] *Linforth's Route from Liverpool*, 108. Gen. Wells states that the cost of the Walker war, apart from losses incurred, was $70,000; that this was cut down to $40,000, after special agents had been sent to investigate, and was not paid until ten years afterward. *Narr.*, MS., 25. On Jan. 5, 1853, the committee on territories transferred to the committee on military affairs a memorial of the Utah legislature for an appropriation for the expense of Indian expeditions. *U. S. House Jour.*, 32d Cong. 2d Sess., 104. On Jan. 29, 1855, the committee on military affairs reported that it had not sufficient data to advise on refunding to Utah her expenses in suppressing Indian outbreaks. *U. S. House Com. Repts*, 33d Cong. 2d Sess., 39. On March 2, 1857, the U. S. senate voted against a motion authorizing the secretary of war to settle the accounts of Utah territory for moneys advanced in suppressing Indian hostilities in 1853. *U. S. Sen. Jour.*, 34th Cong. 3d Sess., 298. For copies of memorials, of which two were forwarded to congress, see *Utah, Acts Legisl.* (ed. 1855), 409–10, 416–17.

[78] Garland Hurt, under date G. S. L. City, May 2, 1855, in *Ind. Aff. Repts*, 1857, 305, says he has become satisfied that the saints have accidentally or purposely created a distinction in the minds of the Indian tribes of this territory between the Mormons and the people of the U. S. that cannot act otherwise than prejudicially to the latter. He recommends that the 13th and 14th sections of the 'act to regulate trade and intercourse with the Indian tribes, and to preserve peace on the frontier,' be rigidly enforced. It is true that the Indians made a distinction between Mormons and gentiles, for the former fed and clothed them, while the latter shot them down. Richards, *Narr.*, MS., 47, says that when the saints first arrived in the valley, Brigham assured the Indians that they would be well treated, and told them that they must not behave toward his people as they did toward the Americans. In *Indian Aff.*

except in case of need, and treated their Indian neighbors as human beings. The emigrants had no such scruples.

Repts, 1837, 311, the governor remarks that more liberal appropriations should be made, and that the troops must be kept away, 'for it is a prevalent fact that wherever there are the most of these, we may expect to find the greatest amount of hostile Indians, and the least security to persons and property.' Most of Brigham's reports bear the impress of common sense, but he had not in his hands the appropriation of government funds or the appointment of Indian agents. For further mention of matters relating to Indian affairs, see *House Ex. Doc.*, i. 32d Cong. 2d Sess., pt. i., 299–300, 487–45; *Id.*, i. 33d Cong. 1st Sess., pt i. 441–7; *Utah, Jour. Legisl.*, Joint Sess., 1854–5, pp. 94–7, 102; *Deseret News*, May 1, 1852, Apr. 2, 1853, May 11, June 22, Sept. 7, Oct. 15, 26, Nov. 16, 1854, Oct. 15, 1856; *Front. Guardian*, Oct 3, 1849; *Tullidge's Quart. Mag.*, July 1884, 235–41; *Mackay's The Mormons*, 233, 238–40; *Olshausen's Gesch. de Morm.*, 184–7; *Carvalho's Incidents of Travel*, 188–94; *Ward's Husband in Utah*, 39–60, 64–7; *Marshall's Through Amer.*, 192; *Hunt's Merchants' Mag.*, xxx. 639; *Pacific R. R. Rept*, ii. 26–7; *Sac. Union*, June 16, 1855; *S. F. Bulletin*, Dec. 11, 1855; *S. F. Alta*, July 4, 1854, Dec. 9, 1856; *San José Times*, Nov. 23, 1879; *S. F. Herald*, June 25, 1854.

CHAPTER XVIII.

THE GOVERNMENT IN ARMS.

1853–1857.

Brigham as Dictator—Utah Seeks Admission as a State—Dissatisfaction among the Saints—Conflicting Judiciaries—The New Federal Officials—Disputes with Judge Drummond—Colonel Steptoe
—An Expedition Ordered to Utah—Official Blunders—The Troops
Assemble at Fort Leavenworth—Hockaday and Magraw's Mail
Contract—The Brigham Young Express—Celebration of the Pioneer Anniversary—News of the Coming Invasion—Its Effect on
the Mormons—Arrival of Major Van Vliet—The Nauvoo Legion
—Mormon Tactics.

" I am and will be governor, and no power can hinder it," declared Brigham in a sabbath discourse at
the tabernacle in June 1853; "until," he added with
characteristic shrewdness, "the Lord almighty says,
'Brigham, you need not be governor any longer.'"[1]
After the departure of the runaway officials in September 1851, there were none to dispute the authority
of the governor, and for several years his will was
law. At the opening of the joint sessions of the assembly, a committee was appointed to escort him to
the hall of the representatives, where he took his seat
in front of the speaker's chair, the members and spectators rising in a body as he entered. The message
was then read by his private secretary; it was ordered
that a thousand copies of it be printed for the use of
both houses, and that it be published in the *Deseret
News* for the benefit of the people. The assembly
then adjourned, and at the meetings which followed

[1] *Journal of Discourses*, i. 135.

adopted only such measures as were suggested in the message, or as they knew would find favor with the governor.[2] "Laws should be simple and plain," remarked Brigham, in his message of December 1853, "easy to be comprehended by the most unlearned, void of ambiguity, and few in number."[3]   Most sensible advice.

During the years 1852–3 little of importance occurred in the political history of Utah.   By act approved January 3, 1853, it was ordered that general elections should be held annually in each precinct on the first Monday in August,[4] and in section five of this act each elector was required to provide himself with a vote containing the names of the persons he wished to be elected, and the offices he would have them fill, and present it folded to the judge of the election, who must number and deposit it in the ballot-box; the clerk then wrote the name of the elector, and opposite to it the number of the vote.   This measure,

[2] Officials nominated by the governor were also elected by the assembly, by a unanimous vote. At a joint session held Jan. 17, 1854, Councillor Taylor presented a list of nominations, including an auditor, treasurer, territorial commissioner, surveyor-general, librarian, member of the code commission, a district attorney, a probate judge, and several notaries public. A vote was taken on each nomination, and all were carried unanimously. *Utah, Jour. Legisl.*, 134.

[3] Copies of the message will be found in *Id.*, 1853-4, 111–23; *Deseret News*, Dec. 15, 1853. It contains a statement of the revenue and expenses of the territory for the then current year. The assessment for 1853 was at the rate of one per cent, and should have yielded, including the delinquencies in the previous year's collections, $24,121.09. The expenses were only $14,181.23, of which $12,301.37 was for public improvements; but during the year warrants had been issued on the treasury amounting to $14,834.92, and there were previous warrants, not yet redeemed, amounting to $2,896.66, together with outstanding debts estimated at $6,000, making in all $23,733.58. Of this sum $10,003.66 had been redeemed, and there was a balance in the treasurer's hands of $1,298.41, leaving a debt of $12,431.57, for which there were no available funds. The delinquencies still remaining for 1852, when the assessment was two per cent, were $6,463, and for 1853, $10,523. If these were collected, there would be a balance of $4,554.49 in the treasury. The saints are exhorted to pay their assessments more promptly, and the officers to be more energetic in their collection. Copies of the governor's messages for 1851-2 will be found in *Utah, Jour. Legisl.*, 1851-2, 100–13; *Deseret News*, Jan. 10, 1852.

[4] Copies of the act are in *Utah, Acts Legisl.* (ed. 1855), 232–4; *Utah Pamphlets, Polit.*, xiv. 6–7. The result of the election for 1853 is given in an extra of the *Deseret News*, Aug. 25, 1853, and will be found in the same paper for each succeeding year.

which virtually abolished vote by ballot, gave much
ground of complaint to the anti-Mormons. "In a
territory so governed," writes Benjamin G. Ferris,
who superseded Willard Richards as secretary in the
winter of 1852-3, "it will not excite surprise that
cases of extortion, robbery, murder, and other crimes
should occur and defy all legal redress, or that the
law should be made the instrument of crime." The
remark is unjust. If crime was not punished, it was
from no fault of the legislature, but, as we shall see
later, from want of harmony between the federal and
territorial judiciaries.

In January 1854[5] Utah again sought admission as
a state, a memorial to congress being adopted by the
legislative assembly praying that the inhabitants be
authorized to call a convention for the purpose of

[5] The remaining acts of the legislature for 1852-3 will be found in *Utah,
Acts Legisl.* (ed. 1855), 231-52, (ed. 1866), 64-6. On March 3, 1852, an act
was approved whereby it was made unlawful 'to use with disrespect the
name of the deity,' or to 'become publicly intoxicated so as to endanger the
peace and quiet of the community.' For the former offence the penalty was
a fine of $2 to $10, or one to five days' labor on the public highway, at the
discretion of the court; for the latter, a fine of $1 to $10. On Jan. 17, 1853,
an act was approved incorporating the Deseret Iron Co., Erastus Snow,
Franklin D. Richards, and Geo. A. Smith being among the members of the
body corporate. Acts were also passed incorporating the Provo Canal and
Irrigation Co., of which Orson Hyde, Geo. A. Smith, and Geo. W. Armstrong
were the promoters, power being granted to divert a portion of the waters of
Provo River. Another act bearing this date gives to Dan. H. Wells the
right to erect and control ferries on Green River, the rates of toll being $3
for each vehicle not over 2,000 lbs weight, $4 for any vehicle between 2,000
and 3,000, $5 for those between 3,000 and 4,000, and $6 for those over 4,000
lbs; for each horse, mule, ox, or cow 50 cents, and for each sheep, goat, or
swine 25 cents. Wells was required to pay ten per cent of the proceeds to
the emigration fund. On Jan. 21, 1853, an act was passed incorporating the
Provo Manufacturing Co., of which Orson Hyde, Geo. A. Smith, and others
were members. By other acts of this date the Great S. L. City Water
Works Association was incorporated, Brigham Young, Heber C. Kimball,
Ezra T. Benson, Jedediah M. Grant, Jesse C. Little, and Phineas W. Cook
being the body corporate; to Chas Hopkins and others was granted the right
to build a toll-bridge across the Jordan, to Jos. Busby the privilege of establishing ferries on Ham Fork of the Green River, and to Jos. Young, David
Fullmer, and two others that of establishing ferries at Bear River and building a toll-bridge across the Malad. On the same date an act was passed regulating the mode of procedure in criminal cases. By act of June 4, 1853,
Abiah Wardsworth and two others were granted the right to erect a toll-
bridge across the Weber. The acts, resolutions, and memorials of the legislature were published in the *Deseret News*. In the issues of June 18, 1853,
and Jan. 11, 1855, is a description of festivities held by the members, to
which the federal officials were invited. They were afterward held once or
twice each year.

framing a constitution and state government.[6] As no notice was taken of this request, the convention met in March 1856, and the people again adopted a constitution of their own, under the style of the state of Deseret, resembling, though with some additions, the one framed in 1849.[7] It was signed by every member of the convention, and together with a second memorial, was presented by John M. Bernhisel, who between 1851 and 1859 filled the position of territorial delegate. Both were again ignored,[8] probably on the score of polygamy, for otherwise there were many arguments in favor of the Mormons. If their population was not yet large enough to entitle them to admission, it was larger than that of several of the younger states when first admitted.[9] They were a prosperous and fairly intelligent community; their wars with the Indian tribes had been conducted successfully, and at their own expense; at their own expense also they had constructed public buildings, roads, and bridges; they had conquered the desert, and amid its wastes had founded cities; there could be no doubt of their ability to maintain a state government; and thus far, at least, there was no valid reason to question their loyalty. That under these circumstances their memorial should be treated with contempt gave sore offence to the saints.[10]

[6] A copy of it may be found in *Utah, Acts Legisl.* (ed. 1855), 414–15.

[7] The full text is given in *Sen. Misc. Doc.*, 35th Cong. 1st Sess., iii. no. 240; *Utah Acts*, 1855–6; *Deseret News*, Apr. 2, 1856.

[8] They were tabled in the senate on the 20th of April, 1858.

[9] In 1854 W. Richards estimated the population of Utah at 40,000 to 50,000. In Feb. 1856 Leonard W. Hardy, census agent, gave 76,335 as the number, of whom 37,277 were males and 39,058 females. The peace commissioners sent to the territory in 1858, after the Utah war, reported its population at the figures given by Richards. The census of 1860 was taken under some disadvantages. Gen. Burr was appointed to that duty by Marshal Dotson, a strong anti-Mormon, but as the saints murmured at this selection, a clerk in his store was chosen in his stead. The returns gave 40,295 souls, including 29 apprentices, or so-called slaves, and are probably much within the actual figures. At this date the Mormons claimed a population of 90,000 to 100,000, which is doubtless an exaggeration. In order to show the number that would entitle them to admission as a state, they were accused of counting cattle and unborn children as souls. *Burton's City of the Saints.* 356–8. It is probable that the actual population in 1860 was about 65,000.

[10] For comments on the admission of Utah as a state at this period, see

Another cause of complaint with the Mormons was the impossibility of acquiring a secure title to land. In December 1853 the president of the United States had recommended in his message that the land system be extended over Utah,[11] with such modifications as the peculiarities of that territory might require. About a year later, an act was passed authorizing the appointment of a surveyor-general for Utah,[12] and soon afterward large tracts were surveyed. But the Indian title had not yet been extinguished; the sections were not open to preëmption, and the saints therefore found themselves merely in the condition of squatters in their land of Zion. They were ready to purchase, but the organic act forbade the primary disposal of the soil, and, as it seems, the government, knowing their ability and their eagerness to purchase, still hesitated to make them its permanent owners. Nevertheless, a few years before, this portion of the public domain had virtually been ceded to them as worthless.

Still another reason for dissatisfaction was the failure of congress to make such appropriations as were granted for other territories. With the exception of about $96,000 granted, it will be remembered, as part compensation for an expense of $300,000 in quelling Indian outbreaks, $20,000 for a state-house, and $5,000 for a library, no money was voted specially for the benefit of Utah between 1850 and 1857; for the sums expended on the survey and construction of roads connecting that territory with other parts of the Union cannot, of course, be so regarded. In 1855 the

Deseret News, Apr. 2, May 21, 1856; *Putnam's Mag.*, v. 225–36; *S. F. Bulletin*, Aug. 23, 1856.

[11] And also over New Mexico. *House Ex. Doc.*, 33d Cong. 1st Sess., i. pt 1, p. 12.

[12] *U. S. Public Laws*, 33d Cong. 2d Sess., 611; *House Ex. Doc.*, 46th Cong. 3d Sess., xxvi. p. 971. The appointment was given to David H. Burr, who, according to a writer in the *Internat. Rev.*, Feb. 1882, p. 192, met with such opposition that he was compelled to flee for his life. I find no confirmation of this statement, nor does Mr Burr mention any disagreement with the Mormon authorities in his report, in *House Ex. Doc.*, 34th Cong. 3d Sess., i. pt i. pp. 542-9.

seat of the legislative assembly and of the supreme court was removed to Fillmore, and in 1856 again transferred to Salt Lake City.[13] In the latter year a further appropriation was asked for the completion of the state-house, but the request was refused, and even the expenses of the assembly and other necessary items were not promptly paid.[14]

Meanwhile most of the gentile officials appointed by the authorities were, according to Mormon accounts, political adventurers of the lowest grade—men who, being glad to accept the crumbs of government patronage, were sent to this the cesspool of the United States. The officials, of course, answered with counter-charges, among them that the Mormons combined to obstruct the administration of justice. To attempt to carry out the laws was, they declared, a hopeless task, in a community controlled by an ecclesiastical star-chamber, working out in darkness a sectarian law, and with a grand lama presiding over their suffrages. Complications hence arise, and the conflict known as the Mormon war.

Among the principal causes of the rupture were the frequent disputes between the conflicting judiciaries. By act of 1852 it had been ordered that the district courts should exercise original jurisdiction, both in civil and criminal cases, when not otherwise provided for by law, and should have a general supervision over all inferior courts, to prevent and correct abuses where no other remedy existed. By consent of court,

---

[13] *Taylor's Narr.*, MS.; *Wells' Narr.*, MS.; *Hist. B. Young*, MS.; *Utah Notes*, MS.; *Olshausen, Mormonen*, 163; *Utah, Acts Legisl.* (ed. 1866), 106. In *Richards' Narr.*, MS., 69, it is stated that the extra expense caused to most of the members was the cause of the second removal. Fillmore is about 105 miles south of S. L. City. In the *Deseret News* of Jan. 11, 1855, is a description of the state-house at Fillmore, so far as it was then completed.

[14] Demands were made on congress for the expenses of the assembly in 1856, and for making a survey of the boundaries of Oregon in the same year. *Utah Acts*, 1855–6, p. 47; 1858–9, p. 38. Neither was granted. In 1852 a bill passed the house of representatives in congress, giving to the legislatures of territories the control of appropriations for their expenses. To this was added an amendment 'that the provisions of this act shall not apply to Utah.' *U. S. House Jour.*, 32d Cong. 1st Sess., 780. The bill was thrown out by the senate.

any person could be selected to act as judge for the trial of a particular cause or question, and while in this capacity possessed all the powers of a district judge. The district court judges were, of course, federal magistrates. By the same act it was provided that there should be judges of probate for each county within the territory; that they should be elected for a term of four years by joint vote of the legislative assembly; should hold four regular sessions each year; and that their courts should be considered in law as always open. Besides the powers pertaining to such courts, they had the administration of estates, the guardianship of minors, idiots, and insane persons, and "power to exercise original jurisdiction, both civil and criminal, and as well in chancery as at common law, when not prohibited by legislative enactment."[15] The probate court judges were, of course, Mormons; but appeal lay from their decisions to the district courts. Subject to the revision of the probate courts were the municipal courts, the justices of the peace, and the three 'selectmen' appointed for each county, whose duties were to oversee and provide for the maintenance of the poor, to take charge of the persons and estates of the insane, and to bind apprentice, orphan, and vagrant children.[16]

Thus the probate courts, whose proper jurisdiction concerned only the estates of the dead, were made judges of the living, with powers almost equal to those of the supreme and district courts. These powers were conferred on them, as the gentiles alleged, in order to nullify, so far as possible, the authority of

[15] *Utah, Acts Legisl.* (ed. 1855), 120–1, 123–4. Section 8 of this act, relating to pleadings, is worthy of note, as it shows the tendency of the Mormons to simplify their system of legal procedure. 'Any pleading which possesses the following requisites shall be deemed sufficient: First, when to the common understanding it conveys a reasonable certainty of meaning. Second, when by a fair and natural construction it shows a substantial cause of action or defence. If defective in the former, the court shall direct a more specific statement. If in the latter, it is ground for demurrer; demurrers for formal defects are abolished.'

[16] An act creating the office of selectmen, and defining their duties, approved Feb. 5, 1852, will be found in *Utah, Acts Legisl.* (ed. 1855), 136–7.

the higher courts; and as the Mormons alleged, because justice could not be had at the hands of the federal officials, who were little with them and at such uncertain times that, save for the probate courts, they would have been practically without civil and criminal jurisdiction. To the malevolent representations of the latter the saints mainly ascribed the Mormon war, and, as will presently appear, the violation of some of their most cherished rights and privileges.

After Secretary Harris and judges Brocchus and Brandebury had set out for Washington, taking with them the territorial seal and the territorial funds, Zerubbabel Snow held court,[17] with little heed to gentile law, until succeeded in 1854 by George P. Stiles, W. W. Drummond being appointed associate judge, as will be remembered, and John F. Kinney chief justice, about the same time.

Stiles, a renegade Mormon, who had been counsel for Joseph Smith and the municipality of Nauvoo at the time when the Nauvoo *Expositor* was ordered to be suppressed as a nuisance, was assigned to the Carson district, but soon afterward returned to Salt Lake City, where he held several sessions of the court. And now trouble commenced. The legislature had appointed a territorial marshal, who was to take the place of the United States marshal, impanel jurors, and enforce writs when the courts were sitting as territorial courts; while the United States marshal claimed the right to officiate in all the United States courts, whether they were sitting as territorial or federal courts. To the latter, the judge issued certain writs, which it was found impossible to serve, and when the question of jurisdiction was brought before the court, several Mormon lawyers entered and

---

[17] According to the provisions of 'an act concerning the judiciary and for judicial purposes,' approved Oct. 4, 1851. A copy of it will be found in *Tullidge's Hist. S. L. City*, 93–4. Among other proceedings, Snow tried and convicted several Mexicans for buying Indian slaves. The slaves were forfeited and delivered into the keeping of the Mormons. *Waites' Mormon Prophet*, 23.

insulted the judge, threatening him with violence unless he decided in their favor.[18] Stiles appealed to the governor, but was told that if he could not sustain and enforce the laws, the sooner he adjourned his court the better. A short time afterward the records of the United States district courts were taken from the judge's office during his absence, and a few moments before his return a bonfire was made of the books and papers in his office. He, of course, supposed that the records were also consumed, and so made affidavit on his return to Washington in the spring of 1857. Meanwhile the business of the courts was suspended. The records had, in fact, been removed, and were in safe-keeping; but this silly freak was noised abroad throughout the land with many exaggerations, and excited much adverse comment.

The chief justice was a more popular magistrate than either of his colleagues. In Iowa, where he resided before receiving his appointment, he was better known as a tradesman than as a jurist, and on account of his traffic with the saints at Kanesville was called a jack Mormon. On his arrival at Salt Lake City he added to his judicial functions the occupations of store-keeper and boarding-house proprietor. He never lost the good-will of his patrons, and never refused to drink with them. Rotund, of vinous aspect, and of medium height, dull-witted, brusque in manner, and pompous in mien, he was a man whom Brigham knew well how to use; before taking leave of the Mormons he became an open apologist for polygamy. He remained in the territory until 1856,

---

[18] The names of the lawyers were James Ferguson, Hosea Stout, and J. C. Little. *Id.*, 37. In Dec. 1858 a Mormon grand jury found that 'James Ferguson of Salt Lake City did use language and threats calculated to intimidate Judge George P. Stiles.' S. E. Sinclair, who succeeded Stiles after the arrival of the troops under Johnston, did his utmost to bring to justice those who had intimidated his predecessor. *Stenhouse's Rocky Mountain Saints*, 283, note. Beadle states that Thomas Williams, also a Mormon lawyer, protested against the insult offered to the judge, that his life was threatened in consequence, and that he was murdered while attempting to escape to California. *Life in Utah*, 175.

and four years afterward was reappointed. We shall hear of him later.

The official who did more than any other, and perhaps more than all others, to bring about the Mormon war was Associate Judge W. W. Drummond. Leaving his wife and family in Illinois without the means of support, he brought with him a harlot whom he had picked up in the streets of Washington, and introducing her as Mrs Drummond, seated her by his side on the judicial bench. Gambler and bully, he openly avowed that he had come to Utah to make money, and in the presence of the chief justice declared: "Money is my God"[19] When first he appeared in court he insulted the community by mocking at their laws and institutions, and especially at the institution of polygamy. He also declared that he would set aside the finding of the probate courts in all cases other than those which lay strictly within their jurisdiction. Here was a direct issue, and one that was immediately taken up, for as yet none of the federal judges had declared the powers granted to these courts by the act of 1852 to be of no effect.[20] Nor had any such view of the matter been expressed by the authorities at Washington.

When asking for admission as a state or territory, the Mormons did not suppose that the majesty of the

[19] Adding, 'And you may put this down in your journal if you like.' *Remy's Journey to G. S. L. City*, i. 469. Remy states that he was present when the remark was made.

[20] Judge Shaver tacitly admitted the jurisdiction of the probate courts, but Chief Justice Kinney was the first to render decisions from the bench confirming their jurisdiction. His interpretation of the organic act is noteworthy: 'The court holds that by virtue of that clause of the organic act which provides that "the jurisdiction of the several courts provided for," including the probate courts, "shall be as limited by law," that the legislature had the right to provide by law for the exercise by the probate courts of jurisdiction in civil and criminal cases.' *Burton's City of the Saints*, 379. The clause in section 9 of this act to which Kinney refers provides that 'the jurisdiction of the several courts herein provided for, both appellate and original, and that of the probate courts, and of justices of the peace, shall be as limited by law.' If the phrase 'limited by law' be so interpreted as to extend the right of proving wills to jurisdiction in all other matters, one fails to see the need of federal judges. As well indict a man for murder before a justice of the peace.

law would be represented by a gamester[21] with a strumpet by his side. Drummond soon became even more unpopular than had been Judge Brocchus, and after administering justice for a brief term at Fillmore and Carson, went home by way of California. On handing in his resignation, he addressed a letter to the attorney-general, in which are many groundless accusations and some truths. He complains "that the federal officers are daily compelled to hear the form of the American government traduced, the chief executives of the nation, both living and dead, slandered and abused from the masses, as well as from the leading members of the church, in the most vulgar, loathsome, and wicked manner that the evil passions of men can possibly conceive." He is pained to say that he has accomplished little good while there, and that the judiciary is only a puppet. He states that the records and papers of the supreme court had been destroyed by order of the church, that Brigham had pardoned Mormon criminals, and imprisoned at will innocent men who were not Mormons.[22] He attributes to the saints the Gunnison massacre, the death of Judge Shaver and of Secretary Almon W. Babbitt,[23] who was in fact murdered by Indians during the year 1856, and says that officials are "insulted, harassed, and murdered for doing their duty, and not recogniz-

[21] Remy states that after a gambling quarrel Drummond ordered his negro Cato to assault and ill use a Jew named Levi Abrahams, who had turned Mormon. *Journey to G. S. L. City,* i. 469-70. Mrs Waite's version of the matter is, that when the court was about to be opened at Fillmore, a Jew was hired to quarrel with the judge and strike him. Instead of striking him, the Jew sent an insulting message by a negro belonging to Drummond. For answer, the judge ordered the negro to take a rawhide and lay it on lustily to the back of the Jew. The negro and judge were arrested. *The Mormon Prophet,* 39. See also *Hickman's Destroying Angel,* 111-12.

[22] He mentions the cases of Moroni Green, convicted before Judge Kinney of assault with intent to murder, and of a man named Baker, who murdered a dumb boy. Both were sentenced to the penitentiary, but pardoned on arriving there. Drummond states that on the sabbath after his pardon Brigham accompanied one of them to church. *House Ex. Doc.,* 35th Cong. 1st Sess., x. no. 71, p. 212. He also alleges that five or six men from Missouri and Iowa, who had not violated any criminal law in America, were in the penitentiary.

[23] Who, he says, was murdered by Mormons by order of Brigham Young, Heber C. Kimball, and J. M. Grant. *Id..* p. 213.

ing Brigham Young as the only law-giver and law-maker on earth."

These allegations were denied by the Mormon authorities in an official letter from the deputy clerk of the supreme court of Utah to the attorney-general,[24] except those relating to the treatment of the federal officials, the Gunnison massacre, the death of Shaver, and the murder of Babbitt, which needed no denial. If it was true that the magistrates appointed by the United States were held in contempt, there was sufficient provocation. Two of them, as we have seen, deserted their post, a third was probably an opium-eater, a fourth a drunkard, a fifth a gambler and a lecher.

After the departure of Drummond, the only gentile official remaining in the territory was Garland Hurt, the Indian agent, and none were found willing to accept office in a territory where it was believed they could only perform their duty at peril of their lives. The saints had now few apologists at Washington. Even Senator Douglas, who in former years was their stoutest champion, had deserted them, and in a speech delivered at Springfield, Illinois, early in 1856, had denounced Mormonism as "the loathsome ulcer of the body politic." At least two years before this date it was apparent that matters in Utah were tending toward a crisis, though no measures had yet been taken except a feeble effort to supersede Brigham as governor of the territory. On the 31st of August, 1854, Lieutenant-colonel E. J. Steptoe arrived in Salt Lake City, en route for California with a body of troops. As Brigham's term of office was now about to expire, the governorship of Utah was tendered to the colonel by President Pierce. Knowing, however, that the for-

---

[24] *Id.*, 214–15. Curtis E. Bolton, deputy clerk (in the absence of the chief clerk), solemnly declares that the records, papers, etc., are in safe-keeping. He states that Green, a lad 18 years of age, drew a pistol in self-defence, but did not point it, and was pardoned at the petition of the U. S. officials and influential citizens of S. L. City, and that the statement as to the incarceration of five or six men from Missouri and Iowa without due cause is utterly false.

mer was the people's choice, he refused to accept the
position, and a memorial signed by himself, by the
federal officials, the army officers, and all the prominent citizens, was addressed to the president, asking
for the reappointment of Brigham as governor and
superintendent of Indian affairs.[25] The request was
granted, and the colonel and his command remained
in the valley until the following spring, being on good
terms with the Mormons, except for a fracas that occurred between the soldiers and the saints on new-
year's day.[26]

Orders had been given to Colonel Steptoe to arrest
and bring to trial the perpetrators of the Gunnison
massacre, and after much expense and the exercise of
great tact and judgment, most of them were secured
and indicted for murder. Eight of the offenders, including a chief named Kanosh, were put on trial at
Nephi City; and though the judge distinctly charged
the jury that they must find the prisoners guilty or
not guilty of murder, a verdict of manslaughter was
returned against three of the accused, the rest being
acquitted. The sentence was three years imprisonment in the Utah penitentiary, this being the severest

[25] On Jan. 4, 1855, Bernhisel wrote from Washington to F. D. Richards: ' I
regret to inform you that Prest Pierce finally declined to reappoint Gov.
Young. Lieut-col Steptoe is the appointee.' *Richards' Incidents in Utah
Hist.*, MS. The memorial states that Brigham Young possesses the confidence
of the people of the territory without distinction of party or sect, that he is a
firm supporter of the constitution of the U. S., and that his reappointment
would serve the interests of the territory better than that of any other man,
while his removal would cause the deepest feeling of regret. A copy of it
will be found in *Tullidge's Life of Young*, 239-40, and in *Skelton and Meik's
Defence of Mormonism*, 22. Beadle states that Col Steptoe was entrapped by
two of Brigham's 'decoy women,' and to avoid exposure resigned his commission as governor. *Life in Utah*, 171; see also *Waite's The Mormon Prophet*,
27-8. There are no gounds for such a statement. By Orson Hyde, in *Deseret
News*, March 21, 1555, and by others of the Mormons, the colonel is spoken
of in the highest terms. Memorials for Brigham's reappointment were also
adopted by the legislature, for which see *Utah, Acts Legisl.* (ed. 1855), 419-21.

[26] A quarrel broke out between the troops and the Mormons in some of the
saloons; fire-arms were used, and several men wounded, two of the soldiers
severely. The entire legion turned out and threatened to annihilate Steptoe's
companies, compelling them to intrench and remain under arms for three
days. The matter was settled by mediation. *Olshausen's Mormonen*, 189. See
also *S. F. Herald*, March 14, 1855, and *Hickman's Destroying Angel*, 107,
where it is stated that the brawl occurred on christmas day. No mention
of this matter is made in the official reports of the officers.

punishment prescribed by statute; but after a brief imprisonment, the culprits made their escape, or, as some declare, were allowed to escape.[27]

On the sabbath after the colonel's departure, Brigham repeated in the tabernacle the remark which he had made two years before, commencing, "I am and will be governor;" adding on this occasion: "I do not know what I shall say next winter if such men make their appearance here as some last winter. I know what I think I shall say: if they play the same game again, so help me God, we will slay them."[28]

Such phrase, deliberately uttered at the place and on the day of public worship, at a time when Utah sought admission as a state, was certainly, from an outside standpoint, injudicious, and boded ill for the saints. At this period the slavery question was the all-absorbing topic throughout the country. The sedition in Utah, grave though it was, passed for a time almost unheeded, except by a section of the republican party, which, while criticising the theories of Senator Douglas, added to the venom of its sting by coupling slavery and polygamy as the twin relics of barbarism. After the presidential election of 1856, however, matters assumed a different phase. There was now a temporary lull in the storm which a few years later swept with all the fury of a tornado over the fairest portions of the Union, and the nation had leisure to turn its attention to the Mormon question.[29]

[27] Judge Drummond, in his letter to Mrs Gunnison, in *Gunnison's The Mormons*, ix.-x., says that those who were convicted were old, crippled, and partially blind, while the able-bodied warriors were acquitted, and that Judge Kinney, before whom the trial took place, was so much mortified at the finding of the jury that he at once adjourned the court. He also states that Col Steptoe, Gen. Holman, the government attorney, Garland Hurt, Indian agent, and others were of opinion that those who were found not guilty were acquitted by order of the church. The statement as to the escape of the three who were convicted rests mainly on the authority of Capt. Rufus Ingalls, the quartermaster of Col Steptoe's regiment. In his report to the quartermaster-general, in *House Ex. Doc.*, 34th Cong. 1st Sess., i. pt ii. p. 167, he says that they were at large when he left the valley.

[28] Again, in a discourse delivered at the tabernacle June 17, 1855, he says: 'Though I may not be governor, here my power will not be diminished. No man they can send here will have much influence with this community.' *Journal of Discourses*, ii. 322.

[29] In *Doctrine and Covenants* (ed. 1876), 278-9, is given a remarkable revela-

It was now established, as was supposed, on sufficient evidence, that the Mormons refused obedience
to gentile law, that federal officials had been virtually
driven from Utah, that one, at least, of the federal
judges had been threatened with violence while his
court was in session, and that the records of the court
had been destroyed or concealed. With the advice of
his cabinet, therefore, and yielding perhaps not unwillingly to the outcry of the republican party, President
Buchanan determined that Brigham should be superseded as governor, and that a force should be sent to
the territory, ostensibly as a posse comitatus, to sustain
the authority of his successor.[30]

tion to Joseph Smith, Dec. 25, 1832, and first published by F. D. Richards in
the *Pearl of Great Price* at Liverpool in 1851. 'Verily, thus saith the Lord
concerning the wars which will shortly come to pass, beginning at the rebellion
of South Carolina, which will eventually terminate in the death and misery of
many souls. The days will come that war will be poured out upon all nations,
beginning at that place; for behold! the southern states shall be divided against
the northern states, and the southern states will call on other nations, even on
the nation of Great Britain, as it is called, and they shall also call upon other
nations, in order to defend themselves against other nations; and thus war
shall be poured out upon all nations. And it shall come to pass after many
days slaves shall rise up against their masters, who shall be marshalled and
disciplined for war.' It is somewhat suspicious that this revelation should
appear in the edition of 1876, but not in the one of 1845, or in any other edition published before the war, so far as I am aware. A copy of it will be
found in *Stenhouse's Rocky Mountain Saints*, 420-1. According to *Hist. B.
Young*, MS.; *Carrington's Rem.*, MS., Joseph Smith early in his career
warned the saints that 'some day they would see the United States come
against them in war, and that the Lord should deliver them.'

[30] The above appear to be the main reasons that led to what was termed
the Utah war. Among the best statements as to its causes, apart from the
official documents already quoted, are those contained in *Remy's Journey to
G. S. L. City*, i. 468-73, and *Tullidge's Hist. S. L. City*, 144 et seq., though
the latter is somewhat far-fetched and lays too much stress on the part that
Frémont bore in the matter. 'In the framing of its first platform,' he says
the republican party raised her (Utah) to a kindred association with the
south; and in every campaign where John C. Frémont was the standard-
bearer of the party, there could be read: 'The abolishment of slavery and
polygamy, the twin relics of barbarism.' Mr Tullidge borrows somewhat
closely from Stenhouse, who, in his *Rocky Mountain Saints*, 307-8, makes the
same remark. The causes of the war have, of course, been touched upon by
most writers on Utah, those in favor of the saints claiming that there was no
just reason for it, and others bringing numberless charges against them. During the years 1855-7 newspapers and periodicals throughout the U. S. were
teeming with articles and paragraphs on the Mormon question, most of them
being more or less acrid and unjust in their comments. A writer in the
Atlantic Monthly, March 1859, p. 364, states that Buchanan's idea in ordering the Utah expedition was 'to gag the north, and induce her to forget that
she had been robbed of her birthright, by forcing on the attention of the
country other questions of absorbing interest.' For views and statements of

In a report of the secretary of war, dated December 5, 1857, it is stated that Utah was inhabited exclusively by Mormons; that the people implicitly obeyed their prophet, from whose decrees there was no appeal; that from the day when they had settled in the territory their aim had been to secede from the Union; that for years they had not preserved even the semblance of obedience to authority, unless by doing so they could benefit themselves; that they encouraged and perhaps excited nomad bands of savages to pillage and massacre emigrants; and that they stood as a lion in the path of the gentile communities established on the Pacific seaboard.   Except that the internal government of the saints was nominally theocratic and practically autocratic, these statements are grossly unjust, but not more so than might be expected from a biased and ill-informed official, who was not even aware that the population of Utah contained a considerable percentage of gentiles.   When first the Mormons peopled their desert land they had raised with due respect the Union flag, and as citizens of the nation had, in the name of the nation, claimed the territory as the nation's right; but now, on the 24th of July, 1857, while celebrating the tenth anniversary of the arrival of the pioneers, they were to hear for the first time of the approach of a United States army, and, as they supposed, were to be driven out of their homes at the point of the bayonet.

It has not been alleged, however, except by Mormons, that in ordering the Utah expedition the president had any desire to limit the freedom of the saints in its broadest constitutional sense.   However baneful to gentile eyes their rights appeared, however profane their dogmas, however bigoted their rulers, it was not proposed to interfere with them until it was made to appear by the reports of Drum-

the press on the Pacific slope, see, among others, *S. F. Alta,* Apr. 24, May 21, July 15, Nov. 13, 16, 1857; *S. F. Bulletin,* Apr. 15, 1857; *Sac. Daily Union,* Oct. 27, 1857; *S. L. C. Contributor,* iii.–iv. passim.

mond and others that they came in conflict with the secular authorities, and even then every precaution was taken to avoid, if possible, the shedding of blood. "The instructions of the commanding officer," writes the secretary of war, "were deliberately considered and carefully drawn, and he was charged not to allow any conflict to take place between the troops and the people of the territory, except only he should be called upon by the governor for soldiers to act as a posse comitatus in enforcing obedience to the laws."

Before the departure of the troops an opinion was requested of General Winfield Scott as to the prospects of an expedition during the year 1857. The general's decision was strongly against the despatch of an army until the following season, on account of the distance and the time required for the concentration of regiments. It would have been well if his advice had been taken, but other counsels prevailed, and about the end of May orders were given that a force, consisting of the 5th and 10th infantry, the 2d dragoons, and a battery of the 4th artillery, should assemble as soon as possible at Fort Leavenworth.[31] Several reënforcements were sent forward during the year, and in June 1858 there were more than six thousand troops in Utah, or en route for that territory.[32] The command was given to Brigadier-general Harney, a man of much rude force of character, ambitious, and a capable officer, but otherwise ill fitted for the conduct of an expedition that needed the qualities of a diplomatist more than those of a soldier.

It is probable that no expedition was ever despatched by the United States better equipped and provisioned than was the army of Utah,[33] of which the portion

[31] Circular letter of Winfield Scott, addressed to the adjutant-general and other officers, on the 28th of May, 1857. A copy of it will be found in *Tullidge's Hist. S. L. City*, 121-2.

[32] A statement of the disposition of the troops and the reënforcements en route at this date will be found in the report of the secretary of war, in *House Ex. Doc.*, 2, 35th Cong. 2d Sess., pp. 31-2.

[33] For estimates of supplies and subsistence, see *House Ex. Doc.*, 35th Cong. 1st Sess., ix. no. 33, xii. no. 99.

now under orders mustered about twenty-five hundred men. Two thousand head of beef cattle, together with a huge and unwieldy convoy, were sent in advance, the trains being larger than in ordinary warfare would have been required for a force of ten thousand troops. The price to be paid for the transport of stores, provisions, and munitions of war was at the rate of twenty-two cents a pound; and thus it will be seen that if the Utah war served no other purpose, it made the fortunes of those who secured the government contracts. Through a little dexterous manipulation at Washington, permission was given to the man who secured the flour contract to furnish Utah flour, and this he did at a cost of seven cents per pound, receiving, of course, meanwhile, the money allowed for freight, and netting in a single year the sum of $170,000.[34] The troops remained in the territory for about four years, and no wonder that they often asked one of another, "Why were we sent here? Why are we kept here? What good can we do by remaining here?" No wonder also that the people asked, "Were they retained in Utah in order to fill the purses of the contractors?"[35]

Fortunately for the welfare of the expedition, it happened that the harvest of 1857 was a plentiful one, and though the crop of 1856 had been a partial failure, and that of 1855 almost a total failure,[36] there

---

[34] *Greeley's Overland Journey*, 253. Greeley says that this instance had become quite notorious at Washington.

[35] Stenhouse relates that the man who obtained the flour contract received an order for his money payable at Camp Floyd, but had the choice of receiving in lieu army mules at a certain valuation. He chose the latter, and sending them to California realized a profit of nearly 600 per cent on his money. *Rocky Mountain Saints*, 416. For further specimens of sharp practice, see *S. F. Bulletin*, June 8, Aug. 20, 22, 30, 1859.

[36] *Utah Notes*, MS.; *Hist. B. Young*, MS.; *Richards' Incidents in Utah Hist.*, MS., 79–80; *Stenhouse's Rocky Mountain Saints*, 291. The failure was caused by crickets. In a letter to his son in England, Heber writes from S. L. City Feb. 29, 1856: 'I have been under the necessity of rationing my family and also yours to two thirds of a pound of breadstuff per day each; as the last week is up to-day, we shall commence on half a pound each. This I am under the necessity of doing. Brother Brigham told me to-day that he had put his family on half a pound each, for there is scarcely any grain in the country, and there are thousands that have none at all, scarcely.' This second famine

was now an abundant supply of grain. Neither the famine nor the bountiful harvest which followed appear, however, to have been known to the authorities at Washington. The winter of 1856-7 had been unusually severe. For six months the territory had been shut out from the remainder of the world, no mails having reached the eastern states. To add to their distress, the Mormons were compelled to feed large multitudes of emigrants, who arrived at this period in a starving condition in the hand-cart companies. At the time when the expedition was ordered, there were thousands in the territory who, for more than a year, had not had a full meal; there were thousands of children who had endured the gnawings of hunger until hunger had become to them a second nature. Yet in the orders to Harney, issued while yet the famine was at its sorest, we read: "It is not doubted that a surplus of provisions and forage, beyond the wants of the resident population, will be found in the valley of Utah, and that the inhabitants, if assured by energy and justice, will be ready to sell them to the troops. Hence, no instructions are given you for the extreme event of the troops being in absolute need of such supplies, and their being withheld by the inhabitants. The necessities of such an occasion would furnish a law for your guidance."[37]

But the sequel will show that instead of the troops living on the Mormons, the Mormons lived on the troops, stampeding their cattle, plundering or destroying their provision trains, and only after all fear of active hostilities had been removed, selling them surplus grain at exorbitant rates.

was compared to the famine of Egypt. For months some families knew not the taste of bread, and settlements in which good crops had been gathered in former years were compelled to send their teams several hundred miles for bran and shorts. After 1855 the Mormons stored their surplus wheat at each harvest, until the completion of the overland railroad removed all fear of famine.

[37] Letter of Aide-de-camp George W. Lay to Harney, dated from the headquarters of the army, New York, June 29, 1857. A copy of it will be found in *Tullidge's Hist. S. L. City*, 122-4.

Before the end of June 1857 the first division of the army of Utah was assembled at Fort Leavenworth, and before the end of July was on its march to Salt Lake City, Harney remaining meanwhile with some squadrons of the second dragoons in Kansas, where trouble was anticipated at the forthcoming elections in October. In the instructions issued to the general, it was stated that though the lateness of the season and the smallness of the force presented difficulties, if not danger, it was believed that these obstacles might be overcome by care in its outfit and prudence in its conduct. No expense was to be spared that would insure the efficiency, health, and comfort of the troops; a large discretion was allowed in the purchase of supplies, and no reasonable limit was placed as to the number of guides, interpreters, spies, and laborers to be employed. The men were to be so completely equipped as to act, for a time, as a self-sustaining machine, and to be kept well massed and in hand. Detachments were not to be lightly hazarded, but a small, though sufficient, force was to move separately in charge of the more cumbersome part of the convoy, and in advance of the rest, until overtaken by the main body, when it was to form the rear-guard. Thus no precautions were omitted that might serve to insure the success of the expedition, and it was hoped that its purpose might be attained without the loss of a single life.

Meanwhile, events of some importance had transpired at Washington. The governorship of Utah, after being refused by several persons, was accepted in July by Alfred Cumming, who had recently been superintendent of Indian affairs on the upper Missouri, in which capacity he had displayed tact and executive ability. About the same time D. R. Eckles was appointed chief justice, and John Cradlebaugh and Charles E. Sinclair, associate judges.

During the month of June, also, a contract granted to Hiram Kimball, for the carriage of the United

States mails between Salt Lake City and Independence, Missouri, was annulled, ostensibly on account of their non-arrival within the stipulated time.[38] Between 1851 and 1856 the service had been regularly performed, the contract being held in the autumn of 1856 by the gentile firm of Hockaday & Magraw,[39] the lat-

[38] In a distorted sketch of the Utah expedition, in the *Atlantic Monthly*, March 1859, p. 367, the writer gives, as the actual reason, that the postmaster believed the mails to have been tampered with, by order of Brigham Young, at S. L. City or en route. It is improbable that Brigham would take such risks, for, as we shall see, he now proposed to establish an express company in connection with the mails.

[39] During the winter of 1856–7 no regular mail service was performed, on account of the severity of the season. The postmaster at S. L. City contracted, however, with Messrs Little and Hanks to carry a mail to Independence for $1,500. They made the trip in 78 days, having suffered severely from cold and hunger. *Little's Mail Service*, MS., 35–8. Mr Little had been for several years connected with the mail service. In 1850 Sam. H. Woodson of Independence, Mo., made a contract with the U. S. P. O. department to carry a monthly mail for four years between that point and S. L. City. This was the first government mail service performed between S. L. City and any point east of the Rocky Mountains. Mr Little afterward contracted with Woodson to carry the mail between S. L. City and Fort Laramie, where the mails exchanged, commencing the service Aug. 1, 1851, and associating with himself Ephraim K. Hanks and Charles F. Decker. At that time there was no settlement between S. L. City and Fort Laramie, except the trading post at Fort Bridger. On their first trip Little and Hanks met Secretary Harris and judges Brocchus and Brandebury between Green River and South Pass. They reached Laramie in nine days, without changing their animals, and there procured five unbroken Mexican mules, with which they completed their journey. In Sept. 1851 C. F. Decker and Alfred Higgins set out in charge of a mail, Delegate Bernhisel being a passenger. At Box Elder Creek their party was stopped by 20 Indians, who plundered the wagon. On Oct. 1, 1851, Mr Little started on a second trip eastward, among his passengers being Judge Brandebury, and among his fellow-travellers Judge Brocchus. Mr Little's third trip was made in Nov. and Dec. 1852, Howard Livingstone, of the firm of Livingstone & Kinkead, being one of his passengers. In Feb. 1852 and May 1853 Mr Decker carried the mails to Laramie, having a narrow escape from death at the hands of hostile Indians on his second trip, on which occasion he met with Kit Carson, to whose intercession he ascribes his deliverance. Another trip was made by Mr Little in April 1853. *Id.*, 1–34; *Utah Early Records*, MS., passim. For further particulars on mail routes and services up to 1856, see *U. S. Acts and Resol.*, 31st Cong. 1st Sess., 111; *H. Ex. Doc.*, 1, pt 3, 33d Cong. 1st Sess., pt iii. p. 821; *Burton's City of the Saints*, 5; *Frontier Guardian*, March 7, 1849, Apr. 17, 1850; *Deseret News*, Apr. 8, 1851, Dec. 25, 1852, May 14, 1853; *Fisher's Amer. Stat. Annual*, 1854, pp. 127–8; *Sac. Union*, Apr. 18, 1855. In the *Mail Service across the Plains, by F. Little*, MS. (S. L. City, 1884), are many incidents of travel during the years of which his manuscript treats. The service was performed under great difficulties, the author suffering many hardships and having several narrow escapes from Indians. Ferezmore Little, a native of Cayuga co., N. Y., came to S. L. City in 1850, and joined the Mormon church in 1853. In 1854–5 he superintended the construction of the Big Cottonwood cañon wagon road and the building of the penitentiary. In 1868–9 he was engaged in railroad work on the Union Pacific, and afterward became interested, as we shall see later, in the Utah Central and Utah Southern railroads.

ter of whom, when it was awarded to a Mormon, addressed a malignant epistle to the president. "I have no doubt," he declares, "that the time is near at hand and the elements rapidly combining to bring about a state of affairs which will result in indiscriminate bloodshed, robbery, and rapine, and which, in a brief space of time, will reduce that country to the condition of a howling wilderness." The remainder of Magraw's communication,[40] though containing no specific charges, is in a similar vein.

This despatch was probably the actual reason that led to the withdrawal of the mail contract, and certainly among the reasons that led to the Utah war; for in answer to a resolution asking for details as to the cause of the expedition, the secretary of state reported that the only document on record or on file in his department was the letter of Mr Magraw to the president.[41]

The annual payment on account of Hiram Kimball's contract amounted only to $23,600 a year, a sum barely sufficient to defray expenses; but such a favor, small as it was, had never before been conferred on a Mormon citizen. Brigham resolved, therefore, that all diligence should be used in keeping faith with the government, and for his own benefit established in connection with the mail service the B. Y. Express Carrying Company. In the early spring of 1857 the snow was still deep on plain and mountain, and to build stations and provide draught animals, and forage for the entire distance of more than twelve hundred miles was no easy task. But Brigham had at his call the entire community. Summoning the more enterprising of the brethren, he laid before them his plan, convinced them that the B. Y. Express would develop

[40] See *Utah Notes*, MS.; *Hist. B. Young*, MS.; *House Ex. Doc.*, 35th Cong. 1st Sess., x. no. 71, pp. 2–3.

[41] *Id.*, pp. 1–2. In doc. no. 71 are the reports of the secretary of state, of war, and of the interior, and also that of the attorney-general, relating to the expedition. Reference is frequently made to them in this and the following chapter.

into a good money-making enterprise, and would place
Utah in frequent intercourse with the world long before an overland railroad could be completed. Moreover, it was proposed that Mormon settlements should
be formed along the line of route, and parties were at
once organized and equipped for this purpose.[42]

On the 2d of June, 1857, Abraham O. Smoot, then
mayor of Salt Lake City,[43] set out in charge of the
eastward-bound mail and of the B. Y. Express. Between Fort Laramie and Fort Kearny he encountered the advanced guard of the army of Utah, and,
as he relates, was informed by the commanding officer
that the troops "were reconnoitring the country in
search of hostile Indians." When about a hundred
miles west of Independence freight teams were met,
destined, as the drivers said, for some western post,
but for what particular post they did not know. On
reaching Kansas City, Smoot repaired with one Nich-
olas Groesbeck, who took charge of the mails at that
point, to the office of William H. Russell, and there

[42] *Stenhouse's Rocky Mountain Saints*, 345–6; *Hist. B. Young*, MS.; *Little's Mail Service*, MS.

[43] As successor to Grant, who died Dec. 1, 1856. *Smith's Rise, Progress, and Travels*, 27; *Deseret News*, Dec. 3, 1856. Jedediah Morgan Grant was a native of Windsor, Broome co., N. Y., his parents, Joshua and Athalia Grant, née Howard, removing to Naples, Ontario co., in 1817, about a year after his birth. Here the lad remained until he was 14 years of age, and receiving lit-tle education, was trained to his father's calling, that of a farmer. The family then removed to Erie co., Penn., and two years later Jedediah heard for the first time the doctrines of Mormonism. Being convinced of their truth, he was baptized in 1832, by Elder John F. Boyington, who afterward became an apostle, and, when 18 years of age, accompanied Zion's camp in its migration to Missouri. In the winter of 1835 he was ordained, at Kirtland, a member of the first quorum of seventy, and the following spring started forth on his first mission, his labors as a missionary extending over eleven years, princi-pally in the southern and middle states. At the expulsion from Nauvoo, he was was one of those who crossed the Mississippi in Feb. 1846, and though not a pioneer, was among the earliest settlers in the valley of Great Salt Lake, being one of the captains of hundreds appointed during the migration of 1847. After holding office under the provisional government of the state of Deseret, he was elected speaker of the house of representatives; he was also appointed brigadier-general and afterward major-general in the Nauvoo legion, and in April 1854, after the decease of Willard Richards, was made second council-lor to Brigham. In the funeral sermon of this much esteemed citizen, deliv-ered at the tabernacle Dec. 4, 1856, Brigham remarked: 'He has been in the church upwards of twenty-four years, and was a man that would live, com-paratively speaking, a hundred years in that time.' *Id.*, Dec. 10, 1856; *Lin-forth's Route from Liverpool*, 115–16; *S. L. City Contributor*, iv. 241–5, 281–3.

ascertained that the freight trains were intended for Salt Lake City, that Cumming had been appointed governor, and that orders had been given that no more mails should for the present be delivered to the Mormons. Harnessing his fleetest animals to a light spring wagon, Smoot immediately started homeward, and making the distance from Fort Laramie in about five days, found the brethren celebrating their pioneer anniversary at Little Cottonwood Cañon.[44]

Thus, in part through the stubbornness of the Mormons, but in part also through the malice of a dissolute and iniquitous judge, the spite of a disappointed mail contractor, the wire-pulling of birds of prey at Washington, and possibly in accordance with the policy of the president, who, until the confederate flag had been unfurled at Fort Sumter, retained in the valley of Great Salt Lake nearly all the available forces in the Union army and a store of munitions of war sufficient to furnish an arsenal, was brought about the Utah war.

"Give us ten years of peace, and we will ask no odds of the United States," declared Brigham when the pioneers first entered the valley. And now the ten years had passed, and on the margin of a mountain lake, seven thousand feet above sea-level, under bowers of fragrant pine and fir, twenty-five hundred of the saints were assembled on the 24th of July, 1857. It was a day of feasting and recreation. Hand in hand with little children, who had seen nothing of the great world beyond their native valley, walked silver-haired elders and apostles, who had passed through all the tribulations of Kirtland and Nauvoo. Of the rest, some were strolling among the trees, some were fishing in the lake, some were dancing, some busied with games. Laughter and the noise of merry-making mingled with the songs of Zion. It was now near even-fall, and the western sun had already crimsoned the frosted peaks, when two dust-stained messen-

[44] Letter of A. O. Smoot.

gers rode in hot haste up the cañon, and announced to the brethren the approach of the army of Utah.

All eyes turned at once to Brigham. It was at times like the present, when the hearts of the others sank within them, that his genius rose superior to all obstacles, proving him the born leader that all acknowledged him to be. Gathering the people around him, he repeated the words uttered ten years before, prophesying even now that at no distant day he would himself become president of the United States, or dictate who should be president. Then festivities were renewed, and when the day was far spent the people returned to their homes with trust in Brigham and the God of Joseph.

Then war became the universal theme. Fire-arms were manufactured or repaired; scythes were turned into bayonets; long-unused sabres were burnished and sharpened, and from all parts of the earth the saints were summoned to the defence of Zion. Apostles Lyman and Rich, who were in charge of the saints at San Bernardino, and Orson Hyde, who, as we shall see, had founded a thriving colony in Carson Valley, were ordered to break up their settlements and gather to the defence of Zion. Messengers were sent to the Atlantic states and to Europe to summon home the elders and apostles,[45] and, had it been possible, thousands of converts from all parts of the world would have rallied this year round the standard of the prophet.

On the 8th of September Captain Van Vliet arrived in Salt Lake City,[46] with orders to purchase forage and lumber, and to assure the Mormons that

[45] The elders returning from Europe landed as secretly as possible in New York, fearing that they would be molested by the authorities, and most of them journeyed to Utah overland by various routes. The apostles crossed the Atlantic incognito, and remaining there in disguise until the steamer sailed for Panamá, travelled by way of San Francisco and southern California, accompanied by a small body-guard of elders. *Stenhouse's Rocky Mountain Saints*, 354–5.

[46] According to special instructions, dated army headquarters, Fort Leavenworth, July 28, 1857. See Van Vliet's rept to the acting assistant adj.-general army of Utah, in *H. Ex. Doc.*, 35th Cong. 1st Sess., ii. pt 2, p. 25.

the troops would not molest or interfere with them.
Though informed by parties whom he met en route
that he would not be allowed to enter the territory,
or would do so at the risk of his life, the captain met
with a cordial reception. Brigham, Wells, Bernhisel,
and other leading citizens called at his quarters on the
evening of his arrival, and a formal interview was appointed for the following day[47] at the social hall, when
Van Vliet was introduced to a large number of prominent Mormons, presented to Brigham an official letter
from Harney, and declared the purpose of his mission.
The governor and the captain then retired with a few
others to a private office, where a conversation took
place, from which I give a few extracts that may be of
interest to the reader.

"We do not want to fight the United States," remarked Brigham, "but if they drive us to it, we shall
do the best we can; and I will tell you, as the Lord
lives, we shall come off conquerors. The United
States are sending their armies here to simply hold
us until a mob can come and butcher us, as has been
done before. We are the supporters of the constitution of the United States, and we love that constitution and respect the laws of the United States; but
it is by the corrupt administration of those laws that
we are made to suffer. Most of the government officers who have been sent here have taken no interest
in us, but on the contrary, have tried many times to
destroy us."

"This is the case with most men sent to the territories," Van Vliet replied. "They receive their offices
as a political reward, or as a stepping-stone to the sen-
atorship; but they have no interest in common with
the people. The greatest hold that the government
now has upon you is in the accusation that you have
burned the United States records."

[47] In his *Life of Brigham Young*, 262, Tullidge gives Aug. 12th, and in his
Hist. Salt Lake City, 161, Sept. 12th, as the date of Van Vliet's first formal
interview with Brigham. The correct date is Sept. 9th. See *Deseret News*,
Sept. 16, 1857, where is a description of the captain's visit.

"I deny that any books of the United States have been burned," said Brigham. "I have broken no law; and under the present state of affairs, I will not suffer myself to be taken by any United States officer to be killed as they killed Joseph Smith."

"I do not think it is the intention of the government to arrest you," sa'd Van Vliet, "but to install a new governor in the te.ritory."

"I believe you tell the truth," returned Brigham, "that you believe this—but you do not know their intentions as well as I do. If they dare to force the issue, I shall not hold the Indians by the wrist any longer for white men to shoot at them; they shall go ahead and do as they please. If the issue comes, you may tell the government to stop all emigration across the continent, for the Indians will kill all who attempt it. And if an army succeeds in penetrating this valley, tell the government to see that it has forage and provisions in store, for they will find here only a charred and barren waste. We have plenty here of what you want, but we will sell you nothing. Further than this, your army shall not enter this valley."[48]

In vain Van Vliet remonstrated, stating that though the mountain passes might be defended against the small army then approaching Utah, a force would surely be sent, during the following year, that would overcome all opposition. To this warning, several times repeated, but one answer was returned: "We are aware that such will be the case; but when these troops arrive they will find Utah a desert; every house will be burned to the ground, every tree cut down, and every field laid waste. We have three years' provisions on hand, which we will cache, and then take

[48] *Woodruff's Journal*, MS., in which were originally noted the words spoken a few hours after the interview took place. There is little doubt that, so far as I have quoted them, they are substantially true. In his report, ut supra, Van Vliet says that at this and other interviews Brigham declared that 'the Mormons had been persecuted, murdered, and robbed in Missouri and Illinois, both by the mob and state authorities, and that now the U. S. were about to pursue the same course; and that, therefore, he and the people of Utah had determined to resist all persecution at the commencement.'

to the mountains and bid defiance to all the powers of the government."

During the captain's visit, Brigham, with the apostles, General Wells of the Nauvoo legion, and others, asked him to walk through their grounds, and introducing him to some of the Mormon women, showed him the garden-spots which their hands had fashioned out of the wilderness. "What, madam," he exclaimed to one of the sisters, "would you consent to see this beautiful home in ashes and this fruitful orchard destroyed?" "I would not only consent to it," was the answer, "but I would set fire to my home with my own hands, and cut down every tree, and root up every plant." On the following sabbath the captain attended divine service at the tabernacle, when John Taylor, after referring in his discourse to the approach of the troops, and repeating that they should not be allowed to enter the territory, desired all who would apply the torch to their dwellings, cut down their trees, and lay waste their farms to raise their hands. Every hand was raised in a congregation numbering more than four thousand. "When the time comes to burn and lay waste our improvements," said Brigham in a sermon delivered on the same day, "if any man undertakes to shield his he will be treated as a traitor. ...Now the faint-hearted can go in peace; but should that time come, they must not interfere. Before I will again suffer, as I have in times gone by, there shall not one building, nor one foot of lumber, nor a fence, nor a tree, nor a particle of grass or hay, that will burn, be left in reach of our enemies. I am sworn, if driven to extremity, to utterly lay waste this land in the name of Israel's God, and our enemies shall find it as barren as when we came here."

Captain Van Vliet was astounded. He had expected to find a seditious and priest-ridden community, mouth-valiant and few in number, whom the mere approach of the troops would tame into submission. He found instead this handful of enthusiasts, rising against the might of a great nation. He declared, as the Mormons relate, that if the United States made war on them, he would withdraw from the army. Quitting Salt Lake City a few days afterward, he arrived at Washington in November, and delivered his report to the secretary of war.[49]

On the day after the captain's departure, Brigham issued a proclamation declaring martial law in Utah, forbidding all armed forces to enter the territory under any pretence whatever, and ordering the Mormon militia to be in readiness to march at a moment's notice.[50] It is probable that the Nauvoo legion, which now included the entire militia force of the territory, mustered at this date from four to five thousand men.[51] Though imperfectly armed and equipped, and of course no match for regular troops, they were not to be held in contempt. In July 1857 the legion had been reorganized, the two cohorts, now termed divisions, having each a nominal strength of two thousand. The divisions consisted of two brigades, the brigades of two regiments, the regiments of five battalions, each of a hundred men,[52] the battalion being divided into companies of fifty, and the companies into platoons of ten. Each platoon was in charge of a lieutenant, whose duty it was carefully to inspect the

[49] A copy of it will be found in *House Ex. Doc.*, 35th Cong. 1st Sess., ii. pt 2, pp. 24-7, 37-8. It contains no specific statements not already made, except that Brigham's only objection to the troops entering Utah was that in doing so they would open the door for the rabble of the western frontier, which, as in former days, would persecute and annoy the saints. Copies of the correspondence between Van Vliet and Brigham as to the purchase of forage and lumber for army use will be found in *Id.*, 35-7.

[50] For copies of the proclamation, dated Sept. 15, 1851, and comments thereon, see *Id.*, 32-3; *Stenhouse's Rocky Mountain Saints*, 358-9; *Hist. B. Young*, MS.; *Waite's The Mormon Prophet*, 43-5; *Tucker's Mormonism*, 232-7; *S. F. Alta*, Nov. 25, 30, 1857; *S. F. Herald*, Nov. 25, 1857; *Sac. Daily Union*, Nov. 25, 1857.

[51] In a report of the secretary of war, in *Sen. Doc.*, 33d Cong. 2d Sess., vi. no. 33, the strength of the Utah militia in 1854 is given at 1,744 infantry and 1,004 cavalry, or a total of 2,748 men. In this return it is stated that they had no ordnance except one howitzer, and no ordnance stores; but, as we have seen, some of their forts were mounted with cannon. Brigham, in his message of Dec. 11, 1854, in *Utah, Jour. Legisl.*, 1854-5, anticipates a considerable increase in the new enrolments. In the *Oregon Argus* of Feb. 13, 1858, the Mormon forces are estimated at 5,000.

[52] The brigades contained 1,000 and the regiments 500 men.

arms, ammunition, and accoutrements. Those who failed to provide their equipments were fined, and those who disposed of them were tried by court-martial and doubly fined. Penalties were also imposed for non-attendance at muster and drill.[53] The cavalry arm was for a time abolished[54] as unsuited to mountain warfare, and a corps of topographical engineers organized, together with an ordnance corps.

All able-bodied males in the territory, except those exempt by law, were liable, as we have seen, to military service, and it is probable that the Mormons could put in the field not less than seven thousand raw troops, half disciplined, indeed, but inured to hardship, and most of them excellent marksmen. If Brigham had now carried out his threat of letting loose the Indian tribes of Utah, the United States forces would have been hopelessly outnumbered. Arms and ammunition were supplied in part from San Bernardino,[55] though no considerable reënforcements from southern California arrived until after the crisis was over, and those from Carson Valley did not exceed one hundred men capable of bearing arms.[56]

It was not, of course, the intention of the saints to encounter the army of Utah in the open field, or even behind breastworks, if it could be avoided. In order

[53] *Utah, Acts Legisl.* (ed. 1866), 190–3, where is a copy of an act, approved Jan. 15, 1857, for the organization of the militia, and of the regulations adopted six months later. The regulations were first published in the *Deseret News*, Apr. 1st of this year. Previous acts relating to the militia, approved in 1852, will be found in *Utah, Acts Legisl.* (ed. 1855), 207–22, 231–2. Daniel H. Wells remained lieutenant-general, James Ferguson was adjutant-general, and A. P. Rockwood commissary-general. The names of other officers will be found in *Id.* (ed. 1866), 193; *Deseret News*, Apr. 29, 1857. All the officers were elected except those in the engineers' and ordnance corps. Further items concerning the legion will be found in *Id.*, July 6, 1859; *S. F. Alta*, Aug. 11, 1857; *Or. Statesman*, Oct. 20, 1857.

[54] By general order issued at the headquarters of the legion. A copy of it will be found in the *Deseret News*, July 1, 1857.

[55] In *Hayes' Scraps, San Bernardino*, i. 53, we read: 'Arms and ammunition continue to be forwarded from San Bernardino. The last mail-rider took along—in Nov. 1857—500 revolvers, which passed through this city.'

[56] With the exception of a few persons, the Carson Mormons started for S. L. City Sept. 26, 1857, and arrived Nov. 2d. They mustered about 450 persons, several being from Or. and Cal., had with them 123 wagons, and were in charge of Chester Loveland. *Early Hist. Carson Valley*, MS., 5.

to explain their tactics, I cannot do better than quote a few lines from a despatch addressed soon afterward by the lieutenant-general of the Nauvoo legion to Major Joseph Taylor, and signed, "your brother in Christ, Daniel H. Wells." "On ascertaining the locality or route of the troops, proceed at once to annoy them in every possible way. Use every exertion to stampede their animals and set fire to their trains. Burn the whole country before them and on their flanks. Keep them from sleeping, by night surprises; blockade the road by felling trees or destroying the river fords where you can. Watch for opportunities to set fire to the grass on their windward, so as, if possible, to envelop their trains. Leave no grass before them that can be burned. Keep your men concealed as much as possible, and guard against surprise."[57]

[57] A copy of the letter is given in *Tullidge's Hist. Salt Lake City*, 172. The major was captured, and the letter delivered to Assistant Adjuant-general Porter when 16 miles from Fort Bridger. In a postscript the major is ordered to 'take no life.' In *Lee's Mormonism Unvailed*, 18–19, is a copy of a circular letter, dated S. L. City, Sept. 14, 1857, and signed by Brigham Young and Daniel H. Wells, in which a similar plan of operations is marked out. 'But save life always,' is the injunction, 'when it is possible; we do not wish to shed a drop of blood if it can be avoided.'

CHAPTER XIX.

THE UTAH WAR.

1857-1858.

Opening of the Campaign—Burning of Supply Trains—Strategic Movement of Colonel Alexander—His Retreat—Arrival of Albert
Sidney Johnston—The March to Fort Bridger—Winter at Camp
Scott—Mission of Colonel Kane—Governor Cumming at Salt Lake
City—Pardon Proclaimed—The Peace Commissioners—The Army
of Utah Advances on Zion—The City Deserted—The Mormons Return to their Homes—The Troops Cantoned at Camp Floyd—Conduct of the Soldiery and Camp Followers—Judges Sinclair and
Cradlebaugh—The Reformation in Utah.

" I am ordered there, and I will winter in the valley
or in hell," exclaimed General Harney, who had now
joined the expedition, when Van Vliet on his way to
Washington reported to him the condition of affairs
among the Mormons. With such prospects before
them, it was probably fortunate for the army of Utah
that the command changed hands early in the campaign, the general's services being again required in
Kansas, Colonel Albert Sidney Johnston, then at Fort
Leavenworth, being appointed his successor, and Colonel Alexander, the senior officer, meanwhile assuming command.

About the middle of August, Colonel Robert Burton with seventy men from the first regiment of the
Nauvoo legion, afterward joined by a company from
Provo, had already been sent eastward as a corps of
observation, with instructions to follow the main emigrant trail, protect incoming Mormon trains, ascertain the number, equipments, and materiel of the

United States troops, and report to headquarters. On the 22d of September the colonel, accompanied by three others, the remainder of his command being ordered to return slowly toward Salt Lake City, selecting on their way the best points for a defensive campaign, encountered the vanguard of the army of Utah, in the vicinity of Devil's Gate, thence accompanied them to Camp Winfield, on Ham Fork, and afterward proceeded to Fort Bridger.

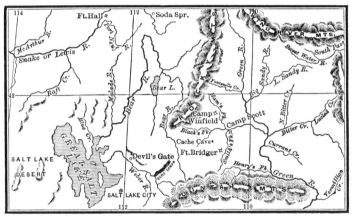

THE UTAH CAMPAIGN.

A few days later General Wells, in command of 1,250 men, supplied with thirty days' rations, established his headquarters at Echo Cañon, a defile some twenty-five miles in length, and whose walls are in places almost within pistol-shot of each other. Through this cañon, the Mormons supposed, lay the path of the invading army, the only means of avoiding the gorge being by a circuitous route northward to Soda Springs, and thence by way of Bear River Valley, or the Wind River Mountains. On the western side of the cañon dams and ditches were constructed, by means of which the road could be submerged to a depth of several feet; at the eastern side stone heaps were collected and bowlders loosened from the overhanging rocks, so that a slight leverage would hurl them on the passing troops, and parapets were built as a protection for sharp-shooters.[1] Leaving his men in charge of staff-officers,[2] the general set forth with a small escort for Fort Bridger, where he was informed by Burton as to the movements and strength of the invading force and the location of its supply trains. It had been ascertained that the army had pressed forward on Fort Winfield to protect the trains, which had been left insufficiently guarded, and it was now feared that the men would be ordered to pack a few days' provisions in their knapsacks and make a forced march on Salt Lake City.

At this juncture a letter from General Wells was delivered to Colonel Alexander, together with copies of the organic act, the laws of Utah, the proclamation forbidding the entrance of armed forces into the territory, and a despatch from Brigham. The last was a remarkable document, and must have been somewhat of a surprise to the colonel, who had proved himself one of the most gallant soldiers of the Mexican war. He was informed that Brigham Young was still governor of Utah, and that he had disregarded his prohibition. He was ordered to withdraw by the same route that he had entered. Should he desire, however, to remain until spring in the neighborhood of his present encampment, he must surrender his arms and ammunition to the Mormon quartermaster-general, in which case he would be supplied with provisions, and would not be molested.[3] The colonel replied in brief and business-like phrase. He addressed Brigham Young as governor; stated that he would

[1] For cut of Echo Cañon, see *Hayden's The Great West*, 313; *Stenhouse's Rocky Mountain Saints*, 363.   The remains of the breastworks and dams were to be seen ten years later. *Kirchoff, Reisebilder*, i. 107-8.
[2] Colonels N. V. Jones and J. D. T. McAllister.
[3] For copies of both letters, see *Secretary of War's Rept House Ex. Doc.*, 35th Cong. 1st Sess., ii. pt 2, pp. 31-3.

submit his letter to the commanding officer immediately on his arrival; that meanwhile the troops were there by order of the president, and that their future movements and operations would depend on orders issued by competent military authority.

On receiving the answer of Colonel Alexander, Wells determined to open the campaign, a plan of which had been before arranged at Salt Lake City. Inviting to dinner Major Lot Smith, who had conveyed the despatches to and from the enemy's camp, he asked him whether he could take some forty men, the only available force then at the Mormon camp at Cache Cave, where Wells was now encamped, and, passing in rear of the foe, turn back or burn the supply trains still on the road. " I think I can," replied Lot Smith; and the next evening he started out. Wells then addressed to Major Joseph Taylor the letter of instructions already quoted.

Riding all night at the head of his detachment, Smith came in sight of a westward-bound government train on the morning of October 3d, and ordered the drivers to go back. This they did, but turned round when out of sight. During the day a party of troops passed them, and relieving the wagons of their freight, left them standing. Smith then started for Sandy Fork, sending a few of his men under Captain Haight in another direction. Soon he observed a cloud of dust in the direction of the old Mormon trail, and was informed by his scouts that a train of twenty-six wagons was approaching. Halting and feeding his men, he approached them at dusk, while encamped at a spot known as Simpson's Hollow, on Green River, and there lay in ambush for several hours. Meanwhile he ascertained, as he relates, that there were two trains, each of twenty-six wagons—there being, in fact, three, with seventy-five wagons in all.[4]

[4] *Rept of Commissary Clarke*, in *House Ex. Doc.*, 35th Cong. 1st Sess., x. no. 71, p. 63. Col. Alexander, however, in his official report to the adjutant-general, dated Camp Winfield, Oct. 9, 1857, says that only two trains were destroyed on Green River, but that one was burned on the Big Sandy, together

It was now near midnight; but a few of the wagoners were still gathered round the camp-fires, some of
them drinking and some smoking, when armed and
mounted men, as it seemed in endless procession,
noiselessly emerged from the darkness, their leader
quietly asking for ' the captain.' Most of the teamsters were asleep, their weapons fastened to the awnings of the wagons, and resistance was almost hopeless.
The captain of the wagoners, Dawson by name, stepped
forward, surrendered his charge, and bade his men
stack their arms and group themselves on a spot
pointed out by Smith, who dealt with the other trains
in like manner. Then, lighting two torches, the major
handed one of them to a gentile in his party, dubbed
Big James, remarking that it was proper for the gentiles to spoil the gentiles. Riding from wagon to
wagon they set fire to the covers, which caught rapidly
in the crisp air of this October night. "By Saint
Patrick, ain't it beautiful!" exclaimed Big James; "I
never saw anything go better in my life." Dawson
meanwhile was sent to the rear of the trains to take
out provisions for his captors. When all the wagons
were fairly in a blaze, the Mormons rode away, telling
their panic-stricken captives that they would return
as soon as they had delivered the spoils to their comrades near by, and instantly shoot any one who should
attempt to extinguish the flames.[5]

with a few wagons belonging to the sutler of the tenth infantry, a few miles
behind the latter. Probably the colonel was for the moment misinformed as to
the train abandoned on the morning of the 4th. The destruction of the sutler's
wagons was perhaps wrought by Haight's party, as Smith states that they
were sent after the convoy of the tenth infantry. Otherwise I find no evidence that this was the case.

[5] Lot Smith's narrative, in *Tullidge's Hist. S. L. City*, 173–5, when stripped
of the braggadocio common to the saints militant—and thus I have given it—
appears to be the best detailed account of this incident. The portions of it
which conflict with the testimony of United States officials I have omitted.
For instance, Smith says: ' His [Dawson's] orders to the train men were from
the commander at Camp Winfield, and were to the effect that the Mormons
were in the field, and that they must not go to sleep, but keep guard on their
trains, and that four companies of cavalry and two pieces of artillery would
come over in the morning to escort them into camp.' The truth appears to
be, that Col Alexander knew nothing about the projected raid. In his report,
ut supra, he mentions that Van Vliet had assured him no armed resistance
would be offered if he did not proceed farther than Fort Bridger and Fort

The army of Utah was now in evil case. Harney had accepted the command reluctantly, and returned to Kansas as soon as possible. Alexander was unfitted for it, and Johnston had not yet arrived. Winter was at hand; forage was almost exhausted; provisions would fail within a few months; and if the troops could not move into quarters within fourteen days, there would be no animals left alive to convey their supplies. The pitiful strait that had now overtaken them is explained in a letter addressed by Colonel Alexander, four days after the Green River catastrophe, to the officers in command of forces en route for Utah. "No information of the position or intentions of the commanding officer has reached me," he writes, "and I am in utter ignorance of the objects of the government in sending troops here, or the instructions given for their conduct after reaching here. I have had to decide upon the following points: First, the necessity of a speedy move to winter quarters; second, the selection of a point for wintering; third, the best method of conducting the troops and supplies to the point selected." A council of war was held, and the point selected was Fort Hall, on Beaver Head Mountain, 140 miles from Fort Bridger. So little did the colonel know even about the disposition of the command, that, at the time and place when he expected to be joined by Colonel Smith, in charge of supply trains, this officer was still at South Pass, with an escort of two hundred men.

On the 11th of October the troops commenced their march. Snow was falling heavily, and for several days they were compelled to cut a path for their

Supply, and that 100 wagons had been parked for three weeks on Ham Fork without being molested. On the other hand, he states in the same report that Col Waite of the fifth infantry, though not anticipating any trouble, was preparing to send a detachment to the trains when he heard of their destruction. For other accounts and comments on the disaster on Green River, see *Hickman's Destroying Angel*, 117–21; *Beadle's Life in Utah*, 189; *Burton's City of the Saints*, 208–9; *S. F. Bulletin*, Dec. 11, 1857; *S. F. Alta*, Dec. 17, 30, 1857; *Sac. Union*, Dec. 11, 1857. The list of stores destroyed is given in *Commissary Clarke's Report*, in *H. Ex. Doc.*, 35th Cong. 1st Sess., no. 71, p. 63.

wagons through the dense brush, their trains being
still of such unwieldy length that the vanguard had
reached its camping-ground at nightfall before the
rear-guard had moved from its camp of the preceding
day. Meanwhile bands of Mormons, under their
nimble and ubiquitous leaders, hung on their flanks,
just out of rifle-shot, harassing them at every step,
700 oxen being captured and driven to Salt Lake
City on the 13th. There was as yet no cavalry in
the force. A few infantry companies were mounted
on mules and sent in pursuit of the guerrillas, but the
saints merely laughed at them, terming them jackass
cavalry. The grass had been burned along the line
of route, and the draught-animals were so weak that
they could travel but three miles a day. When the
point was reached where Smith's detachment was
expected to join the army, the commander, disappointed and sore perplexed, called a second council,
at which many of the officers were in favor of cutting
their way through the cañons at all hazard.

At this juncture a despatch was received from
Johnston, who was now at South Pass, ordering
the troops to proceed to Fontenelle Creek, where
pasture was abundant; and a few days later a second
despatch directed them to march to a point three
miles below the junction of Ham and Black forks,
the colonel stating that he would join them at the
latter point. On the 3d of November they reached
the point of rendezvous, where Johnston arrived
the following day, with a reënforcement of cavalry
and the supply trains in charge of Smith.[6]

Albert Sidney Johnston was a favorite officer, and
had already given earnest of the qualities that he displayed a few years later in the campaigns of the civil
war. The morale of the army was at once restored,
and at the touch of this great general each man put
forth his utmost energy. But their troubles were

[6] Johnston's despatch, in *House Ex. Doc.*, 35th Cong. 1st Sess., no. 71,
pp. 65–6; *Stenhouse's Rocky Mountain Saints*, 369.

not yet ended. The expedition was now ordered to Fort Bridger, and at every step difficulties increased. There were only thirty-five miles to be traversed, but, except on the margin of a few slender streams, the country through which lay their route was the barest of desert land. There was no shelter from the chill blasts of this mountain solitude, where, even in November, the thermometer sometimes sank to 16° below zero. There was no fuel but the wild sage and willow; there was little pasture for the half-frozen cattle.

The march commenced on the 6th of November, and on the previous night 500 of the strongest oxen had been stolen by the Mormons. The trains extended over six miles, and all day long snow and sleet fell on the retreating column. Some of the men were frost-bitten, and the exhausted animals were goaded by their drivers until many fell dead in their traces. At sunset the troops encamped wherever they could find a particle of shelter, some under bluffs, and some in the willow copses. At daybreak the camp was surrounded with the carcasses of frozen cattle, of which several hundreds had perished during the night. Still, as the trains arrived from the rear, each one halted for a day or more, giving time for the cattle to rest and graze on such scant herbage as they could find. To press forward more rapidly was impossible, for it would have cost the lives of most of the draught-animals; to find shelter was equally impossible, for there was none. There was no alternative but to proceed slowly and persistently, saving as many as possible of the horses, mules, and oxen. Fifteen days were required for this difficult operation.[7] Meanwhile Colonel St George Cooke, who arrived on the 19th by way of Fort Laramie, at the head of 500 dragoons, had fared no better than the main body, having lost nearly half of his cattle.[8]

[7] Rept of Col Johnston, dated Camp Scott, Nov. 30, 1857, in *House Ex. Doc.*, 35th Cong. 1st Sess., x. no. 71, p. 77.

[8] *Ibid.* On the 5th the command passed Devil's Gate, and on the following

A length the army of Utah arrived at Fort Bridger —to find that the buildings in and around it, together with those at Fort Supply, twelve miles distant, had been burned to the ground by Mormons, and the grain or other provisions removed or destroyed. All that remained were two enclosures surrounded by walls of cobblestone cemented with mortar, the larger one being a hundred feet square. This was appropriated for the storage of supplies, while on the smaller one lunettes were built and mounted with cannon. A sufficient garrison was stationed at this point; the cattle were sent for the winter to Henry Fork, in charge of Colonel Cooke and six companies of the second dragoons, and about the end of November, the remainder of the troops went into winter quarters on Black Fork of the Green River, two or three miles beyond Fort Bridger, and a hundred and fifteen from Salt Lake City. The site, to which was given the name of Camp Scott, was sheltered by bluffs,

day, while crossing what he terms a four-mile hill, Colonel Cooke writes: 'The north wind and drifting snow became severe; the air seemed turned to frozen fog; nothing could be seen; we were struggling in a freezing cloud. The lofty wall at Three Crossings was a happy relief; but the guide, who had lately passed there, was relentless in pronouncing that there was no grass... As he promised grass and other shelter two miles farther, we marched on, crossing twice more the rocky stream, half choked with snow and ice; finally he led us behind a great granite rock, but all too small for the promised shelter. Only a part of the regiment could huddle there in the deep snow; whilst the long night through the storm continued, and in fearful eddies from above, before, behind, drove the falling and drifting snow.' Meanwhile the animals were driven once more across the stream to the base of a granite ridge which faced the storm, but where there was grass. They refused to eat, the mules huddling together and moaning piteously, while some of the horses broke away from the guard and went back to the ford. The next day better camping-ground was reached ten miles farther on. On the morning of the 8th, the thermometer marked 44° below freezing-point; but in this weather and through deep snow the men made eighteen miles, and the following day nineteen miles, to the next camping-grounds on Bitter Creek, and in the valley of the Sweetwater. On the 10th matters were still worse. Herders left to bring up the rear with the stray mules could not force them from the valley, and there three fourths of them were left to perish. Nine horses were also abandoned. At night the thermometer marked 25° below zero; nearly all the tent-pins were broken, and nearly forty soldiers and teamsters were on the sick-list, most of them being frost-bitten. 'The earth,' writes the colonel, 'has a no more lifeless, treeless, grassless desert; it contains scarcely a wolf to glut itself on the hundreds of dead and frozen animals which for thirty miles nearly block the road.' Rept in Id., pp. 96–9. See also Rodenbough's From Everglade to Cañon with the Second Dragoons, 214–18.

rising abruptly at a few hundred yards distance from the bed of the stream. Near by were clumps of cotton-wood which the Mormons had attempted to burn; but the wood being green and damp, the fire had merely scorched the bark. Tents of a new pattern[9] were furnished to the men, the poles, to which was attached a strong hoop, being supported by iron tripods. From the hoops the canvas depended in the shape of a cone, somewhat in the fashion of an Indian wigwam. Even when the tents were closed fires could be lighted without discomfort beneath the tripods, a draught being created by the opening at the top. The civil officials, who arrived about this time, dwelt apart in structures resembling the Alaskan barabara—holes dug in the ground over which were built huts of mud-plastered logs. To this part of the encampment was given, in honor of the chief justice, the name of Eckelsville.

Though most of the beef cattle had been carried off by Mormons or Indians, a sufficient number of draught-animals remained to furnish meat for seven months during six days in the week, while of bacon there was enough for one day in the week, and by reducing the rations of flour, coffee, and other articles, they might also be made to last until the 1st of June.[10] Parties were at once sent to New Mexico and Oregon[11] to procure cattle and remounts for the cavalry. Meantime shambles were built, to which the starved animals at Fort Henry were driven, and butchered as soon as they had gathered a little flesh, their meat being jerked and stored for future use.

In loading the wagons at Fort Leavenworth the quartermaster had packed into each train such goods as were at hand, taking no trouble to procure for them

[9] The Sibley pattern. Aide-de-camp Lay's despatch to General Harney, in *Rept*, ut supra, 8.

[10] Capt. H. F. Clarke, in *Id.*, p. 105, gives a statement of the supplies stored at Fort Bridger, Nov. 28, 1857. There were 150 days' rations of flour for 2,400 men, 144 of tea or coffee, 217 of sugar, 222 of beans, rice, or desiccated vegetables, 28 of bacon or ham, 137 of vinegar, and 83 of molasses.

[11] The first under Captain Marcy.

their due proportion of other stores. The trains destroyed at Simpson Hollow, for instance, were laden entirely with provisions, while three others that followed contained the tents and all the clothing. Fortunately the latter did not fall into the hands of the Mormons, though when unpacked it was found that they contained more of utterly useless supplies than of what was really needed. For an army of about 2,400 men, wintering in a region 7,000 feet above the sea-level, where at night the thermometer always sinks below zero, there had been provided 3,150 bedsacks—articles well suited for a pleasure camp in summer—and only 723 blankets; there were more than 1,500 pairs of epaulets and metallic scales, but only 938 coats and 676 great-coats; there were 307 cap covers, and only 190 caps; there were 1,190 military stocks; but though some of the men were already barefooted, and others had no covering for their feet except moccasins, there were only 823 pairs of boots and 600 pairs of stockings.[12] One of the wagons had been freighted entirely with camp kettles, but brine could not be had, for at this time there was not a pound of salt in the entire camp, a supply proffered as a gift from Brigham, whom Johnston now termed the great Mormon rebel, being rejected with contempt.[13]

Thus did the army of Utah pass the winter of 1857–8, amid privations no less severe than those endured at Valley Forge eighty-one years before; but this army was composed of seasoned veterans, under able leadership, and the men were confident and even

[12] *Assistant Quartermaster Dickerson's Rept*, dated Camp Scott, Nov. 29, 1857, in *Id.*, pp. 106–7, where will be found a list of all the clothing on hand at that date.

[13] A copy of Brigham's letter, dated S. L. City, Nov. 26, 1857, stating that he has forwarded a load of about 800 lbs, to which Col Johnston is welcome as a gift, but for which payment will be accepted if preferred, will be found in *Id.*, pp. 110–11. Tullidge says that the salt was secretly brought into camp, but that the commander would not eat of it, and that the officers' mess was soon afterward supplied by Indians at the rate of $5 per lb. *Hist. S. L. City,* 196.

cheerful. The festivities of christmas and new year were celebrated with song and dance and martial music, in pavilions for which the timber had been hauled by hand through miles of snow. Over each one waved the regimental colors, and over that of the fifth infantry fluttered the remnants of the flag that had been torn to shreds at Molino del Rey, and borne in triumph up the slopes of Chapultepec.

Meanwhile the Mormon militia had returned to the valley, as soon as the snow had closed up the mountain cañons. The saints of course regarded the disasters of the federal army as a righteous judgment of providence on a nation that took arms against Zion, and welcomed their returning warriors with pæans of triumph,[14] stigmatizing the foe in sorry and insulting doggerel.[15] At the tabernacle elders waxed bold, and all their remonstrances and overtures of peace being now rejected,[16] they openly avowed, sometimes in braggart phrase, their contempt for the United

---

[14] In a song of welcome composed by W. G. Mills, and published in the *Deseret News*, Jan. 13, 1858, are the following lines:

Strong in the power of Brigham's God,
 Your name 's a terror to our foes;
Ye were a barrier strong and broad
 As our high mountains crowned with snows.

. . . . .

Sing! fellow-soldiers in our cause,
 For God will show his mighty hand:
Zion shall triumph, and her laws
 The standard be to every land.

[15] In *Id.*, Jan. 27, 1858, is a song composed by Matthew Rowan of South Cottonwood, commencing:

Who in all Deseret 's afraid
 Of Uncle Sam, and a' that?

A lengthy, and if possible more silly, effusion appears in *Id.*, Feb. 17, 1858. Stenhouse relates that after partaking of the sacrament at the tabernacle the saints concluded divine service with a chorus sung to the tune of 'Du dah day,' and commencing:

Old Sam has sent, I understand,
 Du dah,
A Missouri ass to rule our land,
 Du dah, du dah day.

Rocky Mountain Saints, 372. I find no mention of such a song in the files of the *Deseret News*. In the issue of Oct. 21, 1858, is an adapted translation of the Marseillaise, also rendered by W. G. Mills, who afterward apostatized.

[16] For copies of further correspondence between Brigham and Col Alexander, see *Tullidge's Hist. S. L. City*, 176-84; for letter addressed by John Taylor to Capt Marcy. *Id.*, 184-9. They are also given with some additions in the *Deseret News*, Jan. 13, 1858, and in *House Ex. Doc.*, 35th Cong. 1st Sess., x. no. 71, p. 48 et seq.

States government and its army,[17] and declared that Israel should now be free.

Meanwhile Governor Cumming declared the Mormons in a state of rebellion, warned them that proceedings would be instituted against the ringleaders by Judge Eckels, and bade the militia disband; but throughout the United States and throughout Europe the question was asked, this winter, "What has become of the army of Utah?" The expedition became known as Buchanan's blunder, and there were many who believed that a harsher phrase would have been more appropriate.

In February 1858 a messenger from Washington arrived at Salt Lake City by way of Los Angeles,[18] and introducing himself under the name of Doctor Osborne, asked for an interview with Brigham Young. He was pale and travel-worn, but his request was immediately granted, for he was indeed a welcome visitor. It was Colonel Thomas L. Kane. The council was summoned, and as the elders recognized their old friend of the days of Nauvoo, every eye was fixed on him, for it was hoped that his mission would put a new aspect on affairs. "Governor Young, and gentlemen," he said, "I come as an ambassador from the chief executive of our nation, and am prepared and duly authorized to lay before you most fully and definitely the feelings and views of the citizens of our common country, and of the executive, towards you, relative to the present position of the territory, and relative to the army of the United States now upon your borders.

"After giving you the most satisfactory evidence

[17] In a sermon delivered at the tabernacle Dec. 13, 1857, Lorenzo D. Young remarked: 'If our enemies—I do not mean those few out yonder: a swarm of long-billed mosquitoes could eat them up at a supper spell; I mean the whole United States and the whole world—if they should come upon us, they can not prevail.' *Deseret News*, Dec. 23, 1857. The remarks of other elders, as reported in *Id.*, Dec. 16th, were, however, for the most part rational.

[18] Overtaking in southern California the Mormons who had broken up their settlement at that point and were en route for Utah. *Utah Notes*, MS.

in relation to matters concerning you now pending, I shall then call your attention, and wish to enlist your sympathies in behalf of the poor soldiers who are now suffering in the cold and snow of the mountains. I shall request you to render them aid and comfort, and to assist them to come here, and to bid them a hearty welcome to your hospitable valley. Governor Young, may I be permitted to ask a private interview for a few moments with you?" The purport of this conversation has never yet been ascertained, but at its close the governor remarked: "Friend Thomas, you have done a good work, and you will do a greater work still."[19]

On the 12th of March the colonel arrived at Camp Scott, and was entertained as the guest of Governor Cumming. Being presented to Judge Eckels, he displayed credentials from the president and letters from Brigham authorizing him to act as a negotiator. He came as a peace-maker, but was received almost as a spy. An invitation to dinner from Colonel Johnston was construed by the sergeant who delivered it— whether in malice or mischief does not appear—as an order for his arrest. The blunder was, of course, rectified; but Kane, who was now classed as a Mormon,[20] challenged the commander-in-chief, and a duel was only prevented by the intervention of the chief justice. Nevertheless, he received a fair hearing from the governor. His mission was to induce him to proceed to Salt Lake City under a Mormon escort, and at once

[19] Col Kane arrived Feb. 25th. *Deseret News*, March 3, 1858. On March 2d Major Van Vliet reached S. L. City from Washington at 4 A. M., and started four hours later, probably for Camp Scott. *St Louis Republican*, Dec. 14th, in *Ibid*.

[20] Hyde, *Mormonism*, 146; Waite, *The Mormon Prophet*, 52, and others claim that Col Kane had actually been baptized at Council Bluffs in 1847. The colonel himself never made any such statement; and, as Stenhouse remarks, if this had been the case he would surely have been treated by Brigham with less respect, for implicit obedience was always required from those who embraced the faith. *Rocky Mountain Saints*, 382. The truth appears to be that Kane's Mormon proclivities were due to the kind treatment and excellent nursing which he received from them in 1847, whereby his life was saved when he sojourned in one of their camps near Winter Quarters, as already related. There is no reliable evidence that he was a Mormon.

assume his functions. The officers remonstrated, stating that he would surely be poisoned; but Cumming was a high-spirited man, anxious only that matters should be adjusted, if possible without loss of life. He resolved to trust himself to the colonel's guidance, and on the 5th of April set forth from Camp Scott.

After passing through the federal lines, Cumming was met by an escort of Mormon militia, and on his way to Salt Lake City, where he arrived a week later, was everywhere acknowledged as governor and received with due honors.[21] Several interviews were held with Brigham, during which he was assured that every facility would be afforded him. The territorial seal, the records of the supreme and district courts, and other public property, the supposed destruction of which had helped to bring about the war, were found intact. On the second sabbath after his arrival Cumming attended the tabernacle, where he addressed three or four thousand of the saints, declaring that it was not intended to station the army in close contact with any of the settlements, and that the military would not be used in making arrests until other means had failed. After touching on the leading questions at issue, remembering, meanwhile, that he was ad-

[21] It was arranged with the Mormon officer in charge of the escort that the party should pass through Echo Cañon at night, the object being, as Cumming supposed, to conceal the barricades and defences; but bonfires were lighted by the Mormons, illuminating the valley and the mountain-tops. *Cumming's Rept to General Johnston*, in *House Ex. Doc.*, 35th Cong. 1st Sess., xiii. no. 138, p. 3. According to some accounts of Cumming's journey to S. L. City, Col Kimball, who with Porter Rockwell was in command of the escort, caused a plentiful repast to be prepared for the governor at Cache Cave, the first halting-place on the route. About 150 men of the legion were then ordered out and reviewed; and as the party passed other stations, troops drawn up on both sides of the road saluted the governor. At one point a mock attempt was made to arrest him, but Col Kimball interfered. At Echo Cañon hundreds of camp-fires were lighted, in order to deceive him as to the numbers of the Mormon soldiery. Cumming supposed that there were 2,000 to 3,000 of them in or near the cañon, whereas, in fact, there were but the 150 men whom he had first seen, a portion of them being halted at each stage, while the rest were ordered to pass by unobserved and await him at the next station. When within a few miles of S. L. City, he was met by a strong detachment of the legion, and escorted, amid martial music and salvos of artillery, to the residence of Elder W. C. Staines. *Waite's The Mormon Prophet*, 53–5; *Stenhouse's Rocky Mountain Saints*, 389–90. These statements are not confirmed by Tullidge in his *Hist. S. L. City*,

dressing a people embittered by many real and many imaginary wrongs, he stated that he had come among them to establish the sovereignty of a nation whose laws he was sworn to uphold, and to which he would require their absolute submission. Then followed harangues from certain of the elders, in which were repeated the oft-told story of the prophet's assassination, the services of the Mormon battalion, and the exodus from Nauvoo. One of the speakers declared that the government intended to occupy the territory with its troops, whether they were needed to support the civil officials or not. This remark caused the wildest uproar; and, writes the governor, "I was fully confirmed in the opinion that this people, with their extraordinary religion and customs, would gladly encounter certain death rather than be taxed with a submission to the military power, which they consider to involve a loss of honor."[22]

The tumult was stayed by Brigham, and no further symptoms of rebellion occurred during the governor's visit. About the middle of May he returned to Fort Scott, accompanied by Colonel Kane, and reported that the people of Utah acknowledged his authority, and that, before long, the transit of mails and passengers between the Missouri and the Pacific might be

[22] On the same sabbath Cumming, having been informed that many persons desired to leave the territory but were unlawfully restrained from doing so, caused a notice to be read in the tabernacle asking them to forward their names and places of residence. He states that 160 persons, most of whom were of English birth, claimed his protection, asking to be forwarded to the eastern states. They were sent to Camp Scott, where they arrived in a destitute condition, some of them without apparel except for garments made from the canvas of their wagon-covers. The soldiers shared with them their rations and clothing. In his report the governor also calls attention to the depredations of Indians, and says he has been informed that Garland Hurt had roused to acts of hostility the Indians of Uintah Valley. Hurt, who, as will be remembered, was the only gentile official remaining in Utah after the departure of Judge Drummond, states that when martial law was proclaimed he was unwilling to apply to Brigham for a passport, and, with the aid of Uintah Indians, made his escape, after much privation, to Johnston's camp, then on the Sweetwater. He declares that he was surrounded by Mormons and escaped at great risk of life. Brigham, on the other hand, offered him safe and speedy transportation, and tried to dissuade him from exposing himself to needless risk and hardship. Copies of the correspondence will be found in *House Ex. Doc.*, 35th Cong. 1st Sess., x. no. 71. pp. 205-10, passim.

resumed without fear of interruption. The colonel then took his leave and set out for Washington, to lay before the president the result of his mission. It was admitted that by his mediation he had prevented a collision between the Mormons and the federal troops, and in Buchanan's message to congress in the following December he was thus complimented: "I cannot refrain from mentioning the valuable services of Colonel Thomas L. Kane, who, from motives of pure benevolence, and without any official character or pecuniary compensation, visited Utah during the last inclement winter for the purpose of contributing to the pacification of the territory."[23]

The delay caused by Kane's mission was most opportune. The army was now ready to take the field. At Fort Leavenworth three thousand additional troops[24] had been assembled, and it was intended that the entire force should be concentrated in Utah in two divisions, one under the command of Colonel, now brevet brigadier-general, Johnston, and the other under Harney. As elsewhere mentioned, money without stint had been voted for the expedition, subsistence being provided for eight thousand persons for a period of twenty months.[25] On the 9th and 10th of June Colonel Hoffman arrived with a detachment at Camp Scott, in charge of the supply trains that had been parked at Fort Laramie during winter, and on the 8th 1,500 horses and mules, with an escort of infantry and mounted riflemen, had reached headquarters from New Mexico. The cattle at Henry Fork had thriven

[23] *House Ex. Doc.*, 35th Cong. 2d Sess., ii. pt 1, p. 10. A complimentary letter was handed to the colonel by Buchanan on the eve of his departure for Utah. Whether Kane was intrusted with any direct communication from the president to Brigham, and if so what was its purport, does not appear.

[24] The sixth and seventh infantry, first cavalry, and two batteries of artillery.

[25] At a cost of $1,220,000, the estimate being for 4,880.000 rations, at 25 cents per ration. This, of course, does not include freight. The effective force numbered 5,606, and there were 1,894 employés, 300 servants, and 200 women, for whom rations were also allowed, making 8,000 in all. *Letter from the Secretary of War*, in *House Ex. Doc.*, 35th Cong. 1st Sess., ix. no. 3.). A statement of all contracts made in connection with the expedition for 1858 will be found in *Id.*, xii. no. 99

well, and from that point mules could be furnished
sufficient for a train of 200 wagons. By dismounting
a portion of the cavalry, horses could also be spared
for the field batteries. All was in readiness, and orders were given that the army of Utah should advance.
There could be no longer a doubt, if ever there were
any, that the troops would make short work of the
Mormon militia. Behold, the days of the Utah rebellion were numbered!

But meanwhile events had occurred which promised a peaceable solution of the difficulty. The spir-
ited resistance of the saints had called forth unfavor-
able comments on Buchanan's policy throughout the
United States and throughout Europe. He had
virtually made war upon the territory before any
declaration of war had been issued; he had sent forward an army before the causes of offence had been
fairly investigated; and now, at this critical juncture
in the nation's history, he was about to lock up in
a distant and almost inaccessible region more than
one third of the nation's war material and nearly
all its best troops. Even the soldiers themselves,
though in cheerful mood and in excellent condition, had
no heart for the approaching campaign, accepting, as
they did, the commonly received opinion that it was
merely a move on the president's political chess-board.
In a word, Buchanan and the Washington politicians
and the Harney-Johnston army must all confess themselves beaten, hopelessly beaten, before a blow was
struck. The army was as powerless before the people
it had come to punish as was Napoleon's at Moscow.
All that remained to be done was to forgive the Mormons and let them go.

Through the pressure brought to bear, coupled
with the expostulations of Kane, Van Vliet, and
Bernhisel, Buchanan was induced to stop the threatened war, and on the 6th of April signed a proclamation promising amnesty to all who returned to their

allegiance. After dwelling at length on the past offences of the Mormons and the malign influence of their leaders, he declares the territory to be in a state of rebellion. "This rebellion," he continues, "is not merely a violation of your legal duty; it is without just cause, without reason, without excuse. You never made a complaint that was not listened to with patience. You never exhibited a real grievance that was not redressed as promptly as it could be...But being anxious to save the effusion of blood, and to avoid the indiscriminate punishment of a whole people for crimes of which it is not probable that all are equally guilty, I offer now a free and full pardon to all who will submit themselves to the authority of the government."[26]

The proclamation, though it served its purpose, gave offence to both parties. The Mormons did not regard themselves as rebels; but claimed that when Colonel Alexander was ordered to withdraw his forces no successor to Brigham had been legally appointed and qualified, nor had he been removed by the president, and that in obstructing the entrance of an armed force into the territory he had not exceeded his powers as commander-in-chief of the militia.[27] Moreover, that their complaints had been ignored instead of receiving a patient hearing, and that none of their grievances had been redressed, were among the causes that led to the disturbance. On the other hand, the gentile world declared that if the Mormon question was ever to be settled, now was the time to settle it. If the president had excepted from

[26] For copies of the proclamation, see *House Ex. Doc.*, 35th Cong. 2d Sess., ii. 1, pt 1, pp. 69–72; *Deseret News*, June 16, 1858.
[27] It does not appear that Brigham had been officially notified of Cumming's appointment when he sent his despatch to Alexander by the hands of Wells. In his answer Alexander addresses him as governor, it will be remembered; and in his official report, in *House Ex. Doc.*, 35th Cong. 1st Sess., x. pp. 24–6, Van Vliet also speaks of him as governor. Cumming did not receive his appointment until the 11th of July, 1857, and in view of the interruption of the mails, it is probable that no official intimation had reached S. L. City as early as Oct. 4th, when the baggage trains were burned at Simpson Hollow.

his amnesty the Mormon leaders, this result might
have been accomplished without bloodshed, and the
proclamation would at least have been deemed an act
of judicious clemency; but by purging their leaders
of offence, he had rendered nugatory the purpose of
the expedition, save to imprison the troops, during
'King' Buchanan's pleasure, in this western Siberia.

The document was intrusted to two peace commissioners—L. W. Powell, ex-governor and senator elect
for Kentucky, and Major B. McCulloch, a soldier of
the Mexican war. They were ordered to set out at
once for Utah, circulate the proclamation throughout
the territory, and point out to the Mormons their
unfortunate relations with the government, and how
greatly it would be to their interest to submit promptly
and peacefully to its laws. They were to assure them
that the despatch of the expedition had no reference
to their religious tenets, and that if they resumed
their allegiance no power in the United States had
either the right or the will to interfere with their religion. "To restore peace in this manner," writes the
secretary of war in his instructions, "is the single
purpose of your mission."[28]

On the 29th of May the commissioners arrived at
Camp Scott, where they remained four days, gathering
information as to the condition of affairs. On the 7th
of June they reached Salt Lake City, where Governor Cumming arrived the next day. On the evening
of the 10th they held an informal interview with
Brigham Young, Heber C. Kimball, and Daniel H.
Wells, who constituted the first presidency of the
church. During the two following days conferences
were held, some in private, and some in public at the
council-house, the apostles and many leading citizens
being present at the latter. The result was that the
Mormon authorities admitted the burning of the army
trains and the stampeding of cattle, and for those acts
accepted the president's pardon. All other charges

[28] *Sen. Doc.*, 35th Cong. 2d Sess., ii. p. 161.

they denied.[29]   At the same time they avowed their esteem for the constitution and government of the United States, and declared that under this constitution they desired to dwell in peace.

This concession, slight as it was, the commissioners accepted, and, at the close of the conference, Powell addressed a large number of Mormons, expressing his gratification at the result, and declaring that the army, which would arrive in the valley within a few days, had strict orders to molest no peaceable citizens in person or property.[30]   On the same evening a despatch was sent to Johnston stating the result of the negotiations, and suggesting that he issue a proclamation to the people of Utah and march to the valley at his earliest convenience.   An answer was immediately returned, in which the general expressed his surprise

[29] The commissioners' rept to the secretary of war, in *Id.*, 168–72. The Mormon version of these negotiations, as given in the *Deseret News*, June 23, 1858, confirms that of the commissioners.   A concise statement of what was said at the conference on the 11th and 12th, addressed by the commissioners to the secretary of war after their return to Washington, in the report, pp. 175–7, is also signed by Brigham, who declares it to be substantially correct.   Tullidge, *Hist. S. L. City*, 215–6, has a sensational account of the matter, in brief as follows: During the conference of the 11th he relates that O. P. Rockwell entered the council-chamber and whispered to the ex-governor. Brigham rose and said sharply, 'Governor Powell, are you aware, sir, that those troops are on the move towards the city?' 'It cannot be,' exclaimed Powell. 'I have received a despatch that they are on the march for this city. My messenger would not deceive me.' The commissioners were silent. 'Is brother Dunbar present?' inquired Brigham. 'Yes, sir,' was the response. 'Brother Dunbar, sing "Zion."' Zion was sung—a favorite song with the Mormons—in which occur the lines:

> 'Sacred home of the prophets of God;
> Thy deliverance is nigh,
> Thy oppressors shall die,
> And the gentiles shall bow 'neath thy rod.'

Cumming and McCulloch then withdrew. 'What would you do with such a people?' asked the governor, 'Damn them! I would fight them if I had my way,' answered the major. 'Fight them, would you? Did you notice the snap in those men's eyes to-day? They would never know when they were whipped!' The 'gentile yoke' recurs ad nauseam in Mormon song and hymn. In their national anthem we read:

> 'Hosanna, hosanna, to God! He has broke
> From off our necks the gentile yoke.'

and in their national hymn:

> 'All hell has combin'd with this world's bitter hatred
> Usurped men's best rights, all our freedom supprest.'

Snow's Poems, i. 261, 265.

[30] On the 16th the commissioners addressed a large number of people at Provo, and on the 17th at Lehi. *Rept*, ut supra, 171. Their speeches at Provo are given in the *Deseret News*, July 14, 1858.

at' the uneasiness felt by the Mormons as to their treatment at the hands of the troops, and enclosed a proclamation wherein he assured the Mormons that none would be molested, but that all would be protected in person, rights, and the peaceful pursuit of their vocations. This proclamation, together with one from Governor Cumming, declaring that peace was restored, and that the laws, both federal and territorial, must be strictly obeyed by all, was immediately published.[31]

The army had marched from Camp Scott on the 13th of June in three columns, a sufficient garrison being left at Fort Bridger, near which a score of tents and a few stacks of turf chimneys still marked the site where the men had passed the winter. On the 14th the command was encamped on Bear River, where the express arrived from the peace commissioners, and thence moved slowly forward.

The scene is impressive, and not without elements of the picturesque. At Fort Bridger the westward-bound traveller has passed only the portal of the Rocky Mountains. Between that point and the valley of Great Salt Lake there is scenery of surpassing loveliness. The ridges that divide the cañons are richly carpeted with wild flowers, among which, in midsummer, still linger traces of snow. Thence appear glimpses of the Bear and Weber rivers, their streams, though swollen and turbulent at this season, flowing through valleys whose tranquil beauty recalls the fabled realm of Rasselas. Thence also the silver-crested lines of the Wasatch and Uintah ranges can be distinctly traced, while on every side snow-capped peaks are seen in endless perspective, so that one asks, Whither hurry the swift running rivers? Along the gorges the path winds here and there through densely interlaced thickets of alder, hawthorn, and willow,

---

[31] For copies of both proclamations, see *Sen. Doc.*, 35th Cong. 2d Sess., ii. pp. 113, 121; *Deseret News*, June 23, July 7, 1858; and of Johnston's proclamation, *New York Herald*, July 15, 1858, in *Millennial Star*, xx. 532.

where silence reigns unbroken, save for the rush of waters and the twittering of birds, whose nests are built in the crevices of cliffs high overhead.

Now all is astir throughout this solitude. Among the cañons and ridges appears for the first time the gleam of sabres and rifle-barrels, and the stillness of the valley is broken by the measured tramp of armed men and the rumble of artillery-wagons. Up the steep mountain sides bands of horsemen are seen spurring to the summit, whence they can observe the advance of the troops; while groups of half-clad Indians stand gazing at the pageant, or gallop to and fro with the wonderment of astonished children.

On the 26th of June, 1858, the army of Utah enters the valley of the Great Salt Lake. The day following is the sabbath, and the fourteenth anniversary of the assassination of Joseph and Hyrum Smith. "We will go far enough into the wilderness," said Brigham before the expulsion from Nauvoo, "so far that never again will we come in conflict with our persecutors." They had journeyed some two thousand miles, subsisting at times on herbs and roots, seeking but to be left alone. After years of patient toil and self-denial they had built up their new Zion, a city in which, whatever the faults of its denizens, there was less of gross dissipation, of lewdness and drunkenness, than among the gentiles. They had seen their wives and daughters coerced by a militia rabble. They had not as yet forgotten the days of Nauvoo and the posse comitatus of Governor Ford. And now the posse comitatus of Governor Cumming was debouching from the mouth of Emigration Cañon, the spot whence, twelve years before, the president of their church had selected for them an abiding-place.

The rays of the rising sun slant athwart the bayonets of the 5th infantry as, forming the van of the Union army, it approaches the outskirts of Salt Lake City. At dusk is still heard in its streets the rumble of caissons and baggage-wagons. But no other sound is heard, save the murmur of the creek; nor is there sign of life in the city of the saints. Zion is deserted![32]

Thirty thousand of the Mormons had left their homes in Salt Lake City and the northern settlements, taking with them all their movable effects, and leaving only in the former a score of men, with instructions to apply the torch if it should be occupied by the troops. The outer doors were locked, and in the vacant dwellings were heaps of straw, shavings, and wood ready for the work of destruction. In April, when Cumming first arrived in the city, he reported that the people were already moving from the northern settlements. The roads were filled with wagons laden with provisions and household furniture. By their side women and children, many of them so thinly clad that their garments barely concealed their nakedness, some being attired only in sacking, some with no covering but a remnant of rag-carpet, and some barefooted and bleeding,[33] tramped through the deep snow, journeying they knew not whither, no more than at the exodus from Nauvoo; but it was "the will of the Lord," or rather of their prophet.[34] Returning with the peace commissioners, the governor repaired to the house of Elder Staines, and found the

[32] Johnston's despatch, in *Sen. Doc.*, 35th Cong. 2d Sess., ii. p. 122. Tullidge says that Colonel Cooke, who had commanded the Mormon battalion in 1847, rode through the city bareheaded. *Hist. S. L. City*, 224.

[33] *Jennings' Mat. Progr. in Utah*, MS., 2, where it is stated that, during the spring of 1858, the stock of clothing became exhausted and there were no means to replenish it. Among those who set forth from S. L. City was Mrs Jos. Horne, who started on the 1st of May for Parowan, her husband being employed in raising cotton about 100 miles to the south of that settlement. She had two teams for herself, her ten children, and her husband's second wife and baby. They were one month on the journey, sleeping in their wagons, and cooking at the roadside, were scantily clad and provisioned, and almost without money. On arriving at Parowan Mrs Horne earned the means for clothing her children comfortably by sewing, a party of Mormons having arrived there from San Bernardino, with a load of dry goods. *Horne's Migr. and Settlem. L. D. Saints*, MS., 36.

[34] Cumming states that at the tabernacle, on Apr. 11th, Brigham mentioned Sonora as their goal. *House Ex. Doc.*, 35th Cong. 1st Sess., xiii. p. 6, note. I find no mention of this in the files of the *Deseret News*. Between May 12 and Sept. 1, 1858, this paper was published at Fillmore City.

place abandoned,[35] Brigham and those who took part
in the conference with the peace commissioners being
summoned from some unknown point to the southward.

"What has become of the Mormons?" was a question asked throughout Europe and America when this
second exodus became known. "We are told that
they have embarked for a voyage over five hundred
miles of untracked desert," said the London *Times*.
"We think it would be unwise to treat Mormonism
as a nuisance to be abated by a posse comitatus," declared the *New York Times*. Meanwhile the Mormons were quietly sojourning at Provo, some sixty
miles to the south of Salt Lake City. That they
would have followed their prophet implicitly whithersoever he might have led, does not admit of doubt;
but after some further negotiation, Brigham with the
members of the first presidency and certain of the
elders returned to their homes on the 1st of July,[36]
followed, soon afterward, by the remainder of the
community, and the Utah war was practically at an
end. Two days later the commissioners started for
Washington, having faithfully carried out the spirit
and letter of their instructions.

After remaining for three days on the banks of the

[35] Tullidge relates that at the elder's house a cold lunch was spread for
the governor, and in the garden loads of straw were significantly heaped up.
Inquiring the cause of the silence that pervaded the city, Mrs Cumming was
told that the Mormons had resolved to burn it if the army should attempt its
occupation. 'How terrible!' she exclaimed, 'it has the appearance of a city
that has been afflicted with a plague. Every house looks like a tomb of the
dead. For two miles I have seen but one man in it. Poor creatures! And so
all have left their hard-earned homes.' Bursting into tears, she turned to
her husband: 'Oh Alfred!' she said, 'something must be done to bring them
back! Do not permit the army to stay in the city. Can't you do something
for them?' 'Yes, madam,' he replied, 'I shall do all I can, rest assured.'
A few days after the conference with the commissioners Cumming followed
the Mormons 50 miles to the southward, pleaded with them, at first in vain,
but finally induced them to return. *Hist. S. L. City*, 213, 225–6.

[36] *Deseret News*, July 14, 1858. The peace commissioners, whose last report from S. L. City is dated July 3d, also mention that the ex-governor and
other leading Mormons had then returned with their families. *Sen. Doc.*, 35th
Cong. 2d Sess., ii. 173. Stenhouse, *Rocky Mountain Saints*, 399, and Tullidge, *Hist. S. L. City*, 226, state that Brigham did not start from Provo till
the 5th.

Jordan, the troops were removed to Cedar Valley, where a site had been selected for an encampment about midway between Salt Lake City and Provo,[37] from which the forces could operate in either direction. To this was given the name of Camp Floyd.[38] In the valley there were but two small settlements, one of them, which was near the camp, containing only ten families. "I was desirous," writes Johnston, "to avoid proximity to any settlements, if possible; but this was not practicable, for every suitable position where there is water is occupied."

During the march of the army not a house was disturbed, not a citizen harmed or molested, and during its sojourn of nearly two years in the territory, instances were rare indeed of gross misconduct on the part of the soldiery.[39] The Mormons, who had before been eager to fight the troops, were now thankful for their arrival. Many of the former were still very poor; they had a few cattle, and a few implements of husbandry, but little else of this world's goods save their farms and farm-dwellings. They were ill clad and fed, their diet consisting chiefly of preparations of corn, flour, and milk, with beet molasses, and the fruits and vegetables of their gardens. Now they had an opportunity to exchange the products of their fields and dairies for clothing, for such luxuries as tea, coffee, sugar, tobacco, and for money— an article still scarce among them.

Accompanying the troops, however, was the usual crowd of hucksters and camp-followers, and a more

---

[37] Salt Lake City was 36 miles north and Provo about the same distance south-east of the camp. Johnston's despatch in *Sen. Doc.*, 35th Cong. 2d Sess., ii. 122. Grass was abundant in Cedar Valley, and also in Rush and Tintic valleys near by.

[38] So named after John B. Floyd, then secretary of war.

[39] The men were seldom allowed to leave camp, and only one serious affair occurred, a sergeant named Pike being accused of cracking the skull of a Mormon with his musket. During the sergeant's trial in Salt Lake City he was shot on the public street, and afterward died. His assassin escaped. *Stenhouse's Rocky Mountain Saints*, 419. Waite, *The Mormon Prophet*, 73, says that the culprit, whose name was Spencer, was lauded for his courage in the next issue of the *Deseret News*. I find no mention of it in the files of that paper.

villanous throng was never gathered from the sweep-
ings of the frontier states. At Camp Scott and on
the march they were kept under strict surveillance,
but here they found a safe field for their operations.
Many of the younger Mormons were corrupted by
their example, and in 1859 gambling, theft, drunkenness, and even murder were as common in Salt Lake
City as they became in later years among the mining
towns of Nevada and Colorado. Seldom were the
offenders brought to justice, the authorities being only
too glad to let these desperadoes kill each other off
during their drunken carousals; but if arrests were
made, resistance to an officer or any attempt to escape were considered a sufficient pretext for a free use
of the revolver. Thus the community was relieved
from the cost of the prisoner's trial and his support at
the penitentiary, compared with which the expense
of a coroner's inquest was an insignificant item. This
was the anti-polygamous civilization which Buchanan
and his army introduced into Utah!

The Utah war was an ill-advised measure on the
part of the United States government. In this,
as in other crises, from the time when the latter-day
saints mustered six members until now when they
counted nearly sixty thousand, the Mormons, hated as
they were by their fellow-men, won the respect and almost the esteem of a large portion of the gentile world.
The Utah war cost several hundred lives, and at least
$15,000,000, at a time in the nation's history when
men and money could least be spared, and accomplished practically nothing, save that it exposed the
president and his cabinet to much well-deserved ridicule. That the Mormons had displayed contempt for
Judge Drummond, who had made himself altogether
contemptible, that their treatment of Judge Stiles
was verging on sedition, that they intermeddled
with politics and strove to gain political ascend-
ancy, that they pushed forward their settlements

vigorously,[40] cannot be disputed; but here was no cause for a military expedition to uphold the authority of the government.

With the army of Utah came also the recently appointed officials, Chief Justice Eckles taking up his quarters at Camp Floy l, Judge Sinclair being assigned to the first, or as it is now termed the third, district, which included Salt Lake City, and Judge Cradlebaugh to the southern counties.[41] Alexander Wilson of Iowa had been chosen United States attorney, and Jacob Forney of Pennsylvania superintendent of Indian affairs, which office was now separated from that of governor. John Hartnett as secretary and Peter K. Dotson as marshal completed the list of officials.

Convening his court in November 1858, Sinclair, in his charge to the grand jury, urged the prosecution of Brigham Young, Daniel H. Wells, and other leading Mormons for treason, polygamy, and intimidation of the courts. The district attorney refused to present bills of indictment for treason, on the ground that pardon had been proclaimed by the president and accepted by the people. To ask a Mormon grand jury to indict the leading dignitaries of their church for polygamy was, of course, little better than a farce; while as to the charge of intimidation, referring to the occasion when Judge Stiles held court at Salt Lake City in 1854, all the bills were thrown out, with one excep-

[40] Tullidge, *Hist. S. L. City*, 138–9, says it was feared they would settle territory which ' would come within the political boundaries of half a dozen states, in which they would cast their potent united vote,' and that immigration and the rapid increase of offspring would, within the century, give them a million of people. In a leading article, the *New York Herald* stated that the Mormons held the whip-handle over the U. S., Fillmore and Pierce having given it into the hands of Brigham. Much similar nonsense may be found by turning over the newspaper files of this period.

[41] By act approved Dec. 27, 1865, the judicial districts were altered, Millard, Piute, Sevier, San Pete, Juab, Utah, and Wasatch counties forming the first district; Kane, Washington, Iron, and Beaver counties the second; and Great Salt Lake, Tooele, Summit, Green River, Davis, Morgan, Weber, Box Elder, Cache, and Richland, afterward Rich, counties the third. *Utah Acts Legisl.* (ed. 1866), 194.

tion.[42] Thus Sinclair's judicial career resulted in failure, and to this day he is only remembered in Utah as the judge who appointed a Sunday for the first execution of a white man that had occurred as yet in the territory.[43]

To Judge Cradlebaugh belonged a wider sphere of operations; but, as will presently appear, his proceedings and those of his colleague wellnigh brought about a renewal of the Utah war, hostilities being prevented only by the timely interference of the government. The matters which he proposed to investigate included several outrages, commonly ascribed to the Mormons, among them being the Mountain Meadows massacre.[44]

Before presenting this episode, it may be well to make some mention of a religious movement known in Utah as the reformation, though more in the nature of a revival, and attended with all the excitement and bitterness of denunciation common to such movements elsewhere in the world. On the 13th of September, 1856, Jedediah M. Grant, Joseph Young, and a few others held a conference at Kaysville, at which the saints were exhorted to repent, and to bring forth fruits meet for repentance, to pay their tithing faith-

[42] That of James Ferguson. See chap. xvii., note 18, this vol.

[43] That of Thomas H. Ferguson for murder. The execution was, of course, postponed, and took place on Friday, Oct. 28, 1859. An account of it will be found in the *Deseret News*, Nov. 2, 1859, and the *Sac. Union*, Nov. 17, 1859.

[44] Stenhouse, *Rocky Mountain Saints*, 402-3, states that the judges were supported by the *Valley Tan* newspaper, the first number of which appeared Nov. 5, 1858. This was the first gentile newspaper published in Utah; it ran for only about a year and a half. The phrase 'valley tan' was first applied to leather tanned in the valley, and afterward to other articles of home production. Taylor, *Reminiscences*, MS., 14–15, says that the term was applied to crockery, medicines, whiskey, furniture, and even to gold coin made in S. L. City. In fact, it became synonymous, as I have said, with home-made or Utah-manufactured. As to the manufacture of whiskey, President Taylor states that alcohol was first made by the saints for bathing, pickling, and medicinal purposes, and was little used for drinking. Stills were afterward obtained from emigrants, and the manufacture and sale of alcohol were later controlled by the city councils. The first bar-room in S. L. City, and the only one for years, was in the Salt Lake House, owned by President Young and Feramorz Little. It was opened for the accommodation of travellers, whose requirements would be supplied by some one, and it was thought by the brethren that they had better control the trade than have outsiders do so.

fully, to dedicate themselves and their substance to the Lord, to set their families in order, to purify their houses, their persons, and their lands.[45]

At the bowery in Salt Lake City, on the morning of the 21st, the day being a sabbath, Brigham declared that he would no longer dwell among a people filled with contention, covetousness, pride, and iniquity. Unless they put away their sins a separation must take place, and the righteous be forever parted from the ungodly. At the beginning of his discourse he requested that all who desired to obey the Lord Jesus and live to his glory, denying themselves of worldly lusts, would signify their intention by rising to their feet. As a matter of course, the entire congregation responded. He then asked if there was a man among them who knew how to handle this world's goods without setting his heart upon them, using and distributing them only to the glory of God, that that man would stand up. There was no response. "I tell you," he said, "that this people will not be suffered to walk as they have walked, to do as they have done, to live as they have lived." He was followed by Jedediah M. Grant who declared that there were some among them who, having received the priesthood, dishonored their cause by committing adultery, and every other abomination under heaven.

For many weeks the reformation was preached at the bowery and the tabernacle, the saints being ordered to renew their covenants, and many of them were rebaptized by the elders under the direction of Grant, who, on one occasion, remained so long in the water that he contracted the disease of which he died toward the close of the year.[46] Meetings held by the home missionaries throughout the territory were crowded, and full and frank confession was made, followed in most instances by amendment. Some bene-

[45] For proceedings of conference, see *Deseret News*, Sept. 24, 1856. 'Saints, live your religion,' was the text of a sermon delivered by Brigham at the tabernacle.
[46] For a description of his obsequies, see *Deseret News*. Dec. 10, 1856.

fit was wrought by the movement, especially with regard to cleanliness; but as in other religious agitations,
the effect was mainly emotional, the people being
worked up to a state of frenzy, and most of them
believing that the coming of Christ was at hand.
The revival lasted well into the following year, and
coupled with the excitement of the approaching war,
may serve to explain the abnormal condition of the
community at this critical period.[47]

[47] In *Stenhouse's Rocky Mountain Saints*, 292–305, and *Stenhouse's Tell It
All*, 310–23, are sensational accounts of the reformation, the former by an
eye-witness, who appears to have witnessed things which no one else
observed. He states that teachers were appointed for each ward, whose duty
was to pry into every secret, and learn the private history of every family,
men, women, and children being asked the most indelicate questions about
private actions and secret thoughts. He declares that a catechism of an
obscene nature was printed by authority of Brigham and put into the hands
of every elder, bishop, missionary, and teacher, those who refused to answer
the questions being in danger of the ban of the church, and those who answered them being reported to the authorities and roundly abused at the
public meetings. At a gathering held at the social hall, attended only by
men, Brigham bid all who had been guilty of adultery to stand up. More
than three fourths of the audience rose to their feet. This Mr Stenhouse
explains on the supposition that the crime was admitted as having occurred
at any time during the whole course of their lives as Mormons. He also
states that during his twenty-five years' connection with Mormonism he
knew only of two or three cases of adultery. The account of the reformation as given in the text is taken principally from the files of the *Deseret
News*.

CHAPTER XX.

THE MOUNTAIN MEADOWS MASSACRE.

1857.

An Arkansas Emigrant Party Arrives at Salt Lake City—Assassination of Parley P. Pratt—Ill Feeling against the Emigrants—Alleged Outrages—Their Arrival at Mountain Meadows—They are Attacked by Indians—A Flag of Truce—Plan of the Massacre—Surrender of the Emigrants—The Butchery—Burial of the Slain—The Survivors—Judge Cradlebaugh's Investigation—The Aiken Massacre—John D. Lee on Trial—The Jury Disagree—The Second Trial—Lee Convicted and Sentenced—His Confession and Execution.

The threat uttered by Brigham during his interview with Captain Van Vliet, on the 9th of September, 1857, was speedily fulfilled—so speedily that, at first sight, its execution would appear to have been predetermined. "If," he declared, "the government dare to force the issue, I shall not hold the Indians by the wrist any longer." "If the issue comes, you may tell the government to stop all emigration across the continent, for the Indians will kill all who attempt it." Two days later occurred the Mountain Meadows massacre,[1] at a point about three hundred miles south of Salt Lake City.

[1] In Forney's Rept, in *Sen. Doc.*, 36th Cong. 1st Sess., ii. no. 42, p. 79, and the *Hand-Book of Reference*, p. 75, Sept. 9th is given as the date of the massacre. Forney, as superintendent of Indian affairs, made a close investigation into the details of this tragedy, the result of which is given in his report ut supra, pp. 87–9, and elsewhere in this document, which occupies 139 pages, and contains all the official information then to be had on the subject. His reports are dated Salt Lake City, 1859. He states that the attack began on Monday, Sept. 5th, and lasted till Friday, Sept. 9th, when the massacre occurred; but Friday of that week fell on Sept. 11th. Burton, *City of the Saints*, 411–12, note, also quotes an official report, in which Sept. 4th or 5th is given as the date of the first attack. See also Lee's confession in *Mormonism Un-*

(543)

The threat and the deed came so near together as to lead many to believe that one was the result of the other. But a moment's reflection will show that they were too nearly simultaneous for this to be the case; that in the absence of telegraph and railroad, it would be impossible to execute such a deed three hundred miles away in two days. Indeed, it may as well be understood at the outset that this horrible crime, so often and so persistently charged upon the Mormon church and its leaders, was the crime of an individual, the crime of a fanatic of the worst stamp, one who was a member of the Mormon church, but of whose intentions the church knew nothing, and whose bloody acts the members of the church, high and low, regard with as much abhorrence as any out of the church. Indeed, the blow fell upon the brotherhood with three-fold force and damage. There was the cruelty of it, which wrung their hearts; there was the odium attending its performance in their midst; and there was the strength it lent their enemies further to malign and molest them. The Mormons denounce the Mountain Meadows massacre, and every act connected therewith, as earnestly and as honestly as any in the outside world. This is abundantly proved, and may be accepted as a historical fact.

I will now proceed to give the incidents as they occurred. In the spring of 1857 a party of one hundred and thirty-six Arkansas emigrants,[2] among whom were a few Missourians,[3] set forth for southern California.

railed, 218, 237, 239, where Lee states that the massacre occurred on Friday, and that the attack began on Tuesday. At Lee's trial James Haslem testified, as we shall see later, that he was sent from Cedar City by Isaac C. Haight, with a letter to Brigham, on Monday, Sept. 7th, and that he reached S. L. City at 11 A. M. on Thursday. *Deseret News*, Sept. 20, 1876. The next day was the 11th. Other accounts differ slightly as to date.

   [2] U. S. Attorney Wilson, in his report in *Sen. Doc.*, 36th Cong. 1st Sess., ii. no. 42, p. 102, states that 119 were killed, and it is certain that 17 children were rescued. Forney and Burton say that 115 to 120 were massacred; Waite, *The Mormon Prophet*, 66, that the party consisted of 150 men and women, besides a number of children. Stenhouse, *Tell It All*, 324, mentions 120 to 130. Other reports vary from 120 to 150.

   [3] Stenhouse, *Rocky Mountain Saints*, 424-8, says that the Arkansas and Missouri emigrants formed two separate parties, the latter naming themselves

It included about thirty families, most of them related by marriage or kindred, and its members were of every age, from the grandsire to the babe in arms. They belonged to the class of settlers of whom California was in need. Most of them were farmers by occupation; they were orderly, sober, thrifty, and among them was no lack of skill and capital.[4] They travelled leisurely and in comfort, stopping at intervals to recruit their cattle, and about the end of July arrived at Salt Lake City,[5] where they hoped to replenish their stock of provisions.

For several years after the gold discovery the arrival of an emigrant party was usually followed, as we have seen, by friendly traffic between saint and gentile, the former thus disposing, to good advantage, of his farm and garden produce. But now all was changed. The army of Utah was advancing on Zion, and the Arkansas families reached the valley at the very time when the Mormons first heard of its approach, perhaps while the latter were celebrating their tenth anniversary at Big Cottonwood Cañon. Moreover, wayfarers from Missouri and Arkansas were regarded with special disfavor; the former for reasons that have already appeared, the latter on account of the murder of a well-beloved apostle of the Mormon church.

Missouri 'wild-cats,' and that the Arkansas party was advised by a friend of his to keep clear of the Missourians while passing through the Utah settlements and the portion of that territory occupied by Indians. I find no confirmation of this in other authorities, though, according to Mrs Stenhouse, *Tell It All*, 325, her husband's friend, whose name was Eli B. Kelsey, 'said that the train was divided into two parts, the first a rough-and-ready set of men—regular frontier pioneers; the other a picked community.' The truth appears to be, that there were a few Missourians in the Arkansas party, as stated in *Hutchings' Cal. Mag.*, iv. 345.

[4] They had about 600 head of cattle, 30 wagons, and 30 horses and mules. *Forney's Rept*, ut supra, p. 75. Stenhouse mentions that they had also several travelling-carriages. *Rocky Mountain Saints*, 424. At least $30,000 worth of plunder was collected after the massacre, besides what was appropriated by the Indians. Cradlebaugh estimated the value of their property at $60,000 to $70,000.

[5] I find no mention of their arrival in the files of the *Deseret News*, although the names of passing emigrants were registered in that paper at a nominal charge; and when the party was a large one, its passage was usually noticed among the local items of news.

In May of 1857 Parley P. Pratt was arraigned before the supreme court at Van Buren, Arkansas, on a charge of abducting the children of one Hector Mc-Lean, a native of New Orleans, but then living in California. He was acquitted; but it is alleged by anti-Mormon writers, and tacitly admitted by the saints, that he was sealed to Hector McLean's wife, who had been baptized into the faith years before, while living in San Francisco, and in 1855 was living in Salt Lake City.[6] McLean swore vengeance against the apostle, who was advised to make his escape, and set forth on horseback, unarmed, through a sparsely settled country, where, under the circumstances, escape was almost impossible. His path was barred by two of McLean's friends until McLean himself with three others overtook the fugitive, when he fired six shots at him, the balls lodging in his saddle or passing through his clothes. McLean then stabbed him twice

[6] The account given in the *Millennial Star*, xix. 417-18, is that McLean, after treating his wife in a brutal manner for several years, turned her into the streets of San Francisco, and secretly conveyed the children on board a steamer for New Orleans, where the woman followed him; but finding that her parents were in the plot, set forth for Salt Lake City. Returning to New Orleans in 1856, she rescued her children and fled to Texas; but was followed by her husband, who had previously returned to California, and now regained possession of the children. Parley, who had already befriended Mrs McLean, had written to inform her that her husband was in pursuit. Hence the prosecution. McLean and his wife finally separated in San Francisco in 1855. See also *Autobiog. of Parley P. Pratt*, app. Stenhouse relates that Mrs McLean was married or sealed to Pratt in Utah, that she met Pratt in Arkansas on her way to Utah, and that the apostle was acquitted on account of her assuming the responsibility for the abduction. He admits, however, that the apostle did not abduct the children. *Rocky Mountain Saints*, 429. Burton says that Pratt converted Mrs McLean and took her to wife, but on what authority he does not state. *City of the Saints*, 412. The fact, however, that Mrs McLean arrived on the scene of the apostle's assassination just before his death, as mentioned in the *Millennial Star*, xix. 478, wears a suspicious look. In the *S. F. Bulletin* of March 24, 1877, it is stated that the apostle made the acquaintance of Mrs McLean while engaged in missionary work in San Francisco; that her husband, who was a custom-house official and a respectable citizen, ordered him to discontinue his visits, and kicked him out of the house for continuing them surreptitiously; and that the woman was so infatuated with the Mormon elder that she devoutly washed his feet whenever he visited her. On arriving at Fort Smith (near Van Buren), McLean found letters from Parley Pratt addressed to his wife, one of them signed ' Your own,—— ——.' The McLean residence in San Francisco, on the corner of Jones and Filbert streets, was in 1877 a dilapidated frame building, a story and a half in height. As to the apostle's assassination, the *Bulletin* merely states that he was overtaken by McLean and shot within eight miles of Van Buren, and that he died of his wounds an hour afterward.

with a bowie-knife under the left arm, whereupon
Parley dropped from his horse, and the assassin, after
thrusting his knife deeper into the wounds, seized a
derringer belonging to one of his accomplices, and shot
him through the breast. The party then rode off, and
McLean escaped unpunished.[7]

Thus, when the Arkansas families arrived at Salt
Lake City, they found the Mormons in no friendly
mood, and at once concluded to break camp and move
on. They had been advised by Elder Charles C. Rich
to take the northern route along the Bear River, but
decided to travel by way of southern Utah. Passing through Provo, Springville, Payson, Fillmore,
and intervening settlements, they attempted everywhere to purchase food, but without success. Toward
the end of August they arrived at Corn Creek,[8] some
fifteen miles south of Fillmore, where they encamped
for several days. In this neighborhood, on a farm
set apart for their use by the Mormons, lived the Pah
Vants, whom, as the saints allege, the emigrants attempted to poison by throwing arsenic into one of the
springs and impregnating their own dead cattle with
strychnine. It has been claimed that this charge
was disproved; and what motive the Arkansas party
could have had for thus surrounding themselves with
treacherous and blood-thirsty foes has never been
explained. In the valleys throughout the southern
portion of the territory grows a poisonous weed, and
it is possible that the cattle died from eating of this

[7] This account of Parley's murder is based on the testimony of Geo. Hig-
ginson and Geo. Crouch, whose letter, dated Flint, Arkansas, May 17, 1857,
was first published in a New York paper. Copies of it will be found in the
Millennial Star, xix. 478, and *Burton's City of the Saints*, 412-13, note.
They state that the tragedy occurred close to the residence of a farmer
named Win, and was witnessed by two men who were in the house at the
time, and from whose evidence at the coroner's jury the above version is
taken. Pratt lived long enough to give instructions as to his burial and the
disposition of his property. The account given by Stenhouse, in *Rocky Mountain Saints*, 429-30, does not differ materially, except that he makes no mention of any accomplices.

[8] In his deposition at the trial of John D. Lee and others, George A. Smith,
the prophet's cousin, states that he found them at Corn Creek on Aug. 25th.
Millennial Star. xxxvii. 675; *Lee's Mormonism Unvailed*. 307.

weed.[9] It has been intimated that those who accused
the emigrants of poisoning the Pah Vants were not
honest in their belief, and that the story of the
poisoning was invented, or at least grossly exaggerated, for the purpose of making them solely responsible for the massacre.[10]   The fact has never been so
established, notwithstanding the report of the superintendent of Indian affairs, who states that none of
this tribe were present at the massacre.

Continuing their journey, the emigrants proceeded
to Beaver City, and thence to Parowan.   Grain was
scarce this year, and the emigrants were unable to
purchase all they desired for their stock, though for
their own immediate necessities they obtained what
they required at this place.   Arriving at Cedar City,
they succeeded in purchasing about fifty bushels of
wheat, which was ground at a mill belonging to John
D. Lee, formerly commander of the fort at Cedar,
but then Indian agent, and in charge of an Indian
farm near Harmony.

It is alleged by the Mormons, and on good authority, that during their journey from Salt Lake

[9] *Sen. Doc.*, 36 Cong. 1st Sess., ii. no. 42, p. 76.   Forney mentions that
an ox belonging to a Dr Ray of Fillmore died from this cause while the emigrants were in that neighborhood, that his wife was taken ill while rendering
the tallow, and that a boy who was assisting her died a few days afterward.   One or two Indians who ate some of the meat were also poisoned.

[10]   John D. Lee, living 150 miles south of Fillmore, informed me that
about twenty Indians and some cattle died from drinking of the poisoned
water, and Indians from eating the poisoned meat.' *Forney's Rept*, in *Id.*,
p. 75.   This report was dated S. L. City, Aug. 1859.   In a letter to Brigham,
dated Harmony, Nov. 20, 1857, Lee writes: 'The company there [at Corn
Creek] poisoned the meat of an ox, which they gave the Pah Vant Indians to
eat, causing four of them to die immediately, besides poisoning a number
more.   The company also poisoned the water where they encamped, killing
the cattle of the settlers.   This letter was used in evidence at Lee's trial in
1876.' *Mormonism Unvailed*, 254-5.   At this trial was also placed in evidence
a letter from Brigham to the commissioner of Indian affairs, dated Jan. 6,
1858, in which Lee's statement is repeated almost verbatim. *Id.*, 313-15.   In
his confession, made a few months after his trial, Lee declares that President
Isaac C. Haight told him of the poisoning and other atrocities committed by
the emigrants, and gave him instructions as to the part he should take in the
massacre.   After that event Lee states (still in his confession), 'I thought
over the matter, and made up my mind to write the letter to Brigham Young
and lay it all to the Indians.' *Id.*, 254.

City to Cedar the emigrants were guilty of further gross outrage. If we can believe a statement made in the confession of Lee, a few days before his death, Isaac C. Haight, president of the stake at Cedar, accused them of abusing women, of poisoning wells and streams at many points on their route, of destroying fences and growing crops, of violating the city ordinances at Cedar, and resisting the officers who attempted to arrest them. These and other charges, even more improbable,[11] have been urged in extenuation of the massacre; but little reliance can be placed on Lee's confession, and most of them appear to be unfounded.[12] It must be admitted, however, that rather than see their women and children starve, they perhaps took by force such necessary provisions as they were not allowed to purchase.

Near Cedar City the Spanish trail to Santa Fé branched off from what was then known as Frémont's route. About thirty miles to the south-west of Cedar, and within fifteen of the line of the route, are the Mountain Meadows, which form the divide between the waters of the great basin and those that flow into the Colorado. At the southern end of the meadows, which are four to five miles in length and one in width, but here run to a narrow point, is a large stream, the banks of which are about ten feet in height. Close to this stream the emigrants were encamped on the 5th of September, almost midway between two

---

[11] 'They proclaimed that they had the very pistol with which the prophet Joseph Smith was murdered, and had threatened to kill Brigham and all of the apostles. That when in Cedar City they said they would have friends in Utah, who would hang Brigham by the neck until he was dead, before snow fell again in the territory. They also said that Johnston was coming with his army from the east, and they were going to return from California with soldiers, as soon as possible, and would then desolate the land, and kill every damned Mormon man, woman, and child that they could find in Utah.' *Lee's Mormonism Unvailed*, 218–19.

[12] 'Conflicting statements were made to me of the behavior of this company,' says the superintendent of Indian affairs. 'I have accordingly made it a matter of material importance to make a strict inquiry to ascertain reliable information on this subject...The result of my inquiries enables me to say that the company conducted themselves with propriety.' *Forney's Rept*, ut supra, p. 88.

ranges of hills, some fifty feet high and four hundred yards apart. On either side of their camp were ravines connected with the bed of the stream.

MOUNTAIN MEADOWS.

It was Saturday evening when the Arkansas families encamped at Mountain Meadows. On the sabbath they rested, and at the usual hour one of them conducted divine service in a large tent, as had been their custom throughout the journey. At daybreak on the 7th, while the men were lighting their camp-fires, they were fired upon by Indians, or white men disguised as Indians, and more than twenty were killed or wounded,[13] their cattle having been driven off meanwhile by the assailants, who had crept on them under cover of darkness. The survivors now ran for their wagons, and pushing them together so as to form a corral, dug out the earth deep enough to sink them almost to the top of the wheels; then in the centre of the inclosure they made a rifle-pit large enough to contain the entire company, strengthening their defences by night as best they could. Thereupon the attacking party, which numbered from three to four hundred, withdrew to the hills, on the crests of which they built parapets, whence they shot down all who showed themselves outside the intrenchment.

The emigrants were now in a state of siege, and though they fought bravely, had little hope of escape. All the outlets of the valley were guarded; their am-

---

[13] Seven were killed and sixteen wounded. *Lee's Confession*, in *Mormonism Unvailed*, 226–7; see also *Forney's Rept*, in *Sen. Doc.*, 36th Cong. 1st Sess., ii. no. 42, p. 88.

munition was almost exhausted; of their number, which included a large proportion of women and children, many were wounded, and their sufferings from thirst had become intolerable. Down in the ravine, and within a few yards of the corral, was the stream of water; but only after sundown could a scanty supply be obtained, and then at great risk, for this point was covered by the muskets of the Indians,[14] who lurked all night among the ravines waiting for their victims.

Four days the siege lasted; on the morning of the fifth a wagon was seen approaching from the northern end of the meadow, and with it a company of the Nauvoo legion. When within a few hundred yards of the intrenchment, the company halted, and one of them, William Bateman by name, was sent forward with a flag of truce. In answer to this signal a little girl, dressed in white, appeared in an open space between the wagons. Half-way between the Mormons and the corral, Bateman was met by one of the emigrants named Hamilton, to whom he promised protection for his party on condition that their arms were surrendered, assuring him that they would be conducted safely to Cedar City. After a brief parley, each one returned to his comrades.

By whose order the massacre was committed, or for what reasons other than those already mentioned, has never yet been clearly ascertained; but as to the incidents and the plan of the conspirators, we have evidence that is in the main reliable. During the week of the massacre, Lee, with several other Mormons, was encamped at a spring within half a mile of the emigrants' camp; and, as was alleged, though not distinctly proven at his trial, induced the Indians by promise of booty to make the attack; but, finding the resistance stronger than he anticipated, had sent for

[14] 'Thursday morning I saw two men start from the corral with buckets, and run to the spring and fill their buckets with water, and go back again. The bullets flew around them thick and fast, but they got into their corral in safety.' Lee's *Mormonism Unvailed*, 230.

aid to the settlements of southern Utah.[15]   Thus far
the evidence is somewhat contradictory.   There is
sufficient proof, however, that, in accordance with a
programme previously arranged at Cedar, a company
of militia, among whom were Isaac C. Haight and
Major John M. Higbee, and which was afterward
joined by Colonel William H. Dame, bishop of Parowan,[16] arrived at Lee's camp on the evening before
the massacre.

It was then arranged that Lee should conclude
terms with the emigrants, and, as soon as they had
delivered themselves into the power of the Mormons,
should start for Hamblin's rancho, on the eastern side
of the meadows, with the wagons and arms, the young
children, and the sick and wounded.   The men and
women, the latter in front, were to follow the wagons,
all in single file, and on each side of them the militia
were to be drawn up, two deep, and with twenty
paces between their lines.   Within two hundred yards
of the camp the men were to be brought to a halt,
until the women approached a copse of scrub-oak,
about a mile distant, and near to which Indians lay in
ambush.   The men were now to resume their march,
the militia forming in single file, each one walking by
the side of an emigrant, and carrying his musket
on the left arm.   As soon as the women were close to
the ambuscade, Higbee,[17] who was in charge of the
detachment, was to give the signal by saying to his
command, "Do your duty;" whereupon the militia
were to shoot down the men, the Indians were to

---

[15] See the district attorney's opening address to the jury, in the *Deseret
News*, Sept. 2, 1877.   Lee states that his object in sending for aid was to protect the emigrants. *Confession*, in *Mormonism Unvailed*, 229.

[16] A full list of the company is given in *Id.*, 379–80, and a list of all the
Mormons who took part in the massacre in the *S. L. City Tribune*, June 2,
1877.   See also the speech delivered by Judge Cradlebaugh in the house of
representatives, Feb. 7, 1863. *Cong. Globe*, 1862–3, app. 119.   The speech
was afterward published in pamphlet form, one copy of it being entitled *Mormonism*, and another *Utah and the Mormons*.   The former was reprinted
from the *S. L. Daily Tribune*, Apr. 8, 1877.   The parts of it relating to the
massacre will be found in *Waite's The Mormon Prophet*, 65, and *Stenhouse's
Rocky Mountain Saints*, 447–50.

[17] First councillor to Haight.

slaughter the women and children, sparing only those of tender age, and Lee with some of the wagoners was to butcher the sick and wounded. Mounted troopers were to be in readiness to pursue and slay those who attempted to escape, so that, with the exception of infants, no living soul should be left to tell the tale of the massacre.

Entering the corral, Lee found the emigrants engaged in burying two of their party who had died of wounds. Men, women, and children thronged around him, some displaying gratitude for their rescue, some distrust and terror. The brother played his part well. Bidding the men pile their arms in the wagons, to avoid provoking the Indians, he placed in them the women, the small children, and a little clothing. While thus engaged, one Daniel McFarland rode up, with orders from Major Higbee to hasten their departure, as the Indians threatened to renew the attack. The emigrants were then hurried away from the corral, the men, as they passed between the files of militia, cheering their supposed deliverers. Half an hour later, as the women drew near the ambuscade, the signal was given, and the butchery commenced. Most of the men were shot down at the first fire. Three only escaped from the valley; of these two were quickly run down and slaughtered, and the third was slain at Muddy Creek, some fifty miles distant.[18]

The women and those of the children who were on foot ran forward some two or three hundred yards, when they were overtaken by the Indians, among whom were Mormons in disguise. The women fell on their knees, and with clasped hands sued in vain

[18] *Forney's Rept*, ut supra, 89; *Burton's City of the Saints*, 412, note. Lee also says that three escaped, but were overtaken and killed before reaching the settlements in California. *Mormonism Unvailed*, 244. Cradlebaugh states that two escaped and were overtaken in the desert 150 miles distant. *Mormonism*, 12. Beadle mentions three, one of whom starved to death in the desert, another was murdered by Indians, 90 miles south of the desert, and a third was killed on the Colorado River by persons unknown. *Life in Utah*, 184.

for mercy; clutching the garments of their murderers, as they grasped them by the hair, children pleaded for life, meeting with the steady gaze of innocent childhood the demoniac grin of the savages, who brandished over them uplifted knives and tomahawks. Their skulls were battered in, or their throats cut from ear to ear, and, while still alive, the scalp was torn from their heads. Some of the little ones met with a more merciful death, one, an infant in arms, being shot through the head by the same bullet that pierced its father's heart. Of the women none were spared, and of the children only those who were not more than seven years of age.[19]

To two of Lee's wagoners, McMurdy and Knight, was assigned the duty, as it was termed, of slaughtering the sick and wounded. Carrying out their instructions, they stopped the teams as soon as firing was heard, and with loaded rifles approached the wagons where lay their victims, McMurdy being in front. "O Lord, my God," he exclaimed, "receive their spirits, it is for thy kingdom that I do this." Then, raising his rifle to his shoulder, he shot through the brain a wounded man who was lying with his head on a sick comrade's breast. The Mormons were aided in their work[20] by Indians, who, grasping the helpless men by the hair, raised up their heads and cut their throats. The last victim was a little girl who came running up to the wagons, covered with

[19] In the official report quoted by Burton, *City of the Saints*, 412, it is stated that a girl 16 years of age knelt before one of the Mormons imploring mercy, but he led her away into a thicket, violated her, and then cut her throat. Beadle attributes this deed to President Haight, and says that after violating the girl he beat out her brains with a club. He also accuses Lee of selecting one of the young women for his harem, and relates that, when he made known his purpose, she attempted to stab him, whereupon he shot her through the head. *Life in Utah*, 183-4.

[20] Lee, in his confession, denied having killed any of them, but admits that he intended to do his part. He says: 'I drew my pistol and cocked it, but somehow it went off prematurely, and I shot McMurdy across the thigh, my pistol-ball cutting his buckskin pants. McMurdy turned to me and said: "Brother Lee, keep cool; you are excited."' *Mormonism Unvailed*, 242. As we shall see later, it was clearly proved at his trial that he killed several of the wounded.

blood, a few minutes after the disabled men had been murdered. She was shot dead within sixty yards of the spot where Lee was standing. The massacre was now completed, and after stripping the bodies of all articles of value,[21] Brother Lee and his associates went to breakfast,[22] returning after a hearty meal to bury the dead.

[21] Lee states that only a little money and a few watches were found on them. *Id.*, 244. This is improbable, and other accounts show that the Mormons gathered considerable booty.

[22] 'After breakfast,' says Lee, 'we all went back in a body to the meadows, to bury the dead and take care of the property that was left there.' The above account of the Mountain Meadows massacre is taken mainly from *Forney's Rept*, in *Sen. Doc.*, 35th Cong. 1st Sess., ii. no. 42, pp. 87-9; *Cradlebaugh's Mormonism*, 12; the affidavit of Philip Klingon Smith (Klingensmith), bishop of Cedar City, who was present at the massacre, made in 1871 before the clerk of court of the seventh judicial district of Nevada, in *Stenhouse's Rocky Mountain Saints*, 439-42; the confession of Lee, in *Mormonism Unvailed*, 244, and his trial in *Id.*, 302-78. In the *S. F. Call*, July 30, 1881, it is stated that Bishop Klingensmith was murdered in Mexico. There is no important discrepancy in the several versions. Forney and Cradlebaugh officially investigated the matter in 1859. The statements of both are very brief, and why the investigation was not made sooner does not appear. News of the massacre was first received in Washington in Feb. 1858. See letter of C. E. Mix, acting commissioner of Indian affairs, to Senator W. K. Sebastian, and of the secretary of war to Representative A. B. Greenwood, in *Sen. Doc.*, 35th Cong. 1st Sess., ii. no. 42, pp. 4, 42. On the 18th of this month Senator Gwin of California moved that the secretary of war be called upon to report what steps had been taken to bring the offenders to justice. *Gwin's Memoirs*, MS., 138 a, 138 e. No steps had been taken, and for reasons that will presently appear, none were taken—or none that were effectual—until nearly 20 years later. For other accounts of the massacre, see *Stenhouse's Rocky Mountain Saints*, 435-9; *Stenhouse's Tell It All*, 328-37; *Beadle's Life in Utah*, 180-4; *Waite's The Mormon Prophet*, 60-9; *Beadle's Western Wilds*, 306-7, 496-501; *Young's Wife No. 19*, 228 et seq.; *Bowle's Our New West*, 266-8; *Rusling, Across America*, 188-90; *Hayes' Scraps, Los Angeles*, viii. 228-31, xvii. 3-7; *Hutching's Cal. Mag.*, iv. 345-9; *Utah Review*, Feb. 1882, 243-6. The story of the massacre has, of course, been related thousands of times in the magazines and newspapers of Europe and America. Some of these accounts are substantially correct and some are absurd. One writer, for instance, attemps to throw new light on the subject by giving what is claimed to be a copy of the original order for the massacre, signed ' Daniel G. Wells,' and dated S. L. City, Apr. 9, 1858. The massacre occurred, as we have seen, on Sept. 11, 1857. For statements and comments of the press of the Pacific slope, see, among others, the *Deseret News*, Dec. 1, 1869; *S. L. City Tribune*, Jan. 3, Aug. 22, Oct. 3, Nov. 28, 1874; Aug. 14, 1875; Sept. 9, 1876; Apr. 23, 1879; *S. F. Bulletin*, Oct. 12, 27, Nov. 12, 1857; Apr. 13, May 14, Aug. 12, 1858; Apr. 23, Aug. 25, Oct. 28, 1859; Sept. 23, 27, Nov. 27, 1872; Nov. 17, 1874; July 26, 1875; March 24, Apr. 12, 1877; *S. F. Call*, July 21, 1866; May 23, Sept. 23, 1872; Oct. 14, 1874; July 18, 22, 25, 1875; Feb. 16, March 9, 24, 25, May 29, 1877; *S. F. Alta*, Oct. 12, 21, 1857; Aug. 13, 1858; Jan. 6, May 8, June 26, 1859; Feb. 9, 1873; July 28, Aug. 23, 1875; March 24, Apr. 7, 1877; *S. F. Chronicle*, March 22, 23, 31, Apr. 8, 1877; *S. F. Post*, March 22, 23, 1877; *S. F. Herald*, Oct. 12, 27, Nov. 2, 1857; *Mining and Scientific Press*, July 31, 1875, March 31, 1877; *Pacific Rural Press*, March 31, 1877; *Oakland Tribune*, Apr. 9, 1877; *Sac. Daily Union*, Oct. 13, Dec. 18, 1857; March 1, Aug. 14, 1858; Apr. 14, 25,

It was a ghastly sight that met them at this Wyoming of the west, amid the peaceful vales of Zion, and one that caused even the assassins to sicken and turn pale. The corpses had been entirely stripped by the Indians, who had also carried off the clothing, provisions, wagon-covers, and even the bedding of the emigrants. In one group were the naked bodies of six or seven women, in another those of ten young children, some of them horribly mangled and most of them scalped. The dead were now dragged to a ravine near by and piled in heaps; a little earth was scattered over them, but so little that it was washed away by the first rains, leaving the remains to be devoured by wolves and coyotes, the imprint of whose teeth was afterward found on their bones. It was not until nearly two years later that they were decently interred by a detachment of troops, sent for that purpose from Camp Floyd. On reaching Mountain Meadows, the men found skulls and bones scattered for the space of a mile around the ravine, whence they had been dragged by wild beasts. Nearly all the bodies had been gnawed by wolves, so that few could be recognized, and their dismembered skeletons were bleached by long exposure. Many of the skulls were crushed in with the but-ends of muskets or cleft with tomahawks; others were shattered by fire-arms, discharged close to the head. A few remnants of apparel, torn from the backs of women and children as they ran from the clutch of their pursuers, still fluttered among the bushes, and near by were masses of human hair, matted and trodden in the mould.[23]

1859; Jan. 29, 1867; Nov. 28, 1872; Nov. 24, 1874; *Cal. Mercantile Journal*, 1860, pp. 183–4; *Stockton Independent*, June 11, 1879; *San José Weekly Argus*, Dec. 5, 1874; *Santa Cruz Sentinel*, May 12, 1877; *San Buenaventura Signal*, June 23, 1877; *Winnemucca Silver State*, July 19, 1875; *Antioch Ledger*, Nov. 21, 1875; *Austin Reese River Reveille*, July 12, 1864; *Gold Hill News*, Sept. 21, 1872; Feb. 1, 1875; Sept. 12, 1876; *Carson State Register*, Sept. 26, 1872; *Prescott Miner*, Dec. 12, 1874, Apr. 11, 1879; *Idaho World*, Oct. 1, 1875; *Portland Weekly Standard*, Apr. 6, 1877; *Or. Argus*, Dec. 12, 1857, July 16, 1858; *Or. Statesman*, Nov. 3, 1857. For cuts of the massacre, see *Beadle's Western Wilds*, 498; *Beadle's Life in Utah*, facing p. 183; *Stenhouse's Rocky Mountain Saints*, facing p. 424; *Lee's Mormonism Unvailed*, facing p. 240.

[23] Rept of Assistant Surgeon Brewer, dated Mountain Meadows, May 6,

Over the last resting-place of the victims was built a cone-shaped cairn, some twelve feet in height, and leaning against its northern base was placed a rough slab of granite, with the following inscription: "Here 120 men, women, and children were massacred in cold blood, early in Sept. 1857. They were from Arkansas." The cairn was surmounted by a cross of cedar, on which were inscribed the words: "Vengeance is mine: I will repay, saith the Lord."[24]

The survivors of the slaughter were seventeen children, from two months to seven years of age, who were carried, on the evening of the massacre, by John D. Lee, Daniel Tullis, and others to the house of Jacob Hamblin,[25] and afterward placed in charge of Mormon families at Cedar, Harmony, and elsewhere. All of them were recovered in the summer of 1858, with the exception of one who was rescued a few months later, and though thinly clad, they bore no marks of ill usage.[26] In the following year they were

1859, in *Sen. Doc.*, 36th Cong. 1st Sess., ii. no. 42, pp. 16–17; Captain Campbell's rept, in *Mess. and Doc.*, 1859–60, pt 2, p. 207; *Hutchings' Cal. Mag.*, iv. 346–7. A correspondent of the *New York Herald*, writing from S. L. City, Nov. 8, 1874, states that William H. Rogers, Indian agent, was ordered to proceed from Camp Floyd with a party of cavalry and bury the remains in the summer of 1858. I find no mention of this in the official documents, though the massacre was known to Sup. Forney at least as early as June 22d of that year. See his letter to C. E. Mix, in *Sen. Doc.*, ut supra, pp. 44–5.

[24] Cuts will be found in *Stenhouse's Tell It All*, 335; *Hutchings' Cal. Mag.*, iv. 347. The cairn, cross, and slab are said to have been destroyed by order of Brigham. *Cradlebaugh's Mormonism*, 14.

[25] Forney's rept, in *Sen. Doc.*, 36th Cong. 1st Sess., ii. no. 42, pp. 79–80, where their names are given; see also p. 87; *Lee's Mormonism Unvailed*, 243. Bishop Smith's statement, in *Stenhouse's Rocky Mountain Saints*, 441–2. In giving the result of his investigation, Forney states (p. 76) that Hamblin had left his home several weeks before the massacre, and did not return until several days after it occurred. This statement was confirmed, at the trial of Lee, in the deposition of George A. Smith, who alleged that Hamblin was encamped with him at Corn Creek on Aug. 25, 1857. *Millennial Star*, xxxvii. 675. See also *Little's Jacob Hamblin*, 45. Nevertheless Hamblin was accused of complicity. Affidavit of Capt. Jas Lynch, in *Sen. Doc.*, 36th Cong. 1st Sess., ii. no. 42, p. 83.

[26] 'I succeeded in getting sixteen children, all, it is said, that remain of this butchering affair. I have the children with me; they seem contented and happy; poorly clad, however.' Forney's letter to General Johnston, in *Sen. Doc.*, ut supra, p. 8. 'The seventeenth child was recovered last April.' (1859.) 'It is proper to remark that when I obtained the children they were in a better condition than children generally in the settlements in which they lived.' *Forney's Rept*, in *Id.*, pp. 87, 89. On the other hand, Captain James

conveyed to Arkansas, the sum of $10,000 having been appropriated by congress for their recovery and restoration.[27]

To Brigham Young, as governor and superintendent of Indian affairs, belonged the duty of ordering an investigation into the circumstances of the massacre and of bringing the guilty parties to justice. His reasons for evading this duty are best explained in his own words. In his deposition at the trial of John D. Lee, when asked why he had not instituted proceedings, he thus made answer: "Because another governor had been appointed by the president of the United States, and was then on the way here to take my place, and I did not know how soon he might arrive; and because the United States judges were not in the territory. Soon after Governor Cumming arrived I asked him to take Judge Cradlebaugh, who belonged to the southern district, with him, and I would accompany them with sufficient aid to investigate the matter and bring the offenders to justice."[28]

Lynch, who accompanied Forney's party, states under oath that when he first saw them the children were 'with little or no clothing, covered with filth and dirt.' *Id.*, p. 81. Judge Cradlebaugh says nothing about their being ill treated. It was at first supposed that the children had been left in the hands of Indians, but this is denied by all the officers and officials whose reports are given in *Id.*, passim. 'No one can depict the glee of these infants,' remarks Cradlebaugh, ' when they realized that they were in the custody of what they called "the Americans"—for such is the designation of those not Mormons. They say they never were in the custody of the Indians. I recollect one of them, John Calvin Sorrow, after he found he was safe, and before he was brought away from Salt Lake City, although not yet nine years of age, sitting in a contemplative mood, no doubt thinking of the extermination of his family, saying: "Oh, I wish I was a man! I know what I would do: I would shoot John D. Lee. I saw him shoot my mother." I shall never forget how he looked.' *Mormonism*, 13.

[27] For further particulars as to the treatment and disposition of the children, see *Sen. Doc.*, 36th Cong. 1st Sess., ii. no. 42, passim; *S. F. Alta*, Feb. 23, March 12, May 29, July 10, 20, 1859; *S. F. Bulletin*, May 30, 31, June 6, Aug. 13, 1859; *Sac. Union*, July 19, 1859. Cradlebaugh says that on their way back they frequently pointed out carriages and stock that had belonged to the train, and stated whose property they were. *Mormonism*, 14.

[28] *The Lee Trial*, 37; *Lee's Mormonism Unvailed*, 305–6; *Millennial Star*, xxxvii. 675; *Tullidge's Hist. S. L. City*, 243. In a conversation with Governor Cumming, George A. Smith remarked: ' If the business had not been taken out of our hands by a change of officers in the territory, the Mountain Meadows affair is one of the first things we should have attended to when a U. S.

The Mormons concerned in the massacre had pledged themselves by the most solemn oaths to stand by each other, and always to insist that the deed was done entirely by Indians. For several months it was believed by the federal authorities that this was the case; when it became known, however, that some of the children had been spared, suspicion at once pointed elsewhere, for among all the murders committed by the Utahs, there was no instance of their having shown any such compunction. Moreover, it was soon ascertained that an armed party of Mormons had left Cedar City, had returned with spoil, and that the Indians complained of being unfairly treated in the division of the booty. Notwithstanding their utmost efforts, some time elapsed before the United States officials procured evidence sufficient to bring home the charge of murder to any of the parties implicated, and it was not until March 1859 that Judge Cradlebaugh held a session of court at Provo. At this date only six or eight persons had been committed for trial, and were now in the guard-house at Camp Floyd,[29] some of them being accused of taking part in the massacre and some of other charges.

Accompanied by a military guard, as there was no jail within his district and no other means of securing the prisoners, the judge opened court on the 8th. In his address to the grand jury he specified a number of crimes that had been committed in southern Utah, including the massacre. "To allow these things to pass over," he observed, "gives a color as if they were done by authority. The very fact of such a case as the Mountain Meadows shows that there was some person high in the estimation of the people, and it was done by that authority... You can know no law but the laws of the United States and the laws you have here. No person can commit crimes and say

court sat in southern Utah. We should see whether or not white men were concerned in the affair with the Indians.' *Little's Jacob Hamblin*, 57.

[29] Cradlebaugh's letter in *Mess.* and *Doc.*, 1859–60, pt ii. 140.

they are authorized by higher authorities, and if they have any such notions they will have to dispel them."[30] The grand jury refused to find bills against any of the accused, and, after remaining in session for a fortnight, were discharged by Cradlebaugh as "a useless appendage to a court of justice," the judge remarking: "If this court cannot bring you to a proper sense of your duty, it can at least turn the savages held in custody loose upon you."[31]

Judge Cradlebaugh's address was ill advised. The higher authority of which he spoke could mean only the authority of the church, or in other words, of the first presidency; and to contemn and threaten to impeach that authority before a Mormon grand jury was a gross judicial blunder. Though there may have been cause for suspicion, there was no fair color of testimony, and there is none yet, that Brigham or his colleagues were implicated in the massacre. Apart from the hearsay evidence of Cradlebaugh and of an officer in the army of Utah,[32] together with the statements of John D. Lee,[33] there is no ba s on which to frame a charge of complicity against th m. That the massacre occurred the day after mart l law was proclaimed, and within two days of the th eat uttered by Brigham in the presence of Van Vliet, that Brigham, as superintendent of Indian affairs, failed to embody in his report any mention of the massacre;

[30] A copy of the judge's charge will be found in *Stenhouse's Rocky Mountain Saints*, 403–6.

[31] *Cradlebaugh's Mormonism*, 11; *The Lee Trial*, 6.

[32] Major Carleton, of the first dragoons. In a despatch to the assistant adjutant-general at San Francisco, dated Mountain Meadows, May 25, 1859, he says: 'A Pah Ute chief of the Santa Clara band, named Jackson, who was one of the attacking party, and had a brother slain by the emigrants from their corral by the spring, says that orders came down in a letter from Brigham Young that the emigrants were to be killed; and a chief of the Pah Utes, named Touche, now living on the Virgin River, told me that a letter from Brigham Young to the same effect was brought down to the Virgin River band by a man named Huntingdon.' A copy of the major's despatch will be found in the *Hand-book of Mormonism*, 67–9. Cradlebaugh says that after the attack had been made, one of the Indians declared that a white man came to their camp with written orders from Brigham to 'go and help to whip the emigrants.' *Mormonism*, 11.

[33] Lee's confession, in *Mormonism Unvailed*, passim.

that for a long time afterward no allusion to it was made in the tabernacle or in the *Deseret News*—the church organ of the saints—and then only to deny that the Mormons had any share in it;[34] and that no mention was made in the *Deseret News* of the arrival or departure of the emigrants;—all this was, at best, but presumptive evidence, and did not excuse the slur that was now cast on the church and the church dignitaries. " I fear, and I regret to say it," remarks the superintendent of Indians affairs, in August 1859, "that with certain parties here there is a greater anxiety to connect Brigham Young and other church dignitaries with every criminal offence than diligent endeavor to punish the actual perpetrators of crime."[35]

The judge's remarks served no purpose, except to draw forth from the mayor of Provo a protest against the presence of the troops, as an infringement of the rights of American citizens. The judge replied that good American citizens need have no fear of American troops, whereupon the citizens of Provo petitioned Governor Cumming to order their removal. Cumming, who was then at Provo, was officially informed by the mayor that the civil authorities were prepared and ready to keep in safe custody all prisoners arrested for trial, and others whose presence might be necessary. He therefore requested General Johnston to withdraw the force which was then encamped at the court-house, stating that its presence was unnecessary. The general refused to comply, being sustained in his

---

[34] The massacre is thus mentioned for the first time in the *Millennial Star*, xxxix. 785 (Dec. 3, 1877). 'The reader cannot fail to perceive that any overt act—much less the terrible butchery at Mountain Meadows—was farthest from Brigham Young's policy at that time, to say nothing of humanitarian considerations. There can be but one just view of that melancholy event—that it was an act of retaliation by the Indians.' The emigrants are then accused of the poisoning at Corn Creek, and blamed for taking the southern route contrary to the advice of the Mormons. Forney states that the names of the guilty parties were published in the *Valley Tan. Sen. Doc.*, 36th Cong. 1st Sess., ii. no. 42, p. 86.

[35] Letter to the commissioner of Indian affairs, in *Sen. Doc.*, 36th Cong. 1st Sess., ii. no. 42, p. 74. Capt. Lynch, *Id.*, p. 84, calls Forney 'a veritable old granny,' but, with the exception of Gov. Cumming, he appears to be the only one who kept his head at this juncture.

action by the judges;[36] and on the 27th of March
Cumming issued a proclamation protesting against
all movements of troops except such as accorded
with his own instructions as chief executive magistrate.[37] A few days later the detachment was withdrawn.

Notwithstanding the contumacy of the grand jury,
Cradlebaugh continued the sessions of his court, still
resolved to bring to justice the parties concerned in
the Mountain Meadows massacre, and in crimes committed elsewhere in the territory. Bench-warrants,
based on sworn information, were issued against a
number of persons, and the United States marshal,
aided by a military escort, succeeded in making a few
arrests.[38]

Among other atrocities laid to the charge of the
Mormons was one known as the Aiken massacre, which
also occurred during the year 1857. Two brothers
of that name, with four others, returning from California to the eastern states, were arrested in southern
Utah as spies, and, as was alleged, four of the party
were escorted to Nephi, where it was arranged that
Porter Rockwell and Sylvanus Collett should assassinate them. While encamped on the Sevier River
they were attacked by night, two of them being killed

[36] Copies of all the correspondence in this matter, which is somewhat
voluminous, will be found in Mess. and Doc., 1859-60, ii. 139 et seq. The
action of Cumming was afterward sustained by the secretary of war, in a
letter addressed to Johnston, in Id., p. 157. The judges also received a sharp
rebuke at the hands of Attorney-general Black, who thus sums up the case:
'On the whole, the president is very decidedly of opinion: 1. That the governor of the territory alone has power to issue a requisition upon the commanding general for the whole or part of the army; 2. That there was no
apparent occasion for the presence of the troops at Provo; 3. That if a
rescue of the prisoners in custody had been attempted, it was the duty
of the marshal, and not of the judge, to summon the force which might be
necessary to prevent it; 4. That the troops ought not to have been sent to
Provo without the concurrence of the governor, nor kept there against his
remonstrance; 5. That the disregard of these principles and rules of action
have been in many ways extremely unfortunate.'
[37] For copy of protest see Deseret News, March 30, 1859, where is also
a protest from the grand jury against their dishonorable discharge.
[38] Cradlebaugh relates that when these arrests were made a general
stampede occurred among the Mormons, especially among the church dignitaries, who fled to the mountains. Mormonism, 11.

and two wounded, the latter escaping to Nephi, whence they started for Salt Lake City, but were murdered on their way at Willow Springs. Although the guilty parties were well known, it was not until many years later that one of them, named Collett, was arrested, and in October 1878 was tried and acquitted at Provo.[39] All the efforts of Judge Cradlebaugh availed nothing,[40] and soon afterward he discharged the prisoners and adjourned his court sine die, entering on his docket the following minute: "The whole community presents a united and organized opposition to the proper administration of justice."

This antagonism between the federal and territorial authorities continued until 1874, at which date an act

[39] *Deseret News*, Oct. 16, 23, 1878, where is a report of Collett's trial. A sensational account of this affair is given in *Hickman's Destroying Angel*, 205-9. It is there stated that the party had with them money and other property to the amount of $25,000. See also *Young's Wife No. 19*, 270-6; *S. F. Bulletin*, May 30, 1859; *S. F. Post*, Oct. 11, 1878; *S. L. City Tribune*, Oct. 12, 1878. In the report of the trial I find no mention of the murdered men's property.

[40] Among others, an attempt was made to investigate what were known as the Potter and Parrish murders at Springville, an account of which is given in *Stenhouse's Rocky Mountain Saints*, 462-7. The proceedings in these cases will be found in the *Deseret News*, Apr. 6, 1859. In his address to the grand jury, Cradlebaugh states that three persons were killed on this occasion, and that young Parrish, who was among the intended victims but made his escape, could certainly identify the parties. The judge also mentions the cases of Henry Fobbs, murdered near Fort Bridger while on his way from California, and of Henry Jones, said to have been castrated at S. L. City, and afterward shot at Pond Town, near Payson. *Stenhouse's Rocky Mountain Saints*, 404-5. This writer relates that the marshal and his posse approached Springville before daylight and surrounded that settlement, but on entering the houses, it was found that the culprits had already escaped, and after searching the cañon some few miles farther on, the party returned, having accomplished nothing. See also *Deseret News*, Apr. 6, 1859. For reports of other murders committed about this period, some of them being attributed to Mormons, see *Sen. Doc.*, 36th Cong. 1st Sess., xi. no. 42, passim; *Burton's City of the Saints*, 274; *Hickman's Destroying Angel*, 122 et seq.; *Bowles' Our New West*, 266. At this date the newspapers of the Pacific coast were teeming with accounts of atrocities said to have been committed by Mormons, for which I refer the reader to the *S. F. Bulletin*, May 20, Nov. 26, Dec. 21, 1858; Jan. 4, 24, Apr. 25, May 9, 30, Aug. 8, 24, 25, 30, 1859; *S. F. Alta*, May 15, Oct. 28, Nov. 1, 1857; Jan. 25, Nov. 4, 1858; Jan. 13, May 9, Aug. 30, 31, Sept. 14, Nov. 20, 1859; *Sac. Union*, May 15, 1857; Jan. 6, 18, May 11, 14, Sept. 8, 1859; Jan. 16, 1860. Most of the murders committed appear to have been those of desperadoes who defied the law. On May 17, 1860, for instance, two men of this stamp were shot in the streets of Salt Lake City. Commenting on this affair, the *Deseret News* of May 23d remarks: 'Murder after murder has been committed with impunity within the precincts of Salt Lake City, till such occurrences do not seemingly attract much attention, particularly when the mur-

was passed by congress "in relation to courts and judicial officers in the territory of Utah," and commonly known as the Poland bill,[41] whereby the summoning of grand and petit juries was regulated, and provision made for the better administration of justice. The first grand jury impanelled under this law was instructed by Jacob S. Boreman, then in charge of the second judicial district, to investigate the Mountain Meadows massacre and find bills of indictment against the parties implicated. A joint indictment for conspiracy and murder was found against John D. Lee, William H. Dame, Isaac C. Haight, John M. Higbee, Philip Klingensmith, and others.[42] Warrants were issued for their arrest, and after a vigorous search Lee and Dame were captured, the former being found concealed in a hog-pen at a small settlement named Panguitch, on the Sevier River.[43]

After some delay, caused by the difficulty in procuring evidence, the 12th of July, 1875, was appointed for the trial at Beaver City in southern Utah.[44] At eleven o'clock on this day the court was opened, Judge Boreman presiding, but further delay was caused by the absence of witnesses, and the fact that Lee had promised to make a full confession, and thus turn state's evidence. In his statement the prisoner detailed minutely the plan and circumstances of the

dered have had the reputation of being thieves and murderers or of associating with such characters.'

[41] Approved June 23, 1874. See *Deseret News*, July 8, 1874.

[42] *The Lee Trial*, 6. Forney states that Smith, Lee, Higby, Bishop Davis, Ira Hatch, and David Tullis were the most guilty. Letter to the commissioner of Indian affairs, in *Sen. Doc.*, 36th Cong. 1st Sess., ii. no. 42, p. 86.

[43] A detailed account of the arrest of John D. Lee by Wm Stokes, deputy U. S. marshal, is given in *Lee's Mormonism Unvailed*, 293–301. See also *Beadle's Western Wilds*, 490–2, where is a cut showing the scene of this incident. The two versions differ somewhat, Beadle stating that the arrest was made by Marshal Owens.

[44] More than 100 subpœnas had been issued, but though many obeyed the summons, several material witnesses were not forthcoming—among them being Philip Klingensmith, Joel White, and William Hawley, all of whom were present at the massacre. Klingensmith, who had promised to make a confession, arrived a day or two later, in custody of a deputy, and Joel White was induced to trust himself to the notorious Bill Hickman, then acting as special deputy marshal. *The Lee Trial*, 8.

tragedy, from the day when the emigrants left Cedar City until the butchery at Mountain Meadows. He avowed that Higbee and Haight played a prominent part in the massacre, which, he declared, was committed in obedience to military orders, but said nothing as to the complicity of the higher dignitaries of the church, by whom it was believed that these orders were issued.[45] The last was the very point that the prosecution desired to establish, its object, compared with which the conviction of the accused was but a minor consideration, being to get at the inner facts of the case. The district attorney[46] refused, therefore, to accept the confession, on the ground that it was not made in good faith. Finally the case was brought to trial on the 23d of July, and the result was that the jury, of whom eight were Mormons, failed to agree, after remaining out of court for three days.[47] Lee was then remanded for a second trial, which was held before the district court at Beaver City between the 13th and 20th of September, 1876, Judge Boreman again presiding.[48]

[45] Portions of this first confession will be found in *Id.*, 8–9; *S. F. Call*, July 21, 1875; *S. F. Bulletin*, July 21, 1875.

[46] William C. Carey, who was assisted by R. N. Baskin. Sutherland and Bates, Judge Hoge, Wells Spicer, John McFarlane, and W. W. Bishop appeared for the prisoner. Sutherland and Bates were the attorneys of the first presidency.

[47] For names of jurors, see *The Lee Trial*, 11. On p. 52, it is stated that the foreman, who was a gentile, sided with the Mormons, the three remaining gentiles being in favor of a conviction. In *The Lee Trial*, published in pamphlet form by the *S. L. Daily Tribune-Reporter* (S. L. City, 1875), we have a fair account of the proceedings at the first trial, except that the publishers seem unduly anxious to cast the onus of the charge on the first presidency. Other reports will be found in the files of the *Deseret News*, commencing July 28, 1875; *Beadle's Western Wilds*, 504–13; *Young's Wife No. 19*, 256–60; the *Elko Independent*, Aug. 7, 1875; the *Helena Independent*, July 29, 1875.

[48] For names of jurors, see *Deseret News*, Sept. 20, 1876. Lee had been cut off from the church in 1871, and among anti-Mormon writers it is stated that the church authorities now withdrew all assistance and sympathy, and determined to sacrifice him. *Lee's Mormonism Unvailed*, 32; *Beadle's Western Wilds*, 515. In his introduction to the *Mormonism Unvailed*, W. W. Bishop says that the attorneys for the defendant were furnished with a list of jurymen, and that the list was examined by a committee of Mormons, who marked with a dash those who would convict, with an asterisk those who would probably not convict, and with two asterisks those who would certainly not convict. The names of the jurors accepted were, of course, marked with two asterisks, but they found Lee guilty, as directed by the church authorities.

The court-room was crowded with spectators, who cared little for the accused, but listened with rapt attention to the evidence, which, as they supposed, would certainly implicate the dignitaries of the church. They listened in vain. In opening the case to the jury, the district attorney[49] stated that he came there to try John D. Lee, and not Brigham Young and the Mormon church. He proposed to prove that Lee had acted in direct opposition to the feelings and wishes of the officers of the Mormon church; that by means of a flag of truce Lee had induced the emigrants to give up their arms; that with his own hands the prisoner had shot two women, and brained a third with the but-end of his rifle; that he had cut the throat of a wounded man, whom he dragged forth from one of the wagons; and that he had gathered up the property of the emigrants and used it or sold it for his own benefit.[50]

These charges, and others relating to incidents that have already been mentioned, were in the main substantiated. The first evidence introduced was documentary, and included the depositions of Brigham Young and George A. Smith, and a letter written by Lee to the former, wherein he attempted to throw the entire responsibility of the deed upon the Indians. Brigham alleged that he heard nothing about the massacre until some time after it occurred, and then only by rumor; that two or three months later Lee called at his office and gave an account of the slaughter, which he charged to Indians; that he gave no directions as to the property of the emigrants, and knew nothing about its disposal; that about the 10th of September, 1857, he received a communication from Isaac C. Haight of Cedar City, concerning the Arkansas party, and in his answer had given orders

---

[49] Sumner Howard, who was assisted by Presley Denny. The prisoner's counsel were Wells Spicer, J. C. Foster, and W. W. Bishop. The trial of John Lee, in *Mormonism Unvailed*, 302.

[50] A summary of Howard's opening address to the jury, which was forcible and well studied, will be found in the *Deseret News*, Sept. 20, 1876.

to pacify the Indians as far as possible, and to allow this and all other companies of emigrants to pass through the territory unmolested. George A. Smith, who had been suspected of complicity, through attending a council at which Dame, Haight, and others had arranged their plans, denied that he was ever an accessary thereto. He also deposed that he had met the emigrants at Corn Creek, some eighty miles north of Cedar, on the 25th of August, while on his way to Salt Lake City, and that when he first heard of the massacre he was in the neighborhood of Fort Bridger.

The first witness examined was Daniel H. Wells, who merely stated that Lee was a man of influence among the Indians, and understood their language sufficiently to converse with them. James Haslem testified that between five and six o'clock on Monday, September 7, 1857, he was ordered by Isaac C. Haight to start for Salt Lake City and with all speed deliver a letter or message to Brigham Young. He arrived at 11 A. M. on the following Thursday, and four hours later was on his way back with the answer. As he set forth, Brigham said to him: "Go with all speed, spare no horse-flesh. The emigrants must not be meddled with, if it takes all Iron county to prevent it. They must go free and unmolested."[51]

Samuel McMurdy testified that he saw Lee shoot one of the women, and two or three of the sick and wounded who were in the wagons. Jacob Hamblin alleged that soon after the massacre he met Lee within a few miles of Fillmore, when the latter stated that two young girls,[52] who had been hiding in the underbrush at Mountain Meadows, were brought into his presence by a Utah chief. The Indian asked what should be done with them. "They must be shot," answered Lee; "they are too old to be spared."

[51] *Ibid.* Haslem's testimony, together with other evidence tending to exculpate the dignitaries of the church, is omitted in the account of the trial given in *Lee's Mormonism Unvailed.*

[52] From 13 to 15 years of age.

"They are too pretty to be killed," answered the chief. "Such are my orders," rejoined Lee; whereupon the Indian shot one of them, and Lee dragged the other to the ground and cut her throat.[53]

On the testimony which we have now before us I will make but one comment. If Haslem's statement was true, Brigham was clearly no accomplice; if it was false, and his errand to Salt Lake City was a mere trick of the first presidency, it is extremely improbable that Brigham would have betrayed his intention to Van Vliet by using the remarks that he made only two days before the event. Moreover, apart from other considerations, it is impossible to reconcile the latter theory with the shrewd and far-sighted policy of this able leader, who well knew that his militia were no match for the army of Utah, and who would have been the last one to rouse the vengeance of a great nation against his handful of followers.[54]

Lee was convicted of murder in the first degree, and being allowed to select the mode of his execution, was sentenced to be shot. The case was appealed to the supreme court of Utah, but the judgment was sustained, and it was ordered that the sentence should be carried into effect on the 23d of March, 1877.[55] William H. Dame, Isaac C. Haight, and others who had also been arraigned for trial, were soon afterward discharged from custody.

A few days before his execution, Lee made a con-

[53] *Deseret News*, Sept. 20, 1876; confirmed in the trial of John D. Lee, in *Mormonism Unvailed*, 361, 365-7.

[54] In a sworn statement made at S. L. City, Oct. 24, 1884, Wilford Woodruff states that he was present when Lee had an interview with Brigham Young in the autumn of 1857; that the latter was deeply affected, shed tears, and said he was sorry that innocent blood had been shed. A copy of it will be found in *The Mountain Meadows Massacre*, 51-3, a republished lecture by Elder C. W. Penrose (S. L. City, 1884).

[55] Reports of the proceedings at the second trial will be found in *Lee's Mormonism Unvailed*, 302-78; *The Deseret News*, Sept. 20, 27, 1876; *Beadle's Western Wilds*, 515-19. In passing sentence, Judge Boreman remarked: 'The men who actually participated in the deed are not the only guilty parties. Although the evidence shows plainly that you were a willing participant in the massacre, yet both trials taken together show that others, and some high in authority, inaugurated and decided upon the wholesale slaughter of the emigrants.'

fession,[56] in which he attempts to palliate his guilt, to throw the burden of the crime on his accomplices, especially on Dame, Haight, and Higbee, and to show that the massacre was committed by order of Brigham and the high-council. He also makes mention of other murders, or attempts to murder, which, as he alleges, were committed by order of some higher authority.[57] "I feel composed, and as calm as a summer morning," he writes on the 13th of March. "I hope to meet my fate with manly courage. I declare my innocence. I have done nothing designedly wrong in that unfortunate and lamentable affair with which I have been implicated. I used my utmost endeavors to save them from their sad fate. I freely would have given worlds, were they at my command, to have averted that evil. Death to me has no terror. It is but a struggle, and all is over. I know that I have a reward in heaven, and my conscience does not accuse me."

Ten days later he was led to execution at the Mountain Meadows. Over that spot the curse of the almighty seemed to have fallen. The luxuriant herbage that had clothed it twenty years before had disappeared; the springs were dry and wasted, and now there was neither grass nor any green thing, save here and there a copse of sage-brush or of scrub-oak, that

[56] It will be found entire in *Lee's Mormonism Unvailed*, 213–92; and in part in *Beadle's Western Wilds*, 519–23, *Stenhouse's Tell It All*, 633–48, the last of these versions being somewhat garbled. For other accounts and comments, see *Deseret News*, March 28, 1877; *S. F. Post*, March 22, 23, 24, 1877; *San Buenaventura Signal*, March 31, 1877; *Sonoma Democrat*, March 31, 1877; *Napa County Reporter*, Apr. 7, 1877; *Los Angeles Weekly Express*, March 24, 1877; *Los Angeles Herald*, March 24, 1877; *Anaheim Gazette*, March 24, 1877; *Western Oregonian*, Apr. 7, 1877; *Portland Weekly Oregonian*, Apr. 7, 1877.

[57] He mentions the case of an Irishman, whose throat was cut by John Weston, near Cedar City, in the winter of 1857–8; of Robert Keyes, whose assassination was attempted about the same time by Philip Klingensmith; of three California-bound emigrants, who were suspected of being spies and were slain at Cedar in 1857. An attempt was made, he says, to assassinate Lieut Tobin in the same year. A young man (name not given) was murdered near Parowan in 1854. At the same place William Laney narrowly escaped murder, his skull being fractured with a club by Barney Carter, son-in-law to William H. Dame. Rosmos Anderson, a Dane, had his throat cut at midnight by Klingensmith and others near Cedar City. Lee's Confession, in *Mormonism Unvailed*, 272–83. Some of these cases are imputed to the Danites, but I find no mention of them in *Hickman's Destroying Angel*, whose narrative covers the period 1850–65.

served but to make its desolation still more desolate.
Around the cairn that marks their grave still flit, as
some have related, the phantoms of the murdered
emigrants, and nightly reënact in ghastly pantomime
the scene of this hideous tragedy.

About ten o'clock on the morning of the 23d **a**
party of armed men alighting from their wagons
approached the site of the massacre. Among them
were the United States marshal, William Nelson, the
district attorney, a military guard, and a score of
private citizens. In their midst was John Doyle Lee.
Over the wheels of one of the wagons blankets were
placed to serve as a screen for the firing party.
Some rough pine boards were then nailed together in
the shape of a coffin, which was placed near the edge
of the cairn, and upon it Lee took his seat until the
preparations were completed. The marshal now read
the order of the court, and, turning to the prisoner,
said: "Mr Lee, if you have anything to say before
the order of the court is carried into effect, you can
do so now." Rising from the coffin,[58] he looked calmly
around for a moment, and then with unfaltering voice
repeated in substance the statements already quoted
from his confession. "I have but little to say this
morning," he added. "It seems I have to be made a
victim; a victim must be had, and I am the victim.
I studied to make Brigham Young's will my pleasure
for thirty years. See now what I have come to this
day! I have been sacrificed in a cowardly, dastardly
manner. I cannot help it; it is my last word; it is
so. I do not fear death; I shall never go to a worse
place than I am now in. I ask the Lord my God, if
my labors are done, to receive my spirit." A Methodist clergyman,[59] who acted as his spiritual adviser,
then knelt by his side and offered a brief prayer, to
which he listened attentively. After shaking hands

[58] He first requested one James Fennemore, who was taking photographs
of the group in which Lee formed the central figure, to send a copy to each
of his three wives, Rachel, Sarah, and Emma. Fennemore promised to do so.
[59] The Rev. George Stokes.

with those around him, he removed a part of his clothing, handing his hat to the marshal, who bound a
handkerchief over his eyes, his hands being free at
his own request. Seating himself with his face to
the firing party, and with hands clasped over his
head, he exclaimed: "Let them shoot the balls through
my heart. Don't let them mangle my body." The
word of command was given; the report of rifles
rang forth on the still morning air, and without a groan
or quiver the body of the criminal fell back lifeless on
his coffin. God was more merciful to him than he
had been to his victims.[60]

[60] The body was afterward interred by relatives at Cedar City. Accounts
of the execution will be found in *Lee's Mormonism Unvailed*, 383–90; *Sten-
house's Tell It All*, 627–31; *Stenhouse's Western Wilds*, 524–5; *S. L. City
Tribune*, March 31, 1877; *S. L. Herald*, March 28, 1877; *S. F. Bulletin*,
March 24, 1877; *S. F. Post*, March 24, 1877; *Oakland Tribune*, March 24,
1877; *Los Angeles Weekly Express*, March 31, 1877; *Los Angeles Reporter*,
March 23, 24, 1877; *Sonoma Democrat*, March 31, 1877; *Anaheim Gazette*,
March 31, 1877; *Mariposa Gazette*, March 31, 1877; *Jacksonville (Or.) Dem.
Times*, March 31, 1877. Portraits of Lee will be found in the frontispiece
of *Lee's Mormonism Unvailed*, and in *Stenhouse's Tell It All*, facing p. 632;
cuts representing the execution in *Id.*, facing p. 630; *Beadle's Western Wilds*,
525; *Lee's Mormonism Unvailed*, facing p. 384.

John Doyle Lee was a native of Kaskaskia, Ill., where he was born in
1812. After engaging in the several occupations of mail-carrier, stage-driver,
farmer, soldier, and clerk, he joined the Mormon church at Far West in 1837.
At Nauvoo he was employed as a policeman, one of his duties being to guard
the person and residence of Jos. Smith. After the migration he was one of
those who laid out and built up the city of Parowan. He was later appointed
probate judge of Iron co., and elected a member of the territorial legislature,
holding the former position at the time of the massacre.

CHAPTER XXI.

POLITICAL, SOCIAL, AND INSTITUTIONAL.

1859–1862.

Brigham Threatened with Arrest—The Federal Judges Reproved—Departure of Governor Cumming—And of the Army of Utah—Population of the Territory—Mortality—Wealth—Industries—Prices—Wages—Trade—Salt Lake City in 1860—The Temple Block—Social Gatherings—Theatricals—Scientific and Other Institutions—Character of the Population—Carson Valley—San Bernardino—Summit County and its Settlements—Purchase of Fort Bridger—Wasatch County—Morgan County—Cache Valley—Settlements in Southern Utah.

During the disputes between Governor Cumming and General Johnston, the latter being aided, as we have seen, by the federal judges, there was constant fear that the troops would come into collision with the territorial militia. Though the Mormon authorities had no cause for complaint as to the conduct of the soldiery, they regarded their presence as a menace, and condemned the proceedings of the general and the judges as a personal insult to the governor.

After the arrival of the army, Brigham never appeared in public without a body-guard of his own intimate friends;[1] and for many months he attended no public assemblies. At the door of his residence sentries kept watch by day, and at night a strong guard was stationed within its walls. Nor were these precautions unnecessary. About the end of March 1859 a writ was issued for his apprehension on a groundless charge of complicity in forging notes on

---

[1] *Stenhouse's Rocky Mountain Saints*, 419–20; *S. F. Alta*, Sept. 29, 1858.

the United States treasury.[2] The officers deputed to make the arrest repaired to the governor's quarters and besought his coöperation, but were promptly refused, Cumming protesting against the measure as an unjustifiable outrage,[3] whereupon they returned in discomfiture to Camp Floyd.

But the trouble was not yet ended. In May, Judge Sinclair was to open his court at Salt Lake City, and threatened to station there a detachment of troops. On Sunday the 17th of April it was reported that two regiments were on their way to the city for the purpose of making arrests, whereat General Wells at once ordered out the militia, and within a few hours five thousand men were under arms.[4] It was now ex-

[2] Stenhouse says that a counterfeit plate was engraved at S. L. City, resembling the one used by the quartermaster at Camp Floyd for drafts drawn on the assistant U. S. treasurers at New York and St Louis. When the fraud was discovered the culprit turned state's evidence, and testified that a person in the employ of Brigham had furnished the paper. It was supposed that the latter was implicated, and thereupon the writ was issued. *Rocky Mountain Saints*, 410-11. Cradlebaugh says that the plate was seized by Marshal Dotson, by order of Judge Eckles, and that Brigham afterward obtained judgment against the former for $2,600 damages, the marshal's house being sold to satisfy the judgment. *Mormonism*, 15. See also *Burton's City of the Saints*, 507. I find nothing about this matter in the files of the *Deseret News;* but the fact that the writ was issued is mentioned by Tullidge, *Hist. S. L. City*, 228, and in the *Hand-book of Reference*, 77. Peter K. Dotson, a native of Virginia, came to Salt Lake City in 1851, and was first employed by Brigham as manager of a distillery, afterward becoming express and mail agent. In 1855 he was appointed U. S. marshal for Utah, and in 1857 proceeded to Washington, returning with the army during that year. *Dotson's Doings*, MS.

[3] In a conversation with Stenhouse, the governor stated that, in case of resistance, the wall surrounding Brigham's premises was to be battered down with artillery, and the president taken by force to Camp Floyd. So, at least, said the officers. 'I listened to them, sir, as gravely as I could,' continued Cumming, 'and examined their papers. They rubbed their hands and were jubilant; "they had got the dead-wood on Brigham Young." I was indignant, sir, and told them, "By ——, gentlemen, you can't do it! When you have to take Brigham Young, gentlemen, you shall have him without creeping through walls. You shall enter by his door with heads erect, as becomes representatives of your government. But till that time, gentlemen, you can't touch Brigham Young while I live.' *Rocky Mountain Saints*, 411. Wells, *Narr.*, MS., 63-5, states that Brigham attended court, though his followers were very unwilling to allow it, as they feared a repetition of the Carthage-jail tragedy, but that no proceedings were taken against him.

[4] A correspondent of the *New York Herald*, writing from S. L. City, May 23, 1859, says that the governor notified Wells to hold the militia in readiness to resist the troops. A copy of his letter will be found in *Tullidge's Hist. S. L. City*, 228-30. See also *Hand-book of Reference*, 77. It is very improbable that Cumming would have taken such an extreme measure, and I find no mention of it in his official despatches, in those of General Johnston, or in the files of the *Deseret News*. Gen. Wells himself gives the following

pected and almost hoped that the Nauvoo legion would measure its strength with the army of Utah, but by a little timely forbearance on both sides the threatened encounter was averted. Soon afterward the judges were instructed as to their duty in an official letter from the attorney-general, and were ordered to confine themselves within their official sphere, which was to try causes, and not to intermeddle with the movements of the troops—the latter responsibility resting only with the governor. " In a territory like Utah," he remarked, "the person who exercises this power can make war and peace when he pleases, and holds in his hands the issues of life and death for thousands. Surely it was not intended to clothe each one of the judges, as well as the marshal and all his deputies, with this tremendous authority. Especially does this construction seem erroneous when we reflect that these different officers might make requisitions conflicting with one another, and all of them crossing the path of the governor."[5] The judges were superseded a few months later;[6] and thus the matter was finally set at rest, the action of the governor being sustained, although he became so unpopular with the cabinet that for a time his removal was also under consideration.[7] Though his resignation was not de-

account of the matter: ' I told Cumming myself that we didn't intend the Carthage scene reënacted, and he knew that we intended to resist the troops, which we did. I went to see Cumming frequently, and talked the matter over with him, and he declared himself that he could not recommend Gov. Young to trust himself to that military mob; but he did say he could not see how bloodshed could be hindered. I told him we would not let them come; that if they did come, they would never get out alive if we could help it. He said he did not know what to do.' 'They knew that if they did come, we were ready for them, and that we were ready to cut off their retreat. It gave us a good deal of trouble, and anxiety as well, to prepare against it, as it occurred at a time when we were putting in our crops.' *Narr.*, MS., 63–4.

[5] Soon after a mass-meeting of gentiles was held at Camp Floyd, at which the judges took a prominent part. An address was drawn up, rehearsing all the crimes imputed to Mormons, stating that they were still disloyal to the government, and censuring the president for his interference.

[6] Their successors are mentioned in the next chapter. Cradlebaugh, refusing to recognize the right of the president to remove him, continued in office for a short time, but finding himself unsupported by the government, left Utah and settled in Nevada, whence he was twice sent as delegate to congress. *Waite's The Mormon Prophet*, 75–6.

[7] *Stenhouse's Rocky Mountain Saints*, 413; *Tullidge's Hist. S. L. City*, 233.

manded, he set forth from Salt Lake City in May 1861, about two months before his term of office expired. He had entered that city amid a forced display of welcome, but he left it with the sincere regrets of a people whose hearts he had won by kind treatment.[8]

In 1860 most of the troops were removed to Mexico and Arizona, and about a year later, war between north and south being then almost a certainty, the remainder of the army was ordered to the eastern states. The government stores at Camp Floyd, valued at $4,000,000, were sold at extremely low prices, greatly to the relief of the saints, who could now purchase provisions, clothing, wagons, live-stock, and other articles of which they were in need, at their own rates. Flour, which had cost the nation $570 per ton, sold for less than $11 per ton, and other stores in the same proportion; the entire proceeds of the sale did not exceed $100,000, or little more than two per cent of the outlay; and of this sum $40,000 was contributed by Brigham.[9]

At the sale at Camp Floyd some of the leading

Both these authorities claim that Cumming was aided by Col Kane, who about this time delivered a lecture before the historical society of New York on the situation of Utah, in which he spoke of Cumming as a clear-headed, resolute, but prudent executive, and the very man for the trying position. Stenhouse was present at the lecture as reporter for the *New York Herald,* and notices of it were widely published throughout the country.

[8] Before his departure the citizens desired to show their respect by some public demonstration, but this he declined, slipping away so quietly that his departure was not known until it was published in the *Deseret News* of May 22d. His conduct received the approval of the territorial legislature. *Utah Jour. Legisl.,* 1860–1, p. 161.

Gov. Cumming was a native of Georgia, his wife being the daughter of a prominent Boston physician, and an accomplished lady. In 1836 he was mayor of Augusta, Ga, and during the cholera epidemic of that year used his utmost effort to save the lives of the citizens. During a portion of the Mexican war he was attached to the staff of Gen. Scott, and was afterward appointed by government to visit several Indian tribes in the far west. *Waite's The Mormon Prophet,* 75.

[9] Through his business agent, H. B. Clawson. As Horace Greeley remarks in his *Overland Jour.,* 254, the live-stock would have brought much better prices had it been driven to California, or even to Fort Leavenworth. He states that, in 1859, 30,000 bushels of corn, which could have been bought in Utah for $2 per bushel, were sent from the eastern states at a cost of more than $11 per bushel. Greeley visited the territory in this year, but his observations, apart from his account of an interview with Brigham, already mentioned, contain little of historical value. His reception at S. L. City is described in the *Deseret News,* July 20, 1859.

merchants of Salt Lake City laid the basis of their fortunes; to the rest of the community its main bene-fit was that it gave them a good supply of warm cloth-ing at cheap rates.   For years afterward the members of the Nauvoo legion were attired in military uniforms, which now took the place of the sombre gray clothing that the saints were accustomed to wear.   The ammunition and spare arms were de-stroyed, some of the cannon being exploded and others thrown into wells, though the latter were recov-ered by the Mormons, and are still used on the 4th and 24th of July, and other of their festivities.[10]

We have now arrived at a period in the history of Utah when it may be of interest to give a brief description of the industrial and social condition of the Mormons.   Between the years 1850 and 1862 they had increased in number from 11,380 to about 65,000, a gain that has seldom been equalled in any of the states or territories of the republic.[11]   They were a very healthy community, the number of deaths recorded in the census report for the year ending June 1860 being little more than nine per thousand,[12] though this is doubtless a mistake, the actual death rate being proba-bly at least twelve per thousand.[13]   Of the mortality,

[10] For descriptions of public festivities, between 1855 and 1865, see *Deseret News*, Jan. 4, July 18, 1855; July 9, 30, Aug. 6, 1856; July 8, 15, 22, 1857; July 11, Aug. 1, 1860; July 10, 1861; July 9, 30, 1862; July 8, 1863; July 6, 20, 27, 1864; July 5, Aug. 5, 1865; *Tullidge's Life of Young;* 247-9, *Burton's City of the Saints*, 424-5; *S. F. Alta*, Sept. 10, 1856; *S. F. Bulletin*, Dec. 2, 1858; *Sac. Union*, July 11, 1861.   A thanksgiving proclamation issued by Gov. Harding in 1862 was ignored throughout the territory.   'The non-observance of this thanksgiving day,' remarks Tullidge, 'brought Stephen S. Harding to the full realization of the fact that, though he was governor of Utah, Brigham Young was governor of the Mormon people.'

[11] I have already mentioned that the census report for 1860 gives the pop-ulation at only a little over 40,000, and stated my reasons for supposing this to be an error.   Beadle says that a judge who travelled extensively through-out the territory about 1864-5 estimated it at 85,000, and thinks the judge's estimate too low.   He himself places it, in 1867, at 100,000. *Life in Utah*, 483.   Bowles, *Our New West*, about the same date, at 100,000 to 125,000. See also *S. F. Herald*, Jan. 30, 1861; *Sac. Union*, Feb. 11, 1860.   In the census of 1870 the population is given at 86,786.

[12] *U. S. Census Rept*, for 1860, li. 43.   The total number of deaths re-ported is 374.

[13] For the year ending June 1, 1850, it was about 22 per 1,000, the rate

about twenty-six per cent occurred among infants,[14] the most prominent diseases among adults being consumption and enteritis. It is worthy of note that up to this date there occurred in the territory but one case of suicide among the Mormons.[15] There was little pauperism in their midst, and there was little crime, or such crime as was punished by imprisonment.[16]

The saints were now a fairly prosperous community. The value of their real and personal property was reported in 1860 at $5,596,118, of improved farm lands at $1,333,355, of farming implements $242,889, of live-stock $1,516,707, and of manufactures $900,153. To these figures about 50 per cent must be added in order to obtain the actual value. Among the list of premiums bestowed in this year by the Deseret Agricultural and Manufacturing Society,[17] we find prizes and diplomas awarded for agricultural and gardening implements of all kinds, for steam-engines and fire-engines, for leathern manufactures of every description from heavy harness to ladies' kid boots of many

being then greater on account of the hardships and exposure incidental to new settlements. The following extracts from the sanitary report of Assistant-surgeon Robert Bartholow of Utah terr., dated Sept. 1858, and published in *Sen. Doc.*, 36th Cong. 1st Sess., xiii. 301–2, may serve as a specimen of the prejudice of U. S. officials on matters relating to the territory, and help to account for their blunders: 'The Mormon, of all the animals now walking this globe, is the most curious in every relation.' 'Isolated in the narrow valleys of Utah, and practising the rites of a religion grossly material, of which polygamy is the main element and cohesive force, the Mormons have arrived at a physical and mental condition, in a few years of growth, such as densely populated communities in the older parts of the world, hereditary victims of all the vices of civilization, have been ages in reaching. If Mormonism received no addition from outside sources, these influences continuing, it is not difficult to see that it would eventually die out.'

[14] From cholera infantum 4, croup 23, infantile 57, measles 1, scarlatina 2, teething 11. *Id.* 43.

[15] After the railroad connected the territory with the Altantic and Pacific states, suicides became not infrequent.

[16] In *Compend. Ninth Census*, 533, the table of pauperism and crime shows only one person receiving support as a pauper, and eight criminals. At the time of Burton's visit, in 1860, there were only six prisoners in the penitentiary at S. L. City, of whom two were Indians. *City of the Saints*, 329. In the *Deseret News* of June 18, 1856, it is stated, however, that there were many beggars among the women and children.

[17] Incorporated by act approved Jan. 17, 1856, 'with a view of promoting the arts of domestic industry, and to encourage the production of articles from the native elements in this territory.' A copy of it will be found in *Utah Acts Legisl.* (ed. 1866), 111.

HIST. UTAH. 37

buttons, for woollen and cotton goods, including car-
pets, blankets, flannels, jeans, linseys, kerseys, and
cassimeres, for many articles of furniture, and for the
most needed articles of cutlery and hardware.[18]

The prices of most necessaries of life were moderate throughout the territory, but on account of high
freights—averaging from the eastern states about $28
and from the Pacific seaboard $50 to $60 per ton—
imported commodities were inordinately dear.[19]   The
cost of luxuries mattered but little, however, to a
community that subsisted mainly on the fruits and
vegetables of their own gardens, and the bread, milk,
and butter produced on their own farms.

Wages were somewhat high at this period, common
laborers receiving $2 per day and domestic servants
$30 to $40 per month.   Lumbermen, wood-choppers,
brick-makers, masons, carpenters, plasterers, and painters were in demand at good rates; though until 1857,
and perhaps for a year or two later, their hire was
usually paid in kind, as there was still but little money
in circulation.   Thus, a mechanic might be required
to receive his wages in hats, boots, or clothing, whether
he needed such articles or not, and must probably
submit to a heavy discount in disposing of his wares
for cash or for such goods as he might require.   Some
commodities, however, among which were flour, sugar,
coffee, and butter, could usually be sold at their par
value, and some could not even be bought for cash in
large quantities.   Most of the stores divided their
stock into two classes of wares, which they termed
cash-goods and shelf-goods, and the tradesman objected to sell any considerable amount of the former
unless he disposed, at the same time, of a portion of

[18] For list of premiums and diplomas, see *Burton's City of the Saints*, 384–7.
[19] From the list of prices-current at the tithing-office in 1860, we learn
that cereals were rated in Salt Lake City at $1.50 per bushel, butcher's meat
at 3 to 12½ cents per pound, chickens and ducks at 10 to 25 cents each, eggs
at 18 cents per dozen, milk at 10 cents per quart, and butter at 25 cents per
pound; but sugar worth in New York about 6 cents per pound cost in Utah
35 to 60 cents, while tea ranged in price from $1.50 to $3.50, and coffee from
40 to 60 cents per pound, or at least fivefold their cost in the Atlantic states.

the latter. If, for instance, one should tender $50 for a bag of sugar without offering to make other purchases, the store-keeper would probably refuse; "for," he would argue, "if I sell all my cash-goods for cash, without also getting rid of my shelf-goods, I shall not be able to dispose of the latter for cash at all. I must dole out the one with care that I may be able to get rid of the other."[20]

In some of the shop windows on Main Street were displayed costly imported commodities—silks, velvets, and shawls of diverse pattern, jewelry, laces, and millinery;[21] near by were less pretentious stores, where home-made and second-hand articles were retailed. In some of the latter might be seen a curious collection of dilapidated merchandise, and people almost as singular as the wares over which they chaffered. Here was a group of women holding solemn conclave over a superannuated gown that to other eyes would seem worthless; there a sister in faded garb cheapening a well-battered bonnet of Parisian make that had already served as covering and ornament for half a dozen heads.

Approaching Zion from the direction of Fort Bridger, after days of travel through sage-brush and buffalo-grass, the traveller would observe that within a score of leagues from Salt Lake City nature's barrenness began to succumb to the marvellous energy of the saints. The cañons had been converted by irrigation into fertile lands, whose emerald tint soothed the eye wearied with the leaden monotony of the desert land-

---

[20] William Chandless, who visited Salt Lake City in the winter of 1855-6, states that, if one wanted to sell anything, he could get nothing for it, because of the scarcity of money; while if an offer were made to buy the same article for cash, a very high price must be paid on account of the rarity of the article. *Visit to S. L. City*, 223. For many years afterward, this system of traffic prevailed in a measure. Thus, in the *Deseret News* of Feb. 22, 1860, J. C. Little advertises that he will exchange his store of furniture for wheat and flour; George B. Wallace that he will give five gallons of molasses per cord for wood; and Felt and Allen that they pay cash and store goods for wheat delivered at the Jordan mills.

[21] In 1860 there were three milliner's stores, thirteen dry-goods and two variety stores. *Burton's City of the Saints*, 277-8.

scape. The fields were billowing with grain, the cattle sleek and thriving, the barns well filled, the windmills buzzing merrily. Nevertheless, among these smiling settlements a painful deficiency might be noticed. Everything that industry and thrift could accomplish had been done for the farm, but nothing for the home. Between the houses of the poor and the rich there was little difference, except that one was of logs and the other of boards. Both seemed like mere enclosures in which to eat and sleep, and

SALT LAKE CITY IN 1860.

around neither was there any sign that the inmates took a pride in their home. One might pass three dwellings enclosed by a common fence, and belonging to one master, but nowhere could be seen any of those simple embellishments that cost so little and mean so much—the cultivated garden plat, the row of shade trees, the rose-bush at the doorway, or the trellised creeper at the porch.

The city itself wore a different aspect. The streets,

though unpaved and without sidewalks, were lined
with cotton-wood and locust trees, acacias, and poplars.
Most of the private houses were still of wood or
adobe, some few only being of stone, and none
pretentious as to architecture; but nearly all were
surrounded with gardens in which fruit and shade
trees were plentiful. Many of them were of the
same pattern, barn-shaped, with wings and tiny case-
ments, for glass was not yet manufactured by the
Mormons. A few of the better class were built on a
foundation of sandstone, and somewhat in the shape
of a bungalow, with trellised verandas, and low flat
roofs supported by pillars. Those of the poor were
small hut-like buildings, most of them one-storied,
and some with several entrances. At this date the
entire city, except on its southern side, was enclosed
by a wall some ten or twelve feet high, with semi-
bastions placed at half musket-range, and pierced here
and there with gateways.[22]

In driving through the suburbs the visitor would
find the thoroughfares in bad condition, dusty in summer, and in winter filled with viscid mud. On either
side were posts and rails, which, as the heart of the
city was approached, gave way to neat fences of
palings. On Main Street were the abodes of some
of the leading Mormon dignitaries and the stores of
prominent gentile merchants. On the eastern side,
nearly opposite the post-office, and next door to a
small structure that served for bath-house and bakery,
stood the principal hostelry, the Salt Lake House, a
large pent-roofed building, in front of which was a ve-
randa supported by painted posts, and a sign-board
swinging from a tall flag-staff. Here fair accommoda-

[22] *Woodruff's Journal*, MS.; *Richards' Hist. Incidents of Utah*, MS., 28–9;
Wells' Narr., MS., 60; *Chandless, Visit to S. L.*, 153; *Sloan's Utah Gazetteer*, 25. The wall was built in 1853. Chandless remarks that for defensive
purposes it would be useless, as any one could climb it with ease. Burton,
City of the Saints, 245, states that it was built as a defence against Indians,
though gentiles said that it was constructed only because the people wanted
work. It was of mud mixed with hay and gravel; in 1860 it had already begun to crumble, and in 1883 there were few traces of it remaining.

tion could be had at very moderate charges.[23]   Even in its business portion, Main Street had at this date many vacant lots, being then in the embryo condition through which all cities must pass, the log building standing side by side with the adobe hut and the stone or brick store, with here and there a few shanties, relics of the days of 1848.

Among the principal attractions was the temple block, surrounded in 1860 with a wall of red sandstone, on which were placed layers of adobe, fashioned in imitation of some richer substance, and raising it to a height of ten feet.   On each face of the wall were thirty pilasters, also of adobe, protected by sandstone copings, but without pedestals or entablatures.   Up to the year 1860 the cost of the wall and the foundations of the edifice already amounted to $1,000,000, a sum equal to the entire outlay on the temple at Nauvoo.   The block was consecrated on the 3d of February, 1853, and the corner-stones laid with imposing ceremonies on the 6th of the following April.[24]   In August 1860, the foundations, which were sixteen feet deep and of gray granite, had been completed, but no further progress had been made.   I shall reserve until later a description of the building as it now stands.   Of the tabernacle which occupied the southwest corner of the block, and the bowery immediately north of the tabernacle, mention has already been made.[25]   In the north-west corner, and separated from

[23] Burton relates that at the time of his visit, in Aug. 1860, the Salt Lake House was kept by a Mr Townsend, a Mormon convert from Maine, who had been expelled from Nauvoo, where he sold his house, land, and furniture, for $50. *City of the Saints*, 248.   His charge for 24 days' board and lodging was $34.25.   The bill, which is curiously worded, is given in full in *Id.*, 537. Among its items are '14 Bottle Beer 600' (cents), '2 Bottles Brandy 450.'

[24] The original plans will be found in the *Millennial Star*, xvi. 635, and *Linforth's Route from Liverpool*, 109–10.   Those given by Truman O. Angell, the architect, in the *Deseret News*, Aug. 17, 1854, differ somewhat from the above, but both agree that the edifice was to cover a space of 21,850 sq. feet, or about half an acre.   For descriptions of the consecration and laying of the corner-stones, see *Woodruff's Journal*, MS.; *Tucker's Mormonism*, 222; *Ferris' Utah and the Mormons*, 167–9; *S. L. City Contributor*, iii. 79; *Deseret News*, Feb. 19, Apr. 16, 1853.   Seven thousand four hundred and seventy-eight tons of rock were used for the foundation. *Richards' Incidents in Utah Hist.*, MS., 81.

[25] Burton describes the tabernacle, in 1860, as an adobe building, capa-

the tabernacle by a high fence, stood the endowment house,[26] where, as evil-minded gentiles declared, human sacrifices were offered. The ceremonies that actually took place within its walls have been described elsewhere in this volume.

In the blocks adjacent to the tabernacle were the residences of Brigham, Heber, Orson Hyde, George A. Smith, Wilford Woodruff, John Taylor, and Daniel H. Wells, the first two occupying entire blocks.[27] South of temple block was the council-house,[28] south of Brigham's dwelling and adjoining that of Wells was the historian's office, where the church records were kept, and in the next plat to the east was the social hall,[29] where the fashion of the city held festivities.

Balls held at the social hall were extremely select, and sometimes a little expensive, tickets for the more pretentious fêtes costing ten dollars for each couple, and the invitations, which were difficult to obtain even at that price,[30] being issued on embossed and bordered

ble of accommodating 2,000 to 3,000 persons, the interior of which was spanned by an elliptical arch. Over the entrances were carvings in wood, 'representing the sun with his usual coiffure of yellow beams, like a Somali's wig, or the symbol of the Persian empire.' City of the Saints, 270. A few years later the tabernacle was enlarged, and had a seating capacity of 7,000. Utah Notes, MS., 2.

[26] Cuts of the tabernacle and endowment house will be found in City of the Saints, facing p. 271.

[27] The residences of Young, Kimball, and Wells were on Main St, properly East Temple St, which runs past the temple block. Remy says that one of Brigham's houses was 80 x 40 ft, built of granite and other kinds of stones, with long salient ogives, that adjoining it being the dwelling which he usually occupied. Near by were the governor's offices, the tithing-office, and the court-house. Jour. to S. L. City, i. 193–4. In Id., i. 193–200; Greeley's Overland Jour., 206–7; Atlantic Monthly, iii. 573–5; Schiel, Reise durch Felsengebirge, 100–2, are descriptions of S. L. City about this date.

[28] This building, which was begun in 1849, and has already been described, was afterward destroyed by fire. Nebeker's Early Justice, MS., 3. Except for a small structure used as a post-office, this was the first public building erected in S. L. City. See also Wells' Narr., MS., 42.

[29] The opening of the social hall is described in the Deseret News, Jan. 22, 1853. Among other buildings worthy of note were the arsenal, built on the bench north of the city, the penitentiary in the south-eastern suburb, and the hall of seventies on the 'states road.' Linforth's Route from Liverpool, 110; Burton's City of the Saints, 279–80. The court-house was yet unfinished. Atlantic Monthly, iii. 574.

[30] They were issued on special occasions only for 75 or 80 guests, including a few of the more prominent gentiles.

paper. Dancing commenced about four P. M., the president of the church pronouncing a blessing with uplifted hands, and then leading off the first cotillon. All joined vigorously in the dance, and the prophet, his apostles, and bishops set the example, the saltations not being in the languid gliding pace then fashionable in other cities, but elaborately executed steps requiring severe muscular exercise. At eight came supper, a substantial repast, with four courses,[31] after which dancing was resumed, varied at intervals with song until four or five o'clock in the morning, when the party broke up, the entertainment closing with prayer and benediction.

Besides these fashionable gatherings held from time to time by the élite of Zion, there were ward parties, elders' cotillon parties, and picnic parties, the last being sometimes held at the social hall, where rich and poor assembled, bringing with them their children, and setting their own tables, or ordering dainties from an adjoining kitchen provided for that purpose. Here, also, until 1862, when the first theatre was built, theatrical entertainments were given in winter,[32] and these of no mean order, for among the Mormons there was no lack of amateur talent.[33] Among those who par-

[31] Copies of the card of invitation and the ménu at a 'territorial and civil ball' held at the social hall, Feb. 7, 1860, will be found in Burton's City of the Saints, 231-2. Among the dishes are bear, beaver-tails, slaw, mountain, pioneer, and snowballs. What the names all signify I am unable to state. Otherwise the bill of fare contains a large and choice variety of viands.

[32] Cooke's Theatr. and Soc. Affairs in Utah, MS., 9. In summer they were held at the bowery. The S. L. theatre, or as it was usually termed the opera-house, was dedicated March 6th of this year. Sloan's Utah Gazetteer, 1884, p. 28. A gentleman who visited the city two or three years later states that its interior resembled the opera-house at New York, having seats for 2,000 and capacity for 500 more. Externally the building was a plain but not ungraceful structure of stone, brick, and stucco. Atlantic Monthly, Apr. 1864, p. 490.

[33] Among others Burton mentions H. B. Clawson, B. Snow, and W. C. Dunbar. During his stay the 'Lady of Lyons' was performed. City of the Saints, 280. See also Deseret News, March 2, 1864; Busch, Gesch. Morm., 311-12, 330; The Mormons at Home, 149-51. Chandless, who visited the social hall one evening in the winter of 1855-6, when the third act of Othello and a two-act drama were performed, mentions that the parts of Othello and Iago were fairly rendered, but that the other characters were beneath criticism. Desdemona, he says, 'was a tall, masculine female, with cheeks painted beyond the possibility of a blush. Even worse was Emilia—an old dowdy, she looked, who might have been a chambermaid at a third-rate hotel for a quarter of a

ticipated were several of the wives and daughters of Brigham.[34] All the actors attended rehearsal each night in the week, except on Wednesdays and Saturdays, when the performances took place; most of them found their own costumes, and none received any fixed remuneration.[35]

While the amusements of the people were thus cared for, there was no lack of more solid entertainment. All had access to the public library under proper restrictions, and in the council-house was opened, in 1853, the first reading-room, which was supplied with newspapers and magazines from all parts of the world. Among the scientific associations may be mentioned the Universal Scientific Society, established in 1854, with Wilford Woodruff as president, and the Polysophical Society, over which Lorenzo Snow presided.[36] The musical talent of Salt Lake City formed themselves, in 1855, into the Deseret Philharmonic Society, and in June of that year a music hall was in course of construction.[37] In the same

century...The afterpiece was, on the contrary, very well performed.' *Visit to S. Lake*, 224.

[34] Three of Brigham's daughters, Alice, Emily, and Zina, were on the stage. Hepworth Dixon, who was well acquainted with Alice, the youngest wife of Elder Clawson, says that she remarked to him one day at dinner, 'I am not myself very fond of playing, but my father desires that my sister and myself should act sometimes, as he does not think it right to ask any poor man's child to do anything which his own children would object to do.' *New America*, 144.

[35] *Cooke's Theatr. and Soc. Affairs in Utah*, MS., 9–10; *Stenhouse's Tell It All*, 380–1. Mrs Cooke states that the performers often remained at rehearsal until 12 or 1 o'clock, and that after a hard day's work. Occasionally a benefit was given to the lady actors, and the proceeds divided among them. Her share during the twelve years that she played amounted to $150. In *Theatrical and Social Affairs in Utah, by Mrs S. A. Cooke*, MS., we have, besides the information which the title-page suggests, a number of items relating to church matters and the workings of polygamy. Mrs Cooke was well acquainted with the wife of Heber C. Kimball, Eliza Snow, and other prominent women among the Mormons. Of English birth, she was for eight years a teacher of music in the city of New York, and in 1852 set forth for California, reaching S. L. City in July, where she purposed to remain only until the following spring, but was converted to Mormonism. For 16 years she was employed as a teacher, among her pupils in Zion being the children of Brigham Young.

[36] There was also a horticultural society, organized in connection with the American Pomological Society, and the Deseret Typographical Association formed for the advancement of their art. *Linforth's Route from Liverpool*, 111.

[37] By the members of Capt. Ballo's band. *Deseret News*, June 27, 1855.

year the Deseret Theological Institute was organized, its purpose being to make known the principles of light and truth which its members claimed to have received from the priesthood, in the belief that "the science of theology embraces a knowledge of all intelligence, whether in heaven or on the earth, moral, scientific, literary, or religious"!

Prominent among the charitable associations was the Relief Society, originally organized by Joseph Smith at Nauvoo in 1842, and discontinued after his assassination until 1855, when it was reëstablished in Salt Lake City. After that date its operations gradually extended from ward to ward and from settlement to settlement, until it became a powerful influence for good throughout the land. Its main purpose was the relief of the poor, and by its efforts it prevented the necessity for poor-houses, which are still unknown among the latter-day saints, and otherwise it rendered good service—by educating orphans, by promoting home industries, and by giving tone and character to society through its moral and social influence.[38]

To the student of humanity there were few richer fields for study than could be found at this period in the Mormon capital, where almost every state in the union and every nation in Europe had its representatives. There were to be seen side by side the tall, sinewy Norwegian, fresh from his pine forests, the phlegmatic Dane, the stolid, practical German, the dapper, quick-minded Frenchman, the clumsy, dogmatic Englishman, and the shrewd, versatile American. So little did the emigrants know of the land in which their lot was cast that some of them, while crossing the plains, were not aware that they trod on American soil, and others cast away their blankets and warm clothing, under the impression that perpetual summer reigned in Zion. A few years' residence

---

[38] In 1880 this society had nearly 300 branches. *Snow's Brief Sketch of Organizations*, MS., 1–2.

ın the land of the saints accomplishes a wonderful change, the contrast in mien and physique between the recruits and the older settlers being very strongly marked. Especially is this the case among the women. " I could not but observe in those born hereabouts," writes an English traveller in 1860, "the noble, regular features, the lofty, thoughtful brow, the clear, transparent complexion, the long, silky hair, and, greatest charm of all, the soft smile of the American woman when she does smile."[39]

Much has been said about race deterioration aris-

[39] *Burton's City of the Saints*, 278. Burton attributes this improvement in the race to climate. In amusing contrast with Burton's remarks are those of Surgeon Bartholow, who in his sanitary report says: 'It is a curious fact that Mormonism makes its impress upon the countenance,...an expression compounded of sensuality, cunning, suspicion, and a smirking self-conceit. The yellow, sunken, cadaverous visage; the greenish colored eyes; the thick, protuberant lips; the low forehead; the light yellowish hair; and the lank, angular person—constitute an appearance so characteristic of the new race, the production of polygamy, as to distinguish them at a glance. The women of this territory, how fanatical and ignorant soever, recognize their wide departure from the normal standard in all christian countries, and from the degradation of the mother follows that of the child.' *Sen. Ex. Doc.*, 52, 36th Cong. 1st Sess., 302.

The City of the Saints, and across the Rocky Mountains to California, by Richard F. Burton, London, 1861, ranks among the best of gentile works on Mormonism. Less philosophical than that of Gunnison, it is equally impartial, and gives many details as to the social and industrial condition of the Mormons for which one may search in vain elsewhere. His stay in S. L. City lasted less than four weeks (from Aug. 25 to Sept. 20, 1860), excursions being made during his visit to points of interest in the neighborhood, but he saw more during that time than many others have done in four years. Travelling in company with Lieut Dana of the U. S. artillery, and procuring introductions to Gov. Cumming, Brigham Young, and several of the church dignitaries, he had every opportunity to note the different phases of Mormon life. The first and last portions of the work are taken up with his travels from St Joseph, Mo., to San Francisco, the middle chapters only relating to Utah. In style and tone the writer is sketchy and interesting, good-natured, but somewhat disposed to regard matters in their ludicrous aspect, for which he offers in his preface the excuse—*sic me natura fecit.*

A Visit to Salt Lake; being a Journey across the Plains and a Residence in the Mormon Settlements at Utah, by William Chandless, London, 1857, is the title of a less entertaining and reliable work. As Mr Chandless remarks in his preface, even at that date, 'fictions enough have been written about the Mormons;' but it does not appear that his own work is less fictitious than those of which he complains. There are chapters about religion, government, settlements, morals, institutions, and some that appear to be about nothing in particular, unless it be Mr Chandless. Nevertheless, items of interest may be gleaned from them, as the author made a tour of the principal counties in 1855, and travellers in those parts were rare at this period. After informing us where he slept, and where he dined, and what he had for dinner, he occasionally finds time to tell us something about the condition of the settlements through which he journeyed.

ing from polygamous unions. It has never been
shown that physical development suffers from the
polygamous system, especially when regulated by religion, as in the case of the Mormons. The children
of saints are much like other children. In the streets
of the capital, however, during the period under review,
might be seen youths of eighteen or twenty, some of
them the children of church dignitaries, whose highest ambition was satisfied when they could ride through
the streets, hallooing and shouting, fantastically attired
in fringed and embroidered buckskin leggings, gaudily
colored shirt, and slouched hat, and with the orthodox revolver and bowie-knife conspicuously displayed.[40]
They resembled somewhat the cow-boy of the present day; but their presence was barely felt amid this
staid and order-loving community,[41] the forwardness
of the second generation of the saints being attributed,
not without show of reason, to the corrupting influence of the gentiles.

In order to estimate fairly the character of the population of Salt Lake City, which numbered in 1860
about 14,000,[42] the visitor should attend the bowery
or tabernacle, where according to the season of the
year about 3,000 of the populace assembled on Sunday. The men appeared, in warm weather, without
coats and with open vests, but always in decent and
cleanly garb, most of them being clad in gray tweed,
though some of the elders and dignitaries wore black
broadcloth.[43] The women wore silks, woollen stuffs,

[40] *Jennings' Mat. Progr. of Utah*, MS., 3–4. Mr W. Jennings, ex-mayor
of S. L. City, who supplied me with the above MS. in 1884, says that this
condition of affairs came to an end when the railroad reached Utah.

[41] 'There were no lamps in any but Main Street, yet the city is as safe as
St James Square, London. There are perhaps not more than 25 or 35 constables or policemen in the whole place.' *Burton's City of the Saints*, 273.
'The few policemen that have been on duty during the summer were discharged on Monday last.' *Deseret News*, Sept. 12, 1860.

[42] In 1863 Brigham stated its population at 16,000. *Atlantic Monthly*, Apr.
1864, p. 492; Burton, in 1860, 9,000. *City of the Saints*, 284; Bowles, in
1865, 25,000 to 30,000. *Our New West*, 227. The last two are wide of the
mark.

[43] Before this date Brigham attempted to lead the fashion, appearing in a
yellow slouched hat, much too large for his head, green frock-coat, pants

or calicoes, as they were able to afford, usually of plain pattern and dark color, though a few were dressed in gaudy attire, and with a little faded finery.[44] The congregation was seated on long rows of benches opposite the platform, from which they were separated by the space allotted to the orchestra, then consisting of a violin and bass viol, vocal music being rendered by two female and four male singers. The oratory was somewhat of the Boanerges stamp, and contained much round abuse of the gentiles; but looking at the audience, which consisted, in the main, of a thriving, contented, and industrious class of people, light-hearted and ever ready to laugh at the somewhat broad jokes of the church dignitaries, it was impossible to believe all the hard things spoken and written of them by their enemies. Moreover, about one third of the population consisted at this date of emigrants from Great Britain, and at least two fifths were foreigners of other nationalities, most of them Danes, Swedes, or Norwegians. They were fair types of their race, and it is not very probable

large and loose, and white socks and slippers. His fashion was followed by some of the elders. *Ward's Husband in Utah*, 34-5. Burton says that the prophet was dressed in gray homespun, and wore a tall steeple-crowned hat, as did most of the elders. Describing one of his addresses, he writes: ' Brigham Young removed his hat, advanced to the end of the tribune, and leaning slightly forward upon both hands, propped on the green baize of the tribune, addressed his followers. The discourse began slowly, word crept titubantly after word, and the opening phrases were hardly audible; but as the orator warmed, his voice rose high and sonorous, and a fluency so remarkable succeeded falter and hesitation, that although the phenomenon is not rare in strong speakers, the latter seemed almost to have been a work of art. The manner was pleasing and animated, and the matter fluent, impromptu, and well turned, spoken rather than preached; if it had a fault, it was rather rambling and disconnected...The gestures were easy and rounded, not without a certain grace, though evidently untaught; one, however, must be excepted, namely that of raising the forefinger...The address was long. God is a mechanic. Mormonism is a great fact. Religion has made him, the speaker, the happiest of men. He was ready to dance like a shaker. At this sentence the prophet, who is a good mimic and has much of the old New English quaint humor, raised his right arm, and gave, to the amusement of the congregation, a droll imitation of Anne Lee's followers.' *City of the Saints*, 317.

[44] For many years after their arrival in the valley the women dressed in homespun linseys, as there was nothing else to wear. At one time Brigham, in order to discourage extravagance, decreed that the men must not dance with women who were dressed in other than homespun garments. *Jennings, Mat. Progress*, MS., 1.

that they had so quickly changed their national characteristics as already to forfeit the good opinion of their fellow-men.

Such was Zion in 1860, and such its population. Of the progress and condition of other settlements established soon after the Mormon occupation, and the founding of which has already been mentioned, I shall have occasion to speak later. During the thirteen years that had now elapsed since first they entered the valley, the saints had pushed forward their colonies in all directions almost to the verge of their territory. Especially was this the case toward the west, where, at an early date, they came into antagonism with settlers from California. In 1850 a few persons from that state had settled in Carson valley for trading purposes, the migration of gold-seekers, some of whom wintered in that region, being then very considerable. During the following year several Mormons entered the valley, John Reese, who arrived there in the spring with thirteen wagon-loads of provisions, building the first house, known for several years as the Mormon station, on the site of the present village of Genoa.[45] Reese first came to the valley alone, his nearest neighbor, James Fennimore, living in Gold Cañon, some twenty-five miles distant, in a "dug-out," or hole scooped out of the bank, the front part covered in this instance with rags and strips of canvas, the man being thriftless and a dram-drinker. He was nicknamed Virginia, and after him was named the city whence more bullion has been shipped in a single year than would now replace the floating capital of the states of California and Nevada.[46]

[45] It served as hotel and store, and was a two-story log building, 50 x 30 ft. *Reese's Mormon Station*, MS.; *Taylor's Rem.*, MS.

[46] Reese states that Virginia had a flume in the cañon for gold-washing, and that Comstock, who came to Carson Valley in 1856, bought him out, the latter living but a short time afterward. *Id.*, 5. In *Jennings' Carson Valley*, MS., 3, it is related that Comstock came to the valley in the autumn of 1856, in charge of a herd of sheep, but in a destitute condition. In 1852 Reese was engaged in farming on a considerable scale, selling his produce

By an act of the Utah legislature, approved January 17, 1854, the limits of Carson county were defined,[47] and the governor was authorized to appoint for it a probate judge whose duty it should be to organize the county, by dividing it into precincts, holding an election, filling the various offices, and locating the county seat. The choice fell on Orson Hyde, who with Judge Styles, the United States marshal, and an escort of thirty-five men, reached the settlement of John Reese in June 1855, other parties of Mormons arriving during this and the following year. Meanwhile miners, farmers, and herdsmen from California and the Atlantic states had settled in the valley and elsewhere on the eastern side of the Sierra Nevada in such numbers as to alarm the Mormons, who now desired them to leave the territory. This they refused to do, and some pretended fears of a resort to force. The gentiles fortified themselves, and assumed an aggressive attitude, and for two weeks the opposing forces were encamped almost within sight of each other, but without coming to blows. News of the disturbance reached the mining camps on the other side of the mountains, and numbers prepared to go in aid of their comrades. The aggressors now feared that they would be themselves expelled from the country, and proposed a truce, under which all should be allowed to remain on their lands.

As soon as the matter became known to the authorities, the county organization was repealed, the probate judge recalled, and the records, which contained several criminal indictments of a serious

readily and at high prices to emigrants who, as he says, would pay almost any price for provisions, a small bunch of turnips selling for a dollar. Reese lived later at S. L. City, while S. A. Kinsey, his former partner remained at Genoa. *Van Sickles' Utah Desperadoes*, MS. Among the earliest settlers were three persons named Lee, and others named Condie and Gibson. *Early Hist. Carson Valley*, MS., 1. The place was first known as 'the Mormon station,' Genoa being laid out in 1856. *Id.*, 3.

[47] It was bounded on the north by Deseret co., east by the 118th meridian, south by the boundary line of Utah, and west by California. *Utah Acts Legisl.* (ed. 1855), 261.

nature,[48] were removed to Salt Lake City. When
news arrived of the approach of the army of Utah,
the Carson Mormons were ordered, as we have seen,
to return to Zion and aid in its defence, though a
few remained in the valley. In 1859 the gentile
inhabitants, after several fruitless appeals to congress, formally declared their independence,[49] and demanded admission as a territory. Two years later
the request was granted, and the territory of Nevada
was cut off from Utah, its eastern limit being fixed
at the thirty-ninth meridian, but extended by act of
1862 to the thirty-eighth, and by act of 1866 to the
thirty-seventh meridian. Reluctantly the Mormons
relinquished these portions of the public domain.

In Eagle and Washoe valleys they had also established small settlements in 1854 and 1855, remaining
until recalled in 1857, at which latter date, as will be
remembered, the colony at San Bernardino in California was also abandoned. During the Mormon
occupation the county of San Bernardino was cut off
from that of Los Angeles, the former assuming its
proportion of the liabilities. A city was built, with
substantial dwellings, saw and grist mills, and sur-

[48] A letter of James B. Crane, dated Washington, Jan. 17, 1859, and of
which copies will be found in *Waite's The Mormon Prophet*, 31–5, and *Tucker's
Mormonism*, 226–9, gives a detailed account of the Carson-valley troubles.
The letter, which is somewhat bitter in tone, was written with a view to the
admission of Nevada as a territory. Life and property were somewhat insecure in Carson valley about this date, and vigilance committees were constantly on the alert. See *Sac. Union*, Aug. 26, 1857, June 17, 22, July 2,
Aug. 2, Dec. 21, 1858, June 1, 1859, Sept. 24, 1860. On the 14th of June,
1858, William Thorington, better known as 'Lucky Bill,' Luther Olds,
William Edwards, and four others were arrested by a party of 30 men, and
tried for the murder of a Frenchman named Godier, at Honey Lake. Lucky
Bill was hanged, Olds was released on payment of $1,000 fine and promis-
ing to leave the valley never to return, and Edwards probably escaped by
bribing his captors. The rest were released. *Van Sickles' Utah Desperadoes*,
MS.; *Placerville Tri-weekly Register*, June 24, 1858; *Popular Tribunals*, this
series.
[49] The declaration contains a number of charges against the Mormons,
which will be found in *Remy's Jour. to G. S. L. City*, i. 493–4. On May 6,
1856, joint resolutions of the California legislature were read in the U. S.
senate, setting forth that a large number of settlers in Carson valley had, for
good reasons, petitioned congress that this portion of Utah be attached to
California, and had asked the coöperation of the California legislature, that
the latter body acquiesced, and urged the passage of a law to that effect.
Cong. Globe, 1855–6, 1089.

rounded with thriving farms;[50] a road was constructed as far as the timber belt in the neighboring mountains, each man working incessantly until it was completed, and all this was accomplished without incurring debt, a small balance remaining in the county treasury when the settlers were ordered by Brigham to Salt Lake City.[51]

Of Elder Samuel Brannan's party which arrived in San Francisco, as will be remembered, in the summer of 1846, mention is made in connection with my *History of California.*[52] During this year, a settlement named New Hope was founded by a portion of the company on the north bank of the Stanislaus River, near its junction with the San Joaquin, but was abandoned when news was received that the brethren had resolved to remain in the valley of Great Salt Lake. Most of the Mormons still remained, however, in California, betaking themselves to farming and lumbering until the time of the gold discovery, when they gathered at the mines on Mormon Island. Between 1848 and 1850 about a hundred and forty of them found their way to Utah; the remainder cast in their lot with the gentiles, and most of them, among whom was their leader, apostatized, though a few afterward joined the Mormon communities at San Bernardino and in Arizona.[53]

[50] Elder Rich, who arrived at S. L. City from San Bernardino in April 1852, reported 1,800 acres in grain, and about 1,000 in vegetables. *Deseret News*, May 1, 1852.

[51] *Shepherd's Colonizing of San Bernardino*, MS. See also letter of Amasa Lyman, in *Millennial Star*, xiv. 491-2; and extract from *N. Y. Herald*, in *Id.*, xv. 61; *Richards' Hist. Incidents of Utah*, MS., 23; *S. F. Herald*, Aug. 21, 1852; *Hughes*, in *Hastings' Or. and Cal.*, 96; *Utah Scraps*, 11.

[52] Vol. v., 544-54. On pp. 543-4 (note 35) is a list of the members.

[53] Frisbie states that after the gold discovery the Mormons, many of whom had now become wealthy, refused to pay tithes, whereupon Brannan appealed to their sense of duty, but finding them fixed in their resolve, frankly told them they were sensible, and had been damned fools for paying tithes so long. From that time he ceased to be an elder. *Rem.*, 33-4. For further details as to Brannan's party, see *Glover's Mormons in Cal.*, MS., passim; *Larkin's Doc.*, MS., iv. 55; *Olvera Doc.*, MS., 14-15; *Larkin's Off. Corresp.*, MS., ii. 42; *Millennial Star*, ix. 39-40, 306-7; *Times and Seasons*, vi., 1126-7. Sutter spoke of them in the highest terms. 'So long as these people have been employed by me,' he says, 'they have behaved very well, and were industrious and faithful laborers.' *Hutchings' Cal. Mag.*, ii. 196. In Jan. 1847

Within the territory of Utah many new colonies were established. In 1853 the first settlement was made in Summit county by one Samuel Snider, who built a number of sawmills in Parley Park. In 1861 the county was organized, and soon became noted for

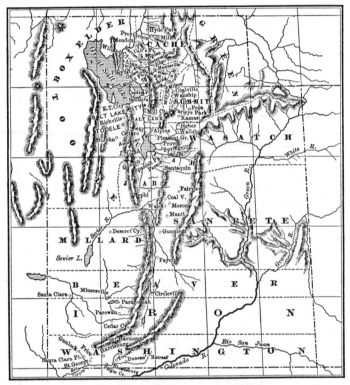

PRINCIPAL SETTLEMENTS IN 1862.

its mineral resources, among them being gold, silver, lead, copper, coal, iron, and mica. Its coal-fields first

Brannan had established a newspaper styled the *Yerba Buena California Star*, with the press, type, and fixtures brought from the office of *The Prophet*, in New York. It was continued until the close of 1848. See *Hist. Cal.*, v. 552, this series. *Richards' Bibliog. of Utah*, MS., 12–13. In Feb. 1856 Geo. Q. Cannon commenced the issue in San Francisco of a weekly paper named the *Western Standard*. It was discontinued in Sept. 1857, when the brethren were recalled to Utah, *Id.*,14.

brought it into prominence, and to aid in their development a short line of railroad was built,[54] but afterward dismantled and abandoned. Coalville, the present county seat, was first settled in 1859.[55] In 1858 the site of the present town of Kamas was occupied as a grazing ground by Thomas Rhoads, and was then known as Rhoads Valley. Two years later a few families settled there, and in 1862 a ward was organized, with William G. Russell as presiding elder.[56]

About seven miles north-west of Kamas, and on the east bank of the Weber, the village of Peoa was founded in 1860 by a party of ten settlers.[57]

In 1853 Fort Bridger, with its Mexican grant of thirty square miles of land, on which stood a few cabins, was sold for $8,000 to the Mormons,[58] who during the following year expended an equal sum in improvements. This was the first property owned by the saints in Green River county. At Fort Supply, in this neighborhood, a settlement was formed about the same time by John Nebeker, Isaac Bullock, and about fifty others from Salt Lake and Utah counties. In 1862 the first settlement was made in Wasatch county, south of Green River and Summit counties, on the site of the present village of Wallsburg.[59] Situated for the most part at an elevation of about seven thousand feet, with a heavy snow-fall and prolific of streams, this section of the territory was and is yet mainly used for stock-ranges, though in the

[54] The Summit County Railroad.

[55] By H. B. Wild, A. B. Williams, W. H. Smith, and others. It was incorporated in 1867. *Sloan's Utah Gazetteer*, 1884, 149. Summit co. was so named from the fact that it included the summit of the Wasatch range. *Richards' Utah Misc.*, MS., 1.

[56] The settlers lived in a fort until 1870, when a city survey was made, and they moved out to their lots.

[57] The first house was built by Henry Barnum and Jacob M. Truman. *Id.*, 150.

[58] The deeds are now in the possession of the church officials at S. L. City. *Trans. Wyom. Acad. Sciences*, 1882, pp. 81-2. Miles Goodyear, the owner, was married to a sister of the Indian chief Walker. *Young's Early Exper.*, MS., 5.

[59] By Wm Wall, E. Garr, and Jas Laird. *Sloan's Utah Gazetteer*, 1884, p. 158. In 1866 Wallsburg was organized as a ward.

north-western portion there is farming land of good quality.

Morgan county, west of Summit, was named after Jedediah Morgan Grant, who with Thomas J. Thurston and others first occupied it in the spring of 1855. In 1862 it was organized, the county seat, Morgan City, being incorporated six years later. The village of Milton was settled by Thurston in 1856, and Enterprise, which together with Morgan is now on the line of the Union Pacific, in 1862.

In 1856 a party of six brethren settled in Cache Valley on the site of the present town of Wellsville, Cache county, north of Weber, being organized during the following year. Except toward the north, the valley is surrounded by mountains, on which the snow lingers late into autumn, thus affording water for irrigation throughout the year. Though the first attempt at agriculture resulted in failure on account of the severity of the climate, excellent crops were afterward raised, and soon this section became known as the granary of Utah. Amid the ranges are vast belts of timber, so dense that there are places where the sunlight never penetrates, and where the foot of man has never trod. Minerals are also abundant, though little utilized at present. During the year 1856 a fort was built at Wellsville, the site of the town being laid out in 1862, when a hundred and fifty families were gathered there.[60] Logan City, about six miles north of Wellsville, and the capital of Cache county, was located by Peter Maughan in the spring of 1859, the spot being selected on account of its rich soil and pasture, and the ample water power afforded by the Logan River. The first settlers drew lots for their

[60] Cache co. was so called from the fact that certain trappers or emigrants cached some goods there as they passed through; Wellsville was named for Gen. Wells. *Richards' Utah Miscell.*, MS., 4. The first house was built at Wellsville by Peter Maughan, the first saw-mill by Esaias Edwards, Francis Gunnell, and Wm H. Maughan, and the first grist-mill by Dan. Hill & Co. A school-house, which served also for meeting-house, was constructed in 1857. *William H. Maughan*, in *Utah Sketches*, MS., 33.

land,[61] and in 1860 the site was surveyed, the city being divided into four wards in 1861, and incorporated five years later. About five miles to the west of Wellsville the settlement of Mendon was commenced in 1857,[62] the settlers removing to Wellsville in the winter of 1858–59 for protection against Indians, and returning the following year in greater number. The first buildings were of logs, with roofs and floors of mud, timber being scarce in that neighborhood.[63]

In 1859 Seth and Robert Langton, Robert and John Thornley, travelled northward from Salt Lake City in search of an agricultural site. Arriving at Summit creek, they settled within half a mile of the present town of Smithfield, Cache county. In November the settlement was organized as a ward, with John G. Smith as bishop, and in March 1860 a survey was begun. A few weeks later troubles arose with the Indians,[64] compelling the settlers to build and take refuge in a fort, in which they remained until late in the following year. At the close of 1861 there were in operation a lumber-mill, a molasses-mill, and a tannery,[65] and the town had then been laid out in its present form. Other settlements in Cache county were Hyde Park, five miles north of Logan, and now on the line of the Utah and northern railroad, where, in 1860, sixteen families were gathered;[66] Providence, two miles south of Logan,

[61] The first house was built by W. B. Preston and John and Aaron Thatcher. who have since been the prominent men in Cache Valley. *Sloan's Utah Gazetteer*, 1884, p. 332. Hezekiah, the father of the Thatchers, had made money at the mines in California, and was then esteemed the richest man in Utah, next to Brigham. In 1879 his son Moses was ordained an apostle.

[62] The first settlers were Wm Gardener and Alex. and Robt Hill. Walter Paul, in *Utah Sketches*, 41.

[63] The first stone dwelling was begun in 1866 by Jos. Baker; others soon followed. *Id.*, 41–2.

[64] Caused by their stealing a horse. In a fight which ensued, Ira Merrill of Smithfield and an Indian chief were killed. Another of the settlers was wounded.

[65] In 1861 a lumber-mill was completed, and in 1864 a grist-mill. *Francis Sharp*, in *Id.*, 117.

[66] At this date they lived in a fort. The town site was laid out in 1864. *Robt Daines*, in *Id.*, 120.

where the first settlers[67] took up their abode in April
1859; Millville, two miles farther south, located in
June 1860;[68] Paradise, at the southern extremity of
the valley, containing in 1861 about thirty inhabitants,[69] and Hyrum, settled in 1860 by about twenty
families.[70]

Thus far the progress of Mormon colonization in
the north, east, and west. Toward the south, the
first settlement in Beaver county, between Millard
and Iron counties, dates from 1856, at which time
Simeon F. Howd, James P. Anderson, and Wilson
G. Mowers arrived in Beaver Valley, commenced to
build a log cabin, and made preparations for farming
and stock-raising. Soon afterward they were joined
by others, making in all some thirty or forty families,
and in the spring of 1858 the site of Beaver City
was laid out.[71] The appearance of the valley was
not inviting. Situated at an altitude of 6,500 feet,
frosty and barren, its surface covered in parts with
sage-brush and its soil everywhere impregnated with
alkali, it was at first considered unfit for occupation.
Its main attraction was the volume of water afforded
by Beaver River, which courses through the valley from east to west, its source being at an alti-

[67] Ira Rich, John F. Maddison, and five others. *Sloan's Utah Gazetteer*,
1884, p. 128.
[68] By Ezra T. Benson, P. Maughan, and several others. George O. Pitkin,
the present bishop, was appointed March 12, 1862. *Ibid.*
[69] A. M. Montierth from Box Elder co. was the first settler in Paradise.
H. C. Jackson built the first saw-mill in 1860, and the first grist-mill in 1864,
in which latter year the town site was laid out under the direction of Ezra T.
Benson. A log meeting-house was built in 1861. In 1868 the settlement
was removed three miles farther to the north, for better protection against
Indians. *Orson Smith*, in *Utah Sketches*, MS., 1–2.
[70] Those of Alva Benson, Ira Allen, and others. It is related that the settlers brought the waters of Little Bear River to their farms in 21 working-days,
by means of a canal eight feet wide, which afterward furnished the water supply of Hyrum. While at this work many of them lived on bread and water,
and their tools consisted only of a few old shovels and spades. Some of them
dwelt for several years in holes or cellars dug in the ground.
[71] In the winter of 1856–7 the first log school-house was built, but gave
place in 1862 to a brick building known as the Beaver Institute. In 1867, also,
the first saw-mill was erected on the site now occupied by the coöperative
woollen-mills. *Jas H. Glines*, in *Utah Sketches*, MS., 18. Beaver city and
co. were so named from the beaver dams found there. *Richards' Utah Misc.*,
MS., 7.

tude of nearly twelve thousand feet. Within recent years, as we shall presently see, this district has proved itself rich in minerals. Next in importance to Beaver City, and about twenty miles to the southwest, was Minersville, first settled in 1859, with J. H. Rollins as bishop of the ward.

The principal settlement in Kane county, which lay south of Iron and east of Washington county, and at one time included a portion of the latter, was Virgin City, founded in 1858, on the upper Virgin River.[72] Its site is in a valley about seven miles in width, and enclosed by mountains, their foothills, seamed and broken by the rains, leaving but a narrow margin for cultivation on the banks of the stream, covered with a dense growth of cotton-woods and an undergrowth of sage and rabbit brush. Five or six miles west of Virgin City was the town of Toquerville, established in 1858 by several families from Cedar City.[73]

In 1854 Jacob Hamblin and two others were sent as missionaries to the Lamanites in the valley of the Virgin and Santa Clara rivers in Washington county, with orders to establish a settlement in that neighborhood. They found the Indians peaceably disposed, and in a measure civilized, many of them being engaged in planting corn, wheat, and squashes, but depending mainly for bread on the seeds of wild grasses.[74]

[72] The city was laid out by Nephi Johnson and others. The first school was organized in 1860, and the first meeting-house built in 1861. John Parker, in *Id.*, 8. Kane co. was so named after Col Thos L. Kane. *Richards' Utah Misc.*, MS., 7.

[73] Among them was the family of Phillip Klingensmith, of Mountain-Meadows fame. John Steele, in *Utah Sketches*, MS., 9. Mr Steele went to Southern Utah in 1850, in company with Geo. A. Smith.

[74] On account of the warm climate, it was supposed that cotton might be raised in the valley of the Santa Clara. About one quart of cotton-seed was planted in the spring of 1855, yielding enough to produce 30 yards of cloth. The ginning and spinning were done by hand, and the weaving on a treadle-loom. James G. Bleak, in *Utah Sketches*, MS., 69. In 1857, 30 lbs were planted, but the crop was a failure, the seed being bad. In 1858-9 other experiments were made, the cotton raised the first year costing $3.40 per lb., and the second year $1.90. The industry was found to be unprofitable. *Id.*, 70-1; *Jennings' Mat. Progress of Utah*, MS., 1. The attempt was made with a view to producing in the territory all that was needed for its population. *Harrison's Crit. Notes on Utah*, MS., 25.

In 1857 other missionaries joined the party, together with a number of families from Salt Lake City, and in May of this year a settlement was formed, to which was given the name of Washington.

In October 1861 three hundred of the saints, under the direction of Orson Pratt and Erastus Snow, were ordered to proceed to this district, and build a city, to be named St George, near the junction of the Virgin and Santa Clara rivers in Washington county. In January 1862 a site was selected and surveyed, the city incorporated,[75] though yet unbuilt, and the people took possession of their lots. Before doing so it was decided by unanimous vote that the first building erected should be a social hall, to be used for educational and other purposes.[76] In September Brigham visited the settlers, and advised them to build, as soon as possible, a substantial, commodious, and well-finished meeting-house, or tabernacle, large enough to seat at least two thousand persons, and one that would be an ornament to their city and a credit to their enterprise. The foundation stones were laid on the 1st of June, 1873, the prophet's birthday, and the building completed eight years later, at a cost of $110,000. Before its settlement, the valley of St George presented a barren appearance, its surface being strongly impregnated with mineral salts, even the bottom-lands of the Virgin and Santa Clara showing large strips of alkaline soil. Its climate was mild, and, with irrigation, crops of many kinds could be raised; but water was scarce, an artesian well sunk in 1862, at a cost of $5,000, being abandoned as a failure, after attaining a depth of more than two hundred feet.[77] Notwithstanding these drawbacks, the city be-

---

[75] By act approved Jan. 17, 1862. See *Utah Acts Legisl.* (ed. 1866), pp. 166–7. It was named St George after Pres. Geo. A. Smith. *Richards' Utah Misc.*, MS., 4.

[76] The foundation stone was laid March 22, 1862, and when completed, at a cost of more than $6,000, it was named St George Hall. James G. Bleak, in *Utah Sketches*, MS., 73–4.

[77] The people farmed on the joint enclosure system, the first enclosed field, named the St George, being irrigated by the 'Virgin ditch,' the cost of which between Dec. 1861 and Aug. 1866 was $26,611.59. *Id.*, 76.

came the county seat of Washington, and is to-day the leading town in southern Utah.[78]

Of the counties organized between 1850 and 1852, and the settlements founded therein up to the latter date, mention has already been made.[79] During the next decade many small villages and towns were located in the older counties,[80] and I shall describe later

[78] Other settlements in Washington co. were Santa Clara, on the river of that name, and about five miles north-west of St George, settled in 1853 by Jacob Hamblin and a company of missionaries; Gunlock, founded by W. Hamblin on the Santa Clara, in 1857; Price, occupied in 1858 as a cotton plantation, submerged by the flood of 1861, and reoccupied for general farming purposes in 1863; Harrisburg, twelve miles north-east of St George, settled in 1860 by Moses Harris and 13 others; Duncan's Retreat, on the north bank of the Virgin, first settled in 1861 by Chapman Duncan, who abandoned it, and resettled by William Theobald and six others; and Shoensburg, also on the Virgin, located in Jan. 1862, by Oliver De Mill and others. *Sloan's Utah Gazetteer*, 1884, 161–2. In this and other counties, settled between 1852 and 1862, were numerous small settlements, some of which will be mentioned later.

[79] See chaps xiii. and xvii., this vol.

[80] In 1852 Call's Fort, in Box Elder co., now on the line of the Utah and Northern railway, was built by Anson Call and two others. In 1883 it contained about 35 families. Deseret, near the centre of Millard co., now having a station on the Utah Central, was founded in 1858, abandoned in 1867, and reoccupied in 1875 by J. S. Black and others. Scipio, in the north-eastern part of the same county was settled in March 1860 by T. F. Robins and six others. Circleville, in what is now Piute co., was settled about the same time, several previous attempts having failed, on account of trouble with Indians. In the same year, also Fort Gunnison was founded in the south-western part of San Pete co. In 1861 it was organized as a ward, with Jacob Kudgerson as bishop. About 30 miles to the north was Moroni, so called after the prophet of that name in the book of Mormon, located in March 1859 by G. W. Bradley and others, and incorporated in 1866. Fairview, farther to the north, and first known as North Bend, was founded in the winter of 1859 –60 by James N. Jones and others, and was incorporated in 1872. Wales, the present terminus of the San Pete railway, was first settled in 1857 by John E. Rees and others, Rees being bishop of the ward in 1883; Fayette, on the west bank of the Sevier, but still in San Pete co., in 1861, by James Bartholomew and four others, Bartholomew being now ward bishop. In Tooele co., St John was founded in 1858 by Luke Johnson, and Lake View in 1860 by Orson Pratt, George Marshall, Moses Martin, and four others, Martin being the present bishop. In Utah co., Spanish Fork, now on the line of the Utah Central railroad, was incorporated in 1855; Salem, a little to the north-east of Payson, and first known as Pond Town, was founded in 1856 by Robt Durfee and six others; and Goshen, in the south-western part of the county, in the same year by Phineas Cook and a few others. The present site of Goshen was located in 1869 by Brigham, a few miles south of the old settlement. In Weber county, Plain City was located in March 1859 on the Weber River, about nine miles north-west of Ogden, by J. Spiers and a few others; West Weber, a little farther south, about the same date, by Wm McFarland and 14 others; Eden, ten miles north-east of Ogden, in 1860, by John Beddle and Joseph Grover; and Huntsville, twelve miles east of Ogden, in the same year, by Jefferson Hunt and others. *Taylor's Rem.*, MS.; *Woodruff's Journal*, MS.; *Hist. B. Young*, MS.; *Sloan's Utah Gazetteer*, 1884, 122–65; *Utah Sketches*, MS., passim; *Hand-Book of Reference*, 71–8. In July 1855 a settlement was founded on the left bank of the Grand River, in the Elk Mountain region, by Alfred N. Billings. *Richards' Incidents in Utah Hist.*, MS., 80.

those that afterward attained prominence.   They differed but little in outward appearance from the pioneer settlements in other parts of the United States,
except in one particular.   Throughout the entire territory, there was rarely to be seen, except in Salt Lake
City, a store or a mechanic's sign, traffic being carried
on from house to house, and the few extraneous wants
of the settlers being mainly supplied by peddlers.[81]

[81] Among other works consulted in this chapter are the *Route from Liverpool to Great Salt Lake Valley: Illustrated with Steel Engravings and Wood-cuts
from Sketches made by Frederick Piercy, together with a Geographical and Historical Description of Utah, and a Map of the Overland Routes to that Territory
from the Missouri River.   Also an Authentic History of the Latter-Day Saints'
Emigration from Europe from the Commencement up to the Close of 1855, with
Statistics.   Edited by James Linforth.*   Liverpool and London, 1855.   Though
this book was written mainly for the purpose of giving a review of the
latter-day saints' emigration from Liverpool to Salt Lake City, together with
statistics to date, it contains much historical and statistical information on
other subjects, drawn, as the editor says, 'from sources far and wide.'   Mr
Linforth acknowledges that he was assisted in his work by missionaries, whose
position and acquaintance with affairs gave him access to many valuable
documents.   In chap. xvii., we find a description of Nauvoo, of the Carthage-
jail tragedy, the persecutions in Missouri and Illinois, and many details concerning the life of the prophet.   In chaps xxi.–xxii. is an account of the
territory and its settlements, and the industrial condition of the saints.   In
the last chapters are brief biographies of some of the leading elders.   All of
this information is contained in notes, the text merely relating the travels of
the artists by whom the sketches were made.   The engravings are well executed, and among them are portraits of several church dignitaries.

    *A Journey to Great Salt Lake City, by Jules Remy and Julius Brenchley,
M. A.: With a Sketch of the History, Religion, and Customs of the Mormons,
and an introduction on the Religious Movement in the United States, by Jules
Remy.*   2 vols.   London, 1861.   In addition to incidents of travel and descriptions of the places visited, we have in these volumes a sketch of Mormon history to 1859, together with chapters on the Mormon church and
hierarchy, polygamy, education, and propagandism.   At one time it was
considered the standard gentile authority on Mormonism, and is freely quoted
by other writers, though greatly inferior to Burton's work published two
years later.   'The greater part of the matter,' remarks the author, 'was
written from day to day, often in the open air, upon the slopes or the crests
of mountains, in the heart of deserts, among the occupations and frequently
the perils which are the necessary accompaniments of so long a journey.'
Hence Mr Remy lays no claim to literary finish, a defect which he hopes may
be atoned for by superior accuracy.   Though there are many interesting
passages and some interesting chapters, one cannot but feel that he might
have said twice as much in half the space.

    *The Husband in Utah; or Sights and Scenes among the Mormons: With
Remarks on their Moral and Social Economy, by Austin N. Ward.*   Edited
by Maria Ward.   New York, 1857.   Here and there in this work will be
found some interesting sketches of Mormon life as Mrs Ward observed it in
1855.   Among them are descriptions of the industrial and social condition of
the Mormons, the stores, manufactures, streets, street scenes, costumes, the
theatre, the tabernacle.   In style the work is sketchy and entertaining, and
written in more friendly mood than could be expected from one who, as
Mrs Ward declares, 'escaped from Mormondom.'   At the end of the work is

Nevertheless the traveller who might chance to visit any of the larger settlements in 1862 could purchase, at reasonable rates, all the necessaries of life, and could perhaps supply himself with luxuries, provided he were willing to pay from three to five fold their value. Though there was no indication that trade in its ordinary sense existed among these communities, and one might search in vain for a hotel, or even for a bath-house or a barber's shop, most of the ordinary crafts were represented, and all that was needful could be obtained for money.

'Joseph's Smith's revelation on polygamy,' and several discourses by leading elders. Another edition was issued in 1863, under title of *Male Life among the Mormons.*

CHAPTER XXII.

PROGRESS OF EVENTS.

1861-1869.

THE first appointments made by President Lincoln
for the territory of Utah were John W. Dawson
as governor,[1] John F. Kinney as chief justice, R. P.
Flenniken and J. R. Crosby associate judges, Frank
Fuller secretary, and James Duane Doty superintendent of Indian affairs. A few weeks after his
arrival, the governor was accused of making improper
advances to one of the Mormon women, and on new-
year's eve of 1861 was glad to make his escape from
Zion, being waylaid at Mountain Dell on his return
journey and soundly beaten by a party of saints.[2]

[1] After Cumming's departure, Secretary Wooton became acting governor,
but resigned as soon as the southern secession was announced. *Stenhouse's
Rocky Mountain Saints*, 445, 591.

[2] In *Waite's The Mormon Prophet*, 76; *Beadle's Life in Utah*, 201; *Stenhouse's
Rocky Mountain Saints*, 592, it is stated that Dawson was entrapped into this
affair; in *Tucker's Mormonism*, 239; *Tullidge's Hist. S. L. City*, 249; *Deseret
News*, Jan. 1, 1862, that it was of his own seeking. In *Id.*, Jan. 14th, is a
letter from Dawson to the editor of the *Deseret News*, dated Bear River
Station, Utah Terr., wherein the governor states that he was badly wounded
in the head and kicked in the chest and loins. A copy of his first and only
message to the legislature will be found in *Utah Jour. Legisl.*, 1861-2, 12-26.

A month later the associate judges also left the territory, Thomas J. Drake and Charles B. Waite, appointed in their stead, with Stephen S. Harding as governor, arriving in July. Meanwhile the secretary, by virtue of his office, became the chief magistrate.[3]

Now came an opportunity for Brigham to put forth once more the claim which he had several times asserted: "I am and will be governor." At this period another effort was being made to obtain admission as a state, and on the 17th of March, 1862, the legislature being then in session, a proclamation was issued, in which, styling himself governor-elect, Brigham convened the general assembly and ordered the election of senators to congress.[4] Soon afterward he telegraphed to Washington that no assistance was needed in subduing the Indians, who, as will presently appear, were somewhat troublesome at this date; for "the militia were ready and able, as they had ever been, to take care of them, and were able and willing to protect the mail line if called upon to do so." Fuller meekly indorsed this statement, and was authorized by the war department to call out ninety men for three months' service between forts Bridger and Laramie. General Wells was ordered to take command of the party, and in three days it was ready to march.

The choice for senators fell on William H. Hooper and George Q. Cannon. The former had been elected delegate in 1859, when he obtained a partial settlement of the outstanding claims of the territory, including a portion of the expenses for the Indian war of 1850, and for the sessions of the assembly under

---

[3] For the second time, as he arrived before Gov. Dawson, and on the resignation of Wooton filled the vacancy. In *Utah Jour. Legisl.*, 1861-2, is a joint resolution approving his first administration, which was, however, in fact a nullity. A day or two before Cumming left the territory Stenhouse asked him, 'How will Wooton get along?' 'Get along?' he replied; 'well enough, if he will do nothing.' *Rocky Mountain Saints*, 445, note. Some years later he was elected a representative conditional upon the admission of Utah as a state. *Harrison's Crit. Notes on Utah*, MS., 29.

[4] A copy of it will be found in the *Deseret News*, March 19, 1862.

the provisional government. He was at once despatched to Washington, with a memorial and constitution of the inchoate state of Deseret, and Cannon, who was then in England, was instructed to join him without delay. The two elders labored diligently in their cause, but failed of success.[5] It was claimed, however, on the part of the Mormons, that they won the respect of congress by accepting their defeat and adhering to the union at a time when it was believed throughout Europe that the war would result in favor of the south, and when the sympathies of England and France were strongly in favor of the southern states. Moreover, the attitude of the saints throughout this struggle, and especially the tone of their church organ, the *Deseret News*, were not adverse to the union cause. On the Sunday preceding the surrender at Appomattox their prophet foretold in the tabernacle that there would be yet four years of civil war.

Though the saints may have had some few friends in congress at this time, it is certain that they had numerous and bitter enemies, who were constantly working against their interests. In April 1862 a bill was introduced by Justin S. Morrill of Vermont "to punish and prevent the practice of polygamy in the territories of the United States, and for other purposes, and to disapprove and annul certain acts of the territorial legislature of Utah." The objectionable acts referred to included all those which tended to establish or support polygamy, and especially an

[5] It would appear that the Mormons hoped to succeed on this occasion. In a letter to Cannon, dated Dec. 16, 1860, Hooper writes: 'I think three-quarters of the republicans of the house would vote for our admission.' For copies of the memorial and constitution, see *House Misc. Doc.*, 78, 37th Cong. 2d Sess.; *Deseret News*, Jan. 29, 1862. They were referred to the committee on territories. In the *Millennial Star*, xxiv. 241-5, 257-61, is a synopsis of the proceedings relating to the constitution and state government. See also *Deseret News*, Jan. 22, 1862; *Sac. Union*, Feb. 14, 17, 1862. Meetings in favor of this measure were held at Provo, Santaquin (a small settlement in Utah co.), Spanish Fork, Grantsville, and Tooele, for an account of which, see *Id.*, Jan. 15, 1862. Prominent among those who opposed the admission of Utah was Judge Cradlebaugh, afterward representative from Nevada, whose speech in the house, on Feb. 7, 1863, has already been mentioned.

ordinance incorporating the church of Jesus Christ of Latter-day Saints, passed in 1851, and reënacted in 1855, whereby all members of the church were included in the body corporate, trustees being appointed to control the church property, and the church empowered to make laws with regard to marriage.[6] It was further provided by the same act of congress that no corporation or association for religious purposes should hold real estate in any of the territories of a greater value than $50,000.[7] In other respects the proceedings of the Utah legislature at this period and for many years afterward contained few objectionable features, most of them relating to municipal affairs, as did those of previous sessions. In 1854 and 1855 acts were passed providing for the construction of canals between Utah Lake, Big Cottonwood Creek, and Great Salt Lake.[8]

[6] And regulations as to solemnities, sacraments, ceremonies, consecrations, endowments, tithings, fellowship, and all matters relating to 'the religious duties of man to his maker.' *Utah Acts Legisl.* (ed. 1855), 104.

[7] A copy of the act will be found in *Cong. Globe*, 1861–2, app. 385. In 1855 a bill was introduced for the suppression of polygamy and in the debates which ensued Morrill took an active part. It was referred to a committee of the whole. See *Cong. Globe*, 1855–6, pp. 895, 1491, 1501. In 1859 a bill passed the representatives. *Id.*, 1859–60, pp. 1559. For other measures and discussions in congress between 1853 and 1862, relating to roads, surveys, mails, appropriations, boundaries, public buildings, Indian troubles and other matters, see *Cong. Globe*, 1853–4, pp. 286, 1437, 1440, 1472, 1621, 1701, 2236–9, passim; *Id.*, 1854–5, pp. 5, 341, 540, passim; 1855–6, pp. 19, 39, 1451–2, 1473, 1491, 1495, 1497; 1856–7, pp. 284, 392, 408, 418, 608; 1857–8, pp. 553, 564, 572–3, passim; 1858–9, pp. 119, 335, 341, 658, 1066; 1859–60, pp. 187–98, 474, 486, 500; 1860–1, pp. 326, 336, 840, 1132, 1159, 1195, 1197, 1288, 1302; *Sen. Jour.*, 33d Cong., 1st Sess., 1003; *Id.*, 33d Cong., 2d Sess., 574–5; 34th Cong., 2d Sess., 943; 34th Cong., 3d Sess., 63; 35th Cong., 2d Sess., 450, 590, 660; 36th Cong., 1st Sess., 1041, 1045–6; 37th Cong., 2d Sess., 1161; *H. Jour.*, 33d Cong., 1st Sess., 1563; *Id.*, 33d Cong., 2d Sess., 723; 34th Cong., 1st Sess., 1837; 34th Cong., 3d Sess., 376; 35th Cong., 1st Sess., 1325, 1366; 35th Cong., 2d Sess., 323, 745, 759, 761; 36th Cong., 1st Sess., 1410, 1455–6; 36th Cong., 2d Sess., 580; 37th Cong., 2d Sess., 1271, 1318–19. In *H. Misc. Doc.*, 100, 35th Cong., 1st Sess., is a memorial stating the grievances of the Mormons, and asking that they be allowed a voice in the selection of their rulers. In the senate, resolutions were submitted that committees should inquire into the propriety of the Mormons electing thei· own officials and no longer submitting their enactments to congress *Sen. Misc. Doc.*, 12, 36th Cong., 1st Sess. The committees reported adversely.

[8] The first was to commence above the rapids of the Jordan, where a dam was to be built, and thence following the base of the mountains, on the east of G. S. Lake Valley, to S. L. City, with depth sufficient for boats drawing two and a half feet of water. *Utah Acts Legisl.* (ed. 1866), 175–6. The

In 1862 an ordinance was approved, regulating the fisheries of the Jordan River. In 1865 laws were enacted amending the charter of Salt Lake City,[9] and prescribing the mode of assessing and collecting territorial and county taxes, which must not exceed one per cent of the assessed value of property.[10] In 1866 statutes were framed defining the boundaries of counties, locating the county seats,[11] and providing for the establishment and maintenance of common schools.[12] Between 1854 and 1866 numerous acts were also passed incorporating agricultural, manufacturing, irrigation, and road companies,[13] and

Cottonwood canal was to divert half the waters of the creek and conduct them to S. L. City. *Id.* (ed. 1855), 277–8.

[9] Among other matters, the city council was empowered to build and control hospitals, and to direct the location of medical colleges, railroad tracks, depot-grounds, gas-works, canals, and telegraph-poles within the city limits; and to collect taxes on real estate for grading, paving, repairing, and lighting streets, and for drainage purposes. *Id.* (ed. 1866), 119.

[10] One half per cent for territorial tax, and for county tax a rate to be prescribed by the county court, but not exceeding a half per cent. *Id.*, 84.

[11] *Id.*, 207–9. The following is a complete list of the county seats in 1866, some of which have already been mentioned. Grafton was the county seat of Kane co., St George of Washington co., Parowan of Iron co., Salt Lake City, Beaver, and Tooele of the counties of the same name, Circleville of Piute co., Fillmore of Millard co., Richfield of Sevier co., Nephi of Juab co., Manti of Sanpete co., Provo of Utah co., Heber City of Wasatch co., Farmington of Davis co., Ogden of Weber co., Brigham City of Box Elder co., Wanship of Summit co., Littleton of Morgan co., Logan City of Cache co., St Charles of Richland co., and Fort Bridger of Green River co. A portion of Richland, later Rich, co., including the site of St Charles, Paris, Bloomington, and other settlements, was afterward included in Idaho. The county was first settled in 1863 by C. C. Rich. *Sloan's Utah Gazetteer*, 1884, 29, 141.

[12] *Utah Acts Legisl.* (ed. 1866), 219–23. For school purposes, a tax not exceeding one fourth per cent was to be levied by the trustees of each district; but this might be increased to as much as three per cent by vote of two thirds of the tax-payers.

[13] By act of 1856, the Deseret Agricultural and Manufacturing Society was incorporated, 'with a view of promoting the arts of domestic industry, and to encourage the production of articles from the native elements in this territory.' The society was required to hold an annual exhibition of the agricultural products, live-stock, and articles of domestic manufacture. By act of 1862, amended in 1865, the Jordan Irrigation Company was incorporated, with power to construct dams across the Jordan, and divert its waters at any point not more than twelve miles above Jordan bridge. By acts of 1865 and 1866, the Ogden Cañon, Uintah, and Logan Cañon road companies were incorporated; the first with the right of building a toll-road from the mouth of the cañon to Ogden Valley, with privilege for thirty years; the second with permission to construct a similar road from Utah Lake, through Uintah Valley, to the eastward boundary of the territory, connecting with the road to Denver, Colorado; the third with power to build a toll-road from Logan City to the summit of the mountains

granting to individuals certain water and grazing rights, and the privilege of building toll-roads and bridges.[14]

In July 1862, Governor Harding, with judges Waite and Drake, arrived in Salt Lake City, and for the first time in his career Brigham declared himself satisfied with the United States officials. Matters worked smoothly until the meeting of the legislature in December, when the saints took offence at the governor's message, wherein he reproved them sharply for disloyalty and the practice of polygamy, and called their attention to the recent act of congress. "I am aware," he said, "that there is a prevailing opinion here that said act is unconstitutional, and therefore it is recommended by those in high authority that no regard whatever should be paid to the same...I take this occasion to warn the people of this territory against such dangerous and disloyal council."[15]

dividing Cache and Rich counties, their rights lasting 14 years. Ben. Holladay, Wm H. Hooper, and W. L. Halsey were the body corporate of the Uintah Road Co., with privilege for 15 years. By act of 1865 the Overland Mail Company was authorized to make a road across the Dugway Mountain, 105 miles west of S. L. City, and to erect a toll-gate at or near the eastern base of the mountain, with privilege for ten years.

[14] By act of 1854, repealing acts of the previous year, Brigham Young was empowered to establish and control ferries and bridges at the Weber and Bear rivers for an indefinite term. *Utah Acts Legisl.* (ed. 1855), 267-8. By acts of 1855 Parley Park and an adjacent valley to the south were granted for 20 years as herd-grounds to Heber C. Kimball, Jedediah M. Grant, Sam. Snyder, and their associates, and certain lands in Utah co. to Miles and Franklin Weaver for the same purpose. By acts of the same year, Kimball and his partners were authorized to make a toll-road from Big Cañon, S. L. co., to Kamas prairie, Utah co., passing through Parley Park, and Orson Hyde and others to build a toll-road and bridges in Carson co., which were to become the property of the territory after five years. *Id.*, 284-6. In 1857 John L. Butler and Aaron Johnson were granted the control of one fourth of the waters of the Spanish Fork River for irrigation purposes, during the pleasure of the legislative assembly. *Id.* (ed. 1866), 179. In 1866 Alvin Nichols and Wm S. Godbe were allowed to establish toll-bridges across the Bear and Malade rivers, the privilege being for eight years. Other proceedings of the legislature between 1854 and 1866 will be found in *Utah Acts Legisl.*, and *Utah Jour. Legisl.*, passim, and in the files of the *Deseret News.* The names of members are also given in *Utah Jour. Legisl.*, for each year.

[15] A full copy of the message will be found in *Utah Jour. Legisl.*, 1862-3, app.; and of parts of it in *Waite's The Mormon Prophet*, 79-82. It was at first suppressed by the Utah legislature. *Sen. Misc. Doc.*, 37, 37th Cong. 3d Sess.; but a senate committee ordered it printed. *Sen. Com. Rept.*, 87, 37th Cong. 3d Sess. Other messages of the several governors will be found in the

Thus was aroused afresh the antagonism of the Mormons, and the trouble was further increased by the action of Judge Waite, who was appointed to the second, or southern district,[16] Drake being assigned to the first, or central district, and the chief justice to the third, or northern circuit. Early in 1863 Waite drew up a bill amending the organic act, providing that juries be selected by the United States marshal, authorizing the governor to appoint militia officers, and restricting the powers of the probate courts to their proper functions, though with a limited criminal jurisdiction. The bill was approved by the governor and by Judge Drake, and, being forwarded to congress, was referred to committee. On hearing of this measure, Brigham called a meeting at the tabernacle for the 3d of March, when many inflammatory speeches were made, and resolutions passed, condemning the governor's message and the action of the judges. A committee was appointed to wait on the officials and request their resignation, and a petition drawn up requesting the president to remove them.[17]

To the committee, among whom was John Taylor, Drake replied: "Go back to Brigham Young, your

Utah Jour. Legisl., for each year. See also Deseret News, Dec. 14, 1854, Dec. 19, 1855, Dec. 23, 1857, Dec. 22, 1858, Dec. 14, 1859, Apr. 16, 1862, Jan. 21, Dec. 16, 1863, Jan. 25, Dec. 11, 1865; S. F. Alta, March 10, 1854; Sac: Union, Feb. 12, 1855, Feb. 12, 1856.

[16] In Waite's The Mormon Prophet, 85-6, it is stated that the legislature ordered court to be opened at St George on the third Monday in May, but as they did not wish the session to take place until autumn, passed a second bill, appointing the third Monday in October for the beginning of the term. Waite preferred to open court in May, and having occasion to examine the bill, found that the word 'May' had been erased and 'October' substituted. This had been done by a clerk in the house, and presumably by the order of members. The governor, who had inadvertently returned the bill, ordered the record corrected, and sent a message to the legislature, calling their attention to the forgery. Issue was taken with him on the matter, one member producing a paper which, he averred, was the original draught, and where October was the month appointed. In the Deseret News, March 25, 1863, Waite is sharply censured for holding court in the third district, where he had no jurisdiction.

[17] For copies of some of the speeches, the resolutions, and petition, see Waite's The Mormon Prophet, 88-95; Tullidge's Hist. S. L. City, 307-11. The petition was signed by several thousand persons. A counter-petition, signed by the officers of Connor's command, will be found in Waite's The Mormon Prophet, 95-7.

master—that embodiment of sin and shame and disgust—and tell him that I neither fear him, nor love
him, nor hate him—that I utterly despise him. Tell
him, whose tools and tricksters you are, that I did
not come here by his permission, and that I will not
go away at his desire or by his directions. I have
given no cause of offence to any one. I have not entered a Mormon's house since I came here; your wives
and daughters have not been disturbed by me, and I
have not even looked upon your concubines and lewd
women." "We have our opinions," remarked one of
the committee as they rose to depart. "Yes," replied
Drake, "thieves and murderers can have opinions."
The governor made answer to the committee in language hardly less injudicious, though somewhat uneasy
as to his own personal safety, but Waite responded in
more seemly and temperate phrase.[18]   The Mormons
resented the conduct of the judges as an outrage.
Men gathered in groups at the street corners and
discussed the matter with angry gestures; one of the
judges was threatened with personal violence, and it
is probable that an émeute was only prevented by the
fact that a party of California volunteers was now
encamped near Salt Lake City.

Ostensibly for protection against Indians, though
in fact because the mail route and telegraph line were
not considered secure in the hands of the saints, and
perhaps also for the purpose of holding the territory
under military surveillance, Colonel Connor was ordered to Utah in May 1862, his command consisting of
the third California infantry and a part of the second
California cavalry, afterward joined by a few companies
from Nevada, and mustering in all about seven hundred
strong.   The men had volunteered in the expectation
of being ordered to the seat of war, and great was their
disgust when it became known that Zion was their
destination.[19]   In October the troops reached Camp

[18] The answers of the governor and judges will be found in *Id.*, 97–9.
[19] A correspondent of the *S. F. Bulletin* writes under date Sept. 24, 1862:

Floyd, or, as it was now termed, Fort Crittenden.[20] Here it was supposed that the volunteers would encamp, and their commanding officer was informed that no nearer approach to the capital would be permitted. The colonel paid no heed to this warning. "He would cross the Jordan," he declared, "though all hell should yawn beneath it." On the next day his men, after passing through Salt Lake City with fixed bayonets, loaded rifles, and shotted cannon, encamped on the brow of a hill[21] east of the city, their artillery being pointed at Brigham's residence. To this spot was given the name of Camp Douglas, the site being afterward declared a military reservation.[22]

The presence of the volunteers, though they were not sufficient in number to overawe the populace, and could have been readily annihilated by the Nauvoo legion, was a source of constant irritation. The Mormons were not backward in their denunciations, while mischief-makers were constantly spreading reports that served to increase the mutual distrust. An elder who was passing Waite's residence, while the judge was in

'The third infantry California volunteers wants to go home—not for the purpose of seeing the old folks, but for the purpose of tramping upon the sacred soil of Virginia, and of swelling the ranks of the brave battlers for the brave old flag.' About $25,000 was subscribed by the men on condition that they were sent east, one private named Goldthaite, in company G., contributing $5,000. On the same date Colonel Connor wrote to General Halleck, stating that the men had enlisted for the purpose of fighting traitors, that the infantry was of no service in the territory, as cavalry alone could act effectually against Indians, and there were enough men of that arm to protect the mail route. 'Brigham Young,' writes the colonel, 'offers to protect the entire line with 100 men. Why we were sent here is a mystery. It could not be to keep Mormondon in order, for Brigham can thoroughly annihilate us with the 5,000 to 25,000 frontiersmen always at his command.'

[20] By order of Col Cook, his purpose being to disconnect it with the name of Floyd, who was a secessionist. Stenhouse mentions a story current among the volunteers to the effect that Brigham, on hearing of their approach, had ordered the flag-staff at Fort Crittenden to be cut down and left on the public road. This was not the case. The flag was hoisted on the brow of a hill east of Brigham's residence. *Stenhouse's Rocky Mountain Saints*, 422, 602.

[21] Termed the bench.

[22] *Stenhouse's Rocky Mountain Saints*, 603; *Harrison's Crit. Notes on Utah*, MS., 20; *Rae's Westward by Rail*, 140; *Gazetteer of Utah*, 182. The site at first included one square mile, but was afterward enlarged to 2,560 acres. The men passed the winter of 1862-3 in dug-outs—in this instance holes dug in the earth and covered with a frame-work of logs—permanent quarters being built the following summer, without expense to the government, except for the nails and shingles.

conversation with Colonel Connor, overheard the latter remark: "These three men must be surprised." "Colonel, you know your duty," answered the judge. It was now believed that the first presidency was in danger;[23] a flag was hoisted over Brigham's residence as a signal, and within an hour two thousand men were under arms, the prophet's dwelling being strongly guarded, scaffolding built against the surrounding walls, to enable the militia to fire down on the volunteers, and cannon planted on the avenues of approach.

Night and day for several weeks armed men kept watch over the prophet, for it was now rumored that Connor intended to seize him at night and carry him off to Camp Douglas before the saints could rally to his aid.[24] The citizens were instructed that, if the attempt were made, alarm guns would be fired from the hillside east of Brigham's residence. On the night of the 29th of March they were roused from sleep by the booming of cannon, and, as quickly as they could don their garments and seize their weapons, all ran forth from their homes, intent on exterminating the foe. As they rushed through the streets, the strains of martial music were heard, to which, as was supposed, the troops were marching on Zion. The alarm was unfounded, the music and salute being in honor of the colonel's promotion to the rank of brigadier-general, of which news had just arrived at Camp Douglas.

Although it is probable that Connor never intended

[23] Letter of David O. Calder in *Millennial Star*, xxv. 301-2; *Harrison's Crit. Notes on Utah*, MS., 20. Colonel Connor denied that he had any designs against the first presidency. In *Stenhouse's Rocky Mountain Saints*, 607, it is related that one of the parties to whom Waite referred was a Mormon, who had recently married the three widows of a wealthy merchant in S. L. City. It was thought that this would furnish a good test of the law against polygamy. No arrest was made, however, as it was feared that difficulties might arise if Waite should try a case that lay within Kinney's jurisdiction.

[24] The Mormons feared that Brigham might be taken to Washington for trial. For several days hundreds of men kept watch in and around his residence. Elders were also instructed to visit the various wards and warn the saints of the danger to person and property, from the lawless conduct of the troops. Parties patrolled the streets at night to protect the citizens; the movements of the soldiery were carefully watched, and all trade with the camp was for a time forbidden. *Harrison's Crit. Notes on Utah*, MS.

to risk his slender force in an encounter with the territorial militia, there was a possibility of a collision, and it is probable that hostilities were prevented by the prevailing of better counsels on both sides. Brigham was always strongly opposed to the shedding of blood, though he wished these men out of the city limits, on which the reservation slightly intrenched.[25] The grand jury had already voted the camp a nuisance,[26] and on the mayor devolved the duty of seeing it abated. But before taking action that official began to count the cost. To rid the city of the volunteers might be no difficult task, but if their blood was shed, others would come in tenfold numbers to take their place.[27] By a little judicious delay the mayor gave time for the prophet's cooler judgment to assert itself, and thus averted an issue which might have resulted in the final dispersion of his people.

The condition of affairs was now similar to that which had obtained during the presence of the army of Utah, Judge Kinney shielding the church dignitaries from molestation by his colleagues, as Governor Cumming had done from the measures of judges Sinclair and Cradlebaugh. When it was believed that the arrest of Brigham was contemplated, on the ground that he had recently married another wife, the chief justice, as a safeguard, and at his own request, ordered him into custody for violating the act for the suppression of polygamy. The writ was served by the marshal, without the aid of a posse, and the prisoner, attended by a few intimate friends, promptly appeared at the state-house, where an investigation was held,

[25] Though its centre was two and a half miles from the city hall, it lapped over the municipal boundary. *Id.*, 609, note.

[26] It was reported that the waters of Red Butte cañon had been purposely fouled, being passed through the stables of the volunteers. The troops were stationed near the head of the stream, but it was denied that they had been guilty of any such act, though doubtless the Mormons believed it. Later in the year there may have been cause for complaint, as the supply for irrigation was curtailed during the dry season.

[27] When Connor heard of Brigham's order, he remarked to Stenhouse: 'I know, sir, that Brigham Young could use up this handful of men; but there are sixty thousand men in California who would avenge our blood.' *Ibid.*

and the accused admitted to bail, awaiting the action of the grand jury. Although the prophet's recent marriage was well known throughout the city, and had long furnished food for gossip, the judges afterward refused to find a bill against him, on the ground that there was no sufficient evidence.[28]

During its session the grand jury indicted, for armed resistance to the laws, certain apostates known as Morrisites. In November 1860 an ignorant and simple-minded Welshman, Joseph Morris by name, made his way to the capital on foot, from an obscure settlement in Weber county. He had two letters, the contents of which were, as he claimed, inspired, their purport being to warn Brigham of his sin.[29] His despatches were unheeded, or answered in befitting phrase,[30] whereupon this new seer and revelator turned his face homeward. Reaching Kington Fort, on the Weber River, some thirty miles north of the city,[31] he found favor with the bishop and certain of his neighbors, who embraced the new doctrine, believing that Morris was appointed by the Lord to deliver Israel from bondage, and that the Lord's coming was nigh at hand. Other proselytes gathered from far and near, and all held their effects in common, for Christ was about to descend and would provide for his elect.[32]

[28] In his *Crit. Notes on Utah*, MS., 18–20, Harrison states that the anti-polygamy act was considered by the Mormons as directed mainly against Brigham Young and the heads of the church. 'I will take the wind out of their sails,' the former remarked, and at once caused himself to be arrested and taken before Judge Kinney. The witnesses were all his friends, among them being some of his own clerks, and he was simply bound over, to appear when called upon. It was not until nine years later that Brigham's name appeared again in any case of the kind, and the act of 1862 had then become void by virtue of the statute of limitations. See also *Deseret News*, March 11, 1863; *S. F. Alta*, March 11, 14, 1863; *Sac. Union*, March 12, 1863.

[29] Waite says that Morris had received many previous revelations, which he had communicated to Brigham and the apostles, that his life had been threatened, and that he now appealed to the prophet for protection. *The Mormon Prophet*, 122.

[30] *Ibid.; Stenhouse's Rocky Mountain Saints*, 594. Stenhouse also says that Brigham answered them with a brief and filthy response.

[31] Near the point where the Union Pacific railroad issues from Weber Cañon.

[32] Waite says that when the Morrisites increased in number, Brigham ordered John Taylor and Wilford Woodruff to investigate the matter. Summon-

But the Lord tarried; and meanwhile provisions ran short and the enthusiasm of the converts began to wane, some desiring to withdraw, demanding a restitution of their property, and refusing to contribute anything to the common stock, even for their own support. It was decided to let the dissenters go in peace; but some of them selected from the common herd the choicest cattle, and laying in wait for their brethren's teams, pounced on them while on their way to the mill laden with wheat. Three of the offenders were seized and imprisoned at Kington Fort, their friends in vain asking the interference of the sheriff and of Brigham. An appeal was then made to Judge Kinney, who at once issued warrants for the arrest of the Morrisite leaders, and writs of habeas corpus for the men held in custody. No heed was paid to these documents, for Morris had already appointed the day for the second advent, assuring his followers that there would no longer be seed-time or harvest, and that meanwhile they had grain and cattle sufficient for their needs. Colonel Burton, sheriff of Salt Lake county, was then ordered to enforce the writs, and on the 13th of June, 1862, appeared on the heights above their camp at the Weber settlement with a posse of three hundred or four hundred men and five pieces of artillery.

A summons was now sent to the leaders,[33] demanding their surrender within thirty minutes, and warning them of the consequences if they should refuse. Morris withdrew to his dwelling, to consult the Lord, and a few minutes later returned with a written revelation, promising that not one of his people should be harmed,

---

ing a meeting at South Weber, they asked whether there were any present who believed in the new prophet. Seventeen persons arose and declared their faith, stating that they would adhere to it though it should cost them their lives. They were excommunicated, but nevertheless the number of converts increased rapidly, and in a few months mustered about 500 persons. *The Mormon Prophet*, 122–4.

[33] Joseph Morris, John Banks, Richard Cook, John Parsons, and Peter Klemgard. A copy of the summons is given in *Stenhouse's Rocky Mountain Saints*, 596–7.

but that their enemies should be smitten before them. The faithful were then assembled, and after prayer and reading of the revelation were told to choose which part they would take. A moment later the report of artillery was heard, and two women were struck dead by a cannon-ball, the lower jaw of a young girl being shattered by the same shot. The firing was continued almost without intermission, the assailants opening with musketry as they approached the camp.

At first the Morrisites, both men and women, took refuge in their cellars, or wherever else they could find cover, all being unarmed and the attack unexpected; but presently, recovering from their panic, the men seized their weapons and organized for defence. The camp consisted mainly of tents and covered wagons, with a few huts built of willows, woven together and plastered. Behind this frail protection the besieged maintained for three days an unequal fight, the cannon and long-range rifles of their assailants raking the enclosure,[34] while their own weapons consisted only of shot-guns and a few Mexican firelocks. At intervals Morris was besought to intercede with the Lord, but his only answer was: "If it be his will, we shall be delivered, and our enemies destroyed; but let us do our duty." On the evening of the third day a white flag was raised, whereupon he exclaimed: "Your faith has gone and the Lord has forsaken us. I can now do nothing more."

After the surrender, the Morrisites were ordered to stack their arms, the men being separated from the women, and most of the former placed under arrest. The prophet, his lieutenant, and two of the women were shot, as the survivors relate, by the sheriff,[35] ten

[34] The cannon were loaded with musket-balls, which tore down the huts and pierced the sandy hillocks, wounding some of the women and children, who had taken refuge behind them. *Beadle's Life in Utah*, 417.

[35] In a sworn statement made before Judge Waite, Apr. 18, 1863, Alex. Dow deposed: 'In the spring of 1861 I joined the Morrisites, and was present when Joseph Morris was killed.' 'Robert T. Burton and Joseph L. Stoddard rode in among the Morrisites. Burton was much excited. He said: "Where is the man? I don't know him." Stoddard replied, "That's him,"

of their party and two of the posse having been killed
during the fight.[36]   The camp was then plundered,
and the dead conveyed to Salt Lake City, where the
bodies of Morris and his lieutenant were exposed at
the city hall, the robe, crown, and rod of the former
being laid in mockery by his side, and his fate regarded
by the saints as the just punishment of one who "had
set himself up to teach heresy in Zion, and oppose the
Lord's anointed."   The prisoners were brought before Judge Kinney, placed under bonds, and at the
next session of court, in March 1863, seven were convicted of murder in the second degree and sentenced
to various terms of imprisonment, while sixty-six
others were fined $100, being committed to jail until
the fines were paid, and two were acquitted.[37]   Against

pointing to Morris.   Burton rode his horse upon Morris, and commanded
him to give himself up in the name of the Lord.   Morris replied: "No, never,
never!"   Morris said he wanted to speak to the people.   Burton said: "Be
damned quick about it."   Morris said: "Brethren, I've taught you true
principles"—he had scarcely got the words out of his mouth before Burton
fired his revolver.   The ball passed in his neck or shoulder.   Burton exclaimed: "There's your prophet!"   He fired again, saying: "What do you
think of your prophet now?"   Burton then turned suddenly and shot Banks
(the prophet's lieutenant), who was standing five or six paces distant.   Banks
fell.   Mrs Bowman, wife of James Bowman, came running up, crying: "Oh!
you blood-thristy wretch."   Burton said: "No one shall tell me that and
live," and shot her dead.   A Danish woman then came running up to Morris
crying, and Burton shot her dead also.'   Stenhouse's Rocky Mountain Saints,
598–9; Waite's Mormon Prophet, 127; Beadle's Life in Utah, 418–19.   Beadle
throws doubt on portions of Dow's testimony, and says that according to the
statements of members of the posse, Morris was killed because, after the
surrender, he ordered his followers to take up their arms and renew the fight.
Stenhouse relates that Banks was wounded at the time of Morris' death,
but not fatally.   In the evening he was well enough to sit up and enjoy his
pipe, but died suddenly, though whether by poison, pistol, or knife is
doubtful.

   [36] Waite's The Mormon Prophet, 126.   Stenhouse says, six of the Morrisites killed and three wounded.   Rocky Mountain Saints, 599; Tullidge, six casualties only.   Life of Brigham Young, 339; Beadle, ten killed and a very large
number wounded.   Life in Utah, 420.

   [37] A nolle prosequi was entered against one of the accused.   Those condemned to the penitentiary were loaded with ball and chain, and made to
work on the roads.   Harding, in Hickman's Destroying Angel, 215.   A detailed, but condensed account of the Morrisite massacre, and perhaps one of
the best, will be found in Waite's The Mormon Prophet, 122–7.   For other versions, see A Voice from the West, 5–12; Stenhouse's Rocky Mountain Saints,
593–600; Beadle's Life in Utah, 413–21; Tullidge's Life of Brigham Young,
336–9; Hickman's Destroying Angel, 211–14; Virginia City (Mont.) Madisonian, Nov. 24, 1877; Deseret News, June 18, 1862, March 12, 1879; S. L. City
Tribune, Aug. 11, 18, 1877.   There are few material discrepancies in the above
accounts, except in the one given by the Deseret News, though Beadle's work

the sheriff and other members of the posse no proceedings were taken at this date, though it was alleged by the Morrisites that his course was severe, and that the arrests might have been made without the loss of a single life. In 1879, however, Burton, who in consideration of his services had meanwhile been promoted to offices of trust, holding among others the post of collector of internal revenue for Utah,[38] was indicted for the murder of one of the women.[39] He was acquitted after a trial lasting several weeks, for he was a good and responsible man in every respect, and there was no evidence that he was guilty of the crime alleged.

To Governor Harding and judges Waite and Drake the law appeared to have been strained against the Morrisites, even though they may have been guilty of resisting a legal process, and petitions for their pardon being signed by the federal officials, the officers

contains some details that do not appear elsewhere. He states, for instance, that when the prisoners were first brought before Judge Kinney, only five of them would sign bonds, and of the rest only a few could speak English, the latter protesting against the entire proceedings, and declaring that they would 'lie in jail till the devil's thousand years were out' before they would admit that they were legally dealt with. The account given in *A Voice from the West*, San Francisco, 1879, is written by one of the sect, and is purely from a Morrisite standpoint. In the *Deseret News*, March 12, 1879, it is stated that Morris had been excommunicated for adultery, that his followers boasted that they would soon occupy the houses and farms of the Mormons, and that Burton took command of the posse with great reluctance, after the Morrisites had frequently defied the officers of the law. 'The Morrisites,' says the church organ, 'commenced to fire upon the posse with their long-range rifles, and having torn up the floors of their log cabins and wickeups, dug up the earth and threw it against the walls. They lay in these cellars firing through port-holes at the posse. There were very close upon 200 men in these fortifications.' After the arms were stacked, Burton, Stoddard, and some fifteen others entered the camp, and Morris, being allowed at his own request to speak to the people, cried out: 'All who are for me and my God in life or in death follow me.' A rush was then made for the arms, whereupon the posse opened fire, the sheriff firing two shots at Morris, Stoddard also firing two or three shots, and two women being killed, though by whom is not stated.

[38] Beadle states that when he visited Utah in 1868, Burton was also assessor of S. L. co., a general in the Nauvoo legion, a prominent elder in the church, and one of the chiefs of the secret police. *Life in Utah*, 398.

[39] He was arrested in Aug. 1876, and his bail fixed at $20,000. *Deseret News*, March 12, 1879; in July 1877, with bail at $10,000. *S. L. City Tribune*, July 28, 1877. A former indictment had been found in the Sept. term of 1870, but the constitution of the grand jury was declared illegal by the U. S. sup. court.

at Camp Douglas, and other gentiles,[40] the chief magistrate released the prisoners and remitted the fines.[41] For thus turning loose on the community a number of persons whom the Mormon rulers classed as dangerous criminals, only three days after conviction, and before any investigation had been made, Harding was severely censured by the grand jury. "Therefore we present his 'Excellency' Stephen S. Harding, governor of Utah, as we would an unsafe bridge over a dangerous stream—jeopardizing the lives of all who pass over it—or as we would a pestiferous cesspool in our district breeding disease and death." Meanwhile the bonds of such offenders as had failed to appear for trial were declared forfeited by the chief justice, and execution issued against their property. The homestead of one of them named Abraham Taylor was sold for a trifling sum,[42] and his family turned into the street. By the advice of Judge Waite, who investigated the matter, and found that no judgment had been recorded, Taylor applied to the chief justice for an injunction. The application was refused, on the ground that "if there was no judgment, he could render one, as the court had not permanently adjourned, but only to meet on his own motion."

Of the further career of the Morrisites it remains only to be said that a few who were possessed of means at once left the territory, while most of the remainder found refuge and employment at Camp Douglas. A few weeks later Connor established a military post at Soda Springs, on Bear River, imme-

[40] And by some of the Mormons. *Beadle's Life in Utah*, 421; *Hickman's Destroying Angel*, 163. Harding, in *Id.*, 216, says that no Mormon signatures except that of Hickman appeared on the petitions, but that several of the saints called at his quarters after dark to intercede for the Morrisites.

[41] Beadle states that Bishop Woolley called on Harding to remonstrate against the pardon, saying, as he took his leave, that if it were granted, 'the people might proceed to violence.' *Life in Utah*, 421. On pp. 423–5, he relates an improbable story of a visit paid to the governor by Banks' widow, to warn him of a plot against his life.

[42] To Joseph A. Johnson, clerk of Kinney's court, for $200. *Beadle's Life in Utah*, 425. In 1868 Taylor recovered his property, with back rents for five years.

diately beyond the northern limit of Utah,[43] offering to furnish conveyance for all who wished to form a settlement at that point. More than two hundred of the Morrisites availed themselves of this offer, removing with their effects under the escort of a company of volunteers.

This feud between the saints and the federal officials was brought to an end in June 1863, Harding being superseded as governor[44] by James Duane Doty, with Amos Reed as secretary, and John Titus of Pennsylvania being appointed chief justice in place of Kinney, who at the next general election was chosen delegate to congress.[45] Thus the president endeavored to restore peace by making concessions on both sides. In the spring of 1864 Judge Waite resigned in disgust, after holding a term of court, at which there was not a single case on the docket.[46] His successor was a Missourian, named Solomon McCurdy. Judge Drake still remained at his post,[47] though merely going through the form of holding court, all attempts to administer justice proving futile among a community that had never willingly submitted, and had not yet been compelled to submit, to gentile domination.

The administration of Governor Doty lasted only for two years, and during this period little worthy of note is recorded in the annals of Utah, this being perhaps the best evidence that some degree of har-

---

[43] At a point about 175 miles north of S. L. City and now in Idaho Ter. It was named Camp Connor.

[44] He left S. L. City on June 11th, being appointed consul at Valparaiso. *Deseret News*, June 17, 1863. Harding was a native of Milan, Ind., and when appointed governor of Utah was about 50 years of age. He was an able lawyer, and a man of energy and personal courage; but during his administration he labored rather to win the approval of the American people than to deal out strict justice. *Waite's The Mormon Prophet*, 107.

[45] *Tullidge's Hist. S. L. City*, 325; *Stenhouse's Rocky Mountain Saints*, 609, where it is stated that Kinney's removal was caused by his subservience to the will of Brigham. In the *Deseret News*, Apr. 27, 1864, are reports of his first speeches in congress.

[46] He afterward followed his profession in Idaho City. *Waite's The Mormon Prophet*, 105, 111.

[47] Before his appointment to Utah, Drake had lived for many years at Pontiac, Mich. At this date he was a man of thin, wiry frame, aged about sixty, of nervous temperament, vigorous mind, and blameless life.

mony at length prevailed between the federal and
territorial authorities. The new magistrate was a
conservative ruler, liberal and tolerant in his policy,
an able and experienced statesman, and on terms of
friendship with many of the most eminent men of
his day. His youth had been passed among the
frontier settlements of Wisconsin and Michigan, and
in early manhood he had held prominent positions
in state and national councils.[48] During his residence
in the territory he had made many friends and scarcely
a single enemy, his intercourse with the citizens being
always marked by the cordiality and freedom from
constraint characteristic of western life and manners.
At his decease, which occurred, after a painful illness,
on the 13th of June, 1865, a city draped in mourning
gave token of the respect in which he was held by
the Mormon community.[49]

Governor Doty was succeeded by Charles Durkee,
a native of Wisconsin, who held office until late in
1869.[50] At the time of his appointment he was aged
and infirm, and was selected perhaps for that reason,
his orders being to pursue a negative and conciliatory
policy. "I was sent out to do nothing," he once remarked to an intimate friend,[51] and his instructions
were faithfully executed.[52]

During Durkee's administration the territory of

[48] Doty, a native of Salem, N. Y., was admitted to the supreme court of
Michigan in 1818, in which year he began to practice law at Detroit, being
then only 19 years of age. In 1819 he was appointed secretary to the Mich.
legislature; in 1834–5 he was a member of the Mich. legislative council, and
introduced a measure providing for a state government, which was adopted by
the council; in 1837 he was elected delegate to congress, and in 1849, representative in congress from Wisconsin. *Waite's The Mormon Prophet*, 108–9;
Beadle's Life.in Utah, 214–15; *Deseret News*, June 21, 1865.
[49] On the day of his funeral business was suspended in S. L. City. *Deseret
News*, June 21, 1865.
[50] In the first half of 1869 Secretary E. P. Higgins acted as governor, during
Durkee's absence. His message to the legislature, while in that capacity,
was regarded as one of the most able ever presented to that body.
[51] J. H. Beadle author of *Life in Utah*.
[52] Gov. Durkee was born at Royalton, Vt, in 1802. He was one of the
earliest settlers and most prominent men in Wisconsin, and a member of its
first legislature. In 1855 he was elected U. S. senator, and was a stanch ad-
herent of the anti-slavery party. He died at Omaha on the 14th of Jan., 1870.
Deseret News, Jan. 26, 1870; *Beadle's Life in Utah*, 215.

Wyoming was organized,[53] and included the portion of Utah north of the 41st parallel and east of the 111th meridian, a surface of 8,000 square miles. Idaho, admitted in 1863, also contained, on its southern border, a narrow belt claimed by the Mormons, though merely by right of possession.[54] In 1861, on the organization of Colorado, the eastern boundary of Utah was placed at the 109th meridian.[55] By these partitions the area of the latter was reduced to about 85,000 square miles, its limits being identical with those which now exist.[56]

The antagonism between General Connor and the Mormon authorities [57] was for the moment relieved,

[53] For organic act, see *Laws of Wyoming*, 1869, 18–24.
[54] In the organic act, the southern boundary of Idaho was fixed at the 42d parallel. *Idaho Laws*, 1863–4, p. 28. In 1850, when Utah was defined, it was bounded on the north by Oregon, of which the southern boundary was the same parallel.
[55] *Colorado Laws*, 1861, p. 23.
[56] In 1865 memorials of the Utah legislature were presented to congress for the annexation of territory in Colorado and Arizona. *Utah Acts*, 1865, pp. 91–2; *H. Misc. Doc.*, 53, 38th Cong. 2d Sess. For further proceedings in congress relating to Utah, see *H. Jour.*, 37th Cong. 3d Sess., 737; *Id.*, 38th Cong. 2d Sess., 562; 39th Cong. 1st Sess., 1339, 1383; *Sen. Jour.*, 37th Cong. 3d Sess., 618; 38th Cong. 1st Sess., 1009, 1029, 1159; 38th Cong. 2d Sess., 503; *Cong. Globe*, 1862–3, 26, 60, 166, 210, 228–9, 1121; *Id.*, 1864–5, 117, 124, 157, 596, 942, 967, 996, 1028, 1172; 1865–6, 1494, 3509, 3522, 4190.
[57] Hickman states that in the autumn of 1863 Brigham offered him a large bribe to assassinate Connor. *Destroying Angel*, 167. The ill feeling had been considerably intensified by the appearance in *The Union Vedette*, a newspaper first published at Camp Douglas, Nov. 20, 1863, of a number of circulars signed by Connor and relating to the mining interests of the territory. The general states his belief that Utah abounds in rich veins of gold, silver, copper, and other minerals, invites miners and prospectors to explore and develop them, and threatens the Mormon leaders with martial law in case of interference. In a letter to Col Drum, asst adjt-general at San Francisco, he writes: 'My policy in this territory has been to invite hither a large gentile and loyal population, sufficient by peaceful means and through the ballot-box to overwhelm the Mormons by mere force of numbers, and thus wrest from the church—disloyal and traitorous to the core—the absolute and tyrannical control of temporal and civil affairs.' *The Daily Telegraph*, the first number of which appeared July 4, 1864, with T. B. H. Stenhouse as editor and proprietor, waged fierce war with the *Vedette*, which was issued at Camp Douglas in Jan. 1864, as a daily paper. Early in 1865 Gen. Connor stopped its publication. *Stenhouse's Rocky Mountain Saints*, 612; *Sloan's Utah Gazetteer*, 1884, p. 29. It was again published, however, in June of this year at S. L. City, and continued till Nov. 27, 1867. The *Telegraph* was afterward moved to Ogden, where the last number appeared in July 1869. *Richards' Bibliog. of Utah*, MS., 15. In Aug. 1859 a newspaper named *The Mountaineer* was published in S. L. City by Seth M. Blair, James Ferguson, and Hosea Stout, being in-

when, in 1865, all joined in celebrating the second in-
auguration of Abraham Lincoln and the success of
the union arms. Though his party was strongly opposed to Mormonism, Lincoln had little to say on the
so-called Mormon question, and that little was expressed in three words: Let them alone. To be left
alone was all that the people asked and all that they
had struggled for, since Utah was first admitted as a
territory. The occasion was therefore one of rejoicing,
honest and heart-felt, and the pageant more imposing
than anything that had yet been witnessed in the city
of the saints.[58] In the centre of Main Street a platform was erected, and here, on the morning of the 4th
of March, the federal officers, civil and military, exchanged greetings with the church dignitaries. Past
them filed a procession of tradesmen and working men,
a mile in length, the sidewalks, the windows, and
house-tops being crowded with an eager and boisterous throng. The buildings were draped with flags,
the carriages and sleighs decorated with streamers,
the men and women with rosettes, while the bands of
the 3d infantry and the Nauvoo legion furnished
music, and Mormon banners, with their manifold de-
vices, appeared side by side with the stars and stripes.

Later the concourse assembled in front of the stand,
the provost guard[59] facing the platform, the militia
companies forming in the rear, and the volunteers
drawn up on their right, four deep and with arms at
rest. Addresses were delivered, the bands playing
and the multitude cheering lustily during the intervals.
The troops were then escorted to their camp by the
cavalry of the legion, and General Connor and his staff

---

tended for secular news and for general circulation, though friendly in its
tone toward the saints. It lasted only one year. *Ibid.*

[58] A meeting of officers and prominent citizens was held at Camp Douglas
on the 28th of Feb., and a committee of arrangements appointed.

[59] Organized by Connor with a view, as Tullidge says, to establishing a
military dictatorship in Utah. In a strongly anti-Mormon report to J. Bidwell, rep. from Cal., dated Feb. 1867, Gen. Hazen admits that Connor was
unduly harsh toward the saints, remarking that his zeal as a catholic may
account for his rigor. *House Misc. Doc.*, 75, 39th Cong. 2d Sess., 4.

invited to a banquet at the city hall, the invitation being accepted, although the general, who had now received orders to take charge of the department of the Platte, was unable to attend in person.[60] In the evening the party again met at the theatre, and the festivities concluded at a late hour, with a display of fire-works, the federal officials being well pleased, and perhaps a little surprised at the exuberant loyalty of the Mormons.

A few weeks after this gala-day citizens and soldiers again united in fraternal gathering to mourn the loss of their president.[61] When news of his assassination was first received, the volunteers could with difficulty be controlled from venting their fury on the inhabitants, who, as they imagined, were exulting over this deed of infamy. Soon, however, they were forced to acknowledge themselves in error, for Lincoln had ever been friendly toward the Mormons, and by none was he more respected. On the 19th of April, the day set apart for the funeral solemnities at Washington, business was suspended in Salt Lake City; the flags on the public buildings were hung at half-mast and covered with crape; many of the stores and residences were dressed in mourning, and long before the appointed hour more than three thousand persons, among them being many gentiles, were assembled at the tabernacle. The platform was occupied by the civil and military functionaries and a number of promi-

---

[60] Stenhouse mentions that before his departure a ball was given at the social hall, which Brigham and his councillors declined to attend, the officers' wives of Camp Douglas also refusing to meet the Mormon women. *Rocky Mountain Saints*, 612. Gen. P. Edward Connor, an Irishman by birth, came to the U. S. early in life, and enlisted in the regular army, serving for five years as a private soldier on the frontier. During the Mexican war he raised a company of volunteers in Texas, and led them as their captain at Buena Vista, where he was wounded, and received honorable mention in the official despatches. At the close of the war he settled in California, where in ten years he accumulated a fortune. At the beginning of the civil war he was offered the colonelcy of the third Cal. volunteers. *Waite's The Mormon Prophet*, 112-13.

[61] On the 18th of April a meeting of federal, civil, and military officers was held at S. L. City, when arrangements were made for the funeral exercises. It is worthy of note that Col Burton was appointed one of the committee of arrangements. See *Tullidge's Hist. S. L. City*, 335.

HIST. UTAH. 40

nent citizens, the stand and organ being draped in black. The exercises commenced with an anthem by the choir, followed by a prayer from Franklin D. Richards. Then came an eloquent address from Amasa Lyman, and an impressive eulogy on the life, character, and services of Lincoln by Norman Mc-Leod, the chaplain at Camp Douglas, the funeral rites concluding with a benediction by Wilford Woodruff.

Soon after the departure of Connor, orders were received to disband the volunteers; but the alarm caused among gentile citizens by further Mormon troubles caused a portion of them to be retained until they could be replaced by regular troops. Of the many crimes laid to the charge of the saints at this period, and by some ascribed to the agency of the church, the murders of Newton Brassfield and King Robinson were the most notorious.[62] In the spring of 1866 Brassfield, formerly a citizen of California and more recently of Nevada, married the wife of one of the elders, then employed on a foreign mission. Application was made and granted for a writ of habeas corpus to obtain possession of the children, the case being still pending when the assassination occurred. On the 2d of April he was shot dead by some unknown person while about to enter his hotel.[63] A reward of $4,500 was offered by the

[62] Gen. Hazen remarks in his report: 'There is no doubt of their murder from Mormon church influences, although I do not believe by direct command.' He recommends that in future the commanding officer at Camp Douglas be ordered to send one of the Mormon leaders to the state prison at Jefferson, Mo., for each man that is assassinated, and that he be retained there until the culprit is surrendered. *House Misc. Doc.*, 75, 39th Cong. 2d Sess., 4. Beadle states that, when most of the volunteers had been withdrawn, all gentiles who had taken up land west of the Jordan were whipped, tarred and feathered, or ducked in the Jordan, and their improvements destroyed, and that Weston of the *Union Vedette* was seized, carried to the temple block by night, and cruelly beaten. *Life in Utah*, 203-4. See also *The Union Vedette*, in *Virginia and Helena (Mont.) Post*, Oct. 9, 1866.

[63] *Deseret News*, April 5, 12, 1866. In the former number it is stated that two other cases of shooting had occurred within less than three weeks, one of the parties, named Mayfield, being dangerously wounded by a soldier who mistook him for a gambler with whom he had had some difficulty. The account of Brassfield's murder and its cause as related in the *Deseret News* agrees

gentile community, but without success, for the arrest of the murderer, who was probably a relative of the elder's, as the sentiment of the Mormon community required that the nearest of kin should avenge the wrongs of an absent husband.[64]

King Robinson, a native of Maine, and in 1864 a resident of California, was appointed in that year assistant surgeon at Camp Douglas.[65] When the volunteers were mustered out of service he practised his profession in Salt Lake City, and in the spring of 1866 married the daughter of a physician, Dr Kay, who in his life-time had been a pillar of the church, but whose wife and children were apostates. The doctor was an intimate friend of Norman McLeod, and at the time of his assassination a superintendent of the gentile Sunday-school.[66] While at Camp Douglas, he ascertained that certain ground in the neighborhood of Warm Springs was unoccupied, and supposing it to be a portion of the public domain, took possession of it, and erected a building thereon. The city council claimed that the land belonged to the corporation, and ordered the marshal to destroy the improvements and eject the claimant. The doctor brought the matter before the court, but the chief

essentially with the one given in *Stenhouse's Rocky Mountain Saints*, 615, except that according to Stenhouse's version no attempt was made to arrest the murderer, while in the *Deseret News* it is stated that he was pursued and several shots fired at him. Beadle, *Life in Utah*, 204–5, says that the woman had repudiated her former marriage, that Brassfield, who had taken her trunk and clothing from her former residence, was arrested for larceny, and a day or two later, while in the street in custody of the marshal, was shot in the back by a hidden assassin, no special effort being made to arrest him.

[64] Stenhouse relates that General Sherman, on hearing of the assassination, telegraphed to Brigham that he hoped to hear of no more murders of gentiles in Utah, and reminded him that there were plenty of soldiers, recently mustered out of service, who would be glad to pay him a visit. Brigham replied that Brassfield had seduced a man's wife, and that life in S. L. City was as safe as elsewhere if people attended to their own business. *Stenhouse's Rocky Mountain Saints*, 616. See also *The Dalles Daily Mountaineer*, May 17, 1866.

[65] He was afterward sent to Camp Connor. *The Union Vedette*, Oct. 25, 1866, in *Beadle's Life in Utah*, 206.

[66] McLeod was at this time preaching at Independence Hall in opposition to Mormonism, and the doctor no doubt shared his sentiments. Both were heartily disliked by the Mormons. *Stenhouse's Rocky Mountain Saints*, 616–17.

justice decided against him.[67]   Soon afterward other
property belonging to Robinson was destroyed at
midnight by a gang of twenty or thirty men, some of
them in disguise, Alexander Burt, of the police force,
with several others as accomplices, being accused,
though not identified.   By the advice of his counsel,
Robinson gave notice that he intended to hold the
city responsible for damages.   Two days later he was
aroused near midnight to attend a patient, and when
a short distance from his dwelling was struck on the
head with a sharp instrument, and then shot through
the brain.   The murder was committed at a corner of
Main Street in bright moonlight, the doctor's cries
were heard by his neighbors, and seven persons were
seen running away from the spot, but no arrests were
made,[68] the verdict of the coroner's jury being that
the deceased had died by the hands of parties unknown.[69]   By the gentiles the doctor's assassination
was attributed to his contest with the city authorities, though in fact the murder may have been neither
ordered nor premeditated.   If it were so, it would
seem improbable that seven persons should have been
intrusted with the secret, and that such time and
place should have been selected.

Other murders and outrages were ascribed to the
Mormons about this date, some of gentiles and some
of their own apostate countrymen.[70]   So great was

[67] During the trial Robinson's counsel raised the point that the city, on
account of the non-performance of certain acts, had no legal existence. *Deseret News*, Nov. 14, 1866.

[68] Parties were indicted for the murder by the grand jury, in 1871, but
there was no evidence against them except that they had been seen in the
neighborhood. *Stenhouse's Rocky Mountain Saints*, 617–18.

[69] *Deseret News*, Nov. 14, 1866; *Stenhouse's Rocky Mountain Saints*, 616–
20, 735–41, where are copies of the speeches of counsel.   In commenting on
the case, the *Deseret News* remarks that the investigation was conducted without the least effort to discover the assassins, unless it could be shown that
they were Mormons.   For other accounts, see *Beadle's Life in Utah*, 206–9;
Richardson's Beyond the Mississippi, 363; *Rusling's Across America*, 183–9;
Virginia and Helena Post, Oct. 30, 1866; *Boisé City Statesman*, Nov. 3, 1866;
Austin, Reese River Reveillé, Oct. 29, 1866; *Virginia City Post*, Nov. 3, 1866.
A large reward was subscribed for the arrest of the murderers, at the head
of the list being the name of Brigham Young for $500.

[70] Among the latter, Beadle mentions the cases of three apostates named
Potter, Wilson, and Walker—the first a brother of those murdered at Spring-

the alarm among gentile merchants, that, with a few exceptions, they signed an agreement to leave the territory, on condition that their property should be purchased by the authorities at a low valuation. The answer was that they had not been asked to come, and were not now asked to depart; they could stay as long as they pleased, and would not be molested if they did not molest others. No further deeds of violence occurred, the excitement gradually died away, and with the approaching completion of the overland railroad a better feeling prevailed. Contracts had been awarded without distinction to Mormon and gentile; travel had increased, and with it traffic and the circulation of money, and for a brief space all felt a common interest in the country's prosperity.

Not least among the benefits caused by the building of the railroad was the gradual cessation of Indian hostilities, which had continued, with little intermission, from the date of the Mountain Meadows massacre. The natives had no alternative but to steal or starve; the white man was in possession of their pastures; game was rapidly disappearing; in the depth of winter they were starving and almost unclad, sleeping in the snow and sleet, with no covering but a cape of rabbit's fur and moccasons lined with cedar bark; even in summer they were often compelled to subsist on

ville in 1857—who were arrested at Coalville, Weber co., for stealing a cow, and placed in charge of a party of policemen, one of them a Danite named Hinckley. Walker escaped to Camp Douglas, but Wilson and Potter were killed by the officers. The murderers were arrested, but escaped from the marshal. Soon afterward a colored man, known as Negro Tom, called on the federal officials to state that he could give important evidence concerning certain murders. A few days later he was found with his throat cut and his body horribly mangled, about two miles east of the city. *Life in Utah,* 211–12. See also *Stenhouse's Rocky Mountain Saints,* 621. The latter relates that Judge Titus caused the arrests, in consequence of which one of the apostles, to mark his contempt for the judge, had a chemise made, about ten feet in length, and ordered it to be handed to the judge as a present. Titus regarded the matter as a threat, as well as an insult, considering that the night garment was intended as a shroud. In 1866 a man named Beanfield, fron· Austin, Nev., had some difficulty with the Mormons and was shot. *Bowles, Our New West,* 266. See also *S. F. Call,* Nov. 1, 16, 1866, April 14, 1867; *S. F. Times,* Aug. 15, Oct. 25, 1867; *Sac. Union,* Oct. 31, 1866.

reptiles, insects, roots, and grass seeds. Farm reservations had been opened for their benefit,[71] and in 1859 it was stated by the superintendent of Indian affairs that an appropriation of $150,000 would enable him to provide for all the destitute among the 18,000 natives then inhabiting the territory. No appropriation was made at this date, though, as will presently appear, liberal provision was made a few years later for certain of the Utah tribes.

Between 1857 and the close of 1862 outbreaks were of frequent occurrence,[72] and until the arrival of the

[71] Among them the Spanish Fork reservation, including nearly 13,000 acres, was opened in 1855 in Utah Valley. Here about 2,500 bushels of wheat were raised in 1859. There were others on Sanpete Creek, in the valley of that name, on Corn Creek, in Fillmore Valley, and at Deep Creek and Ruby valleys. On each there were about 25 acres in wheat, and a small quantity of vegetables were raised. J. Forney, in *Ind. Aff. Rept*, 1859, pp. 367–9. In these reports for the years 1856–63, and in *Sen. Doc.*, 36th Cong. 1st Sess., xi. no. 42, are many statements and suggestions as to the character of the Indians, their condition, treatment, reservation work, and intercourse with the white population. As they were little heeded, it is unnecessary to mention them in detail. The names of the various superintendents of Indian affairs and Indian agents will be found in the *American Almanac*.

[72] For troubles in southern Utah in 1857–8, see Little's *Jacob Hamblin*, 47 et seq. In Oct. 1858, Hamblin with eleven others left the Santa Clara settlement to visit the Moquis on the eastern side of the Colorado, thus paving the way for Mormon colonization in that direction. On Feb. 25, 1858, a descent was made on one of the northern settlements by 250 Shoshones. Two settlers were killed, five wounded, and a large number of cattle and horses driven off. On the 1st and 9th of March the herds of the settlers in Rush Valley were raided and a quantity of stock stolen. On the 7th, 100 horses and mules were taken from the farm of John C. Naile at the north end of Utah Lake. *House Ex. Doc.*, 35th Cong. 2d Sess., ii. pt ii. pp. 74–5, 80–2. On Sept. 10th, Utah Indians violated the persons of a Danish woman and her daughter, near the Spanish Fork reservation. *Id.*, 152; *Ind. Aff. Rept*, 1859, p. 362. In the summer of 1859 an emigrant party, en route for California, was surprised in the neighborhood of the Goose Creek mountains, and at least five men and two women killed, the massacre being caused by the slaughter of two Indians who entered the camp for trading purposes. *Ind. Aff. Rept*, 1859–60, pt ii. 210–11. On Aug. 14th, this body of Indians was attacked by Lieut Gay with a company of dragoons, and about 20 of them killed. In his message to the Utah legislature, dated Dec. 12, 1860, Gov. Cumming states that though a suitable force had been appointed for the protection of the northern emigrant route, many persons had been murdered presumably by roving bands of Shoshones and Bannacks. *Utah Jour. Legisl.*, 1859–60, p. 8. In the summer of 1860, Mayor Ormsby, with a party of Carson Valley militia, was decoyed into a cañon and perished with all his command, the cause of the outbreak being the slaying by emigrants of a chief, named Winnemucca. *Burton's City of the Saints*, 582. See also *Moore's Pion. Exper.*, MS., 15–19. For further Indian depredations up to 1863, measures taken to prevent and punish them, and remarks thereon, too voluminous to be mentioned in detail, see *Ind. Aff. Rept*, 1859–60, pt ii., 231–44, 1861, 21, 1862, 210–14, 1863, 419–20; *Sen. Doc.*, 36th Cong. 2d Sess., ii. no. 1, pp. 69–73; *House Ex. Doc.*, 37 Cong. 3d Sess., iv. no. 3, pp.

volunteers, no effectual curb was placed on the hostile tribes. On the 29th of January, 1863, the battle of Bear River was fought, twelve miles north of Franklin, between some three hundred of the Shoshones and Bannacks, under their chiefs Bear Hunter, Pocatello, and Sanpitch, and about two hundred men of Connor's command, its result effectually putting a stop to hostilities in Northern Utah. For fifteen years the northern tribes had infested the overland mail route, slaughtering and plundering emigrants and settlers, until their outrages had become unbearable. Reaching Franklin by forced marches, during an intensely cold winter, the snow being so deep that their howitzers did not arrive in time to be of service, the troops approached the enemy's camp at daylight on the 29th, and found them posted in a ravine through which Battle Creek enters Bear River. Their position was well chosen, the ravine being six to twelve feet deep, about forty in width, with steep banks, under which willows had been densely interwoven, and whence they could deliver their fire without exposing themselves. Attacking simultaneously in flank and front, Connor routed them after an engagement lasting four hours, and, their retreat being cut off by cavalry, the band was almost annihilated.[73] Among the slain was Bear Hunter,[74] the other chieftains making their escape. Had the savages committed

78–80, 82–5, v. no. 30; *Hayes' Scraps, Los Angeles*, iv. 96; *Deseret News*, March 17, Apr. 14, July 7, Nov. 3, 17, 1858, Feb. 16, Aug. 3, 24, 31, Sept. 21, Nov. 16, 1859, May 30, Aug. 1, Oct. 3, 1860, Feb. 13, 1861, Apr. 16, June 11, Aug. 13, Sept. 17, 24, Oct. 8, Nov. 26, Dec. 10, 31, 1862; *S. F. Alta*, May 11, Aug. 16, 17, Sept. 6, Oct. 20, 28, 29, 1858, Jan. 18, March 29, 30, July 6, Sept. 8, 12, 16, 21, 22, 28, Oct. 6, 28, 1859; *S. F. Bulletin*, May 8, Aug. 18, Oct. 28, 29, Nov. 26, 1858, Aug. 24, 30, Oct. 31, Nov. 19, 1859, Oct. 4, 8, 1862; *Sac. Union*, Aug. 10, 12, Sept. 28, Oct. 2, 5, 12, 19, 31, Nov. 2, 11, 14, Dec. 7, 1857, March 3, July 21, 29, Aug. 17, Sept. 4, Oct. 20, Nov. 16, 25, 31, 1858, Feb. 18, 23, March 16, Apr. 15, May 10, Aug. 11, 31, Sept. 17, 19, 22, 30, Oct. 5, 7, 27, Dec. 2, 19, 1859, Apr. 6, May 4, 9, 10, 11, 14, 15, 21, 23, 24, 28, 30, 31, June 1, 4, 5, 8, 9, 12, 14, 16, 20, 26, July 6, 7, 9, 12, 13, 14, 21, 31, Aug. 1, 21, 23, Oct. 2, 1860, Apr. 4, 24, 29, May 8, 9, 31, June 7, 11, Aug. 15, 18, Sept. 3, 18, 22, Oct. 2, Dec. 26, 1862.

[73] Connor states that he found 224 bodies on the field, and how many more were killed he was unable to say. A copy of his official despatch will be found in *Tullidge's Hist. S. L. City*, 283–6.

[74] And two inferior chiefs, named Sagwitch and Lehi. *Id.*, 286.

this deed, it would pass into history as a butchery or a massacre.

Of Connor's command, which consisted of 300 volunteers, but of whom not more than two thirds were engaged,[75] fourteen were killed and forty-nine wounded. A number of rifles and nearly 200 horses were captured, and more than seventy lodges, together with a large quantity of provisions, destroyed. This defeat completely broke the power and spirit of the Indians, and the result was immediately felt throughout Northern Utah, especially in Cache county, where flocks and herds were now comparatively safe, and where settlements could be made on new and favorable sites hitherto considered insecure.[76]

During the spring of this year an outbreak occurred among the Utahs in the neighborhood of the Spanish Fork reservation. A party of volunteers, under Colonel G. S. Evans, defeated them in two engagements.[77] In April 1865 an Indian war broke out in Sanpete county, spreading to adjacent districts, and lasting without intermission until the close of 1867, under the leadership of a chieftain named Blackhawk. Although the militia of the southern counties were constantly in the field, and reënforcements were sent from Salt Lake City under General Wells, the California volunteers being then disbanded, more than fifty of the Mormon settlers were massacred, an immense quantity of live-stock captured,[78] and so wide-

[75] Seventy-six were disabled by frozen feet. Letter of General Halleck in *Id.*, 287.

[76] In addition to the official despatches of Col Connor and Gen. Halleck, Tullidge gives in his *Hist. S. L. City*, 289–90, two other accounts of the battle at Bear River, one copied from a historical note in the Logan Branch records, and the other from Col Martineau's sketch of the military history of Cache co. Both differ from the official reports as to the number killed, the former placing it at 200, and a great many wounded, the latter stating that the dead, as counted by an eye-witness from Franklin, amounted to 368, besides the wounded who afterward died, and that about 90 of the slain were women and children. For other versions, see *Hayes' Scraps, Indians*, v. 214–17.

[77] The volunteers numbered 140. Among the killed was Lieut F. A. Teale. *Sloan's Utah Gazetteer*, 1884, 29.

[78] Accounts of the various massacres and depredations will be found in *Wells' Narr.*, MS.; *Smith's Rise, Progress, and Travels*, 29–30; *Utah Sketches*, MS., 13–14, 43, 136–48, 153–7; see also *Robinson's Sinners and Saints*, 162–5;

spread was the alarm that many of the southern settlements were for the time abandoned,[79] the loss to the
community exceeding $1,100,000.[80] Of this sum no
portion was voted by congress, the memorials of the
Utah legislature asking for reimbursements being
ignored, although the militia had served for more
than two years without pay, and the governor had
declared that their claims were just and their services
necessary.[81]

Codman's Round Trip, 219-20, 243-5. The leading incidents are briefly as
follow: On the 9th of April, 1865, Blackhawk and his band visited Manti,
where they boasted of having stolen some cattle at a neighboring settlement,
and wanted to hold a 'big talk.' On the next day some of the Manti citizens,
who rode forth to ascertain the truth of the matter, were fired upon and one
of them killed, the Indians retiring up Salt Creek Cañon in Sevier co., where
they killed two herdsmen. A party sent in pursuit a few days later was overpowered with the loss of two men. On May 29th the savages massacred a
family of six persons at Thistle Valley in Sanpete co., slaying two others
about the same time. In July three settlers were murdered, and several
wounded. Many cattle had now been driven off, and the people of Sanpete,
Sevier, Millard, Piute, Beaver, Iron, Washington, and Kane counties kept
guard over their stock with armed and mounted men. Between Jan. and the
beginning of April 1866 several raids were made in Kane co., five settlers being killed, and a man named Peter Shirts with his family sustaining a siege
for several weeks until relieved by militia. Between April 22d and the end of
June six persons were killed and others wounded in Sanpete and Piute counties, two of them while attempting to recover cattle driven off from the Spanish Fork reservation. Early in 1867 James J. Peterson with his wife and
daughter were killed near Glenwood, Sevier co., and their bodies mutilated.
The vigilance of the militia kept the Indians in check for the remainder of
this year, and only three other settlers were killed, the soldiery also losing
three of their number. F. H. Head, sup. of Indian affairs, in *Ind. Aff. Rept*,
1866, p. 124, states that the number of marauders was not more than 50 or 60.

[79] Sevier and Piute counties were entirely abandoned, together with the
settlements of Berrysville, Winsor, upper and lower Kanab, Shunesburg,
Springdale, Northup, and many ranches in Kane co., and Pangwitch and Fort
Sanford in Iron co. *Smith's Rise, Progress, and Travels*, 30. Six flourishing
settlements in Piute co., four on the borders of Sanpete, and fifteen in Iron,
Kane, and Washington counties, were entirely abandoned. Joint memorial of
legislature, in *Laws of Utah*, 1878, p. 167.

[80] For newspaper reports of Indian depredations, difficulties, expeditions,
and battles between 1863 and 1867, see, among others, *The Deseret News*, Jan.
21, 28, Feb. 11, March 18, Apr. 8, 15, 22, May 13, 20, July 1, 1863, June 7,
1865, May 10, 1866, June 5, 12, 1867; *Union Vedette*, July 8, 13, 31, Aug. 4,
17, Nov. 5, 9, 1865; *S. F. Bulletin*, Jan. 26, Apr. 14, 15, May 4, June 9, July
10, 1863, Aug. 8, 1864, Apr. 20, 1866; *S. F. Alta*, Feb. 17, 19, May 8, June
11, 12, July 6, 7, 1863, Aug. 12, Sept. 3, 1864, July 8, 1865, May 1, 16, 22,
June 10, 14, 15, July 31, Aug. 8, 1867; *S. F. Call*, Jan. 5, March 22, June 8,
14, 21, Aug. 10, 11, Oct. 29, 1865, May 14, June 2, 4, 5, 9, 11, July 24, Aug.
1, 3, 8, 9, 1867; *Sac. Union*, Jan. 31, Feb. 12, 13, 17, Apr. 14, 28, May 16, 30,
June 13, 1863, Apr. 20, July 30, Aug. 20, 31, 1864, Feb. 7, June 9, Aug. 4,
26, 31, 1865, Aug. 5, 1867; *Gold Hill News*, March 17, July 8, 1865; *Carson
Appeal*, June 10, Aug. 2, 1865; *Boisé Statesman*, June 8, Dec. 12, 1865, Nov.
2, 1867; *Watsonville Pajaro Times*, May 16, 1863.

[81] See the certificate of Gov. Charles Durkee, appended in 1869 to the joint

After the affair of Bear River treaties were concluded with the Shoshones and Bannacks on the 12th and 14th of October, 1863,[82] whereby travel on the principal routes to Nevada and California was rendered secure, the stipulations being faithfully observed, and the Indians receiving in return annuity goods to the value of $21,000 for a term of twenty years.[83] In June 1865 a treaty was made with a number of the Utah tribes, whereby they agreed to remove within one year to a reservation in the Uintah Valley, relinquishing their claim to all other lands within the territory, receiving as compensation $25,-000 annually for the first ten years, $20,000 for the next twenty years, and $15,000 for thirty years thereafter.[84] Annuities were also to be granted to the chiefs, dwellings erected for them, and lands ploughed, enclosed, and supplied with live-stock and farming implements. A school was to be maintained for ten years, during nine months in the year; grist and lumber mills and mechanics' shops were to be built and equipped at the expense of the government, and $7,000 voted annually for ten years in aid of various industries. The Indians were to be protected on their reservation; must not make war except in self-defence; and must not steal, or if they did, the stolen

memorial, in *Laws of Utah*, 1878, p. 167. Geo. W. Emery, who was governor in Feb. 1878, stated that he knew nothing of the facts, and had no recommendation to make. Two former memorials had been forwarded, the first in 1868. *House Misc. Doc.*, 99, 40th Cong. 2d Sess., 19; the second in 1869. *Id.*, 41st Cong. 1st Sess.

[82] The first in Tooele Valley and the second at Soda Springs. They were confirmed by the senate, but with amendments which were forwarded to Gov. Doty, with instructions to obtain the consent of the Indians. *Ind. Aff. Rept*, 1864, p. 16. On the 30th of July, 1863, a treaty had been made with Pocatello and others whereby the roads to the Beaver Head and Boisé River gold mines and the northern California and southern Oregon roads were made secure. Another treaty was concluded with the western Shoshones at Ruby Valley, Oct. 1st. *Rept of James Duane Doty*, in *Id.*, 1864, p. 175.

[83] *Id.*, 176. In his message to the legislature, dated Dec. 12, 1864, Gov. Doty remarks: 'These are the first treaties ever made by the U. S. with the bands of Shoshones; and it is somewhat remarkable that they have adhered to their stipulations with a fidelity equal to that of most civilized nations.' *Utah Jour. Legisl.*, 1864–5, pp. 11–12.

[84] The appropriations were to be made on the supposition that the Indian tribes would muster 5,000 souls, and were to be increased or diminished in proportion to their numbers. *Ind. Aff. Rept*, 1865, p. 151.

property must be returned, or its value deducted from their annuities.[85] Under these stipulations, though the treaty was not formally ratified, many of the Utahs, among whom was the chief Blackhawk, were gathered and dwelt in peace on the reservation.

In 1864 a memorial had been presented by the Utah legislature, asking that the Indians be removed from their smaller reservations,[86] and in the same year acts were passed by congress authorizing the appointment of a surveyor-general for Utah, providing that the Indian title to agricultural and mineral lands be extinguished, and the lands laid open to settlement, ordering the superintendent of Indian affairs to collect as many of the tribes as possible in the Uintah Valley, and appropriating for agricultural improvements the sum of $30,000.[87] The site was well selected, being remote from routes and settlements, and enclosed by mountain ranges, which were impassable for loaded teams during nine or ten months in the year. It contained at least two millions of acres,[88] portions of it being well adapted for agriculture and grazing, and was well supplied with timber and water-power. In the summer of 1868 about 130 acres were under cultivation, and it was estimated that the value of the produce would reach $15,000; but on the 1st of July swarms of grasshoppers settled

[85] A synopsis of the provisions of this treaty, which was negotiated by O. H. Irish, superintendent of Indian affairs in 1865, will be found in *Id.*, 150–1. See also *Deseret News*, June 14, 1865.

[86] *Utah Acts*, 1863–4, pp. 7–10, 13.

[87] *U. S. Acts*, 38th Cong. 1st Sess., 67–8; 38th Cong. 2d Sess., 16–17; *House Ex. Doc.*, 46 Cong. 3d Sess., xxvi. 971–3. The salary of the surveyor-general was to be $3,000 a year, and his powers and duties similar to those of the surveyor-general of Oregon. The usual school reservations were made. By act of July 16, 1868, it was ordered that the public lands of the territory should constitute a new land district, to be named the Utah district, and that the preëmption, homestead, and other laws of the U. S. should be extended over it. *Id.*, 973–4. In 1862 this district was merged with that of Colorado. *U. S. Acts*, 37th Cong. 2d Sess., 51, 100–1. In *Ind. Aff. Rept*, 1864, p. 16, Commissioner Wm P. Dole states that the Uintah Valley had been set apart for an Indian reservation as early as Oct. 1861, but that on account of the imperfect geographical knowledge of the country its exact limits could not then be defined.

[88] *Id.*, 17. The tract enclosed the whole region drained by the Uintah River and its upper branches, as far as its junction with the Green River.

on the land, and within a week nine tenths of the crop were destroyed. In other years the result was fairly encouraging, when it is considered that the Indian is by nature a hunter, averse to all manual labor, and subsists mainly on meat. For the year ending June 30, 1869, the amount appropriated for the Uintah agency was but $5,000.[89] Small as this sum was, it served to prevent any serious depredations,[90] for a bale of blankets or a few sacks of flour, distributed in proper season, accomplished more than their weight in gold expended in military operations and military surveillance.

[89] Pardon Dodds, in *Ind. Aff. Rept*, 1868, 156. Dodds, who was then Indian agent at Uintah, states that at least $20,000 was needed.

[90] During the summer of 1868 a few unimportant raids were made in Sanpete co., whereupon Col Head and others repaired to Strawberry Valley, Uintah, and a treaty of peace was concluded. *Deseret News*, Aug. 26, 1868. Among the most recent works on Utah is *The History of Salt Lake City and its Founders, by Edward W. Tullidge*. The first volume, which is a reprint from *Tullidge's Quarterly Magazine*, was issued in 1884, and relates the leading incidents of Mormon history between 1845 and 1865, the purpose being to continue it to a more recent date, adding thereto the records of other towns and counties, and forming when completed a history of the entire territory. The work is somewhat in the nature of a compilation, and consists largely of copies of official reports and documents, together with numerous extracts from other works, more especially from *Stenhouse's Rocky Mountain Saints*. Mr Tullidge follows the text of Stenhouse very closely in portions of his work, though writing from a different standpoint, and sometimes borrows his language with very slight alterations and without acknowledgment. The chapters relating to the Utah war occupy a large portion of the first volume. They are carefully considered, and contain much that is not found elsewhere. The work is published by authority of the city council, and under supervision of its committee on revision.

The Rocky Mountain Saints: A Full and Complete History of the Mormons, from the First Vision of Joseph Smith to the Last Courtship of Brigham Young, by T. B. H. Stenhouse. New York, 1873. This work, as its title indicates, carries the story of Mormonism from its earliest inception up to within a few years of the death of Brigham. Besides giving a complete outline of the political history of the latter-day saints, it contains chapters on the Mormon theocracy and priesthood, on polygamy, and on the book of Mormon, together with descriptions of the domestic and social condition of the Mormons, and of the various outrages commonly ascribed to them, more especially of the Mountain Meadows massacre. The book is profusely illustrated, entertaining in style, and though containing 761 pages of printed matter, can be read with interest throughout. The author was for 25 years a Mormon missionary and elder, during which period he was on familiar terms with the apostles, and for twelve years held daily intercourse with the president of the church. As he relates, he 'has no pet theories to advance, no revelations to announce, no personal animosity to satisfy. He has simply outgrown the past.' Though at times unduly severe, it is in the main one of the most impartial works yet published by anti-Mormon writers. Stenhouse, a Scotchman by birth, was converted to Mormonism in 1846, being then 21 years of age. He afterward labored as a missionary in England, Scotland, and various parts of Europe, founding the Southampton conference, and being for three years president of the Swiss and Italian missions. In 1869 he apostatized, and soon afterward removed to the city of New York, where he found employment as a journalist and wrote the above work. His decease occurred in 1882. See *Stenhouse's Tell It All*, preface; *Burton's Rocky Mountain Saints*, 272; *S. F. Bulletin*, March 7, 1882.

Exposé of Polygamy in Utah: A Lady's Life among the Mormons, by Mrs T. B. H. Stenhouse. New York, 1872. *Tell It All: The Story of a Life's Experience in Mormonism. An Autobiography; by Mrs T. B. H. Stenhouse.* Hartford, Conn., 1879. *An Englishwoman in Utah: The Story of a Life's Experience in Mormonism. An Autobiography; by Mrs T. B. H. Stenhouse.* London, 1880. The last two of these works are almost identical, except that one or two chapters of the former are omitted in the latter volume. Beginning with her first introduction to Mormonism about the year 1849, until the date of her own and her husband's apostasy, some 20 years later, the authoress gives what is claimed to be a plain, unvarnished record of facts which have come under her own notice. A few months after the publication of the *Exposé of Polygamy*, Mrs Stenhouse was asked to lecture on that subject, and wherever she spoke was requested to give her narrative more circumstantially and in more detail. Finally she accepted the suggestion of a gentile newspaper, published at S. L. City, to 'tell it all.' Hence the title and subject-matter of this work. Though claiming no literary merit, it is well told, and certainly tells enough, while containing nothing that can be termed positively indelicate.

The Mormon Prophet and his Harem: or, An Authentic History of Brigham Young, his Numerous Wives and Children, by Mrs C. V. Waite. Cambridge, 1866. Apart from the opening chapter, which contains the early life of Brigham, the first half of this work is devoted to the political history of Utah. Its main interest centres, however, in the information given in the latter portion, as to the family and social relations of the Mormon leader. There is the inevitable chapter on polygamy, written, the authoress remarks, as dispassionately as the writer's utter abhorrence of the system will permit. There is also a chapter where the mysteries of the endowment house are described in the form of a burlesque, and others where Brigham is set forth as prophet, seer, revelator, and grand archee. The volume is compact and well written; but though many of the facts may have been gathered, as is claimed, from original sources, they contain little that is not well known at the present day.

Life in Utah: or, The Mysteries and Crimes of Mormonism, being an Exposé of the Sacred Rites and Ceremonies of the Latter-Day Saints, with a Full and Authentic History of Polygamy and the Mormon Sect from its Origin to the Present Time, by J. H. Beadle. Philadelphia, etc., 1870. Though the author claims to have had access to valuable personal records and other private sources of information, his book has no special value. There are chapters on Mormon society, Mormon theology and theocracy, Mormon mysteries, theoretical and practical polygamy, but all these matters have been better treated by others, while the historical portions of the work are far inferior to those of Stenhouse. In relating the crimes of the Mormons, Mr Beadle claims that the statements for and against them have been equally presented. The reader need only turn to his account of the Mountain Meadows massacre to find that this is not the case. Here, and elsewhere, in the usual vein of looseness and exaggeration, crimes are alleged against the saints that have never been sustained, and all extenuating circumstances are omitted. Murders are laid to their charge of which there is no evidence, and which are not even mentioned by the leading authorities. The volume forms one of the many works that have been written on Mormonism with a view to pander to the vicious tastes of a certain class of readers rather than to furnish information.

The following is a more complete list of the authorities consulted in the preceding chapters: *Taylor's Rem.*, MS.; *Wells' Narr.*, MS.; *Utah Notes*, MS.; *Jennings' Mat. Progr.*, MS.; *Early Hist. Carson Valley*, MS.; *Little's Mail Service*, MS.; *Incidents in Utah Hist.*, MS.; *Nebeker's Early Justice*, MS.; *U.*

S. Acts and Res., 31st Cong. 1st Sess., 53-8, 111, 307, 453-8; 33d Cong. 2d Sess., 611; 35th Cong. 1st Sess., 368, app. iii.-iv.; 37th Cong. 2d Sess., 51, 100-1; 38th Cong. 1st Sess., 67; *Id.*, 2d Sess., 16-17; 46th Cong. 3d Sess., *H. Ex. Doc.*, 47, pt 3, 947, 972-3; *H. Jour.*, 31st Cong. 1st Sess., 458, 1804; *Id.*, 2d Sess. 602; 32d Cong. 2d Sess., 72, 104, 232, 243-4, 780; 33d Cong. 1st Sess., 1563; *Id.*, 2d Sess., 164, 246; 34th Cong. 3d Sess., 253, 376; 35th Cong. 1st Sess., 1325, 1366; *Id.*, 2d Sess., 323, 745, 759, 761; 36th Cong. 1st Sess., 1455; 37th Cong. 2d Sess., 1271, 1318-19; *Id.*, 3d Sess., 737; 38th Cong. 2d Sess., 562; 39th Cong. 1st Sess., 1339, 1383; *H. Misc. Doc.*, 31st Cong. 1st Sess., no. 18; 33d Cong. 1st Sess., no. 58; 35th Cong. 1st Sess., no. 100; 36th Cong. 1st Sess., no. 32; *Id.*, 2d Sess., no. 10; 37th Cong. 2d Sess., no. 78; 38th Cong. 2d Sess., no. 53; 39th Cong. 2d Sess., no. 75; 40th Cong. 2d Sess., no. 99; 41st Cong. 1st Sess., no. 19; *H. Ex. Doc.*, 31st Cong. 1st Sess., no. 5, 1002-4; 32d Cong. 1st Sess., no. 2, 272, 444-6; *Id.*, no. 25, 1-4, 7-8, 14-33; *Id.*, 2d Sess., no. 1, 299-300, 437-45; 33d Cong. 1st Sess., no. 1, pt 1, 12, 441-7, pt 3, 821; *Id.*, no. 18; *Id.*, 2d Sess., no. 1, pt 1, 224, pt 2, 63; 34th Cong. 1st Sess., no. 1, pt 1, 504, 515-26, 568-76, pt 2, 166-8; *Id.*, 3d Sess., no. 1, 6-7, no. 37, 2-3, 128, 142-3; 35th Cong. 1st Sess., no. 2, pt 1, 23-6, pt 2, 6-9, 21-38; *Id.*, no. 33, passim; no. 71, passim; no. 93, 40-9, 77, 86-96; no. 99, passim; no. 138, passim; *Id.*, 2d Sess., no. 2, pt 1, 8-10, 69-92, 77; pt 2, passim; pt 3, 780-2; 36th Cong. 1st Sess., no. 1, pt 2, 14-15, 121-256, 608; *Id.*, no. 78; 37th Cong. 2d Sess., no. 58, no. 97; *Id.*, no. 3, 78-85, no. 30, passim; 39th Cong. 2d Sess., no. 1, pt 2, 14-26; no. 20, 7-10; 41st Cong. 2d Sess., passim; *Id.*, 3d Sess., no. 1, pt 2, ii. 72; *H. Com. Rept*, 33d Cong. 2d Sess., no, 39, passim; 36th Cong. 1st Sess., no. 201, passim; *S. Jour.*, 31st Cong. 2d Sess., 406; 33d Cong. 1st Sess., 1003; *Id.*, 2d Sess., 574-5; 34th Cong. 1st and 2d Sess., 943; *Id.*, 3d Sess., 63, 298; 35th Cong. 1st Sess., 338, 1007-8; *Id.*, 2d Sess., 450, 590, 660, 36th Cong. 2d Sess., 521-59; 37th Cong. 2d Sess., 1161; *Id.*, 3d Sess., 618; 38th Cong. 1st Sess., 1009, 1029; *Id.*, 2d Sess., 503; *S. Ex. Doc.*, 32d Cong. 2d Sess., no. 33, passim; 33d Cong. 2d Sess., no. 33, 1-11; 35th Cong. 1st Sess., no. 67; passim; *Id.*, 2d Sess., no. 36, 68-73; 36th Cong. 1st Sess., no. 32, passim; no. 42, passim; no. 52, 301-6; *Id.*, 2d Sess., no. 1, 69-73, 224; 37th Cong. 1st Sess., no. 1, 58; *S. Misc. Doc.*, 35th Cong. 1st Sess., no. 201, passim; no. 240, passim; 36th Cong. 1st Sess., no. 12, passim; 37th Cong. 3d Sess., no. 37; *S. Com. Rept*, 37th Cong. 3d Sess., no. 87, passim; 45th Cong. 2d Sess., no. 142, passim; *Cong. Globe*, 1849-50, 1850-1, 1851-2, 1853-4, 1854-5, 1855-6, 1856-7, 1857-8, 1858-9, 1859-60, 1860-1, 1861-2, 1862-3, 1863-4, 1864-5, 1865-6, passim; *Sec. Inter. Rept*, 40th Cong. 2d Sess., 10-11, 173-89, 361-95; *Sec. Treas. Rept*, 1865, 326; 1866, 391; 1867, 442-3; *Com. Ind. Aff. Rept*, 1856, 227-9, 267; 1857, 306-8, 324, 380; 1859, 22, 365-73; 1861, 21; 1862, 210-14; 1863, 419-20; 1864, 16, 175-8; 1865, 143-4, 147-53; 1866, 124-5, 128-9; 1868, 5-6, 151-2; 1869, 270-1; 1870, 141-4, 191-2, 330-59; 1871, 545-51, 606-51, 683; *Wilson, Ind. Agt at G. S. L.*, *Rept*, Sept. 4, 1849, passim; *Chart. and Const.*, ii. 1236-40; *Stat. 8th Census*, passim; *Rept Com. Land-Office*, 1864, 20; *Millen. Star*, xx. 107-9, 125, 186-9, 532, xxii. 348, 453-4, xxiv. 241-5, 257-61, xxvii. 118-20, 133-6, 150-2, 165-6, xxxii. 744-5, xxxvii. 673-6; *S. Jour. (Cal.)*, 1850, 429-42, 1296; 1853, 645; *S. Jour. (Nev.)*, 1867, 64-5; *Utah Gov. Mess.*, 1870, 7-18; *Jour. Legis.*, 1851-68; *Acts*, 1855-68; *Tullidge's Hist. S. L. City*, 5, 24-32, 56-8, 63, 336; *Id.*, *Quart. Mag.*, i. 190-8, 479, 526-8, 536-7; *Id.*, *Life of Young*, 30-1; 196-212, 239-318, 329-55, 385-7; *Id.*, *Women*, etc., 244, 353-8, 414-22, 441-8; *Stenhouse's R. M. Saints*, p. xxi., 262-471, passim, 591-621, 713; *Id.*, *Les Mormons*, 39-41, 148-50, 172-202; *Stenhouse's (Mrs) Tell It All*, 248, 266-9, 324-39, 380-5, 462-3, 486-7, 496-8, 500-26, 548-9, 627-52; *Id.*, *English-woman*, passim; *Burton's City of the Saints*, 2, 5, 21-5, 209-32, 265-99, 304-59, 406-32, 506-82; *Lee's Morm.*, 16-35, 132-3, 218-50, 232, 240, 269-87, 379-84; *Remy's Journey to G. S. L.*, i. 189-200, 214-18, 446-52, 470-95, ii. 212-14, 240-5; *Richards' Narr.*, MS., 22-4, 35, 123-4; *Richards' (Mrs) Remin.*, MS., 39-46; *Revue des Deux Mondes*, 194-211; *Rusling's Across Amer.*, 183-90; *Robinson's Sinners and Saints*, 162-5, 180; *Rae's Westward by Rail*, 127-8, 140, 169-82; *Paddock's La Tour*, 301-2, 323, 348-9; *Hunt's Merch. Mag.*, xxx.

639; *Hickman's Dest. Angel*, 57–68, 107–12, 118–49, 158, 166–7, 205–9; *Hyde's Morm.*, 28–49, 121–3, 147–50, 177–82; *Greeley's Overland Jour.*, 206–57; *Gunnison's Morm.*, vii.–xiv., 83, 141–3, 146–7; *Gwin's Mem.*, MS.; *Green's Morm.*, 453–4; Glines (J. H.), in *Utah Co. Sketches*, MS., 21–2; Llewellyn, in *Id.*, 43; Jones, in *Id.*, 54–6; Morrison, in *Id.*, 136–48; McFadyen, in *Id.*, 153–7; Teasdale, in *Id.*, 109–11; *Olshausen's Gesch. Morm.*, 153–89, 237–44; *Ferris' Utah and Morm.*, 167–9, 185–90; *Kirchoff's Reisb.*, etc., i. 107–8; *Marshall's Through Amer.*, 177, 192; *McClure's Three Thousand Miles*, etc., 150, 435; *Waite's The Morm. Prophet*, 23–59, 60–113, 122–31, 214–46, 266–72, 278; *Murphy's Min. Res.*, 87; *Little's Jacob Hamblin*, 45–7, 56–7, 75, 140; *Linforth's Route*, etc., 75–77, 104–16; *Ludlow's Heart of Cont.*, 301–2; *Mackay's The Morm.*, 176, 199–200, 233, 238–48, 258–9, 276; *Ebey's Jour.*, MS., i. 146, v. 154, 219; *Carvalho's Incid. of Trav.*, 141–3, 151–9, 188–99; *Beadle's Life in Utah*, 168–266, 390–485; *Id.*, *Western Wilds*, 300–9, 490–530; *Id.*, *Undevel. West*, 646–53; *Codman's Round Trip*, 171–2, 210–45; *Cradlebaugh's Speech*, passim; *Bertrand's Mem. Morm.*, 97–133, 246–8; *Busch, Die Morm.*, 53–5; *Id.*, *Gesch. Morm.*, 46–158, 307–30; *Dana's Great West*, 271; *Schiel's Reise*, etc., 81–94, 100–2; *Bowles' Our New West*, 226, 266–8; *Young's Wife No. 19*, 228–61, 270–6, 341–8, 382–4; *Townsend's Morm. Trials*, 32–4; *Wadsworth's Wagon Road*, 12; *Campbell's Idado*, 11–12; *Corr. Hist. Soc. Mont.*, 44–5; *Comittant's Civili. Inconnues*, 29; *Clark's Statement*, MS., 10; *Dixon's White Conquest*, i. 188–98; *Siskiyou Co. Affairs*, MS., 21; *Revue Orient. et Amer.*, v. 299–306; *Cradlebaugh's Nev. Biog.*, MS., 1; *Kinney's (J. F.) Speech*, Mar. 17, 1864; *Doc. Hist. Mex.*, 3d ser., 100–12; *Moore's Pion. Explor.*, MS., 15–19; *Marcy's Thirty Years*, 267–75; *De Lacy's Montana as It Is*, 81; *Brackett's U. S. Cavalry*, 177–9; *Hutchings' Cal. Mag.*, ii. 196, iv. 345–9; *Hygiene U. S. Army*, 332–3; *Atlantic Monthly*, iii. 573–84; *De Smet's West. Missions*, 396; *Boadicea's The Morm. Wife; Frisbie's Remin.*, MS., 32–4; *Chandless' Visit to Salt Lake*, 154, 157 et seq.; *Trans. Wyom. Acad. Sciences*, 1882, 81–2; *Simpson, Explor.*, 23; *Life among the Morm.*, 186–93; *Smith's Rise, Prog.*, etc., 19–30; *Saxon's Five Years*, 292–4; *Snow's Poems*, i. 225–6, 265–6; *Stansbury's Explor. and Surv.*, 130–5, 148–50; *Spence's Settler's Guide*, 251, 259–60; *Tucker's Morm.*, 222–46, 277, 280–7; *Times and Seasons*, v. 692; *Utah Pamph., Polit.*, no. 14, 6–8; *Stanford's Weber Co.*, MS., 23; *Ward's Husband in Utah*, 19–60, 178–290; *Hughes' Voice from West*, passim; *Lee (J. D.), Trial*, passim; *Smith's Mystery and Crime*, 30; *Hollister's Resour. of Utah*, 8; *Huntington's Vocab. Utah and Shoshone Dialects*, 27–9; *Hand-book on Morm.*, 67–72; *Hittell's Scrapbook*, 94; *Hayes' Scraps, Cal. Pol.*, vii. 57; *Id.*, *Indians*, v. 214–17; *Id.*, *Los Angeles*, iv. 96, viii. 228–31, xvii. 3, 7; *Id.*, *S. Bernardino*, i. 53, 58, 60; *Id.*, *Utah*, passim; *Rodenbough's Second Dragoons*, 172–3; *Richardson's Beyond the Mississ.*, 347–8, 362–3; *Skelton (R.) and Meik's Def. of Morm.*, passim; *Cram's Topog. Mem.*, 25–32; *Crimes of L. D. Saints*, 48–82; *Möllhausen's Tagebuch*, 429–30; *Id.*, *Reisen*, etc., 25, 141, 410; *Id.*, *Das Mormon.*, 35–7, 102–7; *Pratt's Autobiog.*, 483; *Morse's Wash. Ter.*, MS., ii. 15–18; *Smucker's Hist. of Morm.*, 216; *Rinehart's Mem.*, MS., 3; *Harper's Mag.*, xliv. 602; *Pac. R. R. Repts.*, ii. 26–7; *Putnam's Mag.*, ii. 263, v. 225–36; *Utah Rev.*, Feb. 1882, 243–6; *Trib. Alman.*, 1850, 51; 1854, 67; *Amer. Alman.*, 1850, 109; 1851, 297; 1852, 116; 1853–61, passim; *Fisher's Amer. Stat. Ann.*, 1854, 120; *Sloan's Utah Gazett.*, 24–8; *Amer. Quart. Reg.*, iii. 588–95; *S. L. Direc.*, 1869, 64, 173; *Des. News*, 1855–77, too numerous to quote; *Vidette*, July 31, 1865; *Review*, Jan. 27, 1872; *Contributor*, v. 312–13, 446; *S. F. Alta*, 1849–76, too numerous to quote; *Chronicle*, June 17, 1877; Jan. 13, 1881; *Examiner*, Nov. 8, 1871; Jan. 10, 1872; July 21, 1875; *Times*, 1867, Feb. 2, June 4, 6, 13, Aug. 9, 15, Oct. 25; 1868, May 8, July 13, Sept. 29, Oct. 10, Dec. 17; 1869, Jan. 4, Mar. 23, May 20, Sept. 16; *Post*, 1877, Mar. 13, 22, 23, 24; 1878, Oct. 11; *Herald*, 1851, Nov. ?, 4; 1852, Aug. 21; 1853, June 12, Sept. 30, Dec. 3, 24; 1854, Feb. 22, May 3., June 25, Aug. 23, Oct. 1, 19; 1855, Mar. 14, Apr. 6, May 7, July 3; 1856, May 12, Nov. 11, 13; 1857, Feb. 5, May 14, June 19, Oct. 6, 12, 27, Nov. 2, 12, 25, 30, Dec. 1, 7, 17, 30; 1858, Jan. 12, 15, Mar. 11, Apr. 1, May 11, 27, June 29, July 10, Aug. 13; 1861, Jan. 30; *Bulletin*, too numerous to quote; *Call*,

1864, June 25, Aug. 17; 1865, Jan. 5, Mar. 3, May 6, June 1, July 29, Aug. 10, Oct. 3, Nov. 1; 1866, Nov. 1; 1867, Apr. 14, May 14, June 2, July 24, Aug. 1; 1869, Sept. 3; 1872, May 23, Sept. 23, Oct. 14, Nov. 19; 1875, July 18, 21; 1877, Feb. 16, Mar. 9, Apr. 1, May 3; 1881, July 30; *Stock Rept,* 1874, July 30, Nov. 27; 1875, July 24, 31; 1876, Sept. 23; 1879, May 2; *Stock Exchange,* Mar. 24, 1877; *Californian,* Jan. 26, 1848; *Min. and Scien. Press,* July 31, 1875; Mar. 31, 1877; *Courier de S. F.,* Mar. 26, 1869; *Spirit of the Times,* July 14, 1877; *Pac. Rural Press,* Mar. 31, 1877; *Wide West,* Jan. 3, 1858; *Cal. Star,* Jan. 29, 1848; *Golden Era,* May 18, 1856; *Oakland Tribune,* Mar. 24, 1877; *Appleton's Jour.,* xi. 592–3, 623; *Cal., Its Past History,* 211–16; *Cal. Mercant. Jour.,* 1860, 183–4; *Sac. Union,* 1855–67, too numerous to quote; *Bee,* May 24, Nov. 2, 1869; *Antioch (Cal.) Ledger,* Nov. 21, 1875; June 12, 1877; *Napa Co. Reporter,* Apr. 7, 1877; *Calaveras Chron.,* Mar. 31, 1877; *Mariposa Gazette,* Mar. 31, 1877; *Wilmington Jour.,* Dec. 9, 1866; *Havilah Courier,* Apr. 27, 1867; *Copperopolis Courier,* Mar. 23, 1867; *Watsonville, Pajaro Times,* May 16, 1863; *Petaluma Argus,* Mar. 16, 1877; *Sonoma Democrat,* Mar. 31, 1877; *Stockton Herald,* Sept. 28, 1871; *Independent,* June 15, 1867; Nov. 4, 1875; June 11, 1879; *San José Argus,* Dec. 5, 1874; *Herald,* June 6, 1877; *Times,* Nov. 23, 1879; *Lassen Advocate,* Mar. 31, 1877; *Anaheim Gazette,* Mar. 24, 31, 1877; *Sta Cruz Sentinel,* May 12, June 30, 1877; *Los Angeles Express,* Mar. 24, 31, 1877; *Herald,* Mar. 24, 1877; *Republican,* Mar. 23, 24, 1877; *San Buenaventura, Ventura Signal,* Mar. 31, 1877; June 24, 1877; *Free Press,* Apr. 7, 1877; *Winnemucca (Nev.) Silver State,* July 19, 1875; *Eureka Sentinel,* July 17, 1875; *Belmont Courier,* Oct. 28, 1873; May 5, 1877; *Prescott Miner,* Dec. 18, 1874; Apr. 11, 1879; *Austin, Reese Riv. Reveil.,* July 12, 1864; Aug. 18, 1865; Oct. 29, 1866; Jan. 2, 1867; *Gold Hill News,* 1864, Dec. 20; 1865, Mar. 17, July 8; 1872, Sept. 21; 1875, Feb. 1, Apr. 10, July 21, Aug. 4; 1876, Sept. 12; 1877, Mar. 12, May 25; *Dayton, Lyon Co. Sentinel,* July 16, 1864; *Times,* Mar. 24, 1877; *Elko Independent,* Aug. 7, 1875; Apr. 15, 1882; *Carson Appeal,* June 10, Aug. 2, 1865; Nov. 19, 1874; July 18, 1875; Oct. 27, 1876; *State Register,* Sept. 10, 1871; Sept. 26, 1872; *Kanesville (Iowa) Front. Guard.,* 1849, Feb. 7, Oct. 3, 17, 31, Nov. 14; 1850, Mar. 6, May 29, June 26, Aug. 21; 1851, Mar. 21, Apr. 18, Aug. 22, Sept. 22; 1852, Feb. 6, 20, Mar. 4, 11, 18, 25; *Boisé (Idaho) News,* Dec. 5, 1863; Feb. 20, Mar. 5, 1864; *Statesman,* 1865, June 8, Dec. 12; 1866, Nov. 3; 1867, June 16, Sept. 14, Nov. 2; *Idaho City, Idaho World,* Oct. 1, 1875; *Honolulu (Hawaii) Friend,* July 1, 1846; *Virginia (Mont.) Madisonian,* Nov. 24, 1877; *Post,* 1866, Oct. 8, 30, Nov. 3; *Helena Independent,* July 29, 1875; Apr. 5, 1877; *Herald,* Jan. 6, 1876; *Walla Walla (Wash.) Statesman,* Oct. 10, 1863; *Olympia Pion. and Democ.,* Aug. 8, 1856; *Puget Sound Courier,* Sept. 22, 1876; *Seattle, Puget Sound Herald,* Sept. 15, 1858; *Whatcom, Bellingham Bay Mail,* Apr. 3, 1875; *Portland (Or.) Standard,* Apr. 6, 1877; *Bee,* Oct. 31, 1878; *Oregonian,* 1859, Oct. 15; 1863, June 10; 1865, Feb. 7, July 8, 13, Aug. 4, 17, Oct. 6, Nov. 9, 11; 1877, Apr. 7; *Salem, Oregon Statesman,* 1854, Jan. 24, May 2; 1857, July 28, Aug. 11, 18, Sept. 15, 29, Oct. 20, Nov. 3, Dec. 1, 29; 1858, Jan. 5, 12, Feb. 16, Mar. 16, 30, June 15, July 13, Oct. 12; 1862, Apr. 14, June 30; *Jacksonville Democ. Times,* Mar. 31, 1877; *Oregon City, Oregon Argus,* 1857, Feb. 27, Dec. 12, 26; 1858, Jan. 2, 23, Feb. 13, 20, 27, Mar. 6, 13, Apr. 24, June 19, July 16, 30, Aug. 7, 14, 28, Sept. 11; 1866, Dec. 22; 1868, Sept. 11; *Spectator,* 1846, Aug. 6, 20; *Astoria Astorian,* July 20, 1878; *Roseburg Plaindealer,* Apr. 28, 1877; *The Dalles Mountaineer,* 1866, May 17, June 8; 1867, Feb. 22.

CHAPTER XXIII.

SCHISMS AND APOSTASIES.

1844-1869.

THE STRANGITES—THE GATHERERS—BRANNAN'S FOLLOWERS —THE GLAD-
DENITES—THE REORGANIZED CHURCH OF LATTER-DAY SAINTS—ALEX-
ANDER AND DAVID HYRUM SMITH—THE UTAH MAGAZINE—TRIAL OF
GODBE AND HARRISON—SUCCESS OF THE GODBEITE MOVEMENT—THE
STRUGGLE FOR COMMERCIAL CONTROL—PERSECUTION OF GENTILE MER-
CHANTS—ZION'S COÖPERATIVE MERCANTILE INSTITUTION—EXTENT OF
ITS OPERATIONS—DISASTROUS EFFECT ON GENTILE TRADE—REACTION IN
FAVOR OF THE REFORMERS.

DURING the life-time of Joseph Smith there was
but one organized secession from the church, though,
as we have seen, apostasies were frequent during his
later years. If the words of the prophet were not
the living truth, then could no faith be placed in
Mormonism, for he and none other was regarded as
the fountain-head of inspiration. But with his death
the source of infallibility was removed, and thus the
way was opened for schism and dissension, few of the
diverging sects, however, having sufficient faith in
their leaders to preserve them from final dissolution.

The saints who followed Sidney Rigdon to Pittsburgh in 1844 became gradually scattered among
the gentiles, a few of them, with William Marks at
their head, afterward rejoining the church. To J.
J. Strang, a prominent elder, were vouchsafed, as he
claims, numerous revelations that in Wisconsin was
the true Zion, and several thousands accompanied him
to that state. Strang afterward settled at Beaver
Island, in Lake Michigan, where he retained a small

following until the time of his death. Parties also accompanied William Smith, the only surviving brother of the prophet, to northern Illinois, Elder Brewster to western Iowa, Bishop Heddrick to Missouri, and Bishop Cutler to northern Iowa. All of them were soon afterward dissolved, the remnants of Brewster's and Heddrick's disciples forming themselves into a new sect, under the name of the Gatherers, and settling in Jackson county, where they published a weekly periodical, styled the *Truthteller*. During the year 1846 a large Mormon settlement was made in Texas; and under the leadership of Apostle Lyman Wight the colony prospered and increased rapidly. Until 1852 they acknowledged allegiance to the first presidency, but when the doctrine of polygamy was proclaimed, they separated from the church. After the death of Wright, which occurred a few years later, his flock was scattered. A small portion of the members of most of these sects found their way to Salt Lake City, while others joined the reorganized church, as will be mentioned later, and the remainder cast in their lot with the gentiles.

Of the party that sailed with Brother Sam. Brannan for California, in the *Brooklyn*, in 1846, about one fourth apostatized; their leader laying the basis of a fine fortune by investing in real estate funds, to a great extent at least, belonging to the Latter-day Saints.[1] Of the Mormon colony, founded, as we have seen, at San Bernardino, in 1851, a considerable number fell into apostasy, though many joined the parent organization, and a few became members of the reorganized church.

In addition to the various sects already mentioned and to be mentioned, numerous parties and individ-

---

[1] Beadle, *Life in Utah*, 404–5, states that Brannan afterward repaid the money with interest, but it would be difficult to make the early Californians believe it. About 45 adults and 65 children of the *Brooklyn* party remained in California, a few afterward joining Mormon communities at San Bernardino or in Arizona. Nearly 100 adults and some 40 children reached Utah, most of them in 1848–50. See *Hist. Cal.*, v. 544, this series.

uals fell away during the migration from Nauvoo, many of the stakes becoming settlements of recusant Mormons, while numbers of the saints settled at Omaha, Nebraska City, and other towns on the Missouri and its tributaries. Some, as I have said, merely remained in the western states to obtain means for their journey to Zion, but of the twenty thousand persons who followed the apostles from Nauvoo, it is probable that nearly one third were eventually absorbed among gentile communities.

In Utah, between 1852 and 1869, four distinct and organized attempts were made to throw off the yoke of Brigham, and establish what the apostates claimed to be a more perfect faith. These were the Gladdenite secession in 1852, the Josephite schism in 1860, the Morrisite movement in 1861, and the Godbe-Harrison schism in 1869.

When the doctrine of polygamy was openly avowed in 1852, some of the saints were sorely offended, and accusing the hierarchy of having fallen from grace in other respects, formed themselves into a new sect, appointing as their leader Gladden Bishop, whence the name of Gladdenites. Together with other recusants, Gladden, who was several times disfellowshipped and readmitted on profession of repentance, had again rejoined the church,[2] but being now disgusted with this new feature in the policy of the church dignitaries, worked with heart and soul against them. Among his followers was one Alfred Smith from St Louis, a man of great tenacity of purpose, and a bitter foe of Brigham, by whom, as he alleged, he had been stripped of his property. For a time the cause flourished, but on Sunday, the 20th of March, 1853, while Smith was holding services in front of the council-house, the gathering, though orderly and peaceable, was dispersed by the city marshal. Another meet-

[2] Ferris states that Gladden was cut off and rebaptized nine times. *Utah and the Mormons,* 326. See also *Olshausen, Mormonen,* 182.

ing called for the following sabbath was dispersed, Smith being taken into custody, and detained until he promised to desist. On the same day Brigham spoke a few words concerning the apostates in the tabernacle. The whole matter was regarded of no great consequence by the church; nevertheless it was deemed best to shun the very appearance of evil, and consequently the president gave the people clearly to understand that there must be no more of it.[3] Such warnings from the president of the church were never uttered in vain, and now the days of the Gladdenites were numbered. A few months later most of them set forth for California, the rest recanted, and after the year 1854 we hear no more of this apostasy.

The most successful of the recusant sects was the one established by Joseph Smith, the prophet's son, who, with his brothers Alexander H. and David Hyrum, remained at Nauvoo after the exodus.[4] A few years later the remnants of the Strangites and Cutlerites, being in search of a leader, organized a new church and requested Joseph to become their head. He at first refused, but in 1860, the number of members being then considerably increased by the breaking-up of other parties, he accepted the call as prophet, and began to preach the faith of his father, as he affirmed, in its original purity, repudiating the claims of Brigham and the doctrine of polygamy. The schism spread rapidly throughout Illinois, Missouri, and Iowa, the apostates being termed Josephites by the followers of Brigham, but styling themselves the Reorganized

---

[3] *Jour. of Disc.*, i. 82; *Deseret News*, Apr. 2, 1853; *Waite's The Mormon Prophet*, 120–1; *Beadle's Life in Utah*, 408–9; *Ferris, Utah and the Mormons*, 328–30. Brigham was followed by Parley Pratt, who said that he had known Gladden for 20 years, and had seldom heard his name mentioned, except in connection with some imposition or falsehood in the name of the Lord.

[4] Beadle says that the prophet left a considerable fortune, mostly in houses and lands at Nauvoo. *Life in Utah*, 428. Even if this is true, we well know that the houses and lands of the Mormons in Nauvoo were worth little to them when the expulsion came.

Church of Latter-day Saints. In Utah it was checked by fear of persecution, and not until the summer of 1863 did the movement become pronounced. In July of that year two Josephite missionaries, named E. C. Briggs and Alexander McCord, arrived in Salt Lake City, having crossed the plains, they said, as heralds of the gospel, and calling on Brigham, told him the object of their mission, and asked permission to preach in the tabernacle. This was, of course, refused;[5] nor were they allowed the use of any other public building, whereupon the missionaries visited from house to house, offering up prayers for the inmates, and exhorting them to join the true faith.

At first singly, then by dozens, and afterward by scores, converts were gathered into this fold, and in the spring of 1864 the Josephites in Zion mustered more than three hundred, the number of proselytes elsewhere being at this date between two and three thousand.[6] Persecution followed, as they claimed; and in early summer about one half of the Josephites in Salt Lake City started eastward, so great being the excitement that General Connor ordered a strong escort to accompany them as far as Green River. To those who remained protection was also afforded by the authorities.

The excitement caused by the evangelism of Briggs and McCord was renewed in the summer of 1869, when Alexander H. and David Hyrum Smith arrived at Salt Lake City as advocates of the reformed faith. Their meetings were held at Independence Hall, then the principal public building belonging to the gentiles, and at the first service a vast audience assembled, among the number being several of the wives of Brigham. At first the followers of Brigham trembled

---

[5] In *Waite's The Mormon Prophet*, 129, it is stated that Brigham said he would not be responsible for Briggs' safety if he remained in the city.

[6] Bowles, *Our New West*, 263, his work being published in 1869, incorrectly places the entire number at 1,500. In *Waite's The Mormon Prophet*, 129 (published in 1866), we read: ' In the states, those who have gone back to their first love are to be numbered by thousands.'

for the supremacy of their leader, and opposition meetings were organized under the management of Joseph F., the son of Hyrum Smith.[7] But the mantle of the prophet had not fallen on his offspring; they were men almost without force of character, of lamb-like placidity, and of hopelessly mediocre ability; not shrewd enough to contend with their opponents, and not violent enough to arouse the populace. They accomplished little for the cause of the reorganized church.

In 1860 the headquarters of the Josephites were established at Plano, Illinois, where, between 1860 and 1875, was published by this sect *The True Latter-day Saint's Herald*, and where in 1877 their leader still resided,[8] Joseph being at that date president of the church, and Briggs the president of the twelve. A branch was also established at Malad in Idaho; a few of the sect gathered at Kirtland,[9] and the remainder were scattered throughout the states. They rapidly increased, mustering in 1870 not less than twenty thousand in the United States, while in Europe entire churches joined the reformed faith, the name of the sect, and the more conventional morality of its doctrines, being among the causes of its success.[10]

---

[7] Stenhouse says that debates between the two parties were held in public. *Rocky Mountain Saints*, 629 (note).

[8] *S. Lake Herald*, June 6, 1877.

[9] *Ibid.; McClure's Three Thousand Miles*, 435.

[10] The Josephite creed will be found in *Waite's The Mormon Prophet*, 130–1; *Utah Scraps*, 16. It contains the following: 'We believe that the church in Utah, under the presidency of Brigham Young, have apostatized from the true order of the gospel. We believe that the doctrines of polygamy, human sacrifice, or killing men to save them, Adam being God, Utah being Zion, or the gathering place for the saints, are doctrines of devils.' In other respects their creed was almost identical with the Mormon articles of faith. Codman, who attended their services, remarks: 'They use the same religious books in their worship, and argue from them the prohibition of polygamy with as much earnestness as Orson Pratt displays in its advocacy.' *The Round Trip*, 210.

The second Joseph Smith, junior, was born at Kirtland Nov. 6, 1832. His early life was spent in Missouri and Illinois, whither he went with his parents. F. G. Mather received a letter from him in 1879, saying: 'I am now pretty widely recognized as the leader of that wing of the Mormon church declaring positive Mormonism, but denying and opposing polygamy and Utah Mormonism.' I give herewith a copy of an inscription on one of the pillars of the temple at Kirtland, as reported by Mather, *Lippincott's*

While the controversy between the prophet's sons and the prophet's nephew was at its height, an article appeared in the *Utah Magazine*, a periodical first issued in 1867, and of which elders W. S. Godbe and E. L. T. Harrison were proprietors, wherein appeared the following passage: "If we know the true feeling of our brethren, it is that they never intend Joseph Smith's nor any other man's son to preside over them simply because of their sonship. The principle of heirship has cursed the world for ages, and with our brethren we expect to fight it till, with every other relic of tyranny, it is trodden under foot." While speaking thus boldly, the magazine essayed the part of umpire between the disputants, and otherwise gave sore offence to the church dignitaries.[11] About the same time an article was published urging the development of the mineral resources of Utah, a measure which found no favor with Brigham, for thus would the flood-gates be opened to the gentiles, while the saints might be tempted to worship at the shrine of Mammon. "I want to make a wall so thick and so high around the territory," he once exclaimed in the tabernacle, "that it would be impossible for the gentiles to get over or through it."[12] Finally the elders were summoned before the school of prophets, by

Mag., Aug. 1880. 'The Salt Lake Mormons. When Joseph Smith was killed on June 27, 1844, Brigham Young assumed the leadership of the church, telling the people in the winter of 1846 that all the God they wanted was him, and all the bible they wanted was in his heart. He led or drove about two thousand people to Utah in 1847, starting for upper California and landing at Salt Lake, where in 1852 Brigham Young presented the polygamic revelation to the people. The true church remained disorganized till 1860, when Joseph Smith took the leadership or presidency of the church at Amboy, Illinois. We [thirty thousand] have no affiliation with the Mormons whatever. They are to us an apostate people, working all manner of abomination before God and man. We are no part or parcel of them in any sense whatever. Let this be distinctly understood, we are not Mormons. Truth is truth, wherever it is found.' For further particulars as to apostate sects before the year 1869, see *S. F. Alta*, May 21, 1857, July 3, Aug. 2, 1867; *S. F. Bulletin*, May 22, 1857, Aug. 10, Nov. 15, 1867; *Sacramento Union*, Apr. 22, May 20, June 8, Sept. 3, 18, 1857, Dec. 3, 1859, June 28, Aug. 5, 1867.

[11] In the *Deseret News* of Nov. 3, 1869, is a notice signed by the members of the first presidency and three other apostles, cautioning the saints against its teachings, and stating that it is unfit for perusal.

[12] *Godbe's Statement*, MS., 2.

which offenders are examined before being sent for
trial by the high council, and though the most serious
charge against them was the publication of the article
on mineral developments, both Godbe and Harrison
were expelled from the church.[13]

That the elders should have openly advocated the
development of the rich mineral resources of Utah
may appear from a gentile standpoint a slight provocation for so extreme a measure; but it should be remembered that from the earliest occupation of the
territory mining for the precious metals had been
strongly discountenanced by the priesthood.   This
was in fact a most essential part of the policy in accordance with which the Mormons had sought for
seclusion in the vales of Deseret, in order to preserve
their liberty and individuality as a religious community.   From the day when news arrived of the gold
discovery, their leaders had denounced all emigration
to California.   Gold-seekers were indiscriminately
classed as worldlings and apostates, or at least held
to be weak in the faith.   Nevertheless, the accounts
received from members of the Mormon battalion, who
had witnessed the discovery and shared in the excitement which followed it, produced a crisis that threatened their very existence as a people, and one which,
perhaps, none but the Mormons could have withstood.
When, in later years, mineral prospects were disclosed
in Utah, and prospecting largely carried on by gentiles, all such efforts were discouraged; for they could
result only in drawing into the territory a class of
men dangerous to its institutions, and might even seduce from their allegiance the members of the church.
Thus in the light of its full history must the policy
of the Mormon hierarchy be considered in excluding
from its fold this disturbing element.

No attempt was made, however, by either of the
elders to excuse this portion of the charges brought
against them.   Their defence was confined merely to
the question of their alleged apostasy, and to the au-

[13] *Ibid.; Harrison's Crit. Notes on Utah*, MS., 48.

thority of the priesthood. When their case was handed to the high council, the recusants, instead of pleading their cause, merely read a series of resolutions touching measures of church reform, Godbe denying Brigham's right to enforce obedience, whether in matters secular or spiritual, and Harrison stating that if it was apostasy to differ conscientiously from the priesthood, then he must be considered an apostate. "We claim," they said, "the right of respectfully but freely discussing all measures upon which we are called to act. And if we are cut off from this church for asserting this right, while our standing is dear to us, we will suffer it to be taken from us sooner than resign the liberties of thought and speech to which the gospel entitles us; and against any such expulsion we present our solemn protest before God and angels." It remained only to pass sentence of excommunication, and in due form the elders were delivered over to the buffetings of Satan for a thousand years.

But a few days later there appeared in the *Utah Magazine* an account of the trial, together with a protest and appeal to the brethren, afterward copied in the *New York Herald* and other leading journals. "It had been argued," remarked the recusants, "that we must passively and uninquiringly obey the priesthood, because otherwise we could not build up Zion. A nation built up on such a principle could be no Zion. The only glory or beauty there could be in a Zion must result from its being composed of people all of whom acted intelligently in all their operations." Supported as it was by a portion of the wealth and intelligence of Utah, the Walker brothers, the Tullidge brothers, Stenhouse, Lawrence, and Eli B. Kelsey,[14] the reformation gathered weight. On Sunday, the 19th of December, 1869, services were held for the first time by the reformers, in the chapel of the assembly-rooms in the thirteenth ward, and in the

[14] Kelsey, who voted against their expulsion, was also excommunicated. *Stenhouse's Rocky Mountain Saints*, 640.

evening at the Masonic hall.[15]   Before a dense audience, was sung by the choir the first hymn in the
Mormon hymn-book, composed by Parley P. Pratt:

> "The morning breaks, the shadows flee,
>   Lo! Zion's standard is unfurled;
> The dawning of a brighter day
>   Majestic rises on the world."

Then followed speeches by Godbe, Harrison, and
Lawrence, in which the gentiles, who formed one-third
of the audience, were assured that the reformation
would be continued with a purpose that would swerve
not before Brigham and his apostles.

The so-called Godbeite movement, however, though
for a time it excited considerable interest in business
circles, was a matter of small moment to the church
generally, producing little effect on the masses of the
members.   The movement in its incipiency was the
immediate occasion rather than the real cause of
Godbe and his adherents leaving the church.   No man
can consistently be continued a member of any church
if he persists in refusing to submit to the final decisions
of the church authorities.   His arrival at that point
of insubordination is almost always the result of a
growth of greater or less rapidity, and occupying
more or less time in development.   Godbeism at first
professed to be an attempt to reform and purify the
church, in part by the aid of spiritualism, but the
reform pretensions were evanescent, quickly fading
away, so that for many years nobody has looked upon
the movement as a religious one in any respect.   In
fact with the fleeting religious pretensions the very
name of the movement soon died out, and the prominent persons connected with it early manifested a skeptical spirit toward religion of every kind, and directed
their energies more completely into channels of business and money-making.   "I have been instrumental," writes Godbe in 1884, "in establishing and
conducting enterprises that have required an outlay of

[15] For account of secret, benefit, and benevolent societies in Utah, see
Utah Gazetteer, 1884, 218–26.

$1,000 a day for ten years, and have given employment to many hundreds of people." [16]

The struggle for the commercial control of Utah began at an early date in its history. Among the Mormons there were few men of business training, and until the advent of the overland railroad made it certain that Salt Lake City would become a commercial centre, the policy of Brigham was to discourage commerce and commercial intercourse. Nevertheless, gentile merchants, by whom traffic was mainly conducted, as late as 1860 were subject to a running fire of ridicule and condemnation directed against them from the tabernacle. The objection to them was twofold: first, the dislike to the presence of gentiles, in whatever capacity; and second, the fact that they absorbed the small amount of floating capital that the brethren possessed. He who should hold traffic with a gentile was considered weak in the faith, but as goods could be purchased from gentile mer-

---

[16] *Godbe's Statement*, MS., 29. For further mention of the Godbe schism and incidents connected with it, see *Tullidge's Mag.*, i. 14–55; *Stenhouse's Exposé of Polygamy*, 132–45; *Dixon's White Conquest*, i. 208–12.

William S. Godbe, an Englishman by birth, began his career as a sailor; but after being twice shipwrecked, tired of seafaring life, and while yet a lad, betook himself to America. Having made the acquaintance of several Mormons, and being charmed with the story of their adventures, he decided to cast in his lot with them, and journeyed nearly the whole distance on foot between New York and Salt Lake City, where he arrived in 1851, and found employment with a merchant named Thomas Williams, in a few years becoming himself a leading merchant. Between 1857 and 1884 Mr Godbe crossed the Atlantic 21 times, and the plains over 50 times. After his excommunication from the church, and the consequent loss of his business, finding himself, as he says, $100,000 in debt, whereas a year before he had been worth $100,000, he followed mining as an occupation, and in 1873 organized in London the Chicago Silver Mining Co., one of the few English companies that have proved successful in Utah. Of his ventures in mining, mention will be made later. Of Mr Harrison, he remarks that he is 'a man of unusual mental qualities, of earnest nature, and has an overruling love of truth, honesty, and straightforwardness.'

The *Statement of William Godbe*, MS., contains, in addition to matter relating to the Godbeite movement and personal memoirs, some valuable information on mining, together with much adverse comment on the Mormon hierarchy, terse and well put, though hurriedly written. 'They don't make many converts in the United States,' he remarks; 'they don't look for them. They make a few in the south, where the condition of things is analagous, more or less, with that which exists in Europe; but they make most of their converts in the latter country.'

chants to advantage, the saints were tempted sometimes to trade with them, and frequently did so, and
that without the severe censure on the part of the
church, which has been often alleged.

Among those who had transactions with gentile merchants were the Walker Brothers, who in 1868 were
among the prominent merchants of Salt Lake City, and
had contributed in no small degree to its commercial
prosperity. The firm subscribed liberally for all the
purposes to which the church funds were applied, but
refused to pay tithes or to recognize the right of the
church to collect tithing.[17]

During this year, and partly with a view to placing
the trade of Utah under church control, so far at least
as the brethren were concerned, the Zion's Coöperative Mercantile Institution was organized.[18] Aside
from such motives, however, there were good reasons
for securing to the country the benefits of the co-
operative system, for, as we shall see later, the prices
of imported commodities were still extravagantly
high.[19] To protect the people from these high prices
by importing from first hands and in large quantities
was the professed, and perhaps the main, purpose of
the promoters. After passing through some financial
difficulties, the enterprise seems to have obtained a
permanent foothold, and is yet a successful competitor
with gentile tradesmen, supplying at wholesale many
of the settlements in Utah, in addition to its local
and retail trade. In 1883 the total sales exceeded
$4,000,000, a half-yearly dividend of five per cent be-
ing paid in October of that year. At this date the
association had a reserve fund of about $125,000, and

[17] *Walker's Merchants and Miners of Utah*, MS., 2.
[18] On the 16th of October. Business was opened March 1, 1869, and the
company was incorporated Dec. 1, 1870. *Zion's Coöp. Merc. Inst.*, MS., 1.
Brigham Young was the principal stockholder, and Geo. Q. Cannon, Geo. A.
Smith, Wm Jennings, H. S. Eldredge, and Wm H. Hooper were among the
first directors. For constitution, by-laws, form of certificates of stock, and
incorporation, see *Utah Religious Pamphlets*, 9, 10.
[19] See cap. 28, notes 29 and 31, this vol.

a capital of $1,000,000, divided into $100 shares, and distributed among 700 or 800 stockholders.[20] The head of the church continued president of the institution after it was no longer under control of the church, but managed simply on business principles, representing Mormon as against gentile trading interests.[21] Branches were established at Ogden, Logan,[22] and Soda Springs, and, as we shall see later, the coöperative movement spread rapidly throughout the country, though most of these ventures resulted in failure, many of the stores being compelled to close during the commercial panic of 1873.

[20] *Deseret Ev. News*, Jan. 2, 1884. The main building, on East Temple street, S. L. City, was 318 by 100 ft, the front being of iron, and the roof fireproof. It was furnished with hydraulic elevators, fire and burglar proof vaults, and all modern appliances. *Zion's Coöp. Merc. Inst.*, MS., 1-2. In connection with the institution was a tannery and shoe-factory, in which about 170 hands were employed in 1883.

[21] *Harrison's Crit. Notes on Utah*, MS., 58-9. For further mention of the institution and its origin, see *Marshall's Through Amer.*, 176-7; *Stenhouse's Englishwoman*, 371-3; *Townsend's Mormon Trials*, 41-2; *Tullidge's Mag.*, i. 363-8; for cut of buildings, *Id.*, facing p. 385. In connection with it, it may be mentioned that Horace S. Eldredge, who has been connected with the institute from its inception, was appointed president in 1872, and in 1884 was superintendent. Mr Eldredge, a native of New York, arrived in Utah in 1848, after passing through all the tribulations of Far West, Nauvoo, and Winter Quarters. In 1868, being then in partnership with H. B. Clawson, he sold out his stock of goods to the institute.

Hiram B. Clawson, a native of Oneida co., N. Y., was educated at the Utica academy. In 1841, his father being then deceased, and the rest of the family having joined the Mormon church, he moved with them to Nauvoo, and in 1848 to the valley of Great Salt Lake. Though only 22 years of age, he was looked upon as a man of mark, and was employed in superintending the construction of some of the first buildings erected by the church in Salt Lake City. During the Utah war he figured prominently as adjutant-general of the Nauvoo legion, and just before the departure of the troops from Camp Floyd effected a complete reconciliation between the military and the church authorities. Appointed superintendent of Zion's Coöperative Mercantile Institute, in 1873 he was sent east in company with H. S. Eldredge to ask for an extension of credit, in view of the panic then prevailing in commercial circles. He met everywhere with a favorable response, and within eight months the company redeemed its obligations, amounting to $1,100,000. During his management Mr Clawson states that the losses of the institution by bad debts did not exceed a quarter of one per cent. In 1875 he resigned the superintendency, having purchased from the directors the agricultural department of the Z. C. M. I., to which he added a machinery department, furnishing grist and saw mills and steam-engines complete, together with all the different kinds of machines commonly in use throughout the territory. During the earlier part of his career Mr Clawson took a leading part in theatrical affairs, and to him and John T. Caine are largely due the success and prosperity of the Salt Lake theatre. *Tullidge's Mag.*, i. 678-84.

[22] For 1883 the sales of the Ogden branch were about $800,000, and of the Logan branch, of which Aaron Farr was manager, about $600,000.

The first effect of this movement on the trade of
gentile merchants was disastrous, the sales of the
Walker Brothers, for instance, decreasing in a brief
space from $60,000 to $5,000 per month,[23] while those
of the Auerbach Brothers fell off in like ratio,[24] these
two firms, among others, offering to dispose of their
entire property to the directors of the Zion's Coöperative Institute for fifty cents on the dollar, and leave
the territory.[25] The offer was refused. Hence, perhaps, as will presently appear, the rapid development of
the mining resources of the country after 1869, toward
which purpose several prominent merchants, among
them Godbe and the Walker Brothers, applied the
remnants of their fortunes. Soon, however, even the
Mormons began to disregard the warnings of their
leaders against trading with gentiles or apostates.
The spell was broken, and during the conference of
1870 the stores of the latter, and especially of the
Walker Brothers, were so crowded with purchasers
that it was almost impossible for them to serve their
patrons. The reformers preached against and wrote
against the president, and the better to support their
cause, established a newspaper named the *Salt Lake
Tribune*, at first a weekly and afterward a daily pub-

---

[23] *Walker's Merchants and Miners of Utah*, MS., 3. Samuel Sharp, Joseph
Robinson, David, Frederick, and Matthew Henry Walker were in 1883 the
members of this firm. Englishmen by birth, being the sons of a Yorkshire
squire, possessed in 1846 of a considerable landed estate, but who, like
thousands of others, suffered financial shipwreck during the railroad panic of
the following year, they arrived at S. L. City in 1852, at which date there
were only five business houses on Main street. They laid the basis of their
fortune during the presence of the army at Camp Floyd, soon making their
mark among the commercial community, and being classed a few years later
among the leading merchants of Utah. After 1869 their attention was chiefly
given to mining, in which connection further mention will be made of the
firm. *Autobiog. of the Walker Bros.*, MS.

[24] The Auerbach Bros., a dry-goods firm, state that at this time ruin stared
them in the face, and but for the mining developments which followed almost immediately afterward they could not have remained in the territory.
Fred. H. and Sam. H. Auerbach, natives of eastern Prussia, came to S. L.
City in 1864, after suffering heavy business reverses in Austin, Nev., where
they afterward paid their debts in full in gold coin. Their sales for 1885
amounted to about $500,000. *Auerbach's Edmunds Bill*, MS.; *Utah Biogr.
Sketches*, MS., 9–10.

[25] *Harrison's Crit. Notes on Utah*, MS., 52; *Walker's Merchants and Miners
of Utah*, MS., 3.

lication, in which the church dignitaries and their policy were severely criticised. Thus of all the apostasies the Godbeite movement, with its attendant incidents, was the most formidable, and wrought more harm in Zion than any which had preceded it, appealing, as it did, to the common sense and the self-interest of the community.

CHAPTER XXIV.

THE LAST DAYS OF BRIGHAM YOUNG.

1869-1877.

Visit of Schuyler Colfax—Godbe's Interview with President Grant —Governor Shaffer—Military Riot at Provo—Governor Woods —Judge McKean—Burlesque of Justice—Arrest of Brigham Young and Others—George Q. Cannon Chosen Delegate—Axtell's Administration—Governor Emery—Death of Brigham—His Obsequies—His Character—His Will.

"Will Brigham Young fight?" inquired Schuyler Colfax of Elder Stenhouse, during his sojourn at Salt Lake City in 1869.[1] "For God's sake. Mr Colfax." answered the elder, "keep the United States off. If the government interferes and sends troops, you will spoil the opportunity, and drive the thousands back into the arms of Brigham Young who are ready to rebel against the one-man power. Leave the elders alone to solve their own problems. We can do it; the government cannot." But with the exception of Abraham Lincoln, none of the presidents were of the opinion that it was best to leave the Mormons alone. At this date there is little doubt that Grant was resolved on the suppression of polygamy, even if need be at the cost of war. Meanwhile the famous Cul-

---

[1] Colfax also visited Utah in 1865. For reception and purpose of visit, see Richardson's *Beyond the Miss.*, 345-6, 348-9; Bowles' *Our New West*, 203-4; Tullidge's *Life of Brigham Young*, 355-8; Stenhouse's *Rocky Mountain Saints*, 613-15. For speech of Colfax, in 1869, in which, probably, the sentence most acceptable to the Mormons was the concluding line, 'I bid you all good night and good by,' see *The Mormon Question* (S. L. City, 1870), wherein is also a reply by John Taylor, an article on the Mormon question by the vice-president, published in the *New York Independent*, and a rejoinder by Taylor.

lom anti-polygamy bill[2] was before the representatives, and the honorable Thomas Fitch was amusing congress with his speeches on the prospect of another Mormon war.[3] Early in 1870 mass-meetings were held at the tabernacle, by men and women, to protest against the bill, and to draw up a remonstrance against its provisions. A memorial was also prepared and forwarded to congress, setting forth the revelation on polygamy and the duties of the Mormon church in that connection, wherein it was declared that the church would stand by its faith and polygamy institutions in spite of all human will and law.[4] During this year, also, an act was passed by the territorial legislature, granting the right of suffrage to women, but the measure subsequently adopted in Wyoming and elsewhere seemed to be in advance of the times,[5] or was in some way unpopular, and little use has ever been made of the privilege.[6]

Among those who realized the danger of the situation were the leaders of the Godbeite movement, who well knew that, in the event of another Mormon war, the dramatic farce of Buchanan's administration could not be reënacted, and that if the United States government again entered into the controversy, it would never withdraw from it until it had cut with its sword the Gordian knot of Mormonism.

[2] For debate and amendments when the bill passed the representatives, see *Cong. Globe*, 1869–70, 2180–1.

[3] For career of Thomas Fitch in Utah, see *Elliott & Co.'s Hist. Arizona*, 289.

[4] For copy of memorial and resolutions, see *Sen. Misc. Doc.*, 41st Cong. 2d Sess., no. 112, *The Utah Bill*, 33–40, wherein is a speech by delegate W. H. Hooper, delivered before the representatives March 23, 1870, and published in pamphlet form, as was also the speech of Aaron H. Cragin before the senate, May 18, 1870, the two forming nos. 4 and 5 in *Utah Pamphlets, Political.* The memorial and resolutions were referred to a committee which of course reported adversely. *H. Com. Rept*, 41st Cong. 2d Sess., i. no. 21.

[5] *Woods' Recollections*, MS., 67. See, for report in favor of female suffrage, *Utah Jour. Legisl.*, 1870, 81–2; for act granting right of suffrage, *Utah Acts Legisl.*, 1870, p. 8; *Utah Pamphlets, Polit.*, no. 14, 8; *Deseret News*, Feb. 16, 1870.

[6] At the municipal election held two days after the passage of the act only a few of the women voted, the first one being Seraph Young, a niece of the president. *Tullidge's Women*, 498.

HIST. UTAH. 42

Already the apostles had declared their intention of laying the settlements of Utah in ashes and leading their people in another exodus; but an effort was made to save them, and from a source somewhat unexpected. It was resolved by the leaders of the Godbeite faction that William Godbe should proceed to Washington and state to the president the true condition of affairs. "Mr Godbe," remarked the latter, after listening to his arguments, "I am as solicitous as you can possibly be to preserve the Mormon people;" and then he declared that he would save them from their leaders by checkmating their policy. During his visit Godbe also sought an interview with Cullom, and discussed with him the provisions of the bill, section by section, pleading his cause with such warmth and earnestness that all the animus of the congressman gave way, and the bill was not brought up for action in the senate. The substance of the policy recommended by the emissary of the liberal party in Utah was to establish over Utah a firm and efficient federal rule, rather than resort to special legislation or armed interference; and in these views the president heartily concurred.

J. Wilson Shaffer of Illinois, an old comrade of Rawlins, then secretary of war, was the man selected for the occasion, and on the resignation of Durkee, was appointed in his stead.[7] At this time Shaffer was suffering from an incurable disease, and knew that he had but a few months to live. Nevertheless he accepted office as a trust from the president. "Never after me," he declared, "shall it be said that Brigham Young is governor of Utah." On the 15th of September, 1870, the annual muster of the Nauvoo legion being then at hand, he issued a proclamation forbidding all musters, drills, or gatherings of the militia, and all gatherings of armed persons of what-

[7] The interregnum between Durkee's resignation and the arrival of Shaffer was filled by secretaries Edwin Higgins and S. A. Mann, to the latter of whom the women of Utah tendered their thanks for signing the female-suffrage bill. See *Deseret News*, March 2, 1870. For complimentary resolutions from legislature, see *Utah Jour. Legisl.*, 1870, 183.

ever description, except as a posse comitatus ordered forth by himself or by the United States marshal.[8]

After some correspondence with General Wells, the musters in the various districts were postponed until further notice, by command of the latter, though they had been regularly held for eighteen years, and returns duly made, in accordance with an act of congress approved in 1803. In 1870 the militia, which has never since been assembled, included about 13,000 men, most of them efficiently armed, drilled, and equipped, while the United States troops stationed at Camp Douglas, Camp Rawlins in Utah county, and elsewhere in the territory, numbered only a few hundred.[9]

The proclamation was ill-advised, and for what purpose it was issued, save as a puerile expression of the

[8] For copy of proclamation, see *Millennial Star*, xxxii. 668; *Smith's Rise, Progress, and Travels*, 63.

[9] In 1875 the U. S. government called for bids for the rebuilding of Camp Douglas, or as it is now termed, Fort Douglas. The contract was awarded to the Watson Brothers. For description of buildings, see *Surgeon-Gen. Circ. 8*, 1875, 332–46. In 1872 a military post was established near Beaver City. For reasons and descriptions, see *H. Ex. Doc.*, 42d Cong. 2d Sess., xv. 285; *Sen. Doc.*, 42d Cong. 2d Sess., i. 12. For list of military reservations in 1882, see *H. Ex. Doc.*, 47th Cong. 2d Sess., xviii. no. 45, p. 1181. For military organization for protection against Indians in Cache county in 1859–76, see *Tullidge's Mag.*, ii. 122–31. For Indian raid on Kanarra, Iron co., see *Utah Hand-book of References*, 81; for Indian depredations in 1870, *Utah Co. Sketches*, MS., 78–80; *S. F. Bulletin*, June 30, July 6, 8, 1870; for troubles in San Juan co. on account of miners' encroachments, *H. Ex. Doc.*, 43d Cong. 1st Sess., xii. pt 2, p. 193; *Ind. Aff. Rept*, 1872, p. 93; *Sacramento Union*, Oct. 1, 1872; *S. L. C. Tribune*, Sept. 14, 1872; *Deseret News*, Sept. 25, 1872. A brief report on the condition of Indians at this date, with statistics, will be found in *U. S. H. Com. Rept*, 42d Cong. 3d Sess., 365–72, 246–56, 325–6, 414–58. For remarks on the condition, management, and wants of Indians in 1872, see *Wheeler's Surveys, Progress Rept*, 1872; *H. Ex. Doc.*, 43d Cong. 1st Sess., xii. no. 157; for condition and treatment of Indians on reservation in 1873–4, *Sen. Doc.* 43d Cong. 1st Sess., no. 42; *Ind. Aff. Rept*, 1874, 3–4, 52–3, 104–79, 270–1, 276–7; for Indian uprising at Corinne in 1875, *S. F. Chronicle*, Aug. 2, 3, 12, 1875, Sept. 1, 2, 3, 4, 5, 7, 8, 9, 17, 1875; for cause, *Id.*, Sept. 6, 1875; for Indian outbreak in 1875, *S. F. Alta*, Aug. 11, 1875; *Chico (Butte) Record*, Sept. 4, 1875. Reports of agents on reservation Indians in 1876 –7 will be found in *H. Ex. Doc.*, 45th Cong. 2d Sess., viii. 550–60, 577–82. 642–62, 677–717. In 1878 congress paid to Ben Holladay $526,789 for property destroyed by Indians and losses sustained by change of mail-route. *Portland Oregonian*, June 21, 1878. For Indian troubles in 1879, see *Or. Deutsche Zeitung*, Oct. 25, 1879; in 1881, *Deseret News*, July 6, 1881; for information relating to Indian tribes and reservations in 1881–2, see *H. Ex. Doc.*, 47th Cong. 1st Sess., x. 327, 344. For acts concerning Indians in 1882, see *Utah Laws*, 1882, pp. 32, 40. In August 1884 Gov. Murray made a requisition for troops to protect citizens against Utes. *S. L. C. Tribune*, Aug. 14, 1884.

governor's authority, does not appear. The result, however, was most unfortunate; for the soldiery, among whom discipline appears to have been somewhat lax at this period, now supposed themselves masters of the situation. At midnight on the 23d of September a party of forty or fifty men from Camp Rawlins entered the town of Provo, armed with needle-guns, bayonets, and revolvers, and crazed with whiskey. Surrounding the residence of Alderman W. Miller, they fired several shots into his bedroom window, smashed in his doors, and dragged him from his chamber. Thence passing up Centre street, they tore down the sign and stove in the doors of the coöperative store, and then proceeded to the house of Councillor A. F. McDonald, which they completely demolished, scattering its contents on the sidewalk. After some further outrages, as parading defenceless citizens through the streets, beating them with rifles and pricking them with bayonets, yelling, meanwhile, as they passed along the thoroughfares, "Come out, you God damned Mormons and Mountain Meadows massacreers," they returned to camp.[10]

The only provocation for this disturbance appears to have been the fact that Miller refused to grant the soldiers, at their own terms, the use of a hall in which to hold a social gathering, and that the bishops had counselled the people of their wards, and especially the young women, not to hold intercourse with them. An effort was made to bring the offenders to justice, but, as during the administration of Governor Cumming, there was no harmony between the chief magistrate and the commander of the forces. After waiting several days for action to be taken by the military, Shaffer despatched to General De Trobriand, at Camp Douglas, a letter, in which he stated that if the soldiery could not be restrained, it were better for

---

[10] A despatch from A. O. Smoot, mayor of Provo, giving an account of the outrage, together with the depositions of the injured parties, will be found in the *Deseret News*, Sept. ?8, 1870.

the territory to be left to itself. To this the general replied that he was perfectly agreed; that it would be the best thing for all if the territory, its governor, legislature, municipalities, and militia, were left to themselves; and that if the troops had also been left alone, instead of being poisoned physically with bad whiskey and morally with bad influences, there would have been no trouble with them. Both letters were published in the *Deseret News*,[11] and of course drew forth much comment from the saints, who were probably of opinion that, if the soldiers had such proclivities, it was at least the business of their commanding officer to restrain them.

No further incident remains to be chronicled as to the career of Governor Shaffer, whose decease occurred in October 1870,[12] his successor being Vernon H. Vaughan,[13] a mild and conservative ruler, concerning whose brief administration there is nothing worthy of record.[14] To him succeeded George L. Woods, a Missourian by birth, a pronounced anti-Mormon, and one who, as a ferryman in Idaho,[15] and judge and politician in eastern Oregon, had accumulated and lost a considerable fortune. He was a man who, though by no means of the highest and purest morality himself, was, it seems, exceedingly jealous

[11] Of Oct. 5, 1870, and also in the *Deseret Evening News*, the publication of which will be mentioned later. De Trobriand states that, as there was no organization of military districts in the department of the Platte (which included Utah), the commanders of the several posts must communicate with the department headquarters, and that as soon as he received the requisite authority he proceeded to Provo and held an investigation. His letter is extremely insulting and indecorous.

[12] On the 24th of this month Wm H. McKay, with whom the governor had resided, and two others, robbed the U. S. mail about 100 miles south of S. L. City, in Juab co. They were captured the next day, and McKay was sentenced to five years' imprisonment. This was the first mail-coach robbery in Utah. *Smith's Rise, Progress, and Travels*, 64. For argument between J. P. Newman and Orson Pratt at the tabernacle on the polygamy question during the autumn of this year, see *Millennial Star*, xxxii. 599–604, passim.

[13] Shaffer's secretary, and about a month after his decease appointed governor. Geo. A. Black, secretary to Woods, was also acting governor in 1871. *Paul's Utah Incidents*, MS.; *Harrison's Crit. Notes on Utah*, MS.

[14] *Harrison's Crit. Notes on Utah*, MS., 32.

[15] At Lewiston, where he and his two partners made from $250 to $300 a day. *Woods' Recoll.*, MS., 3.

for the morality of the nation.   On the 10th of March, 1871, Woods took the oath of office, and about six weeks later arrived at Salt Lake City, James B. Mc-Kean of New York being appointed about this date chief justice, with C. M. Hawley of Illinois and O. F. Strickland of Michigan as associate judges.[16]

The administration of Governor Woods lasted for about four years, but during that period he sought no opportunity of making the acquaintance of Brigham Young.   When invited by the first councillor to call, as had been the custom with his predecessors,[17] he replied that the lowest subordinate in the United States ranked higher than any ecclesiastic on earth, and that he should not call until the president first called on him.   The reader may judge the chief magistrate by his own words.   "My first conflict with the church occurred," he says, "July 4, 1871.   The organic act of the territory made the governor com-mander-in-chief of the militia.   The Mormon legis-lature, prior to that time, usurped that authority, and invested it in Daniel H. Wells, the third in the church.   (They had a pantomime, in which B. Young played God the Father, Daniel H. Wells God the Son, and John H. Smith the Holy Ghost.)   That law was in force on my arrival.   On July 1, 1871, Wells issued an order as commander-in-chief to the militia of the territory to assemble at Salt Lake City July 4th to participate in the celebration.   I resented this usurpation, and forbade them to assemble, but my prohibition was disregarded.   Thereupon I or-dered to the rendezvous three companies of infantry, one of cavalry, and a battery of artillery, and dispersed them at the point of the bayonet.   This practically ended the Nauvoo legion.   Immediately thereafter,

---

[16] Chas C. Wilson succeeded Titus as chief justice. *Harrison's Crit. Notes on Utah*, MS. Geo. C. Bates, who in 1870 succeeded C. H. Hempstead, ap-pointed in 1868, was now district attorney.   For his argument in the Baker habeas corpus case on the jurisdiction of probate courts, see *Utah Pamphlets, Political*, no. 12.   A list of federal officials between 1851 and 1884 is given in *Utah Gazetteer*, 254–8.

[17] With the exception of Shaffer. *Woods' Recoll.*, MS., 45.

by concerted action of the federal officials, an effort was made to punish judicially the church criminals."[18]

The governor was ably seconded by the chief justice. In October Brigham Young, George Q. Cannon, and others were arrested for lascivious cohabitation. Motion made to quash the indictment was overruled by McKean; "for," he remarked, "while the case at bar is called the people versus Brigham Young, its other and real title is Federal Authority versus Polygamic Theocracy." In the indictment were sixteen counts, extending back to the year 1854, thus attempting to give an ex post facto interpretation to the act of 1862. The president's health was feeble at this time, and on the application of his attorney, a continuance was granted until the March term. One Thomas Hawkins, however, was convicted during this term, on the evidence of his first or legal wife, sentenced under this act to three years' imprisonment with hard labor, and fined $500. But the severest portion of the sentence was the homily. "Thomas Hawkins," commenced the chief justice, "I am sorry for you—very sorry. You may not think so now, but I shall try to make you think so by the mercy which I shall show you...The law gives me large discretion in passing sentence upon you. I might both fine and imprison you, or I might fine you only or imprison you only...It is right that you should be fined, among other reasons to help to defray the expense of enforcing the laws."[19]

Two or three days before sentence was passed on Hawkins, this being of course a test case, Daniel H. Wells and Hosea Stout were arrested on a charge of murder, Brigham Young, William H. Kimball, and others being indicted on a similar charge.[20] Wells

[18] *Id.*, 46–7.

[19] *Deseret News*, Nov. 1, 1871. For adverse comments of the press on the Hawkins case, see *Austin Reese River Reveillé, Carson Daily Register, Sacramento Reporter, Omaha Alta,* in *Millennial Star,* xxxiii. 764–5. In *Townsend's Mormon Trials* is an impartial account of McKean's anti-Mormon crusade.

[20] Wells and Stout were arrested for the murder of Rich. Yates, at the mouth of Echo cañon; Young, Kimball, Wm A. Hickman, O. P. Rockwell,

was admitted to bail,[21] Stout and Kimball were handed over to the authorities at Camp Douglas, and Brigham, hearing that his case was set for the 8th of January, 1872, immediately set out from southern Utah, where he was sojourning, and travelling over 350 miles of mountainous country in midwinter, delivered himself into custody. He was placed in charge of the marshal, bail being refused even in the sum of $500,000, and detained a prisoner in his own house, until discharged on the 25th of April, by Justice White, on a writ of habeas corpus.[22]

In sore disgust, the people of Utah adopted yet another constitution, which was forwarded to congress, together with a memorial for admission as a state, but without result.[23] A bill was passed appropriating $50,000 toward the expenses of the constitutional convention, but was vetoed by the governor, who gave, among other reasons, the open violation of the act of 1862, and the crimes committed against law and public decency in the name of religion.[24] So far, indeed, did the governor push his privilege, that he insisted even on nominating the territorial librarian and the superintendent of common schools.[25]

Meanwhile the condition of affairs in the superior courts of Utah was simply lamentable. During a

G. D. Grant, and Simon Dutton, for the murder of a man named Buck, at Warm Springs. *Woods' Recoll.*, MS., 47; *Millennial Star*, xxxiii. 744, 808–9.

[21] The prosecuting attorney asked that the bail be fixed at $500,000, but the judge said he would be satisfied with two sureties each of $50,000. *Deseret News*, Nov. 1, 1871.

[22] *Millennial Star*, xxxvii. 788–91. In the case of Clinton et al. vs Englebrecht et al., the judgment rendered for $60,000 against the municipal officers of S. L. City for suppressing an unlicensed liquor store was reversed by the supreme court. *Millennial Star*, xxxiv. 296. For grounds, see *Smith's Rise, Progress, and Travels*, 68–9. This decision annulled indictments against more than 120 persons.

[23] A copy of the memorial and constitution is contained in *Utah Pamphlets, Political,* no. 8. See also *Deseret News*, March 6, 1872; *House Misc. Doc.*, 42d Cong. 2d Sess., iii. no. 165. For counter-petitions, see *Id.*, iv. no. 208; *Sen. Misc. Doc.*, 42d Cong. 2d Sess., ii. no. 118.

[24] *Woods' Recoll.*, MS., 50; *Millennial Star*, xxxiv. 117–80; *Deseret News*, Jan. 31, 1872; *House Misc. Doc.*, 42d Cong. 2d Sess., iii. no. 155; *Utah Jour. Legisl.*, 1872, pp. 85–7. For resolution censuring veto, and in favor of convention and election of delegates, see *Id.*, 1872, pp. 104–5.

[25] *Utah Jour. Legisl.*, 1872, p. 36.

portion of McKean's term of office there were no funds wherewith to defray expenses, and the so-called administration of justice was openly burlesqued. In 1872 the removal of the chief justice was urged by the legislature.[26] This was not yet to be; but after some further judicial blunders,[27] he was finally superseded in March 1875 by David T. Lowe.[28]

For ten years William H. Hooper had been delegate to congress, and was in need of rest. He had done his duty faithfully; more acceptably, perhaps, to members of congress than any of his predecessors, and it was no easy task to fill his place. George Q. Cannon was the man selected, although an apostle and a practical polygamist. The election of Cannon was contested by George R. Maxwell, registrar of the land-office,[29] who in 1870 had received a few hundred votes, as against 26,000 in favor of Hooper; but in that year and again in 1874 had no well-grounded hope of success, save his reliance on popular prejudice. At the first session of the forty-third congress he prevailed on one of the members from New York to introduce a resolution embodying a number of charges against the apostle. The reading of his certificate was then demanded, in which it appeared that he had a majority of 20,000 votes, and thereupon he was admitted.[30]

[26] *Utah Jour. Legisl.*, 1872, p. 231.

[27] In his charge to the grand jury, October term, 1874, McKean, after quoting Montesquieu, 'I shall first examine the relation which laws have to the nature and principle of each government,' 'and if I can but once establish it, the laws will soon appear to flow from thence as from their source,' stigmatizes the Mormons in more vile and insulting phrase than had been used even by judges Brocchus and Drummond. See *Deseret News*, Oct. 14, 1874; *Millennial Star*, xxxiii. 550.

[28] *Harrison's Crit. Notes on Utah*, MS., 38. See, for opinions of press on McKean's removal, *Millennial Star*, xxxvii. 282–5; for message of the president on judicial administration in Utah, *Sen. Doc.*, 42d Cong. 3d Sess., no. 44; for act in relation to judiciary, *House Ex. Doc.*, 46th Cong. 3d Sess., xxvi. 997.

[29] Maxwell entered the union army when 17 years of age, and at 21 was a brigadier-general. During the war he had both legs broken, his right arm fractured, lost three fingers of his left hand by a sabre-cut, and had his collar-bone broken by grape-shot, besides receiving several flesh wounds. *Woods' Recollections*, MS., 39–40.

[30] For further particulars as to the Cannon-Maxwell contest, see *House Misc.*

The contest between Cannon and Maxwell was
sharp but decisive, a thorough canvass being made by
the latter, and its results showing how completely
the saints were in unison with their church leaders.
Many persons could have been found better qualified
than the apostle, notwithstanding his great ability,
but Brigham had so willed it.   At this election, if
we can believe the chief magistrate, freedom of speech
was first used in Utah, and by Governor Woods.
Here as on other occasions[31] he intermeddled, playing

Doc., 43d Cong. 1st Sess., no. 49; *House Com. Rept*, 43d Cong. 1st Sess.,
484; Argument of Halbert E. Paine, in *Utah Pamphlets, Political*, no. 13;
Millennial Star, 99–100, 104–6; *Paddock's La Tour*, 292; *S. L. C. Tribune*,
Nov. 30, 1872.   In 1867 Hooper's election was disputed by William McGrorty.
For papers in the case, see *House Misc. Doc.*, 40th Cong. 2d Sess., no. 35;
for comments, *Deseret News*, May 27, 1868.   At the opening of the 44th
congress Cannon's seat was also disputed by a man named Baskin.

   William H. Hooper was born at the old homestead known as Warwick
Manor, Eastern Shore, Md, in 1813, his father, who died during William's
infancy, being of English descent, and his mother of Scotch extraction.   When
14 years of age he obtained a position in a store; and from this beginning rose
step by step, until in 1836 we find him a member of a leading commercial firm
at Galena, Ill.   During the crash of 1838 the firm suspended, their debts,
amounting to $200,000, being afterward paid in full.   In 1850 he moved to
Salt Lake City under engagement to Messrs Holliday & Warner, commencing
business on his own account some four years later.   In 1856 he was temporarily appointed secretary of the territory after the death of Almon W. Babbitt, and in 1859, as we have seen, was chosen delegate for Utah at the 36th
congress, serving in the same capacity during the 39th, 40th, and 41st con-
gresses.   In 1868 Mr Hooper was appointed a director of Zion's Coöperative
Mercantile Institution, and in 1877 became its president, retaining that position until his decease at the close of 1882.   For further particulars, see *Tullidge's Mag.*, i. 369–85, 427–30; *Contributor*, iv. 184–6, suppl. 25–7; *Beadle's
Western Wilds*, 91–2; *Deseret News*, Feb. 8, 1860.   Hooper was an able
speaker, terse, to the point, and forensic.   'If,' he replied in answer to a memorial of the Salt Lake gentile lawyers, ' congress declined to enact a law
that would have enabled Chief Justice Chase to pick out a jury that should convict Jefferson Davis of treason, ought it now to enable Chief Justice McKean
to pick out a jury to convict Brigham Young of polygamy ?   It seems to me
that the law would be a greater offence against the spirit of democratic republican institutions than is the existence of the evil thus sought to be
reached.'
   [31] In consequence of the military riot above mentioned, the police were
instructed to arrest disorderly or drunken soldiers on slight provocation, and
fine them or put them to work in chain-gangs.   After protesting without
avail, Woods reported the matter to the war department, and thereupon
a general order was issued to the commanders of military posts, instructing
them not to allow the arrest of their men except for violation of the known
laws of the land.   Soon afterward a soldier was arrested on a trifling charge,
whereat, his release being refused, the governor proceeded to the jail with
Major Gordon and a detachment of troops, knocked out the wall with a bat-
tering-ram, and 'amid hurrahs for the American flag, set the prisoner free.'
Woods' Recoll., MS., 53–5.

the part rather of a sergeant of militia than of a ruler. A woman who appeared at the polls and offered her ballot was refused, and insisting on her privilege, was removed by the police, by order of Jeter Clinton, judge of election. Woods protested, whereupon Clinton threatened to arrest him, but after an unseemly altercation, the latt r, according to the governor's account, narrowly escaping being lynched by the gentiles, was dragged fainting by the chief magistrate into a gentile store, while the life of Woods was also threatened by the Mormons. The matter was settled without bloodshed.[32] What business the chief magistrate had at the polls he does not explain, though he closed the proceedings by a defiance of the Mormons and their threats, while illustrating what he considered freedom of speech in phrase which contained at least considerable freedom of language.

At the close of 1874 Woods retired from office,[33] his successor being S. B. Axtell of California, whose policy brought on him the censure of the gentile press, by which he was accused of complicity with the Mormon leaders in their political and other designs.[34] He was removed in June 1875, his successor being George B. Emery of Tennessee, who held office until January 1880. Emery's policy was strictly neutral,

---

[32] *Id.*, 55–9.

[33] See for the memorial presented by the gentiles, setting forth the immorality and despotism of the Mormons and the insecurity of life among the gentiles, *House Misc. Doc.*, 43d Cong. 1st Sess., no. 120; for opinion of various newspapers on the Mormon question, *Deseret News*, Jan. 17, 1872; for denial by gentile merchants of the disturbed condition of affairs, as alleged in various newspapers, *Id.*, May 8, 1872. In 1867, and again during the administration of Woods, it was proposed to annex Utah to Nevada without consulting much the wishes of either. For reports of committee of the senate of Nevada on the matter, see *Nev. Jour. Ass.*, 1867, 183–4, 195–7; *Nev. Jour. Sen.*, 1871, 160–2; *Millennial Star*, xxxiii. 161–2.

Samuel Paul, a native of Londonderry, Ireland, who served for four years as a volunteer during the war, and came to Utah in 1865, says that while the Mormons would render no assistance to the governor or his so-called ring, he was well treated in all the settlements which he visited. *Paul's Utah Incidents*, MS. For description of and comments on the political ring from a Mormon standpoint, see *Millennial Star*, xxxiv. 68–70; xxxvi. 120–2; for Vorhees' and Wheeler's bill, introduced April 1, 1872, 'to aid the enforcement of the laws of the territory of Utah,' see *Deseret News*, April 17, 1872.

[34] *Harrison's Crit. Notes on Utah*, MS., 32.

and therefore he was roundly abused by the gentile press.[35] It is worthy of note, however, that as
the Mormons were now for the first time left un-
disturbed, there was little which needs record in their
annals as a body politic,[36] except that from their midst
passed one whose place never could be filled. At
the obsequies of the great president who had cut the
cords of slavery, and being asked to banish its sister
institution, said "Let them alone," believing that in
time it would banish itself, none felt the nation's
loss more grievously than did the Mormons. And
now on the 29th of August, 1877, Brigham Young
was summoned to render his account at the great
tribunal before which all must appear.

Although for several years he had been in feeble
health, he was able to attend to his manifold duties
until six days before his death. Retiring at eleven
o'clock on the night of Thursday, the 23d of August,
after delivering an address before the bishops' meeting in the council-house, he was seized with an attack
of cholera-morbus, and suffered severely till the morning of the following Saturday, when he obtained a few
hours' sleep, opiates being administered to relieve the
pain caused by cramping of the muscles. During the
afternoon, however, inflammation of the bowels set in,
and throughout this and the following day he continued
to moan at intervals, though when asked whether he
was in pain he invariably replied, "No, I don't know
that I am." On Monday morning there were strong
symptoms of nervous prostration, among which was a
constant moving of the hands and twitching of the

[35] See *S. L. C. Tribune*, April 14, June 2, 1877.
[36] On the 22d of April, 1876, Dom Pedro, emperor of Brazil, visited Salt
Lake City on his way eastward; and on October 3, 1875, President Grant,
this being the first occasion on which a president of the United States set
foot in the territory. For account of these visits, and also those of General
Sheridan, Henri Rochefort, Jay Gould, and William Hepworth Dixon in
1874, James G. Blaine in 1873, generals Garfield and McClellan and the
Japanese embassy in 1872, see files of the *Deseret News; Utah Jour. Legisl.*,
1872; *Ventromiles' Tour*, 74–5; *Tullidge's Life of Young*, 441. Sheridan's
visit was mainly for the purpose of establishing another military post in Utah,
Provo being the point selected.

muscles. During all this time his only nourishment was a tablespoonful of milk and brandy, administered at brief intervals, in the proportion of one ounce of the latter to eight of the former. At 10 o'clock on Monday night he sank into a comatose condition, from which he was aroused with difficulty by stimulating injections, and early on the following morning he sank down on his bed apparently lifeless. Artificial respiration was resorted to, and hot poultices were placed over the heart to stimulate its action.[37] Thus his life was preserved for a few hours longer; but at five o'clock on the afternoon of the 29th of August, 1877, being then in his seventy-seventh year, he passed away quietly, surrounded by his family and intimate friends, the last rites of the church being administered by several of the apostles, to whom he responded in a clear and unfaltering voice, "Amen!"[38]

At eight o'clock on the morning of the 1st of September the remains of President Young, escorted by members of his own family, by members of the twelve, and by others of the priesthood, were conveyed to the tabernacle, the coffin being enclosed in a metallic case draped in white and wreathed with flowers. The funeral rites were appointed for noon on the following day, and during each hour of the interval a constant stream of visitors, numbering in all some twenty-five thousand, passed through the great aisle of the building, all being allowed to stop and gaze for a moment

[37] On the evening of Tuesday a consultation was held by his physicians, S. B. Young, W. F. Anderson, J. M. Benedict, and F. D. Benedict, and it was resolved to fill up the lower portion of the bowels by injection, for the purpose of causing an action through the alimentary canal; but this treatment was discontinued on account of fainting symptoms. The coma was attributed to the pressure of the swollen bowels, which checked the circulation to the heart and lungs. *Deseret Ev. News*, Aug. 31, 1877.

[38] Francis Dorr, who crossed the plains in 1850, and rendering assistance to the Mormon trains, was told by Brigham that he would ever be welcome to Salt Lake City, paid the Mormons a visit in 1877, and was kindly received by their prominent men. He is of opinion that Brigham's last illness was partly caused by fear of being arrested and tried for complicity in the Mountain Meadows massacre. *Dorr's Statement*, MS., 3. I find no confirmation of this theory, which is extremely improbable, in view of the evidence and the statements of the counsel for the prosecution at the Lee trial. See pp. 566-8, this vol.

on the features of him who had been to them for so
many years as their God on earth, their faithful guide
and counsellor.   Throughout the territory flags were
hung at half-mast, and civic and religious societies
united in rendering tribute to one who had gained
the respect and almost outlived the hatred of the civilized world.   It was indeed a day of mourning in
Israel, of grievous and heart-felt mourning, for to all
his followers he had been a friend and benefactor, so
far as they would accept his aid and receive his teachings.   From Europe, also, and from various portions
of the United States, came messages of condolence,
and in every quarter of the globe the death of Brigham Young excited more remark than would that of
a great monarch.

Throughout the entire day clouds lowered in heavy
masses over the city of the saints, and from them fell
light but frequent showers, as if in sympathy with
the multitudes that thronged the tabernacle; but on
the morning of the 2d the sun rose over a clear, unruffled sky, ushering in one of the calmest and brightest sabbaths that had ever been seen in Zion.   Long
before the hour appointed for the services, more than
thirty thousand persons were gathered in or around
the tabernacle, the aisles, the doorways, and every
inch of space being occupied.   The building was
tastefully decorated.   From the immense arch which
spans the interior depended strands and garlands of
flowers grouped in rich profusion, in their midst being
a massive floral centre-piece.   Under the entire gallery wreaths were festooned between the pillars with
baskets pendent, the front of the platform, the stands,
and the organ being draped in black.   The coffin,
constructed according to the late president's orders,[39]

[39] Nearly four years before his death, Brigham gave instructions as to his
funeral, and at the same time a number of elders gave orders as to their own
interment.   'I, Brigham Young, wish my funeral services to be conducted
after the following manner: When I breathe my last I wish my friends to put
my body in as clean and wholesome state as can conveniently be done, and
preserve the same for one, two, three, or four days, or as long as my body
can be preserved in a good condition.   I want my coffin made of plump 1¼-

decked with chaplets, but stripped of its case and drapery, stood on a plain catafalque in view of the congregation. On the president's stand were his councillors, John W. Young and Daniel H. Wells. The apostles, of whom ten were present, occupied their accustomed seats, the north side of the platform being set apart for the bishops and councillors of stakes, and the south front for the city council, the band, and glee club; while to the family of the deceased were allotted the seats immediately facing the stands, his four brothers being in front.

Precisely at noon the vast assemblage was called to order by George Q. Cannon, who, at the request of the president's family, presided over the ceremonies. First was sung by a choir of two hundred voices the hymn commencing:

"Hark from afar a funeral knell,"

to a tune composed for the obsequies of George A. Smith, whose decease occurred in 1875,[40] and now

inch redwood boards, not scrimped in length, but two inches longer than I would measure, and from two to three inches wider than is commonly made for a person of my breadth and size, and deep enough to place me on a little comfortable cotton bed, with a good suitable pillow for size and quality; my body dressed in my temple clothing, and laid nicely into my coffin, and the coffin to have the appearance that if I wanted to turn a little to the right or left I should have plenty of room to do so.' After giving instructions as to the services and place and method of interment, he concludes: 'I wish this to be read at the funeral; providing, that if I should die anywhere in the mountains, I desire the above directions respecting my place of burial to be observed; but if I should live to go back with the church to Jackson county, I wish to be buried there.' Address of Geo. Q. Cannon, in *Deseret News*, Aug. 31, 1877.

[40] George Albert Smith, cousin to the prophet on the father's side, his mother being descended from the Lymans of revolutionary fame, was born at Potsdam, N. Y., in 1817. In the spring of 1833 the family started for Kirtland, where they were heartily welcomed, and during the summer George was employed in quarrying and hauling rock, and other duties in connection with the building of the Kirtland temple. He was also one of those who went up to redeem Zion in Jackson co., Mo., returning three months later after travelling some 2,000 miles, most of the way on foot. Of his missionary labors mention has already been made. Ordained a member of the first quorum of seventies in 1835 and an apostle in 1839, he was one of the pioneer band at the exodus from Nauvoo, and almost until the day of his death took a prominent part in settling and redeeming the vales of Deseret. Elected member for Iron co. under the provisional state government, he was afterward appointed church historian, and represented the same constituency during several sessions of the territorial legislature. After the death of Heber C. Kimball in 1868, he was appointed first councillor to Brigham, having previously been elected president of the legislative council, which latter office he held during

used for the second time. Then followed prayer by
Franklin D. Richards, after which addresses were
delivered by Daniel H. Wells, Wilford Woodruff,
Erastus Snow, George Q. Cannon, and John Taylor.
A second funeral hymn was sung,[41] a benediction pronounced by Orson Hyde, the congregation was dismissed, and the remains of Brigham Young were
conveyed to their resting-place at his private cemetery
in the suburbs of the city, where thousands gathered
to witness the closing ceremonies.[42]

Some thirty years had now elapsed since the president of the church, stricken with mountain fever and
seeking for the remnant of his followers an abiding-
place, had stood enwrapped in vision on the Pisgah of
the west, and as he gazed for the first time on the
desert and dead sea that lay beneath, forecast the
future glory of Zion.[43] And who shall say that he
had not lived to see his vision realized ? During these
years, which compassed scarce the span of a single
generation, he had built cities and temples; he had
converted the waste lands of Deseret into gardens and
grain-fields; he had laid the basis of a system of manufactures and commerce that was already the envy
of older and more favored communities; he had sent
forth his missionaries to all the civilized countries of
the earth, and gathered the chosen of Israel from many
nations; he had rescued myriads from the sorest
depths of poverty, giving to all a livelihood, and to

six consecutive sessions.   For further particulars as to his life, character, and
abilities, see *Utah Jour. Legisl.*, 1876, pp. 65-8; *Richards' Narr.*, MS., 94;
Deseret News, Aug. 11, 18, 1858, June 16, Sept. 8, 1875; *S. L. C. Tribune*, Sept.
4, 11, 1875; *Tullidge's Life of Young*, suppl., 7, 13; *Townsend's Mormon Trials*,
47; *S. L. C. Contributor*, 1882, passim; *Codman's Round Trip*, 230-3; *Beadle's
Western Wilds*, 92-3 (with cut).   In 1860 the son of Geo. A. Smith was killed
by Navajos. *Deseret News*, Dec. 5, 1860.
   [41] Composed for the occasion by Charles W. Penrose.
   [42] In accordance with his father's instructions, a stone vault had been built
by John W. Young in the south-east corner of the cemetery.   It was of cut
stone, dowelled and bolted with steel and laid in cement.   The interior was
also cemented and whitened. *Deseret News*, Aug. 29, 1877, where is a full
description of the obsequies, afterward published in pamphlet form, and entitled *Death of President Brigham Young.*
   [43] See pp. 261-2, this vol.

the deserving and capable a competence. All this he had accomplished, beginning wellnigh without a dollar,[44] and in a region forsaken by mankind for its worthlessness, struggling at times almost hopelessly against the unkindliness of nature and the unkindliness of man.

Esteemed by his followers as an angel of light, and considered by his foes as a minister of evil, an impostor, a hypocrite, a murderer, he was in fact simply an enthusiast, a bigoted and egotistical enthusiast, as the world believes, but a practical and far-sighted man, one who by his will, ability, and intuitive knowledge of human nature was fitted to combat the difficulties that beset each step in his path of life, and to give cohesion to the heterogeneous elements of which his people was composed. "As I sat near his bed," remarked George Q. Cannon, "and thought of his death, if it should occur, I recoiled from the contemplation of the view. It seemed to me that he was indispensable. What could we do without him? He has been the brain, the eye, the ear, the mouth, and hand for the entire people of the Church of Jesus Christ of Latter-day Saints. From the greatest details connected with the organization of this church down to the smallest minutiæ connected with the work, he has left upon it the impress of his great mind."[45]

Not least among the traits in the character of Brigham was the faculty for accumulating wealth; and this he did, not, as his enemies have asserted, by

---

[44] He had about $50, then almost the only money in Utah.

[45] For sketches of the character, physique, and policy of Brigham Young, see, among others, *Hist. Brigham Young*, MS.; *Utah Early Records*, MS., passim; *Richards' Rem.*, MS., 15; *Richards' Narr.*, MS., 83–4; *Burton's City of the Saints*, 290–4, 300; *Hyde's Mormonism*, 137–8; *Tullidge's Life of Young*, 456–8; *Utah Pamphlets, Religious*, no. 3, p. 19; *Bowles' Across the Continent*, 86–7; *Mackay's The Mormons*, 286; *Stenhouse's Englishwoman*, 163–7; *Young's Wife No. 19*, 162–5; *Beadle's Life in Utah*, 265–7, 362; *Richardson's Beyond the Mississippi*, 352–3; *Rae's Westward by Rail*, 106–7; *Ludlow's Heart of the Continent*, 366–9, 371–3; *Rusling, Across America*, 177–8. Mention is made of these points in more detail on pp. 200–6, this vol. A history of Brigham Young is published in the *Deseret News*, commencing with the issue of Jan. 27, 1858, and continued in subsequent numbers.

foul means,[46] but by economy and close attention to
his business interests. Of all the business men in
Utah he was perhaps the most capable, but in the art
of making money he had no set system; merely the
ability for turning money to account and for taking
care of it. He purchased saw-mills and thrashing-
machines, for instance, and let them out on shares;
he supplied settlers and emigrants with grain and
provisions; from the lumber and firewood which he
sold to the troops at Camp Floyd he is supposed to
have netted some $200,000, and from other contracts
a much larger sum. By many he is accused of enriching himself from the appropriations of tithes, and
by plundering alike both saint and gentile, whereas
none paid his church dues more punctually or subscribed to charities more liberally than did the president. That with all his opportunities for making
money honestly and with safety he should put in
peril his opportunities and his high position by stoop-
ing to such fraud as was commonly practised among
United States officials of exalted rank, is a charge
that needs no comment.[47] He had a great advantage
in being able to command men and dictate measures,
but he did not rob the brethren, as many have asserted. At his decease the value of his estate was
estimated at $2,500,000,[48] though as trustee for the
church he controlled a much larger amount.

[46] Stenhouse, for instance, relates that in 1852 he balanced his account
with the church, amounting to $200,000, by directing his clerk to place this
sum to his credit for services rendered, and that in 1867 he discharged his
liabilities, amounting to $967,000, in a similar manner. *Rocky Mountain
Saints*, 665. Such statements are pure fiction.

[47] In the records of the internal revenue office at Washington his total
income for 1870 is stated at $25,500, in 1871 at $111,680, and in 1872 at
$39,952.

[48] It has been stated in several books and many newspaper paragraphs that
Brigham had large deposits in the Bank of England, the amount being placed
as high as $20,000,000. This is entirely untrue. Stenhouse, for instance,
says that a New York journalist who visited him in 1871 inquired as to this
report, the sum being then stated at $17,000,000. Brigham replied that he
had not a dollar outside of Utah, but that the church had some small amount
abroad for its use. The following extract from *Richards' Narr.*, MS., may
serve to explain the matter: 'The rumor that President Young ever had any
money in the Bank of England is entirely false. When I was in Liverpool I

Brigham was certainly a millionaire, but his fortune barely sufficed to provide for his family a moderate competence, for he had married twenty wives,[49] and unto him were born more than fifty children, of whom 16 boys and 29 girls survived him. In the body of his will the wives were divided into classes, and to each of them was given a homestead, the sum of $25, payable one month after his decease, and such amount payable in monthly instalments as in the opinion of his executors might be needed for their comfortable support.[50]

opened an account with the branch of the Bank of England in that city, but finding their charges too high, transferred it to the Royal Bank of Liverpool, where it remained between 1850 and 1867. On the failure of the bank I was fortunate enough to get my money. There was a time in our business when there was $20,000, or $30,000 to our credit. This money came from the profits on publications, and from the deposits of people who wished to emigrate. Donations were also remitted to us from Utah, and the company's fund was sustained by the emigration business.' Franklin D. Richards, the author of this manuscript, was nephew to Willard Richards, who, as will be remembered, was appointed secretary of the Perpetual Emigration Fund Company. See p. 415, this vol.

[49] In 1869, at which date the Boston board of trade visited S. L. City, Brigham said that he had 16 living and 4 deceased wives, and 49 surviving children. This was the first time that Mormon or gentile knew how many his family mustered. *Utah Notes*, MS., 1–2. In *Waite's The Mormon Prophet*, 191–214, is a burlesqued description of some of his wives, and of their treatment. *Wife No. 19, or the Story of a Life in Bondage, being a Complete Exposé of Mormonism, by Ann Eliza Young*, is, though the writer affects to be impartial, rather a discharge of venom by a woman scorned. She was of mature age when married, and if she had not then sense enough to understand the responsibilities she was assuming, one would think that, some years later, she ought at least to have had discretion enough to abstain from inflicting her book and lectures on the public. The most valuable part of the work, if it can be said to have any value, is the chapter on the case of Young vs Young, in which Judge McKean awarded to the plaintiff $500 a month as alimony, and committed defendant to jail for refusing to pay it. His decision was reversed by Judge Lowe.

[50] For copy of will, see *S. L. C. Tribune*, Aug. 19, 1883. It has been alleged that Brigham claimed to be a prophet. This he distinctly denied. In *Utah Notes*, MS., it is stated that the lame, halt, and blind flocked to him to be healed, and that he used great tact in dealing with them. One man who had lost a leg came to him to be made whole. Brigham said it should be as he wished; but those created with two legs would have two legs in heaven; hence, if he caused a new one to be framed, the man would have three for all eternity.

Patriarch and President John Young, brother to Brigham, died April 27, 1870. For biographical sketch, see *Deseret News*, May 4, 1870. The decease of Joseph A., Brigham's eldest son, occurred Aug. 10, 1875. For biography, see *Utah Jour. Legisl.*, 1876, pp. 206–8. On July 10th of this year died Martin Harris, one of the three witnesses to the authenticity of the book of Mormon. His age was 92. Among others whose decease occurred during the period to which this chapter refers may be mentioned Ezra Taft Benson, a native of Mendon, Mass., who worked on his father's farm until he was 16 years of age, afterward becoming hotel-keeper, and later proprietor of a cot ton-mill in the same state.   In 1839 we find him at Quincy, Ill., whither he had gone in search of a home, and where, during the following year, he was converted by the preaching of Orson Hyde and John E. Page.   In the autumn of 1840 he was ordained an elder, and in the summer of 1845 an apostle, most of the interval being passed in missionary work in the eastern states. In April 1847 he accompanied the pioneers, finally settling in the valley two years later.   After some further missionary work, he was appointed, in 1860, brigadier-general of militia in the Cache Valley district, where he lived until the date of his decease, Sept. 3, 1869, his death being probably caused by heart disease.   When the provisional government was established he repre- sented Salt Lake county in the legislature, and when Utah was made a terri- tory was chosen a member, first of the representatives for Salt Lake county, and for the last ten years of his life, of the council for Tooele county.   *Deseret News*, Sept. 8, 1869.   At his death joint resolutions were passed in the as- sembly as a tribute of respect, for which see *Utah Jour. Legisl.*, 1870, 185–6.

CHAPTER XXV.

CHURCH AND STATE.

1877-1885.

Many years before the death of Brigham Young it was predicted that whenever that event should hap- pen dissensions would occur among the Mormons, if not entire disintegration of the sect; for die when he would, or succeed him who might, such absolute power as he possessed would never be tolerated in another. He was elected at a time when his people were in distress, and accepting him as their deliverer, they had almost sunk their individuality, vesting him with all the powers of pope and potentate. But now, it was said, all was changed. Contact with the gen- tile world, the establishment of gentile schools and churches, together with other influences that had long been at work, were telling gradually upon their faith. Already they had grown weary of the yoke, and once Brigham was laid in the tomb, his followers would no longer exist as a people. Never was anticipation so ill-founded. The world was now to learn that the inherent vitality of Mormonism depended not on the existence of any one man or body of men, not even on the existence of the twelve. "If every apostle was slain but one," remarked George Q. Cannon at the October conference of 1877, "that one had the right and authority to organize the church, and ordain other apostles and a first presidency to build up the kingdom of God."

On the decease of the president of the church, there was for the second time in its history no quorum of the first presidency, to which authority, and to no other, as the prophet Joseph had declared, the twelve were subject. Once more, therefore, until the presidency was reorganized, the apostles must step forward and take its duties upon themselves.[1] At a meeting of the quorum, held two days after the obsequies of Brigham, ten of the number being present,[2] it was unanimously resolved that John Taylor, the senior apostle and acting president of the apostles, should be sustained in his office, and that the quorum should be the presiding authority of the church.[3] But this resolution, as well as the election of all the authorities of the church, from the twelve down to the deacons and teachers, must be indorsed by a vote of each quorum of the priesthood and of the people assembled in conference.

The forty-eighth semi-annual conference of the church was held, as was now the custom, in the great tabernacle;[4] and in addition to the general congregation, there were present more than five thousand of the priesthood. First was presented the name of John Taylor; then in their order and separately those of each member of the twelve, together with councillors John W. Young and Daniel H. Wells,[5] the

[1] At the conference above mentioned, George Q. Cannon remarked that some had been much exercised about the organization of a first presidency, 'but he wished them distinctly to understand that whenever God commanded a first presidency to be appointed it would not be revealed through any one but his servant, who was now God's mouthpiece.' *Deseret News*, Oct. 10, 1877.

[2] Apostles Orson Pratt and Joseph F. Smith were in England at the time. *Millennial Star*, xxxix. 682. They arrived two or three weeks later. See *Deseret News*, Oct. 10, 1877.

[3] General Epistle of the Twelve, in *Millennial Star*, xxxix. 680–4. See also *Deseret News*, September 12, 1877; *Mormon Pamphlets, Religious*, no. 16.

[4] Completed in 1870. A description of it is given elsewhere in this vol.

[5] Daniel H. Wells was a native of Oneida co., N. Y., his father, who was a direct descendant of the fourth governor of Connecticut, having served in the

patriarch of the church,[6] the presidents of the seventies, and other church dignitaries, concluding with the lesser priesthood. The votes were cast first by the twelve, then by the patriarchs, presidents of stakes, and high councils, after whom followed the high priests, the seventies, the elders, the bishops, with their councillors, the priests, deacons, and teachers,

war of 1812, while his mother, née Catherine Chapin, was the daughter of a revolutionary soldier who fought under Washington. In the spring of 1834, being then in his twentieth year, he settled at Commerce (Nauvoo), and purchased a tract of 80 acres, a portion of which he afterward donated to the Mormons as a site for their temple. He was among the foremost to aid and welcome the saints after their expulsion from Nauvoo, and indignation at their maltreatment, rather than sympathy with their sect, caused him to join the church a few weeks before the commencement of the exodus. Arriving in the valley of Great Salt Lake in September 1848, he was appointed superintendent of public works, and was chosen a member of the legislative council of the provisional state of Deseret. In 1857 he was elected second councillor to Brigham Young. In 1864-5 he was in charge of the European missions, and was afterward mayor of Salt Lake City for several terms. The part that he played in the history of Utah as lieut-gen. of the Nauvoo legion is mentioned elsewhere in these pages. *Wells' Narr.*, MS., 1–8; *Tullidge's Life of Brig. Young*, suppl. 13–17; *The Mormons at Home*, 114–15; *Beadle's Western Wilds*, 93.

[6] John Smith, son of Hyrum Smith, was a native of Kirtland, where he was born in 1832. Nearly two years after the assassination of his father in Carthage jail the boy set forth from Nauvoo in company with Heber C. Kimball's family. Reaching the encampment on the Little Papillon, he became acquainted with Col Thos L. Kane, whom he nursed through a dangerous sickness, probably saving his life. In April 1848 he started for Great Salt Lake in company with his brothers and sisters, and though only 15 years of age, performed a man's work, or rather the work of several men, driving a team composed of wild steers, cows, and oxen, with two wagons tied together, standing guard sometimes day and night, bringing in wood and water, herding cows, or assisting other teams as occasion needed. In the spring of 1850 he was enrolled in the battalion of life-guards, and for several years thereafter was frequently called on at dead of night to set forth in pursuit of marauding Indians. In 1852 occurred the decease of his step-mother, whereby he was left alone to provide for a family of eight persons, three of them being aged and infirm. In 1855 he was ordained patriarch, this being the only office in the church which is handed down from father to son in direct lineage. Ten years later he was sent on a mission to Scandinavia, and arriving in Liverpool with a single guinea in his pocket, about sufficient to procure him a meal and pay his railroad fare to London, borrowed the money for the remainder of his passage. After two years of missionary labor he returned to Salt Lake City, taking charge of a company of 300 emigrants on board the ship *Monarch of the Sea*. During his journey across the plains he had under his care a large party of Scandinavian emigrants, and was frequently urged by the officers at government posts which he passed en route to remain with them for a season, as the Indians were at that time extremely troublesome. His answer was: 'I am used to Indian warfare, and have only provisions enough to take us home if we keep moving. We had better run the risk of fighting Indians than starve on the plains.' After his return the patriarch was engaged in the duties of his calling and in attending to his business interests. *Autobiog. of John Smith*, MS.

and finally the entire congregation. During the proceedings there was no haste. Ample time was allowed
for objection to be made to any of the names proposed
or to any of the propositions offered; but throughout
this vast gathering there was not a dissenting vote.
As the quorums rose to their feet, and with uplifted
hand vowed to sustain those whom their leaders had
chosen, the choice was in every instance confirmed by
assembled Israel. It was evident that, as yet, the
church was in no danger of dissolution.[7]

Addressing the congregation, President Taylor remarked that the apostles were thankful for the confidence and faith that had been manifested. For several reasons he had said little since the death of the
president, who for thirty-three years had stood prominently before the church. In common with the rest
of the community, he felt sad at heart. Moreover, a
multiplicity of cares now devolved upon the twelve,
and, so far as his position was concerned, he did not
wish to say anything that might influence their
choice, but desired to leave the minds of all perfectly
unbiased. "If," he said, "we could carry out in our
lives what we have made manifest this day by our
votes, the kingdom of God would roll forth, and the
favor and blessing of God would rest upon us." "No
man need think this work would stop. It would go
on and increase until the purposes of Jehovah were
accomplished, and no power on earth or in hell could
stay its progress." Three years afterward[8] John Taylor was elected president of the Church of Jesus Christ
of Latter-day Saints, with George Q. Cannon and
Joseph F. Smith as councillors. The vacancies which
thus occurred in the quorum of the twelve were partially filled by the election of Francis M. Lyman[9] and

[7] For account of this conference, see *Deseret News*, Oct. 10, 17, 1877.
[8] At the general conference, commencing on the 6th of October, 1880.
[9] Francis Marion, the eldest son of Amasa Lyman, a pioneer, who was
excommunicated in 1870, was but seven years of age at the date of the exodus
from Nauvoo. As an instance of the experience of Mormon evangelists, it
may be mentioned that when ordered on mission to England in 1859, he was
compelled to leave his newly married wife almost destitute, building for her

John Henry Smith,[10] George Teasdale and Heber J. Grant being chosen to the apostolate on the death of Orson Pratt, which occurred in October 1881.[11]

with his own hands a log hut of green timber. In the spring of 1863 he settled at Fillmore, and there remained until 1877, when he was appointed president of the Tooele stake. In 1860 he was elected a member of the legislature, and on the death of Orson Pratt was appointed speaker of the house of representatives.

[10] The son of George A. Smith, and a native of Winter Quarters, where he was born Sept. 18, 1848. The first portion of his life was spent mainly at Provo, where he worked on a farm until 1874, when he was sent on a mission to Europe, returning the following year on account of the sickness of his father, whose decease occurred a few days after his arrival. In 1875, also, he was ordained bishop of the 17th ward at S. L. City, in which capacity he served until called to the apostolate. For six years he was a member of the city council, and in August 1881 was elected a member of the legislature, where he soon became one of the most prominent debaters.

[11] Orson Pratt, in 1881 the only surviving member of the first quorum of the twelve, was accounted one of the most eloquent preachers in the church; and for his championship of the cause, as a speaker and writer, was known as the Paul of Mormonism. At a general conference held in 1874 he was appointed church historian and recorder, retaining this position until his decease, and was also speaker of the legislative assembly. He was well versed in the sciences, including that of the pure mathematics, and in addition to several elementary works, published *A New and Easy Method of Solution of the Cubic and Biquadratic Equations*, and left in MS. a treatise on the differential calculus. *S. L. C. Contributor*, iii. 58-61. For resolutions of respect to his memory, see *Utah Jour. Legisl.*

George Teasdale, a native of London, and an episcopalian by training, joined the church in 1852 being then in his 21st year. After several years of missionary labor, during which he was appointed in 1858 to the pastoral care of three English conferences, and in 1859 to the charge of the Scottish mission, which comprised the Edinburgh, Glasgow, and Dundee conferences, he was ordered to set forth for Zion. Borrowing the necessary funds, he took a steerage passage for New York, and journeying over the plains from Florence, accompanied by his wife, a refined and delicate woman, arrived in Salt Lake City in 1861, and looked about him for something to do. He was offered the 20th ward school, a position which he at once accepted, laboring faithfully for nearly a twelvemonth, after which he accepted a position as manager of one of Brigham Young's stores, under the direction of Hyrum B. Clawson. In 1867 he was intrusted with the charge of the general tithing office, but the following year was ordered on a mission to England, in company with Albert Carrington, and, among other duties, filled that of sub-editor to the *Millennial Star*. Returning to Utah in 1869, he narrowly escaped death from a railroad accident, in which several persons were killed or fatally injured. After further labors as merchant, missionary, and contractor, being chosen meanwhile a high-priest, he was elected a member of the legislative council for the sessions of 1882 and 1884. In 1885, being then in his 56th year, he was still actively engaged in forwarding the interests of his church. *Autobiog. of Geo. Teasdale*, MS., passim.

Heber Jeddy Grant, the son of Jedediah M. Grant, whose decease occurred when the former was but nine days old, is a native of S. L. City, where he was born in 1856. At fifteen, the family being then in straitened circumstances, he obtained a position in an insurance office, and four years later started an agency for himself. Since that time he has been engaged in various enterprises, in all of which he has been successful, his income ranging from $3,000 to $8,000 a year, though in 1881 he met with a serious reverse

Says Mr Burton in 1861: "Austin Ward describes John Taylor as 'an old man, deformed and crippled,' and Mrs. Ferris as a 'heavy, dark colored, beetle-browed man.' Of course I could not recognize him from these descriptions—a stout, good-looking, some-what elderly personage, with a kindly gray eye, pleas-ant expression, and a forehead of the superior order."[12] When I was introduced to him in 1884, Mr Taylor being then in his seventy-seventh year, there stepped forward with a quick, decisive, nervous tread, greeting me with a smile and a cordial shake of the hand, a white-haired, benevolent-looking man of medium height and well-knit figure, long, oval face, gray, deep-set, penetrating eye, square, broad forehead, and firmly clasped lips, displaying a fixed determination, slightly tinged with melancholy, such as might be expected from one who had passed through many trying scenes, not the least among which was the escape, as by a miracle, from the tragedy of Carthage jail, and who knew that he had still many trials to undergo.[13]

Days of tribulation were indeed at hand. The saints, who for so many years had been buffeted, afflicted, tormented for opinion's sake, were again, after a brief respite, to be subjected to so-called chris-tian influence. The anti-polygamy law of 1862 was, as we have seen, inoperative, although declared con-

through the destruction by fire of the Utah vinegar-works at Ogden, of which he was proprietor. In 1884 he was a member of the legislature and of the S. L. City council. After being called to the apostolate, he travelled exten-sively, in the interest of the church, in Arizona, Idaho, Colorado, and New Mexico. Though still but 30 years of age and in feeble health, his average weight being only 145 lbs, while in stature he was considerably over six feet, Mr Grant affords a striking example of the energy displayed by the descend-ants of the Mormon patriarchs. *Autobiog. of Heber J. Grant,* MS.

[12] *City of the Saints,* 328.

[13] Descriptions of President Taylor's appearance will be found in many of the books written on Mormonism, some of them fair and accurate, as is Bur-ton's, and others varying in degrees of absurdity from that of Lady Duffus-Hardy, who speaks of him as a man 'with a rather large, loose mouth, and cunning gray eyes, which look as though they would never let you see what was going on behind them,' down to the one given by a correspondent of the *New York Sun,* who in 1879 stated that he was six feet high, and that his appearance, manner, and speech were those of a member of the British parlia-ment. See *Duffus-Hardy's Through Cities and Prairie Lands,* 117; *Deseret News,* Nov. 12, 1879.

stitutional by the supreme court of the United States. Under the Poland bill only one conviction was made, that of George Reynolds, private secretary to Brigham, the man being sentenced to fine and imprisonment.[14] Both these measures were sufficiently ill-advised, and rank, perhaps, among the clumsiest specimens of legislation as yet devised by man; but it remained for the Edmunds bill to cap the climax of absurdity by virtually setting aside the statute of limitations, and providing for the punishment of persons living at any time with other than their legal wives.

By the provisions of this bill, approved March 22, 1882, and of which brief mention has already been made,[15] polygamists were made liable to punishment by fine not exceeding $500 and imprisonment not exceeding five years, the president being authorized to grant amnesty on such conditions as he saw fit to those who might have offended before the passage of the act, provided the conditions were afterward complied with. Cohabitation with more than one woman in any territory of the United States, whether in the marriage relation or otherwise, was declared a misdemeanor, punishable by a fine of not more than $300, or by imprisonment for not more than six months, or by both, at the discretion of the court. In all prosecutions for bigamy, polygamy, or unlawful cohabitation—the three offenses being classed together, though differing widely in law—it was to be deemed sufficient cause for challenge that a juryman lived or had ever lived in these practices, or believed it right for one so to live. No polygamist was to be entitled to vote at

---

[14] He was indicted and convicted at S. L. City in 1874. An appeal was taken to the supreme court of Utah, and the case dismissed on the ground that the grand jury had been illegally constituted. In October 1875 he was again indicted, convicted, and sentenced to two years' imprisonment and fine of $500. After a long but useless struggle, the case being argued before the supreme court by the attorney-general for the prosecution, and by Sheeks & Rawlins of S. L. City for appellant, Reynolds was finally committed to jail in Jan. 1879. For review of the decision of the supreme court by George Q. Cannon, see *Utah Pamphlets, Political*, no. 19.

[15] See p. 395, this volume.

any election, or to hold any position of public trust, honor, or emolument.

All the registration and election offices throughout the territory were declared vacant, and all duties relating to the registration of voters, the conduct of elections, the receiving, rejection, canvassing, and return of votes, and the issuing of certificates, were to be performed by persons selected by a board of five commissioners, of whom three might belong to the same political party.[16] After scrutiny by the board of the returns of all votes for members of the legislative assembly, certificates were to be issued to those who had been legally elected, and on or after the first meeting of an assembly, the members of which had been so elected, that body might make such laws as it saw fit concerning the offices declared vacant, provided they were not inconsistent with the organic act and with the laws of the United States.[17]

The Edmunds act, intended to be supplementary to the act of 1862 and to the Poland bill, is virtually a penal statute, as indicated by its title, "A bill to amend section 5352 of the revised statutes of the United States, in reference to bigamy, and for other purposes." It is also an ex post facto law, a bill of pains and penalties, wherein the judicial function, after being misinterpreted, is usurped by the legislature and the executive—one that might not have

[16] The secretary of the territory was to be the secretary of the board, keep a journal of its proceedings, and attest its action.

[17] For copy of the Edmunds act, see *United States Statutes*, 47th Cong. 1st Sess., 30–2; *Utah Commission*, 1–5; *S. F. Call*, Feb. 17, 1882. As soon as its passage became known in Utah, petitions asking congress to send a deputation to investigate matters before enforcing hostile legislation were signed by 75,000 persons, some refusing to sign the petition, among them Fred. H. and Sam. H. Auerbach, who, though declining merely on the ground that they did not wish to interfere with politics, suffered in consequence. On the other hand, a mass-meeting called by the anti-polygamy society was held at the methodist church, among the speakers being Gov. Murray and Judge Boreman. For resolutions, see *Hand-Book of Mormonism*, 87. For principles adopted by the liberal party at their convention in October 1882, see *Important Doc. Bearing on Polit. Quest. in Utah*, 10–13; for declaration of principles by people's party, *Id.*, 7–9. The speeches of Vest, Morgan, Call, Brown, Pendleton, and Lamar against the bill during the final debate in the senate were afterward published in the form of a pamphlet entitled *Defence of the Constitutional and Religious Rights of the People of Utah*.

been amiss in the days of the star-chamber, but is directly at variance with the spirit and letter of the American constitution; and the more so when we consider that the Mormons, driven by persecution out of the United States, settled in what was then no portion of the territory of the United States, though aiding in the conquest and settlement of that territory, as did the colonists of Rhode Island, in 1636, when they fled from the sectional intolerance of Massachusetts.

But not only were the Mormons to be judged as criminals by an ex post facto law—one that barred the statute of limitations, and if strictly enforced would bring within its pale no inconsiderable portion of the adult male population of the United States— they were also to be stripped of the franchise, and made ineligible for office. It was argued in the senate that this was no penalty, and it may be admitted that, as a rule, to deprive men of the suffrage, and disqualify them for office, is not a severe punishment; but in Utah, where at least five hundred lucrative positions would have been laid open to a hungry horde of gentile office-seekers, the suffrage was worth more than houses and lands, for by the ballot alone could be held in check the greed of demagogues, who sought the control of the territory as a field for plunder and oppression. The bill virtually proposed to disfranchise a people, and to govern them by a committee of five men, or at least to create a government by a minority over a large majority; for it was not to be expected that these five men, of whom a quorum belonged to the same political faction, would decide impartially on the electoral qualifications of the people. It was so expressed, and its measures were indorsed by the congress and president of the United States, the question being not whether congress had power to repeal any or all of the laws in each of the territories, and intrust the legislative, executive, and judicial functions to whomsoever it pleased—this was not disputed—but whether it was at liberty to violate for any purpose the rights guaranteed in the constitution.

If there be anything sacred in the American constitution, or in the annals of American jurisprudence, it is that in criminal prosecutions the accused should be tried by an impartial, and not by a packed, jury— by men opposed to him through interest or prejudice, and on whom a religious test is imposed as a qualification. Under the Poland bill it was ordered that grand and petit juries should, if possible, be composed in equal proportions of Mormons and gentiles, or non-Mormons. The latter included, in 1874, about twenty-two per cent of the entire population, and as this measure gave to them the same representation in juries as was allowed to the remaining seventy-eight per cent, its injustice is sufficiently apparent. But under the Edmunds act juries might be composed entirely of gentiles, thus giving to twenty-two, or at that date perhaps twenty-five, per cent of the population the control of the entire criminal proceedings in Utah, although more than seven eighths of the arrests made in the territory were among gentile citizens.[18]

Before striving to regenerate the Mormons, it would seem that congress should have attempted the regeneration of the gentile portion of the population of Utah. At the time when the Edmunds bill was passed, all the keepers of brothels, and nearly all the gamesters and saloon-keepers, were gentiles. Two hundred out of the two hundred and fifty towns and villages in the territory contained not a single bagnio.[19] Until gentiles settled in Salt Lake City there were seldom heard in its streets or dwellings oaths, imprecations, or expletives; there were no place-hunters or beggar-politicians; there was no harlotry;

[18] For criminal statistics, taken mainly from the census of 1880, see p. 394, this vol.

[19] *Utah and its People*, 21. Of the gamblers 98 per cent were gentiles, and of the saloon-keepers 94 per cent.

and there was neither political nor judicial prostitution. The Mormons were a people singularly free from vice —unless that can be called a vice which forms part of the tenets of their church—and they were one of the most industrious, sober, and thrifty communities in the world.

Partly with a view to avoid the operation of the Edmunds act, the Mormons once more asked that Utah be admitted as a state. Seventy-two delegates from the different counties met at Salt Lake City, and during a nine days' session drew up a constitution,[20] which was duly presented by Delegate John T. Caine, but with the usual result; and now the Mormons were left to the tender mercies of the commission. The members[21] went to work vigorously; between 1882 and 1884 some twelve thousand persons were disfranchised,[22] and at the latter date all the municipal and other officers in the territory living in polygamy or unlawful cohabitation were superseded, each elector being also required to swear that he was not so living. It would be a curious subject for speculation to estimate how many voters would be disqualified if the law against illicit cohabitation were enforced in other portions of the United States.

The commission was seconded by Governor Eli H. Murray, who succeeded Emery, arriving in Salt Lake

---

[20] For copy, see *Constit. State of Utah.* Its provisions were directed mainly against the Edmunds bill.

[21] Their names were Alex. Ramsey of Minnesota, Algernon S. Paddock of Nebraska, G. F. Godfrey of Iowa, Ambrose B. Carleton of Indiana, and James R. Pettigrew of Arkansas. For brief biographical sketches of these men, see *Contrib.*, iii. 315–16.

[22] *Special Rept Utah Commission*, 1884, p. 18. In *Barclay's Mormonism Exposed*, 18, the number is erroneously given at 16,000. *Mormonism Exposed, The Other Side, an English View of the Case, by James W. Barclay,* is a pamphlet originally published in the *Nineteenth Century Magazine,* and containing a brief and impartial statement of affairs. Mr Barclay was a member of the British parliament. Though, as he admits, he went to Utah with strong prejudices, he comes to this conclusion: 'Mormonism, apart from polygamy, which seems to me a temporary excrescence, will, in my opinion, grow, and probably be the religion of the settlers or farming classes in the mountainous country between the great plains east of the Rocky Mountains and California on the west.'

City on the 28th of February, 1880, and in 1884 was
again appointed. His message for 1882 was in the
mood of former governors of Utah. "In no sense,
even in the slightest degree," he remarked, "is the
sovereignty of church over state in unison with the
language or spirit of the constitution, or your country's
laws. That political power is wielded by church
authority throughout Utah is a fact; that officers of
the church exercise authority in temporal affairs is a
fact; that the sovereignty of the church is supreme,
and its practices followed, the laws and courts of the
United States to the contrary, is a fact.   These being
true in whole or in part, I submit: Do you believe
that the government of the United States, with all
its humanity, will much longer forbear to assert its
authority in support of its absolute and undoubted
sovereignty? Abiding peace, so much needed, and
abundant prosperity, with its attendant blessings, can
never belong to the good people of Utah until the
symbol of the United States is universally regarded
as the symbol of absolute sovereignty." Touching
the matter of tithing, he said: "The poor man who
earns a dollar by the sweat of his brow is entitled
to that dollar.   It is the reward of honest toil, and he
should be protected in the full enjoyment of it.   Any
exaction or undue influence to dispossess him of any
part of it, in any other manner than in payment of a
legal obligation, is oppression."[23] One would think
that after two years' residence in Utah the governor
ought to have learned at least that, among the saints,
the payment of tithes is an optional matter.

Among the first important acts of Governor Murray was to grant to Allan G. Campbell a certificate
of election as delegate to congress, although he received only 1,350 votes as against 18,568 polled for
George Q. Cannon,[24] and to declare that the latter

[23] The governor's messages for each year will be found in *Utah Jour.
Legisl.*, and of late years have been printed in pamphlet form. See also the
files of the *Deseret News*, and other Utah journals.

[24] *Barclay's Mormonism Exposed*, 18–19. The certificate was rejected by

was not a citizen of the United States,[25] notwithstanding that he held a certificate of citizenship.   Thus the chief magistrate took upon himself a function alto-

congress.   For papers in the case, see *House Misc. Doc.*, 47th Cong. 1st Sess., no. 25.   The seat was declared vacant, and in 1882 John T. Caine was elected. In 1884 he was reëlected.   Mr Caine was a native of Kirk Patrick, in the Isle of Man, where he was born in 1829.   Arriving in New York in 1846, not as a proselyte, but as an emigrant, he joined the church in the spring of 1847, about the time when the pioneers set forth from Council Bluffs.   In September 1852 he reached Salt Lake City, and found occupation as a school-teacher at Big Cottonwood.   Soon afterward he was employed in the office of the trustee in trust, and in that capacity won the confidence of Brigham Young. Sent on a mission to the Sandwich Islands in 1854, he was appointed after his return assistant secretary of the legislative council.   In 1874 he was elected a member of that body, being reëlected for the three ensuing terms.   *Tullidge's Mag.*, ii. 468–73.

For laws regulating elections, see *Utah Election Laws*, 1878, 1882.   In 1884 the Utah legislature consisted of 12 counsellors and 24 representatives, elected biennially on the first Monday in August of every odd year, the sessions commencing on the second Monday in January of every even year, and lasting for not more than 60 days.   For list of members elected in 1883, see *Utah Gazetteer*, 1884, p. 268.   In 1878 a criminal procedure act was passed, and in 1870 a civil practice act, the text of which is given in *Utah Laws*, 1878, 60–165; *Utah Acts Legisl.*, 17–124.   For further acts, proceedings, and memorials of the Utah legislature, see *Utah Laws* and *Utah Acts Legisl.*, 1870, pp. 11–12, 133, 146, 148; 1872, 25–6, 41–2; 1878, 27–37, 169–70; 1880, 45, 95–6; 1882, 106, passim; *Utah Jour. Legisl.*, 1872, pp. 23–4, 1876, 24–5, 31, 104–5; 1878, 36, 45–6, 225–6, 339, passim.

[25] *S. F. Call*, Jan. 9, 1881.   As the reader is probably aware, the Edmunds act was declared constitutional by the supreme court of the United States. For decision, see *S. F. Call*, March 24, 1885.   For arguments against the act, see, among others, the speech of Gen. Jos. E. Brown of Georgia, Jan. 11, 1884, in *Cong. Globe*; *Utah Defence Constit. and Religious Rights; Stillman's The Mormon Question; Barclay's Mormonism Exposed; Utah and its People* (by an ex-U. S. official); *Goodrich's Mormonism Unveiled; Black's Federal Jurisdiction in the Territories.*   Senator Brown's argument is very forcible, though perhaps a little strained.   Quoting the clause in the constitution, which reads, 'Nor shall any person be deprived of life, liberty, or property without due process of law,' he cites *Blackstone's Comm.*, 36, 'Offices which are a right to exercise a public or private employment, and to take the fees and emoluments thereto belonging, are also incorporeal hereditaments,' etc.   So the chief justice in 2 Ala., N. S., p. 31, remarks, 'An office is as much a species of property as anything else capable of being held or owned.'   Comparing other provisions of the act with the U. S. constitution, he quotes Judge Strong in the case of Huber vs Reily, in *Smith's Pennsylvania Repts*, iii. 117.   'There are, it is true, many things which they [judges of election] may determine, such as age and residence of a person offering to vote, whether he has paid taxes.' 'But whether he has been guilty of a criminal offence, and as a consequence forfeited his right, is an inquiry of a different character.   Neither our constitution nor our law has conferred upon the judges of elections any such judicial functions.'   Thus with other features of the bill.   As the senator remarks, 'There are probably twenty times as many persons practicing prostitution, or illegal sexual intercourse, in the other parts of the union as the whole number who practice it in Utah.'   For arrests, prosecutions, and convictions under the Edmunds act, and cases of persons committed for contempt for refusing to answer questions under Chief Justice Zane's ruling, see *S. L. C. Tribune*, Nov. 4, 7, 1884; *S. F. Alta*, Oct. 4, 8, 1884; Jan. 25, Apr. 14, 1885; *S. F. Chronicle*, Jan. 31, Apr. 30, May 10, 23, 1885; *S. F. Call*, Nov. 8, May 23,

gether outside the intent of the national legislature as expressed in the Edmunds act, which was at best but a temporary and ill-judged measure, and one that in the opinion of some of the ablest lawyers in the United States was unconstitutional.

Not content with this puerile display of authority, the governor, at the conclusion of what he terms "the faithful labors of the commissioners appointed under the Edmunds act," recommended that the legislature be abolished, and that Utah be placed entirely under control of a commission to be selected by the president, not as was done with the territory of Louisiana and the District of Columbia, but to reduce its inhabitants to the condition of serfs; "for," he remarks, "I confidently believe that from such action by congress and a council composed of men loyal to the constitution and the laws, there would come that adjustment of wrongs and termination of contentions so earnestly prayed for by those in Utah who possess the intelligence and one third of the wealth of the territory."[26] To the Mormons, as it would seem, he denied the attribute of intelligence; and by such rulers, with scarce an exception, has this people been misgoverned—a people which to impartial observers has been subjected to abuse, calumny, and persecution such as are almost without parallel, even in their Hebrew prototype.

1884, May 11, 26, 1885; *S. F. Bulletin*, Apr. 21, 1885; *Sacramento Rec.-Union*, Apr. 25, May 23, Oct. 7, 1884; Jan. 21, 22, 30, Feb. 6, 9, 11, March 13, 16, Apr. 27, 28, 30, May 1, 12, 14, 15, 20, 21, 22, 29, 30, June 4, 29, 1885. For prosecutions in Arizona, see *Id.*, Sept. 29, Nov. 28, 1884; Apr. 8, 13, 1885. At Paris, Id., polygamists resisted arrest. *Id.*, May 12, 15, 21, 1885. In 1880 further alterations were made in the first and third judicial districts, for which, see *Utah Laws*, 1880, pp. 67–8.

[26] *S. L. City Tribune*, Nov. 28, 1883. The governor's policy was indorsed by President Arthur, and of course by the gentile community of Utah. See *Id.*, Dec. 23, 1883.

CHAPTER XXVI.

SETTLEMENTS, SOCIETY, AND EDUCATION.

1862–1886.

IN all the stages of her existence, Utah has been constantly expanding, her growth, far from depleting her resources, only adding to her strength. Originally one of the most barren spots on the face of nature, with nothing to attract even attention, the land has become as fruitful a field, and her people as busy a commonwealth, as can be found, with few exceptions, elsewhere on the Pacific slope. With her unkindly soil, her extremes of temperature, the thermometer varying between 110° above and 20° below zero,[1] her slight and uncertain rainfall, without foliage, except such as was found here and there in narrow, rock-ribbed gorges, with fuel almost inaccessible at points where habitation was possible, with no nearer sources of general supply than the small and scattered communities on the Pacific coast, and with all sources of supply often practically cut off—amid this forbidding and

---

[1] On Feb. 5, 1849, the mercury stood at 33° below zero at S. L. City. The mean temperature for 19 years was 51° 9′, and the highest 104° in 1871. For meteorological tables, see *Meteor Reg.*, passim; *Surgeon-Gen. Circ. 8*, 1875, pp. 339–40, 345; *Wheeler's Surveys*, ii. 535 et seq.

inhospitable region, the Mormons built up their settlements, which, nevertheless, grew with a steady and stalwart growth. As year followed year, the magic wand of progress touched into life these barren and sand-girt solitudes, and in their place sprang up a country teeming with the wealth of gardens and granaries, of mines and mills, of farms and factories. To show how this has been accomplished, and more especially to explain the industrial and social condition of the people during the first years of the present decade, will be my task in the concluding chapters of this volume.

At the close of 1883 the population of Utah was estimated at 178,121, of whom 92,081 were males, 86,040 females, 123,506 of native and 54,615 of foreign birth.[2] In 1880 there were 14,550 persons employed in agriculture, 4,149 in trade, and 10,212 miners, mechanics, and factory operatives; though notwithstanding the industrial activity of the settlers, the percentage of bread-winners was smaller than in any state or territory of the union with the exception of West Virginia, this fact being due mainly to the large proportion of women and young children. A noteworthy feature in the community was the small amount of debt, crime, and pauperism, the entire public debt, city, county, and territorial, being in 1879 only $116,251, and the number of criminals and paupers being, as elsewhere noticed, much below the average throughout the United States.[3] The death-rate for a series of years averaged about sixteen per thousand, though for 1880 it was somewhat higher on account of the prevalence of diphtheria.[4]

---

[2] *Utah Gazetteer*, 1884, p. 300, where the population is given by counties. In the census report for 1880 the total population is given at 143,963, nearly 20,000 of the foreigners being English, and about 8,000 Scandinavians.

[3] In 1879 there were 33 paupers and 60 criminals. The number of prisoners at the Utah penitentiary for each year, with various statistics, will be found in the reports of the warden and directors in *Utah Jour. Legisl.*, passim. In later years we hear little of such outrages as were alleged to have been committed about the time of the Utah war.

[4] In 1877-8 diphtheria was also common. See *Utah Sketches*, MS., 27. *Description of Huntsville*, MS., 6. For mortality in S. L. City between 1870

Of the progress of settlement up to the close of 1862 mention has already been made.[5] At that date nearly all the available land in Utah had been taken up, and in 1883 colonies had been pushed forward into adjoining territories, until they extended from north to south in an unbroken line of about 1,000 miles, all of them under the religious and political control of the Mormon priesthood.[6]

and 1878, see *Deseret News*, Jan. 8, 1879. In 1870 there were 281 deaths in S. L. City, in 1878, 497, the latter being the largest number recorded during the interval. The principal hospitals at S. L. City were the Deseret, Holy Cross, and St Mark's, the last two being mainly supported by the contributions of miners, who are entitled to its benefits. It was not until 1880 that a territorial insane asylum was established, though one was projected in 1869. See *Utah Laws*, 1880, 57–65; *Utah Jour. Legisl.*, 1869, 124–5; and for grand jury report on asylum, which is built on a high bluff of the Wasatch near Provo, *S. L. C. Tribune*, Nov. 22, 1884.

[5] See caps. xiii. and xxii., this vol.

[6] In 1880 there were, according to the census report, 3,205 Mormons in Idaho, 1,338 in Arizona, 800 in Nevada, 234 in Washington Terr., and 241 in Colorado. There were also 1,131 in California, 451 in Wyoming, 554 in Montana, 394 in Iowa, 208 in Nebraska, and 260 in New York. These are probably below the actual figures at that date, and certainly much below the figures for 1885. The Bannack stake, in the Snake River country, Idaho, alone contained, for instance, on January 31, 1885, 1,770 souls, being divided into eight wards —Louisville, Menan, Lyman, Rexburg, Teton, Wilford, Parker, and Salem. The first Mormon who visited the Snake River country with a view to settlement was John R. Poole of Ogden, who went there in Feb. 1879, and on his return reported favorably to Franklin D. Richards. The first family to settle there was that of Jos. C. Fisher, who in March 1879 located at Cedar Buttes Island, being joined soon afterward by Poole and others. *Ricks, Bannack Stake*, MS., passim. For account of Mormons in Oneida co., see *Silver City Avalanche*, Sept. 17, 1870, March 27, 1875; in Bear Lake Valley, *Boisé City Statesman*, Oct. 16, 1879; for agitation on the polygamy question in Idaho, *Id.*, Sept. 3, 1870, Dec. 6, 19, 1879; *Ogden Freeman*, Feb. 28, 1879. The first attempt to settle the country bordering on the Little Colorado in Arizona was made in 1873, but the party returned, discouraged by the forbidding aspect of the place. Some three years later missionaries were ordered to make permanent settlements in this region, and at a meeting held at Salt Lake City in January 1876, companies were organized and captains appointed for this purpose. The first teams arrived at the Sunset crossing of the Little Colorado on the 23d of March, and after the brethren had explored the neighborhood, W. C. Allen and his company resolved to form a settlement about 20 miles to the south-east of the crossing, to be named after the captain; Geo. Lake and his band settled on the opposite side of the river, two miles to the south-west of Allen, on a spot which they called Obed, near which were springs and meadow-land; Lot Smith and his company formed a colony three miles north-east of the crossing, at a place which was called Sunset, and Jesse O. Ballinger, with his party, settled about four miles north of the crossing on the west side of the river, the settlement being named Ballinger. The brethren proceeded to plough, construct dams, and put in crops, but encountered many difficulties, the river-bottom being treacherous and full of quicksands. At Obed chills and fever prevailed, the settlers being forced to abandon the place and join the other colonies. In November 1877 a number of proselytes arrived from the southern states in a destitute condition; but

As Paris is said to be France, so it has been said of
Salt Lake City that it is Utah, for there the com-

though all the camps were scantily supplied, their wants were at once relieved.
During this season sufficient grain had been raised to last with economy until
the following harvest, and meanwhile other settlements had been started, one
25 miles up the river from Allen, to which was given the name of Woodruff, and one 50 miles south of Woodruff, which was called Forest Dale, the
name Ballinger being now changed to Brigham City, and Allen to St Joseph.
In this year, also, the colonies of eastern Arizona were divided into two presi-
dencies, those on the Little Colorado being west of the dividing line.   According to a stake report, dated Aug. 31, 1878, there were at Sunset 114 souls, at
Brigham City 230, at St Joseph and Woodruff each 67, and including other
small settlements, a total of 587.   The harvest of 1878 was severely damaged
by floods, but that of 1879 was a bountiful one.   In 1880 the crops again suffered from excessive rains and freshets. *Settlements on the Little Colorado.*
MS.   The St Joseph stake at Pima, Ar., was organized in Feb. 1883, the
place being first settled in 1879 by families from eastern Arizona.   St David
was founded in 1878, Philemon C. Merrill being the first settler; Curtis in
1881 by the Curtis family; Graham, so named from the peak a few miles to
the south, in 1881; Thatcher, named after Apostle Moses Thatcher, in 1882,
by John M. Moody; Central, in the same year, by Joseph Cluff and others;
McDonald, named in honor of A. F. McDonald, president of the Maricopa
stake, by Henry J. Horne and others; Layton, named after President C.
Layton, by John and Adam Welker, Ben. Peel, and a few others.   All these
settlements are in Arizona.   The Mesa settlement, belonging to the Maricopa
stake, was founded by companies from Bear Lake co., Id., and S. L. co.,
Utah.   Leaving S. L. City immediately after the death of Brigham Young,
they reached Salt River in Jan. 1878, and soon afterward began the construction of a canal to the present site of the town.   After a year's labor, only a
small stream of water was obtained, barely sufficient for planting gardens, as
the ditch was cut through a very difficult formation.   The settlers persevered,
however, their labors diminishing as their numbers increased, and in 1885 a
canal had been built carrying 5,000 inches of water, at a cost of $43,000.   Lehi,
formerly Jonesville, also near Salt River, was founded in 1877 by a party of
71 settlers.   In the autumn of this year a few members of the company became
dissatisfied with the location, and set forth for San Pedro River, where they
founded the settlement of St David, so named by Prest A. F. McDonald after
David Patten, whom the Mormons regard as a martyr. *Maricopa Stake*, MS.
In the Gila Valley the settlers bought squatter claims of Mexicans, and in
1885 had constructed over 60 miles of canals from 8 to 16 feet wide, besides
a number of smaller ditches.   The soil is a fertile, sandy loam, producing
two crops or more a year, excellent for grapes and fruit, and of fair quality
for all farm products.   Sorghum produces three cuttings from one planting,
and lucern is cut five or six times a year.   Not more than five per cent of the
land is arable, the remainder being grazing-land. *Martineau's Settlements in
Arizona*, MS.   For monogamic settlements in Montana, see *Galveston News*,
Dec. 1, 1884.   In the fall of 1877 Elder John Morgan led a colony of saints
from the southern states to Pueblo, Colorado, where they wintered.   In
March of the following year, James G. Stuart, being ordered to visit the colonists, found them living as best they could, and working at whatever they
could find to do.   Mainly through the elder's efforts, two settlements were
founded, to which were afterward given the names of Ephraim and Manassa.
Stuart's Colonization in Colorado, MS.   In 1884 the Mormons established a
colony at Las Cruces, Sonora, Mex.   At the same time their leaders issued
a proclamation stating that no general migration to Mexico was intended.
The Mexican Financier, Jan. 31, 1885.   In *La Nueva Era*, Paso del Norte,
Chihuahua, Apr. 8, 1885, p. 2, it is stated that 200 Mormons had established
a colony at Corralitos, Galeana, in that state.

merce, arts, industries, and interests of the territory are mainly centred. In 1883 the capital contained a fixed population of about 25,000, its corporate limits including about fifty square miles,[7] divided into five municipal and twenty-one ecclesiastical wards. The city was well supplied with all modern comforts and conveniences, including gas and electric lights,[8] street-railroads,[9] hotels,[10] markets, libraries, theatres,[11] clubs, and saloons, where men might drink, smoke, and discuss politics and religion. Through all the streets, which were about double the usual width, ran the limpid waters of City Creek, the Jordan, Red Butte,

[7] Ten from east to west, and five from north to south, allowing for two square miles occupied by the Fort Douglas reservation. By act of Jan. 18, 1867, the western boundary was removed from the banks of the Jordan to a line running due north and south about two miles west of the river. By act of 1872 the south line was removed to Tenth South street.

[8] In 1877 George Erb organized the Rocky Mountain Electric Light Co. at Salt Lake City, afterward extending his operations to Ogden, Albuquerque, Cheyenne, Silver City, and Tucson, where, in 1884, all the works were in successful operation. *Erb's Electric Lights*, MS. Erb, a native of Penn., enlisted as a volunteer in the union army in 1861, being then 18 years of age. After serving for three years he removed to southern Utah, and in 1877 to S. L. City. For account of city gas-works, see *Deseret News*, Aug. 27, 1873. The city was first lighted by gas July 7, 1873.

[9] In 1872 the S. L. C. Street Railroad Co. was organized. It was in running order in June of the same year, its length being about seven miles. R. R. Anderson, in *Utah Jottings*, MS. In 1883 horse-cars ran every half-hour in eight different directions. *Graham's Utah Direct.*, 1883-4, 184.

[10] Among the principal hotels in S. L. City in 1883 were the Walker House and the Continental, formerly the Townsend House. The former was built in 1872, at a cost of $140,000. *Walker's Merchants and Miners of Utah*, MS. For description, see *Deseret News*, Sept. 4, 1872; *S. L. C. Tribune*, Sept. 7, 1872; *Sala's America Revisited*, 290-4; for mention of the Gardo House, sometimes nicknamed the Amelia Palace, see *Dall's First Holiday*, 101-3; *Duffus-Hardy's Through Cities and Prairie*, 113.

[11] An account of the various libraries is given later in this chapter. The theatre at the corner of First South and First East streets was 175 by 80 ft, with a stage 62 by 32 ft. It was of rock and adobe, with granite finish, fluted pillars, and massive cornices, cost $200,000, and had a seating capacity of at least 1,500. In 1882 the Walker Bros built the opera-house, at a cost of $136,000, within a few yards of their bank. Its dimensions were 167 by 67 feet, with a height of 60 feet. The interior was tastefully decorated and upholstered, and the stage well supplied with scenery and appointments, the drop-scene being remarkably handsome. *Walker's Merchants and Miners of Utah*, MS.; *Graham's Utah Direct.*, 1883-4, 193. For further mention of theatres and theatricals, see p. 584-5, this vol.; *Cooke's Theatr. and Soc. Affairs in Utah*, MS.; *Ward's Lectures*, 40; *Hubner's Round the World*, 80; *Bowles' Our New West*, 229-31; *Richardson's Beyond the Mississippi*, 358-9; *Rusling's Across Amer.*, 178-81; *Beadle's Life in Utah*, 245-6; *Ludlow's Heart of the Continent*, 334-7, 365-7; *Rae's Westward by Rail*, 108-10; *Millennial Star*, xxix. 70-3; *Deseret News*, March 27, 1867; *Overland Monthly*, v. 276-9.

and Emigration cañons,[12] cooling the air, cleansing
the thoroughfares, and giving life to verdure. The
adjacent lands were cultivated, and most of the
houses were surrounded with orchards, so that in
early summer Zion wore the appearance of Eden in
bloom. The flowers were full of beauty and fra-
grance, surpassing, if possible, in this respect, the
ancient towns of Mexico, or the modern capital in the
days of Cortés.

Aside from the temple and the tabernacle, Salt
Lake City thus far had little to boast of in the way
of architecture, nor was that little interesting. The
temple, when finished, was to cost several millions,[13]
and the walls of gray granite, more than six feet in
thickness, with a length of 200 and a width of 100
feet, were to reach a height of 100 feet.[14] It was
determined that this building should be of elegant
design, magnificent proportions, and unique pattern,
a marvel of beauty, strength, and solidity.[15] As a
structure in which a vast assemblage can see and
hear, the new tabernacle, west of the temple, completed in 187C, is a remarkable edifice. It is elliptical
in shape, with a primitive diameter of 233 feet, a con-
jugate of 133 feet, and a height of 70 feet, its huge
dome-shaped, or as some term it, dish-cover roof of
heavy, bolted lattice-work resting on sandstone pil-

----

[12] By act of Feb. 20, 1880, in *Utah Laws*, 1880, 55–6, amending the city
charter, the city council was authorized to borrow $250,000 for the construc-
tion of a canal, tapping the Jordan at a point 25 miles south of the city, for
irrigation purposes, thus releasing nearer and better sources of supply for
domestic use. It was finished in 1881, at a cost of $200,000. In 1884 there
were 13 miles of main pipes, which were tapped at regular intervals by hy-
drants, so as to insure a sufficient supply in case of fire. The city had a very
efficient fire department. See *Utah Direct. and Gaz.*, 1874, 177, 1879–80, 56.

[13] In 1886 it had already cost some $2,500,000.

[14] In 1884 they were over 60 feet above the ground.

[15] Under President Taylor's administration more work in the same time
was done on the temple than ever before. *Utah Notes*, MS. For condition of
the temple building in 1860, see p. 582, this vol.; at other dates, *Deseret News*,
Nov. 20, 1867, Aug. 20, 1873, May 27, 1874, Aug. 23, 1876, July 3, Nov. 20,
1878; *Millennial Star*, xxxvi. 273–5; *Harper's Mag.*, Aug. 1883. In quarrying the granite at Little Cottonwood cañon, the workmen dislodged huge
bowlders from the mountain side, and sent them crashing down to the railroad track, a descent of 700 feet. One of these bowlders weighed 21,000 tons.

lars. Its seating capacity is about 9,000,[16] and in the building are twenty doors, some nine feet in width, and all of them opening outward, so that in case of fire a full congregation can make its exit in three or four minutes. As was the case in the old tabernacle,[17] the acoustic properties are remarkably good, and it is said that one standing in the east end of the gallery and uttering a few words in his lowest tone can be distinctly heard in the amphitheatre where the church dignitaries are seated, at the opposite end of the building.[18]

On the site of the old tabernacle now stands the new assembly hall,[19] which is also the stake house for the Salt Lake stake of Zion. It is built of rough-hewn granite, the rock being taken from the same quarry that supplies material for the temple, and with frescoed ceiling, representing important events in church history. Though church-like in appearance, it is considered one of the most sightly structures in the city.[20] Of the endowment house and other buildings on temple block mention has been made elsewhere.

On South Temple street is the museum, where are specimens of home art, in painting and sculpture, also home products and manufactures, as in cotton, wool, silk, cloth, paper; gold and silver bullion and coins, with samples of the ores and minerals of Utah;

[16] *Richards' Utah Miscell.*, MS. In *Utah Notes*, MS., 2, it is given as low as 7,000. Other authorities say 12,000 to 13,000, but recent estimates show this to be an exaggeration, though including standing-room, the former figure is about correct.

[17] For mention of the old tabernacle and its organ, see p. 292, this vol.

[18] For further descriptions of this tabernacle, see, among others, *Sala's Amer. Revisited*, 296-8; *Bonwick's Mormons and Silver Mines*, 10-17; *Marshall's Through Amer.*, 1658; *Duffus-Hardy's Through Cities and Prairie*, 113-15; *De Rupert's Cal. and Morm.*, 138-46; *Deseret News*, May 4, 1870, on which date were delivered the inaugural addresses.

[19] The corner-stones were laid Sept. 28, 1877, and it was dedicated Jan. 9, 1882, though public meetings were held in it as early as Apr. 4, 1880. Until Apr. 1879 it was called the new or little tabernacle, its name being changed at that date to the Salt Lake Assembly Hall. It is 120 by 68 feet, and can seat 3,000 people. *Richards' Utah Miscell.*, MS.

[20] *Utah Notes*, MS., 2; *Sloan's Utah Gazetteer*, 1884, 204. The building is 120 by 68 ft, the height of the tower which rises from the centre being 130 ft. It has excellent acoustic properties, contains a large organ, rich and sweet in tone, and was dedicated in the spring of 1880.

petrifactions, fossils, and obsidian; Indian weapons, scalps, ornaments, pottery, wampum, and the boat in which Kit Carson crossed the waters of great Salt Lake—the first craft launched by white man into the Dead Sea of the West.[21]

Other prominent buildings in Salt Lake City, and many points of interest within easy reach of the capital, as Great Salt Lake, the mineral springs, Fort Douglas, Parley's park, the Cottonwoods, Ensign and Twin peaks, Echo cañon, American Fork cañon—the so called Yosemite of Utah—have been described for the most part in other portions of this volume, and in many of the countless volumes that have been written concerning the Mormons.

In order to see Salt Lake City at its best, one should stroll about three o'clock in the afternoon through Main and Temple streets, which are to this city what Market and Kearny streets are to San Francisco. At that time the spacious sidewalks are crowded with well-dressed women passing to and fro among the shops, prominent among which stands out the Zion's coöperative store, or, as it is usually termed, "Zion's Coöp." In no part of the city, or elsewhere in Utah, are there signs of abject poverty, and there are few beggars, tramps, or drones, the idle and dissolute being discountenanced by the community.[22]

[21] *Sala's America Revisited*, ii. 295; *Bonwick's Mormons and Silver Mines*, 18–21; *Gaz. of Utah*, 1874, 178; *S. L. C. Tribune*, Jan. 1, 5, 1878; *S. L. C. Herald*, Sept. 13, 1878. In 1882 occurred the death of Joseph L. Barfoot, for several years curator of the museum. Born at Warwick Castle, England, and, as he claimed before his decease, legitimate heir to one of the greatest earldoms in the realm, his ancestry being traced back on the father's side to Robert Bruce of Scotland, and on the mother's to Bishop Ridley, he enlisted in the marines, probably on account of some family quarrel. His discharge being procured, he joined his father, who was superintendent of the Mormon Mission in London, and in 1856 Joseph joined the Mormon church. *S. L. City Contributor*, iii. 250–2; Campbell, *Circular Notes*, i. 62, states that his father was merely tutor at Warwick Castle.

[22] For descriptions of S. L. City in 1883–4, see *The Mormon Metropolis;* in 1881, *Sala's Amer. Revisited*, 290–317 (with cut); *Hollister's Res. and Attract. of Utah*, 73–6; in 1879, *N. Y. Observer*, in *Portland Wkly Christ. Advoc.*, Feb. 6, 1879; in 1878, *Marshall's Through Amer.*, 163–82; in 1877, *Boyer's from Orient to Occident*, 61–3; *Musser's Fruits of Mormonism*, 3, 11; *Leslie's Cal.*, 74–5, 91–5, 103; *Taylor's Summer Savory*, 20–1; in 1876, *Jackson's Bits of Travel at Home*, 19–22; in 1875, *Williams' Pac. Tourist*, 132–40, 150–2;

While not communists, the elements of socialism enter strongly into all their relations, public and private, social, commercial, and industrial, as well as religious and political. This tends to render them exclusive, independent of the gentiles and their government, and even in some respects antagonistic to them. They have assisted each other until nine out of ten own their farms, while commerce and manufacturing are to a large extent coöperative. The rights of property are respected; but while a Mormon may sell his farm to a gentile, it would not be deemed good fellowship for him to do so.

Salt Lake county contained, in 1883, nearly one fifth of the population of Utah, the eastern side of the valley, where the streams of the Wasatch Mountains are utilized for irrigation, being the principal farming section; while the western portion, in the neighborhood of the Oquirrh Range, was but sparsely settled. In this county were found, with the exception perhaps of coal, nearly all the minerals that contribute to the wealth of communities. Alta, the mining town of Little Cottonwood, contained a considerable population until the spring of 1878, when it was almost destroyed by fire. Bingham, about thirty miles south-west of the capital, was surrounded by productive mines; and Sandy, where the Bingham cañon and Cottonwood ores were forwarded for sampling, was a thriving village.[23]

Curtis' Dottings, 18–28; in 1872, Bonwick's Mormons and Silver Mines, 8–10; Washington Star, in Deseret News, July 10, 1872; Oakland Monthly Rev., i. no. 1, 18–19; in 1871, Hubner's Round the World, 76–80; Greenwood's New Life, 137–8, 142–4; in 1870, Nordhoff's Cal., 40–2; Nelson's Pict. Guide-Book, 19–25; Kneeland's Wonders of Yosemite, 19–21; Overland Monthly, v. 270–3, 275; in 1869, Rae's Westward by Rail, 104–12; in 1868, Goddard's Where to Emigrate, 152–3; Bowles' Pac. Railroad, 40–51; Ludlow's Heart of the Continent, 315–28; Beadle's Life in Utah, 240–7; in 1867, Hepworth Dixon's New Amer., 133–41; McClure's 3,000 Miles Through the Rocky Mts, 165–6 (with cut); in 1866, Rusling's Across Amer., 163–6; Life among the Mormons, 88–97; in 1865, Bowles' Our New West, 202–3, 206, 219–22 (with cut); Barnes' From Atlantic to Pacific, 54–5; Richardson's Beyond the Mississippi, 347 (with cut); in 1860–2, pp. 577–90, this vol. (with plan).

[23]Among other growing settlements in Salt Lake co. at this time were

Of the establishment and progress of other settlements, up to the close of 1862, mention has already been made.[24] Davis county, north of Salt Lake, was settled by quiet pastoral and agricultural communities of the old-fashioned type. Farmington, Centreville, Kaysville,[25] and the three towns named Bountiful,[26] were, in 1886, reasonably prosperous, resembling somewhat small English villages, except for the fact that no ale-houses were to be seen in their midst.

Ogden, or, as it was sometimes erroneously called, Junction City, the site of which was purchased, as the reader will remember, in 1848, for some $2,000 or $3,000, ranked in 1883 next to Salt Lake City in population.[27] In the centre of a network of railroads and of a prosperous agricultural region, with excellent

Mill Creek, East Mill Creek, Big Cottonwood, South Cottonwood, Union, North Jordan, South Jordan, West Jordan, Brighton, Butlerville, Granite, Draper, Herriman, Mountain Dell, and Pleasant Green.

[24] See caps xiii., xxi., this vol.

[25] So called after a bishop and early settler named William Kay, who owned a large portion of its site. About the year 1857 the bishop's interest was purchased by John S. Smith, an Englishman by birth, who, landing in Canada in 1841, afterward proceeded to Nauvoo, and was one of those who took part in the exodus. Mr Smith is now one of the principal farmers in Davis co. Among other prominent men in that county may be mentioned the following: Joseph Barton, a native of St Helens, Lancashire, England, settled at Kaysville, his present home, in 1862, being then only 14 years of age. In 1869 he was elected county surveyor, and since that date has held the appointments of city recorder of Kaysville, county clerk, and prosecuting attorney, the last two of which offices he filled in 1885. In 1884 he was a member of the territorial legislature, and almost throughout his career in Utah has occupied positions of trust, though they have come to him unsought, and somewhat against his will. N. T. Porter, a native of Vermont, was one of the first settlers in Centreville, where he took up his abode in 1849, after suffering all the hardships of the expulsion, and of a long residence at Winter Quarters. Jos. Egbert, a native of Salina co., Ind., was a pioneer, sharing the blanket of Orson Pratt during the journey, and driving the first team that entered the valley. John R. Baines of Kaysville, a native of Bedfordshire, England, arrived in Utah with a capital of 10 cents, and afterward accumulated a fortune of $100,000 by farming and traffic. The president of the Davis stake was W. R. Smith, who was for several years a member of the legislature, and for nine years probate judge. He was born in Ontario, Canada.

[26] South, East, and West Bountiful. The last was sometimes called Wood's Cross. Bountiful was a city in the book of Mormon. *Richards' Utah Misc.*, MS., 4–5. Prominent among the citizens of West Bountiful was W. S. Muir, a Scotchman by birth, who, accepting the Mormon faith, set forth for Nauvoo, and in 1847 was a corporal in the Mormon battalion. In the following year he started, in connection with Sam. Brannan, the first store ever opened at the mines of California.

[27] In 1883 it contained about 8,000 inhabitants.

manufacturing facilities, and with many of the attractions and conveniences of modern cities, including a theatre[28] and one of the best hotels in the country, with gentile churches and schools, both protestant and catholic, the western terminus of the Union Pacific was probably the most cosmopolitan town in Utah.[29] Among the other settlements of Weber county the most prominent were North Ogden,[30] Harrisville, Huntsville,[31] Lynne,[32] Slaterville, Uintah, Plain City, Hooperville, and West Weber.[33]

[28] Opened Jan. 4, 1870. *Stanford's Ogden*, MS., 10.

[29] For act to incorporate Ogden, see *Utah Compiled Laws*, 746–54; *Deseret News*, Jan. 30, 1861. For act amending charter of incorporation, see *Utah Laws*, 1880, 4–5. In 1885 the mayor of Ogden was David H. Peery, a Virginian, who during the civil war served as assistant commissary under General Marshall. In 1864, after being honorably discharged from the confederate army, he arrived in Utah with the sum of $1,400, saved from the wreck of his property. In 1885 he was the owner of several blocks of business buildings, and was worth about $150,000, being at that date a member of the territorial legislature. In 1880 the city and county built a bridge over the Weber, at a cost of $16,000, and in the same year the city constructed a reservoir on Court-house hill to collect the waters of several small springs which were conveyed in pipes to Main street. *Stanford's Ogden*, MS., 15–16. For sketch of the business growth of Ogden, see *Tullidge's Mag.*, i. 478–84. For description of town at various dates, see *Bonwick's Silver Mines*, 22–3; *Millennial Star*, xxxi. 518; *S. L. C. Tribune*, Jan. 1, 1878, July 6, 1879, Jan. 1, 1881; *Telegraph*, May 18, July 8, Dec. 19, 1869; *Herald*, Dec. 12, 1877. Topographical plan, in *Wheeler's Surveys*, ii. 471.

[30] With a population in 1880 of 956. *Stanford's Ogden*, MS., 8; about 900. Amos Maycock, in *Utah Sketches*, MS., 115. In 1883 it was about 1,200, and in 1886 some 1,500.

[31] Harrisville was an agricultural settlement containing in 1880 about 60 families, most of them Scandinavians. Though subject to early frosts, cereals were raised, with the exception of wheat, and in the neighborhood was good pasture. A considerable income was also derived from the sale of shingles and railroad ties. *Stanford's Weber Co.*, MS., 5, 11–12. In the *Description of Huntsville*, MS., 1–6, and *Utah Sketches*, MS., are particulars as to the resources and growth of Huntsville from 1860, when it was founded, until 1880.

[32] An agricultural settlement two miles north of Ogden, containing in 1880 about 500 inhabitants. *Stanford's Weber Co.*, MS., 1.

[33] Slaterville was organized as a county precinct in 1864. Population in 1880 about 400. Uintah, at the western entrance of Weber cañon, was first known as East Weber, the name being changed to Easton early in 1867, and in the same year to Uintah. At Plain City the raising of fruit and vegetables, especially strawberries, was the principal industry. Hooperville, settled in 1869, had in 1880 about 100 families. West Weber, organized as a ward in 1877, mustered at the same date nearly 700 inhabitants. There were also small settlements at Mound Fort, a mile north of the Weber; Eden, near Huntsville; Marriotsville, three miles north-west of Ogden; Riverdale, two miles south of Ogden; and several others. *Id.*, passim.

In the *Brief Historical Sketch of the Settlements in Weber County, by Joseph Stanford*, MS., are given in minute detail the leading incidents in the history of all the principal settlements of Weber co. from their foundation until the year 1880. The *Historical Sketch of Ogden City*, MS., by this author, covers

In Cache county were added to the settlements already mentioned Richmond, a farming town[34] on the line of the Utah and Northern railroad; Lewiston on the west bank of Bear River, opposite Richmond; Benson, eight miles south-west of Logan; and Newton, a thriving village a little to the north-west of the same town.[35]   The corner-stones of the Logan temple were laid in 1877, its site being chosen by Brigham a few weeks before his death.   The structure is of stone, painted and plastered in variegated tints, and capped with an iron roof.[36]

Rich, or as it was first termed Richland, county, in the north-eastern corner of the territory, was organized in 1864, being carved out of Cache county,[37] Randolph, the county seat, near its centre, and surrounded with excellent pasture-land, Garden City at its extreme north-west, and Woodruff[38] on Bear River, being now the principal settlements.   The limits of Summit county on the south were extended in 1872 by an act of the Utah legislature, and in 1886 it was bounded on the north by Wyoming and Morgan county, and on the south, east, and west by Uintah, Wasatch, Morgan, and Salt Lake counties.   In 1883 Park City, the centre of supply for the Ontario and other mines, was the most considerable town.[39]

Brigham City, the county seat of Box Elder, west of Cache county, and on the line of the Utah and

the same period, commencing with the time when its site was purchased by Captain Brown from Miles Goodyear.

[34] Incorporated Feb. 6, 1868.

[35] At the southern end of Cache Valley is the town of Paradise, and scattered throughout the valley are several small settlements.   For descriptive sketch of Cache co. settlements, see *S. L. C. Herald*, Nov. 3, 10, 1877.   In 1880 Paradise had 490 inhabitants. Orson Smith, in *Utah Sketches*, MS., 1-2.

[36] See, for ceremony of laying the corner-stones, *Deseret News*, Sept. 26, 1877; for dedication, *Biog. Lorenzo Snow*, 452-3; for act incorporating Logan City, *Utah Compiled Laws*, 711-18; for description of the city, *Deseret News*, Oct. 15, 1873, July 23, 1879; *S. L. Weekly Herald*, March 31, 1881.

[37] For organic act, see *Utah Acts Legisl.*, 1863-4, 18-19.   The county was named after Apostle Chas C. Rich.

[38] Named after Apostle Wilford Woodruff. *Richards' Utah Miscell.*, MS., 4.

[39] The other principal settlements besides those mentioned elsewhere were Echo and Wanship, both on the line of the Utah Eastern railroad.   Wanship was named after an Indian who was much respected. *Richards' Utah Miscell.*, MS., 3.

Northern railroad, together with Willard City, seven miles farther to the south, had in 1886 become places of note. The site of the former was remarkably picturesque.[40] Tooele and Grantsville, in Tooele county, south of Box Elder, had each in 1880 a population of about 1,200, and Corinne, incorporated in 1870, about 400.[41] Nephi, the county seat of Juab county,[42] contained in 1880 a thriving population of about 2,500, most of them farmers, though the manufacturing interests of this town were not inconsiderable, the Tintic mines furnishing a market for surplus lumber and produce.[43]

Utah county, with two lines of railroad,[44] excellent farming-lands[45] and manufacturing facilities, and the largest fresh-water lake in the territory,[46] ranked second in population to Salt Lake county,[47] and first in its yield of cereals and fruits. By persistent effort, the

[40] Willard City is named after Willard Richards. *Richards' Utah Miscell.* MS., 7; Brigham, of course, after President Young. Both were incorporated in 1867. See *Utah Compiled Laws*, 737-9, 743-5. At Brigham City choice fruit was raised in abundance. In 1880 there was a large tannery and a woollen factory in operation. Near Willard City grain, fruit, and vegetables were raised, but the facilities for manufacture were meagre. A. Christensen and G. W. Ward, in *Utah Sketches*, MS., 45-104. For descriptions of Brigham City at various dates, see *McClure's 3,000 Miles beyond the Rocky Mountains; Deseret News*, July 24, 1862, Jan. 16, 1878. In 1883 Call's Fort, already mentioned, had only 35 families. Among other settlements were Honeyville on the line of the Utah and Northern railway, organized as a ward in 1877, and Snowville, a stock-raising centre, fifty miles north-west of Corinne, settled by A. Goodliffe and others in 1876.

[41] For acts incorporating these towns, see *Utah Compiled Laws*, 740, 843-52. Grantsville was named after Col. Geo. D. Grant. *Richards' Utah Miscel.*, MS., 6. In the neighborhood of Tooele many kinds of farm and orchard products were raised. At Grantsville, also a farming settlement, there were 25 artesian wells. F. M. Lyman, John Rowberry, and Harrison Severe, in *Utah Sketches*, MS., 29, 151. For historical sketch of Corinne, see *Tullidge's Mag.*, ii. 243-6.

[42] Juab is Indian or Spanish-Indian for flat. For acts defining and extending the limits of the county, see *Utah Acts Legisl.*, 1868, pp. 41-2; 1870, 127.

[43] Mona, eight miles north of Nephi, Juab, on the Utah Central, and Levan, seven miles east of Juab, were also promising settlements. At Nephi there were in 1880 two hotels, a furniture factory, and a large coöperative store. Geo. Teasdale, in *Utah Sketches*, MS., 112.

[44] The Utah Central and Denver and Rio Grande.

[45] In 1880 there were over 40,000 acres in tilth.

[46] Utah Lake is 40 miles in length, with an average width of 10 miles.

[47] In 1883 Salt Lake co. had 41,890 and Utah co. 23,472 inhabitants. *Utah Gazetteer*, 1884, 300.

inhabitants of Provo, the county seat, built up a settlement that ranked among the leading towns of Utah, with handsome public and private buildings, a theatre, a large tabernacle, and, as will presently be mentioned, the largest woollen-mill in the territory. Prominent among its industries was the drying of fruit, of which several hundred tons were forwarded yearly to market.[48] In 1883 the other principal towns were fairly prosperous, several of them, as Payson,[49] Spanish Fork,[50] and Springville,[51] having wealth and population sufficient to support a number of schools and churches, a theatre,[52] and the inevitable young men's and young women's mutual improvement associations.[53]

Uintah county, in the eastern portion of Utah, was organized in 1880,[54] with Ashley as the county seat.

[48] See, for act incorporating Provo, *Utah Acts Legisl.*, 1866, 120–5; for names of municipal officers between 1861 and 1877, see *Provo City Revised Ordinances*, iv.–v.; in 1880, *Utah Sketches*, MS., where is a brief historical sketch of the town. Among the most prominent men in Provo may be mentioned Abraham O. Smoot, a native of Owen co., Ky, who joined the church in 1835, being then in his 21st year, and a few months later was ordained an elder. Of his missionary labors, and the part that he played during the exodus and the Utah war, mention has already been made. Chosen mayor of Salt Lake City in 1857, he was reappointed to that office at each election until 1866, when, declining the mayoralty, he served for twelve years in the legislature. In 1868 he removed to Provo, where he was also elected mayor, holding that office for twelve years, and receiving no pay for his services in that capacity in either city. In 1884 he was president of the Provo Manufacturing Company, the Provo Bank, the Provo branch of Zion's Coöperative Mercantile Institute, and the Utah county stake. *Utah Early Scenes in Church Hist.*, 17–31; *Tullidge's Mag.*, iii. 297–9.

[49] At Payson there was a coöperative store established, mainly by the efforts of Wm Douglas, who arrived in Utah in 1848. See for act incorporating Payson, *Utah Acts Legisl.*, 1865, 42; for act extending limits, *Utah Laws*, 1882, pp. 18–19.

[50] Among the prominent citizens of Spanish Fork may be mentioned the bishop of ward, Geo. D. Snell, a descendant of one of the pilgrim fathers and a native of New Brunswick, whence he removed to Utah in 1854. In 1878 he was elected a member of the legislature. Wm Creer of the same city, and an Englishman by birth, was also a member of the legislature in 1883, and served on some of the most important committees. In 1882 the limits of Spanish Fork City were altered. *Utah Laws*, 1882, 8.

[51] The first mayor of Springville was G. D. Wood, who came to Utah in 1848, and in 1884 was still mayor, though 76 years of age. His son, L. S. Wood, was also one of the prominent men of Springville.

[52] The Payson theatre was the second largest in Utah, and had a seating capacity of 800.

[53] Midway between Payson and Utah Lake, on the line of the Utah Central, the settlement of Benjamin was founded in 1870. *Utah Gazetteer*, 1884, 156.

[54] For organic act, see *Utah Laws*, 1880, 11–12.

ln the same year Emery and San Juan counties, and in 1882 Garfield county, were organized, with Castle Dale, Bluff City, and Panguitch as their several seats.[55] Emery county was noted as an agricultural and mineral district, full of inherent wealth and resource. In Garfield county, below the junction of the Green and Grand rivers, is first encountered the weird scenery of the Colorado. Toward the south and in San Juan county the traveller, standing on the cliffs that overhang its banks, after making his way over leagues of sandstone, where there is no blade of grass or drop of water, sees below him the stream which Captain Cárdenas discovered in 1540,[56] still gliding peaceably, after a lapse of more than three centuries, through valleys as yet untrodden by man. Near the point below which the waters of the Green and Grand are named the Colorado, ran the eastern boundary line of Piute county, organized in 1865,[57] and of which Junction was the county seat.[58] Beaver City, in the county of that name west of Piute, had in 1883 a population of about 2,000, and was one of the principal manufacturing centres of southern Utah.[59]

In Sanpete county,[60] south of Utah and Uintah counties, Manti was in 1883 the largest and one of the most prosperous towns. Built on a solid rock near its suburbs, and at an elevation of several hundred feet, stood the walls of an unfinished temple, facing toward the west, and destined when finished to be one

[55] For organic acts, see *Utah Laws*, 1880, 4–5, 10–11, 1882, 98–101. Emery co. was named after Gov. Emery, and Garfield after President Garfield. Emery and San Juan were both bounded on the east by Colorado.
[56] See p. 1–5, this vol.
[57] *Utah Acts Legisl.*, 1865, 16.
[58] *Utah Laws*, 1878, 48. Circleville, settled in 1860, was the county seat until 1868, when it was removed to Bullion. *Utah Acts Legisl.*, 1874, 6; thence to Marysville, and again to Junction.
[59] Beaver was incorporated in 1867. *Utah Acts Legisl.*, 1867, 4–5. For plan, see *Wheeler's Geog. Surveys*, ii. 491.
[60] For act changing the limits of Sanpete, Utah, and Wasatch counties, see *Utah Laws*, 1880, 18–19. By act of 1864 the county seat of Sanpete co. was removed from Manti to Moroni, and by act of 1865 again fixed at Manti. *Utah Acts Legisl.*, 1863–4, 21; 1865, 16.

of the finest in existence.[61]   Ephraim City, incorporated in 1868,[62] contained in 1883 about 2,500 inhabitants, and rivalled the county seat in aggregate wealth,
all its citizens being men of means, though none very
rich.   Among other towns and villages may be
mentioned Spring City, nine miles north-east of
Ephraim, incorporated in 1870; Mount Pleasant, second to Manti in population, incorporated in 1868; and
Fairview, in the northern section of the county, incorporated in 1872, with an area of twenty square miles.[63]

In 1864 Albert Lewis and ten other citizens from
Manti pitched their tents on a spot later forming a
portion of Main street in Richfield, Sevier county,
Lewis soon afterward building a hut of cottonwood
logs, cedar posts, and mud.   During this and the
following year it is related that 600 bushels of wheat
were harvested from 10 acres of land.   In 1865, the
settlement being then reënforced, a canal was made,
eleven miles in length, tapping the waters of the
Sevier.   In this year, also, Sevier county was organized.[64]   After the cessation of Indian raids in 1865–6,
of which mention has already been made, other portions were occupied, several villages, among them
Salina, Glenwood, Vermilion, and Joseph, being built
on the banks of the river.

Parowan, the seat of Iron county, south of Sevier,
had in 1883 a population of 800, the leading interests
being farming and lumbering.   Cedar City had about
the same number,[65] and Summit, six miles south-west
of Parowan, and Kanarra, formerly in Washington

---

[61] The site of Manti temple was chosen by Brigham, and ground was broken
Apr. 30, 1877.   The corner-stones were laid Apr. 14, 1879. *Deseret News*,
May 7, 1879.   For condition in 1882, see *Robinson's Sinners and Saints*, 163–5.
[62] *Utah Compiled Laws*, 828.
[63] Chester, about four miles west of Spring City, was settled in 1882 by R.
N. Allred and others; Mayfield, ten miles south of Manti, by families from
Ephraim and Fort Gunnison in 1873–5.   In 1880 there were 16 considerable
towns and villages in Sanpete co.   J. B. Maiben, in *Utah Sketches*, MS., 173.
[64] Wm Morrison, Paul Poulson, and James M. Peterson, in *Utah Sketches*,
MS., 134–6; *Utah Acts Legisl.*, 1865, 16.
[65] For acts incorporating Parowan and Cedar, see *Utah Compiled Laws*,
1868, 808–11.

county, were prosperous farming villages. In Kane
county, south of Iron, the first settlement, named
Kanab, was established in 1870.[66] St George, the
county seat[67] of Washington, and a few miles north of
the Arizona line, was in 1886 one of the principal
cities in southern Utah, and though built on alkaline
sands and artificial soil, was one of the garden spots of
the country. In its suburbs was a temple built of red
sandstone, and dedicated in 1875, its baptismal font
being presented by Brigham.[68]

In common with all the leading towns of Utah, St
George was well supplied with schools, containing in
1883 no less than five school-houses, one of which
belonged to the presbyterian mission. At that date
there were in the territory 411 district schools,[69] and
the total expenditure for school purposes was in 1879
about $293,500, or some $6 per capita of the school
children,[70] the term lasting on an average little more
than four months in the year.

Upon the establishment of schools belonging to
other religious denominations, or as they were usually
termed in Utah, mission schools, educational results
were more satisfactory, and if much was professed,
much was actually taught. The Saint Mark's grammar-school, founded in 1867 in connection with the

[66] *Utah Sketches*, MS., 100. Among other settlements were Johnson, some
ten miles east of Kanab, Pahreah, near the junction of Pahreah River and
Cottonwood Creek, settled in 1872, and Orderville, on the west bank of the
Virgen, in 1875. In 1869 the seat of Kane co. was removed from Rockville to
Toquerville. *Utah Acts*, 1869, 17.

[67] For act to incorporate St George, see *Utah Compiled Laws*, 814–20. It
was made the county seat in 1863. *Utah Acts Legisl.*, 1862-3, 5–6.

[68] For dedication and description, see *Millennial Star*, xxxvi. 252–5; *Deseret News*, Apr. 8, 1874, Jan. 17, Apr. 26, Sept. 13, 1876. For plan of St George,
see *Wheeler's Geog. Surveys*, ii. 491. Six miles from St George was the village
of Washington, and three miles north of Harrisburg the town of Leeds, first
settled in 1868-9 by R. H. Ashley and others. Pinto, in the northern part of
the county, was settled by Jacob Hamblin and others in 1856. The mining
camp of Silver Reef was about one mile from Leeds.

[69] Of these 111 were primary, 60 intermediate, and 240 mixed. *Utah Gazetteer*, 1884, 293.

[70] *Rept Dist Schools*, 1880, p. 11. The value of district school property
was in 1879 $393,984.57, of private school property $175,000.

episcopal church, the Salt Lake seminary, established by the methodists in 1870, and others founded later by various denominations,[71] received so much of patronage that it became necessary for the Mormons to bestir themselves in the matter, and there was afterward more efficiency in the school system, private institutions being also founded by the saints, among them the academy at Provo,[72] and the Brigham Young college at Logan.[73]

For many years a great advantage to Mormon as against gentile schools was the fact that they were allowed to use their meeting-houses for public school purposes. In 1880, when the legislature passed an act creating school districts,[74] and authorized a tax for the erection and repair of school buildings, these meeting-houses were constituted legal district schools, though retained for religious purposes, the gentiles, none of whose children, with rare exceptions, attended them, being also taxed for this purpose. Hence, legal conflicts arose, the decision of the courts being that Mormon school trustees could not collect such taxes

[71] Presbyterians, congregationalists, and catholics. *Harrison's Crit. Notes on Utah*, MS., 63. Among them was the Salt Lake Collegiate Institute founded by the presbyterians, the Salt Lake Academy by the congregationalists, and St Mary's Academy by the catholics. The presbyterians a one had in 1883 33 schools and 2,200 pupils. *Utah Gazetteer*, 1884, 280.

[72] Opened Jan. 1876, burned Jan. 1884, and rebuilt the same year. *Id.*, 278-9, Albert Jones, in *Utah Co. Sketches*, MS., 59-60, 64, states that it was founded for the children of members of the church in good standing, though others are admitted, and that in 1880 it had 431 pupils. See also, for faculty, course of instruction, etc., *Contributor*, ii. 179-80, 241-2, 272-3; *Deseret News*, April 17, 1878, Feb. 5, 1879; *Utah Jour. Legisl.*, 1880, 461-5, 489-93. Among the professors in 1883 was Elder Karl G. Mæser, formerly of the Budig institute, Dresden. While presiding over the European mission in 1855, F. D. Richards heard that he was desirous of being informed as to the faith and doctrine of the saints, and a few months later visited that city by invitation in company with elders Wm H. Kimball and Wm Budge, baptizing eight persons and organizing the first branch of the church in Saxony. Mæser was left in charge, and when the government banished the saints from fatherland, as we have seen, he and most of the other converts gathered to Utah. *Richards' Miscell.*, MS. Mr Richards states that the B. Y. academy is one of the best and most popular educational institutes in the territory.

[73] Opened in Sept. 1878, the number of pupils in 1880-1 being 160. In 1877 a tract of nearly 10,000 acres south of Logan City was deeded for this purpose to a board of trustees by Brigham. *Utah Gazetteer*, 1884, 283-4. In 1883 Mariner W. Merrill presided over the educational affairs of Logan temple.

[74] A copy of it will be found in *Rept Dist Schools*, 1880. 71-80.

while the buildings stood on record as church prop-erty. Many of the ward meeting-houses, therefore, were transferred to school trustees.[75] The University of Deseret, founded, as we have seen, in 1850, and incorporated the same year,[76] the curriculum of which was to include all living lan-guages and sciences, had but a nominal existence until 1869. At the former date there were no efficient private schools in the territory, no public-school law had as yet been passed by the legislature, and there were few competent teachers. As the university

[75] *Harrison's Crit. Notes on Utah*, MS., 67-71. The first gentile elected school trustee in Utah was Benjamin Grundy Raybold, a native of Birming-ham, England, who came to Utah in 1862. Finding no other occupation, he began his career among the saints as a hod-carrier; then he turned carpenter; then postmaster; then journalist; and finally, in 1866, found employment with the Walker Bros, to whom in 1885 he was confidential clerk. A brief history of the Mormon school system from 1850 to 1875 will be found in *U. S. Educ. Rept*, 44th Cong. 2d Sess., 458-60. See also, for further information, *Id.*, 42d Cong. 2d Sess., 21, 383-4, 600-4; 42d Cong. 3d Sess., 377-80, 416, 608-13, 942-97; 43d Cong. 1st Sess., xxii.-cxxiii. 460-3, 475, 510-12, 728; 43d Cong. 3d Sess., xiii., cxxv., 500-2, 507, 526-34, 733; 44th Cong. 1st Sess., xxvi.-ccxxiii. 510-14, 548-54; 44th Cong. 2d Sess., passim; *H. Ex. Doc.*, 46th Cong. 2d Sess., vol. xi., cxxvii.; *Utah Jour. Legisl.*, 1859-60, 22-6; 1860-1, 78-9; 1861-2, 65; 1863-4, 96-9; 1864-5, 110-14; 1865-6, 17-18, 170 -3; 1869, 14-15, 108, 176-8; 1870, 191-9; 1872, 228-30; 1876, 28-9, 78-9; 1878, 33-4, 345-80; 1880, 442-60; *Utah School Repts*, passim; *Bien. Rept Supt Dist Schools*, 1880, 1882, 1884; *Utah Sketches*, MS., passim; *Stanford's Weber Co.*, MS., 1-23; *Linforth's Route from Liverpool*, 104, 110-11; *Remy's Jour. to G. S. L. City*, ii. 177-94; *Burton's City of the Saints*, 512-16; *Gunni-son's The Mormons*, 80-1; *Ward's Husb. in Utah*, 264-6; *Hollister's Res. of Utah*, 72-3; *Utah Pioneers*, 33d ann., 30-4; *Utah Resources*, 55-8; *Todd's Sunset Land*, 179; *Utah Gazetteer*, 39-40, 175-6; 1884, 278-94; *Contrib-utor*, i. 84; ii. 240, 270; iv. 182-3, 352-3; *Millennial Star*, xxxiii. 551; *Deseret News*, Oct. 19, Nov. 16, 1850, Feb. 22, 1851, March 19, 1853, Jan. 11, 1855, Apr. 1, 1857, Apr. 11, Oct. 24, Dec. 5, 1860, Jan. 15, 1868, Apr. 17, 1872, Feb. 13, 1878, March 26, 1879; *S. L. C. Tribune*, Nov. 1, 1873, March 25, Aug. 29, 1876, March 3, 20, Apr. 21, 1877, March 20, Sept. 21, 1878, Apr. 23, May 22, Sept. 6, Nov. 20, 1879; *Herald*, Jan. 30, Apr. 13, 1878. For disbursement of school revenue, see *Utah Jour. Legisl.*, 1880, 469-81; for evening-schools, *Deseret News*, Dec. 28, 1854, Dec. 5, 12, 1860; Sunday-schools, *Harrison's Crit. Notes on Utah*, MS., 71-3; *Cannon's Sunday-schools in Utah*, MS., 3; *Juv. Inst.*, xv. 89; *Deseret News*, Apr. 14, 1869. Mr Harrison states that un-til there were gentile churches in Utah the Sunday-school was almost un-known. This the Mormons deny, saying that Sunday-schools have been taught in Salt Lake City since 1857, the Sunday-school Union being established in 1866. For gentile churches and missionary work in Utah, see *Hand-Book of Mormonism*, 77-86; *Utah Gaz.*, 208-11; *Marshall's Through Amer.*, 230.

[76] With Orson Spencer as chancellor, Dan. Spencer, Orson Pratt, Jno. M. Bernhisel, Sam. W. Richards, W. W. Phelps, Albert Carrington, Wm I. Appleby, Dan. H. Wells, Robt L. Campbell, Hosea Stout, Elias Smith, and Zerubbabel Snow as regents, and David Fullmer as treasurer. *Des. Univ.*, MS., 3.

could be of little service without preparatory schools,
and the grant of $5,000 a year had been made from
an empty treasury, it was converted into a parent
school, of which mention has before been made,[77] the
attendance being invited of all who wished to qualify
themselves as teachers, or for other reasons to acquire a somewhat liberal education.[78] In 1852 the
parent school was closed for lack of funds,[79] and from
that date until fifteen years later nothing further was
attempted, although meanwhile valuable tracts of
land had been set apart for the future state by congress for the establishment of a university.[80] During
most of this interval, however, the board of regents
exercised a general supervision over the schools of the
territory.[81]

In the autumn of 1867 an educational institute
was established by the board, and conducted at the
council-house, mainly as a commercial academy,[82] until 1869, when classical, scientific, and normal departments were added, though at this date it was in fact
rather a high-school than a university.[83] Students of

[77] See p. 324, this vol.
[78] It was opened Nov. 11, 1850, at the house of Mr Pack, in the 17th ward
of S. L. City, Cyrus Collins being appointed teacher, but succeeded the same
year by Orson Spencer and W. W. Phelps. The terms were $3 a quarter.
Id., 6, 10; *Utah Gazetteer*, 1884, 287.
[79] *Des. Univ.*, MS., 24; *Utah Jour. Legisl.*, 1853–4, 115.
[80] By act of 1855 a grant was confirmed of nearly a section of land lying
east of S. L. City. By contributions of labor and produce, nearly all of it
was enclosed with a stone wall. A building was also commenced in the 13th
ward for the use of the parent school. *Des. Univ.*, MS., 8–9; *Utah Acts Legisl.*,
1866, 110. By act of congress, approved Jan. 21, 1855, two sections, including 46,080 acres, were reserved for a university, said lands to be disposed
of under the direction of the territorial legislature. *Utah Laws*, 1878, 172.
In 1859 the legislature passed an act to provide for the selection of two townships for this purpose. *Utah Acts Legisl.*, 1866, 93–4.
[81] By act of 1851 the chancellor and board of regents were authorized to
appoint a superintendent of primary schools, to be under their control, his
salary not to exceed $1,000 a year. By act of 1866 the right of making such
appointment was transferred to the legislature. *Des. Univ.*, MS., 4–5, 24.
[82] Of which David O. Calder was principal.
[83] The course lasted four years in the classical and two in the normal department. In connection with the normal department was a 'model school,'
where pupils were prepared for the college course. The charges were $20 per
term for the classical, $15 for the normal and commercial, and $8 for the preparatory course, with extra charges for modern languages, music, etc. The
rates for tuition were afterward reduced. For studies and faculty, see *Catal.
Univ. of Deseret*, 1868–9, 5, 14–16; for list of text-books, *Id.*, 1869–70, 25–6.

both sexes were admitted, the total attendance in 1870 being 546,[84] while in 1884 the number was but 298, the decrease being due to want of sufficient appropriations, suitable buildings,[85] and preparatory schools. In 1882 the university included an academic, a normal, and a preparatory department. In the first the courses included elementary mathematics, a little Greek and Latin, and a smattering of ancient, mediæval, modern, and natural history, physical science, political economy, logic, and English literature. On completing any one course, and keeping only three terms, the student was entitled to a certificate of graduation. In the normal department the curriculum, apart from the theory of teaching, was about the same as in the junior classes of a San Francisco high-school, and in the preparatory department almost identical with the subjects usually taught in the lower grades of a grammar-school.[86] Although the standard is somewhat low, it is probable that in the University of Deseret more has been accomplished, at an average cost for each pupil of $50 or $60 a year per capita, than in many similar institutions, where the pretensions were greater and the expense in proportion.[87]

[84] There were 307 males and 239 females. *Id.*, 1869-70, 21. *Des. Univ.*, MS., 27.

[85] At the session of 1879-80 the legislature appropriated $20,000 for the university, and soon afterward the city council donated to the regents the finest public square in the city. A building was at once commenced, but the appropriation was almost expended before the basement was finished, under the expectation that the legislature of 1881-2 would vote a sum sufficient to complete it. Such a bill was passed, but failed to receive the governor's signature. At the beginning of 1884 the walls and roof had been completed, and a portion of the building was ready to be occupied, the money being raised by contribution. For the two years ending Dec. 31, 1879, the receipts were $18,151.44, of which $9,200 was from territorial appropriations, and $5,986.80 from tuition fees. The salary of the president, J. R. Park, was $2,400 a year. At this date the institution was $5,384.14 in debt. *Bienn. Rept Chancellor Univ. Deseret*, 1878-9, 11-13. In 1854 Orson Hyde was appointed chancellor, in 1857 and 1861 Albert Carrington, the interim being filled by Orson Pratt, elected in 1858; in 1869 Dan. H. Wells and in 1878 Geo. Q. Cannon were appointed. *Des. Univ.*, MS., 35.

[86] See *Circ. Acad. Dept Univ. of Deseret*, 1880-2, 9-10.

[87] In 1870 a school in connection with the university was established at Provo, with Myron Tanner of that city, A. K. Thurber of Spanish Fork, and L. E. Harrington of American Fork as executive committee, and Warren

At a meeting of the board of regents, held in October 1853, Parley P. Pratt, Heber C. Kimball, and George D. Watt were appointed a committee to prepare a small school-book in characters founded on some new system of orthography, whereby the spelling and pronunciation of the English language might be made uniform and easily acquired. A further object was exclusiveness, a separate people wishing to have a separate language, and perhaps in time an independent literature. After some previous discussion, it was agreed that each regent should prepare an alphabet of his own contrivance and present it to the board. Parley Pratt was in favor of adopting one in which each letter should represent a single sound, but as some of the letters represent no sound except when in combination with other letters, and others are of uncertain sound, depending on such combination, the task would seem a difficult one. Finally, at a session held in December of this year, characters were adopted, under the style of the Deseret alphabet, the number of letters, or rather sounds, being thirty-two, of which the so-called vocal sounds were eleven, including six long, with short sounds to correspond, four double and one aspirate, and twenty-one articulate sounds. Thus the long sound of the letter *e* in meter was represented by a character resembling the Greek *sigma* reversed, the double sound of *woo* in wood by one resembling *omega*, the aspirate by *phi*, and the articulate sound of *f* by *rho*. While these characters are apparently borrowed from the Greek, this is also the case in the plates

Dusenberry principal. It lasted only a few years. *Deseret Univ.*, MS., 27-8. In 1884 a deaf-mute department was opened in connection with the university. *Annual of Univ. of Deseret*, 1884-5, 36-7. For further items concerning the university, see the circulars and reports above quoted. *Deseret Univ.*, MS., passim; *Utah Jour. Legisl.*, 1870, 168-72, 1876, 121-7, 1878, 295-6, 355-7, 381-91; *Ann. Univ. Deseret*, 1884-5, 7-38; *Smith's Rise, Progress, and Travels*, 24-5; *S. L. C. Contributor*, ii. 13-16, 48, 82, 110, 142; *Deseret News*, June 9, 1869, Jan. 5, 1871; *S. L. C. Tribune*, Aug. 13, 1876, March 9, 1878; *Herald*, Nov. 17, 1877, Nov. 22, 1878, Jan. 30, 1881.

Most of the details given in the text are taken from the *Deseret University*, MS., 1-35, which, besides a brief historical sketch of that institution, contains some valuable items concerning the district schools and the district school system of Utah.

𐐔𐐯𐑅𐐯𐑉𐐯𐐻 𐐈𐑊𐑁𐐲𐐺𐐯𐐻.

Long Sounds.			
Letter.	Name.		Sound.
𐐔	..e..	.as in..	eat.
𐐀	..a	"	ate.
𐐖	..ah	"	art.
𐐤	..aw	"	aught.
𐐃	..o	"	oat.
𐐭	..oo	"	ooze.

Short Sounds of the above.

Letter			Sound
𐐮	..as in..		it.
𐐲		"	et.
𐐱		"	at.
𐐳		"	ot.
𐐴		"	ut.
𐐷		"	book.

𐐵	..i..	.as in..	ice.
𐐶	..ow	"	owl.
𐐶	..woo		
𐐷	..ye		
𐐸	..h		

Letter.	Name.	Sound.
𐐹	..p	
𐐺	..b	
𐐻	..t	
𐐼	..d	
𐐽	che...as in.... cheese.	
𐑀	..g	
𐐿	..k	
𐑅	..ga...as in..... gate.	
𐑁	..f "	
𐑂	..v	
𐑃	..eth...as in.... thigh.	
𐑄	..the " thy.	
𐑅	..s	
𐑆	..z	
𐑇	..esh.... as in ..... flesh.	
𐑈	..zhe " vision.	
𐑉	..ur " burn.	
𐑊	..l	
𐑋	..m	
𐑌	..n	
𐑍	..eng...as in ....length.	

CHARACTERS OF DESERET ALPHABET.

from which the book of Mormon is said to have been translated, where the letters *pi, rho, tau, phi, chi,* some of them as in manuscript. and others as in printed Greek, can be distinctly traced.

Type was ordered, and with a view to durability, made so as to contain neither the top nor tail extensions of the letters. At a meeting of the board of regents, held in March 1854, some of it was presented to the members; and between that date and 1869 were published in the Deseret alphabet a primer, the book of Mormon, and the first book of Nephi. Some attempt was made to introduce into the public schools books thus printed, but without success. The tailless characters, and the monotonous evenness of the lines, made the words difficult to distinguish, and it was found impossible to insure uniform pronunciation and orthography. Within a few years the alphabet fell into disuse, and is now remembered only as a curiosity.[88]

In connection with the university may also be mentioned its library, containing at the close of 1875 about 10,000 volumes, later reserved for the use of students, but for many years open to the public.[89] The territorial library, for which, as we have seen, an appropriation was made by congress in 1850, further grants being made by the Utah legislature from time to

[88] *Richards' Utah Misc.*, MS., 13–16; *Des. Univ.*, MS., 16–18; *Richards' Incidents in Utah Hist.*, MS., 63. The preparation and use of the alphabet were ordered, or at least suggested, by Brigham Young, who, in his address to the legislature of 1853, thus gives his reasons: 'While the world is progressing with steam-engine power and lightning speed in the accumulation of wealth, extension of science, communication, and dissemination of letters and principle, why may not the way be paved for the easier acquisition of the English language, combining, as it does, great extension and varied expression with beauty, simplicity, and power, and being unquestionably the most useful and beautiful in the world. But while we freely admit this, we also have to acknowledge that it is perhaps as much abused in its use, and as complex in its attainment, as any other.' In the *Deseret News*, Aug. 19, 1868, the weeding-out of objectionable literature is stated as an additional reason. In 1855 $2,500 was voted by the legislature for the new type and for printing books in the Deseret characters. *Utah Acts Legisl.*, 110–11. In 1859–60 the Deseret alphabet was used in keeping Brigham's ledger, and to some extent in the historian's office and in journalism. In 1877 an attempt was made to have the book of Mormon printed in Pitman's phonotype, and Orson Pratt started for England for this purpose, but returned at the death of Brigham in August of that year. No further effort was made.

[89] *Des. Univ.*, MS., 29; *Utah Gazetteer*, 228.

time,[90] contained in 1883 about 4,500 volumes. At the same date the masonic library, established in 1873, contained nearly 6,000 volumes, the odd-fellows' about 1,500, and there were smaller libraries in connection with various literary, benefit, secret, and mutual improvement societies.[91]

Like citizens of the United States elsewhere, the settlers of Utah have always been patrons of newspapers—and except that their columns are cumbered with church matters, interesting only to the saints, their journals compare very favorably with others published on the Pacific slope. The news is fairly reliable, but the editorial and other comments must be taken at the reader's own valuation. In freedom from journalistic scandal-mongering, they certainly rank among the foremost, and if sometimes dull, they are never silly or obscene. As a rule, the Mormon journals are less rabid in politics and religion than the gentile newspapers. Of several of the former mention has already been made. In 1867 was first published and issued daily the *Deseret Evening News*, the weekly having been first issued in 1850. The *Daily Telegraph* first appeared on the 4th of July, 1864, under the parentage of T. B. H. Stenhouse,[92] and in 1869 was removed to Ogden, where it expired during that year. The *Juvenile Instructor*, an illustrated Sunday-school periodical published semi-weekly at Salt Lake City, was established by George Q. Cannon, the first number appearing January 1, 1866. The *Salt Lake Daily Herald* came into existence in June 1870,

[90] The last one in 1882.

[91] For mention of such societies, see *Contributor*, ii. 27-9, 31-2, 61, 92-4, 159, 222, 287, 350; *Deseret News*, Aug. 7, Nov. 20, 1878; *Utah Gazetteer*, 1884, 218-25. For further details as to libraries, see *Id.*, 228-30; *Burton's City of the Saints*, 286-7; *Deseret News*, Aug. 20, 1862; *S. L. C. Tribune*, March 15, Nov. 22, 1873, Dec. 18, 1875; *Reno Gazette*, Dec. 6, 1880; *Bonanza City (Id.)*, *Yankee Fork Her.*, Sept. 25, 1879; observatories, *Wheeler's Geog. Surveys*, ii. 7-9, 461-7, 469-71. The office of superintendent of meteorological observations created by act of 1857 was abolished by act of 1876. *Utah Jour. Legisl.*, 1876, 179-80.

[92] The author of *Rocky Mountain Saints*. His decease occurred in 1882.

Edward L. Sloan being the first editor. The *Woman's Exponent*, a semi-monthly woman's-rights paper, was first issued June 1, 1872, under the care of Mrs Louise L. Green Richards, and afterward transferred to Mrs Emeline B. Wells. The *Salt Lake Daily Times*, a theatrical and advertising sheet of which John C. Graham was editor and proprietor, commenced December 24, 1875, and in March 1881 its publication ceased. The first number of *Tullidge's Quarterly Magazine* appeared in October 1880. This publication is embellished with steel engravings, and has been favorably received, not only in Utah, but in the eastern states and in England. Considerable sums have been subscribed for the publication therein of city and county histories.

The *Ogden Junction* was first issued as a semi-weekly in charge of F. D. Richards on the 1st of January 1870. Mr Richards associated with himself C. W. Penrose, to whom he resigned the editorship, subsequent editors being John Nicholson, Joseph Hall, and Leo Haefli. Soon after its first appearance the paper became a daily and its name was changed to the *Ogden Herald*.[93] The *Provo Daily Times*, which started into being August 1, 1873, has had a varied experience, being successively called the *Provo Tri-Weekly Times*, the *Utah County Times*, the *Utah County Advertiser*, and the *Territorial Inquirer*, the last being its present name.[94] The *Beaver Enterprise* was instituted early in 1874, Joseph Field being editor; the *Southern Utonian* was also published at Beaver City in March 1881, with F. R. Clayton as editor,[95] and the *Beaver County Record*, at first a

[93] Among those who early took an interest in newspapers may be mentioned Sidney Stevens, who in 1885 was still one of the largest proprietors of the *Herald*. Mr Stevens, a native of Somersetshire, England, came to Utah in 1863, settling two years later at North Ogden, where, and at Ogden City, he has ever since been actively engaged in business. Among other ventures, he has been largely interested in the shipment of produce to the eastern states, forwarding as many as 470 car-loads in a single year. To his enterprise the terminus of the Union Pacific is in no small degree indebted for its recent growth.

[94] It has been edited at various dates by R. T. McEwan, R. G. Sleater, J. T. McEwan, and John C. Graham. *Richards' Bibliog. of Utah*, MS., 18.

[95] Later Dan. Tyler became editor. *Ibid.*

weekly and afterward a semi-weekly, in 1883, with
F. R. Clayton and R. Maeser as editors. In addition
to the above, and to those already mentioned, numerous daily, weekly, monthly, semi-weekly, and semi-
monthly publications were issued at the capital and
elsewhere in the territory, some of them having but
an ephemeral existence, and some being in existence
to-day. For an account of them, I refer the reader
to the note subjoined,[96] where it will be seen that

[96] Additional list of publications, showing name, where located, frequency
of issue, and, where possible, date of establishment and suspension:

Location.	Name.	Established.
Alta City	Cottonwood Observer, s.w.	1870 et seq.
Beaver	Enterprise, w	1873.
"	Beaver County Record, s.w.	June 8, 1883, et seq.
"	The Southern Utonian, w.	March 1881 et seq.
Bear Lake	Democrat, w. (Mor. pub., but pub. in Idaho)	Oct. 1880 et seq.
Bloomington	The Union and Village Echo, m	1882.
Camp Douglas	Union Vedette, d. (trans. to S. L. City)	1864–7.
Corinne	Daily Reporter, d	1867.
"	Daily Journal, d	1871.
"	Mail, d	
"	Utah Reporter, d., s.w. (changed to)	
"	Corinne Republican, t.w., w.	
Diamond	Rocky Mountain Husbandman, w	
Frisco.	Times, w	
Logan	Leader, w. (changed to)	Sept. 1879–82.
"	Utah Journal, s.w	Aug. 1, 1882, et seq.
"	The Northern Light, w.	May 1879.
	(Transferred and changed to)	
Oxford, Id.	Idaho Banner, w	1879.
Ogden	Amateur	
"	Daily Morning Rustler, d	
"	Evening Dispatch, d	
"	Ogden Herald, d., s.w	1881 et seq.
"	Ogden Freeman, d., s.w.	
"	Ogden Junction, d., s.w	Jan. 1870.
"	Ogden Pilot, d.	
"	Ogden Telegraph, s.w	
"	Ogden Times, s.w	
"	Utah Talsmand	
Park City	Record, w	
Provo City	Territorial Inquirer, s.w	
"	Times, d	
"	Utah County Times, t.w	
"	The Utah County Advertiser	Jan. 13, 1876.
Richfield	Sevier Valley Echo, w	Aug. 1884 et seq.
Salt Lake City	Anti-Polygamy Standard, m	Apr. '80 to Sept. '82.
"	Bikuben, w	Aug. 1, 1876 et seq.
"	Circular, w	1874.
"	City Review	
"	College Lantern, m	May, 1870.
"	Deseret News, d., s.w., w	June 1850 et seq.
"	Deseret Home, m	Jan. '82 to Aug. '84.
"	Diogenes	Jan. 1871.

about one hundred newspapers and periodicals have
been published since June 15, 1850, when the first

Location.	Name.	Established.
Salt Lake City	....Enoch's Advocate	1874.
"	....Evening Chronicle, d	
"	....Evening Mail, d	
"	....Foot-Lights	
"	....Grocer and Trade Journal, m	May 1, 1881, et seq.
"	....Juvenile Instructor, s.m	Jan. 1, 1866, et seq.
"	....Keep-a-Pitchin-in, s.m	1869.
"	....Kirk Anderson's Valley Tan, w	Nov. '58 to Feb. '60.
"	....Life and Home, m	Aug. 1884.
"	....Mining Gazette, w	1873 et seq.
"	....Monthly Record, m	
"	....Morgenstjernen, s.m	1882 et seq.
"	....Mormon Expositor	
"	....Mormon Tribune, w	
"	....Mountaineer, w	Aug. 27, 1859.
"	....Mormonen Zeitung, w	Aug. 26, 1882.
"	....New Endowment, d	Feb. 17, 1873.
"	....Parry's Literary Journal, m	Oct. 1884 et seq.
"	....Peep O'Day, w	Oct. 20, 1864.
"	....Press, d	1874.
"	....Real Estate Circular	
"	....Real Estate and Min'g Gazette, s.m., m.	
"	....Rocky Mt Christian Advocate, m	1876.
"	....Salt Lake Herald, d., s.w	June 5, 1870, et seq.
"	....Salt Lake Independent, d	
"	....Salt Lake Journal, d	1872.
"	....Salt Lake Leader, w	
"	....Salt Lake Reporter, d	May 11, 1868.
"	....Salt Lake Review, d	1871.
"	....Salt Lake Telegraph, d., s.w., w	July 4, 1864.
"	....Salt Lake Times, d	
"	....Salt Lake Tribune, d., w	1870 et seq.
"	....Skandinav	
"	....The Contributor, m	Oct. 1879 et seq.
"	....The Utah Farmer, m	Feb. '80 to Sept. '81.
"	....Tullidge's Quarterly Magazine, qty	1880 et seq.
"	....Union Vedette, d., w	1864.
	(Trans. fr. Camp Douglas in 1867.)	
"	....Utah Commercial, m	
"	....Utah Educational Journal, m	July 1875.
"	....Utah Mail, d	
"	....Utah Magazine, w	1867.
"	....Utah Miner	
"	....Utah Mining Journal, d	June, 1872.
"	....Utah Posten	Dec. 1873.
"	....Woman's Exponent, s.m	June 1, 1872, et seq.
Silver Reef	....Silver Reef Echo, s.w	
"	....Silver Reef Miner, s.w., chgd to w	1879.
Spring Lake Villa	.Farmer's Oracle, s.m	May 22, 1863.
St George	....Cactus, w	1862.
"	....Enterprise, m	1869.
"	....Our Dixie Times, w. (changed to)	Jan. 22, 1868.
"	....Rio Virgen Times, w	
"	....Pendogist, m	
"	....Pomologist and Gardener, m	1870.
"	....The Union	1878.

number of the *Deseret News* announced to the saints
the death of John C. Calhoun.[97]

[97] For further mention of Utah journalism, see *Richards' Bibliog. of Utah*,
MS.; *Millennial Star*, xxxvi. 731–2; xxxix. 127; *Remy's Jour. to G. S. L.
City*, i. 189–90; *Beadle's Life in Utah*, 534–8; *Richardson's Beyond the Mis-
sissippi*, 351; *Smith's Rise, Progress, and Travels*, 27; *Bonwick's Mormons and
Silver Mines*, 160–2; *Tucker's Mormonism*, 246–7; *S. L. C. Contributor*, ii.
209–10, iv. 352; *Pettengell's Newsp. Direct.*, 1856.

In connection with Utah literature may be mentioned Eliza R. Snow, the
sister of Apostle Lorenzo Snow, and the second of the seven children of Oliver
Snow, a native of Mass., and a farmer by occupation, though one much occupied by public business and holding many responsible positions. While still
almost a young girl, Sister Snow commenced writing for various publications,
under an assumed signature, and later in life published nine volumes, two of
them being of poetry, and several reaching a second edition. Miss Snow was
baptized as a Mormon in 1835, and the following year removed to Kirtland,
residing in the family of Joseph Smith and teaching his children. After a
brief residence at Adam-on-Diahman and Quincy, she repaired to Nauvoo,
and, at the expulsion, crossed the Mississippi with the first parties, reaching
the valley of Great Salt Lake with Parley P. Pratt's companies. *Snow's Autobiog.*, MS., passim; *Richards' Narr.*, MS., 116–7; *Tullidge's Mag.*, 116–17.

In connection with the press of Utah may be mentioned Chas W. Penrose,
who was called to the ministry at the London conference of 1850, being then
only in his 18th year. Mr Penrose commenced his literary career as a contributor to the *Millennial Star*, of which he was editor about 1867, having
before that date passed several years in Utah, where, however, he found
little encouragement as a journalist. Returning in 1870, he was appointed to
the editorial charge of the *Ogden Junction*, which position he filled for seven
years, after which he became editor of the *Deseret News*. In 1876 he was
elected member of the legislature for Weber co., in which body he was for
several sessions a tireless worker. Among the measures that he introduced
was one to remove the political disabilities of women, which passed both
houses, but failed to receive the governor's signature. *Tullidge's Mag.*, ii.
27–30.

CHAPTER XXVII.

AGRICULTURE, STOCK-RAISING, MANUFACTURES, AND MINING.

1852–1886.

AGRICULTURAL PRODUCTS AND YIELD PER ACRE—IRRIGATION—CHARACTER
OF THE SOIL—FRUIT CULTURE—VITICULTURE—SERICULTURE—TIMBER
AND TIMBER-LANDS—BUNCH-GRASS—CATTLE-RAISING—DAIRY PRODUCTS
—HORSES—SHEEP—WOOLLEN MANUFACTURES—LEATHER—OTHER MAN-
UFACTURES—IRON-MINING—COAL-MINING—COPPER—SULPHUR—GYPSUM
AND MICA—OTHER MINERALS—BUILDING STONE—GOLD AND SILVER—
THE WEST MOUNTAIN DISTRICT—THE RUSH VALLEY DISTRICT—THE
COTTONWOOD DISTRICT—THE AMERICAN FORK DISTRICT—THE TINTIC
DISTRICT—THE ONTARIO MINE—OTHER MINING DISTRICTS—MINING
PRODUCTS—MILLING, SMELTING, AND REDUCTION-WORKS.

THE progress of agriculture in Utah will best be
understood from the following figures: In 1849, as
we have seen, nearly 130,000 bushels of cereals were
raised from about 17,000 acres of land,[1] then valued
at $6.50 per acre. In 1883, which was by no means
a favorable year, more than 1,600,000 bushels of
wheat, and some 722,000 of oats, 305,000 of barley,
193,000 of corn, together with 215,000 tons of hay,
and 800,000 bushels of potatoes, were produced from
about 215,000 acres,[2] the value of which varied according to location from $25 to $100 per acre; the yield

---

[1] See p. 328, this vol. Three fourths of the crop was wheat, and there
were 10,000 bushels each of corn and oats. Most of it was produced on the
banks of Jordan River and its affluents, and in the neighborhood of Utah Lake.
In *Utah Sketches*, MS., passim, it is stated that land was cultivated in Sanpete co. in 1848, and in Tooele and Utah cos. in 1849. Some 45,000 bushels
of potatoes were also raised in 1849, besides other vegetables, together with
40 pounds of hops and 70 of tobacco.
[2] For tabulated statement of cereal and farm products for each county in
1883, see *Utah Gazetteer*, 1884, 297–8.

of wheat being in 1883 about 20 bushels, of oats 33, of barley 25, and of corn 16 bushels, to the acre; though in Willard county the average of wheat was 57,[3] of oats in Cache and Utah counties 53 and 58 bushels, and of barley in the latter nearly 41 bushels.[4] When the pioneers entered the valley in 1847 their hearts sank within them at the hopeless prospect. The land seemed barren beyond redemption; but from less than seventeen acres of its soil were raised, in 1880, more than 1,250 bushels of grain.[5]

According to the census returns for 1880, there were 9,452 farms in Utah, with a total area of 655,-524 acres, of which 416,105 were in tilth, their value, including improvements, being estimated at $14,015,-178; the total value of all farm products at $3,337,410, and of farming implements and machinery at $946,-753. The agricultural products of Utah in 1883 more than sufficed for her needs,[6] and as there was no very reliable market for the surplus, there was little incentive to further exertion in this direction. It was claimed, however, that with more careful cultivation the yield could be at least doubled on the same acreage, and it is certain that there were several million acres of farming land untouched and almost unthought of, on

[3] Utah co. produced over 30 and Cache over 29 bushels per acre.

[4] Agricultural statistics for Utah will be found in the census reports for 1850, 1860, 1870, 1880. For intervening years, see the files of the *Utah Directory and Gazetteer; Utah Gazetteer; Deseret News; Smith's Rise, Progress, and Travels*, 23; *Fabian's Utah*, 6, 8-9; *Utah Resources and Attractions*, 18-19; *Sac. Union*, Jan. 9, 1873; *S. L. C. Tribune*, March 30, 1879; *Deseret News*, Nov. 9, 1881; *House Ex. Doc.*, 46th Cong. 2d Sess., 46, 503.

[5] By S. A. Woolley. Of wheat, 426 bushels were obtained from 6¾ acres, 517 of barley from 5¾ acres, and 310 of oats from 3½ acres. *Sloan's Utah*, 4. For an essay entitled *Utah: Her Attractions and Resources, as Inviting the Attention of Tourists and Those Seeking Permanent Homes*, a prize was awarded in 1881 by a committee of Mormons, among whom were Joseph R. Walker and Wm Jennings, to Robt W. Sloan of the *S. L. C. Herald*. It was afterward published as a pamphlet, and contains much reliable information in a compact form. Mr Sloan is also the compiler of the *Utah Gazetteer, and Directory of Logan, Ogden, Provo, and Salt Lake Cities for 1884*, in which is a valuable compendium of the agricultural, manufacturing, mining, railroad, and commercial interests of Utah, together with a chronological table and a description and brief historical sketch of the various counties and settlements.

[6] The consumption of wheat was estimated at 900,000 to 1,000,000 bushels a year, or about 6¼ bushels per capita of the population.

HIST. UTAH. 46

account of an insufficient rainfall,[7] or through lack of irrigation.

There are few parts of the world where irrigation has been pushed forward more systematically and with better results than in Utah. In 1865, 277 canals had already been constructed, at a cost, including dams, of $1,766,939, with a total length of 1,043 miles, irrigating 153,949 acres; and there were others in progress at this date, the cost of which was estimated at $877,730.[8] During each succeeding year thousands of acres, before considered worthless, were brought under cultivation, canals being built in all directions, the waters that had run to waste down the mountain sides and through the cañons deposit-

[7] The average annual precipitation at several places and periods covered by observation is as follows: S. L. City and Camp Douglas 15.72 inches for 19 years; Harrisburg 13.74 inches, 2 years; Saint George 11.39 inches, 3 years; Camp Floyd 7.33 inches, 2½ years. Consult *Sloan's Utah Gazetteer*, 1884, p. 189; *Powell's Lands of the Arid Region*, in *H. Ex. Doc.*, 45th Cong. 2d Sess., 73, 49, 79; also *Schott's Tables of Precipitation*, 72, 116. In the year ending June 30, 1879, 37.71 inches of rain are reported at S. L. City. *U. S. Signal Officer*, in *H. Ex. Doc.*, 46th Cong. 2d Sess., i. pt 1, 92. The greater rainfalls at S. L. City and Camp Douglas are due to the modifying influence of G. S. Lake, which is only local. From May to October there is almost a total absence of rain. *Stansbury's Expedition*, 140. Burton, who visited Great Salt Lake City in 1860, says the rain that year extended to the middle of June, and attributes the change to cultivation and settlement. *City of the Saints*, 335. About two thirds of the districts under cultivation require irrigation. *Utah Direc.*, 1879-80, 17.

[8] *Smith's Rise, Progress, and Travels*, 23. For act incorporating the Big Cottonwood Canal Co., see *Utah Acts Legisl.*, 1855, 277-9; for progress of work, *Deseret News*, Aug. 29, 1855, March 25, 1857. In 1856 the Davis Co. Canal Co. was incorporated. *Utah Acts Legisl.*, 1855-6, 34-5. For an account of the Weber River canal, see *Deseret News*, Aug. 20, 1856, Oct. 10, 1860; of the Logan canal, *Tullidge's Mag.*, i. 534-5; and of the Jordan cañon canal, *Id.*, Sept. 21, 1864. In this year it was first proposed to bring the waters of Utah Lake into Salt Lake co., where there was not one third of the water needed for irrigation. The cost of making a canal for this purpose, 32 miles in length, 20 feet broad at the bottom, 3 feet deep, and capable of irrigating about 30,000 acres per week, was estimated at $485,580. *Id.*, Nov. 30, 1864. The enterprise was termed the Deseret Irrigation and Navigation Co. The governor refused to grant a franchise. See *Utah Jour. Legisl.*, 1864-5, 116-17; but it was incorporated in 1867. The act of incorporation will be found in *Utah Acts Legisl.*, 1867, pp. 30-2. See, for statistics of irrigation for each county in 1865, *Pac. Coast Direct.*, 1867, 151-3; for reports on extent, cost, and value of canals at this date, with other statistics, *Utah Jour. Legisl.*, 1864-5, 130-3, 1865-6, 149-53; for various acts regulating irrigation, *Utah Compiled Laws*, 879; for act to provide right of way for S. L. City canals, *Utah Laws*, 1880, 85-8; for act regulating water rights, *Id.*, 36-41; for other acts concerning irrigation, *Id.*, 1882, 119; for names, length, and cost of canals in Weber co., *Stanford's Brief Hist. Sketch of Weber Co.*, MS., 22.

ing on the farm-lands rich particles of fertile soil.[9] Two or three waterings a year would, in most localities, secure good crops, and the millions devoted to purposes of irrigation throughout the territory paid better interest, directly and indirectly, than capital invested in any other description of enterprise. Nevertheless, the supply was insufficient, more water being still allowed to run to waste during the spring and winter months than was utilized.[10]

The winter rains swell the streams, sometimes to overflowing, when considerable damage occurs to farming-lands along the river-bottoms. Snow falls to a depth of from two to twenty-five feet, but does not usually melt before summer is well advanced. Wind-storms are often violent, and occasionally destroy growing crops.[11] The altitude of Utah renders the high lands liable to night frosts during the summer months, and on the more elevated plateaus no attempt is made to plant, the surface being devoted entirely to grazing purposes. At times in winter a very low temperature is registered. Often the valleys are colder at night than the more elevated adjacent regions, and

[9] The necessity for irrigation of course reduces the size of farms, which in 1883 probably did not average more than 25 acres. See *Hollister's Res. and Attract. of Utah*, 16.

[10] See, for remarks on facilities for irrigation, *Wheeler's Surveys, Progress Rept*, 1872, 28–33; for report on water supply, character and quantity of irrigated and irrigable land, etc., in 1876, *House Ex. Doc.*, 45th Cong. 2d Sess., 73, passim; for report on existing system of irrigation and needed improvements, *Powell's Lands of the Arid Region*, passim.

[11] The Kings of Kingston, in Piute county, one year sowed 300 acres with wheat, and the wind blew the crop away. What was not actually displaced was kept cut close to the ground by the perpetual passage of waves of sand. They planted an orchard, but some gooseberry bushes alone remained. Shade trees were set out about their houses, but the wind worked them around so that they could not take root. *Robinson, Sinners and Saints*, 209. In 1880 occurred the most violent storm ever known in Utah. A description of it is given in the *S. L. C. Herald*, July 29, 1880. For account of flood at Parowan in 1857, see *Deseret News*, Sept. 30, 1857. In Nov. 1860 there was a violent hurricane which caused great destruction of property. See *Deseret News*, Nov. 21, 28, 1860; *Sac. Union*, Dec. 1, 1860. In 1860 there were heavy floods in various parts of Utah. See *Little's Jacob Hamblin*, 75–7; *Deseret News*, Jan. 15, 22, Feb. 12, May 7, July 9, 1862; *Utah Jour. Legisl.*, 1863–4. For other remarkable storms, see *S. F. Bull.*, May 25, 1877; *S. F. Chron.*, Apr. 25, 1883. The prevailing winds are westerly. *Powell's Lands of the Arid Region*, in *H. Ex. Doc.*, 45th Cong. 2d Sess., 73, 68.

growing crops are occasionally nipped by frost when
those on the bench-lands escape altogether.[12]

The havoc wrought, as we have seen, by crickets
and grasshoppers among the growing crops of the
first settlers, and again in 1855–6,[13] was repeated at
brief intervals in later years. Seldom was a harvest
gathered in Utah that was not more or less injured
by this scourge.[14]

Of the nature of the soil, slight mention has already
been made.[15] The early settlers discoursed in glowing
terms of its fertility, though passing emigrants spoke
of it as a "mean land," hard, dry, and fit only for the
plodding, thrifty, sober Mormon. The main drawback was the alkaline matter, which was so abundant
in spots as to form a white efflorescence on the surface,
and wherever this efflorescence appeared, vegetation
died. Otherwise its composition was favorable to
fertility, being formed principally of the disintegrated
feldspathic rocks of the mountain ranges, mingled with
the débris and decomposed limestone of the valleys.[16]

At the annual fairs held by the Deseret Agricultural and Manufacturing Society, discontinued after
1881 on account of inability to secure permanent
grounds and buildings, prizes were awarded for nearly
all the varieties of grain, fruits, and vegetables that

[12] Says Burton: 'The spring vegetation is about a fortnight later on the
banks of Jordan than above them;' and he also asserts that the presence of
saleratus or alkaline salts is another cause of cold. *City of the Saints*, 345.

[13] See pp. 279–81, 498 (note 36), this vol.

[14] In 1859 great injury was done to the crops in Juab co. and elsewhere.
Deseret News, June 29, 1859; and in Carson Valley. *Sac. Union*, June 23, 1859.
For damage by crickets and grasshoppers in other years, see *Deseret News*,
May 2, 1860; *S. F. Call*, July 22, 1864; *Deseret News*, Aug. 7, 14, Sept. 4, 1867;
May 13, 1868; *S. F. Bull.*, May 21, June 30, 1868; *Huntsville, Descript. of*,
MS., 6; *Utah Sketches*, MS., 27; *S. F. Times*, Aug. 10, 1869; *S. F. Call*,
Aug. 18, 1869; *Deseret News*, June 29, 1870, May 17, 1871; *S. F. Bull.*, Oct.
4, 1872. In the *Second Rept Entomol. Comm.*, 45th Cong. 2d Sess., there is
also a report on their ravages, with suggestions as to their extermination.

[15] See p. 322, this vol.

[16] For further mention of the soil of Utah, see *U. S. Agr. Rept*, 1869, p.
617, 1870, 557 et seq., *H. Ex. Doc.*, 42d Cong. 2d Sess., 325; *Mess. and
Doc.*, 1868–9 (abridg.), 831; *U. S. Land-Off. Rept*, 1869, 170–1; *King's Geol.
Survey*, v., p. xlviii.; *Ludlow's Heart of the Continent*, 202–3; *Marshall's
Through Amer.*, 237; *S. L. Wkly Tribune*, Feb. 14, 1880; *Musser's Fruits of
Mormonism*, 27.

were raised in California and Oregon.[17] With the exception of Indian corn, all the cereals raised in Utah thrive vigorously when under irrigation, fall wheat requiring only one watering a year. In the basin of Great Salt Lake the fruits of the temperate zone grow to good size, and are of excellent flavor, the crop being remarkably sure. The value of orchard products in 1883, including apples, of which there were at least ninety varieties, pears, quinces, cherries, peaches, currants, plums, and berries of many descriptions, was estimated at $157,000. The yield of apples was about 90 bushels to the acre, of pears 75, of peaches 120, of plums 165, and of cherries 75.[18] Production was largely in excess of the demand, most of the surplus being dried for shipment, though for want of a market thousands of tons were fed to hogs, or allowed to rot on the ground.[19]

On the Rio Virgen and elsewhere in southern Utah below the rim of the basin were, in 1883, a few vineyards, but viticulture was not a profitable industry, as both grapes and wine were slow of sale, the latter

[17] See, for list of prizes awarded in 1879, *Deseret News*, Oct. 22, 1879; for report of directors in 1860, *Id.*, Oct. 17, 1860; for exhibition in that year, *Sac. Union*, Oct. 20, 1860; for condition, operations, and financial exhibits, *Utah Jour. Legisl.*, 1863-4, pp. 59-60; 1864-5, 79-81; 1865-6, 82-4, 123; 1870, 177 -8; 1876, 133-4; for rules and regulations, *Deseret Agr. and Man. Soc.—List of Premiums; S. L. Dy Herald*, July 19, Aug. 9, 1879; for description of last fair, *S. L. Wkly Herald*, Oct. 6, 1881; for agricultural fair held at Provo in 1870, *Deseret News*, Oct. 12, 1870; for Utah co. fair in 1860, *Id.*, Oct. 3, 1860; for fairs at various settlements and prizes awarded, *Id.*, Oct. 8, 1862; for complete list of agricultural societies, *Id.* Aug. 21, 1872. In 1865 lands and funds were appropriated for an agricultural college. See *Utah Jour. Legisl.*, 1865-6, p. 40; *Utah Acts Legisl.*, 1865, p. 88.

[18] *Utah Gazetteer*, 1884, p. 46. These figures are for 1875. Of late years apples, peaches, vegetables, and grain have been infected with worms, and the trees with noxious insects, four or five large worms being sometimes found in a single ear of corn. *Jennings' Mat. Progr. of Utah*, MS., 7; *Hollister's Res. and Attract. of Utah* (1882), 18.

[19] See, for review of fruit culture in Utah, *Deseret News*, March 20, 1861; for tables showing area under fruit, product, yield per acre, and sketch of fruit-growing interest for 1875-9, *S. L. C. Tribune*, Apr. 2, 1879; for other statistics and reports on horticulture, *Deseret News*, Dec. 31, 1856; *Utah Jour. Legisl.*, 1866-7, pp. 159-62; 1868, 163-8. Among the leading men engaged in the wholesale fruit business may be mentioned H. L. Griffin, who commenced operations in 1881 and met with fair success. Mr Griffin, a Pennsylvanian by birth, came to Utah in 1879, having previously resided for many years in Kansas, to which state he removed after his father was crippled in the war of the rebellion. *Griffin's Fruit Cult.*, MS.

on account of its inferior quality, and because the
Mormons seldom use stimulants.   In 1875 there were
only 544 acres in grapes, the total yield being about
1,700 tons, and the average a little more than three
tons per acre.[20]

In 1883 nearly 700,000 bushels of potatoes were
raised from about 8,500 acres of land, the value of
market-garden produce for this year being less than
$65,000.   The small volume of business in these and
in orchard products is due to the fact that most of
the settlers raised their own fruit and vegetables.

Of experiments in the raising of cotton in southern
Utah between 1855 and 1859, mention has already
been made.[21]   Of flax fibre there were raised in 1879
a few thousand pounds in Washington county, and of
flax straw about 1,170 tons in various counties.

That sericulture will eventually become a leading
feature in the industries of Utah seems almost beyond
a peradventure, as portions of the country are well
adapted to this industry, and nowhere else in the
United States can the labor of women and children be
obtained so cheaply and in such abundance.   In 1868
a large cocoonery was built some four miles south of
Salt Lake City,[22] and about thirty acres planted in
mulberry-trees, but through mismanagement, and also
on account of the dampness of the building, which
was of adobe, the first experiments resulted in failure.
After some further efforts, a company was organized,
styled the Utah Silk Association, and incorporated
under the laws of the territory.[23]   Ground was leased

[20] Sloan, *Utah*, 11, says that grapes yield five tons to the acre, but this is
doubtless an exaggeration.   For grape culture in Utah, see *Ogden Freeman*,
Feb. 21, 1879; for wine-making, see *Sac. Union*, Nov. 2, 1861; for viticulture
at St George in 1882, see *Robinson's Sinners and Saints*, 218.

[21] See p. 599, note 74, this vol.   A little cotton was raised until 1864. See
Deseret News, Oct. 9, 1861; *Sac. Union*, March 4, 1862; *Cal. Farmer*, March
11, 1864; but after that date its culture seems to have been practically discontinued.

[22] Experiments were made before this date.   In the *S. F. Bulletin*, Aug.
21, 1863, a correspondent states that he saw the first silk fabric made in Utah
—a small scarf—from silk raised at Centreville.

[23] In 1880 William Jennings was president, Eliza R. Snow vice-president,
A. M. Musser secretary, and Paul A. Schettler treasurer, the first three being

at the mouth of City Creek, where a neat brick building was erected and fitted with machinery for the manufacturing purposes. Samples of raw silk were sent to New York, to Florence in Italy, and Florence in Massachusetts, and were found to be well reeled and of good strength and quality. Though the industry is as yet in its infancy, the Mormons are confident that it will soon develop into a source of wealth.[24]

One of the main drawbacks to the industries of Utah has been the scarcity of timber for hard and finishing woods. In the mountains and cañons there was a fair supply of common timber for ordinary use, though in the valleys and plains there was no forest growth, sage-brush having been often used for fuel during the first years of settlement, willow brush for fencing, and adobes for building. In later times the black balsam and red pine, indigenous to the Oquirrh and other ranges, were largely used for posts and railroad ties, the scrub cedar and piñon pine, found in many portions of southern and western Utah, being made to serve the same purpose. Though the people were not allowed to acquire title to timber-lands, and were even nominally forbidden to use the timber except on mineral lands, and then only for domestic purposes, they obtained all that they needed without even paying stumpage, except in a few localities. In 1883 there were a hundred or more saw-mills in operation in various parts of Utah, the price of building and fencing lumber generally ruling at from $20 to $25, and of flooring and finishing lumber $40 to $45, per thousand feet.[25]

directors. The other members of the board were Wm H. Hooper, Zina D. Young, Alex. C. Pyper, and M. I. Horne. *S. L. C. Contributor*, ii. 115. In 1878 $1,500 was appropriated by the legislature for the purchase of machinery. *Snow's Autobiog.*, MS.; *Utah Laws*, 1878, 56.

[24] For further mention of sericulture in Utah, see *Id.*, 115–16; *S. L. Dy Tel.*, Dec. 5, 1868; *S. F. Bulletin*, July 22, 1868; *Sac. Union*, Nov. 25, 1868.

[25] *Hollister's Res. and Attract. of Utah*, 18; *Utah Gaz.*, 11. See, for remarks on the scarcity of timber, *Utah Early Records*, MS., 20; *House Ex. Doc.*, 46th Cong. 2d Sess., xxii., p. 504; *Beadle's Life in Utah*, 461–2; for extent, character, and statistics of timber-lands, *Powell's Lands of the Arid*

Bunch-grass, on which the countless flocks and herds of Utah mainly subsist, first makes its appearance on the western slope of the Black Hills, and thence is found at intervals as far as the eastern slope of the Sierra Nevada. Growing in clumps, as its name implies, and on the most unkindly soil, in thirsty sand or on barren hills, it gives value to millions of acres which would otherwise be absolutely worthless. Its growth commences in early spring, and though in May or June it dries up, it is still nutritious, having then the appearance of a light-yellow straw. Within its withered stalk it puts forth a green shoot after the first autumnal rains, and its pyriform seed, resembling the oat but of smaller size, is the favorite food of cattle. In winter it gathers juice and nourishment beneath the snow, and except in the late summer months, when it is still of fair quality on the mountains and high in the cañon ravines,[26] serves as pasture for stock the year round, producing large, sinewy limbs and strong, elastic muscles, and giving to the beef and mutton an excellent flavor.[27]

As elsewhere on the Pacific slope, before 1886 the range for cattle decreased, lands once common for grazing[28] being taken up for agriculture, while sheep-raising was found to be a more profitable industry. Hence the introduction of alfalfa, in which many thousands of acres were seeded, the yield being three to four tons on inferior and poorly irrigated land, and ten tons under more favorable conditions.

Region, in *House Ex. Doc.*, 45th Cong. 2d Sess., xiii. no. 73, pp. 14–19, 27–8, 98–102; *U. S. Agr. Rept*, 1875, 331–2; for tenure of timber-lands, *House Ex. Doc.*, 46th Cong. 2d Sess., xxii., pp. 497–8; for depredations committed on timber-lands, *S. L. C. Tribune*, June 26, 1875.

[26] L. B. Adams, in 1884 a resident of Ogden and the owner of one of the best winter ranges for stock about 20 miles south of Rozel, says that feed is plentiful throughout the summer.

[27] *Burton's City of the Saints*, 171–2; *Beadle's Life in Utah*. For further mention of pasture-lands in Utah, see *House Ex. Doc.*, 42d Cong. 2d Sess., 325, 233 et seq., no. 326, 243 et seq. In 1877 the islands of Great Salt Lake were used as herd-grounds.

[28] In 1856 several acts were passed granting 'herd-grounds' to various parties. See *Utah Acts*, 1855–6, passim. In 1860 more than 30 of these grants were revoked. *Id.*, 1856–60, 26–30.

The herds which the Utah settlers brought with them from Illinois were largely increased, as we have seen, during the California-bound migration, especially between 1849 and 1854, when thousands of steers and cows, broken-down and sore-footed, but of excellent breed, were bartered for provisions, mules, and Indian ponies. The emigrant roads from the Sweetwater to the Humboldt were lined with enterprising traders, who secured this lame stock on their own terms; and after fattening their cattle on the rich grasses of Utah, sent them to California, where they were exchanged for gold-dust or for Mexican mustangs, which were again traded off for cattle. Thus herds multiplied rapidly in the land of the saints; moreover, the natural increase was enormous, for as yet pasture was abundant and the inhabitants consumed but little meat. There was no difficulty, however, in disposing of the surplus. When California became overstocked, large numbers were driven to Nevada,[29] afterward to Idaho and Montana, and still more recently to Wyoming and Colorado. Gradually, however, some of these markets became glutted, though there was still a considerable demand, and in later years farmers who had before paid little attention to grading, as they found that an inferior beast sold for almost as much as a well-bred animal, made some effort toward raising better and larger stock, such as would find ready sale in eastern cities.[30] Short-horn, Devon, Hereford, Jersey, or Ayrshire cattle crossed with other breeds were then to be found on most of the principal ranges. In 1883 the total number of cattle was estimated at about 160,000,[31] and their value, at an average of $30 per head, at $4,800,000. At that

[29] As early as 1856 cattle were driven to Truckee. *Huffaker's Early Cattle Trade*, MS., 1–2.

[30] *Stock-Raising in Utah*, MS., 5. Burton remarks that stock-breeding was one of Brigham's hobbies, and that the difference between Utah cattle and the old Spanish herds of California was very remarkable. *City of the Saints*, 285.

[31] According to a carefully compiled table in *Sloan's Utah Gazetteer*, 1884, 296. In the governor's message of 1882 the number was placed at 200,000, probably too high; in the census report for 1880 at 93,581, certainly too low.

date there were fewer cattle in Utah than for several preceding years,[32] the operations of large stock companies[33] having forced the price to a maximum figure, and caused large droves to be sent out of the country.[34]

The dairy products of Utah for 1883 were about 630,000 gallons of milk, 1,300,000 pounds of butter, and 125,000 pounds of cheese. Of eggs the yield was more than 1,100,000 dozen, of honey more than 130,000 pounds, and of wax about 2,300 pounds. The home consumption of all these articles was very large, yet heavy consignments of eggs were made to San Francisco, where they sold at much higher rates than eastern eggs. Some of the butter found a market in Idaho and Montana, though imports of eastern butter were still considerable.

The number of horses and mules in the territory at this date was estimated at not less than 75,000,[35] the most prominent breeds of horses being the Norman, Clydesdale, and Hambleton. From the cross of the mustang with the American horse were produced ani-

[32] According to statistics compiled by order of the legislative assembly in 1875, there were at that date over 170,000 head. *Utah Jour. Legisl.*, 1876, 285.

[33] Among them may be mentioned the Weber Co. Land and Live-Stock Co., organized in 1884 by J. M. Langsdorf, of which F. A. Hammond was president, and J. W. Guthrie vice-president, with Langsdorf as secretary and treasurer. They secured a large tract some 15 miles from Ogden, intending to raise the Hereford breed of cattle. *Langsdorf's Stock-Raising in Weber Co.*, MS.

[34] For further particulars as to the cattle interests of Utah, see *Stock-Raising in Utah*, MS., passim; *Land-Office Rept*, 1869, 173; *Utah Gazetteer*, 1884, 47–8; *Hollister's Res. and Attract. of Utah*, 19–20; for cattle-raising on Green River, in northern Utah, and Tooele co., see *House Ex. Doc.*, 46th Cong. 2d Sess., xxii. 500, 509, 514–16; in eastern Utah and Col., *Id.*, 42d Cong. 2d Sess., xv. 248–57; for general sketch of cattle and sheep interests, *S. L. C. Tribune*, Apr. 2, July 18, 1879; for act equalizing taxes on passing herds, *Utah Laws*, 1878, 49. In 1860 there was a recorder of marks and brands, who rendered annual accounts to the legislature. *Utah Jour. Legisl.*, 1869, 68. In 1874 the church owned large herds of stock. *Tullidge's Mag.*, i. 560. In 1879 church sales of stock amounted to $58,557.85. *S. L. C. Tribune*, Apr. 7, 1880. In 1873 the epizootic appeared in Utah. *S. F. Alta*, Jan. 25, 1873. Among the prominent stockmen of Utah may be mentioned Ezra T. Clark of Farmington, Davis co. Mr Clark came to Utah in 1848, crossing the plains in charge of a company, and the same year settled on his farm. About 1869 he engaged in stock-raising in Idaho. He was the owner of a flouring mill in Morgan co. He crossed the plains eleven times, and travelled 50,000 miles as a missionary, always paying his own expenses.

[35] In *Stock-Raising in Utah*, MS., 4, the number of horses alone is given at 70,000.

mals with remarkable powers of endurance; and it was claimed that those raised in Utah had better lungs, hoofs, and muscles than could be found in most parts of the United States. The lungs gain strength from the mountain air, the hoofs from the dry climate, and the muscles from the distance to be travelled for grass and water.[36]

Until 1870 most of the sheep gathered in Utah, apart from the few herds which the early settlers brought with them, came from New Mexico. Since that date ewes of the Spanish-merino breed have been introduced from California, together with long-wool bucks from Canada, and fine-wool rams from Ohio, the Cotswold, Kentucky, and other breeds being also represented.[37] Though Utah wool sold at higher rates than that produced in neighboring states, the breed still might be better. The fleece was dry and dusty, readily absorbing alkali, though after the introduction of the merino the wool improved considerably as to fineness of texture. In value it usually ranged from 15 to 20 cents a pound, and as the number of sheep in Utah was estimated, in 1883, at not less than 450,000,[38] the clip, allowing five pounds per fleece,[39] may be estimated at about $500,000. For many years sheep were exempt from taxation, and hence large amounts of capital were invested in this industry, some of the largest ranges being in Cache Valley, where they get little fodder in winter, and under favorable conditions this industry yielded a profit of 40 per cent a year.[40]

[36] In a letter of H. J. Faust to the *Spirit of the Times*, it is stated that one of these horses travelled 113 miles in 14 hours, over plains and mountains where there was no road; another made 65 miles in 6½ hours, and a third, belonging to the pony express, 22 miles in 1 hr 20 min. *Stock-Raising in Utah*, MS.

[37] In 1869 $5,000 was appropriated for importing improved breeds. *Utah Compiled Laws*, 186.

[38] *Utah Gazetteer*, 1884, 296. *Hollister's Res. and Attract. of Utah*, 1882, 20, places the number at about 400,000; the governor, in his message of 1882, at 600.000. In *Stock-Raising in Utah*, MS., 6, 800,000 is given as the number.

[39] Although there are many herds that shear 10 ℔s to the fleece. *Id.*, 6, where the average is placed at 6 lbs. For wool-clip of 1884, see *S. L. Dy Tribune*, Aug. 16, 1884.

[40] In former years, especially in 1860-1, sheep were sometimes almost de-

About one fourth of the total clip was used for manufacturing purposes, supplying not more than one eighth of the demand for textile fabrics, most of the remaining three fourths being sent out of the territory, not only unworked but even unwashed, to be returned in the shape of clothing and blankets, with all the added charges of freight, commissions, and manufacture. In 1882 Utah possessed ten woollen-mills, which were worked only to half their capacity, one of which—the Rio Virgen Manufacturing Company—also produced cotton fabrics. They contained at that date about twenty sets of cards, with 120 looms and perhaps 5,000 spindles, the value of goods produced being estimated at $300,000. For several years the Provo Manufacturing Company had the largest woollen-mill west of the Missouri. It was built in 1872, on the coöperative plan, the people of Utah county being asked to contribute money or labor for the purpose, and the material obtained at small expense.[41] Utah also claims to have established the pioneer woollen-mill of the Pacific slope, for in the *Deseret News* of April 19, 1853, we read that Mr Gaunt "has commenced weaving satinets at his factory at Western Jordan, and very soon he will full and finish some cloth."[42]

stroyed in winter. Later, people learned how to take care of them. *Jennings' Mat. Progr. of Utah*, MS., 3. For clip and value between 1875 and 1879, see *Hollister's Res. and Attract. of Utah*, 1879, 21–2; for account of the sheep industry between 1870 and 1879, *S. L. Dy Tribune*, Apr. 2, 1879; for sheepraising on White River, *House Ex. Doc.*, 46th Cong. 2d Sess., xxii., p. 495; for damage done by wolves, *Deseret News*, March 12, 1862. In 1871 the Utah Cashmere Goat Company was organized. For description of its operations, see *Deseret News*, Oct. 28, 1874.

[41] For further mention of the Provo Manufacturing Company, see *Stanford's Ogden*, MS., 7; *Hittell's Com. and Ind. Pac. Coast*, 447–8; *Utah Sketches*, MS., 60–1; for grant of water rights, *Provo City Revised Ordinances*, 129–30.

[42] For further mention of woollen-mills, see *Deseret News*, Sept. 14, 1881. In *Sloan's Utah Gazetteer*, 1884, 53, it is stated that Brigham brought the first carding-machine into Utah in 1849. Others were imported between 1852–4. After the latter date they were manufactured in the country. The Deseret mills, located in Parley Cañon, were built by Brigham Young; the Wasatch woollen-mills by A. O. Smoot, John Sharp, and R. T. Burton. In 1870 mills were built at Brigham City and Beaver. John R. Murdock took a prominent part in establishing the latter. Mr Murdock came from California in 1847, having been honorably discharged from service in the Mexican war. In 1883 he was president of the Beaver stake. In 1871 there was

The volume of manufactures in Utah increased from about $300,000 in 1850 to at least $5,000,000 in 1883, the value of all materials used at the latter date being estimated at about $2,400,000, of labor at $700,-000, the number of hands employed at 2,500, and the amount of capital invested at $3,000,000. The chief items apart from textile fabrics were flour, lumber, furniture, leather and leathern products, machinery, lead and leaden pipes, and malt liquors.[43] There were at least seventy-five flour and grist mills, 100 lumber-mills, eighteen furniture factories, twenty boot and shoe factories, and seven founderies and machine-shops.[44]

A great drawback to the leather interests is that nearly all the materials used for tanning have to be imported in the shape of extracts, at a cost that leaves

a factory in operation at Ogden, owned by Randall, Pugsley, & Co. There were also mills in Cache co., in which John Stoddard was largely interested. Mr Stoddard, a Scotchman by birth, came to Utah in 1850, settling in Iron co., whence he moved to Cache Valley in 1860, where he also engaged in the lumber business, removing to Ogden in 1884, to follow the same business. During his career he was four years employed in fighting Indians, suffering great hardships, and was also one of those who went out to meet Johnston's army in June 1858.

[43] The Utah breweries by 1886 made about 20,000 barrels a year. In 1864 Henry Wagener started the first large brewery in the territory, about a mile and a half from Fort Douglas. The first year he made only 400 barrels, and in 1884 7,000 barrels. Mr Wagener, a German by birth, came to Utah in 1864, having previously resided in California and Nevada.

[44] According to the census returns between 1850 and 1880, which cannot, however, be accepted as the exact figures, there were in the former year 14 manufacturing establishments, with 51 hands, $44,400 of capital, and $291,-223 of products; in 1860, 48 establishments, with 389 hands, $443,356 of capital, and $900,153 of products; in 1870, 533 factories employing 1,534 hands, $1,491,848 of capital, and producing $2,248,519 of goods; and in 1880, 1,066 factories, 3,221 operatives, $2,839,463 of capital, and $4,217,434 of products. See, for list of saw-mills in 1865, *Pac. Coast Direct.*, 1867, 153–4; of grist-mills in 1869, *Id.*, 1871–3, 151–2; for further mention of saw and grist mills and lumber manufactures, *Utah Sketches*, MS., passim; *S. L. Dy Tel.*, Dec. 16, 1868; *Tullidge's Mag.*, i. 558–9, iii. 34–6. As early as 1850 there was a machine-shop in the temple building. *Deseret News*, Sept. 14, 1850. For account of the Deseret Iron Co. in 1852, see *Bertrand's Mem. Morm.*, 81–2; of wagon and carriage manufactory in 1868, *S. L. Dy Tel.*, Dec. 12, 1868; of soap factory in 1878, *S. L. C. Herald*, Dec. 29, 1878; of boot and shoe fac-tories, *Deseret Ev. News*, Jan. 2, 1884; *S. L. C. Herald*, May 2, 1879; *Tullidge's Mag.*, i. 205–8. The first nail factory in Utah worthy the name was built under the superintendence of James Finlayson in 1859, a little south of S. L. City. Before this date nails sold at 50 cents a pound. Mr Payson, a Scotch-man by birth and a millwright by occupation, came to the country during this year and settled at Payson, of which town he was elected mayor in 1882.

little profit for the manufacturer. Pine barks are used to a small extent, but chestnut, oak, hemlock, and sumac are not found in Utah. Nevertheless there were in 1883 about 25 tanneries in operation, producing leather valued at $250,000. During this year some 200 car-loads of hides and pelts were shipped to the eastern states, sufficient to supply almost the entire demand of Utah for leathern products. The leather used for harness and saddlery, trunks and valises, of which the manufacture amounts to not less than $150,000, is almost entirely imported. The same condition of affairs exists among the furniture and carriage and wagon factories, which import nearly all of their material, paying for it the same rates of freight as on imported vehicles and furniture, while labor is considerably higher than in the eastern states.[45]

Under such disadvantages, it was greatly to the credit of the settlers that they undertook to compete to any considerable extent with eastern manufacturers, and that the production of goods should increase steadily from year to year, with occasional set-backs caused by dull markets and over-production. Manufacturing is seldom a profitable industry in new countries, even from materials native to them, and under the most favorable conditions. It is doubtful whether this branch of enterprise, throughout the Pacific slope, yielded, on an average, six per cent on the entire capital invested, and it is doubtful whether even this average was obtained in Utah.

The production of iron—not only of pig-iron, but of iron and steel rails—and of mill, mining, smelting, and railroad machinery, bids fair in 1886 to be foremost

---

[45] Nevertheless James B. Glass, who opened a carriage manufactory and repository at S. L. City in 1879, reports that between that date and 1884 his sales increased eightfold. For further general mention of Utah manufactures, see *Hollister's Res. and Attract. of Utah* (1882), 55–6; *Gov. Message*, 1882, pp. 7–8; *S. L. Wkly Herald*, Nov. 17, 1881; *Dy Telegraph*, Dec. 1, 1868; *Tribune*, May 3, 24, 1873; *Sloan's Utah*, 7, 13–14; *Utah Gazetteer*, 1884, 50, 299. In March 1882, $5,000 was appropriated by the legislature as a premium to be paid to the producer of 7,000 ℔s of merchantable brown sugar, made in Utah from material produced in the country. *Utah Laws*, 1882, 44–5.

among the manufactures of Utah. In 1883 the product of her founderies and machine-shops was esti-mated at over $360,000, being second only to that of her flouring and grist mills. With suitable and abun-dant fuel, there is probably no state west of the Mis-souri with better facilities in this direction, among them being a great variety of rich and pure ores, labor and supplies at moderate rates, a climate that seldom interferes with out-door work, a central location, a net-work of railroads, a fair demand, and a freight tariff[46] that almost prohibits the shipment of crude or manufactured iron from more distant sources of sup-ply, whether to Utah or the surrounding states.

At a very early date it was ascertained, as will be remembered, that there were immense deposits of iron in various parts of Utah. At Smithfield, in Cache county, there were beds of hematite sixty feet in thickness. On the Provo near Kamas, on the Weber in the neighborhood of Ogden, on the Wasatch near Willard and Bountiful, at Tintic, at City Creek cañon in the Cottonwoods, on many of the mountain slopes, and on much of the desert land, ores were found in almost every variety except in the form of carbonates. The largest deposits were in Iron county, and in what may be termed the southern prolongation of the Wa-satch Range, about two hundred miles south of Salt Lake City. The most remarkable outcrops were in the neighborhood of Iron Springs, Iron City, and Oak City. In the Big Blowout, as it is termed, a solid mass of magnetic ore near Iron Springs, with a length of 1,000 feet and half that width, it is esti-mated that there are 3,000,000 tons near the surface. Other deposits have each 1,000,000 in sight, and in this district there are probably some 50,000,000 tons above or near the surface, while the ledges are prac-tically inexhaustible and of excellent quality.[47]

[46] Varying from $20 to $40 per ton.

[47] Blodgett Brittan, a prominent Philadelphia iron-master, who analyzed five specimens of ore from this district, the analyses being only for iron, phos-phorus, and sulphur, reports that they averaged 64 per cent of iron, 12 per

Between 1872 and 1882 about 70,000 tons of coke were brought into Utah at a cost of $1,800,000, and during the same period 500,000 tons of coal were brought from Wyoming at a cost of nearly $4,000,000. The future of the iron interests of Utah appears to depend mainly on the question whether coking coal can be produced of sufficient consistency for the smelting of pig-iron. As yet it has not been produced, or not in considerable quantity; but the coal regions are of vast extent, have been but slightly explored, and it would seem almost a certainty that deposits will somewhere be found that answer the purpose. It is well known that the best coal for coking is that which has been subjected for ages to pressure under the application of heat. The coal-beds of Utah are of recent and not of what is termed the true coal formation, but such coal sometimes makes excellent coke. At Wales, in Sanpete Valley, in Pleasant and Castle valleys to the east and south, on Cedar Mountain, and elsewhere, coking coal has been found which serves for the smelting of lead, but not for iron,[48] though it is believed that coke will soon be produced that can bear the weight of the charges in pig-iron smelting.

In January 1854 the Utah legislature offered a reward of $1,000 to any resident who would open a vein of coal not less than 18 inches thick within 40

cent of phosphorus, and of sulphur a trace. W. A. Hodges of S. L. City obtained from a specimen of magnetic ore 62.60 of iron, .12 of sulphur, and 4.8 of silica; from a specimen of hematite, 60.90 of iron, .08 of sulphur, and 5.7 of silica. *Hollister's Res. and Attract. of Utah*, 45. For description of Great Western iron-works at Iron City, incorporated in 1873, see *Deseret News*, Oct. 13, 1875; of the Ogden iron-works, at which operations were commenced systematically in 1882, *Hollister's Res. and Attract. of Utah*, 51; for further mention of iron deposits in Utah, see *Deseret News*, Aug. 26, 1874, Aug. 17, 1881; *S. L. Wkly Herald*, June 23, 1881; *S. L. C. Tribune*, Oct. 24, 1874, Apr. 10, 13, 17, Nov. 2, 1879, Dec. 3, 1880, Jan. 1, 1881; *S. F. Bull.*, Jan. 17, 1882; *S. F. Alta*, Sept. 4, 1873; *Austin Reese River Reveille*, Nov. 21, 1866; *Murphy's Min. Res. of Utah*, 8.

[48] From an analysis of Castle Valley coal, Mr Brittan reported 48.21 per cent of fixed carbon, 1.88 of ash, and 40.61 of volatile matter; from coke produced from this coal, 94.05 of fixed carbon, 3.25 of ash, and 2.70 of volatile matter. From an analysis of Sanpete Valley coal, the samples being taken 40 feet below the surface, A. P. Bouton obtained 50.7 per cent of coke, 34.2 of bitumen, 13.3 of ash, and 1.8 of moisture. *Hollister's Res. of Utah*, 47.

miles of Salt Lake City, and where it could be profitably worked.[49] Between that date and 1880, 126,000 acres of coal-lands had been surveyed in various counties,[50] and in 1883 the total area of such lands was estimated at 20,000 square miles. The largest deposits are found on the eastern slope of the Wasatch, extending at intervals from the Uintah reservation through Sanpete, Pleasant, and Castle valleys, as far south as Kanab, and its vicinity. In considerable areas the formation is broken or destroyed by erosion, among others, in the neighborhood of Iron City, where veins are plentiful, though too small to be profitably worked. On the Weber and its tributaries in Summit county, for 12 or 15 miles above Echo City, there is coal of fair quality for household and steam-making purposes, which has been worked since 1867, some of the mines being opened in 1883 to a depth of 1,100 or 1,200 feet. From the Coalville mines, a few miles south of Echo, were drawn until recent years most of the supplies needed for Salt Lake City and the northern settlements. At Evanston, also in Summit county and on the line of the Union Pacific, there is a vein of bituminous coal from 17 to 19 feet in thickness. In 11 out of the 24 counties of Utah coal-lands had been surveyed in 1880, varying in extent from 120 to 35,696 acres, and in several others it was known that coal existed. Perhaps the most valuable deposits are in the Sanpete Valley, where the seams vary from 6 inches to 6 feet of bituminous coal, which, when a better plant is used in the mines, may produce a serviceable coke, while in the mountains to the

---

[49] *Utah Acts Legisl.*, 1855, 393. The reward was claimed in 1860 by Wm H. Kimball and John Spriggs, whose petition was referred to a committee and refused, on the ground that the mine was more than 40 miles distant and the coal of inferior quality. See *Utah Jour. Legisl.*, 1860-1, 73, 1862-3, 65-6. In 1863 a mine had been opened 40 miles from the capital, the coal selling at $40 per ton.

[50] For list of counties, locations, and number of acres in each, see *Utah Gazetteer*, 1884, 62. For coal-lands taken up in 1876-9, according to the surveyor-general's report, see *S. L. C. Herald*, Nov. 26, 1879.

south and east veins are being worked from 10 to 12 feet in width.[51]

In estimating the value of these deposits, it must be remembered that veins less than three or four feet wide can seldom be worked at a profit, except when near to market and under favorable circumstances, and that the Utah veins are of smaller average width. Thus the yield for 1869, though there were several mines in operation at that date, was but 4,500 tons, in 1876 and 1877 45,000 tons, and in 1878 60,000 tons,[52] or little more than one half of the consumption, even for the last of these years. It will be observed, however, that there are large coal-beds in close proximity to the principal iron deposits; and with a ready market, cheap and reliable labor and supplies, access by railroad, and other advantages, it is probable that the coal and iron industries of the territory, far removed as it is from the manufacturing centres of Europe and America, will rank among the foremost.

There are few of the metals or minerals known to science which are not represented in Utah.[53] Copper is found, usually in connection with other metals, in

[51] For act incorporating the Sanpete Coal Co., see *Utah Acts*, 1855-6, 33-4; for further mention of Sanpete mines, *S. L. C. Tribune*, May 29, 1875; for report on condition of Utah coal mines in 1859, *Utah Jour. Legisl.*, 1859-60, 32, 64-5; for discovery of coal near Provo, *Deseret News*, March 14, 1860; near Ogden, *Id.*, Aug. 13, 1862; at Farmington, *Id.*, May 16, 1860; for extent of coal strata in Green River basin, *King's Surveys*, iii. 455-8; for mines opened at Coalville and their operations in 1870, *Id.*, iii. 467-73; for Pleasant Valley mines, *Reno Gazette*, Nov. 12, 1881; for additional details as to coal mines, lands, discoveries, and interests, *Murphy's Min. Res. of Utah*, 8; *Hollister's Res. and Attract. of Utah*, 45-51; *Utah Gazetteer*, 1884, 61-2; *S. L. C. Tribune*, Jan. 18, 1873, Oct. 27, 1879; *S. L. C. Herald*, May 12, Dec. 22, 1877, March 30, 1878, Jan. 28, 1880; *Herald*, Nov. 17, 1881; *S. L. Mail*, May 17, 1876; *S. F. Bull.*, Jan. 17, 1882; *Alta*, March 15, 1873, April 6, 1875; *Stock Report*, April 26, 1875; *Sac. Union*, May 30, 1860, Dec. 19, 1863; *Austin Reese River Reveille*, July 19, 1864.

[52] *House Ex. Doc.*, 46th Cong. 1st Sess., 3, 157. In *Balch's The Mines, Miners, and Mining Int. of the U. S. in 1882*, 1040, the output for 1880 and 1881 is given at 275,000 tons. This statement is taken from *Saward's Coal Trade*, and is no doubt very much above the actual figures.

[53] In *Utah Gazetteer*, 1884, 67-8, is a complete list of the minerals and metals found in Utah. It does not include tin, which, however, is said to have been discovered near Ogden in 1871. See *S. L. Rev.*, Oct. 27, 1871; *S. F. Call*, Oct. 10, 24, 1871; *Scient. Press*, Oct. 28, 1871. Other lists will be found in *Wheeler's Surveys*, iii. 652-61; *S. L. Semi-Wkly Herald*, Jan. 3, 1880; *Silver Reef Miner*, Jan. 10, 1880.

most of her mining districts, from the Weber to the
Colorado, where, in the sandstone formations, some
very rich ores have been discovered. It is most
abundant in southern Utah, but the only mines developed in 1883 were in the extreme north-western portion of the territory, where veins averaging seven or
eight feet in width, enclosed in micacious shale and
intermingled with porphyry, yielded in spots as much
as fifty per cent of metal.[54]

Beds of sulphur were found both in northern and
southern Utah, the largest, with an area of about 300
acres and a depth of not less than twenty feet, being
in Millard county. In the hills of Beaver county,
some fourteen miles south of Frisco, there are also
large deposits of singular purity among fissures of
silicious flint; but though much of it would yield fifty
per cent, and some even 98 per cent, of pure brimstone,
it has no commercial value, and is not even utilized
for local consumption. Near Brigham City there are
sulphurets of antimony, averaging at least four feet in
thickness, and yielding from twenty to thirty per
cent of metal. In Piute and Garfield counties are
purer and larger deposits. Gypsum and mica abound
in southern Utah, the latter being found also in Salt
Lake and Davis counties. East of Nephi, in Juab
county, is a vein of gypsum 1,200 feet long and 100
in width. In Washington and Sanpete counties it is
also encountered, both in the crystallized and oxydized
state. Cinnabar, cobalt, and bismuth, the last in paying quantities, are met with in Beaver county and at
Tintic.[55] Near Salt Lake is a solid mountain of rock
salt.[56] West of the lake are large deposits of saleratus.

[54] Among other localities, copper was found in the San Francisco district,
Big Cottonwood, the Snake district, Copper gulch, Red Butte and Bingham
cañons, Antelope Island in G. S. Lake, in many parts of Beaver co., and in
the granite range between Ogden and S. L. City. For account of copper mines
near Milford and at Grand gulch, see *Silver Reef Miner*, June 8, Oct. 15, 1881.
Murphy states that in 1872 the only places where it would pay to work were
in the Bingham, Tintic, and Lucin districts, the last being partly in Box
Elder co. and partly in Nevada. *Min. Res. of Utah*, 8.
[55] For further mention of bismuth deposits, see *S. F. Bulletin*, Apr. 27, 1872.
[56] For description, see *Niles' Register*, lxxv.

At Emigration cañon carbonate of soda is found on
the surface, and was used by the first settlers for
making bread.   In the iron-beds red and yellow ochre
are abundant.   Under the shale-beds, which cover a
surface of 1,000 square miles, occurs what is termed
mineral wax, some of it being rich in gases and paraf-
fine.[57]   At Promontory Range, so called because it
projects into Great Salt Lake, and in Sanpete county,
are vast beds of alum shale, alum in combination with
other minerals being found in all parts of Utah,
though as yet without value.

Building stone is exceedingly plentiful throughout
the territory, and in great variety.   At Little Cottonwood there is granite; at the Red Buttes near Salt
Lake City there is red sandstone; in Sanpete county
is white sandstone; and at Logan, limestone, easily
quarried and strongly impregnated with iron.   Marbles, black, white. gray, cream-colored, variegated,
and some of them capable of receiving a fine polish,
are found among other points on the islands of Great
Salt Lake, near Provo, at Logan, Tooele, Frisco,
Alpine City, and Dry cañon, the Logan marbles being in most demand.   On Antelope Island, also in
Great Salt Lake, there is a large quarry of green and
purple slate, which for some purposes is preferred to
eastern slate.   Clays of various descriptions, as brick
clays, potter's clays, and porcelain clays, are found in
Beaver, Davis, and Sevier counties, west of Utah
Lake, and at several of the mines.

Mining of most descriptions, and especially of gold
and silver, was discouraged, as we have seen, by
the dignitaries of the church, partly with a view to
prevent the rush of gentiles which would surely follow the discovery of gold, and also because the very
existence of the Mormons as a community depended
on their unremitting exertions in producing the neces-

[57] *Hollister's Res. and Attract. of Utah*, 52; *S. L. C. Tribune*, May 27, 1879;
S. F. Post, March 18, 1879; *Silver Reef Miner*, Jan. 10, 1880.

saries of life. The first systematic efforts at prospecting, made by permission of General Connor, when in command at Camp Douglas, were ridiculed in the tabernacle;[58] and later, when mining projects were brought forward by gentiles, they were steadily discountenanced. In 1863 Captain A. Heitz and a party from Camp Douglas discovered argentiferous galena and copper in Bingham cañon, on the east slope of the Oquirrh Range, near the Jordan, and about thirty miles south of Salt Lake City. A mine was located in September of that year by a man named Ogilbie, and in December following, a mining district was established, named the West Mountain, and including the portion of the range between Black Rock, at the southern end of Great Salt Lake, and the fortieth parallel. In 1871 this district contained thirty-five mines.[59]

The first shipment of ore from Utah was a car-load of copper ore from Bingham cañon, hauled to Uintah on the Union Pacific, and forwarded by the Walker Brothers to Baltimore in June 1868. In 1864 free gold was discovered in this district by a party of Californians returning from Montana to pass the winter in Salt Lake City. Between 1865 and 1872 the production of gold was estimated at $1,000,000, and up to 1882 the total product was 500,000 tons of ore and 100,000 of bullion, from which was extracted $1,500,000 in gold, $8,800,000 in silver, and $5,000-000 in lead. The surface was a broken quartzite formation, the mineral belt broad and containing many fissure veins believed to be permanent, the ore being partly galena, largely silicious, and decomposed on or near the surface.[60]

---

[58] *Harrison's Crit. Notes on Utah*, MS., 48. In 1857, and perhaps at an earlier date, it was known that there were silver mines near G. S. Lake. See *Surgeon-Gen. Circ. 8*, 1875, 338-9; *Sac. Union*, Nov. 30, 1858.

[59] A list of them with particulars will be found in *Murphy's Min. Res. of Utah*, facing p. 14.

[60] For further information as to this district, see *Id.*, 2; *Hollister's Res. and Attract. of Utah*, 28-30; *S. L. C. Tribune*, July 13, Aug. 3, 13, 1879, Jan. 3, 1880; *S. L. C. Herald*, July 18, 1879; *Mining and Scientific Press*, July 17, 1875.

On the western side of the Oquirrh Range, on the margin of Rush Lake, in Tooele county, the Rush Valley district was organized in 1863, being segregated from the West Mountain district, and two years later about 400 claims had been taken up, 40 of them being in what was afterward known as the Ophir district, though both were more commonly termed the Stockton mines, from the town built near their location.[61] The ores were sulphurets and carbonates of argentiferous lead, with occasionally a trace of gold, selected specimens assaying over $1,200 per ton, and the average being $50 to $60. In the Ophir district rich chloride ores, assaying in spots $500 to $5,000, were afterward discovered.[62]

The first discovery of silver-bearing rock in the Wasatch Range was made by General Connor in person, at the head of Little Cottonwood cañon. The first ore encountered was galena, and afterward carbonate of lead, both being found in chimneys. The first shipment was made by the Walker Brothers in July 1868; but it was not until the completion of the Utah Central to Salt Lake City, early in 1870, that the mines were systematically opened. Among them were the Emma, of evil fame, and the Flagstaff, the latter producing up to the close of 1882 more than 100,000 tons of ore, averaging $30 to the ton.[63] The former was located in 1869, the vein for the first 100 feet being only eight to twelve inches wide, but increasing with depth to thirty-five feet, and yielding from $135 to $250 per ton in silver, the output for the eighteen months ending with the close of 1872 being over $2,000,000.[64] The unsavory transactions con-

[61] For list and plan, with developments, etc., in 1872, see *Murphy's Min. Res. of Utah*, facing p. 20.

[62] For further mention of the Rush Valley and Ophir district, see *Id.*, 20–1, 29–31; *Hollister's Res. and Attract. of Utah*, 31; *Utah Gazetteer*, 1884, 89-91. In 1882 the town of Stockton was destroyed by fire. *S. F. Call*, Sept. 5, 1882.

[63] In 1872 the production was about 80 tons a day. *Paul's Utah Incid.*, MS.

[64] The first year it paid in dividends $1,000,000. *Godbe's Statement*, MS., 4–5. The Walker Bros purchased a fourth-interest for $30,000, and furnished money and supplies for opening it. *Walker's Merchants and Miners of Utah*, MS., 4.

nected with it after its sale to a party of English capi-
talists, for the sum of $5,000,000, have no parallel in
the history of mining swindles, except perhaps in
connection with the Comstock lode.[65] The Big Cottonwood district lay immediately to the north of its
namesake, both being near Alta, in Salt Lake county,
and from 8,000 to 9,000 feet above the sea-level. In
1871 none of the mines promised well, but a year
later several were yielding largely, and some hundreds
of claims were located.[66]

In the American Fork district, south of Little
Cottonwood, many locations were taken up in 1870
and 1871, some of considerable value—one mine,
named the Pittsburg, being afterward sold for $20,000,
and one called the Miller for $190,000. The most
prominent mine in 1882 was the Silver Bell, in which
a strong vein of milling ore was encountered at a
depth of 300 feet. In geologic features this district
resembled the Cottonwoods, and was on the same mineral belt.[67] In connection with it may be mentioned
the Silver Lake district, on Deer Creek, containing
several promising locations, and now merged in the
American Fork district.

On the extreme southern end of the Oquirrh
Range, and on its western face, was the Tintic district,
overlooking the Tintic Valley, where the first mine,
named the Sunbeam, was located in 1869, the district
being organized a few months later. On the Sun-

[65] See further, for history and description of Emma mine, *Beadle's Western Wilds*, 120; *S. F. Call*, March 11, 1876; *S. L. C. Tribune*, Jan. 11, 1872, March 25, April 8, 1876; of swindle, *Id.*, Nov. 30, 1875; of lawsuit, *Coast Rev.*, 1872, vol. ii., no. 5, 192, no. 6, 230–1; *S. F. Bull.*, Jan. 7, 1875; *S. F. Post*, June 8, 1872.

[66] For further mention of the Cottonwood mines, see *Godbe's Statement*, MS., 4–5; *Paul's Utah Incid.*, MS.; *S. L. C. Tribune*, Jan. 1, 1881; *Tribune*, Jan. 3, 1880; *S. L. Herald*, Jan. 3, 1880; *S. F. Alta*, Feb. 9, 26, 1873; *Hayden's Geol. Surv. Rept*, 1872, 106–8.

[67] For further details, see *Murphy's Min. Res. of Utah*, 32–4. In this work are descriptions of all the mining districts of Utah up to 1872, and of the leading districts to 1882, in *Hollister's Res. and Attract. of Utah*, 1882, 22–41. In the former are also the names of the productive mines in each district, with no. of feet, assays, etc. In *Utah Gazetteer*, 1884. 73–104, there is also a description of the various districts.

beam ledge there were in 1882 nine locations, selected ores from all of them carrying 80 to 100
ounces of silver, besides gold, copper, and lead.
Among the leading mines at that date were the Crismon, Mammoth, and Eureka Hill, the former with an
ore-chimney 100 feet wide, averaging about $35 per
ton in gold and silver, and 7 or 8 per cent of copper,
the latter producing ores of several descriptions,
which yielded about the same average, and paying
occasional dividends.[63]

In the Uintah and Blue Ledge districts, both at
Park City, near tributaries of the Weber and Provo
rivers, is the famous Ontario mine, discovered in
1872,[69] and in 1883 developed to a depth of 800 feet.
The vein is in a quartzite formation, the pay-chute
being several hundred feet in length, and about three
in width. Up to the close of 1883 the total output
exceeded $17,000,000, of which about $6,250,000 had
been disbursed in dividends, the ore producing on an
average about $106 per ton in silver, and the yield
being remarkably uniform. The cost of mining and
milling, with other expenses, was $33 to $34 per ton,
and was largely increased by the flow of water, which
was at the rate of 2,000 gallons per minute. A huge
pumping-engine of the Cornish pattern had been
erected at the mine, with power to drive a double
line of 20-inch pumps at a depth of 2,000 feet.[70]

In the San Francisco district in Beaver county,
fifteen miles west of Milford and about 240 south of
Salt Lake City, the leading mine was the Horn Silver,
the outcrop of which resembled the top of a hay-cock,

[63] The Tintic mines are further described in the *S. L. C. Tribune*, Aug. 5,
19, 1871, Feb. 29, 1880, Jan. 1, 1881; *Wkly Tribune*, March 6, 1880.
[69] For account of discovery, see *Balch's The Mines, Miners, and Mining
Int. of the U. S. in 1882*, 788; *S. L. Wkly Tribune*, Dec. 4, 1880.
[70] In Aug. 1885 this mine paid its 110th monthly dividend, the amount
being $75,000, and the total to that date $6,650,000. *S. F. Bulletin*, Aug. 28,
1885. Additional items relating to the Ontario mine will be found in *Rept
Ontario Silver Mg Co., Apr. 1, 1881, to Nov. 30, 1883; Robinson's Sinners and
Saints*, 249–59; *Utah Gaz.*, 6; *Vallejo Chronicle*, May 14, 1880. For other
mines in these districts, see *S. L. Tribune*, Jan. 3, 1880.

and was discovered by accident.[71] In 1882 it had been opened to a depth of 500 feet, the ore being a decomposed argentiferous galena, some 50 feet in thickness, from which at the close of that year about $6,000,000 worth of silver and lead had been extracted,[72] and $1,500,000 paid in dividends. The Frisco Mining and Smelting Company, in the same district, owned the Carbonate mine at the town of Frisco, the Cave, Bigelow, and other locations in Granite Range, and a large tract of auriferous ground in Osceola county, Nevada. The vein of the Carbonate was found to be composed of one part of rich argentiferous galena to three or four of trachyte, and it was of course necessary to concentrate the ores. The Cave mine, which was in the neighborhood of the Horn Silver, and consisted of a series of limestone caves, containing limonite ore near the surface and argentiferous galena at greater depth, produced a considerable amount of bullion, and in 1884 was capable of yielding 100 tons a day, but was not worked to its full capacity pending the construction of a branch railroad.[73] The mine in Osceola county covered an area of 700 acres, and was believed to contain very rich deposits of gold, but lay idle for lack of water, the nearest supply being 17 miles distant. During the year 1885 it was expected that arrangements would be made for working the ground by the hydraulic process.[74]

The Harrisburg or Silver Reef district was in Wash-

[71] The discovery of this mine is mentioned in the *Silver Reef Miner*, July 30, 1879.

[72] J. E. Dooly, express agent at S. L. City, gives as the product for 1881, 1,259,903 oz. of silver and 16,343,995 lbs of lead, valued at $1,807,092.20. After losing his property, W. S. Godbe obtained a contract for smelting ore from this mine, reducing in all some 20,000 tons. *Godbe's Statement*, MS., 7.

[73] The Cave mine originally belonged to Mr Godbe, who in 1885 was still largely interested in it. *Id.*, 7, 9. In 1884 there were 300 men employed by the Frisco company. Rock was shipped to the reduction-works near Salt Lake City, and most of the bullion to Chicago. *Hill's Mines and Mg in Utah*, MS. In 1881 the company's mines at Frisco produced 221,846 oz. of silver and 2,023,213 lbs of lead, worth $330,329.38. For further particulars, see *S. L. Wkly Tribune*, Jan. 3, 1880.

[74] The owners of this mine were W. S. Godbe and three others, the former being confident that the deposit was worth several millions of dollars. *Godbe's Statement*, MS., 10-11.

ington county, south of Milford, and in the basin of
the Colorado. The town of Silver Reef in this district was so named from a silver-bearing sandstone
reef 100 miles in length, and yielding in places $30 to
the ton. The Leeds Silver Mining Company, a San
Francisco organization, was the pioneer location of
this district, and from its ground about $800,000 have
been extracted. From the Christy Mill and Mining
Company's locations, 16 in number, about 50,000 tons
were taken out during the four and a half years ending with the close of 1882, the yield of bullion being
over $1,275,000. At that date the Stormont Silver
Mining Company and the Barbee and Walker Mill and
Mining Company, both New York organizations, had
produced each a round million, the former having disbursed $145,000 in dividends. The silver-bearing part
of the reef was at least 15 miles in length, and there
were hundreds of locations as yet unworked, which, if
consolidated and provided with mills, could probably be
developed into dividend-paying properties.[75]

[75] Silver Reef City was incorporated in 1878. *Utah Laws*, 1878, 23–6. For
further mention of Silver Reef mines, see *S. L. C. Tribune*, March 30, 1879;
Wkly Tribune, Jan. 3, 1880; *Ruby Hill Mg News*, Sept. 19, 1881; *S. F. Chronicle*, Nov. 14, 1880. In the Lucin district, on the dividing line between Utah
and Nevada, there were several good locations. Among other gold and silver
mining districts in Utah may be mentioned the Lincoln, where was discovered
the first silver mine in Utah, named the Rollins, and containing a heavy deposit of argentiferous galena. The Star District, a few miles west of Milford,
formerly produced considerable bullion, but the exhaustion of the surface deposits, distance from railroads, and the fall in the price of lead caused smelting
operations to be suspended, though in 1883 development was still progressing
with good results. The Rocky and Beaver Lake districts, north of the Star,
abounded in ores containing gold, silver, and copper, the O. K. and Old Hickory
being the prominent mines in 1882. In the Timmons or Nebo district in Juab
county there were large bodies of low-grade galena ore. At the Pine Grove
district, 30 or 40 miles west of Frisco, the Carrie Lucille mine had been opened
at that date to a depth of 200 feet and showed strong veins of high-grade ore.
In the Ohio and Mount Baldy districts, at Marysvale, in Piute county, the
leading mine was the Deer Trail, at which there were 100,000 tons of ore in
sight in 1882, averaging about an ounce of gold and 15 oz. of silver to the ton.
There were several other good mines and prospects, but capital was needed
for their development. For further mention of this district, see *Silver Reef
Miner*, May 14, 1879; for account of Clifton mining district, *S. L. C. Tribune*,
Aug. 15, 1874; of Camp Floyd district, *Utah Gazetteer*, 1884, 80–1; of
Walker River placer mines in 1857–9, *Sac. Union*, Aug. 1, 29, Sept. 7, 1857;
Apr. 26, 29, May 24, 26, Dec. 11, 17, 1858; July 23, 1859; of Ruby mines, *S.
F. Alta*, Apr. 4, 1873; for gold discoveries on Bear River, *S. F. Bulletin*, Apr.
30, 1864; on New River, *Sac. Union*, Apr. 5, 1858; on the Sweetwater,

For 1869 the product of all the Utah mines in gold, silver, and lead did not exceed $200,000. In 1871 it had risen to $3,000,000, and in 1875 to $7,000,000. For 1883 it was $7,017,682. Between 1870 and 1883 there were produced $2,150,000 in gold, $45,790,272 in silver, 258,000 tons of lead, worth at the Atlantic seaboard $23,220,000, and 1,000 tons of copper which sold in New York for about $300,000. The total output for this period was $71,502,772, or an average of more than $5,500,000 a year.[76] At the close of 1883 there were at least 95 districts in Utah where mining of various descriptions was in progress, all of them contributing more or less to the total yield, though the great volume of production was confined to a few. The entire annual expense of these districts may be roughly estimated at $10,000,000, while the output is far below that figure. It does not follow, of course, that this industry has proved unprofitable, for the amount of capital invested was trifling when compared with other states on the Pacific slope, and the difference between output and outlay may be fairly considered as so much money expended on

Deseret News, Sept. 11, 1867; for description of Willard mines, *S. L. C. Tribune*, Aug. 8, 1880; of silver mines near Pahraganat Valley, *U. S. Ind. Aff. Rept*, 1865, 156–7. For historical sketches of mining in Utah, see *Tullidge's Mag.*, i. 179–90; *Stenhouse's Rocky Mountain Saints*, 713–34; for lists and reports of various districts between 1870 and 1880, with operations, prospects, etc., *Wheeler's Surveys, Progress Rept*, 1872, 13–26, 51; *Sec. Int. Rept*, 42d Cong. 3d Sess., pt i. 166–7; *Fabian's Utah*, 4–5, 7–8; *Raymond's Stat. of Mines*, 1873, 242–64; *Coast Rev.* 1872–9, passim; *Utah Direct. and Gaz.*, 1879–80, passim; Raymond's ann. repts, in *House Ex. Doc.*, 42d Cong. 1st Sess., no. 10, 218–23; 43d Cong. 1st Sess., 141, 218–23; 43d Cong. 1st Sess., 141, 255–83; 43d Cong. 2d Sess., 177, 328–57; 44th Cong. 1st Sess., 159, 269–81; Professor Newberry's reports, in *S. L. C. Tribune*, Aug. 21, 26, 1879; Aug. 28, 1880; Delegate Cannon's statement, in *House Misc. Doc.*, 45th Cong. 2d Sess., 54, 97–100; *Wheeler's Geog. Surveys Rept*, 1878, 90–1; *Codman's Round Trip*, 185–93, 203–6, 222–3, 250–1. For Utah mines placed on the London market, see *London Times*, July 24, 1871; for legislation concerning mines, see *Utah Laws*, 1878, 8, 42.

[76] Professor J. E. Clayton, in *Utah Gazetteer*, 1884, 56. In *Gov. Mess.*, for 1882, 8, the average output of gold, silver, and lead between 1870 and 1882 is given at $6,500,000. This is probably too high, as between 1870 and 1874 inclusive it was less than $3,000,000 and in no year did the product much exceed $7,000,000. For other estimates during portions of this period, see *Balch's The Mines, Miners, and Mining Int. of the U. S. in 1882*, passim; *Hayden's Gt West*, 317–18; *New Mex. My World*, Dec. 1, 1882, 83, Nov. 1, 1884, 136; *S. F. Bulletin*, Jan. 3, 1882; *Utah Direct. and Gaz.*, 1879–80, 36.

developments. That as a rule "it requires a mine
to develop a mine," of whatever nature, is, however,
no less true of Utah than of other mineral sections.

Of mining at Carson Valley and other districts in
Nevada which were formerly portions of Utah, mention is made in my *History of Nevada*. It is worthy
of note that from the tailings of the Raymond and
Ely mine, near Pioche, W. S. Godbe and his associates had extracted bullion to the amount of $750,-
000 up to the close of 1884, and it was believed that
the value of that which remained in the pit exceeded
$1,250,000. The tailings were worked by Russell's
leaching process, the distinctive feature of which is
the use of sulphate of copper as an extract solution.
By this process, which has now been in use for several
years, it is claimed that a very high percentage of
metal can be extracted, and that ores of low grade can
be profitably worked.[77] At an earlier date Kustel's
process of leaching chloridized ores with a solution
of hyposulphide of soda was somewhat in favor, and
it is the opinion of many practical miners that the
leaching process will eventually be substituted for
the usual pan amalgamation.[78]

At the close of 1883 there were seventeen smelting
and reduction works in Utah, producing more than
2,000 tons of bullion per month, and twenty quartz-
mills, with at least 350 stamps, the cost of a chloridiz-
ing-mill being $3,000 to $4,000 per stamp, and of a
gold-mill perhaps $1,000 per stamp.[79] All of the

[77] *Godbe's Statement*, MS., 8–9. Mr Godbe is of opinion that the leaching
process will, when its merits are better known, be of vast benefit to the
mining world.

[78] In 1871 Joshua R. Nichols, who came to S. L. City with the exclusive
right for Krom's patent separating and concentrating machinery, organized a
company for the introduction of this process in connection with smelting,
amalgamation, and chlorination. Mr Nichols, a native of Onondaga co., N. Y.,
followed at Detroit, Mich., the several occupations of farm-boy, errand-boy,
clerk, and store-keeper until 1865, when he engaged in the railroad-supply
business until July 1869, being then appointed assistant superintendent on
the Union Pacific. Removing to Utah in 1871, he became engaged in mining
and railroad enterprises. *Nichols' Mining Mach.*, MS.

[79] The Pioneer quartz-mill of 15 stamps, for the reduction of silver ore, the

smelting and reducing works were of modern pattern, and with modern improvements, their capacity varying from 20 to 250 tons of ore per day. The largest in operation at this date were the Germania lead-works, where most of the base bullion was refined, and the Francklyn smelting-works. The former were at South Cottonwood, seven miles from Salt Lake City, and on the line of the Utah Central and Denver and Rio Grande railroads. Their refining capacity was forty tons a day, and they contained all the apparatus needed for converting galena ores into Doré bars, litharge, and marketable lead.[80] The refining capacity of the Francklyn works, a mile distant, was 55 tons a day, or about 250 tons of crude ore.[81]

The average cost of mining and hauling in Utah, including dead-work, up to 1884, was probably not less than $10 per ton; and of milling silver ore at least as much, though there were districts where it did not exceed $4 per ton.[82] When purchased at the smelting-works, the silver and lead in the base bullion were estimated at New York prices. Five per cent on silver and ten per cent on lead were deducted for loss in smelting; $10 to $12 per ton for the cost of smelting, $16 to $18 for refining, and about $25 per ton for freight to New York. When it is remembered that

first one in Utah, was built by Walker Bros, at the Ophir mining district. When that district was considered a failure the mill was removed to the Alice mine in Montana, five stamps being added, and a 60-stamp mill erected by its side. *Walker's Merchants and Miners of Utah*, MS., 5. Nevertheless, at the close of 1883 there were three mills in this district, named the Pioneer, Enterprise, and Fairview. At this date the Ontario mill, at Park City, Uintah district, had 40 stamps, and the Marsac mill at the same city, 30 stamps. Among others may be mentioned the McHenry mill at Parley Park, the Stewart mills in the West Mountain district, and one belonging to the Tintic Mining and Milling Co., the last with 10 stamps.

[80] Including common, refined, white, sheet, pipe, shot, and test lead. *Hollister's Res. and Attract. of Utah*, 43. For further mention of the Germania works, see *S. L. C. Tribune*, Dec. 14, 1872, Jan. 4, 1873.

[81] For description of other smelting and refining works, see *Utah Gazetteer*, 1884, 70–1. The first smelting furnace was erected by Gen. Connor at Stockton in 1864. *Murphy's Min. Res. of Utah*, 2. Among the sampling-works may be mentioned those of J. C. Conklin at S. L. City, and Scott & Anderson at Sandy, the former with a capacity of 200 and the latter of 500 tons a day.

[82] As in the Silver Reef district

the average yield of galena ores, which form the bulk of the deposits, is less than $30 per ton, it will be seen that they could not be worked at a profit. With the exception of the Ontario, Horn Silver, and perhaps one or two others where the ore was exceptionally rich, none of the mines paid steady dividends of any considerable amount.

CHAPTER XXVIII.

COMMERCE AND COMMUNICATION.

1852-1885.

Common Roadways—Railroads—The Union and Central Pacific—The Utah Central—The Utah Southern—The Utah and Northern—The Utah Eastern—The Salt Lake and Western—The Utah and Nevada—The Denver and Rio Grande Western—Imports and Exports—Commerce and Trade—Banking—Insurance—Taxation and Revenue—Mails and Mail Services—The First Telegraphic Message—The Deseret Telegraph Company.

In 1860 the principal route from the Missouri to Utah was still the old emigrant-road which had been mainly used during the Utah and California migrations, and which was traversed by the army of Utah in 1857. Between Utah and California there were three principal lines of travel—the northern, the central, and the southern. The first skirted the upper edge of Great Salt Lake, and thence after crossing an intervening stretch of desert followed the valleys of the Humboldt and Carson rivers, being, in fact, almost identical with the Frémont route of 1845. Notwithstanding its length, it was still preferred by travellers, as pasture and water were fairly plentiful, and only two small tracts of desert land were met with.[1] The central, better known to the settlers of Utah by the name of Egan's and to the California-bound emigrants as the Simpson route, though the two were by no means coincident, varied but a few miles from the fortieth parallel until reaching the

[1] For descriptions of this route, see *Horn's Overl. Guide; Kelly's Excurs. to Cal., Remy's Jour. to G. S. L. City*, passim.

Hastings pass in the Humboldt Mountains, where it branched off in a south-westerly direction toward Carson lake and river, and from Carson City south to Genoa.[2] The southern route was by way of the Sevier, Santa Clara, and Vírgen rivers, striking the Frémont trail near Las Vegas, thence partly across desert tracts to the junction of Indian River and the Colorado, and from that point to San Bernardino.[3] On neither of the last two were grass and water abundant, but the southern route had the advantage of being rarely blocked with snow, except for the portion of it that lay between Salt Lake and the Rio Vírgen.

At the close of 1883 there were more than 3,000 miles of common roadway in Utah,[4] and 1,143 miles

[2] In 1859 J. H. Simpson of the topographical engineers received instructions from Gen. Johnson to explore the great basin, with a view to find a direct wagon route from Camp Floyd to Genoa, in Carson Valley. An account of the expedition will be found in his *Rept Explor. Gt Basin.* For about 300 miles his route was identical with Egan's, except for a few unimportant deviations; but soon after reaching Ruby Valley it tended more toward the south. Egan's line was preferred, however, as on the one taken by Simpson grass and water were scarce. Howard Egan, a major in the Nauvoo legion, and a well-known guide and mountaineer, was for some years engaged in driving stock to Cal. in the service of Livingston & Kinkead, and afterward became a mail agent. *Burton's City of the Saints,* 550. See, for an account of the explorations of E. F. Beales between Fort Defiance and the Colorado, and F. W. Lander between Green and Bear rivers in 1857, Warren's mem. in *Pac. R. R. Rept,* xi. 91; for remarks on the advantages of different routes, *Wheeler's Surveys, Progress Rept,* 1872, 33–6; for J. W. Powell's exploring and surveying expeditions, *Appleton's Jour.,* xi.; *Smithsonian Rept,* 1877, 67–82; for further matters relating to government roads, *House Ex. Doc.,* 34th Cong. 1st Sess., i., pt 2, 504–7; 35th Cong. 2d Sess., ii., pt 2, 12, 149–51, 202–6, pt. 3, 1300–3; 36th Cong. 1st Sess., Mess and Doc., pt 2, 13–15, 131–2, 194–5, 200–4, 221–30; *House Rept,* 34th Cong. 1st Sess., i. 185; *Sen. Doc.,* 35th Cong. 2d Sess., nos. 39, 40. Appropriations were made at various dates for the building and repair of bridges, for which see *Utah Jour. Legisl.* and *Utah Laws,* passim. In 1882 the sum of $5,000 was appropriated toward building a bridge across the Weber at Riverdale, and $1,000 for a bridge across the Provo at Provo City. For description of Provo cañon bridge in 1858, see *Deseret News,* Oct. 13, 1858; for condition of bridges and roads in 1859, *Id.,* July 6, 1859.

[3] Portions of this route were traversed by Chandless and Remy, by whom it is described in their respective works.

[4] For reports of commissioners, appropriations, work done, condition, and other matters relating to local roads, see *Utah Acts,* 1855–6, 44–6; *Utah Jour. Legisl.,* 1859–60, 96–8; 1860–1, 58–9, 113–14, 149, 165, 168; 1861–2, 59, 70, 73, 104, 116–17, 121, 132, 144; 1862–3, 29–30, 45, 51, 63; 1863–4, 54–5, 85, 108, 131–2; 1864–5, 53–6, 73, 140–1; 1865–6, 20–3, 29, 53, 70–1, 102, 122, 156–7; 1866–7, 20, 23–5, 28–9, 61–3, 66; 1868, 21–2, 25, 44–6, 75–6, 92, 116–18, 129; 1869, 20–1, 23–4, 55–6, 71–2, 79–80, 82–3, 88, 93–4, 102, 112,

of railroad,[5] of which 297 belonged to the Union Pacific, 150 to the Central Pacific, 386 to the Denver and Rio Grande, 280 to the Utah Central, and 30 to the Sanpete Valley.

In 1854, as we have seen, a memorial was addressed to congress by the territorial legislature, urging the construction of an overland railroad. In 1860 a second memorial was presented, to the same purport,[6] and though neither of them was regarded, none rejoiced more heartily over the advent of the railroad than did the settlers of Utah. They felt now strong enough to have let in on them the advancing tide of civilization without being swept away by it. Brigham had long foreseen that the railroad would bring with it a new and manifest destiny to his people. Being himself a man of destiny, he quickly adapted himself to the altered condition of affairs, and declared that he believed in it. As all Utah believed in Brigham, it followed that his people would do their utmost to help it to completion. They were for the most part too poor to subscribe money, but whatever of aid or material their land and labor could supply was cheerfully furnished.

In May 1868 a contract was made between Brig-

172; 1870, 63-4, 79, 84-8, 108, 118; 1876, 29-30; *Utah Laws*, 1878, 57; 1882, 102-4; *Deseret News*, Nov. 23, 1859, Jan. 22, 1862; *Rae's Westward by Rail*, 99.

[5] In 1860 there was a weekly stage to S. L. City, conducted by Russell & Waddell, who during the same year started a pony express. In 1861 they were bought out by Ben Holliday, and in that or the following year a daily line was established to S. L. City. In 1866 Wells, Fargo, & Co. purchased Holliday's interest, believing that the railroad would not be completed for six or seven years. They lost by the transaction, among their purchases being $70,000 worth of new coaches which they never used, and afterward sold to Gilmer & Salisbury for one fourth of the cost. John T. Gilmer commenced staging in 1859 under Russell & Waddell. In 1864 he was appointed division agent at Bitter Creek by Ben Holliday. About 1876 he began mining in the Black Hills, Utah, and afterward in Nev., Id., Ariz., and Cal. He was also connected with the Stewart mine in Bingham cañon, and others. In 1884 he was conducting a staging business in Utah, Id., Ariz., and Cal. *Gilmer's Mails and Staging in Utah*, MS. Descriptions of stage-coach travel in Utah in the years before the opening of the railroad will be found in almost every book that treats of Mormonism up to that time. Among others, see *Burton's City of the Saints; Remy's Jour. to G. S. L. City; Chandler's Visit to S. Lake; Bowles' Across the Continent; Dilke's Greater Britain; Greeley's Overl. Jour.*

[6] See *Utah Acts*, 1858-9, 37-8; *House Misc. Doc.*, 36th Cong. 2d Sess., 34.

HIST. UTAH. 48

ham and a superintendent of construction on the
Union Pacific, for grading and other work on the
road between the head of Echo cañon and the terminus of the line, yet to be located. At Weber cañon,
through which point it entered the valley, there was
much tunnelling, blasting, and mason-work to be done,
including the heavy stone-work of the bridge abut-
ments. The contract amounted to about $1,000,000,
gave employment to 500 or 600 men, and, according
to its terms,[7] eighty per cent of the payments were
to be made monthly as the work progressed, and the
remainder when it was completed and accepted. As
soon as the contract was closed, the superintendent
urged that the work be commenced immediately,
promising that if men and teams were collected he
would have the line surveyed and made ready for
them within a few days. On this understanding,
workmen were concentrated at various points on the
line, but weeks passed, and still the line was not surveyed. Many of the sub-contractors were thus compelled to wait until the cost of their operations was
largely increased by the severity of the weather, and
to incur debt from bankers, merchants, and farmers,
who supplied them with funds, goods, grain, and material, thinking that the money due from the promoters of the Union Pacific would be promptly paid;
but the payments were not made as specified.

Notwithstanding these drawbacks, the contracts
were faithfully executed, and it was acknowledged by
all railroad men that nowhere on the line could the
grading compare in completeness and finish with the
work done by the people of Utah. Before the last
tie was laid,[8] all the contracts with the Union and

---

[7] Particulars will be found in the *Deseret News*, May 27, 1868. See also
S. F. Call, May 22, 1868; *S. F. Times*, May 22, 1868. At this date it was yet
uncertain where the junction between the U. P. and C. P. R. R. would be
located. For act to fix the point of junction, see *House Ex. Doc.*, 46th Cong.
3d Sess., 973.

[8] For celebration at S. L. City on the completion of the railroad, see *Deseret
News*, May 12, 1866. On March 8th a railroad celebration was held at Ogden,
an account of which is given in *Id.*, March 8, 1869; *Tullidge's Mag.*, i. 476-7.

Central Pacific, including forty miles of road between Ogden and the promontory, had been completed and accepted; but on the 10th of May, 1869, it was claimed by the saints that the former company was indebted to them in the sum of $1,000,000, and the two companies about $1,250,000. Toward the close of the year John Taylor, Joseph A. Young, and John Sharp[9] went eastward, with a view to bringing the

In 1868 Gen. Connor built and launched a small steamer, named the *Kate Connor*, for carrying railroad ties and telegraph poles from the southern to the northern shore of the G. S. Lake. *Res. and Attract. of Utah*, 63. The ties were for the Union Pacific. This appears to have been the first steamer that navigated the lake, though in the *S. F. Bulletin*, July 29, 1856, it is stated that there was one at that date. In 1869 an excursion steamer was built, and in 1870 a boat costing $45,000, first named the *City of Corinne* and then the *General Garfield*. In 1879 the latter was still used mainly for excursions, as there was little freight to be had. At this date there was a considerable yachting fleet on the lake, the first, and for some years the only yacht, being built by the Walker Bros. For description of excursions on G. S. Lake in 1879, see *Marshall's Through Amer.*, 191; for navigation on the Colorado in 1865, *Austin Reese River Reveillé*, June 27, 1865; in 1873, *Prescott Miner*, Jan. 18, 1873.

[9] Bishop Sharp, known in Utah also as the railroad bishop, was born in 1820 at the Devon iron-works, Scotland, and when eight years of age went to work in a coal-pit. In 1847, being then a coal-miner in Clackmannanshire, he was converted to Mormonism, and the following year sailed for New Orleans with his two brothers, who had also joined the faith. They reached S. L. City in 1850. Here Sharp was first employed in quarrying stone for the tabernacle and tithing-office, and was soon afterward made superintendent of the quarry. In 1854 he was ordained a bishop, and ten years later was appointed assistant superintendent of public works. When the contract was made with the Union Pacific by Brigham, as above mentioned, Sharp was one of the principal sub-contractors. In 1871 he became superintendent of the Utah Central, and in 1873 president, having previously been elected vice-president of the Utah Southern. While employed as purchasing agent for the latter company in the eastern states, he became associated with the directors of the Union Pacific, by whom he was afterward elected a member of the board. Among those who were awarded contracts by the Central Pacific was Lorin Farr, who, with Benson and West as partners, graded 200 miles of the road, Aaron F. Farr being employed as superintendent. Lorin Farr also took an active part in the building of the Utah Central and Utah Northern, of which more later, and was one of the prime movers in bringing the Denver and Rio Grande into Ogden. In 1868 he built the Ogden woollen-mills in conjunction with Randall Pugsley and Neil, and for 20 years was mayor of that city. Aaron F. Farr was for six years probate judge of Weber co., and was elected a member of the Utah legislature.

In connection with the Central Pacific may be mentioned the name of James Forbes, their agent at Ogden between 1869 and 1884, and in connection with the Union Pacific, A. G. Fell, at the latter date superintendent of division in the same city. Forbes, a native of Conn., came to Cal. when 16 years of age, and after being engaged in mining for several years, was appointed agent for the C. P. R. R. at Elko, Nev., soon after the line was opened, removing thence to Utah a few months later. Fell, a native of Ontario, Can., and in 1867 employed in the train-despatcher's office at Montreal, also removed to Utah in 1867.

Joshua R. Nichols, appointed assist super. U. P. R. R. in July 1869, says

matter to an issue, and so vigorously and adroitly did
they press their claim, that, in the absence of funds,
rolling stock and material to the value of $600,000
were assigned to them in payment.

On the 17th of May, one week after the completion
of the transcontinental railroad, ground was broken
near the Weber River for a line between Ogden and
Salt Lake City, to be named the Utah Central.[10]
The road was built and equipped mainly with the
material and rolling stock transferred from the Union
Pacific; for even at this date there was little money
in Utah, mining and traffic being as yet undeveloped,
and the entire floating currency of the community was
probably less than $5,000,000.   This, the pioneer line
of Utah, is the only one which has preserved its
original identity, and that it has done so is perhaps
due to the fact that it forms the main connecting link
between the route of transcontinental traffic and the
principal distributing point for the country.

In May 1871 ground was broken at Salt Lake City
for the Utah Southern,[11] the line being pushed forward at intervals both north and south through some
of the richest lands in Utah, until, in June 1879, its
northern terminus was at Provo,[12] and its southern
limit at Juab, 105 miles south of the capital.[13]   Later

that for three months after that date no director or manager dare travel on the
line without a body-guard. *Nichols' Mining Mach.*, MS.

[10] For act granting right of way, see *House Ex. Doc.*, 46th Cong. 3d Sess.,
xxvi. 974; *Cong. Globe*, 1870–1, p. 329; *Zabriskie's Land Laws*, 1877, suppl. 10;
Grant's Rights and Priv. Utah Cent. R. R. Co., in which last are the articles
of association, by-laws, and a copy of the mortgage executed by the company
to secure its first-mortgage bonds.   Brigham Young was president, W. Jennings vice-president, Dan. H. Wells treasurer, and John W. Young secretary;
the first three, together with Feramorz Little and Christ. Layton, forming
the board of directors.   The original capital was $1,500,000, divided into
15,000 shares of $100 each.   It does not appear that the directors had much
faith in the undertaking, for none of them, except Brigham, subscribed for
more than twenty shares, while Layton took only 10, and Little 5 shares.   For
celebration when ground was broken, see *S. F. Bulletin*, May 19, 1869; *Tullidge's Mag.*, i. 477; for ceremonies, etc., when the road was completed, *Deseret News*, Jan. 12, 1870; *S. F. Abend Post*, Jan. 12, 1876; *Scientific Press*,
Jan. 15, 1870; *Tullidge's Life of Young*, 362–3.

[11] *Deseret News*, May 3, 1871.

[12] For bill granting right of way, see *Cong. Globe*, 1874–5; for special privileges, *Provo City Revised Ordin.*, 127–9.

[13] For further items as to the Utah Southern, see *Williams' Pac. Tourist,*

during this year the Utah Southern Extension was commenced at the latter point, completed during the following spring as far as Milford,[14] and a few weeks later to Frisco, the location of the Horn Silver mine, its distance from Juab being 138 miles.[15] In 1881 both these lines were incorporated with the Utah Central.[16]

The Utah and Northern was organized in 1871, ground being broken at Brigham City in September of that year, and the road completed to Logan at the close of January 1873, and to Franklin, Idaho, by way of Ogden, early in the following year.[17] The means for building this line were raised by the people of northern Utah with great difficulty, and after being maintained for years, first at a loss and then with meagre returns, it was sold to the Union Pacific for an insignificant sum, in February 1877,[18] extended through Idaho into western Montana, and in 1883 had become one of its most profitable branches.

During Emery's administration a bill passed the legislature authorizing the counties of Salt Lake, Davis, Summit, and Tooele to issue bonds for the purpose of constructing a road from Coalville to

131-2; *Deseret News*, Dec. 3, 1873, Jan. 27, 1875, Jan. 26, 1876; *S. L. C. Herald*, March 20, 1878; *S. F. Alta*, May 11, 1872; *S. F. Post*, Nov. 11, 1873; *Prescott Miner*, Jan. 26, 1877.

[14] The first train ran through to Milford in May. *S. L. Wkly Tribune*, May 22, 1880.

[15] *Utah Gazetteer*, 1884, 108. See also *S. L. Herald*, Jan. 1, 1879; *S. L. C. Tribune*, July 8, 1879.

[16] In the *Contributor*, iv. 182, is a report of freights received and forwarded over the Utah Central for eleven and a half months in 1882.

[17] The road from Ogden to Franklin was built entirely by the settlers. *Doddridge's U. & N. R. R.*, MS. For act granting right of way through public lands of Utah, Idaho, and Montana in 1873, see *Zabriskie's Land Laws*, suppl., 1877, p. 57; *House Ex. Doc.*, 46th Cong. 3d Sess., 47, pt 2, 976-7. In 1772 an act was passed granting right of way through to the Utah, Idaho, and Montana road, which was to connect with the Utah and Northern. *Id.*, 975.

[18] During 1879 the income had increased to about $80,000 a month. *Deseret News*, July 16, 1879. For further items concerning the Utah and Northern, see *Id.*, Oct. 10, 1877; *S. L. C. Herald*, Nov. 21, 1877; *Portland Ev. Telegram*, May 3, July 24, 1879; *Utah Gazetteer*, 1884, 108-9; *Doddridge's U. & N. R. R.*, MS. W. B. Doddridge, a native of Circleville, O., came to Ogden in 1867, and though only 19 years of age, readily obtained employment on the U. P. R. R. In 1882 he was appointed to the charge of the Idaho division.

Salt Lake City, the main object being to obtain a supply of coal at cheaper rates than was charged for fuel taken from the Wyoming mines of the Union Pacific. The bill was vetoed by the governor; but in 1880 an effort was made to build the line by private enterprise, among the subscribers being many who could ill afford such a venture. Like others of the Utah lines, it was thus commenced on a slender capital, but through the aid of wealthy stockholders in the Ontario mine, it was completed as, far as Park City, a distance of twenty-five miles from Coalville. Soon afterward a parallel branch, named the Echo and Park City, was built by the Union Pacific, and in 1883 the control of the former, which was known as the Utah Eastern, fell into the hands of the latter.[19]

The Salt Lake and Western, fifty-seven miles in length, and later a branch of the Union Pacific, was built in 1874–5 from Lehi junction, a mile north of Lehi City, to the Tintic mines. It was at first intended to push the line through to California, tapping some of the rich mining districts of Nevada; but this project was abandoned. In 1883 it was used mainly for hauling gold, silver, and iron ore.[20] The Utah and Nevada, first named the Salt Lake, Sevier Valley, and Pioche Railroad, was commenced in 1872, the intention being to build the line through the mining and agricultural lands of the Sevier Valley as far as Pioche, in south-eastern Nevada. After some twenty miles had been completed, work was abandoned in 1873, but resumed later, and the road completed as far as Stockton, in Tooele county, its terminus in 1883, at which date it was also under control of the Union Pacific. On account of the failure of the Pioche mines, and for other reasons, there seems little prospect of the original project being executed. The Sanpete Valley Railroad, built in 1880, between Nephi, in Juab

---

[19] *S. L. C. Tribune*, Dec. 28, 1879.
[20] *Williams' Pac. Tourist*, 147; *S. L. C. Tribune*, Dec. 19, 1874; *S. F. Bulletin*, July 6, 1881; *Utah Gazetteer*, 1884, p. 110.

county, and Wales, in Sanpete county, its length
being thirty miles, was constructed by an English
company for the purpose of securing a market for the
output of its coal mines.[21]

The Denver and Rio Grande Western, the Utah
division of the Denver and Rio Grande system of
railroads, first began work here in 1881, and in 1883
had 386 miles of road in operation, running through
Emery, Utah, Salt Lake, Davis, and a portion of
Weber counties, with branch lines named the Little
Cottonwood and Bingham Cañon, the former running
east into the Wasatch Mountains and the latter west
into the Oquirrh Range, both being built solely to
facilitate mining operations.[22]   Ninety miles of the
Denver and Rio Grande Western were built entirely
by local enterprise, including fifty miles of the main
line extending through Spanish Fork cañon, completed by the citizens of Springville, and first known
as the Utah and Pleasant Valley Railroad.[23]

During the years immediately preceding the completion of the overland railroad, the imports of Utah
seldom exceeded 12,000 tons, while the exports were
of trifling amount.   Commerce with the east and west
was entirely insignificant, supplies being drawn mainly
from St Louis and San Francisco, and paid for in part
with the money received for surplus grain, stock, and
garden produce from passing emigrants, who, together
with the soldiery and the stage lines, furnished almost

[21] *S. L. C. Herald*, June 17, 1880; *Utah Gazetteer*, 1884, 110.
[22] Companies were organized to build both these roads in 1872, and they
were constructed by local enterprise, afterward becoming tributary to the
Denver and Rio Grande.
[23] In addition to the above roads, there were two short lines, formerly in
operation, and known as the Summit County and American Fork.   Both have
been abandoned.   For further particulars as to the Utah railroads, see *Hollister's Res. and Attract. of Utah*, 58–65; *Utah Gazetteer*, 1884, 105–11; *Crofutt's
Overl. Tourist*, 126–42; *Utah Res.*, 43–8; *Hayden's Gt West*, 319; *Duffus-Hardy's
Through Cities*, 97; *Utah Laws*, 1878, 13, 1882, 12–18; *Utah Jour. Legisl.*,
1880, 135–7; *Sec. Int. Rept*, 42d Cong. 3d Sess., pt i., 167; *Sen. Ex. Doc.*,
45th Cong. 2d Sess., 40.   In 1883 the bonded debt of the Utah Central was
$4,900,000, of the Utah Eastern $400,000, of the Utah and Northern $972,000,
of the Salt Lake and Western $1,080,000, of the Sanpete Valley, $750,000.
The Utah and Nevada had no bonded debt.

the principal cash receipts of Utah.[24]   In 1871 the
volume of domestic imports and exports had increased
to 80,000 tons, and since that date has averaged about
125,000 tons, of which two thirds were imports, and
nearly one half consisted of material needed for mining
operations.

The total value of imports for 1882 was estimated
at $11,410,000, and of exports at $11,525,000, the
chief items among the former being dry goods, groceries, clothing, lumber and other building material,
agricultural implements, leather and leathern manufactures; among the latter, gold, silver, lead, copper
matte, live-stock, beef, wool, hides, pelts, furs, and
tallow,[25] the exports of metals alone amounting to
$9,000,000.   The shipment of iron ore and charcoal
to Utah, which at one time were important factors in
the imports, has now practically ceased; but the territory must always import more or less of lumber,
agricultural implements, wagons, and furniture; for
there are no hard or finishing woods of native growth,
and lumber of good quality cut from native timber is
scarce and difficult to obtain.   Imports of leathern and
woollen goods will doubtless decrease with the growth
of manufactures, though for reasons that are explained
elsewhere, the leather produced in Utah is of inferior
quality.

While Utah could without difficulty produce a large
surplus of many agricultural products, distance from
market and an exorbitant freight tariff make it almost
impossible for her to compete with the Pacific and
western states.   Several efforts have been made in
this direction, but the results were not satisfactory,
and it is doubtful whether Utah has yet sent away in
all more than 1,000,000 bushels of grain.   The ex-

[24] Flour, meat, and vegetables were also exchanged for groceries, clothing,
etc. *Brown's Statement*, MS., 3.   In 1849 the settlers were anxious to open a
highway to San Diego, whence they intended to obtain supplies.   In 1867 it
was proposed to use the Colorado route for traffic. See *Hayes' Scraps, San
Diego*, ii. 171-93.

[25] *Hollister's Res. and Attract. of Utah*, 67-8; *Utah Gazetteer*, 1884, 113,
where are tables of imports and exports for 1882.

periment was first tried on a large scale in 1878, when a ship was laden at San Francisco with 64,000 bushels of Utah wheat, the cargo being sold before the vessel put to sea. A few months later a ship was chartered for England with 78,000 bushels,[26] but though a small profit was realized, it was not sufficient to encourage further operations.

If to the $11,410,000 of imports there be added 25 per cent as the profits of jobbers and retailers, we have a total of about $14,250,000, which represents approximately the general business of Utah. It is worthy of note that while this large amount of business is transacted, the average number of failures for the eight years ending 1883 did not exceed fourteen, with liabilities averaging about $11,000.[27] The credit of Utah merchants is for the most part exceptionally good; not that they are considered more upright than other merchants, but because a very large proportion of cash is now employed in their transactions; and while many import on a small scale, the bulk of the business is done by a few large firms, which trade on a sufficient capital and do not require much credit.

In 1883 it was estimated that the Zion's Coöperative Mercantile Institution, with its 800 stockholders, its cash capital of $1,000,000, its surplus of $150,000, and its branches at Ogden and Logan, imported at least one third of all the merchandise consumed in Utah. Soon after this association was established, coöperative stores were opened in every large town, and in nearly every village and farming settlement, all of them purchasing from the so-called parent institution, and through its agency disposing of the produce received in barter. Every one who could purchase or earn a share of stock contributed his labor or capital, and though many of them succumbed through opposition or over-anxiety to dis-

[26] The names of the vessels were the *Maulsden* and *Ivy*, both being chartered by S. W. Sears.
[27] See reports of R. G. Dun & Co.'s agency.

burse large dividends, it is probable that at least two thirds of the settlers patronize them at this day.[28]

The progress and development of trade in Utah from the days of 1848, when probably the entire cash capital of the community did not amount to $3,000, present some interesting and anomalous features. At first, as we have seen, the Mormons desired to avoid all traffic with the outside world; but as emigrants passed over their roads and through their settlements, goods were exchanged with advantage to both sides. It was not until two years after the pioneers entered the valley that the first store was opened at an adobe house, in the seventeenth ward of Salt Lake City, by the firm of Livingston & Kinkead,[29] whose stock was worth some $20,000. In 1850 the firm of Holliday & Warner established a branch of their business in the capital, through their agent, William H. Hooper, who opened a store in a building erected for school purposes, on the block occupied by Brigham Young, thence removing to the structure later occupied by the museum.[30]

Soon the unerring scent of commerce discovered the direction which business must take, and Main

[28] For further details as to commerce in Utah, and the development of the coöperative system, see *Hollister's Res. and Attract. of Utah*, 48–52, 67–9; *Tullidge's Mag.*, Apr. 1881, passim; *Contributor*, iv. 182; *Fabian's Utah*, 11–13; *S. L. C. Tribune*, Jan. 4, 1872; *S. L. Herald*, in *S. F. Call*, Feb. 24, 1872; *S. F. Alta*, Apr. 10, 27, May 13, 1872; *S. F. Bulletin*, Feb. 22, 1872; *S. F. Chronicle*, Oct. 6, 1873; *S. F. Post*, Apr. 12, 1875; for commercial law, *Utah Gazetteer*, 1884, 273–7.

[29] *Richards' Reminiscences*, MS., 31. At this date the firm occupied what was considered the most convenient house in the city. Later it was pulled down. In the *Deseret News* of Sept. 28, 1854, it is stated that Capt. Grant of Fort Hall was the first outsider who brought goods to the Utah market for sale, offering sugar and coffee at $1 a pint, calico at 50 to 75 cents a yard, and other articles in proportion. Livingston & Kinkead, who came with the intention of trading for five years, realizing a certain net profit, and then returning to Egypt, which they did, sold coffee and sugar at 40 cents a pound (a little more than a pint), calico at 25 cents a yard, etc. At this date there were few eastern, or, as they were termed, states goods in the market; and if we can believe *Beadle's Life in Utah*, 197, the firm took in $10,000 in gold the first day their store was opened. As this amount then probably represented almost the entire floating capital of the Mormons, the statement must be taken for what it is worth.

[30] In 1851 David Smith and E. N. Cook, bound for Oregon with a large band of stock from St Joseph, stopped at Salt Lake City for three weeks, trading dry goods, etc., for additional cattle. *Clark's Sights*, MS., 11.

street, then dubbed Whiskey street, the denizens of
which were often rebuked in the tabernacle for their
iniquities, rapidly became the business quarter of the
city, John and Enoch Reese, the third firm in historic
date, building a store on the ground later occupied by
the express office, and J M. Horner & Co., the fourth,
occupying a portion of the premises of the *Deseret
News.*[31] Among the men who had become prominent
at the time of the Utah war were Gilbert & Gerrish
and William Nixon, the latter being still termed the
father of Utah merchants.[32]

Before the Utah war and for several years afterward, internal trade was conducted mainly by barter
and the due-bill system. At this period the settlers
had little use for money, and preferred taking in exchange for their commodities something that they
could eat, or drink, or wear, and which could not be
had at home. Thus scores of well-to-do farmers, with
families to clothe and educate, while living in greater
comfort perhaps than those of the western or Pacific
states, seldom possessed a dollar in coin. Should one
of them, for instance, require clothing for wife or
child, he consulted the store-keeper, who agreed, perhaps, to supply him for so many loads of wood. If
he should have no spare wood, he searched out some
neighbor who had a surplus and offered him its equivalent in butter or poultry. Perhaps, however, this
neighbor did not need butter or poultry, but required
a few loads of gravel or adobes. In that case the
farmer must find some one who was willing to exchange

[31] Horner & Co. reduced the price of sugar to three pounds for $1, where-
upon Livingston & Kinkead sold it at 30 cents a pound, calico at 18¾ cents a
yard, and marked all their goods 25 per cent below former prices, giving a
guarantee never to exceed these rates. *Deseret News*, Sept. 28, 1854. In 1855,
however, coffee and moist sugar were still selling at 40 cents per lb., and
domestics at 25 cents a yard, tea being worth $2.25 per lb., flour $6.25 per
100 lbs., bacon and cheese each 30 cents, and butter 36 to 40 cents. *Chandler's
Visit to S. Luke*, 345. Horner & Co. continued but a short time in business,
being succeeded by Hooper & Williams.

[32] Gilbert & Gerrish were a gentile firm, and William Nixon was a Mormon of English descent, who began his commercial career at St Louis.
Among his pupils were the Walker brothers.

for his poultry or butter, gravel or adobes, which he delivered in return for wood, hauled the wood to the store, and thus, at length, wife and child were clad. For the tuition of his children he would pay, perhaps, so many dozens of eggs per quarter; for admission to the theatre, a score of cabbages; for the services of a laborer or mechanic, a certain number of watermelons per day; and his tithes were usually, but not always, paid in kind.

In this primitive fashion, until the advent of the railroad, trade was for the most part conducted in Utah; and notwithstanding the wisdom and economic system of their rulers, there were times, as will be remembered, when the settlers were really needy. The country was relieved only by a train of fortunate, or as the settlers believed providential, circumstances. These were, first, the presence of the army of Utah, which after disbursing large sums among the community sold them its substance at nominal rates; second, the arrival of a second army under Colonel Connor, with the interchange of traffic and demand for labor thereby occasioned; third, the needs of the overland mail and telegraph lines.

In part through such adventitious aid, the merchants of Utah, putting forth their might, built up a commerce as wonderful in its growth and development as that of any of the states on the Atlantic or Pacific seaboard. As early as 1864 there were several houses in Salt Lake City that purchased in New York, St Louis, or Chicago goods to the value of $250,000 or more at a time, among them being William Jennings,[33] Godbe & Mitchell, the Walker Broth-

[33] Isaac, the father of William Jennings, a wealthy butcher of Yardley, Worcester, England, was better known to fame as one of the claimants in the Jennings chancery suit, in which millions of pounds were at stake; but though he proved himself a lawful claimant, his efforts won for him no substantial result. In 1847 William Jennings, then some 14 years of age, took ship for New York, where, during the ensuing winter, he was employed by a pork-packer at a wage of $6 a week. After some adventures, being at one time robbed of his all and glad to find work as a journeyman butcher, and on another occasion attacked with cholera, which left him with a shattered constitution and $200 in debt, he chanced to make the acquaintance of a catholic

ers, and Kimball & Lawrence, than whom few firms throughout the United States, outside, perhaps, of Boston, ranked higher as to commercial integrity. After the founding of Zion's Coöperative Mercantile Institution, mentioned elsewhere, and the development of its banking system, the trade and commerce of Utah assumed a more homogeneous character.[34]

In 1883 there were twelve private and five national banks in operation in Utah, of which six were at the capital, three at Ogden, two at Logan, and one each at the several towns of Provo, Corinne, St George, Richfield, Silver Reef, and Park City. Their aggregate paid-up capital was estimated at $1,000,000, their loans at $3,000,000, their deposits at $3,500,000, and the amount of their exchange business at from $12,000,000 to $15,000,000.[35]

priest, from whom he borrowed $50. With this capital Jennings made his first real start in life, and turning every dollar to account, soon paid off his debt and laid the basis of his fortune. In 1851 we find him at St Joseph, where he was married to Jane Walker, a Mormon emigrant girl. In the autumn of 1852 he arrived at Salt Lake City, having first invested all his means in three wagon-loads of groceries, from which he realized a considerable profit. Joining the church, he engaged in business as a butcher, and in 1855–6 as a tanner, boot and shoe manufacturer, and saddle and harness maker. In 1856 he was sent on a mission to Carson Valley, and, returning in the summer of 1857, commenced business some three years later as a dry-goods merchant in Salt Lake City, soon becoming the leading business man in Utah. In 1864 his purchases in New York and St Louis amounted to $500,000, and in Salt Lake City to $350,000, his business thereafter averaging about $2,000,000 per annum. Mr Jennings assisted in organizing the Utah Central R. R., of which he became vice-president, and succeeded Brigham as president of the Utah Southern. He was also one of the founders and directors of the Deseret National Bank, and a member of the legislature under Governor Doty.

[34] Until the advent of the railroad, the prices of all commodities continued extremely high. At a convention held at the Bowery, S. L. City, Oct. 4, 1864, the price of flour was fixed at $12 per 100 lbs, of wheat, corn, and beans at $5, $4, and $10 per bushel respectively, of pork at 30 cents, and of dried apples at 75 cents per lb., all in gold. *Deseret News*, Oct. 19, 1864. Bowles says that in June of the following year lumber was worth $100 per thousand feet, sugar 75 to 85 cents, coffee $1 to $1.1Q and tea 3.50 to $5 per ℔. *Across the Continent*, 101–2. These prices were in currency.

[35] *Utah Gazetteer*, 1884, 115. The firm of Hooper, Eldredge, & Co.—W. H. Hooper, H. S. Eldredge, and L. S. Hills—commenced business at S. L. City May 1, 1869, with a capital of $40,000. They were succeeded by the Bank of Deseret, incorporated under territorial law Sept. 1, 1871, with a capital of $100,000, Brigham Young being president, H. S. Eldredge vice-president, and W. H. Hooper, W. Jennings, F. Little, and J. Sharp the remaining directors. L. S. Hills was cashier. This institution was again succeeded by the Deseret National Bank, organized under the act of Nov. 1,

At this date there were some fifty insurance agencies having business with Salt Lake City and Ogden, their risks on buildings amounting to $500,000, and on merchandise in stock to $3,500,000.[36]

Thus with her 1,143 miles of railroad, her agricultural and stock-raising interests, now valued at $12,-000,000 a year, her manufactures at $5,000,000, her mining output at $7,000,000 or $8,000,000, her commerce at $23,000,000, and her seventeen national and commercial banks, it will be seen that Utah compares

1872, with a capital of $200,000, and with the same directors and officials, its deposits in 1880 being about $500,000. The Walker Bros' bank was established in 1871, the firm having at that date large deposits of cash and bullion to their credit, notwithstanding the losses caused by the coöperative movement and by the opposition of the church dignitaries. *Walker's Merchants and Miners of Utah*, MS., 4. The remaining banks at S. L. City in 1873 were those of Jones & Co., McCornick & Co., Wells, Fargo, & Co., and the Zion's Savings Bank, the last having a capital of $50,000, and of which John Taylor was president.

The Ogden banks were the Commercial National Bank, the Utah National Bank of Ogden, and the First National, of which last H. S. Eldredge was president in 1885. The business of the Commercial National was purchased from J. M. Langsdorf and H. O. Harkness, the former organizing the firm of J. W. Guthrie & Co. at Corinne in 1874. J. M. Langsdorf, a native of Pittsburg, Pa, came to Utah in 1869. His first occupation was to sweep out the bank at Corinne, of which he was soon made book-keeper, and afterward manager. *Langsdorf's Stock-raising in Weber Co.*, MS. Guthrie & Co.'s business afterward fell into the hands of R. M. Dooly, by whom the Utah National Bank of Ogden was organized in 1883. Dooly, a native of Ill., came to Cal. in 1872, removing to Utah the following year, and being employed by Wells, Fargo, & Co. until Oct. 1881. In 1878 he was married to Mary Eliza Helfrich, a native of Grass Valley, Cal. *Dooly's Ogden Banks*, MS. Among the bankers of Ogden may also be mentioned Watson N. Shilling, a native of Ohio, where he was born in 1840. Removing to Michigan when he was twelve years of age, he enlisted in 1861 in the 1st Michigan cavalry, serving throughout the war, and being mustered out, in 1865, at Fort Collins, Col. Two years later he proceeded to Oneida co., Id., where he engaged in farming, trading, and stock-raising, and where in 1884 he still retained his interests, his residence in Ogden being mainly with a view to the education of his family. In 1883 he was a delegate to the national republican convention, throwing in his influence to secure the nomination of Blaine. *Utah Biog. Sketches*, MS., 56. The Logan banks were those of Charles Frank and Thatcher Bros & Co., the latter having a capital of $75,000. The bank at Provo was named the First National, its capital being $50,000, with A. O. Smoot as president; the one at St George was conducted by Woolley, Lund, & Judd; the one at Richfield by Jas M. Peterson; and the one at Silver Reef by R. T. Gillespie. For further particulars concerning Utah banks, see *Tullidge's Mag.*, i. 522-3; *House Ex. Doc.*, 46th Cong. 3d Sess., cxciii. 713; *Deseret News*, Nov. 6, 1872, Aug. 27, 1873; *S. L. C. Tribune*, Jan. 11, 1873; *S. F. Post*, Aug. 9, Oct. 21, 1873; *S. F. Chronicle*, July 17, 1877; *Silver Reef Miner*, Jan. 21, 1883.

[36] Alex. Daul of Ogden opened the first fire-insurance agency in Utah. Mr Daul, a native of Germany, came to the U. S. in 1862, and on arriving at S. L. City was for the most part employed as a missionary until 1873.

not unfavorably with the states of the Pacific slope. She is practically free from debt, and nowhere is taxation lighter or more equitably adjusted. In 1865, as we have seen, the territorial and county taxes were not allowed in any case to exceed one per cent of the assessed value of property, while for school purposes they seldom exceeded one fourth of one per cent.[37] In 1883 the rate was but six mills on the dollar for both territorial and school purposes,[38] counties being allowed discretion as to their rate of levy, provided that it should never exceed six mills on the dollar.[39] Cities were limited to five mills on the dollar for municipal expenses, and five mills for the making and repair of streets. The assessed value of all property in the territory was, in 1883, $30,834,425,[40] and this was considerably less than 50 per cent of the real value, the total revenue from territorial and school tax being $185,000,[41] or little more than $1 per capita of the population. That this sum was expended economically for the public benefit is shown by the number of public buildings, roads, bridges, and other improvements in the cities and counties of Utah.[42]

[37] See p. 608, this vol.

[38] A property tax, not exceeding two per cent, might be levied, however, for school buildings and improvements.

[39] For amount of property and taxes, and financial reports of the several counties at various dates, see *Utah Jour. Legisl.*, 1859–60, 12–15; 1860–1, 19; 1861–2, 29; 1862–3, 35; 1865–6, 24; 1866–7, 22–3; 1868, 20, 66–73, 135 –6, 141–2; 1869, passim; 1876, 35–6, 45–6, 271–7; 1878, 51–2, 403–64; 1880, 151–205; *Utah Fin. Repts of Cos.; Mess. of Gov.*, 1870, 10.

[40] As shown in the office of Auditor Clayton. *Utah Gazetteer*, 1884, 116. In *S. L. C. Contributor*, Feb. 1883, 183, it is given at $34,000,000.

[41] Mines and mining products were exempt, though machinery and improvements were liable to taxation. The county assessors were allowed to make their own standard, the result being that the tax was but 20 to 50 per cent of the cash valuation. Thus a steer was valued in one county at $15, in another at $6 or $8, whereas the cash value of cattle was in 1883 $25 to $30 per head. Roads bonded at $20,000 per mile were assessed at about $2,000, and others in the same proportion, the rate never exceeding one sixth of the indebtedness.

[42] For governors', auditors', and treasurers' reports and statements as to territorial revenue, expenditure, and appropriations, see *Utah Jour. Legisl.*, 1851–2 (joint sess.), 110–13; 1853–4 (joint sess.), 118–20; 1854–5, 94, 100–1, 109–12; 1859–60, 9–16; 1860–1, 16–25; 1861–2, 27–33; 1862–3, 33–9, app. xiii. –xv.; 1863–4, 21–6; 1864–5, 14–19; 1865–6, 23–33; 1866–7, 22–31; 1868, 20– 7; 1869, 20–7; 1876, 35–48, 266–79; 1878, 51–64, 316, 321–2; 1880, 23–46; *Utah Acts Legisl.*, 1866, 84–6; *Utah Laws*, 1878, 11–23; 1880, 41–4; *Mess.*

This amount does not of course include the income from tithes, which in 1880 was estimated at $458,-000,[43] a sum not larger in proportion to population than is expended for religious and charitable purposes in other states and territories of the union.

The receipts of the United States internal revenue from Utah were for 1883 about $48,000, and for the twenty preceding years averaged about $40,000. Neither tobacco nor spirituous liquors were manufactured in the country, though 230,000 cigars and some 18,000 barrels of malt liquors made during the fiscal year ending June 30, 1883, yielded revenue to the amount of $18,097. Apart from these items, most of the internal revenue receipts were derived from license taxes.[44]

The United States land-office at Salt Lake City was opened in the year 1869. Up to the 31st of March, 1884, the total payments made through this office were $831,209.08, this amount representing almost the entire sum paid for lands disposed of by government. During this period 6,388 homestead entries were made, covering an area of 844,159 acres, and 2,773 final proofs. The number of mineral-land entries was 1,023, and their area 8,656 acres; of coal-land entries 72, with an area of 10,423 acres.[45]

of Gov., 1870, 9–15. For miscellaneous matters relating to taxation and revenue, see *Utah Jour. Legisl.*, 1860–1, 76–7, 83–8; 1870, 111–13; 1876, 254–6; *Utah Acts*, 1859–60, 33; 1872, 2; 1878, 11–12; *Deseret News*, Feb. 1, 1855, Feb. 13, 1856, Dec. 21, 1865; *Utah Directory*, 1869, 67; *S. L. C. Directory*, 1869, 67.

[43] *Utah Hand-Book of Mormonism*, 6, 40, where it is stated that the total income of the priesthood exceeded $1,000,000.

[44] *Utah Gazetteer*, 1884, 117. For other matters relating to internal revenue, see *Rev. Rept Com.*, 1863, 1864, passim; *Deseret News*, March 8, 1871. In 1862 a memorial was presented for a remission of direct federal taxation, for which see *Utah Acts Legisl.*, 1861–2, 59–60. In 1878 a memorial was presented to congress asking that a mint be established in S. L. City. *H. Misc. Doc.*, 45th Cong. 2d Sess., 54, 97. In 1868 the Mormons again issued a currency of their own. *S. F. Call*, Nov. 29, 1868; *Gold Hill News*, Nov. 14, 1868; *S. F. Bulletin*, April 12, 1872.

[45] *Utah Gazetteer*, 1884, 117. For list of Utah land-offices in 1882, see *H. Ex. Doc.*, 47th Cong. 2d Sess., x. 42. For patents issued to gentile as against Mormon applicants, see *Sen. Doc.*, 46th Cong. 2d Sess., v., no. 181. The total number of acres disposed of in each year will be found in *H. Ex.*

The receipts of the post-office at Salt Lake City
for the year ending March 31, 1884, amounted to
$39,294, and the expenses to $12,871, leaving a surplus in this department of $26,423. The first post-
office was established in March 1849, letters being
usually delivered before that date at the conclusion
of divine service on the sabbath at the several places
of worship. Of mail contracts and services up to the
close of 1856 mention has already been made.[46] At
that date, it will be remembered, there was a monthly
service, when not interrupted by severity of weather
or unforeseen casualties, connecting eastward with
Independence and westward with Sacramento. After
the reopening of postal communication, interrupted
by the Utah war, there was little regard to regularity
or promptness in the delivery of the mails, letters
and papers being often lost, mail-bags wetted, thrown
carelessly to the ground, and sometimes purposely de-

Doc., 47th Cong. 2d Sess., xix., no. 72, 146. For town sites patented in
1878–80, see *H. Ex. Doc.*, 47th Cong. 1st Sess., ix., pt 5, 187. For surveys
and statistics between 1869 and 1880, see *U. S. Land-Off. Rept*, 1869, 168–74,
225–42, 256–62, 326–31, 400–5; *Sec. Interior Repts*, 42d Cong. 2d Sess., pt i.,
42, 219–23; 42d Cong. 3d Sess., pt i., 12–13, 18; 43d Cong. 1st Sess., i. 149–
57, 257–93; 43d Cong. 2d Sess., i. 155–68, 268–84, 300–3; 44th Cong. 1st
Sess., 37–40, 248–60, 377–424; 44th Cong. 2d Sess., 32–3, 36–39, 130–52, 166–
85, 277–93; *H. Ex. Doc.*, 45th Cong. 2d Sess., viii. 69, 155–217, 299–311;
45th Cong. 3d Sess., p. x., x.–xvi., 18–19, 55, 86–7, 95–6, 161, 213, 215, 319–33;
Id., 46th Cong. 2d Sess., v. 2206–8, 2213–15; *Sen. Doc.*, 46th Cong. 3d Sess.,
no. 12, 50, 67. For portions of surveyor-general's reports touching Utah, see
H. Ex. Doc., 46th Cong. 2d Sess., ix. 871–897; 47th Cong. 1st Sess., ix., pt
5, 141, 882–915; 47th Cong. 2d Sess., x. 75–7. For legislation of congress
upon which title to land in Utah depends, see *Id.*, 47th Cong. 2d Sess., xviii.,
no. 45, 971–8. For laws relating to preëmption, homestead, timber-land,
desert, and other lands, see *U. S. Stat.*, 44th Cong. 2d Sess., 377; 45 Cong. 2d
Sess., 88–9; *Stayner, Farmers' and Miners' Manual*. For further discussions,
measures, proceedings, and appropriations of congress for Utah, see *Cong.
Globe*, 1868–9, 687, 754, 781; 1869–70, passim; 1872–3, cclv., iii.–ix., ccxc.,
221, 353; 1873–4, 21, 51, 84–5, 187, 204, 506, 1838; *U. S. Acts*, 40th Cong. 3d
Sess., 224; 42d Cong. 2d Sess., 40, 223, 363, 530; *House Jour.*, 40th Cong. 3d
Sess., 617; 41st Cong. 1st Sess., 317; 41st Cong. 3d Sess., 624–5, 650–1; 42d
Cong. 2d Sess., 657, 699, 701, 713, 725, 1219, 1290, 1302–5, 1345–7; 43d Cong.
1st Sess., 1545, 1559, 1582–3; 43d Cong. 2d Sess., 793, 800, 810, 812; 44th
Cong. 1st Sess., 1736, 1775; 45th Cong. 1st Sess., 408, 431; 45th Cong. 2d
Sess., 1654–5, 1708; *Sen. Jour.*, 41st Cong. 2d Sess., 1490, 1527–8; 41st Cong.
3d Sess., 603, 673; 42d Cong. 1st Sess., 239, 249, 266, 277, 279; 42 Cong. 2d
Sess., 1234, 1380–2, 1419–20; 42d Cong. 3d Sess., 856, 870, 886; 43d Cong.
1st Sess., 1121, 1141–2; 45th Cong. 1st Sess., 168; 45th Cong. 2d Sess., 977–
8, 990, 1021; *H. Comm. Rept*, 45th Cong. 2d Sess., iv., no. 708, v., no. 949.
    [46] See pp. 500–502, this vol.

stroyed. As for magazines and newspapers, the saints considered themselves fortunate if they received them four months after date. The establishment of the pony express in 1860, and the persistence with which the Mormons advertised their grievances, improved matters considerably; and with the building of railroads, lines of postal route were of course established throughout the territory. In 1879 there were 109 routes, the subsidies for which amounted to nearly $200,000,[47] and about 200 postmasters, whose compensation varied from 18 cents to $2,800 a year.[48]

On October 18, 1861, a message from Brigham Young was received by the president of the Pacific Telegraph Company at Cleveland, Ohio, of which the following is a portion: "Utah has not seceded, but is firm for the constitution and laws of our once happy country."[49] The message was courteously answered. The same day Secretary and Acting Governor Frank Fuller thus saluted President Lincoln: "Utah, whose citizens strenuously resist all imputations of disloyalty, congratulates the president upon the completion of an enterprise which spans a continent... May the whole system speedily thrill with the quickened pulsations

[47] For list, with annual payments to each, see *U. S. Off. Reg.*, 1876, ii.; *P. O. Dept*, 118–19.

[48] Names of post-offices, postmasters, and the compensation paid to each will be found in *Id.*, 351–2. For further items concerning mail services, see *Richards' Incidents of Utah Hist.*, MS., passim; for statistics, *House Ex. Doc.*, 35th Cong. 2d Sess., ii., pt iv., pp. 757, 783, 819, 833; 37th Cong. 3d Sess., iv. 152–5, 170, 214; 38th Cong. 1st Sess., v., pt ii., 73; 38th Cong. 2d Sess., v. 802, 822, 829–30, 861; 41st Cong. 2d Sess., i. 43, 66, 88–9, 104, 114; 41st Cong. 3d Sess., i., pt iii., vol. iii., 46, 73, 147–9, 156, 169–71; 42d Cong. 3d Sess., i., pt iv., vol. iv., 54, 136, 140, 228, 237–43; 45th Cong. 2d Sess., vii., pt ii., 6–7, 20, 56, 65, 218; *Sen. Ex. Doc.*, 36th Cong. 1st Sess., i., vol. iii., pt i., 1432–1440; 37th Cong. 2d Sess., i., vol. iii., 585–6, 601–3, 621, 644; *Mess. and Doc.*, 36th Cong. 1st Sess., pt iii., 1432–72; 39th Cong. 1st Sess. (abridged), 48–53; 39th Cong. 2d Sess., *P. M. Gen'l Rept*, 18–19, 24, 50, 87; 40th Cong. 2d Sess. (abridged), 772–9. For routes, expenses, subsidies, etc., see *Postmaster-Gen. Rept*, 1858, pp. 45, 69, 71, 121; 1859, 46, 54, 86; 1860, 74, 76, 140; 1865, 25, 40, 58–9, 83–4; 1868, 42, 64, 261–2, 278; 1871, 17, 40, 47, 85–6, 116, 126–8; 1873, 33, 69, 184–5, 198, 208–20; 1875, 77, 83, 210, 230, 241–51; 1876, 20, 41–5, 81, 89, 182–3, 198, 204–9; *H. Ex. Doc.*, 47th Cong. 2d Sess., xxii., no. 93, pp. 255–7; *Id.*, 48th Cong. 1st Sess., pt 4, no. 2, pp. 252, 292, 612.

[49] *Deseret News*, Oct. 23, 1861.

of the heart, as the parricide hand is palsied, treason
is punished, and the entire sisterhood of states join
hands in glad reunion around the national fireside."
The president answered: "The government recipro-
cates your congratulations."[50]   In the autumn of this
year the line was completed westward to California.[51]
The charge for messages to New York was in 1861
at the rate of $7.50 for 10 words, as against $1.50 in
1880.[52]

At the former date Brigham had already resolved
to connect the leading settlements of Utah by means
of a home telegraph system.   It was not, however,
until the autumn of 1865 that the matter was brought
prominently before the people.   They responded
cheerfully and promptly, as they ever did to his be-
hests, contributing funds and labor, and about a year
later the Deseret Telegraph Co. was in operation, the
line opening for business in December 1866, connecting first with Ogden, and soon afterward with Brigham City and Logan, its northern terminus.   In
January 1867, 500 miles of wire had been laid, extending northward to Cache Valley and southward to St
George, with a branch line running through Sanpete
Valley.[53]   During this month the company was organized under charter from the legislature, with a capital
of $500,000.[54]   The line was afterward continued

[50] Id.   See also Tullidge's Hist. S. L. City, 249–51; S. F. Bulletin, Oct.
21, 1861; S. c. Union, Oct. 25, Nov. 2, 1861.

[51] Deseret Tel. Co. Mem., in Utah Jottings, MS.   In 1859 an act was passed
to incorporate the Placerville, Humboldt, and S. L. C. Tel. Co.   See Utah
Acts, 1858–9, 26.

[52] For day rate.   The night rate was 75 cents. Deseret Tel. Co. Mem., in
Utah Jottings, MS.

[53] Id.   On this the first circuit 320 pounds of wire were used per mile, the
cost being 35 cents per lb and $150 per mile. Tullidge's Life of Brigham
Young, suppl. 67.   In the Deseret News of Jan. 23, 1867, the line is termed
the Deseret State Telegraph.

[54] The officers were Brigham Young president, Dan. H. Wells vice-president, Geo. Q. Cannon treasurer, and Wm Clayton secretary, the two first
being ex officio members of the board; the remaining directors were Edward
Hunter, Geo. A. Smith, A. O. Smoot, A. H. Raleigh, John Sharp, Jos. A.
Young, Erastus Snow, Ezra T. Benson, and A. M. Musser, the last named
being appointed superintendent. Deseret Tel. Co. Mem., in Utah Jottings,
MS.

Amos Milton Musser, a Pennsylvanian by birth, joined the Mormons in

through Sevier county to Monroe, and from Toquerville to the Kanab country in south-eastern Utah, to
Tintic, Cottonwood, and Bingham, and to Pioche and
other towns in south-eastern Nevada. In 1880 it
had been further extended to Paris, Idaho, to the
mining towns of Frisco, Silver City, and Alta, and
toward the south-east as far as Ordenville, touching
Arizona in its route. At this date there were 955
miles of pole line, 1,130 of wire, and 68 offices in operation. The capital stock was held entirely by Mormons, and though much of the route lay through a
sparsely settled country, where the expenses were out
of all proportion to the receipts, the enterprise was
self-supporting.[55]

In 1882 there were 2,647 miles of telegraph and
600 of telephone wire, with 560 instruments in Utah,[56]
and communication with the adjacent states and territories was being rapidly pushed forward.

The people of the United States seem now determined that polygamy shall be suppressed. During the
years 1885–7, fines and imprisonments were of constant occurrence, and hundreds of heads of families
went into hiding. Some voluntarily came forward,
gave themselves up, and stood their trial. Whether
or not the system is destined thus to be wholly rooted
out, it is impossible to say. But in answer to the

1844, and together with his mother and sister settled at Nauvoo in 1846,
remaining in that neighborhood after the expulsion until 1851, in which year
he arrived in Utah and was appointed to the general tithing-office. In 1852
he was sent on mission to Hindostan, where he labored for three years, principally in Calcutta and Bombay, and was afterward employed as a missionary
in England. Returning to Utah in 1857, he took an active part in promoting
the home industries of the territory; he was also travelling agent of the
church, assisted in emigration matters, temple building, the coöperative
movement, and was, in brief, one of Brigham's most trustworthy agents.

[55] In 1880 John Taylor was president, Dan. H. Wells vice-president, Jas
Jack treasurer, and W. B. Dougall secretary, all of them being directors.
The other members of the board were John Sharp, F. Little, Ed. Hunter, H.
P. Kimball, and Geo. Reynolds. Musser having resigned the superintendency
in 1876, Dougall was appointed in his stead. Id. In 1878 the wires were
laid to the houses of many bishops of wards throughout the territory. Conyer's letters to Boston Educ. Jour.

[56] Contributor, iv. 182. For list of telegraph offices, see Utah Gazetteer,
1884, 269.

oft-repeated accusations of those who regard the Mormons merely as an ulcer in the body politic, there are many points which to the impartial observer would seem worthy of being noted in their favor. Laying aside the questions of religion and polygamy, we find recorded in their annals one of the greatest achievements of modern times, and one that sheds a lustre on the dark cloud which, to gentile gaze, hangs like a funeral-pall over the genius of this singular and long-suffering community. Driven from Far West, from Kirtland, from Nauvoo, they found at length, amid the farthest west, an abiding-place—one then as remote from civilization as the wilds of Senegambia. There, within forty years, has been established a thriving community; there has been built one of the most sightly capitals west of the Mississippi, an oasis amid the great American desert, and with hundreds of settlements depending upon it. There farms and orchards, flocks and herds, factories and warehouses, cover the formerly unpeopled solitude, abandoned but a few decades ago to the savage, the coyote, and the wolf. The men and women who compose this community, drawn for the most part from the lower strata of European society, have not been slow to learn the practical lessons which their church has taught them; to learn how to exercise forethought, frugality, and other qualities which lead to success in life.[57]

[57] I give herewith some further biographical notices. Orson Hyde, a native of Oxford, Conn., was born in 1805, commenced life by working in an iron-foundery for six dollars a month, afterward serving for a year or two as clerk to the firm of Gilbert & Whitney of Kirtland. While at Kirtland, Hyde, who was then a stanch methodist, and a class-leader in a camp-meeting at that point, heard that a golden bible had been dug out of a rock in the state of New York. A few months later he was converted to Mormonism, and set forth as a missionary, being a member of the English mission of 1837, when he was accompanied by Heber C. Kimball, Willard Richards, and others. In 1840 he went to Jerusalem, where he held service at the mount of Olives, and consecrated the holy land, being appointed to this duty by the prophet, who declared him to be of the house of Judah. After the prophet's assassination, he again proceeded, in company with Parley Pratt and John Taylor, to Great Britain, where he set the churches in order, having now been chosen one of the twelve. He arrived at Winter Quarters a few weeks after the departure of the pioneer band, and on their return labored to reorganize the first presidency, Brigham Young being appointed Joseph's successor, partly by his efforts. After the saints were gathered in Utah, he

remained in that territory as presiding apostle at various settlements, maintaining robust health until about his 70th year, and continuing to labor in the ministry until his decease in November 1878. For further details, see *Autobiog. of Mrs M. A. P. Hyde*, MS., 4; *Hyde's Travels and Ministry*, passim; *Tullidge's Life of Brigham Young*, 69–71; *Millennial Star*, v. 163; *Deseret News*, May 5, 12, 1858, March 25, 1874, Dec. 4, 11, 1878; *Smucker's Hist. Mormons*, 297; *S. L. Herald*, Nov. 30, 1878; *Prescott Miner*, Dec. 13, 1878.

Edward Hunter, a native of Newtown, Pa, was descended on the father's side from John Hunter, who served as lieutenant of cavalry under William III. at the battle of the Boyne, his mother's lineage being traced back to one Robert Owen, a Welsh quaker, who, refusing to take the oath of allegiance after the restoration in 1685, was imprisoned, and afterward emigrating to America, purchased an estate near Philadelphia. On his father's death, Edward, who was then only 22 years of age, was offered his position as justice of the peace, but refused it on account of his youth. A few years afterward he purchased a farm in Chester co., Pa, where he was visited by three Mormon elders, who were invited to make his house their home, though he had not yet joined the faith. In 1839 he entertained as his guest the prophet Joseph, who was then returning from his errand to Washington. In the following year he was baptized by Orson Hyde, then on his way to Jerusalem. In the summer of 1841 he proceeded to Nauvoo and purchased a farm from the prophet, contributing the first year no less than $15,000 to the church. In 1847 he entered the valley of Great Salt Lake with the first companies that followed the pioneers, and on the death of Newel K. Whitney was appointed presiding bishop of the church.

Of the early career of Franklin D. Richards mention has already been made in these pages. In March 1869 he was appointed probate judge of Weber co., and removed with his family to Ogden, his sons Franklin S. and Charles being in 1885 prosecuting attorney, and county clerk and recorder. With the advent of the railroad Ogden was clearly destined to become a city second in importance only to the capital, and one that must soon contain a large gentile element, whereby the commercial and political control of northern Utah would be imperilled. At this juncture, also, it became advisable that the Weber stake should be raised to the dignity of an apostolic see, and for the purpose no better selection could have been made than that of Franklin D. Richards. Brought into contact with the business world during the many years when he directed the immense European migration to Utah, a man without political ambition, kindly, placable, and tolerant, his administration was no less acceptable to the gentile than to the Mormon community. At the close of 1885, though at that date in his 65th year, he still discharged his manifold duties with all the vigor of a man yet in the prime of life, and throughout his long career he has made not a single enemy. As I have already stated, I am under deep obligations to Mr Richards for his kindness in furnishing much valuable material for this volume that would else have been inaccessible.

Lorenzo Snow, a native of Mantua, Ohio, but of New England parentage, first made the acquaintance of the Latter-day Saints while visiting his sisters at Kirtland, Lorenzo having just completed his course at Oberlin college. Convinced of the truth of their doctrines, he was baptized, ordained an elder, and sent forth to preach. As a missionary, none remained longer in the field, or travelled more, his journeys between 1836 and 1872 extending over 150,000 miles. In Feb. 1846 he crossed the Mississippi in company with the twelve, being himself ordained an apostle some three years later. When Box Elder co. was organized, he was made president of the stake at Brigham City, and afterward member of the council for Box Elder and Weber, both of which positions he held for many years. He was an active promoter of the coöperative movement, establishing in 1863–4 a coöperative store, and afterward a tannery, a woollen factory, and several coöperative farms, the employés having the privilege of counting the value of their labor as so much capital invested in the concern. In the *Biography and Family Records of Lorenzo Snow, Written and Compiled by his Sister, Eliza R. Snow Smith* (S. L. City, 1884), we have an account of his travels and missionary labors, together with a description of various incidents in the early career of the saints. The book was written, however, as the authoress states, for the purpose of being handed down in lineal descent from generation to generation, to be preserved as a family memorial.

Erastus Snow, who, with Orson Pratt, was, as the reader will remember, the first of the pioneer band that entered the valley of Great Salt Lake, joined the Mormon church in 1833, and two years afterward was ordained an elder, though at this time only 17 years of age. Bidding adieu to his parents at St Johnsbury, Vt—his birthplace—he journeyed to Kirtland, and thenceforward became prominently identified with the church, sharing in all its tribulations. In the winter of 1848-9 he was chosen an apostle, filling, with Lorenzo Snow, F. D. Richards, and C. C. Rich, the vacancies caused by the reorganization of the first presidency, and the apostasy of Lyman Wight. Soon afterward he was sent on a mission to Scandinavia, and through the branches of the church which he established in that country it has been claimed that nearly 20,000 converts were gathered into the fold. After the close of his missionary career his labors were directed to the founding and development of various settlements in southern Utah, over which he presided as their spiritual head, being also a member of council in the territorial legislature.

Like Heber C. Kimball, Charles Coulson Rich came of puritan stock, though a native of Kentucky, where he was born in 1809. He was baptized into the church in 1832, receiving his endowments at Kirtland, where he was ordained a high-priest by Hyrum Smith. Moving to Far West in 1836, he rendered good service during the persecutions in Missouri, being afterward forced to flee for his life through the wilderness, and making his way to Nauvoo, where he was appointed a member of the high council. In the winter of 1846-7 he was president of the stake at Mount Pisgah, and set forth from Winter Quarters in June of the latter year in charge of a company of saints. In 1849 he was chosen an apostle, and set out on a mission to California, returning in Nov. 1850, and the following year taking charge of the San Bernardino colony. His first mission to Europe was in 1860, when he labored for two years in England, again reaching Zion in 1863, when he settled in Bear Lake Valley, where he resided for the most part until his decease in 1883, serving for several terms as a member of the legislature. *Contributor*. Dec. 1883, 114-15.

Albert Carrington, a native of Royalton, Vt, and a graduate of Dartmouth college, joined the Mormon church in Wiota, Wis., in 1841, and removed to Nauvoo in 1844, a few weeks before the prophet's assassination. A member of the pioneer band, he returned with Brigham Young to gather up the main body of the saints, and journeyed with them to the valley in 1848. After the admission of Utah as a territory, he was several times elected a member of the council until 1868, when he was sent to England to preside over the European missions. For twenty years, when not on some mission, he acted as private secretary to Brigham, and his ability gained for him among anti-Mormons the sobriquet of 'The Mormon Wolsey.' In 1870 he was ordained an apostle, and for several years afterward presided over the British mission.

Elias Smith, nephew to Joseph Smith, the prophet's father, was born at Royalton, Vt, near the birthplace of the former. Joining the Mormon faith in 1834, being then 30 years of age, he removed in 1836 to Kirtland, and thence to Nauvoo, where he was business manager of the *Times and Seasons* and *Nauvoo Neighbor*, filling the same position on the staff of the *Deseret News* after his arrival in Salt Lake City. In 1851 he was appointed probate judge of Salt Lake county, which office he retained for many years; and throughout his public career it may be said that he was almost without an enemy; in such respect were his decisions held, both in law and in equity, while his private life was also beyond reproach.

In connection with the judiciary of Utah may be mentioned Alexander

Pyper, a native of Ayrshire, Scotland, who in 1874 was appointed police court judge of Salt Lake City. His administration of justice was somewhat in contrast with that which prevailed in the third judicial district, James B. McKean being in office during the same year. At that date the questions asked by the prosecuting attorney of jurors and applicants for citizenship were of such a nature that they frequently excluded persons who were not polygamists but simply believed in the Mormon faith, among them being, 'Are you a Mormon?' 'Have you been through the Mormon Endowment House?' 'Do you believe that polygamy is a divine revelation?' 'My education and religion,' remarked Judge Pyper, 'have taught me to deal fairly and justly toward all men, under the law, irrespective of their conditions or opinions.'

David O. Calder, a native of Thurso, Caithness, Scotland, joined the Mormon church in 1840, and in 1851 started for Utah, accompanied by his mother and her family. A man of excellent business ability, his talents were quickly recognized. In 1857 he was appointed chief clerk to the trustee in trust of the church, and in that position organized a system of accounts and records in all the departments of the church. Between 1859 and 1870 he held office as territorial treasurer, and after a visit to his native country, where he also labored as a missionary, was chosen business manager and managing editor of the *Deseret News*, and a director of Zion's Coöperative Mercantile Institute, which latter position he held until his decease in July 1884.

Among the presidents of the Utah stake of Zion may be mentioned Harvey Harris Cluff, a native of Kirtland, whose ancestors settled at Durham, N. H., a few years after the arrival of the *Mayflower*, and whose father, David Cluff, served in the American army during the war of 1812. Removing from Durham to Ohio in 1830, David and his family joined the Mormon faith, and proceeding thence to Nauvoo, shared in all the hardships of the exodus, arriving in the autumn of 1850 in the valley of Great Salt Lake, where they cast in their lot at Provo. On the 6th of October, 1856, when Brigham Young announced before a general conference of the church the threatened disaster to the hand-cart emigrants, Harvey Cluff, then only in his twentieth year, was one of the first who volunteered to go to their aid. On this occasion he states that the provisions and clothing furnished before nightfall were more than sufficent to load 22 teams. In 1859 Mr Cluff was elected city councillor, and in 1875, after his missionary labors, principally in Europe and the Sandwich Islands, was ordained bishop, and assigned two years later to the charge of the fourth ward of Provo City. *Biog. Sketch of H. H. Cluff*, MS.

Biographies of other prominent men are given in *Richards' Bibliog. of Utah*, MS.; *Utah Biog. Sketches*, MS.; *Contributor; Tullidge's Mag.; Deseret News; S. L. C. Tribune; S. L. C. Herald*, passim.

For further references to authorities consulted in the last chapters of this volume, see 34th Cong. 1st Sess., *H. Ex. Doc.*, 1, pt 2, 504–7; pt 3, 375, 431; *Doc.*, 10, 235; *H. Rept*, 185; *S. Doc.*, 96, vol. xviii., 559; *Id.*, 3d Sess., *S. Doc.*, 5, 837, 877; 35th Cong. 1st Sess., *H. Ex. Doc.*, 2, pt 2, 1053, 1096; *Id.*, 2d Sess., 1, pt 2, 12, 149–51, 202–6; pt 3, 1300–3; pt 4, 757, 783, 819, 833; *S. Ex. Doc.*, 39, 1–73; 40, passim; 36th Cong. 1st Sess., *Mess. and Doc.*, pt 2, 13–15, 121, 131–2, 194–5, 200–4, 207–20, 221–44, 589; pt 3, 1432, 72; *Id.*, *S. Ex. Doc.*, 1, vol. iii., pt 1, 490–2, 556; 52, 417–98; *Id.*, 2d Sess., *H. Misc. Doc.*, 34; *H. Ex. Doc.*, 63, vol. ix.; 37th Cong. 2d Sess., *S. Doc.*, 1, vol. iii., 585–6, 601–3, 621, 644; *Acts and Res.*, 209; *Id.*, 3d Sess., *H. Ex. Doc.*, 1, vol. iv., 152–5, 170, 214; 38th Cong. 1st Sess., *H. Ex. Doc.*, 1, vol. v., pt 2, 73; *Id.*, 45, vol. ix.; *Id.*, 2d Sess., 802, 822, 829–30, 861; 39th Cong. 1st Sess., *Mess. and Doc.*, 48–53; *H. Com. Rept*, 96; *Id.*, 2d Sess., *Mess. and Doc.*, 18–19, 24, 50, 87; *H. Jour.*, 523, 733–5, 765; *S. Jour.*, 624; *Acts and Res.*, 303; 40th Cong. 1st Sess., *S. Jour.*, 307; *H. Jour.*, 365; *H. Misc. Doc.*, 26; *Id.*, 2d Sess., *Mess. and Doc. Abridg.*, 772–6; *H. Misc. Doc.*, 35; *Doc.*, 153, 25–8; *H. Com. Rept*, 8, 79; *H. Jour.*, 1407; *S. Jour.*, 1240–1; *Cong. Direc.*, 41; *Id.*, 3d Sess., *H. Jour.*, 671; *Mess. and Doc. Abridg.*,

829–34, 1109, 1114, 1130, 1134, 1220–1; *H. Ex. Doc.*, 54, 168; *S. Jour.*, 617, 621; *Acts and Res.*, 224; 41st Cong. 1st Sess., *H. Jour.*, 317; *H. Misc. Doc.*, 20; 22; 23; *Id.*, 2d Sess., *H. Ex. Doc.*, 1, pt 1, 43, 66, 88–9, 104, 114; *Doc.* 68; *Doc.* 207, 319–21; *Doc.* 230; *H. Com. Rept*, 21, pts 1 and 2; *S. Jour.*, 1490, 1527–8; *S. Misc. Doc.*, 112; *S. Com. Rept*, 72; *H. Jour.*, 1539, 1542–3, 1600–1; *Id.*, 3d Sess., *H. Jour.*, 624–5, 650–1; *H. Ex. Doc.*, 1, pt 3, 46, 73, 147–9, 156, 169–71; pt 4, iv.; pt 1, 139–45, 443–6; *Doc.* 52; *Doc.* 71; *Rept Com. Educ.*, 328–83, 351, 558; *S. Jour.*, 603, 673; *S. Com. Rept*, 302; 42d Cong. 1st Sess., *H. Jour.*, 279; *H. Ex. Doc.*, 10, 218–23; *S. Jour.*, 239, 249, 266, 277, 279; *Id.*, 2d Sess., *H. Jour.*, 1219, 1270, 1302–5, 1345–7; *H. Ex. Doc.*, 211, 300–30; *Doc.* 256; *Doc.* 258; *Doc.* 325, 179–86; *Doc.* 326; *Rept Sec. Int.*, pt 1, 51–2; *H. Misc. Doc.*, 155; *Doc.* 165; *Doc.* 208; *Rept Com. Educ.*, 21, 383–4, 600–4; *S. Jour.*, 1234, 1380–2, 1419–20; *S. Ex. Doc.*, 12; *S. Misc. Doc.*, 118; *Doc.* 126; *Acts and Res.*, 40, 223, 363, 530; *Id.*, 3d Sess., *H. Jour.*, 657, 699–701, 713, 725; *H. Ex. Doc.*, 1, pt 4, 54, 136, 140, 228, 237–45, 21; *H. Misc. Doc.*, 95; *H. Com. Rept*, 98, 246–56, 325–6, 365–7, 377, 414–58; *S. Jour.*, 856, 870, 886; *S. Ex. Doc.*, 44; *S. Misc. Doc.*, 73; *Rept Com. Educ.*, 24–41, 55; 379–80, 416, 608–13, 942–97; 43d Cong. 1st Sess., *H. Jour.*, 1545, 1559, 1582–3, *H. Ex. Doc.*, 96; *Doc.* 141, 255–83; *Doc.* 157; *Doc.* 193; *Doc.* 197; *Doc.* 193; *Rept Com. Educ.*, xxii.–cxxiii., 460–3, 475, 510–12, 728; *Id.*, 2d Sess., *H. Jour.*, 793, 800, 810, 812; *H. Misc. Doc.*, 49; *Doc.* 120; *Doc.* 139; *H. Com. Rept*, 484; *S. Jour.*, 593, 1121, 1141–2; *S. Ex. Doc.*, 42; *Id.*, 2d Sess., *H. Ex. Doc.*, 177, 328–57; *Rept Com. Educ.*, xiii.–cxxv., 500–2, 507, 526–34, 733; *P. M. Genl Rept*, 69, 264–5, 278, 287–300; 44th Cong. 1st Sess., *H. Jour.*, 1775, 1736; *H. Ex. Doc.*, 159, 267–81; *Rept Com. Educ.*, xxvi.–cxxiii., 510–14, 548–54; *H. Misc. Doc.*, 42; *Sec. Intr Rept*, 591–2, 606–44, 675–80, 859–62; *Sec. War Rept*, 44, 119–20, 148; *Id.*, 2d Sess., *H. Jour.*, 871; *S. Jour.*, 552–3; *Rept Com. Educ.*, xx.–xxix., lix.–clv., 458–61, 500–7, 760; *S. Com. Rept*, 608; *Sec. Intr Rept*, 532–5, 604, 610–58, 675–85; *Sec. War Rept*, 48, 67; 45th Cong. 1st Sess., *S. Jour.*, 168; *Id.*, 2d Sess., *H. Jour.*, 431, 408, 1654–5, 1708; *H. Ex. Doc.*, 45, 971–8; *Doc.* 72, 146; *Doc.* 73, 1–163; *H. Misc. Doc.*, 54, 97–100; *H. Com. Rept*, 708, 949; *S. Jour.*, 977–8, 990, 1021; *S. Ex. Doc.*, 40; *Entom. Com. Second Rept*, 322, 380; *Id.*, 3d Sess., *H. Ex. Doc.*, 88, passim; 46th Cong. 2d Sess., *H. Ex. Doc.*, 46, 475–522, 632–7; *H. Com. Rept*, 1710; *S. Ex. Doc.*, 181; *Id.*, 3d Sess., *S. Ex. Doc.*, 12, 50, 67; 47th Cong. 1st Sess., 79, 94; *H. Misc. Doc.*, 38, 98–9, 126, 197–9; *Id.*, 2d Sess., *H. Ex. Doc.*, 45, 1181; *Doc.* 72, 153–5, 158; *Doc.* 77, 64; *Doc.* 93, 255–7, 1157–74; *H. Misc. Doc.*, 44, 4–7; *H. Com. Rept*, 1865; *S. Ex. Doc.*, 45; *S. Misc. Doc.*, 8, pt 2, 86; *Doc.* 46, 70; 48th Cong. 1st Sess., *H. Misc. Doc.*, 1, pt 4, no. 2, 252, 292, 612; *Poore's Cong. Direc.*, 97, 102; *Census Rept*, 1870; *Indus.*, passim; *Id.*, 1880, i. 3–45, 351–3, 378–456; *Id.*, iii. 3–10, 25–9, 94, 136, 173, 208, 244, 318; *Sec. Intr Rept*, 1871, pt 1, 166–7, 219–20; *Id.*, 1873, pt 1, 150–1; *Id.*, 1874, pt 1, 44–50, 156–60; *Id.*, 1875, pt 1, 89–100, 251–3; *Cong. Globe*, 1868–9, 687, 754, 781, 1364, 1620; *Id.*, 1869, 83, 86, 195; *App.*, 47; *Id.*, 1869–70, 41; *Id.*, 1870–1, 329; *Id.*, 1871–2, 127, 300; *Id.*, 1872–3, clviii.–ix., clx–i., clxxvi.–lxxxii., cclxvi.–lxxii., ccxc., 221, 353; *App.*, xxxii.; *Id.*, 1874, 21, 43, 51, 85, 187, 204, 2183, 2838; *Id.*, 1874–5, 144; *Id.*, 1875–6, 44; *Id.*, 1877–8, 176, 529; *Id.*, 1878–9, 45–53, 565, 1873; *Ind. Affrs Rept*, 1869, 20–1, 226–34, 270–6, 460–532; *Id.*, 1871, 683; *Id.*, 1872, 78, 91, 93; *Id.*, 1873, 336–46; *Id.*, 1874, 52–4, 104–79, 270–1, 276–7; *Com. Genl Land-Office Rept*, 1869, 168–74, 225–42, 256–62, 326–31, 400–5; *Direc. Mint Rept*, 1881, 19; *Id.*, 1882, 14; *Surg.-Gen. Circ.*, no. 8, 1875, 328–32, 338–40, 345; *Hayden, Geolog. Surv.*, 1872, 106–8, 659–792; *Hague*, in *King's Surv.*, iii., 455–73; *King's Surv.*, v., passim; *Gilbert's Rept*, in *Powell's Geolog. Surv. Rocky Mtns*, 1876, passim; *Wheeler's Surv.*, 1872; *Progress Rept*, passim; *Id.*, 1878, ii., iii., passim; *Smithsonian Inst. Rept*, 1877, 67–82; *Meteorol. Regis.*, 1843–54; *U. S. Offic. Register*, 1877; *Id.*, 1879; *Comptr of Currency Rept*, 1878, 52, 759; *Id.*, 1881, 94–107, 112–19, 212; *Id.*, 1884, 128–41, 250; *Com. of Educ. Rept*, 1871, 8, 21, 383, 404; *Id.*, 1875, 510–14; *Id.*, 1875, 510–14; *Id.*, 1877, 291–2; *Id.*, 289–91; *Id.*, 1879, 285–6; *Id.*, 1880, 282–5; *Id.*, 1881, 301–2; *Id.*, 1882–3, 302–3. Utah Pub. Doc., as follows: *Jour. Legis.*, 1869, 13, 28–9, 101–2, 131–4; *Id.*, 1869, 158–9; *Id.*, 1870, 81–2, 183, 185–7; *Id.*, 1872, 36, 85–7, 104–5, 122, 149, 182, 231, 237–9; *Id.*, 1876, 24–5, 31, 65–8, 104–5, 112–15, 197, 199–201, 206–8, 213, 239, 292; *Id.*, 1877, 31, 35–6, 39–40, 161–4, 323, 392–402; *Id.*, 1878, 339; *Id.*, 1880, 1–8, 21–2, 241–3; *Acts and Res.*, 1869, 2, 7, 17, 20–2; *Id.*, 1870, 2, 4, 8, 12, 127–8; *Id.*, 1872, 2, 28–33, 40–2; *Id.*, 1874, 6; *Id.*, 1878, 8, 11–26, 38, 41, 43, 48; *Utah Laws*, 1878, i., 28–37, 46, 60–105, 167–8; *Id.*, 1880, iv., 2–5, 10–19, 26–44, 55–65, 67–81, 84–8, 95–6; *Id.*, 1882, 2–3, 23–4, 30–6, 40, 102, 106–7; *Compiled Laws*, 184–896, passim; *Gov. Message*, 1869, passim; *Id.*, 1870, 6–7, 9–15; *Id.*, 1876, 5–8, 10, 12–13, 20–2, 23–4, 26–7; *Utah Election Laws*, 1878, 1882, passim; *Com. Rept on Gov. Mess.*, 1882, passim; *Constitution State of Utah*, passim; *Memors of Legislature*, 1882, 1–8; *Memor. to Congress*, 1882, passim; *Supt Schools, Rept*, 1867–9, passim; *Id.*, 1874–5, 1–42, 61–70; *Id.*, 1876, 1878, passim; *Finance Rept of Counties*, 1869, passim; *Supm. Court Decis.*, 1879, in *Reynolds' Case*, passim; *Black, Argument for Utah*, 1883, passim; *Hopt vs People of Utah*, 1884, passim; *Cannon*, in *House of Rep.*, 1–15; *Defence Constit. and Relig. Rights*, passim; *Bigamy and Polygamy*, passim; *Relief Soc. L. D. Saints*, 1884, passim; *Burchard's Rept*, 1880, 127–32; *Id.*, 1881, 237–48; *Id.*, 1882, 253–69; *Id.*, 1883, 617–41. Other authorities as mentioned below: *Taylor and Woodruff, Reminiscences*, MS., passim; *Richards' Crime in Utah*, MS., 1–15; *Id.*, *Europ. Emigration*, MS., passim; *Id., Narrative*, MS., 59–60, 64–6, 74, 78, 82–6, 94, 96–105, 110–18; *Id.*, *Utah Miscellany*, MS., passim; *Id.*, *Bib. of Utah*, MS., 15–23; *Incidents in Utah History*, MS., 5, 81; *Richards, Mrs, Reminiscences*, MS., 9, 11, 15, 17, 30, 44, 50–1; *Godbe, Statement*, MS., 12, 15, et seq., 19, 20; *Id.*, *Mining Mem.*, MS., 7–11; *Smoot, Margaret S., Experience of a Mormon Wife*, MS., 8–9; *Cluff's Overland in Winter*, MS., 1–14; *Tracy, Mrs N. N., Narrative*, MS., 8; *Glidden's Statement*, MS., 1, 6–7, 11–12; *Utah Biog. Sketches*, MS., 1–55, 60–1; *Harrison's Critical Notes*, MS., 30–42, 51–9; *Woods' Recollections*, MS., 39, 52–5, 59–60, 66–70; *Utah Notes*, MS., passim; *Hoyt's Arizona*, MS., 29–31; *Stanford's Brief Historical Sketch*, etc., MS., passim; *Woodruff, Phebe, Autobiog. Sketch*, MS., passim; *King, Hannah T., Brief Memoir*, etc., MS., passim; *Cobb's Mormon Problem*, MS., passim; *Bleak*, in *Utah Co. Sketches*, MS., 78–80; *Madsen*, in *Id.*, 12–13; *Powers*, in *Id.*, 19; *Huntsville Described*, MS., 6; *Utah Miscellany*, MS., 12; *Brown, Statement*, MS., 3–4; *Hill, Mines and Mining*, MS., 1; *Stanford, Ogden City*, MS., 1–16; *Id.*, *Brief Hist. Sketch of Weber Co.*, MS., 1–23; *Id.*, *Hist. Deseret University*, MS., passim; *Dotson's Doings*, MS., 1–2; *Dalton's Autobiog.*, MS., 4; *Ebey's Journal*, MS., i. 177; *Clark's Sights*, MS., pt 4, 7–9, 11–12; *Cradlebaugh's Nev. Biog.*, MS., 4; *Chambers' Hist. Ft Bridger*, MS., 2; *Barfoot, Brief Hist. of Des. Museum*, MS., passim; *Utah Sketches*, MS., 27, 47–100; *Utah Early Records*, MS., 5, 12, 17, 20, 24–9; *Description of Huntsville*, MS., 6; *Jones, Albert*, in *Utah Co. Sketches*, MS., 1–170; *Anderson, R. R., Letter on Salt Lake City Street-Railroad*, MS., passim; *Statistical Report of the Stakes of Zion*, MS., passim; *Huffaker, Early Cattle-Trade*, MS., 1–4; *Rept of Stakes*, etc., 1880, MS., passim; *Utah Merchants and Mines*, MS., passim; *Cannon, Geo. Q., Sunday-schools in Utah*, MS., passim; *Id., Life of Nephi*, passim; *Snow, Eliza R., Incidents in My Life*, MS., passim; *Deseret Telegraph Co.*, MS., passim; *Dorr's Statement*, MS., 3; *Millennial Star*, ii. 1–5, v. 195; *Id.*, viii. 176; *Id.*, xii. 159–60; *Id.*, xvi. 109; *Id.*, xviii. 315, 319; *Id.*, xix. 8–9; *Id.*, xxv. 743, 760, 792, 819; *Id.*, xxix. 70–3; *Id.*, xxxi. 518–19; *Id.*, xxxii. 120, 400, 467, 624, 668; *Id.*, xxxiii. 529–35, 550–1, 643–4; *Id.*, xxxiv. 6–7, 68, 70, 177–80, 296–8, 334–5; *Id.*, xxxv. 68–70, 72–4, 99–100, 104–6, 122, 135–8, 148–9, 191, 527, 580–3, 587–8, 671; *Id.*, xxxvi. 11–12, 88–90, 93–5, 252–5, 263, 273–5, 424–6, 741–2; *Id.*, xxxvii. 204–5, 282–5, 510–11, 532–3, 545–54, 576, 788–91; *Id.*, xxxviii. 366; *Id.*, xxxix. 127; *Id.*, xli. 196–8, 666, 698, 811; *Times and Seasons*, i. 32, 96, 120–3, 139–40, 168, 179, 469; *Id.*, ii. 467; *Id.*, iii. 585, 710; *Id.*, iv. 162–3, 288, 360–61; *Id.*, v. 398–9; *Id.*, vi. 850, 914–15, 989; *Id.*, vii. 63; *Pratt, P. P., Autobiog.*, 334–5, 374, 376, 387–93, 498–502; *Id., Voice of Warning*, passim; *Id.*, **in**

Times and Seasons, i. 64, 111; iv. 162–3; *Id., Key to the Science of Theology,* passim; *Provo City, Rev. Ordinances,* iii.–v. 1–145; *Powell's Lands of the Arid Region,* passim; *Pacific R. R. Report,* ii. 77–88; *Murphy's Mineral Resour.,* 1–7; *Niles' Register,* lxxv. 383; *Zabriskie's Land Laws,* sup. 19, 43, 57, 86; *Warren's Mem.,* in *Pac. R. R. Rept,* xi. 91; *Burton's City of the Saints,* 5, 15–17, 171–2, 187–8, 200–87, passim; 300–54, 426, 433, 509–50, 600–24; *Browne's Min. Resources,* 130–1, 240, 256, 482–6; *Greeley, Horace, Overland Journey,* 191–257; *Gunnison, The Mormons,* 26, 80–1, 84–160; *Simpson, Explorations,* 44–55; *Id., Shortest Route to Cal.,* 30–3; *Schott, Distribution and Variation,* etc., 82–3; *Id., Precipitation,* etc., 62–73, 116; *Smith, Rise, Progress,* etc., 23–6, 27, 33–4, 36–7, 59–62, 65; *Stenhouse, Mrs, Exposé of Polyg.,* 132–45, 181, 198–205; *Id., Englishwoman in Utah,* 107–8, 122, 209–23, 368–73; *Id., Tell It All,* 59, 186–8, 251–2, 269–70, 272, 291–4, 338–9, 387–9, 552–3, 554–5, 577, 608–9; *Stenhouse, T. B. H., Rocky Mtn Saints,* 567–80, 613–15, 622–68, 671–88, 691–6, 698, 701–6, 741–6; *Green, Mormonism,* 465, 468, 470; *Todd, Sunset Land,* 178, 181–2, 184–5; *Townsend's Mormon Trials,* 16–27, 29–30, 46–9; *Tucker, Mormonism,* 156–8, 246–7, 250–9, 299–302; *Tullidge, Women of Mormonism,* 265, 278–82, 498–9, 501–15; *Id., Hist. S. L. City,* 247, 249–59; *Id., Life of Brig. Young,* 99, 203–4, 207–8, 359–82, 406–34, 436–40, 442–4, 448–9, 456–8; *Supplement,* 37, 66–8; *Id., Quart. Magazine,* i. 1–6, 14–86, 96–110, 111–17, 177–90, 201–28, 244–50, 353–432, 475–84, 496–501, 522–3, 529–75, 534–5, 537, 539–43, 548–52, 558–91, 654, 664–72, 678–84; *Id., 1882,* 1–8, 21–32, 34–8, 42–52, 62–7, 79–85, 91–2, 122–34, 187–232, 243–6, 260–2, 265–84, 399–413, 426–54; *Id., 1883,* 3–25, 34–7, 49–60, 456–80, 493–6, 506–8, 577–600, 662–4, 675–6; *Id., 1884,* 113, 137–70, 176–7, 225–86, 294–7; *Utah, Resources and Attractions,* 9–38, 43–69; *McCabe, Our Country,* 1106–16; *Prime, Around the World,* 30–1; *Joureaux, L'Amérique,* 228–30, 234–42; *Ward, Husband in Utah,* 163–8, 261–8; *Id., Male Life among the Mormons,* passim; *Rae, Westward by Rail,* 108–92; *Dall, My First Holiday,* 84, 88–91, 97–103, 105–9; *Scribner's Magazine,* 1880, 613–16; *Chandless, Visit to Salt Lake,* 345; *Paddock, Fate of Madam La Tour,* 286–92, 294–300, 308–30, 336–41; *Quigley's Irish Race,* 545–6; *Waite, Mrs, The Mormon Prophet,* 31–5, 132–52, 177, 276–7, 279–80; *Nordoff, Northern Cal.,* 38–43; *Nelson, Pictorial Guide-Book,* 14–25; *National Almanac,* 1863, 531; *Nat. Quart. Rev.,* ix., 2d Ser., July 1879, 80–94; *Nicholson, The Preceptor,* passim; *The Mining Industry,* ii. 22; *The Mines, Miners,* etc., 365, 489, 507, 512–13, 569, 571, 574–5, 591, 597–682, 788–9, 959, 962–6, 984–95; *New Mexico, Pointers on S. W.,* 54–5; *New Mexican Mining World,* Dec. 1882, 83; *Id.,* Nov. 1884, 136; *Mackay, The Mormons,* 48–51, 189, 237, 286, 292–8, 307; *McClure, Three Thousand Miles,* etc., 144, 146, 155, 165–6, 186, 446; *Marshall, Through America,* 150, 160, 163–82, 191, 195–7, 206–12, 219, 227–8, 231–4, 237, 394–6, 409–24; *Utah, Mercantile and Manuf. Estab. of Z. C. M. I.,* 3–13; *Miller, First Families,* etc., 63; *Wentworth, Great West,* 269–76; *Mormon Politics and Policy,* passim; *Mormons at Home,* 215–16; *Lyon, Harp of Zion,* 23–7, 29–30, 31–3, 39–40, 44–9, 67–8, 79–81, 84–7, 93–4, 116–17, 135–42, 156; *Ludlow, Heart of the Continent,* 302–3, 307–8, 315–22, 322–5, 328–32, 333–7, 341–3, 365–73; *Linforth, Route from Liverpool,* 69–75, 78, 97, 99–101, 103–4, 110–15; *Life among the Mormons,* 88–103, 179–80; *Leslie, Overland Trip to Cal.,* 74–5, 78, 91–5, 103; *Little, Jacob Hamblin,* 36; *Young, Ann Eliza, Wife No. 19,* 266–7, 349–51, 371–2, 378–82, 446–52, 522–4, 532–6, 603; *Kelly, Excursion to Cal.,* ii. 231; *Kneeland, Wonders of Yosemite,* 19–21; *Lydia Knight's History,* passim; *Kirchhoff, Reisebilder,* i., passim; *Jaques, John, Catechism for Children,* passim; *Goddard, George,* in *Juvenile Instructor,* xv. 89; *Olshausen, Mormonen,* 149–51, 154–8, 163, 166–70; *Worthington, Women in Battle,* 587–8, 590–5; *Wolfe, Mercantile Guide,* 185–200, 202–57, 327–41; *Williams, Pac. Tourist,* 116–72, 295; *Wells, Fargo, and Co., Statement,* 1883, passim; *Western Monthly,* i. 290–3; *Ward, Artemus, Chas F. Brown, Lectures,* 20–40; *Utah Miscel. Pamphlets,* no. v., vi., vii., viii., ix., passim. *Mormon Pamphlets,* as follows: *Circular from the Twelve Apostles,* no. 3, passim; *Epistle of the Twelve Apostles and Counsellors,* no. 4, passim; *Hughes, Elizabeth, Voice from the West*, etc., no. 7, passim; *Musser, Fruits of Mormonism*, no. 8, 3-11, 32-5; *Young, History of the Seventies*, no. 10, passim; *Circular of the First Presidency*, no. 12, 5-9; *Utah, Pamphlets, Political*, no. 3; *Fitch, Thos, Speech*, passim; *Id.*, no. 5, *S .eech of A. H. Cragin*, in *U. S. Senate*, 1870; *Id.*, no. 6, *Correspondence Relating to Expenses of U. S. Dis. Courts*, passim; *Id.*, no. 7, *Fitch, Course of Judge McKean*, 3-15; *Id.*, no. 8, *Constitution of State of Deseret*, passim; *Id.*, no. 9, *Hooper, W. H., Vindication of the People of Utah*, passim; *Id.*, no. 10, *Clayett, W. H., Speech against Admission of Utah as a State*, passim; *Id.*, no. 12, *Bates, Geo. C., Argument on Jurisdiction of Probate Courts*, passim; *Id.*, no. 13, *Opinion of U. S. Justice Bradley*, etc., passim; *Id., Paine, H. E., Argument in Case of Contested Election*, passim; *Id.*, no. 14, *Woman Suffrage, Act Relating to*, 8; *Id., U. S. Marshals and Deputies, Duties of*, 11-14; *Id.*, no. 16, *Int. Rev. Tax and Z. C. M. I.; Id., Religious*, no. 3, *Read, L. H., Character of Brig. Young*, 19; *Id.*, 9, *Z. C. M. I., Constitution and By-laws*, passim; *Id.*, no. 10, *Articles of Incorporation*, passim; *Id.*, no. 11, *Legislation Concerning Railroads*, 1-40; *Vetromile, A Tour*, etc., 72-5; *Busch, Mormonen*, 64-71; *Id., Gesch. Mormon.*, 299, 314, 327-32, 334-9; *Appleton, Guide*, 357; *Id., Illus. Hand-Book*, 1861, 1867, passim; *Id., Journal*, 1874, passim; *Atlantic Monthly*, iii. 571, 583-4; *Annals of University of Deseret*, 1884-5, passim; *Bowles, Across the Continent*, 100-102; *Id., Our New West*, 202-3, 206-70; *Id. Pac. Railroad*, 49-5; *Bonwick, Mormons and Silver Mines*, 1-219, 283-97, 339-41, 357-62; *Boadicea, The Mormon Wife*, passim; *Bertrand, Mem. Mormon.*, 70-1, 76-7, 81-2, 84-90, 219-20, 261-2; *Beadle, Life in Utah*, 59, 196-200, 222-50, 281-8, 435-70, 508-16, 532-8; *Id., Undeveloped West*, 108-690, passim; *Id., Western Wilds*, 53-5; *Utah Pioneers, 33d Anniv.*, 1-40; *Utah Review*, Feb. 1882, 243; *Crocheron, Augusta J., Women of Deseret*, 1-9; *Brown, J. E., Speech in U. S. Senate*, 1884, passim; *Annals University of Deseret*, 1882-3, 1883-4, 1884-5, passim; *Bennett's Hist. of the Saints*, passim; *Clemens, S. C. (Mark Twain), Roughing It*, 120-6; *Culmer*, in *S. L. Grocer*, ii., no. 2, 1, 3; *Daly's Address*, in *Amer. Geog. Soc. Repts*, 1873, 15; *Dixon's White Conquest*, i. 198-200, 206-14; *Del Mar's Hist. Prec. Metals*, 168; *Elliott & Co., Hist. Arizona*, 1, 87, 151-2, 206, 282-4, 289; *Faithful's Three Visits to Amer.*, 159 et seq.; *Goodrich's Mormon Kingdom*, 6-12; *Green's Mormonism*, etc., passim; *Stillman, J. W., Speech at Boston*, 1882, passim; *Harris, L., Faith of the Zuñis*, in *Spencer's Labors in the Vineyard*, 61-4; *Internat. Review*, Feb. 1882, 181; *Kimball, A. A., Finding a Father*, in *Do's Gems for Young Folks*, 1-18; *Lee, John D., Mormonism*, etc., 276, 294, 318; *McClellan's Golden State*, 586-7, 592; *Merewether's By Sea and by Land*, 264-71; *Musser, A. M., Defence of Our People*, passim; *Nelson's Pict. Guide-Book*, passim; *Head, Frank H.*, in *Overland Monthly*, v. 277; *Oakland Monthly Review*, i. 16-22; *Pratt, Orson, and Newman, J. P., Public Discussion*, 1877, passim; *Player-Frowd, Six Months in California*, 36-7; *Proceedings First Natl Conv. Cattlemen*, 12-13; *Preble's Hist. Steam Navigation*, 244; *Pilling's Bib. of N. Amer. Languages*, nos. 84, 217, 266, 267, 508, 509, 527, 528, 840, 1391, 1924, 1955, 2212, 2216, 2645, 2859, 3079, 3084, 3085, 3088, 3575, 3608, 3609, 3610, 4272; *Pop. Science Monthly*, lii. 486-90; *Id.*, lvi. 156-62, 171; *Porter's Census of the West*, 1880, 437-46; *Ross' From Wis. to Cal.*, 29-32, 37-44, 48; *Gary, The Roaming Badger*, in *Id.*, 91-5, 117-23; *Sturgis' The Ute War of 1879*, 7-8; *Smyth, John H., Law of Homestead and Exemptions*, 467; *Spencer, Orson, Letters*, etc., passim; *Stayner's Farmers' and Miners' Manual*, 1-20; *Colfax's Mormon Question*, passim; *Young, Brig., Death*, etc., 2-9, 12-35; *Woodruff's Leaves from My Journal*, passim; *Wells' Woman's Exponent*, Sept. 1, 1884, 53; *Id.*, 15th, 63-4, 90-102, 117-28, 164-81, 333, 470-606; *Barclay, Mormonism Exposed*, 13, 15-16, 20, 25-6; *Id., New View of Morm.*, 25-6; *Hyde, Mormonism*, 115-35, 137-8, 185-6; *Hubner, Round the World*, 72-125; *Hollister, Resources of Utah*, passim; *Hickman's Destroying Angel*, 48, 112-17; *Hittell, Wash. Scrap-Book*, 75-6; *Head*, in *Overland Monthly*, v. 270-9; *Hayes, Scraps, Emigrant Notes*, 653; *Id., Los Angeles*, ii. 186-7, viii. 416, xvii. 45, xviii. 13-16; *Id., Mining*,

i. 19, 61-3, xi., passim; *Id., Railroads*, ii. 7, 17-19, 25, iv. 16-17, 53; *Id.*, *San Bernardino*, i. 47-9; *Id., San Diego*, i. 202, 213, 215, ii. 171-93; *Riggs*, in *Bienn. Rept Terrtl Supt Educ.*, 1874-5, 43-60; *Bienn. Repts Terrtl Supt Schools*, 1874-5, 1878-9, 1880-1, 1882-3, passim; *Brigham Young Academy, Circular*, 1880, passim; *Hayden, Great West*, 86, 316-19, 325-8; *Duffus-Hardy, Lady, Through Cities and Prairie*, 97-100, 108-9, 113-15, 117-19; *Harper's Magazine*, Oct. 1876, 642-4, 650-1; *Id.*, Oct. 1883, 795; *Id.*, Aug. 1884, 388; *Jackson, Helen, Bits of Travel*, etc., 17-22; *Boyer, From Orient to Occident*, 58-63; *Barnes, From Atlantic to Pacific*, 54-60; *Prieto, Viage*, etc., i. 551-3; *Hall, Great West*, 19-93; *Greenwood, Grace, New Life*, etc., 137-8, 140-4; *Sala, America Revisited*, 274-317; *Simonin*, in *Revue des Deux Mondes*, Nov. 1875, 305; *Seward, Wm II., Travels*, etc., 16-25; *Smith, Joseph, Doctrine and Covenants*, passim; *Smith, Mystery and Crime*, etc., passim; *Snow, Eliza R., Hymns and Songs*, passim; *Id., Recitations*, etc., i., passim; *Id., Biog. of Lorenzo Snow*, 167-8, 449-53; *Id., Poems*, i., ii., passim; *Utah, Scraps*, 1-5, 11-14, 24; *Rept Ontario Silv. Ming Co.*, passim; *Univ. Deseret, Annual*, 1884-5, passim; *Id., Circulars*, 1868-71, 1874-5, 1878-9, 1880-2, passim; *Smucker, Hist. of Mormons*, 1, 83-4, 131, 174-5, 263-6, 273, 321-3, 349, 355, 433-5; *Sacred Hymns*, etc., passim; *Sandette, My Queen*, passim; *Taylor, Summer Savory*, 17-30; *Culmer, Tourist's Guide-Book*, passim; *Garden of the World*, 274; *Goddard, Where to Emigrate*, 148, 152-5; *Codman, Round Trip*, 173-4, 176, 182-255 et seq.; *Cole, California*, 16-9; *Curtis, Dottings*, 18-28; *Coyner's Letters*, etc., i.-v., passim; *Id., Hand-Book of Mormonism*, passim; *Campbell, Circular Notes*, i. 61-3; *Cornaby, Autobiog. and Poems*, passim; *Camp, Year-Book*, 1869, 502-4; *Cradlebaugh, Mormonism*, passim; *Crofutt, Overland Tourist*, 55, 65, 114-51; *Froiseth, Women of Mormondom*, 315-16, 327, 372-9, 382, 384-9, 392-3. 396, 398, 412-16; *Ferris, Utah and the Mormons*, 34-7, 39-40, 45-6, 75, 117, 204, 264-84, 289-302; *Tanner, Mary J., Fugitive Poems*, passim; *Fabian, Utah*, 4-15; *Emerald Hill Ming Co., By-laws*, passim; *Dilke, Greater Britain*, i. 122-7, 131-2, 142; *Deseret Sunday-school Music-Book*, passim; *Deseret Agric. and Manufac. Soc., List of Premiums*, 1878, passim; *Dickeson, Amer. Numismatic Manual*, 225; *De Rupert, California and Morm.*, 123-46; *Hand-Book to Salt Lake Museum*, passim; *Mormon Metropolis*, 7-16; *Horn Silver Ming Co. Rept*, 1884, passim; *University of Deseret, Catalogue*, 1850, passim; *Cummings, B. F.*, in *Utah Pion 33d Anniversary*, 30-4; *Robinson, Sinners and Saints*, 71-3, 110-30, 137, 139-43, 177, 183-4, 186-7, 189-90, 193-5, 234, 239, 243-5, 249-59; *Richardson, Beyond the Mississippi*, 347, 351, 358-9, 364; *Rusling, Across America*, 163-6; *Richards, Willard*, with *Taylor's Govt of God*, no. 26, passim; *U. P. R. R., Rept of Sam. B. Reed*, passim; *Remy, Journey to G. S. Lake City*, i. 53-4, 176, 189-90, 268-75, 450, 453-70; *Id.*, ii. 177-94, 239, 264-8, 283-4, 323-4, 336, 343-4, 360-4; *Raymond, Min. Resources*, passim; *Id., Statistics of Mines*, 1873, 242-64; *Sloan, Gazetteer of Utah*, 1874, 1884, passim; *Salt Lake Contributor*, i., passim; *Id.*, ii. 13-16, 27-32, 48-86, 92, 94, 110, 115-16, 142, 159, 179-80, 209-10, 222, 239-46, 270-3, 287, 302, 333, 350, 367-9; *Id.*, iii. 61-3; *Id.*, iv. 181-3, 276-8, 320, 352-3, 383-8; *Juvenile Instructor*, 1869, et seq.; *California Ann. Mng Review*, 154; *Cal. and Nev. R. R. Prospectus*, 9; *Cal. State Register*, 1857, 116; *Coast Review*, 1872-9, passim; *Mining Review*, 1876, 25; *Fisher, Advertiser's Guide*, 100-1; *Id., Amer. Statis. Annual*, 1854, 101, 103, 114; *Directory Salt Lake City*, 1869, passim; *Id., Utah*, 1879-80, passim; *Graham, Utah Directory*, passim; *Directory Pac. Coast*, 1871-3, 38-42, 149-53, 413-29; *Histor. Magazine*, iii. 85; *Price, Two Americas*, 259-63; *Patterson, Who Wrote the Book of Mormon?* *Pettengill, Newspaper Directory*, 185-6. From hundreds of newspapers, I select the following: S. L. City, *Deseret News*, 1869-81; *Tribune*, 1871-84; both too voluminous to be quoted in detail; *Herald*, 1877, Mar. 24, May 12, June 13, 16, Sept. 12, 29, Oct. 31, Nov. 3, 7, 17, 21, Dec. 12, 22; 1878, Jan. 9, 16, 30, Mar. 20, 23, 30, Apr. 13, 17, Sept. 10, 13, 14, 26, Oct. 3, Nov. 22, Dec. 8, 15, 22, 29; 1879, Jan. 1, Apr. 1, 3, 6, May 2, 24, 29, June 21, July 18, 19, Aug. 9, Sept. 2, 6, 7, 21, 24, 25, 26, Oct. 14, 17, 18, 22, Nov. 9, 12, 26, Dec. 6, 16,

19, 28; 1880, Jan. 1, 3, 10, 17, 28, Feb. 4, 12, June 17, July 29, Aug. 12, 19, 22, 26, Sept. 16; 1881, Mar. 17, 24, 31, June 2, 23, 30, July 28, Oct. 6, Nov. 17; 1882, Jan. 12; *Daily Independent*, 1878, Feb. 22; *Daily Telegraph*, 1869, Jan. 21, Mar. 22, May 16, 18, 29, July 8, 20, 25, Nov. 30, Dec. 19; 1870, Mar. 23, Apr. 14; 1878, Jan. 1; *Western Mining Gazette*, 1880, Aug. 25, Sept. 1, 8, 15, 29, Oct. 6, 20, 27, Nov. 10, 20, Dec. 25; *Daily Mail*, 1876, Jan. 6, 15, 25; *Anti-Polygamy Standard*, June 1, 1880; *Grocer*, 1882, June 1, 3; *Utah Review*, 1871, May 9, 10, Aug. 1, Sept. 2, 4, 5, 13, 16, 18, 21, 23, 24, 25, 26, Oct. 27; 1872, Jan. 4, 11, 30, Feb. 10, 13; *Corinne, Utah, Reporter*, July 17, 1869; *Ogden Freeman*, 1879, Feb. 21, 28; *Junction*, 1879, Aug. 27, Sept. 30; *Silver Reef Miner*, 1879, May 14, June 1, 4, 14, 25, July 9, 19, 30, Aug. 13, Dec. 27; 1880, Jan. 10, 17, Feb. 14, 28; 1881, June 8, Oct. 15, 29, Dec. 31; 1882, Jan. 21, Mar. 15; San Francisco, *Alta*, 1869-85; *Bulletin*, 1869-85; *Call*, 1869-85; all too voluminous to quote in detail; *Chronicle*, 1860, Jan. 23, 30; 1872, Aug. 25, Sept. 29; 1873, Oct. 6; 1878, July 17; 1880, July 24, Oct. 14, Nov. 6, 14, 28; 1881, Sept. 4; 1882, Jan. 1, 17, Feb. 25, Aug. 22; 1883, Apr. 25, Aug. 28; 1884, Jan. 16, 27, Feb. 21, June 2, Nov. 28; 1885, Jan. 13, 20, 31, Feb. 3, 15, Mar. 5, 24, Apr. 21, 30, May 3, 10, 23; *Examiner*, 1869, Jan. 30, June 11, Oct. 24, 30, Nov. 1, 4, 18; 1871, Feb. 1, 17, 21, Mar. 2; 1872, Jan. 27, Mar. 4, 7; 1874, Nov. 13, Dec. 19; 1877, Nov. 30; 1879, Mar. 6, May 7; *Daily Herald*, 1869, Jan. 25, Feb. 5, 11, 21, May 5, 9, 13, 19, June 26, Aug. 17; *Golden Era*, 1869, July 17, 24; 1871, Oct. 8; 1872, Mar. 31, Sept. 22; 1874, Sept. 27; 1878, Jan. 12; 1879, Dec. 27; 1880, May 15; *Monitor*, 1869, Mar. 27; *News Letter*, 1869, May 15; 1870, Dec. 17; 1874, June 27; *Abend Post*, 1869, Feb. 19, June 10; 1870, Jan. 12; 1872, May 25, June 8, Dec. 24; 1873, Jan. 15, Apr. 23, Aug. 9, Sept. 8, 16, 26, Oct. 2, 7, 17, 21, Nov. 11, Dec. 29; 1874, Jan. 29, Apr. 4, June 3, Sept. 22; 1875, Jan. 22, Mar. 18, Apr. 12, May 28, June 10; 1876, Mar. 9, Apr. 6, Dec. 15; 1877, Feb. 21, 1878, Feb. 18, Nov. 13, 30; 1879, Mar. 18, Dec. 22; *Occident*, 1876, Apr. 29; *Stock Report*, 1874, Aug. 4; 1875, Apr. 26; 1876, Sept. 17; 1879, Jan. 17, Aug. 9, Nov. 13, 27; 1880, Jan. 1, Feb. 5, June 8, July 21; 1881, Feb. 10; *Times*, 1869, Jan. 1, 8, 12, 15, 26, Feb. 11, 19, Mar. 2, 6, 10, 11, 17, 23, 30, Apr. 21, May 8, 10, 11, 15, 17, 18, 19, 20, 21, 22, 24, 25, 26, June 9, July 6, 9, 28, 30, Aug. 10, 17, 19, 24, Sept. 6, 17, 29, Oct. 9, 15; *Courier de San Francisco*, 1869, Dec. 15; 1870, June 11; 1871, Mar. 4; *Journal of Commerce*, 1876, Nov. 8; *Pacific*, 1873, Mar. 13, Apr. 3; *Pacific Rural Press*, 1879, May 3; *Directory*, 1873, 36-7; *Scientific and Mining Press*, 1870, Jan. 15, Sept. 3, Nov. 26; 1871, Oct. 8, 28; 1872, Feb. 3, Mar. 9, 30, Apr. 13, Oct. 19; 1873, Jan. 18, Feb. 15, 22, Mar. 1, 8, Apr. 5, May 31, July 17, Aug. 9, Oct. 4, 11; *Commercial Herald and Market Review*, 1871, Mar. 24, Aug. 11; 1874, June 18; 1877, Sept. 6; *Pacific Baptist*, 1875, May 6, 13, 20, Nov. 11; *Pacific Churchman*, 1870, Aug. 25; *Christian Union*, Jan. 14, 1875; *Pac. Advertiser*, Dec. 21, 1872; *Pioneer*, 1872, Aug. 15, Nov. 21, Dec. 5; *Post*, 1872, Apr. 11, 12, May 8, July 3; 1873, Apr. 9, Aug. 7, 16, Sept. 25, Oct. 9; 1875, Jan. 22, Mar. 11, Apr. 13, 24; 1876, Jan. 11, Apr. 1, May 3, July 15, 1877; Apr. 4, May 3, 4, Aug. 30, Sept. 1, 17, 29; 1878, Apr. 4; 1879, May 17, Nov. 24, Dec. 30; 1884, Mar. 27; *Stock Exchange*, Apr. 10, Sept. 6, 1877; *Vanity Fair*, Nov. 12, 1881; *Visitor*, May 24, 1873; *Cal. Christ. Advocate*, 1869, Nov. 11; 1870, Apr. 28, Aug. 4; 1871, Jan. 19; 1872, Aug. 15; 1874, Aug. 27, Sept. 3; *Sacramento Union*, 1869-85, too voluminous to be quoted in detail; *Sacramento Bee*, 1869, May 24, 25; 1878, Nov. 2; 1879, Dec. 6; 1880, Feb. 28; *San Rafael Wy Herald*, 1877, Jan. 11; *Sonora Union Democrat*, Nov. 15, 1879; *San José Mercury*, Nov. 23, 1871; *Id., Pioneer*, Mar. 3, 1877; Dec. 11, 1879, Jan. 1, 1880; *Id., Herald*, 1877, Apr. 12, 13, 16, May 8, Aug. 29, 30; *Castroville Argus*, Mar. 27, 1869; *Independence Inyo Independent*, Nov. 2, 1878; *Mariposa Gazette*, Apr. 3, 1875, Sept. 8, 1877, Oct. 12, 1878, Jan. 25, 1879; *Vallejo Daily Chronicle*, May 14, 29, 1880; *Truckee Republican*, May 11, 1872; *Bakersfield Californian*, Nov. 25, 1880; *Chico Butte Record*, Sept. 4, 1875; *Crescent City Courier*, 1879, Feb. 19, Dec. 17; *Dutch Flat Forum*, Sept. 6, 1877; *Gilroy Advocate*, May 12, 1877, Nov. 2, 1878; *Healdsburg En-*

terprise, Feb. 9, Sept. 6, 1867; *Id.*, *Russian River Flag*, Sept. 13, 1877; *Lakeport Lake Democrat*, 1877, Sept. 6, 22; *Los Angeles Wy Star*, Sept. 8, 1877; *Id.*, *Wy Express*, 1877, May 26, Sept. 1; *Id.*, *Evening Express*, 1879, Sept. 18; 1884, Jan. 2, Mar. 31, Apr. 5; *Marin Co. Journal*, Aug. 21, 1879; *Marysville Dy Appeal*, Sept. 6, 1879; *Monterey Democrat*, Sept. 1, 1877; *Napa Register*, 1877, Sept. 1, 8, 29; 1878, Feb. 9; *Oakland Tribune*, Jan. 9, 1877; *Petaluma Argus*, July 27, 1877; *Id.*, *Courier*, Sept. 6, 1877; *Red Bluff Sentinel*, Sept. 8, 1877, Jan. 26, 1878; *San Buenaventura Free Press*, Sept. 8, 1877, Jan. 19, 1878, June 28, 1879; *San Diego News*, 1877, Apr. 17, May 7, Aug. 25, 30, Sept. 6, 11; *Id.*, *Union*, Dec. 25, 1873, May 31, 1877; *Santa Cruz Courier*, Sept. 7, 1877; *Id.*, *Sentinel*, Sept. 8, 1877; *Santa Rosa Wy Times*, Sept. 6, 1877; *Sonoma Democrat*, June 29, 1878, July 19, 1879; *Stockton Independent*, 1877, May 12, June 16, July 14, Aug. 4, Sept. 1, Nov. 24, 1878, June 29; 1879, Apr. 2, Aug. 8, Nov. 18, Dec. 6; 1881, Sept. 30, Oct. 3, Nov. 1; 1883, Jan. 1; *Suisun Republican*, Sept. 6, 1877, Sept. 4, 1879; *Ukiah Democrat*, 1877, Sept. 8, 29; *Yuba Wy Banner*, Nov. 2, 1878; *Anaheim Gazette*, 1877, May 12, June 2, Sept. 8, 15; *Antioch Ledger*, 1874, Nov. 14; 1877, May 12, 26, Sept. 1; *Jackson Amador Ledger*, 1877, Sept. 8, 22; *Roseburg Plaindealer*, 1877, May 26, Oct. 6; 1879, Aug. 16; *Yuma Sentinel*, Sept. 8, 22, 1877, July 26, 1879; *Quincy Plumas National*, July 16, 1870; *Austin, Nev., Reese Riv. Reveille*, Sept. 13, 1872, Aug. 9, 1879; *Lyon Co. Times*, Sept. 4, 1877; *Carson Valley News*, May 30, 1879; *Carson Appeal*, 1873, Feb. 9, Mar. 21, Apr. 20; 1874, June 3; 1875, Mar. 18, July 27; 1880, Apr. 1; *Belmont Courier*, Nov. 11, 1876; *Carson State Register*, 1871, Mar. 4, 11, Oct. 27, Nov. 12, 23; 1872, Feb. 6, Apr. 16, Oct. 11, Nov. 8; *Id.*, *City Tribune*, Sept. 26, 1879; *Cherry Creek White Pine News*, Mar. 19, 1881; *Como Sentinel*, July 9, 1864; *Dayton Lyon County Sentinel*, July 16, 1864; *Elko Independent*, 1869, Aug. 18, Sept. 22, Oct. 6, 13, Nov. 10; 1870, Jan. 26, May 4, June 4, 25; 1871, July 15, Sept. 9, 30, Nov. 11, Dec. 23; 1872, Mar. 2, Aug. 10, Dec. 28; 1873, Jan. 18, June 22; 1879, Jan. 31, Aug. 17; *Eureka Daily Leader*, 1880, June 28; *Id.*, *Sentinel*, 1871, June 13, 27, Oct. 31; 1872, Mar. 17; 1875, Jan. 23; 1878, Nov. 9; 1879, Jan. 30; 1882, Feb. 11, Mar. 7, July 14; *Gold Hill News*, 1869, June 5; 1871, May 8; 1874, Jan. 30; 1875, Feb. 24, Mar. 14; 1876, Apr. 10; 1877, Apr. 7, 16, May 17, June 1, 8, July 17, Aug. 29, 30, Sept. 1, 19, 27; 1878, Mar. 15, Apr. 22, July 31; 1881, June 24, July 19, Oct. 23; *Pioche Journal*, July 29, 1875; *Id.*, *Daily Record*, 1873, Feb. 18, 25; *Reno Gazette*, 1877, May 5, Sept. 15, 22; 1878, Jan. 4, Nov. 14; 1880, Dec. 6; 1881, Nov. 12; 1882, Jan. 24, Mar. 30, Apr. 13, Aug. 5, 26; 1883, Jan. 24, 31, Apr. 17; *Id.*, *State Journal*, 1876, Dec. 23; 1877, Sept. 22; 1879, June 18; 1880, Aug. 3, 20; *Ruby Hill Mining News*, Sept. 19, 1881; *Tuscarora Times-Review*, 1879, Feb. 1, 2, 3, 4, 23, May 10, June 17, Aug. 29; *Unionville Silver State*, Dec. 23, 1871; *Virginia City Eveng Chronicle*, 1877, May 4, 15, Aug. 30, Sept. 3, 8, 10; *Territorial Enterprise*, Nov. 25, 1869; *Winnemucca Silver State*, Apr. 3, 1876, Mar. 1879, Aug. 1882; 1878, Nov. 16; 1879, July 11, Aug. 29; *Boisé, Id., Republican*, Sept. 20, 1884; *Id.*, *Statesman*, 1870, June 25, Sept. 24; 1872, Jan. 6, June 1; 1873, Jan. 4, Feb. 1, 15, July 12; 1874, July 31; 1876, Mar. 18; 1879, Mar. 4, Aug. 16, Nov. 29; *Bonanza City Yankee Fork Herald*, Sept. 25, 1879; *Oxford Idaho Enterprise*, 1879, Sept. 11, 18, Oct. 16, 30; *Silver City Avalanche*, 1870, Sept. 17; 1872, May 4; 1873, Dec. 6; 1875, Mar. 2; 1876, Feb. 22, 26; 1877, Sept. 8, 15; *Omaha, Neb., New West*, Dec. 1879; *Prescott, Ariz., Miner*, 1872, May 4; 1873, Jan. 18, 25, Mar. 8, May 17; 1875, June 4, Aug. 27; 1876, Dec. 22; 1877, Jan. 26, May 18, June 15, Aug. 31, Sept. 14, Oct. 26; 1878, Dec. 13; 1879, May 9; *Tucson Fronterizo*, Jan. 27, 1882; *Galveston, Tex., Daily News*, Dec. 1, 1884; *Id.*, *Herald*, in *Watsonville Pajaronian*, Apr. 4, 1878; *Walla Walla Statesman*, May 24, 1879; *Port Townsend Democ. Press*, Sept. 4, Oct. 3, 1879; *Seattle Intelligencer*, Nov. 15, 1869; *Puget Sound Wy Courier*, Sept. 7, 1877; *Olympia, Wash., Standard*, Sept. 8, 1877, Aug. 15, 1879; *Id.*, *Transcript*, Aug. 15, 1874; *Vancouver Register*, June 11, 1875; *Portland, Or., Deutsche Zeitung*, 1871, Sept. 23, Oct. 28; 1872, Aug. 31; 1876, Oct. 21;

1877. Apr. 28, June 2, 23, July 14, Oct. 6; 1879, Mar. 8, Oct. 25, Dec. 13, 20; *Id.*, *Wy Standard*, 1877, Apr. 27, Sept. 7; *Id.*, *Herald*, July 10, 1870, Mar. 21, 1872, Oct. 27, 1874, June 29, 1878; *Id.*, *Eveng Telegram*, 1879, Sept. 8, Dec. 8; *Id.*, *Pac. Christ. Advocate*, July 24, 1879; *Ashland Tidings*, Sept. 7, 1877, Nov. 15, 1878; *Astoria Astorian*, 1880, Apr. 23, Oct. 20; *Eugene City, Or.*, *State Journal*, Aug. 23, 1879; *Jacksonville Democ. Times*, 1877, Sept. 7, 28, Oct. 5; *Albany States Rights Democ.*, Sept. 5, 1879; *Salem, Or.*, *Statesman*, Mar. 13, 1875, May 18, 1877, May 12, 1879; *Virginia City, Monta, Madisonian*, June 23, 1877; *Deer Lodge New Northwest*, 1870, Sept. 23; 1873, Feb. 22; *Helena Dy Gazette*, 1872, Feb. 17, Apr. 30, May 1; 1873, Nov. 25; *Id.*, *Herald*, 1873, Dec. 11; 1876, Mar. 23, Sept. 14; *N. Y. Tribune*, in *Calaveras Chronicle*, Oct. 6, 1877; *N. Y. Herald*, 1882, Jan. 30, Feb. 13; *Id.*, in *Independence Independent*, Aug. 16, 1879; *Panamá Star and Herald*, Nov. 18, 1869, June 7, 1873, Apr. 1, 1875, Nov. 14, 1877; *Mexico Diario Oficial*, 2d fol., 1880, passim.

INDEX.